JOHANN NIKOLAS BÖHL VON FABER (1770–1836)

Johann Nikolas Böhl von Faber (1770–1836)

A German Romantic in Spain

CAROL TULLY

UNIVERSITY OF WALES PRESS
CARDIFF
2007

© Carol Tully, 2007

All rights reserved. No part of this book may be reproduced, stored in a retrieval system, or transmitted, in any form or by any means, electronic, mechanical, photocopying, recording or otherwise, without clearance from the University of Wales Press, 10 Columbus Walk, Brigantine Place, Cardiff, CF10 4UP.
www.uwp.co.uk

British Library Cataloguing-in-Publication Data
A catalogue record for this book is available from the British Library.

ISBN 978-0-7083-2001-3

The right of Carol Tully to be identified as the author of this work has been asserted by her in accordance with sections 77 and 78 of the Copyright, Designs and Patents Act 1988.

The publishers wish to acknowledge the financial support of the Higher Education Funding Council for Wales in the publication of this book.

Typeset by Columns Design Ltd, Reading
Printed and bound in Great Britain by Cambridge Printing, Cambridge

*In memory of my father
John Gill Tully*

Contents

Acknowledgements	ix
Bibliographical Note	xi

LIFE AND WORK

Introduction:	Spanning Cultures, Shifting Ideologies	3

Part One
From Campe to Calderón: Böhl's Early Intellectual Development

1	Campe, Faith and Reason	23
2	New Influences: Doña Francisca and Spain	40
3	Critical Beginnings: 'Reflexiones sobre la poesía'	59
4	Romantic Rebirth	73
5	Catholic Conversion	88

Part Two
The Calderón Polemic

6	Settled in Spain	101
7	Böhl's Translation of Schlegel	110
8	The Polemic: Phase One (1814)	128
9	The Polemic: Phase Two (1817 to 1820)	142
10	New Voices in the Final Battle	160

Part Three
Romantic Philologist and Man of Letters

11	The Ominous Decade	175
12	Böhl's Mature Romantic Ideals	186
13	Böhl and the Genealogy of Romantic Philology	204
14	Böhl's Transcultural Philology	218
15	The Reception of Böhl's Philology	234
Conclusion:	Böhl von Faber: A Transcultural Pioneer	251

LITERARY CORRESPONDENCE

Letters	259
Editor's Notes	505
Select Bibliography	583
Index	591

Acknowledgements

The completion of this project would have been an impossible task without the help and support of a number of individuals and organisations.

I would first of all like to thank the Arts and Humanities Research Council, the British Academy and the University of Wales Bangor for their financial support in providing me with research leave and the opportunity to undertake archival work in Germany and Spain.

A large proportion of the time spent on this project was dedicated to the transcription and annotation of Böhl's correspondence. I am extremely grateful to Professor Hinrich Siefken for his tireless efforts in assisting me with the transcription of the material and to Frau Marion Sommer of the *Handschriftenabteilung* of the *Staats- und Universitätsbibliothek Hamburg* for her support and advice over the years. I would also like to thank Dirk Moldenhauer for his advice on the Perthes *Nachlass* and Anke Lindemann-Stark for her generosity in providing transcriptions of Böhl's letters to Joachim Heinrich Campe. I am extremely grateful to the *Staats- und Universitätsbibliothek Hamburg* and to the *Staatsarchiv Hamburg* for granting me permission to publish Böhl's correspondence. Unfortunately, my efforts to gain access to his papers in the Osborne archive in El Puerto de Santa María were less successful.

In writing Böhl's biography, I have been fortunate to be able to draw on the advice and expertise of a number of scholars. I am, as ever, indebted to Professor Jeremy Adler for reading my work as it developed and also to Professor Andrew Ginger for his enthusiasm and suggestions. Professor Siefken was also more than generous in reading the early drafts of many chapters. I was also fortunate enough to benefit from the support of Professor Anthony J. Harper in the early stages of my work. Sadly, he passed away before the project was completed.

My thanks also goes to Professor Helen Chambers and Professor Catherine Davies for their support and to Dr Milagros Fernández Poza and Professor Nigel Glendinning for the provision of essential material. Particular thanks must go to the family of the late Dr María Guadalupe Reyes Ponce for granting me access to her papers and to Dr Judith Purver for her encouragement in the early stages of the project.

Over the last few years, I have benefited from the holdings of a number of libraries and archives. Scholarship would be impossible without the help of librarians and archivists and I would particularly like to thank Jennie Green at Bangor for her help in tracking down some most unlikely inter-library loan

Acknowledgements

requests. Thanks also to Dr Bill Abbey of the Institute of Germanic and Romance Studies, London and to the staff at the British Library, the *Biblioteca nacional*, the *Real Academia Española*, the *Staats- und Universitätsbibliothek Hamburg* and the *Staatsarchiv Hamburg*.

Finally, I would like to thank my colleagues in the School of Modern Languages at Bangor for their indulgence, my family in Germany and friends in London for their hospitality and my nearest and dearest for taking the strain.

Carol Tully
Bangor, 2007

Bibliographical Note

Original orthography, including the use of diacritics, from sources cited has been respected throughout. Translations have been provided by the author unless otherwise indicated.

References to Böhl's writings during the Calderón polemic are taken from the collected documents as published in *Vindicaciones de Calderón* (1820) and abbreviated as follows, adopting the system employed by Pitollet (1909):

- V   'Vindicaciones de Calderón' (Calderón vindicated; also known as 'Sobre el teatro español' [On Spanish theatre]).
- IP   *Pasatiempo crítico en que se ventilan los méritos de Calderon* (Critical musings in which the merits of Calderón are discussed; also known as *Primer pasatiempo*).
- AIP 'Apéndice' (Appendix).
- IIP *Segunda parte del pasatiempo crítico que trata de lo mismo* (Second part of the critical musings which deal with the same; also known as *Segundo pasatiempo*).
- AIIP 'Apéndice. Respuesta á los mismos' (Appendix. Response to the same).
- IIIP *Tercera parte del pasatiempo crítico en defensa de Calderon y del teatro antiguo español* (Third part of the critical musings in defence of Calderón and old Spanish theatre; also known as *Tercer pasatiempo*).
- AIIIP 'Apéndice de algunas lecciones al editor de la Crónica' (Appendix to some lessons for the editor of the Chronicle).

Unless otherwise indicated, reference to Böhl's correspondence in the text is made according to the date of the letter. Correspondence with the Campe family, Nikolas Heinrich Julius and Friedrich Perthes forms the second part of the work. Correspondence with Agustín Durán and Martín Fernández de Navarrete is taken from the following sources:

1. H. Juretschke, 'Die Deutung und Darstellung der deutschen Romantik durch Böhl in Spanien. Mit einem Anhang von Briefen an Martín Fernández de Navarrete', *Spanische Forschungen der Görresgesellschaft* (1956), 147–191.
2. L. Romero Tobar, 'Textos inéditos de Agustín Durán, Gallardo, Böhl, Quintana y Martínez de la Rosa', *Revista de archivos, bibliotecas y museos* (1975), 409–428.
3. P. Sainz Rodríguez, 'Documentos para la historia de la crítica en España. Un epistolario erudito del siglo XIX', *BBMP* (1921), 27–43; 87–101; 155–165; 251–262.

Bibliographical Note

The following studies constitute the key texts in Böhl scholarship to date and are referred to throughout this volume using the abbreviations provided in parenthesis:

VL   Elise Campe, Johann Nikolas Böhl von Faber: *Versuch einer Lebensskizze nach seinen eigenen Briefen* (Leipzig: [no publ.], 1858).

O   Guillermo Carnero, *Los orígenes del romanticismo reaccionario español: el matrimonio Böhl de Faber* (Valencia: Universidad de Valencia, 1978)

Vk   Johann Dornhof, *Johann Nikolas Böhl von Faber: ein Vorkämpfer der Romantik in Spanien* (Hamburg: Seminar für romanische Sprachen und Kultur, 1925)

SR   Derek Flitter, *Spanish Romantic literary theory and criticism* (Cambridge: CUP, 1992)

DD   Hans Juretschke, 'Die Deutung und Darstellung der deutschen Romantik durch Böhl in Spanien. Mit einem Anhang von Briefen an Martín Fernández de Navarrete', *Spanische Forschungen der Görresgesellschaft* (1956), 147–91.

QC   Camille Pitollet, *La querelle caldéronienne de Johan Nikolas Böhl von Faber et José Joaquín de Mora reconstituée d'aprés les documents originaux* (Paris: Alcan, 1909)

A   María Guadalupe Reyes Ponce, 'Spanish and German Antecedents to Agustín Durán's *Coleccion de Romances Castellanos Anteriores al Siglo XVIII* (1828–1832)', unpublished doctoral thesis, University of Manchester, 1991.

Life and Work

Life and Work

Introduction
Spanning Cultures, Shifting Ideologies

The aim of this study is to examine the intellectual development and transcultural significance of a key cultural mediator in the age of Romanticism. A sometimes controversial, but also highly respected figure in his own age, the German merchant, scholar and Hispanist, Johann Nikolas Böhl von Faber (1770–1836), has yet to receive the recognition he deserves. The current climate of interest in interdisciplinary studies and what Dieter Henrich calls *Konstellationsforschung* – examining the detailed links that connected the major thinkers and writers of the period to their teachers, professors and other formative influences in order to embed them in their cultural context – is particularly appropriate to this task. Recognizing the role played by education, aesthetics, philology, even trade in the spreading of Romanticism enables a more just appreciation of this complex and interesting personality.

The European Romantic age has long been recognised as an interdisciplinary, international phenomenon. Indeed, it is the diverse nature of its many aspects and influences which makes it so hard to define, on the one hand revolutionary in its questioning of Enlightenment aesthetics, on the other tending towards reactionism with its proto-nationalist, medievalising values. At its best, however, the period was a celebration of cultural diversity and aesthetic freedom, the impact of which still marks our cultural landscape today. Neo-Classical principles were taken to task as the interdisciplinary spirit of the age opened new perspectives and reset the European canon to value cultures and writers once consigned to the margins. The translation and emulation of works from other literatures became a central focus for many scholars as a thoroughly European aesthetic began to replace the Classical ideal driven by France. In the context of this contemporary cultural transfer, there are few figures who can claim to have played a truly transcultural role in the development of European letters. By this, I mean to have taken in equal measure from two very different cultures, functioned critically and creatively within each and performed a mediatory role to the benefit of both. Instead, many thinkers, including some of the most prominent, functioned solely within their own cultural sphere, observing other cultures as interpreters for their fellow countrymen, but with very little lived experience of the subject of their interest. Whilst exile was a common experience in such politically unstable times – one need think only of the Spanish Liberals in London's Sommers Town – it rarely led to assimilation and often to marginalisation and alienation. Those who ventured out voluntarily onto the open road tended to limit their travels to the well-worn paths leading from one cultural centre to another. Even those who undertook a more ambitious trip or a longer sojourn in Paris, London or the Italian Riviera would eventually return to the security of a familiar landscape. The examples are many: Goethe and Byron in Italy, Tieck in England, Scott and Coleridge in Germany and Wilhelm Humboldt in Spain. New experiences brought new influences and whilst these were evaluated and absorbed, emerging as new aspects in the thought and art of the individual's native culture, they were generally defined in relation to that culture as a point of reference for self-determination in the face of the dominant neo-Classical tradition. Writers and artists from abroad were absorbed into the individual national psyche almost as a possession – the German reception of Shakespeare is a case in point. As this suggests, whilst mediation between cultures certainly took place, it was very often exploitative, taking the form of reception rather than interanimation. Few scholars can claim to have taken that mediatory role to a level which drew two cultures together, securing a mutual influence whilst defending the individuality of each. Some may have played an important role in the development of a European aesthetic – Herder, Scott, the Schlegel brothers and Chateaubriand to name but a few – but can they truly be said to occupy a transcultural position as individuals? One figure who might lay claim to such a status is Böhl.

A biographical study of this nature generally has one of two objectives: either to reappraise with new insights and information the life and work of a prominent figure or to salvage from obscurity one who is significant, but has been overlooked for various reasons. It is perhaps indicative of the dichotomous nature of the subject matter – the narrative of a life split across two cultures at a time of ideological revaluation – that the present study falls somewhere between the two. The problems encountered in tackling such a dichotomy are not unusual. As David Gies emphasises in his introduction to *The Cambridge History of Spanish Literature* (2004), such projects in literary history struggle with two interrelated dilemmas: the need to select material in order to remember, a process which itself somewhat perversely encourages an element of forgetting, and the appropriate use of that material in the construction of a literary past, an act which creates a version of reality intended to underpin our cultural identity, but which is itself necessarily incomplete and subjective. In the case of Böhl, both dilemmas are apparent. Born in Hamburg and brought up under the tutelage of the Enlightenment pedagogue, Joachim Heinrich Campe, Böhl went on to travel Europe as a young man, became a titled landowner in Mecklenberg and then settled in Cadiz as a merchant and man of letters in 1813. The narrative of his life, told here by the author of this work, but also in Böhl's own words through his correspondence, straddles two cultures: that of his native Germany and that of his adopted homeland, Spain. His work as a scholar saw him contribute to the contemporary cultural framework of both these cultures, yet what survives of his life and work in modern literary historiography provides only a fragmented account of the breadth and value of a life dedicated to transcultural mediation. Indeed, Böhl's treatment in the literary histories of Germany and Spain illustrates quite clearly the issues raised by Gies.

In a German context, Böhl has been all but forgotten, subsumed into the invisible cement which binds together the construct of German literary history, one of many receivers and conveyors of aesthetic trends who are overlooked, perhaps for their lack of poetic genius in such a fecund period, but who are central to the cultural framework of the age. Böhl was certainly conscious of his role within that framework as a mediator, keen to defend the Romantic cause, both in Germany and further a field. Yet, despite having carefully constructed for himself the identity of a Romantic thinker, he has all but vanished from the literary historical narrative in a German context, this despite connections with some of the foremost writers, thinkers and publishers of his day including Campe, Perthes, Uhland and Kerner, his work attracting the attention of no lesser figures than Jacob Grimm, the Schlegel brothers and even Goethe. Indeed, Böhl's fate in his native context is that of his entire family. Despite their prominence as one of Hamburg's most successful trading families, the family name remains absent from the streets of the city whilst fellow mercantile dynasties are honoured on any number of urban landmarks. It seems strange that the Böhl family, who still featured alongside such worthy contemporaries as the Sievekings in the Hamburg genealogies of the early twentieth century, should have vanished from the cityscape a hundred years later, record of their achievements now hidden in archives and library catalogues.[1] This absence is made all the more ironic when one considers the impact which that family, through Böhl and his novelist daughter, Cecilia (pseudonym Fernán Caballero; 1796–1877), would have on the development of Spanish letters and European culture in general, in many ways far exceeding the contribution of those more prominently remembered. In a German context, then, the issues pertaining to the narrative of Böhl's life and work are those encumbered by forgetting.

In a Spanish context, his fate has been a different one. Here, he is undoubtedly remembered, but that remembering is often incomplete, attention focused on selected landmarks in his scholarly career. In Spain, Böhl has become part of the literary historical construct, established as a marker in Spanish literary historiography, almost depersonalised as the 'moment' when Spain's literary elite first encountered the revolutionary aesthetics of the German Romantics. This is not to undermine the importance of this key event, which will also be discussed in detail in the current work. Indeed, it would be impossible to discuss the development of Romanticism in Spain without some reference to his introduction to the Iberian peninsula in 1814 of key aspects of Schlegelian thought and the highly politicised and often unpleasant polemic which followed. However, as Derek Flitter's seminal study, *Spanish Romantic literary theory and criticism* (1992), has shown, Böhl's contribution consisted of far more than the reactionary literary agitation often ascribed to him in accounts of the period. As Flitter has demonstrated, Böhl's influence continued to shape the more conservative strain of aesthetics in nineteenth-century Spain during his lifetime and beyond, albeit often in modified form as his conservative German Romantic ideals were received into the complex cultural landscape of a politically polarised nation. His mediation of German Romantic theory secured him a place in Spain's literary establishment from which he was able to exert further influence on the development of Spanish letters. A member of the Royal Spanish Academy from 1820, Böhl's philology was particularly instrumental, reviving interest in the ancient *romance* (Spanish ballad) and exerting a profound influence on the monumental work of Agustín Durán in the same field. Furthermore, as the father of Spain's first female novelist of note, Fernán Caballero, he exerted an immeasurable influence on his favourite, like-minded daughter and her work, an ideological inheritance which would help shape the emerging realist novel in the mid-century. Despite this prominence, the appraisal of Böhl as a scholar in a Spanish context is subject to lacunae. Whilst many focus on his polemical activities as a herald of German Romantic thought in Spain, most make only passing reference to his early intellectual development, his critical career in Spain and Germany before the polemic and his philological work in the last decades of his life (his influence on Durán notwithstanding). In a Spanish context, then, dealing with Böhl's life and work involves detaching him from the literary historical construct in order to evaluate his contribution in terms which acknowledge his position within the cultural framework of the age, but also enable a broader understanding of his scholarship.

This dual fate, polarised between near oblivion and intellectual disenfranchisement, masks the reality of a complex figure, the study of whose life brings the reader into contact with the aesthetic and political ideologies which shaped the development of European culture at the turn of the eighteenth and nineteenth centuries. Disillusioned with much of Enlightenment thought and by his own admission a 'convert' to both Romanticism and Catholicism, Böhl's experiences and shifts in stance present the changing values of the age in microcosm, his life and work representative of the myriad figures who functioned on the periphery of the emerging canon and whose advocacy and scholarship ensured the prosperity of a revolutionary aesthetic. Although this was an age when the artist took centre stage, there was also am important shift towards a new concept of philology with figures such as Humboldt and the Brothers Grimm redefining the parameters of scholarship. Böhl was part of this shift. He was a scholar rather than a poet, yet his work, like that of other similar figures, was driven a by an intense aesthetic appreciation, one which provided the creative genius of the period with the means to flourish in an intense dialogue between the intellectual strata. That such a dialogue is essential to the evolution of any culture requires no reiteration and figures like Böhl, who encourage that dialogue to continue, should themselves not be forgotten. In responding to new ideas, they are just as responsible for the shifting zeitgeist as those who provide the creative impetus. To understand that response fully, we need to consider the reasons for their participation in the cultural dialogue of the age and the rationale behind the attitudes they adopt. This is particularly true of Böhl who occupies a unique position, straddling two cultures. His efforts, increasingly influenced by a conservative political stance, have often been dismissed as reactionism, yet not enough attention has been paid to the impact of personal and cultural context on his thought and scholarship. Born into a Protestant family in northern Germany and imbued with Enlightenment principles as a child, he died at the southernmost tip of Spain a staunch, conservative Catholic clinging to the vestiges of a Romantic age which he could not bear to see decline. The personal trajectory this suggests is both dramatic and tortuous and its impact on the development of European and in particular Spanish letters remains underestimated.

Böhl's self-definition as a Romantic thinker and his conservative political stance suggest a level of cultural and self-awareness which locates him ideologically within what can be regarded as the second phase of Romanticism in Germany. This emerged during the Napoleonic occupation of the German lands from the ideals of the earlier, less politically driven phase and saw the development of the new aesthetic in a highly politicised atmosphere coloured by disillusionment with reason, revolution and the cultural dominance of France. Böhl's 'conversion' to Romanticism took place in this context and he was undoubtedly attuned to the ideal of German Romanticism proffered retrospectively by Joseph von Eichendorff in his *Geschichte der neueren romantischen Poesie in Deutschland* (History of more recent Romantic poetry in Germany, 1846), which, as Littlejohns explains, distorted the concepts of early Romanticism in particular by shifting attention away from the aesthetic complexities of a productive engagement with Enlightenment thought towards a far more politicised, antagonistic vision of these early thinkers as 'Ritter des Christenthums wider den herrschenden Rationalismus' (knights of Christendom against the prevailing rationality).[2] Whilst this image of early Romanticism has long since been tempered by more subtle readings, it holds a marked significance in the context of Böhl's own scholarship for this is precisely how he interpreted his own efforts and those of his more prominent contemporaries. In keeping with the experience of many intellectuals at this time, his rationalist upbringing resulted in a questioning of rationality itself, in particular the Classical principles governing art. The doubts this raised in relation to the aesthetic dominance of French taste found their political counterpart in the anti-French sentiment in the aftermath of the Terror and horrors of the Napoleonic invasion. Engagement with this reaction, both political and aesthetic, saw Böhl undertake a similar journey to others, also including key first generation Romantics such as the Schlegel brothers and Tieck, which led him away from the values of his youth towards a highly politicised, but at the same time deeply existential understanding of the new aesthetic as a means of defence in the face of cultural and political dominance by France and the threat of Liberalism. The biographical section of this work will explore this journey and assess its impact on Böhl's scholarship as a Hispanist and philologist, drawing together existing scholarship and new perspectives to provide the first detailed, comprehensive study of Böhl's life and work. Böhl's correspondence with the Campe family, his friend, Nikolas Heinrich Julius, and his publisher, Friedrich Perthes, published here in full for the first time, is presented in the second section, providing Böhl's own narrative of a life characterised by shifting ideals and changing environments. What emerges is the story of an archetypal Romantic *Zerrissener*, someone struggling to reconcile practical realities with poetic sensitivity in an age of change. Such figures are emblematic of the age and typical in German letters in particular, with Novalis, the poet and mining engineer, and E. T. A. Hoffmann, at once writer, composer and lawyer, among the more prominent examples.[3] For his part, Böhl continually finds himself torn between the daily duties of the merchant and the intellectual drive of the scholar, struggling to locate his shifting world view in a cultural context as the environment around him changes against a backdrop of political upheaval. His *Zerrissenheit* is further emphasised by physical and cultural dislocation as he travels the length of Europe repeatedly before eventually settling in Spain at the age of forty-three with much of his scholarly career still before him. This results in what Gustav Siebenmann refers to negatively as a 'Zwiespalt zwischen zwei Kulturen' (conflict between two cultures).[4] Taking a more positive stance, María Guadalupe Reyes Ponce draws attention to this aspect of Böhl's development in her admirable, but sadly unpublished, doctoral thesis, acknowledging in particular Böhl's presence in the critical discourse of both German and Spanish Hispanism. In so doing, she ascribes to Böhl a 'double critical nationality' (A:147). This apposite description could, I would argue, be extended to encompass the context of his scholarship itself, endowing Böhl with what is effectively a dual cultural identity, something underlined, as Reyes Ponce also notes, by the fact that, once settled in Spain, Böhl oscillated between two forms of his name: the correct German 'Böhl von Faber' and the Hispanised version, 'Bohl de Faber'. As this duality might suggest, Böhl's is a life which occupies the spaces between cultures and spans ideologies and it is perhaps that peripherality and transitionality which has resulted in the fragmented reception of his work.

This is not to suggest, however, that Böhl was in any way an outsider. In social terms, he was quite sure of his status and although there is little direct reference to Böhl's family history in his surviving correspondence, there can be little doubt that much of his self-assured approach to his commercial duties and also his attitudes to society stem from the secure knowledge that, as a member of the merchant bourgeoisie and later as a titled landowner, he had a significant role to play in contemporary affairs. An intellectually modest man, he may have occasionally questioned his ability to deal with the philosophical issues of the day, but he never questioned his right to do so. The desire for knowledge and self-improvement were befitting of his station, an inalienable right of the increasingly confident European bourgeoisie, as valid in the established civic circles of Hamburg as amongst the nascent middle classes of mercantile Spain. The security of Böhl's social position is of fundamental importance to his intellectual development in a number of ways. It afforded him the opportunities of education and travel in his youth, furnished him with the means to further his studies and reassess his ideological standpoint in early adulthood and provided him the security of a respectable family existence upon which to found his reputation as a man of letters in his latter years. The family business and Böhl's own financial stability may have been threatened or even destroyed during the harsh days of the Napoleonic Wars, but even in the worst of times, he led a privileged, unchallenged existence with an assured position in the social hierarchy of the day.

The stability afforded by his social status was one of the few certainties in a life which was characterised by change. Politically, the period was certainly one of upheaval. Europe was in a state of flux and at war with itself. Böhl lived, worked and travelled against a background of disruption, fear and economic uncertainty. Journeying to and fro on family business between Germany and Spain in the decades spanning the turn of the century, Böhl experienced the upheaval of conflict and the resultant political insecurities as the continent struggled to deal with the fallout from revolution and war. His life was marked by a series of significant events. Born in 1770 into a Europe still reeling from the effects of the Seven Years War (1756–63), as a young man he witnessed the beginnings of Prussian domination in the German lands and the establishment of an Austro–Prussian power axis. His formative years saw the introduction of social and political reforms as his native Hamburg finally gained full independence. However, just as this autonomy began to foster a prosperous civic and urban culture, more ominous events in France began to shape Böhl's life, leaving an indelible mark on his own ideological development. He spent the years of revolution and terror in Spain and subsequently many of his travels through Europe were undertaken against a background of war as Napoleon took hold of much of the Continent. Following Napoleon's demise, the Böhl family firm fell into ruin along with many others as the Congress of Vienna set about planning a new political landscape in 1815. Having eventually settled with his family in Spain in 1813, Böhl found the political climate there no less disrupted. The restoration of the monarchy in 1814 saw the intensification of a struggle between Liberals and conservative Monarchists which would characterise the remainder of the century in Spain. Böhl, by now defending an absolutist stance, watched the Liberal return to power in 1820 with dismay and welcomed the return of Fernando VII in 1823 with open approval, continuing to support the regime throughout the repressive years of the Ominous Decade (1823–33). Böhl's death in 1836 spared him the worst excesses of the Carlist Wars and the political chaos which dogged Spain for well over a century to come. The staunchly conservative political stance which Böhl came to adopt in the second half of his life emerges as a response to these events. His views are typical of the conservative reaction to Enlightenment political thought and the Liberalism which it fostered. For Böhl, the stance adopted was a defensive one aimed at ensuring the survival of a way of life which he felt had been betrayed by the failed promises of revolution and reason. As the situation worsened, Böhl found himself drawn ever closer to an arch-conservative, Catholic world view which was the very antithesis of his upbringing. His responses to the aftermath of 1789 and the economic and political instability wrought by the Napoleonic Wars were highly personal and manifested themselves in an existential abhorrence of Enlightened thought, the very foundation of his education under Campe. Consequently, in Böhl's writing, reason and Enlightenment come to represent the very opposite of their accepted meaning, heralding chaos and undermining age old social values.

It is this political stance which underpins Böhl's scholarship as his world view changes. In this respect, the aesthetic and the political are inextricably intertwined as Böhl's defensive stance extends to the salvation of a literary past which is representative of a lost golden age. His approach can be located amongst the more extreme responses to rapid change outlined by Virgil Nemoianou in his recent study, *The Triumph of Imperfection. The Silver Age of Sociocultural Moderation in Europe, (1815–1848)* (2006), in which he describes how '[p]hilosophers and poets, political leaders, and fairly large and diverse strata of the population responded with sullen or brutal enmity to all that was happening and tried more than once to stop and reverse the trends of history'.[5] One side effect of the social and ideological dislocation which this suggests was the tendency towards sacrality in a rejection of what Nemoianou refers to as 'rationalist structures of religion' and the recourse to 'oppositional modes of religiosity', a move which was paralleled by the creation of 'supplementary or adversarial canons that faced the classical and neo-classical traditions' (241). Both are evident on Böhl's development as he absorbs the conservative spirit of the age, described by Nemoianou in its European breadth:

> While there are sometimes hesitations as to the centrifugal lines fleeing from romanticism towards the world of left-wing ideas, it is rarely denied that a whole range of conservative views (whether moderately reformist or hard-line right wing) sprang from the same romanticism. [. . .] Indeed romantic writers [. . .] tended to seek a return to the origins, to primal, happier state of affairs. This search could lead to a

more or less imaginary past (as in Arnim's *Kronenwächter* for instance), but it could more specifically zoom in on the Middle Ages not as a kind of vernacular but as an actual model to be reconstructed in the contemporary world. Thus romanticism could become open reaction. Joseph de Maistre's acid and pitiless proclamations come to mind. Adam Müller developed an aesthetic politics that strayed far from its purported Burkean roots. Friedrich Schlegel, Coleridge, Wordsworth, and Southey were disliked for their later views, but these views were deeper and more eloquent than their shallow enthusiasms as young people. Chateaubriand was perhaps more constant in his inconsistency throughout his life, but on the whole what his contemporaries decided to choose and maintain out of his writings was stark conservatism. Perhaps the same can be said about Schelling. (247)

Nemoianou's assessment of this European trend might just as easily describe Böhl's own intellectual development. The writers and thinkers mentioned are those with whom Böhl engaged time and time again, from early adulthood to the final years in El Puerto de Santa María. Apparent here too is the transcultural nature of the contemporary dialogue, one within which Böhl is fully integrated, remarkably, however, in the context of two cultures simultaneously.

The literary historical context of Böhl's scholarship underlines the uniqueness of his position. Unusually, he can be located quite firmly within the Hispanist and philological traditions of both Germany and Spain. Central to this is his interest in Spain's literary heritage, which, like that of many other thinkers of the period, emerged in response to what was regarded as the dogma of Enlightenment aesthetics. During the early part of the eighteenth century, sixteenth and seventeenth-century theatre – Spain's Golden Age – was universally condemned as unrefined and reactionary, a by-word for poor taste and excess. Once the pinnacle of Baroque culture, Calderón, Cervantes and Lope de Vega were cast aside by the eighteenth-century literary elite in favour of Molière, Racine and Voltaire as Enlightenment values, Aristotelian principles and humanist rationality gathered sway. The influence of a French Bourbon monarchy in Madrid meant that, even in Spain itself, the work of the nation's once feted dramatists was maligned and neglected. The critical tone emerging from Paris was one of derision. Montesquieu's *Lettres Persannes* (Persian letters, 1721) were typical, mocking Spain's culture as backward and famously claiming with reference to *Don Quijote* that '[l]e seul de leurs livres qui soit bon est celui qui a fait voir le ridicule de tous les autres' (the only book of theirs which is good makes clear how ridiculous all the others are).[6] Contemporary critical opinion in Spain tended to echo that from beyond the Pyrenees and was expressed most forcefully by the prominent neo-Classicist, Ignacio de Luzán (1702–54) in his hugely influential *Poética* of 1737 which defended Classical notions of relevance and utility.[7] Further unequivocal criticism came from the pen of Blas Antonio Nasarre (1689–1751) in the prologue to his 1749 edition of Cervantes' *Ocho comedias y ocho entremeses*, where he claimed that Lope and Calderón were no less than arch corruptors of the Spanish stage.⁸ In addition to such aesthetic criticism, the Golden Age was also attacked for presenting Spain in an unfavourable light. The eminent Liberal thinker José Clavijo y Fajardo (1730–1806) saw the resultant image of Spain as one of 'una nación intratable' (an impossible nation) where 'en cada esquina piensan se encuentra un asesino armado de rejones y puñales' (at every corner they think one will meet a murderer armed with lances and daggers).⁹

The negative view of Spain's Golden Age was not confined to France and its satellite court in Madrid. In the German-speaking lands, once enthusiastic in their support of Spanish theatre during the Baroque period, the theatrical reforms introduced by Johann Christoph Gottsched (1700–66), who advocated the adaptation of the German stage to the principles of French neo-Classical taste, had been devastating for all forms of popular theatre and led to a shift in the perception of Spanish culture. No longer considered the domain of conquering heroes and chivalric quests, Spain was now thought of in terms of the 'Black Legend', harking back to the age of Felipe II and portraying the nation as one perpetually riven with intrigue and intolerance, the negative character traits central to works such as Schiller's *Don Carlos* (1787) and Goethe's *Egmont* (1788).¹⁰ Indeed, given the supposed predominance of such irrational extremes, it is not hard to see why the negative image of Spain should prove so rich a source for writers of the *Sturm und Drang* in their reaction to the constraints of Classicism. Yet, somewhat perversely, the negative image acquired by Spain was the very thing which made it so attractive to audiences who still had a taste for the high colour and complexity of the Baroque age, whatever the literary elite might wish to impose upon them. Consequently, as Sullivan has shown, the advocates of neo-Classicism could do little to dampen the wide popular appeal of Golden Age theatre itself, in particular that of Calderón.¹¹ The public still clamoured for the drama and excitement of his works, which provided a contrast to the often bland characterisation and forced unity of the neo-Classical stage.

Using this continued popular appeal to bolster their argument, other thinkers in Germany and Spain began to voice a defence of the Golden Age as part of an emerging counter-trend which fostered an appreciation of individual national literatures as an alternative to neo-Classicism. In Germany, the revival of interest in Spanish culture was closely linked to the wider rejection of Gottsched's prescriptive reforms. As the eighteenth century progressed, other views began to make themselves heard, including those of Swiss literary critics Johann Jakob Bodmer (1698–1783) and Johann Jakob Breitinger (1701–76) who, influenced by Addison, advocated cultural pluralism and began to demand a less restrictive approach to literary appraisal. The ideas of the Zürich school were reflected in the work of a number of German thinkers, in particular Gotthold Ephraim Lessing (1729–81) whose positive appraisal of Spanish Golden Age literature is voiced in his influential *Hamburgische Dramaturgie* (Hamburg dramaturgy, 1767–8). Lessing's views did much to shape the new appreciation of Spanish culture in Germany and his influence is particularly notable in the work of Johann Gottfried Herder (1744–1803) who studied Spain's literature in the context of other national literatures, drawing on works such as James Macpherson's *Ossian* (1760) and Bishop Percy's *Reliques of Ancient English Poetry* (1768). Herder was enchanted by *Don Quijote* and included translations of Góngora in his *Stimmen der Völker in Liedern* (Voices of the peoples in song, 1778–9). Spain's culture provided Herder with a rich source of material for his study of folk literature which is evident in his familiarity with the *Cancioneros* and his study of the influence of Moorish culture in his so-called *Araberthese* (Arab theory).[12] The Herderian appreciation of Spanish culture was significant in opening up a range of material to German scholars unfamiliar with the breadth and variety of Spain's literary heritage. Another follower of Lessing, Johann Andreas Dieze (1729–85), also furthered Hispanist interests with his translation of Luis Joseph Velázquez's *Orígenes de la poesía castellana* (Origins of Castilian poetry, 1754) in 1769.[13] The text, published in Göttingen, was hugely influential as the only German language study of Spanish literature available at the time. It was not until 1804 that it was superseded by Bouterwek's study of Spanish literature which formed part of his ambitious *Geschichte der Poesie und Beredsamkeit seit dem Ende des dreizehnten Jahrhunderts* (1801–19) and was published in the same town.

Such publishing milestones underline the central role of Göttingen to German Hispanism at this time.[14] Under the tutelage of eminent scholars including Bouterwek, Thomas Christian Tychsen (1758–1834) and the poet Gottfried August Bürger (1747–94), students such as the Brothers Grimm, Tieck and the Schlegels studied Spanish language and literature to an advanced level. It is perhaps no coincidence, given the integral role of Spanish Golden Age literature in the development of the Romantic aesthetic, that this group of students in Göttingen should form the core of the German Romantic movement itself. Indeed, it was with the emergence of Romanticism in Germany that the Hispanist trend reached its peak and Spain's Golden Age truly experienced a revival. Almost every key figure of the Romantic age engaged on some level with the literature of Spain, including Tieck, who published a seminal translation of *Don Quijote* (1799–1801), E. T. A. Hoffmann, who staged Calderón at Bamberg, and Jacob Grimm, who published an anthology in Spanish entitled *Silva de romances viejos* (Collection of ancient romances) in Vienna in 1815. Providing this surge of activity with a theoretical foundation were perhaps the most vigorous apologists of Spain's culture at this time: August Wilhelm (1767–1845) and Friedrich Schlegel (1772–1829). Friedrich's *Geschichte der europäischen Literatur* (History of European literature, 1803–4) and, in particular, August's *Wiener Vorlesungen* (Vienna lectures, 1808, published 1809–11) were seminal in the formulation of a new critical approach to Spanish literary culture which lay at the heart of the new aesthetic. Prompted by Tieck, the Schlegels were first drawn to the work of Cervantes and his epic chivalric novel *Don Quijote*. They saw the text as the epitome of Romantic literature, unfettered by literary rules and merging diverse genres. It was August Wilhelm, however, who was most influential in bringing the theatre of the age to the attention of a new audience. He was widely read in the field of older Spanish literature and published a number of related pieces, including a two-volume selection of Calderón's plays with the title *Spanisches Theater* (Spanish theatre, 1803–9).[15] In terms of drawing attention to Golden Age theatre, however, it is perhaps Schlegel's theoretical writings which are most significant. His seminal piece is undoubtedly the essay 'Über das spanische Theater' which appeared in his brother's periodical, *Europa*, in 1803 and was then delivered in revised form in his *Wiener Vorlesungen*. This was a significant moment in the reception of Spanish literature in Germany and Europe as a whole. As Sullivan observes, Calderón and Spain's once maligned Golden Age now had the weight of intellectual opinion in Germany on their side. Building on the views of Lessing and Herder, Schlegel's translations and the publication of the *Wiener Vorlesungen* in 1809 combined with the support of Goethe fostered a growing interest in the literature of the period with the publication of numerous translations of Calderón, Cervantes and Lope de Vega, as well as *romances* and works by less well-known authors. Critical and philological interest was also on the increase. Georg Bernhard Depping (1784–1853) followed Jacob Grimm's *Silva* with his *Sammlung der besten alten spanischen historischen Ritter- und Maurischen Romanzen* (Collection of the finest ancient Spanish historical chivalric and Moorish ballads) in 1817 with further collections by a number of scholars appearing at regular intervals throughout the period, including the immensely popular *Altspanische Romanzen* (Ancient Spanish ballads, 1821) translated by Friedrich Diez (1794–1876). Böhl forms part of this group, responding to the late eighteenth-century and subsequent Romantic apotheosis of Spain's literary heritage. Through his scholarship, he became an acknowledged expert on Spanish culture with a respected place in the emerging genealogy of German Romantic philology.

What marks Böhl out in the context of German Hispanism at this time, however, is the fact that, through his work, he reversed the flow of ideas, taking both the Schlegelian apotheosis of the Spanish stage and the methodology of German Romantic philology and redirecting them at Spain itself. Initially, he struggled to find a point of reference for the new aesthetic in a culture still guided by neo-Classical principles. However, as his knowledge of the literary debate in Spain deepened, he was able to cite in his favour a modest, but nevertheless persistent, eighteenth-century campaign in support of Golden Age literature. The indigenous change in attitudes towards Spain's literary heritage was, however, confined to the margins. José Carrillo took Nasarre directly to task in his *La sinrazón impugnada y beata de Lavapiés* (The refuted and hypocritical injustice of Lavapies, 1750) and, in the same year, the pseudonymous Tomás de Erauso y Zavaleta launched a defence of literary freedom in his *Discurso crítico* (Critical discourse). Further claims for the validity of the national theatre came from Juan Cristóbal Romea y Tapia (1732–66) who published a series of eleven discourses defending national theatre in 1763. He emphasised the consideration of national individuality in establishing literary principles as the best means to secure the appreciation of the audience, itself representative of that nation and its character. Romea y Tapia was joined in the same year by the journalist, Francisco Mariano Nipho (1719–1803), who, whilst a staunch advocate of technical advance, nevertheless extolled the virtues of a national literary tradition, praising the work of Calderón in particular. The correlation between this home-grown defence of Spain's literary heritage with the Schlegelian apotheosis of Calderón communicated with such vigour by Böhl is clear. His introduction of the new aesthetic in 1814 and his ongoing defence of older Spanish literature drew him into the debate in Spain at a crucial juncture, just as the modest questioning of neo-Classical values collided with the political fallout from the Napoleonic Wars, an event which placed in doubt the role of France as an aesthetic and ideological model. Through his scholarship, Böhl helped lay the foundations of what Philip Silver, in his 1997 study *Ruin and Restitution. Reinterpreting Romanticism in Spain*, has termed a historical Romanticism in Spain. Silver's revisionist reading, partly derived from the argument put forward by Hans Juretschke, redefines Spanish Romanticism as one driven by conservative ideals. This is a view, however, which itself requires some reconsideration. Whilst agreeing with the need to acknowledge this aspect of Romanticism in Spain, one which is linked inextricably to Böhl's own contribution, it is impossible to ignore the significance of Liberal thought so carefully outlined by other critics, including Navas-Ruiz, Vicente Llorens and, most recently, Andrew Ginger in his *Political Revolution and Literary Experiment in the Spanish Romantic Period (1830–1850)* (1999). Reflecting the broader political debate, it is possible, I would argue, to see both Liberal and conservative engagement with the new aesthetic as thinkers of either persuasion respond to a changing world once forced to question the values of the past. Convinced, therefore, of the dual nature of Romanticism in Spain, both ideologically and aesthetically, it seems more appropriate to adopt the stance defended recently by Donald Shaw:

> It is not only a case of tracing a gradual evolution from one world view to another, or from neo-Classical forms and diction to more specifically Romantic ones. It is also a case of recognising that some of the Romantics chose to clothe their Romanticism in

a traditional garb, while others preferred to flaunt the novelty of their innovations. Both groups were Romantic.[16]

The choices made reflect the concerns and political leanings of those engaged in the debate: the ideal at the heart of the matter is the revival of Spanish culture and the revaluation of a national heritage as a foundation for progress and stability. The more traditional strain alluded to by Shaw owes a great deal to Böhl whose introduction of ideas grounded in Herderian-based Romantic historicism provided a new perspective on Spain's literary past. This perspective, which, as Flitter has argued, underpins Böhl's own critical agenda, later informs the development of a historical Romanticism through the mid-century, not least in the work of Böhl's daughter, Fernán Caballero.

Böhl can, then, be located within the aesthetic debate in both cultures as an active participant and a link between the two at a time when both nations were beginning to turn away from France as the dominant force towards other models. Böhl fully understood this dialectic and was an active apologist of both German and Spanish culture as a means of national self-definition, seeking to encourage recognition of Spain's heritage in Spain itself by presenting the German Romantic revival of both German and Spanish national literatures as an alternative paradigm. In so doing, he would contribute to a change of attitude to Spanish letters in Spain which paralleled the revaluation already completed in Germany, whilst simultaneously enriching the debate in his native culture through the dissemination of previously unknown material.

The validity of Böhl's contribution duly noted, a survey of scholarship to date presents the reader with the odd situation of a figure whose significance is widely acknowledged, but of whom relatively little is known or, perhaps more accurately, a great deal has been forgotten. Successive critics have called for a comprehensive study of Böhl's life and work, but this has not been forthcoming until the current work. However, there have been a number of studies which focus extensively, if not exclusively, on Böhl and his scholarship. Interest has been consistent since the mid-nineteenth century, but the coverage is fragmented. The first accounts came from within Böhl's own circle with two biographies appearing in the 1850s, the first by his great friend and correspondent, Nikolas Heinrich Julius, who appended an essay on Böhl to his 1852 translation of George Ticknor's *History of Literature in Spain* (1849). Julius' analysis of Böhl's scholarly activities is quoted at length in the far more influential work of another friend, Elise Campe, who published her *Johann Nikolas Böhl von Faber: Versuch einer Lebensskizze nach seinen eigenen Briefen* in 1858. The text has become the central source of information pertaining to Böhl, providing much of the material contained in subsequent studies, her narrative filtering into Hispanist criticism via Camille Pitollet's extensive, but often impenetrable, study, *La querelle caldéronienne de Johan Nikolas Böhl von Faber et José Joaquín de Mora reconstituée d'aprés les documents originaux* (1909). This is problematic as Campe's account lacks any degree of critical distance, contains a number of factual errors and distorts archival material. She also focuses on Böhl's early life and career to the detriment of a more balanced investigation. This selectivity is not uncommon. With the exception of Johann Dornhof's brief study, *Johann Nikolas Böhl von Faber: ein Vorkämpfer der Romantik in Spanien* (1925), which, despite its brevity, can at least boast coverage of all aspects of Böhl's career and a sensitive appraisal of the early years, even those with a particular interest in his work often approach that work from a secondary angle. Typical are Javier Herrero, *Fernán Caballero: un nuevo planteamiento* (1963) and Santiago Montoto, *Fernán Caballero, algo más que una biografía* (1969), who, as their titles suggest, discuss his life and work in relation to that of his daughter, basing much of what they say about Böhl on Campe via Pitollet. Pitollet himself covers a vast range of material, building a picture of Böhl's life through his correspondence. His examination of archival and rare published material provides an invaluable resource, as does the overview he provides of the critical reception of Böhl during his own lifetime. However, as the title of his 1909 study suggests, Pitollet's ultimate focus is on the Calderón polemic and he makes no reference to Böhl's later career as a philologist. A broader range of material is covered by the eminent German Hispanist, Hans Juretschke, who examines Böhl's work in a number of studies. Particularly salient is the article 'Die Deutung und Darstellung der deutschen Romantik durch Böhl in Spanien' (1956), which presents an overview of Böhl's life and work and is intended to promote further investigation of a figure who, Juretschke feels, has been underestimated in both a Germanist and Hispanist context. Juretschke's work benefits from his grounding as a scholar of German letters, but examines Böhl's work in a fragmentary fashion within the context of a broader mission to outline the interrelation of German and Spanish culture during the nineteenth century. Guillermo Carnero's 1978 study, *Los orígenes del romanticismo reaccionario español: el matrimonio Böhl de Faber*, is the latest to tackle the archival material in any depth. Much of the material relevant to Böhl is held by the Osborne family in El Puerto de Santa María and they have not regularly opened their archive to researchers since the late 1970s. Like Pitollet, Carnero provides invaluable, previously unpublished material, as well as a detailed listing of the material held in the Osborne archive and a chronology of the documents pertaining to the Calderón polemic. His discussion of Böhl considers his life and work in its entirety, but the detail is limited with an emphasis on proving Böhl's reactionary stance.[17] A more sympathetic appraisal is presented by María Guadalupe Reyes Ponce in her 1989 doctoral thesis, 'Spanish and German Antecedents to Agustín Durán's *Colección de romances castellanos anteriores al siglo XVIII* (1828–32)', which offers a pertinent discussion of the polemic, but centres primarily on Böhl's influence as a philologist. She provides a detailed account of his efforts in securing the revival of the *romance* in the 1820s, but makes little reference to Böhl's early development or political motivations. Reyes Ponce's work benefits from an understanding of Böhl in a mediatory role, a view which echoes that espoused by Juretschke some years earlier, and, as she points out, has been more readily acknowledged, albeit in passing, by German Hispanists such as Tiemann, Pabst and Brüggemann (A:144). The most recent study to deal with Böhl in any depth is Flitter's *Spanish Romantic literary theory and criticism* (1992), which focuses on his work in the context of emerging Romantic theory in Spain and presents a convincing argument for his continued influence throughout the nineteenth century. Flitter's work has been central to a clearer understanding of Böhl's contribution of Spanish culture, although some critics have been reluctant to acknowledge the extent of the conservative strain of Romanticism which he has identified. Whilst the arguments presented are convincing in the context of Böhl's contribution, again the focus is on one aspect of his career with minimal discussion of the early years.

Whilst each of these approaches is perfectly valid, they fail to provide a comprehensive analysis of Böhl's intellectual, personal and political development from his youth to maturity. Yet, without such an analysis, his contribution to Spain's cultural framework is in danger of misinterpretation. This has often been the case in more general studies of Spanish Romanticism where there is a tendency to take Böhl's arrival in Spain in 1813 as a point of departure, completely ignoring the fact that following his conversion to Catholicism and permanent move to Spain, Böhl remained a German, deeply influenced by his native culture and the experiences of his compatriots. The most recent study of Spanish Romanticism, Michael Iarocci's *Properties of Modernity. Romantic Spain, Modern Europe, and the Legacies of Empire* (2006), is typical in its treatment of Böhl, introducing him as '[a] reactionary German immigrant who was familiar with the writings of the Schlegel brothers'.[18] None of this is untrue. By the time he was forty, in 1810, Böhl did defend a reactionary political stance. He did emigrate to Spain and he was familiar with work of the Schlegel brothers. What Iarocci fails to ask is how Böhl arrived at this point. Admittedly, it does not fall within the remit of his study to do so, but the fact that he takes these characteristics for granted is typical of the majority of critics of the period, including major commentators such as Tubino and Menéndez y Pelayo in the nineteenth century and, more recently, Alborg, Navas-Ruiz, Kirkpatrick and Silver. Böhl's origin as a German is referred to in passing and then forgotten. He appears instead in the Spanish cultural landscape as if from another world, bringing with him an aesthetic ideal – that of German Romanticism – which is interpreted as a political statement, a reactionary tool to be raised in anger against the *afrancesado* Liberal cause. This contribution to the debate duly noted, Böhl is then at best ignored as attention refocuses on Schlegel or, in the worst cases, categorised or even simply dismissed as a Fernandine reactionary.

What fails to emerge from such cursory treatment is the complexity of Böhl's world view and the torturous path which led him there. If German Romanticism was, as Dennis F. Mahoney suggests, 'a manifestation of the seismic shocks striking at a civilisation on the fracture line between tradition and modernity',[19] then surely the impact of those shocks on this herald of the new aesthetic must be understood in order to comprehend the impulses which drove him to disseminate the material in the first place. Had his life experiences been different, would his presentation of Schlegel and subsequent defence of Spanish culture have been different too? The answer is almost undoubtedly affirmative. In the context of Böhl scholarship, then, the current work is in many ways a retrospective. As stated, arguments for Böhl's influence have been well made by Pitollet, Juretschke, Carnero, Reyes Ponce and, in particular, Flitter. What is lacking is a fundamental understanding of his development as an individual and the thoroughly transcultural nature of his scholarship. This requires a detailed analysis of the complex set of circumstances, both personal and historical, which led this figure to develop a conservative Romantic world view and in so doing engage fully in the interdisciplinary dialogue of the age, choosing his native Germany and adopted homeland Spain as the axis, an act which places Böhl at the heart of the Romantic aesthetic revolution.

NOTES

[1] The following information is based on that provided by E. L. Meyer and O. L. Tesdorpf, *Hamburgische Wappen und Genealogien* (Hamburg: Im Selbstverlag der Verfasser, 1890). According to Meyer and Tesdorpf, the Böhl family hailed from Stralsund on the Baltic coast. Böhl's grandfather, Johann Jacob Böhl, was originally known by the surname Wohlgast and was born c.1690. He and his wife Gertrud had four sons who went on to establish a trading house in Hamburg in the mid-eighteenth century and the Böhl family soon numbered among the elite group of successful families who dominated the commercial life of the city. The most successful member of the family was the eldest of the four sons, Johann Jacob Böhl (1727–86). His ambition led to the founding of a further trading house in the cosmopolitan Andalucian city of Cadiz, then the preferred Spanish base for foreign trade with the Americas following the easing of the Sevillian monopoly in 1679. The expansion into Spain established the Böhl enterprise as one of the major European trading houses, alongside Hoppe of Amsterdam and Baring of London. In 1769, Johann Jacob married Cecilia Isabel, the daughter of Hamburg senator Nicolaus Gottlieb Lütkens, and the couple had seven children. Johann Nikolas, the eldest, was born on 10 December 1770 and baptised on 13 December in the Katharinen-Kirche in the heart of Hamburg's mercantile quarter. There followed Anton Gottlieb (1772–1800), Johann Friedrich (1773–1844), Peter (1777–92), Cecilia (1778–1852), Carl Wilhelm (1779–1800) and Ferdinand (1780–7). All scholars of Böhl's life and work have cited this record as their source of information about Böhl's family. It is therefore inexplicable that all erroneously claim that Böhl was one of either four or five children. Not a great deal is known of the life of these siblings, apart from Anton Gottlieb who married Sophie Therese, daughter of Hamburg senator Johann

Valentin Meyer, in 1797. Both he and Carl Wilhelm fell victim to the outbreak of yellow fever in Cadiz in 1800. Johann Friedrich, known as Fritz, was elevated into the nobility in 1818, carrying the name von Böhl, and spent most of his days managing his estate at Cramonshagen in Mecklenburg. Both Peter and Ferdinand died at a young age. Cecilia married the son of an established Hamburg family, Bernhard Philip Berckemeyer, who also turned to farming at Thürow near Schwerin. She outlived all six of her brothers.

2   Quoted in Richard Littlejohns, 'Early Romanticism' in Dennis F. Mahoney (ed.), *The Literature of German Romanticism*, The Camden House History of German Literature 8 (Rochester NY: Camden House, 2004), pp. 61–77 (p. 61).

3   This theme is explored in detail in Theodore Ziolkowski, *German Romanticism and its institutions* (Princeton: Princeton University Press, 1990).

4   Gustav Siebenmann, 'Johann Nikolaus Böhl von Faber (1770–1836): Ein deutscher Wahlspanier zwischen Selbst und Entfremdung', in Thomas Bremer and Jochen Heymann (eds.), *Sehnsuchtsorte. Festschrift zum 60. Geburtstag von Titus Heydenreich* (Tübingen: Stauffenberg, 1999), pp. 119–34 (p. 125). Despite the promising title, Siebenmann's essay lacks depth and contains a number of factual errors.

5   Virgil Nemoianou, *The Triumph of Imperfection. The Silver Age of Sociocultural Moderation in Europe, 1815–1848* (Columbia: University of South Carolina Press, 2006), p. 233. Further references appear in the text.

6   Charles de Secondat, Baron de Montesquieu, *Lettres persannes*, 2 vols (Paris: Bure, 1824); II: Lettre LXXIII, 237.

7   Ignacio Luzán, *La Poetica, ò reglas de la poesía en general, y de sus principales especies* (Zaragoza: Francisco Revilla, 1737); 'Libro segundo de la utilidad, y del Deleite en la Poesía', p. 110.

8   Blas Antonio Nasarre (ed.), *Comedias y entremeses de Miguel de Cervantes Saavedra, el autor de Don Quijote, divididas en dos tomos con una disertacion, o prologo sobre las Comedias de España*, 2 vols (Madrid: Antonio Marin, 1749).

9   José Clavijo y Fajardo, 'Pensamiento LXV', *El pensador*, 1762.

10 See B. Becker-Cantarino, 'Die "Schwarze Legende". Zum Spanienbild in der deutschen Literatur des 18. Jahrhunderts', *ZfdP*, 94 (1975), 183–203.

11 Henry W. Sullivan, *Calderón in the German lands and the Low Countries: his reception and influence, 1654–1980* (Cambridge: Cambridge University Press, 1983), Chap. 5.

12 See Wolfgang Kayser, *Die iberische Welt im Denken J. G. Herders* (Hamburg: Ibero-Amerikanisches Institut, 1945); Reyes Ponce (A: Chap. 1).

13 Luis Joseph Velázquez, *Geschichte der Spanischen Dichtkunst. Aus dem Spanischen übersetzt und mit Anmerkungen von Johann Andreas Dieze* (Göttingen: Victorianus Bassiegel, 1769).

14 The other main centres for the study of Spanish language and literature were Hamburg and Weimar.

15 A. W. Schlegel, *Spanisches Theater*, 2 vols (Berlin: Julius Eduard Hitzig, 1803–9). He also attempted translations of poetry and published a collection of works by Italian, Spanish and Portuguese poets in 1804 entitled *Blumensträusse* (Bouquets of flowers).

16 Donald L. Shaw, 'Time and History in Spanish Romantic Poetry' in *Romantic Poetry*, Angela Esterhammer (ed.) (Amsterdam/Philadelphia: John Benjamins, 2002), pp. 287–303 (p. 301).

17 Carnero revisits his argument in subsequent articles including 'El teatro de Calderón como arma ideológico en el origin gaditano del romanticismo español', *Cuadernos de Teatro Clásico*, 5 (1990), 125–39

18 Michael Iarocci, *Properties of Modernity. Romantic Spain, Modern Europe, and the Legacies of Empire* (Nashville, Tenn.; Vanderbilt, 2006), p. 22.

19 Dennis F. Mahoney (ed.), *The Literature of German Romanticism*, 'Introduction', pp. 1–24 (p. 7).

PART ONE

*From Campe to Calderón:
Böhl's Early Intellectual Development*

Chapter 1
Campe, Faith and Reason

The privileged position of the Böhl family amongst the merchant bourgeoisie meant that Johann Nikolas and his two oldest brothers, Anton Gottlieb and Friedrich (Fritz), enjoyed a high standard of education from an early age. Their father, Johann Böhl, took an enthusiastic interest in his children's progress and was well informed on the latest pedagogical developments. Keen to ensure the best for his sons, Böhl senior joined forces with two fellow enthusiasts, the merchant Johannes Schuback and the publisher August Polycarp Leisching, to secure the services of the renowned pedagogue and philologist, Joachim Heinrich Campe (1746–1818), who had made his name as a teacher at the *Philanthropin* at Dessau.[1] For reasons which were never fully explained, Campe suddenly left Dessau in 1777 and made for Hamburg, a flourishing city republic which held many attractions for a disciple of Enlightenment thought.[2] There, he took up the position as tutor to a small group of boys comprising Nicolas Schuback, Dietrich Leisching, and Johann Nikolas, Gottlieb and Fritz Böhl.[3] The boys, of whom Johann Nikolas was the eldest, were sent to board with Campe at Billwerder on the outskirts of Hamburg, in a property which had been leased for the purpose by Böhl's father. This arrangement meant that, as a child, Böhl was effectively blessed with two sets of parents: his natural parents, Johann and Cecilia, and his *Pflegeeltern* (foster parents), Campe and his wife, Dorothea. Both couples played a key role in shaping his attitudes and beliefs, but it is the influence of Campe and his wife which lies at the heart of Böhl's early intellectual and personal development, stretching far beyond the formative years. This imbalance can be explained by a dramatic change in family circumstances during Böhl's adolescent years. Johann Böhl's death in 1786 at the age of fifty-eight, when Böhl was fifteen years old, was followed a year later by Cecilia's decision to marry the Protestant canon and Prussian privy councillor, Martin Jakob Ritter und Elder von Faber (1752–1827), a man several years her junior. The absence of a father and somewhat strained relations with his mother following her plans to remarry meant Böhl's relationship with the Campes gained an importance which was in many ways disproportionate to the limited time he actually spent in their care. Both during and after the Billwerder days, he referred to them simply as *Vater* and *Mutter* and turned to them for support until he left Hamburg for Spain for the last time in 1813 at the age of forty-two. Although he had by then moved away from the values of his youth, the role played by the Campes in educating and encouraging the young Böhl cannot be underestimated and provided a solid intellectual and moral grounding upon which he was able to build, albeit eventually taking a direction of which Campe himself would never have approved.

In keeping with the ethos of the Philanthropist movement, the boys' education under Campe followed the ideals of Rousseau, with an emphasis on intellectual freedom and physical activity. Rousseau's social vision, developed from Hobbes and Locke and elaborated in *Du Contrat Social* (1762), was underpinned by a set of pedagogical values which the Genevan thinker described in his educational novel *Émile, ou de l'Éducation* (Emile, or on education) published in the same year. Rejecting more traditional, classroom-based methods, Rousseau valued practical learning over that centred around books. Indeed, he claimed to hate them, declaring that 'ils n'apprennent qu'à parler de ce qu'on ne sait pas' (they only teach people to talk about things which they do not understand).[4] Only once a child had reached adolescence should they be encouraged to read as by then they would have amassed enough experience and understanding to evaluate texts with a critical eye. Until then, their education should be empirical with a focus on lived experience. However, this rejection of the written word as a means to educate the very young allowed one exception, Daniel Defoe's *Robinson Crusoe* (1719), which, Rousseau suggested, offered an object lesson in experiential learning as the protagonist is forced to depend on his own observations and newly learned skills in order to survive. Rousseau's appreciation of Defoe's work is significant in the context of Campe's teaching in providing the inspiration for one of his own major educational treatises, *Robinson der Jüngere* (The new Robinson, 1779), written whilst at Billwerder. The work, one of a flood of Robinson-related texts in the eighteenth century following the success of Defoe's novel, maintains the basic desert island theme of the original and depicts the possibilities open to the individual to acquire an understanding of social values through the experience of isolation and the subsequent creation of a new society. The moral of the tale is made explicit through a guided interpretation which encourages autonomous learning according to Rousseau's ideal. Publication of the text was intended to bring these educational principles to a wider public otherwise unable to afford to educate their children in this way. It also provided parents with a suitable book to give to children for, in Campe's opinion, many other texts lacked any pedagogical foundation and were likely to lead the young astray.[5]

Robinson der Jüngere was particularly significant for Johann Nikolas. Not only was the text central to his education, but in it Böhl, aged only nine, also made his first appearance in a literary context. Campe based his main characters, the children Johannes and Gotlieb, on Johann Nikolas and his younger brother.[6] The prominent role occupied by the fictional Johannes in the popular book placed the young Böhl unexpectedly in the limelight and the enduring popularity of the character amongst Campe's young readers meant that as late as 1812, when Böhl visited a Madame Pauli in Bückeberg, the unsuspecting lady's house was surrounded by schoolchildren eager to see the 'real Johannes'.[7] Campe's depiction is coloured by the impression the Böhl boys made on their mentor; their eagerness to learn and their intellectual promise enrich the text. The fictional Johannes is lively and sensitive, receptive to the Rousseauian ideal, but also precocious. He writes to the imaginary castaway:

Hochedelgeborner Robinson,

Ich bedaure dich sehr, daß du so ganz von allen lebendigen Geschöpfen abgesondert bist. Ich glaube wol, daß du es jezt selbst bereuen werdest. Lebe wohl! Ich wünsche von ganzem Herzen, daß du einmahl wieder zu deinen lieben Aeltern kommen mögest. Vertrau künftig ja immer Gott; der wird schon für dich sorgen. Nochmahls: lebe wohl! Ich bin Dein getreuer Freund Johannes.

Hamburg, d. 7ten Febr. 1779.[8]

(Most noble Robinson,

I feel very sorry that you find yourself so isolated from all other living creatures. I do believe that you regret it yourself by now. Farewell! I hope from the bottom of my heart that you will one day be reunited with your dear parents. Always have faith in God, he will surely look after you. Once more: farewell! I am your true friend, Johannes.

Hamburg, 7 February 1779.)

Here is a child imbued with the exemplary values of his society: piety, reason and respect for the prevailing social order. The influence of Campe's teaching on the 'real Johannes' is equally marked and continued even after Böhl left his care in 1782, when Campe was forced to give up the running of his institute due to ill health. Upon his return from Billwerder, Böhl's education was placed in the more conventional hands of Lorenz Andreas Noodt (1743–1809),[9] after which he was sent to England in 1784 to spend a year in Andover at the institute run by Dr Tay. Böhl's journey to Andover via Amsterdam and his education in England are documented in a series of letters to Campe in the summer of 1784, in which the young traveller describes visits to Amsterdam and Utrecht and expresses his enthusiasm for English life. The fullness and eagerness of his reports to Campe are telling. Despite the respect shown to his natural father and the many new experiences and opportunities afforded by his generosity, it is Campe's influence and approval which are most important. This continued dependence on his mentor is further illustrated by a series of references to Campe's most recent pedagogical guide, published in 1783, which had been written during the final months at

Billwerder. The work, *Theophron oder der erfahrene Rathgeber für die unerfahrene Jugend* (Theophron, or the experienced advisor to the inexperienced youth), is intended for the benefit of his young charges as the subtitle makes clear: 'Ein Vermächtniß für seine gewesenen Pflegesöhne und für alle erwachsene junge Leute welche Gebrauch davon machen wollen' (A legacy for his former foster sons and for all young adults who wish to make use of it).[10] The text consists of three parts, each recounting the advice of a father to a son on the threshold of manhood. Campe explained in the foreword that he saw the work as one of his final duties to his pupils at Billwerder in which he sought to provide them with a guide for life, to carry with them after he had gone. The work contains an eight-page dedication in which Campe takes leave of his pupils and calls upon them to carry his teaching into adulthood. This was something which Böhl found impossible to do and it is pleas of this nature which perhaps help to explain the extent of Böhl's discomfort in later years as his views began to diverge from those of his mentor. As a young adolescent travelling through unfamiliar lands, however, Böhl was deeply affected by the text and assured Campe that he found advice and inspiration in its pages on a daily basis, taking comfort in the words as a surrogate for his absent mentor.

Towards the end of Böhl's time in England, plans were made for the next stage of his journey. Following in the footsteps of a number of family members, he was to make his way to the south of Spain. Böhl had intended to travel to Andalucia via Paris and Marseilles, thus providing an opportunity to improve his French further. However, the plan was placed in doubt by harsh weather at the beginning of 1785 and was eventually abandoned. After a short stay in London, Böhl sailed instead from Gravesend in the early summer that same year. At the age of fourteen, he took up his first post in his father's offices in Cadiz, where he would remain for three years. The experience was not a happy one and his letters to the Campe family describe the monotony of his daily routine:

Meine Lebensart ist hier sehr einförmig, und es hört Geduld und Vernunft dazu, sich darin zu schicken. Von des Morgens um 8 bis 1½ Uhr ist man auf dem Comptoir, dann wird gegeßen. Nach Tische schläft man, läßt sich frisieren (Sie werden wohl schon wissen, daß ich leider! gezwungen worden bin, es zu thun) und um 4 Uhr ist jeder wieder auf dem Comptoir. Um 6 Uhr geht man spazieren biß 8. Dann habe ich meinen Spanischen Sprachmeister, Klavier Meister etc: so daß ich wenig Zeit für mich selbst übrig habe. (2 August 1785)

(My life here is very monotonous and it requires patience and reason to resign oneself to it. One is at the office from 8 o'clock in the morning until half past two, then it is time to eat. After lunch, one sleeps, has one's hair done (you will be well aware that I had to be forced to do this) and then at 4 o'clock everyone is back at the office again. At 6 o'clock, one takes a stroll until eight. Then my Spanish master, piano teacher, etc. comes, so that I have little time left for myself.)

The ordered, indoor life must have come as something of an unpleasant surprise to this young product of Enlightenment pedagogy, used to fresh air and intellectual variety. Indeed, it is that very education which Böhl draws upon to deal with the new demands placed upon him, relying on reason as well as patience as he stoically follows his father's wishes. The security of this rational world view seemed unassailable, yet there was soon evidence of a change.

In 1788, at the age of eighteen, Böhl returned to Hamburg for the first time since his father's death in 1786.[11] He spent time with Campe in Braunschweig and felt immediately at ease in the familiar cultured atmosphere reminiscent of his Billwerder days. This made the inevitable return to Spain in 1789 all the more painful. Not only was he once more separated from his family and his beloved Campe, but the turbulent political situation, with an imminent break in Anglo–Spanish relations,[12] meant that trade was poor and there was little chance of a prompt return to Germany. Forced to stay in Cadiz, Böhl continued to feel uncomfortable in an essentially alien environment. The resultant melancholy suggests a growing self-awareness which foreshadows the deliberations of subsequent years and offers the first indication of the *Zerrissenheit* which would characterise Böhl's transition to maturity throughout the 1790s and early 1800s. Writing to Campe on 1 May 1790, he reveals the full extent of his unhappiness and confusion, aware of his responsibility towards his brothers and the family firm, but nevertheless conscious of a need for more intellectual depth in his life. Significant is a proto-Romantic longing for self-realisation which, judging by his defensive tone, Böhl clearly feels to be at odds with Campe's values. Whilst seeking to avoid accusations of idleness, he expresses the desire for a better life centred on 'Vergnügen und Verbesserung meines Ichs' (pleasure and self-improvement) and tries to reconcile the conflicting emotions which this desire provokes by placing his apparently self-seeking urges in the social context of Campe's teaching:

Ich mögte für mein Theil eine gänzlich von menschlicher Gesellschaft unabhängige Lebensart, mit Beruf od[er] Bestimungs Pflichten verbinden; allein mir däucht daß nur alsdann jemand solcher Ruhe zu genießen berechtigt ist, wenn er der menschlichen Gesellschaft lange genug seinen Kräften gemäß, gedient hat, und dieses, däucht mir, kann er nur thun wenn er einen Stand hat od[er] ein Amt bekleidet. – Helfen Sie mir hierin meine Gedancken berichtigen!

(I would, for my part, like to combine a way of life independent of human society with the duties of career and purpose; however, it seems to me that one is only entitled to enjoy such peace when one has served human society to the best of one's abilities for long enough and this, it seems to me, can only be done when one has followed a profession or held office. – Help me to order my thoughts on this matter!)

The Rousseauian ideal of social responsibility underpins Böhl's understanding of his role as a merchant and member of the bourgeois class.[13] Yet, this ideal is often at odds with his desire for personal fulfilment. It is perhaps in response to this struggle that Böhl seeks to place his studies in a practical context. His quest for knowledge and stimulation does not, he claims, stem from a desire for individual greatness. Instead, even at this young age, Böhl consciously limits himself to the role of mediator, styling himself as a scholar whose aim it was to understand and promote the work of those more gifted than himself. This self-effacing stance, given Böhl's undeniable talents and sensitivity, is perhaps evidence that he was never quite able to shake off the ideals of social purpose instilled in him as a young man. Indeed, his approach to learning is one derived from a work ethic which, for all its appreciation of the creative process, leaves Böhl little room to participate in that process itself:

> Nicht als wenn ich mich schmeichelte, mich als ein Gelehrter hervorzuthun, und die Wissenschaften mit neuen Entdeckungen bereichert zu haben, nein! – die schöpferischen Genies müssen gebohren werden! – meine Begierde diesen Punkt betrefend schränken sich nur auf das <u>verstehen</u> deßjenigen ein, was andere hervorgebracht haben und noch hervorbringen, und dieses würde mir doch wohl durch anhaltenden Fleiß gelungen seyn. (July 1790; to Dorothea Campe)
>
> (It is not as if I flatter myself that I could distinguish myself as a scholar and enrich the sciences with new discoveries, no! – creative geniuses must be born! My desires in this area limit themselves to understanding that which others have created and are still to create and I would only be able to achieve this through constant diligence.)

Such modest denials of talent notwithstanding, Böhl's leaning towards and, indeed, his ability to follow an academic path were apparent to all who knew him, not least Campe. In 1792, Böhl spent a year in Montpellier to take a cure for an eye complaint and it was here, with time for contemplation, that he gained his first real taste of the scholarly existence which would become his ultimate goal.[14] Lacking a university education – perhaps the one thing he held against his father's otherwise unquestioned judgement – Böhl was determined to pursue his studies upon his return to Spain. This desire was no doubt further fuelled by a need to escape the daily routine of the trading house and combat his dislike of a country in which he still felt culturally isolated, despite the regular shipments of books from Campe and other friends in Germany. It was in this atmosphere of perpetual *Zerrissenheit* – torn between mercantile duty and scholarly stimulation – that Böhl began to doubt the values of his youth.

Central to this process of revaluation was the issue of faith. Upon his departure for Spain in 1784, the young merchant was still very much determined by childhood influences. In terms of religious conviction, his understanding of faith was firmly grounded in the Protestantism espoused, traditionally, by his family and, more forcefully, by his mentor. Whilst the influence of Böhl's family was undoubtedly important, it was Campe who set the ideological and intellectual tone. The guidance offered by the pedagogue was aimed at ensuring his pupils found a faith grounded in reason, an ideal which did not preclude a certain degree of bias. As Leyser makes clear, despite his Rousseauian belief in freedom in learning, Campe's views on religious practice accepted only one true path:

> Campe war ein protestantischer Christ, nicht bloss durch den Zufall der Geburt, sondern aus innerster Ueberzeugung. Die Freiheit des Glaubens hat er stets hochgehalten, die Freiheit der Lehre durch Wort und Schrift. Jeder Aberglaube, jede priesterliche Bevormundung dünkte ihm unerträglich. Aber mit Glaubensfreiheit verband er Glaubensinnigkeit, ein Gewissen, fromm, demüthig, opferbereit.[15]

> (Campe was a Protestant Christian, not merely by accident of birth, but from the deepest conviction. He always held freedom of religion in the highest regard, the freedom of teaching through the spoken and the written word. All superstition, any imposition of priestly will, was intolerable in his eyes. However, he associated freedom of religion with deep personal conviction, a conscience, pious, humble, ready to make a sacrifice.)

In emphasising Campe's Protestant conviction, Leyser's assessment suggests a specifically Lutheran standpoint, with echoes of the reformer's *Von der Freiheit eines Christenmenschen* (On the liberty of a Christian, 1520) informing Campe's deep aversion to the unhappy, clearly Catholic, union of authority and superstition. Anxious, however, to reconcile his faith with the light of reason, Campe was also influenced by developing Enlightenment theology and drew chiefly from two related sources: Deism and Neology. Deism was in many ways the extreme of Enlightenment theology. It centred on the notion that reason itself was the enabling factor in allowing man to believe in God as 'the Intelligent Author of Nature' and 'the Moral Governor of the World'.[16] Building on John Locke's *Reasonableness of Christianity* (1695), which argued that divine revelation was only necessary as a supplement to man's reason, the English Deists, in particular Matthew Tindal in his *Christianity as Old as Creation* (1730), proposed that it therefore ought to be possible to discard revelation altogether as a needless alternative when truth could be perceived just as effectively by means of reason. Although Deism per se was mostly confined to England and North America, it also made inroads into France where it resulted in Rousseau's notion of natural religion, as expressed in both *Émile* and *Du Contrat Social*, the former in particular rejecting the notion of revelation. The potential impact of such radical ideas on the credibility of Christian doctrine is clear and for many Deists the natural consequence of their beliefs was a move towards pantheism or even atheism. Campe, however, remained a committed Christian throughout his life and, as Leyser points out, his continued faith owes much to his awareness of the emerging revolutionary notion of historical consciousness, promoted in the work of Burke and Herder.[17]

Such an awareness of historical progression perhaps also explains Campe's open approbation of the ideals of Neology, which have their origins in the work of Christian Freiherr von Wolff (1679–1754). Wolff, a student of Leibnitz, acknowledged aspects of Deist thought, but maintained a far more optimistic approach towards Christianity as a historic faith. He set out to show that the insights of the Bible and the claims of reason were effectively the same, each the characteristic product of a given age. Maintaining an essentially Pietist stance, he argued that man finds happiness in submitting to a natural law created by God. It is therefore rational to adhere to that law and out of such rational behaviour will follow harmony between man and God; conversely, rejection of that law will result in sin, which is irrational. God is therefore simultaneously the creator of reason and of revelation and the two cannot contradict one another. As Stoeffler points out, the popularity of such a view in an age of transition was assured:

> It is not difficult to see that during an incipiently humanistic age this was an understanding of the Christian message which was felt to have a great deal to commend it. It made it possible for theologians, pastors, and laity alike to regard themselves as being faithful to the Christian tradition, on the one hand, while on the other they could pride themselves upon being utterly relevant to the new age that was dawning.[18]

The appeal for the devout Campe of Wolff's tempering of Deist thought is certainly understandable. Indeed, Wolff's work was widely recommended by orthodox theologians. Wolff's ideas were also adopted by the Neologists, a group of Berlin theologians, including the influential Johann Joachim Spalding (1714–1804), who promoted a positive approach to rational faith, which Stoeffler describes in the following terms:

> Christian piety had thus become a confident and complete adjustment to a stoic understanding of the general rightness of things, which in this life and the next will necessarily bring the happiness for which man was created. It was based on an utterly optimistic faith which simply averted its gaze from the darker aspect of human existence and made man alone the captain of his ship. (240)

Campe was well acquainted with this group and echoes of their thinking can be found in a number of his works, including *Robinson der Jüngere*. It was Spalding who recommended the publication of Campe's first treatise on religion, *Philosophische Gespräche über die unmittelbare Bekanntmachung der Religion und über einige unzulängliche Beweisarten derselben* (Philosophical discussions on the direct announcement of religion and on some insufficient means of proof of the same), which appeared anonymously in Berlin in 1773.[19] The *Gespräche*, which consist of four dialogues between Agathokles and Hermogenes, discuss the relationship of reason and revelation. Spalding's stoicism is much in evidence in Campe's advocacy of a pragmatic approach to faith, made explicit in the concluding dialogue:

> Wenn wir also vernünftig sein wollen: so bleibt uns in dieser ganzen Sache nichts weiter übrig, als zu sehen, was Gott wirklich gethan hat, und nicht, was er unserer Einsicht gemäss, hätte thun können, oder thun müssen. Und zu dieser vernünftigen Bescheidenheit bei allen unseren Untersuchungen dieser Art, braucht es weiter keiner Beweggründe als der Erinnerung: dass die Wege des Herrn nicht unsere Wege, und seine Gedanken nicht die unserigen sind. (98)
>
> (If we are therefore to adopt a reasoned approach, there remains only one thing for us to do in all of this and that is to see what God has truly done and not what he, in our opinion, could or should have done. And to attain this reasoned modesty in all our investigations of this type, no other motive is necessary other than to remember that the ways of the Lord are not our ways and his thoughts are not our thoughts.)

Campe acknowledges the inadequacy of human reason to understand God's work fully. However, such acknowledgement is reasoned in itself, demonstrating a stoical awareness of God's unfathomable greatness. This pragmatic argument is developed further in Campe's *Versuch eines Leitfadens beim christlichen Religionsunterricht für die sorgfältiger gebildete Jugend* (Suggested guidance for the Christian religious instruction of the more carefully educated youth, 1791), where he argues that every religion is based upon reason. Indeed, Campe suggests that reason is a necessary prerequisite to faith as God can only make us aware of faith through our ability to think rationally. In keeping with this stance, religious instruction should take the simplest, clearest form possible. This is made explicit in his *Schreiben aus Algier* (Letter from Algiers, 1801), in which Campe takes the simple clarity of Christ's own teaching as his role model:[20]

> Dieser sperrte seine Jünger, wenn er von Gott und göttlichen Dingen mit ihnen reden wollte, in kein dumpfes Lehrzimmer ein, sondern ging mit ihnen ins freie Feld, wo Gott in jeder Pflanze, in jedem Grashalme, nicht bloss ihrem Verstande, sondern auch

ihren Sinnen gegenwärtig war; oder er erstieg eine Anhöhe mit ihnen, wo sie die wundervollen Werke desselben, welche Weisheit und Liebe verkündigen, übersehen konnten. Er liess sie nicht auswendig lernen, nichts gelerntes herplappern, sondern gab ihnen nur ein Beispiel, des kindlichen Geistes und der Einfalt, womit sie beten sollten, indem er ihnen vorbetete, ohne von ihnen zu verlangen, dass sie seine Worte nachsagen und auswendig lernen sollten.[21]

(He did not lock his followers in a stuffy classroom when he wanted to talk to them about God and godly things, but instead took them out into an open field, where God was in every plant, every blade of grass, present not just in their minds, but in their senses too; or he climbed a hill with them, where they could look out over the wonderful works of the Lord, which herald wisdom and love. He did not have them learn by heart, simply churn out things they had learned, but instead gave them only an example of the childlike spirit and the simplicity with which they should pray. This he did by praying before them without demanding that they repeat his words and learn them by heart.)

There is clearly no role for the catechism here, but rather an emphasis on freedom and learning by example, as both reason and the senses are opened up to experience the vastness of God's creation. As this suggests, the notion of Christianity as a *Vernunftreligion* (rational religion) was central to Campe's teaching. The harmony of creation is appealing to reason and the beauty intended by the divine creator is perceivable through the senses, which are in turn informed by rational judgement. To appreciate this, a balance between reason and faith had to be achieved, a quest made clear in Campe's *Seelenlehre für Kinder* (Guidance for the souls of children, 1780), which once more features Johannes, Gotlieb and other characters from *Robinson der Jüngere*.[22] In this text, Campe employs a series of terms and concepts intended to form a bridge between reason and faith.[23] Using the psychological terminology of the period, these terms and concepts are understood as *Triebe* (drives) which are in harmony with the reasonable view of God's creation and which govern human behaviour. Each is related to faith and social propriety, once again emphasising the benefits of rational adherence to a God-given natural law. It is this value system, instilled during the years at Billwerder, which provided the young Böhl with his first understanding of the relationship between faith and reason and laid out the parameters of social responsibility and citizenship which underpinned Campe's enlightened pedagogy. As his responses to the early, unhappy years in Spain show, following his departure from Billwerder, Böhl adhered to these values unquestioningly, convinced of their validity and accepting of the stoicism they advocated.

However, as Böhl grew in experience and read more widely, Campe's encouragement ironically began to draw him away from the ideals of Enlightenment theology. There is a foretaste of this in the autumn of 1794 when Böhl refers to the attempts he and his brother Gottlieb have made to broaden their religious and philosophical understanding of the world, the outcome of which he fears may have offended his mentor:

> Wir waren ungewiß, was Sie uns auf unsere unchristlichen Gesinnungen antworten würden; wir hätten uns auch nicht gewundert, wenn Sie uns allenfalls der Leichtigkeit und Unbesonnenheit beschuldigt und uns vermahnt hätten, die Vernunft gefangen zu nehmen und anzubeten. Ich habe dieses selbst manchem neumodischen jungen Zweifler angerathen. – Jetzt aber urtheilen wir aus etlichen gesandten Schriften, daß Sie uns nicht verkennen, und dieses ist uns sehr angenehm. (24 October 1794)
>
> (We were unsure what you would have to say about our unchristian beliefs; we would not have been surprised if you had perhaps accused us of frivolity and rashness and had warned us to grasp hold of reason and worship it. I have given this advice myself to many a fashionable young doubter. – Now we see from numerous letters sent that you do not disown us and this pleases us greatly.)

This shows Böhl testing the intellectual boundaries, pulling away from Campe, albeit with a great deal of caution for fear of falling into the same trap as 'manch neumodischer junger Zweifler' (many a fashionable young doubter). Significantly, his mentor still commands respect as a touchstone for evaluating new ideas and it is in the context of Campe's teaching that any judgements are to be made. The response, which Böhl and his brother were half expecting, 'die Vernunft gefangen zu nehmen und anzubeten' (to grasp hold of reason and worship it), highlights the continuing role of Enlightenment thought as a benchmark for philosophical legitimacy. Interesting too is Böhl's clear need to reconcile his new, albeit tentative, intellectual explorations with the demands of enlightened society:

> Manchen langen und traurigen Kampf haben uns die jugendlichen Vorurtheile gekostet, den es war nicht Uebermuth welche uns ihr Joch abzuwerfen antrieb, sondern heißer Durst Bedürfniß nach Wahrheit – Endlich hat uns ein kleiner Stral ihres Lichtes erquickt; wir sind nun so ruhig und glücklich als es unsere eigenen Unvollkommenheiten zulassen, und indem wir an der Veredlung unsres Geistes arbeiten, glauben wir zu gleicher Zeit nützliche Mitglieder der menschlichen Gesellschaft zu seyn.
>
> (Our youthful prejudices have cost us many a long and miserable struggle. For it was not pride which drove us to cast off their yoke, but rather a great thirst, a need for truth – Finally, a brief shaft of her light has satisfied us; we are now as peaceful and happy as our own shortcomings will allow and as we work towards the refinement of our minds, we believe ourselves to be at the same time useful members of human society.)

Böhl's self-defence is telling and typical of the tone of his correspondence during these years of early maturity as he treads the fine line between adhering to Campe's teaching and establishing his own opinions. Consequently, any deviation from the proscribed rational path is excused as the result of a quest for ultimate truth and Böhl is at pains to confirm that the widening of his intellectual horizons is compatible with his role as a useful member of society. Yet despite the desire to ensure his mentor's approval, Böhl displays a clear need to revise certain attitudes adopted in his youth which he now sees as impeding the quest for truth which he has identified as his intellectual and existential goal.

An important catalyst for this reappraisal was Böhl's interest in the work of theologian and political theorist, Andreas Riem (1749–1814).[24] Riem was a radical Enlightenment thinker, European in outlook, a supporter of Jewish emancipation and thoroughly anti-Catholic. His work covered a wide range of theological and political issues and came to Böhl's attention via his mentor. Campe followed the career of this reformed thinker closely and was undoubtedly aware of certain affinities between them. Riem shared much with the Neologists, in particular the rejection of the notions of original sin, predestination and the belief in the Trinity, and, like Campe, sought the reconciliation of reason and faith through the rational interpretation of important biblical myths in a modern context. For Riem, the purity of the word of Christ was the key to faith and the struggle to attain this was central to the Enlightenment debate as he understood it. Inspired by Kant and Montesquieu, Riem condemned unenlightened theologians as a 'Pestilenz der Menschheit' (plague of humanity)[25] and advocated 'eine im eigenen Denken gewonnene Privattheologie' (a private theology derived from one's own thought).[26] One of Riem's most radical essays, *Christus und die Vernunft oder Prüfung der Wahrheit und Göttlichkeit der Lehre Jesu Christi des christlichen Lehrbegriffs und der symbolischen Bücher* (Christ and reason or an examination of the truth and godliness of the teaching of Jesus Christ of Christian teaching and the symbolic texts, 1792), was amongst the material sent by Campe to Böhl and his brother. The text equates Christian institutions with those of the Judaic Essene sect:

> Die strengen Grundsätze der Essäer, welche ihrer Moral das finstere Ansehen klösterlicher Disciplin gab, und im Aeußern einen gewissen Schein der Heiligkeit verlieh, diese scheinen Christhum einigermaßen bei seinen Forderungen vom sittlichen Verhalten, geleitet zu haben. Bei näherer Zusammenhaltung der Institute der Essäer und des Christenthums werden wir finden, daß das Letztere wol schwerlich etwas mehr, als der völlige Essäismus sey.[27]

> (The strict principles of the Essenes, which lent their morality the dark appearance of monastic discipline and outwardly a certain façade of piety, seem to have guided Christianity to some extent in its requirements of moral behaviour. Closer

comparison of the institutions of the Essenes and Christianity will show us that the latter can surely be nothing other than total Essenism.)

The 'moral behaviour' referred to is the defence of human rights, which Riem understands to be at the core of Essenism, and which has been subsumed into Christian ideology. As Becker explains, by equating Christianity with this Judaic sect, Riem identifies a pure form of the Christian faith which was altered in form once St Paul opened the Church to the heathens.[28] Although Campe no doubt intended his young pupils to engage positively with this by encouraging them rationally to consider the development of the faith from its origins, the negative potential of Riem's appraisal is clear, effectively suggesting the superiority of a pure, ancient Church, now lost through human manipulation. This complex text unsettled the young Böhl and presented him with a wealth of new ideas, as he explains to Campe:

> Das Buch Chr[istus] und die Vernunft hat uns auch viel Vergnügen gemacht, nicht sowohl der bündigen uns unnützen Widerlegungen halber, sondern wegen der neuen Aussichten die es in dem weiten Gebiete der Philosophie manchesmahl eröffnet. (24 October 1794)
>
> (The book Christ and Reason brought us much pleasure too, not because of the concise refutations, which were of no use to us, but rather because of the new vistas which it sometimes opened in the wide field of philosophy.)

Significant here is Böhl's dismissal as superfluous of Riem's carefully argued defence of the role of reason in faith. This is by now a well-worn path and Böhl seems weary of the arguments of the *Aufklärer*. Instead, he focuses on other aspects of Riem's work which foster a growing desire to explore new areas of interest and an impatience to take on fresh intellectual challenges. This is further underlined by Böhl's response to Riem's later work, *Reines System der Religion für Vernünftige* (Pure system of religion for the rational, 1793). The text, which was also radical in nature, responding to the ideals of the French Revolution, suggested, amongst other things, the division of wealth and eventually led to the author's expulsion from Prussia in 1795, having been condemned by the censor as an affront to Christian teaching. Böhl seems fascinated by the issues raised:

> Jetzt hat besonders mein Forschungstrieb einen neuen Sporn durch das uns gesandte Reine System der Religion von Riem erhalten; ich bemühe mich jetzt, das viele darin auffallend neue, dem ich meine Zustimmung nicht versagen kann, mit den Resultaten

meines bißherigen Nachdenkens zu vereinigen – Sagen Sie uns doch, ob Sie diesem System Ihren Beyfall geben? (3 February 1795)

([M]y drive for inquiry has now received further encouragement upon receipt of Riem's Pure System of Religion; I am now endeavouring to unite the many things in it which are quite new to me, and which I cannot disagree with, with the results of my deliberations to date – please tell us whether you applaud this system.)

Once more, the young scholar can be seen attempting to balance his own intellectual curiosity with the ideological values of his mentor. New ideas interact with established views as Böhl tries to construct his own intellectual framework. This is a significant juncture in Böhl's ideological and intellectual development, for although his comments on Riem are limited and provide only minimal insight into his views on the content of the theologian's work, this is the first indication in Böhl's correspondence of independent reception of contemporary thinkers. Riem's radical stance triggers a questioning of the core values related to faith, fostering a revision of Böhl's understanding and acceptance of the Church and the wider theological debate. The ramifications of this still modest shift carry with them a degree of irony. Böhl's study of Riem's work, intended by Campe to strengthen his protégé's faith in Enlightenment ideals, would lead him instead to continue the search for an ultimate truth, the validity of which Campe would never acknowledge. The brief mention of an interest in 'neue Aussichten' (new vistas) alluded to in relation to *Christus und die Vernunft* marks the beginning of a process of disillusionment with Enlightenment theology which would culminate in Böhl's conversion to Catholicism in 1813.

During the early 1790s, however, Campe cannot have suspected that his protégé would one day follow this path. Böhl's letters from Spain show him to recoil in the first instance from the demands of commercial life, but also, and more significantly for his later development, from the very land and its culture. The young merchant felt stifled by what he perceived to be restrictive social structures and a backward-looking intellectual climate. This country and its society had no place in Böhl's youthful, enlightened world view and his understanding of it owes much to the received opinion of the 'Black Legend'. Writing to Campe on 27 August 1793, Böhl, aged twenty-three, makes his aversion to Spanish life abundantly clear, focusing in particular on the role of the Catholic Church:

Wenn ich einmahl nach Deutschland käme, so würde ich mich gerne für die hier in erzwungener Verstellung verlebten Jahre durch freimüthige Äußerung meiner Meinungen schadlos halten wollen. [. . .] In meinem jugendlichen Eifer würde ich vielleicht alle weltliche und geistliche Hierarchie für unrechtmäßig erklären, gegen Religions Meynungen die mir einen schädlichen Einfluß auf Moralität und Wircksamkeit zu haben scheinen reden. [. . .] Wir sind alle drey so glücklich unsere

Pflichten oder Glückseeligkeit Lehre auf schlichte angewandte Vernunft zu gründen; wir können nicht umhin zu glauben, daß die menschliche Vernunft sich durch sich selbst auf diesen Grad von Einsicht erheben kann; unter dessen mag eine durch Gott veranstaltete Belehrung immer den Schwachen gerne zu Hülfe kommen: wir schmeicheln uns daß sie für uns überflüßig ist.

(If I were to return to Germany one day, then I would very much like to take advantage of the ability to express my opinions openly to compensate for the years spent here in enforced pretence. In my youthful enthusiasm, I would perhaps declare all worldly and spiritual hierarchy to be unjust, speak out against religious opinions which seem to me to have a damaging influence on morality and effectiveness. We are so fortunate to base our ideas of duty or happiness on simple, applied reason, we cannot believe otherwise than that human reason can raise itself to this level of understanding of its own accord; admittedly, instruction provided through God can of course always assist the weak; we like to think that it is superfluous for us.)

Campe's influence is clear, both in the advocacy of reason and in the almost imperious tone, which sees Böhl firmly occupying the intellectual and moral high ground over an entire people who have not had the benefit of his modern, enlightened education. Böhl feels hampered in his intellectual endeavours by 'erzwungene Verstellung' (enforced pretence) and is straining at the leash to give vent to the new ideas gleaned from his studies. He rails against the hypocrisy of a social system, dictated by religion, which forces the outsider to conform to a way of life which he clearly despises. Böhl is frustrated that his new environment is not sympathetic towards 'schlichte angewandte Vernunft' (simple, applied reason) and displays a sense of moral and intellectual superiority which all but relegates religion to the role of comfort for the uneducated masses. In so doing, Böhl distances the rational Protestant 'we', represented by himself and his brother, from the irrational Catholic 'they' of Spanish society. The views expressed by Böhl must have pleased his mentor whose attitude towards Catholicism was thoroughly negative. The Neologists' aversion to the 'darker aspect of human existence' underpinned an active discouragement in his teaching of any tendency towards the superstitious in religion and, consequently, Campe bore great antipathy towards what he regarded as the nefarious obscurity of the Catholic Church. This is made particularly clear in the letters describing his *Reise von Braunschweig in die Schweiz* (Journey from Braunschweig to Switzerland). In a letter dated 22 July 1789, addressed to his daughter Lotte, Campe observes in the area around Paderborn 'der plumpste und abergläubischste Katholizismus mit allen den schädlichen Mißbräuchen, welche gewöhnlich damit verbunden sind' (the crudest and most superstitious Catholicism, with all the nefarious abuses which are usually associated with it).[29] In his text, Campe depicts Catholicism as an ill requiring remedy, a plague of ignorance to be cured by means of rational thought. However, the main target of his criticism is not so much the Catholic faith itself, but instead the complex establishment which has grown up around it, one fostering an atmosphere of superstition and institutional intrigue. In his *Reise durch England und Frankreich* (Journey through England and France, 1803), he states quite clearly that he hopes the day will come when Catholicism will be free of 'menschliche Zusätze' (human additions) to serve once again as comfort for those in need.[30] For now, however, he adopts a sympathetic, if rather condescending, stance in relation to those who adhere to the Catholic faith as lost souls requiring pity. This echoes the view of Catholicism as a medieval manifestation, a by-product of the Dark Ages, juxtaposed in Campe's argument with Protestantism, heralding religious enlightenment, progress and liberation. Upon reading Campe's clear disapproval of Catholicism, often expressed with almost missionary zeal, it is not hard to see how Böhl's subsequent defence of both the Catholic faith and its institutions would severely undermine their relationship, the dynamic of which was inextricably linked to Campe's teaching and to his model of a parent–child or teacher–pupil relationship. Any divergence on Böhl's part from these parameters would necessarily threaten its foundations and, indeed, these close ties would be gradually loosened as Böhl began to explore alternative understandings of faith, a process which would eventually lead him towards a world view far removed from that instilled by Campe.

NOTES

[1] The institution was established by the educational reformer, Johann Bernhard Basedow (1723–90).

[2] Having finally secured independence from Denmark with the treaty of Gottorp in 1768 and recently established as a republic, Hamburg was regarded by many as an exemplary enlightened society. From 1713, *Der Vernünftler* (The Rationalist), Germany's first moral weekly, was published there and the presence of Gotthold Ephraim Lessing (1729–81) at the city's theatre and publication of his *Hamburger Dramaturgie* (1767–9) placed the city at the centre of German intellectual life. Hamburg was home to an influential bourgeois avant-garde with figures such as Friedrich von Hagedorn (1708–54), Friedrich Gottlieb Klopstock (1724–1803) and Matthias Claudius (1740–1815) commanding the literary scene. Education was taken very seriously by the merchant bourgeoisie of the fledgling republic with educators such as the founder of the *Hamburger Handelsakademie*, Johan Georg Büsch (1728–1800), and grammar school teacher Christoph Ebeling (1741–1817) at the forefront of pedagogical advancement.

[3] Elise Campe (VL: 7) erroneously states that three of Böhl's brothers were also taught by Campe. Peter, Carl Wilhelm and Ferdinand were, however, too young to have been sent to Billwerder.

[4] Jean Jacques Rousseau, *Émile, ou de l'Éducation* (Paris: Guarnier, [n.d.]), p. 359.

[5] Campe was not alone in his assessment of contemporary literature for the young and *Robinson der Jüngere* emerged as one of the foremost texts in the growing trend which called for a more open approach to education. Indeed, many of the views and values put forward in Campe's immensely popular work were echoed a year later by the renowned Swiss educationalist, Johann Heinrich Pestalozzi (1746–1827), in his 1780 work, *Die Abendstunde eines Einsiedlers* (A hermit's evening hour).

[6] The Böhl children made an appearance in a number of other texts by Campe, including *Die*

7 Campe (VL: 76–77n).
8 *Sämmtliche Kinder- und Jugendschriften von Joachim Heinrich Campe. Vierte Gesamtausgabe der letzten Hand*, 39 vols (Braunschweig: Verlag der Schulbuchhandlung, 1831–6); X and XI: *Robinson der Jüngere*; X: 401.
9 Noodt was a private tutor and headmaster of the city's prestigious *Johannaeum*.
10 Joachim Heinrich Campe, *Theophron oder der erfahrene Rathgeber für die unerfahrene Jugend* (Tübingen: Schramm and Balz, 1786 [1783]).
11 Elise Campe suggests (VL:12) (and subsequently Pitollet (QC: 9) and Herrero (*Planteamiento*, p. 31)) that this return was at the behest of Böhl's father. This is clearly an error as Johann Böhl died in 1786.
12 Relations between Great Britain and Spain had been strained since the pact signed between Carlos III and the French Royal house in 1761.
13 The plight of the poor is often mentioned in Böhl's correspondence during these early years and results in a number of charitable donations, made at Campe's behest, to the *Hamburger Versorgungs Anstalt* (Hamburg Welfare Institute), an offshoot of the Hamburg *Patriotische Gesellschaft* (Patriotic Society), founded in 1765 by a number of wealthy merchant families for the benefit of public welfare and cultural promotion. See Mary Lindemann, *Patriots and Paupers (Hamburg, 1712–1830)* (New York: Oxford University Press, 1990).
14 The details of this visit are recorded in Böhl's diary, which is held in the Osborne archive. See Montoto, *Algo más*, pp. 22–3.
15 Johann Leyser, *Joachim Heinrich Campe. Ein Lebensbild aus dem Zeitalter der Aufklärung*, 2 vols (Braunschweig: Vieweg, 1877); I:127.
16 Alan Richardson (ed.), *A Dictionary of Christian Theology* (London: SCMP, 1969), p. 89.
17 Leyser, *Lebensbild*, pp. 109–10.
18 F. Ernst Stoeffler, *German Pietism During the Eighteenth Century* (Leiden: Brill, 1973), p. 238.
19 Campe's views and writings on religion are discussed in Leyser, *Lebensbild*; I: Chap. 2, 'Zur Religion und Theologie', pp. 89–134. Some of the texts referred to are now extremely rare. Consequently, quotations have been taken from Leyser's study where necessary and page references appear in the text.
20 This text was inspired by a letter from Anton Gottlieb Böhl.
21 *Sämmtliche Kinder- und Jugendschriften*; XXIX: *Neue Sammlung merkwürdiger Reisebeschreibungen. Erster Theil* (1832), 109.
22 Ibid.; VIII: *Seelenlehre für Kinder* (1831), iii–xiii, 'Vorrede zur ersten Auflage'.
23 Leyser, *Lebensbild*, p. 117.
24 See K. H. L. Welker (ed.), *Andreas Riem. Ein Europäer aus der Pflaz*, Schriften der Siebenpfeiffer-Stiftung 6 (Stuttgart: Thorbecke, 1999).
25 Katharina Becker, 'Andreas Riem als Theologe' in Welker, pp. 61–77 (p. 73). Quoted from Riem's pamphlet *Ueber Aufklärung*, written in opposition to the religious edicts introduced by Prussian minister Johann Christian Wöllner in 1788.
26 Quoted in Becker, p. 64.
27 Quoted in Becker, p. 74.
28 Becker, pp. 74–5.
29 *Sämmtliche Kinder- und Jugendschriften*; XXIV: *Erste Sammlung merkwürdiger Reisebeschreibungen für die Jugend. Achter Theil* (1831), *Des Herausgebers Reise von Braunschweig in die Schweiz*, 19–20.
30 Ibid.; XXXII and XXXIII: *Neue Sammlung merkwürdiger Reisebeschreibungen. Vierter Theil* (1832), *Reise durch England und Frankreich in Briefen an einen jungen Freund in Deutschland*, XXXIII: 168.

Chapter 2
New Influences: Doña Francisca and Spain

Böhl's dependence on Campe as a source of intellectual guidance would be expected to wane with maturity as he made his own discoveries and was exposed to new stimuli. Campe, following Rousseau, could have wished for nothing less for his young pupil. However, that this shift in focus should, at least in part, be directed both by and towards a woman was probably less foreseeable, especially given the limited role assigned to women and their intellectual abilities in Campe's own work. Nevertheless, Böhl's susceptibility to influences other than those endorsing Enlightenment ideals – the 'neue Aussichten' evoked by Riem – is closely linked to the relationship with his wife, Doña Francisca Ruiz de Larrea (1775–1838), the daughter of a Spanish merchant, Antonio Ruiz de Larrea, and a mother of Irish descent, Francisca Javiera Aherán y Malone, which began in 1790.[1] His interaction with her, in particular during the late 1790s and early 1800s, provided Böhl with a new set of challenges as he set out to shape his wife's world view, a process which forced him to review his own beliefs in order to justify them to his wife. This revaluation extends to issues of faith, culture and environment, effectively questioning the values established during the Billwerder years and introducing a new cultural framework which would underpin Böhl's subsequent career. Francisca's significance in her husband's intellectual development has been acknowledged by some, notably Herrero and Carnero, and emphasised by others, in particular Antonio Orozco Acuaviva and Milagros Fernández Poza,[2] but there has been a tendency to focus on her political and religious views. Whilst this is justifiable, in particular in the context of the Calderón polemic, it fails to acknowledge her notable influence on Böhl as a cultural mediator. Through her, Böhl gains a deeper understanding of a culture which contemporaries still tended to view as a quasi-oriental other. Marriage to Francisca and their increasingly shared *Weltanschauung* drew Böhl into that culture on a very tangible level, not just as an expatriate observer, but as someone with a lived experience of Spanish culture.

Böhl's choice of bride was driven, not unusually for the time, by practical as well as emotional reasons and his somewhat ambivalent attitude towards both his wife and mother-in-law is expressed in typical fashion in a letter to the Campes on 28 March 1797, in which he claims that 'Mutter und Tochter sind in den Gesichtszügen von der Natur vernachläßigt worden, von Körper aber wohlgebildet, wenngleich nicht groß' (Mother and daughter have been neglected by nature in terms of their facial features, but are nevertheless physically well-formed, if not tall). Despite this rather passionless appraisal, Böhl appears to have been a persistent suitor and embarked upon the duties of marriage with typical stoicism, aware of the benefits as well as the potential drawbacks. Although he acquired improved trading rights through marriage to a Spaniard, Francisca's widowed mother was unable to provide her with a dowry and the groom had to pay the dowry himself. Relations were further complicated by the vexed issue of faith. Francisca's mother was uncomfortable with the idea of her daughter marrying a Protestant and would not give permission for the union until Böhl agreed that his children be brought up in the Catholic faith, something which was still abhorrent to him at this stage. Once these matters were settled, the couple married on 1 February 1796 and set off for Germany accompanied by Böhl's mother-in-law. They travelled overland through Switzerland and spent the following winter in Morges in the canton of Berne where their first child, Cecilia, was born on Christmas Day.[3] The couple had made plans to set up home near the Campes in Braunschweig and Böhl rather nervously hoped that his wife and mother-in-law would be able to settle in this unfamiliar land with its foreign ways and changeable climate. As his correspondence shows, the full implications of his decision to marry were becoming clear. He had not made things easy for himself in choosing a Catholic bride who spoke no German, a woman with her own mind and the willpower to match. Already accustomed to the demands of familial responsibility in relation to the family firm, Böhl now saw a further restraint being placed on his personal freedom. It would take Böhl some time to accept this fully and this first trip to Germany saw the beginning of a power struggle which would characterise the Böhl marriage until the end. Despite the best efforts of all concerned, neither Francisca nor her mother were able to settle in Germany, alienated by the language and the culture and suffering from the vagaries of the climate. They disliked Hamburg and Braunschweig in equal measure and Böhl, admitting the folly of his attempt to settle them there so soon, made plans for a return to Cadiz before the winter set in. The departure was sudden, much to the dismay of family and friends alike, but Böhl promised his mother that he would return to Germany in six years' time, hoping that by then his wife would have mastered the language.

Upon their return to Spain in 1797, the family were forced to remain in Chiclana for over a year as it proved difficult to find a house near to the family offices in Cadiz. The situation in the city itself was desperate. Spain, seeking to re-establish favour with the French following the post-revolutionary war of 1793–5 and outraged at British colonial policies, had declared war on Great Britain in 1796. The war, which lasted until the Peace of Amiens in 1802, was hugely detrimental to Spain's economy and especially that of Cadiz, which was at the centre of the British campaign to cripple Spanish trade with the Americas. Böhl and his family found the practicalities of life extremely difficult, especially as all the possessions sent from Hamburg had been impounded by the British at Malaga. Family pressures were further heightened as Böhl began to suffer the draining effects of recurrent attacks of malaria. These events seem to have unsettled Böhl and, spurred on by the news that both his brother Fritz and his brother-in-law Berckemeyer had bought country estates in Germany, he once more began to ponder a return home. He had long entertained the notion of running his own estate, thinking first of Switzerland and even the United States, and now the idea of finding a property near his brother, within reasonable distance of both Campe and Hamburg, seriously began to occupy his mind. Plans were, however, hindered by a combination of his wife's reluctance to leave her home and the precarious political situation. The frustration this caused was, however, soon dwarfed by a profound personal tragedy. In 1800, yellow fever swept through Cadiz, killing thousands. The victims included Böhl's brothers, Gottlieb and Carl Wilhelm, as well as Gottlieb's wife, Therese, and her two brothers. Böhl and his immediate family took refuge from the epidemic in Chiclana and thus managed to emerge unscathed from the worst outbreak of the disease for over a century.[4] The impact was immense, affecting trade and decimating Cadiz society. Böhl's personal loss was immeasurable, losing a brother whose friendship and support had been central to his life ever since childhood. There were also far-reaching consequences for the future. Following Gottlieb's death, Böhl found himself duty bound to take full responsibility for the family firm, a task which occupied the majority of his time. Trading activity soon intensified with the lifting of the British blockade following the brief Peace of Amiens and a year later Böhl's involvement in mercantile life further increased as he took up the post as Hanseatic Consul, a position he would hold until his return to Germany in 1804.[5]

Despite the numerous disruptions and distractions, the Böhls pursued a full intellectual life. Francisca was as active as her husband. She was well-read, fluent in English and French and, during the late 1790s, established her own salon in Cadiz. Whilst appreciative of his wife's desire for intellectual advancement, Böhl was perturbed by her independence and, referring to himself as her 'zweiter Erzieher' (second educator), sought to guide her development in accordance with his own upbringing and away from what he perceived to be her somewhat unenlightened views. The dynamic of their early relationship is perhaps best illustrated by their diverging responses to the work of Rousseau, which in turn reflect the Genevan thinker's role in the European transition from Enlightenment thought to the ideals of the Romantic age. Böhl saw Rousseau's work as an affirmation of Enlightenment values. He embraced the social teachings of *Émile* and was in full agreement with Rousseau's view of women as intellectually inferior. Expressing his horror at the very existence of 'gedrukte Apologien der Weiber' (printed apologies of womankind), he comments with some irony on his inability to deal with such texts having read so much of Rousseau (letter to the

Campes, 3 February 1795). His wife, however, saw Rousseau in a more romantic light, preferring the sentimentalism of *Julie: oú La nouvelle Heloïse* (1761). Dismayed by this, Böhl criticised Francisca for throwing herself into 'die Arme einer gewissen eingebildeten Rousseauschen Natur' (the arms of a certain, imaginary Rousseauian nature; letter to Campe, 21 January 1797). Not that Francisca, a mere woman, was herself to blame. Reflecting the value assigned to the female intellect in the teaching of both Rousseau and Campe, Böhl saw his wife's failings as the consequence of his own pedagogical shortcomings and not as the result of independent thought on her part:

> Ich habe diese Periode in dem Gemüthe meiner Frau schon lange vor unserer Heirath selbst herbeygeführt, allein sie hat diese Natur mit solcher Heftigkeit ergriffen ihre gründlich reine Seele hat sich diese Natur so untadelhaft gebildet, daß es mir noch nicht völlig geglückt ist ihr das Joch der Vernunft aufzulegen, die mehr oder weniger immer über Neigung gebieten muß. (21 January 1797)
>
> (I myself encouraged this stage in my wife's emotional development long before we were married, but she has embraced this nature with such passion and it has shaped her thorough, pure soul so impeccably that I have not yet been able to place her under the yoke of reason, which must curb inclination to some degree.)

Böhl's adherence to contemporary gender bias is apparent in the ambivalent use of language which highlights the natural purity of Francisca's character, whilst simultaneously describing her education in terms befitting the breaking in of a stubborn mare. His responses to his wife's education are also revealing in the context of his own intellectual and existential struggle during early adulthood. The resultant battle of wills illustrates both the impact of Campe's teaching and the extent of Böhl's crisis of faith in Enlightenment values as a dichotomy develops between his attitude towards his wife's education and his own need for reassurance. His efforts to draw his wife into the orbit of his own value system force him to reflect upon those very values at a time when his ideological framework is showing the first signs of collapse. This results in a degree of inconsistency. In dealing with Francisca, Enlightenment values are an unquestionable benchmark, promoting reason in the face of feminine emotionality. Crucial is Böhl's role as moral and intellectual guide:

> Sie hat Anlagen zu allen vortrefflichen Eigenschaften. Doch wird die Ausbildung bey einzelnen schwer durch die Macht etlicher eingewurzelten romantischen Ideen. Sie hat Verstand genug um mich zu verstehen und um meine Ueberlegenheit einzusehen;

kurz es fehlt ihr nur an Willen, an beständiger Vernunft Unterwerfung des betrügerischen Gefühls, um dem Ideal einer Frau für mich zu entsprechen. (28 March 1797)

(She has a tendency towards all the best characteristics, but the development of some is made difficult by the power of numerous deep-rooted romantic ideas. She has enough intelligence to understand me and to recognise my superiority; in short, she merely lacks the will, the constancy of reason and domination of treacherous emotion, to represent my ideal woman.)

The sense of frustration is palpable. Böhl argues simultaneously as the husband who resents his wife's insubordination and, adopting the role of mentor learned from Campe, as the representative of a more enlightened and reasoned attitude. The juxtaposition of the negative influence of 'etliche eingewurzelte romantische Ideen' (numerous deep-rooted romantic ideas) with the positive values of 'beständige Vernunft' (the constancy of reason) makes clear Böhl's stance at this time, his reference to the notion of a 'romantic' world view suggesting an irrational, emotional set of responses. The criticism of Francisca also extends to the world she represents and is to be understood in close association with his wife's upbringing in the culture of Roman Catholic Spain. The pejorative tone of his comments dismisses her ideals as inferior to his own reasoned understanding.[6] The fact that Böhl has been unable to curb his wife's 'eingewurzelte, romantische Ideen', but feels that it is imperative for reason to prevail, suggests that he is still fully convinced of the values of his youth. This assuredness, however, masks a crisis of faith which is given voice in a letter written only two months prior to that outlining his battle with his wife's 'romantic' tendencies. The difference in tone is remarkable as Böhl invites Campe to play for him the role of the rational educator who will convert him back to reason, thus paralleling the role which Böhl seeks to adopt in relation to his wife:

Es giebt ja viele Sachen besonders in Rücksicht eines künftigen Zustandes, worüber wir nichts wissen können, und warum dann nicht ahnden und träumen? Wir tragen ein Herz im Busen daß im Schooße der Liebe immer noch mehr will, nie befriedigt ist, warum nicht das Reich der Möglichkeit mit Gegenständen dieser überströmenden Liebe bevölkern? – Ich weiß wie viel hierauf zu antworten ist, ich antworte es andern selbst. Meine Vernunft ist überzeugt, aber mein Gefühl widerspricht ihr. Ich denke die Rolle mit Ihnen zu spielen die meine Frau gegen mich spielt, gebe Gott mit gleich gutem Erfolge: der Bekehrung zur Vernunft! (21 January 1797)

(There are so many things, particularly in reference to the future, about which we can know nothing and so why not sense and dream? We carry a heart in our breast which desires ever more in the lap of love and is never satisfied. Why not fill the realm of possibility with objects of this overflowing love? – I know how much there is to say in answer to this; I advise others on the matter myself, my reason is convinced, but my emotion contradicts it. I intend to play the role with you that my wife plays with me; God willing, with the same success: the conversion to reason!)

Böhl's confessional outburst reveals a susceptibility to 'romantic' emotionality quite alien to the reasoned emphasis of his upbringing. The resultant anguish is obvious. He seems at a loss as to how to deal with the situation and knows only too well the arguments against it. Indeed, he often gives such advice to others facing a similar dilemma. Yet, in his own case, 'Gefühl' (emotion) cannot be silenced. Long imbued with the values of Enlightenment thought, Böhl feels it is his duty to pass those ideals on to Francisca, yet is himself somehow unsure of their validity. Although he views the concept of 'Bekehrung' (conversion) as something which should eventually lead him back to an enlightened world view, knowledge and reason are under threat as Böhl resorts to 'ahnden und träumen' (sens[ing] and dream[ing]) in his quest for understanding.

Forced to reassess his own values in an attempt to justify them to his wife, Böhl also demonstrates a shift in attitude towards his environment which sees his negative attitude to Spain recede. There is evidence of a gradual realignment in his cultural framework and although he continues to express frustration at certain attitudes and restrictions, there is a growing fascination with the country and its traditions. The extent of this shift is made dramatically apparent in the record provided by Wilhelm von Humboldt (1767–1835), who encountered Böhl on his journey through Spain in 1799. His description provides some unexpected insights:

Gottlieb Böhl und sein Bruder Nicolas, die, welche im Robinson figuriren. Der erste, der ältere, ist mehr Kaufmann, trocken, und scheint sich sonst mit nichts anderem zu beschäftigen. Der andre, ein ächter Zögling Campens, aber im besten Sinn. Gross, stark, derb, sehr gesund an Leib und Seele, moralisch, religiös, doch naiv und in nichts übertrieben, von viel Lecture und mancherlei Kenntnissen. Er ist ein Freund des Commissarius des heiligen Gerichts, und hat diesem versprochen, mit Sorgfalt dafür zu haben, dass keine unzüchtigen Bücher gelesen würden. Er hat ihm auch wirklich einige aufgefundene angezeigt und eingeliefert. Eine wunderbare Allianz eines Inquisitors mit einem protestantischen Kaufmann.[7]

(Gottlieb Böhl and his brother Nicolas, the ones who appear in Robinson. The first, the elder, is more of a merchant, dry and does not seem to occupy himself with anything else. The other, a true pupil of Campe in the best sense. Tall, strong, gruff, very healthy in body and spirit, moral, religious, yet naive and reserved, well-read with a reasonable breadth of knowledge. He is a friend of the Commissioner of the Inquisition and has promised him to take care that no indecent books are read. He has even reported and handed in some he found. A strange alliance between an inquisitor and a Protestant merchant.)

Humboldt's record reveals a conflict of interests within Böhl himself and brings the issues at stake into sharp focus. The description of Böhl as 'ein ächter Zögling Campens' (a true pupil of Campe) jars with the reference to the 'wunderbare Allianz eines Inquisitors mit einem protestantischen Kaufmann' (strange alliance between an inquisitor and a Protestant merchant) and mention of the latter is absent from Böhl's correspondence with Campe, perhaps unsurprisingly as his mentor would hardly have approved. However, if Humboldt's account is to be believed, by the end of the 1790s, Böhl's ideological value system had already undergone a major shift, the extent of which is only obliquely visible in his correspondence. Here, the focus is on more subtle changes of an existential rather than an ideological nature. This is manifested in a collection of six letters, which Böhl referred to as his 'Peculiaridades de España' (Characteristics of Spain). These were written on his return to Spain in 1798 and describe various aspects of Spanish life and in particular that of Cadiz and Andalucia.[8] Still cautious of the power of emotion over reason, the first of these begins with a discussion of the dangers of too great or too lacking an affinity with one's surroundings. This done, Böhl then goes on to describe the climate, environment, character, social mores and forms of entertainment of Andalucia. Unlike earlier commentaries, the tone does not suggest any particular antipathy, but instead a growing fondness.[9] Yet Böhl's own response to the letters is ambivalent. Referring to his travelogue in a letter to Dorothea Campe in 1798, Böhl at first insists that he has no idea 'wodurch Spanien überhaupt interessieren kann, als durch den Reitz der Neuheit' (what interest Spain could possibly offer, other than the charm of novelty). Nevertheless, in writing to Dorothea, Böhl reveals a puzzling attitude to Spain and its people. His description of the landscape in particular is negative:

Nächstdem führt der große Weg von Cadiz nach Bayonne durch den traurigsten Theil des Landes. Nur Biskayen bietet Naturschönheiten dar. In ganz Andalusien und den beiden Kastillen sind Bäume eine Seltenheit. Die Städte sind alle gleich traurig, oede und verfallen, und die Menschen gleich verschloßen, zurückstoßend und gefühlloß. (16 October 1798)

(Then the long road from Cadiz to Bayonne passes through the most miserable part of the country. Only Biscay offers any natural beauty. Trees are a rarity in the whole of Andalucia and in both Castiles. The towns are all just as miserable as each other, desolate and derelict and the people are all similarly reserved, unapproachable and devoid of feeling.)

New Influences: Doña Francisca and Spain

Although largely critical in content, the melancholic tone of Böhl's description hints at a developing affinity with his adopted home which echoes the response of other contemporary writers, including Christian August Fischer (1771–1829) in his *Reise von Amsterdam über Madrid und Cadiz nach Genua in den Jahren 1797 und 1798* (Journey from Amsterdam via Madrid and Cadiz to Genoa in the years 1797 and 1798, 1799):

> Wir erblicken beym Eintritte in Altcastilien eine ganz neue Landschaft vor uns. Einförmige Flächen, mit entlegenen Ortschaften, magere Felder, hie und da mit Weinranken und überall mit Steinen bedeckt; eine Menge Schaafherden, aber wenig Rindvieh; keine Wiesen, keine Waldungen, keine Gärten noch Landhäuser; im Allgemeinen eine todte verödete Gegend. Die wenigen Dörfer, welche wir antreffen verkünden nichts als Elend.[10]

> (Upon entering Old Castile, we see a quite new landscape before us. Monotonous open spaces with isolated settlements, poor fields, vines here and there and stones lying everywhere; any amount of flocks of sheep, but few cattle; no meadows, no woodland, no gardens or large farm houses; all in all a dead, barren land. The few villages we come across present nothing but misery.)

Fischer visited Böhl in Cadiz and the similarity of their descriptions suggests a shared experience. Both writers are drawn to the melancholy beauty of the landscape, a beauty somehow enhanced by the misery housed there and which contrasts markedly with the lush landscape of northern Europe. This harsh terrain is one which Böhl is coming to know well, for good or for ill, and as his letter to Dorothea shows, elicits a highly emotive and perhaps unexpected response:

> Eines Theils dieser Empfindungen aber auch, schäme ich mich schon jetzt weil sie einen Anstrich von Ueberspannung und von Schwärmerey haben, der bei blos vernünftigen Menschen den Argwohn der affectation sogar erregen könnte. Doch nicht bei Ihnen, bin ich überzeugt, die mich kennen. Daß ich aber damahls so fühlte, und jetzt nicht mehr, ist die Frucht der Erfahrung. Bey unserer Art Absonderung hier in Cadiz von Natur und Kultur gewinnt die Einbildungskraft den größten Spiel Raum. In unsern Muße Stunden leben und weben wir in den Elysäischen Feldern mit nur gebildeten Seelen. Die ersten Eindrücke also sind sehr heftig, wenn wir diesem Ziele zuzueilen glauben. Die Wirklichkeit und die Gewohnheit entzaubern uns nachher sehr bald, allein wir schämen uns es zu gestehen. – Viel mag das clima dazu beitragen, welches hier der Empfänglichkeit besonders günstig ist; Natur und Kunst brauchen nur einen geringen Aufwand, um die angenehmsten Empfindungen zu erregen und dieses habe ich auch nach meiner Rückkehr erfahren. (16 October 1798)

(I am already partly ashamed of these impressions because they have an element of eccentricity and passion to them, which might arouse suspicions of affectation in mere rational people. Not in you, however, who know me well, I am sure. That I no longer feel as I did then is the fruit of experience. The kind of isolation in which we find ourselves here in Cadiz, away from nature and culture, allows the imagination the greatest freedom. We spend our leisure hours in the Elysian fields with only cultured souls for company. Reality and habit seem almost disenchanting afterwards, but we are ashamed to admit it. The climate here, which is particularly favourable for sensitivity, must have a lot to do with it. Nature and art only need the slightest extravagance to arouse the most pleasurable sensations and I have experienced this since my return.)

The impact of environment on individual responses is significant in suggesting a concession to elemental forces which undermines the rational self-perception taught by Campe. In assessing his travelogue in this way, Böhl reveals an awareness of a susceptibility to the irrational which provokes an uncertain response. Yet, despite cautiously blaming the extremes of the Andalucian climate for such uncontrolled outbursts, there is no doubt that Böhl's relationship to Spain is changing, clearly influenced more by his wife's 'eingewurzelte romantische Ideen' than his once lauded reason.

His marriage in 1796, as well as heralding new responsibilities as a husband and father, sees Böhl looking out, albeit tentatively, beyond his enlightened world view towards a future no longer anchored in the security of reason. A year later, looking back over the previous decade, Böhl evaluates his development in a manner which questions implicitly the values established by Campe and demonstrates a growing intellectual independence. Whilst still using the language of Luther's Bible, here echoing the text of *Corinthians*, Böhl expresses himself in powerfully loaded terms which describe a transition from mere knowledge to an almost visionary appreciation of the world:

Der Saame des Guten lag etliche Zeit verborgen, ehe er keimte. Endlich ward der Buchstabe lebendig, oder das Wissen ging in Schauen über, wie eigentlich und wodurch, weiß ich selbst nicht recht. Bei meinem letzten Besuch a[nn]o 1788 hatte ich noch keinen Sinn für was Gut ist und Schön. (21 January 1797)

(The seed of goodness lay hidden for a very long time before it sprouted. Finally, the characters came to life or knowledge changed to observation – how and why, I am not too sure myself. When I last visited in 1788, I still had no sense of what was good and beautiful.)

Böhl, at the age of twenty-eight, would seem to be emerging from an intellectual stasis and describes his experience in terms of a revaluation. His comments highlight an openness to new ideas and a revitalised approach to learning. No longer content to rest upon the laurels of acquired knowledge, but rather prepared to open his mind to new ideas and experiences, he seems ready to embark upon a new phase in his life. Indeed, Böhl's return to Spain in 1798 marked the end of an era in terms of his relationship with Campe and his wife, Dorothea. Although his affection for them remained undiminished, other influences now held sway in determining Böhl's intellectual development. Whilst he continued to seek Campe's advice and opinion, increasingly the support sought was of a more personal, practical nature, rather than intellectual or philosophical. For example, following the death of his brother Gottlieb in 1800, he longed for the comfort of the 'ruhige und glückliche Augenblicke' (peaceful and happy moments)[11] which he had been accustomed to spend with Campe. The days at Billwerder and in Braunschweig had begun to lose their significance in underpinning Böhl's intellectual views and served ever more to symbolise an idyllic existence free from the constraints of commercial life. Böhl, it would appear, had finally opened himself up to his wife's Rousseauian sentimentality.

Böhl's desire for learning and his changing relationship with Spain are underlined by the emergence of what would become a lifelong interest in Spanish literature, in particular the poets and dramatists of the Middle and Golden Ages. His interest in these works, much maligned as contrary to Classical, Aristotelian principles, and deeply imbued with Catholic taste and culture, seems to some extent as incongruous in the context of his upbringing as his alleged association with the Inquisition. However, it represents a more palatable engagement with Spanish culture and is reported in detail to his *Pflegeeltern*. Böhl is keen to emphasise the scholarly worth of the material and highlights his interest in the language itself. This is expressed in the most positive of terms:

Das zweite Interesse an diesem Studium entsteht aus der so vortrefflichen Sprache, die sich zu jeder Gattung von Komposition schickt und zu einer jeden andere Wörter und andere Wendungen hat; ihre Redensarten (lebhafte Bilder für gewöhnliche Gedanken) bewundere ich noch mehr als ihre Sprichwörter, weil sie natürlicher anzubringen sind: im Komischen besonders sind sie darin unerschöpflich, sowie an aller Art Wort und Witzes Spielen. (19 August 1803)

(The second area of interest in these studies stems from the quite splendid language which lends itself to every type of composition and which offers an alternative to every word and turn of phrase; their idioms (lively images for simple thoughts) amaze me even more than their proverbs because they can be used more naturally, there is no end to their use in humour, as well as in all types of word games and jokes.)

His appreciation of the Spanish language forms part of a new cultural framework which develops as Böhl's understanding of Spanish culture deepens. This in turn enables further engagement with established values. The works of the late medieval period in particular offer a fresh perspective and potential solutions to the questions raised by Böhl's dissatisfaction with Enlightenment thought. Evidence of this can be found as early as 1803 when Böhl enthuses on the subject of medieval Spain in the same letter to Dorothea Campe:

> Die damahlige spanische <u>Art zu seyn</u> ist etwas unendlich großes, und den neueren völlig unbekanntes: wer sich in das Wesen derselben, durch tiefes Studium der Sprache und durch natürliche Empfänglichkeit hinein zu setzen versteht, findet eine neue Welt: anstatt einer flachen Empfindsamkeit zu fröhnen, huldigte man nur dem Verstande; man liebte positiven Edelmuth und Geistesgröße und wußte nichts von unserer heutigen negativen Tugend alias Unvermögen, und war nicht der beruhigende Schlaf der Vernunft besser, als unsere kränkelnde Vernünfteley?

> (The Spanish <u>way</u> at that time is something unceasingly grand and quite unknown to the modern way: whoever is able to adapt themselves to this, by means of intense study of the language and through natural receptiveness, will find a new world: instead of indulging a shallow sentimentality, only understanding was honoured: positive nobility and genius were loved and nothing was known of our current negative virtue alias inability and was not the reassuring sleep of reason better than our ailing petty rationalising?)

Böhl's emerging interest in Spain's cultural heritage is clearly inspired by an understanding of the past, which is presented in positive comparison with the 'flache Empfindsamkeit' (shallow sentimentality) of the modern nation. Yet the appreciation of Spain's culture remains ambivalent and betrays a continued reliance on Enlightenment values typical of this transitional phase. Consequently, Böhl's criticism is not directed at the principles of reason themselves, but takes issue instead with their misapplication and the pedantry associated with it.[12] That Böhl is able, however, to adopt this critical stance in relation to the values which shaped his education in the context of an increased engagement with Spanish culture is significant. It almost appears that in his endeavours to educate his wife, she has simultaneously managed to educate him, awakening an appreciation of Spain's environment and heritage which would permanently colour his scholarship and self-perception. He is certainly far better disposed towards her culture and its values. This did not, however, signify an end to the fraught nature of their marriage as the issues of old soon re-emerged.

In 1805, Böhl finally realised his long-cherished dream when he began negotiating the purchase of a property at Görslow in Mecklenburg on the banks of the Schweriner See. He was eventually able to secure the deeds to this feudal estate, having been elevated into the nobility in July 1806 following his formal adoption by his stepfather.¹³ Such was his enthusiasm to establish his rural idyll that the purchase of Görslow had not actually been settled when Böhl set off from Spain for Hamburg at the beginning of the summer of 1805 with his wife and two of their four children – Cecilia and Juan – in what would be a second attempt to settle them in Germany. Hamburg was rife with speculation surrounding the developing political situation as Napoleon's troops advanced through Germany. At this time, Böhl was one of many who supported Napoleon, as a number of letters to his mother-in-law demonstrate. He felt that a French victory would usher in a period of peace and would far rather see Napoleon succeed than Pitt. In later years, he would gloss over this and the relevant correspondence, still held in the Osborne archive, has been badly mutilated. Carnero suggests this may have been the result of a subsequent attempt to destroy politically damaging material. Such views would certainly have blackened Böhl's reputation in the reactionary climate following Fernando VII's return to the throne in 1814.¹⁴ However, Carnero offers another potential reason for this apparent act of self-censorship: Böhl and Francisca were on the verge of a marital crisis and Böhl may have been highly critical of his wife in these letters, leading to a subsequent removal of the offending passages either by himself or another family member. Feelings were certainly running high. It had become clear that Francisca would not agree to stay in Germany for any length of time. Böhl was at his wit's end, but faced with an otherwise intolerable situation for both parties, had no choice but to allow his wife to return to Spain in the spring of 1806. He had to concede that life on the estate at Görslow would leave her lonely and miserable, but this is not to say that he was happy to see his wife leave, neither on a personal level nor in terms of social propriety. In an undated letter written after Francisca's departure for Spain, Böhl expressed his concerns to his mother-in-law, by now his ally in the battle to contain his wife's wilful behaviour:

> Vous avez bien raison avec Vos anciens principes: une femme ne doit jamais laisser son mari, mais pour la lettre de Madame que Vous m'envoyés, ce sont des *phrases*: il est inutile de parler d'avantage la dessus: je me rapporte a mes lettres: si ma femme a eu l'inconcevable folie de s'imaginer, que telle quelle *est maintenent*, elle est nécessaire a mon bonheur, elle s'est furieusement trompée. Si elle ne peut être autre, ella a fait fort bien de partir: quand elle se convertira, quand elle deviendra humble, docile, obéissante, complaisante et économique, elle sera reçue par moi les bras ouverts [. . .]¹⁵

> (You are quite right with your old principles: a wife should never leave her husband, but as for the letter from Madame which you sent me, these are just *words*: it is useless to speak of having the advantage over her: I refer to my letters: if my wife has had the inconceivable insanity to believe that she is necessary to my happiness in her

current state, then she is tremendously mistaken. If she cannot be otherwise, then she has done the right thing in leaving: when she converts, when she shows herself to be humble, docile, obedient, compliant and economical, then I will receive her with open arms [. . .])

Böhl's views were traditional yet thoroughly contemporary: a wife should be subordinate to her husband. Any other mode of behaviour could only be construed as disrespectful and disruptive. A later epistle points towards a possible source of Francisca's perceived stubbornness: 'Le petit billet de ma femme est doux et amer en même temps, comme composé de nature et de caractère. Que ne peut elle congédier le caractère et bruler Mad: Wollstonecraft!' (The little note from my wife is sweet and bitter at the same time, as if composed by nature and by character. Can she not dismiss the character and burn Mad. Wollstonecraft!).[16] The influence of Wollstonecraft is mentioned by Böhl in relation to his wife on more than one occasion and certainly merits consideration. For a woman of her time to be allowed such a level of self-determination as to choose to live separately from her husband, not to mention in another country, was extremely unusual and points to a character unwilling to accept subservience. The separation was painful, but inevitable. Intended as a short-term solution to an otherwise insurmountable problem, the couple would remain apart for almost seven years, their reunion impeded by the upheaval of the Napoleonic Wars.

During the years at Görslow, Böhl was often troubled by the reports he received from his wife which painted a worrying picture of the situation in Andalucia, itself under threat of French occupation. At first, Francisca's life in Chiclana was one of relative tranquillity. She felt much happier than she had done in Germany, despite the prospect of a lengthy separation from her husband and two of her children and, like Böhl, she devoted a great deal of time to her studies. This peaceful life was, however, disturbed at the beginning of 1810 when the French forces finally took Andalucia. Only Cadiz, with its natural defences, remained free. Francisca was trapped at Chiclana and did not have time to escape to the safety of Gibraltar. She watched with dismay and anger as the French troops took control of her beloved homeland. Cut off from any source of income, she soon found herself in financial difficulty and was forced to sell much of Böhl's Spanish library. Furthermore, she suffered the indignity of quartering foreign troops, although she was rather fortunate in being ordered to house a French General, Eugene Villate. A cultured man, he proved to be a respectful and sympathetic character and used his influence to enable Francisca's escape to Cadiz in 1811. Once settled there, Francisca continued to display independent spirit by re-establishing her own salon meetings. These *tertulias* became popular as monarchist meetings, the participants voicing their opposition to the French occupation. Francisca was long remembered for these gatherings, reference to them even appearing in the first series of Benito

Pérez Galdós' *Episodios nacionales* (National episodes).[17] A first hand account is provided by Alcalá Galiano who remembers Francisca's salons in his *Recuerdos de un anciano* (Memoirs of an old man; 1862–4):

> En esto apareció una tertulia de igual naturaleza, pero en la que predominaban opiniones diametralmente opuestas: la de la señora Doña Francisca Larrea, mujer del ilustrado alemán D. N. Bohl de Faber, literato, buen escritor en nuestra lengua y apreciabilísimo, visto á todas luces. Su mujer, á quien acababan de dar licencia los franceses para pasar á Cadiz desde Chiclana, donde residía durante los meses primeros del sitio, era literata y patriota acérrima, pero de las que consideraban el levantamiento de España contra el poder francés como empresa destinada á mantener á la nación española en su antigua situación y leyes, así en lo político como en lo religioso, y aún volviendo algo atrás de los días de Cárlos III, únicos principios y sistema, según su sentir, justos y saludables.[18]

> (A salon of the same type emerged, but one which was largely driven by views diametrically opposed to the other: that of Doña Francisca Larrea, wife of the learned German Don N. Böhl de Faber, man of letters, gifted in our language and honourable by any reckoning. His wife, who had just been granted passage by the French to move to Cadiz from Chiclana, where she spent the first months of the occupation, was a woman of letters and staunch patriot, but one of those who saw the Spanish uprising against the French as an action destined to ensure the continuation of Spain's old ways and laws, in political as well as religious terms, even going back to the days before Carlos III, the only principles and system which she considered to be just and worthy.)

Alcalá Galiano's testimony places Francisca at the reactionary extreme of the political spectrum, a view justified when read in the context of her contemporary writings. Her experiences and views at the time of the French occupation are recorded in the earliest of a series of letters, memoirs and essays which she would continue writing until the early 1820s and which are referred to as the *Pensamientos españoles* (Spanish thoughts).[19] This collection provides a great deal of insight into Francisca's understanding of the world and, indeed, herself and reveal an unlikely synthesis of proto-feminist, proto-Romantic, but in many ways thoroughly reactionary, political views. The following, from the first piece entitled 'Una aldeana española a sus compatricias' (A Spanish villager to her countrywomen; 260–1) is typical:

> Una vez fué noble la inercia de nuestra Nación – pues más noble es el reposo que una vana agitación por pequeños intereses. – Pero hoy que el entusiasmo se ha despertado, y que combatimos por nuestra Religión, nuestra independencia y nuestro Rey; hoy que podemos desplegar las virtudes que la naturaleza ha vinculado en

nuestra Patria; hoy, en fin, nos será fácil levantarnos del abatimiento en que el mundo entero nos ha visto abismados. No nos aterren las armas del desolador universal; no nos acordemos de las victorias que más debe a sus seducciones que al valor de su brazo. Los Españoles no se compran. (260)

(There was a time when the inertia of our nation was noble – for repose is more noble than pointless activity in pursuit of small gains. – But now that enthusiasm has awakened and we are fighting for our religion, our independence and our king; now that we are able to display the virtues which nature has joined together in our nation; now it will be easy for us to rise from the dejection in which the whole world has seen us languish. We are not afraid of the weapons of the universal destroyer; we do not recall the victories which owe more to his seductions than to his bravery. Spaniards will not be bought.)

This call to arms against the French presents a vehement defence of the throne and altar axis so crucial to the reactionary politics of the Fernandine period and pre-empts the tone of Francisca's writings at the time of the restoration of Fernando VII in 1814. It is this exalted style which earned her the reputation which has succeeded in overshadowing other aspects of her work. Whilst her political stance is an important cornerstone of her world view, it is only a part of a complex set of opinions which see her engage with a number of social and cultural issues. This has often been overlooked or dismissed. Herrero, for example, sees her views as a superficial version of those expressed by her husband.[20] This fails to take into account her independence and is typical of the approach which has placed her in a subordinate role to both her husband and her daughter, Cecilia.

However, as both Orozco Acuaviva and Fernández Poza demonstrate, some of Francisca's views were quite revolutionary. Already possessed of an independent nature and inspired by the work of Wollstonecraft, she clearly saw the need for a level of female self-determination quite out of step with prevailing gender stereotypes. However, this progressive view is oddly combined with an otherwise reactionary stance which baulks at any evidence of liberal influence or social change. The first two *Pensamientos*, 'Una aldeana española a sus compatricias' and 'Saluda una andaluza a los vencedores de Austerlitz en los campos de Baylen' (An Andalucian woman greets the victors of Austerlitz in the fields of Baylen; 261–2), illustrate this contradiction. Both texts voice forthright political views in support of the reactionary cause which are in keeping with those expressed by any number of conservative commentators of the period, not least Böhl himself. However, the significance of these texts lies less in the views expressed and more in the specifically female voice employed. This is a radical strategy for the time, one which Francisca's own daughter felt unable to adopt almost half a century later, choosing instead the safety of a male pseudonym for her work. Francisca, on the other hand, would retain a more forthright approach throughout her polemical career, choosing a female pen name, *Cymdocea* (often given in the still clearly feminine form 'C......a'). Reading her work, it becomes apparent that she felt the feminine voice had a right to be heard and that it could offer a valid contribution to contemporary debate. This is underlined in a later example from the *Pensamientos* written in 1817 and entitled 'La razón y el sentimiento: diágolo entre una Dama, un Filósofo y un Labrador' (Reason and sentiment: dialogue between a lady, a philosopher and a peasant).[21] The dialogue rehearses a debate between a supporter of Romantic views, the *Dama*, and a follower of Enlightenment values, the *Filósofo*. The pro-Romantic views expressed clearly echo those being defended by Francisca and Böhl at the time and show the intellectual superiority of the *Dama* in arguing her case. Böhl's response to the *Pensamientos* is interesting in the context of his previous disapproval of his wife's proto-feminist tendencies. He seems to have been impressed with his wife's efforts as his annotations, provided for Julius and reproduced by Becher, demonstrate. 'La razón y el sentimiento' is described as 'vorzüglich' (exquisite) and another text, also written in 1817 and entitled 'Un sueño' (A dream), is described as 'sehr gut' (very good). Indeed, it is unlikely that he would have taken the trouble to send the pieces to Julius had he not felt them to be of some worth. At odds with his earlier dismissal of female intellectual endeavour, his views in 1821 were formed with the benefit of a decade of close co-operation with his wife and mark the culmination of a convergence in world view which developed during the Görslow years. This saw Böhl begin to occupy similar political and aesthetic ground to that defended by his wife and led him to respect her intellect and patriotic views. Central to this convergence is the exchange and subsequent dissemination of shared material and ideas.

This becomes particularly clear in the context of their scholarship. Writing to her husband in December 1810 at the height of the French occupation, Francisca takes defiant consolation in the work of a writer whose defence was soon to occupy their leisure hours:

> Me ocupo de Calderón y de nuestros antiguos poetas para procurarme algún consuelo. En los poetas es que se puede percibir el espíritu, los modales y el carácter de las Naciones. Los historiadores nos cuentan crímines y la historia es tristísima lectura. ¡Cómo pinta Calderón esa nobleza, esa generosidad, ese excesivo pundonor que caracterizaba a los españoles de su siglo! Pues todavia es lo mismo a pesar de la corteza viciosa que los vecinos, desde tanto tiempo, han echado sobre esta Nación y los siglos venideros lo dirán![22]

> (I try to find some solace by busying myself with Calderón and our ancient poets. It is in the work of the poets that one is able to perceive the spirit, manners and character of nations. Historians tell us of crimes and history makes for very sad reading. How Calderón depicts the nobility, the generosity, the overwhelming pride

which characterised the Spaniards of his century! And it remains the same despite the appearance of depravity which the neighbours have cast over this nation for so long and the centuries to come will testify to it.)

This excerpt, with its clear association of older literature and patriotic fervour, gives some indication of the impact Francisca would have on her husband's intellectual development, exposing him to a thoroughly conservative reading of Spanish culture which found its echo soon after in the Schlegelian apotheosis of Calderón which would inform the subsequent polemic. Indeed, the couple were involved in an intense dialogue throughout their years of separation, which laid the foundations for their polemical writings. Francisca's own knowledge of German culture was fostered by her correspondence with her husband. Böhl would write describing his own reading and recommend texts to her. Some of the letters failed to pass the censorship of Villate, but those that did were read aloud at Francisca's salon meetings. This, combined with her translating activity during this period, which later extended to Wollstonecraft's *Letters written during a Short Residence in Sweden, Norway and Denmark* (1796) and Byron's *Manfred* (1817),[23] show Francisca herself in the role of cultural mediator, emulating the example set by her husband. There is undoubtedly a developing commonality of purpose which emerges despite their physical separation, and which would culminate in their joint attack on neo-Classicism during the Calderón polemic a decade later.

Whilst Francisca was not solely responsible for changing her husband's *Weltanschauung*, this forceful and intelligent woman, along with the culture and ideals she represented, provided Böhl with a counterpoint, and indeed an alternative, to the values of his youth in relation to faith, literature and society. Indeed, he would later concede in a letter to Julius of 28 February 1813 shortly before his final departure for Spain, '[d]aß durch den Umgang einer solchen Erzspanierin als meine Frau ist, meine Studien wieder eine spanische Wendung genommen haben' (that, in the company of such an arch-Spaniard as my wife, my studies have again taken a Spanish turn). Whilst the years of separation placed a strain on their marriage, it nevertheless provided both Böhl and Francisca the opportunity to pursue their own intellectual path. Whilst Böhl retreated into introspection at Görslow, his wife was able to exercise her own judgement and establish a definitive stance for herself, one which would colour both the Calderón polemic and her own writings. What is astonishing is the similarity of their emergent world view, enabled only by irregular correspondence, but indicative of a shared ideological conviction. Böhl's increasingly intense relationship with his wife and Spain enables a shift in perspective which prefigures the transcultural nature of his scholarship and provides the foundation for his conversion to Catholicism and Romanticism during the relative isolation of the Görslow years. Having once thoroughly rejected Spain and its customs, Böhl can now be seen to function effectively between two cultures. This places him in a unique position as his world view shifts towards the inherent interdisciplinarity of Romanticism.

NOTES

1. The exact details of the young couple's early relationship remain unclear. There are hints in a letter from Böhl's brother, Gottlieb, dated 3 February 1795 that the couple met during Böhl's year in France in 1792, a view supported by Elise Campe and Pitollet. This view would seem to be further strengthened by Böhl himself. He states in the same letter (the brothers often wrote joint letters to their foster parents) that he was no longer emotionally unattached. However, Montoto places their first meeting earlier, in Cadiz sometime in 1790. Again, there is evidence from Böhl himself to support this claim. He states in a letter to Campe after his marriage, dated 22 March 1797, that he had known his wife for some six years before their wedding, which would place their first meeting in 1790.
2. Antonio Orozco Acuaviva, *La gaditana Frasquita Larrea, primera romántica española* (Jerez de la Frontera: Graficas del Exportador, 1977); Milagros Fernández Poza, *Frasquita Larrea y 'Fernán Caballero'. Mujer, revolución y romanticismo en España 1775–1870* (El Puerto de Santa María: Ayuntamiento de El Puerto de Santa María, 2001). Both texts also provide an overview of Böhl's life, relying in both cases on Campe via Pitollet and Carnero.
3. The Böhls had another three children, all of whom survived into adulthood: Aurora (1799), Juan Jacobo (1801) and Angela (1803).
4. There is a gap in the correspondence between Böhl and the Campes at this time which is probably due to the fact that any letters arriving from the infected city would have been immediately destroyed (VL: 38). This would also explain why the death of Carl Wilhelm, Böhl's younger brother, seems to go unreported.
5. Böhl was highly regarded in this capacity and would later become Consul for Hamburg in 1816. See Guillermo Carnero, 'Documentos relativos a Juan Nicolás Böhl de Faber en el Ministerio Español de Asuntos Exteriores', *Anales de Literatura Española*, 3 (1984), 159–86.
6. This is a typical usage of the term *romantisch* before 1798 and its first appearance in the German Romantic periodical, *Athenaeum*. Then, the term referred to anything associated with the *romance* lands or languages which had a clearly negative connotation for Böhl at this time. See Hans Eichner (ed.), 'Germany / Romantisch – Romantik – Romantiker' in *Romantic and Its Cognates/The European History of a Word* (Manchester: Manchester University Press, 1972), pp. 98–156 (p. 98).
7. Wilhelm von Humboldt, *Gesammelte Schriften*, 17 vols (Berlin: Behr, 1903); XV: Albert Leitzmann (ed.), *Wilhelm von Humboldts Tagebücher, Zweiter Band 1799–1835* (1918), pp. 252–3. Humboldt confuses the seniority of the two brothers.
8. The documents are in the possession of the Osborne family. The comments made here rely on the information provided by Carnero (O: 136–9), which are based on translations from the original German.
9. Böhl was later asked by Julius to submit these letters, written in German, for publication in the *Vaterländisches Museum*, but he declined, describing them as 'eine heitere Ansicht der geselligen Verhältniße, ohne tieferes Eindringen' (a light-hearted view of social relations, with no particular depth; 16 August 1810).
10. Christian August Fischer, *Reise von Amsterdam über Madrid und Cadiz nach Genua in den Jahren 1797 und 1798* (Berlin: [n. publ.]. 1799), pp. 216–17.
11. This letter is no longer extant in the *Campe-Sammlung* but is quoted by Elise Campe (VL: 40).
12. This locates Böhl at a significant cultural crossroads which emphasises a clear affinity with avant-garde aesthetics. As well as echoing the proto-Romanticism of Francisco de Goya's celebrated work 'El sueño de la razon produce monstruos' (The dream of reason produces monsters, 1799) in his reference to 'der beruhigende Schlaf der Vernunft' (the reassuring sleep of

reason), Böhl betrays a lexical and theoretical debt to Schiller, who employed similar terminology in the sixth of his *Ästhetische Briefe* (1794).

13 Martin Jakob von Faber had been Privy Councillor to the Prussian king since 1794 and was ennobled by Emperor Franz II in 1803. Böhl joked with Campe in a letter dated 27 September 1806, after receiving the privileges associated with his title, that he was now known as Böhl von Faber in Mecklenburg, but still plain Böhl everywhere else.

14 Carnero (O: 79); see also Montoto, *Algo más*, p. 45.

15 Böhl's letters to his mother-in-law are held in the Osborne archive; see Carnero (O: 80).

16 Quoted in Carnero (O: 81).

17 *Benito Pérez Galdós, Obras completas*, Federico Carlos Sainz de Robles (ed.), 6 vols (Madrid: Aguilar, 1950); I: *Episodios nacionales*, pp. 849–958 (p. 903).

18 Antonio Alcalá Galiano, *Recuerdos de un anciano* (Madrid: Biblioteca Clásica, 1907), pp. 176–7.

19 Copies of these *Pensamientos españoles* (Spanish thoughts) were sent to Julius by Böhl in 1821 and are now held in the *Österreichische Nationalbibliothek* in Vienna as part of the estate of the renowned Hispanist Ferdinand Wolf who later obtained the fragments from his friend Julius. The originals remain in the Osborne archive and have been published along with the rest of Francisca's writings by Orozco Acuaviva. References appear in the text.

20 Herrero, *Planteamiento*, p. 118.

21 This document is not reproduced by Orozco Acuaviva but appears instead in Hubert Becher, 'Pensamientos españoles de Da. Francisca de Larrea Böhl de Faber', *BBMP*, 1931 (316–35); 1932 (1–45), 1932: 20–8.

22 Quoted in Becher, 1932 (45).

23 It is not known when Francisca translated Byron's text but her version appeared posthumously in 1858, 'Manfredo. Drama en tres actos, traducido del original ingles de Lord Byron, por la madre de Fernán Caballero', *Revista de Ciencias, Literatura y Artes* 4 (1858), 429; 555; 626; 755. Her translation of Wollstonecraft is reproduced by Orozco Acuaviva who wrongly identifies the text as Francisca's own. Again, the date of the translation is unknown.

Chapter 3
Critical Beginnings: 'Reflexiones sobre la poesía'

Böhl's first public attempt at cultural mediation was the result of intense study following his return to Spain in 1798. Setting the pattern for future years and following the example set by Campe, Böhl was keen to keep abreast of the most recent developments in aesthetics and regularly received material from Hamburg. One parcel, supplied by the father of his friend and colleague, Valentin Meyer, and mentioned in a letter to Campe on 15 August 1799, is typical in its breadth and variety. It contained amongst others the rationalist Garve's *Grundsätze der Sittenlehre* (Principles of the theory of manners, 1798), Goethe's journal *Propyläen* (1798) and Gentz's *Historisches Journal* (1799), as well as the Schlegel brothers' *Athenaeum* (1798). The contents encapsulate the literary and cultural debate of the period and show the extent of Böhl's exposure to the contemporary flow of ideas at a time of intellectual and ideological revaluation. These ideas provide the foundations for Böhl's early work as a critic and pave the way for his first article in the Spanish press, 'Reflexiones sobre la poesía' (Reflections on poetry), which appeared in the periodical *Variedades de ciencias, literatura y artes* (Miscellany of sciences, literature and arts),[1] edited by Liberal thinker and poet, Manuel José Quintana (1772–1857). Although Quintana would later become the object of Böhl's censure during the 1820s, the writer provided the young critic with his first public forum, allowing him to introduce a set of ideas previously unknown in Spain. Quintana's own work is characterised by an openness to literary experimentation and an interest in the adaptation of traditional forms, an attitude illustrated by his willingness to showcase new poetics in a cultural environment still largely governed by neo-Classical ideals. This included an open interest in ideas emerging from other cultures and Böhl's article is one of a number included in the periodical, which appeared from 1803 to 1805, which discuss works from abroad. These include a review article on a translation of the first volume of Campe's *Reisebeschreibungen* and excerpts from a new translation of *Ossian*.[2] The latter in particular highlights Quintana's interest in traditional forms which would later drive his own philological work. His interest in Böhl's article, however, was undoubtedly driven by its contribution to the debate surrounding neo-Classical poetics. Indeed, Böhl himself may have intended to introduce the conceptual framework of contemporary German aesthetics into the existing Spanish debate surrounding the challenge to the neo-Classical canon by the more lyrical, sentimental poetry of Meléndez Valdés, although there is no suggestion of this in the article itself, nor does the poet merit mention in Böhl's literary correspondence at the time.

Böhl's text is primarily an introduction to Schiller's reading of Kantian aesthetics, mainly taken from Schiller's two major aesthetic treatises, *Über die ästhetische Erziehung des Menschen* (On the aesthetic education of man, 1794), often referred to as the *Ästhetische Briefe* (Aesthetic letters), and *Über naive und sentimentalische Dichtung* (On naive and sentimental poetry, 1795–6).[3] The article constitutes possibly the earliest attempt to introduce Schiller's critical writings to Spain.[4] Koch, in his extensive study of Spanish reception of Schiller, offers no earlier example and cites as the first Spanish translation of the *Ästhetische Briefe* that provided by Manuel García Morente in 1920.[5] Furthermore, he rather oddly rejects Böhl's efforts as a first attempt to draw Schiller into the aesthetic debate in Spain on the grounds that the article was written by a German. This overlooks the transcultural nature of Böhl's work and ignores the willingness of a Spanish editor to publish a text which epitomises the complex relationship between Enlightenment and Romantic thought in Germany, focusing on or at the very least echoing the ideas of thinkers whose work is crucial to this cultural axis: Kant, Herder and Schiller.

This short text is, however, rather frustrating for the modern reader intent on tracing its role in Böhl's intellectual development, due for the most part to his own questionable methodology. His claim in the introduction that the text comprises extracts can only be understood in the very loosest sense. There is no use of direct quotation nor any attempt at a systematic exposé. The reader is instead presented with a summary of selected key points from Schiller's treatises which are discussed without any attempt at contextualisation as Böhl moves from one to the other without warning. His use of terminology is also problematic. As Juretschke points out, the exposition of Schiller's ideas is hampered by Böhl's attempts to render certain key terms in Spanish (DD: 152). For example, the concepts of 'naiv' and 'sentimentalisch' are greatly simplified as representing reason, grounded in the abstract, and sensuousness, based on intuition and reflection. These are then rendered respectively as 'didáctico' (didactic) and 'lírico' (lyric). This choice of terminology is certainly more transparent, if not immediately clear, to an audience already familiar with Schiller's development of Kant, but must have made for confusing reading to a Spanish readership unversed in the contemporary literary debate in Germany. The reference to source is also vague with no indication as to the original text beyond the names Schiller and Kant. Other thinkers are alluded to, but not named. This practice, dubious even by the standards of the day, foreshadows Böhl's technique in disseminating the ideas of August Wilhelm Schlegel in 1814. However, in contrast to the forthright nature of Böhl's later polemic, this article opens with an introductory paragraph which is almost apologetic in tone. The author seems aware that the views he is about to put forward might not meet with the approval of his audience: 'remito las adjuntas reflexiones sobre la Poesía extractadas de Schiller y otros discípulos del célebre Kant: si merecen la aprobacion de vmds, enviaré otros extractos de los mismos autores' (I offer the following reflections on poetry taken from Schiller and other disciples of the famous Kant: if they merit your approval, I will send other extracts by the same authors; 247). This self-effacing opening informs the reader on two levels, drawing attention explicitly to the area of aesthetics under discussion whilst alluding implicitly to the process of selection which has shaped the article. The text before the reader is, then, as much an anatomy of Böhl's developing world view as it is an exploration of contemporary German aesthetics.

Böhl's approach to Schiller's work is clearly informed by his reception of the material received regularly from Hamburg and owes much to two seminal periodicals which were central to the cultural debate of the period. The first of these is Schiller's own journal, *Die Horen*, which appeared from January 1795 until April 1798, and to which Garve, Goethe and Gentz all contributed. Inspired by Enlightenment philosophy and assuming an enlightened consensus, the publication was intended to educate the reading public in current literary debate and was to include contributions from key figures of the period. Although unable to obtain a contribution from Kant, Schiller was nevertheless successful in securing the collaboration of emerging talents such as August Wilhelm Schlegel, as well as prominent figures such as Fichte, Herder and Goethe. The latter's involvement was crucial in order to lend the publication intellectual weight as the organ of a self-proclaimed 'Societät der Schriftsteller' (society of writers), suggesting a literary republic of like-minded thinkers. Unlike Schiller's earlier publication, *Neue Thalia*, the journal was aimed at a wide audience and was set up in direct competition to Wieland's *Teutscher Merkur* (German Mercury). Unfortunately, Schiller failed to secure the competitive edge and whilst Wieland's periodical continued until 1810, *Die Horen* ceased publication after three years amidst a certain degree of animosity, especially between the editors, Schiller and Fichte, as the 'Societät der Schriftsteller' began to crumble. Despite this collapse and a mixed response in intellectual circles, the publication left an indelible mark on the literary landscape of the period. For Böhl, the periodical was crucial in introducing him to the contemporary avant-garde of aesthetic thought. The inclusion of Schiller's *Ästhetische Briefe*, which were to play a key role in the development of early Romantic aesthetics, was particularly significant. Böhl received copies of *Die Horen* from Campe and was greatly impressed by Schiller's contributions. Writing to Campe on 21 January 1797, Böhl comments on the relationship between Goethe and Schiller and praises the latter in terms which emphasise his pivotal role:

> Von Schiller besonders hatte ich eine große Idee gefaßt, seitdem ich seine Aufsätze in den Horen gelesen habe. Was halten Sie besonders von seinen Briefen über die

> ästhetische Erziehung? Ist überhaupt diese Zeitschrift so interessant, wie sie mir scheint? Ich finde so viel Neues und Anziehendes für mich darin, daß ich gewißermaßen damit geitze, und noch lange nicht den ersten Jahrgang erschöpft habe: manches auch kostet mir Anstrengung um es zu faßen, und leider faße ich es nur in dem Augenblicke wo ich es lese; es haftet nicht in meinem Gedächtniß wenigstens nicht nach erstem und zweitem Lesen. Besonders angenehm ist mir endlich, daß ich fast nichts darin finde, was sich nicht mit meinem jetzigen Gedanken System kombiniren läßt und vieles was Gefühle in Gedanken umwandelt.
>
> (I had acquired a particular interest in Schiller since reading his essays in Die Horen. What do you make of his letters on aesthetic education in particular? Is the periodical really as interesting as it seems to me? There are so many new and attractive things in it for me that I am somewhat sparing with it and still have not finished the first volume: some of it also requires some effort in order to understand it and unfortunately I only grasp it when I am reading it, it does not remain in my memory, at least not after the first or second reading. I am, however, most pleased that I find almost nothing in it which cannot be combined with my current mode of thinking and much which transforms emotion into thought.)

These comments serve to emphasise the tension and sought resolution between reason and emotion which underlies Böhl's revaluation during the 1790s and demonstrate the extent to which Böhl's personal intellectual journey reflects the wider cultural shift at a time when faith in the power of reason was beginning to falter.

The relevance of Schiller's periodical, both as a repository for contemporary ideas and in the context of Böhl's development, is further underlined by the involvement of August Wilhelm Schlegel, who would go on to co-found the *Athenaeum*, the key periodical of early Romanticism. Böhl's interest in Schiller's aesthetics ensured a predisposed fascination with the content of this new publication which was launched in 1798 just as the Schlegel brothers were coming to prominence. August Wilhelm was writing for Schiller and Friedrich, having been turned down for *Die Horen*, was writing for the rival publications, *Deutschland* and *Lyceum der schönen Künste* (Lyceum of the fine arts). Breaking away from the literary power axis created by Goethe and Schiller, the *Athenaeum* was a development beyond *Die Horen*. It was intended as the vehicle for a new aesthetic and effectively presents emergent Romantic theory as work in progress. The contributors included the poet, Novalis (Friedrich von Hardenberg, 1772–1801) and the theologian and philosopher, Friedrich Schleiermacher (1768–1834), and, of course, the Schlegels themselves.[6] Instead of focusing on a 'Societät der Schriftsteller', the *Athenaeum* was inspired by the far more intimate notion of 'Verbrüderung' (avowal of brotherhood) following the Romantic ideals of *Symphilosophie* and *Sympoesie*. The relevance of the journal to Böhl's development is reflected in Friedrich Schlegel's discussion of the publication in 1803 in his own periodical, *Europa*, where he highlights the transfer in early Romantic thought from 'Kritik und Universalität' (criticism and universality) to the 'Geist des Mystizismus' (spirit of mysticism).[7] This conceptual shift recalls Böhl's personal struggle and his emerging critical stance in the 1790s and early 1800s. His article in Quintana's periodical represents a crucial stage in this process and the dilettante nature of the piece exemplifies the difficulties facing a young, inexperienced scholar anxious to present new ideas to others as a self-appointed cultural mediator, but yet still struggling to steady his own uncertain *Weltanschauung*. The tensions created by exposure to both Schiller's ideas in *Die Horen* and the revaluation of aesthetics presented in the *Athenaeum* are apparent in Böhl's choice of material and critical emphasis.

'Reflexiones sobre la poesía' can be divided into three main sections. The first of these opens with the following statement: 'Para juzgar con fundamento de la Poesía, es preciso ántes de todo formarse de ella ideas exâctas y cabales' (to enable a reliable judgement of poetry, it is first of all necessary to establish an exact and proper idea of what it is). This might suggest an introduction to Schiller's second aesthetic treatise, *Über naive und sentimentalische Dichtung*, but is instead followed by an argument which is clearly indebted to the Kantian dualism elaborated in his *Über die ästhetische Erziehung des Menschen*. The length of Böhl's article precludes an exhaustive discussion of Schiller's ideas and Böhl is indeed selective. He ignores Schiller's introduction to Kantian aesthetics and bypasses too Schiller's initial discussion of the interaction between the political and the aesthetic, moving forward instead to concentrate on the discussion of man's aesthetic understanding of the world contained in letters eleven to fifteen. First, Böhl outlines the thesis put forward by Schiller in letters eleven and twelve, which describe the two key intellectual resources of the individual as being formal and material. In terms already familiar to Böhl through Campe, Schiller explains these in terms of 'drives' (*Triebe*): the 'formal drive' (*Formtrieb*) and the 'sensuous/material drive' (*Stofftrieb*). The former gives order and coherence to our otherwise arbitrary sensual perception of the world, whereas the latter turns what is mere form into the reality which we experience as emotional beings. These 'drives' are grounded in Kant's notions of *a priori* and *a posteriori* and denote our means of relating to the world around us, based either on a rational (analytic) or sensual (synthetic) response, thus defining our experience of the world as something which, in Wordsworth's terms, we 'half-create and [half] perceive'.[8] Böhl focuses on the drives described by Schiller as a prerequisite to an understanding of poetry and summarises his complex argument in the following terms:

> Si nos exâminamos atentamente, reducirémos todas las afecciones de nuestra alma á dos inclinaciones radicales, á la una llamarémos inclinacion *material*, y á la otra *formal*. Es indudable que ambas son sumamente análogas á nuestra naturaleza, la

qual siendo compuesta de *materia* y *espíritu*, se ha considerado siempre como *doble ó mixta*, es indudable tambien, que la inclinacion *material* nos acerca á los animales, y nos hace desear las sensaciones agradables; al contrario la *formal*, distinguiéndonos de ellos, es la fuente y orígen de nuestros pensamientos. (248)

(If we examine ourselves carefully, we will reduce all the affects of our soul to two radical inclinations, one we will call the *material* inclination, the other the *formal*. There is no doubt that both are extremely analogous with our nature, which, being composed of *matter* and *spirit*, has always been considered *double* or *mixed*, there is also no doubt that the *material* inclination places us close to animals and makes us crave agreeable sensations; conversely, the *formal* distinguishes us from them and is the source and origin of our thoughts.)

Böhl's reductive approach, perhaps unavoidably given his journalistic medium, emphasises and exaggerates the divide between the rational and the sensual. This necessarily robs Schiller's argument of a good deal of its subtlety and threatens to leave the reader with the impression that his aesthetic theory is founded on the basis of an insurmountable polarity. Böhl does seek to redress the balance by then moving forward to Schiller's thirteenth letter, which warns against excess, but this too leads to a simplification of Schiller's ideas. Whereas Schiller's original argument emphasises containment and balance, Böhl instead dwells on the extreme. In his view, both 'drives' must be balanced in us, for to submit to the material drive is to be brutalised, just as to submit to the spiritual drive is to be overwhelmed. Either extreme is to be seen in a negative light: 'En efecto vemos gran número de sabios, que abusando de la facultad de pensar, viven tan lejos de la felicidad destinada á los humanos, como los hombres sensuales anegados en sus desmedidos apetitos' (in fact we see a great number of wise men who, abusing the faculty of thought, live as far from the happiness which is man's destiny as those men of a sensual nature drowning in their own disproportionate appetites; 248). To appreciate life to the full, we must satisfy both 'drives' and seek 'un modo conciliatorio' (a conciliatory mode). Just such a solution is identified in Schiller's third principle, outlined in letter fourteen, the so-called 'play drive' (*Spieltrieb*) or aesthetic inclination, which Böhl describes as 'una manera de explicarse en que igualmente se *piensa* y *siente*' (a means of expressing oneself which involves *thought* and *sensation* in equal measure; 249). In Schiller's terms, as outlined in letter fifteen, whereas the 'form drive' provides 'Gestalt' or form, the 'play drive' strives for 'lebende Gestalt' or living form. Focusing on the aesthetic dimension of this holistic outcome, Böhl rather misleadingly defines this third principle 'Arte', the means by which 'los Filósofos modernos' (modern thinkers) hope to realise living form and of which poetry is one of the main branches.

Having thus introduced the concepts informing Schiller's three principles, Böhl moves on, albeit unannounced, to a discussion of Schiller's other major treatise on aesthetics, *Über naive und sentimentalische Dichtung*, which provides the focus of the second section of the article. He begins with a definition of two types of poetry:

> La poesía producirá este efecto de dos maneras ó dando un cuerpo á lo que solo es espíritu, ó espiritualizando la materia. La Poesía, pues, será didáctica ó lírica. La primera tiene mas relacion con el pensamiento, la segunda con las sensaciones; pero precediendo en nosotros las sensaciones al pensamiento, del qual son aquellas el único tesoro de sus riquezas intelectuales, se sigue de aquí ser los hombres mas inclinados á sentir que á pensar, é igualmente mas amantes de la Poesía lírica que de la didáctica.
>
> (Poetry produces this effect in two ways, either by giving body to that which is spirit or spiritualising matter. Poetry is then didactic or lyric. The former relates more to thought, the latter to the senses; but as our senses precede our thoughts, and senses are the only treasury of thought's intellectual riches, it follows that men are more inclined to feel than to think and equally more enamoured of lyric than didactic poetry.)

This passage opens with the notion of duality outlined earlier as Böhl concentrates on poetry's mediating function, helping to balance the material with the spirit and vice versa, evoking therefore the 'play drive' and underlining Böhl's emphasis on the holistic aspect of Schiller's aesthetics. There is then something of a disjuncture in Böhl's argument as he claims that poetry will therefore be either didactic or lyric, the former related to thought, the latter to the senses, an assertion which suggests divergence rather then convergence. The focus then shifts back to the reciprocity of these two categories, which are further extrapolated to parallel Schiller's notions of 'naiv' and 'sentimentalisch'. However, Böhl once more begins his exposition of Schiller's ideas from the middle rather than the beginning, forgoing the detailed argument which Schiller puts forward for the existence of these two categories and, indeed, the subtle divisions within the latter, which forms the bulk of the treatise. Such eclecticism aside, the main problem here is Böhl's choice of terminology. Schiller does indeed use the term 'didaktische Poesie' (didactic poetry; 732), but does not juxtapose it with one referring to lyrical poetry. In referring to didactic poetry in his critique of Haller, Schiller is discussing a specific genre, which he then defines as a 'Lehrgedicht' (didactic poem), which to his mind has never been successfully attempted. Whether Böhl chose his term from this section remains unclear, but it would seem unlikely given its peripheral position in the context of Schiller's wider argument. Instead, it seems far more likely that Böhl is attempting, albeit it with limited success, to distil Schiller's thesis to a few key points. In poetic terms, Böhl thus ascribes to the rational notion of *Formtrieb* the characteristic of didacticism and to the sensuous notion of *Stofftrieb* that of lyricism.

Böhl's reading of Schiller is weighted towards an appreciation of the lyrical, which clearly foreshadows a Romantic world view. The claim that man is more inclined towards the lyric summarises a central aspect of Schiller's argument for sentimental or reflective poetry. However, Böhl takes a stance which goes further than Schiller in its appreciation of the lyric. Whereas Schiller claims that 'von dem naiven Dichter wendet man sich mit Leichtigkeit und Lust' (one turns with ease and joy from the naive poet) and that 'wir versinken lieber betrachtend in uns selbst' (we would rather sink into self-observation; 753), Böhl's judgmental summary of Schiller's views emphasises a subjective emotionality which denies the universal and tends toward the emerging Romantic aesthetic as expressed in the *Atheneaum*:

> Si á lo dicho añadimos que la poesía lírica enoblece la situación mas ordinaria de nuestro ser, y que la didáctica degrada de un cierto modo el mas sublime entusiasmo, confesarémos tambien que la primera merece la preferencia. (249)
>
> (If we add to this that lyric poetry ennobles the most ordinary state of being and that the didactic degrades to some extent the most sublime enthusiasm, we must confess that the former deserves preference.)

Böhl's formulation clearly recalls Novalis' words of 1798: 'Indem ich dem Gemeinen einen hohen Sinn, dem Gewöhnlichen ein geheimnisvolles Ansehen, [. . .] gebe, so romantisiere ich es' (by endowing that which is common with a deep meaning, by endowing that which is ordinary with a mysterious appearance, I thus romanticise it).[9] As well as adopting this marked Romantic stance, Böhl also juxtaposes the two categories of poetry far more crudely. His definition of the lyric remains close to Schiller's view of reflective poetry as the 'Geburt der Abgezogenheit und Stille' (product of seclusion and calm; 753) by evoking a conciliatory middle way: 'Si llamamos sentimiento el estado medio entre la sensacion y el pensamiento, podrémos decir por consequencia que la Poesía lírica produce este sentimiento' (if we are to call sentiment the state midway between sensation and thought, then we can therefore say that lyrical poetry produces this sentiment; 249). However, the rhetorical 'No así la didáctica' (not so the didactic [poetry]) carries an almost disapproving tone, the grounds for which are then explained: 'lo primero porque parte del punto enérgico del pensamiento, al qual no podemos elevarnos siempre, y lo segundo porque las formas de que se sirve distan demasiado de las nuestras' (first, because it emerges from the life force of thought, to which we are not always able to raise ourselves and, secondly, because the forms it uses are too far removed from our own). Again, however, the sense of Schiller's original idea is reproduced; this time his claim that 'die naive ist das Kind des Lebens, und in das Leben führt sie auch zurück' (naïve [poetry] is the child of life and leads back into life too; 753) is paralleled in Böhl's idea that the didactic 'parte del punto enérgico del pensamiento' (emerges from the life force of thought). Böhl ends his discussion by focusing on the ability of the lyric to relate to man, again placing the didactic in a negative position which suggests a degree of alienation: 'al contrario la lírica amoldándose á nuestro estado habitual, solo usa materiales que exîsten siempre en nuestro contorno' (on the contrary, the lyric moulds itself to our habitual state, only using materials which always exist around us; 249). Whilst lyric poetry centres on that which is familiar to us, bringing us comfort in a context we know, didactic poetry is abstract and rational. Here lies the crux of Böhl's Romantic reading of Schiller: the need for poetry to communicate individualised emotion.

The Romantic emphasis of Böhl's reading of Schiller's aesthetics was not unusual. Connections between Schiller's argument and the emerging Classic–Romantic dichotomy were soon made, a point underlined by Goethe's famous claim made in conversation with Eckermann:

Der Begriff von klassischer und romantischer Poesie, die jetzt über die ganze Welt geht und soviel Streit und Spaltungen verursacht [. . .] ist ursprünglich von mir und Schiller ausgegangen. Ich hatte in der Poesie die Maxime des objektiven Verfahrens und wollte nur dieses gelten lassen, Schiller aber, der ganz subjektiv wirkte, hielt seine Art für die rechte, und um sich gegen mich zu wehren, schrieb er den Aufsatz über naive und sentimentalische Dichtung.[10]

(The concept of classical and romantic poetry, which is now spreading all over the world and causing so much conflict and division [. . .] originated with myself and Schiller. In poetry, I was guided by principles of objectivity and wanted to recognise this method only. Schiller, however, whose method was wholly subjective, maintained his way was the right one and in order to defend himself against me, he wrote the essay about naïve and sentimental poetry.)

As Lesley Sharpe makes clear in her study of the reception of Schiller's aesthetic writings, Goethe's assertion is rather misleading, mainly because the terms 'naïve' and 'sentimental' do not correspond to 'classical' and 'romantic'. Nevertheless, his view is evidence of the nature of contemporary reception of Schiller's work and 'the very fact that Goethe runs together the pairs *naïve–sentimental* and *classical–romantic* indicates how quickly Schiller's distinction was adapted by Romantic critics and became part of people's mental furniture'.[11] Böhl is clearly part of this reception process, engaging with Schiller's work at a time when he is himself subject to the broader cultural shift, receiving the development of Kantian aesthetics as part of an Enlightenment tradition, but sharing the doubts experienced by others of his generation which fostered the emergence of the new Romantic aesthetic. In fact, in publishing his article, Böhl paid Schiller's work a good deal more attention than most of the Romantic school, who, Sharpe adds, effectively ignored his work 'in accordance with their policy of elevating Goethe and keeping a telling silence on Schiller'. Although Böhl, in line with many other Romantic thinkers including August Wilhelm Schlegel, would later conform to the criticism of Schiller's categorisation of certain poets such as Shakespeare and Goethe among the 'naiven Dichter' (naïve poets), at this early stage in his development, the step beyond Kant's vigorous rejection of *Neigung* found in Schiller's aesthetics provides a suitable staging post in his experimentation with new ideas.

Böhl's absorption of ideas central to the contemporary aesthetic debate is further underlined in the third and final section of his 'Reflexiones' article, where he briefly discusses poetry in the context of national character and its impact on the creation of literature. Here, he brings together two uncomfortable bedfellows in Kant and Herder. Their influence is, however, clear. In discussing national character, for example, elements of Böhl's argument bear a striking similarity to Kant's depictions of national characteristics in relation to aesthetic taste found in his *Betrachtungen über das Gefühl des Schönen und Erhabenen* (Observations on the beautiful and sublime, 1764).[12] Kant's view of the Spaniards as 'phantastisch' (visionary; 876) and of Spain as a land where 'die Unterweisung der gesunden Vernunft [. . .] große Hindernisse zu überwinden haben [wird]' (the instruction of sound reason will encounter great obstacles; 877) is echoed in Böhl's depiction of Spain's literature as one which has produced 'una metafisica de pasiones' (a metaphysic of passions). Similar parallels are apparent in relation to German character. In examining the nature of the Germans, Kant claims the following:

Er hat eine glückliche Mischung in dem Gefühle so wohl des Erhabenen und des Schönen; und wenn er in dem ersteren es nicht einem Engländer, im zweiten aber dem Franzosen nicht gleich tut, so übertrifft er sie beide, in so ferne er sie verbindet. (874)

(He has a fortunate combination of feeling, both in that of the sublime and in that of the beautiful; if in the first he does not equal an Englishman, nor in the second a Frenchman, he yet surpasses both in so far as he unites them.)

This view is echoed by Böhl who claims that the Germans are 'alimentados con las grandes obras de todas Naciones' (nourished with the great works of all nations) and thus appreciative of many cultures. The echoes of Kant in Böhl's argument are to be expected given their currency at the time. Interesting is the apparent willingness to disseminate further ideas central to the 'Black Legend' in Spain itself, something which would lend weight to the criticism levelled by the likes of Clavijo in assessing the negative reception of Spanish culture abroad. However, the notion of a nation whose artistic efforts are driven by sheer emotion is perhaps less negative than it might at first appear as the Kantian view of Spain is tempered by Böhl's allusions to the work of Herder. Although clearly no 'disciple' of Kant, as Böhl's introductory comments might suggest, there is much in Herder's notion of a national literature which is suited to Böhl's argument and his influence, although not acknowledged in name, seems probable. Building on Schiller, Böhl traces the development of literature from the Classical to the modern age and draws attention to the manner in which individual nations have managed to combine the material and formal drives in order to suit the aesthetic needs of their individual characters. Read in this context, it is the very emotionality of Spanish culture which helps to delineate its individuality, thus appropriately reflecting the character of the people. This underlines the communicative significance of poetry as a means of historical and cultural record which is a central principle of Herder's theory of cultural organicism as elaborated in his essays 'Briefwechsel über Ossian und die Lieder alter Völker' (Correspondence concerning Ossian and the songs of the ancient peoples) and 'Shakespeare' (both 1773). Adopting this Herderian stance, Böhl's article carries a further significance, constituting his first, albeit brief, defence of Spanish literature:

> Los Españoles aunque llenos de ideas, no pudiendo extenderlas por varias circunstancias agenas de mi asunto, al dominio de la razon, las aplicáron al sentimiento. De aquí resultó una metafisica de pasiones, que si fué contraria al buen gusto, no por eso dexó de abrir un campo anchuroso para que se desarrollasen grandes qualidades y sublimes talentos. (251)
>
> (The Spaniards, although full of ideas, being unable to develop them for various reasons outside of my subject, in line with reason, applied them to sentiment. This resulted in a metaphysic of passions, which although contrary to good taste, nevertheless did not stop them from opening up a wide field in which they could develop great qualities and sublime talents.)

These comments pre-empt Böhl's later vehement defence of Spain's national literature and are notable for their emphasis on Romantic excess. The absence in his appraisal of any harmonising tendencies displays a tacit willingness to defend a literature which clearly defies the rules of good taste. Following this line of argument, Böhl's article ends with a call to appreciate the virtues of each national literature, which is undoubtedly Herderian in tone:

Por último, concluyo diciendo, que es preciso estimar sobre manera los poetas Españoles é Italianos, divertirse con los rimadores Franceses, admirar los bardos Ingleses, y amar los romancistas Alemanes. (252)

(Finally, I conclude by saying that it is necessary to value the Spanish and Italian poets greatly, to find amusement in the French rhymesters, admire the English bards and love the German balladeers.)

Böhl's declaration amounts to an outright rejection of Enlightenment universality, showing unequivocal support for the cultural pluralism at the heart of Herderian theory, which sees Böhl move ever closer to the Romantic aesthetic in a celebration of cultural diversity. This is typical of the broader reception of Herder's work which, although still part of the Enlightenment debate, heralded Romanticism and came to be understood as Romantic by many European critics.

The validity of Böhl's reading and presentation of contemporary German aesthetics is clearly open to question, not least because the result is eclectic and hampered by problems in translating key terms. It is impossible to know how he might have continued the proposed series of articles, as this was the first and last article by Böhl to appear in Quintana's periodical. (The text actually appeared in the final volume of the publication.) However, Böhl's emphasis on the 'Romantic', holistic aspects of Schiller's aesthetics combined with a Herderian appreciation of national literature represent another major milestone in his literary revaluation. Central to his reception of both thinkers is the notion of art as a means of communication and it this which characterises his own drive to mediate between cultures. This early attempt at cultural mediation had little impact, something alluded to by Böhl himself some years later during the Calderón polemic, but is significant as an early attempt – possibly the first – to provide a Spanish readership with an overview of contemporary German thought.

NOTES

1 *Variedades de ciencias, literatura y artes, obra periódica*, 8.22 (1805), 247–52. References appear in the text.
2 The texts referred to are the following: *Biblioteca geográfica, ó Colección de viages para la juventud: escrita por el Sr. Campe y traducida por Don Juan Corradi, Tom. I. Madrid, en la Imprenta de Don Josef Collado. Año de 1804*, 2.8 (1804), 120–8; *De Osian, y de una nueva traducción española de sus poemas*, 4.16 (1804), 248–54; 4.17 (1804), 307–19; 4.18 (1804), 375–8.
3 References to these two works are to the following edition: Gerhard Fricke and Herbert G. Göpfert (eds.), *Friedrich Schiller, Sämtliche Werke*, 9th edn., 5 vols (Munich: Hanser, 1959 [1993]); V: *Erzählungen/Theoretische Schriften*. References appear in the text.
4 Whilst the 'Reflexiones' article is now widely acknowledged to be by Böhl, there has been some confusion surrounding the original date and indeed the authorship of the piece. In a letter to Dorothea Campe on 19 August 1803, Böhl refers to an early foray into the world of literary

criticism, announcing that he has written 'einige Briefe' (some letters) in Spanish on the theatre. He then goes on to explain that the first of these has been published anonymously by a friend without his knowledge in a Madrid periodical, but that despite some positive response from intellectual commentators who, he claims, accredited the piece to the finest thinkers in the land, he has been discouraged by the unkind reaction of his mercantile peers and therefore decided that the remainder must remain 'im Pulte', 'biß zu einer besseren Gelegenheit' (in the desk, until a better opportunity). He has, however, had some success, in keeping with his self-appointed role as cultural mediator, in bringing the ideas of key German thinkers to the attention of his friends and acquaintances: 'Es mangelt nicht an einzelnen guten Köpfen sogar hier in Cadiz und verschiedenen Freunden habe ich die neue Aesthetik von Kant und Schiller sehr goutiren machen' (there is no lack of good individual minds, even here in Cadiz, and I have been able to bring a number of friends to look most favourably on the new aesthetic from Kant and Schiller). The reference here to Kant and Schiller would certainly seem to indicate an overlap between Böhl's letters on the theatre and the *Variedades* article. However, his letter to Dorothea Campe precedes the article by over two years, the latter not appearing until November 1805. Consequently, critics are in disagreement as to the provenance of the piece. Pitollet takes the view that the article was written by one of the 'einzelnen guten Köpfen' who Böhl mentions in his letter to Dorothea (QC: 86n). Juretschke, however, points out that, during the polemic, Mora makes reference to the *Variedades* piece, citing it as an early example of Böhl's misguided views (DD: 152n). Böhl himself revisits the argument put forward in the article almost word for word in the first *Pasatiempo* in his lengthy response to Mora's attack. Carnero also argues for Böhl's authorship of the article and suggests that the letter refers instead to another, as yet undiscovered, article or to a publication which did not see the light of day. As he points out, although the article did not appear until November, it is dated 'Chiclana y Julio 12 de 1805', at which time Böhl was still in Spain, about to depart for Germany. Given that one of his earlier pieces on the theatre clearly must have been published in order to provoke the negative response it did from his peers, I would agree with Carnero's second suggestion that Böhl is referring to another, as yet undiscovered, text (O: 153–5). Böhl's description of this early piece further supports this view. The reference to Kant and Schiller in his letter to Dorothea Campe would certainly tally with the content of the *Variedades* article, but the emphasis in the published text is on poetics rather than theatre. The fact that there would appear to be two texts would also suggest that Böhl had been actively considering a career as a critic for some time, but was put off by the response of his fellow merchants. It makes sense, then, that he should choose to take advantage of his departure for Germany to voice his opinions once more, this time out of earshot of those who might mock him.

5   Herbert Koch, *Schiller und Spanien*, Münchener Romantische Arbeiten 31 (Munich: Hueber, 1973), p. 122.
6   Notable also were the female contributors Caroline Schlegel-Schelling (1763–1809), Dorothea Schlegel (1763–1839) and Sophie Bernhardi-Tieck (1775–1833). Interestingly, both Tieck and Schelling had contributions rejected, as the Schlegel brothers were unsure of their compatibility with the notion of 'Verbrüderung' which underpinned the ethos of the journal. The journal appeared twice a year over a period of three years, published initially by Vieweg the elder (whose son later married Lotte Campe) and then by Frölich, who took over Vieweg's business in 1799.
7   *Europa. Eine Zeitschrift*, I/I (1803), 52.
8   Stephen Gill (ed.), *William Wordsworth. A Critical Edition of the Major Works* (Oxford: Oxford University Press, 1984), p. 134. From 'Lines written a few miles from Tintern Abbey' (1798). Wordsworth borrowed the notion from Young's *Night Thoughts* (1742–5).
9   Paul Kluckhohn and Richard Samuel (eds.), *Novalis Schriften. Die Werke Friedrich von Hardenbergs*, 2nd edn., 4 vols (Stuttgart: Kohlhammer, 1968); II: 545. The fragment first appeared in *Novalis Schriften* (1802).
10 Karl Eibl et al (eds.), *Johann Wolfgang von Goethe Sämtliche Werke, Briefe, Tagebücher und Gespräche*, 40 vols (Frankfurt am Main: Deutscher Klassiker Verlag, 1999); Abt. II, 12: 395.
11 Lesley Sharpe, *Schiller's Aesthetic Essays: Two Centuries of Criticism* (London: Camden House, 1995), p. 10.
12 Wilhelm Weischedel (ed.), *Immanuel Kant. Werke in sechs Bänden*, 6 vols (Darmstadt:

Johann Nikolas Böhl von Faber (1770–1836): A German Romantic in Spain

Wissenschaftliche Buchgesellschaft, 1983); I: *Vorkritische Schriften bis 1768; Betrachtungen über das Gefühl des Schönen und Erhabenen. Vierter Abschnitt: Von den Nationalcharaktern, in so ferne sie auf dem unterschiedlichen Gefühl des Erhabenen und Schönen beruhen*. References appear in the text.

Chapter 4
Romantic Rebirth

In the years following his return to Germany in 1806, Böhl found himself questioning the very essence of his existence. The value systems of his youth had been under attack for some time. Enlightenment truths had been thrown into question by the Terror which followed the French Revolution, whilst the Napoleonic Wars had shattered illusions of French beneficence. His family idyll had been torn apart by his wife's departure and Görslow, for all the contemplative peace it provided, was proving a drain on his finances at a time when the family firm stood on the verge of ruin. Little wonder that Böhl, left to his own devices on his country estate, should begin to question in earnest the values which governed his life. Already aware of new influences through Campe, Francisca and Spain, the next few years were spent wrestling with old beliefs and new ideas as Böhl explored fresh horizons in terms of faith, political ideology and aesthetics, areas which saw him engage with current thinking on topics ranging from philosophy to medieval literature in an attempt to reground his world view. This process was undertaken on a conscious level which Böhl referred to from the very beginning as his 'Wiedergeburt im Norden' (Rebirth in the north; letter to Dorothea Campe, 22 January 1807) and which saw issues relating to religious belief, political stance and aesthetic judgement become thoroughly intertwined in a period of intense introspection.

This quest for rebirth was played out against a backdrop of perpetual crisis. Daily life was far from straightforward. Böhl's country idyll proved far more testing than he had initially expected. Much of his time was taken up with the care and education of his two young children and the first summer was plagued by illness and a poor harvest. Furthermore, the relative tranquillity of Görslow stood in sharp contrast to the political events of the day. The Napoleonic occupation was underway and the effects of war were soon felt uncomfortably close to home threatening the stability of life on the estate, as well as the fortunes of the family firm in Spain. It is indicative of the complexity of contemporary politics that, in this tense situation, France was not the only foe. Böhl was particularly outraged by the actions of the British government in establishing an anti-French naval blockade in May 1806 and gave vent to his anger in an article published in the Hamburg-based *Nordische Miszellen* on 31 August 1806.[1] His article 'Auch etwas über Handels-Monopol und Handels-Bedrückung' (Further comment on trading monopolies and trade restrictions) is a response to the situation following the defeat of the French at Trafalgar, which saw British dominance of maritime trade further strengthened at the expense of her trading partners. The British navy kept trade routes open for Britain and her allies whilst blockading the French coast and that of any nation allied or subordinate to France, leaving any neutral states, such as Hamburg, defenceless in the face of such a power. This aggressive British protectionism eventually led to the establishment of Napoleon's Continental System in November 1806 in a plan intended to suffocate British trade in turn. Böhl was angered by the notion that the individual merchant should suffer for the advancement of a belligerent leader's cause. The circumstances of war should not, in his view, impact upon the rights or property of neutral powers or citizens. He supports his argument with examples from the moderate British press and, in particular, the views expressed by one commentator in *Bell's Weekly Messenger* on 5 May 1805 who supported a less heavy-handed policy by highlighting the fact that trading nations are in fact co-dependent. An earlier article by the same commentator makes the case for seeking to contain the enemy rather than destroy him, depicting modern war as a rational means to an end, which should now be free from the traits of barbarity. Maintaining trade is part of this rational war and the role of neutral traders as mediators is crucial. Böhl calls for British policy to take this into account and again bemoans the fate of the unfortunate merchant 'dessen Herrscher mit dem englischen Ministerium in Krieg liegt' (whose rulers happen to be at war with the English ministry; 131). The liberal views expressed by Böhl are tinged with a sense of disappointment that 'diese einst so große Nation [. . .] den Geld-Erwerb zum höchsten Zweck ihrer Existenz macht' (that this once great nation [. . .] has made the acquisition of money its highest goal; 133) and reflect both the ideals of Enlightenment political thought and the early Romantic cosmopolitanism which it fostered. Such greed had no place in Rousseau's social vision nor could it have arisen in Novalis' vision of *Europa*. This article, which contrasts markedly with the vehement nationalism of later years, was Böhl's only attempt to engage openly in the political debate during the Napoleonic Wars. The absence of further interventions was probably the result of increased French aggression. Like many others, Böhl was horrified by the execution by Napoleon's troops of the patriotic Nuremberg bookseller, Johann Philipp Palm (1766–1806), and immediately pulled back from all political comment for fear of bringing those close to him into danger.

In December 1806, with political tension running high, Böhl went to stay with his mother in Hamburg for the winter, establishing a tradition which would continue throughout his years in Germany and which fostered a series of lifelong friendships. He became a regular visitor at the home of his mentor's nephew, August Campe (1773–1836) and his wife Elise (née Hoffmann, 1786–1873). Friendship with the young couple provided Böhl with an opportunity to discuss his changing literary and ideological values and his letters to them reveal a close personal relationship with Elise in particular. 1810 also saw the beginning of Böhl's correspondence with Nikolas Heinrich Julius (1783–1862). Julius, a doctor and the son of a Jewish banker from Altona, had recently returned to Hamburg to set up in practice. A natural philanthropist, he converted to Catholicism in 1809 and dedicated his medical work to the poor. In later years, he also campaigned for prison reform, calling on the support of his many distinguished friends and acquaintances, including a great friend from his student days in Heidelberg, the Romantic poet, Joseph von Eichendorff. Böhl and Julius first met at book auctions, both often bidding for the same lots, but they became properly acquainted through August Campe. Böhl's relationship with Julius was central to his scholarly work and their correspondence continued until Julius left for a visit to the United States in 1834. By the time he returned in 1836, Böhl was dead. For over twenty years, the two bibliophiles provided each other with support and material, Böhl in particular benefiting from Julius' generosity during his years in Spain after 1813. Indeed, in some respects, the relationship became rather one sided. In later years, no longer quite so convinced of his social purpose, Böhl had little time for his friend's charitable campaigning, but was happy to make use of Julius as a constant source of information and material, in addition to his role as proofreader and literary agent whenever Böhl sought to publish in Germany. During the early years of their acquaintance, Böhl and Julius were familiar figures in the intellectual circles of Hamburg, along with the publisher Friedrich Perthes (1772–1843) and members of the major Hamburg patrician families including the Sievekings and Pohls. In the heightened, patriotic atmosphere of war, literary discussions centred on the reception of Romantic aesthetics as a response to the political and cultural threat from France. Moving in such circles after 1806, Böhl was exposed to a debate which he had previously only been able to follow from a distance and, as his correspondence demonstrates, his engagement with the issues raised was intense, their impact almost immediate. Indeed, the views expressed in his critique of Pitt's protectionism represent the last public defence of a more moderate political stance. Tending instead towards the reactionary stance suggested in Humboldt's testimony, Böhl soon subscribed wholeheartedly to the prevailing proto-nationalist sentiments emerging from his new intellectual environment, establishing a set of conservative political values which would remain constant throughout his life.

The worst fears of the patriotic Hamburg intelligentsia were soon to be realised. On 13 December 1810, Napoleon's forces reached the mouth of the Elbe and Hamburg became part of the French Empire. The impact on the intellectual life of the city was immediate and many sacrifices had to be made, including Perthes' patriotic *Vaterländisches Museum*, edited by Julius, which was forced out of circulation. Family life was disrupted too. Cecilia was sent to live with her aunt and uncle Berckemeyer at Thürow and Böhl, having spent the winter with his mother, returned to Görslow with Juan in the spring of 1811. Even here, they were not spared the effects of the wars raging around them and were soon faced with the indignity of quartering foreign troops. Böhl, now a sworn enemy of the once vaunted Napoleon, complained bitterly that men from every nation seemed to be fighting for the French: Poles, Hungarians and even Germans. He singled out the unruly Piedmontese for particular criticism, horrified by their lewd and reckless behaviour as the environs of Hamburg were ravaged by the advancing troops. Nothing seemed sacred as even his childhood idyll at Billwerder fell victim to the onslaught. His father's legacy was under threat too with the trading house in Cadiz on the point of ruin, ground down by the relentless struggle against blockades and the disruptions of war. The financial concerns which had plagued Böhl since his arrival at Görslow now overwhelmed him, but selling the estate was impossible in such unstable times. He applied, unsuccessfully, for a diplomatic post to keep his head above water and was forced to sell much of his library. These were dark days indeed. Where Napoleon's campaign had once promised peace and stability, it now seemed to undermine everything Böhl and his family held dear. It would take Böhl a long time to forgive the nation who had inflicted this misery upon them.

Despite the severity of the political and economic situation during the Görslow years, Böhl pursued his studies with enthusiasm. In fact, his scholarship provided a refuge from the misery which surrounded him. In keeping with his new intellectual environment, the focus was increasingly and consciously Romantic with a growing appreciation of popular poetry and an avid fascination for British writers such as Wordsworth and Scott. Initially, however, Böhl's attention remained firmly focused on furthering awareness – both his own and that of others – of Spain's literary heritage. Anxious to defend the culture he had come to appreciate so greatly, Böhl published an article entitled 'Ueber die Spanische Literatur' (On Spanish literature) in the *Nordische Miszellen* in March 1808.[2] The piece constitutes a firm defence of Spain's literary heritage and shows Böhl enter into a fully transcultural dialogue, reversing the flow of ideas already initiated through his 1805 dissemination of Schiller's aesthetics. The timing of the text's publication in the spring of 1808 is significant too in emphasising Böhl's awareness of contemporary issues. His article appears in advance of two more widely noted studies, Adam Müller's appraisal of August Wilhelm Schlegel's defence of Spanish theatre, 'Vom Charakter der spanischen Poesie' (On the character of Spanish poetry), published in Kleist and Müller's journal *Phöbus* in July 1808 and Schlegel's revised version of his defence of Spain's literary heritage which appeared in the *Wiener Vorlesungen*, delivered in 1808. Assessing Böhl's engagement with these texts is problematic. There is no mention of Müller in his correspondence until a much later date and no reference whatsoever to his essay on Spanish poetics. Böhl's response to Schlegel's lectures is also much later, forming the basis of his argument during the Calderón polemic. This suggests that he had no direct knowledge of the piece when compiling his own article in 1808. His correspondence would seem to support this. Böhl makes no reference to Friedrich Schlegel's *Europa*, where August Wilhelm's essay on Spanish literature first appeared in 1803, and first mentions the second volume of the *Wiener Vorlesungen*, which contained the revised version of Schlegel's defence, in a letter to Julius on 24 May 1810. Had Böhl known of its existence in 1808 whilst composing his article in defence of Spain's literature, he might have greatly strengthened his argument and quite possibly raised his critical profile as a Romantic acolyte. There is nevertheless a clear affinity in Böhl's work with the Romantic reception of Spanish literature which, if not itself a direct response to the *Wiener Vorlesungen*, certainly builds on the numerous positive references to Cervantes in the *Athenaeum* and the growing appreciation of Calderón in the German periodical press following August Wilhelm Schlegel's translations. Böhl's article, although not widely known, sees him engaging fully in this aspect of contemporary aesthetic debate and locates him within the emergent tradition of German Hispanism, stretching back to Lessing and Herder. Central to Böhl's appreciation of Spanish culture, and something he shared with contemporaries such as the Schlegels, was the reception of Spain as an essentially Romantic nation.

Opening his discussion, there are echoes of Böhl's 1805 article, as he rejects the claim made by a previous contributor to the *Nordische Miszellen* that Spain's literature was inferior to that of Portugal, praising it instead as the equal of that of Germany, France, Britain and Italy. Merging Herderian pluralism with Kant's assessment of the German national intellect, Böhl claims that each national literature has its own value, but only the German literary mind has been able to absorb the ideals and influences of other cultures and thus truly appreciate Spanish culture. He attacks those who claim that Spain has only produced one text of note, *Don Quijote*, and points out that very few writers are well known outwith their own national context. He then goes on to highlight the seminal role of *Don Quijote* as an example of Romantic art rather than a simple satire of the chivalric novel. In so doing, Böhl adopts a well-attested Romantic stance, repeating the defence of Cervantes' novel found in the work of the Schlegel brothers, Tieck and others and evoking Friedrich Schlegel's description of the text as 'der einzige durchaus romantische Roman' (the only completely romantic novel).[3] Continuing his own assessment of the novel genre in similar terms, Böhl adopts the Schlegelian definition of the term and goes on to qualify the prose works of the Golden Age, including *Lazarillo de Tormes* and the work of Marcos de Obregón, as 'romantisch' per se. Such texts are, however, far inferior to the poetry of the period whose beauty he attributes to 'die Fülle der südlichen Phantasie' (the fullness of the southern imagination) which is carried by 'die so bilderreiche, wohlklingende Spanische Sprache'(the vivid, pleasing Spanish language) which '[sich] fast von selbst in Versen ergießt' (forms verses almost of its own accord; 162). This praise is, however, not unqualified. There are no direct parallels to be made with the great prose writers of Enlightenment France, the 'Schön-Redner Bossuet und Massillon' (silver-tongued Bossuet and Massillon) – although one senses that Böhl sees this as a positive thing – nor can one speak of a truly national intellect. Despite these apparent shortcomings, there is a great deal to be found which is worthy of praise, including the sixteenth-century mystical poets, Fray Luis de Granada, Pedro de Ribadeneira and Teresa de Avila, who are singled out for their devotional work in an early indication of Böhl's appreciation of the mystics.

Continuing his description of Spain's literary landscape, Böhl makes brief mention of the pastoral novel, which he identifies as a transitional genre, linking prose and poetry through its liberal use of both and mention is made, amongst others, of Cervantes' *Galatea* and Montemayor's *Diana*. Böhl then turns his attention to poetry. Displaying his wide knowledge, he lists those poets he deems to be most worthy of praise: Boscán, Garcilaso, San Miranda and Villegas for their lyrical work; León, Herrera and Argensolas for their odes; Mendoza, Rioja and Esquilache for their epistles and Castillejo, Quevedo and Góngora for their satires. As far as true poetry is concerned, Böhl claims that no other nation can boast such 'klassische Dichter' (classical poets). Pre-empting any misunderstanding, he immediately clarifies his terminology, warning the reader away from the narrow French definition of Classical and citing instead that of Bouterwek in his *Geschichte der spanischen Poesie und Beredsamkeit* (History of Spanish poetry and rhetoric, 1804):

[Aber] so lange sich die Phantasie in ihren aesthetischen Bildungen nur nicht mit der Vernunft und der Natur überhaupt entzweit, kann sie weit über die Schranken der Griechischen und andern Formen hinausschweifen, ohne das höchste Gesetzt der Schönheit zu übertreten. Und dahin eben soll uns ja die wahre Geschmackslehre führen, über alle zufälligen Beschränkungen des schaffenden und bildenden Geistes hinauszusehen, um einen Standpunkt der Kritik zu finden, der nur von der Vernunft und Natur überhaupt getragen wird.[4]

([But] as long as imagination does not split entirely away from reason and nature in its aesthetic form, it can range well beyond the limits of Greek and other forms without overstepping the highest law of beauty. And it is in this direction that the true theory of taste should lead us, to look out beyond all the arbitrary limitations of the creative and educational mind in order to find a critical standpoint carried by reason and nature alone.)

Böhl's interpretation amounts to a reappropriation of Bouterwek which focuses on the possibility of an aesthetic independent of regulation, grounded instead in creative freedom, but attaining poetic harmony. If, by rejecting Aristotelian principles, this is the valid definition of Classical, it is impossible, Böhl argues, to deny the value of Spanish poetry. Böhl's readers are, then, presented with an explicit juxtaposition of 'klassisch' and 'romantisch' based on genre lines. Poetry is 'klassisch' because, following Bouterwek's definition, it clearly achieves harmony between nature and reason. This is also reflected to some degree in the pastoral novel and the idyll, both of which have a transitional role. The novel, epitomised by *Don Quijote* and the picaresque tradition, does not strive for such harmony and is therefore 'romantisch'. In constructing this argument, Böhl reveals the dual influences at work on him at this time. There is a clear tendency towards key Romantic values, in particular the appreciation of the novel as a Romantic genre, whilst at the same time a need to accommodate a revised understanding of established aesthetic principles in order to incorporate them into a revised cultural framework.

Interestingly, having categorised poetry and prose in such terms, Böhl stops short of any categorisation for the theatre. He settles instead for an unapologetic apotheosis of the Spanish stage. This further reveals his extensive knowledge of the primary material and a close affinity with the Romantic reception of Calderón's work. He begins by pointing out the debt which other nations owe to the inspiration offered by Spanish theatre. Böhl praises 'die poetische Behandlung, die geniale Verschmelzung, das kühne Aneinanderreihen aller Elemente des äußern und innern Lebens' (the poetic analysis, the brilliant fusion, the daring combination of all elements related to internal and external life). Whilst his interpretation of the harmonious nature of these works once more evokes his reading of Schiller, Böhl also echoes Friedrich Schlegel's concept of *Universalpoesie* with its appreciation of diversity and experiment. The emerging influence of the Schlegel brothers is then confirmed explicitly as Böhl recommends August Wilhelm's 1803 translation of Calderón. Bringing his assessment of Spanish literature to a close, Böhl highlights the success of Spanish lyrical satire and bemoans the demise of the *entremeses* in Spain itself in a critique of the rejection of national literature in Spain which pre-empts his polemical stance in defence of Calderón. For now, however, the apparently still limited impact of Schlegelian thought is highlighted by Böhl's closing recommendation, which directs the interested reader not to Schlegel, but to Bouterwek's study. The fact that Böhl felt compelled to make use of the latter as a point of reference for both his own argument and his reader's edification is significant. Bouterwek was an outspoken critic of the new Romantic aesthetic, dismissing it in his *Neues Museum der Philosophie und Literatur* (1803–5) as 'die phantastischen Auswüchse der neueren Philosophie und der neueren Aesthetik und Poesie' (the fantastical excesses of the new philosophy and the new aesthetics and poetry).[5] As such, much of what Bouterwek believed went against Böhl's developing world view. Indeed, the Göttingen scholar would soon be the subject of Böhl's censure in relation to his work on English literature in an attack which centred specifically on Romantic writers. Böhl's reliance on Bouterwek's study in 1808 is, then, further evidence that he had not yet encountered Schlegel's article, the content of which would prove so significant in years to come.

Böhl's article on Spanish literature is an important milestone in his intellectual development. Just as 1798 marked the break from Campe, 1808 sees Böhl's first public defence of key Romantic ideals and is indicative of the ongoing cultural revaluation of the period. Böhl is now fully engaged in this process and the Herderian appreciation of national literatures and traditional forms which underpins the Romantic appreciation of Spain's national literature also prompts him to reassess his own literary heritage. In so doing, he was particularly drawn to the work of German poets from the sixteenth and seventeenth centuries and managed, with Campe's help, to borrow from the extensive collection of literary historian and writer, Johann Joachim Eschenburg (1743–1820), director of the *Collegium Carolinium* in Braunschweig. This interest in older German culture is underlined by Böhl's enthusiastic response to one of the key publishing events of the year, the appearance of the second and third volumes of Arnim and Brentano's seminal ballad collection, *Des Knaben Wunderhorn* (The boy's magic horn). This anthology of ancient ballads constitutes the first example of an essentially Romantic approach to philology and inspired a number of similar collections of older, often popular material, including the monumental contributions of the Brothers Grimm and Böhl's own efforts in the 1820s and 1830s. The rationale for the collection was as much political as it was aesthetic and Böhl's enthusiasm accords with the broader Romantic view, prevalent in particular in the second generation of writers, which saw the collation and preservation of such popular material as a means of defiance at a time of extreme anti-French sentiment. Böhl's reception of the collection also marks the beginning of an intense engagement with the work of Goethe. Following the publication of the first volume of the collection in 1806, Goethe published an extensive review in the *Jenaische Allgemeine Literaturzeitung*. This was followed in 1810 by a review of volumes two and three by Friedrich von der Hagen which appeared in the same periodical. Böhl's correspondence with Julius includes an undated list of his favourite pieces from the collection with commentaries taken from these reviews. He focuses on comments which are very much in keeping with his own positive and deeply personal appraisal of the collection with evaluations ranging from 'christlich zart, anmuthig' (Christian, tender, charming) to 'deutsch romantisch, fromm-sinnig, gefällig' (German-Romantic, pious in character, pleasing).[6] The interrelation of patriotism, poetry and faith highlighted here reflects the nature of Böhl's own concerns at this time. Also apparent is the influence of mystical thought as Böhl strives for an immanent, experiential relationship to God. This colours his appraisal of others and in a criticism which becomes typical in his reception of Goethe, he adds a note which explains the rationale behind his choices, commenting that '[i]ch unterschreibe zwar die meisten aber doch nicht alle diese

Aussprüche; dem grossen G[oethe] [. . .] fehlt der Sinn fürs tiefe oder innere Christenthum' (I subscribe to most but not all of these statements; the great Goethe lacks the sense for deep or inner Christianity). The ancient poets themselves, however, are described in a postscript to von der Hagen's comments as possessing 'die bewegliche Fantasie des Naturdichters' (the agile imagination of the natural poet). This marks a development from Böhl's earlier appropriation of Bouterwek. Nature is no longer compelled to a synthesis with reason in the creation of great poetry. Instead, the emphasis is on freedom and imagination.

Böhl may have been critical of some of Goethe's evaluations, but he was inspired to act by the suggestion made in the latter's 1806 review that the *Wunderhorn* material should be set to music. Taking Goethe at his word, Böhl set about compiling a selection of songs from the collection and setting them to traditional melodies for piano accompaniment. Böhl's *Vier und zwanzig deutsche Lieder aus des Knaben Wunderhorn mit bekannten meist älteren Weisen beim Klavier zu singen* (Twenty-four German songs from the Boy's Magic Horn set to mostly familiar melodies for piano accompaniment) was published anonymously in 1810 in Heidelberg. The preface quotes directly from the Jena review and promises to take up Goethe's challenge to find and publish similar works in other languages. Sadly, Böhl's plans for further volumes did not come to fruition (although he did try to persuade August Campe to take on the project following his return to Spain in 1813) and the volume itself has become something of a rarity. It is nevertheless significant as a first example of Böhl's direct engagement with the Romantic aesthetic on its own terms, beyond the parameters of literary criticism and the constant conflicts with Enlightenment thought. The tone of his preface is confessional:

> Der Herausgeber, der sich zu den Liebhabern bekennt, fühlte ein Bedürfniß gewißen Liedern schickliche Weisen anzuschmiegen; sie sind ihm dadurch doppelt werth geworden, und wenn er sie hiemit öffentlich darlegt, geschieht es aus der reinen Absicht, auch andere dieses Genußes theilhaftig zu machen.
>
> (The editor, who counts himself amongst the enthusiasts, felt the need to adapt appropriate tunes to certain songs; they are now worth twice as much to him and if he now presents them here publicly, it is with the pure intention to share this pleasure with others.)

It seems that Böhl is simply enjoying the material and wants others to share in his pleasure. Whilst the purpose of this collection is to respond to Goethe's call to pay further homage to these songs as musical pieces, it is an emotive rather than a reasoned response which underlies Böhl's preface as he fulfils a 'Bedürfniß' (need) to work with the *Wunderhorn* material. In so doing, he reveals a marked affinity with the prevailing Romantic mood and contributes actively to the renewed appreciation of older literature which lies at the heart of contemporary aesthetics. By 1811, he was steeped in the ideals of Romanticism and eagerly devoured all he could relating to Romantic thought, supplementing his engagement with the aesthetic theories of the early school with an appreciation of the medieval apotheosis of later writers: Fouqué's *Undine* (1811) with its fairytale depiction of a medieval idyll was a particular favourite.

Böhl's developing network of contacts in the publishing world, including the Campes, Julius and Perthes, might lead one to question why he did not become a more prominent figure in the contemporary debate. He was clearly in tune with the zeitgeist and not afraid to make his views known, even openly criticising a literary historian of Bouterwek's standing. Although his financial concerns at Görslow and the turmoil of the Napoleonic Wars had a role to play, Böhl's reputation might have been greatly enhanced were it not for the failure of another collaboration, this time with Swabian poet, Justinus Kerner (1786–1862). Böhl's contact with Kerner was indirect, made via Elise and August Campe. Kerner hoped to publish a second volume of his *Poetischer Almanach*, which had first appeared in 1811, before falling foul of the ongoing political upheaval.[7] He intended the second volume as a platform for new material in order, as he explained in a letter to Elise, 'daß die Poesie nicht blos gewissen großen Namen und kunstfertigen Leuten in Deutschland als Monopol angehört' (that poetry in Germany is not just monopolised by certain well-known names and skilful people).[8] Elise clearly saw this as an opportunity for her friend Böhl and wrote to Kerner with a description of the material which he would be able to provide. The contact must have been made early in 1812 as Kerner replied in April that year, welcoming the offer of Böhl's contribution. Elise forwarded Kerner's letter to Böhl, who responded with an enthusiastic promise to select 'einige altdeutsche Blumen' (a few old German flowers) for the periodical, expressing the hope that there are some 'altdeutsche Nasen' (old German noses) able to enjoy them. By June 1812, Böhl wrote to Elise Campe that he had some pieces ready for inclusion in the almanac, including also translations of Wordsworth and some Spanish folk songs. These suggestions were passed on to the editors of the planned journal for their consideration and, as Kerner and Uhland's correspondence demonstrates, the response was positive.[9] Having apparently thus secured an outlet for his work, Böhl was bitterly disappointed as the plans fell by the wayside, a victim once more of the political upheaval of the period. The failure of Kerner's project was significant as it deprived Böhl of the opportunity to publish alongside prominent Romantic writers, including Uhland, Fouqué and Chamisso, a prospect which he would have relished.

The range of material Böhl hoped to contribute to Kerner's publication reflects his main literary and aesthetic interests during the Görslow years and once more highlights his growing determination to disseminate works and ideas from other cultures. His wide knowledge of contemporary literary trends meant that he was well versed in the literature of other European nations beyond Germany and Spain and he was particularly fascinated by the poetry of the British Romantics, especially William Wordsworth (1770–1850), whom he describes, echoing his praise of the *Wunderhorn* poets, as 'ein systematischer Naturdichter' (a systematic natural poet). This interest inspired Böhl's final contribution to the literary debate before his return to Spain in 1813: an article entitled 'Von der neuesten englischen Poesie' (On recent English poetry), which appeared in 1811 in the *Vaterländisches Museum*.[10] The text, which marks the final step in Böhl's Romantic rebirth, sees his work appear alongside that of Friedrich Schlegel, Jacob Görres and Fouqué. Böhl's piece comprises a survey of the most recent developments in English literature and is intended to supplement Bouterwek's recently published two-volume *Geschichte der englischen Poesie und Beredsamkeit* (History of English poetry and rhetoric, 1809–1810). Böhl, now substantially less reverential towards the renowned scholar, finds fault with Bouterwek for failing to include any reference to new poetic trends which were presumably at odds with the latter's anti-Romantic tastes. Echoing his private comments on the *Wunderhorn* material, Böhl picks up Bouterwek's argument in the mid-eighteenth century, agreeing that the influence of Pope had by then begun to decline and that there was once more an emphasis on the natural in poetry. However, the concept of nature at that time was a sterile scholarly notion whose chief concern was 'die äußere Politur' (superficial polish; 101). This superficiality was to be overcome as poetry was reclaimed by the people in what amounted to a popular literary revolution. This signalled a breaking away from literary stricture and fostered the recognition of previously maligned poets. They had only been neglected, Böhl argues somewhat melodramatically, because people had been pressured into accepting the rules imposed upon them in an attempt to seek favour or, even worse, out of base instincts such as hatred or self-importance. The first poet to break the mould, according to Böhl, was William Cowper (1731–1800), whose poetry is extravagantly described as the antithesis of Enlightenment reserve:

Es sind planlose Ergüsse eines tief ergriffenen Gemüthes, in schlecht gereimten Jamben, bald didaktisch trocken, bald hinreißend belebt und schön, bald geschroben witzig, bald innigst gefühlt, aber immer mit auffallender Vernachlässigung der Vollkommenheit und Ründung des Versbaues. (103)

(They are unplanned outbursts of a deeply moved soul, in poorly rhymed iambs, sometimes didactically dry, sometimes captivatingly lively and beautiful, sometimes cuttingly humorous, sometimes deeply felt, but always with an obvious neglect of the completeness and roundness of the structure.)

This was the epitome of 'eine andere Natürlichkeit, als die gelehrte' (a different kind of naturalness from the scholarly; 103) and provided new insights and possibilities. Cowper, according to Böhl, paved the way for the acclaim achieved by Robert Burns (1759–96) and the attempts by Robert Southey (1774–1843) to revive the ancient ballad form. The central focus of Böhl's article is, however, Wordsworth's *Lyrical Ballads* (1798). That Böhl should be attracted to this collection, the work of a poet now truly disillusioned with the realities of revolutionary France and the ruins of the Age of Reason, is not surprising. He is particularly impressed by the introduction to the work, revised for the 1802 edition, which presents Wordsworth's poetics. Coming to Wordsworth's treatise almost a decade after it was written, Böhl finds confirmation of a number of the aesthetic values he has chosen to defend. For example, Wordsworth's decision 'to choose incidents and situations from common life, and to relate or describe them throughout, as far as was possible, in a selection of language really used by men; and at the same time, to throw over them a certain colouring of imagination, whereby ordinary things should be presented to the mind in an unusual way'[11] reflects the notion of 'romantisieren' at the heart of early German Romantic thought. Similarly, Wordsworth's defence of prose as the equal of poetry – 'the same human blood circulates through the veins of them both' (69) – underlies the core principle of Romantic aesthetics with its appreciation of all literary genres. Crucially, however, there are also key ideas in Wordsworth's preface which relate directly to Böhl's personal development. Discussing his own work, Wordsworth argues for the role of emotion as a driving force in the literary process, insisting 'that the feeling therein gives importance to the action and situation, and not the action and situation to the feeling' (64). The poet is nevertheless at pains to point out that thought too has an important role to play in achieving a balance:

> Poems to which any values can be attached were never produced on any variety of subjects but by a man who, being possessed of more than usual organic sensibility, had also thought long and deeply. For our continued influxes of feeling are modified and directed by our thoughts, which are indeed the representatives of our past feelings; and as by contemplating the relation of these general representatives to each other we discover what is really important to men, so, by the repetition and continuance of this act, our feelings will be connected with important subjects, till at length, if we be originally possessed of much sensibility, such habits of mind will be produced that, by obeying blindly and mechanically the impulses of those habits, we shall describe objects, and utter sentiments, of such a nature and in such connection with each other, that the understanding of the being to whom we address ourselves, if he be in a healthful state of association, must necessarily be in some degree enlightened, and his affections ameliorated. (62–3)

Wordsworth associates two key elements that will have appealed to Böhl. First, he places emotion in a central position as the lynchpin upon which reason must hang. Thought is required to make sense of emotion, but emotion itself is the defining element in the human character. This provides Böhl with a comforting validation of his own revised appreciation of the evaluative reliability of 'Gefühl'. For Böhl, Wordsworth's aesthetic seems to take Schiller's development of Kant a step further, placing the sensuous above the rational. It is this shift which underlies Böhl's own inner development. Also significant is Wordsworth's affinity with the philosophy of Schelling whose work Böhl was reading at this time in the context of his engagement with the work of the mystics. Schelling's view parallels that of Wordsworth, and indeed Coleridge, in identifying emotion, which he calls 'Gemüth' (emotive soul), as enabling effective thought.[12] The parallel is important for Böhl's engagement with Schelling in the context of his subsequent struggle to redefine his relationship to faith and, in keeping with the earlier critical appraisal of Goethe's response to the *Wunderhorn* material, this demonstrates the immediacy of Böhl's religious and aesthetic revaluation. This is underlined in a letter to Elise on 17 August 1811 in which Böhl criticises 'eigentliche Vernunftmenschen' (truly rational people) as 'kalt und streng' (cold and strict) and praises instead what he regards as the opposite, Christian way of thinking which knows how to value everything on its own terms, claiming that 'letztere Ansicht hängt mit dem poetischen Gefühl zusammen' (the latter point of view is linked to poetic emotion).[13]

The correlation between poetry and emotion identified by Böhl relates to a second key issue dealt with in Wordsworth's text: the communicative role of art. The poet, 'possessed of more than usual organic sensibility', is the archcommunicator. This notion underlies Wordsworth's vision of the poet as a mediator, 'a man speaking to men' (71):

In spite of difference of soil and climate, of language and manners, of laws and customs, in spite of things silently gone out of mind and things violently destroyed, the Poet binds together by passion and knowledge the vast empire of human society, as it is spread over the whole earth, and over all time. (77)

Although unwilling to see himself in such grand terms, this represents the ideal envisaged by Böhl for the poet and his work: to communicate through art, respecting the plurality of national cultures and the centrality of emotion and faith. Echoing his reading of Schiller's aesthetics, this is reflected in Böhl's personal appraisal of the English poet. For Böhl, Wordsworth is himself a mediator, bringing together man and nature, 'kurz, in ihm waltet der alles verbindende, alles versöhnende Geist der ewigen Liebe' (in short, he is driven by the all-combining, all-appeasing spirit of eternal love; 105). As such, he was bound to meet with the disapproval of the 'Kunstrichter' (judges of art). Outraged by their inability to see beyond sterile rules, Böhl closes the article with a clear attack on Enlightenment aesthetics, which demonstrates the extent to which his ideals have been consolidated through his reading of German and English Romantic writers:

> Dieses wird hinlänglich seyn, um zu beweisen, daß in der englischen Poesie, fast zu gleicher Zeit mit der ihr verwandten deutschen, derjenige alte Sinn wieder erwacht ist, der sich getrieben fühlt, die Musen von den willkürlichen Fesseln pedantischer Regeln zu erlösen, sie von dem Katheder wieder in das freye Feld, von dem Kanape unter das Strohdach zurückzuführen, um von frischen Menschen aufs neue belebt, diejenige goldene Zeit wiederzubringen, wo Poesie mit dem täglichen Leben innigst verwebt, alles Niedrige zu veredeln wußte, alles Rauhe abzuschießen verstand, alles Irdische mit dem Ewigen in Beziehung brachte, und so den Menschen unter Sang und Klang von der Wiege bis zum Grabe begleitet. (105–6)

> (This will be sufficient to prove that English poetry, almost at the same time as related German poetry, saw a reawakening of that old way of thinking which feels compelled to release the muses from the arbitrary shackles of pedantic regulation, to lead them from the lectern back into the open field, from the chaise longue back under the thatched roof, in order to return, revived by revitalised people, that golden age, where poetry, inextricably woven into the fabric of everyday life, was able to ennoble all that was ordinary, to destroy all that was rough, to bring all earthly things into relation with the eternal and thus to accompany the people singing and playing from the cradle to the grave.)

An affinity with Romantic thought is once more apparent. The echoes of Novalis are clear as Böhl once more evokes the concept of 'romantisieren' with his description of poetry at the heart of everyday life. Furthermore, he harks back to a golden age similar to the medieval ideal depicted in the former's *Die Christenheit oder Europa* with its evocation of 'eine einzige, ewige, unaussprechlich glückliche Gemeinde' (a single, eternal, indescribably happy community).[14] Böhl may not have had access to Novalis' work, which remained unpublished until 1826, but his new *Weltanschauung* possessed a clear affinity with certain of the ideas expressed there. The idealisation of the medieval age it proffered, whilst advocating quasi-Rousseauian structures based on mutual responsibility, also depended to a large degree on the overarching, unifying power of a single, effectively Catholic religion. This appealed to the increasingly conservative political stance of a number of Romantic thinkers, not least the Schlegel brothers, and Böhl's call for a regeneration of 'diejenige goldene Zeit' (that golden age) certainly parallels the paternalistic ideal of Novalis' 'schöne glänzende Zeiten' (beautiful, glittering times; 507). The dismissal of a more moderate, progressive world view which this suggests is then underlined by an assessment of reason which marks the final rejection of Böhl's enlightened education. His reference to 'die willkürlichen Fesseln pedantischer Regeln' (the arbitrary shackles of pedantic regulation) could not be further from his youthful admiration for an aesthetic grounded in 'schlichte angewandte Vernunft' (simple, applied reason). Now fully immersed in the Romantic aesthetic and defending a conservative political stance, the publication of 'Von der neuesten englischen Poesie' in 1811 marks the end of a process of revaluation. With it, Böhl's Romantic rebirth is complete.

NOTES

1. The full title of the article is 'Auch etwas über Handels-Monopol und Handels-Bedrückung; bei Gelegenheit des im 58 und 59sten Stück der Hamb. Addr. Comp. Nachrichten abgedruckten Fragments aus den Dialogen über Krieg und Handel'; references appear in the text.
2. The full title of the article is 'Ueber die Spanische Literatur, in Bezug auf die fragmentarischen Bemerkungen darüber, in den Nordischen Miszellen vom 7. und 14ten Februar 1808' (On Spanish literature, in relation to the fragmentary comments made on the matter in the Northern Miscellany of 7 and 14 February 1808); references appear in the text.
3. Friedrich Schlegel, *Literary Notebooks 1797–1801*, H. Eichner (ed.) (London: Athlone, 1957), p. 117, fragment 1096.
4. Friedrich Bouterwek, *Geschichte der Poesie und Beredsamkeit seit dem Ende des dreizehnten Jahrhunderts*, 12 vols (Göttingen: Johann Friedrich Röwer, 1801-19); III: *Geschichte der spanischen Poesie und Beredsamkeit* (1804), 'Beschluß der Geschichte der spanischen Poesie und Beredsamkeit', 613–18 (615).
5. Friedrich Bouterwek (ed.), *Neues Museum der Philosophie und Literatur*, 3 vols (1803–5), II/2, 'Nachschrift des Herausgebers', [no page numbers].
6. Siegfried Seidel (ed.), *Goethe. Berliner Ausgabe*, 22 vols (Berlin: Aufbau, 1970–8); XVII: *Kunsttheoretische Schriften und Übersetzungen. Schriften zur Literatur I. Aufsätze zu Schauspielkunst und Musik. Aufsätze zur deutschen Literatur* (1970), 390–405, (pp. 392–3).
7. Kerner did eventually publish a second volume in 1813 with the title *Deutscher Dichterwald*.
8. The letter is quoted by Elise Campe (VL: 70–2). Pitollet (QC: 41) wrongly assumes the letter to be from Kerner to Böhl, rather than to Elise Campe.
9. Julius Hartmann (ed.), *Uhlands Briefwechsel*, 4 vols (Stuttgart/Berlin: Cotta, 1916); I: 320.
10. *Vaterländisches Museum*, II/I (1811), 101–6. Böhl had originally hoped to place the piece in either the *Heidelberger Jahrbücher* or one of the Viennese periodicals. Julius instead decided to place the piece in his own publication.
11. William Wordsworth, *Lyrical Ballads*, Michael Mason (ed.) (London: Longman, 1992), p. 59. Further references appear in the text.
12. See E. D. Hirsch, *Wordsworth and Schelling. A Typological Study of Romanticism* (Hamden: Archon Books, 1970), pp. 133ff; also Rosemary Ashton, *The German Idea in four English writers and the reception of German thought 1800–1860* (Cambridge: Cambridge University Press, 1980).
13. Campe (VL: 66).
14. Kluckhohn and Samuel (eds.), *Novalis Schriften*; III: 523; further references appear in the text.

Chapter 5
Catholic Conversion

As well as allowing him to devote time to his literary scholarship, the years at Görslow saw Böhl engage in a very private struggle surrounding the matter of his faith, one which would lead to his conversion to Catholicism in 1813.[1] Closely linked to his Romantic rebirth and fostered by his reading of key Romantic texts, the period saw the culmination of a process of introspection which can be traced back to the first encounter with Riem. The extent of Böhl's deliberations is reflected in his first letter to Julius on 6 April 1810, in which he opens his heart to his friend:

> [I]ch [. . .] habe längst mein Ziel in Hinsicht der Bedürfniße des Herzens, in eine andere schönere Welt gesetzt. Nur möchte ich wissen wie ich (und vielleicht auch Sie) dazu gekommen bin, dieses Bedürfnis zu verspüren? Ich habe diese Sehnsucht des Herzens nicht von meinen Eltern, meine Erziehung ist ganz praktisch gewesen, ganz irreligiös, meine Umgebungen in der großen Welt ganz die gewöhnlichen, und doch hat von der frühesten Erinnerung an, mein Herz gebrannt, bald von düstrer, trüberer, bald von hellerer wärmerer Flamme! Mein innerstes Wesen ist also etwas bestimmtes, angeborenes, dem (der gemeinen Meinung zuwider) kein Äußeres hat Abbruch thun können.
>
> (I [. . .] have for some time placed my aims in relation to the needs of the heart in another, more beautiful world. But I would like to know how I (and perhaps you too) came to feel this need? This heart-felt longing does not come from my parents, my upbringing was quite practical, quite irreligious, my surroundings in the wider world quite ordinary, and yet for as long as I can remember my heart has burned, sometimes with a dim, dull flame, sometimes with a brighter, warmer one! My innermost self is then something specific, inherent, which (contrary to popular opinion) no external force has been able to dislodge.)

Acknowledging the longstanding nature of his inner struggle, Böhl quite categorically denies his intellectual and ideological roots. The assertion that there is a greater, inner force, 'etwas bestimmtes angeborenes' (something specific, inherent), rejects the omnipotence of rationality and highlights a darker, unfathomable side to the self over which the individual has no control. Campe's teaching, alluded to obliquely, has not managed to dislodge what Böhl now sees as his essential self and he is finally finding the courage to express himself, free from any constraints. This passage describes an angst-ridden search for self-knowledge, phrased in highly emotive, quasi-mystical terms – 'die Bedürfniße des Herzens' (the needs of the heart), 'diese Sehnsucht des Herzens' (heart-felt longing) and 'helle, wärmere Flamme' (brighter, warmer flame) – which echo the *Herzensergiessungen* (outpourings from the heart) characteristic of the early Romantic period.[2] There is a palpable sense of liberation as Böhl gives vent to a sense of disquiet which has troubled him for some time:

> Lange habe ich dieses geahnet, aber nicht gewagt es auszusprechen, biß sich in den unvergleichlichen Wahlverwandtschaften S[eite] 310 fand: Und so finden wir die Menschen, über deren Veränderlichkeit so viele Klage geführt wird, nach vielen Jahren zu unserm Erstaunen unverändert, und nach äußern und innern unendlichen Anregungen <u>unveränderlich</u>. – daß diese innerliche Unveränderlichkeit vollkommen wohl bey sehr verschiedenen Erscheinungs und Äußerungs-Arten bestehen könne, brauche ich <u>Ihnen</u> nicht zu sagen.[3]

> (I have sensed this for a long time, but did not dare to say it out loud, until I found this in the incomparable Elective Affinities, p. 310: thus we find people, whose changeability is ever the subject of complaint, after many years much to our surprise unchanged and following endless external and internal stimuli, <u>unchangeable</u>. – that this inner, unchangeable nature could remain intact even with the most varied means of appearance and expression is something I do not need to tell <u>you</u>.)

As Böhl makes explicit, this personal revelation marks another episode in his engagement with the work of Goethe, triggered by a passage in the recently published *Die Wahlverwandtschaften* (Elective Affinities, 1809). The novel provoked a great deal of debate and Böhl's highly personal response was not unusual. As Fröschle explains, the reactions of Romantic writers were mixed, but certainly not ambivalent. Tieck and Brentano expressed disquiet, whilst Fouqué claimed it to be the most beautiful Goethe had written. A more extreme response was that of Zacharias Werner (1768–1823) who was prompted to convert to Catholicism after reading the text.[4] Werner's experience presents an interesting parallel to Böhl's own actions, but it is important to interpret the latter's response to Goethe's text in the context of the interrelated influences at work on him at this time. His reading of *Die Wahlverwandschaften* forms part of a broader debate. For many contemporaries with a vested interest in the new aesthetic, Goethe's novel could be interpreted as coded vindication of the Romantic ideal, an analogy of the Classic versus Romantic debate. This was the reading adopted by Böhl. The idea of 'innerliche Unveränderlichkeit' (inner, unchangeable nature), which echoed the notion present in Schiller's aesthetics of a 'niemals wechselndes Ich' (never changing I),⁵ led Böhl to reconsider the autonomy of human nature. His revaluation centres on the concept of 'Neigung' (inclination), a central motif of Goethe's text. In his earlier correspondence with Campe, Böhl saw 'Neigung' as something which must forcibly submit to reason. Now, drawn in to Böhl's revised *Weltanschauung*, 'Neigung' is to be considered an enriching factor, part of the complex and impenetrable weave of the poetic self. This sees Böhl engaging further with the idealist revaluation of Kantian dualism found in the work of Fichte and, in particular, Schelling. Both thinkers held that reality was not confined to the bounds of mere reason, but that the 'I' could only attain a finite understanding of the world, thus conceding the existence of an unknown, chaotic element at the heart of the self. It is in such terms that Böhl, no longer anchored in reason, continues to struggle with the issue of his faith.

Central to this struggle is his engagement with the writings of a number of German mystics in particular whose work exerted a brief, but profound, influence on Böhl around 1810. The quasi-mystical tone of his first letter to Julius is symptomatic. At this time of inner turmoil, their concept of faith seemed to reach out to Böhl from the core of humanity itself, replacing the rationality of the Deist creed with a wealth of imagery and unashamed emotion. The central concepts of mystical thought provided a theological justification for the previously uncomfortable shift in Böhl's relationship to faith and, writing to Dorothea in March 1810, he reveals a new perspective, defining 'eigentliche Christenthum' (true Christianity) as a 'Gefühlsreligion' (religion of emotions). Böhl's study of early German and Spanish works had already brought him into contact with a number of mystical poets and his correspondence with Julius is full of his latest discoveries as he sets about collecting with customary zeal. Böhl's engagement with this contemplative approach to Christianity, with its quest for an introspective, intuitive experience of faith beyond the bounds of human understanding, is typical of the Romantic turn towards mystical thought. Drawn initially to the aesthetic qualities in the work of St Martin and Teresa de Avila, Böhl expands his reading to encompass theological works, in particular those of the Protestant mystic, Jakob Böhme (1575–1624).⁶ Böhme's theosophy of God as the basis of all things, including both good and evil, and of nature as the 'Leib Gottes' (the body of God) presents Böhl with an alternative concept of deity, one which inextricably links nature and emotion, and he is able to locate Böhme's thought within his current frame of reference. In particular, this signals once more the presence of Herder whose notion of cultural organicism is underpinned by the Böhmian concepts of an inner force (God) and a series of outer signatures (nature). Herder's notion of cultural diversity – each nation as a self-defining organic whole and its literature as an expression of that self – develops this relationship in aesthetic and political terms which inform Böhl's Romantic scholarship. Furthermore, Böhme's assertion of an inner force also equates with Böhl's understanding of the inner self as an unchanging core: a mystical antecedent to Goethe's 'innerliche Unveränderlichkeit' which explains the power of 'Neigung' in theosophical terms.

Böhl's awareness of Böhme influences much of his reading in 1810. His correspondence reveals a somewhat erratic journey through the reception of mystical thought as Böhl struggles to understand the complexities of the original texts and locate them within his own understanding and that of the Romantic writers whose work is increasingly vital to his quest for aesthetic and philosophical truth. In so doing, his efforts to trace the tradition span the centuries, ranging from seventeenth-century thinkers such as the hymnist, Paul Gerhardt (1607–76), and the Catholic convert and poet, Angelus Silesius (1624–77), to the eighteenth-century Pietist, Friedrich Christoph Oetinger (1702–82). Böhme's legacy in the eighteenth century is particularly significant in presenting Böhl with a contemporary ideology which runs counter to his Deist, Lutheran upbringing. The reception of German mysticism in the eighteenth century produced a reaction to doctrinal hegemony of which Herderian organicism was the cumulative, but not the only, outcome and which Weeks refers to as 'German pluralism'.[7] As Weeks explains, post-1700, the pansophic mysticism derived from Böhme becomes allied to biblicalism in a struggle against reason as Pietism and Deism entered public battle over the work of Wolff, whose interpretation of Deist theology had so greatly influenced Campe. Exposure to and engagement with the ideas which fostered this counter to Deist thought encouraged Böhl to question the validity of Campe's teaching further, resulting in his brief condemnation, expressed in the first letter to Julius, that his upbringing had been 'irreligiös'. Whilst clearly a rather unfair appraisal of Campe's approach, which was after all grounded on solid Lutheran foundations, the comment illustrates how Böhl's understanding of the relationship between the individual and faith is changing.

This change is reflected in the shifting value of key terms employed by Böhl in his correspondence, which in turn echo the emerging Romantic reception of mysticism. Böhme's legacy, apparent primarily in Pietism and Herderian thought, combines with the new sciences and the philosophy of Idealism in the early Romantic mind. Having absorbed these ideas, the Romantic interpretation of mysticism gradually moves away from the doctrinal, tending instead towards an aesthetic appreciation enlivened by mystical experience. This is epitomised in the work of Friedrich Schlegel who develops the early Romantic pantheistic-Idealistic stance, again via Böhme, into a full-blown Christian philosophy which employs mysticism as an interpretative key. This is taken to its extreme by Jacob Görres who exhibits what Weeks terms a 'narrowly Catholic mystagogy' (227). Böhl follows closely this contemporary synthesis of ideas and, as his first letter to Julius shows, he is aware of the importance of the terminology of mysticism in creating a set of ciphers for a new philosophical framework. This is evident in his responses to Schelling, whose work Böhl devoured with a mixture of fascination and frustration. Central is Schelling's *Über das Wesen der menschlichen Freiheit* (On the nature of human freedom, 1809), often referred to as the *Freiheitsschrift* (Treatise on freedom). Writing to Julius on 6 April 1810, Böhl locates Schelling in his deliberations surrounding the issue of faith and the individual's relationship to God. In so doing, he is clearly seeking affirmation of his reading of the mystics as much as he is an understanding of Schelling's philosophy:

> Ich lese jetzt Schelling seine Abhandlung zum zweitenmahl; es sind wunderbare Sachen darin. Einzeln verstehe ich jeden Satz ganz wohl, aber mein Kopf ist nicht stark genug den Faden zu behalten. Was mich am meisten darin freut, ist seine Übereinstimmung mit den Mystikern, obwohl er dem Zeitgeist huldigend an andern Stellen auch die Religion des Gefühls schimpft. Seine meisten Resultate sind mystische Aussprüche, nur daß er sie auf einer anderen sehr scharfsinnigen Weise deduzirt.
>
> (I am now reading Schelling's treatise for the second time; there are wonderful things in it. I can understand each individual sentence well enough, but my mind is not strong enough to follow the argument. What pleases me most about it is his concordance with the mystics, although in keeping with current thought, he does criticise the religion of emotion elsewhere. Most of his conclusions are mystical statements, only he arrives at them in another very quick-witted way.)

In a subsequent letter to Julius on 24 May, Böhl admits to finding Schelling's ideas hard to grasp and claims to have read his works in reverse order in an attempt to come to grips with the content. Commenting on the difficulties he has experienced, he is as ever modest in his self-appraisal:

> Bey meinem geringen Maaße von Verstand bin ich befriedigt, wenn nur bewiesen wird, daß auch für den höheren Verstand nichts absurdes und sich selbst widersprechendes in den reinen mystischen (eigentlich christlichen) Ideen liege, für deren Wahrheit <u>mir</u> mein Gefühl bürgt.
>
> (With my limited understanding, I am satisfied if it is proven simply that even for the higher intellect there is nothing absurd and self-contradictory in the purely mystical (truly Christian) ideas, the veracity of which is vouched for <u>for me</u> by my emotions.)

Böhl's comments show how the ideological value of 'Gefühl' (emotion) has shifted. In his letter to Campe in 1797 calling for a 'Bekehrung zur Vernunft' (conversion to reason), emotion was regarded as an infiltrating, negative force threatening the foundations of Böhl's rational ideal. Now truth and emotion are inextricably linked in a new relationship with God and faith. 'Gefühl', like 'Neigung', has become the new touchstone in Böhl's self-evaluation and that of the world around him. Interesting too is the comment, made almost as an aside, that the mystical is the true manifestation of Christianity, an assertion which marks the height of Böhl's engagement with mystical thought.

Whilst Böhl associates Schelling's ideas with mysticism, he maintains enough distance to find fault. The irritation expressed at what he perceives to be Schelling's tendency to belittle the work of the mystics is typical of Böhl's attitude towards the contemporary reception of their work, in particular amongst German Idealist philosophers. He is annoyed by the lack of respect accorded them by modern thinkers who, he felt, often borrowed from their work without acknowledgement. In his letter to Dorothea on 24 March 1810, he is particularly critical of Fichte and Schelling whose work he feels owes much to the early fifteenth-century *Theologia Teutsch* which, along with the *Book of Spiritual Poverty*, set the tone for the latter stages of the Rhineland Mysticism associated with Meister Eckhart.[8] The *Theologia Teutsch* – a text which exercised a profound influence on the young Luther – promoted a notion of Divine Will and suggested that the enactment of evil came through a denial of that Divine Will in the form of 'self-will'. Böhl sees an echo of the mystical text in Schelling's Kant-derived concept of *Wille*, which seeks to avoid a slide into Spinozist determinism by arguing for the existence of human freedom with the choice for the individual to do good or to do evil. As his reading progresses, Böhl's critical stance in relation to the Romantic reception of mysticism leads him to adopt a defensive position in the face of any criticism or neglect of mystical thought. On 16 August 1810, he mentions to Julius an impassioned sermon by the reformed preacher, Pastor Geibel, which came 'aus dem Herzen und ging zu Herzen' (from the heart, to the heart) and expresses concern that others present may not have understood it 'in dem rechten Sinn' (in the right way). According to Böhl, the appropriate interpretation was grounded in a mystical understanding and, indeed, he becomes quite protective of his new religious ideal, encouraging Julius to publish in the *Vaterländisches Museum* an essay on mysticism which explains 'die Gründe des Haßes gegen diese stille innere Religion, die niemandem im Wege stehen kann' (the reasons for the hatred of this peaceful, inner religion, which no one can impede). Significantly, in the same letter, he also defends Catholicism. The defence is brief, but perhaps provides a hint that he has already chosen his future path. By the end of 1810, he certainly seems ready to move on.

The sheer intensity of Böhl's emotive response to mysticism means this encounter is short lived. Ever conscious of his own limitations, he admits to Dorothea: 'aus der Mystik bin ich so ziemlich wieder heraus: es ist eine wunderbar große Erhebung, derer ich mich nicht fähig fühle' (I am more or less over my mystical phase: it requires one to raise oneself up to such a wondrous extent, something of which I do not feel capable; 1 September 1810). This marks too the end of his engagement with German Idealism. Despite Böhl's observations, his correspondence does not reveal any further engagement with contemporary philosophy and, indeed, the nature of his comments suggests a quest for confirmation of the validity of mysticism as a pathway to God, rather than any serious attempt to enter the philosophical debate. His reading of Schelling and the mystics is incomplete and the conclusions he draws necessarily eclectic. Böhl's unsystematic analysis notwithstanding, the discovery of the mystics and the apparent affirmation of their ideals in the modern philosophical debate feeds a growing desire for a more immediate relationship to faith. This leads Böhl even further from Enlightenment ideals, almost, one feels, against his own better judgement. Indeed, he even describes this as a feminine tendency of the type he might once have associated only with his wife. The comment is telling and once more highlights the interrelation of influences in Böhl's shifting world view. Although the encounter with mysticism and Schelling had been brief, its impact was great, opening Böhl's mind to a new experience of religion which sat more comfortably with the thoroughly Catholic influence of his wife and the culture she represented.

Perhaps unsurprisingly (particularly given the latent sympathies suggested in Humboldt's testimony of 1799), exposure to these multiple stimuli encouraged Böhl to reappraise his approach to Catholicism. A key influence in this process was Friedrich Leopold Stolberg's *Geschichte der Religion Jesu Christi* (1806–18), the early volumes of which are mentioned in a letter to Julius on 3 April 1811. Stolberg was not a follower of Romantic thought and actively rejected aspects of Romantic aesthetics and philosophy. However, his conversion, described by Joshua as 'a reaction against the increasing secularisation and atheism of the time',[9] set an example for many prominent thinkers. Friedrich Schlegel praised his actions as 'ein öffentliches Ereignis, das jeden berührte, der an den höheren Fragen in Kirche und Staat irgend Anteil nahm' (a public event which touched everyone who had an interest in the higher matters of Church and state)[10] and the very public nature of his conversion and the polemical responses it provoked, not least from his fellow poets of the *Göttinger Hain*, heightened interest in Catholicism. This was intensified by the publication of the first volumes of his *Geschichte der Religion Jesu Christi*, which outlined Stolberg's ecclesiastical views, adopting a thoroughly pro-Catholic position. Once more, Böhl had discovered a text which confirmed his new framework of values. Echoing his appreciation of mystical thought, he found in Stolberg further expression of the centrality of *Wille* in relation to faith. The concept was a cornerstone of Stolberg's thought, as is made clear in the dedication included in the first volume of his monumental work:

> Die Wahrheit desjenigen, was wir glauben sollen, muß so einleuchtend seyn, daß wir gewiß glauben, wofern nur unser Wille der Ueberzeugung nicht widerstrebt. In

unserm kranken Willen liegt das Wehe unsrer Natur. In der Genesung unsers Willens unser Heil. [. . .] Unser Wille ist in unserem Herzen. Darum redet Gott uns an's Herz.[11]

(The truth of that which we should believe must be so plausible that we are sure to believe, provided that our Will does not contradict our conviction. In our diseased Will lies the misery of our nature. In the recovery of our Will our salvation. [. . .] Our Will is in our heart. That is why God speaks to our heart.)

For Stolberg, the positive aspect of *Wille* is associated with the heart, the seat of emotion, whilst the negative brings only misery and the rejection of truth. Underpinning this is the idea of revelation and it is to a revealed God that Stolberg turns as a guide in the struggle of the Will between good and evil:

Weil der Mensch durch Sünde sich von Gott entfernt, also seiner Urbestimmung zuwider handelt, so fühlt er sogleich inneres Mißbehagen. Mit Recht nennen wir es Gewissen. Der Mensch *weiß*, auch wenn niemand ihn belehrte, daß er durch Sünde sein Inneres zerrüttet; und wollte er es läugnen, so würde seine Schaamröthe ihn der Lüge zeihen. [. . .] Im Gewissen offenbart sich Gott. (260)

(Because man distances himself from God through sin, that is to say, acts against his original character, he therefore immediately feels an inner discomfort. Quite rightly, we call this conscience. Man *knows*, even if he is never taught it, that he destroys his inner self through sin and were he to deny it, then his red-faced shame would indict him. [. . .] God is revealed in our conscience.)

Stolberg's reference to the concept of 'Urbestimmung' parallels the notion of 'innerliche Unveränderlichkeit' which so attracted Böhl to Goethe's *Wahlverwandschaften* and confirms the centrality of 'Neigung', one of the novel's central themes, to his understanding of revelation with the belief that there is an inherent inclination in man to please a revealed God. Whilst embracing this aspect of Stolberg's work, Böhl rejects his claim, also grounded in mystical thought, that God reveals himself in nature. Writing to Julius, he now appears to reject the Böhmian concept in favour of the ministry of Christ. In so doing, Böhl quotes directly from Goethe's poem, 'Das Göttliche':[12]

Der May ist schön: seitdem ich aber den geoffenbarten Gott näher kennen gelernt habe, ist mir die Natur nicht mehr was sie war. Unsere Naturliebe ist wahrlich nur Täuschung – <u>denn unfühlend ist die Natur; es leuchtet die Sonne über Bös' und Gute, und dem Verbrecher glänzen wie dem besten der Mond und die Sterne.</u> (5 May 1811)

(May is beautiful, but ever since I have come to know the revealed God better, nature no longer means the same to me. Our love of nature is truly deception – <u>for nature is without feeling. The sun shines on good and evil alike and the moon and the stars sparkle for the criminal just as they do for the best of men</u>.)

Böhl's move away from the mystics is significant in illustrating the nature of the tortuous deliberations surrounding his faith at this time. The extent of these becomes clear when one compares his position in 1813, the year of his conversion, with that once defended as a young man following his initial departure from Germany and during the first years in Spain. The ideals of Campe's teaching, based upon a Protestant ethic, but inquiring into the ideals Deism and Neology, which guided the young Böhl through adolescence and the first years of adulthood, have been superseded, after many years of inner torment and deliberation, by a secure belief in a revealed God and an acceptance of Catholic doctrine. Whilst much of that torment centred on the issue of faith itself, it was further heightened by a sense of betrayal. Given Campe's staunch anti-Catholic views, it is hardly surprising that Böhl felt unable to confide in him the extent of his disaffection with the religious values of his youth. Although he clearly does feel able to convey some of his feelings in his correspondence with Dorothea, in particular his appreciation of mystical thought, in a letter to Julius on 3 April 1811, Böhl alludes to the fact that he is finding it increasingly difficult to maintain contact with his *Pflegeeltern*, 'weil mein Herz zu voll ist und ich mich doch nicht mittheilen darf' (for my heart is too full and yet I may not give account of myself). Having once turned to the Campes for advice on all matters of a personal nature, he is now increasingly reliant on Julius and Francisca. His wife in particular plays an important role as a confidante and Böhl opens his heart to her much earlier than he did to any of his German friends. As early as 14 February 1808, he reveals a state of mind which leaves the reader in little doubt as to the eventual outcome of his inner struggle:

Tu conoces los delirios de mi juventud y los ideales que sucesivamente me han encantado: el amor perfecto, la Suiza, la vida campestre, en fin algún objeto que pudiera revestir con los colores de mi fantasía [. . .] mi corazón me impelía a buscar lo infinito; la identidad del pensamineto con el sentimiento; la reunión del amor y de la justicia; en una palabra, Dios. Entonces empecé, a barruntar que el Dios de los filósofos nada era para mí, y que yo necesitaba de un Dios-hombre para consuelo de mi corazón. Hoy en dia ya los talentos mas distinguidos se han declarado por el Cristianismo, y ya puede uno intitularse cristiano sin pasar por beato, hipócrita y tonto.[13]

(You know the ravings of my youth and the ideals which enchanted me one after the other: pure love, Switzerland, rural life, in fact, anything which I might dress up in the colourful trappings of my imagination [. . .] my heart compelled me to seek the infinite; to identify thought with emotion; the fusion of love and justice; in a word, God. Then I began to suspect that the God of the philosophers was not for me and that I needed a God-man to console my heart. Nowadays, the most distinguished talents have come out in favour of Christianity and already one can call oneself a Christian without being regarded as overly devout, hypocritical and stupid.)

In one single paragraph, Böhl calls into question and rejects the ideological foundations of his early years as he traces the shift away from the Rousseauian ideal and the concept of a rational Christian faith towards a world enlivened by unfettered imagination and the consolation of a revealed God. It is in this context that the dual aspects of Böhl's 'Wiedergeburt im Norden' merge as his reading of the Romantics during the Görslow years runs parallel with his encounter with mystical thought. However, whilst Böhl's conversion and his relationship to religion has some marked parallels with the experience of other Romantics, he does not display what Weeks terms the typically 'Catholic-nostalgic sentiments of the Protestant Romantics' (220), nor was he 'halfway Catholic' as August Wilhelm Schlegel was accused of being. Instead, he underwent a complete and sincere conversion, which was the result of many years of silent anguish. He remained faithful to them and, with the exception of a short period of melancholy during the late 1820s, he never voiced any regret or doubt at his decision. Describing his feelings to Julius shortly after his formal conversion, Böhl expresses himself in terms which confirm the sincerity and validity of his views:

Ich finde mich seitdem innerlich einig und beruhigt und rathe jeder liebenden und suchenden Seele ein Gleiches zu thun. Hätte ich Zeit wie viel Wunderbares würde ich Ihnen über diese Bekehrung mittheilen können! Daß sie <u>aus dem Herzen</u> kommt brauche ich Ihnen der mich kennen, wohl nicht noch besonders zu versichern. (9 August 1813)

(Since then, I feel at one with myself and calm inside and advise every loving, searching soul to do the same thing. If I had time, how many wonderful things I would be able to tell you about this conversion! I do not really need to assure you, who know me, that they come <u>from the heart</u>.)

On the eve of his return to Spain in 1813, Böhl had completed a personal journey from a child of Enlightenment pedagogy to a convinced Romantic. His clear affinity with a number of Romantic thinkers – the Schlegel brothers, Novalis, Schelling and Wordsworth – and his interest in ancient German and Spanish texts and the work of the mystics place him at the heart of a pan-European revaluation of culture. Böhl's publishing activities during the Görslow years see him engage fully with the Romantic debate on all levels – creatively, critically and, perhaps most importantly, as a cultural mediator. His role might have been more prominent had it not been for the failed collaboration with Kerner and, for the time being, his scholarly efforts would succeed only in securing him a place on the periphery of the Romantic debate in Germany. Nevertheless, the years at Görslow had set the course for Böhl's future endeavours. His closing comments in the article on English poetry, comparing English and German literary trends, typify the transculturalism which would characterise his subsequent critical and philological career. Indeed, he was already making plans for a collection of ancient Spanish poetry which would eventually be published in Germany as his three-volume *Floresta de rimas antiguas castellanas*. This collection, which would influence Spanish philology for decades to come, would not see the light of day for another ten years, hampered by financial, commercial and political circumstance. Moreover, there was another battle to fight first – for the honour of Calderón.

NOTES

1. Although a number of commentators have placed Böhl's conversion to Catholicism at the time of his return to Spain in 1797, citing the influence of Fray Diego José de Cádiz (1743–1801), the popular missionary and orator made famous by his defence of the power of Rome and criticism of Carlos III, it seems more likely, as both Montoto and Carnero suggest, that this period instead saw the beginnings of Böhl's disaffection with Protestantism which would lead to his subsequent crisis of faith, something which he did not begin to confront fully until the Görslow years.
2. Most notably in the *Herzensergießungen eines kunstliebenden Klosterbruders* (Outpourings of an art-loving monk) published by Ludwig Tieck and Wilhelm Heinrich Wackenroder in 1796.
3. Böhl quotes from part two, Chap. 17; *Goethe. Berliner Ausgabe*; XII: 261.
4. Harmut Fröschle, *Goethes Verhältnis zur Romantik* (Würzburg: Königshausen und Neumann, 2002), p. 144.
5. Schiller, *Sämtliche Werke*; V: 602.
6. See Pierre Deghaye, 'Die Natur als Leib Gottes in Jacob Böhmes Theosophie' in J. Garewicz and A. M. Haas (eds.), *Gott, Natur und Mensch in der Sicht Jacob Böhmes und seiner Rezeption* (Wiesbaden: Harrassowitz, 1994), pp. 71–111.
7. Andrew Weeks, *German Mysticism. From Hildegard of Bingen to Ludwig Wittgenstein. A Literary and Intellectual History* (NY: SUNY, 1993), p. 212; further references appear in the text.
8. Oliver Davies, *The Rhineland Mystics. An Anthology* (London: SPCK, 1989).
9. Eleoma Joshua, *Friedrich Leopold Graf zu Stolberg and the German Romantics*, British and Irish Studies in German Language and Literature 36 (Bern: Lang, 2005), p. 138.
10. Ernst Behler et al (eds.), *Kritische Friedrich-Schlegel-Ausgabe* (Paderborn: Schönigh, 1961–); VIII: CLX.
11. *Gesammelte Werke der Brüder Christian und Friedrich Leopold Grafen zu Stolberg*, 20 vols (Hamburg: Perthes, 1827); XX: 'Zueignung der Geschichte der Religion Jesu Christi von Fr. Leop. Graf zu Stolberg an seine Söhne und Töchter' (1806), 261.
12. *Goethe. Berliner Ausgabe*; I: 'Poetische Werke; Gedichte und Singspiele I', 331–3.
13. Quoted in Fernández Poza, p. 99.

PART TWO

The Calderón Polemic

Chapter 6
Settled in Spain

Francisca's independent life in Spain could not continue indefinitely. Anxious to see her family again and driven by political and financial circumstances, Böhl's wife began to make plans for a return to Germany. The period of marital separation came to an end in 1811 when, having finally obtained passports from the French authorities, Francisca set off with her mother and daughters, Aurora and Angela, on the long and perilous journey to Görslow, one which Böhl's aging mother-in-law would not survive. Once reunited in 1812, the couple sought refuge from the political upheaval which surrounded them by retreating into their studies. Böhl, at the height of his Romantic rebirth, was both inspired by the reconnection with Spanish culture which his wife's presence signified and relieved to see his children together once more with their mother after an absence of seven years. The scholarly existence at Görslow could not, however, mask the dire reality of the situation and despite having finally realised his dream of family life on the estate, Böhl knew it could not be permanent. By now, it was clear that any plans for the future would have to centre on Cadiz. His wife's aversion to the German language and climate combined with the demands of the family firm meant that Böhl had no choice in the matter. The summer of 1813 was spent preparing for the family's return to Spain, their plans postponed several times due to the war. These delays only served to heighten Böhl's growing anguish. Already in the throes of great personal upheaval, he was deeply troubled at the thought of leaving all his friends and family behind and felt uncomfortable abandoning his beloved estate to financial ruin. When it finally came, the family's departure was abrupt, made just in time to avoid the return of French troops advancing once more through Mecklenburg. Böhl wrote to Julius from Görslow on 9 August to bid him farewell and the family set off two days later. This journey, one of so many undertaken by Böhl and his family, was a turning point in their lives. The finality of the situation cannot have been apparent to them at the time, but Böhl would never see any of his German friends or family again. This would also be the last major journey of his life. Having travelled the length and breadth of western Europe from childhood, from now on, Böhl would lead a far more settled existence, never moving far from the environs of Cadiz.

Despite the prevailing political uncertainties and the atmosphere of general upheaval, these first years of reunion, at Görslow and then in Spain, were perhaps the happiest of Böhl's marriage. The convergence in world view which had developed through mutual encouragement in the face of adversity during the years of separation meant that once reunited, the couple could share their interests, no longer at loggerheads over issues of faith or location. Böhl now held his wife's religious conviction and had come to appreciate the customs and culture of her home almost as much as she did. He certainly seemed far better disposed towards her intellectual activities and, even before the polemic commenced, their writings displayed a set of similar values. As well as concurring in their aesthetic appraisal of Spain's literary heritage and sharing an interest in contemporary English works, there is a marked similarity in political stance which saw both husband and wife defend an absolutist, anti-French position in the face of both the internal Liberal threat in Spain and the external danger presented by Napoleonic France. Fuelled by the bitter experiences of recent years, the stance adopted is defended vehemently in both private correspondence and published material, the exalted tone of which at times exceeds that of the Calderón polemic. There is a sense throughout that both Böhl and Francisca view their contributions as part of a crusade against the forces which have destroyed much of what they held dear, part of the battle to preserve and revive that which remained. This lends an immediacy to their writings in the years from 1813 to 1815 which conveys the depth of feeling and, indeed, fear experienced in the face of such a palpable threat. There is no doubt that this was a battle for both self and nation, one which others must be persuaded to join. Francisca, in particular, adopts an evangelical tone, spreading the word through her salon, which, once re-established, soon regained popularity amongst the more conservative supporters of the monarchy. In keeping with the tenor of the period, much of her work at this time centred on political issues, arguing in particular against the Liberal Constitution of 1812 and eulogising the monarch following the restoration of Fernando VII in the spring of 1814. Indicative is the pamphlet 'Fernando de Zaragoza. Una Vision' (Fernando of Zaragoza. A vision) which appeared in 1814 under her customary pseudonym *Cymdocea*.[1] Describing in elaborate terms a vision of Fernando's return to power, the text ends with an exalted adoration of throne and altar intended to speak to the heart of every patriotic Spaniard:

Postrado el trémulo monarca al pie de los altares, el genio ciñó sus sienes reales con la corona de las Españas, y poniendo en su augusta mano la palma, desapareció envuelto en una armonia celestial. (O: 24)

(The quivering monarch prostrate at the foot of the altars, the spirit encircles his royal temples with the crown of the Spains and placing the palm in his august hand, disappeared enveloped in a celestial harmony.)

Despite this vociferous appreciation of the newly restored king, depicted in terms which border on deification, the author of the pamphlet found herself at the centre of a bitter wrangle with the authorities. Francisca, enthused by the apparent return to the values of old, was a little premature in publishing the piece before Fernando VII's repudiation of the Constitution on 4 May. Consequently, her association of throne and altar with patriotism, which, it must be noted, also ran counter to the constitutional ideal espoused by more moderate monarchists, was deeply offensive to the stauncher adherents of the still valid Constitution, themselves now under threat and forced to adopt an equally trenchant position. This left the censors with little option but to act against the piece. Had the pamphlet appeared only a few weeks or even days later, it would have met with at least measured approval. Instead, it was banned and its author officially reprimanded.

In this tussle with the censors, Francisca received support from an unexpected source. In June 1814, the theologian, critic and poet, José María Blanco White (1775–1841), who had occasionally attended Francisca's salons before leaving for exile in London in 1810, published a brief defence of her pamphlet in the last edition of his periodical, *El Español* (The Spaniard).[2] In an article entitled 'Conclusion de esta obra' (Conclusion of this work), Blanco voices his disillusionment with the *Cortes*, which he feels has allowed the opportunity for just government in Spain to dissolve into extremism and revolution. Whilst not adhering to Francisca's views, Blanco regarded the censors' treatment of her as symptomatic of this and feels compelled to defend her right to express her opinions. This defence was, however, short lived. Blanco was a supporter of constitutional monarchy, equally opposed to both the tyranny of absolutism and the excesses of 1812 *Cortes*. Ever the enemy of religious and political extremes, he must have found the Böhls' increasingly reactionary stance abhorrent and his correspondence with Francisca ended abruptly in the summer of 1814. The change of political mood in Spain following the return of Fernando VII meant that Francisca was anyway soon able to draw support from closer to home. Now in tune with the new regime, her enthusiasm in defending the faith and the crown did not go unnoticed and she was awarded with special recognition by the *Junta Patriótica de Cádiz* (Cadiz Patriotic Committee) in 1815. In a development which highlights the complexities and fluidity surrounding notions of patriotism at this time of rapid political change, she was also elected into the progressive *Real Sociedad Económica de Cádiz* (Cadiz Royal Economical Society) as a member of the *Clase de Damas* (Class of Gentlewomen) in 1818.[3]

Recognition by such societies, whilst itself evidence of their standing in Cadiz society, presented the Böhls with a dilemma. The conservative views they espoused were undoubtedly shared by others, but were not the norm in a city which had come to be seen as the heartland of Liberal Spain. Bound to the area by family and business ties, there was an inevitable need to compromise. Böhl was himself a founder of the *Real Sociedad Económica de Cádiz*, which was established in 1814. Although he fundamentally disagreed with many of their progressive principles, he had no choice but to become involved in order to protect his fragile financial interests. He regarded much of what the society stood for as unpatriotic, modern and overly influenced by France. That Böhl should have agreed to have anything to do with an organisation so alien to his own beliefs simply in order to help maintain the family's business reputation is an indication of the severity of the financial situation in which he found himself upon his return to Spain. Already encumbered by the difficulties in disposing of his Görslow estate, Böhl now had to deal with what remained of the family firm. It was, as he had always expected, in ruins and was finally put into liquidation on 29 May 1815. Böhl spent the next few years trying to settle the family's affairs in a way which would safeguard the dowry which he had provided for Francisca and also the inheritance he expected to receive from his mother and stepfather. Böhl joined some associates in setting up an insurance company and took on a number of commissions from various other trading houses, ventures which enabled him to keep his head above water until the family's debts had been cleared, but it was not a life which he enjoyed. He felt torn in two and commented in a letter to Elise Campe on 6 April 1816 that he could hardly believe that the philosopher of Görslow and the businessman in Spain were one and the same person.

However, whilst the Spanish businessman might find himself forced to compromise, the philosopher of Görslow was determined to defend a hard won set of values and did so with a passion which emphasises the correlation between Böhl's revised world view and his responses to the political threats which sought to undermine it. In so doing, perhaps having learnt from his wife's experience, he was aware of the problematic reception which his absolutist, anti-French views might attract and resigned himself to making those views known only privately, either in his correspondence or in the context of Francisca's salon meetings. He makes reference in a letter to Julius on 15 July 1817 to a number of pieces written following his return to Spain which he feels to be too conservative for prevailing taste there. Convinced, however, of a more receptive audience in Germany, he did make some effort to see at least one such piece published in Hamburg. A short essay entitled 'Auch eine Stimme über Bonaparte' (Another opinion of Bonaparte) was sent to Johann Daniel Runge (1767–1856), brother of the artist, Phillip Otto Runge (1777–1810), on 10 August 1815. The piece, held amongst the papers of the Campe collection, is a vehement attack on '[d]er Lügengeist, welcher seit der Verbreitung der französischen Philosophie alles verkehrt, alles entstellt und alles beschmutzt hat' (the dishonest spirit, which, following the spread of French philosophy, has twisted, displaced and besmirched everything).[4] Böhl takes great issue with what he sees as the failure of Napoleon's enemies to punish him adequately, calling into question their judgement when compared to the treatment

Settled in Spain

of other heads of state, including Louis XVIII. Long regarded by Böhl as the arch-enemy of Catholicism, the defeated emperor should not have been rewarded with land and privilege. This has merely enabled his resurgence. Instead, the solution is clear:

> So lange Bonaparte athmet bleiben die Seinigen hoffnungsvoll. Er ist der Mittelpunkt alles Schlechten, alles Jakobinismus, alles Religionshasses; er ist der Anker aller Unzufriedenen aller Verräther, aller diejenigen die durch Ordnung und Rath gezügelt werden. Diese Hoffnungen sind durch Bonapartes öffentliche Hinrichtung abzuschneiden.
>
> (As long as Bonaparte breathes, his followers have hope. He is the centre of all evil, all Jacobinism, all hatred of religion; he is the anchor for all the dissatisfied, all the betrayers, all of those who are bound by order and wisdom. These hopes can be cut off by Bonaparte's public execution.)

These words convey the extent of Böhl's anger towards Napoleon and the French, drawing together in his attack the extremes of republicanism, religious intolerance and social disorder, the impact of which on his own life and that of his family he is now trying to contain. Anxious for an outlet, he offered the essay to Runge with the comment 'Sie werden beurteilen ob es noch an der Zeit ist vorstehendes zu verbreiten' (you can judge whether it is still appropriate to make known the above). Runge must have seen some value in the piece which was proofread and altered slightly before presumably being sent on to August Campe for consideration.[5] However, the text never appeared in print, its content no doubt too extreme for the delicate political atmosphere surrounding the Congress of Vienna.

As the tone of Böhl's essay suggests, during the first years in Spain, he was still very much affected by the experiences of the Napoleonic invasion and the extreme patriotism which this inspired heightened his interest in both German and Spanish culture. He continued to receive the latest material from Germany through August Campe, although, conscious of the limits placed on him by cost and time, he asked his friend to send only the very best in new publications, mostly drawn from Romantic writers such as Tieck and Arnim. His enthusiasm for Goethe's work also continued and he was greatly impressed by the third part of *Dichtung und Wahrheit* (Poetry and Truth) which appeared in 1814. Whilst able to follow such new developments with relative ease, his study of older German literature was hampered by circumstance. The hasty departure from Görslow had meant that his collection of older material had to remain with his brother Fritz in Germany. Böhl was deeply affected by this, plagued with a sense of disconnection from his own literary heritage, and he sought to keep his interest alive by asking Campe if he might like to take on the compilation of a second volume of *Volkslieder* to complement the earlier edition based on the *Wunderhorn*. August does not appear to have accepted the challenge, however, and Böhl eventually had the manuscript forwarded to him in Cadiz so that he might remember his homeland by playing the old songs for himself and his family.

Unable to maintain any physical links with his native Germany and restricted in his study by the absence of key materials, Böhl's interest in Spanish culture intensified. The intellectual energy once devoted to his deliberations surrounding matters of faith and the defence of Romantic values in Germany was now refocused on Spain as the nation gradually took on the mantle of surrogate homeland in the years after 1813, becoming the object of Böhl's cultural and political patriotism as the work begun at Görslow was advanced with vigour to map out further a new Romantic, now essentially Hispanophile identity. This shift did not, however, lessen the transcultural nature of Böhl's scholarship. Driven by political and aesthetic motives, there was a continued emphasis on the cultural mediation which had characterised Böhl's work in Germany, with a desire to advance the cause of Romantic thought to the betterment of Spain's beleaguered national literature. Indeed, whilst reticent to seek publication in Spain for his political views, Böhl had no such qualms when it came to mounting a Romantic defence of Spain's literary heritage. Already well known in Cadiz and assured access to the literary elite by virtue of his wife's continued profile as a salon hostess, Böhl was able to establish links with the Spanish publishing world almost immediately and the periodical press of Cadiz and Madrid soon provided the battleground for much of the literary skirmishing which later became known as the Calderón polemic.

The debate centred on Böhl's patriotic attempt to defend Calderón and the literature of his age in the face of the prevailing *afrancesado* neo-Classical trend.[6] Böhl's main ally in the debate was his wife, Francisca, but he also received support from the historian, José Vargas Ponce (1760–1821), and later, the polemicist, Juan Bautista Cavaleri Pazos, of whom little is known beyond his controversial literary activities. Böhl's adversary, erstwhile family friend, José Joaquín de Mora (1783–1864), was briefly supported by the well-known Liberal author and critic, Antonio Alcalá Galiano (1789–1865). Although Francisca's own voice plays a limited role in the polemic, featuring in only a fraction of the papers published, she provided her husband with both practical and moral support throughout, copying and proofing texts. In addition, she was able to furnish Böhl with valuable ammunition in the battle to discredit his opponent. During her time alone in Spain, Mora had been one of her closest associates and their correspondence continued even after Mora had been imprisoned by the French at Autun following the uprising of 1808. Testimony to the intimacy of their friendship is to be found in an album owned by Francisca, now held in the Osborne archive, in which Mora wrote the following message in April 1807:

Los recuerdos de una amistad fundada sobre la simpatia, y la virtud, resisten a los años y a las revoluciones del tiempo; nos dan placeres tranquilos y disminuyen el sentimiento de nuestras penas. Frasquita ha deseado mi felicidad; me ha querido ver en el número de sus amigos ¿como podra borrarse jamas de la memoria y gratitud de J. J. de Mora?[7]

(The memories of a friendship founded on sympathy and virtue resist the passing of the years and the revolutions of time; they give us quiet pleasure and lessen our sense of suffering. Frasquita wished for my happiness; she wanted me to number among her friends. How can the memory and gratitude of J. J. de Mora ever be erased?)

The irony of these words in the light of the vehement exchanges which followed is clear. In a further ironic twist, in 1813, just before the polemic began, Francisca sent three *romances* penned by Mora to August Wilhelm Schlegel who responded with approval.[8] Little did the two friends realise that they would soon be at war with each other over the ideas of the German theorist whose Romantic reading of Spain's literary past formed the backbone of Böhl's argument. Equally ironic is the fact that Francisca should elicit a response from Schlegel on this matter when all Böhl's subsequent efforts to gain any acknowledgment failed.[9] The renowned critic was, however, aware of Böhl's efforts in disseminating his views, commenting to the publisher Cotta in 1841 that his work had been widely translated 'von Cadiz bis Sct. Petersburg' (from Cadiz to St Petersburg).[10] Carnero (O: 162) suggests that Böhl's views simply became too extreme for Schlegel, but it is just as likely that by the time the Böhl rendition of the *Wiener Vorlesungen* was published and news of this had made its way back to Germany, Schlegel's attention was focused elsewhere, the emphasis of his work having shifted towards the study of oriental languages. This was certainly the explanation which Böhl identified for the lack of recognition received for his efforts.

The polemic can be divided into two phases which fall either side of the ban imposed on the Cadiz press following the return of Fernando VII.[11] The first phase, of 1814, involved the Cadiz periodical, the *Mercurio gaditano* (Cadiz Mercury), whilst the second, from 1817 to 1820, drew into the fray the Madrid-based *Crónica científica y literaria* (Scientific and Literary Chronicle) and two Cadiz periodicals, the *Minerva* and the *Diario mercantil de Cádiz* (Cadiz Daily Commercial). Both sides in the debate also produced pamphlets, all of which are now either unavailable or extremely rare. Their scarcity perhaps reflects the embarrassment with which many of those concerned would later view the vehement nature of the debate. Böhl was, in fact, alone in attempting to preserve his argument for posterity, publishing a collection of his polemic documents in 1820 which included all of his periodical contributions as well as the four pamphlets, *Donde las dan, las toman* (Give as good as you get), the *Pasatiempo crítico* (Critical musings), the *Segunda parte del pasatiempo crítico* (Second part of the critical musings) and the *Tercer parte del pasatiempo crítico* (Third part of the critical musings). The collection, entitled *Vindicaciones de Calderon y del Teatro antiguo español contra los afrancesados en literatura. Recogidas y coordinadas por D. Juan Nicolas Böhl de Faber, de la Real Academia Española* (Vindications of Calderón and of ancient Spanish theatre against the literary Francophiles. Collected and co-ordinated by D. Juan Nicolas Böhl de Faber of the Royal Spanish Academy), which is itself now extremely rare, presents the documents chronologically with some alterations, omissions and additions.

Study of the collection soon reveals the significant nature of the debate. Although there was a good deal of petty and unedifying name calling, at the core of the polemic lay the first attempt to introduce a Romantic ethos into Spain following the specifically German model proposed by August Wilhelm Schlegel, which sees Böhl offer his new audience an alternative appreciation of Spain's national literature grounded in a new and complex aesthetic which promoted a move away from Classical precepts. The polemic appears upon first examination to have been a straightforward ideological struggle between the Romantic, conservative Böhl and the Liberal, neo-Classicist Mora, a struggle which resulted in a victory for the German, his views vindicated, so he claimed, by his admission to the Royal Spanish Academy in 1820. The clarity of the debate is, however, clouded by Mora's shifting stance. As a poet and thinker, Mora was ideologically torn, on the one hand partially sympathetic towards many of Böhl's aesthetic ideals, whilst on the other utterly at odds with the thoroughly conservative political import of the German's pro-Calderón campaign. Therefore, whilst for Böhl the debate seamlessly combined the political and the aesthetic in an argument which encompassed both Herderian historicism and Schlegelian Romantic theory, Mora, defending a Liberal position, was forced to argue against the aesthetic in order to condemn the political. His pre- and post-polemic stance as a moderate Liberal with an unequivocal understanding of the value of national literature as a cornerstone of Spain's cultural identity meant he ought to have been able to pick up on subtle connections between his own aesthetic values and those inherent in Schlegelian thought. Indeed, these connections might have been more fruitfully expanded had Böhl's initial, highly politicised presentation of Schlegel's views been of a different hue. Instead, Mora was compelled to contradict certain views compatible with Romantic thought which he expressed both before and after the polemic took place. It is this division which lies at the heart of the polemic. Whilst Böhl's historical Romanticism defended the nation's culture – a sentiment with which no patriotic Spaniard of the day would have found fault – on a secondary level, it also justified and promoted a thoroughly reactionary political system quite out of step with the enlightened, Liberal ideals of the Constitution of Cadiz. Consequently, even the less scholarly content of the debate can be seen as illustrative of the underlying political tensions in contemporary Spain as Liberals and Absolutists battled for ideological supremacy in a nation in a state of flux. Liberal thinkers like Mora, constrained by the return of Fernando VII in 1814, might not be able to voice their condemnation of the absolutist regime freely, but they could certainly take up their pens in the face of a foreign appraisal of Spain's cultural heritage which seemed to apotheosise everything for which that regime stood. It is this aspect of the debate, as much as the reputation of Calderón, which made the polemic into a battle between old and new, tradition and progress; the prize was the right to define the nation's cultural soul.

NOTES

1. Carnero reproduces the full text in his introduction (O: 21–4 (p. 24)).
2. *El Español*, 8 (1814), 297–8.
3. See Carnero (O: 93–4).
4. SUBHH, CS 1: Böhl von Faber.
5. The most significant change is to the title where the words 'aus Nordamerika' (from North America) have been added, perhaps to add an extra dimension to what were by 1815 well-worn arguments.
6. Use of the term *afrancesado* in this context is restricted to that defining the adherence of writers and thinkers to French cultural taste and does not relate the alternative meaning denoting to a pro-Napoleonic political stance.
7. See Carnero (O: 85).
8. The three *romances* are reproduced by Pitollet (QC: 77–9): 'Las granadinas de la Reyna Isabel' (The Granadan ladies of Queen Isabel), 'Bustos' and 'Zaide'; two of these later appeared in Mora's *No me olvides* (Forget me not; Christmas 1824).
9. The letters are reproduced by Carnero (O: 160–2).
10. Quoted in Dorota Masiakowska, *Vielfalt und Einheit im Europabild August Wilhelm Schlegels* (Frankfurt am Main: Lang, 2002), p. 41.
11. See Ramón Solis, *Historia del periodismo gaditano 1800–1850* (Cadiz: Instituto de Estudios Gaditanos, 1971), pp. 83–127.

Chapter 7
Böhl's Translation of Schlegel

The catalyst for the polemic was Böhl's anonymous publication in the *Mercurio gaditano* on 16 September 1814 of an article entitled 'Reflexiones de Schlegel sobre el teatro, traducidas del Aleman' (Reflections of Schlegel on the theatre, translated from the German). Böhl's purpose in publishing the piece was to defend Calderón against the criticisms of his neo-Classical detractors by showing the appreciation of modern German critics for the work of the Golden Age dramatist. The article purported to be a translation, but was in effect a combination of selective summary and paraphrase, highlighting key aspects of Schlegel's *Wiener Vorlesungen* (Vienna lectures). The lectures were first delivered in the Austrian capital in 1808 and their publication caused a furore throughout Europe. Schlegel's main intention, clearly historicist in inspiration, was to provide a survey of dramatic art over the ages in different nations in order to develop a means to judge each in a manner appropriate to its location and period. Although the lecture series contained some thirty essays, including those which outline the basic tenets of Schlegel's seminal theory of Romantic literature, it was the twelfth and fourteenth lectures and their discussion of the Spanish stage in particular which drew Böhl's attention. The material Schlegel provided, based on his 1803 *Europa* article, was ideally suited to Böhl's plan to continue his transcultural scholarly defence of Spain's literary heritage, begun five years earlier with his essay, 'Ueber die spanische Literatur' (On Spanish literature). Having engaged in the Hispanist debate whilst in Germany, he now sought to disseminate the views of those Hispanists in Spain itself. Schlegel's seminal role in that debate meant Böhl felt he was offering his Spanish readership the benefit of a true authority and at the same time an object lesson in the patriotic appreciation of their own neglected culture.

Böhl's article draws from two sources: Schlegel's twelfth lecture, which offers a comparison of English and Spanish drama, both regarded as individual and unsullied by universalist ideals, and ends with a lengthy analysis of Shakespearian theatre, and his fourteenth lecture, which examines the development of Spanish drama, with a particular emphasis on the work of Calderón.[1] Böhl's translation contains elements of both, assembled on an apparently eclectic basis and with no indication to the reader as to source or *modus operandi*. Such an approach may seem confused and untenable, but it was not unusual for the time. Nor was it without a certain logic within the context of Böhl's own critical agenda. In her 1989 article comparing Böhl's piece with Schlegel's original, Reyes Ponce provides an insightful explanation for Böhl's idiosyncratic methodology which further underlines the extent to which he is now steeped in Romantic aesthetics. According to Reyes Ponce, Böhl is effectively reproducing Schlegel's own practice of 'case analysis' by using the study of Shakespeare in the *Wiener Vorlesungen* as a model for his defence of Calderón.[2] It is for this reason that Böhl chooses elements from the first section of lecture twelve before switching to the argument presented in the latter part of lecture fourteen. In so doing, he combines Schlegel's examination of an organically developing national theatre from lecture twelve and the discussion of the Spanish stage found in lecture fourteen. The two elements are then brought together in a defence of Calderón. Such an eclectic approach, although intentional, necessarily creates a confusing and incomplete presentation of Schlegel's ideas. Whilst Böhl remains faithful to the spirit of the original, he blatantly disregards the form, effectively editing Schlegel's texts in order to construct an argument intended to support his own views. The resultant confusion is further compounded by weaknesses in Böhl's actual translation which blur the clarity of the original argument. In agreeing with Reyes Ponce's interpretation, however, it must be stressed that Böhl's eclecticism is not arbitrary, but part of a careful selection of salient material, intended to highlight the key concepts behind Schlegel's approach to drama, whilst shifting the original Schlegelian emphasis on Shakespeare towards a defence of Calderón. Böhl's *modus operandi* in assembling this piece parallels the eclectic approach adopted for his 1805 article on Schiller's Kantian aesthetics, 'Reflexiones sobre la poesía', and, indeed, the two pieces are linked. The Schlegel translation follows on from the earlier text and constitutes Böhl's second attempt to introduce contemporary German aesthetics to a new audience in Spain. Furthermore, the content of the two pieces is closely related. In his defence of Calderón, Böhl follows Schlegel's development of Kant's ideas and there are grounds to argue that Schlegel may have been one of the 'disciples of the famous Kant' referred to alongside Schiller in the introduction to the 1805 article. Böhl was certainly familiar with the work of both thinkers by the time his article appeared in Quintana's journal and there is a clear progression in Böhl's choice of material which reflects the growing Romantic emphasis of his studies during the Görslow years.

The questions which inevitably arise from Böhl's treatment of his subject matter mean that evaluation of his contribution to the contemporary debate is fraught with difficulty. The fact that Böhl limits himself to a selectively summarised version, instead of providing the full translation undoubtedly required to elucidate such complex ideas, is clearly problematic. His method might have had more success in Germany where the concepts of Romanticism were already common currency, but his elliptical presentation of Schlegelian thought to a Spanish audience unversed in the ideas of the German Romantic theory was bound to cause controversy. Particularly contentious was Schlegel's apotheosis of throne and altar, which, taken out of context in Böhl's piece, appeared utterly reactionary at a time when the validity of that political axis was under the severest scrutiny. It was perhaps this aspect which most offended Mora. Further confusion was caused by a misprint in the title, which, according to Böhl, ought to have read 'extractos' rather than 'reflexiones'. Had the correct title been given, then Böhl's readership might at least have known they were dealing with a partial version of Schlegel's ideas rather than a full translation.

Reyes Ponce's close textual comparison highlights the contentious issues raised by Böhl's approach. Often severely reducing key passages, Böhl discards any information which is of no relevance to his cause. One of the central issues in Schlegel's twelfth lecture is the comparison of English and Spanish poetry, which the Romantic critic highlights as worthy examples of national literature. Böhl's treatment of this subject is typical as he refines and modifies it to suit his own ideological requirements, which demand a negative appraisal of neo-Classical theatre and its *afrancesado* associations. Comparison of key passages reveals the extent of Böhl's alterations. For example, Schlegel argues the following in his defence of those works which fall outside the strictures of the ancients, responding to the assertion that these are the only valid rules governing taste. Note, however, the careful advocation of an alternative, culture-specific set of rules: this is not a call for literary anarchy:

Wäre die Behauptung richtig, so würde Alles, was die Werke der vollendetsten englischen und spanischen Dramatiker, eines Shakspeare und Calderón, unterscheidet, sie bloß unter die Alten herabsetzen; sie würden auf keine Weise für die Theorie wichtig sein, und könnten höchstens durch die Annahme merkwürdig scheinen, der Eigensinn dieser Nationen, sich durchaus nicht nach den Regeln bequemen zu wollen, möchte den Dichtern desto unbeschränkteren Spielraum gelaßen haben, ihre angestammte Originalität, wiewohl gleichsam hinter dem Rücken der Kunst, zu offenbaren. Allein selbst diese Annahme dürfte bei näherer Beleuchtung sehr zweifelhaft werden. Der dichterische Geist bedarf allerdings einer Umgränzung, um sich innerhalb derselben mit schöner Freiheit zu bewegen, wie es alle Völker schon bei der ersten Erfindung des Silbenmaßes gefühlt haben; er muß nach Gesetzen, die aus seinem eignen Wesen herfließen, wirken, wenn seine Kraft nicht ins Leere hinaus verdunsten soll. (109)

(If the assertion be well founded, all that distinguishes the works of the greatest English and Spanish dramatists, a Shakespeare and a Calderón, must rank them far below the ancients; they could in no way be of importance for theory and would at most appear remarkable, on the assumption that the obstinacy of these nations in refusing to comply with the rules may have afforded a more ample field to the poets to display their native originality, though at the expense of art. But even this assumption, on closer examination, appears extremely questionable. The poetic spirit needs to be limited, that it may move with becoming liberty, within its proper precincts, as has been felt by all nations on the first invention of metre; it must act according to laws derivable from its own essence, otherwise its strength will evaporate in boundless vacuity. [339–40])[3]

Schlegel's view is quite clear: poetry must have form. That form, however, ought to be dictated by a process of organic development within the culture of each nation and not imposed by unrelated arbiters of taste whose ideals are founded on ancient precepts as alien to each nation as they are to the modern world. Böhl's response to this pragmatic defence of national literature is to realign the key arguments presented by Schlegel. He is clearly aware of the significance of Schlegel's positive appraisal of the parallels between Spanish and English drama in illustrating his argument in favour of an organically developed national literature. Indeed, Böhl uses it to open his rendition of Schlegel's work (beginning his translation, therefore, *in medias res*). However, although he mentions the comparison in his own version, it is given markedly less attention than it ought to receive. In fact, Böhl shifts the emphasis away from the value of the dramatic works themselves, drawing attention instead to the negative impact of those critics who only value 'modelos antiguos' (ancient models). This gives his version a far more critical slant than Schlegel's original, which advocates adherence to indigenous rules. Whilst the latter is at pains to emphasise the originality and individuality of writers such as Shakespeare and Calderón, Böhl turns the argument to underline the constraining nature of the ancient rules and critics who uphold them. Moreover, Böhl's version, whilst respecting the overall sense of Schlegel's passage, is clearly much shorter:

Es muy natural que los criticos que solo estudian los modelos antiguos, menosprecien el teatro inglés y español. Admirarán quizás algunos de sus rasgos brillantes, pero no por eso dejará de parecerles bárbara y absurda la economía del conjunto. En vano procurarán reducir a sus reglas estas creaciones originales, y más bien las condenarán por heréticas, que poner en duda la infalibilidad de Aristóteles. Muy lejos estamos de querer quitar toda traba a la fantasía del poeta; el ritmo, compañero inseparable del verso, es también el primer símbolo de una sujeción. (V: 1)

(It is quite natural that the critics who only study the ancient models should undervalue English and Spanish theatre. They might admire some of its brilliant traits, but the economy of the whole will still seem barbaric and absurd to them. In vain, they will try to reduce these original creations to their rules and even condemn them as heretical for placing in doubt the infallibility of Aristotle. We are far from wishing to remove every constraint upon imagination; rhythm, inseparable companion of verse, is also the first symbol of a subjection.)

Böhl has reduced the text to a summary which supports his own argument, polemicizing in the process through the insertion of the religiously loaded term 'herética' (heretical) and the explicit mention of Aristotle, both of which intensify Schlegel's more measured assessment. Böhl also lessens the emphasis on 'Silbenmaß' (metre). This is described by Schlegel as emerging naturally from the creative responses of the *Völker* and is a concept central to the influential Herderian notion of an organically developing national literature. Böhl instead offers a far more general appraisal which reduces the comparatist element of the original text, typified by the odd omission of the dramatists' names, and which consequently fails to convey the organicist notion of poetry's self-regeneration. Furthermore, his rather weak definition of metre – or 'ritmo' (rhythm), as he translates it – places far more emphasis on the role of metre as a means of constraint than on the concept of freedom within a set of specifically national, organic rules which is central to Schlegel's original.

Further problems arise when dealing with another key Romantic concept, that of *Universalpoesie*, the merging of genres and contrasting elements within a poetic text. Echoing his brother Friedrich's famous 'Athenaeumsfragment 116', Schlegel contrasts Romantic and Classical poetry:

Die antike Kunst und Poesie geht auf strenge Sonderung des ungleichartigen, die romantische gefällt sich in unauflöslichen Mischungen; alle Entgegengesetzten, Natur und Kunst, Poesie und Prosa, Ernst und Scherz, Erinnerung und Ahnung, Geistigkeit und Sinnlichkeit, das Irdische und Göttliche, Leben und Tod, verschmilzt sie auf das innigste mit einander. (111–12)

(Ancient art and poetry rigorously separate things which are dissimilar; the romantic delights in indissoluble mixtures; all contrarieties: nature and art, poetry and prose, seriousness and mirth, recollection and anticipation, spirituality and sensuality, terrestrial and celestial, life and death, are blended together by it in the most intimate combination. [342])

In selecting this passage for translation, Böhl has clearly identified the centrality of *Universalpoesie* within the Romantic aesthetic and provides his own essentially faithful version:

El arte antiguo separaba con severidad todas las especies; el arte moderno pretende combinar todos los opuestos, y asi se complace en amalgamar la naturaleza y la compostura, la poesía y la prosa, la memoria y la esperanza, el alma y los sentidos, lo terrestre y lo divino, la vida y la muerte. (V: 2–3)

(Ancient art separated all genres with severity; modern art seeks to combine all opposites and thus takes pleasure in merging nature and composition, poetry and prose, memory and hope, soul and senses, earthly and divine, life and death.)

This passage provides clear evidence that Böhl was fully aware of the import of Schlegel's ideas, although his success in conveying key concepts is mixed. His choice of the term 'moderno' to translate the German 'romantische' was probably intended to avoid the potentially pejorative connotations of the terms 'romántico' or 'romancesco' in Spanish.[4] In choosing such a solution, Böhl shows he has clearly grasped Schlegel's meaning which reflects the wider European zeitgeist in demanding a revaluation of the boundaries of literary acceptability in order to acknowledge art produced outwith the prescriptions of the Ancients. Romantic literature, with its roots in the Middle Ages, is modern in its denial of these constraints. Seeking to defend Calderón in this context, Böhl is clearly keen to convey the dramatist's inspirational value within the Schlegelian vision of modern, Romantic aesthetics, where his work is regarded as an exemplary fusion of often contrasting elements. In so doing, however, Böhl risks presenting these elements as incompatible rather than merely contrasting and, whilst his translation remains close to the original in spirit, it cannot be denied that Schlegel's 'unauflösliche Mischungen' (indissoluble mixtures) have far more subtlety than Böhl's blunt 'combinar todos los opuestos' (combine all opposites).

Böhl's attempts to convey other key concepts in Spanish are also open to criticism. Reyes Ponce highlights his version of Schlegel's notion of Romantic chaos. Whereas Schlegel describes the concept as '[das] nach neuen und wundervollen Geburten ringende Chaos' (chaos [. . .] perpetually striving after new and marvellous births; 112 (343)), which suggests the attainment of an order beyond the first throes of genesis, Böhl offers the rather mundane and effectively damning explanation that the fragmentary nature of Romantic poetry 'a veces no ofrece más que un caos' (at times offers little more than chaos; V: 3). Elsewhere, other key aspects are glossed over. For example, the revolutionary comparison of Greek and Romantic art, which precedes Schlegel's discussion of Shakespeare towards the end of the lecture, is alluded to only briefly. Böhl then switches abruptly to lecture fourteen. In fact, his selective summary of lecture twelve only occupies the first two of his ten-page article (as it appears in *Vindicaciones*). Despite this relative brevity, these carefully chosen excerpts lay the theoretical foundation for the ensuing defence of national literature by highlighting the negative nature of Ancient rules in order to juxtapose them with the following discussion of the positive characteristics of Spain's national theatre, represented primarily by Calderón.

Böhl recommences his translation in the middle of lecture fourteen with Schlegel's idealisation of the Spanish Middle Ages, a vision which fails to adopt any measure of critical distance in its apotheosis of throne, altar and chivalry and which constitutes a complete rejection of the prevailing 'Black Legend'. Böhl fully supports this new depiction of Spain as a final bastion of Christendom in the face of the infidel and seeks to bolster Schlegel's argument by adding some extra detail gleaned from his own knowledge of the material by including references to Pelayo and the *Reconquista*. Having thus established the historical context, albeit in a selective and uncritical form, Böhl at last turns to the crux of the matter: Schlegel's appreciation of Golden Age theatre. Central to Schlegel's reading is the notion that Spain's literature is inextricably linked to the character of the nation itself. The medieval ideal forms the backdrop for the development of a national literature imbued with the values of a bygone chivalrous age. Böhl subscribes wholeheartedly to this idea and makes it the focus of his presentation of Schlegel's views. In so doing, he selects those sections of Schlegel's treatise which are devoted to pure hyperbole, eulogising Spain as the very pinnacle of piety, chivalry, honour and love:

Wenn Religionsgefühl, biedrer Heldenmut, Ehre und Liebe die Grundlagen der romantischen Poesie sind, so mußte sie in Spanien, unter solchen Auspizien geboren und herangewachsen, wohl den höchsten Schwung nehmen. Die Phantasie der Spanier war kühn wie ihre Tatkraft, kein geistiges Abenteuer schien ihr zu gefährlich. Schon früher hatte sich in den Ritterromanen die Vorliebe des Volkes für das ausschweifendste Wunderbare kund gegeben. Dieß wollten sie auf der Bühne wieder sehen, und da nun ihre Dichter, ganz auf der Höhe der künstlerischen und gesellligen Bildung stehend, es darnach umschufen, ihm eine musikalische Seele einhauchten, es ganz von grober Körperlichkeit gereinigt zu Farbe und Duft hinauf läuterten, so entsteht eben aus dem Kontrast des Stoffes und der Form ein unwiderstehlicher Reiz. (263)

(If a feeling of religion, loyal heroism, honour and love be the foundation of romantic poetry, it could not fail to attain to its highest development in Spain, where its birth and growth were cherished by the most friendly auspices. The fancy of the Spaniards, like their active powers, was bold and venturesome; no mental adventure seemed too hazardous. The popular predilection for surpassing marvels had already shown itself in its chivalrous novels. And they also wished to see wonders on the stage when their poets, standing on the lofty eminence of a highly polished state of art and society, gave it the requisite form, breathed into it a musical soul and refined its beautiful hues and fragrance from all corporeal grossness, there arose, from the very contrast of the matter and form, an irresistible fascination. [500–1])

Seldom can Spain have been more favourably presented. For Schlegel, this is truly a nation apart and he is at pains to point out the unsuitability of ideals inspired by Classical taste in a land driven by action and imagination. Instead, a lively, colourful theatre emerges, full of wonder and experiment, clearly intended to stand out in comparison with the dull regularity of the modern neo-Classical stage. Notable here also is the approbation of Spain's ancient axis of throne and altar, underpinning the 'Höhe der künstlerischen und gesalligen Bildung' (lofty eminence of a highly polished state of art and society), which is portrayed as enabling the development of this national theatre. This highlights the ideological abyss separating Böhl from much of his readership in Spain. The German Romantic enthusiasm for chivalric values, which lies at the heart of their idealisation of the medieval world, recalled quite different emotions in the context of Spain's absolutist past where, to the Liberal mind, feudal rule equated with inquisitorial oppression, backwardness and indignity. Whilst the depiction of a passionate, poetically-inspired land might fit happily with the appraisal of patriotic moderate Liberals such as Quintana, the German Romantic vision of Golden Age Spain, even in its less exalted moments, here simply listing characteristics in an oft-repeated apotheosis, could not help but offend Liberal sensitivities by lending credence to an absolutist political system. Given such prominence in Böhl's rendition of Schlegel, the value of chivalry emerged as a recurrent theme as the polemic developed, Mora in particular unable to countenance the value of such an apparently retrograde character trait.

This passage was to create offence in another way, this time drawing attention to the difficulties faced by Böhl in translating such complex ideas. Keen to transmit the glorification of Spain's literary past, with its emphasis on colour and vivacity, Böhl begins his version with a close translation, but then begins to waiver, becoming lost in Schlegel's exalted reverie:

> Si la poesía moderna se funda sobre los sentimientos religiosos, sobre el heroísmo, el honor y el amor, en España precisamente había de adquirir su más alta perfección nacida y desarollada bajo esos auspicios. Ninguna hazaña del entendimiento arredraba la imaginación española, no menos arrojada que lo eran sus paladines. Su predelicción hacia lo maravilloso se había ya manifestado en sus libros de caballería. Faltábale a su teatro alguna cosa semejante, y cuando los grandes poetas de aquel tiempo, adornados con todas las galas de la más noble civilización, trasladaron a la escencia el carácter caballeresco purificado de toda liga material, y sublimando hasta la semejanza aérea de un perfume matizado (si se nos permite la expresión), el espectador quedó contento. (V: 5–6)

> (If modern poetry is based on religious feeling, heroism, honour and love, then it is in Spain that it was to realise its most perfect form, born and developed under such auspices. No deed of learning frightened the Spanish imagination, itself no less daring than their champions. Their preference for the marvellous had already emerged in their chivalric novels. They lacked something similar in their theatre and when the great poets of the day, adorned with all the trappings of the most noble civilisation,

transferred the chivalric character to the stage, purified of all material ties and as sublime as the hint of perfume (if we may use such an expression), the spectator was happy.)

The apology in parentheses is enough in itself to demonstrate Böhl's own dissatisfaction with his rendition of Schlegel's inspired evocation of the arrival of chivalric values on the Spanish stage, their natural home. In fact, this excerpt would cause Böhl a great deal of discomfort as the polemic developed. Mora was particularly offended by the vagueness of 'un perfume matizado' (hint of a perfume) and recalled the metaphor repeatedly as an example of Schlegel's incomprehensible metaphysics. (It is fair to say that Schlegel too may well have been dismayed by Böhl's clumsy effort.) Despite the obvious flaws, Böhl does nevertheless succeed in conveying Schlegel's depiction of Spain as a nation whose character and culture combine with religious faith in a manifestation of the German Romantic ideal, one not only limited to the Schlegelian vision of Spain, but an extension of the wider idealisation of the Middle Ages found in the work of Novalis, Tieck, Brentano and other contemporary German writers. Böhl's emphasis, however, tends towards the more reactionary aspect of this ideal, something emphasised by Reyes Ponce who argues that Böhl's translation technique severely confused the issue by effectively making Calderón the symbol of a glorious past. This is underlined by Böhl's careful modification of those elements of Schlegel's depiction of medieval Spain which might undermine his own view of the period. This is particularly the case with Schlegel's critical references to the Habsburg monarchy, the central players along with the Inquisition in the 'Black Legend'. The nature of Böhl's editing of Schlegel's text is shown in his rendition of what was originally a fairly harsh criticism of Felipe II. Whereas Schlegel refers to his reign as one marred by 'verderbliche Fehltritte' (damaging errors; 262), Böhl simply mentions 'el tiempo de Felipe II' (the time of Felipe II; V: 5). Reyes Ponce sees this as a 'most grievous' act as publication of Böhl's text coincided with the re-establishment of a repressive Bourbon monarchy and, she argues, 'Böhl's tacit endorsement of the Habsburg kings could effectively place Schlegel's name in the middle of a virulent political controversy' (117). This is particularly pertinent when one considers that the Constitution of Cadiz was itself drawn up to reflect the existence of ancient Spanish freedoms cast asunder by the foreign influence of Habsburg and Bourbon rule. This highlights a degree of critical naivety in Böhl's approach which characterises this first phase of the polemic.

The poetic, Romantic credentials of the Spanish nation and its literature now firmly established, Böhl's attention turns to Schlegel's examination of Calderón himself. It is odd, as Reyes Ponce comments, that Böhl should not have translated Schegel's hyperbolic description of Calderón as 'ein Dichter, wenn je einer den Namen verdient hat' (a poet if ever any man deserved that name [257 (494)]), but he does include the definition of Calderón as 'demasiado español para identificarse con individualidad agena' (too Spanish to identify with any foreign character; V: 7). Schlegel's praise of Calderón's religious dramas as the pinnacle of his work is emphasised by Böhl, something which reflects the latter's own recent personal development as much as it does Schlegel's understanding of Romantic art as inherently Christian. Böhl's personal agenda is also to the fore as he moves on to Schlegel's discussion of the recent reception of Calderón's work, selecting Schlegel's concluding negative appraisal of the impact of Enlightenment aesthetics to end his own translation:

> Gewisse Geisteskrankheiten sind so epidemisch in einem Zeitalter, daß eine Nation niemals vor einem Anfalle davon sicher ist, bis man sie ihr inokuliert hat. Indessen sind die Spanier, wie es scheint, in Absicht auf die leidige Aufklärung des letzten Geschlechts mit den Windpocken abgekommen, während die entstellenden Blattergruben in den Zügen andrer Nationen nicht zu verkennen sind. In ihrer etwas insularen Existenz haben sie das achtzehnte Jahrhundert verschlafen, und wie konnte man im Grunde seine Zeit besser anwenden. Sollte die spanische Poesie im alten Europa oder in der andern Hemisphäre wieder aufwachen, so würde sie allerdings einen Schritt vom Instinkt zum Bewußtsein zu tun haben. Was sie bis jetzt aus angeborner Neigung geliebt, müßten die Spanier mit klarer Erkenntnis verehren lernen, und, unbekümmert um die dazwischen aufgekommene Kritik, aus Grundsatz im Geist ihrer großen Dichter zu schaffen fortfahren. (267–8)

> (In particular ages, certain mental maladies are so universally epidemic that a nation can never be secure from infection until it has been inoculated with it. With respect, however, to the fatal enlightenment of the last generation, the Spaniards it would appear have come off with the chicken pox, while in the features of other nations the disfiguring variolous scars are but too visible. Living almost in an insular situation, Spaniards have slept through the eighteenth century and how in the main could they have applied their time better? Should Spanish poetry ever again awake in old Europe or the New World, it would certainly have a step to make, from instinct to consciousness. What the Spaniards have hitherto loved from innate inclination, they must learn to revere on clear principles and, undismayed at the criticism to which it has in the mean time been exposed, proceed to fresh creations in the spirit of their greatest poets. [505])

Schlegel's analogy is rather harsh and effectively denies a whole century of Spanish culture a place in the history of that nation's letters, but his forthright criticism of the impact of the Enlightenment in Europe as a whole must have pleased Böhl greatly. He certainly makes the most of Schlegel's derision, once more embellishing his translation with added details so that his Spanish readers would have no difficulty placing his argument in context:

Hay enfermedades del entendimiento tan epidémicas, que no se puede librar de ellas una nacion, sino por la inoculacion. Tal es la filosofía moderna. Los españoles parecen haberse liberado con solo unas viruelas volantes ó locas, mientras que las señales de una irrupcion maligna desfiguran las fisonomías de las demas naciones. En su existencia peninsular han pasado en modorra el siglo XVIII; y en efecto, ¿qué mejor podían haber hecho? Si la poesía española despierta algún día, sea en Europa, sea en las Indias, no hay duda que sólo un paso tendrá que dar desde el instinto ciego al conocimiento meditado. Los españoles admirarán entonces por convencimiento lo que han amado hasta aquí por inclinación; y sin hacer caso de la crítica bastarda del siglo filosófico, pondrán todo su conato en componer en el mismo sentido que los grandes modelos de su siglo de oro. (V: 9–10)

(There are illnesses of the mind so epidemic that it is only possible to free oneself of them by means of inoculation. Such is modern philosophy. The Spaniards seemed to have escaped with only a few light or errant blemishes, whilst the signs of a malignant outburst disfigure the faces of the remaining nations. In their peninsular existence, they spent the eighteenth century dozing and, indeed, could they have done any better? If Spanish poetry awakens one day, be it in Europe or the Americas, there is no doubt that it will only have to take one step from blind instinct to carefully considered knowledge. The Spaniards will then admire with conviction everything which they have loved instinctively until now and without paying attention to the bastard criticism of the philosophical century, they will make every effort to create the same feeling as the great paragons of their golden age.)

Whilst Böhl once more remains true to the critical tone of the original, certain aspects of Schlegel's argument are intensified. The specific reference to 'las Indias' (the Americas) and the inclusion of the controversial term 'siglo de oro' (golden age), neither of which features in the Schlegelian original, effectively personalises the text, drawing the Spanish reader into a familiar cultural landscape. The polemical aspect is also revisited: where Schlegel describes the prevailing taste in Spain as 'die dazwischen aufgekommene Kritik' (the criticism to which it has in the mean time been exposed), which is marring appreciation of the national literature, the same taste is described rather more vehemently in Böhl's translation as 'la crítica bastarda' (the bastard criticism). Once again, Böhl is guilty of intensifying Schlegel's views to advance his own critical cause.

Böhl's translation is undoubtedly problematic and clearly fails to provide an impartial rendition of Schlegel's texts. Echoing his 1805 article on Schiller, Böhl is using the theories of others to support his own critical agenda. There is, of course, nothing unusual in this. The problem is that both the 1805 article and the Schlegel piece purport to offer extracts and translations and presumably, therefore, ought to be faithful to the original texts. They are instead summaries tending towards paraphrase which attempt to distil the essence of the original whilst serving Böhl's own interests as a critic. By failing to acknowledge this adequately, Böhl has attracted a great deal of criticism from scholars of the period. This critical stance in turn fails to take into account the currency of such practices during the early century in particular where the dividing line between translation and paraphrase was thoroughly blurred. Whilst acknowledging this, however, it remains the case that such paraphrasing inevitably coloured the reception of ideas as they were disseminated between cultures, something which has provoked a great deal of comment from scholars with an interest in Böhl's work.

Pitollet, the critic responsible for coining the term 'la Querelle caldéronienne' in the title of his 1909 study of the polemic, condemns Böhl's translation of Schlegel as 'beaucoup moins d'une traduction que d'un résumé assez arbitraire' (much less a translation than a rather arbitrary summary). He regards Schlegel's original as 'déjà médiocre' (already mediocre), only to be rendered 'franchement paradoxal' (frankly paradoxical) by Böhl's translation. He is also critical of Schlegel for seeking all aspects of Spanish theatre in the work of one poet and feels that Mora was fully justified in taking issue with Böhl for propagating these ideas within Spain itself (QC: 93). Pitollet claims Mora's understanding to have been hampered by what he sees as Böhl's less than subtle rendition of the difference between Classic and Romantic (QC: 97–8). Schlegel's understanding of the two as individual periods in the history of art, not opposing genres or different degrees of perfection, has been blurred in Böhl's version, forcing Mora to see things in terms of opposites. The confusion created by Böhl is highlighted elsewhere.

Juretschke criticises 'seine manchmal unangemessenen und einander widersprechenden Formulierungen' (his sometimes inappropriate and self-contradictory formulations) and goes on to suggest that he was simply out of his depth (DD: 155). However, claims that Böhl simply did not understand Schlegel's original fail to take into account his very specific agenda in mounting a defence of Spain's literary heritage grounded in Herderian historicism. Furthermore, Juretschke's assertion that the area was 'ihm im Grunde fremd und unvertraut' (basically strange and unfamiliar to him) seems quite incongruous against the background of Böhl's intellectual development, especially during the Görslow years. In his otherwise pertinent contextualisation of Böhl's ideological development, Juretschke himself exhibits a degree of eclecticism in his own comments on Böhl's piece, failing to address the second section dealing with Spanish theatre in any depth at all, whilst dwelling at length on the short theoretical selections from Schlegel's twelfth lecture. This imbalance points to Juretschke's reluctance to acknowledge the true significance of Böhl's critical emphasis, one made clear by the revised title given to the second and third published versions of his translation, 'Sobre el teatro español' (On Spanish theatre), as well as Böhl's choice of title for his collection of polemic documents, *Vindicaciones de Calderón*. These headings leave the reader in no doubt as to the purpose of the piece. Yet, Juretschke even objects to Pitollet's naming of the polemic 'la Querelle caldéronienne' (DD: 154), claiming that the term is too narrow and does not emphasise the Schlegelian content adequately. In so doing, he continues to overlook Böhl's main intention, which was to defend the honour of Calderón in the context of his Romantic world view. To a large extent, Schlegel's involvement was as a tool of war, representative of Böhl's new stance. The debate was not intended to focus on Schlegel's work per se, but rather to revive interest in the type of literature he was defending within the wider Romantic reappraisal of national cultures.

This view is advanced by Flitter, who sees in Böhl's approach a strategy driven by Herderian historicism, claiming that 'Böhl's intention had not been to provide a systematic presentation of the totality of A. W. Schlegel's Vienna lectures, but to vindicate Calderón and early Spanish literature generally' (SR: 11). Reyes Ponce is similarly sympathetic. Whilst agreeing with Juretschke that Böhl may have been out of his depth in some areas, she acknowledges that his eclectic approach was part of a specific plan and criticises Pitollet for judging Böhl too harshly (A: 110). She pleads for a more nuanced reading of the piece before underlining the transcultural value of Böhl's scholarship:

> [...] it is impossible not to acknowledge the vision which Böhl's personal introduction to Spain of the most up-to-date aesthetic thinking in Europe implied. In this context, the assessment by various Hispanists of Böhl as 'retrograde' loses its force. Böhl was bringing into Spain the body of thought of one of the most visionary group of thinkers. Schlegel used Kantian and Fichtean philosophies, combined them with art history and thereby arrived at a new system of art criticism. His method was 'state of the art' aesthetics. (A: 123)

These recent, more charitable appraisals of Böhl's contribution to the debate highlight the significance therein of contemporary German thought beyond that of Schlegel himself. Flitter's identification of Herderian historicism, along with Reyes Ponce's reminder of the broader import of Schlegel's development of Kant and Fichte, highlight the aesthetic importance of Böhl's efforts in drawing Spain into the wider sphere of developing Romantic thought. Both his 1805 article on Schiller's Kantian aesthetics and his translation of Schlegel constitute pioneering attempts to introduce new ideas to the cultural debate in Spain. As Flitter has demonstrated, the introduction of Schlegelian thought in particular had a continued impact on aesthetics in Spain throughout the nineteenth century. Unfortunately, such crucial aesthetic aspects of the polemic have all too often been overlooked or undervalued in the fraught discussion over Böhl's political motivation.

This highlights one of the key problems in Böhl reception in which there is a marked tendency to discuss his aesthetics and his politics as separate issues. A more pertinent approach would be to question the validity of any attempt to separate two areas which became inextricably linked as Böhl's Romantic world view developed during the Görslow years. The divergence in critical opinion illustrates the problematic nature of the debate. Flitter echoes Reyes Ponce in suggesting that Böhl's intentions in publishing these extracts were rooted in his love of Spain as a symbol of the Romantic ideal and not the result of a reactionary political agenda, as has been argued, perhaps overzealously, by Carnero. Böhl's own explanation of his motives, as expressed to Galiano in the appendix to the second *Pasatiempo* in 1818, would seem to support the former view: 'A mi vuelta a Cádiz (1813), pensé dar un testimonio de amor a España y a los españoles publicando algunas reflexiones de aquél excellente crítico' (Upon my return to Cadiz (1813), I wanted to bear testimony to my love for Spain and the Spaniards by publishing some reflections by that excellent critic; AIIP: 4). There is, nevertheless, some legitimacy to Carnero's argument. It is hard to countenance that Böhl could have been unaffected by the political events of the period in his choice of material. Schlegel's very argument is based on the enduring values of throne and altar in the literature of a nation which has apparently been able to resist the pernicious effects of French cultural hegemony. Having just witnessed the havoc wreaked in his beloved north German landscape and the downfall of the Cadiz merchant classes, including his own family, in the economic crisis caused by the Napoleonic invasion, Böhl's choice of material has a charged political significance. Here, however, the political is undoubtedly personal, an inevitable product of the times and of Böhl's origins in a disparate German nation which was increasingly aware of the notion of national identity, both cultural and political. Also significant are the changes experienced by Böhl during the first decade of the nineteenth century. His elevation into the nobility in 1806, his dream of being a landowner at Görslow and his conversion to Catholicism, as well as his abandonment of the Enlightenment teaching of his youth, all contributed to an essentially conservative, absolutist world view. It was the threat to these new values posed by French influence, the seat of revolution, secularism and republicanism, coupled with a growing love of Spain and its culture, which drove Böhl to react against them by defending Calderón. Böhl's association at this time of Enlightenment thought and republican ideals is made explicit in the original version of *Donde las dan, las toman*, in which he claims that 'los principios enciclopédicos en general [. . .] pretenden introducir el despotismo en la república literaria al mismo tiempo que quieren al republicanismo en el orden social' (encyclopaedic principles in general [. . .] are attempting to introduce despotism to the literary republic, at the same time as they wish to see republicanism in the social order).[5] The inseparable nature of the aesthetic and the political in Böhl's mind is clear. Consequently, Juretschke's criticism that the first appearance of German Romantic thought in Spain was given 'eine politische Färbung und Bedeutung' (a political hue and meaning; DD: 162) presents Böhl in an overly negative light. It is arguable whether the political could ever be separated from the aesthetic in the discourse of a movement whose aesthetic ideals, particularly in the wake of the Napoleonic invasion, centred on the revival of a national literature and freedom from neo-Classical precepts imposed by French arbiters of taste. For many, the once-vaunted Classical aesthetic had ceased to be the object of productive engagement with the new Romantic ideal and come to symbolise instead the cultural and political hegemony of a nation whose worst excesses had all but destroyed Europe in a mockery of the very values of a revolution intended to bring Enlightenment to all. It is in the context of this cultural patriotism that Böhl's Schlegel translation must be considered. Upon his arrival in Spain in 1813, Böhl was essentially a second generation German Romantic, imbued with the same values and ideals as many of his fellow countrymen. Whilst agreeing, therefore, that Böhl is in part politically motivated, it must be made clear that this motivation is not grounded in Fernandine reactionism. The rationale is far more complex and must be traced back to Böhl's intellectual development during the years at Görslow, which saw the parallel development of a *Weltanschauung* steeped in Romantic ideology and a personal journey culminating in Catholic conversion. The interrelation of Böhl's many concerns is highlighted by Reyes Ponce, who claims that 'Böhl's defence of German Romantic ideas, of Calderón and of traditional Spanish literature is intertwined (in best Romantic fashion) with aspirations of cultural, social and even political reform' (A: 110). She goes on to point out that Böhl was defending 'a spiritual as much as an aesthetic system', one which he had endured a long inner struggle to attain. The presence of Herderian historicism in this development, which, as Flitter argues, manifests itself in a nationalist stance, highlights the inseparable nature of the literary and the political in Böhl's defence of Calderón. In his view, respect for the nation's literature signified respect for the nation itself and Spain was to be admired as a nation blessed with a glorious past and a rich cultural heritage. It was this appreciation which underpinned the German Romantic vision of Spanish culture as a paradigm of nationhood, a vision central to the Schlegelian apotheosis favoured and elaborated by Böhl. Consequently, Böhl's dissemination of this vision in Spain itself sees the transferral to Spanish soil of the developing nationalist ideal in Germany which centred on a regenerative, but essentially defensive, nationalism voiced by Fichte, Görres and others, and which was intent on the revival of indigenous culture as a means to unity and political stability. It is therefore difficult at this early stage in the polemic to criticise Böhl in terms specific to the contemporary debate in Spain when the ideas and, to a certain extent, the emotions which drove his pro-Calderón campaign were deeply embedded in the political and cultural insecurities of his native Germany.

It is Böhl's position as a German Romantic critic which also underlies the problematic contemporary reception of his Schlegel translation in Spain. Through Schlegel, Böhl was addressing a number of issues simultaneously – political, aesthetic and cultural – but without sufficient understanding of his new audience and its belief systems. He had, after all, been away from Spain for almost a decade and had relied in the interim on information from his conservative wife. Having once abhorred the culture and attitudes of traditional Andalucia as a young man imbued with Campe's enlightened teaching, he perhaps presumed that his new Romantic world view would assimilate seamlessly into the Spain he expected to find upon his return. Indeed, if Schlegel could be believed, then he was returning to the very nation which epitomised the essence of the Romantic ideal. Spain, however, had moved on. Age-old values were being questioned: the monarchy had caved in to Napoleon's demands and the uprising of 1808, far from recalling a chivalrous past, had become a symbol for a progressive patriotism driven by the people. In intellectual circles, neo-Classicism held sway as Spain sought to conform to a universal aesthetic regarded as evidence of modernity and progress. Emerging in the aftermath of these developments, Böhl's Schlegelian idealisation of Spain's past and its literature was out of step with much of current opinion, both politically and aesthetically. Coming from abroad, his unprefaced presentation of Schlegel's ideas must have seemed like a bolt from the blue which amounted to an apotheosis of an age and a writer long out of vogue in Spain, expressing what appeared to be wholehearted approval for a regime which the nation, under more enlightened Bourbon rule, had spent almost a century trying to overcome by means of gradual reform. Instead, Spain stood once more on the threshold of absolutism, the Liberal dream of a constitutional monarchy dashed by Fernando VII's rejection of the Cadiz Constitution in May 1814. Consequently, to publish Schlegel's views in Cadiz, the very heartland of Spanish Liberalism, was unlikely to prove anything other than controversial.

Whether or not Böhl intended to create a stir is impossible to tell. On the one hand, he perhaps expected no more of a response than the silence which followed his 1805 article, especially given the ongoing political upheaval which busied the essayists and commentators of the day. On the other, he must surely have been aware that much of Schlegel's argument would be likely to offend those still hopeful of a return to the Constitution of Cadiz and keen to defend the neo-Classical tradition. Taken in this context, Böhl's decision to publish displays a degree of naivety in assuming the values of German Romanticism would find an immediate welcome in Spain. For all his good intentions and love of Spain, he does not seem to have taken account of the fact that he was no longer voicing opinions in tune with the prevailing trend, as he had been with his critical pieces in Germany, but was instead to all intents and purposes a stranger in a strange land, bringing essentially alien ideas to an unprimed audience. Had he, perhaps, presented Schlegel's ideas in more coherent form, including material from the first of the *Wiener Vorlesungen* which sets out the basic premise of the German Romantic aesthetic ideal or at least prefaced his piece with an explanatory paragraph, then the ensuing debate might have been very different indeed. There were, after all, those in Spain who might have welcomed a more detailed elaboration of Schlegel's ideas as an adjunct to their own. Moderate Liberals such as Jovellanos and Quintana, as well as more conservative thinkers like Capmany, had already begun to echo concerns expressed earlier by eighteenth-century thinkers including Iriarte and Cadalso which pointed to the need for a reassessment of the nation's cultural heritage. Böhl, newly arrived from Germany, seems to have been unaware of the subtleties involved, knowledge of which might have aided his cause. As Ginger has argued, there was a complex debate surrounding the role of nationalism which focused on some of the issues raised by Schlegel in relation to the existence of a national literature.[6] Crucial was the co-existence of Spanish neo-Classicism and an appreciation – influenced particularly by Blair – of the sublime, which entered Spain in the late eighteenth century and fostered a new understanding of older Spanish literature. For many thinkers, neo-Classicism and the existence of a national literature were not necessarily contradictory concepts and certainly did not preclude the measured appreciation of older Spanish literature. Consequently, those who acknowledged the sublime were happy to appreciate aspects of Golden Age drama as compatible with empirical philosophy's demands by relating them to psychological responses to aesthetic objects. These responses were driven by inherent national character traits which deserved expression, but must be constrained to some degree. In this context, neo-Classical thought was not regarded as an anathema to national cultural pride, but rather a means of refining and promoting a national poetic essence. In assessing this, Ginger identifies a progressive debate which has at its heart national advancement and cultural rebirth, the terms of which are not necessarily out of step with the Schlegelian ethos. After all, the 1812 Constitution was that of a constitutional monarchy, not a republic. The notion that the sovereignty of the nation lay with the people, whilst clearly rejecting an absolutist model, nevertheless presented ample scope to adapt key ideas brought by Böhl to the constitutional argument, in particular the concept of a monarchy based on popular consent. Indeed, the whole interpretation of *Volkspoesie*, which lies at the heart of German Romantic aesthetics, rests on the notion of the people expressing national selfhood, a concept thoroughly in keeping with the ideals which underpin the 1812 Constitution in Spain. The fact that Liberal critics, in responding to Böhl's rendition of Schlegel, were unable to identify these affinities lays bare the flawed nature of Böhl's intermediary efforts. Had the tone and political import of Böhl's presentation of Schlegel been more measured, his efforts might have met with a more immediate sympathetic reception as part of the ongoing cultural revaluation within Spain. Instead, the underlying conservative political tone – heightened by Böhl – of the German Romantic aesthetic meant that, initially at least, Schlegel's views, via Böhl, became the subject of the severest Liberal censure.

NOTES

1. E. Lohner (ed.), *A. W. Schlegel, Kritische Schriften und Briefe*, 7 vols (Stuttgart: Kohlhammer, 1967); VI: *Vorlesungen über dramatische Kunst und Literatur – Zweiter Teil* (1967); references appear in the text.
2. María Guadalupe Reyes Ponce, 'August Wilhelm Schlegel's *Wiener Vorlesungen* and Böhl von Faber's *Sobre el teatro español*', *Bulletin of the John Rylands University Library of Manchester*, 71/3 (1989), 105–24; references appear in the text.
3. Translations of Schlegel's lectures are taken from *A Course of Lectures on Dramatic Art and Literature by Augustus William Schlegel*, translated by John Black, revised by A. J. W. Morrison (London: Bohn, 1846); references appear in the text.
4. See D. L. Shaw, 'Spain/Romántico – Romanticismo – Romancesco – Romanesco – Romancista – Romántico' in Eichner (ed.), *'Romantic' and its Cognates*, pp. 341–71.
5. Quoted in by Pitollet (QC: 110–11). In his much-criticised study, Carnero (O: 172) highlights this section as proof that Böhl was attempting to shift the emphasis of the polemic towards the political and implicitly suggests the suppression in the later edition of the text of a reference to the Inquisition, replaced by the rather vague 'censura arbitraria' (arbitrary censorship), as evidence of Böhl's approval for the *Santo oficio*. Intent on proving his argument that Böhl was a Fernandine reactionary, Carnero also claims that Böhl places his opponents in danger by leading the discussion towards the issues surrounding political orthodoxy (O: 171) and shows how he persistently focused on what he perceived to be Mora's anti-patriotic attitudes (O: 248). Juretschke also highlights Böhl's association of neo-Classical and republican ideals and depicts Böhl as retrograde and 'unzeitgemäß' (anachronistic; DD: 162).
6. Andrew Ginger, *Political Revolution and Literary Experiment in the Spanish Romantic Period (1830–1850)* (Lewiston, NY: Mellen, 1999), pp. 120–1.

Chapter 8
The Polemic: Phase One (1814)

Whatever Böhl's hopes for his translation, it would prove to be the first document in a long running polemic which would eventually make his name in Spain and attract attention from all over Europe. It is unlikely that this would have been the case had it not been for the efforts of Mora, erstwhile correspondent and acquaintance of Francisca, who was quick to respond to Böhl's translation of Schlegel with a series of three articles in the *Mercurio gaditano* in September and October 1814.[1] It is unclear whether Mora was initially aware that the offending text had been shaped by Böhl and therefore possible that the former regarded this first phase of the polemic as a direct attack on Schlegel himself, assuming, as he must have, that he was dealing with a faithful translation. This early salvo certainly lacks the more personal jibes found in later polemic documents. Equally unclear are Mora's motives in attacking the piece. A staunch patriot and fervent admirer of Shakespeare, he would upon initial consideration seem an unlikely opponent for an apotheosis of Spanish national literature. Furthermore, the views expressed by Mora during the years of his close friendship and correspondence with Francisca from 1808 to 1813, later to be exploited ruthlessly by Böhl and his wife, would be far more likely to suggest an affinity with Schlegel than disagreement. This is underlined by the interest Mora had earlier shown in the work of a number of Romantic writers such as Chateaubriand. His later literary career also reveals a sympathy for Romantic aesthetic values. He went on to edit a number of periodicals, at home and in exile, which featured Romantic works, as well as publishing his own poetic versions of popular literature, including the 1840 collection *Leyendas españolas* (Spanish legends). Mora later befriended Böhl's daughter, Cecilia, and both were at pains to distance themselves from the more unseemly side of the polemic. These pre- and post-polemic positions would suggest that following the publication of Böhl's translation, Mora found himself far more at odds with the potential political import of Schlegel's views than he was with the aesthetic principles upon which they were based. The conservative tone of German Romantic thought promoted by Böhl meant that a convinced Liberal of Mora's standing found himself compelled to reject the political aspect of the debate, an action which severely impeded his appreciation of the broader aesthetic argument with which he might have had more sympathy. For Mora, however, the difficulty lay in the glorification of a bygone age which he saw as politically repressive.[2] As the polemic began, the close association of political and aesthetic in Böhl's presentation of Schlegelian thought coupled with the context of a newly restored absolutist monarchy in Spain meant Mora had no choice but to respond in a negative fashion. The significance of Böhl's ideologically motivated presentation of Schlegel cannot be underestimated and, indeed, many of the points Mora raises relate to those sections of Schlegel's work where Böhl's translation and summary skills have made most of an impact, a fact which prompts Pitollet to comment that 'Mora se fût exprimé d'autre sorte s'il eût eu sous les yeux la tenuer exacte des Conferences de Schlegel' (Mora would have expressed himself differently had he had the exact content of Schlegel's lectures before him; QC: 97).

Mora's immediate response to Böhl's translation was published under the pseudonym 'El Mirtilo gaditano' (The Cadiz Myrtle)[3] and appeared in the *Mercurio gaditano* on 22 September with the title 'Crítica de las reflexiones de Schlegel sobre el teatro insertas en nuestro número 121' (Critique of Schlegel's reflections on the theatre published in our number 121). Possessed only of Böhl's eclectic translation and with no knowledge of the theoretical basis of German Romantic aesthetics laid down in the first *Wiener Vorlesung*, elements of which he might have been happy to accept, Mora is unaware of the context within which Schlegel is developing his appraisal of Spain's literature. This lack of information colours Mora's subsequent argument and the tone of his criticism is often quite sharp. Picking up on the debate surrounding the validity of the precepts of ancient theatre, which are discarded far more forcefully in Böhl's translation than in Schlegel's original, Mora expresses outright disgust at the very idea that art should be liberated from regulation:

La moda de desacreditar las reglas eternas del gusto, y de sacudir el yugo de los preceptos, es un contagio tanto mas facil de comunicarse, cuanto mas halagos presenta á la mediocridad [al] verse libre de trabas y poder abandonarse á todos los desórdenes de la imaginacion. (QC: 94)

(The fashion for discrediting the eternal rules of taste and discarding the yoke of precepts is an infection all the more easily spread the more flattery is paid to mediocrity at seeing itself free of restriction and able to abandon itself to all the disorder of the imagination.)

This is a clear example of the impact of Böhl's presentation on Mora's understanding of Schlegelian thought. At no point does Schlegel advocate disorder. Romanticism is a means to a higher order, not the path to chaos or, indeed, mediocrity. He had been quite insistent on the need for form in poetry, albeit within a culture-specific context. Reading Böhl's version of Schlegel outwith the wider Romantic context, Mora has no choice but to adopt a condemnatory stance. In so doing, however, he is himself guilty of further distortion by highlighting isolated phrases and subjecting them to derision. Typical is the attack on the deployment of individual words launched in relation to the key terms 'orgánica' and 'mecánica', explained in Schlegel's twelfth lecture and summarised with reasonable accuracy by Böhl. Ignoring the argument put forward, based on Kantian duality, that the organic presents a natural, innate form whereas the mechanical is that which adheres to regulation, Mora mocks the terms as a gross simplification of the chemical process. It is, however, difficult to be too critical of Mora here. As Juretschke notes, this application of scientific terms to literary concepts was quite alien to a Spanish audience, whereas the German public were already accustomed to such analogies, in particular Gottsched's use of 'mechanisch' in relation to the theatre (DD: 154). This confusion surrounding terminology remains central to Mora's argument in this first phase of the polemic and provides further evidence of the difficulty Böhl faced initially in finding a point of reference for the new aesthetic within the contemporary Spanish debate.

Mora encounters particular difficulty in trying to come to terms with the notion of Romantic poetry, the complexities of which he must try to unravel by means of Böhl's flawed translation. Consequently, Mora's fiercest attack in this first article is reserved for Schlegel's apparent claim that he has discovered a new type of poetry which combines opposites and succeeds in uniting nature and art. Mora derides this, saying that this is precisely what Classical poetry achieves and that art has no need of what he terms 'la fantasmagoria germánica' (Germanic phantasmagoria; QC: 95) proposed by Schlegel and his followers. The impact of Böhl's rendition of 'romantisch' as 'moderno' can be felt here. Despite its conceptual accuracy, correctly equating the Romantic aesthetic with a modern, non-Classical approach, the translated term suffers from a lack of context in Böhl's version, giving Mora the impression that Schlegel's ideas have no established aesthetic foundation, but are instead the product of some strange modern whim. The Schlegelian glorification of Spain's past is certainly not in keeping with Mora's contemporary understanding of 'modern' as 'enlightened' and he is unaware of the broader definition of Romantic aesthetics upon which Schlegel's argument is based. The resultant misunderstanding leads to a widening of the divide between ancient and modern, which was never Schlegel's intention, and ignores the whole notion of organic development in a nation's literary heritage, itself the indispensable link between old and new. Schlegel's actual call for a new evaluation of poetry is lost as Mora focuses his criticism on the misconstrued notion of a completely new poetry which results from Böhl's translation. This then affects Mora's understanding of Schlegel's appraisal of Calderón, which he decries 'una perversion mas completa del gusto' (a complete perversion of taste; QC: 96). Although Mora admits to a certain value in the latter's work, he criticises Schlegel for praising those elements of Calderón's theatre which others regard as flawed. In so doing, Mora fails to grasp that, according to Schlegel, the prevailing, essentially Classical values are an inappropriate means of evaluation for Spain's ancient theatre. The values of one age should not be applied to the art of another, the product of a different phase in the organic development of national culture. The historicist element of Schlegel's evaluation is therefore overlooked as Mora clings to neo-Classical ideals in an attempt to combat the underlying absolutist tone of Böhl's translation.

There is little attempt at originality in Mora's first response to Böhl's translation. He simply picks up on anomalies in Böhl's wording and calls upon the established rules of good taste to support his criticism of Schlegel's ideas. The impatient tone of the later polemic is already in evidence as the article ends by damning Schlegel's views as mere 'paradoxas germánicas' (German paradoxes; QC: 97). Mora's response elicited a brief riposte in the *Mercurio gaditano* from 'el traductor de Schlegel' (Schlegel's translator) on 24 September in which Böhl explains that he feels compelled to defend Schlegel's honour, claiming that his ideas will not be to everyone's taste, only to those with an innate understanding of poetry and not to those whose only interest is the adherence to rules.[4] Böhl juxtaposes two sets of names as representative of these diverging positions: Dante, Calderón and Shakespeare on the one hand and Boileau, Alfieri and 'algunos modernos españoles' (some modern Spaniards) on the other, thus directly contrasting the freedom of the Romantic world view, inspired by national literature, with the alien austerity of neo-Classical rules. Clearly unaware of the political rationale behind Mora's attack, Böhl seems taken aback by his adversary's forceful rejection of Schlegel's ideas and seems to want to help him out of his unhappy misconception by pointing out some printer's errors which may have impeded his reading of the text. The most significant of these is Böhl's insistence on the terms 'extractos' (extracts) rather than 'reflexiones' (reflections) in the title, the latter having appeared in his original manuscript only to be altered during the printing process. Böhl argues that it must nevertheless have been clear to the reader that the text was a selection of extracts because so many paragraphs ended with 'etc.'. He then draws attention to a second error. In his rendition of Schlegel's discussion of the role of metre, the printer had inserted the word 'rima' (rhyme) instead of the intended 'ritmo' (rhythm). This, Böhl claims, alters the sense of his translation immeasurably, thus challenging Mora's criticism of Schlegel's poetics as one founded on error. Mora had responded vehemently to Schlegel's defence of the individuality of metre in national literature, an argument already drastically summarised by Böhl, by selecting the phrase 'la rima compañera inseparable del verso' (rhyme, inseparable companion of verse), claiming that 'es difícil amontonar mayor número de disparates en menor número de palabras' (it is difficult to accumulate more nonsense in fewer words; QC: 94).

Had Böhl hoped to convert Mora on the basis of these amendments, he was to be sadly disappointed. There followed an article in the *Mercurio gaditano* on 27 September purporting to be written by a third party who signed himself 'El

Imparcial' (The Impartial). Given the tone, however, there is little doubt that the author of this article was Mora himself. The text has little to recommend it, pre-empting as it does the later, rather puerile tone of the polemic. However, there is one salient comment which is worthy of mention. Referring to Böhl's insistence on the term 'extractos' rather than 'reflexiones' in describing his text, Mora insightfully points out that the problem may therefore lie with the translator himself, rather than the critic, given that the published text is per force the result of a series of choices made by the translator 'para que sus observaciones tengan apoyo' (in order to support his observations; QC: 99). This comment serves to heighten the ideological tone of the debate, highlighting the role of the translator in deliberately reshaping Schlegel's original to support a specific agenda, one which Mora views as politically unacceptable.

Mora follows this attack with another, more measured critique on 8 October, which displays far more originality. In this anonymous article, Mora introduces his argument as one intended as an enlightened, patriotic defence of Spain's literary achievements, claiming that there is no merit in praising works simply because they are Spanish. This would merely devalue the great achievements of the past and stand in the path of progress. His criticism continues to be levelled at Schlegel himself, the German's views regarded as nefarious in the extreme:

> Asegurarle como Schlegel que ha creado un género nuevo en la poesía dramática, por el hecho mismo de haberse apartado de los principios, que es lo mismo que separarse de la naturaleza, seria proponerse pervertir su gusto para siempre, empeñarla en forjar quimeras brillantes por la fuerza y fecundidad de la imaginacion española, y ponerla á vergüenza en el mundo culto é ilustrado. (QC: 101)
>
> (To assure as Schlegel does that he has created a new genre in dramatic poetry by the very fact of having separated himself from the principles, which is the same as separating oneself from nature, would be to propose to pervert its taste forever, forcing it to forge brilliant chimeras by means of the strength and fertility of the Spanish imagination and putting it to shame in the cultured and enlightened world.)

Mora's analogy, comparing a lack of aesthetic principles to an abandonment of nature, shows the degree to which the subtleties of Schlegel's argument have been lost. Mora fails to grasp, or rather has not been told, that, according to Schlegel, nature is reflected in Romantic art by virtue of its organicism and thus itself provides a framework for the development of poetry. The natural progression of poetry is by means of imaginative freedom, not constraint. Unable to engage with the wider Romantic debate in his appraisal of Schlegelian thought, Mora instead accuses Schlegel of trying to force Spain backwards in its cultural development, leaving the nation out of step with the progressive trend. By breaking away from the rules, Schlegel's theories, with their intention to 'espiritualizar la poesía' (spiritualise poetry; QC: 101), will only render poetry incomprehensible, instead of fostering clarity and reason. Further defending the structures of neo-Classicism, Mora feels that Schlegel has lost his way in his enthusiasm for Spanish literature and ought to have limited his praise to its imagination and variety without proclaiming it as the inspiration for a new type of poetry. It is, he feels, pure folly to deny the value of regulation within poetry. Adherence to rules is the sign of a developing culture and to praise a nation for failing to have any amounts to an insult. This overlooks Schlegel's own demand for indigenous rules within any national literature and highlights the often unintentionally contradictory content of Mora's anti-Schlegel campaign which at times finds him in agreement with the German critic in spite of himself.

In similar vein, Mora's final paragraph is also somewhat contradictory with an attempt to define modern patriotism which simultaneously defends key ideals inherent in Romantic nationalism. He begins by conceding the value of Golden Age literature, but only within the context of its own age. The chivalric spirit which inspired the poets of the period has long been superseded by a far more effective sense of enlightened patriotism, akin to that found in ancient Greece and Rome. Consequently, he ascribes the valour of the 1808 uprising against Napoleon to the Spanish hatred of foreign domination and their love of freedom. This is an argument which, if applied to aesthetic values, rather contradicts his previous defence of neo-Classicism, a trend itself led by French taste. Mora goes on to claim that the actions of the Spanish people in the face of the French invasion had been inspired by a sense of national honour and devotion to the monarch, not some vague notion of quixotic chivalry. Yet, it is not chivalry alone which informs the German Romantic idealisation of medieval Spain. Each of the traits Mora mentions has an equal part to play. Indeed, the 1808 uprising was itself one of the reasons for Spain's popularity in terms of the German Romantic ideal, regarded as a manifestation of the apparently prevailing characteristics of patriotism, honour and loyalty which were seen as the foundations upon which the great Spanish nation and its culture had been built. Mora is, then, albeit unwittingly, once more in partial agreement with the Schlegelian view. He is certainly appreciative of the very traits which inform the Romantic apotheosis of his homeland, but defines their source as a different, Classical one. This serves to highlight once more the complexities of contemporary concepts of nationhood and national identity, which are here effectively exploited in terms suited to opposing political agenda.

Mora's initial intervention in the polemic shows the inherent difficulty he faces in defending his position: how to combine his patriotism with his Liberal ideals. Imbued with the values of the Constitution of Cadiz, he is keen to defend Spain's honour as a progressive nation. He is also proud of the nation's past and of her cultural heritage, but he cannot approve of an overvaluation of that past at the expense of the political future. The image of Spain he finds in Böhl's representation of Schlegel's views is politically regressive, a threat to the values and hopes which Liberals had for the modern nation. For Mora, in the context of this debate, neo-Classicism represents the new Liberal Spain – forward looking and enlightened – the Golden Age embodies the past – obscurantist and repressive. That the spectre of that past is itself looming large in the guise of Fernando VII must have added a certain urgency to Mora's sense of dismay upon reading Böhl's translation. It was unthinkable for a Liberal to approve of such a glorification of Spain's absolutist past at such a delicate juncture in the nation's political development. Equally abhorrent was the public justification from abroad of a regime whose name was synonymous throughout Europe with intrigue, injustice and intolerance. Monguió astutely identifies this as the reason for Mora's vehement response to Böhl's translation of Schlegel and his uncompromising defence of neo-Classical precepts:

[F]rente a la censura fernandina, esa preceptiva constituía algo así como un oportuno camoflage de su línea de defensa humanista, racionalista y liberal contra el fanatismo religioso y el absolutismo político que en la interpretación de Böhl parecían ir involucrados en el romanticismo, en su visión del pasado español y del antiguo teatro calderoniano.[5]

(In the face of Fernandine censorship, these precepts constituted something of a welcome camouflage for his humanist, rational and liberal line of defence against the religious fanaticism and political absolutism which, in Böhl's interpretation, appeared inextricably linked to Romanticism, his vision of Spain's past and of the ancient theatre of Calderón.)

Any notion that Mora might have been overreacting in his abhorrence of Böhl's vision is soon dispelled when one considers the repression inflicted upon the nation upon Fernando's return to power following the failed Liberal Triennial of 1820 to 1823. For now, however, Mora's desire to see Spain flourish means he is able to overlook the inconsistency of adhering to French cultural taste in the battle to see Spain hold rank with other progressive European nations. This highlights the significance of the political situation in shaping the polemic. Böhl's exalted anti-French sentiment, which informed his presentation of Schlegel's ideas, was met with an equally fervent anti-absolutist argument from Mora. In the context of this debate, neo-Classical aesthetics remain an anathema to the former, as the symbol of French hegemony, whilst representing a cultural panacea of enlightened progress to the latter.

Böhl took some time in responding to Mora's attack, but when he did so in October 1814, it was in characteristically tenacious fashion with the pamphlet

The Polemic: Phase One (1814)

Donde las dan, las toman: en contestacion á lo que escribieron Mirtilo y el Imparcial en el Mercurio gaditano, contra Schlegel y su traductor (Give as good as you get: in response to that written by Myrtle and the Impartial in the Cadiz Mercury against Schlegel and his translator).[6] In many ways, the document constitutes Böhl's own manifesto of Romantic historicism, building on Schlegel, but with a clear debt to Herder's historicist theories. In it, Böhl adopts an unequivocal stance in opposition to Mora's Liberal, neo-Classicist ideals. The pamphlet also resolves the previously muddied issue of authorial identity. The close-knit nature of Cadiz society meant that anonymity could not be maintained for long and Böhl makes it quite clear that he is now aware of the true identity of his assailant by the insertion of the epithet 'Et tu, Brute!' Consequently, the debate now entered new territory with open warfare between two individuals, once friends, as well as two ideologies. The version of *Donde las dan, las toman* reproduced in *Vindicaciones* has a number of alterations, most notably the omission of a contribution to the original pamphlet by the historian, José Vargas Ponce, signed 'El Bóreas español' (The Spanish north wind), which simply revisits arguments already discussed by Böhl and Mora.[7] Despite its limited polemical worth, Vargas Ponce's contribution is nevertheless significant in raising Böhl's standing. It would certainly not go unobserved that his new supporter was a member of the prestigious Royal Academy of History and supporter of the 1812 Constitution. Vargas Ponce's intervention is significant in demonstrating that Böhl's argument, dismissed by Mora as an anachronistic offence to modern Spanish values, did in fact strike a chord within Spanish intellectual circles, now beginning to digest the import of Böhl's Schlegelian argument. No longer merely a commentator working on the periphery of Spanish letters in his native Hamburg, Böhl's views could now be placed in the context of the ongoing revaluation of Spain's literary heritage in Spain itself. Vargas Ponce's involvement shows that the modest defence of national literature mounted in the eighteenth century by Romea y Tapia, Nipho and others also had support in contemporary intellectual circles as critics began to reappraise the nation's literary heritage in a debate already reignited by Jovellanos and Quintana. The earlier apologists may have taken a more ideologically measured approach, but the quest for cultural autonomy is as important in their appraisals as it is in the context of German Romantic thought. For Böhl, however, the task of defending the nation's culture was theoretically easier than it had been for his predecessors. As Flitter astutely observes, whereas eighteenth-century defenders of the Golden Age in Spain were struggling against the tide of Enlightenment aesthetics, Böhl could exploit the sea change in European thought and call upon the greatest thinkers of his age to support his argument in favour of national literature (SR: 7). That Böhl was aware of his position within the current European debate is made clear in his first piece in the pamphlet, entitled 'Contrastes que me ocurrieron al leer la crítica de Mirtilo, inserta en el Mercurio Gaditano, núm. 127' (Contrasts which occurred to me upon reading Myrtle's critique in the Cadiz Mercury no. 127). Responding to Mora's first article attacking Schlegel, Böhl's riposte begins in rhetorical fashion:

¡Un aleman realza la gloria de España en armas y letras, y un español le impugna! El primer crítico de la Europa, el profesor de tantas lenguas cultas, el traductor por excelencia se entusiasma del teatro de *Calderón* despues de haber dedicado años á su estudio, y *Mirtilo gaditano* le moteja! El norte brota volcanes, y un hijo de la adusta Andalucía trata de apagarlas con un poco de agua de nieve alambicada de *Boileau* y consortes! (V: 10)

(A German highlights Spain's glory in arms and letters and a Spaniard impugns him! Europe's foremost critic, the professor of so many cultured tongues, the excellent translator enthuses over the theatre of *Calderón* having spent years studying it and the *Cadiz Myrtle* derides him! Volcanoes erupt in the north and a son of severe Andalucia tries to put them out with a little water from melting snow distilled from *Boileau* and friends!)

This attack on Mora's audacity, clearly a defence of Schlegel and not Böhl himself, sets the tone for later polemic texts in drawing on Mora's inferiority in relation to Schlegel and focusing on the issue of patriotism. Any attempt to question Mora's patriotic credentials was, as Carnero points out, potentially dangerous in such politically unstable times (O: 171). Undaunted by or, indeed, oblivious to this fact, Böhl steers the literary aspect of the debate towards the issue. Once more, his argument centres on the problematic notion of chivalry. Mora's denial in his initial response to Böhl's translation of the prevailing chivalric spirit in Spain amounts to a slight on the bravery of his countrymen in 1808 and is highlighted in contrast to the visionary approach adopted by Schlegel. Clearly allying himself with the wider Romantic debate, Böhl claims that the rest of Europe quite rightly views Schlegel as 'un profeta' (a prophet; V: 11). He had, after all, recognised the inherent chivalry of Spain long before 1808, even when the nation was still governed by what Böhl terms 'un gobierno relajado' (a dissolute government; V: 11), a criticism of the years under Godoy. It is that very chivalric spirit which serves to inspire the nation's poets and Schlegel's views are validated by the opinion of the populace who have maintained their appreciation of Spanish poetry through an inherent love of land and culture. The critics should follow this lead and turn away from French values to the glories of their own national literature and in particular Calderón. As for Mora's fears for the morality of those subscribing to such ideas, Böhl responds at his polemical best, claiming that lovers of poetry in Germany and in particular those with a love of Spanish poetry are 'muy religiosos, muy morales y muy adictos á toda clase de órden' (very religious, very moral and very addicted to every type of order; V: 12).

The second text in the pamphlet, 'Contestacion á la crítica de Mirtilo gaditano, inserta en el Mercurio gaditano, núm. 127' (Response to the critique by the Cadiz Myrtle in the Cadiz Mercury, no. 127), also responds to moral objections voiced in Mora's first piece. Again, the issue of cultural diversity is key as Böhl sets about debunking the myth of Classical superiority. He begins by refuting the claim made by Mora that modern foreign literature is somehow corrupt. Calling once more on public opinion, he points out that the reading public are quite happy with the writers of the day. Echoing his 1811 article 'Von der neuesten englischen Poesie' (On recent English poetry), he lists Scott, Burns, Southey, Wordsworth, Byron and Campbell as successful writers in Britain, mentioning in turn Goethe, Schiller, Schlegel and Tieck in Germany. The focus here is clearly on the success of Romantic or at the very least proto-Romantic writers. Public taste is naturally drawn towards the work of such indigenous poets who represent the nation's own culture, not that laid down by ancient prescription. Continuing his critique of Mora's defence of the Classical, Böhl then goes on to discuss the relationship between art and nature. In discussing the possible unity of the two concepts, he attacks the sterility and lack of imagination in neo-Classicism which, he claims, has proven itself incapable of approaching art and nature simultaneously. He borrows again from Schlegel, this time exploiting a key argument from the twelfth *Wiener Vorlesung* all but ignored in his earlier translation, by drawing a parallel between Greek sculpture and the heroes of French theatre. Both are presented as the result of a process of refinement which has removed all individuality in the pursuit of the aesthetic ideal which is the ultimate aim of art within the neo-Classical school. Böhl also attacks the work of Kotzebue, Iriarte and Moratín for their slavish imitation of human nature, claiming that 'en tales producciones todo es naturaleza' (in such productions, everything is nature; V: 15). By adhering to the sterile rules of neo-Classical art, these playwrights fail to convey the intricacies of human experience in all its imaginative variety. Böhl sees the German Romantic aesthetic succeed where the neo-Classicists fail. Romantic success stems from a revised understanding of art which welcomes diversity and innovation. The value of Calderón and Shakespeare can only be truly understood in this context. According to Schlegel, they are able to unite art and nature in such a way as to reflect the true beauty of life: 'han producido carácteres ideales sin despojarlos de su individualidad y carácteres naturales que nunca carecen de poesía' (they have produced ideal characters without divesting them of their individuality and natural characters which never lack poetry; V: 16). Despite emphasising the value of Romantic ideals in this way, Böhl also makes it clear that Schlegel has never criticised Classical art per se. It is much appreciated in Germany, not least by Schlegel himself, as his work on Homer demonstrates. The message is that each nation has its own great writers and its own great periods, but appreciation of these ought not be exclusive. This comment marks the introduction of a more moderate tone in Böhl's argument, one which Mora seems to ignore as the polemic progresses. This acknowledgment of the validity of Classical literature within its own period is crucial to Schlegel's original and Böhl's decision to highlight this aspect now sees him begin a gradual move away from the exalted tone of the first polemic documents towards the more balanced view which he will adopt in the second phase. This emerges in conjunction with his plans to approach the Royal Spanish Academy and can be seen as the first strategic step in his plan to establish himself as a man of letters. In this first phase, however, such conciliatory remarks remain few in number.

Seeking a wider context for his views, Böhl steers the debate towards the concept of nationhood. Considering Schlegel's appreciation for national literature, Böhl ponders whether such insight 'tal vez no le es dado sino á un aleman á quien le falta una patria verdadera, por ser la Alemania una aglomeracion de diferentes estados, gobiernos, religiones y costumbres, siendo el idioma lo que únicamente tienen en común' ([. . .] is perhaps only possible for a German who lacks a true fatherland, as Germany is a conglomeration of different states, governments, religions and customs, with the language as the only common factor).[8] This is one of a number of occasions where Böhl is able to bask in the reflected glory of perceived Schlegelian superiority by virtue of a shared nationality. More significantly, however, this comment provides an accurate assessment of the contemporary divided German cultural and political landscape, as well as a distillation of the origins of Romantic nationalism in Germany which sought to overcome such division. Once more, Böhl's criticism demonstrates how deeply entrenched he is in the political mood of his homeland and, consequently, how that mood informs his defence of national literature in Spain. The underlying message is almost a rebuke: the Spaniard should think himself lucky to have the benefit of such an illustrious heritage enabled by national unity and not seek to besmirch its honour through the introduction of nefarious foreign ways.

Painfully aware that such influences have nevertheless been allowed to flourish on Spanish soil, Böhl sets about explaining the import of the concluding paragraph of Schlegel's fourteenth lecture with its criticism of neo-Classicism and the vision – essentially inaccurate – of Spain as a nation unaffected by the universalising effects of Enlightenment aesthetics. Neo-Classicism has indeed been allowed to take hold in Spain, but Böhl is keen to depict it as an unnatural presence. He recalls the general outcry at the first performances in Spain of 'las piezas arregladas á la francesa' (plays regulated in the French style) and ridicules the notion of 'progreso del entendimiento humano entre los vecinos' (progress of human understanding amongst the neighbours), which he equates with 'la crítica francesa' (French criticism) and 'la mania sentimental alemana' (German sentimental mania; V: 19), both of which he cites as examples of the negative impact of Enlightenment aesthetics on contemporary letters. Böhl lends further support to Schlegel's negative appraisal of neo-Classicism by highlighting the fact that many French writers are themselves now following a similar path away from the strictures of neo-Classical theory, mentioning among others Madame de Staël and Chateaubriand. Ignoring this trend, Spain has continued to reject its own literature and Böhl ends this piece with a vehement attack on the stubborn and unpatriotic nature of Spain's so-called 'buenas cabezas' (wise heads) who, having once been forced to turn their backs on their own national literature, are now too set in their ways to consider a return to its appreciation as anything other than a backward step. Schlegel's ideal of a slumbering nation, blissfully unaware of the cultural deviation brought by French domination, is uncovered by Böhl as something of a delusion: had it only been thus, then this terrible neo-Classicist plague might have been avoided.

The final piece in Böhl's pamphlet responds to Mora's third article, signed 'El Imparcial', and is entitled 'Contestacion al artículo comunicado, inserto en el Mercurio Gaditano, núm. 143' (Response to the article in the Cadiz Mercury, no. 143). Again, Herderian ideas dominate as Böhl emphasises once more the need for an appreciation of national individuality in the appraisal of great literature. Such literature, he argues, preceded rules and, indeed, great writers have no need of rules. These are instead created for the benefit of second-rate writers and remain valid only until another great talent comes along. As such, rules must develop with taste, instead of governing it. The Spanish *comedia* is one of the great periods of literature, like ancient Greece and the Shakespearian age, and each of these periods offers a different set of rules for those attempting to write in a certain way. Having stated his case once more, Böhl now calls for a halt to the polemic, arguing that although the public might be interested in Schlegel's views, they are less likely to wish to read those of Böhl and his adversary. Mora's views are anyway not worthy of any consideration, bent as he is on misunderstanding what Böhl feels to have been clearly explained. Böhl closes the argument by saying that Schlegel is only attempting to praise Calderón, not detract from the value of others. Having thus emphasised his own moderation, Böhl calls for silence with the following plea, aimed at highlighting Mora's incompetence:

Por Dios señor Mirtilo, antes de mandar sus críticas á la imprenta, que las revise algun amigo de cabeza madura, y zeloso de la reputacion de Vm.; y no nos haga desperdiciar tanto tiempo, papel y tinta en enmendarle las planas. (V: 25)

(For God's sake, Mr Myrtle, before you send your critical pieces to the printers, please find someone with a little sense and concern for your reputation to check them over and do not have us waste so much time, paper and ink in correcting your papers.)

With this, the first phase of the polemic drew to a close. Characterised by personal insult and misunderstandings, as well as flaws in translation and methodology, it would not be surprising to find the interlude consigned to the vaults of literary history. Looking beyond these issues, however, it remains clear that Böhl had achieved something not attempted before in Spain. He had drawn to the attention of Spanish literary circles the existence of a new means of approaching literature, which questioned the validity of the prevailing neo-Classical trend and in so doing placed a renewed value on Spain's own literary heritage. This was indeed the introduction of state of the art aesthetics, as Reyes Ponce claims, and places Böhl in the context of a debate being carried out in the salons of Europe's major literary centres. Entering the debate in Spain as a German Romantic and driven by a love of Spain, both cultural and patriotic, he may have intended to encourage his new countrymen to revise their understanding of their national literature, but the impact of his translation in the context of European Romanticism extends far beyond the individual expression of cultural patriotism. With Böhl's intervention, Spain finally enters the debate surrounding the German Romantic aesthetic, bringing German thought directly from Germany itself and pre-empting its reception via the more usual conduit of French translation. This direct mediation of Schlegelian thought accords with the existing reappraisal of Spain's literary heritage within Spain itself and offers a new aesthetic framework from within which to re-establish pride in Spanish national literature. This was precisely Böhl's intention.

NOTES

1. All three are reproduced by Pitollet (QC: 94–103). References appear in the text.
2. Central to this repression was the influence of the Church and the Inquisition and, as Monguió notes, Mora's main criticism of Schlegel in years to come would remain the interrelation of religion and literature which underpinned his theories; Luis Monguió, *Don José Joaquín de Mora y el Perú del Ochocientos* (Madrid: Castalia, 1967), p. 34; p. 60.
3. Pitollet (QC: 97) suggests that Mora was inspired by the pseudonym of Nicolás Tap y Núñez, known as 'El Mirtilo Sicuritano', whilst Carnero (O: 168) also suggests as a source the title of Pedro Montengón's 1795 pastoral novel *El Mirtilo, o los pastores transhumantes*.
4. Böhl's response is reproduced by Pitollet (QC: 99).
5. Monguió, *Don José Joaquín de Mora*, p. 33.
6. The pamphlet is now extremely rare, with only one known extant copy held by the Boston Public Library as part of the bequest of Hispanist George Ticknor. Quotations are taken from the version included in *Vindicaciones*.

The Polemic: Phase One (1814)

7 Vargas Ponce's authorship is confirmed by evidence from his correspondence and the style. See Carnero (O: 170–1).
8 This section was omitted from the version included in *Vindicaciones*, presumably given the criticism of Germany which Böhl's comments implied. Quoted by Carnero (O: 171).

Chapter 9
The Polemic: Phase Two (1817 to 1820)

Böhl's plea for Mora's silence was, in fact, unnecessary. The ban imposed on the Cadiz press by the returning absolutist regime in 1814 made any further debate impossible until 1816 when limited press freedom was restored. Early the following year, the polemic re-emerged. The instigator of the renewed hostilities appears to have been Böhl himself, although he would later claim that Mora had attacked him 'de repente [. . .] del modo mas violento' (suddenly in the most violent fashion; AIIP: 22). In April 1817, Mora had taken on the editorship of the new Madrid periodical, the *Crónica científica y literaria*. News of this reached Böhl in Cadiz and he was quick to react, no doubt seeing the chance to revive his career as a critic. The resultant war of words would last until 1820. The tone was often far more vicious than the earlier phase and, although Böhl's own contributions are characterised by an increasingly measured, scholarly approach, a substantial number of controversial documents were also published by both parties. These appeared in a variety of periodicals, pamphlets and other privately funded publications. Mora, and later Alcalá Galiano, relied for the most part on the *Crónica*, whilst Böhl exploited brief associations with the Cadiz-based *Minerva* and *Diario Mercantil* before opting to provide his own forum. His decision was prompted by the difficulties he faced in securing agreement to publish his pieces. Journal editors seem to have been unsure how to approach the polemic, torn between interest in the argument and fear of offending prevailing taste and the censors. Consequently, Böhl suffered a mixed reception in his dealings with both Cadiz publications.

The editor of the *Minerva*, Pedro de Olive, a rival of Mora, refused to publish a number of Böhl's documents, presumably given their insulting tone, but was happy to include an amended version of his Schlegel translation which appeared on 26 February 1818, albeit with a caveat. In an editorial note, Olive made it clear that he did not necessarily subscribe to the Schlegelian view, but was nevertheless impressed by 'el honor que hace á nuestra nacion' (the honour it pays our nation).[1] As this note of caution suggests, the involvement of the *Minerva* in the polemic was brief. Keen to maintain a moderate stance, the periodical did not publish anything further by Böhl.[2] However, Olive did provide Böhl's translation with a wider readership, including many who had known nothing of the first phase of the polemic, and thus allowed an opportunity to refresh the topic which had become rather obscured by the vehement exchanges of 1814. A new audience for Böhl was also provided by the *Diario mercantil de Cádiz*, which published a number of contributions by the German from April to July 1818. However, having given him almost free rein, the editors of the *Diario* suddenly withdrew support, a result, Böhl would later claim, of *afrancesado* pressure.

Böhl's relations with the *Diario* are an interesting example of the extreme strategies adopted at this time by editors striving to adapt to an ever-changing political landscape. The publication had been founded in 1811 under the editorship of the satirist, Pablo de Jérica (1781–1841), and the poet and translator of Boileau, Juan Bautista de Arriaza (1770–1837).[3] Originally Francophile in tone, the periodical was banned by decree in 1815, but later reinvented itself somewhat dramatically as a Catholic, royalist daily. As this new stance might suggest, the editors had at least some sympathy for the ideals of German Romantic thought being promoted by Böhl in his defence of Calderón. Arriaza, a close friend of Francisca, was one of a number of Spanish poets who were beginning to voice unease at the restrictions imposed on imaginative freedom by neo-Classical ideals and in the preface to his *Fragmentos de la Silvia* (Fragments of Silvia, 1811) he highlights 'la imposibilidad que hay siempre de suplir con frías añadiduras el primer ardor de la imaginación' (the impossibility of always substituting the initial ardour of the imagination with cold additions).[4] The affinity with Romantic thought which this suggests was, however, not enough to secure Böhl continued support from the periodical in the face of Liberal criticism and the *Diario*'s withdrawal from the debate in July 1818 finally forced him into private publication. This resulted in the three *Pasatiempos*, the first of which appeared in August 1818 with the grand title *Pasatiempo crítico en que se ventilan los méritos de Calderon y el talento de su detractor en la Crónica científica y literaria de Madrid por el autor de las noticias literarias del Diario de Cádiz* (Critical musings in which the merits of Calderón and his detractor are discussed in the Madrid Scientific and Literary Chronicle by the author of the literary notices in the Cadiz Daily). The pamphlet consists of twelve texts, which, as the title suggests, are aimed at discrediting Mora whilst further glorifying Calderón and include two vicious contributions from Francisca. The rationale behind the publication is described in Böhl's 'Introduccion':

> Los siguientes papeles yacian arrumbados en la carpeta de su Autor, pues hallándose en directa oposicion con el espíritu de estrangería que predomina en el dia en la literatura Española, no fueron admitidos en ningun periódico, y no había medios para costear su impresion por separado. Algunos amantes de su pais, viendo que el principal propagador del despotismo literario de los Franceses (el editor de la Crónica de Madrid, alias Martilo [sic] Gaditano) seguía impunemente zahiriendo á Calderon, al teatro antiguo Español, y á los Alemanes que le hacen justicia, han resuelto costear la impresion del presente cuaderno, juzgándolo útil y aun necesario

para que el Público venga en conocimiento de los resortes que mueven esta contienda, de la pericia del crítico de Madrid y de la conexion que existe entre el amor á la literatura nacional, y el verdadero patriotismo. (IP: 4)

(The following papers lay neglected in the desk of their author, having been refused publication in any periodical given the direct opposition they expressed to the alien spirit which currently dominates Spanish literature and there being no funds to publish them separately. A few lovers of their country, observing that the principal propagator of French literary despotism (the editor of the Madrid Chronicle, alias Cadiz Myrtle) continued to attack with impunity Calderón, ancient Spanish theatre and the Germans who do it justice, decided to fund the publication of this pamphlet, judging it to be useful and even necessary in order that the public come to realise the concerns which motivate this struggle, the astuteness of the Madrid critic and the connection which exists between the love of one's national literature and true patriotism.)

Böhl presents himself as the victim of an unofficial censorship, driven by the *afrancesado* literati, but is at pains to show that he has support, providing a list of initials of those who have helped fund his venture (although the identities of these supporters remain unclear). Notable is the still explicit connection made between the political and the aesthetic, as Böhl highlights the interrelation of an appreciation of national literature with a love of one's country. The reference to Mora as 'el principal propagador del despotismo literario de los Franceses' (the principal propagator of French literary despotism) places the Madrid critic outwith this patriotic axis and depicts him as little short of a public menace and certainly as a traitor. In this second phase of the polemic, Böhl may have wished to present himself in a more moderate light, but as such comments demonstrate, he found it very hard to contain his contempt for his adversary as personal insults continued to fly.

The polemic recommenced in the spring of 1817 when Böhl launched his initial response to the prospectus announcing the publication of Mora's new venture, the *Crónica*. His article, dated 18 March, appeared in the third issue of the periodical on 8 April and is initialled 'B de T', suggesting either an unfortunate typographical error or a poor attempt by Böhl to maintain anonymity. There is, however, little doubt that Mora knew very well with whom he was dealing. Indeed, he may have welcomed the revival of the polemic. He certainly took the decision to publish the piece rather than simply ignoring it. Böhl's article responds to Mora's new publication in what appear, initially, to be positive terms. However, he expresses concern at the use of the term 'ilustración' (enlightenment) in relation to material published in the periodical, complaining that the term is often abused. He offers instead his own definition in an open attack which seeks further to bolster his defence of Romanticism as a valid world view by realigning certain key Enlightenment principles and drawing them into a Herderian historicist discourse. Böhl states that he is quite happy with the notion of Enlightenment as a means of human advancement in relation to science and technology. This is what he understands to be universal Enlightenment and he assumes, with more than a hint of irony, that this is the type of enlightened thought which drives the editors of the *Crónica*. He then goes on to argue against the prevalence of so-called Enlightenment thought in the field of philosophy, citing the French Revolution as evidence of its nefarious influence. Seeking an alternative, Böhl points to a specifically national type of 'ilustración', one which is, in his view, the most important of all. This is not universal, but instead related to the character of a given nation. In England, this manifests itself in the form of a governmental system which has enabled commercial success; in Germany, there is the union of knowledge and innovation which strives towards a sublime spirituality and in France, notably less lofty in its endeavours than its neighbours, there is the ability to embellish physical existence and social life with trivial amusements. Each nation plays to its individual cultural strengths in order to advance and improve. Following this pattern, it is natural to conclude that the true manifestation of enlightened thought in Spain ought to be anchored in the heroic virtues found in its ancient literature. Bearing this cultural pluralism in mind, Böhl argues, any recourse to universal Enlightenment should only be undertaken in order to benefit from technological advancement and ought not to threaten the individuality of the nation's culture. In making such a claim, Böhl rather daringly alters the definition of Enlightenment to suggest one based solely on national character and cultural heritage, which, as Flitter observes, 'is at marked variance with its more accustomed usage' (SR: 16). This is a defensive strategy which, far from narrowly propagating, as Carnero suggests, 'esa xenofobia nostálgica de la España Imperial' (this nostalgic xenophobia of imperial Spain; O: 179), effectively suggests a Romantic redefinition of Enlightenment, based on Herderian historicism, which, following Schlegel, draws the nation's cultural heritage into the contemporary aesthetic debate. The stance which Böhl adopts may be ironic, making fun of Mora's *afrancesado* views, but this does not detract from the seriousness of his intention which is openly to call into question the principles of universality upon which Enlightenment aesthetics are based.

Perhaps unsurprisingly, this elicited an immediate response from Mora, who published his own article in a supplement to the *Crónica* on 25 April 1817, following Böhl's lead in feigning anonymity with the pseudonym 'G. J. G.'[5] Mora's approach is defensive. Adopting his own patriotic stance, he insists that his compatriots do understand the true meaning of Enlightenment. Mora claims that 'B de T' is unrepresentative and, perhaps justifiably, accuses him of distorting the meaning of the word. He points out that revolution is not an inevitable consequence of Enlightenment and that revolutions, such as those in England and Switzerland, had taken place long before the Age of Reason. As for Böhl's notion of national Enlightenment, Mora mocks this as a naive confusion of enlightened thought and national stereotype and closes with the cutting remark: 'Es verdad que para hablar de ilustracion, es menester ser ilustrado' (It is true that to speak of enlightenment, it is necessary to be enlightened; QC: 115). Clearly outraged, there is a sense that Mora is now squaring up in earnest for battle. In his next piece, entitled 'Extravagancias literarias' (Literary extravagances),[6] he counters Böhl's attack on Enlightenment values with an equally vicious condemnation of contemporary German thought which Pitollet quite rightly describes as his 'déclaration de guerre' (declaration of war; QC: 116). In the text, he mounts an attack on the fundamental values which inform the German Romantic ethos and points to the negative impact on European culture of 'los ossiánicos alemanes' (the German Ossianists; QC: 117). However, perhaps most significant is Mora's lengthy, but critical, elaboration, which outlines and questions, albeit without acknowledgement, the basic tenets of Kantian aesthetics as developed by Schiller, which as both Par and Juretschke argue, is clearly taken from Böhl's presentation of these ideas in 1805 and is further evidence of Mora's once close links with the Böhls, as well as confirmation of Böhl's authorship of the piece.[7] Mora does not name his source, nor is the text rendered verbatim from Böhl's original, but familiar phrases such as 'el sentimiento es un estado medio entre el pensamiento y la sensacion' (sentiment is midway between thought and feeling; QC: 117) and a discussion of poetry as 'didáctica' or 'lírica' point to the 1805 article as the origin.[8] Although Böhl must have been pleased to have his article on Schiller acknowledged, the potential for further debate was wasted. In a move which characterises his approach in this second phase, Mora, rather than attempt a theoretical counter-argument to the ideas put forward by Böhl, simply dismisses the new aesthetic as nonsense.

Böhl responded to the appearance of 'Extravagancias literarias' with a series of three texts which he hoped to publish in Olive's *Minerva*. However, Olive refused to co-operate, vaguely citing 'motivos que impiden su publicacion' (reasons which prevent publication)[9] and Böhl was forced to wait until he published his first *Pasatiempo* in August 1818 before he could bring these texts into the public domain. Much of the emphasis is on Mora's weakness as a critic, but one of the contributions, given the enquiring title '¿De qué medios se valen los Mirtilos para desacreditar á Calderón y sus panegristas?' (What means do the Myrtles use to discredit Calderón and his eulogists?), continues the debate surrounding the definition of Enlightenment. In it, Böhl also employs satire to defend his position further, citing a 'letter' purporting to come from the 'Alcalde de Daganzos' (Mayor of Daganzos) – a character borrowed from Cervantes' *Entremeses* – which had been sent to the editor of the *Crónica*. The letter describes the interest provoked by the polemic in the mayor's village and, in particular, the impact of events on the local priest. Once again, the significance of the term 'Enlightenment' is challenged. The mayor, 'gran partidario de la ilustracion' (very much in favour of enlightenment), agrees with the notion of scientific advancement, but this is expressed with a self-deprecating irony which doubts the ability of the Spanish – 'unos ignorantes' (an ignorant bunch) – to move with the times and fears that 'estamos a pique de quedarnos sin escuelas a lo Lancaster, sin alumbrados de gas, y sin litografia' (we are on the verge of finding ourselves without Lancastrian schools, gas lighting and lithography; IP: 15). As Pitollet notes, these references may initially seem to indicate approval and a desire for progress, but are in fact loaded against the whole notion of Enlightenment (QC: 120). Attempts to introduce John Lancaster's Quaker system of primary education had failed miserably in Spain and all three innovations were warmly supported by the *Crónica*, thus forcibly an anathema to Böhl. The sub-text of the mayor's letter is therefore clear. This is not to be a defence of Enlightenment, but is instead a satirical attempt to undermine it, which echoes Böhl's previous redefinition of the term in his response to the *Crónica* prospectus. The mayor complains that he is unconvinced by the Enlightenment evaluation of old literature. He finds it impossible to countenance that the cultural output of Spain's era of world domination should be so poor as to meet with the disapproval of contemporary scholars. He expresses these doubts by pointing out the contradictions in Mora's argument, citing a positive assessment of national drama expressed in number twelve of the *Crónica* which is completely at odds with the harsh criticism of Calderón in 'Extravagancias literarias'. The mayor then makes reference to a copy of Böhl's 1814 translation of Schlegel, which has been preserved by the local priest and has proved very popular in the village. He reports an incident in which the priest defends Schlegel – 'nuestro buen Aleman' (our good German; IP: 18) – who, he claims, displays a more patriotic attitude towards Spain than the majority of home-grown thinkers. The priest then chastises Mora for ridiculing and misquoting the 1814 translation. How, he asks, can such errors equate with the professed enlightened and scholarly views of the *Crónica*? In contrast, Böhl depicts the Church, represented by the priest, to be both patriotic and open to new ideas. The choice of the priest as a popular conduit for Schlegel's ideas is significant in once more drawing Schlegel and Romantic aesthetics into the throne and altar debate. This would seem to be mollified by the mayor's self-professed pro-Enlightenment views, but it is interesting to note that even this apparently open mind is unable to come to terms with Mora's ideas when it comes to the denigration of the nation's cultural heritage. Instead, the mayor voices Böhl's Herderian redefinition of Enlightenment, one which encourages a pluralist as opposed to a universalist approach, and closes his letter with a request for clarification from the editor of the *Crónica* as to 'el medio de combinar el amor á mis paisanos con mi querida ilustracion' (the means to combine my love of my compatriots with my beloved enlightenment; IP: 21), a plea which, for Böhl, encapsulates the very dilemma faced by Mora in maintaining his polemical stance.

Böhl's satirical attack helps to redirect the emphasis of the debate away from his redefinition of Enlightenment to Mora's credibility as a critic, an issue which begins to dominate this later phase of the polemic. Unfortunately for the editor of the *Crónica*, his opponents were well aware of his apparent shift in stance in the years from 1808 when he first befriended Francisca. At the very least, they were able to exploit certain apparent inconsistencies in his argument. An article entitled 'Carta de un español residente en Francia á un amigo suyo residente en Madrid' (Letter from a Spaniard resident in France to a friend living in Madrid), which appeared in the *Crónica* on 26 September 1817, is typical in highlighting the changes in ideological stance which characterise Mora's contribution to the debate.[10] Here, Mora criticises the nascent Romantic Movement in France with an attack on the extremes adopted by Chateaubriand, sadly, he feels, now representative of 'la secta romancesca' (the romantic sect), and also an attack on the reactionary ideas of de Bonald. Now a critic of Chateaubriand, in 1814, Mora had translated the latter's essay on Napoleon, referring to the author in the preface as 'el inmortal autor del genio del cristianismo' (the immortal author of the spirit of Christianity).[11] Such praise for the French writer and his seminal text would further suggest that for Mora the aesthetic ideals of Romanticism are not wholly distasteful, an observation which once more places Böhl's presentation of those ideals in question.[12]

Apparently unaware of his own role in Mora's ambivalence, Böhl was keen to exploit his opponent's shifting stance and did so in another of his responses to Mora's 'Extravagancias literarias'. This takes the form of a letter dated 7 November 1817 which purports to be from 'El apasionado de marras al Revisor general' (The aforementioned passionate admirer to the editor of the General Reviser) and which is given the alternative, enquiring title: '¿Por qué odian los Mirtilos á Calderon?' (Why do the Myrtles hate Calderón?). The letter recalls Mora's defeat in 1814 – clearly Böhl's perception of the outcome – and criticises him for giving a false impression of Schlegel, reiterating the fact that Schlegel is himself an admirer of Classical poetry and that truly at fault are those who refuse to recognise anything other than Classical values when judging the merits of a work. This is further evidence of Böhl's developing moderation vis-à-vis Classical art itself, proposing a balance or at least the freedom to appreciate both ancient and modern works. Continuing in the same vein, 'El apasionado' then revisits the discussion of Kant and highlights the inherent philosophical divide, with some thinkers more inclined to the spiritual, others the material, the divide between imagination and logic. Both strains of human endeavour are to be admired, but Böhl is keen to defend the former, saying that if one is to disregard 'el entusiasmo poético' (poetic enthusiasm) as mere extravagance, then one must disregard a good deal more besides, including mysticism, platonic love and self-denial; in other words, to deny the validity of Romantic thought is to deny all of these. Consequently, Böhl argues, Mora does not actually hate Calderón, but instead hates the spiritual, imaginative aspect of man per se and, along with it, Böhl's Romantic world view:

> No es Calderon á quien odian los Mirtilos; es el sistema espiritual que está unido y enlazado al entusiasmo poético, la importancia dá á la fé, los límites que impone al raciocinio, y el poco aprecio que infunde de las habilidades mecánicas y económicas, único timbre de sus contrarios. (IP: 11)

> (The Myrtles do not hate Calderón; they hate the spiritual system which is united and entwined with poetic enthusiasm, the importance it accords faith, the limits which it imposes on reason and the little appreciation it shows for the mechanical and economic abilities which are the only distinguishing mark of its opponents.)

This once more highlights the ideological divide underlying the entire polemic as faith, the spiritual and imagination are pitted against reason, materialism and science. Again, the aesthetic is linked to the political as the traditional values which underpin the old order are juxtaposed with those which inform the new. Clearly hoping thoroughly to discredit his opponent, Böhl then makes explicit reference to the *romances* by Mora which had been sent to Schlegel by Francisca in 1813, describing them as the product of 'una imaginacion florida, tierna y risueña' (a florid, tender and bright imagination; IP: 12). In a rather underhand move, he also quotes from a private letter sent by Mora to Francisca from France in 1813, the content of which contradicts Mora's current views. In so doing, Böhl takes particular issue with Mora's claim in his article 'Extravagancias literarias' that the two nations most notable for their participation in the Romantic 'carrera de extravios' (misguided chase; IP: 12) have been the English and the Germans. How different, Böhl points out, were Mora's views in April 1813 when he wrote the following:

> Añadiré que he leido estos dias algo de *Shakespear* y que lo creo el mas hermoso genio que jamas ha exîstido y de todos los poetas el que mas se acerca á la region de la belleza ideal, ¿que son las reglas y las *convenances y las trabas de estos monos* junto á sus sublimes arrebatos? Yo gozo cuando oigo decir que es un bárbaro, un salvage, un grosero: porque si estos hombres lo entendiesen y alabasen ¿sería lo que es? Mientras mas se aleja en sus poesias de todo lo que huele á dramatico en este pais mas me gusta. Es el *mayor de los poetas*. No tuvo otra regla sino la inspiracion, creó otra naturaleza, penetró la humana como si se hubiera hallado en su creacion, y

nadie ha sabido como él encerrar en un verso una serie de ideas que dan materia para meditar horas enteras. (IP: 12–13)

(I add that in recent days I have read something of *Shakespeare* and I believe him to be the most beautiful spirit that has ever existed and of all the poets the one who comes closest to the region of ideal beauty. What are the rules and the *conventions and the constraints of these jokers* when compared to his sublime raptures? I take pleasure in hearing him called barbaric, savage, crude, for if these men were to understand and praise him, would he be what he is? The further he distances himself in his work from everything to do with drama in this country, the more I like him. He is the *greatest poet of all*. He had no rule other than inspiration, he created another nature, he penetrated humanity as if he had been there at its creation and no one can equal him in enclosing in verse a series of ideas which provide material for hours of contemplation.)

There are several points worthy of note here for the contradictions they present to Mora's polemical stance: his reference to the rules of ancient theatre as 'las reglas y las convenances y las trabas de estos monos' (the rules and the conventions and the constraints of these jokers), his pleasure in hearing Shakespeare described as 'un bárbaro, un salvage, un grosero' (barbaric, savage, crude), not as an insult, but in celebration of his freedom from regulation, his praise of writing without 'otra regla sino la inspiracion' ([any] rule other than inspiration) and the creation of 'otra naturaleza' (another nature). Not only does this clearly fly in the face of Mora's position in the polemic itself, but much of it also accords with Böhl's stance and is clearly in line with the Schlegelian appraisal of both Shakespeare and Calderón. If one is to believe the authenticity of this excerpt, then it is quite understandable that Böhl should find his opponent's revised view and subsequent attack on Schlegel and himself so hard to accept. He tries to explain this change of stance in charitable terms, but cannot contain his condescension, suggesting that Mora has somehow lost his way, lured from 'el paraiso de la imaginacion' (the paradise of the imagination) to 'el desierto de la filosofía' (the desert of philosophy; IP: 14).

In his third response to Mora's 'Extravagancies literarias', Böhl launches an unsigned attack on Mora's misrepresentation of German literary theory. This text, entitled 'Ensayo de Análisis' (Analytical essay) or '¿Cual es el sentido de las llamadas paradojas Germánicas?' (What is the meaning of the so-called German paradoxes?), picks up on Mora's reference in 'Extravagancias literarias' to Böhl's 1805 article on Schiller. Böhl cleverly reverses Mora's attempt to turn his own words against him by praising his opponent for including such eloquent views in his argument. The irony employed must have infuriated Mora greatly, especially when he found himself depicted as an apologist of German ideas. Once more at pains to present himself as a moderate in the debate, Böhl's article begins with an attack on all extremes, be they the pedantic application of neo-Classical rules or the paradoxes flooding in from Germany. The latter is, however, not a criticism of contemporary German aesthetics, but instead Böhl's response to Mora's misrepresentation of these ideas which has tended to overemphasise those aspects which might be deemed excessive or detrimental. This leads Böhl to conclude that not even he could condone the ideas as presented by Mora. Instead, he sets about re-examining these 'ideas tan claras' (very clear ideas; IP: 22), which are of course those of Kant and Schiller as presented by Böhl himself in 1805. Whilst this text furnishes Böhl with the opportunity to explain and strengthen the views he had put forward anonymously some twelve years earlier, its primary purpose is to undermine Mora's argument. In defending Kant and Schiller, Böhl makes much of the use of metaphor in poetry, which is, of course, a further veiled reference to Mora's repeated mocking of 'perfume matizado' and other metaphors used in Böhl's translation of Schlegel (the subject is, rather predictably, revisited in 'Extravagancias literarias'). Böhl argues that metaphor is a perfect example of art 'espiritualizando la materia' (spiritualising the material) and is a technique which, far from being the sole domain of Romantic literature, has been employed by poets with indisputable Classical credentials such as Virgil and Racine. Metaphor is not therefore a sign of literary excess, as Mora would seem to suggest through his constant mocking of Romantic aesthetics, but rather an indispensable tool in the creation of art. Böhl's somewhat convoluted logic therefore suggests that Mora is not only criticising Romantic art, but also the Classical ideal he holds in such high esteem.

More convincing evidence of Mora's precarious position is found in the satirical attack entitled 'Relacion de lo acaecido en la última reunion de figuras poeticas en el Imperio de la Imaginacion' (Narrative of events which occurred at the last meeting of poetic figures in the Empire of the Imagination). Here, Böhl humorously depicts a meeting of characters who represent various tropes and figures associated with Classical literature.[13] Their dialogue reveals that Mora has offended a number of them and as a result he is to be punished by having poor and bland writing skills. Revenge is exacted at the disastrous premier of Mora's translation of Charles Brifaut's *Ninus II* (1813) staged at the *Teatro del Príncipe* in Madrid on 2 June 1818. This is the first mention of Mora's translation of Brifaut (1781–1857) in the polemic, but the drama would soon become a regular weapon in Böhl's literary arsenal. Further on in the *Pasatiempo crítico*, Böhl revisits Mora's translation in a pedantic critique entitled 'Setenta faltas cometidas contra la pureza de la diccion Castellana en la traduccion de Nino II' (Seventy errors committed against the purity of Castillian diction in the translation of Ninus II). Whilst Böhl's attack on the play is perhaps somewhat ill-conceived in tone, the issues it raises concerning Mora's shifting stance are nevertheless pertinent. The play, translated at the behest of the famous actor, Isidoro Máiquez, and published by Repullés, carries a prefatory note by Mora explaining the rationale behind his translation technique. This echoes his letter of 1813, previously cited by Böhl, and sees him once more contradict much of what he is arguing for in the polemic:

> Al presentar al público la traduccion de una de las Tragedias modernas que mas aplausos han recibido en el teatro francés, creo de mi deber disculpar el atrevimiento con que he alterado en muchas partes las espresiones y aun las situaciones y escenas del original. Para esto, no solo he consultado las críticas que se hicieron de la tragedia francesa cuando salió á luz, mas tambien el gusto del público español que exige mas movimiento y rapidez en la accion que el francés, y sobre todo, el género en que sobresale el inimitable actor que me confió este trabajo. Guiado por esta última consideracion he procurado suprimir algunas monólogos que no me parecen convenientes en la situacion de Nino; dar à este carácter colores mas sombrios, un lenguage mas conciso y enérgico, y mas violencia y calor á los sentimientos que lo agitan y lo conducen al suicidio.[14]

> (In presenting the public with the translation of one of the modern tragedies which has been most lauded in the French theatre, I feel obliged to excuse the audacity with which I have in many places altered the expression and even the situations and scenarios of the original. In so doing, I have not only consulted the reviews of the French tragedy when it first appeared, but also the taste of the Spanish public which demands more movement and speed of action than the French and, above all, the genre in which the inimitable actor who commissioned the work excels. Guided by this last consideration, I have tried to remove some monologues which to me did not seem appropriate to Nino's situation; to give this character darker colours, a more concise and energetic language and more violence and fire to the emotions which agitate him and lead to his suicide.)

Not only does Mora happily admit to altering various aspects of the play to bring it into line with Spanish taste, therefore making a mockery of the notion of universal good taste, he also embellishes the work in a manner befitting the most vivid depictions of the *Sturm und Drang*. Böhl's attack on the piece was prompted by Juan Bautista Cavaleri, whose discussion of Mora's translation appeared while Böhl was preparing the first *Pasatiempo* for the press. Once alerted by Cavaleri to the content of the play and presumably its preface, the German fell upon the translation with almost rabid glee. Böhl makes use of Cavaleri's existing critique of Mora's work, referred to as 'notas de otra mano' (notes by another hand; IP: 52), to support his own lengthy and detailed attack which dwells on a number of perceived offences such as 'gongorismos' and 'galicismos' and is clearly intended to undermine Mora's credentials as a linguist and scholar. The translation would provide such a rich seam of material for Böhl that he would return with another thirty errors in the appendix to the second *Pasatiempo* some six months later,

'Otras treinta faltas de diccion que se hallaron en un segundo repaso de la traduccion de Nino II' (Another thirty errors of diction found during a second reading of the translation of Ninus II), the inclusion of which does little to support Böhl's oft-repeated argument that it is Mora who oversteps the bounds of honourable conduct.

Mora, undaunted by the fate of his Brifaut translation, continued to defend Classical taste without any attempt to clarify his current position in relation to his previous stance. His next direct contribution to the polemic was an article in the *Crónica* on 12 June 1818, signed 'Heleno-filo'. As the pseudonym suggests, this is a defence of Classical values, although the strategy employed relies almost exclusively on an open attack on Romantic literature, old as well as new. The author makes a comparison between Calderón and Chateaubriand, a move which places both in a negative light as proponents of literary excess. There is also a lengthy attack on the audacity of 'un aleman' (a German; QC: 137), Schlegel, who has dared to try to impose foreign ideas on Spain. Böhl responded quickly with two further texts which appeared as an 'Apéndice' to the *Diario* on 21 June. Both are reproduced in modified form in *Vindicaciones*. The first text, entitled 'Debido aplauso al numero 126 de la Crónica' (Praise due to no. 126 of the Chronicle), attacks 'Heleno-filo' for his lack of originality in simply revisiting old arguments. On the matter of a German defending Spain's literature, he reminds his correspondent that many Spaniards have done the same. This argument is strengthened in a second text in the 'Apéndice', entitled 'Sencillas verdades contra los retumbantes sofismas de las variedades de la Crónica N. 126' (Simple truths against the bombastic sophisms in the miscellany of the Chronicle no. 126), in which Böhl asserts that Mora's views are not representative. Indeed, he is an oddity in Europe: such criticism of national literature elsewhere would simply be ignored. These comments serve further to highlight Böhl's growing confidence and awareness of his position within the wider European debate, one which allows him to argue that Mora is both out of touch and inconsistent.[15] As the year wore on, Böhl's relentless tirade began to wear Mora down. Pitollet suggests that the latter simply began to realise that his adversary would stop at nothing and that the polemic could severely damage his reputation, especially given the revelations concerning his pre-polemic position (QC: 142). On 23 June 1818, Mora published a 'Crítica' in the *Crónica* which claims to be his last word in the debate. Whilst not surrendering to Böhl's views, which he ridicules once more, he claims he is growing tired of the polemic and vows to remain silent on the matter from now on.[16] There can, however, be no doubt that his reputation had suffered a severe blow. Whilst Böhl had endeavoured to present himself in an ever more moderate light, the German's continued references to Mora's pre-polemic views, coupled with the latter's own persistent reliance on satire and insult, meant that Mora's position as a credible critic was in danger of becoming untenable.

Whilst Mora's position was steadily weakened during this second phase, Böhl's development is marked by a shift in tone. Although he undoubtedly sharpens criticism of his adversary, aided and abetted enthusiastically by his wife, he also moderates his critical stance. Now presumably able to gain some distance from the emotive outbursts of the first phase and keen to establish a reputation for himself as a man of letters, there is less emphasis on the outright condemnation of neo-Classical aesthetics and more attention paid to the need to revaluate older and contemporary works in the context of a national culture. Accordingly, Böhl's contribution to this second phase consists of two types of document: those already discussed, which relate specifically to the polemic and are largely devoted to discrediting Mora, and those of a more scholarly nature, intended to foster the dissemination and discussion of developing European aesthetics. Whilst markedly different in tone, the latter are also pertinent to the polemic and are carefully selected to add credence to Böhl's Schlegelian argument. They include a series of essays on literature in the *Diario mercantil de Cádiz*, published under the rubric 'Noticias literarias originales',[17] and a number of discursive pieces and translations presented in the three *Pasatiempos*. The highly personal nature of the debate meant that these more scholarly contributions were often ignored by Mora and therefore had limited impact on the polemic itself. They are, however, significant in defining Böhl's growing stature as a man of letters and represent a conscious attempt on the part of the critic to place his work in a European context.

Böhl's self-contextualisation involves the elaboration of two key themes: the praise for Spanish literature emanating from respected literary figures outside of Spain and the presence in European intellectual circles of critical opinions which undermine the validity of neo-Classical thought. Tackling the first of these themes in the second of the 'Noticias literarias originales', Böhl supplies a translation of an extract from a letter to Julius of 30 April 1818 which is intended to demonstrate the high regard for older Spanish literature in his native Germany in particular, with reference to recent translations of Calderón, Cervantes and Lope de Vega, as well as the publication of Jacob Grimm's *Silva de romances viejos*. Evidence of similar appreciation in Great Britain is provided in the third 'Noticia' with a review of Lord Holland's recently republished *Some account of the lives and writings of Lope Felix de Vega Carpio and Guillen de Castro* (1817). Böhl then draws a number of well-known thinkers into his argument in a review of a recent anthology of Spanish theatre published in London, in which the English editor pays homage to the great German Hispanists whose work has helped uncover the treasures of Spain's literary past: Dieze, Sulzer, Bouterwek and Schlegel.[18] Böhl shows his familiarity with all of these and having demonstrated that he and Schlegel are not alone, he turns his attention to the critical appraisal of Schlegel's views. As well as citing the praise for German scholars and Romantic aesthetics in Madame de Staël's *De l'Allemagne* (1810–13), Böhl is able to draw on a number of influential sources for support. He focuses first of all on Simonde de Sismondi's *De la littérature du midi de l'Europe* (1813), which follows Bouterwek in much of its detail. Whilst making clear that he might not agree wholeheartedly with the Swiss scholar (who he erroneously states is French), Böhl draws attention to the fact that Sismondi relies heavily on German sources with a lengthy quotation from his work which praises Schlegel and his fellow countrymen for their dedication to the study of Spain's literature. The passages chosen reflect Sismondi's affinity with Schlegel in ascribing to Spain Oriental qualities and emphasising the chivalric aspect of its national character, as well as denouncing the rigidity of French neo-Classical drama.[19] The validity of Schlegelian thought is then further emphasised with the review of John Black's English translation of Schlegel's *Lectures on Dramatic Literature* (1815) which appeared in the *Edinburgh Review*. Here, Böhl reverts to a familiar policy of selection which ensures that the Scottish journal is on his side. In truth, aspects of the review of Black's translation would have ruined Böhl's case. The reviewer was enthusiastic in his praise of Schlegel's reading of Shakespeare and expressed admiration for the development of Kantian aesthetics and the elaboration of Romantic theory. However, the response to Schlegel's views on Spanish drama was far less positive:

We cannot go into our author's account of the Spanish drama [. . .] Neither can we agree in the praises which he lavishes on the dramatic productions of these authors. They are too flowery, lyrical and descriptive. They are pastorals, not tragedies. They have warmth, but they want vigour.[20]

This seems a rather risky strategy for Böhl to adopt. After all, it would not have been difficult for Mora to seek out the review in question and thoroughly undermine Böhl's case. He was, however, in luck and the solid reputation of the *Edinburgh Review* stood behind him. Even without this rather questionable tactic, Böhl's strategy appears successful. By drawing on figures of authority such as de Staël and Sismondi, Böhl demonstrated quite clearly that he and Schlegel were in tune with current European thought and not the purveyors of mere 'paradoxas germanicas' as Mora would have it.

The Romantic aesthetic is given further credence as Böhl tackles a second key theme: the questionable status of neo-Classical thought. Here, Böhl once more relies on established thinkers to validate his views as he assembles an eclectic mix of supportive opinions. A like-minded figure is Prussian historian, Johann Peter Friedrich Ancillon (1766–1837), whose treatise on national literature in his *Essais philosophiques ou nouveau mélanges de littératures et de la philosophie* (Philosophical essays or new miscellany of literature and philosophy, 1817) provides Böhl with ample ammunition in his defence of both Schlegel and Spain's national literature.[21] This does require some sleight of hand, however. Although Ancillon is critical of uniformity, he does believe in universal or absolute beauty. Böhl mollifies this in a note, agreeing that this may be the case with sculpture, but not with poetry. However, Ancillon's view that absolute perfection incorporates national colour meets with Böhl's unreserved approval, as does his call for the acknowledgement of national identity as a means of self-defence. Further sources of compatible opinion are found in the work of Samuel Johnson in the preface to his edition of Shakespeare with its criticism of the unities when applied out of context and in the success of Thomas Moore's narrative poem, *Lalla Rhook* (1817), which had been widely praised despite is lack of adherence to regulation. Finally, Böhl turns once more to the *Edinburgh Review* and its discussion of the merits of Romantic poetry and in particular Byron. The periodical is unequivocal in its praise of the vibrant, passionate modern poet and places his work in direct, positive comparison to the sterility of much eighteenth-century work.

These negative appraisals of neo-Classical thought pave the way for Böhl's own critical discussion, 'Del gusto en la poesia' (On taste in poetry), which appears in the third *Pasatiempo*. The text is a substantial study of an issue at the heart of the polemic: whether imagination should be subject to rules or allowed to function independently. Böhl counters La Harpe's criticism of modern attempts to divide the inseparable ideals of antiquity and puts his own case against Enlightenment ideals. He points to the failed attempts by Boileau, Batteux and Blair to reconcile rules and emotion, claiming that such rules are opposed by the 'sentido poético' (poetic sense; IIIP: 54). Art will please with or without reason and this is how the public judges. Even La Harpe agrees with this. Imagination has more in common with poetry and the poetic sense has no rules, but is guided by sentiment and character. The result is a national poetry. Böhl is critical of La Harpe's suggestion that works by great poets such as Dante and Shakespeare are only appreciated because they contain a limited amount of material which conforms to the rules, ridiculing this as an idea 'que solo puede nacer de una cabeza francesa' (which could only come from a French mind; IIIP: 57).

Having established his own position and that of Schlegel in the contemporary European critical landscape, Böhl turns his attention in the 'Noticias literarias originales' to the ongoing defence of Golden Age theatre in Spain itself. As well as providing further evidence of Böhl's own awareness of recent scholarship, this succeeds in placing the domestic debate on the value of Spain's literary heritage in its European context. Böhl's argument, which summarises eighteenth-century criticism with an emphasis on the positive appraisal of indigenous forms, is elaborated in the final five 'Noticias', which are reproduced in full with minor modifications in *Vindicaciones*. In the first of these (7 June), Böhl notes that there have been apologists of Calderón since the reign of Felipe V when the preference for French thought was established, in particular with Luzán's *Poetica*. Despite disagreeing with Luzán and the views of his age in general, Böhl is at pains to point out that some eighteenth-century critics were prepared to recognise the value of Golden Age works. He refers to volume four of the influential *Diario de los literatos de España* (Spanish literary daily) which, despite being one of the main conduits for French ideas, contains criticism of the rigidity of neo-Classical rules and voices concern at certain aspects of Luzán's criticism of Spanish theatre and poetry.

The following 'Noticia', published on 14 June, begins by attacking the francophile views of Blas Antonio Nasarre, whose 1749 edition of Cervantes' *comedias* went so far as to claim that the rules proposed by French neo-Classical theory had already been in practice in the time of Lope and Calderón, but that these playwrights had chosen to ignore them.[22] Böhl is pleased to note that this assertion was refuted by Erauso y Zavaleta, whose *Discurso crítico sobre el origen, calidad y estado presente de las Comedias de España* (Critical discourse on the origin, quality and present state of the Spanish *comedia*, 1750) was written in defence of the *comedia* and criticised the pedantry of the three unities. The rejection of Classical principles continues in the following 'Noticia' (21 June), which begins with an attack on Clavijo's *El Pensador* (The Thinker) for espousing French views. Keen to undermine the authority of this influential figure, Böhl draws attention to Francisco Mariano Nipho's critique of Clavijo in his *La Nacion Española defendida de los insultos del «Pensador» y sus sequaces* (The Spanish nation defended from the insults of the 'Thinker' and its followers, 1764). Böhl quotes extensively from Nipho's text before claiming that the latter's wide knowledge of European culture gave him a perspective denied many of his fellow Spaniards, one which led him to refute the association of the *comedia* with the 'Black Legend'. Another of Clavijo's adversaries is mentioned in the next 'Noticia', which appeared on 28 June, highlighting the views of Juan Cristóbal Romea y Tapia, alias 'el escritor sin título' (the writer without title), who wrote in response to an attack on Calderón published in *Las noticias de la moda* (Report of current trends) of *El Pensador* in 1763.[23] Having traced the defence of Spain's national literature to the late eighteenth century, in the last of the 'Noticias' Böhl mentions other, more recent apologists of Golden Age theatre, listing several including Vicente García de la Huerta, in the prologue to his *Teatro español* (Spanish theatre, 1785), García de Arrieta, in his *Principios filosóficos de la literatura de Charles Batteux* (Charles Batteux's philosophical principles of literature, 1801), and Juan Francisco de Masdeu, in the first volume of his monumental *Historia crítica de España* (Critical history of Spain, 1783–1805). Böhl ends this overview of eighteenth-century criticism in typical fashion, claiming that Spain's literature has always been defended by patriots and that it is no coincidence that these are the very thinkers who also criticise Enlightenment thought. Pitollet allows himself a wry reflection at this point: how might Mora have responded had he had access to the letters written by Böhl to Campe as a young man (QC: 135)?

NOTES

1. *Minerva*, 26 February 1818, p. 11. There is, however, some debate surrounding this development. Carnero reproduces a letter dated 16 January 1818, held in the Osborne archive, in which Olive responds to one Rafael Álvarez, who had apparently supported republication of Böhl's text. It would appear that Olive's correspondent was very interested in the polemic and hoped to make his views known (O: 188–9). However, like Böhl, Álvarez was refused publication because of the personal nature of his comments. Olive explains his stance, declaring himself to be a follower of the Classical school, but nevertheless interested in other ideas. Olive's letter is particularly interesting, not just because it gives an insight into his views on Böhl, Schlegel and the wider debate, showing his reluctance to involve his periodical in the less seemly side of the polemic, but also because it suggests a third party, Álvarez, either acting for Böhl or at least keen to support him. It may even suggest that the republication of the Schlegel translation was done without Böhl's knowledge, although there is no reference to this in his correspondence.
2. Carnero claims that Böhl penned an article which appeared in Olive's *Minerva* in July 1818 entitled 'De la pureza del lenguaje' (On the purity of language) which attacked neologisms (O: 199–200), but there is no evidence to support this. Pitollet (QC: 182–3) sees Olive himself as the author and the ensuing battle between the *Minerva* and the *Crónica* as the result of an antagonism between Olive and Mora. This is hard to explain given Olive's professed adherence to the views espoused by Mora.
3. There was also a personal link between the German polemicist and the editorial board of the *Diario mercantil*. Arriaza had been a close friend of Francisca during her years in Spain whilst her husband was at Görslow and they also met during her brief sojourn in London on her way to Germany in 1812.
4. Juan Bautista Arriaza, *Ensayos poéticos* (Palma: [no publisher], 1811), p. 55.
5. The text is reproduced by Pitollet (QC: 114–15), who does not credit Mora with authorship, viewing it instead as the work of a third party. Carnero, however, is convinced of Mora's involvement (O: 179). The style and content of the piece certainly speak for Mora's authorship.
6. *Crónica*, 28 October 1817; reproduced by Pitollet (QC: 116–18).
7. Alfonso Par, *Shakespeare en la literatura española*, 2 vols (Madrid/Barcelona: Suárez/Balmes, 1935); I: 153; Juretschke (DD: 152).
8. Pitollet (QC: 116) suggests another source for the article, drawing attention to Saint-Chamand's *Anti-Romantique* of 1816. Böhl himself refers to Mora's article as 'las traducciones literales de chistes franceses' (literal translations of French jokes; IP: 7), which would further support this view.
9. Quoted by Carnero (O: 186).
10. Quoted by Carnero (O: 185).
11. *De Buonaparte y de los Borbones por F. A. de Chateaubriand. Traducido al castellano por José Joaquin de Mora* (Cadiz: Ramon Hovve, 1814), 'Advertencia del traductor', 4pp. s.n. (p. 1).
12. There is limited approbation of Chateaubriand in a review article in the *Crónica* on 17 October 1817, which further develops Mora's apparently revised opinion of the French writer. He praises his *Veleda* for being 'privado de los atavios á veces estravagantes de Atala y de Renato' (lacking the at times extravagant tendencies of Atala and Renato); quoted by Carnero (O: 185).
13. This strategy appears to have been inspired by Nipho's *sainete*, *El tribunal de la poesía dramática* (The tribunal of dramatic poetry, 1763).
14. *Nino II. Tragedia escrita en francés por Mr Brifaut, traducida al castellano por Don José Joaquin de Mora, y representada en el Teatro del Principe en la noche del 2 de junio de 1818* (Madrid: Repullés, 1818); 'El traductor', no page numbering.
15. The seventh text in the *Pasatiempo crítico* also relates Mora's appearance as 'Heleno-filo'. This really rather vicious piece is the work of Francisca and bears her hallmark signature, 'C......a'.

The text takes the form of a letter entitled 'Implicaciones y contradicciones del No 126 de la Crónica' (Implications and contradictions of no. 126 of the Chronicle). Clearly intended to damage Mora as much as possible, the text dissects his argument in the 'Heleno-filo' article, mocking inconsistencies and misconceptions relating to Romantic ideas and quoting once more from private correspondence with Mora, in particular relating to the *romances* sent to Schlegel.

16 According to a short note appended to the final text to appear in the first section of *Vindicaciones*, 'el profundo silencio' (profound silence; V: 72) promised by Mora was to last only three weeks. In fact, it would appear to have lasted even less. A review of the Italian translation of Schlegel's lectures appeared in the *Crónica* only three days later on 26 June. This lengthy review, ostensibly taken from the *Bibliothèque Universelle de Genève*, claims that the French version of the *Wiener Vorlesungen*, from which the Italian was taken and which was corrected by Schlegel himself, is far clearer than the original and benefits from being more moderate. This is clearly damning with faint praise and, indeed, Mora could not have chosen a more negative review to reproduce. His choice mirrored that of Böhl in choosing to highlight only the positive response of the *Edinburgh Review* to Schlegel's work in the 'Noticias literarias originales' on 31 May 1818.

17 The 'Noticias literarias originales' appeared as a regular series of literary commentaries in the *Diario mercantil* from April to July 1818. The texts are reproduced in summarised form in *Vindicaciones* under the title 'Resumen de las noticias literarias publicadas en el Diario de Cádiz en Abril, Mayo, Junio y Julio de 1818' (Summary of the . . .). Pitollet's study proves invaluable in providing a commentary on the original, unabridged texts which are extremely rare.

18 Böhl refers to the collection published by Ángel Anaya, *El Teatro Español ó coleccion de dramas escogidos* (Spanish theatre or collection of selected plays), 3 vols (London: Smallfield, 1817). Anaya refers in his prologue to 'algunos criticos alemanes' (some German critics) and names Schlegel specifically (p. xvi).

19 This praise is undermined somewhat by a comment in a letter to Julius (13 March 1818) which criticises Sismondi for his lack of knowledge of the Spanish language and literature. The version published in the *Tercer pasatiempo* was modified and Pitollet highlights one significant alteration, namely the omission of Böhl's claim that 'hasta en la lengua francesa, anti-poética en su esencia, empiezan á resonar los elogios debidos á la antigua poesia castellana' (even in the French language, anti-poetic in essence, due praise is beginning to emerge for older Spanish literature). Pitollet explains this omission on the grounds that it contradicts the foundations of German Hispanism which took its lead from France (QC: 131). The fact that Romantic thought was becoming ever more popular in France itself seems an equally likely reason for Böhl's removal of this potentially offensive claim.

20 The review appeared in the *Edinburgh Review*, 26 (1816), 67–107; quoted by Pitollet (QC: 132).

21 Friedrich Ancillon, *Essais philosophiques ou nouveau mélanges de littérature et de philosophie*, 2 vols (Paris: Paschoud, 1817); II: 'Analyse de l'idée de littérature nationale' (Analysis of the notion of national literature), pp. 39–81.

22 The original addresses Nasarre as 'señor académico'. By 1819, as Böhl was angling for membership of the Academy, the text read 'señor Nasarre', thus removing any potential insult to the body of the Academy.

23 Pitollet suggests Böhl must have been unaware of yet another critic of Clavijo, Francisco Nieto de Molina, whose *Discurso en defensa de las comedias de Frey Lope Félix de Vega Carpio* (Address in defence of the *comedias* of Friar Lope Felix de Vega Carpio, 1768) would have further supported his views (QC: 134n).

Chapter 10
New Voices in the Final Battle

Had Böhl sensed victory following Mora's promised silence, then he was to be disappointed. Mora's withdrawal was brief and certainly did not mark the end of the polemic. Instead, the debate was about to widen to include the views of others on both sides. The first to intervene was Antonio Alcalá Galiano, who entered the debate with a brief article in support of Mora in the *Crónica* on 21 July 1818. As had been the case with Vargas Ponce's intervention on Böhl's behalf in 1814, Galiano's early contributions to the polemic are less significant in terms of their content than they are in demonstrating the existence of wider support for Mora. Galiano was also a moderate Liberal who, like Mora, would later go into exile following the failure of the Liberal Triennial in 1823. Consequently, he too must have been concerned at the political tone of Böhl's argument and his intervention highlights once more the ideological complexity of the debate. Galiano's later approbation of Romantic literature and open regret at his involvement in the polemic show how political motives continued to underlie this ostensibly literary debate. Although he would later claim that he had taken Mora's part 'más por celo de la fe de clasicismo profesada entónces por mi en su pureza, que por otras razones' (more in defence of the deep belief in pure Classicism, which I held at that time, than for other reasons), he also recalls his concern at Böhl's preference for 'la monarquía al uso antiguo' (old style monarchy).[1] Galiano's criticism of Böhl's absolutist tendencies is unequivocal and his belief in neo-Classicism, like Mora's, must be understood in the context of the broader Liberal desire to see Spain develop along more democratic, modern lines, away from the repression of the past which, under Fernando VII, now stood to regain a hold over both nation and culture. In gaining Galiano's support, then, Mora essentially finds an echo of his own views, albeit often in more considered form.

Less easily assessed is the support received by Böhl. This emerged from two very different sources. The first was the publication on 27 July, only a few days after Galiano's first intervention, of a pamphlet entitled *Artículo remitido al editor del Diario Mercantil de Cadiz, quien no ha juzgado conveniente insertarlo por mantener la palabra que tiene dada, aunque no en letra de molde, de guardar el mas profundo silencio sobre la cuestion suscitada acerca del mérito ó demérito de los autores dramáticos, clásicos y romancescos* (Article submitted to the editor of the Cadiz Daily Commercial, who did not consider it appropriate to publish it due to having to keep his word, albeit it not in writing, to maintain the deepest silence on the matter raised of the merit or otherwise of Classical and Romantic dramatists). The author was Cristóbal Zulueta, an otherwise unknown figure, possibly the son of a prominent merchant family in Cadiz, who clearly felt compelled to add his voice in an attempt to settle the debate, but who, like Böhl, appears to have experienced difficulty in negotiating with the capricious Cadiz press.[2] The reference in Zulueta's lengthy title to the *Diario*'s self-censorship is substantiated by the facts and parallels Böhl's own experience. The final edition of the periodical to publish anything by the German was number 703, dated 5 July 1818, and Böhl later complained in a letter to Julius on 7 October that the editors, who remained close friends, had been bribed by the 'Madriter'. In fact, the publication ceased to include any material criticising Liberal values, perhaps once more tailoring output to suit circumstance as Liberal groupings in Cadiz began to strengthen their hold. Although annoyed at their refusal to publish his own contribution, Zulueta would seem to be in accordance with the editorial decision to withdraw from the polemic. He claims to have been looking forward to silence in the debate and to the discussion of other, more interesting matters. He criticises Galiano for having revived the issue and calls for moderation. Whilst claiming that the debate was pointless, having already been settled in the time of Horace, and asserting that art should of course be governed by universal rules of taste, he also posits as the only guiding maxim of dramatic art the need to capture the audience's imagination, something which Calderón had clearly achieved. Consequently, whilst not exactly professing unstinting support for Böhl, Zulueta does at least seem to agree with his argument by acknowledging Calderón's value and suggesting the need to consider national character when defining taste.

However, as Carnero points out, Zulueta was never actually allied with Böhl (O: 120). The association was made by Mora who wrongly assumed a collaboration. This is borne out by the fact that Zulueta's text is critical of both sides in what he considers to be a superfluous debate and also by Böhl's own response to Zulueta's intervention, which appeared in the second *Pasatiempo*, published in January 1819, with the title 'Anotaciones á una carta firmado C.Z., remitida al Editor del Diario Mercantil de Cádiz' (Notes on a letter signed C.Z., sent to the editor of the Cadiz Daily Commercial). Given that Zulueta had been identified by Mora as one of Böhl's supporters, the tone of the piece is rather more critical than one might expect and perhaps indicates that Böhl was not prepared simply to exploit the meagre approval of Calderón offered by this unsolicited source of assistance, but rather remained intent on putting his case across in the terms he demanded. The piece, dated 16 August 1818, begins by praising Zulueta's moderation, but then goes on to point out some minor errors in his argument. This mild and essentially good-natured revision of Zulueta's views is then superseded by an angry postscript, dated 9 December 1818, which responds to a second pamphlet published by this enigmatic figure, *Yo solo a uno de los mismos* (I alone to one of the same), which was written in response to Galiano and Mora's joint production of November 1818, the nonsensically titled *Los mismos contra los propios* (The same against the same). Böhl criticises Zulueta, who, despite earlier attempting to present a moderate argument in praising Calderón, now seems to have adopted some of the views espoused by the *Crónica*. Böhl accuses him of misrepresenting the content of the 'Noticias literarias originales' by depicting German theory as a threat to good taste and to the Spanish language itself. Expressing his regret at the content of Zulueta's second text, Böhl declares that, unlike his adversaries who are forever announcing their imminent silence, he will not stop unless it can be proven that Classical values are truly superior. Perhaps taken aback by Böhl's forthright response, Zulueta withdrew from the polemic. His intervention remains something of a mystery, especially given his somewhat ambivalent stance, and it is hard to assess his contribution as his motives are unclear. He may already have been a figure in the literary salons of Cadiz or someone keen to make a name for himself amongst the city's literati. Whilst Pitollet describes his contribution as being notable 'par son remarquable bon sens' (for its remarkable good sense; QC: 199), praising him for his conciliatory efforts, it is hard to overlook the inconsistencies in his argument.

More resolute, and apparently welcome, support came from the pen of Juan Bautista Cavaleri, who, as well as drawing Böhl's attention to Mora's ill-fated Brifaut translation, had begun writing to Mora in support of Böhl under the pseudonym 'Serafina Rubio'.[3] By allying himself with Cavaleri, Böhl reveals what might, with hindsight, be regarded as a severe lack of judgement. Now largely forgotten, Cavaleri made his mark on Spain's literary history as a troublemaker with often inconsistent views. Over the years, he acquired a reputation for involving himself in literary wrangles, including a scuffle with Böhl's later friend, Gallardo.[4] Undaunted by controversy, he was not afraid to voice his criticism of the great names of the age and was highly critical of a number of eighteenth-century writers, including Moratín and García de la Huerta, in the preface to his edition of Cervantes' *Entremeses* (Interludes) in 1816. He was also extremely harsh in his criticism of developments in Spanish Romanticism in the 1840s, reacting to the notable influence of the French Romantics and their apocalyptic world view. In so doing, he was keen to defend the German Romantic aesthetic. In his 'Ensayo filosófico sobre el Romanticismo' (Philosophical essay on Romanticism), published as a prologue to Aguado's 1840 edition of *Juan de Mena*, Cavaleri defends the honour of Schlegel, claiming that the German critic cannot be held responsible for the abuses of his so-called literary heirs who have simply succeeded in perverting his ideals. Similar views were also expressed in the prologue to an edition of Lope de Vega's *El dómine Lucas* (Schoolmaster Lucas), also published in 1840, where Cavaleri attacked Spanish Romantic writers, alleging that those who now claimed to represent Romanticism in Spain were not worthy of the name.[5]

Cavaleri's first contribution to the Calderón polemic was the pamphlet *Tres producciones plebeyas, en que los Editores de la Crónica Científica y Literaria verán sacadas á plaza su crítica destreza y su buena fé, sin que por eso se corran* (Three plebeian productions in which the editors of the Scientific and Literary Chronicle will see their skilful critique and good faith put in their place without their humiliation). This contained little of value other than the critique which drew Böhl's attention to Mora's Brifaut translation.[6] More significant, however, was Cavaleri's second intervention in October 1818, entitled *Discurso en razon de la tragedia Á secreto agravio secreta venganza* (Address with regard to the tragedy secret revenge for a secret offence). This was published as a pamphlet on the occasion of the performance of Calderón's play in Cadiz on 17 October for the benefit of two travelling German scientists, Baron d'Alton, a colleague of August Wilhelm Schlegel in Bonn, and his associate, Dr Pander. Böhl was indirectly involved with this publication in as much as he had befriended his two countrymen and supported the rescheduling of the performance of Calderón's play.[7] Cavaleri claims that this had been done at the behest of the famous actor, Juan Llonín, who was to play the lead role and was horrified that the travellers had been unable to see any works by Calderón during their time in Spain. Cavaleri's text explains that there had been no time to prepare a play which would have been familiar to the visiting Germans through Schlegel's translation, knowledge of which the author presumably gained via Böhl. Sure, however, that they will appreciate what they are about to see, Cavaleri mounts a general defence of Calderón which takes particular exception to accusations of immorality within the play. Adopting a historicist stance, he claims that any apparent breaches of good taste are merely the result of differences in social and moral values from the sixteenth to the nineteenth centuries. This moderate tone then gives way to a long and pompous diatribe, which reveals the author's extreme reactionary views on matters relating to anti-Semitism, the meting out of justice and the definition of heroism. Somewhat unexpectedly given the cause he purports to support, Cavaleri also suggests the removal of certain elements from Calderón's plays, citing the playwright's own dissatisfaction as justification.[8]

The intervention of Cavaleri saw the pace of the debate quicken to an almost frantic exchange of personal insults. His *Discurso* provided an opportunity to respond to the personal criticism levelled at him in a 'Crítica' (Critique) signed 'Juan Gil' which had appeared in the *Crónica* on 14 August. Cavaleri believed the author to have been Galiano, but it was in fact Mora, who used the pseudonym on other occasions when controversy required a façade of discretion. The text was a condemnatory response to *Tres producciones plebeyas* which attacked Calderón as 'el Padre del Gerundismo dramático, nata y espuma de la poesía romántico-vándala' (the father of dramatic gerundism, the pinnacle of romantic-vandal poetry).[9] Cavaleri's response is equally vicious, turning the accusation of 'vandalism' against the critics of the *Crónica*. Then, as tension continued to escalate, Mora and Galiano issued what amounted to a joint refutation in the *Crónica* on 27 October 1818. In a letter written mainly in response to Cavaleri's *Discurso*, Galiano reiterated his previous stance and vehemently denied being 'Juan Gil', whilst Mora provided an introduction to the letter which, echoing Clavijo, claimed that the Cadiz production of Calderón would simply have given the travellers the impression that Spain was once riven with intrigue.

Böhl's own response to the intervention of 'Juan Gil' is reserved for the second *Pasatiempo*. The second text (number 14) addresses the intervention of Mora's pseudonymous alter ego and identifies a number of errors in the piece. According to Juan Gil's claims, Böhl argues, the only way to make the Enlightenment work in Spain would be to convince the people that the nation is barbaric and therefore in need of reform. Böhl, on the other hand, is not so extreme and once more presents himself as a moderate who has been forced to argue against the ignorance of his opponents. He reiterates his understanding of true Enlightenment as one based on balanced views and respect for each nation and supports this by highlighting the interest in old literature shown in England, Germany and Denmark, pointing out that this had also been the case in Spain some thirty years previously before the nation had been gripped by 'galomania'. The intention is once more to show Mora to be out of step with developments in the aesthetic debate within Spain and carefully to position Böhl once more in the context of an alliance with an earlier generation of Spanish critics such as Romeo y Tapia and Nipho, whose work he had already highlighted in the 'Noticias literarias originales'. Böhl ends by gently amending Schlegel's own suggestion that the nation had slept through the last hundred years, refuting the accusation that he is trying to depict Spain as a nation which has failed to develop culturally since the sixteenth century. It would surely not be in his interest to do so, given his patriotic views. Again, Böhl presents himself as a moderate voice whose values stand out in stark comparison to Mora's apparently extreme and unfounded stance.

Mora did little to counter Böhl's efforts to depict him in a negative light. In fact, his approach in the final months of the polemic simply added weight to Böhl's argument as his contribution descended into repeated name-calling and ridicule. Mora ceased to contribute anything of value and focused instead on publishing a variety of anti-Romantic, anti-German snippets in the 'Variedades' section of the *Crónica*. The material chosen was often less than credible and ranged from literary commentary to malicious gossip – including reports of human sacrifices in Dresden and student revolt in Göttingen – intended to depict the German lands in the grip of Romantic excess.[10] In November 1818, Mora and Galiano published their final joint production, *Los mismos contra los propios ó respuesta al folleto intitulado Pasatiempo crítico* (The same against the same or response to the pamphlet entitled Critical Musings),[11] which appeared in Barcelona, having been rejected by the Madrid censors. The publication was not only a response to the *Pasatiempo crítico*, but also takes account of Zulueta's letter to the editor of the *Diario mercantil* and Cavaleri's first pamphlet. Unfortunately, much of the content of *Los mismos* does little more than further propagate the already well-rehearsed stream of insults and accusations. The second text, a satirical verse dialogue entitled *Escena calderoniana* (Scene in the style of Calderón), is typical, depicting a mock baroque dialogue between two characters named Bolonio and Calvurino, the new, thinly veiled nicknames coined for Böhl and Cavaleri. The appearance of such material marked a low point in the debate and, perhaps understandably, those involved began to retreat. Publication of *Los mismos* was followed by a brief and insulting correspondence between Galiano and Cavaleri, after which both fell silent.[12] Zulueta's second contribution, *Yo solo a uno de los mismos* in December 1818, marked the end of third party intervention in the polemic. The interlude had been ugly and for the most part unscholarly. Indeed, it is questionable whether these third parties really brought anything other than infamy. Perhaps aware that there was little left to say, Galiano, Cavaleri and Zulueta now withdrew to leave Böhl and Mora to battle it out alone.

What Böhl made of this flurry of critical activity can be found in the first text to appear in the appendix to the second *Pasatiempo*, 'Carta de J. N. B. al señor D. A. A. G.' (Letter from J. N. B. to Mr A. A. G.). Addressed to Galiano, the text is a review of the polemic as a whole and includes some comments on the various third party interventions. The text underlines the extent of Böhl's attempt to moderate his stance in this second phase, no longer merely voicing the emotive responses of an exalted patriot, but offering instead the considered opinion of a man maturing in his new world view. The initial tone of the document is one of grudging respect, but this soon gives way to a more critical approach. Alluding to his abandonment by the *Diario*, Böhl begins by explaining that he has been forced to write a letter because, unlike Galiano, he has no publishing outlet for his views. He then sets about explaining his position, beginning with information on his background and how he came to know Schlegel's work. Böhl explains that he wanted to translate Schlegel's defence of Calderón as a homage to Spain's literature and expresses his surprise at having been suddenly attacked by Mora for so doing. Böhl feels that he has been misrepresented, his views made to appear extreme. Reiterating instead his moderate position, the central feature of Böhl's defence is the claim that he is not suggesting that Classicism is a purely negative cultural force, but is instead simply calling for an acknowledgement of other aesthetic values beyond those approved by current dogma, assuring his correspondent that '[r]espeto todo gusto en materia de poesía, menos el exclusivo'

(I respect all kinds of taste in relation to poetry, except that which is exclusive; AIIP: 16). Instead, he argues that in order to appreciate art fully, critics and poets must be prepared to question neo-Classical values and supports this by referring to his previous pluralist argument surrounding the definition of Enlightenment. Alluding to the words of the fictional Alcalde de Daganzos, Böhl condemns what he terms 'ilustración á la violeta' (violet enlightenment), in other words 'afrancesamiento' (Frenchification) and the rejection of Spanish culture. Böhl goes on to present his perspective on the polemic, one which provides some insight into his interpretation of the third party intervention in the debate. He clearly feels he has been wronged by his opponents, having battled without hope of material gain and with the simple aim of doing some good. His intentions are unquestionably honourable, whereas, he feels, Mora has often overstepped the mark. Furthermore, if Mora himself now feels ill done to, he has no one but himself to blame. Indeed, the third parties who intervened on Böhl's behalf were inspired to do so by 'el desenfreno loco' (mad lack of self-control) of the *Crónica*, not by any particular literary conviction. This was itself limited, as Böhl himself admits:

> El Señor C. Z. es todo clásico, como lo manifiesta mi impugnacion de su carta. El humanista gallego (ó Serafina Rubio) es todo clásico; y con un rigor que no temo culparle de excesivo en muchisimas ocasiones. Es unitario cerrado. No tenemos en literatura mas punto de conformidad, que nuestra comun admiracion de las bellezas de Calderon y de la antigua poesía castellana. (AIIP: 25–7)

> (Mr C. Z. is an out and out classicist, as my refutation of his letter shows. The Galician humanist (or Serafina Rubio) is an out and out classicist and with a rigour for which I do fear to criticise him much of the time. He is a confirmed advocate of the unities. We have nothing more in common in matters of literature than our shared admiration for the beauties of Calderón and ancient Spanish poetry.)

Here, the tone again suggests a more moderate stance as Böhl deliberately tempers the role of Spanish literature in the political issues of the day, replacing the once central emphasis on the connection between neo-Classicism and republicanism with one centred on the value of Calderón to neo-Classicists and Romantics alike. It was this reasoned tone which perhaps convinced Galiano to withdraw from the debate, unable to argue with views which were similar in essence to those he held himself. Indeed, the views expressed by Böhl in the latter stages of the polemic constitute a far fairer representation of Schlegelian thought than the highly politicised rendition of the first phase. The emphasis on plurality and historicism is tempered ideologically to foster an open debate on the value of older literature, which sits far more easily with the ongoing Liberal revaluation of Spain's literary heritage emanating from thinkers such as Quintana and Jovellanos.

Whilst the more moderate tone of Böhl's later interventions lacks the absolutist affiliation which so enraged Mora as the polemic commenced, this does not mean that Böhl's political beliefs had altered; he would maintain a staunchly conservative stance throughout the rest of his life. Instead, the defence of Spain's literary heritage, which had become Böhl's main intellectual aim, was driven by a complex set of impulses. The aesthetic and ideological arguments which filled the pages of the polemic documents were of course central, but perhaps just as significant in the second phase was Böhl's own ambition to become an authority in matters of literature. The highest goal he could set himself in this context was to be admitted into the ranks of the *Real Academia Española* and, having drawn attention to himself through the polemic, his preliminary work on the *Floresta*, already underway by 1817, was to be the key. Consequently, the second phase of the polemic formed part of a wider strategy to gain recognition for his work as a scholar and in which Böhl displays a canny understanding of the workings of the Academy. He soon established contact with a series of useful figures, the most important being Navarrete who had been appointed librarian to the Academy in January 1817.[13] This marked the beginning of a fruitful relationship, each providing the other with material and assistance, although Navarrete always maintained a careful distance from the polemic, despite the fact that Böhl sent him copies of the *Pasatiempos*. The latter seems to have overlooked this, far more concerned with the support Navarrete could provide in gaining access to the Academy. Writing to his new friend on 18 Feburary 1819,[14] Böhl seeks advice as to whether, given the great expense involved in publishing, a manuscript submission would be considered by the Academy. The response was clearly positive as Böhl submitted the manuscript for the first volume of the *Floresta* to the Academy at the beginning of 1820, along with three studies concerning metre, rhyme and the history of poetic forms and language. His submission was supported by a letter of recommendation from Vargas Ponce and was delivered to 'los Srs. Don Francisco Antonio González, Don Diego Clemencín y Don Ramón Cabrera' for their consideration.[15] Böhl's endeavours were promptly rewarded in April 1820 with notification that he had been admitted to the Academy as an honorary member, the highest honour which could be given to non-residents of Madrid. This was the crowning moment in his ongoing polemic and Böhl finally felt able to claim victory. Proud of his achievement, he inserted the following in the *Diario mercantil de Cádiz*, clearly unable to resist a side-swipe at his detractors in so doing:

> D. Juan Nicolás Bohl participa á sus amigos que la Real Academia española le ha hecho la distinción de asociarle á su cuerpo en calidad de académico honorario. Con este se evidencia que si existen algunos españoles que han llevado á mal que un estrangero aprecie y alabe la poesia nacional antigua, el cuerpo mas esclarecido de la

nacion y los jueces mas competentes en la materia han tenido á bien recompensar su celo y aplicacion con el premio mas digno de la ambicion de un amante de las letras. Cádiz 3 de Mayo 1820.

(Don Juan Nicolas Böhl advises his friends that the Spanish Royal Academy has done him the honour of awarding him membership of the body in the capacity of honorary academician. This proves that, even though there do exist some Spaniards who are offended when a foreigner appreciates and praises their ancient national literature, the most educated body in the land and the most competent judges in the field have had the good grace to award his enthusiasm and diligence with the prize most befitting the ambitions of a lover of literature. Cadiz, 3 May 1820.)

Keen to make the most of his success, Böhl proclaimed his affiliation to the academic body on the frontispiece of *Vindicaciones*, the publication of which in 1820 marked the end of the polemic. Having preserved his contributions for posterity and been rewarded for his efforts by the highest intellectual authority in the land, Böhl felt he could move on. His future plans to collate and edit anthologies of ancient Spanish verse and theatre were taking shape, now with the added sanction of the Academy. The motivation was scholarly, but the love of Spain which had driven the emotive reaction of the first phase of the polemic still underpinned Böhl's choice of material and his approach to it. There is no clearer testimony to this than the prologue to *Vindicaciones*, which provides a retrospective assessment of his polemical stance, as well as a philological and ideological manifesto for Böhl's subsequent career:

No hay verdadero patriotismo sin amor á la literatura nacional, y sin predileccion hácia aquellos sublimes ingenios, que por el medio de la poesía ennoblecen el alma y recrean el entendimiento. Ninguna nacion tiene mas motivo de gloriarse en sus poetas que la española. Sin embargo solo la España ha producido hijos, que se han empeñado en ajar las glorias poéticas de su madre. Contra los dicterios y sofisterías de semejantes ilusos se dirigen estos papeles, satisfecho su colector si en algo puede contribuir á consolidar el aprecio tan debido al grande *Calderon* y sus ilustres contemporáneos.

(There is no true patriotism without a love of national literature and without a preference for those sublime talents who by means of poetry ennoble the soul and divert the mind. No nation has more reason to glory in the work of its poets than Spain. However, only Spain has produced sons who have insisted on undermining the poetic glories of their mother. These papers are directed against the dictates and sophisms of such misguided men, their collector satisfied if he is in some way able to contribute to the consolidation of the acknowledgement due to the great *Calderón* and his illustrious contemporaries.)

It was in this essentially Romantic spirit that Böhl would embark upon the philological projects which would occupy the final years of his life.

That Böhl considered himself the victor in the polemic is not in doubt. His election to the Royal Spanish Academy was the final vindication of his actions and one of which he was immensely proud. However, it is the subsequent response of his adversaries which is perhaps the most interesting outcome of the debate. Both Mora and Galiano would go on to voice approbation of Romantic thought and, in so doing, display a degree of acceptance of the German Romantic aesthetic promoted by Schlegel. Mora's stance would shift once more after the polemic, returning to a more sympathetic appraisal of Romantic aesthetics in keeping with the views expressed in his pre-polemic days. In exile from 1823, first in London and then in Latin America, his work reveals a thinker appreciative of poetry on a broad level. Vicente Llorens highlights in particular the views espoused by Mora during his years in London and sees his wide-ranging appreciation as the result of a character which 'pudo tender hacia la novedad romántica después de haberla combatido, mas sin librarse nunca del todo de su herencia clasicista' (could tend toward the novelty of Romanticism after having battled against it, but without ever really breaking free of his Classical heritage).[16] The continuity with Mora's pre-polemic position is made apparent through one of his London publications, *No me olvides* (Forget me not, 1824–7), published by Ackermann, which is regarded as one of the earliest manifestations of Spanish Romanticism and which includes two of the *romances* which found their way to Schlegel in 1813. There is also evidence of an increased aesthetic understanding approaching that of Böhl in an article published by Mora in the *European Review* in 1824 in which he assesses the current state of literary criticism in Spain and offers a new perspective:

> Quintana, who is the only one that has written upon the subject to any extent, considers the first productions of Spanish poetry rather as a French littérateur than as a national judge. [. . .] The Germans have been more just towards a nation to which they are strangers. Schlegel and Bouterwek, though often overlooking the respective merit of authors, penetrate the spirit that inspired them, and know how to appreciate the striking beauties of their first attempts. We shall pursue a new course. We shall trace the dominant qualities of the first epoch of Spanish poetry, forgetting that we have studied Horace or Boileau. The heart and the imagination must be the touchstone by which we try those treasures which art has not adulterated, and which were not the produce of either abstract theories or of self-love.[17]

Again, just as Mora's pre-polemic attitudes had contradicted his argument in the years after 1814, here, after the polemic, he is found even praising Schlegel, albeit grudgingly. Furthermore, he is prepared to countenance an appreciation of Spanish poetry which ignores the Classical strictures of Horace and Boileau, favouring instead 'the heart and the imagination'. This is surely an echo of Böhl's later, more moderate argument, which, following Schlegel, asked for Spain's national literature to be considered on its own terms. This is done without necessarily condemning Classical precepts which are valid in their own sphere. This parallel appreciation of essentially Romantic ideals and Classical precepts would continue throughout Mora's exile in Latin America. There is, however, a growing emphasis on a Romantic aesthetic in Mora's work as the decade progresses. In 1829, writing in the *Mercurio chileneo* (Chilean Mercury), in an essay entitled 'Poesía. Ensayo sobre el hombre, de Mr Pope. Version de D. J. J. Olmeda, Lima, 1823' (Poetry. An essay on man, by Mr Pope. Translated by D. J. J. Olmeda, Lima, 1823), Mora expresses the desire to see Latin American poets 'saliendo algún tanto del senderon trillado de los latinos y de los franceses' (moving away a little from the well-trodden path of the Romans and the French).[18] Monguió sees in this the influence of English literature in exile, but the views expressed by Mora clearly echo those voiced before the polemic.[19] By adopting a position diametrically opposed to that taken during the polemic, Mora effectively returns to his original stance before 1814. This *volte-face* can be seen as both a vindication of Böhl's efforts in attempting to introduce German Romantic thought into Spain and also as a criticism of his manner of so doing, given Mora's readiness to engage productively with the new Romantic ideas once distanced from the heat of the polemic and its underlying political import. Mora's apparent agreement with Böhl's later, more moderate stance shows how damaging Böhl's initial naive presentation of Schlegel's ideas had been. Such was the ideological fallout from that initial presentation that Mora either did not notice or was unable to accept the later more moderate tone, despite its affinity with his own aesthetic beliefs.

Galiano's views also changed markedly during his years in exile. This is made particularly clear in his *Introductory Lecture Delivered at the University of London* (1828), delivered upon taking up the first Chair in Spanish, where he outlines his tentative acceptance of the Schlegelian apotheosis of Calderón.[20] Later, in his *Atheneaum* articles of 1834, he admits his change of stance, but will not accept Schlegel's views without reservation, qualifying them as 'more ingenious and fanciful than just'.[21] He does, however, accept and support Schlegel in highlighting the difference between the Romantic and Classical forms of literature. Galiano further demonstrates his increasing commitment to the new aesthetic in his 1834 prologue to the Duque de Rivas's *El moro expósito* (The foundling moor) in which he refers to Germany as 'la cuna del romanticismo' (the cradle of Romanticism), praising the efforts of German intellectuals in developing new ideas.[22] There are echoes of both Herderian and Schlegelian theory in the text, in particular Galiano's emphasis on the difference between northern and southern Europe and the fact that the literature of a nation should reflect the character of its people instead of merely following universal rules.

Given the apparent change of heart on the part of both Mora and Galiano in the years following the polemic, it might seem just to lay the blame for the entire episode at Böhl's door. He had, after all, launched Schlegelian theory on an unprepared audience, reworking the text in such a way as to make it seem utterly reactionary to the Liberal intellectual circles of Cadiz. However, the response of his adversaries was just as immersed in the political and historical events of the period. Where Böhl was responding in the first instance from a conservative, absolutist position to the devastating treatment of homeland and culture at the hands of the French, Mora and Galiano, confirmed Liberals, were railing against the threat of absolutism and repression as moderate thinkers hoping desperately to reinvent the nation as a modern constitutional monarchy, a goal partially achieved under the regency of María Cristina following Fernando VII's death in 1833. Yet, despite these ideologically opposed positions, both sides shared a fundamental appreciation for the literature of Spain, one which eventually emerged from the muddied waters of the polemic and secured the beginnings of a Romantic movement in Spain which inspired poetic as well as philological trends throughout the nineteenth century. The issues raised by Böhl would soon be taken up by others within Spain, in particular in the pages of the Barcelona periodical, *El Europeo* (1823–4), and, as Flitter has shown, found their way into the aesthetic framework of the century via Durán, Donoso Cortes and Larra, continuing through to the mid-century in the work of Böhl's own daughter, Fernán Caballero. Following the polemic, Böhl's own scholarship went on to find a new focus, moving away from theoretical arguments towards the practical collation and salvaging of the material so lauded by Schlegel and his German Romantic contemporaries. It is in this context that he enters the final phase of his intellectual development.

NOTES

1. A. Alcalá Galiano (ed.), *Memorias de Don Antonio Alcalá Galiano publicados por su hijo*, 2 vols (Madrid: Rubiños, 1886); I: 418–19.
2. Pitollet was unable to uncover any further information on Zulueta (QC: 154–5), nor is he mentioned by Fernán Caballero as one of her father's supporters.
3. Mora responded to this letter in his 'Crítica' of 4 August 1818.
4. See A. Rodríguez-Moñino, *La polémica entre Gallardo y Cavaleri-Pazos sobre el asonante (1824)* (Badajoz: Imprenta provincial, 1959).
5. See Carnero (O: 115–20).
6. The three *producciones* are a letter attacking Mora's pedantry (presumably that referred to by Mora himself), a critique entitled 'Notas á varias cláusulas del artículo intitulado Crítica en el número 141 de la Crónica C. y. L.' (Notes on various clauses in the article entitled Critique in no. 141 of the S. & L. Chronicle) and a discussion of Mora's translation of *Nino II*, 'Herir por los propios filos, aunque con un tantíco mas de hidalguia' (Wound with your own arrows, but with a little more nobility). The first two pieces continue the bitter tone of the polemic and contain little worthy of comment. The third piece is significant as it provided Böhl with ample

7   Böhl also appears to have sanctioned further support from Cavaleri when compiling the appendix to the second *Pasatiempo*. According to Pitollet and Carnero, Cavaleri was responsible for the piece entitled 'El aspirante Bolonio al señor Moralla' (The aspiring Bolonio to Mr Moralla), another vicious attack on Mora; (QC: 223–4; O: 120).

8   Cavaleri would later publish an edition entitled *Teatro expurgado de Calderón* (The theatre of Calderón expurgated, 1845) in which he realised the suggested changes. Perhaps surprisingly, Böhl seems to have approved of Cavaleri's proposed editing of Calderón. In the third *Pasatiempo*, in his essay on the figure of the 'gracioso' (fool), he makes reference to the Cadiz performance of *Á secreto agravio, secreta venganza* and praises the ability of those staging the work in 'ciñéndose á cercenar las superfluidades, sin faltar al respeto debido á los originales con añadiduras é interpolaciones de propia cosecha' (managing to excise the superficialities without showing disrespect to the original through the addition and interpolation of their own material; IIIP: 47). He justifies such intervention on the grounds that some works are simply so devoted to the tragic that the role of the fool becomes incongruous and therefore in need of modification. That modification, however, must be executed with the utmost care and respect for the overall tone and content of the play.

9   Quoted by Carnero (O: 199).

10 Quoted by Pitollet (QC: 197–8).

11 The title plays on Cavaleri's third *Produccion plebeya* which also refers to the defenders of Calderón as 'los propios'.

12 The correspondence is reproduced in Montoto, *Algo Más*, pp. 122–124n.

13 The two men shared other mutual friends and acquaintances, in particular Vargas Ponce and Antonio Van Halen. Juretschke (DD: 153) refers to links to Quintana, Lista and Reinoso, the latter having apparently frequented the Böhl house in Cadiz.

14 The letters are held in a private collection in the archive of the *Palacio de Abalos*. The correspondence lasted from 1817 to 1833 and consists of 23 letters, all from Böhl to Navarrete. There is a gap in the correspondence from 1822 to 1826. Both H. Janner, 'Algunos datos nuevos acerca de J. N. Böhl de Faber', *Boletín de la Real Academia Española* (1945), 229–39 (p. 232), and Juretschke (DD: 167) suggest that some letters must have been mislaid as there are indications in later letters that the correspondence had been ongoing. Juretschke also cites a note from English Hispanist, John Bowring to Navarrete that supports this view.

15 Don Francisco Antonio González was confessor to Fernando VII and secretary to the Academy from 1814 to 1833, Don Diego Clemencín (1765–1834) was an influential philologist, well known for his commentary on *Don Quijote*, and Don Ramón Cabrera (1754–1833) was a priest and philologist and director of the Academy from 1814. Both Clemencín and Cabrera were friends of Navarrete.

16 Vicente Llorens, *Liberales y románticos*, 2nd edn. (Valencia: Castalia, 1979), p. 206.

17 Quoted in Llorens, *Liberales y Románticos*, pp. 309–10.

18 Quoted in Monguió, *Don José Joaquín de Mora*, p. 18.

19 Monguió, *Don José Joaquín de Mora*, pp. 14–16.

20 Antonio Alcalá Galiano, *An Introductory Lecture Delivered in the University of London on Saturday, November 15, 1828* (London: John Taylor, 1828), p. 24.

21 Antonio Alcalá Galiano, 'Literature of the Nineteenth Century: Spain', *The Atheneaum*, 7 (1834), 290–5; 329–33; 370–4; 411–14; 450–4 (p. 414).

22 Ángel Saavedra, Duque de Rivas, *El moro expósito*, A. Crespo (ed.), 2 vols (Madrid: Espasa-Calpe, 1982); I: 'Prólogo', 7–34 (p. 23).

PART THREE

Romantic Philologist and Man of Letters

Chapter 11
The Ominous Decade

Böhl may have claimed victory in the battle with Mora, but his struggle for the salvation of Spain's literary heritage was still very much work in progress. Despite having made his mark by defending Calderón and proving his worth as a scholar in the process, there was still, he felt, much to be done. Typically, however, Böhl's efforts were hampered by circumstance as family and business commitments intervened once more to disrupt his studies. Mercantile life presented a particular challenge. In 1818, Böhl had taken up employment with the British sherry exporters, Duff Gordon, and although an experienced merchant, the wine trade was relatively unfamiliar and took up much of his energy. He was eventually able to secure more time away from the demands of work in 1820 when Duff Gordon transferred their offices from Cadiz to their *bodega* in El Puerto de Santa María. This meant Böhl no longer needed to spend hours every day writing letters to his foreman, able instead to summon him in person. However, whilst undoubtedly pleased to have more time to devote to his scholarship, there was another reason why Böhl was glad to be away from Cadiz. The city was the seat of a resurgent radical Liberalism, which Böhl viewed with extreme suspicion, fully aware of the implications of Liberal government for the survival of the throne and altar axis. Given his own trenchant political views, it is not hard to imagine his dismay at witnessing the revival which eventually led to the Liberal Triennial of 1820 to 1823. Writing to Julius on 15 July 1817, he expressed his disgust at the anti-Catholic, anti-monarchist tone which was current in Cadiz. A few months later, on 19 October, he wrote despairingly: 'Die gute Sache gebe ich hier immer mehr auf, da sich die filosofische Parthei täglich stärkt, und den wohlmeinenden (leider aber kurzsichtigen) König völlig umstrickt hat' (I am increasingly giving up on the good cause here, as the philosophical party is gaining strength every day and has fully enmeshed the well-meaning (but sadly short-sighted) king). Powerless to act, Böhl felt himself to be totally at odds with prevailing opinion in Cadiz, referring again in a subsequent letter on 30 April 1818 to a number of essays he had written, but could not hope to publish because of their monarchist, anti-Liberal, anti-Enlightenment tone.[1] Unable to voice such views himself, he seeks out similar ideas in the work of other, mostly pre-1814 commentators such as 'El Filósofo rancio' (The old philosopher), pseudonym of Francisco Alvarado (1756–1814), whose *Cartas críticas* (Critical letters) had staunchly defended the Inquisition and the monarchy in the years prior to the Constitution of Cadiz. Also potentially significant for Böhl in this context was Antonio de Capmany (1742–1813). This anti-Enlightenment, Gallophobic reactionary railed against French cultural corruption in a number of treatises, including his well-known *Centinela contra franceses* (Sentinel against the French, 1808). Juretschke, Carnero and Reyes Ponce all argue for the presence of Capmany in Böhl's world view, alongside Herder and Schlegel, although, as is the case with Herder, Böhl never actually mentions him in his correspondence.[2] It is likely, however, that Böhl would have known Capmany's defence of Spanish literature as presented in the 'Discurso preliminar' of his *Teatro histórico-crítico de la eloquencia española* (Historical-critical theatre of Spanish eloquence, 1776–9) which offers a notion of cultural identity similar to that proposed by Herder in its insistence on the value of popular culture as a means to cultural self-definition and organic development. Furthermore, dismayed at the demise of 'die gute Sache', Capmany's staunch anti-French stance would certainly have appealed to Böhl as a voice of conservative sense in a country which seemed doomed to Liberalism and revolution. The views of men like Capmany provided evidence of the existence in Spain of a national Enlightenment of the kind described by Böhl in the *Pasatiempos*. Reading their work, he could feel that his was not a lone voice in Spain's political wilderness. He must have been aware, however, that both Alvarado and Capmany were dead, their ideals now swept aside by an apparently unstoppable wave of Liberalism.

Observed from the safety of El Puerto, the Liberal advance must indeed have seemed unstoppable. Led by General Riego and a number of prominent figures from the 1812 *Cortes*, including Quintana, the Liberal rebels eventually forced Fernando VII to accept the Constitution for a second time in March 1820. Political turmoil ensued before the king was finally driven into exile in France by General Mina's troops in 1822. As the Liberal cause gained momentum, Böhl watched events unfold with a mixture of trepidation and disgust. Writing to August Campe on 5 August 1820, he is barely able to contain his contempt:

Sie werden leicht ermessen, daß ich mich jetzt (wo nicht in Spanien) doch in Cadiz außer meinem Elemente befinde, da hier die allerseichteste Aufklärerei an der Tagesordnung ist, da Alles, was gedruckt wird, keinen andern Zweck hat, als die Machthaber und die Klerisei zu verunglimpfen, und sogar das Theater sich nur mit Verspottung der Mönche, Nonnen und der sogenannten Serviles beschäftigt; [. . .]

Es ist nicht übel, daß die Liberales wenigstens kein Blatt vor den Mund nehmen und geradezu auf eine Trennung von der römischen Kirche antragen. So weiß man, woran man sich zu halten hat. Auch den Juden steht eine ehrenvolle Aufnahme in Spanien bevor. Die Welt soll innewerden, daß sie künftig in Spanien die rechte Aufklärung suchen muß. Da Neapel jetzt die spanische Constitution angenommen hat, so erwartet man zuversichtlich, daß Preußen ein Gleiches tun werde. Dann bleibt nur die

Kleinigkeit übrig, Rußland zu bekehren und das System der Zweikammern in England und Frankreich umzuwerfen; dann ist Europa frei und glücklich.³

(You will easily be able to appreciate that I am currently most uncomfortable (if not in Spain per se) in Cadiz, for here the most shallow Enlightenment nonsense is the order of the day, for everything that is published has the sole purpose of disparaging those in power and the clergy, and even the theatre only concerns itself with mocking monks, nuns and the so-called *serviles*; [. . .]

It is no bad thing that the Liberals are at least quite honest and openly propose a split from the Church of Rome. At least one knows what one is dealing with. The Jews can also expect an honourable welcome in Spain. The world should be aware that in future true Enlightenment is to be found in Spain. Now that Naples has accepted the Spanish Constitution, one can confidently expect Prussia to do the same. Then there is only the small matter of converting Russia and overturning the two-chamber system in England and France; then Europe will be free and happy.)

Böhl's sardonic tone echoes his critique of Enlightenment thought during the polemic and highlights the specific role of Cadiz in enabling the resurgence of such a nefarious political force. The frequent attacks on the Church and Spain's literary heritage which he reports show the extent to which more radical Liberal values undermined everything he held dear.

By 7 July 1820, the situation had reached crisis point. Writing to Julius, he complained in terms which illustrate the ingrained nature of his Romantic nationalism: 'Es geht mit Riesenschritten auf den Jakobismus loos, und wäre das Volk nicht so schlicht und wohl so würde es schon an allen Ecken brennen' (There are giant leaps towards Jacobinism and if the people were not so pure and good then there would be fire on every corner). This firm belief in the people as the true representatives of the nation places their natural sense of honour and justice above the revolutionary tendencies of the intellectually driven Liberal cause. The people represent the true Spain and it is in them and their devotion to the monarchy that her salvation lies. Their apparent rejection of republicanism serves as a justification for the traditional values promoted by Böhl, values which are inextricably linked to his patriotic reading of the nation as one guided by a benevolent monarch and an unshakeable faith and which would later find their echo in Böhl's engagement with the ideals of the *Wiener Romantik* (Viennese Romanticism).

The trenchant nature of Böhl's political views is further demonstrated in his correspondence with the publisher, Friedrich Perthes. In a letter dated 17 December 1819, he refers to Perthes and Fouqué's epistolary dialogue *Ueber den deutschen Adel, über Ritter-Sinn und Militair-Ehre* (On German nobility, chivalry and military honour), which appeared in 1819. The slim volume presents a debate on the role of the nobility in the German lands which explores the possibilities open to that class in a changing society. Fouqué, true to his aristocratic origins, defends the status quo and hankers after a golden past, whereas Perthes tries to suggest moderate change which would prove more productive for society as a whole. Fouqué opens the debate, responding to Perthes' review of his 1818 *Jäger und Jägerlieder. Ein kriegerisches Idyll* (Hunters and hunting songs. A belligerent idyll). He defends the traditions of the nobility and describes the Germans as 'ein altbegründetes, tief eingewurzeltes Volk' (a long-established, deep-rooted people).[4] He enthuses over a time when 'Adel, Bürger- und Bauernstand' (nobility, bourgeoisie and peasant) will live harmoniously with mutual respect and responsibility. Such harmony is, he claims, everyone's duty. Perthes argues instead for a wider role for the nobility. Whereas Fouqué is critical of the loss of land rights for younger sons, Perthes argues that this gives them the opportunity to contribute to the military and civil service, a role they could share with the bourgeoisie, thus pre-empting the development of German society towards the end of the nineteenth century. Böhl responds to the debate with interest. Perhaps predictably, he takes Fouqué's side and is particularly impressed with his criticism of the French Constitution as a product of whim which displays no continuity with the past and which effectively nullifies the nation's history. Fouqué argues that whereas German culture and scholarship have developed organically, French culture has suffered from experimentation and the adoption of Classical principles. This is reflected in the country's political development which has seen 'gesetzloses Willkür' (lawless capriciousness) lead to 'starren Despotismus' (rigid despotism).[5] Böhl reinforces this view in aesthetic terms, claiming that the *Aufklärung* undermined cultural identity and heralded the death of poetry. In agreeing with Fouqué's argument, both aesthetically and politically, Böhl expresses views diametrically opposed to those driving the political agenda in Spain at the time and which place him instead at the extreme of the retreating *servile* position. The reactionary stance he adopts explains the lack of criticism he voiced when faced with the realities of the so-called Ominous Decade following the restoration of the Bourbon monarchy in 1823. Fernando VII reclaimed the throne with French support and immediately repudiated the Constitution for a second time, annulling all legislation passed during the Triennial. Censorship laws were tightened and many, including Mora and Galiano, fled into exile to escape political persecution. For his part, Böhl was greatly relieved to see the monarchy restored, pleased to see himself and his family 'in das vormalige biedere Spanien versetzt' (returned to the old, decent Spain; 22 June 1823). Events also provoked a change in attitude towards the French. Delighted by the advance of the Duke of Angoulême's army – the 'Hundred Thousand Sons of St Louis' – Böhl wrote to Julius on 12 August 1823, describing his 'unbeschreibliche Vergnügen den ersten Franzosen einrücken zu sehen' (indescribable pleasure at seeing the first Frenchman moving in), a sentiment which would have seemed quite impossible a decade earlier.[6]

At ease with the restored regime, now in a world seemingly in accordance with his political ideals and settled in his new mercantile role, Böhl might have been expected to enjoy his mature years in an atmosphere of scholarly peace. However, the 1820s were to prove ominous for Böhl on a quite different level as his home life began to take a disturbing turn for the worse. Francisca had begun to show the first signs of a nervous condition which would plague her for the rest of her life and which made her irascible and generally difficult to live with. A constant source of support for Böhl since their return from Germany in 1813, Francisca now became the cause of great worry and distress. On 26 March 1824, Böhl wrote to Julius: 'Meine Frau leidet viel an Nerven & ist in allerlei unfruchtbaren Grübeleien versunken' (My wife suffers greatly from her nerves and has sunk into all manner of fruitless brooding). Efforts later that year to alleviate her condition through convalescence in the quiet village of Bornos were unsuccessful and she was constantly at odds with her family. She took particular exception to the marriage plans of her two younger daughters. Aurora's choice, the English-born merchant, Thomas Osborne, did not hold suitable political beliefs, whereas Angela's choice, the Baron Chatry de la Fosse, a general in the French army, was too old and not well enough educated. Much to her disgust, Francisca's views were ignored and the weddings went ahead with their father's blessing in 1825. The departure of his two younger daughters meant that Böhl was now alone with his wife for the first time in their marriage. Whereas this might once have provided a wealth of opportunity for further joint scholarship, it was instead marred by Francisca's illness. Although her condition had begun to stabilise, her intolerance and criticisms often made Böhl's life a misery and he was always happy to see his wife in residence elsewhere. Unsettled by this domestic strain, towards the end of the decade, Böhl's thoughts turned once more to Germany. He planned to visit Hamburg in order to spend a few months with his aging mother, but was forced to cancel the trip due to his heavy workload. Sadly, this would be his last opportunity to see her as she died soon afterwards on 27 February 1828, only a few months after her husband. Made aware by these events of his own mortality, Böhl was even more desperate to visit Hamburg, keen to see old friends and attend his son's wedding, but his plans were dealt a final blow on 13 June 1829 when he fell down a staircase in the *bodega* and badly dislocated his right leg. He was forced to remain in bed for a month and needed crutches to walk thereafter, never fully regaining his mobility.

Despite the constraints placed upon him by his health and family cirsumstances as the decade progressed, Böhl nevertheless continued to play a prominent role in cultural life. The recognition of the Academy in 1820 was a great inspiration and motivated Böhl to pursue in earnest the publication of his long-planned 'Parnaso español' (Spanish Parnassus), which, like the polemic before it, became part of a crusade in defence of Spain's threatened culture and resulted in his two major anthologies, *Floresta de rimas antiguas castellanas* (Selection of ancient Spanish verse) and *Teatro antiguo anterior á Lope de Vega* (Ancient theatre before Lope de Vega). The necessity for such action was underlined during a visit to Seville's cathedral library in 1819 and relayed in an article entitled 'Korrespondenz-Nachrichten. Cadix' (News by correspondence. Cadiz) published with Julius' assistance in Cotta's *Morgenblatt für gebildete Stände* (Morning paper for the educated classes) in January 1820.[7] The piece records a trip from Cadiz to Seville undertaken in September 1819 with the purpose of taking his son, Juan, and daughter, Cecilia, to board the ship which would carry them to Hamburg. His discoveries in the library, far from providing him with fresh material, leave him utterly aghast:

> Von den 20,000 Bänden, aus denen die Sammlung ursprünglich bestand, ist der größte Theil, durch nicht zu entschuldigende Nachlässigkeit, ein Raub der Motten und des Moders geworden; 5000 sind noch vorhanden. Der fleißige Sammler hat ein alphabetisch geordnetes Verzeichniß seines Schatzes hinterlassen, wovon mehrere Bände dem Verderben entronnen sind. Aus ihnen lässt sich die Unersetzlichkeit des Verlustes ermessen. Ich griff sogleich nach einem dieser Bände, und forderte die spanischen Dichterwerke, auf die ich stieß. Urtheilen Sie über meinen Verdruß, als mir der Aufseher trocken erwiederte: daß ich mich nicht nach spanischen Dichtern umsehen möge, da gerade diese alle fehlten.

> (The majority of the 20,000 volumes which made up the original collection have been lost to moths and mould due to unforgivable neglect; 5,000 are still available. The conscientious collector left an alphabetical catalogue of his treasures of which several volumes have escaped destruction. They show the full extent of the loss of irreplaceable material. I immediately took hold of one of these volumes and requested the works of Spanish poetry I found there. Imagine my horror when the librarian responded that I need not look for Spanish poets as these were the very volumes which were all missing.)

This physical evidence of the neglect of Spain's culture heightened Böhl's determination and, with the weight of the Academy now behind him, he took up his philological work with renewed vigour. In so doing, he was still very much a Romantic thinker, a fact underlined in a letter to Julius on 24 September 1819 describing his experiences on the trip to Seville in which Böhl exhibits a readiness to embark on a new challenge, but also pays homage to those who have influenced his personal and intellectual development:

> Anstatt daß das Alter mich abstumpfen sollte wird mein Gemüth allen schönen Eindrücken stets offener. Diese Fertigkeit auch dem Gemeinsten das Edle abzuziehen verdanke ich Wordsworth und Göthe.

(Rather than being deadened by age, my spirit is ever more open to all beautiful impressions. This ability to see the nobility in even the basest things I owe to Wordsworth and Goethe.)

The sentiment expressed could be an allusion to Novalis or the Schlegel brothers, but it is telling that the two writers mentioned are those to whom Böhl became most attached before and during his Romantic rebirth. This underlines the importance of the Görslow years for Böhl's subsequent development and, indeed, his post-polemic philological career, throughout which he would continue to engage with Romantic thought. He was by now established in Spain as a herald of the new aesthetic and seemed reluctant to relinquish this role even as taste in his native Germany, the anchor of his revised world view, began to change.

Böhl's reputation as a man of letters following the polemic is highlighted by the number of visits received from travelling writers and scholars, including the English Hispanist, John Bowring (1792–1872), and the German philologist, Friedrich Diez. Established as something of a landmark on the grand tour of Spain, Böhl was always delighted to receive such visitors and was at great pains to offer whatever assistance he could. Typical was the visit in April 1828 of the American writer, Washington Irving, who had been in Spain since 1826 researching his works *The Conquest of Granada* (1829) and *Tales of the Alhambra* (1832). Böhl admired his work and visited Cadiz in order to make his acquaintance, soon persuading him to come to El Puerto. In terms of aesthetics, Irving and Böhl were like-minded men and the stay in El Puerto gave rise to long discussions and debates on the value of Spain's literature. The visit was marred by the death of Irving's travelling companion, John Nadder Hall, and the American writer was grateful to Böhl, who undertook the funeral arrangements, describing him in a letter to Hall's cousin as 'a German gentleman, [. . .] (distinguished in the literary world), who during the whole time of our residence in that neighbourhood showed us the most hospitable civilities'.[8] Washington Irving, whose friendship would prove just as fruitful to Böhl's daughter, Cecilia, was not, however, the only prominent writer of the period with whom the German scholar had close ties.

During the last decade of his life, Böhl developed a close and fruitful friendship with the Spanish Romantic writer and philologist, Agustín Durán (1789–1862). Contact was sought by the German following the publication of Durán's 1828 *Discurso sobre el influjo que ha tenido la crítica moderna en la decadencia del teatro antiguo español y sobre el modo con que debe ser considerado para juzgar convenientemente de su mérito peculiar* (Address on the impact of modern criticism upon the decline of ancient Spanish theatre and on how it should be judged to appreciate its individual merit best). The text displays a number of attitudes in relation to both aesthetic and political thought which seem to echo Schlegel and which must have appealed immediately to Böhl. Politically, Durán promoted a Christian, monarchical view which eulogised Spain's Christian past and continuing Christian values, whilst condemning France for falling prey instead to republicanism and anti-religious tendencies. Durán was a moderate Liberal and a staunch monarchist who saw the salvation of the nation in wise execution of monarchical duties within a constitutional framework. This meant he could not agree with many of Fernando VII's policies, although, like many of his fellow writers and thinkers, he found himself obliged to praise the king in public. Such public praise of the incumbent monarch combined with the pro-Christian message of the *Discurso* must have been reassuring to Böhl, providing a welcome change from the extreme Liberal rhetoric of the early 1820s. However, this was not the only aspect of Durán's work which appealed to Böhl. He was equally enthused by the aesthetic content of the *Discurso*, which continued along markedly Schlegelian lines, presenting a defence of Spain's ancient theatre in terms reminiscent of those employed by Böhl a decade earlier, albeit with less vehemence, and linking it in no uncertain terms to the Romantic character of the nation as a whole.

Böhl first became aware of Durán through their mutual friend, the critic, Bartolomé Gallardo (1776–1852).[9] Böhl's friendship with Gallardo was an unlikely match as they held differing views on a number of matters. There was, however, a deep mutual respect and, like Julius, the Spanish critic would show his admiration for Böhl after his death, cataloguing his library after its purchase by the *Biblioteca Nacional* in Madrid.[10] The idiosyncratic Gallardo wrote to Durán on 11 January 1829 to congratulate him on the publication and content of his *Discurso*, noting the surprise expressed by others, in particular the *Diario de Cádiz*, that he had not made explicit reference to Böhl or the Calderón polemic and hinting that Böhl himself was a little put out by this. Perhaps at Gallardo's suggestion, and no doubt in order to raise awareness of his own work, Böhl approached Durán, writing to him from El Puerto on 13 January 1829. In his letter, Böhl expresses his approval for Durán's work, which he praises 'por fundarse en los mismos principios que durante cinco años he defendido' (for being founded upon the same principles which I defended for five years) – the five years referred to being those of the polemic – and introducing himself and his own efforts in salvaging Spain's literary heritage. As these parallels might suggest, these were, in many, but not all, respects, two liked-minded men and what survives of their correspondence reveals a warm and fruitful relationship. Böhl's friendship with Durán and Gallardo, as well as his continued relations with Navarrete, place him at the centre of Spain's cultural life. He had become a recognised expert on Spain's literary heritage – 'distinguished in the literary world', as Irving puts it – and was highly respected for his philological pursuits. Any negative impression left by the uglier outbursts of the Calderón polemic had begun to fade.

Despite his literary activities and success as a man of letters, as the 1830s began, the mood in the Böhl household was sombre. In 1831 he had resumed in earnest his correspondence with August and Elise Campe. Despite the obvious joy this occasioned, the renewed contact reawakened Böhl's desire to return to Hamburg. However, his longing was tempered by the fear of seeing so many friends ravaged by old age and a city he might no longer recognise. Böhl and his wife were themselves suffering from the advance of their years. Francisca's health remained unstable and Böhl's immobility worsened his own state of mind. The family situation was made worse in March 1835 when Cecilia was widowed for the second time. Her husband, the Marqués de Arco Hermoso, whom she had married in 1821, had been ill since 1825. Cecilia had cared for him tirelessly and was devastated by his death, her sadness heightened by the knowledge that her father's health was failing too. Böhl had been suffering from severe bowel problems since 1834 and this, coupled with the pain in his leg, led to a rapid deterioration in his health from the spring of 1836 which forced him to neglect his duties at Duff Gordon. On 5 July 1836, Böhl altered his will, originally drafted in 1826. The revised terms ensured that all of his children and his wife were amply provided for after his death. He also requested that his library be donated to the *Stadtsbibliothek* in Hamburg. The terms of this bequest would never be fulfilled, prevented by an ancient Spanish law which forbade the export of rare books. The library was eventually sold to the *Biblioteca Nacional* in Madrid for 100,000 *reales*.

Böhl's final letters reveal a man whose lust for life is beginning to wane. On 24 March 1836, he wrote to Elise Campe:

Ihre so schön ausgedrückten melankolischen Gefühle bei dem Hinscheiden der gewohnten Umgebung berühren harmonische Saiten auch in meiner Seele. Nur finde ich mich leider nicht so vollkommen resignirt als Sie es sind. Ich fühle mich immer gedrungen, mit unserm Klopstock auszurufen: Warum muß gerade ich solange zurückbleiben? Warum vielleicht der Letzte sein? – Es wäre indessen undankbar zu verkennen, daß mir die periodische Umgebung von Kindern und Kindeskindern, ein schöner Ersatz für den Abgang der Zeitgenoßen ist, und daß meine Niedergeschlagenheit mehr leiblich als geistig ist. Der Zustand meiner Beine hat sich leider seit 6 Monathen sehr verschlimmt. Ich habe offene Wunden, die beim Verbinden sehr schmerzhaft sind und mir den nöthigen Schlaf rauben, Magen und Kopf ist bisjetzt gut, und wenn es Gott gefällt und mir dienlich ist, wird er mir die letzten Lebensjahre mildern.

(The melancholy emotions you express so beautifully in response to the demise of old friends touch harmonious chords in my soul too, but I find that I am unfortunately not completely resigned as you are. I always feel compelled to cry out with our Klopstock: 'Why must I remain behind for so long? Why even be the last one?' – It would, however, be ungrateful not to acknowledge that the periodic company of children and grandchildren is a pleasant replacement for departed contemporaries and that my despondency is more physical than spiritual. The state of my leg has deteriorated greatly in the last six months, I have open sores which are very painful and which rob me of much needed sleep. Stomach and mind remain in good order and if it so pleases God to help me, then he will ease my last years.)

Unsettled by the loss of friends, Böhl's boundless enthusiasm for learning and literature also seemed to be diminishing rapidly, commenting to Elise that the work of Goethe, Schiller and Tieck had been the pinnacle of German literature. Everything since was poor in comparison. The new *Jungdeutschland* (Young Germany) movement offered no solutions: writers such as Heine and Börne might be amusing, but that was all. Böhl also expressed disappointment at the development of French Romanticism. Having initially been quite interested in it, he now felt that it had not really come to anything, serving only to upset the Paris establishment. Instead, he sought comfort in the work of English writers who he felt best reflected his own love of 'die gute Sache'. In his final letter to August Campe on 30 April 1836, he asked that no more books be sent from Germany as he had no interest in German literature at all. The letter ends on a morbid note, asking God to release them both and reunite them in more peaceful surroundings. Sadly, his prayer would soon be answered.[11] Surrounded by his family, Böhl died on 9 November 1836. He was buried the next day in the cemetery of Santa Cruz. Francisca attempted to soldier on, but Böhl's death only served to worsen her condition. She continued to hold her salons, but produced no further literary or critical work. She passed away two years later on 14 November 1838 and was buried with her husband.

NOTES

[1] A possible example of these is found in a text published posthumously in 1856. Taken presumably from Böhl's literary estate by his daughter, Cecilia, 'Creer y obrar' (Belief and labour) appeared in the *Revista de ciencias, literatura y artes* as part of a proposed series of texts by 'el colector de la Floresta de rimas antiguas castellanas' (the collector of the Floresta). The piece presents a Catholicising diatribe on the value of faith in society and a vicious condemnation of the Age of Reason (*Revista de ciencias, literatura y artes*, II (1856), 5–7).

[2] See Hans Juretschke, 'La presencia del ideario romántico alemán en la estructura y evolución teórica del romanticismo español', *Romanticismo I. Atti del II congresso sul romantcismo spagnolo e ispanoamericano* (Genova: Biblioteca de Letterature, 1982), pp. 11–24 (p. 12); Carnero (O: 250); and Reyes Ponce (A: 109ff).

[3] This would be the last known letter to Campe for some time. There is a gap in the correspondence from 1820 to 1831. This letter is no longer extant in the Campe Collection, but is quoted by Elise Campe (VL: 92–3).

[4] Friedrich de la Motte Fouqué and Friedrich Perthes, *Ueber den deutschen Adel, über Ritter-Sinn und Militair-Ehre* (Hamburg: Perthes und Besser, 1819), p. 8.

[5] Ibid., p. 5.

[6] A further softening of his approach towards the French is also found in a letter to Julius, dated 30 May 1819, in which Böhl refers to De la Mennais and the Catholic order, the Brothers of Christian Instruction, which provokes the following, previously unthinkable response: 'Eine solche Empfänglichkeit für dergleichen, hätte ich in der französischen Zunge nicht vermuttet und ich gestehe daß ich aus diesem Grunde die Franzosen jetzt weniger haße und verachte' (Such

receptiveness to this kind of thing I would never have expected in the French tongue and I admit that for this reason I now hate and disrespect the French less).

7   *Morgenblatt für gebildete Stände*, 12 January 1820, p. 40; 13 January 1820, p. 44; and 14 January 1820, p. 48.

8   Pierre M. Irving (ed.), *The Life and Letters of Washington Irving*, 3 vols (London: Richard Bentley, 1862); II: 292–3. Further references appear in the text, denoted by the date of the letter. The correspondence between Böhl and Irving continued once the latter had taken up his post at the American Consulate in London, but eventually ceased following his return to the United States.

9   The precise beginnings of the relationship between Böhl, Gallardo and Durán remain rather clouded. Gallardo's letter of 11 January would appear to refer to the first contact between Gallardo and Böhl. However, the reference to the poet Arriaza and 'una Sa. amiga suya i mia' (a lady friend of his and mine) may suggest that Francisca also had a role to play. It would appear from a letter sent to Durán by Gallardo on 1 February 1829 that Gallardo, responding to Böhl's annoyance at not having been mentioned in the *Discurso*, supplied the latter with Durán's details and that Böhl then approached Durán. Gallardo refers to Böhl as 'el Aleman' (the German) during the early exchanges and there are previous instances in his correspondence where he may be referring to Böhl: on 30 November 1828, he refers to 'un Consul de Estranjis' (a foreign consul) who has written to him on the matter of Spanish literature and on 4 December 1828, referring to the content of the *Discurso*, he alludes to 'el changûí alemancesco i filosofal' (the German philosopher chap) which may equally be a reference to Böhl or Schlegel. Gallardo's idiosyncratic style precludes more precise interpretation.

10 *Catálogo formado por D. Bartolomé José Gallardo de los principales artículos que componían la selecta librería de D. Juan Nicolás Böhl de Faber perteneciente en el día a la Biblioteca Nacional de Madrid enmendado y anotado por D. Cayetano Alberto de la Barrera* (Madrid: Revista de Archivos, 1923).

11 August Campe died on 22 October 1836.

Chapter 12
Böhl's Mature Romantic Ideals

In many respects, the final decades of Böhl's life were the most productive. Analysis of the years from 1818 to 1836 reveals a life dedicated to scholarship and the continued struggle for the salvation of Spain's literary heritage, the rationale for which is inextricably linked to the consolidation of his mature world view. Whereas Böhl's intellectual development in his youth had centred on change and a quest for self-knowledge, his energies in maturity were focused on the defence and intensification of the value system worked out during the years at Görslow. Whilst careful to ensure that his public pronouncements remained focused on scholarly matters in his quest for entry to Spain's literary establishment, from the second phase of the Calderón polemic onwards, Böhl can be seen to revise and strengthen key values, shifting in the process towards an increasingly conservative, Catholic stance. Although perturbed by political developments in his native Germany, this shift was primarily undertaken in response to cultural and political changes in Spain. Living in Cadiz, the seat of Spanish Liberalism, Böhl's values were under palpable threat just as they had been during the Napoleonic Wars. Now, however, the emphasis had changed. Whereas the reading of early Romanticism which had driven the Calderón polemic had been fuelled by a disillusionment with alien *afrancesado* Enlightenment principles and a reaction to events in Germany and Spain during the wars of liberation, by the end of the polemic, the focus had narrowed. The political threat no longer came from France, but existed solely within Spain itself, in the guise of Liberal activism. Böhl now felt the need to defend against an enemy within and was greatly relieved to see them thwarted by the return of the king in 1823. Following the restoration, his support for Fernando VII's strict regime was unstinting. Although its censorship laws often impeded his own work, at least under the king Böhl was safe in the knowledge that the throne and altar axis he supported was no longer under threat. As the 1820s wore on, he adopted an ever more trenchant stance, simply ignoring any aspect of Spanish literary and political debate which did not relate to his own world view. This pro-Catholic, monarchical position, shored up by intense philological study of Spain's literary past, saw Böhl withdraw into the ivory-towered existence of the man of letters. In so doing, he effectively created for himself the Romantic Spain he desired, whilst ignoring the reality of a nation riven by political division, labouring under the iron rule of a king and government who had little in common with the Romantic vision of patriarchal beneficence.

Ironically, just as Spain seemed to offer monarchical stability after years of Liberal agitation, Böhl found himself increasingly disillusioned with his native Germany. The political climate there had changed since his departure in 1813, attention no longer focused on the repulsion of a common enemy. As his correspondence shows, political developments in Germany were of constant concern. He was anxious to see his Romantic ideals survive in their native environment in order to preserve the values he held so dear and felt very strongly that the axis of throne and altar was the only feasible form of government for a modern nation, be it Spain or the numerous kingdoms and principalities of his native Germany. Whilst Böhl's ideals remained anchored in the defensive nationalism of the Napoleonic era, the political landscape in the German lands had changed following the Congress of Vienna. Not only was the mood somewhat becalmed, a state of affairs promoted initially by relief at the defeat of Napoleon and then effectively enforced by the restrictions imposed by the Carlsbad Decrees, there was also a creeping tendency towards Liberalism which Böhl viewed with extreme suspicion. Whilst he was undoubtedly opposed to the theoretical strain prevalent in the southern German states, where support for the ideals of the French Revolution drove a constitutionalist agenda of the sort promoted by Liberals in Spain, he might have been expected to show more of an affinity with the historical Liberalism emerging in the north. This owed more to the values of late Romanticism in rejecting the ideals of 1789 and held up the medieval paradigm as an ideal manifestation of the organic state with the notion of limited constitutional monarchy as an ultimate aim. However, as the 1820s wore on, Böhl, unable to countenance any suggestion of constitutionalism, merely saw in this a gradual erosion of what he termed 'die gute Sache' (the good cause) and by the time the writers of the *Jungdeutschland* group emerged in the early 1830s, he had utterly rejected modern German culture and taken refuge in his philological study and the remnants of British Romanticism. These responses to developments in both Germany and Spain are central to Böhl's work from 1818 onwards and his scholarship must be understood in this political, ideological context, as a reaction to Liberalism and a defence of 'die gute Sache'.

Despite a level of conscious self-censorship which saw Böhl's more vehement pronouncements consigned to the writing desk in the knowledge that they would be too much for prevailing taste, some evidence of his mature stance had already begun to emerge during the second phase of the Calderón polemic. A shift in emphasis is apparent as the debate widens to include issues which are not directly related to the value of Golden Age theatre, but which instead form part of Böhl's defence of that theatre as the aesthetic representation of a specific world view. There are a number of documents in the *Pasatiempos*, including the 'Noticias originales literarias', which reveal this process, but perhaps the most significant in demonstrating the correlation between Böhl's aesthetic and political ideals is his translation in 1818 in the second *Pasatiempo* of extracts from August Wilhelm Schlegel's first *Wiener Vorlesung*, 'Lo que entiende Schlegel por poesía romancesca, extractado de su obra sobre el arte y literatura dramática, impresa en Heidelberg 1809' (What Schlegel means by romantic poetry, extracted from his work on dramatic art and literature published in Heidelberg in 1809).[1] In presenting the text, Böhl employs a technique similar to that used in his 1805 exposition of Schiller's Kantian aesthetics and Schlegel's later lectures, selecting the material most relevant to his argument, whilst glossing over or ignoring other topics. Although, on this occasion, he does carefully state that the work offered is in extracted form, there is nevertheless a marked editorial emphasis. In presenting Schlegel's text, Böhl focuses on the definition of Romanticism, the problematic nature of Classicism in the modern world, the role of Christianity and the significance of chivalry to patriotism. That Böhl sought to emphasise these issues is underlined by his omission of Schlegel's comments relating to music, architecture and the plastic arts, thus keeping the focus of his translation firmly on the subject of literature and its relation to the nation and faith.

Böhl's eclectic approach is immediately evident. Bypassing Schlegel's prefatory comments, which describe his intentions and terminology, Böhl opens his translation with the Schlegelian attack on universal rules and its discussion of how the revival of Greek in the Middle Ages eventually led to the current fixation with the unities. Here, Böhl's translation remains quite faithful to the original, omitting only one small section comparing superficial rules to the transience of a child's garden made of picked flowers. (This omission was perhaps judicious, given Mora's vicious response to other, less fanciful comparisons earlier in the polemic.) As the piece progresses, however, Böhl's translation technique begins to display some familiar characteristics. Particularly significant is his approach in dealing with Schlegel's comments on the role of Christianity which follows the translator's own ideological agenda by emphasising the value of faith within the cultural framework of the new aesthetic. Schlegel views Christianity as a reviving force in an essentially moribund Europe:

Und dies ist denn auch im neueren Europa durch die Einführung des Christentums geschehen. Diese ebenso erhabene als wohltätige Religion hat die erschöpfte und versunkene alte Welt wiedergeboren; sie ist das lenkende Prinzip in der Geschichte der neueren Völker geworden; und noch jetzt, da viele ihrer Erziehung entwachsen zu sein wähnen, werden sie in der Ansicht aller menschlichen Dinge weit mehr durch deren Einfluß bestimmt, als sie es selbst wissen. (24)

(And this is what has actually taken place in modern Europe through the introduction of Christianity. This sublime and beneficent religion has regenerated the ancient world from its state of exhaustion and debasement; it is the guiding principle in the history of modern nations and even at this day, when many suppose they have shaken off its authority, they still find themselves much more influenced by it in their views of human affairs than they themselves are aware. [24–5])

In this critical appraisal of the ancient world, Schlegel highlights the positive, all-pervasive influence of the Christian faith, something which Böhl is keen to underline. His translation generalises and summarises, removing all reference to specific geographic regions. Whilst this may detract from Schlegel's original argument by partially divesting it of its context, Böhl's sweeping translation also effectively broadens the claimed impact of Christianity by erasing all boundaries. Schlegel's references to Europe and the ancient world are lost as Böhl endows his comments with a general, global significance:

El Cristianismo reconcentró al hombre. Esta Religion tan sublime como piadosa, ha regenerado al mundo, y es el registro que dirige la historia moderna; y aun, en el dia, cuando muchos imaginan haberse substraido á su imperio, se hallan influidos por ella, sin percibirlo, en todas sus opiniones. (IIIP: 80)

(Christianity brought man back to his centre. This religion, as sublime as it is kind, regenerated the world and it is the regulator which directs modern history; even now, today, when many imagine they have been able to escape its authority, they still find themselves influenced by it, without knowing, in all of their opinions.)

Generalisations then give way to apparently intentional ambivalences as the rendition of individual terms becomes crucial. Böhl's choice of 'piadosa' to render 'wohltätig' (beneficent) is telling. Meaning 'kind' or 'merciful', it can also be read as 'pious' or 'devout', thus heightening the religious import of the text. Similar tactics are employed later in rendering Schlegel's term 'eine höhere Weisheit' (a superior wisdom), which remains open to interpretation, as 'la revelacion' (revelation), a concept central to Böhl's own experience, which carries added Christian significance and which places far greater emphasis on the issue of faith.

The importance of faith to the chivalric character of the medieval ideal is also central to Böhl's vision. Consequently, Schlegel's attempt to justify the less morally correct actions inherent in chivalry is also subject to Böhl's editorial bias. Schlegel's original text depicts chivalric honour as a manifestation of human independence:

Da das Christentum sich nicht, wie der Götterdienst der alten Welt, mit gewissen äußern Leistungen begnügte, sondern den ganzen inneren Menschen mit seinen leisesten Regungen in Anspruch nahm, so rettete sich das Gefühl der sittlichen Selbstsändigkeit in das Gebiet der Ehre hinüber: gleichsam einer weltlichen Sittenlehre neben der religiösen, die sich oft im Widerspruche mit dieser behauptete, aber ihr dennoch insofern verwandt war, daß sie niemals die Folgen berechnete, sondern unbedingt Grundsätze des Handelns heiligte, als Glaubenswahrheiten über alle Untersuchung grübelnder Vernunft erhaben. (24–5)

(As Christianity did not, like the heathen worship, rest satisfied with certain external acts, but claimed an authority over the whole inward man and the most hidden movements of the heart, the feeling of moral independence took refuge in the domain of honour, a worldly morality, as it were, which subsisting alongside, was often at variance with that of religion, but yet in so far resembling it that it never calculated consequences, but consecrated unconditionally certain principles of action, which, like the articles of faith, were elevated far beyond the investigation of a casuistical reasoning. [25])

Schlegel sanctions a sphere of activity beyond faith which acknowledges humanity's drive to act independently. Although this is tempered through association with a set of guiding principles, grounded in honour, such activity outwith the legitimising guidance of Christian doctrine does not accord with Böhl's specifically Catholic understanding of chivalry. Instead, in his version, this independence is ascribed only to the hero, almost as a negative trait, untamed by faith and found in only a few. Böhl shortens Schlegel's portrayal and renders it in far less sympathetic terms, removing the moral emphasis of the original:

La parte de independencia característica del héroe que no podia ser domada por la Religion, se refugió en la esfera del honor, formando una legislacion mundanal en oposicion á la cristiana, pero parecida á ella en cuanto á no calcular las consecuencias materiales, y á sancionar máxîmas de conducta independientes de las cavilaciones de la reflexîon. (IIIP: 81)

(The part of the characteristic independence of the hero which could not be dominated by religion took refuge in the sphere of honour, forming a worldly legislation in opposition to the Christian, but similar to it in as far as it did not calculate consequences and sanctioned principles of conduct independent of the ruminations of reflection.)

The emphasis of Böhl's translation is clear. He makes a virtue of the denial of reason, whilst glossing over the potential moral argument for an independent set of values beyond those of Christian teaching. In so doing, he once more realigns Schlegel's original argument in order to preserve his own view of the Christian, chivalric values inherent in both Spain's national literature and the character of the people.

The tenor of Böhl's translation of Schlegel's first lecture is echoed in two further texts which appear, perhaps significantly, at the end of the third *Pasatiempo*. Each places an emphasis on the value of religious belief for art and the individual, thus leaving the reader with a lasting impression of Böhl's traditional values as the polemic draws to a close. In the first of these texts, 'De la moralidad del teatro' (On morality in the theatre), Böhl argues that morality is central to any theatrical masterpiece, although this is a different morality from that of the pulpit. Böhl describes the latter as direct, whereas the moral message of the theatre ought to be implicit. To explain the value of morality, itself grounded in the Catholic faith, Böhl outlines the various types of moral to be found in different types of theatre. In so doing, he maintains his polemical stance, consistently depicting modern theatre in a negative light, whilst levelling criticism at a number of prominent playwrights including Jovellanos. According to Böhl, tragedy is a struggle between passion and dignity which teaches us to suffer. This message has, however, lost its impact in the new sentimental genre which rewards good and punishes evil, an approach which Böhl finds dishonest in its superficial optimism: 'quisieramos que esos profundos moralistas nos indicasen á donde se hallan ese recompensar de virtudes que nos pintan' (we would like the profound moralists to tell us where to find this reward of virtue which they show us; IIIP: 65). It does not take long for Böhl to trace this degeneration to the Enlightenment, as he turns his attention to moral comedies, which, he claims, began to emerge with the rise of the Encyclopaedists:

> Era consiguiente que cuando se trataba de socabar la Religion se procurase substituirle una especie de moralidad natural envuelta en retóricas retumbantes, para persuadir al hombre que con ella sola podria ser virtuoso y feliz. Esta moralidad despojada de la autoridad cristiana, y ataviada de la molicie y blandura que modernamente ha usurpado el nombre de bondad, seducía á los incautos, y minaba sordamente la veneracion debida á las verdades reveladas. Mas daño han hecho á la fé religiosa las comedias morales oidos por concursos numerosos, que las impiedades metafísicas de Spinosa, Mirabaud y La Metrie, que pocos tienen proporcion y paciencia de leer. (IIIP: 66–7)

> (It followed that when they tried to undermine religion, they tried to substitute it with a kind of natural morality wrapped in bombastic rhetoric in order to persuade man that with it alone he could be virtuous and happy. This morality, divested of Christian authority, and endowed with the softness and blandness which has usurped the name of goodness in modern times, seduced the unwary and silently undermined the veneration owed to the revealed truths. More damage has been done to religious faith by the moral comedies heard at any number of contests than by all the metaphysical impieties of Spinoza, Mirabaud and La Metrie, who few have the opportunity or patience to read.)

This launches a double criticism, attacking those thinkers who alienate even the educated, whilst decrying too the modern theatre which poisons the minds of the populace by virtue of its facile depiction of morality. Böhl's fears for the survival of his world in the face of such threats are clear and the emphasis placed on the value of revealed truths highlights the continued immediacy of his faith. This is further underlined in the final text to appear in the third *Pasatiempo*, 'Del entusiasmo, segun la Baronesa de Stael' (On enthusiasm, according to Baroness de Staël). Taken from the concluding chapters of *De l'Allemagne*, this plea for a high Romantic, emotive appreciation of life, art and faith focuses less on morality and more on the divine presence in the individual. Böhl's rendition of de Staël emphasises the religious and moral tone of her argument at the expense of other elements, although he is also careful to exploit her argument in order to draw attention once more to the value of tradition and popular culture, as well as to criticise the dominance of reason. Using the authority of de Staël's text to draw together the threads of his own argument, Böhl then ends his translation with a catechising paragraph of his own which highlights the centrality of faith to all aspects of life:

> En fin, siendo los elementos del entusiasmo la admiracion, el amor y el desprendimiento, afectos todos tan íntimamente unidos á la Religion, es indudable que como fé, caridad y esperanza, nos consolarán hasta en los umbrales de la muerte. (IIIP: 74)

> (So, given that the elements of enthusiasm are admiration, love and generosity, all aspects intimately linked to religion, there is no doubt that like faith, hope and charity, they will console us unto the threshold of death.)

These are the closing words of the third *Pasatiempo* and it is telling in the context of Böhl's development that the defence of Calderón, an undertaking which began with such revolutionary, albeit reactionary, drive, should end in such a moralistic fashion. Yet, these words indicate the extent of Böhl's disquiet and his need to see his values securely drawn together in a coherent defence of the Romantic cause as he has chosen to understand it.[2]

Given this continued Romantic emphasis, it is no surprise that Böhl, dismayed by events in Spain in the years leading up to and including the Liberal Triennial, should turn once more to the stalwarts of German Romanticism for confirmation of his views. This time, it was Friedrich Schlegel who seemed to provide the solace and inspiration Böhl required. Just as events were reaching crisis point in Liberal Cadiz, a group of conservative thinkers were forming around Schlegel in Vienna. These men, whose particular brand of high Romantic political thought would become known as *Wiener Romantik* (Viennese Romanticism), included prominent theological and sociological thinkers such as Adam Müller (1779–1829) and Karl Ludwig von Haller (1768–1854). Anxious for a forum, Schlegel founded the periodical *Concordia*, which appeared in six parts from 1820 to 1823. Many of the contributors, including Schlegel himself, were Catholic converts and Böhl found his own views reflected in theirs. Significantly, the appearance of *Concordia* coincides almost precisely with the Liberal Triennial in Spain. In such a context, this pro-Catholic, pro-monarchist publication must have seemed like an oracle of sense and wisdom to Böhl, faced with the prospect of constitution and Liberalism in his adopted homeland. In it, he found a number of texts and treatises which supported his political, religious and aesthetic ideals, including Schlegel's review of the religious poems of La Martine, a poet often praised by Böhl in his correspondence with Julius, and Franz Baader's appreciation of Stolberg's late writings. Also to Böhl's taste were Adam Müller's contributions outlining a domestic governmental policy based on theological foundations. Perhaps the key text, however, for both the *Wiener Romantik* group and Böhl himself, was Schlegel's lengthy assessment of the age, 'Signatur des Zeitalters' (Signature of the age).[3] This was an extreme work, but it provided Böhl with a palatable counterpoint to the arguments prevailing in his adopted homeland. Suggesting clear approval for the absolutism favoured by Böhl, Schlegel attacks the Protestant church, the Enlightenment, Liberalism and constitutionalism, whilst advocating a return to feudalism and the values of the Middle Ages as the foundation for political stability and a just society. The affinity between Schlegel's thought and that of Böhl is reflected in the apparent currency of Böhl's favoured phraseology. His much vaunted 'gute Sache' echoes Schlegel's notion of 'das gute Prinzip' (the good principle) as polar opposite to 'das böse Prinzip' (the evil principle) which had emerged from the Enlightenment:

Wir wollen dieses gute Prinzip zuerst nicht nur im ganz allgemeinen Umriß auffassen und bezeichnen, als das lebendige Positive; denn dieses ist in allen Dingen des Lebens und in allen Verhältnissen der Gesellschaft, das innerlich und äußerlich Feste, das dauernd Gewisse, das wirksam Reelle; dagegen das Absolute, gleich der blinden Elementarkraft in der Natur, den organischen Zusammenhang zerschneidend, geradeaus, oder 'Rücksichtslos', wie man im praktischen Leben sagt, schrankenlos und isoliert herausgerissen, aller Ruhe feind ist, und doch sein Ziel nie erreichen kann, mithin durch und durch zerstörend wirkt. (279–80)

(We want first of all not only to understand and describe this good principle in general terms as the living positive, for this is the internal and external permanence, the lasting certainty, the effective actuality in all areas of life and in all social relations; in contrast, the absolute, just like the blind elemental power of nature, which tears apart organic coherence, directly or 'thoughtlessly', as one says in practical life, ripped out, unconstrained and isolated, is the enemy of all peace and yet cannot reach its goal and therefore has a thoroughly destructive effect.)

This round condemnation of the abstract absolute rejects Enlightenment universality and the political ideals which underpin it as Schlegel rails against the dismantling of feudal structures and the introduction of republicanism. He supports his argument by tracing the degeneration of society through the ages since the Reformation in an argument which parallels that put forward by Novalis some twenty years earlier. Böhl's approval of this late Romantic political ideal and his enthusiasm for the return of Fernando VII in 1823 are symptomatic of his unshakable faith in the axis of throne and altar. In both Schlegel's text and the iron rule of the Ominous Decade, Böhl finds confirmation of the political beliefs which underpin his understanding of aesthetics and philology during the last decade of his life. In the years following the restoration of the monarchy, Böhl is increasingly drawn to writers and works of a conservative nature, whilst revisiting the work of writers previously considered exemplary in order to revalue their work with a conservative, Catholic emphasis which further underlines his ideological affinity with the *Wiener Romantik* group.

Indicative of this is Böhl's revised reception of early Romantic thought. The ideas which once informed Böhl as he broke free from Campe's influence now find themselves the subject of re-emphasis and reinterpretation as he seeks to legitimise and consolidate his mature stance. This is particularly evident in relation to the Romantic apotheosis of Spain's Moorish past, which Böhl, intent on preserving the nation's Catholic heritage, could not countenance. Despite having earlier included the positive reference to Arab influence in his translation of Schlegel, he later became quite hostile to any material dealing with Oriental topics, commenting to Julius on 23 December 1821 that he was not 'morgenländisch gestimmt' (disposed towards the Orient) and even rejecting Goethe's *West-östlicher Diwan* (Poems from West and East, 1819).[4] Such was Böhl's desire to present a pure, Catholic vision of Spain's past that he even went so far as to reject any Moorish-style designs for the frontispiece of the *Floresta*. Yet this rejection of the Oriental in Spain is clearly at odds with the Romantic reading of the nation and also contradicts the historicist view of Herder. Accordingly, in taking this stance, Böhl placed himself outside the literary historical tradition which had hitherto informed his appreciation of Spanish culture. In Herderian terms, outlined in the *Humanitätsbriefe* (Letters on humanity, 1796), the Arab influence is emphasised as a source of civilisation in southern Europe. Although the Moors were banished from Spain or forced to convert to Christianity following the *Reconquista*, their legends and heroes were assimilated quite quickly into the Spanish cultural consciousness, providing colour and individuality.[5] This aspect of Spain's culture also fascinated the Romantics. Friedrich Schlegel in particular praised the Moorish element in his *Gespräch über die Poesie* (Discourse on poetry, 1800) and reiterated his appreciation in the *Beiträge zur Geschichte der modernen Poesie und Nachricht von provenzalischen Manuskripte* (Contributions to the history of modern poetry and report on Provencal manuscripts, 1803). None of this impressed the staunchly Catholic Böhl. He might have been influenced by Herder and Schlegel, but he could not agree with the view that it was the Arab element which made Spain's culture different. In rejecting both Herder's *Araberthese* and its Romantic reception at this later stage in his career, Böhl is once more seen to focus on those elements of late Enlightenment and early Romantic theory which best suit his specifically Catholic defence of Spain's national culture, adopting and assimilating Herder's love of the *romance*, whilst firmly rejecting the apotheosis of Spain's Moorish past. This foreshadows a broader reappraisal of early Romantic ideals, examples of which begin to appear in his later correspondence. For example, writing to Durán on 17 January 1832, Böhl rejects the notion of a synthesis of Christian and Greek mythologies, one of the cornerstones of the Schlegelian notion of a 'neue Mythologie' (new mythology), and in a subsequent letter, dated 11 May, he also expresses reservations at the mixing of genres, again rejecting a key element in early Romantic theory. These are little more than asides in the context of Böhl's correspondence with Durán, but they show a shift in attitude from the Görslow years, one which consistently seeks a specifically Catholic emphasis.

Böhl's revaluation of early German Romantic theory during the 1820s and 1830s reflects a gradual disillusionment with letters in his native Germany. Although his interest in new German literature continued throughout the 1820s, his responses to later Romantic works were often ambivalent and at times disinterested. Tieck and Fouqué meet with both praise and criticism, whilst Hoffmann is the subject of much superficial interest. Arnim, Brentano and the Brothers Grimm feature in the correspondence with Julius, but no significant comments are passed on their later work. Often, the sense conveyed is one of disappointment, something apparent too in his ongoing engagement with the work of Goethe. Although the latter continues to provide Böhl with stimulation, the response is no longer always positive, as his attitude to the *Diwan* shows. Writing to Julius on 23 December 1821, Böhl gives a damning critique of *Wilhelm Meisters Wanderjahre* (Wilhelm Meister's journey years, 1821):

An Göthes M[eisters] Wanderungen habe ich mich wenig erbaut – Die heilige Familie scheint mir flach und geistloos: das pädagogische Land eine langweilige utopische Fratze: die interessanten Liebschaften des 50Jährigen bleiben leider Fragment: die Verwechslung der Schwestern am Schluß ist sehr gewöhnlich. Kurz nur das Mährchen & die eingestreuten Bemerkungen über Menschen und Dinge haben meinen unbedingten Beifall.

(I took little sustenance from Goethe's M. wanderings – The holy family seemed flat and spiritless to me: the pedagogical land a boring, utopian, ugly creation: the interesting love affairs of the fifty year old sadly remain a fragment: the mix up with the sisters at the end is very ordinary. In short, only the fairytale and the smattering of comments on people and things meet with my unconditional approval.)

These comments show how much Böhl has come to expect from Goethe as a spiritual and intellectual guide. Although later comments show that he still has an affinity with Goethe's work, praising *Faust* (1808) as 'eine hohe Zierde unserer sonst so rauhen Sprache' (a great embellishment of our otherwise rough language; letter to Julius, 6 August 1822), there is nevertheless an air of dissatisfaction with his later work which is further underlined by Böhl's positive reception of the work of Johann Friedrich Wilhelm Pustkuchen (1793–1834). Pustkuchen was a Protestant clergyman who published a number of religious and educational texts, including *Wilhelm Meisters Wanderjahre* (1821–7), the first part of which appeared in the same year as Goethe's own continuation of the Wilhelm Meister theme. Pustkuchen's text was seen by many as a critique of Goethe and unleashed a controversy which saw the priest vilified for attacking such a revered figure.[6] Undeterred, Pustkuchen continued his project, publishing four further volumes, as well as two appendices entitled *Wilhelm Meisters Tagebuch* (Wilhelm Meister's diary, 1822) and *Gedanken einer frommen Gräfin* (Thoughts of a pious duchess, 1822), both of which, like the so-called 'false' *Wanderjahre*, sought to provide moral and religious guidance. Much of what Pustkuchen had to say appealed to Böhl's increasingly trenchant world view. Although perhaps not an obvious choice for someone defending a strictly Catholic stance, the Protestant Pustkuchen had absorbed many of the same influences as Böhl, including Idealism, pantheism and the work of Friedrich Schlegel, Jean Paul and Herder. He had also been a pupil of Bouterwek at Göttingen. Böhl, possibly unaware of Pustkuchen's religious background, clearly felt he had found someone whose views and values echoed his. He was particularly impressed by the two appendices, commenting that 'in dem Tagebuche W. M. habe ich mich ganz wiedergefunden: sie sind so öfters ein Kommentar meiner Pasatiempos' (I found myself again in W. M.'s diary: they are so often a commentary on my *Pasatiempos*) and praising Pustkuchen for attacking Goethe's 'Gottlosigkeit' (Godlessness). The former's staunch beliefs and catechistic style provided Böhl with a fresh perspective on Goethe's work from which to set about the revaluation of an old exemplar according to increasingly conservative criteria. Particularly significant is the continued fixation with Goethe's seemingly questionable religious values, which reflects Böhl's growing dissatisfaction with the moral and religious propriety of contemporary German letters. His faith in the work of his compatriots is shaken to such an extent that, by 1823, he has begun to express fears that the Romantic cause in Germany is in danger of utter demise:

> Wenn ich daran denke daß Schloßers Fievée, Schlegels Konkordia & Tieks Phantasus ohne Fortsetzungen bleiben, so wäre ich geneigt an dem Fortgang der guten Sache in Deutschland zu zweifeln. Dann aber kommt mir der wohlbeliebte Haller in den Sinn dessen vier wenngleich treffliche doch sehr schwerfällige Bände schon eine zweite Auflage erlebten und ich tröste mich. Daß Sie mir die franz[ösische] Uebers[etzung]

der Hallerschen Schrift gegen den Sp[anischen] K[ortes] nicht gesandt haben ist eine arge Uebersicht. Diesen Augenblick wäre sie schon in spanisch uebers[etzt] und thäte sicherlich Wirkung. (21 February 1823)

(When I think that Schlosser's Fievée, Schlegel's Concordia and Tieck's Phantasus all remain without continuation, then I would be inclined to doubt the progress of the good cause in Germany. Then, however, I think of the much loved Haller and his four albeit first class, but nevertheless difficult, volumes and am comforted. That you have not sent me the French translation of Haller's writings against the Spanish [cortes] is an annoying oversight. They would be in Spanish translation by now and would surely do some good.)

The positive appraisal of Haller notwithstanding, by the mid-1820s, Böhl's assessment of contemporary German letters was increasingly negative.[7] On 28 May 1824, he comments to Julius that 'Schuberts Wanderbüchlein ist eine der interessantesten Erscheinungen in unserer jetzt so *matten* deutschen Literatur' (Schubert's Wanderbüchlein is one the most interesting publications in our otherwise so bland German literature), adding later 'im Ganzen jedoch stehen wir weit gegen die jetzt so glänzende britannische Literatur zurück' (on the whole, however, we are so far behind the so brilliant British literature of the day). These comments exemplify the difficulty Böhl had in finding a taste for more recent German writing and his choice of Romantic anthropologist and pupil of Herder, Gotthilf Heinrich von Schubert (1780–1860), as a praiseworthy exponent is telling. The text in question, Schubert's *Wanderbüchlein eines reisenden Gelehrten nach Salzburg, Tirol und der Lombardei* (Diary of a travelling scholar in Salzburg, Tyrol and Lombardy, 1823), is essentially a travel journal which has perhaps more in common with the nascent trend of *costumbrismo* and the depiction of manners than the complex and imaginative works of Goethe and the Romantics. It would appear that Böhl's increasingly conservative taste leads him to seek reassurance in literary mediocrity, apparently unwilling to engage in any depth with new developments which might offend his world view, even if the work in question is aesthetically appealing. This tendency is apparent in his response to Heine, whom he referred to as 'el diablo predicador' (the preaching devil).[8] Writing to Julius on 19 October 1827, Böhl expresses his frustration with the new writer:

Von dem letzten Packet von Perthes haben mich die Schriften des ruchlosen Heine außerordentlich interessirt. Ich ärgere mich blau und blass an ihm & werde nicht müde ihn zu lesen. Die Nordsee sind ganz originale Gedichte und der darin waltende humour spricht mich recht eigentlich an. Wenn er aber den kleinen Byron spielt und seiner abgeschmackten Vergötterung Bonapartes die Zügel schießen läßt, dann ist er um so widerlicher da man es bei seinem Geiste nur als eine bezweckte Verhöhnung des Publikums ansehen kann, gleichsam als wolle er sehen <u>wieviel sich die deutschen Leser bieten lassen.</u>

(From the last package sent by Perthes I was very much interested by the writings of the dastardly Heine. He makes me <u>terribly</u> angry and I do not tire of reading him. The <u>North Sea</u> are most original poems and the <u>humour</u> which characterises them really appeals to me. However, when he plays the little Byron and lets his tasteless deification of Bonaparte run loose, then he is even more disgusting for one can only see this, given his spirit, as a deliberate mockery of the public, as if he wanted to see <u>how much German readers would put up with</u>.)

Implicit here is the correlation between the aesthetic and the personal so typical of Böhl's Romanticism. Heine's *Nordsee* poems must have struck a chord with him, as he once more longed for a return to his north German homeland and faced the prospect of never seeing his mother again. The sense of Romantic longing diminishes when faced with the reality of Heine's political views and religious attitudes. Certainly, his Jewish origins and conversion to Protestantism in 1825 in an attempt to improve his social standing cannot have endeared him to the fervently Catholic Böhl. However, it is Heine's political stance, informed by the nascent French socialism of the Saint-Simonian movement, as well as his professed admiration for Napoleon, which would have offended most. With Heine now lauded as the rising star of the literary world, it seems that German letters have nothing left to offer. Böhl's disgust reaches its peak in 1831. Writing to Julius on 26 January, he explains that he is returning a number of books as he feels himself to be out of touch with the 'zwecklose Grübeleien der Deutschen' (pointless broodings of the Germans).

No longer in tune with thought in his native Germany, Böhl increasingly found himself drawn towards English literature and criticism which he felt had remained faithful to 'die gute Sache'. Indeed, he was pleased to see the influence of German Romanticism spread elsewhere and in a letter to Elise Campe in June 1831 he refers to the changing aesthetic climate in Great Britain and France where German Romanticism is now much admired. It is in his reading of the literary periodicals of the period, however, that Böhl's attitudes to developments in German and British literary taste are most apparent. As early as 18 August 1819, Böhl commented to Julius that he found German periodicals to be far inferior to their British counterparts. Later, on 1 November 1822, he makes the following critical remarks:

Es ist doch sonderbar, daß es niemals in Deutschland zu einem eigentlich litterarischen Journal kommt, einer wirklichen Litteratur Zeitung aber ohne förmliche Rezensionen und in mässigen wöchentlichen oder monathlichen Heften, mit Nachrichten über Bücher, Verfaßer, Nekrologien, Aukzionen etc kurz alles was den bloßen Litteraten interessirt.

(It is rather strange that there is never a proper literary journal in Germany, a proper literary newspaper, but without formal reviews and in measured weekly or monthly editions, with news about books, editors, necrologies, auctions, etc., in short everything which interests the purely literary man.)

Unable to find what he needed on the German market, Böhl turned to the British literary press. On 22 September 1821, his enthusiasm is such that he reports having purchased the entire run to date of the Tory *Quarterly Review*, impressed by its political if not its aesthetic stance. The *Retrospective Review*, with its sympathetic revival of sixteenth and seventeenth-century literature, also draws favourable comment. The Whig *Edinburgh Review*, once a useful source of support during the polemic years, is now deemed utterly unpalatable, its reception quite different from the warm praise reserved for its Tory rival, *Blackwood's Magazine*:

Alle meine Ahnungen und Andeutungen finden sich darin entwickelt. Ich gestehe daß ich nie einen litterarischen Genuß gehabt habe der diesem zu vergleichen wäre! – Erstlich die völlige Anerkennung meines herrlichen Wordsworth, den Blackwood nie müde wird zu erheben und zu loben. Zweitens die tiefen deutschen Ansichten von Geschichte Kunst Poesie und Kritik die unter dem Namen von Lauerwinckel und Kempfershausen diese Zeitschrift zieren. Drittens die einzige unnachahmliche Laune womit Tickler die Verfaßer der Edinburgh Review abstraft. Viertens die Kenntnis der deutschen und dänischen Litteratur & die Vorliebe für dieselben.

(All my presentiments and suggestions are developed in it. I admit that I have never experienced a literary pleasure to compare with it! – First, the full recognition of my wonderful Wordsworth, who Blackwood never tires of elevating and praising. Secondly, the deep, German views on history, art, poetry and criticism which adorn this periodical under the names Lauerwinckel and Kempfershausen. Thirdly, the singular inimitable humour with which Tickler upbraids the editors of the Edinburgh Review. Fourthly, the knowledge of German and Danish literature and the preference for the same.)

Blackwood's approval of Wordsworth provides Böhl with a reflection of his own views which he clearly finds reassuring. This is underlined a month later, when he describes the publication as 'ein Kommentar der Pasatiempos was Litteratur betrifft' (a commentary on the *Pasatiempos* when it comes to literature). However, by 1824, Böhl was beginning to lose faith in *Blackwood's*, mainly due to what he feels to be the editors' inaccurate assessment of Catholic Spain and Fernando VII. The periodical was highly critical of the restored regime, claiming with some insistence that:

> [. . .] the conduct of Ferdinand VII has been consistent with no intelligible principle of any kind, that is worthy of being regarded with any species of tolerance. HE has been guilty of the basest treachery of ALL – and has stamped THE WHOLE of his own character with one dye of unrelieved blackness.⁹

Were this not enough, Böhl was forced to recoil completely when faced with the editors' vehement opposition to Catholic emancipation. His favour turned instead to the new *Foreign Quarterly Review*, which contained a number of essays on German literature by Thomas Carlyle (1795–1881), who was acquainted with Julius. Böhl's interest in the reappraisal of German Romantic literature which was spearheaded by Carlyle in the late 1820s and which centred on older German poetry and the work of Goethe and Schiller, sees him once more crossing national and cultural boundaries in order to find verification of his world view. Ironically, but nevertheless in keeping with his earlier enthusiasm for Schlegel's apotheosis of Calderón, Böhl now finds himself obliged to seek appreciation of German Romantic theory from the pens of British writers and critics, where once he might have been able to rely on German periodicals such as the *Vaterländisches Museum*.

It was not only the periodical press which drew Böhl's attention at this time. As the 1820s unfolded, Böhl spent ever more time reading English literature. He remained critical of Byron, unable to countenance his positive appraisal of Napoleon, but had some sympathy for the work of Sir Walter Scott (1771–1832) and the 'Ettrick Shepherd', James Hogg (1770–1835). It was Wordsworth, however, particularly in his early work, who remained a constant source of inspiration. Responding with open jealousy to Julius' report of a visit to England, Böhl bemoans the fact that he can no longer undertake such a journey. Had he been able to, his destination would have been Cumberland on a pilgrimage to see Wordsworth, commenting that the Lake poet 'für meine Sinnesart noch immer der erste aller Dichter ist, gerade weil er das Gewöhnliche mit dem Allerhöchsten zu verknüpfen weiss' (for my disposition, [he] is still the first among all poets because he knows how to combine the ordinary with the highest of all). Through Wordsworth, Böhl became aware of other writers, including George Crabbe (1754–1832), and as the decade progresses, he became convinced of the superiority of English literature over German works. However, in his quest to identify worthy successors to his hero Wordsworth, his focus is less on the great writers of that age than on the relatively minor exponents of the Lake School. He is particularly impressed by John Wilson (1785–1854), the author of *Light and*

Böhl's Mature Romantic Ideals

Shadows of Scotch Life (1822), *The Trials of Margaret Lindsay* (1823) and *The Foresters* (1825), as well as *Sayings and Doings* (1823) by Theodore Hook (1788–1841). This choice of works is at first glance unusual for a literary man once drawn to the aesthetic intricacies of German Romantic literature and the allegorical depth of Spain's Golden Age. Wilson and Hook are moralists and mannerists of a mediocre nature, their works worthy portraits of rural life with an emphasis on faith and morality. Again, Böhl's taste seems minded towards the *costumbrismo* of the mid-century, shying away from more challenging works, even passing over the work of the later Romantics such as Southey, whose interest in Spain attracts little attention in Böhl's commentary of the period. Instead, he seems deliberately to choose works which will leave his mature world view intact.

This tendency is reflected in Böhl's choice of associates at this late stage in his career. Typical is his relationship with Washington Irving. Böhl had been an admirer of Irving's work for some time, recording in his literary notebooks as early as May 1824 that he found the first volume of Irving's *History of New York* (1809) 'magnífico, y de un humor excelente' (magnificent, and of an excellent humour). Reflecting his taste in English literature, he was most impressed, however, by the depiction of shire life in *Bracebridge Hall* (1822) 'con su gracioso mezcolanza de humor y altos sentimientos' (with its charming mixture of humour and high sentiment).[10] As their correspondence shows, the two men spent a great deal of their time together discussing Spain's literary past and sharing resources. In a letter dated 6 February 1828, a hastily written list, which included *Vindicaciones*, shows that Irving not only borrowed material pertinent to his own studies, but also came to know the work of Navarrete and, of course, Böhl himself. Whilst there is no record of a direct response to *Vindicaciones*, the same letter shows Irving's clear sympathies with Böhl's polemic stance:

> Do you ever see a new literary paper published in Madrid entitled El Correo Literario y Mercantil. I observe that the critics who write for it consider the late dramatic writer Moratín as superior to Calderón, Lope de Vega and all the old school. How little do these degenerate Spaniards know of what they ought to be proud of. When I see them tamely bending the neck to the yoke of French dramatic rule, I despair of ever beholding a renewal of the ancient literary glory of Spain.

Later the same year, on 7 April, Irving revisits the subject, this time with reference to the Spanish translation of Bouterwek's history of Spanish literature which, it was thought, would cause an outcry:

> The Spanish literates seem vexed that one of their number should take pains to translate and augment a history of their literature written by a foreigner. They are

singularly capricious and touchy on this subject. They turn their backs upon their old writers and are then piqued when they find strangers appreciate them more than they do themselves. They are like some husbands who neglect their wives, but are ready to draw the sword the moment they detect a stranger ogling them.

The frustration apparent in Irving's letter echoes a view expressed by Böhl on many occasions during the polemic. The affinity this suggests is, however, limited. As an enthusiastic citizen of the new American republic, Irving makes a clear distinction between the aesthetic value of Spain's older literature and the political ideals which that literature promotes. As Ivan Jakšić has argued, Irving views Spain's past as an example of chivalry and religious extremism at its worst.[11] Rather than serve as a paradigm for future stability, as is the case with Böhl's vision, in Irving's analysis there is a warning of the negative potential of such characteristics as the path to potential decay. The ambivalence of his attitude is made clear in his 1835 *Legends of the Conquest of Spain*:

Spain is virtually a land of poetry and romance, where everyday life partakes of adventure, and where the least agitation or excitement carries everything up into extravagant enterprise and daring exploit. The Spaniards, in all ages, have been of swelling and braggart spirit, soaring in thought, pompous in word, and valiant, though vainglorious in deed.[12]

Here, the very elements of the Spanish character praised by Böhl in his Schlegelian apotheosis are singled out for criticism by Irving as extreme. The nation's poetic nature is not overwhelmingly positive, but rather one which leads the populace into ill-considered action and a tendency towards self-importance. Therefore, whilst the American writer clearly understood Böhl's philological drive and supported the reappraisal and preservation of Spain's literary heritage in aesthetic terms, he would have found it impossible to share his political views. To Böhl, however, these views were an integral element in his philological project: by saving the poetry of the past, he could help salvage the spirit which produced it.

NOTES

[1] E. Lohner (ed.), *A. W. Schlegel, Kritische Schriften und Briefe*; V: *Vorlesungen über dramatische Kunst und Literatur – Erster Teil* (1966); references appear in the text. Translations are taken from Black's edition.

[2] That Böhl felt that these values were under particular threat in Spain itself is apparent in his correspondence. His reading during the period continued to centre on religious as well as literary material and he despairs of the attitude towards faith found amongst Spain's intellectual community. Writing to Julius on 31 October 1820, he comments that Stolberg would find no audience there and expresses disgust at the anti-Catholic campaigning of Olabarrieta, a

polemicist who wrote under the pseudonym *Clararossa*. This figure, who regularly fell foul of the Inquisition, would have been an utter anathema to Böhl. In his *Cartas familiares del Cuidadano José Joaquín de Clararossa á Madama Leocadia* (Intimate letters of the citizen Clararossa to Madame Leocadia), published posthumously in 1822, Olabarrieta includes a satirical dialogue between Jesus, Mohammed and Moses which depicts all three as power-hungry impostors. It is therefore not surprising to find Böhl so offended at such open criticism of the very notion of faith, let alone the approbation of republicanism, which the inclusion of the word *cuidadano* in the title suggests.

3   Friedrich Schlegel, *Kritische Schriften und Fragmente; Studienausgabe in sechs Bänden*, Ernst Behler and Hans Eichner (eds.), 6 vols (Paderborn: Schöningh, 1988); IV: *Kritische Schriften und Fragmente [1812–1823]*, 251–334; references appear in the text.

4   It is also possible that August Wilhelm Schlegel's recent enthusiasm for Sanskrit might have intensified this aversion. Böhl felt sure that Schlegel was simply too buried in his Oriental philology to pay any attention to his efforts in defending Spanish literature.

5   See Werner Brüggemann, *Die Spanienberichte des 18. und 19. Jahrhunderts und ihre Bedeutung für die Formung und Wandlung des deutschen Spanienbildes*, SfdGG, Series I, XII (Münster: Aschendorffsche Verlag, 1956), pp. 30–4.

6   See Thomas Wolf, *Pustkuchen und Goethe. Die Streitschrift als produktives Verwirrspiel* (Tübingen: Niemeyer, 1999).

7   Although not made explicit here, it seems likely that the suggested translation of Haller's *Über die Constitution der spanischen Cortes* (1821) would be undertaken by Böhl himself. Once again, he sees himself as a mediator, keen to avail the Spanish readership of Haller's critique of their ill-conceived Constitution in the hope that his words might change opinion in Spain itself.

8   Böhl is alluding to the play of the same name by Luis de Belmonte Bermúdez (c.1587–1650).

9   'Spain', *Blackwood's Edinburgh Magazine*, 14 (1823), 675–94 (p. 676).

10 Quoted in Montoto, *Algo más*, p. 151.

11 I am very grateful to Professor Ivan Jakšić for allowing me to see his yet unpublished article '"My King, my Country, my Faith": Washington Irving's Writings on the Rise and Fall of Spain'.

12 Washington Irving, *Legends of the Conquest of Spain* (Philadelphia: Caray, Lea and Blanchard, 1835), pp. vii–viii.

Chapter 13
Böhl and the Genealogy of Romantic Philology

Böhl's drive to preserve Spain's literary heritage forms part of a broader philological movement emerging throughout Europe during the late eighteenth and early nineteenth centuries. However, whilst he shares an enthusiasm for older, culture-specific poetic forms with a number of Romantic scholars, his dual critical identity places him in an unusual position, which is both reactive and proactive, absorbing and emulating the ideals of German Romanticism, whilst attempting to revive interest in and realign attitudes towards national literature in his adopted homeland. Böhl was conscious of his role in the development of philology in both nations and this duality lends his scholarship a unique character. His physical, permanent presence in Spain meant he viewed the nation's culture in a way which his German contemporaries could not. Whilst other German Romantic philologists were drawn to Spain's ancient poetry as something exotic, almost otherworldly, which seemed to epitomise the Romantic ideal, for Böhl, its survival was part of the mainstream late Romantic desire to preserve national culture. Scholars such as Herder, Jacob Grimm and Depping may have been enchanted by the forms and cadences of the *romance*, but they dealt with the genre as a foreign literary artefact, its Oriental mystique setting it apart from mainstream European culture. For Böhl, however, the work of Spain's medieval poets was as integral to the notion of national literature as the *Märchen* or *Lied* were in a German context. It is, therefore, with Böhl that one is able to see the German and Spanish literary traditions merge. Not only does he mediate from Germany to Spain with his dissemination of Schiller and Schlegel, he also brings with him the developing ideals of German Romantic philology. Then, having applied those ideals to his own collecting, his work reverses the flow of ideas through the publication in Germany of both the *Floresta* and *Teatro antiguo*. It is this transcultural aspect to his scholarship which sets Böhl apart from his contemporaries and makes his contribution so important to a debate which, for all its nationalist, political fervour in the immediate post-Napoleonic era, was essentially European in nature. This becomes apparent when one considers Böhl in the context of the genealogy of Romantic philology and its role in the literary history of both nations.

The emergence of Romantic philology in Germany paralleled the development of German Hispanism and in many ways the two disciplines are inextricably linked, both in a wider context and in terms of Böhl's own scholarly career. Both emerged from a questioning of Enlightenment aesthetics which encouraged scholars to look to their literary heritage and that of other nations for alternative paradigms. The philological trend of the period has its origins in the wider interest in ancient poetry in the mid-eighteenth century, epitomised by publications such as *Ossian* and the work of Bishop Percy, which in turn led to a revaluation of ancient German and Nordic forms, as well as the rediscovery of the popular literatures of southern Europe.

A key element, common to both philologists and Hispanists alike, was the renewed appreciation of the ancient Spanish *romance*. Although translations of *romances* had already begun to emerge in the mid-eighteenth century, most notably those by Johann Wilhelm Ludwig Gleim (1719–1803) and Johann Georg Jacobi (1740–1814),[1] it was the inclusion of translations from Spanish in Herder's *Stimmen der alten Völker in Lieder* (Voices of the ancient peoples in song, 1778–9) which set the tone for a Romantic appreciation of the *romance* form, introducing a new audience to ancient collections such as the *Cancionero de romances de Amberes* (Collection of romances of Anvers, 1550) and Pérez de Hita's *Guerras civiles de Granada* (Civil wars of Granada, 1608). Herder's initial exploration and defence of ancient genres as examples of national literature informed the theoretical approaches of the *Frühromantiker*, including the Schlegel brothers and Tieck. Both Friedrich and August Wilhelm wrote on the *romance*, praising it as an example of *Volkspoesie*, whilst Tieck integrated the form in his play *Kaiser Octavianus* (1804), the prologue to which is entitled 'Der Aufzug der Romanze' (The parade of the romance).

The early Romantics were certainly enthusiastic about the form and its survival, so much so that Friedrich Schlegel made a call for a historical collection of *romances* in his 1803 *Beiträge zur Geschichte der modernen Poesie und Nachricht von provenzalischen Manuskripte* (Contributions to the history of modern poetry and report on Provencal manuscripts). His brother continued the trend for translation with his 1804 collection of French, Spanish and Portuguese poetry, *Blumensträusse* (Bouquets of flowers), which differed from earlier collections in its adherence to original metre and form. However, it was not until the collecting work of Arnim, Brentano and the Brothers Grimm that the more methodical approach to the collection of ancient material suggested by Friedrich Schlegel began to emerge. Here, the motivations were twofold; first, and in keeping with *Frühromantik* ideals, to highlight popular poetry as an integral part of the Romantic aesthetic and, secondly, the preservation of the nation's culture as a political statement in the face of Napoleonic aggression. Both elements relate to Böhl's reception of Romantic ideals as an apologist of ancient forms driven by political as well as aesthetic beliefs. His interest in ancient poetry, including the *romance*, parallels his defence of Golden Age theatre and places his collecting work in the context of late Romantic philology, the development of which mirrors Böhl's own as he made the transition from follower of

Enlightenment thought to a Romantic world view. His approach reflects the shifts in emphasis and methodology of the period, resulting in a synthesis of Herderian historicism, late Romantic philology and his own specifically conservative, Catholic stance.

In keeping with the Herderian emphasis of the Calderón polemic, Böhl's quest to record and thus salvage the vanishing culture of medieval Spain was grounded in an understanding of ancient poetry as part of an organic national culture. In the third *Pasatiempo*, in the text entitled 'Bosquejo de una historia de la poesía castellana' (Sketch for a history of Castilian poetry), Böhl mounts a defence of ancient poetry which denounces all efforts to introduce foreign precepts and assures the reader that, even if such errors are made, poetry will naturally return to an innate, organic state:

> La poesía nace inocente y sencilla; presume de docta en su juventud; ennoblece los afectos con la instruccion en su edad viril; luego substituye fuegos fátuos á la calor orgánico que le va faltando; pierdese en absurdos, anagramas y laberintos; busca refrigerio en recetas estrangeras, hasta que postrada con socorros mecánicos, que amatan en vez de reanimar, se acuerda de las delicias de su infancia, y construye sobre la base de los primitivos acentos de su naturaleza é índole, la expresion mas adecuada á su situacion actual. (IIIP: 6)

> (Poetry is born innocent and simple; it thinks it is clever in its youth; it ennobles its impact with education in its virile years; then it substitutes with will-o'-the-wisps the organic passion which it is losing; then it becomes lost in absurdities, anagrams and labyrinths; it seeks relief in foreign prescriptions until, exhausted by mechanical assistance, which destroy rather than revive, it remembers the delights of its childhood and constructs upon the foundation of the primitive tones of its nature and disposition the expression most appropriate to its current situation.)

Böhl's words convey an evangelical certainty that the *Volksgeist* will prevail, drawing the nation's culture back to its natural poetic roots. They echo, perhaps with more optimism, the views on ancient poetry expressed by Herder in his 'Briefwechsel über Ossian und die Lieder alter Völker' (Correspondence concerning Ossian and the songs of ancient peoples, 1773):

> Sehen Sie, in welche gekünstelte Horazische Manier wir Deutschen hie und da gefallen sind – Ossian, die Lieder der Wilden, der Skalden, Romanzen, Provinzialgedichte könnten uns auf bessern Weg bringen, wenn wir aber auch hier nur mehr als Form, als Einkleidung, als Sprache lernen wollten. Zum Unglück aber fangen wir hiervon an und bleiben hiebei stehen, und da wird wieder nichts. – Irre ich mich, oder ists wahr, daß die schönsten lyrischen Stücke, die wir schon jetzt haben und längst gehabt haben, schon mit diesem männlichen, starken, festen, deutschen

Ton übereinkommen oder sich ihm nähern – was wäre nicht also von der Aufweckung meherer solcher zu hoffen!²

(Look at the Horatian mannerism which we Germans have adopted here and there – Ossian, the songs of the savages, the skalds, romances, Provencal poetry could all lead us to a better path if we were interested here in learning more than mere form, mere garb, mere language. Unfortunately, however, that is where we begin and that is where we stay and nothing will come of it once again. – Am I mistaken, or is it true that the most beautiful, lyrical pieces, which we already have and have had for a long time, already compare with or come close to that masculine, strong, solid German tone – what could not be hoped for from the awakening of more such things!)

Herder's direct reference to the popular genres of southern Europe as a worthy inspiration for the future of German poetry highlights the significance of the *romance* as an alternative lyrical paradigm. Whilst Böhl undoubtedly accords with this, his comments must be understood in a different context. Whereas Herder's comments are directed towards a revival of the German lyric, Böhl's adaptation of his ideas has transferred the argument to Spain itself and forms part of the debate surrounding the validity of national literature.

Whilst indebted to Herder on a theoretical level, it was the philological example set by the later generation of Romantics in Germany which truly inspired Böhl to begin collecting material. In this respect, he proved to be very much attuned to contemporary taste, something epitomised by his enthusiasm for *Des Knaben Wunderhorn*. However, Arnim and Brentano's often rather incoherent editorial policy, which saw disagreements concerning the reworking and invention of texts,³ did not meet with Böhl's strictly historicist understanding of Romantic philology as an accurate recording of essentially fragile historical material. In this respect, he was far more drawn to the practices advocated, if not necessarily followed, by Jacob (1785–1863) and Wilhelm Grimm (1786–1859). These are made explicit in their 1815 'Zirkular wegen Aufsammlung der Volkspoesie' (Circular concerning the collection of popular poetry) which demanded material in its pure, unadulterated, popular form, 'getreu und wahr, ohne Schminke und Zutat' (loyal and true, without embellishment and addition).⁴ Böhl's affinity with the Grimms further highlights the influence of Herder. As Lichtenstein argued as early as 1928, the Brothers Grimm followed Herder more closely than the early Romantics, especially in their elaboration of the notion of *Naturpoesie* and their developing philological methodology.⁵ Like Böhl, both brothers shared an historicist standpoint, as well as an understanding of *Sagenforschung* (research into legends) as a means to discovering the inner, historical essence of poetry. However, the brothers had differing views when it came to the relationship of *Volkspoesie* to contemporary literary trends. Jacob saw old poetry in an historical context, not to be revived as an art form, but to be recorded, whereas Wilhelm saw the form as an aesthetic paradigm for poetic revival. Convinced of the value of older forms as a vehicle for cultural self-determination, Böhl had an aesthetic as well as an historicist appreciation of ancient poetry and it is possible to see in his work an amalgam of the differing positions adopted by the brothers. Furthermore, Böhl's world view absorbs the Herderian approach to ancient and foreign literatures in similarly heuristic and philological terms to those elaborated by the Grimms in their extensive scholarly work.

Although appreciative of their collaborative efforts, it was in Jacob Grimm in particular that Böhl found a temperament in keeping with his own careful, scholarly approach and although they never met or had any contact, Böhl's indebtedness to Grimm's work is clear.[6] The latter's altruistic approach provided Böhl with a model for his own endeavours and, although delighted with the *Kinder- und Hausmärchen* (Children's and household tales, 1812; 1815–19), it was Grimm's 1815 collection of ancient Spanish poetry, *Silva de romances viejos* (Collection of ancient romances), which Böhl regarded as exemplary in the context of Romantic philology. Grimm's collection broke new ground within German Hispanism. Whereas previous German scholars had dealt exclusively with works in translation, Grimm published entirely in Spanish, including the introduction and notes. Furthermore, his choice of material was far more consequent, only including old *romances*. Earlier collections, including Herder's, had been far less selective and had included alongside examples of ancient popular poetry works by much later, clearly learned poets such as Góngora. Such selection criteria had been met with some criticism, notably from Johann Gottfried Eichhorn (1752–1827) in his *Allgemeine Geschichte der Cultur und Litteratur des neueren Europa* (General history of the culture and literature of modern Europe, 1796), in which he called for a more purist approach:

> In den Sammlungen, welche meist El Romancero oder El Cancionero überschrieben sind, stehen noch die alten und neuern spanischen Romanzen ohne die nöthige Unterscheidung untereinander. Ein Litterator von Geschmack könnte sich durch ihre Trennung ein Verdienst erwerben.[7]

> (In the collections, which are mostly entitled El Romancero or El Cancionero, are included old and new Spanish romances without the necessary differentiation. A literary man with taste could make a name for himself by dividing them.)

As Friemel argues, Grimm was just such a 'Litterator von Geschmack', but his single volume anthology left the task of recording Spain's ancient poetry incomplete.[8] Although a second volume had been planned, it never appeared, nor did the critical apparatus which Grimm had intended to include. Consequently, the *Silva* remained work in progress, awaiting completion by another scholar. Böhl took up the challenge with his *Floresta* and although he also failed to provide the critical apparatus called for by Friedrich Schlegel in 1803, he did succeed in moving the project forward towards its eventual completion by Durán and Ferdinand Wolf (1796–1866) in the late 1820s and 1830s. Böhl's work can, therefore, be seen to bridge the gap between German and Spanish Hispanist philology, introducing new German Romantic practices and fostering the development of new philological work in Spain, whilst simultaneously furthering knowledge of Spanish material in a German-speaking context.

Böhl may have taken up the cause first espoused by Grimm, but the latter remained ambivalent towards his successor. Grimm was aware of the first volume of the *Floresta* and commented on it in response to a review article in the *Leipziger Literatur Zeitung* in 1822 which discussed his own collection as well as those of Böhl and Depping. He refers to 'Böhls treffliche Samml[ung]' (Böhl's first-rate collection), but goes on to characterise its content as 'meist lyrische Stücke' (mostly lyrical pieces), a comment which might have offended Böhl, especially as his collection was still only partially complete.[9] Grimm's assessment seems all the more incongruous when one considers that Böhl wholeheartedly approved of the former's methodology, following it for his own collection. He made use of Grimm's source, the rare *Cancionero de romances de Amberes*, and was particularly impressed by Grimm's use of long lines, combining two lines together on the printed page. Grimm did this in an effort to show the *romance* as part of an epic *Nationalpoesie*, the acknowledgement of which greatly enhanced the canonical standing of texts such as *El Cantar del mio Cid* (The poem of the Cid). Böhl describes his approval of this *modus operandi* in a letter to Julius on 30 April 1818:

> In meiner Ansicht (die in der Einleitung zu meinem Parnaso gehörig ausgeführt erscheint) ist die Hauptbestimmung des Reimes eine metrische Reihe scharf zu begränzen und demnach der Reim in der Mitte der Reihe eine Künstelei die erst spät in der spanischen Poesie erschienen ist, und auch dann nicht den End Reim aufgehoben hat – Der Einschnitt findet sich sehr früh in der spanischen Poesie, sowohl in den jambischen, als den trokäischen Silbenmaaßen; meistens finden sich in den älteren Handschriften die zwei Hälften der Reihe in <u>eine</u> geschrieben, wie in Sanchez und Grimm: einige Beispiele aber auch giebt es wo die zwei Hälften der Reihe in zwei Zeilen geschrieben sind. Auf der ersten Weise findet sich am Ende jeder Reihe ein Reim, welcher sich später in Assonanz verwandelte; nach der anderen Art (welche ohne Zweifel der Bequemlichkeit zu Liebe und um gleiche Form mit den Redondillas zu erhalten, die gewöhnlicher geworden ist) erfolgt der Reim oder Assonanz nur am Ende jeder geraden Zeile, weil der Einschnitt keinen Reim hat, wenn in Romance geschrieben wird, welches der Natur dieser Gattung völlig angemeßen ist, die eben weil <u>derselbe</u> Reim oder Assonanz durchstehend ist, keine so häufige Wiederholung desselben braucht, als die Redondilla und alle ihre Gattungen

– Ich theile übrigens nicht mit Ihnen Ihre Parteilichkeit für die Romanzen; mir besagen nur die alten gereimten der Cancioneros; die späteren mit assonancias, die den Haupt Inhalt der Romanceros ausmachen, sind mir leichte Speise die weder Herz noch Geist erquicken, besonders wenn verliebte Schäfer erscheinen –

(In my opinion (as will appear accordingly in the introduction to my Parnassus), the main purpose of rhyme is to limit a metrical line and therefore the rhyme in the middle of a line is an artifice which did not appear until later in Spanish poetry and even then did not remove the end rhyme – The break appears very early in Spanish poetry, in iambic as well as trochaic metre; in older manuscripts, one usually finds the two halves of the line written as <u>one</u>, as in Sanchez and Grimm: there are, however, some examples where two halves of the line are written on separate lines. In the first manner, there is a rhyme at the end of each line, which later developed into assonance; in the other (which no doubt became usual for the sake of ease and to keep the same form as the redondillas), the rhyme or assonance only appears at the end of every even line because the break has no rhyme when the romance form is used, which is perfectly suited to the nature of this genre, which because <u>the same</u> rhyme or assonance carries throughout, does not require it to be repeated so often, as occurs in the redondilla and its derivatives – By the way, I do not share your preference for romances; I only like the old rhymed ones of the cancioneros; the later ones using assonance, which make up the majority of the content of the romanceros, I find rather superficial, with nothing to inspire heart or spirit, especially when love-struck shepherds are involved –.)

As Reyes Ponce notes, this demonstrates Böhl's intimate knowledge of Spanish metre and an awareness of the subtleties of genre often lacking in works of others (A: 178). Interesting too is his insistence on the value of older *romances*, showing an understanding of the development of popular forms from the medieval age to the Baroque. However, it was not only in terms of methodology that Böhl and Grimm shared a similar standpoint. Böhl fully subscribed to Grimm's belief that the knowledge of a language was the only way to understand a nation's culture fully. This led Grimm to criticise others, including Herder, for attempting to convey knowledge of other cultures through translation. In Grimm's view, this could only ever lead to an inaccurate impression, lacking in true spirit. This firm belief in the individuality of national literature formed part of Grimm's wider political *Weltanschauung* and, in many respects, his collecting in the years following the Napoleonic invasion was politically motivated. Looking back on his life in 1831, Jacob makes an explicit link between his studies and a personal response to the political situation of Germany during the Napoleonic era:

Mögen diese Studien überhaupt manchen unergiebig geschienen haben und noch scheinen: mir sind sie jederzeit vorgekommen als eine würdige, ernste Aufgabe, die sich bestimmt und fest auf unser gemeinsames Vaterland bezieht und die Liebe zu ihm nährt.[10]

(These studies may have seemed and may still seem unproductive to some: to me, they have always seemed a dignified, serious task which is firmly linked to our common fatherland and fosters a love of it.)

These words might just as easily have been written by Böhl, looking back on his philological and critical career in Spain, and demonstrate the depth of affinity between these two scholars at this juncture. Unlike Böhl, however, Grimm's Hispanist work played a relatively minor role in his overall contribution to European philology and the *Silva* was his only foray into the publication of Spanish material. The collection was nevertheless significant in the development of both Hispanism and Romantic philology in Germany, setting a new standard for the collection and treatment of Spanish popular poetry. A number of scholars, including Depping and Diez, followed in Grimm's footsteps by focusing exclusively on older works, but it is arguable that only Böhl did so in the spirit Grimm might have wished, presenting the material in the original, rather than translation, and maintaining a Spanish context for the works. In contrast, Depping's *Sammlung der besten alten Spanischen Historischen, Ritter- und Maurischen Romanzen* (Collection of the best ancient Spanish historical, chivalric and Moorish romances, 1817), whilst presenting the works themselves in Spanish, provided German titles and notes. Diez' *Altspanische Romanzen* (Ancient Spanish romances, 1821) relied solely on translation. In this respect, Böhl must be accredited with a pioneering role, following Grimm's lead, but taking the project a step further by collecting material from within Spain itself. The significance of his work in the context of German Hispanist philology is highlighted by the later collection published by Wolf in 1837, entitled *Floresta de rimas modernas castellanas* (Selection of modern Spanish verse), which takes Böhl's anthology as its starting point and methodological inspiration.

Böhl kept a careful watch on developments in contemporary German Hispanism, which he valued far more highly than any work being carried out in Spain at the time. Although he made the acquaintance of Diez, who visited him in El Puerto, and knew of Wolf through Julius, it was Depping's work which was most important for his own, providing material which would have otherwise remained inaccessible to him, in particular those works available only in the major libraries of Paris. Depping's significance for Böhl is further enhanced by a shared world view which saw the former adopt a Herderian stance similar to both Böhl and

Grimm. In keeping with the prevailing proto-nationalist ideology of the post-Napoleonic era, Depping too saw Spain as an heroic nation, especially following the 1808 uprising against the French. Culture and nation are inextricably linked in Depping's view and Herder's notion of *Volksgeist* is abundantly clear in the following Romantic outburst from the introduction to his collection of *Romanzen*:

> Auch die Nationalunabhängigkeit, die nach so harter Unterdrückung in unsern Tagen so lebhaft wieder zur Sprache gekommen ist, wird in den alten Spanischen Romanzen energisch gelobt und vertheidigt. [. . .] Daß diese Volkslieder dem Charakter der Nation völlig entsprechen, und auf denselben wieder zurückgewirkt haben, leidet wohl keinen Zweifel. So wie sie in den Romanzen geschildert wird, hat sie sich zu allen Zeiten bewährt, selbständig, tapfer, großherzig, rachsüchtig und übermüthig. Ihre Volkslieder sprechen ihre hervorstechenden Eigenschaften aus, und dienen dazu, ihr Nationalgefühl zu nähren. Es ist also nicht zu verwundern, daß heißer Patriotismus in einem Lande glühte, wo die schönsten Züge aus der Nationalgeschichte beständig dem Volke durch Gesang und auch durch Schauspiele vergegenwärtigt wurden.[11]
>
> (National independence, once more a lively topic after such hard repression in our times, is also energetically praised and defended in the old Spanish romances. [. . .] There can be no doubt that these folk songs reflect the character of the nation and have in turn had an impact on it. Just as it is presented in the romances, it has proved itself to be independent, brave, magnanimous, vengeful and high spirited at all times. Their folk songs give expression to their notable characteristics and serve to foster their national feeling. It is therefore no surprise that passionate patriotism burns in a land where the most admirable traits of national history are constantly brought to life to the people through song and also on the stage.)

As well as evoking the Herderian notion of *Volkspoesie*, here Depping echoes much of Böhl's Schlegelian argument surrounding the patriotic Spanish character voiced during the polemic. Böhl's affinity with Herder, Grimm and Depping shows his continued interaction with the aesthetic and political debate in his native Germany in relation to the role of popular forms in the overall context of national literature. His views accord with the mainstream and find their echo in the work of a number of like-minded contemporaries. In seeking to transfer those views to Spain, however, Böhl found himself in a quite different position.

In its native environment, Spain's ancient poetry had essentially suffered the same fate as Golden Age theatre, a demise chronicled by Böhl himself in his 'Noticias literarias originales'. Once more, the perceived value of the *romance* was key. The genre had been popular during the sixteenth and seventeenth centuries through the work of Lope de Vega, Góngora and Quevedo, but interest and approval diminished as the influence of neo-Classical aesthetics began to spread.

The rejection of popular forms reached its height in the eighteenth century following publication of Luzán's *Poetica* and these views prevailed into the early nineteenth century.[12] Whilst some commentators maintained an interest in older works, they were not necessarily positive in their appraisal. Martín Sarmiento (1695–1771), whose *Memorias para la historia de la poesía y poetas españoles* (Notes for a history of Spanish poetry and poets, 1741–5; published in 1775) informed the work of Herder, Grimm and Depping, maintained a rationalist stance and although some of his ideas on national culture pre-empted those of Herder, he remained critical of key popular forms, especially the *romance*, which he felt did not fit the criteria for 'national' poetry. Often fluid in content, these popular creations were not historically accurate and therefore ran counter to Enlightenment notions of truth. Also hostile to popular poetry was Tomás Antonio Sánchez (1723–1802), whose *Colección de poesías castellanas anteriores al siglo XV* (Collection of Castilian poetry from before the fifteenth century, 1779–90) shows the impact of neo-Classicism at its height, evident in his bias towards learned poetry. This trend continues into the late century in the work of Quintana, whose approach would be met with impatient criticism from Böhl. Although far more positively disposed towards popular forms, Quintana's focus was on the 'artistic' *romances* of the *Siglo de oro*, rather than the popular poetry favoured by Grimm. Indeed, Quintana criticised folk ballads. His *Poesías selectas* (Selected poetry, 1796) formed part of Estala's larger collection of poetry, which was published under the pseudonym Ramón Fernández and set the tone for the appraisal of Spain's poetry in Spain itself until the appearance of Durán's collections in the late 1820s and 1830s. However, Quintana's collection had at least acknowledged the *romance* form, unlike López de Sedano's nine-volume *Parnaso español* (Spanish Parnassus, 1768–78), which, following the majority of collections of the period, made no reference to the form whatsoever.

Despite the clear emphasis on neo-Classical ideals within the canon, a more sympathetic, albeit peripheral, approach to popular poetry was also emerging which drew attention to ancient genres as a valuable part of the nation's culture. The critic, Rafael Floranes (1743–18??), although he did not publish his views, adopted a pro-*romance* stance, regarding the form as an historical source, both literary and factual. Floranes' stance is indicative of a shift in attitudes towards popular poetry which parallels developments in Germany. As Reyes Ponce explains (A: 92), the emerging interest in the *romance* in Spain during the late eighteenth century formed part of the Enlightenment pursuit of a true understanding of the history of ideas. As a result, whilst neo-Classical aestheticians derided the form, some philologists and historians, such as Böhl's ally, Vargas Ponce, began to uncover and record it as part of a process of cultural archaeology. The *romance* was seen as part of the medieval world and could offer an insight into its workings. Discussion of the genre began to appear in influential studies including

Johann Nikolas Böhl von Faber (1770–1836): A German Romantic in Spain

Luis José Velázquez' *Orígenes de la poesía castellana* (Origins of Castilian poetry, 1754), later translated into German by Johann Andreas Dieze, and Juan Andrés' ambitious *Origen, progesos y estado actual de toda literatura* (Origen, progress and current state of all literature), the first volume of which appeared in 1784. Consequently, whilst the form was not necessarily approved or appreciated in aesthetic terms by literary archaeologists, it was studied as a valid cultural artefact in the context of literary history. This, to some extent, parallels the view of philologists such as Jacob Grimm and emphasises the emerging historicist nature of collecting. It can also be seen to provide Böhl with a Spanish context from within which to argue for the appreciation of Spain's ancient poetry, able to graft his German Romantic values onto the existing appreciation of the *romance* as an integral part of the nation's literary heritage, just as the work of Nipho and other earlier commentators had done in the context of the theatre.

Whilst this archaeological approach contributed greatly to the revival of popular poetry in philological circles, it was the pre-Romantic poet, Juan Meléndez Valdés (1754–1817), who revived interest in the *romance* as a poetic genre, finally re-establishing it as an aesthetic form, as well as an archaeological concept, highlighting in so doing its moral and artistic value. Although some poets, including Nicolás Fernández Moratín (the Elder, 1737–80) and José Cadalso (1741–82), had experimented with the *romance* form during the eighteenth century, it did not feature regularly in their repertoire. Meléndez Valdés, however, adopted the form with enthusiasm. He mounted a defence of popular poetry in his elaborately entitled *Discurso sobre la necesidad de prohibir la impresión y venta de las jácaras y romances vulgares por dañosos a las costumbres públicas y de ser sustituídas por otras canciones verdaderamente nacionales, con motivo de ciertas coplas mandadas recoger por orden superior* (Address on the need to ban the printing and sale of comic ballads and vulgar *romances* as damaging to public custom and to substitute them with other truly national songs on the occasion of the order from a high authority to seize certain folk songs, 1798). Reyes Ponce highlights the heuristic element in Meléndez's appraisal, describing it as 'that of an Enlightened educator who appreciated the social and educational potential of the *romances viejos* and valued their usefulness in the education of the Spanish masses' (A: 136). This echoes the terms set out by the Brothers Grimm when compiling their *Kinder- und Hausmärchen*, describing it as an 'Erziehungsbuch' (educational guide). Meléndez also focuses on the patriotic value of these ancient texts and in so doing connects with the German Romantic appreciation of ancient forms as part of a national literature. These views clearly parallel many of those espoused by Böhl in the years following his return to Spain and, consequently, Böhl's defence of Spain's ancient poetry can be seen to form part of the ongoing debate within Spain surrounding the validity of popular forms within the context of a national literature. In this respect, it forms a natural adjunct to his defence of Calderón. However, in contrast to his position within the contemporary debate in his native Germany, in Spain he found himself contributing to a campaign in defence of indigenous forms which had been very much consigned to the sidelines, overwhelmed by mainstream discussions over the Spanish assimilation of neo-Classical ideals. The little revaluation there was still adhered to Enlightenment principles and lacked the scholarly rigour of the German revival. Consequently, whilst some Spaniards were able to value these ancient forms as educational and poetic, they stopped short of following the philological approach taken by the Germans in seeking to record and preserve ancient material in its pure form. Böhl's arrival in Spain in 1813 marked a decisive moment in the development of Romantic philology as the principles beginning to be applied to collecting in his native Germany now found their way into Spain itself. Equipped with an intimate knowledge of both cultures, Böhl was able to identify the resultant methodological divide and sought to unite both approaches through an appreciation of the educational and historical, as well as the national, aesthetic aspects of older poetry.

The validity of Böhl's approach is, however, compromised by his increasingly conservative, Catholic stance, in particular his negative reception of Spain's Arab heritage. This saw Böhl adopt a position which set him apart from the majority of his contemporaries. Other philologists were happy to acknowledge the value of Spain's Moorish past. Indeed, it proffered a wealth of vibrant and aesthetically pleasing material. In Germany, Depping and Grimm followed the Schlegelian reading of Herder's *Araberthese*, whilst in London, Bowring even went as far as to claim that only Moorish *romances* were original. This was one area where Böhl found the English Hispanist's views to be utterly unpalatable, his disagreement grounded almost entirely in his conservative, Catholic stance rather than any strictly philological argument. Commenting on Bowring's position in a letter to Julius on 21 January 1823, Böhl makes explicit his association of Catholicism and the true Spain:

Mit Mr Bowring kann ich trotz seines ausgezeichneten Talentes nicht harmoniren. Wir kamen in unserer einzigen Unterredung gleich aneinander weil er behaupten wollte nur das maurische in der spanischen Poesie sei original & achtungswerth. Ich schickte ihm darauf die Floresta und er schrieb diese zeuge für seine Meinung – die ganze Floresta athmet der katholisch-christliche Geist der alle ächte spanische Poesie karakterisirt –

(I cannot harmonise with Mr Bowring, despite his outstanding talent. We came to blows during one single communication because he wanted to maintain that only the Moorish element in Spanish poetry was original and worthy of attention. So I sent him the Floresta and he wrote that this proved his point – the whole Floresta breathes the Catholic, Christian spirit which characterises all genuine Spanish poetry –.)

Such was Böhl's insistence on the importance of 'der katholisch-christliche Geist' (the Catholic, Christian spirit) that he even rejected some of the early philological work produced by his great friend, Durán. In his first *romancero*, published in 1828 and entitled *Romancero de romances moriscos* (Collection of Moorish romances), Durán had, as the title suggests, focused heavily on the Moorish influence. Whilst Böhl was prepared to acknowledge the value of the collection, he was unimpressed by the content. Writing to his young friend on 17 March 1829, Böhl says he is looking forward to the publication of the second *romancero*, hoping he will enjoy it more than the first as he has never been keen on the 'morisco' (Moorish) element of Spain's literature. However, unlike his opposition to Bowring, here Böhl does display philological judgement in rejecting the Moorish influence, aware that, unlike his later anthologies, Durán's first collection contained the predominantly Baroque *romance*. Böhl expressed reservations about this particular type of *romance*, realising, unlike Herder and Friedrich Schlegel, that these were idealised representations of Moorish life and not authentic in the sense of the popular poetry which Böhl himself sought to collate. This blurring of aesthetic boundaries was typical of Herder, who made no distinction between popular and artistic poetry, thus accepting the work of Góngora and Gil Polo alongside so-called 'canciones del pueblo' (songs of the people).[13] Reyes Ponce notes that in preferring the popular style, Böhl was once more simultaneously agreeing and disagreeing with Herder (A: 206), in full accordance with his desire to preserve primitive compositions for posterity, but setting his own criteria by recognising only genuine popular poetry. In so doing, he sought to counter prevailing practice in Spain. Herder's approach found its echo in that adopted by anthologists such as Quintana in Spain and it is testimony to Böhl's influence that, despite the inconsistent nature of his reception of Herderian thought in this regard, his views held sway in persuading Durán to change his approach in order to focus on more authentic material in later collections.

Böhl's intention to reshape philology in Spain is implicit in his reception of his contemporaries there. He despaired of more recent collections of poetry and, in particular, voiced severe criticism of Sedano's *Parnaso español* and Quintana's *Poesías selectas*, describing the former as 'indigesta' (muddled) and the latter as 'ligerísima' (extremely lightweight) (letter to Navarrete, 8 April 1817). This would set the tone for later assessments, becoming in many ways a substitute for the Calderón polemic, with Quintana, in particular, remaining the object of Böhl's derision for years to come (as his correspondence with Durán after 1829 demonstrates). Böhl felt that these collections failed to do justice to the richness of Spanish literature as they contained too much of poor quality whilst omitting other works deserving of attention. As Juretschke notes, the neo-Classical ideals aspired to by scholars like Quintana restricted their appreciation of much of Spain's early poetics, whereas Böhl was approaching it from a far more sympathetic angle based on Herderian historicism and inspired, in particular, by the work of Romantic philologists such as Grimm and Depping (DD: 166). For Böhl, the *Floresta* was a means to educate new generations of Spaniards on the treasures of their national literature, not only highlighting their historical and political, but also their aesthetic and moral value. In this, Böhl displays not only the thoroughly Romantic nature of his philology, but also the continued importance of cultural mediation to his scholarship.

NOTES

1. In 1743, Gleim translated three *romances* by Góngora and in 1756 he published *Romanzen und romanzische Lieder*, a collection which made use of the form, but included no Spanish material. Jacobi's prose version of *Romanzen aus dem Spanischen* appeared in 1767.
2. Wilhelm Dobbeck (ed.), *Herders Werke in fünf Bänden* (Berlin/Weimar: Aufbau, 1969); II: 234.
3. See Heinz Rölleke (ed.), *Des Knaben Wunderhorn. Alte deutsche Lieder gesammelt von Achim von Arnim und Clemens Brentano. Kommentierte Gesamtausgabe*, 3 vols (Stuttgart: Reclam, 1987); I: 'Nachwort', 559.
4. Ludwig Denecke (ed.), *Jacob Grimm. Wilhelm Grimm. Schriften und Reden* (Stuttgart: Reclam, 1985), 'Zirkular wegen Aufsammlung der Volkspoesie', pp. 44–7 (p. 45).
5. Ernst Lichtenstein, 'Die Idee der Naturpoesie bei den Brüdern Grimm und ihr Verhältnis zu Herder', *DVJS*, 6 (1928), 513–47. See also Hermann Bausinger, *Formen der 'Volkspoesie'* (Berlin: Erich Schmidt Verlag, 1968), pp. 17–27.
6. They were certainly moving in similar circles. Mutual associates included the bookseller Hitzig in Berlin, Friedrich Perthes, Friedrich Diez and the exiled Spaniard Liaño, who was asked to proofread Grimm's work.
7. Johann Gottfried Eichhorn, *Allgemeine Geschichte der Cultur und Litteratur des neueren Europa*, 2 vols (Göttingen: Rosenbusch, 1796); I: 134n.
8. Berthold Friemel, 'Zu Jacob Grimms Silva de romances viejos', *Brüder-Grimm-Gedenken*, 9 (1990), 51–88 (62).
9. Quoted in Friemel, p. 74.
10. Denecke (ed.), *Schriften und Reden*, 'Selbstbiographie', pp. 15–34 (p. 33).
11. Georg Bernhard Depping, *Sammlung der besten alten Spanischen Historischen, Ritter- und Maurischen Romanzen. Geordnet und mit Anmerkungen und einer Einleitung versehen von . . .* (Altenburg und Leipzig: Brockhaus, 1817), pp. xxxi–xxxii.
12. Reyes Ponce (A: 85–142) provides a detailed chronology of the reception of the *romance*, to which I am indebted.
13. There is an interesting aside to this entire debate which involves Jacob Grimm's response to Herder's translation technique. Grimm had taken a stance against Herder on the matter of translation and criticised him for suppressing certain Catholic elements in his rendition of Spanish *romances*, in particular those from the *Cid*. This echoes Böhl's stance on Herder's *Araberthese* and shows Grimm also to be jealous of Spain's Catholic past; see Friemel, pp. 56–8.

Chapter 14
Böhl's Transcultural Philology

Böhl's two major anthologies, the three-volume *Floresta de rimas antiguas castellanas* (1821–5) and its sister publication, *Teatro antiguo anterior á Lope de Vega* (1832), provide both an insight into his Romantic philology in practice and evidence of the wealth of knowledge amassed since his time at Görslow. The work undertaken helped further to establish Böhl's reputation in Fernandine Spain, whilst maintaining his profile as a scholar of Spanish letters in his native Germany, contributing simultaneously to European Romantic philology and German Hispanism. As this suggests, Böhl's dual cultural identity is once more to the fore, underpinning his role as a cultural mediator, one which he felt able to tackle with increasing confidence. His involvement in the Calderón polemic and subsequent election to the Academy meant that by the end of the second decade of the century, he was able to assume a more authoritative stance. His correspondence with Julius bears testimony to this. There is a regular exchange of materials, often evading censorship and import legislation, and Böhl's letters are full of comments and advice on Spanish culture, not just intended for his friend, but for the benefit of others too. It is against the background of this private transcultural dialogue between Germany and Spain that the anthologies assume importance as the public manifestation of a campaign to salvage what Böhl felt to be a culture in peril, threatened by neglect and ignorance as his experiences in the cathedral library of Seville had shown. By preserving these works, Böhl felt he was ensuring the survival of 'die gute Sache', its values intact in an aesthetic context unsullied by the prevailing political mood.

The two collections had a lengthy gestation period, both emerging from initial ambitious plans to compile a comprehensive collection of older Spanish literature. Böhl's interest in older Spanish theatre, not least during the Calderón polemic, was equalled by a long-standing love of popular poetry and these two genres became the main object of his collecting zeal, the fruits of which he was keen to share with others. It is possible through his correspondence with Julius and Navarrete to see the plans for both the *Floresta* and the *Teatro antiguo* gradually taking shape. The character of the collections, with their emphasis on popular or neglected material, is determined almost immediately. On 6 April 1810, in his first letter to Julius, Böhl expresses a preference for the *Volkslied*, a view evidenced by his enthusiasm for Arnim and Brentano's ballad collection, *Des Knaben Wunderhorn*. Indeed, Böhl's 1810 *Wunderhorn* selection can be regarded as a forerunner to the later

Spanish collections, especially the first volume of the *Floresta*, with its specific emphasis on Spanish popular poetry. The proposed inclusion, also in 1812, of both German and Spanish material in Kerner's failed *Poetischer Almanach* marks a further development. The close correlation between Böhl's Germanist and Hispanist interests which this suggests is further supported by the collecting plans detailed in his correspondence with Julius. In a letter of 5 September 1810, Böhl mentions the possibility of compiling a German 'Liedersammlung' (collection of songs) in collaboration with Julius. Later, on 15 September, he broadens the scope of his comments to include Spanish material. He makes reference to 'Romanzen', describing them as 'mehr Ergüße des individuellen Gefühls' (more effusions of individual emotion), before going on to mention his own 'innige Bekanntschaft mit der spanischen Poesie' (intimate acquaintance with Spanish poetry). Such comments show the inherently Romantic aesthetic appreciation of the lyrical aspect of ancient poetry at the height of Böhl's 'rebirth', which echoes his emotive response to the *Wunderhorn* material. However, the plans for a 'Liedersammlung', which spans the period from August 1810 to May 1811, eventually give way to more specifically Hispanist interests and, by 1813, now reunited with his wife and reconnected with Spanish culture, the plans for a 'spanischer Parnass' (Spanish Parnassus) are to the fore.

Although still drawn to its aesthetic value, perhaps inevitably, Böhl's relationship to the material appears to shift against the fraught political background of the period. By 1817, when the project is discussed once more, the notion of saving the nation's culture is the central concern, eclipsing the purely aesthetic motivation which inspired the *Wunderhorn* selection. This reflects the broader development of Böhl's scholarship. The growing importance of literary history and the role of a national literature in defining the nation's culture can be seen in a number of philological treatises in the third *Pasatiempo* where Böhl's discussions on theatre overlap with those concerning the history of poetry, as well as metre and taste. These documents were written in parallel with Böhl's work on the *Floresta* and both undertakings are clearly informed by the same Herderian ethos, as well, of course, as Böhl's ardent desire to become a member of the Royal Spanish Academy. Such personal ambition notwithstanding, the vast scope of Böhl's initial plans highlights his commitment to Spain's ancient literature, adding practical substance to the rhetoric of the polemic. Not only does Böhl upbraid the Spanish literary elite for neglecting their literary heritage, he then goes about showing them how to preserve it. The impact of this lesson in philology may not have been immediate, but at least no one could accuse Böhl of failing to meet his own challenges. For him, the act of collecting, categorising and, ultimately, saving Spain's ancient literature was a serious task, one which he approached methodically and with a great deal of deliberation and caution.

Böhl's commitment to his cause becomes clear when one examines the evolution of his plans for the 'Parnassus'. They show a careful scholar at work, fearful of omission or error, hoping to achieve as comprehensive a study as possible in order to do justice to the material in hand. By 1817, Böhl was able to describe his plans for a collection to both Julius and Navarrete, although it is an indication of their still preliminary nature that these vary slightly. In his letter to Julius of 28 February 1817, he outlines the possibility of publishing a 'Parnaso' and also a selection of pre-Lopean theatre, as well as a 'neue Metrik' (new study of metre) and a collection of *romances*. To Navarrete, two months later on 8 April, he also proposes a foreword to the anthology on the history of poetry. By 1818, the plans for the collection have developed further. On 30 April, he writes to Julius that the proposed title of the first volume is to be 'Museo de poesia antigua castellana' (Museum of old Castilian poetry). It will focus on previously unpublished poetry from 1550 to 1650, but still that of an 'educated' nature as public taste cannot cope with 'das Frühere, Einfache' (earlier, simple [material]). The projected collection of pre-Lopean theatre will follow a similar principle. His intention, already outlined to Navarrete in April 1817, was to provide a representative anthology, with examples of all types of poetry. Böhl was, however, aware of the enormity of the task he had set himself, due not least, as he put it to Navarrete, to his own Germanic thoroughness. He also expressed reservations to Julius as to the feasibility of such a project, given his relative isolation in Cadiz, away from the grand libraries of Madrid and the major university towns, let alone the libraries of foreign capitals such as Paris which had proved such a rich source for Depping. In fact, Böhl had great difficulty in accessing resources within Spain, in particular the Royal Library in Madrid, and it was sometimes easier to obtain material from Germany. One of his main sources was the Berlin bookseller, Hitzig, who supplied him with, among others, the rare *Cancionero de Amberes*. That Böhl, a seasoned traveller, did not himself venture to Madrid seems strange. However, his correspondence reveals several plans to visit the Royal Library from as early as May 1819 which never succeeded, thwarted over the years by a combination of business commitments, recurring restrictions due to yellow fever and general political upheaval. These logistical problems had an impact on the eventual content of the collection and its critical apparatus. Initially, Böhl had also spoken of including a substantial introduction to his anthology, the content of which would demonstrate the level of knowledge he had acquired. However, although clearly well informed, Böhl was never satisfied that his work was truly complete, aware of lacunae in his knowledge and collecting. This almost obsessive desire for comprehensiveness undoubtedly had an impact on his scholarly output and most probably cost the *Floresta* its extensive introduction.

Such issues notwithstanding, by December 1819, the carefully copied manuscript of the first volume of the anthology was ready to send to Perthes for publication.[1] Aware that his selection of poems was far from complete, Böhl eventually opted for a title which would convey this, naming his collection *Floresta de rimas antiguas castellanas*. The term *Floresta* was to echo the German notion of *Blütenlese* (florilegium), commonly applied to anthologies of the period, and may also be intended as a homage to Schlegel's 1804 *Blumensträusse*. Böhl's first volume was intended to supplement Sedano's *Parnaso español*, Quintana's *Poesías selectas* and Estala's extensive collection. Clearly revising his plans for the inclusion of 'educated' works, Böhl deliberately excluded well-known poets such as Garcilaso de la Vega, Quevedo, Cervantes and Lope de Vega. Instead, the volume was to contain only popular *romances* and no satires, historical *romances* or sonnets. The result was a substantial tome containing some 380 poems, most of which were previously unpublished, and duplicating only a handful of *romances* included in earlier collections. Writing to Julius on 17 December, Böhl was clearly delighted with the fruits of his labours and emphasised the Romantic nature of the pieces chosen:

> Was sagen Sie zu 380 fast alle unbekannten Gedichte? die die spanische Poesie von einer ganz neuen Seite zeigen, die fast alle das Gefühl ansprechen und deren viele eine Zärtlichkeit athmen die man sonst an der erhabenen Kastilischen Muse vermißt?
>
> (What do you say to 380 all almost unknown poems which show Spanish poetry from a quite different angle, which almost all appeal to the emotions and many of which exude a tenderness which one otherwise finds lacking in the sublime Castilian muse?)

This juxtaposition of the lyrical, emotive, ancient poetry with the staid nature of more modern Spanish works shows that, for all his historicist and philological concerns, Böhl, the Romantic, was still greatly inspired by the aesthetic aspect of this early material. Also evident, however, is his self-perception as a pioneering philologist, able through his endeavours to disseminate new material and seeking to influence taste and literary history by drawing attention to rediscovered writers and genres, previously shunned by established scholars.

With the work on the first volume complete, Böhl realised that there was scope for an even more ambitious collection and he revised his plans once more, outlining them in a letter to Perthes on 17 December 1819. A second volume would contain the work of well-known poets, a third examples of theatre before Lope de Vega, and a fourth would be dedicated to the epic. The intention was to preserve every aspect of Spain's literary heritage. Böhl's plans were, however, still subject to alteration and by 2 June 1820 they had changed again. He had realised that the collection of pre-Lopean theatre could not be compiled on the same basis as the *Floresta*, given the likelihood that it would be a far more comprehensive collection as there was relatively little material to collate. He was also losing interest in the collection of epic poetry, which he regarded as the weakest aspect of Spain's literary heritage. (This project was instead to be left for his retirement, but was never realised.) By 16 February 1821, Böhl had eventually finalised his plans. Leaving his work on the theatre to a later date, he had decided to concentrate on poetry. There would be two further volumes of the *Floresta*, the second volume containing poetry more suited to general taste, the third texts of a more unusual nature. The print run of these would depend on the success of volume one: sadly, this meant reducing the run as sales were slow. Although work was often impeded by personal and logistical problems, the rest of the collection was published relatively quickly. Volume two, containing works by better known poets such as Boscán, Garcilaso and Luis de León, appeared in 1823 and volume three, including Lope de Vega, Quevedo and Góngora, in 1825, with a second edition of the entire collection appearing in 1827.[2]

Böhl was convinced of the importance of his work and saw it as far superior to that being produced by Spanish contemporaries, in particular Quintana. The brief prologue to the first volume of the *Floresta* shows his growing confidence and underlines the issues which had inspired the collection. Böhl explains the genesis and progress of his work and places it in its Spanish context, whilst also drawing attention to the German interest which is presented as the driving force behind publication:

> El editor de estas rimas ha dedicado los ocios de veinte años al estudio de la poesía castellana antigua. Tenia trazado dar de ella un cuadro cumplido, extractado por el órden de los tiempos los poetas mas sobresalientes de cada era, con notas históricas y filológicas, y añadiendo algunas investigaciones sobre la naturaleza del ritmo, metros y rimas. Mas faltándole gran parte de los documentos indispensables para tan vasta empresa, y no morando en la capital, en cuyas bibliotecas tal vez se hallarian, ha cedido á las instancias de sus amigos en Alemania, que desean gozar del fruto de sus desvelos. Publica pues por mano de ellos esta floresta, que es parte de los materiales con harto trabajo por él colectados. Compónense de 371 poesías con unos veinte mil pies de verso, ordenado en sus ramos de sacras, doctrinales, amorosas y festivas. Solo 42 de ellas han visto la luz modernamente en los 31 tomos que componen el Parnaso Español, la coleccion de Don Ramon Fernandez y las Poesías selectas de Don M. J. Quintana, de modo que esta floresta puede servir de suplemento a todas aquellas colecciones.

> (The editor of these poems has devoted the leisure of twenty years to the study of ancient Castilian poetry. He had intended to offer a full description of it, chronologically with the work of the most outstanding poets of each era, with historical and philological notes and adding some studies on the nature of rhyme, metre and verse. However, lacking the major part of the documents necessary for such a huge undertaking and not residing in the capital in whose libraries they might

be found, [the editor] has submitted to the insistence of his friends in Germany who desire to enjoy the fruits of his labours. He is therefore publishing this selection through them, which is part of the material he has collected so laboriously. It consists of 371 poems with some twenty thousand lines of verse, ordered into the categories of sacred, doctrinal, love and festive. Only forty-two of them have been published recently in the thirty-one volumes which make up the Spanish Parnassus, the collection of Don Ramón Fernández and the selected poems of Don M. J. Quintana, this selection therefore providing a supplement to all those collections.)

Böhl's public attitude is interesting. Despite private criticism of previous Spanish collectors, in his prologue he presents his work as secondary to theirs, providing a supplement to existing anthologies. Yet, this self-deprecatory stance only thinly disguises a sense of superiority at having been able to appreciate better the true poetic genius of Spain than the cream of Spanish scholarship and he goes on to claim explicitly that only those with a poetic affinity with the essence of Spain can ever properly appreciate the works on show. Of course, this select group includes Böhl himself, as well as his German friends. The ambitious plans referred to in the prologue can also be seen as an implicit criticism of existing Spanish collections, all of which Böhl had criticised for their lack of scholarly apparatus. Even without the inclusion of extensive historical-critical notes, Böhl felt he had augmented the value of his collection by carefully noting the source and origin of each text. The lack of such information in the work of Quintana and, indeed, Depping had frustrated Böhl greatly. In the prologue to the second volume of the *Floresta*, Böhl continues to draw attention to his collection in the context of contemporary Spanish philology, appraising the latter in veiled critical terms:

Habiéndose propuesto el editor de esta floresta extenderla en términos de abrazar una seleccion de cuantas poesías antiguas han llegado á su conocimiento, no ha podido ceñirse en esta segunda parte á lo desconocido solo. Sin embargo, son tan diversos los gustos que de las 319 poesías que comprende esta parte, cuarenta no mas se hallan en el Parnaso Español y trece en las poesías selectas de Don M. J. Quintana.

(Having proposed the extension of this collection to include a selection of all the ancient poems which he has come to know, the editor has not been able to limit himself in this second part to unknown works only. However, tastes vary to such a degree that of the 319 poems to appear in this part, only forty can be found in the Spanish Parnassus and thirteen in the selected poems of Don M. J. Quintana.)

Here, Böhl emphasises his non-Classical stance, referring to the difference in taste between himself and other collectors, in particular Quintana. Implicit in these comments is the notion that Böhl's approach is better, far more in tune with the qualities of these ancient works. He then underlines his superior scholarship by outlining his plans to include, alongside more familiar names in the third and final volume of the *Floresta*, a number of 'poesías desconocidas ú olvidadas' (unknown or forgotten poems), thus further enhancing the value of his collection when compared to others who have ignored or overlooked valuable material.

The extent of Böhl's contribution to the recording and preservation of Spain's literary heritage is then further emphasised in the prologue to the third volume with the proud declaration: 'No llega pues á su décima parte lo que la Floresta tiene en comun con dichas colecciones' (It does not share a tenth of its content with those other collections). The three prologues may be brief, offering only a minimum of information to a Spanish readership, but they leave that readership in no doubt as to the value of the collection when compared to the less erudite efforts of established scholars such as Quintana. This self-publicising approach may seem crass, but it proves the extent of Böhl's self-belief at this time. Now a member of the Royal Spanish Academy and equipped with a wealth of knowledge, his confidence as a man of letters is growing steadily. There is certainly little evidence of the timid tone found in the introduction to his 1805 article on Schiller published, rather ironically, by Quintana, the very object of his criticism here.

If the work of Quintana and earlier anthologists of Spanish poetry had furnished Böhl with a critical perspective in the compilation of the *Floresta*, it was the work of Leandro Fernández de Moratín (1760–1828) which provided the backdrop to Böhl's later collection, *Teatro antiguo anterior á Lope de Vega*. The neo-Classicist's *Orígenes del teatro español*, published posthumously in his collected works from 1830 to 1831, sought to fill a void in scholarship by providing a representative rather than an exhaustive collection of theatre before Lope, whilst also offering a discussion of more recent developments in the principles of dramaturgy. At the same time, Böhl's interest in his own long-planned collection of pre-Lopean theatre had been reawakened by his correspondence with Durán which began in 1829, following the publication in 1828 of the latter's *Discurso*, and his contact with the young scholar proved to be extremely useful. It was well known that Moratín, with Durán's assistance, had been working on a collection of ancient Spanish theatre, but his death in 1828 left the project shrouded in uncertainty, its fate in the hands of the king. Aware that Moratín's work would set a standard for others to follow, Böhl did not feel that he could publish his *Teatro antiguo* until he had at least seen the unpublished collection. The material became the subject of much conjecture and triggered a series of events worthy of any 'cloak and dagger' plot. The main difficulty lay in gaining access to the material which must have seemed tantalisingly close to Böhl. Moratín's manuscript was in the possession of Navarrete, but he was unable to supply Böhl with a copy because, as he explained in a letter of 13 March 1829, the manuscript was the property of the king and the latter intended to have it published. Navarrete was, therefore, only able to give Böhl brief details of the content. Undeterred by this refusal, Böhl remained persistent in his efforts, hoping to benefit from the influential position of both Navarrete and Durán in order at least to receive a preview of Moratín's work before it was placed on general sale. His tenacity was eventually rewarded in December 1830 when, thanks to Durán's intervention, and having been sworn to secrecy, he finally received a copy which Durán had bound himself.

Writing to Durán on 12 December 1830, upon receipt of the clandestine material, Böhl's response to the collection was mixed. The introduction was, he felt, adequate, but of no outstanding merit. He was, however, impressed by the 'Catálogo', exclaiming that 'nunca crei a Moratín capaz de un trabajo tan puramente literario' (I never believed Moratín to be capable of a such a purely literary undertaking). However, this did not prevent Böhl from bemoaning evidence of 'una infatuación de las reglas' (infatuation with the rules). Having now seen and assessed Moratín's collection, Böhl could continue with his own plans. Rather surprisingly, given his reservations, he at first intended to make use of the introduction to *Orígenes* rather than provide his own, suggesting a title for the volume which would incorporate Moratín's name as well as his own. He outlines his reasons in a letter to Julius on 26 January 1831, displaying in so doing a certain guile which he keeps from his Spanish friends:

Der Name von Moratin wird wahrscheinlich dem Buche mehreren Liebhaber zuführen. Für <u>mich</u> ist sein Discurso ein altes abgeleiertes Lied, und die meisten Kritiken seines Catalogus ausgedroschenes Stroh; doch nur so (meine ich) lassen sich die alten derben kraftvollen ächtspanischen Possen einschwärzen an dem es mir eigentlich gelegen ist.

(Moratín's name will probably attract more enthusiasts to the book. For <u>me</u>, his Discurso is an old, worn out song and the majority of critiques in his catalogue out of date; but this is the only way (I think) to print the old, sturdy, truly Spanish farces which are truly important to me.)

Böhl is quite shamelessly prepared to use Moratín's name for marketing purposes, having paid homage to him in order to obtain the material required. Whether or not his Spanish friends became aware of this ploy is unclear, but soon they had dissuaded him from using Moratín's introduction. Instead, by March 1831, Böhl's plans had developed to include two volumes; the first was to contain works ranging from Juan del Encina to the verse drama of Lope de Rueda and the second was to encompass Lope de Rueda's prose works and the collection of his shorter dramatic works, *El Deleitoso* (The delightful), published by Joan Timoneda in 1567. Again, each was to be furnished with German notes. However, Böhl was once more hampered by lack of material in Cadiz and the planned second volume could not go ahead without Timoneda's work, which he was unable to locate. The first volume was, however, complete and by 5 July the manuscript was on its way to Hamburg where Böhl's *Teatro antiguo anterior á Lope de Vega* was published by Perthes in 1832. The collection contained twenty-four plays by Juan del Encina, Gil Vicente, Torres Naharo and Lope de Rueda and was supplemented by 'Andeutungen für deutsche Leser' (Hints for German readers).

Böhl's two collections were a major achievement of scholarly and philological significance, both for German Hispanism and for the knowledge of indigenous literature in Spain itself. Böhl had succeeded in amassing a wealth of material, some of it on the verge of disappearing, and had preserved it for future generations, just as he had hoped to do. The collections may not have been best sellers in their day and may still remain rather obscure on the periphery of modern philology when compared to the monumental works undertaken by the likes of the Brothers Grimm and Durán. Nevertheless, Böhl's contribution to Romantic philology, grounded in the ideals of Herderian historicism, deserves recognition as part of the contemporary Romantic revaluation of European culture.

This becomes all the more significant when one considers his work in its transcultural context. Here, Böhl's dual cultural identity emerges as the key to his understanding of two cultures at differing stages in their reception of both Enlightenment and Romantic thought. That Böhl's collections should display a dual identity is perhaps inevitable. Compiled by a German living in Spain, containing Spanish material, but published in Hamburg, they are effectively the product of two cultures brought together in close contact by a scholar with an intimate knowledge and a love of both. It is this duality which sets them apart from other collections of the period, in particular those emerging from Hispanists in Germany. Grimm had made no attempt to place his work in any German context, Depping opted for the rather odd combination of German notes and titles with original Spanish texts and Diez followed Herder and Schlegel in opting for German translation only. Böhl's texts take a different approach to all of these and in so doing remain a hybrid. Nowhere is this more apparent than in the critical apparatus added to the collections by the editor. Here, Böhl is clearly addressing two separate audiences. For example, whilst the prologues to the three volumes of the *Floresta* are directed at Böhl's Spanish readership, emphasising the pioneering philological nature of the collection in preserving and categorising Spain's ancient popular poetry, the third volume also carries the following concluding message for German readers, which adopts a quite different tone:

> Hiermit schließt diese Blumenlese, die hoffentlich keine andere als angenehme Eindrücke hinterlassen wird. Möge sie dabei die Ueberzeugung verbreiten helfen, daß ächte Poesie weder an Zeit noch Ort gebunden ist; sondern jedesmal verjüngt

aufersteht, wo die Menschheit, einer höheren Bestimmung eingedenk, ihre irdischen Verhältnisse zu veredeln strebt.

(Herewith ends this selection, which will hopefully leave behind only favourable impressions. May it in so doing have helped to spread the conviction that true poetry is bound neither to time nor place, but rather rises anew wherever humanity, mindful of a higher destiny, seeks to ennoble its earthly existence.)

There is a change of emphasis in this brief note, shifting the focus from the essentially philological concerns of the Spanish prologues to more aesthetic, inherently Romantic values. This concession to a German readership, approaching the collection from a different perspective, underlines the unique position of Böhl's work. The inclusion of separate comments for German and Spanish readers confuses the identity of the collections, reflecting very much the position of the philologist himself, seeking to mediate between two cultures, feeding the German Romantic aesthetic desire for popular material whilst at the same time attempting to educate Spanish taste to appreciate and preserve the literary glories of the nation's indigenous culture. This shows Böhl responding to each culture in the context of its own development, taking into consideration the extent and appraisal of Romantic ideals in each.

As part of this heuristic approach, Böhl was keen to provide a critical apparatus for both collections. This would be founded on a number of earlier works dealing with literary history and genre issues and can be traced back to Böhl's studies at Görslow and the 1808 article, 'Über die spanische Literatur'. Also significant are a number of documents published during the polemic, including the 'Bosquejo' from the third *Pasatiempo*, in which Böhl announces his intention to publish more detailed material in due course, thus effectively announcing the appearance of the *Floresta* in 1821. There are also a series of texts in the third *Pasatiempo* dealing specifically with the theatre: 'De las varias clases de comedias españolas' (On the various types of Spanish comedia), 'Del gracioso en las comedias españolas' (On the fool in Spanish comedias) and 'Del metro de las comedias españolas' (On metre in Spanish comedias). Whilst these relate to the polemic itself in debunking the myth of universal superiority, they also suggest a theoretical engagement with older literature of the kind necessary for the detailed annotation of the material presented in both the *Floresta* and the *Teatro antiguo*. Böhl's studies during the polemic, which focused mainly on Spanish literature, complemented those of a broader nature undertaken at Görslow, thus enabling him to draw upon a knowledge of both cultures. This would prove invaluable when addressing the dual readerships of his two collections, allowing him to tailor his supplementary material to suit their differing tastes. What emerges is a bias towards what is presumed to be a far more appreciative German audience steeped in Romantic values. Böhl's Spanish audience, on the other hand, is presented with a minimum of material, their attention drawn instead to the works themselves and the need to salvage them for posterity. Consequently, whilst the German audience is treated with the respect owed to a connoisseur, the Spanish readership is handled with an almost patronising air.

Böhl's most ambitious plans for a critical apparatus centred on the *Floresta*. Here, the bias towards his German audience is clear. Whilst providing each volume with a brief explanatory prologue in Spanish, from the outset, Böhl was concerned to provide his German readers with something more substantial. Initially, he deliberated whether to add an appendix with German poems, presumably intended as a point of comparison, but this was never carried out. Instead, the collection was furnished with 'Fingerzeige für deutsche Leser' (Pointers for German readers) on separately numbered pages which gave brief information on some of the poems and poets. It is interesting to note how Böhl's own stance colours his commentary, often emphasising the Catholic, religious content and evaluating works according to his own set of ideals. Typical is his brief evaluation of Sor Juana Ines de la Cruz whose poems are, he claims, for the most part mediocre, with some 'als Erzeugungen einer Nonne anstößig' (quite improper for the creations of a nun).[3] He also admits to editing out some material of poor quality. Böhl must have been aware of the negative impression his brief notes might create and his response to Julius' enquiry in June 1820 as to whether the 'Fingerzeige' should be translated into Spanish was a categorical refusal. Böhl commented that they would be of no relevance to a Spanish readership. Reyes Ponce (A: 183) claims that Böhl was too embarrassed to translate them into Spanish for fear of the derision they might attract, just as Herder had been forty years previously when he published his *Volkslieder* anonymously. This does not, however, tally with Böhl's customary tenacity and it seems far more likely, given the partially critical nature of the notes, that Böhl felt a Spanish translation might weaken his argument for the preservation of Spain's literary heritage in Spain itself, playing into the hands of *afrancesado* theorists.

Böhl's ambivalence towards his Spanish audience remained apparent as he continued to make ever more elaborate plans for a critical apparatus for the collection. Writing to Navarrete on 15 November 1821, he announced his intention to produce a supplementary volume entitled 'Spaziergänge durch die Floresta' (Wanderings through the Floresta). This would expand on the 'Fingerzeige' and was to be directed solely at a German audience: Spaniards would have no use for it:

> [. . .] y después ha de seguir un tomito para los literatos donde además de decir de los autores lo poco que se sabe, se dicurrirá sobre los metros y se analizará el mérito de muchas piezas. Esto habrá de ser en idioma alemán por el ningún interés que los españoles del día toman en materias literarias, y también porque el modo de entender

la poesía, generalizado en Alemania y en Inglaterra, está diametralmente opuesto a lo que se opina de esto en Francia y España, como ya lo han indicado los Pasatiempos.

([. . .] and then this is to be followed by a slim volume for scholars in which, as well as the little information which exists on the authors, there will be a discussion of metre and analysis of the merit of many pieces. This will have to be in German due to the total lack of interest which today's Spaniards show in literary matters and also because the current means of understanding poetry in Germany and England is diametrically opposed to opinion in France and Spain, as the Pasatiempos have shown.)

Once more, aesthetic as well as historicist issues dominate as Böhl condemns the lack of critical judgement shown by Spanish contemporaries. The material included in the *Floresta* and any critical commentary which Böhl might succeed in supplying could only be appreciated in Germany or Great Britain where, Böhl feels, the Romantic spirit still informs critical judgement. Discussion of the finer points of poetics would simply be wasted on the Spanish and the French. Despite the obvious passion shown by Böhl for the projected critical volume, the plan was fraught with difficulty as the pressures of everyday life impeded its progress. He felt he needed to see the *Floresta* complete before he could begin work on the 'Spaziergänge' and the project required a prolonged period of peace to reflect, something which was hard to find given the distraction of commercial concerns and his wife's erratic behaviour. Nevertheless, the project continued to occupy Böhl's mind until his death in 1836.

Böhl's failure to complete the 'Spaziergänge' is made all the more frustrating when one considers that much of the material required had already been written long before the first volume of the *Floresta* appeared, forming part of his submission to the Royal Spanish Academy in 1820. It is also ironic, given Böhl's insistence that the critical apparatus to the *Floresta* appear in German only, that these, the only comparable texts which he succeeded in completing, were written in Spanish and never published. Their content would provide a far clearer picture of the depth of Böhl's knowledge, already apparent in his correspondence with Julius and Durán, as well as enabling further investigation of his development as a scholar and thinker during the last decades of his life. Unfortunately, however, these documents remain inaccessible or even lost, inexplicably missing from the holdings of the Academy, but possibly held by the Osborne family in El Puerto.[4]

Despite these difficulties, it is possible to glean some idea of the content of the three studies submitted to the Academy by considering the context in which they were written. The texts are certainly related in some measure to the content of the third *Pasatiempo*, in particular the 'Bosquejo', providing evidence of Böhl's growing critical stature towards the end of the polemic. This is supported by the fact that in a letter to Julius dated 19 February 1820, Böhl mentions the possibility of sending the third *Pasatiempo* as part of his submission to the Academy. The content of the pamphlet does not, however, focus on poetry and, consequently, he appears to have decided to submit instead three new texts specifically related to his philological work, perhaps also hoping to gloss over some of the less seemly side of the polemic when approaching the Academy for approval. (In the end, he did also ensure that members of the Academy received copies of the third *Pasatiempo* on an unofficial basis; their responses are not recorded.) Although the new pieces are absent from the holdings of the Academy, Carnero claims to have located copies of them in the Osborne archive (O: 308). He describes the documents as 'muy ciudada' (very careful[ly written]) with 'abundantes notas a pie de página' (abundant notes at the foot of the page), surmising from this that they were intended to be read by a third party. Carnero lists three documents. The first, a twelve-page manuscript with the title 'Bosquejo historico de las formas de la poesía nacional castellana' (Sketch for a history of forms of Spanish national poetry), would appear, judging by the title, to relate to the 'Bosquejo' contained in the third *Pasatiempo*. A second document, also twelve pages in length, entitled 'Sistema de metros de la poesía nacional española por el cual se prueba el ningun fundamento de las divisiones por numero de sílabas' (System of metre of Spanish national poetry by means of which is proven the lack of foundation for the division by number of syllables) discusses various metres including the iambic, trochaic and dactylic pentameters. The third document, seventeen pages in length, has the title 'Sistema de rimas en las formas nacionales de la poesía castellana' (System of rhyme in the national forms of Spanish poetry) with sections relating to *coplas, estrofas, villancicos* and *glosas*, amongst others.

    Carnero's discovery is supported by other evidence. The letter sent by Böhl to the Academy on 4 April 1820, which is supported by the records of the Academy, lists a set of documents which tally with those found by Carnero, but which no longer exist in the Academy's collection.[5] Whilst the documents held in the Osborne archive would appear to carry far more detailed analysis than those published in the third *Pasatiempo*, there are clear similarities and it may even be the case that Böhl expanded some texts already published during the polemic. There is evidence that Böhl intended the critical essays submitted to the Academy later to form part of the *Floresta*. Writing to Navarrete on 8 April 1817, he mentions the possible inclusion of 'una disertación sobre la parte métrica de las poesías de aquel tiempo, fruto de muchos años de meditación' (a dissertation on the metrical aspect of the poetry of that era, the fruit of many years of thought). Later, writing to Julius in June 1820, he promises to send copies of the essays submitted to the Academy so that his friend might edit them as he best saw fit. It is highly probable, therefore, that the documents submitted to the Academy, having themselves evolved from those published during the polemic, would have formed the basis for the ill-fated 'Spaziergänge'. Sadly, until the material becomes available, it remains impossible to assess this aspect of Böhl's scholarly career fully.

Issues surrounding the critical apparatus for the *Teatro antiguo* are far clearer. Böhl provided the volume with 'Andeutungen für deutsche Leser' (Hints for German readers), but had no plans to augment these, although he did briefly mention in a letter to Julius on 2 June 1820 the possibility of including the essays on the theatre found in the third *Pasatiempo*. However, these relate specifically to post-Lopean theatre and would therefore have less relevance to the planned collection. Accordingly, the issues surrounding the dual identity of the *Teatro antiguo* relate instead to the editorial stance adopted in dealing with Böhl's dual readerships. Addressing his Spanish audience, Böhl's comments echo those of the *Floresta* prologues, highlighting the positive nature of his work to salvage Spain's ancient literature. In so doing, he has been forced to take certain measures and the collection was prefaced by a short prologue which explains the editorial approach adopted:

> Las antiguas impresiones de los primeros ensayos de la Musa dramática en España se han hecho tan raras, que esta reimpresion de la mejor parte dellas no puede dejar de ser grata á los que se interesan en este ramo de la literatura. El editor no ha tenido otra mira, que el reproducir estas antiguallas en su forma original. Solo se ha permitido la supresion de algunas divagaciones pesadas ó impertinentes, y tal cual vez la mudanza de alguna palabra en obsequio del sentido. Estas faltas en los originales son sin duda erratas, de las que rebosan las impresiones poco esmeradas de aquellos tiempos.
>
> (The old editions of the first attempts of the dramatic muse in Spain have become so rare that this reprinting of the majority of them cannot help but be welcome to those who are interested in this branch of literature. The editor has had no other intention than to reproduce these ancient works in their original form. He has only allowed himself to suppress some tiresome or impertinent digressions and, now and then, the removal of a word or two for the benefit of sense. These failings in the originals are doubtless errors of the type which are to be found in the rather unpolished editions of those times.)

Crucial here is the sense that Böhl feels he is preserving works which were at risk of disappearing altogether. This is an ongoing project, in the best sense of Romantic philology, and Böhl confirms his plans to continue the collection 'si el presente merece la aceptacion pública' (if the current volume meets with public approval), something which never came to fruition. More significantly, however, the prologue would also seem to demonstrate Böhl's faith in the writers of ancient Spain and his desire to present them in the most positive light, a desire which sees him compromise his own professed values by effectively editing the works. This faith is, however, open to question when one compares the somewhat bland praise of the prologue with the comments included in the 'Andeutungen', where Böhl is openly critical of the standard of the works he is reproducing. He is particularly scathing in his assessment of Juan del Encina:

Nr. 1 ist also wohl das erste wirklich aufgeführte Drama in spanischer Sprache, und eigentlich nur in dieser Hinsicht merkwürdig. In Nr. 2 finden sich schon mehrere Anklänge eines poetischen Gemüthes. Nr. 3 ist ganz lustig, doch hatte der Archpreste de Hita denselben Gegenstand schon im 14ten Jahrhunderte weit vorzüglicher behandelt: [. . .] Nr. 4 und 5 nähern sich schon dem eigentlichen Drama als Darstellung einer fortschreitenden Handlung. Nr. 6 ist nur ein wohlgesezter Gevatterschnack. Seine übrigen dramatischen Arbeiten sind des Abdruckes nicht werth. Der ehrliche Encina überhaupt war mehr ein Reimer als ein Dichter.

(Number 1 is therefore probably the first drama in Spanish to be properly performed and is only really notable for this reason. In number 2, there are already more echoes of a poetic disposition. Number 3 is very funny, but Archpriest Hita already dealt far better with the same material in the fourteenth century. [. . .] Numbers 4 and 5 are already more in line with true drama as the representation of an ongoing plot. Number 6 is only well-written chitter chatter. His remaining dramatic works are not worth printing. The honourable Encina was indeed more of a rhymer than a poet.)

Böhl is similarly critical of Torres de Naharro, complaining of his 'metrischer Zwang' (metrical compulsion) which leads him to employ almost every possible metre and condemning elements of his work as 'abgeschmackt und ungereimt' (tasteless and unrhymed), something which forces him to leave out large sections. This certainly seems to go far beyond Böhl's intention merely to remove 'errata' from the original texts as he claims in the Spanish prologue. Similar editorial decisions are also applied to Lope de Rueda whose otherwise flawless work is marred, in Böhl's opinion, by the poor quality of his *Coloquios*. Consequently, Böhl opts to reproduce only the comical *entremeses*, the rest of the pieces discarded as 'unausstehlich geschraubt' (unbearably pretentious). Of the four playwrights included in the collection, only Gil Vicente escapes Böhl's critical eye. Here, Böhl's only real complaint is that Gil Vicente had not written more in Spanish, rather than in Portuguese. The difference in tone and level of detail in the prologue and the 'Andeutungen' would suggest that Böhl was again consciously addressing two different audiences. The difference does not lie in the language – he could simply have provided versions of the same text – but is instead rooted in Böhl's perception of the receptiveness, taste and knowledge of a German as opposed to a Spanish audience. Whereas the German reading public were already very well disposed towards Spain's ancient literature and thus able to appreciate criticism of it in the spirit Böhl intended, that of an informed appraisal combined with the philological drive to preserve, a Spanish audience might be more likely to view any criticism of the works as proof of their inferiority, thus simply strengthening the position of those defending *afrancesado* views. Aware of this danger, Böhl plays down his editorial intervention in the prologue, defending it on grounds of taste or correction, whereas in the German text, he is openly judgmental. There is something deeply ironic in Böhl's attitude to his readerships. Having spent five years defending the honour of Calderón in Spain in the periodical press and claiming victory with his election to the Royal Spanish Academy, by aiming his collections at two different audiences in this way, he nevertheless implicitly concedes defeat. Deeply immersed in Spanish life, convinced in his Catholic faith, Böhl must still turn to his native Germany for the aesthetic sanction of his literary ideals and, his Spanish friends notwithstanding, remains unable to find adequate echo for his views in the literary culture of modern Spain. This is not say that his work was in vain – it would yield notable results as the century wore on – but in the final years of his life, Böhl's frustration at the minimal impact of his scholarship is painfully clear.

NOTES

[1] The reasons for choosing Perthes as a publisher were threefold. Firstly, Böhl was well acquainted with the publishing house and Perthes himself following his involvement in the patriotic circles of Hamburg and the *Vaterländisches Museum*, secondly, Böhl was anxious to maintain a reputation in Germany as well as Spain and, thirdly, on a practical level, the cost of publishing in Germany was far lower than that in Spain, an advantage further enhanced by Perthes' willingness to act for Böhl for a minimum cost.

[2] This involved an amended version of volume I and reprints of volumes II and III.

[3] *Floresta de rimas antiguas castellanas ordenado por Don Juan Nicolas Böhl de Faber de la Real Academia Española*, 3 vols (Hamburg: Perthes y Besser, 1821–5); I: 'Fingerzeige', 6.

[4] There are, in addition, a series of documents held in the *Biblioteca nacional* in Madrid (MS2590) in Böhl's hand which provide a detailed bibliography of poets and works from the sixteenth and seventeenth centuries. Inspection of these documents has shown that they are not the materials sent to the Academy.

[5] Camille Pitollet, 'Une lettre inédite de Böhl von Faber à l'éditeur Friedrich Perthes à Hambourg relative à la Floresta de rimas antiguas castellanas', *Revue germanique*, V (1909), 301–18.

Chapter 15
The Reception of Böhl's Philology

The reception of Böhl's collections reflects the multiplicity of his target audiences. Indeed, Böhl's attitude towards his two different readerships would seem to be justified by their differing responses: the Spanish literary world initially all but ignored his work, whilst the German periodical press, along with commentators in Great Britain, were much more receptive, publishing a number of positive reviews often penned by prominent figures. In both cases, attention focused almost solely on the *Floresta*, tapping into the wider appreciation of the ballad form which was popular at the time, thanks to the work of Burns, Moore, Byron and Scott, as well as Arnim, Brentano and the Brothers Grimm. Böhl was particularly pleased by opinion in his native Germany, where the collection was, as he had expected, well received. The climate was certainly favourable for such a venture, especially in the wake of the popular and highly praised Spanish collections of Grimm, Depping and Diez, as well as the literary histories of Dieze, Bouterwek and Schlegel.

Attention was first drawn to the collection by an advertisement placed by Julius in the *Originalien aus dem Gebiete der Wahrheit, Kunst, Laune und Phantasie* (Original pieces from the field of truth, art, recreation and imagination) in Hamburg in 1821. Judging by Böhl's response, voiced in a letter of 23 December 1821, Julius appears to have adopted a rather ostentatious marketing strategy, placing Böhl's work on a par with that of Goethe, something which Böhl understandably denies, excusing Julius' words as the result of an over-enthusiasm born of friendship. This initial announcement was followed by more measured responses from a number of prominent scholars which, although markedly less effusive, nevertheless demonstrate a recognition of Böhl's work which reaches the core of contemporary German letters. This is emphasised by the positive response from Goethe himself, writing to Perthes from Weimar on 12 May 1821:

Der Spanische Lustgarten hat mich aufgeregt dieser herrlichen Sprache und Literatur wieder einige Stunden zu widmen; hätte der treffliche Sammler, von dem ich wohl nähere Kenntniss wünsche, nur das doppelte oder dreyfache an die Fingerzeige für deutsche Leser gewendet so hätte er mich und alle die ohngefähr in demselben Verhältniss gegen das Spanische sich finden sehr gefördert und würde uns ohne Mühe viel Mühe erspart haben.[1]

(The Spanish pleasance encouraged me once more to dedicate a few hours to this wonderful language and literature; had the worthy collector, of whom I would indeed like to know more, only spent twice or thrice as much time on the <u>Pointers for German Readers</u>, then, without much trouble, he would have aided and spared a great deal of trouble for me and all those who are in more or less the same position in relation to the Spanish language.)

Goethe echoes Friedrich Schlegel's earlier desire to see careful annotation as an accompaniment to the collation of such material, the aesthetic appreciation of which would later form the core of his 1823 review of Beauregard Pandin's *Spanische Romanzen* (1823), in which he appraises Spanish *Volkslieder* as the product of a nation 'die eine reiche Wirklichkeit und darin ein geistreiches Leben besaß und besitzt' (which possessed and possesses a rich reality and within it a witty life).[2] Whether Goethe ever pursued his wish to know more of Böhl in the context of this appreciation of Spanish culture is not recorded, but the latter was deeply grateful for his recognition which, although expressed privately, was more than was ever forthcoming from August Wilhelm Schlegel, who continued to maintain a silence on the matter of his exiled acolyte.

Others, however, made more public comment. Bouterwek reviewed the collection in August 1822 in the *Göttinger Gelehrten Anzeigen* (Göttingen scholarly announcements), commenting favourably on the broad selection of material and making passing reference to Böhl's involvement in the Calderón polemic. Writing to Julius, Böhl welcomed the praise of the Göttingen scholar, expressing surprise at the lack of anti-Catholic rhetoric from the 'Verstandsquartier' (rational quarter; 1 November 1822). A further review appeared in 1822, this time in the *Leipziger Literatur-Zeitung* (Leipzig Literary News). The author, the celebrated translator of Calderón, Johann Georg Keil (1781–1857), praised the collection, highlighting Böhl's prominence as member of the Royal Spanish Academy. Böhl's response to Keil's review was mixed, fearing that it might have gone too far in praising the collection, commenting to Julius on 21 January 1823 that '[d]ie Leipziger hat den Fehler daß sie das Günstige übertreibt, sonsten geht sie ganz von dem rechten Gesichtspunkt aus' (the Leipzig paper makes the mistake of exaggerating the favourable, otherwise it views things from the correct standpoint). The enthusiasm for Böhl's work which this suggests secured a positive German reception for the collection throughout the 1820s, although some criticism began to emerge as knowledge of the field developed. Following the publication of the second edition, Friedrich Diez discussed the work in the *Jahrbücher für wissenschaftliche Kritik* (Yearbook for scientific criticism) in 1827, praising Böhl's efforts, but expressing some reservations concerning the treatment of the material, which he considered lacking in suitable care.[3] Nevertheless, he lauded Böhl's work as a major source for future scholars and continued to express his approval, later reviewing the *Teatro antiguo* in similarly positive terms in the same journal in 1833.⁴

These positive assessments of Böhl's efforts, both private and public, illustrate the extent to which he had come to be associated with Spanish letters in Germany. There is no doubt that his name figured amongst those now accredited with the revival of interest in Spain's literary heritage, including Bouterwek, Schegel and Grimm. The decision by Perthes to move to a second edition of the *Floresta* supports this, indicating a level of interest which would elude Böhl in Spain itself during the 1820s. The positive early reception of the collection secured a degree of posthumous continuity which saw the *Floresta* established as a benchmark for future scholarship. Interest in the collection was such that when Viennese Hispanist, Ferdinand Wolf, set about compiling his two-volume *Floresta de rimas modernas castellanas; ó poesias selectas castellanas desde el tiempo de Ignacio Luzan hasta nuestros dias, con una introducción histórica, con noticias biograficas y críticas* (Selection of modern Castilian poems; or selected Castilian poems from the time of Ignacio Luzán to the present day, with an historical introduction, with biographical and critical notes) in 1837, he explicitly intended to supplement Böhl's collection. His decision marks a conscious continuation of the Hispanist work begun by Herder, furthered by Grimm and Depping and expanded by Böhl himself. Using Böhl's collection as a template, Wolf's work collates material from Luzán to the early nineteenth century and plays homage to the Hamburg merchant in the introduction, although acknowledging that Böhl might not approve of the more modern material. This reservation notwithstanding, the importance of Böhl's collection is clear. Wolf opts for a purely Spanish context and supplies a critical apparatus of the type long envisaged for the latter's own collection. Wolf's indebtedness to Böhl is heightened by his close friendship with Julius who kept him informed about Böhl's work and supplied him with copies of documents by both Böhl and his wife. This is typical of Julius' own campaign to ensure his friend was not forgotten. As well as preserving his correspondence, Julius included an essay on Böhl's life and work as an appendix to his 1852 translation of George Ticknor's *Literature of Spain*, a gesture which maintained Böhl's profile in the German Hispanism of the late nineteenth century.⁵

The positive appraisal of Böhl's *Floresta* in Germany was echoed in the British periodical press where all the major literary journals took note of his work. Indeed, it is perhaps fitting, given Böhl's own predilection for English writing in the 1820s, that his work should find a welcome resonance in the literary landscape of late Romantic Britain. Once again, attention focuses mainly on the *Floresta*. The collection was first reviewed in the *Monthly Review* in 1821 in positive terms which Böhl had not expected, commenting to Julius that the views expressed were 'schmeichelhafter als ich sie erwarten konnte' (more complimentary than I could have expected; letter of 14 July 1822). *Blackwood's Magazine* also reviewed the collection briefly in January 1822, although Böhl was disappointed that this would be the only mention of the collection in a periodical which he regarded highly at the time. The rival *Edinburgh Review*, however, made several references to his work. The first was a letter in 1821 from Julius himself, signed 'Eremita hamburgensis', which sought to introduce both collector and collection to a British readership. This was followed in January 1824 by an article which used the *Floresta* and other similar collections as a starting point for a discussion of Spanish poetry in general.[6] Böhl was rather unimpressed with this, commenting to Julius on 26 March 1824 that the article was 'schön geschrieben, mit einigen hellen Ideen, aber im Einzelnen <u>unwissend</u>, <u>ungerecht</u> und <u>unpoetisch</u>' (well written with some clear ideas, but in places <u>unknowledgeable</u>, <u>unjust</u> and <u>unpoetic</u>), his frustration emphasised by the angry underlining. However, as he goes on to explain, such a response was little more than one might expect from such a source:

> Die preisenden Lobeserhebungen meiner Vorrede werden persiflirt, die religiösen Kindlichkeiten verlacht, dennoch wird die Sammlung <u>excellent</u> genannt. Mehr konnte ich von den Verächtern Wordsworth's und Coleridge nicht erwarten.
>
> (The praising commendations of my preface are satirised, the religious childlike qualities are mocked, but then the collection is described as <u>excellent</u>. I could not have expected more from those who disrespect Wordsworth and Coleridge.)

What Böhl fails to note in his disgust is that his collection was reviewed alongside those of Grimm and Depping, thus locating him at the heart of the British reception of German Romantic philology. However, the editors of the *Edinburgh Review* are, as Böhl complains, rather scathing of his efforts and the content of the collection is condemned as repetitive and at times 'egregiously absurd' (422), although some of the love poems, especially the shorter ones, merit being called 'exquisitely graceful' (424). The journal overlooked Böhl's historicist aims in salvaging the material and focused instead on an aesthetic evaluation, thus only partly appreciating the value of the collection. This is perhaps the main reason for his outrage and Böhl's angry comments highlight once more his determination to have both his work and the material properly appreciated. There is no room for compromise, something further underlined in his dealings with the prominent English Hispanist, John Bowring.

The two scholars met briefly when Bowring approached Böhl on a visit to Cadiz in the spring of 1822 with a request for manuscripts of ancient Spanish theatre for publication in London. Despite the acknowledgement of his scholarly credentials which such a visit would suggest, Böhl was rather ungracious in describing the Englishman, presenting him as something of an inconvenience. Indeed, their relationship would remain fraught throughout, Böhl suspicious of Bowring as 'sicherlich ein Freigeist und Radikal' (surely a free thinker and radical; letter to Julius, 21 January 1823).[7] It was this which led Böhl to suspect Bowring to be the author of a further article on Spanish poetry in the *Edinburgh Review* in 1824 which he criticised for mixing poetry with politics (letter to Julius, 8 March 1825).[8] Such antipathies aside, Bowring was clearly impressed by Böhl's work. In 1823, he published an extensive article in the *London Magazine*, later published in *Galignani's Magazine*, which praised Böhl highly, claiming that '[n]o man has probably done so much for the revival of old Spanish poetical literature as Böhl de Faber',[9] although, echoing Goethe, Bowring does bemoan the lack of critical apparatus in the *Floresta*. Nevertheless, the English Hispanist was able to make use of Böhl's scholarship as a valuable resource, just as Diez would later suggest, a fact evidenced by the inclusion of some twenty texts from the *Floresta* (some taken from the manuscript for volume two) in his *Ancient Poetry and Romances of Spain* (1824). Collaboration with Böhl provided Bowring with material unavailable to others such as John Gibson Lockhart whose *Ancient Spanish Ballads Historical and Romantic* had appeared in Edinburgh a year earlier.

Böhl's interaction with Bowring can be seen as particularly significant in widening his European sphere of influence beyond the dual axis of Germany and Spain. This in turn would impact upon the reception of his work in Spain itself and it is indicative of the complex, transcultural context of Böhl's work that his reception in the British press would lead to the first Spanish review of his collection, which emerged, perhaps unexpectedly, from the Liberal Spanish exile community living in London. Their periodical, *Ocios de Españoles emigrados* (Diversions of émigré Spaniards), drew attention to Böhl's work in May 1826 in a review article written in response to the publication of the third volume of the *Floresta*. The piece, which Böhl, whilst aware of positive appraisals of his work in exile circles, may never have seen, takes the collection as a point of departure for a discussion of the development of Spanish poetry and defines the German's intentions as follows:

[S]u intencion ha sido solamente reunir en las tres partes de su *Floresta* lo que basta para vindicar á los antiguos poetas castellanos un eminente lugar en el Parnaso. Puede lisonjearse de haberlo conseguido, y no es trabajo perdido el haberlo intentado, aun despues de la aceptacion que han tenido otras varias compilaciones de esta especie, hechas con el mismo objeto.[10]

([H]is intention has simply been to reunite in the three parts of the *Floresta* that which suffices to vindicate for the ancient Castilian poets an eminent place in the Parnassus. He can flatter himself at having achieved this and it was no waste of time to try to do so, even after the approbation which other similar collections have received, compiled with the same objective.)

The other collections alluded to presumably include those published in Spain and criticised so vehemently by Böhl, but also that of Depping, which was published with translated, augmented notes in London in 1825 by the editor of the *Ocios*, the Valencian bookseller, Vicente Salvá.[11] Aware of its context, the reviewer praises Böhl's collection for the publication of unknown or forgotten material, but is critical of certain omissions, such as excerpts from *El Cantar del mio Cid*. There is also concern at the apparent lack of interest in the epic and historical *romance*, as well as lyrical works included in ancient Spanish theatre. Clearly, the reviewer cannot have been aware of Böhl's grand plan which aimed to fill these very gaps. It would, therefore, have been satisfying for Böhl to see the collections of Ramón Fernández and Quintana criticised for similar omissions, happy in the knowledge that his work would eventually surpass theirs. The conclusion reached by the reviewer is highly complimentary:

> Tenemos pues la mayor complacencia en poder decir: que la Floresta de rimas antiguas castellanas del Sr. Böhl de Faber basta por sí sola para presentar en un punto de vista mui ventajoso las diferentes épocas de nuestra poesía, desde sus primeros ensayos inmediatos á la formacion de la lengua, hasta el fin de la dominacion de la dinastía austríaca. (454)

> (We have great pleasure therefore in saying that the Floresta de rimas antiguas castellanas by Mr Böhl de Faber suffices on its own to present the different epochs of our poetry from a most advantageous viewpoint, from its first attempts following the formation of the language to the end of the period of domination of the Austrian dynasty.)

The response of the editors of the *Ocios* to Böhl's collection, combined with the interest shown in the like-minded Depping, indicates a willingness in Liberal exile circles, having been exposed through the British periodical press to new aesthetic ideas of the sort being defended by Böhl himself, to adopt a more Romantic appreciation of Spain's older literature which begins to approach that already prevalent in other European cultures. Indeed, the interest emerging from exile circles in London pre-empted the first public acknowledgement of Böhl's efforts in Spain itself. The reception of his work there was fraught with difficulty, due in part to the strict censorship and publishing laws introduced by the Fernandine government in 1814, which made the distribution of Spanish books published abroad illegal. This meant that initial dissemination of the *Floresta* was extremely awkward, although Böhl did his best to circumvent the law. When the first volume was published in 1821, he ordered one hundred copies for sale through a Cadiz bookseller. This was a risky undertaking and Böhl must have been aware of the danger it posed. Although the collection itself would appear somewhat benign in terms of its political content, it was nevertheless open to interpretation as supporting the ideals of throne and altar through its emphasis on the glories of the chivalric past. This was at a time when the political landscape was marked by uncertainty as the Liberal government in Cadiz strove to maintain its unconvincing hold on power in the face of the continual threat of a royalist revival. Böhl's conservative stance was no secret following the polemic and his new venture was bound to attract some attention in Liberal circles. Sale of the volume was indeed contested by an otherwise unknown figure named Liaño who expressed concern at the religious content of the volume.[12] The complaint, a copy of which was sent to Julius in October 1821, demanded that the texts be confiscated and the bookseller fined. In the end, the authorities clearly had more pressing issues to deal with as the complaint was ignored. Böhl and his bookseller decided, however, not to aggravate the situation by insisting on further sales in Cadiz and instead sent the copies of the *Floresta* to Madrid in the hope of finding an outlet there,[13] a move which Böhl himself viewed with a degree of scepticism, convinced as he was of the prevailing *afrancesado* attitudes of the capital which would have little time for such a national collection.

Censorship and political motivations notwithstanding, Böhl had initially been hopeful of a positive response from like-minded scholars within Spain. A copy of the *Floresta* was sent to Navarrete in May 1821, along with another from Francisca for her friend, the poet and editor of the *Diario*, Arriaza.[14] Navarrete was duly impressed and in a letter dated 3 July 1821 Böhl thanked him for his praise, hoping too that he has not caused any offence by including the name of the Academy in the title. He goes on to describe other positive responses from fellow German Catholic converts and 'algunos inteligentes' (some intelligent [people]), sadly anonymous, from Spain's literary elite. At this early stage, however, the reception of the *Floresta* in Spain did not extend beyond Böhl's own circle of friends and acquaintances. This presented him with a dilemma. Despite his aversion to their *afrancesado* aesthetics, as the 1820s wore on, Böhl was eager for a wider audience from within the literary establishment. The focus of his attention is Quintana who it was known was preparing a second edition of his *Poesías selectas*. Böhl's response to this highlights both the extent of his frustration at seeing the *Floresta* stranded on the periphery of the modest indigenous revival of Spain's literary heritage and the ambivalent stance which he finds himself forced to adopt in relation to his Spanish contemporaries, at once dismissive of their aesthetic values, but also acutely aware that without their acknowledgement, his Spanish readership would remain limited. This becomes particularly apparent in the context of his relations with Durán.

Writing to Durán on 13 November 1829, Böhl attacks Quintana as one of many detestable modern poets, but nevertheless expresses the hope that the latter would at least have made use of the *Floresta* to enhance the new edition of his *Poesías selectas*. In a subsequent letter, dated 20 November 1829, Böhl further appraises Quintana in the context of a lengthy piece on the *romancero* which provides a further tantalising indication of the depth of knowledge Böhl might have been able to display had the 'Spaziergänge' come to fruition. Steering Durán towards German and English collections as well as those published in Spain, Böhl provides an overview of Hispanist philology to date and identifies two phases in the development of the *romancero*, the first up to 1600, the second from Sedano to the present. In so doing, he compares his *Floresta* with Quintana's collection in an attempt to demonstrate that the poets he has chosen are of a higher standard, the latter having chosen far too many of a classical nature – 'epicos y didacticos' (epic and didactic) – and having omitted 'tantos poetas dignos de nota' (so many poets worthy of note). This relatively mild censure later takes on a more vehement tone once Böhl gained access to the new edition of the *Poesías selectas* from which he quickly deduced that Quintana had paid no attention whatsoever to the *Floresta*, having only added two poems by San Juan de la Cruz to the section dedicated to ancient poetry. Böhl is irate:

Quisiera que alguien (que no fuese yo mismo) preguntara al Sr. Quintana: 1) Si en 23 años que han discurrido entre las dos ediciones de su colección nada ha encontrado digno de añadirse á la parte antigua sino las dichas dos poesías. 2) Si no sabe que de 20 años a esta parte se han publicado varias colecciones de la misma clase mucho mas completas que la suya. 3) Si ignora del todo que en los años de 1820 á 1825 se ha impreso una *Floresta de rimas antiguas castellanas* en Hamburgo de que no faltan ejemplares en manos de los aficionados de Madrid. (15 October 1830)

(I would like someone (if not myself) to ask Sr Quintana: 1) Whether in the twenty-three years which have passed between the two editions of his collection he has found nothing worth adding to the ancient section other than the two poems mentioned. 2) Whether he is unaware that during the twenty years up to now various collections of the type have been published which are far more comprehensive than his. 3) Whether he is completely unaware that in the years 1820 to 1825 a *Floresta de rimas antiguas castellanas* was published in Hamburg, copies of which are not lacking amongst the enthusiasts of Madrid.)

At the core of Böhl's critique is the issue of cultural patriotism. Although he does go on to praise Quintana's introduction and notes, he feels he can only condemn him for failing to inform the Spanish public as to the extent of their literary treasures, a duty which he claims, with some justification, his *Floresta* has performed on Spain's behalf in the literary circles of Germany and Britain. Quintana should, Böhl felt, have made use of the *Floresta* and other collections to complete the second edition of his anthology, thus using his influence as a recognised figure in Spain's literary elite to further the cause of Spanish literature in Spain itself. Instead, he had let his readership down and deeply disappointed Böhl in the process.

As this vehement response suggests, the matter of Quintana's recognition was of great importance to Böhl and led to some friction in his relationship with Durán. Böhl felt he deserved Durán's support and in a letter dated 17 January 1832, criticised the fact that the latter had not alluded to Quintana's ignorance of the *Floresta* in the 'Discurso preliminar' (Preliminary address) to his forthcoming *Romancero de romances caballerescos e históricos* (Collection of chivalric and historical romances, 1832). However, by attacking Quintana in his correspondence with Durán, Böhl seems to be unaware of his friend's reliance on the renowned critic and the long-standing nature of their association. In fact, Böhl may even have Durán to thank for Quintana's ignorance of his work. The new edition of the *Poesías selectas* is discussed in their correspondence on various occasions, but no mention of Böhl's work is ever made. Although much of this dialogue took place before Böhl and Durán became acquainted, Durán seems to have been aware of Böhl's collection whilst preparing his 1829 *Romancero de romances doctrinales*. His failure to mention it to Quintana is unexplained and meant Böhl's immediate impact on Spanish philology was once more confined to his own circle of friends.

This is further highlighted by the first public responses to his collections which were limited in number, partly due, it must also be assumed, to the general lack of publishing activity at a time of strict censorship. Although Böhl mentions having received a number of letters of support in appreciation of his work in a letter to Navarrete on 29 May 1827, the first public recognition in Spain itself of Böhl's efforts in compiling the *Floresta*, excluding, of course, his acceptance into the Royal Spanish Academy, was indeed from Durán, who praised Böhl in the introduction to his *Romancero de romances doctrinales*, referring to the *Floresta* as 'escelente' (excellent). This was later echoed by their mutual friend, Gallardo, who, reviewing Böhl's *Teatro antiguo* with enthusiasm in his periodical *El Criticón* (The harsh critic) in 1836, also praised the *Floresta* in the highest terms, taking the opportunity to criticise Quintana, claiming his collection to be 'mui pobre y seca al lado de la rica y florida del Aleman' (very poor and dry alongside the rich and colourful [collection] of the German).[15] Gallardo's response to the *Teatro antiguo* seems to support Böhl's own view that the collection of theatre was better received than the *Floresta*, aided no doubt by the lifting of restrictions on the sale of foreign books. Böhl certainly felt the collection of early theatre had met with a warmer welcome in Madrid, commenting to Julius on 28 April 1833 that 'man dem Teatro etwas mehr Aufmerksamkeit geschenkt hat als der Floresta' (one has paid more attention to the *Teatro* than the *Floresta*). However, there is little published material to support this with most views emanating once more from Böhl's own circle. Dornhof argues plausibly that the limited public approbation of the *Teatro antiguo* in Spain was due to the almost simultaneous publication of Moratín's *Orígenes* and the rapid appearance of other, more comprehensive anthologies such as that by Eugenio de Ochoa. His *Tesoro del Teatro Español* (Treasury of Spanish theatre) was published in Paris in 1838 and, as Dornhof points out, in many ways carried on the work that Böhl had begun (Vk: 46). This is underlined by the epigraph chosen by Ochoa for his collection:

En nuestro sistema literario no admitimos nada absoluto, y por eso tenemos mas fe en el sentimiento que en las reglas dogmáticas, y quizá arbitrarias, en que los críticos quieren que se busque siempre la belleza.

(In our literary system, we do not admit anything of an absolute nature and therefore we have more faith in sentiment than in the dogmatic and possibly arbitrary rules in which the critics always want us to look for beauty.)

Ochoa's words certainly recall the ideals promoted by Böhl during the polemic and indicate the change in aesthetic attitudes, the realisation of which was gradual in Spain, but to which Böhl undoubtedly contributed and which echoes that already experienced by writers in exile in the 1820s and early 1830s.[16]

The limited nature of the immediate reception of both the *Floresta* and the *Teatro antiguo* in Spain itself did not mean that Böhl was dissatisfied with his efforts, as his attitude to Quintana shows. Writing to Navarrete on 15 November 1821, Böhl places the *Floresta* in a transcultural context, tracing its genealogy back to the work of Bishop Percy in mid-eighteenth-century Britain and the subsequent revival of indigenous literature in Germany.[17] Spain lies beyond this axis – the best efforts of a minority of eighteenth-century critics notwithstanding – such ideas unable to flourish due to prevailing Enlightenment aesthetics. Consequently, his collection is simply too much for current taste. However, Böhl sees a future role for his collection which is almost prophetic in its accuracy:

Cuando haya pasado la fiebre política en España, es dable que también los españoles vuelvan en sí. Entonces tratarán de fundar sus instituciones tanto civiles como literarias sobre un fondo nacional, y entonces la Floresta será una piedra preciosa para los cimientos de esta hermoso edificio.

(Once the political fever in Spain has past, it is conceivable that the Spanish will come to their senses. Then they will try to found their civic as well as their literary institutions upon a national foundation and then the Floresta will be a precious stone for the cement of this beautiful edifice.)

Böhl appraises his own work in Herderian terms as forming part of a cultural continuum, the value of which will be appreciated by generations to come. This certainly accords with Durán's response and predicts the resonance of Böhl's work in subsequent Hispanist philology. Indeed, if Durán had potentially impeded the dissemination of the *Floresta* by failing to mediate between Böhl and Quintana, then his own response to Böhl's collection was crucial to its Spanish reception. As their collaboration on the *Teatro antiguo* shows, their friendship soon developed into one based on mutual appreciation and support. Böhl assisted Durán by supplying him with a copy of the rare *Cancionero de Amberes* and the latter made extensive use of the *Floresta* when compiling his own collections, in particular the *Romancero de romances doctrinales*. Böhl, for his part, was happy to approach Durán, both as a private bibliophile and in his capacity as librarian of the *Biblioteca nacional* after 1834, to locate texts which he had been unable to find. He was happy, too, to promote his friend's work further afield, enlisting the voice of the young scholar in his own campaign. Upon receiving the second of Durán's *romanceros* in October 1829, Böhl was so impressed that he immediately ordered extra copies to send to Germany. He was delighted that Durán had mentioned him in the introduction and saw this as the first positive public acknowledgement of his work by a Spaniard (which would suggest he was unaware of the 1826 review in Salvá's *Ocios de españoles emigrados*). He clearly felt he had found a like-minded scholar and the strength of feeling this provoked is apparent in their correspondence, exemplified by the following excerpt from a letter to Durán on 30 November 1830 in which Böhl expresses his pleasure at the content of his friend's most recent communication:

> Aunque todas las cartas de Vmd son muy apreciables para mi, ninguna ha herido tan intimamente todas las cuerdas de mi alma como su ultima y asi mi contestación solo podria ser una repitición de lo mismo en otras palabras. Gracias á Dios que existen todavía almas del temple que solo lo *espiritual* las mueve, mirando con indiferencia la batahola sobre intereses y adelantos desta tierra, y gracias á Dios que algunas veces nos proporciona el revelarse una á otra, con lo que animamos para lo que queda de la jornada.
>
> (Although all your letters are of great value to me, none has struck a chord so intimately with my soul than your last and as such my reply could only be a repetition of the same in different words. Thank the Lord that there still exist spirited souls who are only moved by the *spiritual*, regarding with indifference the hullabaloo over earthly interests and advancements and thank the Lord that sometimes he allows one of us to recognise [mutual interests] in the other, which then inspires us for the rest of our days.)

This extract shows the empathy which existed between the two scholars. In many ways, Durán, like Böhl, was a Romantic *Zerissener*, bridging two worlds. Whereas Böhl dealt with the commercial machinations of the wine trade, Durán was trained in the dry rhetoric of the law. Like Böhl, however, his unsettled nature soon saw him question certain values. As David Gies explains, Durán had undergone an aesthetic shift in the years following the completion of his law degree in 1817, moving away from the influence of French neo-Classical drama and developing an avid interest in popular poetry and Golden Age theatre.[18] The parallels with Böhl's own development a decade earlier are clear. Indeed, Durán was exposed to many of the same influences as Böhl: Madame de Staël, August Wilhelm Schlegel, Bouterwek and Sismondi. He owned a number of their works in French, many in the first editions of the 1810s, and is known to have discussed the theories of Kant and Schlegel with his father, Don Francisco Durán, and his mentor, Alberto Lista, respectively. Indeed, Gies credits Durán in the late 1820s with tempering Lista's once vehemently condemnatory views on German Romantic thought as expressed in his 1821 article in *El Censor*, which was written at the height of his relations with the young Durán (67).[19] As this suggests, despite his reactionary political stance, Böhl was not seeking to advise his friend in opposition to current trends in Spain. Instead, as the responses of his polemical adversaries demonstrate, many of Böhl's aesthetic and philological ideas began to move ever more towards the mainstream as the decade wore on, echoed initially in the work of Luis Monteggia and Ramón López Soler (1806–36) in the Barcelona periodical, *El Europeo*, and providing a counterpoint, along with Durán's own *Discurso*, to the debate engendered by the reiteration of Classical values in Hermosilla's *Arte* (1826) and Martínez de la Rosa's *Poetica* (1827).

Given this context, it is tempting to add Böhl to the list of mentors who shaped Durán's thinking, including his father, Don Francisco, as well as Lista and Quintana. Whilst there is no doubt that Böhl would later influence Durán's philological work, there is some debate as to the role he played in Durán's early development as a Romantic thinker. Gies makes the tentative suggestion that Durán, in his post at the *Dirección General de Estudios* (General Office for Education), would have been quite likely to follow the latter stages of the Calderón polemic, bound as he was to avail himself of current literary activity (69). In a more forceful assertion, Reyes Ponce suggests that Durán already held Schlegelian views before encountering Böhl and that his *Discurso* introduced early German Romantic theory to Spain in 1828 (A: 235). However, this inexplicably fails to take into the account the impact of Böhl's dissemination of Schiller and Schlegel in 1805 and 1814 respectively, both mediations taking place before the arrival in Spain of Schlegel's work in French translation. It is certainly possible that Durán gleaned his initial knowledge of Romantic theory from reading Madame de Staël's account in *De l'Allemagne*, but then it is surely she who must be accredited with spreading the message, not Durán. It must also not be forgotten that Böhl included extracts from her seminal work in the *Pasatiempos*. Reyes Ponce also argues that Durán imitates Schlegel in his assessment of Spanish drama. This may be true, but it is interesting to note that in so doing he happens to refer only to those of Schlegel's lectures made known by Böhl during the polemic, an observation which would seem to support the case for Böhl's role in Durán's development.

In such a complex context, it would appear most likely that Durán, like many other thinkers of the period, acquired his knowledge of Schlegelian thought from various sources as it filtered through into Spanish culture via Böhl, de Staël and French translations of seminal Romantic texts. As a result of this process, Böhl and Durán came to share a similar aesthetic outlook which drew them together a decade after the polemic had ended. The intervening years had seen Böhl consolidate his conservative aesthetic, whilst Durán had continued to move further away from a neo-Classical position. The result was a shared philological goal underpinned by a similar, but not identical, world view. The subtle differences emerge primarily in terms of tone. Whilst Durán's objective was the same as Böhl's in terms of a revival of ancient Spanish literature, in his *Discurso* he took a more measured approach than Böhl had done during the polemic. This was in many ways a difference born of circumstance. Whereas Böhl had been responding to a very physical French threat at the time of the Napoleonic Wars, a stance he now still defended despite its ultimately anachronistic nature, Durán, in the tense atmosphere of the Ominous Decade, was responding to the less threatening reiteration of French neo-Classical hegemony by Martínez de la Rosa and Hermosilla, whose defence is seen as the final expression of neo-Classical theory in nineteenth-century Spain. This context had an impact on Böhl's dealings with Durán. Against such a background, unable to recommend much of contemporary native Spanish criticism, English and German writing instead provide the evaluative touchstone for Böhl's assessment of contemporary thought and this extends to his assessment of his young friend. In a later letter dated 3 February 1831, Böhl underlines his admiration for Durán, comparing him with German and English scholars; praise indeed, given Böhl's high opinion of many of these. Although his attitude towards the far younger Durán often verges on the paternal, there is also evidence that he holds his young friend in some degree of awe:

> Estamos llamados para cosas diferentes como Vmd bien lo reconoces [sic]: yo para indicar y segregar aquello que mas fielmente reproduce los afectos de las varias clases de hombres, estados y naciones: Vmd para deducir dello lo que á cada cual le caracteriza.

(We are called for different things as you well know: I to point to and classify that which most truly reproduces the effects of the various classes of man, state and nation: you to deduce from it that which characterises each.)

Böhl views himself, still modestly, as a collector and organiser of facts, whereas Durán is capable of analysis. This respect does not, however, preclude an element of quasi-parental disapproval, which creeps into the correspondence as the years go by. The frank tone adopted years previously when making demands and complaints of Julius becomes apparent in Böhl's letters to Durán too, for example when, in January 1833, Böhl learns from a third party that Durán has plans to publish work by Lope de Rueda, one of the key figures in his own collection. The sharp tone he adopts is, however, to be regarded as a sign of intimacy rather than one of disapproval and, indeed, Böhl is soon pacified with the receipt of Durán's latest *romancero*, adopting once more his encouraging tone. He is nevertheless not afraid to criticise his friend's judgement. Durán's plans for a *Romancero historico caballeresco* met with a degree of disapproval from Böhl in a letter of 13 November 1829 and he justifies his criticism, claiming that these *romances* are too long and have been printed too many times. His own plans for such a collection have been abandoned. For his part, Durán was not averse to voicing disagreement with Böhl, notably rejecting Böhl's cherished system of long lines adopted from Grimm's *Silva* in favour of a return to the eight-syllable method.

Such differences notwithstanding, Böhl was undoubtedly a great help to Durán. Although by the end of the 1820s Böhl was steeped in the theatre of the early Golden Age, he was still actively pursuing his plans for the 'Spaziergänge' and had just seen the second edition of the *Floresta* published in Hamburg. The wealth of knowledge he had amassed meant he could provide Durán with advice and material and the two men worked well together, this in spite of the fact that they never actually met, conducting their dealings by means of the laborious system of post coach and personal carrier. The influence of the German on his Spanish partner was marked and, according to Reyes Ponce (A: 200), opened up a new vista on the *romance*, leading Durán away from the restricted appreciation associated with neo-Classicism. As Durán's work progressed, Böhl became a point of reference as each new *Romancero* was sent to him for approval and their intense exchanges involved arriving at a definition of the genesis of the baroque *Romancero general*. Böhl and Durán compared notes for some nine months, focusing on the *Romancero general* and the *Cancionero de romances*. As Reyes Ponce notes, Durán benefited greatly from Böhl's co-operation, learning from him the German methodology which lacked a parallel in Spain, as Quintana's collection had demonstrated, and which, as Juretschke argues, gave Böhl a great advantage over his Spanish contemporaries (DD: 166). In Böhl, Durán had access to a body of knowledge developed from Dieze to Herder, the Schlegels, Bouterwek, then Grimm and Depping and finally Böhl himself. It is a measure of Durán's success and of Böhl's influence on his work that the Spaniard goes on to form part of that philological genealogy in a transcultural context, his own work, alongside Böhl's *Floresta*, providing an essential source of material for Wolf in the late 1830s.

As the various reviews of his work suggest, Böhl's claim to have disseminated knowledge of Spain's poetry in Germany and Britain is valid, if perhaps a little overstated given the small print run of the *Floresta*. However, it is indicative of the spirit of the age that such a modest undertaking was able to elicit such a high level of interest in the literary landscape of both cultures. Böhl and Durán were both aware of this trend and the need to exploit it in order to salvage Spain's threatened literary heritage. Böhl in particular gives voice to his long-held belief that the Spaniards themselves are the least able to appreciate their own culture. In a letter of 8 December 1829, he remarks that it is odd that *rimas sacras* displease the Spanish, but are those most reproduced in translation by the English and Germans, an observation which highlights the popularity of the prevailing Romantic image of Spain as a Catholic bastion which had emerged from the writings of Schlegel and others. Later, on 15 November 1830, he congratulates Durán on the positive response of the British press to his *Romanceros*, adding that even the French are beginning to change their attitudes. Only the Spanish persist in their love of neo-Classicism. This is rather harsh and fails to take into account a gradual shift in approach, apparent not least in Durán's own work.

Böhl's own position within the European cultural dialogue is illustrated in a letter to Durán dated 4 July 1832 from an otherwise unidentified acquaintance named Minero.[20] This friend, residing at the time in Göttingen, reports enthusiastically that Durán's views have been adopted in Germany, which is, of course, rather ironic as he has been heavily influenced by Schlegel, Böhl and a number of German thinkers. Whilst Minero's letter perhaps reveals as much about his own limited understanding of the origins of the German appreciation of Spain's literature as it does Böhl's accurate appraisal of European aesthetic taste in relation to Spanish culture, it raises an important issue in the context of Böhl's reception and the relation of his work to that of Durán in a European context. Writing to Durán, Minero includes summaries of two recent newspaper articles on Spanish literature. The first, from the *Magazin für Literatur des Auslandes* (Magazine for Foreign Literature) of 14 May, is a review of Durán's collections which praises them, but makes no reference to Böhl. The second, from a Cologne newspaper a month later, lists a number of German Hispanophiles, but makes no mention of Böhl either, this despite Durán's openly declared debt to the latter's scholarship. This apparent denial of Böhl, who was after all Durán's point of access to German culture both intellectually and logistically, contrasts starkly with the attention accorded Böhl's work in the 1820s and would seem to suggest that, a decade later, Durán, in many ways Böhl's philological heir, had already begun to eclipse his mentor, even in his native Germany. This is supported by a number of letters to Durán from other Spaniards in Germany or German scholars with an interest in Spain, including Victor Aimé Huber, a native of Bremen and acquaintance of Julius, none of which makes reference to Böhl. To some extent, this absence characterises the reception of Böhl's work in both Germany and Spain as the century progressed, his influence subsumed into the broader culture complex. His collections continued to serve as a resource, as both Diez and Wolf attest, but his name and profile as an individual scholar begin to fade. Indeed, even Wolf, once so openly indebted to his work, fails to include reference to him in later work. His 1853 essay 'Ein Beitrag zur Bibliographie der Cancioneros' (A contribution to the bibliography of Cancioneros) mentions Depping, Durán, Ticknor and Julius, but fails to mention Böhl.[21] It is for this very reason that both Julius and Elise Campe revisit his life and work in the 1850s, fearful that Böhl's contribution might eventually be forgotten.

NOTES

[1] The letter is held in the Perthes collection of the *Staatsarchiv Hamburg*.
[2] *Goethe. Berliner Ausgabe*, XVIII, 251–3 (253); Beauregard Pandin was the pseudonym of Karl Ferdinand von Jariges (1773–1826), erstwhile neighbour of Goethe in Weimar.
[3] Hermann Breymann (ed.), *Friedrich Diez kleinere Arbeiten und Recensionen* (Munich: Oldenbourg, 1883), pp. 49–63.
[4] Ibid., pp. 130–7.
[5] George Ticknor, *Geschichte der schönen Literatur in Spanien. Deutsch mit Zusätzen herausgegeben von Nikolaus Heinrich Julius*, 2 vols (Leipzig: Brockhaus, 1852); II: 'Elfte Beilage. Lebensnachricht über Johann Nikolaus Böhl von Faber, vom deutschen Herausgeber', 641–56.
[6] 'Early Narrative and Lyrical Poetry of Spain', *Edinburgh Review*, 39 (1824), 393–432; references appear in the text.
[7] Bowring published several pieces in the almanac, *Forget me not*, published by Rudolf Ackermann. By coincidence, Böhl's old adversary, Mora, also edited an almanac for Ackermann entitled *No me olvides*, as well as a number of educational works.
[8] 'Lyric Poetry of Spain', *Edinburgh Review*, 40 (1824), 443–76.
[9] 'Spanish Romances', *London Magazine*, 7 (1823), 405–10; 509–14; 605–15; 8 (1823), 47–59; 158–68; 485–92; 593–6 (7, 605).
[10] *Ocios de españoles emigrados*, 5 (May 1826), 449–68 (452).
[11] *Coleccion de las mas célebres romances antiguos españoles, históricos y caballerescos publicada por C. B. Depping y ahora considerablemente enmendada por un español refugiado*, 2 vols (London: Salvá, 1825).
[12] There is some confusion surrounding the figure of Liaño. The name appears in another context in a letter to Navarrete from 3 July 1821. Böhl mentions that 'un Sr. Liaño' has sent him an historical work, published in Spanish in Berlin. According to Juretschke (DD: 181), the gentleman in question is an ex-priest who found a position as a librarian in Berlin. He appears to agree with Pitollet (QC: 37) in suggesting that this is the same Liaño who lodged the complaint against the *Floresta*. This is thrown into doubt on two counts. First, the ex-priest would already appear to be in Berlin when the complaint was lodged and, secondly, he sent Böhl a book which was itself in contravention of the restrictions placed on Spanish books printed abroad.
[13] Böhl had recently quarrelled with his previous Madrid bookseller, Orea, and sought advice from

Navarrete (3 August 1821) as to a replacement. Navarrete suggested Sánchez. He would subsequently complain to Julius that the latter was as unreliable as the former.

14   Copies of each edition were sent faithfully by Böhl to the Academy.
15   'Anuncio literario', *El Criticón, papel volante de Literatura y Bellas-artes*, 4 (1836), 2.
16   See my argument in *Creating a National Identity: A Comparative Study of German and Spanish Romanticism*, Stuttgarter Arbeiten zur Germanistik 347 (Stuttgart: Hans-Dieter Heinz, 1997), pp. 60–76.
17   That Böhl was indeed to some extent successful in his efforts to save the treasures of Spain's literary past from obscurity is underlined in a letter to Navarrete on 24 December 1821, where he mentions having been able to include a poem by Montalvo in the manuscript of the third volume of his collection, the loss of which had been lamented by Mayans.
18   David T. Gies, *Agustín Durán, A Biography and Literary Appreciation* (London: Tamesis, 1975), pp. 12–13; further references appear in the text.
19   The claim for Böhl's affinity with aspects of the broader aesthetic debate is given credence in a letter from Lista to Durán dated 10 May 1831. Lista is discussing Moratín's *Origenes* and praises them, but for the lack of a critical apparatus. He then describes what he would like to see. The result would very much parallel, in spirit and intent, Böhl's projected 'Spaziergange', providing an historical analysis of the theatre in the same way Böhl intended to illuminate the ancient poetry of Spain. It is also notable that, whilst ignoring almost every other aspect of contemporary Spanish literature, Böhl recommends Lista's poems to Julius in a letter dated 17 November 1829.
20   Durán's correspondence with Minero and Huber is reproduced by Sainz Rodríguez, 'Documentos'.
21   Ferdinand Wolf, 'Ein Beitrag zur Bibliographie der Cancioneros und zur Geschichte der spanischen Kunstlyrik am Hofe Kaiser Karls V', *Sitzungsberichte der philosophisch-historischen Classe der kaiserlichen Akademie der Wissenschaften*, X (1853), 153–204; also 'Zur Bibliographie der Romanceros', ibid., 484–516.

Conclusion
Böhl von Faber: A Transcultural Pioneer

In many ways, this study has been less concerned with assessing Böhl's impact than it has been with understanding Böhl himself. Yet that impact has been considerable, especially in the context of Spanish letters, with a complex and sustained legacy stretching far beyond Böhl's own lifetime. Having drawn attention to Böhl in a German context and reappraised his contribution in Spain, these concluding remarks seek to contextualise his work and legacy within the cultural framework of the early nineteenth century by reiterating his transcultural role and highlighting the extent of his contribution in the context of both cultures. What emerges is a network of influence which stretches far beyond the Calderón polemic, the episode for which he is most often remembered.

Key is Böhl's dual cultural identity. His active role in the context of both cultures is at once receptive and revolutionary, engaging with the ongoing aesthetic debate whilst also fostering new dialogue in both Germany and Spain. During the early years of his scholarly career, the transcultural flow of ideas was often marked by shifts in location, bringing German culture to the attention of Spanish intellectuals whilst resident in Spain and vice versa. Far from diminishing once Böhl had settled permanently in Spain, this dialogue continued throughout Böhl's life. Indeed, the pioneering nature of his work in the later years of his career was far more pronounced, driven by the consolidation of a world view which he was determined to defend. This was carried out on a variety of levels. In both cultural contexts, Böhl's sphere of activity ranged from private scholarship to publication to the informal dissemination of ideas and material. Indeed, much of his immediate impact was at an individual level. For some, the interaction was relatively minor: friendship and assistance in the case of Navarrete and Gallardo, contact and hospitality in that of Diez and Keil. For others, Böhl's role was significant at a specific point in their career, his imprint clear on Wolf's and Bowring's collections of *romances* and Irving's engagement with Spanish culture. In a few notable cases, however, Böhl's presence was a defining factor in the establishment or affirmation of a world view: those of Durán, Fernán Caballero and, arguably even, his great antagonists, Mora and Alcalá Galiano. This engagement with other scholars at a European level was a mutually beneficial relationship. These individual contacts shaped Böhl's own self-definition as a Romantic and a man of letters, drawing him into the heart of the contemporary debate and bringing his efforts to the attention of prominent writers and scholars such as Goethe, Jacob Grimm, Bouterwek and the cream of the British periodical press. Such activity at an individual level, much of it unrecorded beyond the pages of personal correspondence, laid the foundations for a lasting contribution to the developing culture complex of both Spain and Germany.

The scant attention paid by scholars of the period to Böhl's contribution to his native culture in particular disguises a pioneering spirit centred on cultural mediation and the reappraisal of his own and other cultures. Drawn towards the ideals of the Romantic aesthetic, he undoubtedly saw himself as a herald of the new world view, one which would revive and revalue national cultures at a politically critical juncture. His critical work in Germany is embedded in the dialogue of the period, with contributions to prominent periodicals including the *Nordische Miszellen*, the *Vaterländisches Museum* and Cotta's *Morgenblatt für gebildete Stände*, as well as the beginnings of a philological career founded on his *Wunderhorn* edition and collaboration on Kerner's ultimately unsuccessful *Poetischer Almanach*. The issues with which Böhl engaged in the course of these various activities lie at the heart of the Romantic debate – the literature of Spain, the revival of popular forms of poetry and the ideals of British Romanticism – and inform the Schlegelian arguments of the Calderón polemic and his enthusiasm for the ideals of Romantic philology. His attempt to bring Schiller's aesthetic theories to the attention of a Spanish audience in 1805 is remarkable in this context. Schiller was virtually unknown in Spain at this time, his aesthetic theories certainly quite revolutionary in a Spanish context. Yet Böhl drew them to the attention of the literary elite only a year or so after their publication in Germany in the year of Schiller's death. The immediate impact was limited, but this can be seen as the first public manifestation of a private mediation already underway in Francisca's salon in Cadiz at the turn of the century. This process, which would continue through his correspondence as well as his published material, meant Böhl was able to bring together two cultures, connecting them through his own engagement with the German Romantic apotheosis of Spain and raising awareness of Schlegelian thought and its Herderian historicist premise well in advance of the arrival of the first French translation of his work.

Equally significant is the introduction to Spain of Romantic philology, the first evidence of which reaches the Royal Spanish Academy directly via Böhl, his first copy of Grimm's *Silva* commandeered upon arrival for the Academy's library. The flow of ideas is then reversed once more as Böhl's own anthologies – thoroughly Romantic in conception – present a receptive German audience with new treasures from Spain's literary past, helping to establish Böhl as an expert in Spanish culture with an immediate impact on the collecting activities of others, notably Ferdinand Wolf. Yet despite this raised profile, achieved quite remarkably from a distance with the help of Julius and Perthes, Böhl's broader legacy in a German context remains hidden and essentially indefinable. Whilst his work as a collector enters the canonical corpus and can be found in libraries and collections, both private and public, Böhl himself disappears from view, attention turning instead to his daughter whose work enjoyed a notable degree of success in translation in Germany. Yet through his own translations, transcultural dialogue and scholarly activity, Böhl was the first to bring the work of Herder, Schiller, August Wilhelm Schlegel and Jacob Grimm to the attention of a Spanish audience. Whether that dissemination was direct, in the case of Schiller and Schlegel, or indirect in the case of Herder and Grimm, what is remarkable is that these figures, who are so central to the German Romantic canon, should first receive attention in Spain not through the monumental works of the great scholars of the age such as de Staël, Sismondi or Bouterwek, nor indeed through the offices of the great literary journals of London, Paris or Vienna, but rather through the efforts of a merchant from Hamburg functioning on the periphery of the Romantic movement in Germany, but with a burning passion for Spain's culture and a heightened sense of cultural patriotism. This is surely a service to German culture and its European profile which should not be forgotten.

Equally remarkable is Böhl's impact on the culture of his adopted homeland after 1813. Here, initially, he was even less well known, familiar perhaps in the mercantile circles of Cadiz, but with little influence beyond the salons of the trading city. By 1820, he was a member of the Royal Spanish Academy and, by 1830, a recognised expert on Spain's literary heritage attracting attention from scholars all over Europe. His actions, driven by ideological as well as aesthetic impulses, may seem audacious, but in a Spanish context Böhl was very much intent on setting a trend rather than following one. His efforts centred on reviving interest in a once immensely popular aspect of Spain's culture against the tide of prevailing aesthetic values and, fortunately, he was able to exploit a modest home-grown revival which provided him with the context for a new aesthetic which eulogised the nation's cultural heritage. The impact was profound. As Diego Saglia notes, Böhl's contribution reaches the heart of Spain's cultural self-perception:

> Böhl de Faber was the first to introduce systematically the image of Spain as an attractive *other* culture. Thus his writings present a displacement of perspective which, by allowing Spanish intellectuals to see their country in the mirror of the *other*, promoted a different awareness of their culture.[1]

That 'different awareness' extended to both areas of activity pursued by Böhl: his polemical campaign in defence of Calderón and his campaign to salvage Spain's threatened literary heritage. The polemic itself triggered a well-documented chain reaction within nineteenth-century Spanish letters which secured Böhl's influence well into the mid-century. Whether one is convinced or otherwise by Flitter's reading of Spanish Romanticism as one dominated by conservative tendencies, his account of Böhl's intellectual and ideological legacy within the broader spectrum of Spanish letters in the nineteenth century is extremely compelling. Flitter summarises his findings in terms which emphasise the cyclical nature of the cultural impact of Böhl's work:

> Romantic literary theory, lent initial impetus by the tenacious endeavours of Böhl von Faber, developed cohesively in the 1820s. This Romantic historicism continued to provide the framework of ideas for Spanish literary criticism during the crucial years 1834–1837, when the advent of a new and radical Romantic approach briefly gained the support of writers. Larra promoted the essential features of the historicist vision even while disagreeing with the ideological associations it had acquired. His more stringent sense of determinism contributed to a change in the emphasis of later Romantic criticism, towards a growing social awareness. With the development of the idea of literature as a stimulant to social regeneration, critics widely canvassed its dynamic potential as a positive moral guide, with the power to inculcate desirable attitudes and valuable emotions and with the ability to provide contemporary society with lessons to be learned by the consideration of past events. A progression from firmly established bases then culminates in the work of Fernán Caballero, in a developing cycle begun by her father Johann Nikolaus Böhl. Spanish Romanticism was therefore longer-lived than most modern critics have suggested, and more consistent in its embodiment of a specific framework of ideas than they have been prepared to recognise. (SR: 175)

The trajectory described, from the polemic itself, through the work of the writer, journalist and moderate Liberal, Mariano José de Larra (1809–37), to that of Fernán Caballero, encompasses within its range a network of influence which associates Böhl with the prominent figures of Spanish Romanticism and the aesthetic debate in Spain throughout the first half of the nineteenth century. As has already been noted, once distanced from the highly politicised atmosphere of the polemic, both Mora and Alcalá Galiano found themselves able to countenance and even recommend many aspects of Böhl's Schlegelian argument. That argument, based, as Böhl was at pains to point out in his third *Pasatiempo*, on the prevailing European aesthetic, gradually shifted from the periphery to the mainstream of the literary debate in Spain itself, notably though the Barcelona-based periodical, *El Europeo*, which defended an aesthetic stance and understanding of Enlightenment close to that espoused by Böhl. As Saglia's comments suggest, major commentators of the age also began to examine the new ideas as they attracted wider interest, both Quintana and Lista realigning their position in relation to popular poetry and the value of neo-Classical principles as the 1820s wore on. The shift in perspective was driven as much by political as it was aesthetic concerns. By the mid-1820s,

Spain was coming to terms with life without the majority of its once vast empire. Despite Fernando VII's best efforts, the success of independence movements in South America meant that, for the first time since 1492, Spain was forced to consider the possibility of an exclusively peninsular identity. The focus shifted away from external to internal influences with an increased interest in older works and regional cultures in particular. Theatre and the ballad lay at the heart of this revaluation. The influence of a younger generation of Spanish intellectuals is apparent here, Durán refocusing the debate with his 1828 *Discurso* and the historicist reading of Spain's literary heritage then explored further by Juan Donoso Cortés (1809–53) in his 1829 *Discurso de apertura en el colegio de Cáceres* (Opening address at the college of Cáceres). This ongoing reappraisal within Spain provides the returning exiles in 1833 with a point of reference for the new ideas absorbed in London and Paris in much the same way as Nipho and other eighteenth-century commentators had done for Böhl twenty years earlier. This debate at the level of aesthetic theory found its practical counterpart in the philological activity of the period. Reyes Ponce's thesis provides a detailed analysis of the increased awareness of Spain's fragile literary heritage as a positive cultural legacy which supports Flitter's argument from another angle, emphasising the impact of Böhl's cultural mediation on the aesthetic and methodological values of Hispanist philology. The convergence of these aspects meant that by the early 1830s the conceptual framework of historicism was firmly established in the Spanish literary debate. As we have seen, Flitter identifies the continuation of the debate in the work of Larra and Fernán Caballero, but also in the responses to French Romanticism voiced by Manuel Milá y Fontanals (1818–84) and Ramón de Campoamar (1817–1901) and in the work of Antonio Gil y Zarate (1793–1861) and Fermín Gonzalo Morón in the 1840s, to name but a few.

The intellectual engagement of Spanish contemporaries with Böhl's 'tenacious endeavours', catalogued by Flitter and, in the context of his philology, by Reyes Ponce, is certainly receptive, but does not preclude a degree of reinterpretation as part of a broader dialogue with European aesthetics. The historicist approach, with its tendency towards Catholic values and anti-rationalist stance, clearly equates with the views advanced by Böhl, but it would be wrong to suggest that he was the only source. The exiles have already been mentioned, but there were other key influences including Scott, de Staël and Chateaubriand. There is also a marked toning down as Böhl's conservative, absolutist ideology is tempered as the debate centres specifically on the notion of a national literature rather than nationalism, with some more extreme concepts surviving in what Flitter terms Fernán Caballero's 'strident *casticismo*' (SR: 159). Böhl's proto-nationalist desire to see an absolutist regime restore the values of a lost golden age in order to preserve 'die gute Sache' shifts once these ideas have entered the mainstream in Spain towards a filtered version of Böhl's Schlegelian historicism, which evokes those aspects of the past which are desirable, whilst rejecting others in a quest for stability, which stands in stark contrast to the political insecurities of the age. In literary historical terms, however, what began as the exalted defence of cultural patriotism in 1814 merges gradually into the mainstream debate and eventual classification of Spain's literary canon. Böhl thus forms part of the literary historical continuum in the best Herderian sense.

What emerges from this study is the extent to which Böhl was integrated into the European cultural landscape, both reactively and proactively. His engagement with the work of a variety of writers and thinkers involved him in the key debates of the age. Once convinced of the need to move away from the value system instilled by Campe, Böhl follows a thoroughly Romantic trajectory, his reading in line with that of the Schlegel brothers, Tieck, Brentano and many others of the period: the literature of Spain's Golden Age, the German mystics, popular genres, Goethe, Schiller and the Idealist philosophers. In addition to this, his interaction with and influence upon a variety of writers and thinkers secured him a proactive role in the cultural dialectic of the age. This is an evaluation which might be applied to any number of scholars at this time, but Böhl's work can boast an added dimension, that of being thoroughly transcultural. His active participation in the cultural debate and production of Germany and Spain is perhaps the most valuable aspect of his legacy, one which has been underestimated thus far. The central feature of his scholarship was the mediation between cultures. From his early private dissemination of ideas in the salons of Cadiz and Hamburg to his 1805 exposition of Schiller's aesthetics, from his work as a critic in Germany, defending the literatures of Spain and Great Britain, to the heady days of the Calderón polemic and finally to his thoroughly transcultural philological work, his efforts were consistently aimed at establishing a productive dialogue between cultural frameworks as a means to foster cultural patriotism. Whether one chooses or not to condemn the political motivation which underpins much of his activity, there is no doubt that, in his scholarship, Böhl was a transcultural pioneer.

NOTES

[1] Diego Saglia, '"The True Essence of Romanticism": Romantic Theories of Spain and the Question of Spanish Romanticism', *Tessarae*, 3 (1997), 127–45 (p. 135).

Literary Correspondence

Letters

1. Joachim Heinrich and Dorothea Campe, Trittow

Amsterdam den 23 July 1784

Theuerste Pflege Eltern

Verzeihen Sie mir daß ich Ihnen nicht schon aus Bremen geschrieben habe, aber meine Zerstreuungen haben es mir nicht erlaubt. Nun aber! Da ich allein und ruhig bin, denke ich an Sie zurück, und alle die glücklichen Stunden die wir miteinander durchlebt haben, und wünsche Sie mir zurück. Jetzt aber sage ich Ihnen noch einmahl dank für Ihren Theophron.[1] Ich habe ihn schon ein paar mahl ganz durchgelesen, und finde doch immer noch neue Lehren drin, die mir jezo vorzüglich nötig sind. Ich hab auch sehr oft Gelegenheit mehr davon in Ausübung zu bringen. Doch genug hiervon.

Ich hatte gerne meine Tour über Lemgow genommen um den lieben H[er]rn Benzler zu besuchen, aber es ist mir nicht möglich gewesen, da ich einen Reise compagnon gehabt habe nachdem ich mich richten mußte. Morgen werde ich nach Ulzeihl gehen und den lieben H[er]rn Haike besuchen. Künftige Woche werde auch zu H[er]rn Ansberg gehen.

Verzeihen Sie mir, beste Pflegeeltern so wohl meine haßliche Schreiberei als auch meine Kürze, aber ich habe keine Zeit mehr, ich muß außgehen. Ich hoffe mich bald einmahl länger mit Ihnen unterhalten zu können. Tausend Grüße an Alle.

Ihr
gehorsamer und dankbarer
Pflegesohn J. N. Böhl

2. Joachim Heinrich and Dorothea Campe, Trittow

Andover den 7. Octobre 1784

Theuerste Pflege Eltern

Endlich habe ich von meinem lieben Vater die Erlaubniß erhalten, Ihnen sowohl von meiner Reise als auch von meinen jeztigen Umständen Nachricht zu geben. Ich hätte Ihnen zwar schon früher davon benachrichtigen müßen, aber habe doch lieber erst meinen Vater um Erlaubniß bitten wollen.

Der Ort wo ich bin ist klein, 64 Engl[ische] Meilen von London 19 d[it]o von Salisbury und 14 d[it]o von Winchester entfernt. Er liegt aber sehr angenhem zwischen vielen ansehnlichen Hügeln, welches mir zu vielen angenehmen Spaziergängen Anlaß gibt. Dr. Tay bei dem ich hier bin ist zugleich ein guter und geschikter Man, ist verheiratet, und hat drei Söhne, wovon der erste in Smirna der zweite in Rotterdam und der dritte noch hier ist. Meine übrigen Camaraden sind 2 kleine van Nollen, und ein Mr Walpok der schon ziemlich erwachsen ist. Uebrigens die Sachen die ich hier ler[ne] bestehen ungefähr in folgenden: die Englische, Holländische und Lateinische Sprache, Schreiben, Rechnen Geographie etc (die französische Sprache versteht sich von selbst, da ich nichts andres hier sprechen kan, daher daß französische mir jezt eben so geläufig als das deutsche ist) zu meinem großen Vergnügen seze auch das Clavier fort.

Uebrigens bin ich kein besonderer Freund des englischen Charakters, da der Engländer jeden verachtet der nicht von seiner Nation ist. Die Engl[ische] Aussprache ist wie jederman weiß sehr schwer, und man moquirt immer über einen Ausländer der es nicht recht ausspricht. Aber ich bin dieß jezo schon gewohnt, und macht mir nichts mehr auß.

Nun will ich einen kurzen Auszug meiner Reisebeschreibung machen: Sonabend, den 10. Jul[i] reißte ich von Hamburg ab, und kam den anderen Tag schon in Bremen, hielte mich hier 3 Tage auf und sahe den Bleikeller, die Wasserkunst und die übrigen Merckwürdigkeiten, und besuchte viele Freunde und Correspondenten meines Vaters. Donerstag, den 15. Jul[i] früh, reißte von Bremen ab, durch Oldenburg, Delmenhorst, Leer, Neuschanz, die 2 Nächte durch und Sonab[end] früh um 3 Uhr in Groningen, wo wir uns nicht aufhalten. Denselben Abend spät kamen in Lemer an und emba[rquirten] uns auf der ZuiderZee Sontag Mittag um 2 kamen mit schlechtem Wind nach Amsterdam. Diesesmahl wurde nicht kranck. In Amsterd[dam] hielt mich 14 Tage auf, in welcher Zeit ich beinahe immer zu Gaste und auf der Börse alle Mittag gewesen bin. Besahe auch daselbst, den botanischen Garten, Hospitäler und Werckhäuser, den Haven, die 2 dasigen französischen Theater, das berühmte Rath- und Stadt Hauß, etliche Particulier Naturalien und Kunst-Cabinetter etc. In dieser Zeit besuchte gleichfalls H[er]r[n] Amsberg und H[er]r[n] Hacke die ich beide wohl antraf. Machte auch eine kleine Tour nach Utrecht wo ich zu der Zeit einen schönen Markt zu sehen bekam. Montag den 2. Aug[ust] reiste aus Amsterdam ab, und kam Dienstag den 3ten Abend in Rotterdam, durch Haag, Harlem, Delft und Leyden. Hier hielte mich 3 Tage auf, in einem derselben ich neue Tour nach Dordrecht machte. Sonabend den 7ten kamen in Helvoetsluys wo wir biß Montag 9. Morgen auf guten Wind warten mussten. Dienstag 10. Abend kamen wir in Harwick, nach einer unangenehmen Ueberfahrt, wo ich außerordentlich kranck gewesen war.

Das übrige schreibe ich Ihnen nächstens. Ich füge nur noch hinzu noch daß sowohl das Land selbst als auch die Art zu leben mir außerordentlich gefällt, und daß ich hoffe Sie, bester Pflegevater, bald hier zu sehen. Meine herzliche Empfehlungen und Grüße an H[e]r[rn] Rudolphi und Ms Rudolphi,[1] Malortie,

Lotte,[2] die kleinen Fräuleins, Hanchen, und ganz Trittow. Gerne schreibe ich Ihnen auch, wenn der Plaz und das theure Porto es erlaubte. Mit inniger kindlicher Liebe und Dankbarkeit verbleibe,

  Ihr gehorsamer Sohn
  J N Böhl

NB. Wir haben viel mit Luft Ballons zu thun. Aus den Zeitungen werden sie wohl vernommen haben, daß in London ein gewißer H[er]r Lunardi[3] aufgegangen ist, dessen Luftballon ich gesehen. Man kann hier allerwärts welche die 9 Fuß im Umfang haben für 2 St[ück] Hamburger Geld kriegen. Vielleicht schicke ich Ihnen einen bei Gelegenheit.

NB. Ihr Theophron duet mir immer sehr gut, und ich schöpfe täglich neue Lehren aus ihm. Desto weiter ich komme desto mehr sehe ich ein wie glücklich ich bei Ihnen war, weniger glücklich schon bei H[er]r[n] Noodt[4] wo innerliche Zwistigkeiten uns beschäftigten, hatte aber doch noch meine Eltern und Freunde – jezt! ganz allein – ohne einen Freund, mit dem ich wenigstens meine Muttersprache reden kan.

3. Joachim Heinrich and Dorothea Campe, Trittow

Andover den 3 März 1785

Theuerste Pflegeeltern

Da ich heute Gelegenheit habe Ihnen zu schreiben, ergreife ich die Feder mit Vergnügen, um Ihnen meiner steten kindlichen Dankbarkeit zu versichern. Ihr lieber Brief hat mir sehr viel Freude verursacht, aber auch manche Trauer gekostet. Wie oft habe ich mich in meine glückliche Lage schon zurückgewünscht, [illeg.] ich ihn loos! Aber alle Wünsche helfen nichts. Gott hat es so gewollt, und ich habe mich schon so früh von meinen lieben Eltern, Lehrern, und Freunden trennen müssen.

Meinen jetzigen Aufenthalt werde ich in der Mitte Aprils verlassen müssen. Sogleich ich die Englische Sprache nicht ganz vollständig sprechen kann, kann ich mich doch so ziemlich ausdrücken, und alles was ich lese und höre verstehen. Und, in so ferne, ist die Absicht meines lieben Vaters erreicht.

Vermuthlich werde ich mich noch 14 Tage in London aufhalten, und dan mit H[er]rn Justus einem Freund meines Vaters, dem ich addressirt und der in London wohnt, nach Paris gehen, der Plan meines Vaters ist, daß ich von da nach Marseille gehen soll, wo ich vermuthlich Gelegenheit finden werde, zu Schiffe nach Cadix zu gehen. Ich hoffe daß dieses geschehen wird, da ich sehr neugierig bin Frankreich zu sehen, und da das mich zugleich in der französichen Sprache zu perfectioniren würde. Aber es ist noch nicht gewiß.

Ihren Ring werde ich stets wie ein Heiligthum ansehen und bewaren, so wie auch Theophron, aus dem ich immer neue Anweisungen schöpfe.

Wir haben hier einen sehr harten unangenehmen Winter gehabt, der noch immer fortdauert. Gestern sogar, lief ich noch auf Schlittschuhe. Der Schnee bedeckte einmahl alle Wege, so daß alle Communication, der eine Stadt mit der anderen, aufhörte.

Meine besten Grüße und Empfehlungen an H[er]rn Rudolphi, dessen Schwester mit ihren kleinen Eleven, H[er]r[n] Ansberg (wenn er schon bei Ihnen seyn sollte) Malortie, Lotte, Hanchen, kurz allen Bekannten, Sagen Sie dem ersteren, daß ich große Progresse auf dem Clavier mache, obgleich die hiesige Musik, in einem ganz anderen Schlüssel ist.

Zuletzt bitte ich um Verzeihung, daß ich mich vielleicht etwas schlecht ausgedrückt habe, und ortographische Fehler gemacht habe. Aber denken Sie, daß ich nun schon länger dan 7 Monathe, kein Wort Deutsche gesprochen habe. Ich muß entweder Französisch od[er] Englisch sprechen.

Leben Sie wohl, und erinnern Sie sich stets meiner. Seyen Sie versichert, daß ich Ihrer Lehren stets eingedenk seyn werde. Indem Abend fort Gott mein Gebeth für Ihre Erhaltung. Ich verbleibe stets
Meiner lieben Pflege Eltern
dankbarer und ergebener Sohn
John Nicolas Böhl

4. Joachim Heinrich Campe, Trittow

Cadiz den 2 August 1785

Theuerster Pflegevater,
Obgleich ich in so langer Zeit, keinen Ihrer lieben Briefe erhalten habe, so halte ich es doch für meine Pflicht Ihnen von Zeit zu Zeit meine Versicherungen der aufrichtigsten Dankbarkeit und Liebe zu erneuern.

Die eigentliche Uhrsache dieses, wird Ihnen wohl unbekannt seyn. Wollen Sie mir aber erst versprechen, meine unverzeihbahre Nachläßigkeit zu vergeben, so will ich sie Ihnen kund thun. Es ist nemlich Ihr Geburtstag. Nehmen Sie denn hierzu meine herzlichsten Wünsche für Ihr beständiges Wohlergehen, und Gebe Gott! daß ich dereinst in 15 oder 20 Jahren denselben mit Ihnen feiern kann. Daßelbe hoffe ich mit meiner besten Pflegemutter und allen andern gemeinschaftlichen Freunden thun zu können, so Gott will!

Den 11. May trat ich meine See Reise von Gravesend an. Wir hatten beständig contrairen Wind, und waren beinah 14 Tage ehe wir England aus dem Gesichte verlohren. Nun aber erhob sich ein schöner günstiger Wind der uns in 9 Tagen biß nach Cadiz bließ. Ich war stark und anhaltend krank.

Meine Lebensart ist hier sehr einförmig, und es hört Vernunft und Geduld dazu, sich darin zu schicken. Von des Morgens um 8 bis 1½ Uhr ist man auf dem Comptoir. Dann wird gegessen. Nach Tische schläft man, läßt sich frisieren (sie werden wohl schon wissen, daß ich leider! gezwungen worden bin, es zu thun) und um 4 ist jeder wieder auf dem Comptoir. Um 6 geht man spazieren biß 8. Dann habe ich meinen Spanischen Sprachmeister, Klavier Meister etc: so daß ich wenig Zeit für mich selbst übrig habe. Manchmahl geht man auch in Gesellschaft oder in die Comödie, und so geht es jeden Tag.

Wie oft springt der Wunsch in mir auf, dazu seyn, wo ich hergekommen bin. Zwischen Eltern, Freunden in seinem Vaterlande, freie Uebung seiner Religion. Hier zwischen Leuten, die jeden Ausländer der nicht katholisch ist, als einen Ketzer betrachten, wo man für Bilder knien muß, an keine Kirche dencken kan etc: Mein Trost aber denn ist, daß dieß alles zu meinem wahren Besten geschieht, und daß mein Vater mich nicht würde hieher geschickt haben, wenn nicht davon gröstentheils meine zeitliche Glückseligkeit abhinge. –

Wie sehr werden mich nicht etliche Zeilen von Ihrer mir stets werthen Hand erfreuen. Ich werde nicht ermangeln, darauf gleich zu antworten. Vieles habe ich noch zu sagen, aber Platz fehlt mir.

Meine herzlichsten Grüße an meine liebe Pflegemutter, Lotten, Malortie, H[er]r[n] Rudolphi, Madame Rudolphi, den kleinen Fräuleins und allen übrigen Hausgenossen. Seyn Sie meiner kindlichen Liebe und Dankbarkeit stets versichert mit welcher

Ihr gehorsamer Sohn
Johan Niclas Böhl

5. Joachim Heinrich Campe, Braunschweig

Cadiz den 1 May [17]90

Theurster Pflegevater,

Meine Zeit erlaubt mir diesesmahl nur, Ihr sehr angenehmes vom 15 Märtz kurz zu beantworten. Ich habe daraus mit Vergnügen die dießjährige Bücher Absendung ersehen, und verspreche mir, den Titeln nach zu urtheilen, recht viel Genuß davon. Nachdem ich dieselben alle werde empfangen und gelesen haben, so sollen meine künftigen Briefe Ihnen mein bestimteres Urtheil überbringen, welches Sie alsdann gütigst berichtigen werden.

Schon von meinem Bruder hatte ich vernommen daß Sie vorigen Herbst Paris besucht haben.[1] Wie sehr es für einen scharfsinnigen Beobachter interessant gewesen seyn muß, Augenzeuge einer Revolution gleich der dort vorgefallenen zu seyn kann ich mir leicht vorstellen. Ich erwarte daher mit Ungeduld Ihre Briefe darüber und auch seiner Zeit die ganze förmliche Reisebeschreibung. Daß Sie nicht biß zu den Säulen des Herkules vorgedrungen sind, thut mir zwar meinentwegen leid, aber ist mir was Ihnen anlangt um desto lieber, den Sie würden für die Unannehmlichkeiten der Reise durch Spanien, durch nichts entschädigt worden seyn, sondern im Gegentheil beständige Ursache zu Aergerniß vorgefunden haben.

Derselbe Schiffer der diesen Brief überbringt, hat ein an meinen Bruder in Hamburg addressirtes Packet mit einem Exemplar des spanischen Robinsons mit.[2] Der guten Kupferstiche habe ich nur ironisch erwähnt, wie Sie solches gleich aus dem ersten ersehen werden, wo Ihr Werthes selbst in altfränkischer Kleidung, mit quacksalbermäßigen gestus, die Geschichte vorträgt – die Vorrede können Sie als ein Muster spanischer Suffisance für merckwürdig annehmen.

Mit meiner Zurückkehr nach Deutschland sieht es leider noch sehr weitläuftig aus. Die Zeiten des rapiden fortune machens sind vorbey, die Handlung ist schlecht und wird immer schlechter, und will ich es mir zum Ziel machen ebenso reich wie meine Vorgänger zurückzukehren, so kann ich lange arbeiten. Indessen ist meine ambition nicht Reichthum, und allein die Begierde denselben zu erringen würde nicht mächtig genug seyn mich hier zu halten, wenn sich nicht Nebenzwecke vereinigten, mich stärcker zu binden. Die hauptsächlichsten sind: daß ich nicht allein für mich sondern auch für meine Brüder arbeite, welche sich durch meine zu zeitige retirade aus den Besitz unseres hiesigen Etablissements gesetzt finden würden: daß ich noch nicht mein eygener Herr bin und daß wenn ich es auch wäre ich doch zweifeln würde ob es sich mit meinen Pflichten vertragen könne, schon so früh dem geschäftigen nutzbringenden Leben zu entsagen. Nicht als wenn meine Absicht wäre ein Müßiggänger zu werden, aber meine Beschäftigungen würden doch hauptsächlich auf Vergnügen und Verbesserung meines ichs abzielen. Ich arbeite zwar anjetzo auch nur für mich, aber ich bin doch ein Rad in dem großen Uhrwercke der menschlichen Gesellschaft, setze viele Leute in Arbeit und gebe vielen etwas zu verdienen, verbessere auch selbst meine zeitlichen Umstände und vermehre dadurch die Mittel andere zu beglücken, welches, ich gestehe es, mir das rühmlichste Ziel auf dieser Erde zu seyn scheint – Wenn ich aber nur von meinen Interessen leben, und ein raffinirter Müßiggänger bin (worunter ich jemand verstehe der nur für sich lebt und nichts zum allgemeinen Besten mit beiträgt) erfülle ich dann meine Bestimmung? – Hierüber muß ich mich Ihre Gedancken ausbitten! – Ich mögte für mein Theil eine gänzlich von menschlicher Gesellschaft unabhängige Lebensart, mit Beruf od[er] Bestimungs Pflichten verbinden; allein mir däucht daß nur alsdann jemand solcher Ruhe zu genießen berechtiget ist, wenn er der menschlichen Gesellschaft lange genug seinen Kräften gemäß, gedient hat, und dieses, däucht mir, kann er nur thun wenn er einen Stand hat od[er] ein Amt bekleidet. – Helfen Sie mir hierin meine Gedancken berichtigen!

Was meine Lebensart und mich selbst überhaupt anlangt muß ich vor diesesmahl aufschieben Ihnen zu unterhalten, aber nächstens soll es desto weitläuftiger geschehen.

Die angeschloßenen Briefe von meiner beste Pflegemutter und der lieben Lotte habe ich wohl erhalten und mit vielen Vergnügen gelesen, muß indeß auch die Beantwortung aufschieben – Meinem Versprechen gemäß habe ich bey Ueberbringer dieses auch 1 Kistel M^{on} I H C mit 1 @ Chocolade geladen, und selbe an meinen Bruder addressirt um sie Ihnen zu spediren. Die Hälfte davon ist mit Vainillas, welches den Geschmack des Chocolades außerordentlich hebt und hier vorgezogen wird und die andere Hälfte ohne. Ich wünsche daß solche Ihrem Geschmack gemäß ausfallen möge, und bitte sich dabey an Ihren Sie alle stets liebenden und verehrenden PflegeSohn zu Cadiz zu erinnern. Gerne hätte auch die Orangen und Zwiebeln gesandt aber es ist anjetzo nicht die Jahreszeit; haben wir hier indessen, gegen FrühJahr Schiffs Gelegenheit, so sollen dieselben ohne Fehl erfolgen.

Mathias Lohmann ist etwas leichtsinnig; sein gutes naturel verläugnet sich indessen nicht; mit zunehmenden Alter wird er gesetzter werden. Er geht diesen Sommer wieder nach Hamburg.

Empfehlen Sie mich bestens allen Freunden die meiner gedencken und glauben mich stets ohne Rückhalt

Ihren danckbaren ergebnen

Pflegesohn

Johan Nic. Bohl

6. Dorothea Campe [Braunschweig]

Cadiz July [17]90

Theuerste Pflegemutter

Daß mir Ihr lieber Brief vom 15 Märtz recht sehr angenehm gewesen ist brauche ich Ihnen wohl nicht zu sagen; jede Zeile deßelben ist mir ein neuer Beweiß Ihres liebenden mütterlichen Herzens, dessen mich würdig zu machen gewiß mein anhaltendes Bestreben ist und seyn werden

Ein Theil von Vaters dießjähriger litterarische Absendung ist schon in meinen Händen, und macht mir viel Vergnügen, so wie ich dann noch immer der alte Freund von Lesen bin. Die Braunschweigischen Journäle habe ich indessen noch nicht erhalten,[1] also auch bis jetzt Vaters interessante Briefe über die Französische Revolution entbehren müssen. Wäre meine Reise nach dorten um ein Jahr später gefallen, so hätte ich vielleicht das für mich so erwünschte Vergnügen haben können, die Reise nach Paris mit Vater zu machen. – Was hätte ich nicht darum gegeben!

Ihre Wünsche mich bald in Deutschland wiederzusehen stimmen sehr mit den meinigen überein, allein —— doch schon in meinem letzten Brief an Vater habe ich mich hierüber geäußert, und seitdem haben sich die Aussichten wo nicht verschlimmert, doch gewiß auch nicht gebessert. Die schon so lange anhaltende

Ungewißheit eines Bruches zwischen Spanien und England, druckt unsere Handlung außerordentlich, und rückt uns das Ziel unseres arbeitsamen Bestrebens immer weiter aus den Augen. So viel kann ich Ihnen indessen nochmahls versichern, daß nichts mich zur Erwerbung eines noch so großen Vermögens wird reitzen können, wenn ich deßhalb den größten und besten Theil meines Lebens in diesem traurigem Lande zubringen müßte. Nach meiner jetzigen Gesinnungen denke ich nicht viel über 30 Jahre hier zu zählen woran mir anjezo noch über 10 fehlen. Nach 15 jähriger schwerer Arbeit denke ich dann auch schon einen kleinen Anspruch auf eine thätige Ruhe machen zu können, wo ohne durch Specielle Societätsconventionen gebunden zu seyn, ich so nach meiner Art den Menschen und Weltbürger spielen kann. Daß ich hinzu vor allem unseren lieben Vater und Sie zu Rathe ziehen werde, versteht sich von selbst, vornehmlich nach den angenehmen Äußerungen dieserwegen, in seinem letzten Schreiben.

Die Nachrichten von einigen meiner gewesenen Mitschüler sind mir zwar traurig aber nicht unerwartet gewesen. Ich habe mich schon etwas in der Welt umgesehen, und sowohl aus Beobachtung als Erfahrung kann ich zuversichtlich sagen, daß ich biß jetzt noch keinen Ort habe ausfindig machen können, wo nicht Vernunft und Tugend lächerlich, hingegen Leichtsinn und modische Laster bon ton sind, und zur feinen Gesellschaft gehören! – Was Wunder daß ein junger Mann, obschon mit den besten theoretischen Grundsätzen, bey seinem Eintritt in der Welt ausgerütscht, von dem allgemeinen Beispiel hingerissen wird! – Er muß sich entweder entschließen für sich allein allen schlichten Urtheilen, Spöttereien und ridiculisationen des großen Haufens, Trotz zu bieten oder auch dem Strom zu folgen – Er hat keinen Freund keinen Rathgeber, keine Stütze, der ihn in Güten bestärkt, der die falschen Vorspiegelungen der modischen Jugend ihm aufdeckt, und seinem schwankenden Glauben an Tugend, den er nirgends findet, neue Kräfte giebt. Verführungen im reizenden Gewand stellen sich ihm von allen Seiten dar ——— doch wozu ein mehreres? – Ihr scharfes Auge muß schon ehe es bis hieher gekommen ist, entdeckt haben daß ich meine eygene Apologie schreibe. Wundern Sie sich nicht daß Sie solches jetzt erst von mir hören. Gott weiß wie viel mir diese lange Verstellung gekostet hat aber ich war entschloßen erst durch Thaten die Aufrichtigkeit meiner Erkenntniß und Reue zu beweisen, und als dann Ihnen mit der Wunde den Beysam zugleich zu ertheilen, indem ich von dem aufrichtigen Antheil so Sie besonders an mein moralisches Wohl nahmen überzeugt bin – Jetzt fodere ich alle Zeugen meiner hiesigen Aufführung seit 1½ Jahren das ich zuviel bin, auf, um mir willkührliche Ausschweifungen zu überweisen. Es schickt sich nicht für mich ein mehreres hierüber zu schreiben; indirecte Nachrichten werden Ihnen hoffentlich das Fehlende ergänzt haben – Nur noch eine, und dann nichts mehr von dieser unangenehmen Sache. Von Ihrer großmuthigen edlen Denkungsart erwarte ich nunmehr nicht allein Verzeihung, dann auf diese kann ja jeder aufrichtiger Reuige Anspruch thun, sondern womöglich Vergessenheit dieses

Flecken meines Lebens der schon genug unangenehme Folgen für mich gehabt hat, daß wenigstens Ihre Liebe zu mich, dadurch nicht geschmälert werde! (Daß ich dieses eben so gut für unsern theuren Vater, wie für Sie beste Pflegemutter schreibe, ist fast überflüßig anzuzeigen)

Herzlich wünsche ich, daß die Brunnenkur des lieben Vaters Gesundheit möge wieder gestärkt, und im Stande gesetzt haben von neue seine Kräfte dem allgemeinen Besten zu widmen – Von Pyrmont aus habe ich Nachricht, daß Sie daselbst alle im Monat Juny gewesen sind. Auch hat mir dieselbe Person ein gewißer Gundelach der in unserem Hause hier gewesen ist, Grüße von Ihnen gebracht für welche ich dankbar bin. Daß es diesem Freunde an gesunde Vernunft fehlt, werden Sie wohl ohne mein Zuthun, durch seine Unterredung errathen haben. Er ist ein guter aber äußerst schwacher Mensch, der durch seine durch Leichtgläubigkeit veranlaßten Unbesonnenheit, sein Glück hier verscherzt hat.

Was Sie mir wegen den Grüßen sagen ist mir so äußerst schmeichelhaft und unerwartet, daß man wirklich bey mir in einem so hohen credit wie Sie, liebe Mutter, stehen muß, um es mir glauben zu machen. Ist es möglich? – So viele große edle Menschen, erinnern sich eines unbedeutenden Jünglings, der kein weiteres Verdienst hat als ein Pflegesohn Campen's zu seyn? – Mir fehlt es an Muth nur einmahl etwas darauf zu erwiedern, da ich bey einer Vergleichung in ein Nichts zurückfinde, welches es mir unmöglich macht mich zu überzeugen daß ich je würdig gewesen bin die Aufmerksamkeit solcher Personen zu fixiren. Glauben Sie nicht daß ich untertreibe; seitdem ich denken kann haben mir Genie und Talente eine Ehrebietung eingeflößt, die mir niemahls ein bebänderter und besternter Alltags-Mensch, Prinz od[er] König hat abgewinnen können. Ich bewundere, beneide und wünsche mir keine andere Größe als Geistesgröße; welches dann auch die Ursache ist, daß mir die Fesseln des ganz mechanischen Kaufmannsstandes etwas schwer fallen. Nicht als wenn ich mich schmeichelte, mich als ein Gelehrter hervorzuthun, und die Wissenschaften mit neuen Entdeckungen bereichert zu haben, nein! – die schöpferischen Genies müssen gebohren werden! – meine Begierde diesen Punkt betrefend schränken sich nur auf das verstehen deßjenigen ein, was andere hevorgebracht haben und noch hervorbringen, und dieses würde mir doch wohl vielleicht durch anhaltenden Fleiß gelungen seyn.

Mathias Lohmann bringt diesen Brief biß nach Hamburg; er hat sich hier nicht zu schicken gewußt, und wird seinem Vater wieder beschwerlich fallen – Seine Jugend macht ihn gar sehr leichtsinnig und unbesonnen handeln, ohne daß ich ihm bißjetzt verderbte Grundsätze angemerckt habe.

Den Chocolade werden Sie hoffentlich erhalten und gut befunden haben. Das übrige versprochene erlaubt mir die Jahreszeit noch nicht zu senden; ich behalte es unterdessen im besten Andenken.

Daß die liebe Lotte Ihnen fortfährt Freude zu machen, ließ sich von deren guten Charakter und vortreffliche Leitung deßelben nicht anders erwarten. Mogten alle Ihre Pflegekinder eben so viel zu Ihrer und Vaters Zufriedenheit beybringen!

Ich hoffe Sie werden mit meinem Brief den vielen Fehlern ohngeachtet von jeder Art zufrieden seyn; meine Kaufmännische Lage muß alles entschuldigen. Sie sehen ja auch wohl mehr auf den guten Willen als auf die Aufführung.

In Erwartung Ihrer angenehmen Nachrichten verbleibe ich nach bester Empfehlung Ihr ergebener Pflegesohn,
Johan Nic. Bohl

7. Joachim Heinrich and Dorothea Campe, Braunschweig (appended to a letter from Anton Gottlieb Böhl)

Cadix den 31 May 1791

Obgleich meine Zeit sehr eingeschränckt ist, kann ich doch diesen Brief meines Bruders nicht weggehen lassen, ohne Ihnen eigenhändig die Versicherungen der volkommenen Liebe und Danckbarkeit zu wiederholen, welche mich Ihr Werthes Andencken stets einflößt. Gerne werden wir von Ihnen von Zeit zu Zeit die Fortdauer Ihrer Zufriedenheit und gegenseitigen Wohlseyns vernehmen, welche uns so sehr am Herzen liegen; uns gehet es beyden wohl; und wir sind so glücklich wie wir es nach Maaßgabe der Umstände verlangen können; nur ist mein eigentlicher Gemüths Zustand durch die vielen Zweifel welche dem denckenden Menschen jemehr er sieht und lernt aufstoßen müssen, manchmahl sehr schwanckend, und giebt mir zu trüben Stunden Anlaß. Grüße an alle Bekante besonders Lotte.
Der Ihrige J N Bohl

8. Joachim Heinrich and Dorothea Campe, Braunschweig

Cadix, den 27 April 1792

Eine angenehmere Ueberraschung konnte uns wohl nicht leichter werden, als die, den in jeder Rücksicht uns schätzbaren Professor Stuve[1] acht und vierzig Stunden lang so unverhoffterweise zu besitzen – desto einsamer und trauriger befinden wir uns jetzt, da das Schif welches ihn trägt unseren Augen schon entrückt, und seine reichhaltige Quelle von belehrender und beruhigender Unterhaltung schon wieder für uns versiegt ist – Wir erwachen von einem Traum, worin, durch Einwirkung eines Individu's, die durch Zeit und Mangel an Nachrichten etwas verdunkelte Idee des Braunschweigischen Cirkels mit verjüngter Lebhaftigkeit und Reitz hervorgegangen ist, und sehnen uns mit verdoppeltem Verlangen nach dem Tage, wo wir uns diesem finsterem Lande entziehen, und uns in dem Schooß unseres Vaterlandes zurückziehen können, um Nahrung für Geist und Herz, mit der Sorge für Beutel und Magen zu verbinden. Leider läßt sich diese Periode aber noch nicht bestimmen – Der liebe Stuve wird Ihnen Theure PflegeEltern von unserer Lebens- und DenckungsArt mehr hinterbringen, als wir auf ellenlange Bogen schreiben könnten; ich Johannes werde mich daher um desto kürtzer fassen, da ich an einem schwachen Auge leide, und mir das Schreiben beschwerlich fällt – Ich ersuche Vater Campen gelegentlich die Fortsetzungen der gesandten Schriften (von der Revision habe ich 13 Bände von dem Br[aunschweigischen] Journal 27 St[üc]k) auch andere besonders merckwürdige Bücher (doch nicht über ein paar Dutzend Bände jährlich) an Nic[olas] Conrad Schuback² in Hamburg für meine Rechnung abzusenden und sich mit demselben über die Bezahlung zu verstehen. Es herrscht hier jetzo etwas mindere Strenge, und einzelne Bände schlüpfen in den Taschen, und unter den Mänteln durch das Thor. – Ich wünsche, daß es Ihnen recht wohl gehe, und Ihnen eine dauerhafte Gesundheit zur Beförderung aller Ihrer menschenfreundlichen Zwecke behülflich sey! Meiner guten PflegeMutter, und der lieben Lotte sind meine angenehmsten Erinnerungen gewidmet – Grüßen Sie auch den braven Pr[ofessor] Trapp,³ und andere sich meiner erinnernde Freunde – Wenn Pr[ofessor] Stuve ankömt so zeigen Sie ihm diesen Brief; er zeugt von dem wahrhaften Eindruck seines Besuchs, der nicht so leicht verlöschen wird

der Ihrige J N Bohl

9. Joachim Heinrich and Dorothea Campe, Braunschweig

Cadiz den 27 August 1793

Nach einem zwölfmonathlichen Aufenthalt in Frankreich meiner Augenkranckheit halber bin ich, Wertheste PflegeEltern, hier seit Monath May zurück, und ob ich gleich den Endzweck meiner Reise nicht gänzlich erreicht habe, ist es den Aertzten doch wenigstens geglückt insofern den sich auf die Augen werfenden humeur zu mildern, daß ich mich schon wieder etliche Stunden am Tage mit Schreiben oder Lesen beschäftigen kann, und es hoffentlich bey zunehmenden Alter immer besser damit gehen werden

Ihre Briefe machen uns immer, wie Sie sich leicht vorstellen können, viel Vergnügen; nur thut es uns leid, daß Sie so viel von den Verfolgungen kleiner Seelen zu leiden haben: wir hatten dieses schon aus dem Braunschweigischen Journale ersehen, und wie Sie leicht glauben werden mit Leib und Seele für die unbescholtenen freimüthigen Menschen und Wahrheitsfreunde Parthie genommen, denn es mag in Fr[ankreich] gehen wie es will, so bleiben darum die Grundsätze dessen politischen Systems nicht weniger wahr, und keine Macht wird sie in unbefangenen Köpfen je auslöschen. Wenn ich einmahl nach Deutschland käme, so würde ich mich gerne für die hier in erzwungener Verstellung verlebten Jahre durch freimüthige Äußerung meiner Meinungen schadloß halten wollen, und dann würden Ihre guten Freunde einmahl eine schöne Gelegenheit haben auf die guten Früchte der neuen Erziehung loßzuziehen. In meinem jugendlichen Eifer würde ich vielleicht alle weltliche und geistliche Hierarchie für unrechtmäßig erklären, gegen Religions Meynungen die mir einen schädlichen Einfluß auf Moralität und Wircksamkeit zu haben scheinen reden, manchen ein sanftes Küßen von Vorurtheilen zu rauben suchen etc. Also biß Sie keine Apologie mehr, wie die eingesandte, brauchen, oder biß ich mich auf zeitlebens unter das Joch der hergebrachten Meynungen schmiegen lerne, müssen wir an keine Vereinigung in Ihrem Wohnort dencken. Doch können sich gegen der Zeit, daß ich an eine Rückkehr nach Deutschland dencken kann, die Umstände noch sehr ändern und ist es hoffentlich zu Gunsten der Toleranz alsdann, . . . doch keine Pläne, da die Umstände alles leiten.

Valentin Meyer,[1] mein Bruder und ich erleichtern uns durch gleichartige Gesinnungen unsere hiesige Ausschließung von Kopf und Herz stärckender Unterhaltung mit Männern wie Sie, Theurer PflegeVater, und Ihres gleichen. Wir lesen und sprechen über das gelesene, und nähren so immer die eingepflanzte Vorliebe uns und andere durch richtige angewandte Einsicht zu beglücken. Ihr christlicher Leitfaden ist uns sehr angenehm gewesen, und würde mir insbesondere noch nützlicher werden wenn eine Korrespondenz gestattete, mich mit Ihnen über die mir nicht einleuchtenden Puncte eines angebornen moralischen Gefühls oder Gewissens, einer besonderen oder mittelbaren Vorsehung etc zu erörtern. Wir sind alle drey so glücklich unsere Pflichten oder Glückseligkeit Lehre auf schlichte angewandte Vernunft zu gründen; wir können nicht umhin zu glauben, daß die menschliche Vernunft sich durch sich selbst auf diesen Grad von Einsicht erheben kann; unter dessen mag eine durch Gott veranstaltete Belehrung immer den Schwachen gerne zu Hülfe kommen: wir schmeicheln uns daß sie für uns überflüßig ist – In Rücksicht auf diese Vordersätze, werden uns die neueren dahin einschlagenden Schriften sehr willkommen seyn, so wie auch etwas ausgezeichnetes im Fach der schönen Litteratur, Geschichte, oder Reisen; auch etwas jetzt so sehr nöthige Geißel auf Sitten Verderbniß und gesellschaftliche Verhältniße im Geschmack von Noldmann,[2] doch mehr ins bürgerliche und allgemeine – Wäre ich oder hätte ich Talent zum Schriftsteller an letzteres würde ich mich machen, und recht aufdecken wie in der jetzigen Gesellschaft alle Laster geehrt vorgezogen und alles Gute verschrien und lächerlich gemacht wird; mir däucht es ist hohe Zeit daß sich alle wohldenckende Menschen aufraffen und den immer mehr einreißenden verderblichen Vorurtheilen in sittlicher Rücksicht laut die Stirne bieten – Addressiren Sie die Bücher an Nic[olas] Conrad Schuback in Hamburg, auf dem Sie gleichfalls den Belauf entnehmen können. Von der vorigen Sendung bleiben noch verschiedene St[üc]ke bey unseren Onkel zurück.

Gerne trage ich mein Theil zu der für Minderung des menschlichen Elends bestimmten Summe bey – bey der Gelegenheit wünsche von Ihnen zu erfahren was Sie von der Hamburger Versorgungs Anstalt halten.[3] Ohne Ihnen wegen der Anwendung im geringsten etwas vorzuschreiben, erwähne ich im vorbeygehen daß mir nützliche Thätigkeit zu befördern, der beste Gebrauch des überflüßigen Geldes zu seyn scheint. Die Arbeit Lustigen zu beschäftigen, den Handwerker zum Einkauf von Materialien Vorschuß zu leisten oder ihm fertige Sache abzunehmen, ist ihm nur dienen ohne ihm Almosen zu geben. – Man muß entweder durch Kranckheit oder Alter absolut unfähig zu aller Arbeit seyn oder den Sinn für Gerechtigkeit unterdrückt haben, wenn man Anspruch auf Almosen machen will. Ich kann unmöglich viel von demjenigen halten der sich zu nehmen erniedrigt; so lange er noch erwerben kann.

Wir besitzen hier jetzt einen Litteraten den Legat[ion]s Rath Sepier aus Altona der uns viel unterhaltendes von den deutschen großen Männern erzählt: von der dänischen Regierung und den Gesinnungen des dortigen Adels spricht er sehr vortheilhaft: vielleicht wird dies kleine Land noch einmahl der Zufluchtsort der Verfolgten. Er hat uns auch gesagt, daß H[er]r Pr[ofessor] Trapp und H[er]r Knigge ihren [damage] wegen der neuern Pädagogik beigelegt haben, und daß letzterer sich durch seinen Noldman über die Mittelmäßigkeit erhoben hat: ich habe Mühe zu glauben daß dieselbe Person seichte LiebesRomane und einen Noldman schreiben kann.

Die Pflanze per Schiff ist nicht gut übergekommen; ich dancke indessen dafür so wie für Vaters guten Rath; meine Kranckheit kömmt von schlechten humeurs, die sich besonders auf ein Auge werfen: durch eine Ableitung dieses humeurs alias cautère wäre mir wohl zu helfen, allein das Mittel ist schlimmer als das Uebel.

Meine besten Grüße an die liebe Lotte, Pr[ofessor] Stuve, Trapp und andere bekannte Haußgenoßen

Ich bin bekantermaßen Ihr aufrichtigliebender
Johan Nicolas Bohl

10. Joachim Heinrich and Dorothea Campe, Braunschweig

Cadiz den 24 October [17]94

Theuerste PflegeEltern

Es ist sehr lange her, daß wir nichts von Ihrer Hand gesehen haben, da leider ein Brief den Sie uns im Anfang dieses Jahres schrieben uns nicht zugekommen ist. Unser Korrespondent Schuback nahm sich erst die unnütze Mühe an uns zu schreiben um zu wissen auf welchen Ort er den etwas dicken Brief absenden sollte; nachher gab er ihn an einen Herrn der in Frankreich aufgebracht ist, sodaß wir diesen Brief spät oder gar nicht erhalten werden – Unterdessen haben wir glücklicher einen Theil der für uns besorgten Bücher, nemlich den Rest der Sendung von 93 und 18 Stück der neuesten Sendung (wovon die übrigen 19 Stück auch schon unterwegens sind) erhalten, und auch schon größtentheils verschlungen. Man muß es empfunden haben was es ist von allen Äußerungen des gebildeten menschlichen Geistes entfernt zu leben, um sich unser Vergnügen bey dieser lecture lebhaft vorstellen zu können. Dank sey es den edlen Männern, die es uns verschaffen!

In meinem letzten Brief vom 17. April schrieb ich Ihnen, daß ich besonders neugierig auf die Uebersetzung der letzten Theile des Emils wäre.[1] Diese habe ich glücklich erhalten und die noten mit besonderem Interesse gelesen. So sehr ich nun auch Ihrem Urtheile darin über Sophie beitreten muß, so wenig kann ich mich jedoch von der Unnatürlichkeit und den Widersprüchen dieses Characters überzeugen. Meine wenigen Erfahrungen über das andere Geschlecht haben mir dieselben Resultate gegeben; ich dencke und fühle über die Weiber wie R[ousseau] – Wenn eine Frau Tugend der Tugend selbst halben übt, so ist es, weil die Tugend schön ist – doch es steht alles im R[ousseau] – In Spanien und in Frankreich, als wo ich observirt habe, ist Eitelkeit oder feine Sinnlichkeit die Triebfeder aller weiblichen Handlungen welche nicht durch Religion oder Menschenfurcht erkünstelt werden.

Das Schleswigische Journal[2] von 93 haben wir auch erhalten – Anstatt März 93 kommt nur leider März 92 – auch fehlen uns die 9 letzten Stücke von 90 und die 8 letzten von 92, die wir, wenn sie einzeln zu haben sind nachzuschicken bitten. Fast alle Aufsätze darin haben uns besonders gefallen, nur der Schluß nicht. Also auch in D[eutschland] fängt Preßzwang an? – Das Buch Chr[istus] und die Vernunft[3] hat uns auch viel Vergnügen gemacht, nicht sowohl der bündigen uns unnützen Widerlegungen, halber sondern wegen der neuen Aussichten die es in dem weiten Gebiete der Philosophie manchesmahl eröffnet. Auch Funk's Praktische Gesch[ichte] des M[enschen][4] hat uns voller interessanten fruchtbringenden Wahrheiten geschienen. Die übrigen Bücher sind außer etlichen erhaltenen Fortsetzungen, noch zurück.

Wir waren ungewiß, was Sie uns auf unsere unchristlichen Gesinnungen antworten würden; wir hätten uns auch nicht gewundert, wenn Sie uns allenfalls der Leichtigkeit und Unbesonnenheit beschuldigt und uns vermahnt hätten, die Vernunft gefangen zu nehmen und anzubeten. Ich habe dieses selbst manchem neumodischen jungen Zweifler angerathen – Jetzt aber urtheilen wir aus etlichen gesandten Schriften, daß Sie uns nicht verkennen und dieses ist uns sehr angenehm – Manchen langen und traurigen Kampf haben uns die jugendlichen Vorurtheile gekostet, den es war nicht Uebermuth welche uns ihr Joch abzuwerfen antrieb, sondern heißer Durst Bedürfniß nach Wahrheit – Endlich hat uns ein kleiner Stral ihres Lichts erquickt; wir sind nun so ruhig und glücklich als es unsere eigenen Unvollkommenheiten zulassen, und indem wir an der Veredlung unsres Geistes arbeiten, glauben wir zu gleicher Zeit nützliche Mitglieder der menschlichen

Gesellschaft zu seyn. – Ich muß Ihnen bey dieser Gelegenheit noch einmahl für Garvens Cicero danken.[5] Dieses Buch hat viel zu meiner Zufriedenheit beigetragen.

Unsere gesellschaftliche Laage hier verbessert sich mehr und mehr. Am Ende dieses Jahres werden wir als gültige compagnons mit der Unterschrift in die Handlungsverbindung eintreten, und zugleicher Zeit wird sich ein älterer compagnon der uns immer entgegen gewesen ist zurückziehen. Hiedurch erlangen wir nicht allein einen größeren Verdienst, sondern auch freie Wirksamkeit – Unsern Freund Meyer und einen andern jungen Mann, werden wir auch das Vergnügen haben fortzuhelfen, indem wir sie zu unsern Nachfolger bestimmen. Nach drei Jahren wird sich auch der letzte ältere associes zurückziehen, und wir sodann die eigentlichen Eigenthümer der Handlung werden. Nachdem werde ich noch drey Jahre bleiben, das ist biß Ende von 1800, und mein Bruder noch drei Jahre nach mir. Dieses sind so menschliche Pläne; da unsere Glückseeligkeit aber nicht an ihre Erfüllung hängt, so hängen wir ihnen geruhig nach – Eigentlich haben wir die Reichthümer die wir so wahrscheinlicherweise erwerben werden für unsere Bedürfniße nicht nöthig; denn ich werde mit dem Schluße dieses Jahres schon 100.000 paister a 2 besitzen, und meines Bruders Vermögen nicht weit davon seyn, aber vor 30 Jahre kann man sich doch auch nicht von den Geschäften abziehen. Man muß einen Beruf erfüllen, und etliche Zeit ein thätiges Mitglied der Gesellschaft seyn; man muß eine Stiftung wie die unseres HandlungHauses für die seinigen und andere Würdige aufrecht erhalten, man muß endlich viel auf eine rechtmäßige Art zu erwerben suchen um sich desto nützlicher machen zu können – demohngeachtet werden wir uns nicht sklavisch an den Schreibpult fesseln, weil es so hergebracht ist, und unsere Gesundheit vielleicht durch zu eifrige Betriebsamkeit untergraben. Nein, wir verstehen es besser zu leben. Mir besonders, dem meine Augenschwäche eine anhaltende Arbeit noch schädlicher macht, und bey dem sich schon unter der körperlich trägen hiesigen Lebensart die Hamburgische Anlage zu einem dicken bürgerlichen Bauch, an zu zeigen fängt, mir besonders, sage ich, convenirt heftige Bewegung und also Reisen. Demzufolge gedencke ich (wenn etliche biß jetzt noch unbestimmte Umstände nach Wunsch eintreffen) auf das nächste FrühJahr von hier zu Schiffe nach Genua zu gehen und von da nach der Schweitz, einem Lande wornach ich lüsterner bin als die Juden nach ihrem gelobten Lande seyn konnten. Vermuthlich werde ich auch in Lausanne meinen Bruder Fritz treffen und dann können wir zu Fuß dieses herrliche Ländchen durchwandern. Ob ich dann am Ufer des Genfer oder des Boden Sees einen kleinen Meyerhof kaufen werde, soll lediglich davon abhängen ob die Wirklichkeit im Thürgau meinem Ideale von diesen Gegenden entspricht. Ist es, so werde ich mit etlichen tausend Thalern einen kleinen Zufluchtsort im Schoße der Natur und der Freiheit nicht zu theuer erkaufen, um vielleicht einmahl meine Laufbahn daselbst zu schließen. Auf alle Fälle werden mir 6 Monath Schweitzer diät und motion für den Körper und ebensolange Muße zum beschauen und überlegen für die Seele sehr zuträglich seyn. Ich weiß was ich in dieser Rücksicht meinem Aufenthalt in Frankreich zu dancken habe – In Gesellschaft meines Bruders Fritz gedencke ich dann im Winter desselben Weges wieder auf hier zu kommen, um im FrühJahr von a[nno] 96 mit ihm mich nach Nord Amerika einzuschiffen. Sie müssen nemlich wissen, daß unser Fritz, den ich nur aus einer sparsamen correspondenz kenne, auch einer von den Verrufenen zu seyn scheint, die unmöglich genießen können während, daß tausende ihrer Brüder um ihnen herum in Elend schmachten. Er hat oeconomie studirt, und wird oft sein Vermögen in Land anlegen. Er denckt daher auf alle Art für sein Interesse zu sorgen, wenn er dieses in Nord Amerika thut, wo Elend selten und Land häufig seyn soll. Ich gehe mit um vor's erste zu observiren; gefällt es ihm, so macht er sich daselbst ansäßig: ich kehre gegen Winter heim, arbeite dann noch etliche Jahre, und wähle nächstdem meinen Aufenthalt zwischen der Schweitz und Nord Amerika – Nach meinem Vaterlande gedencke ich nur besuchend zurückzukehren. Deutschlands rauher Himmel und bunte Verfassung ist mir zuwider. So sehr wie ich die teutschen Männer schätze, welche in diesen bedrängten Zeiten sich zu Märtyrern der Vernunft und des allgemeinen Wohls aufwerfen, so sehr muß die Zahl der Unwürdigen meinen Unwillen reitzen, welche – doch Sie kennen solche besser wie ich. Tröstlich ist es, daß sie gegen ihren Willen zum allgemeinen Besten beitragen, indem sie die schlummernden Kräfte ihrer Gegner wecken, und die Unerschütterlichkeit der Sache der Vernunft wie ihre vergeblichen Angriffe beweisen. Sie werden mich dennoch nicht tadeln, wenn ich mich von einem Schauplatz entferne, wo die Ungewißheit der nöthigen Reife mich hindern würde meine Rolle zu spielen, und wo ich dann als Zuschauer sogar den gezierten Drathpuppen Beyfall zuklatschen müßte, deren niedrige Triebfedern meinen geöffneten Augen nicht verborgen bleiben könnten – dieses kann man wohl in Ländern ansehen, wo der Mangel an irgend eine Gährung, den Beweiß der völligen Thierheit und Nichtswürdigkeit des Ganzen führt, aber nicht in einem Lande wo der edlere Theil ohnmächtig seufzt und ohne sichtbaren Nutzen seine Kräfte verschwendet. Kommt der Zeitpunkt des Hervortretens, der Aufopferung von Gut und Leben mit wahrscheinlichen Nutzen für das Allgemeine sind Meere keine Scheidewände.

Wenn ich dann wieder hier bin, so wird mein Bruder Gottl[ie]b auch reisen, und unsern Sommer Pallast in der Schweitz besuchen – Alles dieses bitte ich indessen nicht aus Ihrem Circel kommen zu lassen, da es biß jetzt nur Projekte sind die sehr leicht durchkreuzt und vernichtet werden können. Da ich indessen gerne Ihre Meinung hierüber vernähme, ehe es zur Ausführung kommt, so bitte ich sobald möglich darauf zu antworten, und den Brief an d[en] H[er]rn Johan Hinrich Ludendorff[6] in Hamburg einzusenden damit dieser Freund mir denselben sogleich per Post zusende. Hoffentlich werde ich auf solche Art im nächsten Januar Monath Ihre Antwort erhalten.

An eben diesen Freund geben wir heute auch ordre Ihnen 1000 Thaler – sage tausend für unsere Rechnung einzuschicken, worüber Sie auf die bewußte Art disponiren werden, und an ihm Ihr Recief darüber zu geben bitten – doch muß er nichts von dem Endzwecke davon wissen – Ihre jährliche Büchersendung fahren Sie gütigst fort an den H[er]rn Franz Jacob Schuback[7] in Hamburg auf dem auch der Belauf anzuweisen ist –

Verdrießlich ist es wirklich, daß wir schon lange nichts von Ihnen gehört haben, nichts von unserer guten Pflege Mutter, nichts von unserer lieben Lotte nichts von unsern braven Trapp und Stuve! – Daß Sie dieses nur sogleich beantworten, und auch so etwas in das künftige hinein, um zu sehen ob wir nicht einen Vereinigungspunkt in der physischen Welt finden. Unsere Geister haben Sie sich Ihnen selbst nachgebildet, und so schließen sie sich an den Ihrigen in allem was deren Fassungskraft angemessen ist. Ueber die Körper haben Sie schon nicht so viel Gewalt; wir müssen also in dieser Rücksicht den Ausschlag der Umstände leider abwarten.

Mit bekannter kindlicher Liebe und Danckbarkeit bin ich beständig
Ihr aufrichtiger Johan Nicolas Bohl
und ich Ihr eben so aufrichtiger
Anton G Bohl

P. S. Wir besitzen hier jetzo einen wahren Philantrop einen böhmischen Grafen Berchtold:[8] sein Umgang gewährt uns viel Vergnügen: er hat wenig Bedürfnisse, sein Zweck ist der Wahrheit durch Verbreitung fruchtbarer wissentschaftlicher Entdeckungen zu nützen: zu dem Ende will er den Orient bereisen –

11. Joachim Heinrich and Dorothea Campe, Braunschweig

Cadiz den 3 Februar 1795

Endlich ist uns gestern per Post Ihr erstes Schreiben seit zwei Jahren vom 9/16 December richtig geworden, und hat uns wie gewöhnlich viele Freude verursacht – Alle Ihre übrigen Briefe haben wir nicht erhalten. H[er]r J[ohann] V[alentin] Meyer hat die ihm addressirten einem Schiffer mitgegeben welcher in Norwegen in Havarie liegt und vielleicht noch lange liegen kann – Viele Herrn Hamburger glauben, daß weil ihnen selbst nichts am Herzen liegt als das Geld, andere nothwendig eben so fühlen müssen, und daß ein Brief der weder Factura noch Connaiß[emen]t enthält, unmöglich das Porto werth seyn kann.

Ich eile sogleich die wichtigsten Punkten Ihres lieben Schreibens zu beantworten – Ausführlicher soll es nächstens per Schiff geschehen. Es freuet mich sehr, daß Sie meine Pläne für die Zukunft billigen, aber noch unendlich mehr, daß Sie sich vielleicht entschließen werden, mich auf die projectirten Reisen zu begleiten. Der Kosten Aufwand soll und kann kein Hinderniß daran seyn. Von Ihrer Freundschaft und Ihrer Kentniß meiner Denckungsart kann ich mit Zuversicht erwarten, daß Sie mir die Unkosten dieser mir so nützlichen und angenehmen Reise, allein werden tragen lassen, die überdem durch einen Reisegefährten wenig vermehrt werden können – Unsere Vermögens-Umstände werden, Dank sey es der Vorsehung, täglich blühender, und erlauben nicht nur diese sondern weit ansehnlichere Ausgaben.

Für nächstes FrühJahr hat sich meine Reise nach der Schweitz vereitelt: mit Ende dieses Jahres aber werde ich gänzlich frei werden, und mich den Geschäften auf beliebige Zeit entziehen können. Ich habe dieses hauptsächlich meinem Bruder zu verdancken der durch seine Einsicht und Fleiß, meine Anwesenheit hier unnöthig macht. Ich dencke mich also im Anfang 1796 aufzumachen, und zu Schiffe nach Genua zu gehen um von da nach der Schweitz zu reisen. Das Stell dich ein wäre dann in Lindau oder wo Sie sonsten wollten im Monath May oder Juny und dann soll es lediglich von unsern weitern Berathschlagungen abhangen, wann und auf wie lange Zeit wir nach America würden gehen wollen – Bruder Fritz ersuche ich dabey, zu Rath zu ziehen, und ihm womöglich zu beide Reisen zu bewegen. Einlage zur Beförderung an ihn.

Wir dancken für die nochmalige BücherAbsendung, hätten aber gerne eine kleine nota von Inhalt und Kosten dabey erhalten, um uns bey den Empfang darnach zu richten. – Das Absterben des guten Stuve haben wir mit Leidwesen vernommen

Es wäre vielleicht zu bewundern, wenn bey mir, der ich mir seit meinem Jünglings Alter mit einem lebhaften Temperament und einem liebenden Herzen beständig selbst überlassen gewesen bin eine reife Vernunft meine Neigungen immer genug beherrscht hätte, um frühzeitige Verbindungen mit dem andern Geschlecht zu verhindern – die ersten Äußerungen des gereitzten Natur-triebes pflegen gewöhnlich bloß sinnlich zu seyn. Schlimme physische Folgen, Uebersättigung oder mehrere Ueberlegung führen den wohlorganisirten Jüngling bald wieder zurück. Er sucht alsdann Befriedigung für das Herz zugleich, oder zu dem bloß thierischen Trieb gesellt sich das Gefühl des Anständigen und des Schönen, alias der gute Geschmack, welchen der Verf[asser] der Lebensl[äufe] in aufst[ehender] Linie irgendwo sehr wohl die Blüthe der Tugend nennt – die Periode wo die Vernunft das Uebergewicht über diese geläuterte Sinnlichkeit erhält, denn wo nur auf moralische Vollkommenheit die Haupt Rücksicht genommen wird, pflegt bey solchen Leuten, nur spät einzutreffen, und gewöhnlich zu spät – Unter dem Siegel der Verschwiegenheit vertraue ich Ihnen hiemit an, daß dieses auch bey mir der Fall ist, und daß ich mich in einer Lage befinde, worin es mir nicht mehr frei steht, eine künftige Gefährtin des Lebens zu wählen.

Sehr angenehm ist es uns, daß Sie die Früchte unseres Nachdenckens mit den Ihrigen übereinstimmend gefunden haben – Jetzt hat besonders mein Forschungstrieb einen neuen Sporn durch das uns gesandte Reine System der Religion von Riem erhalten;[1] ich bemühe mich jetzt, das viele mir darin auffallend neue, dem ich meine Zustimmung nicht versagen kann, mit den Resultaten meines bißherigen

Nachdenckens zu vereinigen – Sagen Sie uns doch, ob Sie diesem System Ihren Beyfall geben? – die übrigen gewiß sehr interessanten Wercke desselben Verfassers, worauf er sich in dem erwähnten Buche bezieht, habe ich mir schon von Hamburg verschrieben.

In Hoffnung einer baldigen Antwort, durch H[errn] Ludendorff, schließe ich für jetzt mit der Versicherung meiner aufrichtigsten Hochachtung und wahrsten Liebe
    Johan Nic. Bohl

Ihren herzlichen Brief, beste Pflege Mutter, kann ich leider für heute nur summarisch beantworten – die geretteten Bücher hatte der Schiffskapitän von Franckreich wieder nach Hamburg zurückgebracht, empfingen wir sie durch ein anderes Schiff. – Eine makellose Konstitution wird wohl das 18 Jahrhundert nicht hervorbringen: es kommt darauf an wo am wenigsten Mängel sind, und in Folge dessen die meisten zufriedenen Menschen leben – Ich hoffe und wünsche, daß wir uns a[nn]o 1796 in der Schweitz sehen werden – Nach America müssen Sie dann auch Vater und uns ziehen lassen – Eins kann gegen das andre aufgehen – Keine Regel ohne Ausnahme, also auch unter der Menge, Personen wie Sie und Lotte – Ueber die größte Anzahl habe ich nur geurtheilt: Die Ausnahmen haben meine herzliche Ehrfurcht und Liebe – Gedrukte Apologien der Weiber würde ich nicht ohne Zwang lesen. Was hilft schwarz auf weiß, wenn die Erfahrung jeden Augenblick wiederspricht – Der Umgang mit Ihnen und Ihres Gleichen wird ungleich mehr fruchten – die Rechte der Weiber in der bürgerlichen Gesellschaft wollen mich noch weniger behagen. Rousseau hat mir vielleicht den rechten Gesichtspunkt verrückt – Ihre kaufmännische Speculation ist gar nicht schlecht: Gottlieb, als der besser in dem Leinen Fach bewanderte, wird Ihnen weitläuftig nächstens darüber schreiben. Für jetzt will ich also nur anführen, daß Sie Ihr Augenmerck hauptsächlich darauf richten müssen, hier bekannte Leinen Sorten nachzuahmen – Wie z. B. die Westphälischen Flechsen oder Crezuelas, d[it]o Stiegleinen oder Casserillos, und d[it]o Bleichtücher oder Cañamaros. Sodann wären solche hier in großen und kleinen Partheien gewiß vortheilhaft abzusetzen – H[er]r Trapp's und seiner Frau Erinnerung ist uns sehr angenehm: wir bitten ihm zu sagen, daß auch er, als ein redlicher Verfechter des freien Gebrauchs unserer Vernunft, öfters der Gegenstand unserer Verehrung Dankbarkeit und Liebe ist – für das abgeschriebene Gebeth dancken wir unsrer lieben Lotte von Herzen; wir stimmen gerne mit ein, und wünschen nur, daß es in Chor mit alle dortige Freunde seyn könnte – Die Chocolade soll nächstens erfolgen – Gottl[ieb] will noch etwas schreiben, also Lebewohl

12. Joachim Heinrich Campe, Braunschweig

Morges den 21 Jan. 1797

Ihr lieber Brief vom 2 dieses ist mir erst gestern geworden, und hat also auf denselben Weg 18 Tage zugebracht, den ihr voriges Schreiben in 13 zurücklegte. Ich beziehe mich in Beantwortung desselben zuförderst an mein Letztes vom 18,[1] welches hoffentlich glücklich in Ihre Hände gerathen ist. Ich bestätigte darin meinen vorigen Auftrag zum Ankauf des bewußten Gartenwesens, und zeigte Ihnen die glückliche Entbindung meiner Frau an – Leider nun sagt mir Ihr letzter Brief, daß mein Auftrag zu spät gekommen ist, ich lebe jedoch noch der Hoffnung, daß es Ihnen glücken wird, für etliche 100 Thaler mehr, das kleine Wesen für mich zu erstehen, die ich als sehr wohl angewandt ansehen würde.

Ich kann Ihnen unmöglich beschreiben, wie viel Vergnügen mir Ihre Briefe machen, wie angenehm es mir ist auf dem Wege den ich so lange Zeit allein oder doch mit Schwächern gekrüppelt habe, endlich einmahl Vorgänger in der That anzutreffen, die meine Schritte durch ihr Beispiel sichern – Was die Ausbildung meiner Frau anlangt, glaube ich verschiedenes zu der Rechtfertigung meiner Behutsamkeit anführen zu können. Es scheint mir edlen Seelen natürlich zu seyn, daß wenn sich ihnen plötzlich die Augen über alle Folgen der künstlichen menschlichen Anstalten eröffnen, sie sich als dann eifrig in die Arme einer gewissen eingebildeten Rousseauschen Natur werfen, wo ihnen das Selbstbewußt- seyn eines guten Herzens und eine daraus entspringende Offenheit und Gradheit die einzige Regel des Betragens wird. Ich habe diese Periode in dem Gemüthe meiner Frau schon lange vor unserer Heirath selbst herbeygeführt, allein sie hat diese Natur mit solcher Heftigkeit ergriffen ihre gründlich reine Seele hat sich diese Natur so untadelhaft gebildet, daß es mir noch nicht völlig geglückt ist ihr das Joch der Vernunft aufzulegen, die mehr oder weniger immer über Neigung gebieten muß. Sie hatte es sich zur Regel gemacht, <u>alle</u> ihre Gedanken laut zu sagen, in allen ihren Handlungen dem gutmüthigen Triebe zu folgen. Daraus entsprang natürlicherweise daß sie von den Schlechten angefeindet und selbst von den Bessern für eine Närrin gehalten wurde. Es glückte mir jedoch bald ihr gegen Fremde Zurückhaltung aufzulegen, aber es blieben die Haußgenoßen es blieb besonders ihre Mutter eine Frau die wie so manche mit den besten Eigenschaften höchst kleinliche Schwächen verbindet. Sie wollte die strenge Wahrheit oder ihr unmaßgebliches Dafürhalten gegen ihre Mutter geltend machen: sie deckte in den kleinen Alterkationen die Schwächen der Mutter unbarmherzig auf und warf sie ihr vor, und erreichte dadurch Zwist schrekliche Ausbrüche von Zorn und Skandal. Die Erfahrung hat sie nach und nach klüger gemacht: doch aber bleibt noch ein Hang zu dieser falschen Freimüthigkeit, den ich nothwendig vertilgen muß, ehe ich weiter gehen kann. Ich kann ihr nie meine Denkungsart anders als indirekt eröffnen, biß ich überzeugt bin, daß sie sich gegen ihre Mutter über alle höhere Erkentniß Stillschweigen auferlegen kann, den diese gute Mutter ist eine eifrige Katholikin, die alles dem Seelenheil hintenansetzt, der ich versprochen habe ihre Tochter bey ihrem Glauben zu lassen, und die vor Zeiten schon genug Thränen über die leichtfertigen Außerungen dieser Tochter in Glaubens Sachen vergossen hat. Jetzt hoffe ich werden Sie meiner Behutsamkeit beistimmen. Wie gerne lasse ich nicht meine andern Gründe fallen! Mit welchem Entzücken werde ich nicht Weiberseelen wie die Ihrige, liebe Mutter und Lotten's in der Nähe betrachten, und um wieviel wird nicht noch mein Glück erhöht werden, wenn ich Ihnen dereinst den Geist meiner Frau zugesellen kann!

Ich hatte Ihnen schon lange mit Fleiß meine Lieblings Bücher angezeigt, um Ihre Meinung darüber zu vernehmen: ob sie nun wohl meiner Neigung nicht entspricht, so ist sie mir doch nicht unangenehm gewesen, denn ich hoffe bey einer nähern Verhandlung noch manches zu retten und die jugendliche Ueppigkeit der Fantasie mit der nüchternen Vernunft des Mannes zu vereinen. Es giebt ja viele Sachen besonders in Rücksicht eines künftigen Zustandes, worüber wir nichts <u>wissen</u> können, und warum dann nicht ahnden und träumen? Wir tragen ein Herz im Busen daß im Schooße der Liebe immer noch mehr will, nie befriedigt ist, warum nicht das Reich der Möglichkeit mit Gegenständen dieser überströmenden Liebe bevölkern? – Ich weiß wie viel hierauf zu antworten ist, ich antworte es andern selbst. Meine Vernunft ist überzeugt, aber mein Gefühl widerspricht ihr. Ich denke die Rolle mit Ihnen zu spielen die meine Frau gegen mich spielt, gebe Gott mit gleich gutem Erfolge: der Bekehrung zur Vernunft.

Es käme vielleicht nur darauf an, daß diese Träumereyen unserer irdischen Thätigkeit keine Schranken setzten, und uns nie den Genuß der Gegenwart verleideten. Das erste mag ich was mich anlangt nicht verbürgen, wohl aber das zweite, den Gott sey Dank ich genieße täglich mit zufriedenem Herzen alte Wohlthaten, die die Vorsehung auf mich häuft. Die vielleicht unvermeidlichen kleinen Perioden von Mißmuth entspringen bei mir mehr aus Furcht von dergleichen bey meinen Haußgenoßen als aus eigner Leere, dennoch würde eine bestimte Richtung der Thätigkeit auch diese Wolken, glaube ich, verjagen.

Ich hoffe daß die Bücher glücklich ankommen werden: der erste große Brief ist indessen immer noch zurück. Sie sagen mir nicht an welche Adresse die Bücher abgesandt sind? Es ist traurig daß G[oethe] und S[chiller] so ausschweifen.[2] Von Schiller besonders hatte ich eine große Idee gefaßt, seitdem ich seine Aufsätze in den Horen gelesen habe.[3] Was halten Sie besonders von seinen Briefen über die ästhetische Erziehung? Ist überhaupt diese Zeitschrift so interessant, wie sie mir scheint? Ich finde so viel Neues und Anziehendes für mich darin, daß ich gewissermaßen damit geitze, und noch lange nicht den ersten Jahrgang erschöpft habe: manches auch kostet mir Anstrengung um es zu fassen, und leider fasse ich es nur in dem Augenblicke wo ich es lese; es haftet nicht in meinem Gedächtniß wenigstens nicht nach erstem und zweitem Lesen. Besonders angenehm ist mir endlich, daß ich fast nichts darin finde, was sich nicht mit meinem jetzigen Gedanken System kombiniren läßt und vieles was Gefühle in Gedanken umwandelt.

Wie gerne überlasse ich mich dem Gedanken unseres Zusammenlebens in Braunschweig! Nur die anfänglichen Unannehmlichkeiten die meine Frau und meine Stief Mutter der Sprache, des Klima's und der Gebräuche halber werden ausgesetzt seyn, und die ich besser wie sie selbst vorhersehe trüben diese heitere Aussicht. Da indessen jetzt in Deutschland so viele Personen Französisch reden, da Ihr Klima, glaube ich doch wenigstens besser wie das Hamburgische ist, indem es bey Ihnen weniger regnet und weniger donnert (In Kadix haben wir nur ein paar mahl im Laufe des Jahres schwache Gewitter) da wir endlich entschloßen sind nur wenige erlesene Freunde zu sehen und auch nur diese wenigen zu unserer Zufriedenheit nöthig haben (denn schon lange leben wir, Höflichkeits Besuche abgerechnet, nur unter uns) so hoffe ich wird alles wohlgehen und der eigne Heerd besonders den ersten Grund zur Anhänglichkeit legen – Gottlieb muß uns am Ende auch werden und unser Herzensfreund Meyer. Mein erster vorzüglichster Genuß soll seyn, Sie von diesen beyden zu unterhalten. Sie sollen Freuden Thränen mit mir weinen über diese Menschen, die aussöhnen mit der Menschen Natur, um die allein es werth wäre zu leben. Sie sollen mitleben in unserer heiligen Freundschaft, über alles irdische Interesse erhaben, die mir das wahre Beste der andern bezweckt. Gottlieb ist mit Geschäften überhäuft: er schreibt mir auch nur selten, ich den beyden desto öfterer, denn ich bin ihnen die Beweise meiner Glückseeligkeit schuldig. Ich werde jedoch nicht allein Ihren Auftrag bestellen, sondern den größten Theil Ihres Briefes in Abschrift nach Kadix senden, so wie ich mit den vorherigen gethan habe. Haben Sie Gottliebs vortrefflich gemahltes und sehr ähnliches Bildnis erhalten? Zu der selben Zeit war ich mit der Vollziehung meiner Heirath beschäftigt: ich fand also nur Zeit zu einem Gemälde von mir, welches meiner Frau geworden ist.

Fritz ist jetzt in Paris und denkt auf das Früh Jahr auch nach Deutschland zurückzukehren. Ein mehr verschloßener Charakter ist mir nie vorgekommen. Eine auf das höchste getriebene Neigung zur Unabhängigkeit scheint den Grund desselben aus zumachen: zu Äußerung von Grundsätzen habe ich ihn nie bringen können. Ich freue mich indessen hinzufügen zu können, daß er mir verschiedentlich Erbietungen gemacht hat, die eben so viel Freundschaft beweisen, als sie eigne Aufopferungen gekostet hätten. Und was er anbot, würde er gethan haben – Er denkt ein Gut im Meklenburgischen, findet er es preiß würdig, zu kaufen; ich glaube der Fleck wäre ihm so ziemlich gleich, wenn er nur sein Geld vortheilhaft anlegen könnte – Es ist doch sonderbar, wie dieselbe Erziehung, so verschieden ausgeschlagen ist. Ich hoffe noch immer es wird allen Ihren ehemaligen Zöglingen so wie mir gehen. Der Saame des Guten lag etliche Zeit verborgen, ehe er keimte. Endlich ward der Buchstabe lebendig, oder das Wissen ging in

Schauen über, wie eigentlich und wodurch weiß ich selbst nicht recht. Bey meinem letzten Besuch a[nn]o 88 hatte ich noch keinen Sinn für was <u>Gut</u> ist und <u>Schön</u>.

Sie wissen nun schon daß Sie getroffen haben, und daß es eine kleine Cecilia gibt, von der sich der kleine Bräutigam Eduard[4] noch nichts träumen läßt. Biß jetzt befinden sich Amme und Kind vortreflich, und alles scheint sich zu einer gesunden Erziehung einzuleiten, den selbst die Groß Mutter hat gute Grundsätze der physischen Behandlung: demnach wird die Kleine in laues Wasser getaucht, hat nichts gebundenes, eingezwängtes, und schläft ohne Wiege.

Schließlich für heute einen Dank wegen des zu leistenden Vorschußes, der mir den Ankauf in meiner jetzigen Laage allein möglich macht, denn ich rechne noch immer darauf. Es sollen hoffentlich keine 6 Monathe vergehen, ohne dieses Geschäft abgemacht zu finden.

Ihr Pflege Sohn

Johan Nicolas Bohl

Was macht Ihr braver Freund Trapp? Welches Buch ist L[udwig] Wagehals[5] wovon eine Anzeige sagte daß wenn alle Bibliotheken vernichtet würden, dieses Buch sie ersetzen wird!

13. Joachim Heinrich and Dorothea Campe, Braunschweig

Morges, den 28 Märtz [17]97

Ihre lieben Briefe vom 12 und 13 dieses habe ich, Werthe PflegeEltern, mit derselben Freude durchgelesen, die ich immer bey Ansicht Ihrer Handschrift empfinde. Ehe ich indessen zu der Uebernahme Ihres Gartens völlig beystimmen kann, muß ich erst von Ihnen vernehmen, ob nicht eine übertriebene Delikateße Sie zu einer Aufopferung verleitet, die natürlicher auf <u>mich</u>, als den Anstifter, fallen müßte: Konvenirt Ihnen aber das größere Wesen wegen Ihrer Kentniß der Landwirthschaft, übernehmen Sie es nicht bloß um mir das Ihrige überlassen zu können, alsdann, gestehe ich gerne, daß ich das Kleinere vorziehe, und Ihnen im voraus für die Ausmittelung desselben recht vielen Dank weiß – Ich sehe vollkommen ein, daß der Genuß Ihres Gartens uns als Freunde und Nachbaren in gleichem Maaße mit Ihnen zu Theil werden wird – Ob mir aber mein Gewissen erlauben wird den Garten zu 4 Thaler zu übernehmen, während jemand anders 5 Thaler bietet, bleibt noch unter uns auszumachen. Gegen Johanni können Sie sicher auf die 4 Thaler rechnen. Wir fangen schon an uns zur Reise zu rüsten, und wenn mein calcul nicht sehr trügt, so müssen wir vor dem 15 May dort eintreffen. Anfang Juny gehe ich dann allein nach Hamburg und verschaffe mir das nöthige Geld.

Gerne werde ich die Bücher zum Behuf der Reise etc empfangen; ich hoffe daß sie nicht zu lange unterwegens bleiben werden. Die Bedienten machen uns schon

Klage genug; desto weniger desto besser. Jetzt sind wir darüber daraus eine Wartfrau für unsere kleine Tochter zu finden, aber keine will reisen, oder auch sie sind zu jung zu neu, zum Fall gekommen etc. Es macht uns wahrlich verlegen!

An Bruder Gottlieb werde ich wieder den Inhalt Ihres Briefes mittheilen; von dem Lauf der Geschäfte in Cadiz hängt es ab, inwiefern wir uns in Rücksicht von Gaben ausdehnen können; von dorten also muß die Entscheidung kommen. Unterdessen lassen Sie keine Gelegenheit von dringenden Noths Erlösung ungegriffen; ich stehe auf alle Fälle vor dem Riß. Ueberdem halte ich es nur für ein Vergessen, daß Gottlieb nicht wenigstens etwas zu dem bewußten Zwecke remittirt hat.

Das Obst Ihres Gartens will ich mir denn, wills Gott, brav schmecken lassen, und der Gedanke, daß Sie die Bäume gepflegt haben, soll mir den Genuß noch vergrößern – Wenn das Haus mir nicht etwas zu klein ist! Vier Zimmer ist nun das höchstnothwendige für uns, eines für meine Schwieger Mutter, eines für meine Frau und ein daranstoßendes für Kind und Wärterin, und ein viertes für mich. Bequem ist es, eine Eßstube noch obendrein zu haben, um den Saal nicht zu verunreinigen und von der einen zu dem andern überzugehen. Bequem auch ein Paar Stuben für besuchende Freunde.

Meine Frau ist Spanierin, ist aber halb in England erzogen worden, ihre Mutter ist Irländerin von Geburt, kam aber sehr jung nach Cadiz, verheirathete sich mit einem spanischen Kaufman, der aber zurückkam, und (ohne jedoch irgend jemand schuldig zu bleiben) arm und als Mäkler starb. Wir haben uns 6 Jahre vor unserer Heirath gekannt und ich kann mich also ihren zweiten Erzieher heißen. Unsere Liebes Geschichte ist lang und nur für uns interessant. Ich habe sie aufgesetzt und etliche hundert Briefe dienen ihr zu Belege; vielleicht, liebe Pflege Mutter, interessiren wir Sie mit der Zeit genug, um Ihnen deren Mittheilung wünschenswerth zu machen – Die Korrespondenz rührt daher, weil die Damen einen großen Theil des Jahres auf dem Lande, zubrachten, wo ich sie nur alle acht oder vierzehn Tage besuchen konnte. Mutter und Tochter sind in den Gesichtszügen von der Natur vernachläßiget worden; von Körper aber wohlgebildet, wenngleich nicht groß. Die Mutter hat sich beständig durch eine besondere Ordnung und Reinlichkeit ausgezeichnet, wodurch [es] die Häßlichen die Schönen oft ausstechen; sie besitzt überdem die meisten Eigenschaften einer guten Hausmutter, die nur durch die Ausbrüche einer leicht zu reizenden Eigenliebe manchmal verdunkelt werden. Doch auch letztere werden immer seltener durch die wachsende Behutsamkeit meiner Frau, und durch die Existenz der kleinen Enkelin. Ihre Gemüths Stimmung ist so ziemlich der Vernunft untergeordnet; sie hat viel gelitten, sie hat in Spanien vierzigjährige Freunde hinterlassen, ihre Söhne haben ihr bißjetzt wenig Freude gemacht und dennoch läßt sie uns fast niemals schwermüthige Klagen hören – Sie hat lange Jahre gegen Armuth gekämpft, einen kränkelnden Mann ernähren und für die Erziehung ihrer Kinder sorgen müssen. Sie hat eine ältere sehr liebenswürdige Tochter die mit einem Kaufman in Lyon verheirathet war an den Folgen des ersten Kindbettes verlohren, ihr ältester Sohn ist nach Amerika gegangen und läßt wenig oder nichts von sich hören. (Der jüngere 14 oder 15 Jahr alt befindet sich jetzt in England.) Sie sah ein, daß sie nur bey der übrigbleibenden noch Tochter Glück finden könnte, und wirklich genießt sie und gestehet ihren Genuß, besonders seit der Geburt Cecilens – Meine Frau ist sehr brunette, hat dunkle und viele Haare, artige Augen, schöne Augenbrauen, eine große und häßliche Nase, einen großen Mund aber rothe Lippen und gesunde Zähne. Die Farbe wird etwas nachgeholfen: übrigens seit ihrer Entbindung etwas unbehilflich an taille und Unterleib, und, dem Saugen ohngeachtet, bey zunehmenden Fleisch – Sie hat Anlagen zu allen vortrefflichen Eigenschaften. Doch wird die Ausbildung bey einzelnen schwer durch die Macht etlicher eingewurzelten romantischen Ideen. Sie hat Verstand genug um mich zu verstehen und um meine Ueberlegenheit einzusehen; kurz es fehlt ihr nur an Willen, an beständiger Vernunft Unterwerfung des betrügerischen Gefühls, um dem Ideal einer Frau für mich zu entsprechen. Ihre Gemüthsstimmung unter uns ist beständig heiter, wenn sie sich nicht durch spitzfindige Zweifel an meiner Liebe beunruhiget fühlt. In Gesellschaft und mit Unbekannten ist sie dagegen still und ernsthaft – Nach dieser Schilderung werden Sie theure PflegeEltern, mit mir den Schluß ziehen, daß der Mutter mit Achtung und der Tochter mit Liebe gedient ist. Ein freundschaftliches Zutrauen welches Sie, beste Pflege Mutter, gewiß in Ihrem Herzen für <u>meine</u> Frau finden werden, wird Ihnen ihr Herz sogleich erobern, und hoffentlich werden Sie es mit der Zeit des Ihrigen würdig erkennen. – Eine schwere Klugheits Regel wird es mich hier noch seyn <u>Ihnen</u> nicht zu viel Achtung und Liebe zu beweisen, um keine Eifersucht rege zu machen.

Von Herzen genehmige ich alle Ihre Vorkehrungen, liebe PflegeMutter und schmeichle mir, daß die Damen auch unsern Geschmack haben werden; es giebt der Grillen in diesem Stück viele und nur sehr helle Köpfe meine ich komen darin überein, daß auch der gute Geschmack seine allgemein gültigen Regeln habe. Ich denke mit Ihnen daß es gerathen seyn wird uns anfänglich durch einen Koch speisen zu lassen; er kann anfänglich uns gut aufschüsseln, nachher werden wir wählen. Auf die zwei kleinern Gärten spekulire ich schon im Geiste – Ich theile Ihre Freude über eine beständige Wohnung. Das Umziehen scheint auch mir höchstbeschwerlich. Ich vernehme mit vieler Freude indirekt, daß Sie auch auf unsere liebe Lotte diesen Sommer rechnen. Die Komißionen an Gottlieb richte ich aus. Vaters kleine höchst ähnliche Büste in Biskuit erhielten wir noch vor meiner Abreise. – Ja wohl! erinnere ich mich der Kopenhagener Reise und auch der noch lustigeren nach Lübeck und Travemünde. Claudius[1] mischt sich sehr in diesen Erinnerungen und es wird mir ganz wehmüthig, wenn ich lese wie sehr er sich verändert hat. Die kleine M[adame] Stuve war mir ganz entfallen. Wieder ein

Genuß und nützliche Vorübung für uns! – Zu meiner Schande bekenne ich, daß ich in Constanz und nicht in Lindau gewesen bin; aber ein verheiratheter Mann taugt nicht mehr zum Reisen: ich habe wenig Genuß auf meiner Schweizertour gehabt, weil die Erinnerung an die Verlassenheit meiner Frau und Schwieger Mutter mir alles verleidete. Sobald unsere vor acht Tagen mekulirte Cecile genesen ist, werde ich jedoch honneur noch einen Abstecher von 10 Tagen nach Luzern und die neuere Schweitz machen, um sagen zu können, daß ich da gewesen bin – Völlig zufrieden bin ich nur zu Hause –

Ihr aufrichtig ergebener
J. N. Bohl

14. Joachim Heinrich and Dorothea Campe, Braunschweig

Chiclana den 8 Febr [17]98

Ich habe seit kurzen vernommen, daß ein langer Brief den ich Ihnen, liebe PflegeEltern unter dem 3 Dec[em]b[e]r per Cap[itain] Hendrick adressirte, vermuthlich wohl für Ihnen verloren ist weil dieser obgleich neutrale Schiffer, von dem schurken Volk von Korsarer in Vigo aufgebracht ist, wo er wohl vor's erste liegen bleiben wird – Ich will also kurz dessen Inhalt wiederholen – die letzte Zeit in Hamburg war die unruhigste und geräuschvollste Periode meines Lebens: zu den Gastmählern gesellte sich die Anschaffung eines völligen Hausraths, für unser separates Hauswesen hier. Nur in Hamburg habe ich die Skizze meiner Gedanken über die mir vorkommenden Gegenstände unterbrochen, und diese Lücke bleibt in mein Reise Journal welches ich mit der Abreise von Hamburg wieder anfing. Ich gab meinem Bruder den Auftrag Ihnen meine Abreise zu verkündigen – Von Hamburg nach Brüssel waren wir 10 Tage unterwegens, und befanden uns in dem verschrieenen Westphalen ganz wohl. Wege, Pferde, Schwager und Bedienung fielen sehr über unsere Erwartung aus. Brüssel fanden wir öde und verlassen. Von Brüssel nach Paris brauchten wir nur 3 Tage. In Paris haben wir uns wohl amüsirt. Die öffentlichen Sitzungen der Volksdeputirten hatten wenig Interesse für mich, theils wegen der Geringfügigkeit der Verhandlungen an sich, theils wegen die unschickliche Verhandlungsart. Desto besser gefielen mir die Schauspiele – das große Fest der Republik am 22 Sept[em]b[e]r war ernst und stille; die Menge zeigte keinen Funken von Enthusiasmus mehr – Von Paris nach Bordeaux waren wir 9 Tage unterwegens; meistens Spatzierfahrt bey schönem Wetter und sehr guten Wegen; alle französischen Städte (außer Paris) fanden wir öde, aber das Land allenthalben zu bebaut und in den Dörfern öfters neue maßive Häuser. Die fatale Strecke Landes von Bordeaux nach Bayonne nahm uns 4 Tage weg – Außer den eigentlichen Vorstehern der gegenwärtigen Ordnung fanden wir keine Zufriedene, aber die Wohnung, Kleidung und Nahrung besonders der niedern Stände stand mit ihren Klagen in Widerspruch – des Menschen Herz ist unersättlich: nur der Nachdenkende weiß sich an der Gegenwart zu halten, dachte ich und wunderte mich nicht. Die Reise durch Spanien war höchstbeschwerlich; nur das schöne Wetter ersetzte uns in etwas die schmutzigen scheußlichen Nachtquartiere, die wir 26 mahl beziehen mussten. Nach so vielen Mühseligkeiten war die Ankunft recht labend. Gottlieb und Therese waren erst seit kurzem angekommen. Wir gingen hier bey einem guten Freund wohnen, und haben erst seit Kurzen ein selbst gemiethetes Haus bezogen. Da meine persönliche Anwesenheit auf dem Comptoir bey dem gänzlichen Mangel an Geschäften völlig entbehrlich ist, so sind wir fast immer in diesem Dorfe 5 Meilen von der Stadt entfernt und legen nur kurze Besuche bey Gottlieb und seiner Frau ab. Wir haben auch noch kein Haus in der Stadt gemiethet, weil sie der betrübten Umständen ohngeachtet sehr schwer in der Nähe des Comptoirs zu finden sind, und weil unser Hausrath, von den Engländern weggewiesen in Malaga liegt –

Sie wünschen nun gewiß zu vernehmen, ob mich diese Rück Reise nicht gereut, und ich muß aufrichtig gestehen, daß ich nicht glaube etwas Klügeres je gethan zu haben. Die Erfahrung lehrt manches neue, und so auch, daß ich eine gewiße Unabhängigkeit von so manchen weiblichen Bedürfnißen, die mir zu ferneren Ausbildung meines Geistes, zur Anspannung meiner Kräfte und zum stillen innern Glück überhaupt, doch so unumgänglich nöthig ist, daß ich diese Unabhängigkeit nur in einem Lande erreichen konnte, wo die Sorge für dergleichen Bedürfniße sich selbst überlassen bleiben kann. In der Schweitz trug die bekante Sprache viel dazu bey meine Vorsorge zu vermindern; die Umstände banden uns an Ort und Stelle; eine andere und eben dadurch schönere Zukunft stand bevor, und auch ich stand allein wie sie. In Deutschland war mir jedes deutsche Wort eine Wunde; wir waren frei zum wählen; die endliche Wahl sollte jede andere Zukunft ausschließen, und ich war von Freunden umgeben, die mich aus dem Hause zogen, während sie in gänzlicher Abgeschiedenheit schmachteten! – Doch dieses alles nur meine Gefühle; auf Ehre kein Wort von ihnen. Ich war in Braunschweig und in Hamburg weit davon entfernt glücklich zu seyn; allein wäre ich es nirgends mehr als ebendaselbst gewesen – Hier bin ich jetzt herzlich zufrieden. Wie es denn aber weiterhin werden soll? Das bleibt der Vorsehung überlassen. Ich habe meiner Mutter heilig versprochen in 6 Jahren wieder zukommen und werde es auch halten. Ich hoffe daß meine Frau während dem wird die deutsche Sprache vollkommen erlernt haben, daß sie mir wird allein folgen wollen, daß sie dem zukünftigen Besten ihrer Kinder mehr wird aufopfern können etc

Uebrigens hat dieses Land viele Annehmlichkeiten, die man nur durch Vergleichung schätzen lernt. Das schöne clima erhöht Körper und Geistes Kraft. Von 80 Tagen die seit unserer Ankunft den 18 Nov[ember] verfloßen sind, sind nur 4 regnigt, 14 bewölkt, und 62 ganz heiter gewesen – Unsere freundschaftlichen Verbindungen zwischen Brüder Frauen und Freunde sind vielleicht einzig, und auch die Kaufmännische Thätigkeit, und Schätzung hat ihren Reitz – Geistes Genuß ist durch seine Seltenheit doppelt anziehend: biß jetzt habe ich noch nichts von meinen in Hamburg gelassenen Büchern habhaft werden können; wenn mich indessen Ihr lieber Neffe[1] auf das merkwürdigste Ihrer Litteratur schriftlich aufmerksam machen will, so werde ich es ihm sehr verdanken –

Unsere Cecile die jetzt über 13 M[ona]th[e] alt ist, hat 9 Zähne und geht sehr behende auf 4 Füßen, sie spricht verschiedene Wörter deutlich aus, hat ihren guten Charakter beibehalten; und trägt dergestalt viel zu unsern Genüßen bey. Wir wünschen sehr von Eduard und seinen lieben Eltern zu hören. Lottens Bekantschaft hat einen bleibenden Eindruck in unserer aller Seelen hinterlassen – Antworten Sie uns bald, und geben uns recht ausführliche Nachrichten von allem was Sie persönlich angeht. Meine Liebe und Achtung kann durch unsere kurze Ansicht nur vermehrt seyn. Das Schicksal hat zwar unsere liebsten Pläne vereitelt, aber Sie sind darum nicht weniger meine würdigsten zweiten Eltern, die beständig mein wahres Bestes gesucht haben, die mir in Liebe und Weisheit vorausleuchten, und also stets die Gegenstände meiner Nachahmung und reinsten Zuneigung seyn werden.

Johan Nicolas Bohl

Cecile wurde mit 11 M[ona]th[en] ohne große Mühe entwöhnt. Meine Frau ist aber seitdem noch nicht wieder schwanger geworden, eben so wenig die Therese, die es heftig wünscht.

15. Dorothea Campe, Braunschweig

Chiclana den 16. April 1798

Ihr liebes Schreiben vom 9 Febr[uar] habe ich schon lange zur Beantwortung vor mir liegen, aber die Zerstreuungen eines gesellschaftlichen Lebens, und die zeitfreßenden Einrichtungen einer neuen Haushaltung haben es biß jetzt verschoben – Sie haben nun schon aus meinem letzten Briefe, verschiedene details meiner Reise und Ankunft vernommen. Gottlob daß wir so weit sind! Das Andenken an die Mühseligkeiten der Reise frischt jedesmahl den Genuß meiner jetzigen ruhigen Lage von neuem auf, und diese ist mir so behaglich, daß mich jede mögliche Veränderung fast erschreckt. Es liegt aber auch ein Zauber in diesem clima in dieser freien Lebensart, der keine schwarze Gedanken aufkommen läßt. Rechnen Sie hierzu meine Ihnen wohlbekannte Familien Verhältniße, und den Umgang meiner beyden Freunde, so müssen Sie mir beystimmen. Es ist doch Schade, daß wir so weit auseinander sind, und daß Sie sich durch BerufsGeschäfte gebunden glauben. Eine Reise nach diesem freundlichen Himmelsstrich, würde Ihnen Gesundheit und FrohSinn für Ihr übriges Leben geben.

Alles was Sie in Rücksicht des Gartens gethan haben und thun werden ist wohlgethan. Sollten Sie darüber ohne großen Verlust disponiren können, so würde ich die KaufSumme Ihrem Neffen August anvertrauen, um damit eine BuchHandlung, nach seinen mir darüber geäußerten Ideen, in Maynz anzulegen. Bemühen Sie sich auch nicht zu sehr um den Verkauf der Möbeln, liebe Pflege Mutter, vielleicht findet sich einmahl Gelegenheit einem guten Freund damit zu dienen; einen Nothverkauf brauchen wir ja nicht zu machen – Meine Reisebeschreibung sende ich Ihnen willig ein, sobald der Friede wieder eine ordentliche Schiffarth zwischen Hamburg, und hier wird hergestellt haben. Sie gefällt mir zwar jetzt selbst schon nicht mehr besonders, allein auch Sie, werden auf eine fortwährende Entwicklung, und hoffentliche Annäherung zur Reise, Rücksicht nehmen, und die Eingebungen des jedesmahligen Augenblicks nicht für Resultate des ganzen Forschens und Strebens halten –

Unsere politische Lage ist immer sehr traurig: Die Feinde aller NichtEngländer schneiden uns Handel und Wandel gänzlich ab, und täglich versinkt der größere Haufen der Einwohner von Kadix (die nur von Handel lebten) in tieferes Elend. Alles was wir aus der Fremde nöthig haben ist ungewöhnlich rar, und theuer biß auf Butter, Hutzucker und Wachs. Gottlob, daß die Räuber uns nicht unser Korn und Wein vorenthalten können – bey diesen Umständen hat meine Frau darein gewilligt, vor's erste kein Haus in der Stadt zu miethen, um unsere Ausgaben einzuschränken, da meine Anwesenheit im Comptoir ganz unnütz ist, so bin ich gerne in diesem Dorfe, wo uns Gottlob nichts fehlt –

Unsere Cecile geht jetzt schon, und ist immer rothbackigt und gesund: in diesem clima trägt sie nur ein Hemde und geht baarfuß. Täglich gewährt sie mir mehr Genuß – Meine Frau ist noch nicht wieder schwanger, übrigens glücklich und gesund. Meine Schwieger Mutter hat periodisch ihre Anfälle, und genießt wenig – Beyde sprechen von Ihnen und noch mehr von Lotten mit einer Art Enthusiasmus, und grüßen tausendmahl.

Ihr Pflege Sohn
J. N. Bohl.

16. Dorothea Campe, Braunschweig

Cadiz den 16. October 1798.

Ihre lieben Briefe vom 31 Aug[ust] haben wir richtig erhalten, und wie gewöhnlich mit dem größten Interesse gelesen. Nur die Nachrichten von Vaters Krankheit waren uns unangenehm; Gottlob, daß eine so merkliche Besserung erfolgt war, die wie wir hoffen von Dauer seyn wird, besonders wenn das Zusammenleben mit den lieben Kindern und Kindeskindern manchen Ansatz zur Hypokondrie wird haben können – Mit dem Verkauf des Gartens bin ich sehr zufrieden, so wie mit allen übrigen Dispositionen; die Anlegung dieses Geldes in Händen Ihres Neffen ist ganz meine eigene Idee. Ich hoffe es wird ihm zu seinem Fortkommen behülflich seyn, und ihn bald in den Stand setzen mir eine kleine Interesse davon zu bezahlen – der Verkauf der Möbeln ist hoffentlich noch nicht zu Stande gekommen. Ich bestimme sie für meinen Bruder Fritz, der wie sie schon lange werden gehört haben, ein Landgut im Meklenburgischen 2 Meilen von Schwerin und 10 von Hamburg gekauft hat. Außer den 6 Stühlen und Kanape also die für Ihnen bleiben, und mit deren Gegengeschenk Frasquita sehr zufrieden ist, halten Sie alles übrige auf den Packwagen zu dessen freien Disposition. Wegen Bezahlung verstehe ich mich direct mit ihm selbst.

Wie angenehm muß es Ihnen nicht seyn, daß sich Ihre Kinder nun bald ganz mit Ihnen vereinigen. Ich hoffe noch der mahleinst Ihr schönes neues Hauß zu bewundern, und unter seinem Dache manche angenehme Stunden zu verleben. Wenn ich mich nicht irre, so ist der Platz derjenige worauf dem berühmten Löwen ein Denkmahl errichtet steht –

Die Beschreibung Ihrer silbernen Hochzeit Feier hat uns viel Vergnügen gemacht. Ja wohl, lieben wir auch Familien Feste, und halten sie für den schönsten Genuß des Lebens. Die dazu gehörigen Stücke sind des Gegenstandes würdig. Schade daß Vater ihm nicht beiwohnen konnte!

Ob wohl ich meine Reisebeschreibung, bey kalter Durchlesung, sehr uninteressant finde, so bin ich dennoch bereit sie Ihnen zuzusenden, sobald die Schiffarth zwischen unsern Haven und Hamburg wieder im Gange seyn wird. Da ich diese Reise für meine Freunde aufschrieb, so war es mir mehr darum zu thun jedesmahl meine Empfindungen zu schildern, als Beschreibungen und Nachrichten zu liefern; sie kann also auch nur meine Freunde interesiren. – Eines Theils dieser Empfindungen aber auch, schäme ich mich schon jetzt weil sie einen Anstrich von Ueberspannung und von Schwärmerey haben der bey bloß vernünftigen Menschen den Argwohn der affectation sogar erregen könnte. Doch nicht bey Ihnen, bin ich überzeugt, die mich kennen. Daß ich aber damahls so fühlte, und jetzt nicht mehr, ist die Frucht der Erfahrung. Bey unserer Art Absonderung hier in Cadiz von Natur und Kultur gewinnt die Einbildungskraft den größten Spiel Raum. In unsern Muße Stunden leben und weben wir in den Elysäischen Feldern mit nur gebildeten Seelen. Die ersten Eindrücke also sind sehr heftig, wenn wir diesem Ziele zuzueilen glauben. Die Wirklichkeit und die Gewohnheit entzaubern uns nachher sehr bald, allein wir schämen uns es zu gestehen –Vieles mag das clima dazu beitragen, welches hier der Empfänglichkeit besonders günstig ist; Natur und Kunst brauchen nur einen geringen Aufwand, um die angenehmsten Empfindungen zu erregen und dieses habe ich auch nach meiner Rückkehr erfahren – So viel ist gewiß, daß diese Briefe auf keine Art gedrukt zu werden verdienen, weil nicht zu begreifen ist wodurch sie andere als Freunde interessiren könnten. Ich weiß eigentlich nicht wodurch Spanien überhaupt interessiren kann, als durch den Reitz der Neuheit;

die Reise die sie gelesen haben ist vermuthlich Bourgoine,[1] der alles Gute was man von dem Lande sagen kann erschöpft hat; eher ließe sich noch überhaupt etwas interessantes aus langjährigen Aufenthalt abgezogenes, über Sitten und Charakter der Nation sagen. Nächstdem führt der große Weg von Cadiz nach Bayonne durch den traurigsten Theil des Landes. Nur Biskayen bietet Naturschönheiten dar. In ganz Andalusien und den beiden Kastillen sind Bäume eine Seltenheit. Die Städte sind alle gleich traurig oede und verfallen, und die Menschen gleich verschloßen zurückstoßend, und gefühlloß – Der Garten Spaniens ist die Provinz Valenzia; Cataluña der Sitz der Industrie und des Fleißes, und die schöne Natur muß man in Granada suchen. Alles dieses aber liegt weit von der Haupt Straße ab.

Ich habe mit meiner Familie bißjetzt noch immer Chiclana bewohnt, und nur kurze Besuche hier abgelegt, weil unsere Handlung leider nicht viele Arbeiter erfordert. Die Sommer Hitze, die wir dort stärker als in der Stadt fühlen, ist mir nicht zuträglich gewesen. Im September litt ich an ein starkes Wechselfieber, bin aber Gottlob jetzt völlig wiederhergestellt; auch Gottlieb hat an Fieber gelitten. – Frasquita fährt in ihrer Schwangerschaft glücklich fort; gegen Ende Janner muß sie ihre Woche halten, wesgegen wir Weihnachten ein kleines StadtHauß, in unserer Nachbarschaft beziehen werden. Cecilia macht uns täglich mehr Freude; ich habe es durch anhaltende Aufsicht dahin gebracht, alles Weinen und Launen in seinem Ursprung zu ersticken; so fällt sie nicht allein niemanden beschwerlich, sondern gewöhnt sich auch an Selbstbeherrschung – Sie ist besonders stark, geht jetzt sehr gut, aber spricht noch wenig, woran mir jedoch nichts gelegen ist, da ich alle Zeichen einer frühen Reife ganz besonders haße –

Im übrigen würden wir recht zufrieden leben, in dem angenehmen Umgang zwischen Brüder, Frauen und wahren Freunde, wenn uns nicht die Sperrung unseres Havens alle Mittel des Verdienstes abschnitte, und auf solche Art die eigentliche Absicht unseres Hierseyns vereitelte. Wir warten sehnsuchtsvoll auf den Frieden, um das versäumte womöglich nachzuholen, und das Elend um uns hier vermindert zu sehen.

Ich hoffe, daß sich Bruder Fritz in seinen neuen Stand gut schicken wird; es scheint als wenn er einen sehr vortheilhaften Ankauf gemacht hat. Sein Gut heißt Crammonshagen; es gehört das Kirchdorf Crammon dazu. Auch hat sich seit kurzen unser Schwager Berkmeyer das Gut Türow nur 2 Meilen von Crammonshagen entfernt gekauft. Beyde Güter sollen schön und einträchtlich seyn. Ich freue mich sehr darüber, weil ich noch immer einen Hang zum Landleben habe, und mir diese Freunde bey meiner Rückkunft zu einem guten Ankauf sehr behülflich seyn werden. Auch ist die Nachbarschaft von Freunde und Verwandten auf dem Lande sehr angenehm – Was halten Sie von den künftigen Schicksalen der Meklenburgischen Länder? – Kann Preußen sie erben, und würden sie sich bey preußischer Verwaltung besser aufnehmen? –Würde Preußen den Gutsbesitzern die ansehnlichen Vorrechte lassen? –

Einlage an Ihren Neffen. Wegen Mangel an Schiffsgelegenheit müssen die so sehnlich gewünschten Bücher vor's erste liegen bleiben – Von Vaters Wörterbuch[2] würde ich gerne etwas näheres vernehmen. Meine herzliche Liebe an Ihre Kinder und Kindeskinder. Frasquita denkt Ihrer aller mit Rührung, und stellt Lotten beständig als Muster auf, wenn von weiblicher Vortrefflichkeit die Rede ist –
Johan Nicolas Bohl

17. Dorothea Campe, Braunschweig

Cadiz den 8. Febr[uar] [17]99.

Obgleich ich Ihren letzten Brief an Gottlieb nicht zur Beantwortung vor mir liegen habe, so kann ich doch nicht länger aufschieben Ihnen die glückliche Entbindung meiner Frau mitzutheilen, die schon seit c[irc]a 3 Wochen unserer Cecile eine Schwester gegeben hat, und jetzt wieder die Pflichten einer guten Mutter durch Selbst Stillen, erfüllt. Die Entbindung ist sehr leicht gewesen, und das Kind Gottlob gesund und wohl. Es hat die Nahmen von Aurora Josefa Rosalia Canuta erhalten.

Gottlieb ist jetzt mit seiner Therese auf dem Lande, wo sie die letzten Karnavals Tage sehr vergnügt zugebracht haben – Da unsere Handlung noch immer darnieder liegt, so denke ich gegen Ende des Monaths auch mit meiner Familie herauszuziehen, da den Kindern besonders das freie Feld so unentbehrlich ist. Cecile ist noch immer ein starkes und gesundes Kind und fängt jetzt endlich an zu sprechen – Mit dem größten Interesse, lesen wir alles was Sie selbst und Ihre liebe Familie betrifft, und erwarten bald Ihre gänzliche Vereinigung zu vernehmen – Was von den Möbeln einmahl verkauft ist, muß verkauft bleiben; ich sehe auch wohl ein, daß voluminöse Sachen des transports nach Mecklenburg nicht werth sind. Nächsten Johanni wird Fritz von seinen Gütern Besitz nehmen. Ich verlange sehr zu hören wie ihm das eigentliche Landleben gefallen wird, da ich nicht umhin kann dasselbe (bey veränderten Umständen) zum letzten Ziel meiner Wünsche zu machen. Uebrigens leben wir hier ruhig und vergnügt und halten uns schlecht und recht an die Gegenwart. Ihr Sohn
J. N. Bohl

An August bitte zu sagen daß es hier keine eigentliche MusikHandlung giebt, und daß ohne konsiderablen Fonds auch schwerlich eine bestehen würde, weil der Abgang langsam ist und die eingehenden Rechte enorm hoch sind

18. Joachim Heinrich and Dorothea Campe, Braunschweig

Cadiz, den 15 August 1799.

Ich hatte just seit etlichen Tagen daran gedacht mich einmahl wieder mit Ihnen, liebe Pflege Eltern, recht ausführlich zu unterhalten, als Ihr lieber Brief vom 15 passto gestern ankömmt, und diesen Vorsatz in That verwandelt. Also schon wieder ein Enkel! Der Herr Schwieger Sohn[1] verliert keine Zeit, wie es scheint. Wenn nur die Gesundheit Ihrer guten Lotte nicht darunter leidet, so ist indessen nichts dagegen einzuwenden – Ich gehe jedoch bedächtiger zu Werke; meine Frau stillt jetzt die kleine Aurora, und soll so fortfahren biß ein Jahr abgelaufen ist, und dann so Gott will wird in weniger als einem Jahre ein kleiner Junge nachkommen; so verfließen fast zwei Jahre zwischen jedes Wochenbette – Cecile ist immer rüstig und stark, spricht schon ziemlich viel französisch, und liebt die kleine Schwester ganz außerordentlich. Letztere ist viel kleiner und feiner, sehr brunett, schwarze Augen, kurz ganz die Mutter, sonsten einen heitern sanften Charakter, der nichts zu wünschen übrig läßt – So viel von den Kleinen. Von den Großen läßt sich nicht so viel gutes sagen. Ich habe einen äußerst beschwerlichen Sommer zugebracht. Heftige Wechselfieber, die Anfang dieses Monaths sogar tägliche Fieber wurden, haben meiner Gesundheit und meiner Heiterkeit heftig zugesetzt. Ich kann nicht begreifen wodurch ich mir diese sonderbare und vorher ganz fremde Krankheit zugezogen habe ... Drey Doktors haben vergebens versucht sie auszurotten; ein vierter hat mich auf eine äußerst strenge Diät gesetzt die ich seit den letzten Anfällen beobachte, und wobey ich mich biß jetzt wirklich ohne Fieber befinde, allein ich befürchte daß mein appetit darauf gehen wird, da nicht allein die qualität der Lebensmittel, sondern auch die quantität auf das äußerste eingeschränckt ist, und ich gewiß nicht mehr Nahrung als der berühmte Corsaro zu mir nehme. Merkwürdig ist es dabey, daß meine Kräfte keine merkbare Abnahme erleiden – Auch sind die daraus entspringenden Uebungen in der Selbstüberwindung gewiß moralisch nützlich und fruchtbringend.

Meine Vorliebe für Spanien hat durch diese Zufälle (die ich auch schon vergangenen Sommer obwohl in geringerem Grade verspürte) sehr abgenommen. Meine Gedanken beschäftigen sich immer lieber mit Deutschland, aber nur leider meine Gedanken. Die fatalen Umstände die mir vor zwei Jahren alle fremde Länder zum Fege Feuer machten, walten auch jetzt noch ob, und ich sehe keinen Ausgang ... Indesen kommt Zeit, kommt Rath. Unsere Lebensart hier ist ganz angenehm, so lange wir den hiesigen Aufenthalt als periodisch ansehen. Sobald aber ein reiferes Alter Ruhe und die möglichste Sicherheit des Vermögens zu beabsichtigen anfängt, sobald auch wünscht man sich ein Landgut in einem ruhigen Revolutionsfreien Lande. Die kritische Lage der Finanzen Spaniens, die Herabwürdigung des Papiergeldes welches fast nur allein zirkulirt, macht uns viele Sorgen. Es war Klugheit und Pflicht etwas zu sichern; nicht allein haben wir ansehnliche Summen in Hamburg, sondern wir hatten auch wirklich schon unserm Bruder Fritz den Auftrag zum Ankauf eines sehr gepriesenen kleinen Landguts gegeben, welches er aus Saumseeligkeit fahren ließ – Es hat sich auch schon unser Schwager Berckemeyer angekauft. Sein Gut soll groß und sehr schön seyn; es heißt Thürow liegt nahe am Schall See im Lauenburgischen oder Meklenburgischen eine TageReise von Hamburg; seit Johanni haußt er mit seiner Familie daselbst. Fritz seine Güter sind im Meklenburgischen in der Nähe von Thürow; sie heißen Crammonshagen und Niemarcken. Er sollte gleichfalls um Johanni haben davon Besitz nehmen; wir haben aber keine Nachricht davon von ihm erhalten – Diese Nachbarschaft ist ein starker Grund für uns das Meklenburgische zu einem Landankauf vorzuziehen; es ist überdem ein fruchtbares Land und hat durch die mächtigen Allianzen seiner Fürsten eine Art Garantie für die Aufrechthaltung seiner Verfassung die den Gutsbesitzern besonders günstig ist. – Wir werden jetzt unserm Schwager den Auftrag geben, gelegentlich und ohne Uebereilung etwas in gute Ländereyen anzulegen –.

Es wäre leicht möglich, daß der so sehnlich erwünschte Frieden den gänzlichen Ruin oder wenigstens eine lange Unthätigkeit in unserer Cadixer Handlung hervorbrächte. Der Krieg, wenngleich für das allgemeine schädlich, giebt den Kapitalisten zu mannichfaltigen Spekulationen Anlaß, und der thätige und feine Handlungs Geist meines Bruders hat denselben vielfach für uns benutzt. Es könnte leicht in den Friedens Artikeln eine direkte Schiffarth fremder Nationen nach dem Spanischen Amerika stipulirt werden, und dann wäre es gänzlich um die Kadixer Handlung geschehen – Durch solche Begebenheiten würden wir geschwinder an unsern Rückzug denken. Soviel kann ich Ihnen über unsere Zukunft mehr andeuten, als sagen. Das eigentliche Bestimmte bleibt der Vorsehung überlassen, die gewiß alles am Ende zu unserm wahren besten lenken wird. Eine gewiße Resignation scheint mir immer nöthiger und beruhigender; eine Art Gleichmuth bey alles persönliche individuelle, wobey man sich am Ende selbst am besten steht. Sind nur meine Haußgenoßen zufrieden, so bin ich es auch, und bin es um so mehr desto weniger Aufwand von Zeit und Geisteskräften es mir kostet, denn unter allen Qualen ist mir die erschrecklichste müßige Damen amüsiren zu müssen – Dieses ist Schlüssel zu manchen Begebenheiten meines verheiratheten Lebens –

Sehr interessant ist uns der ganze Inhalt Ihres Briefes; ich wünsche sehr, daß die Schiffarth wieder frei komme, um die interessanten Werke die Sie mir versprochen zu erhalten; unterdessen sind glücklicherweise in Malaga etliche Bücher die ich Herrn Meyer aufgetragen hatte angekommen und ich hoffe sie bald zu erhalten; es sind Hufeland Kunst etc, d[it]o über die Blattern und Kinder Krankheiten,[2] Garvens Prinzipien der Sittenlehre,[3] Goethe Propyläen,[4] Schlegels Athenäum,[5] Genz Journal,[6] und dann verschiedene Werke über Mathematik, Astronomie und

Architektur, da ich dieses FrühJahr angefangen habe von einem geschikten emigrirten Priester, Stunden zu nehmen, die nur durch die fatalen Fieber unterbrochen worden sind.

Außer diesen können Sie nur immer die interessansten Bücher für mich anschaffen, heften lassen, und an H[er]r[n] Meyer in Hamburg absenden, da sich manches mahl unerwartet eine Gelegenheit auf hier hervorthun kann. Es ist sehr wohl, daß Sie mir den Belauf der verkauften Meubles dagegen gutgeschrieben haben –

Es wäre mir sehr lieb gewesen von unsern August Nachrichten aus Paris zu erhalten; litterarische und politische Angelegenheiten sind von daher gleich interessant. Seit einem langen Brief den er mir den 18 Jan[uar] von dorten aus geschrieben hat, habe ich weiter nichts von ihm vernommen: Da nun das Manuscript der Noten schon seit etlicher Zeit bey Ihnen angekommen seyn muß, verlangt mir sehr zu wissen, wie es mit dem Drucke und den übrigen aufgetragenen Punkten, geht –

Daß die Freude Ihres jetzigen Zusammenlebens unendlich groß seyn muß kann ich mir leicht vorstellen! Wie herzlich stimme ich in Ihren Ausruf ein: Ach! warum so weit von einander . . . allein noch stärkere Hindernisse dringen sich zwischen unsere Vertraulichkeit. Hat sich je ein verheiratheter Mann <u>selber</u> oder <u>seinen</u> Freunden gehört? Darf er Sinne haben für etwas anders als für seine Frau und ihren Anhang? – Und auch diese Erscheinung ist leicht zu rechtfertigen, denn sie führt auf Verengung der Familienbande – doch sollte man sich nicht zu frühe verheirathen.

Ich werde gerne hören, daß das neue Etablissement Ihres lieben Vieweg's guten Fortgang hat, und besonders (wovon Sie gar nichts sagen) wie es mit der Gesundheit Vaters geht, und womit er sich hauptsächlich beschäftigt und was er von der Wendung der politischen und litterarischen Begebenheiten denkt, ob wir Sklaven oder Barbaren werden, Atheisten oder Papisten; und welches von beiden Extremen das minder schreckliche sey –

Ich mögte Ihnen auch wohl etwas von interessanten Menschen und Begebenheiten erzählen können, allein dazu gibt unser Cadiz wenig Stoff

Das angenehme unserer Lebensart besteht in einer geschäftigen Einförmigkeit, während welcher das Leben unbemerkt und reißend verfließt. Und dieses ist viel; denn desto geschwinder desto besser. Nur bewahre uns der allgütige Vater für Schmerz der Tage zu Jahre macht. Der Sontag ist uns nicht recht mit, weil er eine kleine Veränderung in dieser lieben Einförmigkeit hervorbringt. Sonst den Tag über auf dem Comptoir, es mag viel oder wenig zu thun seyn; ein öder Spatziergang gegen Abend, und jeder für sich zu Hause. Jede Dame hat ihren kleinen Hof, und biß 10½ spielt Karten wer Lust hat, und wer nicht konversirt – An Festtagen pflegen beide Familien zusammen zu eßen – Viele Herzlichkeit herrscht im Umgange nicht. Es hat langerprobte Freundschaft und Standhaftigkeit erfordert, um den Grund der Männer Freundschaft aufrecht zu erhalten. Er ist ganz. Gott sey es gedankt, obwohl alle Äußerungen und die Gelegenheiten dazu durch Anstalten der Damen so ziemlich vernichtet sind. Die Damen sehen sich just so viel, als es der Wohlstand erfordert; ohnmöglich können auch ungleichere Charaktere existiren – Nächstdem absorbiren die Geschäfte jede andere Unterhaltung, und es kommt am Ende darauf hinaus, wie es denn auch zu unserm wahren Besten seyn muß: Sich selbst genügen lernen. Also auch mit mir und meinen Büchern alleine handle ich alle geistige Geschäfte ab, und da meine moralische Begriffe immer stätiger werden, so fängt das eigentliche wissentschaftliche an mich mehr zu interessiren, so wie ich denn auch schon einen artigen Fortschritt in der Algebra macht hatte, als das verzweifelte Fieber kam – Ich trieb nemlich auf Rath des Lehrers die Algebra als Introduction zur Geometrie – Nun, das heiße ich geschwatzt. Sie werden merken, daß verschiedenes ganz unter uns gehört, besonders alles was die Verhältniße der beiden Familien betrifft; antworten Sie auch nicht darauf ... es ist nichts darin zu ändern. – Ich umarme Sie alle von ganzen Herzen, und erwarte von der Vorsehung, daß sie die Herzen noch einmahl fügen wird, die füreinander geschaffen zu seyn scheinen. –

J.N.Bohl.

Die Chocolade soll bey erster Schiffsgelegenheit erfolgen – Unser vortreffliche Deutsche Mahler liegt in Madrid krank; kommt er hier, so werde ich mich des versprochenen Portraits erinnern – Apropos. Neulich trafen die sehr hübschen Stammbücher mit etlichen brochuren von Jean Paul ein.[7] – Vielen Dank dafür.

19. Dorothea Campe, Braunschweig

Cadiz den 5 Nov [17]99

Ihren lieben Brief vom 22. Sept[em]b[e]r habe ich die vorletzte Post erhalten und da verschiedene Punkte desselben mir schleunige Beantwortung erfordern, so zögere ich damit nicht – Vor's erste kann ich Ihnen sowohl zu meiner als auch gewiß zu Ihrer Zufriedenheit benachrichtigen, daß mich die bösen Fieber ganz verlassen haben, und daß ich mich, besonders seit dem Eintritt des frischen Wetters, besser wie jemals befinde. Die Diät hat sich auch mit Zunahme der Kräfte von selbst modifizirt, und jetzt hüte ich mich nur für das Uebermaaß, und für gewiße schwerzuverdauende oder schlechtsaftige Speisen – Meine Stimmung ist in eben dem Maaße heiterer geworden, und ich genieße jetzt wieder mit voller Erkentlichkeit alles das unzählige Gute, so mir die Vorsehung zugetheilt hat –

Ich kann es an August kaum vergeben, daß er nicht allein meinen Auftrag der noten halber ganz vernachläßiget, sondern mir auch seit seiner Abreise von Braunschweig nicht einmahl geschrieben hat. Um dieses Versehen nach besten Kräften zu verbessern, gebe ich Ihnen hiemit den Auftrag, sogleich den Stich der übersandten Noten bewerkstelligen zu lassen. August hatte mir versprochen zu bewerkstelligen daß nachdem Druck Exemplare an berühmten Meistern postfrei eingehändiget werden sollten, deren Meinung darüber in ein paar Zeilen zu erfahren, mir höchst angenehm seyn würde; besonders diejenige des berühmten und lautseeligen Haydn[1] in Wien – Auch ein Paar Dutzend Exemplare sollten durch H[errn] Meyer in Hamburg an mich befördert werden; alles dieses könnte nun schon geschehen seyn –

Den jungen Komponisten, dem ich den Druck feierlich zugesagt hatte, muß ich nun mit leeren Versprechungen hinhalten ... Jedes Werk muß besonders <u>gestochen</u> und nicht gedruckt werden; auch nicht in Querfolio, sondern aufrecht stehend – Die Titel müssen genau, als wie verzeichnet, auch mitgestochen werden – Die Zahl der Exemplare eine MittelAnzahl, so wie gewöhnlich dergleichen Auflagen veranstaltet werden; auch in den musikalischen Journalen müßte eine Anzeige geschehen, und dann die Auflage vertheilt und verschiedenen Musikhandlungen in Commißion gegeben werden – Ueber alles dieses hatte ich schon ausführlich an August geschrieben –

Demohngeachtet hätte ich fast Lust mit Ihnen zu hadern, daß Sie nochmahls wegen der Bestimmung des aus dem Garten gelößten Geldes anfragen. Was ich sage thue ich auch, was ich verspreche, daß halte ich auch; und dieses auch ohne die Kaufmännische Konsequenz hoffentlich, womit wir uns manchmahl gegen die Herrn Gelehrten brüsten zu können glauben. Es bleibt also dabey, daß ich den Kaufpreiß des Gartens Augusten anvertrauen will, und daß es ihm frei steht mir davon (durch Ihre Hände) einen von ihm selbst zu bestimmenden Zins zu entrichten, oder auch die ersten Jahre unentgeltlich zu behalten.

Das Verzeichniß der abgesandten Bücher habe ich nicht vorgefunden; da es mir nun aber unumgänglich nöthig ist, um zu wissen was ich zu erhalten und im Nothfall zu reclamiren habe, so bitte ich es mir <u>mit umgehender Post</u> einzusenden, und es doch ja bey ähnlichen Gelegenheiten nie beizulegen vergessen.

Ich glaube nicht, daß ich im wissenschaftlichen Fache so leicht zu viel thun werde. Der Antheil den ich an meine häuslichen Verhältniße und an der Handlung nehme, leitet meine Aufmerksamkeit von einen Gegenstand zum andern. Nebenher ist meine Wißbegierde so groß, daß um nur von vielen <u>etwas</u> zu wissen, ich nothwendigerweise auf das tiefe Eindringen in das einzelne Verzicht thun muß; aber glauben Sie ja nicht das Eitelkeit oder Begierde zu glänzen dieser Wißbegierde zum Grunde liegt. <u>Nie</u> habe ich Gelegenheit auch nur das geringste wissentschaftliche auszukramen; es ist mir nur um eigne Befriedigung zu thun, die ich auch bey jeden Schritt reichlich finde, und noch mehr ebendadurch vorzubereiten hoffe – Ich bin jetzt durch die Elementare Geometrie durch und in der Trigonometrie; dann will ich mit Hülfe der Algebra versuchen, eine Idee der höhern Geometrie zu erlangen, wenigstens so viel als nöthig ist um deutliche Begriffe über die Astronomie mir eigen zu machen – Die übrigen Zweige der angewandten Mathematik werden mir nachher als Erholungen erscheinen – Baukunst gefällt mir immer sehr, besonders da ihre SchönheitsRegeln so leicht zu fassen sind – Nebenher lese ich mit besonderm Interesse medizinische Schriften und habe auch leider einen Hang die neue Chemie von Lavoisier[2] zu studiren – Aesthetik bleibt nicht vergessen; besonders wünsche ich eine Anleitung zur Beurtheilung des Mechanismus der verschiedenen Versarten, zum skandiren, und deklamiren. Wenn Heusingers Handbuch[3] dergleichen enthielte würde es mir sehr willkommen seyn. – Auch wünsche ich ganz besonders das Lateinische wieder bey mir aufzufrischen auch noch Italianisch zu lernen, um Petrarch[4] im original zu lesen etc. Unter so mannichfaltigen Begierden, fließt das Leben reißend dahin; und das ist eine herrliche Sache. Glücklicher fühle ich mich nie, als wenn ich an keine Zeit gedacht habe, und unter dem Streben nach erreichbaren Wünschen, verschwinden Jahre wie Tage –

Wir wollen dann Vaters Besuch, wenn er sich nach America aufmacht, erwarten, oder wenns nicht zu bald ist ihm vielleicht mit einer visite zuvorkommen. Jeder hat so seinen Lieb[lings] Plan. Der meinige bleibt noch immer einmahl 3 Jahre auf eine Universität zu gehen und mich zu einem Doktor schlagen zu lassen, dann ein Gut im Meklenburgischen zu kaufen und mit Vater in der Wette zu pflanzen.

Bey den Bankerotten in Hamburg sind wir biß jetzt noch Gottlob ohne Interesse, Dank sey es der Unthätigkeit unserer Handlung; dennoch verlieren wir ansehnlich durch den immer zunehmenden Verlust des Papier Geldes; nur der Friede kann so viele Uebel heilen.

Sehr gerne werde ich die <u>gereimte Weltgeschichte</u> erhalten. Ist denn, apropos von Versen, der Froschmäußler[5] nicht vollendet? – Von Lotte sagen Sie mir kein Wort, und sehr wenig von den Kleinen; Dieses hat mich sehr verdroßen. Ueber den guten Fortgang des neuen Hauses freue ich mich. – Meine Familie ist recht wohl und seit Mitte vorigen Monaths auf dem Lande, wo sich die Kleinen besonders gut befinden. Die Jüngste hat bey den Zähnen etliche mahl Zuckungen gehabt, die uns schrekliche Stunden gemacht haben. So Gott will wird sie es überstehen, obwohl nicht so robust wie Cecile – Therese hat diesen Sommer mineralische Bäder in der Nachbarschaft gebraucht, allein biß jetzt ist (so viel ich weiß) noch kein Anzeichen von Schwangerschaft da; übrigens leben die Eheleute sehr gut zusammen. Gottlieb immer in Handlungsspekulationen vertieft – Frasquita hat durch meine Schuld das Deutsche leider wieder vernachläßiget, aber nächstens soll es nachgeholt werden – Ich hoffe daß Sie mir eben so promt antworten werden, als ich gethan und bin unterdessen wie immer Ihr Johannes –

20. Dorothea Campe, Braunschweig

Cadiz, den 13 April 1802

Ich habe, beste Pflege Mutter, Ihren Brief vom 16. passto gestern erhalten, und da Sie absolut mit umgehender Post Antwort haben wollen, so müssen Sie sich mit diesen wenigen Zeilen begnügen. Ich weiß nicht ob ich mich über Vaters Augenkrankheit mehr betrüben oder mehr freuen soll, einmahl da daraus eine Hoffnung erwächst ihn hier bey uns zu sehen. Dem sey nun wie ihm wolle, so viel ist gewiß, daß sich hier weiter keine Spur von Epidemie geäußert hat, und daß alle vernünftige Menschen mit mir glauben, daß nur durch eine neue Ansteckung von America das Uebel wieder entstehen könne. Daß wenn Vater auf hier käme, er kein ander Logis als unser Hauß haben muß ist wohl unnöthig anzuführen. Was den Knaben David anlangt so billige ich zum voraus alles, und mag er biß nach Marseille mitgehen und sich daselbst auf hier einschiffen, oder die ganze Reise mit Vater machen, so wie es dem letztern nach näherer Bekantschaft am angenehmsten seyn wird.

Ich hoffe bald das weitere über diese schöne Reise zu vernehmen, und habe nur Zeit hinzuzufügen daß wir alle sehr wohl sind, und daß meine Augen auch durch das viele Arbeiten gelitten haben, und die Geschäfte meinem Geiste manche Nahrung raubten. Ich umarme Sie nebst allen den lieben Ihrigen aus vollem Herzen.
    Ihr PflegeSohn
    Johan Nic. Bohl

21. Dorothea Campe, Braunschweig

Cadiz den 19 Aug[ust] 1803

Es ist mir besonders angenehm gewesen, theuerste Pflege Mutter, nach einem so langen Zwischen Raum einmal wieder Nachricht von Ihnen zu erhalten. Die Knaben Manzuco haben mir nämlich im vorigen Monath Ihr Schreiben vom 7 Juny mit 3 artigen Puppen und einiges allerliebstes Porzellan über liefert, so sämtlich an die Behörde befördert, und mit lautem Beifall aufgenommen worden. Mit dem ältesten Knaben, den ich unter Augen habe, bin ich ganz wohl zufrieden, obwohl mein Verhältniß zu ihm mir nicht erlaubt, seinen Charakter genauer kennen zu lernen; ihn ändern ist anderwärts angebracht. Mit den Rechnungen ist alles wohl an Bartels[1] beordere ich heute Ihre 20 L[i]t[e]r Extra zu übermachen.

Vaters letzte Reisebeschreibung hat mir Wibold zu lesen gegeben, und ich habe mich sehr daran erbaut: ich fürchte jedoch, daß die Kritiker behaupten werden, der alte Sauerteig sey noch immer darin zu verspüren: nach meinem Gefühl kommen die Engländer zu glimpflich weg. Aug[ust] Campe ist übrigens ein sehr nachlässiger unordentlicher Bücherlieferant, den ich auf keine Weise in das Gleis der kaufmännischen Pünktlichkeit habe hineinschieben können.

Nicolas Schuback versprach uns mit seiner Frau auf hier zu kommen; am Ende aber hat er seinen Plan verändert und ist von Bordeaux wieder nach Paris zurückgegangen; Reisende erzählen, daß er die große Schwäche hat eifersüchtig zu seyn, wodurch er zum Greuler an sich selbst und an allen seinen Umgebungen werden muß: wenn dieses wahr ist, so ist es mir lieb daß er uns nicht besucht hat. Daß unser gute John[2] in seiner Wahl so glücklich gewesen ist, freut mich von ganzem Herzen. Wann aber werden diese Schubacks endlich einmal zum Sitzen kommen?

Daß Vater in Paris gänzlich von seinen Uebeln geheilt wurde ist mir eine erfreuliche Nachricht: ich bin aber nicht wenig neugierig das nun zu erfahren, und da nun wohl vors erste alle Schiffahrt unterbrochen ist, so ersuche ich mir die gedruckten Blätter die davon handeln auszuschneiden und in einem Briefe p[er] Post zuzusenden.–

In den Familien müssen leider die ältern abgehen um den jüngeren Platz zu machen: also haben Sie schon 5 Enkel? – Ich erwarte No. 4 im nächsten October, und freue mich dass es nicht so rasch damit geht: in den jetzigen Weltumständen ist nicht viel Glückseligkeit für die nächste Generation abzusehen, besonders für die Mädchen. Die gänzliche Kraft und Saftlosigkeit der reifenden Jünglinge macht ihnen alle Leidenschaftlichkeit fremd, und nur Leidenschaft kann die Berechnungen des Egoismus ertödten, und die Verbindlichkeiten des Familen Vaters auferlegen.

Der Krieg ist für alle Handlung, wie immer, höchst verderblich besonders im Anfange: Da Spanien aber durch Gottes Gnade neutral geblieben ist und den grössten Theil seiner erwarteten Schätze zu Hause erhalten hat, so sind wir wenigstens für zerstörende Verluste in etwas gesichert. Seit Ende May lebe ich aber desswegen in einer so angreifenden Angst, daß ich hundertmahl den Kaufmannsstand verwünscht habe, und allerlei Pläne zum baldigen Zurückziehen aus der Handlung mache, die aber für jetzt noch immer an die Existenz meiner SchwiegerMutter scheitern, die ich weder hierlassen, noch auch mitnehmen kann.

Bey allen diesen Trübsalen haben mich jedoch die rein geistigen Genüße nie ganz im Stiche gelassen und selten hat mir die Kraft gemangelt mich aus der wirklichen Welt in die idealische zu versetzen. Das Studium der alten spanischen Litteratur habe ich mit meiner gewöhnlichen Heftigkeit ergriffen und dieses ganze Jahr darin gearbeitet: ich habe meinen Fleiß reichlich belohnt gefunden besonders in den Dichtern, und Auszüge davon mit einer Charakteristik eines jeden Dichters zu Papier gebracht. Die damahlige spanische Art zu seyn ist etwas unendlich großes, und den neueren völlig unbekanntes: wer sich in das Wesen derselben, durch tiefes Studium der Sprache und durch natürliche Empfänglichkeit hinein zu setzen versteht, findet eine neue Welt: anstatt einer flachen Empfindsamkeit zu fröhnen, huldigte man nur dem Verstande; man liebte positiven Edelmuth und Geistesgröße und wußte nichts von unserer heutigen negativen Tugend alias Unvermögen, und war nicht der beruhigende Schlaf der Vernunft besser, als unsere kränkelnde Vernünfteley? – Dieser hohe, edle, gewandte zierliche, artige, lachende Geist spiegelt sich auch in dem winzigsten Fliegeblatt der damahligen Periode, hauptsächlich aber in den dramatischen Produkten, die von dem heutigen Publikum gar nicht mehr verstanden werden, weder in den Worten noch in dem Sinn, denn auch hier will man nun Kotzebue[3] und sein imitatorum pecus sehn. Madrid besitzt Gottlob davon drey Comella,[4] Zavala[5] und Valladares,[6] die die Stücke gleich wie er aus dem Ermel schütteln, wo jede moralische und sentimentale Armseligkeit von dem Pöbel beklatscht wird, während die Kenner einschlafen. – Ich habe über das Theater einige Briefe spanisch in diesem Sinn geschrieben,[7] und einer meiner Freunde spielte mir den Streich den ersten in Madrid in ein periodisch Papier drucken zu lassen, welcher viel Aufsehen machte und den ersten Köpfen zugeschrieben wurde: da mich aber meine Brüder Kaufleute (nach ihrer Art) zu sehr damit aufzogen, so sind die übrigen im Pulte geblieben biß zu einer besseren Gelegenheit. Es mangelt nicht an einzelnen guten Köpfen sogar hier in Cadiz und verschiedenen Freunden habe ich die neue Aesthetik von Kant[8] und Schiller sehr goutiren machen – Das zweite Interesse an diesem Studium entsteht aus der so vortrefflichen Sprache, die sich zu jeder Gattung von Komposition schickt und zu einer jeden andere Wörter und andere Wendungen hat; ihre Redensarten (lebhafte Bilder für gewöhnliche Gedanken) bewundere ich noch mehr, als ihre Sprichwörter, weil sie natürlicher anzubringen sind: im Komischen besonders, sind sie darin unerschöpflich, so wie an aller Art Wort und Witzes Spielen. Das niedrig Komische (im Gegensatz von le haut comique) habe ich nie so ächt gefunden; was ich über den ästhetischen Werth der bouffoneries und des Burlesken denke, mag ich nicht sagen: genug darin giebt es eine so originale Ausbeute, daß man allein darum die Sprache studiren könnte! Schade, daß so wenige Sinn dafür haben!

Meine häuslichen Verhältniße sind so angenehm als ich es erwarten kann: meine Frau fängt an weniger die Zerstreuungen zu lieben und sich mehr mit ihren Kindern zu beschäftigen. Dabey erinnere ich mich Ihnen wegen eines Hauslehrers oder Lehrerin geschrieben zu haben, von katholischer Religion, der französischen Sprache mächtig, und übrigens so unterrichtet als möglich: Sie haben mir darauf nichts geantwortet – Unterlassen Sie nicht mir zu antworten: Das Porto scheue ich nicht, und Ihre Briefe gewähren mir immer die angenehmste Unterhaltung –

Ihr ergebener Pflegesohn

Johan Nic. Bohl

Noch gehört zu meiner Geschichte daß ich an dem jungen Bokelmann,[9] dem jetzigen dänischen Konsul, einen geistreichen und aufgeklärten Gesellschafter besitze, welches hier zu Lande ein großer Schatz ist, besonders in Rücksicht auf deutsche Litteratur und Patriotismus. –

P. S. Ich umarme mit herzlicher Liebe die gute Lotte ihren Mann und Kinder und habe öfters die Freude zu hören, welchen angenehmen Eindruck ihr ganzes Wesen auf meine Frau und Mutter gemacht hat.

Der schwedische Cap[itain] Enbeck von sein Sch[iff] Minerva hat ein Kistel mit 50lb Chocolade an Bord, wovon hiebey des Steuermanns Recief; vielleicht erreicht er Hamburg, vielleicht Bremen oder Lübeck, so wie es die Herrn Engländer erlauben: nach dem Orte wo er ankommt müssen Sie das Recief senden und die Kiste damit empfangen lassen.

22. August Campe, Hamburg

Görslow 27 Sep[tember] 1806

Ihre Briefe vom 20 und 23 so wie auch die beyden Sendungen habe ich wohl erhalten. Die Brochuren sind mir willkommen gewesen.

Bülow's Feldzug von 1800 habe ich neulich bey meinem Bruder gesehen und er hat mir nicht gefallen; ist es also noch thunlich, so bestellen Sie ihn wieder ab – dagegen sehe ich im Reichs Anzeiger:[1] Blicke auf zukünftige Begebenheiten aber keine Profizeihungen. Von dem Verfaßer des Geistes des neuen Kriegssystems, welches ich zu erhalten wünsche.[2]

Mit den Oeuvres de Luis XIV ist mir nicht gedient;[3] ich erwarte aber das Werk vom Palm,[4] wenn Sie es nemlich auftreiben können –

Ihr ergebener
Bohl v: Faber

Der 5. Theil von Bouterwek's Geschichte der Poesie und Beredsamkeit[5] ist erschienen: ich wünsche ihn broschiert zu erhalten.

23. Dorothea Campe, Braunschweig

Hamburg d[en] 22 Jan[uar] 1807

Die fatalen Zeitumstände haben unsere Korrespondenz leider von neuem unterbrochen: indeßen habe ich doch durch meinen Freund August Campe manchesmahl etwas von Ihnen erfahren: Sie sind gesund, und mit Gesundheit läßt sich allen andern Uebeln so ziemlich die Stirne bieten. Damit wollen wir uns dann auch für getröstet halten.

Daß meine Wiedergeburt im Norden in den Strom der Verwüstung fallen mußte, ist wirklich ominös; meine Frau schreibt, daß sie es nicht begreift wie ich es noch hier aushalte. Ich muß indeß gestehen, daß meine Ansicht der Dinge durch diese Begebenheiten wenig geändert ist, und daß ich für meine Person gerne auf meinem Landgute in Mecklenburg bliebe. Vor's erste muß ich jedoch nach Spanien wieder zurück, und wahrscheinlich werde ich im NächstJahr meine Reise antreten; von meinen Kindern vermag ich es nicht, mich zu trennen: sie werden mich begleiten. Meine Mutter giebt mit Edelmut alle ihre Ansprüche auf, weil sie einsieht wie sehr ich an die Kinder hänge und weil sie sich keine Verantwortung auf dem Halse laden will. Da ich nun wahrscheinlicherweise wieder eine Reihe von Jahren in Spanien werde zubringen müssen so bin ich gesonnen einen Hauslehrer für meine Kinder mitzunehmen, wenn sich nemlich ein für mich paßender dazu anfinden sollte. Ich wende mich desfalls zuerst an Sie, weil ich Ihre Gewißenhaftigkeit und Ihre ausgebreiteten Verhältniße kenne. Es käme mir dabey hauptsächlich auf Moralität, gründliche Kenntniß der lateinischen und deutschen Sprache, Mathematik und Naturkunde (hauptsächlich Botanik) an; Geschichte und Geographie wird vorausgesetzt; als Zugabe würde französische Sprache, Musik oder Zeichenkunde angenehm seyn. Die katholische Religion wäre zwar zu wünschen, aber doch nicht nothwendig. Bey paßenden Qualitäten könnte die beste Behandlung und ein reichliches honorar erwartet werden; man würde sich gegenseitig auf gewiße Jahre binden und bey anerkanntem Verdienst zu fernerem Fortkommen behülflich seyn.

Ich lebe hier, den Umständen zu Trotz, ganz angenehm: ich sehe zwar mein Vermögen von allen Seiten einschmelzen, allein der Herr hat es gegeben der Herr hat es genommen. Für jetzt kann ich es halten; weiterhin kommt Rath. Mit dem Hamburger Jammer kann ich nun gar nicht sympathisiren, und ich muß immer lachen, wenn sie schmögen – daß keine Gastereyen mehr sind, ist mir ganz recht; biß 1 bin ich nun auf meiner Stube, dann treibe ich mich in den Buchläden herum, und bringe den Abend im Schauspielhause zu.[1] Ich lebe also meistens in der idealen Welt, die (wie Rousseau sagt) allein werth ist bewohnt zu werden; mit wie viel mehr Recht können wir nicht jetzt sagen, daß die Wirklichkeit nicht auszuhalten sey! Wann war der göttliche Tod mit mehr Recht ein Erlöser zu nennen! –

Meine Kinder sind nach überstandenem Husten und Schnupfen jetzt ganz wohl und wünsche ich dasselbe von Ihren lieben Kindern und Enkeln.

Ihr Pflege Sohn
J.N.Bohl

24. Dorothea Campe, Braunschweig

Hamburg den 13 Febr[uar] 1807

Gottlob, daß ich endlich einmahl wieder etwas von Ihnen vernommen habe! Und Gottlob, daß Ihr Muth und Ihre Ansicht der Dinge, dieselben geblieben sind! – Man ist das elende Gewinsel und Gestöne so überdrüßig, daß man sich einer Sinnesart doppelt freut, die sich über die Armseligkeiten dieser Spanne sublunarischer Zeit, zu erheben weis. So lange der Himmel nur mir und den meinigen

Gesundheit schickt, lache ich über alles andre; meine innere Welt, meine Empfänglichkeit für alles Schöne und Gute, meine Aussichten in die Ewigkeit, soll mir kein Eroberer entreißen –

Ich gehe sehr ungerne nach Spanien zurück, allein es kann nicht anders seyn; meine Abwesenheit war von Anfang an, auf drey Jahre berechnet, und ich habe niemanden zurücklassen können, dem ich mich ganz anzuvertrauen wagen durfte. Meine Reisekosten werden nicht groß seyn, denn ich gehe zur See. Wollte Gott übrigens, daß mir die Engländer nicht mehr Schaden zugefügt hätten, als die Franzosen! Was sind ein paar tausend Thaler, gegen hundert tausend die bey dem Ueberfall eines Schiffes in Friedenszeiten verloren gehen können? Bey liegenden Gründen verliere ich vielleicht den Ertrag eines Jahres, bey der Handlung steht mein ganzes Vermögen aufs Spiel, so lange es mächtige See Räuber giebt! –

Mit meiner Frau stehe ich in einer regulären wöchentlichen Korrespondenz; sie bleibt dabey, daß sie sich zufrieden fühlt, welches aber den Wunsch nach unserer Vereinigung in Spanien nicht ausschließt. Von einem Freunde aber weis ich, daß sich Mutter und Tochter nach altem Brauch unendlich quälen, daß aber die Tochter ohne zu murren, alles über sich ergehen läßt und ihre Gesundheit darunter leidet. Ich bin überzeugt, sie würde eher sterben, als mir je eingestehen, daß sie die Reise nach Spanien bereue. Ihre übrigen Verhältniße stehen in grellem Kontrast, mit der vormahligen Vergötterung; Schreiber die nicht verdienen ihr den Schuh Riemen aufzulösen, stehen jetzt an ihrer Stelle und empfangen die Huldigungen der Sykophanten, während sie auf dem Lande kaum ihre intimsten Freunde zu bewirthen vermag. Sie fühlt es hart, was es ist ohne Mann dazustehen, und doch kommt keine Klage über ihre Lippen: das heiß ich Karakter! –

Hans Leisching[1] hat auf eines seiner Güter viel gelitten: dieses hat er aber seitdem, gegen ein Holsteinsches Gut bey Kiel verkauft, wo er jetzt seinen Wohnplatz aufzuschlagen denkt. Er glaubt damit einen vortheilhaften Handel gemacht zu haben; er scheint mir ein braver Mensch und ein tüchtiger Wirth zu seyn. Durch ihn habe ich vor kurzem meine Bekanntschaft mit Johannes Schuback erneuert und freue mich, daß es sich so hat fügen wollen: seine Frau scheint mir eine der vernünftigsten die mir je vorgekommen sind und ich glaube daß unser John es unmöglich hätte besser treffen können – Ich glaube, daß August nicht glücklich ist und wünsche seiner Frau[2] nur eine festere Gesundheit: in seiner Handlung vermiße ich noch immer die so nöthige Ordnung und Pünktlichkeit, wodurch sich Perthes[3] so sehr gehoben hat – Mein Bruder Fritz hat durch Klugheit und Geistesgegenwart weniger gelitten als seine Nachbarn: er hat indessen verschiedene Nächte im Holze zubringen müssen und hat am Ende verkleidet, in der anderthalb Meilen entlegenen Stadt Gadebusch, zu eßen gesucht – Mad[ame] Sieveking[4] sehe ich oft, weniger ihre Mutter: ich will aber meinen Besuch erneuern; wenn Sie nur wüßten, wie sehr meine Zeit beschränkt ist! – Ich begreife nicht, wie Sie etwas mich angehendes, haben auf dem Herzen behalten können! Sie kennen

mein Innerstes vielleicht besser, als irgend ein Lebender, und können also auch bestimmt die treuste Aufrichtigkeit von mir erwarten. Fast ist es mir peinlich daß es Ihnen einige Ueberwindung kostet, Ihre so wohl erworbenen mütterlichen Rechte gegen mich gelten zu machen; erlösen Sie mich bald von diesem Uebel.
   Ganz der Ihrige
   J N Bohl

25. Dorothea Campe, Braunschweig

Görslow 20 Juny 1807

Ihren lieben Brief vom 6 dieses habe ich erhalten. Ich gestehe, daß die lange Ungewißheit, worin Sie mich über die wichtige Sache eines Hauslehrers gelassen haben, mir empfindlich gewesen ist. Mit Ihrer Erklärung ist nun aber auch dieser Anlaß gehoben und ich hoffe also, daß auch von Ihrer Seite die alte Zutraulichkeit wieder eintreten würde. Als einen Beweis dessen erwarte ich ungesäumt den Anfang des langen Briefes mit der Beilage unseres Freundes Trapp.
   Wenn sich in Ihrem Kreise gegenwärtig niemand findet, den Sie zum Hauslehrer für mich geschickt halten so muß ich anderwärts suchen. Vielleicht gelingt es durch eine öffentliche Aufforderung im ReichsAnzeiger.
   Ist es mit dem Hagelschlag in dortiger Gegend so arg gewesen, als es die Zeitungen melden? – Hier begünstigt uns das Wetter außerordentlich. Die Roggen Aehren schlagen mir hier im Felde ins Gesicht, und wir werden wahrscheinlich um Jacobi (wie vor Zeiten) ärndten können. Die Landwirthschaft interessiert mich diesen Sommer mehr als den ersten; es ist mehr dabey zu lernen als ich glaubte, die Mecklenburgische Wirthschaft insbesondere eröffnet dem Kombinations Geist ein weites Feld. Nur sehr bedaure ich, daß Sie es nicht möglich machen können mich mit Vater zu besuchen. Die Landwirthschaft im großen, würde gewiß viel Interesse für ihn haben, und seinen rastlosen Geist auf eine zweckmäßige Art zerstreuen – Noch ist es Zeit sich zu ermannen. In der ersten Hälfte des July werde ich die Freunde Leisching und Schuback in Holstein besuchen; später aber bin ich jeden Tag bereit Sie insgesamt willkommen zu heißen
   Ihr Pflege Sohn
   J. N. Böhl

26. Dorothea Campe, Braunschweig

Görslow d[en] 25 Febr[uar] 1810

Ohne mich in weitläuftige Redensarten zu ergießen, die am Ende doch nur meine Nachläßigkeit sehr nothdürftig decken würden, fange ich lieber mit einem aufrichtigen: <u>Herr ich habe misgehandelt,</u> diese meine Epistel an, und füge gleich hinzu, daß meine dankbaren Gesinnungen, mein innigstes Wohlwollen, und meine warme Anhänglichkeit an meine guten Pflegeeltern, sich auch während meines langen Stillschweigens keinen Augenblick verläugnet haben. Von August Campe habe ich mitunterdurch Nachrichten von Ihnen alle erhalten, und Theil genommen an dem Guten und an dem Bösen. Gott gebe, daß alles nur so leidlich bleibe; denn auf ungestörte Ruhe und Frieden, muß das gegenwärtige Menschenalter wohl Verzicht thun.

Ich bin Ihnen Rechenschaft von meine beyden letzten Jahren schuldig. Meine Gesundheit ist gut gewesen, und habe ich den letzten Sommer an dem allgemein in diesen Gegenden wüthenden kalten Fieber, darnieder gelegen. Meine Augen muß ich immer sehr schonen – Ich habe mein Landgut sehr verbessert, und mit Gottes Hülfe dessen Ertrag ansehnlich vermehrt; ich habe für das gute Auskommen meiner Leute gesorgt, und sie in Kranksein und Noth beygestanden – Ich habe einen Theil meiner Zeit dem beschwerlichen Unterricht meines Sohnes gewidmet, weil es mir nicht hat glücken wollen einen Lehrer nach meinem Sinn zu finden – Da es nun aber mein Beruf nicht ist, alle Einzelheiten der Landwirthschaft wahrzunehmen (welches mir ein Inspektor für jährliche 150 Thaler abnimmt) so bleibt mir noch Zeit genug zu meinen litterarischen Streifzügen, worin ich mich, seitdem ich denken kann, am glücklichsten gefühlt habe. Ich bin dann auch wieder recht herumgeschweift, und da mir (wie manchem anderen litterarischen Dilettanten) das nun alt geworden ist, so habe ich wieder in dem alten das neue suchen müssen, und bin ein leidenschaftlicher Liebhaber der Litteratur des 16 und 17ten Jahrhunderts geworden. Mit vieler Mühe und Fleiß habe ich aus Auktionen jetzt schon einige hundert schmutzigen Pergamentbände deutscher Antiken zusammengeklaubt, die mir unendlich viel Freude machen; und da wir doch einmahl ohne Steckenpferd nicht zukommen können, so denke ich daß dieses doch wohl zu den harmlosesten gehört. In meinen Nebenstunden sinne ich nur auf Vervollständigung meiner Sammlung, besonders im poetischen Fach, und so lasse ich den Winter ohne Unlust toben. – In diesem Gebiete mußte ich auch auf mystische Schriften stoßen; ich habe deren verschiedene mit großem Antheil gelesen und lese sie noch. Ich bewundere den Geist der Verfaßer, die kurz gedrungen und deutlich uns dasjenige vortragen, was die Neueren in ungeheurem Wortschwall verhüllt, als das Neueste auftischen. Ein eigentlicher Adept bin ich aber bisjetzt nicht geworden, denn, wie einer von ihnen sagt 'das Studium welches nicht die Ehre Gottes zum einzigen Zweck hat, ist der nächste Weg zur Höllen; nicht von wegen des Studirens selber, sondern wegen der Hoffarth so die Menschen darzu treibet, und dadurch ferner geheget und vermehret wird. Es ist beklägig, daß die meisten Gelehrten der Welt zu keinem andern Ende studiren, als nur der unersättlichen Neugierigkeit ihres alten Menschen ein Genügen zu thun.'[1] Da letzteres nun leider mein Fall so kann ich auch kein ächter Mystiker werden.

Nun wissen Sie mein Aeußeres und mein Inneres. Meine Tochter Cecilia die nun 13 Jahre alt ist macht mir viele Sorgen. Sie ist in Hamburg in einer Pension einer ehemaligen Dame von St Cyr, die wohl nicht schlechter ist, als manch andere, allein doch so vieles zu wünschen übrig läßt!! – Da nun aber meine so lange aufgeschobene Reise nach Spanien dieses Jahr vor sich gehen muß, so denke ich sie ihrer Mutter wieder zuzuführen, die jetzt den Eitelkeiten dieser Welt entsagt hat, und sich nach nichts anders als Vereinigung mit ihrer Familie sehnt. Ob, wie, und wann ich aus Spanien zurückkehren werde, das weiß der liebe Himmel. Mein Wunsch ist es, mich baldmöglichst mit der ganzen Familie wieder hier auf meinem Gute in Ruhe zu setzen; es kommt nur darauf an ob meine Vermögens Umstände es mir erlauben werden.

Ich erwarte jetzt, daß Sie, um Böses mit Gutem zu lohnen, mir diesen Brief recht bald beantworten werden, und bitte um so eben ausführliche Nachrichten von Vater, Ihnen selbst, Viewegs, Ihre Minna, Trapps etc – Unser Land ist bis jetzt glücklich, wer weiß aber wie lange es dauern wird! Die Landgüter sind sehr wohlfeil, da die niedrigen Kornpreise manchen Besitzer drücken.

Seyn Sie, beste Mutter, meiner unwandelbaren Liebe und Achtung versichert.
Ihr Pflege Sohn
Joh. Böhl

27. Dorothea Campe, Braunschweig

Görslow den 24 Märtz 1810

Ich danke Ihnen, beste Pflegemutter, herzlich für die baldige Beantwortung meines Briefes, und freue mich, daß Sie von der Aufrichtigkeit meiner Gesinnungen überzeugt sind. Der erste Unterricht im Lesen, Schreiben und Rechnen ist mir mit meinem Knaben sehr sauer geworden; jetzt aber daß wir darüber weg sind, geht es leichter, um so mehr da er geschwinde begreift und auch ein gutes Gedächtniß hat. Käme die Reise nicht dazwischen, so würde ich das Latein mit ihm bald beginnen, und meine Schuljahre wieder mit durchmachen – Meine Tochter mußte ich, der bey meiner Heirath eingegangenen Verpflichtung gemäß, in der katholischen Religion erziehen lassen, und dieses bestimmte mich für die in St. Cyr erzogene Französin, der ich mehr religiösen Sinn zutraute, als ich nachher bey ihr gefunden habe. Sie hat jedoch daselbst des Unterrichtes eines trefflichen französischen Geistlichen genoßen und da sie nun schon ihre erste Kommunion gehalten hat, so hoffe ich, daß der gute Grund auf lebenslang gelegt ist. Ich würde mich nun zwar leicht von ihr trennen können, allein da ich nicht weiß wie lange meine Abwesenheit dauern kann, so bin ich es der Mutter schuldig sie ihr wieder zuzuführen. Sie ist auch schon in ihrem vierzehnten Jahr, wo die Wachsamkeit einer Mutter immer nöthiger wird, und überdem habe ich es der Mutter und Großmutter seit langer Zeit so versprochen.

Den alten Froschmäusler besitze ich schon, und habe mich manchesmahl daran gefreut; zur Umarbeitung wie Vater es angefangen besitze ich leider nicht Talent genug. Mein Exemplar von dieser Umarbeitung ist in Cadiz geblieben; sollten noch welche vorräthig seyn, so schicken Sie mir doch gelegentlich eines an August Campe in Hamburg – Wer übrigens Schätze in dieser Gattung hat, ist der dortige Prof[essor] Eschenburg;[1] sollte man es ihm wohl anmuthen seyn können, einzelne Bände auf ein Paar Wochen zum excerpiren zu überlassen?

Von der unsinnigen Anklage der Bayern ist mir noch nichts zu Gesicht gekommen; ich habe aber darum geschrieben. Mir ist dieses um so unerklärbarer, da in meinen Augen die katholische Religion nie einen größeren Feind als eben den großen N[apoleon] gehabt hat. Er erschüttert sie recht in ihren Grundvesten, und wenn er lebt, so haben wir sicher noch von ihm eine Vereinigung zu erwarten in welcher unter katholischer Form eine Art Kalvinischer Dogmatismus alles eigentliche Christenthum (GefühlsReligion) zu vernichten streben wird. Die wahren Mystiker werden dann aber, so wie sie es immer gethan haben, das heilige Feuer unter der Arche bewahren, bis es wieder erlaubt seyn wird, auch öffentlich, das Ewige dem Zeitlichen vorzuziehen.

Haben Sie von Schellings Untersuchung über die menschliche Freyheit gehört?[2] Es ist ein wunderbares Ding, und fällt mir hiebey ein, weil die GrundIdeen ganz mystisch sind, und nur auf eine andere Weise deduziert werden. Ich kann mich darüber ärgern, daß die neueren Philosophen immer so vornehm auf die Mystiker herab sehen, da sowohl Fichte[3] als Schelling ihre Grundansichten daraus genommen haben, besonders aus dem uralten Büchlein von der Teutschen Theologia.[4]

Den Tod Ihrer lieben Auguste empfand ich damals sehr schmerzlich; ich erinnere mich des kleinen freundlichen Geschöpfes noch, als wenn es vor mir stünde; möge der Knabe der ihre Stelle ersetzt hat, Sie desto länger erfreuen. Ich freue mich der unermüdeten Thätigkeit des guten Vaters; sein Wörterbuch muß ihn jetzt den deutschen Männern so werth machen, wie seine früheren Schriften der Jugend gethan haben. In Ihre Wünsche für Ihre Minna stimme ich von Herzen ein; unterdessen bleibt Ihnen der Genuß ihrer Liebe. An Trapps Schicksal nehme ich herzlichen Antheil. Ich wiederhole die Versicherung der wärmsten Anhänglichkeit an Sie und alle lieben Ihrigen und unterschreibe mich stets

Ihr liebevoller Sohn
Böhl v: Faber

28. Nikolas Heinrich Julius, Hamburg

Görslow, den 6 April 1810

Ich danke Ihnen herzlich für Ihre Zuschrift vom 27. März; ich fühle innigst was Sie sagen und habe längst mein Ziel in Hinsicht der Bedürfniße des Herzens, in eine andere schönere Welt gesetzt. Nur möchte ich wissen wie ich (und vielleicht auch Sie) dazu gekommen bin, dieses Bedürfnis zu verspüren? Ich habe diese Sehnsucht des Herzens nicht von meinen Eltern, meine Erziehung ist ganz praktisch gewesen, ganz irreligiös, meine Umgebungen in der großen Welt ganz die gewöhnlichen, und doch hat von der frühesten Erinnerung an, mein Herz gebrannt, bald von düstrer, trüberer, bald von hellerer wärmerer Flamme! Mein innerstes Wesen ist also etwas bestimmtes, angeborenes, dem (der gemeinen Meinung zuwider) kein Äußeres hat Abbruch thun können. Lange habe ich dieses geahnet, aber nicht gewagt es auszusprechen, biß sich in den unvergleichlichen Wahlverwandtschaften S[eite] 310 fand:[1] Und so finden wir die Menschen, über deren Veränderlichkeit so viele Klage geführt wird, nach vielen Jahren zu unserm Erstaunen unverändert, und nach äußern und innern unendlichen Anregungen <u>unveränderlich.</u> – daß diese innerliche Unveränderlichkeit vollkommen wohl bey sehr verschiedenen Erscheinungs und Äußerungs–Arten bestehen könne, brauche ich <u>Ihnen</u> nicht zu sagen. Es hängt diese Materie zusammen, mit der Lehre von der Freiheit, der Gnade und Prädestination, womit ich diese letzten Tage beschäftigt habe. Ich lese jetzt Schelling seine Abhandlung zum zweitenmahl; es sind wunderbare Sachen darin. Einzeln verstehe ich jeden Satz ganz wohl, aber mein Kopf ist nicht stark genug den Faden zu behalten. Was mich am meisten darin freut, ist seine Übereinstimmung mit den Mystikern, obwohl er dem Zeitgeist huldigend an andern Stellen auch die Religion des Gefühls schimpft. Seine meisten Resultate sind mystische Aussprüche, nur daß er sie auf einer anderen sehr scharfsinnigen Weise deduzirt. Nachher habe ich gerne ausfinden wollen, worin sich Augustinius[2] oder vielleicht Bossuet[3] nach ihm, von Jansensius[4] und Calvinus[5] in der Lehre von der Gnade unterscheiden: ganz bin ich nicht damit aufs Reine gekommen. Soviel wird mir klar, daß die Päbste ganz richtig sowohl den übertriebenen Rigorismus der Jansenisten und Calvinistischen Lehre, als die zu kecken und stolzen Lehren des Molinos[6] von den natürlichen Kräften des Menschen, vedammt haben.

Ob dieses Sie gerade interessieren wird, weiß ich nicht; ich fühle aber eine Art Bedürfniß mich mitzutheilen. Ich entbehre diese Befriedigung schon lange. Sie brauchen also auch gar nicht darauf zu antworten; es genügt mir davon überzeugt zu seyn, daß Ihre Sinnesart der meinigen analog ist.

Die Ankündigung des Handwörterbuches[7] habe ich gerne gelesen; ich subscribire gerne für mich. Einen zweiten Subscribanten aber wurde ich Ihnen in ganz Mecklenburg nicht nachzuweisen wissen. Das 2te H[e]ft des Museums[8] habe ich mit Vergnügen durchblättert. Ob Docen[9] diese Messe wohl mit seiner Sammlung

Volkslieder herausrücken wird? Er scheint mir ein fleißiger Gelehrter und guter Kritikus, aber seinen poetischen Sinn traue ich nicht recht.

Ich erwarte seiner Zeit meine Leipziger Bescherung und und auch die Anzeige der Kosten um sie anzuweisen. Es versteht sich vom selbst, daß Sie von allen beliebigen Gebrauch machen können. – Mich wundert, daß Ihnen nicht einiges von Wasserhun[10] gefallen hat, in demselben Sinne nemlich wie Schirmer[11] oder Homburg,[12] wo eigentlich der Gedanke herrscht und in lieblichen Reimen und Silbentänzen verkleidet ist. Das mehr lyrische Volkslied steht weit höher; darin sind wir vollkommen einig.

Die Doubletten erfolgen bey Gelegenheit: noch kann ich einen Wernike[13] anbieten, wenn Sie ihn nicht schon haben – von Leander[14] aus Schlesien sagen der H[er]rn Haug und Weißer[15] in ihrer Anthologie: sein wahrer Nahme findet sich nirgends – Die Dissertation von Neumeister[16] habe ich nicht, werde sie aber aus Breslau erhalten, da ich sie unlimitiert aufgegeben – das bey Alberts Arien[17] stehende (In his multe Dachiana) ist wohl so zu verstehen daß viele Lieder von Dach[18] in diesen Arien komponiert stehen, aber nicht separat angebunden. Ich wiederhole daß Sie alles mitgenießen und mitgebrauchen sollen.

Oettinger[19] ist mir ganz unbekannt. Sie wissen jetzt ohngefähr was sich für mich schickt; ist es der Art, so senden Sie es mir gelegentlich mit. Von St Martin[20] habe ich nur die Erreurs [und] de la verité, sein erstes Werk welches nur zu weit ausholt, und seine Oeuvres posthumes in trefflichen einzelnen aber zu abgerißenen Sätzen. Nur dem Nahmen nach kenne ich Le tableau naturel, l'homme de desire, le nouveau homme, l'ecco homo, etc und einige Übersetzungen des J[akob] Böhme,[21] die notirt stehen um sie mir gelegentlich anzuschaffen. Welches Werk lesen Sie von ihm? St Martin ist ein eigentlicher Mystiker; Chateaubriand[22] nur ein gefühlvoller Dogmatiker. Bey Chateaubriand wird mir noch immer manchmahl, als wenn es ihm nicht recht Ernst wäre.

Sie sehen recht in welcher Abgeschiedenheit ich lebe, daß ich noch gar nichts von der bayrischen Sache weiß. Zeitschriften halte ich gar nicht mehr. Jakobi[23] kann doch unmöglich zu der anklagenden katholischen Partei gehören? – Perthes hat mir versprochen, mir bald die Akten zu senden. Meine Meinung über den Kath[olizismus] des großen Kaysers schrieb ich neulich an P[erthes]. In meinen Augen ist N[apoleon] ein arger Feind des Kathol[izismus], der ohne Hierarchie und Klöster bald zur Verstandes Religion hinabsinken wird.

Endlich habe ich nun auch einen Brief aus Kiel, mit vielen Entschuldigungen etc. daß ich <u>alles</u> erhalten habe und mit meinem Kaufe zufrieden seyn werde, und daß er es ehestens absenden würde. Sobald ich es erhalte und die Preise weiß, theile ich Ihnen das nähere mit.

So eben empfange ich Ihre Zeilen vom 4ten mit der unangenehmen Nachtricht, daß mit dem Theurdank[24] eine fatale Verwechselung vorgegangen sey. Ich lege ein Blatt bey, welches Sie so wie es ist nach Leipzig mit dem Buche senden können; es versteht sich, daß ich es auf alle Fälle bezahle. Sollte aber keine Vergütung zu erhalten seyn, so mag H[er]r Weigel[25] das Buch meinetwegen umsonst behalten, weil es wirklich für mich gar keinen Werth hat. Vielleicht ließe sich auch der Belauf bei einer andern Auktion wiederabziehen. Die übrigen Bücher bitte mir sobald möglichst p[er] Post senden zu lassen; ohne denen nemlich, die Sie noch durchzusehen wünschen. Zu der Adelung Gesch[ichte] der Narrheiten,[26] erwarte ich Nachrichten von manchen Weisen zu finden; die Aufklärer stellten alles auf dem Kopf, wie Sie wissen.

Ich weiß nicht, ob ich Ihnen schon von den Schriften der heil[igen] Teresa[27] gesprochen habe, die ich in der orig[inalen] spanischen Sprache besitze und in guten Stunden lese.– Ach! welche himmlische Seele! Es ist das höchste und schönste mystische Werk, welches ich biß jetzt kenne, selbst Molinos ist ein Schatten dagegen. Trauen Sie Ihrem Spanisch genug zu, so will ich Ihnen gerne einen Quartband von [damage] –

Ganz der Ihrige, B. v. F.

P. S. Sollte wohl eine absichtliche Vertauschung des Theurdank vorgegangen seyn?

29. Nikolas Heinrich Julius, Hamburg

Görslow 18 April 1810

Ich hoffe Sie werden mein letztes von 7 dieses wohl erhalten haben. Anbey schicke ich Ihnen von der Kieler Auktion

den Reinicke Voß[1] für	3 Mark,
den Landstörzer[2]	4 Schilling
	3. 4.
Unkosten und Porto	8
	3 Mark, 12 Schilling

Der Anakreon[3] ist nicht erstanden. Zu dem Reinicke Voß glaube ich Ihnen gratulieren zu können, weil er so schön konserviert ist; wenigstens würde ich ihn gerne zu dem Preise behalten. Der Landstörzer sieht schlecht aus, hat aber einen dritten Theil der meiner Ausgabe mangelt. Zugleich erfolgt der versprochene Schuppius[4] und der Liscow,[5] den Lauremberg[6] muß ich erst von einem andern Werke abtrennen lassen. Vielleicht erhalten Sie den mit dem Rachel[7] zusammen für wenige Schilling in dortiger Auktion vom 25 dieses. S[eite] 40 N[ummer] 317 –

Zu dieser Auktion (auf dem Einbeckschen Hause) bin ich so frey einen kleinen Auftrag zu beyzulegen. Wenn Sie selbst nicht hingehen so übertragen Sie die Commiß[ion] wohl an Rueppprecht.[8]

Von Kiel habe ich nur einige alte Reisebeschreibungen, und das heilsame Gewisch Gewasch von Ab[raham] a S[an]ta Clara[9] erhalten welches sich durch schöne eingedruckte Kupfer auszeichnet; sonsten etwas von Swedenborg[10] (in desse Vorrede ich den Würtemberger Oettinger als Liebhaber von Sw[edenborg] lese, und Herausgeber von Sw[edenborg] und anderer irdischen und himmlischen Philosophien. 1765, 2 Th[eile], 8°°[11] – und Frankf[urt] 1771 eingeführt finde) aber nichts poetisches.

Die Einlage bitte an Fr[iedrich] Perthes bitte zu übergeben – In großer Eile.
Ganz der Ihrige,
Böhl von Faber.

30. Nikolas Heinrich Julius, Hamburg

Görslow, den 24 May 1810

Wenngleich Ihre Briefe mir sehr viel Freude machen, so will ich Sie absolut an keine pünktliche Beantwortung binden, weil ich weiß daß Sie nicht allein Berufs Geschäfte haben, sonder auch überdies Ihre Zeit spalten und theilen müssen, um keinem Zweige Ihres vielumfassenden Geistes, seine Nahrung zu entziehen. – Ich möchte wohl eine tüchtige Geschichte des katholischen Lehrbegriffes haben; würde ich Sie wohl in Plank[1] finden? ich kenne nur seine herrlichen Worte des Friedens – die ersten Br[iefe] von Max Leineke[2] in N[ummer]1 des 5 B[andes] der Studien (N[ummer]2 habe ich noch nicht) sind mir sehr willkommen gewesen; es ist zwar nicht ganz was mir dunkel im Sinne liegt, aber es nähert sich doch. Desselben Symbolik aus der jetzigen Messe erwarte ich mit Ungeduld. Die Würdigung des J[akob] Böhme habe ich gerne gelesen; nächstens erhalte ich seine Schriften; ich glaube aber nicht daß ich in den Sinn werde eindringen können – Es ist sonderbar, daß ich wirklich Schellings Abhandl[ung] das erstemahl von hinten an gelesen habe, weil mir mehr um das Resultat, als um die Deduktion zu thun war; das zweitemahl, da ich von vorne anfing, bin ich stecken geblieben. Bey meinem geringen Maaße von Verstand bin ich befriedigt, wenn nur bewiesen wird, daß auch für den höheren Verstand nichts absurdes und sich selbst widersprechendes in den reinen mystischen (eigentlich christlichen) Ideen liege, für deren Wahrheit mir mein Gefühl bürgt. – Aus der dortigen Auktion habe ich just das liebste erhalten. Hauptsächlich den Cyrano,[3] den ich Ihnen nochmals als Lecture nach Tische wegen seines (in der franz[ösischen] Litter[atur] einzigen) fantastischen Schwunges empfehle – Wie ich die liebevolle Empfehlung des Buches der Liebe[4] in den N[ordischen] M[iszellen][5] laaß, fiel ich von selbst auf Sie; ich besitze es natürlich und erbaue mich auch daran – Der Meßkatalog ist seiner Dickleibigkeit ohngeachtet in unserem Sinne mager. Ich hatte auf einen zweiten Theil des Buches der Liebe gehofft, auf die Uebersetzung des Kiämpeviser,[6] auf

Docens Volkslieder, auf v. Seckendorfs Nachlaß;[7] auch vermisse ich Fr[iedrich] Schlegel,[8] Tieck,[9] Kanne,[10] v. Schütz[11] (nicht als Dramatiker sondern als Lyriker wie in den herrlichen Romantischen Wäldern). Außer Ihren Angaben, muß ich noch anzeichnen: v. Arnims Armuth, Reichthum etc.[12] (ich hoffe noch immer daß v. Arnim, nachdem er sich erst selbst wird geläutert haben, etwas vorzügliches leisten wird) Fouqué der Held des Nordens (doch nicht Sigurd in anderer Form?)[13] Hebels Schatzkästlein,[14] Humboldts Versuch über Neu Spanien,[15] Matthisons Erinnerungen[16] (woraus artige Bruchstücke im Morgenbl[att][17] NB. ich ziehe M[atthisons] Prosa seiner Poesie vor), Maler Müller über den Rhythmus,[18] die Uebers[etzung] des Ginez Perez de Hita Guerras de Granada,[19] A[ugust] W[ilhelm] Schlegels Vorlesungen 2 Th[eil], 2 Abt[eilun]g.[20] – Unter den versprochenen werden Sie die endliche Fortsetzung des Bragur von Gräter[21] bemerkt haben.

Ihre Bestellung zu der Schweriner Auktion habe ich bemerkt; ich werde wenn das Wetter gut ist, wahrscheinlich selbst dabei seyn; auf 3 Nummern bin ich Ihr Kompetent, wir werden uns indessen wohl darum vertragen.

Ich habe nun einen ganzen Sammelwurf aus der Stader Auktion erhalten, die nicht das Portho wert sind. Ich glaube nicht, daß ich künftig mehr Bücher nach dem Titel verschreiben werde. Aber stellen Sie sich vor: Erckers unterirdische Hofhaltung,[22] ich dachte an das Teufelskreis, und erhalte eine BergwerksBeschreibung – Bibel der Natur Amst[erdam] 646 eine holländische Uebersetzung der bekannten Vertheidigung des Christenthums von Mornay[23] – die wohlangefüllte Kunstquelle; Rezepten. Miraculoso Glorisonti, eine Uebers[etzung] des Prevot Mem[oir]s d'un homme de qualité[24] – Apollos Geheime Schreibekammer 661 (man hätte nicht Gedichte vermuthen sollen) Uebers[etzung] einer politischen Schrift des Bocalini[25] und sofort. Gute Sachen dagegen sind: Bruckers Ehren Tempel der deutschen Gelehrsamkeit mit 50 trefflichen Küpfern[26] – Spatens Deutscher Sprachschatz 1691[27] – die wegen ihrer Seltenheit so berühmten Pasquillorum tomi duo [illeg.] 1544[28] für 4 Mark – Die Briefe des Guyon[29] 4 Bände für 5 Schilling. Poives Pratique[30] – Koddige en ernstige Upschriften[31] Amst[erdam] 698 – Prätorius Buch des Blocksberges.[32]

Hätte ich Ihren Brief nicht erhalten, so würde ich Ihnen den Schweriner Katalogus gesandt haben; ich hoffe Sie unterlassen nicht mir Bücher Verz[eichnisse] zuzusenden, wenn sie Ihnen vorkommen. Auf d[en] 18 Juny habe ich eines von Lübeck und eines von Bremen. Von alten Sachen kommt nur der Reineke Fuchs die Ausgabe von 1592 mit guten Holzschnitten in beyden vor, und dann der Gänse König,[33] den ich haben muß. Wenn Sie etwas haben wollen, so tragen Sie mir es nur auf, da ich ohne hin komittieren werde, und daselbst Bekannte habe.

Noch immer weiß ich nichts von meinem kleinen Auftrag nach Stuttgardt durch Perthes; der Verkauf war d[en] 1 Febr[uar]; auch nichts von Leipzig durch denselben, zu der Auktion vom 9. April. Haben Sie Gelegenheit, so bringen Sie es in Erinnerung.

Den Gr[af] Moltke auf Nütschau[34] kenne ich gar nicht; da ich aber bald in seiner Nachbarschaft einige Tage zubringen werde, so interessiert es mich sehr etwas von ihm zu wissen, um seine nähere Bekanntschaft entweder zu suchen oder zu meiden; in dieser Hinsicht bitte ich diesen Brief d[en] 1 oder 2ten des nächsten Monaths, wenn auch nur mit ein paar Zeilen, zu beantworten.

Haben Sie eine detail[lierte] Nota der Bücher die für mich den 5 Febr[uar] in Leipzig erstanden sind erhalten, so möchte ich wohl eine Abschrift davon haben, weil ich die Preise gerne anschreibe; wo nicht ist es aber nicht der Mühe werth darum zu schreiben; es soll mich wundern was H[er]r W[eigel] wegen des falschen Theuerdanks antworten wird.

Ganz der Ihrige,
Böhl von Faber

31. Nikolas Heinrich Julius, Hamburg

Görslow den 4 Juny 1810

Ich danke Ihnen für die geschwinde Beantwortung meines letzten Briefes; die Bekanntschaft des Gr[afen] Moltke werde ich nun nicht so geschwinde machen können, als ich glaubte, weil sich meine in dieser Woche nach Holstein projektirte Reise zerschlagen hat. Ich habe gehört, daß da sich dieser geschätzte Mann gänzlich der Erziehung seiner Söhne widmete und dieselben jetzt nach Universitäten begleiten wolle, auch darum sein Gut Nütschau auf 25 Jahren verpachtet habe. Ich gehe nun Morgen mit meinem Schwager nach seinem Gut Thurow bey Ratzeburg, und werde daselbst in Gesellschaft meiner Eltern (die sich von Hamburg dahin begeben) das Pfingstfest zubringen. Mittwoch den 13 bin ich auf Görslow zurück, und werde dann wohl bis Sonnabend allein und mein eigener Herr seyn; wenn Sie nun auf Ihrer Retour von Holstein über Schwerin gehen, und bey mir ein paar Tage zubringen wollten, so würden Sie mir einen ächten Beweis Ihrer Freundschaft geben, und mich sehr glücklich [deletion] machen. In Schwerin finden Sie jeden Augenblick ein Boot, das Sie in ¾ Stunde zu mir bringt; wenn ich Ihre Ankunft zum voraus weiß, kann ich Sie auch abholen lassen. Können Sie jetzt nicht abkommen, so ist es vielleicht später möglich; ich werde Ihnen schreiben, sobald ich meine geräuschvollen Hamburger Gäste wieder loos bin.

S[eite] 277 des Meßkatalogus werden Sie die Ankündigung der Fortsetzung von Bragur finden. Der Tannhaüser[1] ist in dem Wunderhorn[2] aus dem Prätorius biß auf einige orthographische und grammatikalische Änderungen genau abgedruckt; von Liedern findet sich nichts weiter darin; wohl aber noch etliche Reime über den Hexenkram, woran ich nichts finde, und ein Fragment eines Hochzeit Scherzes von Sylvander Philosethus,[3] das besserer Art ist – Aus Kornmanns Mons Veneris[4] (wo der Tannhaüser völlig gleich lautend steht) ist das Lied: Zu Eulsberg hat mich

Kladte Wunderh[orn] 2ter Th[eil] S[eite] 254 ohne Veränderung entlehnt. Ich finde noch darin die Geschichte des Hammelnscher Rattenfängers,[5] die ich mich nicht entsinne im Wund[erhorn] gesehen zu haben, auch einige aus der grimschen Mythologie,[6] die Sie hoffentlich selbst in Augenschein nehmen werden.

Ich habe noch keine Nachricht von Perthes wie es mir mit meinem Auftrage vom 9 April in Leipzig ergangen ist. Den Katalog vom 12 July daselbst wird mir ja Perthes wohl schicken. Den Bremer Catalogus finden Sie hierbey zum behalten, da ich noch meinen habe; auf die angeschriebenen N[ummer] habe ich Auftrag ertheilt. Der Lübecker ist in Hinsicht älterer Sachen ganz unbedeutenden

Eine große Kiste von der Hannover Auktion habe ich nun auch erhalten und bin sehr damit zufrieden. In einzelnen Bändern habe ich nun den Jacob Böhme komplet, die niedliche Amst[erdamer] Ausgabe von 1682 und die schönen Kupfern alle in Pergament gebunden, und wohl konditionirt, zusammen, 3 Thaler 13 Groschen und noch obendrein von derselben Ausgabe Signatura verum, die Apologien und der Weg zu Christo,[7] in einem Lederband für 21 Groschen. Bey der alten weisen Exempel, 1545 fanden sich angebunden Petrarcha Gedankbuch 1541, Frontini Kriegsanschläge[8] 1542, J[ohann] Boccati Hystoribuch[9] 1541 mit schönen Holzschnitten, das Angeli Cherubinischer Wandersmann[10] der mir in [illeg.]heim zu 2 Thaler entging habe ich für 2 Kreutzer erhalten, und sehr gerne gelesen. Arnolds mystische Theologie[11] und viele Werke Poivets haben mir Freude gemacht, so wie das Tersteegens Lebensbeschr[eibung] heiliger Seelen.[12] Zu den perraris gehören: die Pucelle von Chapelain,[13] ein Belon observations,[14] seder olam[15] und verschiedene Jesuitica.

Die Schweriner Auktion ist nun auch über; Sie haben daraus erhalten

Dahnerts Wörterbuch[16]	34 Schilling.	Die in dem beygehenden Packete erfolgen.
Histoire de Louis XI[17]	25 Schilling	
L[ouis]-P[ascale] Jullian[18]	15 Schilling	
Orlando inamorato[19]	47 Schilling	
	7 Mark 9 Schilling	

Von den anderen die Sie beordert haben, ist mir nur den Placcius[20] geworden, den ich 2 Thaler 6 Schilling aufgegeben hatte und den ich zu 46 Schilling erhalten. Für mich habe ich nur noch c[irc]a 8 Thaler angelegt und hauptsächlich dafür erstanden: die Bible de l'Ours[21] (2 Mark) die Wertheimer Bibel[22] (8 Schilling) Seb[astian] Münsters Kosmographey[23] (35 Schilling) Gottfrieds Archontologia[24] (36 Schilling) Garzoni allgemeiner Schauplatz[25] (mit schönen Holzschn[itten] v. [illeg.]) (26 Schilling) Parnaße Satyrique[26] 21 Schilling, Le moyen du parvenir[27] 14 Schilling, Gramondi historia Galliae[28] 36 Schilling und mehrere lateinische rara zum aufstellen.

Ich danke für die Specification der erstandenen Bücher; den Adam und Eva habe ich noch nicht erhalten; sollte es wohl bey Ihnen od[er] Perthes liegen geblieben seyn? – In der angenehmen Hoffnung Sie bald bey mir zu sehen verbleibe ich
Ganz der Ihrige
Böhl v: Faber

32. *Nikolas Heinrich Julius, Hamburg*

Görslow, den 16 Aug[ust] 1810

Ich mag es gar nicht, bester Freund, daß Sie sich wegen Ihres Stillschweigens gegen mich entschuldigen; es würde mich drücken, wenn ich Sie an pünktliche Erwiderungen gebunden glaubte. Auch würden Sie, ohne Ihren lieben Brief, schon wieder etwas von mir gelesen haben, wenn ich nicht 14 Tage in Holstein und Lübeck gewesen wäre. Ich habe von daher nur <u>einen</u> schönen lebendigen Eindruck mitgebracht; nemlich die Predigt des reformirten Pastor Geibels[1] am 5ten dieses: es war eine ächt christliche Rede aus dem Herzen und ging zu Herzen. Die Inbrunst des Gebetes war fast zu ergreifend für den öffentlichen Gottesdienst; dennoch habe ich niemand gefunden der ihn, <u>in dem rechten Sinn</u>, gelobt hätte.

Mit dem Vaterl[ändischen] Mus[eum][2] bin ich sehr zufrieden, und fände es ein großes Publikum, so ließe dieses auf vieles Gute schließen, wenigstens in der Gesinnung. Der Aufsatz N[ummer] 2 hat mich sehr befriedigt, als J[ean] P[aul] Produkte es gewöhnlich thun. N[ummer] 3 ist derb aber tröstlich wahr, und muß jeden denkenden Kaufmann tief angesprochen haben. Als Resultat erscheint mir leider nur, daß auf solcher studierten Schlichtigkeit keine Erlösung hienieden mehr statt finden kann. N[ummer] 4 ist herrlich, nur im Anfang wohl etwas zu spitzfindig und weiterhin ungerecht gegen den Katholizismus. Das <u>Verlorene</u> ist allerliebst. – Im 2ten Stück ist der Aufsatz von Heeren sehr schön und ruht an seiner Stelle, aber die Krone der Ganzen sind <u>für mich</u> die Reflexionen; es scheint mir diesen kräftigen Manier bekannt zu seyn; nur weiß ich nicht von woher. <u>Dürfen</u> Sie den Verf[asser] verrathen, so melden sie ihm mir. Ich sehne mich nach der Fortsetzung besonders nach der Entwicklung von dem was eigentlich <u>deutsche Art und Sitte</u> sey. Denn wenn es so wichtig ist daß sich eine bestimmte <u>öffentliche Meinung</u> über das Deutsche bilde, so muß das ächt Deutsche in jeder Hinsicht hervorgezogen und dem Publikum vorgehalten werden. Für deutsche Kunst, ja für deutsche Poesie ist etwas gethan, was aber für deutschen Karakter, deutsche Sitte, deutsches Leben??? – Dürfen Sie auch alte deutsche Lieder aufnehmen, oder müssen Sie fürchten, die Klassiker zu erzürnen? –

Was ich in früheren Jahren über Spanien aufgesetzt habe, theile ich Ihnen gerne mit, allein Sie werden finden, daß es sich nicht für Ihre Zwecke eignet. Es ist eine heitere Ansicht der geselligen Verhältniße, ohne tieferes Eindringen. Ich habe es umschmelzen wollen, allein bey genauer Prüfung gefunden, daß ich wirklich nichts mehr von Spanien aus eigener Erfahrung weiß; das eigentliche innere Spanien bin ich immer nur durchflogen und meine Ansicht paßt sich nur auf den andalusischen Winkel, der von Fremden bewohnt, auch schon viel fremdartiges angenommen hat. Sie werden sich indessen durchaus von meinen guten Willen überzeugen; es soll baldigst anfolgen.

Meine letzten Analekten aus alten Bücher beziehen sich fast nur auf Mystik. Machen Sie doch einen kleinen Aufsatz über wahre und falsche Mystik, und entwickeln Sie uns die Gründe des Haßes gegen diese stille innere Religion, die niemandem im Wege stehen kann.

Ich gratuliere zu dem Dach; von deutschen Sachen habe ich neuerdings nichts wichtiges erhalten, mehr von Latein[ischen] rarit[a] auch etwas alchemystisches. – Aus der Bützower Auktion hoffte ich manches zu erhalten, wenn (wie zu vermuthen steht) es wohlfeil weggeht. Wenn Sie Auktionsverzeichniße erhalten, so senden Sie sie mir doch zu; von der Göttinger Auktion habe ich nichts gewußt.

Ich habe kürzlich Schubert Ahnungen einer allgemeinen Geschichte des Lebens[3] gelesen: das ist ein gewaltiges Buch, bey dem mir oftmals geschwindelt hat. Ich kann zwar seine Hauptansicht nicht zu der meinigen machen, allein die scharfsinnige Zusammenstellung so mancher facta hat mich sehr ergötzt.

Die sonderbare Lage in welcher sich Cadiz befindet, hat meine Reise dahin vereitelt, und so lange es so bleibt, werde ich auch nicht reisen können. Wir sehen uns also wahrscheinlicherweise diesen Winter in Hamburg wieder und ich freue mich recht darauf, sich einmahl wieder ansprechen zu können. –

Ganz der Ihrige,

B v F

33. Dorothea Campe, Braunschweig

Görslow den 1 Sep[tember] 1810

Ich hoffe, theuerste Pflege Mutter, daß Ihnen mein letzter Brief vom 24 Märtz wird richtig zugekommen seyn – Meine schon so lange entworfene Reise nach Spanien, ist durch die wunderbare Lage von Cadiz bis jetzt aufgehalten worden, und da diese sich wahrscheinlicherweise vor's erste auch noch nicht ändern dürfte, so werde ich diesen Winter wohl noch hier zubringen.

Mein Sommer ist mir sehr angenehm verstrichen; ich und meine Hausgenoßen sind immer wohl gewesen und wir haben uns einer guten Erndte zu erfreuen. Meine Tochter ist bey meiner Schwester, wo bey mehreren Kindern eine Anweiserin zu weiblichen Arbeiten und ein Hauslehrer gehalten werden; auf diese Weise kommen wir öfterer zusammen. Meinen Knaben habe ich fortgefahren zu unterrichten, wenngleich es mir sehr sauer wird. Man hat mir kürzlich zu einem

Hauslehrer den dortigen emigrirten Abbé Lequeue empfohlen, weil der Verlust seiner Pension ihn zwingen wird eine Stelle zu suchen. Ich wende mich deshalb an Sie, um zu erfahren was dieser Mann sey und welche Kenntnisse er besitze. Sie wissen daß ich die Verpflichtung auf mich genommen habe meine Kinder in der katholischen Religion erziehen zu lassen; über diesen Punkt wäre also keine weitere Aufklärung nöthig, sondern nur über gründliche Kenntniße des Lateinischen, sonstige Wissenschaften, musikalische Talente, Alter, Gesundheit, Charakter etc. Wenn Sie ihn auch nicht selbst kennen, so werden Sie doch über Ihre Freunde das Nöthige darüber erfahren können; welches ich mir ungesäumt mitzutheilen bitte.

Meine Frau ist von den Franzosen in Chiclana überrascht geworden, und befindet sich seitdem mitten im Lager; ich erhalte ziemlich öfters Briefe von ihr, durch Vermittelung eines bei ihr einquartirten Generals, der sich sehr artig bezeigt. Grobe Ausschweifungen scheinen daselbst nicht vorgefallen zu seyn; nichtsdestoweniger sind ihre Gesinnungen so patriotisch, daß sie sich mit Leib und Seele aus dem besiegten Lande herauswünscht, und ihre Entfernung mehr wie je bereut. Meine Handelsverhältnisse erlauben mir jedoch noch nicht, der Niederlassung in Cadiz auf immer den Rücken zu wenden. Ich will nicht unterlassen etwas über den Gang meiner Geistesthätigkeit hinzuzufügen; aus der Mystik bin ich so ziemlich wieder heraus: es ist eine wunderbar große Erhebung, derer ich mich nicht fähig fühle. Deutsche Sprache und Litteratur (hauptsächlich des 17. Jahrhunderts) interessiert mich aber immer mehr. Jeden Theil des großen Wörterbuches empfange ich also auch immer mit Jubel und Dank gegen die unermüdeten Verfaßer dieser herkulischen Arbeit – Ob Sie es wohl durch Ihre Freundschaft mit dem Prof[essor] Eschenburg möglich machen könnten, daß er mir einige seiner alten poetischen Schätze zum excerpiren auf einige Wochen überließe, wünsche ich sehnlichst zu erfahren.

Ich bitte alle Mitglieder der Familie und Hausgenoßen bestens zu grüßen, und mich mit unwandelbarer Liebe und Dankbarkeit zu glauben

Ihren treuen PflegeSohn

Böhl v. Faber

In 14 Tagen erwarte ich Johannes Schuback mit seiner Familie zum Besuch; vorigen Herbst war ich bey ihm in Witmold. Wir werden uns Ihrer und der JugendJahre öfters erinnern.

– Der erbetene Neue Froschmäusler ist nicht erschienen. –

34. Nikolas Heinrich Julius, Hamburg

Görslow, den 5 Sept 1810

Ich beantworte Ihr Liebes vom 29 August; es freut mich und macht mich stolz, daß meine Ansicht der erstandenen Aufsätze des N[ordischen] M[iszellen] mit dem

Ihren und P[erthes] seinen übereinkommt. Ich habe in Schwerin mehr Gelegenheit gefunden, als ich es vermeinte, meine Ansicht laut werden zu lassen, und verzweifle nicht an der Zündung manches Funkens. Besonders hatte ich mit dem Minister v. Brandenstein[1] eine Unterredung, wobey mir das Vergnügen ward, auf scheinbarem Einwürfen meinen eignen Sinn in seiner Beantwortung zu vernehmen; er läßt dem Zweck des Vat[erländischen] M[useums] die gänzliche und verdiente Gerechtigkeit wiederfahren, und wird sich sehr dafür interessieren.

Bey den Reflexionen habe ich wohl an G[örres]–[2] gedacht, allein so sehr wie ich ihn liebe, traute ich ihm doch nicht eine solche Klugheit und Bildung zu; gewöhnlich ist mir bey ihm, unter der Menge der herrlichen Bilder der Gedankenfaden verlorengegangen; er war mir mehr Dichter als Philosoph; in den Refl[exionen] ist er beides und das im vorzüglichstem Grade.

Ueber deutsche Lieder müssen wir uns noch näher verabreden ehe wir unser Licht leuchten lassen. Haben Sie einen Plan so theilen Sie mir ihn mit, jetzt oder im Winter in Hamburg. Ich habe einen doppelten Plan 1) von einer Sammlung aller guten alten Lieder, nach Fächern geordnet, in doppelten Kolonnen Gr[öße] 8 wie das Buch der Liebe, auf welche Weise sich in einem Alphabeth 6 a 700 Lieder zusammendrängen liessen; Auslassungen würde ich mir erlauben, auch kleine Änderungen, aber die original Zeile stünde jedesmahl in einer Note darunter. Ich mochte folgende Fächer: Balladen, Romanzen, Liebeslieder, Lebenslieder, Trinklieder, Hirtenlieder, Jagdlieder, Kriegslieder, Oden (in dem Sinne von lehrenden filosophischen Lieder), Scherzlieder, und in einem Anhang Christliche Lieder. Vielleicht etliche Blätter Melodien bloß für die Stimme, theils alte, theils angepaßte, mit Hinsicht auf den heutigen Geschmack. – Mein anderer Plan ist den Specimens of early english poets[3] ähnlich, oder den von Zacharia[4] und Eschenburg veranstalteten, nur leider so geschmacklosen Sammlungen. Von dem Dichtern werden die merkwürdigsten Lebensumstände angegeben, seine Werke verzeichnet, gleichzeitig Beurtheilungen angeführt, und allenfalls ein eigenes Urtheil motiviert. Dann folgen die Specimens oder das beste und eigenste der Gedichte. Anstatt aber mit Z[acharia] dem Opitz[5] allein einen ganzen Band ausfüllen zu lassen, konnte ein mäßiger Band wenigstens ein Dutzend Dichter umfaßen. Zu dem letzten Plan hört aber eigentlich eine sehr vollständige Büchersammlung, die man sobald nicht vorweisen kann.

Von dem trefflichen Fleming[6] habe ich die Ausgaben Jena 1666 und Merseburg 1685. Der Inhalt ist völlig gleich, nur ist der letze größer und besser gedruckt und die Rechtschreibung unverändert; ich erwarte eine Lübecker Ausgabe s. anno. Weiter habe ich von ihm lateinische Epigr[amma], die hiebey anfolgen, und daran weder Zacharia, noch Meister,[7] noch Schmidt[8] erwähnt (Mein Jördens[9] ist leider beym Buchbinder; dieser ist sonst das vollständigste). Sein Rubella[10] ist mir noch nicht vorgekommen – Haben Sie die erwünschten Werke nicht, und wollen mir den Entwurf Ihrer Lebensbeschreibung zusenden, so kann ich nachsehen ob

Umstände daraus nachzuholen sind. Zacharia ist der vollständigste und hat die gute Idee die Schiksale des [illeg] . . . durch Stellen aus seinen Gedichten zu erläutern. Man müßte eigentlich den Olearius[11] und Mandelslo[12] dabey haben, so würde man vielleicht die ganze Reise poetisch erläutern können. Ich hoffe diese Werke wohlfeil aus Bützow zu erhalten.

Ich lege noch bey: Weise[13] drey ärgsten ErtzNarren etc. Dieses hört Puhl in Altona, und können Sie es biß ich es Ihnen abfordere bey sich behalten. Ich wollte Sie auf das letzte angehängte Büchlein ohne Titel aufmerksam machen; vermuthlich ist es: <u>die zwey Hauptverderber</u> etc von Siegismund Gleichviel (unter welchen Nahmen Weise versteckt ist) Leipzig 1671 od[er] 73 od[er] 1710. Mir scheint es ganz geeignet in dem V[aterländisches] M[useum] (verkürtzt) wieder abgedruckt zu werden; mein Geschmack wird nur das Examen S[eite]68/74 auswarzen aber für das große Publikum müßten vielleicht die meisten Gedichte und einige derbe Späße wegbleiben. Ich würde es <u>Strafgeschicht</u> aus dem 17ten Jahrhundert nennen, und den Verf[asser] ganz verschweigen – Mich hat es unendlich vergnügt, mehr noch bey dem zweiten als bey dem ersten Lesen. Da Sie indessen Ihr Publikum besser kennen, so werde ich mich auch nicht wundern, wenn es unabgedruckt bleibt. – Haben Sie Zeit so lesen Sie auch die anderen Romane; die <u>Ertz Narren</u> scheinen mir besonders geglückt – die <u>klügsten Leute</u> haben dagegen schöne Gedichte im S[eite] 26. 234. 347. 362.

In Breslau bin ich wohl glücklich gewesen H[einrich] Alberts Arien sind lauter Lieder von Dach, Roberthin,[14] und andere Preußen mit den Melodien des geschiksten Organisten und Dichter Alberts. Die original Sammlung besteht aus 8 Th[eile] Fol[io]. Ich hoffte nur den ersten beyden in diesen Abruck zu erhalten und habe 6 Th[eile] darin gefunden, und das für 6 Groschen. – Die sehr rare Dissertation von Neumeister (ein alfabetisches Verz[eichniss] der Dichter des 17ten Jahrh[underts]) für 6 Groschen – den Abschatz für 10 Groschen – diesen zwey hatte ich unlimitirt bestellt. Dagegen habe nicht erhalten, das Picardische Gesangbuch[15] wofür ich 2 Thaler gesetzt hatte, die Zürichscher Streitschriften[16] 2 Thaler, Gottsched Neuste aus der anmuthigen Gelehrsamkeit[17] zu 8½ Thaler – Von den anderen erhaltenen Sachen, werde ich Ihnen noch Ansicht schreiben.

Die Ansichten der Nachtseite von Sch[ubert][18] habe ich seitdem gelesen und ist mir dabey die höhere Vollendung nicht entgangen; es hat mich erfreut nicht soviel von Verwesung darin zu finden, auch nicht auf die mir widrigen Gedanken von Gleichheit der Geschlechter zu stoßen. Was steht uns bevor, wenn wir (in der Wissenschaft) so fortgehen? Man schwindelt schon jetzt bey dem leisen Lüften des Vorhanges! – Ich vernehme genau, daß es derselben Sch[ubert] ist der die alten span[ischen] Gedichte hat abdrucken lassen. In dem 2t[en] Theil ist des Berceo[19] sein Ged[ichte] über die heil[ige] Jungfrau besonders schön, auch viele von den Romances – Warum schweigt er jetzt?

Ich danke für die übersandten Verzeichnisse, und hebe sie sorgfältig auf; nächstens werde ich mit einer Kommission beschwerlich fallen und hoffe daß es sowohl Sie als ich noch zeitig seyn werden.

Ich ersah den Inhalt des 3. Th[eil] des V[aterländischen] M[useums] – Wenn Ihre Betrachtungen auf das englische Amerika gehen, so fürchte ich fast daß ich nicht werde mitstimmen können. Es ist mir ein gräßliches Land, auf die schlechte Seite des englischen Charakters gegründet und durch keine englische Bürger Tugend beschönigt.

Von den Heidelb[erger] Jahrb[ücher][20] habe ich jetzt 15 Hefte gesehen, und mich an die beyden Rez[ensionen] v. A[ugust] W[ilhelm] Schlegel gelabt. Welche Ruhe und welche Klarheit! Ich kann mich nicht darin finden, daß er nach Amerika mit der Fr[au] v. Stael[21] gehen sollte, und warum läßt man auch so lange auf den Schluß seiner Wiener Vorlesungen warten? – Auch die Rez[ensionen] mit den Zeilen 11–3 sprechen mich an. Das 25 Heft werde ich bemerken.

Damit will ich mich die für heute Ihnen Andenken empfehlen . . . ja noch wegen des Winters. Mein Winter fängt mit Albertus Magnus den Tag St. Clemens 23 Nov[ember] an, also in der letzten Hälfte des Nov[embers] hoffe ich in der Stadt zu seyn.

Ganz der Ihrige,
Böhl v: Faber

Ich habe so vieles interessante dieser Tagen vogehabt, daß mein Auszug der spanischen Ber[ichte] noch nicht zu Stande gekommen ist, soll aber bald erfolgen.

35. Nikolas Heinrich Julius, Hamburg

Görslow den 15 Sep[tember] 1810

Ich fange an Ihr Liebes vom 12 dieses zu beantworten, worin einiges mich recht erquickt hat. <u>Wir gehen alle von unserem individuellen Gesichtspunkt aus</u>, wenn wir gleich alle nach demselben Ziele streben. Wie wahr und wie schön! Doch wird es mich in Hinsicht der alten Lieder etwas eigensinniger machen. Ich habe zwar noch niemand gefunden, dessen Gefühle und Geschmack so mit dem meinigen harmonisierte als Sie, allein in den feineren Abstufungen wenden wir doch wieder von einander ab. Ich denke eine Liste derjenigen Lieder mitzunehmen, die ich für die Sammlung tauglich halte, und dann können wir über jedes einzelnen debattiren. Ich möchte keine der gedruckten Sammlungen unbenutzt lassen, um in der Vorrede sagen zu können, man liefere hier für 1 Thaler die in einige Dutzend Bände zerstreute Lieder davon Ankauf 50 kosten würde, oder halten Sie es für <u>litterarisch</u> unerlaubt? – Aus dem 1 Theil von Docen besagen mir <u>nicht</u> N[ummer] 5. 6. 9. 10. 11. aus dem 2ten besagen mir <u>nur</u> N[ummer] 24 und 29. – Büschings und v. d[e]r Hagen Samml[ung] hat das große Verdienst der Melodien, sonst schienen sie mir darin mehr der Gemeinheit als der Gelehrsamkeit gefreut zu haben. Das Mission ist nur leider ganz philologisch. – Ihre Fächer stimmen doch mit den meinigen meist überein bis auf die Folge; Gott bewahre uns für scherzhafte Balladen! Balladen sind mir Erzählungen wie: Es spielt ein Graf mit einer Maid, Es ritt ein Ritter wohl durch das Rind, Ulrich und Änchen, Herr Oluf, Es liegt ein Schloß im Oesterreich, Es lauften zwey Sterne am Himmel, Erlkönig etc. Romanzen sind mir mehr Ergüße des individuellen Gefühls, die sich aber nun mittelbar an einem sichtlichen Gegenstand oder Begebenheit anschließen und dadurch zwischen den meist objektiven Balladen und den meist subjektiven Liedern in der Mitte stehen, wie: Sich ein Haas wie Röslein stehe, Es ging ein Mädlein zarte, Ich habs gesagt schon meiner Mutter, Nachtigall ich hör dich singen, Wohl unter einer Linde, Wär ich ein wilder Falke etc. Minnelieder würden gar nicht in meinem Plan gehören. Es ist etwas ganz anderes als was wir Lieder heißen; mit aller meiner Vorliebe für das Alte kann ich sie doch nicht ohne Anstrengung lesen, und schließe daraus auch die Mehrzahl.– Buchner[1] hat gesagt: 'Schlichte Wort und gut Gemuth ist das rechte deutsche Lied'. Dieses müßte das Epigraph der Sammlung seyn. – Die sogenannten Volkslieder bleiben immer das vorzüglichste und man möchte verzweifeln, daß wir von den übrig gebliebenen Sammlungen auch keine einzige zu Händen kriegen können (Ich habe jetzt einen neuen Versuch auf Eschenberg gemacht) Nächstdem folgen die Lieder der Opitzschen Periode, wenngleich schon mehr Reflexionspoesie doch noch ehrlich und ächt deutsch, wie Opitzens Ist irgend zu erfragen, Ich empfinde fast in Grauen, Wer sich auf Ruhm begiebet, mehere von Tscherning[2] etc. Hier glänzen auch die Preußen mit ihren trefflichen Dach und Roberthin. Bey der dritten Art sind es schon nicht mehr schlichte Worte sondern schöne Bilder. Wohlklang und Treibhaus Hitze, doch bey weitem noch kein Lohensteinischer Schwulst. Hier parodieren Schirmer, Leander, v. Abschatz,[3] und zum Theil schon Fleming und Homburg.[4] Wahrscheinlich rüht es von meiner innigen Bekanntschaft mit der spanischen Poesie her, daß mir diese Art wohlgefällt; ich habe es aber schon vorigen Winter gemerkt, daß Sie darin nicht so ganz einstimmten, und wenn Sie mir die Minnelieder opfern, so werde ich Ihnen dagegen alle südlichen Flammen, Sonne und Sterne schenken müssen. – Über die Weisen denken wir eins – Einige Veränderungen, hauptsächlich in Hinsicht der Paßlichkeit zum singen, lasse ich mir nicht nehmen, mit N. B. original Text in einer Note. – Ihre Bedenklichkeit bey den Anthologien verstärkt sich eigentlich auch auf die erste Sammlung, denn alle Opitzsche, Flemingsche, Dachsche etc. Lieder können wir doch nicht geben? Es käme ja aber vors erste nun darauf an den Geschmack an das ältere herzliche Deutsche zu erwecken und zu beleben, und dieses würde durch Vollständigkeit und die damit verbundenen Weitläuftigkeit und Aufwand nicht erreicht werden. –

Das zweite Projekt wäre mehr auf den Litterator berechnet und hat gar keine Eile; die Materialien dazu werde ich fortfahren zu sammeln, wenn auch nur zum Zeitvertreib.

Sie schreiben von Göttingen und München kommen zu lassen: kann man so etwas kommen lassen?, das ist mir ganz neu. Ich hatte schon gedacht einmahl nach Göttingen hinzureisen um zu ekzerpieren. Ich erwarte darüber Ihren Aufschluß.

Die 8 Th[eile] Fol[io] von Alberts Arien müssen sehr dünn seyn; auf jeder Seite ein Lied wie Ihr singende Rosen. In der Herderschen Auktion waren alle 8, die musikalische Kürbishütte[5] und die Sorgenlügnerin[6] in einem Band; glücklich wer ihn verstanden hat! Bey meiner Ausgabe steht bestimmt auf dem Titel daß alle Lieder des 6 Th[eile] Fol[io] darin enthalten sind. Es sind ganz herzliche Sachen darin, von der zweiten vorhin erwähnten Art und die Mel[odien] interessant, wenngleich für unser verfeinertes Ohr zu rauh. Ich werde sie und die erste Ausgabe des Opitz [und] den Logau[7] mitbringen; dagegen bitte ich mir diejenigen meiner Sachen zurückzusenden die Sie nicht mehr brauchen. Nach meinem Weckherlin[8] sehe ich mich schon lange vergebens um – Die Nachricht von Thiess ist mir neu und sehr interessant; was ich von Fleming weiß ist aus Jördens, der die Rubella verführt; sie kommt in der Bützower Auktion vor. Da ich aber nur 4 Schilling darauf gesetzt habe, so weiß ich nicht ob ich sie erhalten werde – das Picardische Gesangbuch habe ich von neuem in zwey Auktionen aufgegeben. Von dem Neumeister ist es gewiß nur ein Exemplar gewesen, welches doppelt aufgeführt war; in der Ungewißheit ob ich ihn erhalten würde und da mir so viel daran gelegen war habe ich ihn wieder nach Halle aufgegeben; wird er mir, so soll er für Sie seyn. Überzeugt bin ich leider in dem Fall, durch die so sehr verspäteten Auktions Berichte manches doppelt zu kaufen. Bey dem Analecten von Wetzel[9] müssen Sie mich überboten haben; ich hatte einen Thaler dafür gesetzt. Ich bin mit dem Breslauer Einkauf sehr zufrieden. Das merkwürdigste ist: Ein alter Thauler und Geyler[10] in einem Band, Weisens Schauspiele,[11] Reinecke Fuchs der Ausg[abe] v. 1662 in allerhand jetziger Zeit üblichen Reimarten, das Narrenschiff mit Geylers Predigten[12] darüber eine schöne Auflage v. 1574 mit trefflichen Holzschnitten, v. Kempii Madrigalen[13] (die ersten die ich habhaft werden kann; nach dem Bredelo,[14] Stockmann[15] und Caspar Ziegler[16] suchte ich vergebens) Anton Ulrich geistl[iche] Lieder,[17] Angeli geistliche Hirtenlieder,[18] letztere besonders schön, beyde mit Melodien; den einzigen herausgekommenen Theil des Opitz v[on] Bodmer,[19] v. Zesens Helikon[20] und seinen poetischen Rosenwälder Vorschmack, mit einigen merkwürdgien Liedern, die erste Edit[ion] des alten Gryph[ius][21] von 1663, vollständiger als die anderen, mit einem plattdeutschen Schauspiel, Hallmanns Schauspiele[22] mehr rar als gut etc. Vieles zur Litteratur der raren Bücher, worin ich mich der Kompletirung nähere. – Einen lateinischen Molinos kann ich Ihnen jetzt anbieten.

V. Abschatz nimmt einen ausgezeichneten Platz zwischen meinen 17 raren ein; er ist zierlich, lieblich, fein, artig und doch nicht ohne Herz; ich besinne mich Ihnen einige seiner kleinen Sachen in der Matthisonschen Anthol[ogie][23] gewiesen zu haben, Sie ergriffen es aber nicht mit meiner Vorliebe.

Ich sende Ihnen nun anbey mein original der spanischen Briefe; zum Abschreiben hätten mich meine alten Deutschen doch nicht kommen lassen. Was nicht zur Sache gehört habe ich durchstrichen. Ich hätte gern das ewige Beziehen auf die Persönlichkeit geändert, allem ohne das ganze umzustoßen, ließ es sich nicht machen, wie Sie es selbst auch finden werden. Ich wiederhole dabey, daß ein so leichtes Produkt sich gar nicht für den Ernst des Museums schickt, überlasse es jedoch Ihrer Willkühr, es ganz, stückweise, so oder geändert, oder gar nicht aufzunehmen, auch einzelne Ausdrücke, Sprachfehler oder Rechtschreibung nach belieben zu ändern. – Ich habe noch einige Briefe über das spanische Theater gefunden, die ich später schrieb und die auch etwas mehr Reife haben; ich muß sie aber erst aus dem spanischen übersetzen.

Hiebey auch meine Komission nach Freysinger und Fürth und da ich doch ein Packet machen muß, so gehen die Verzeichniße zugleich mit zurück mit vielen Dank. Die meisten Lieder haben Sie schon bestellt, und so habe ich mich auf andere Kurios und Holzschnitte gerichtet.

Das 3te Heft des Museums habe ich noch nicht erhalten – Größere Leute wie die Hamburger Philologen haben das neue Licht ersticken wollen und haben ihren Ruhm daran verbrannt. Man läßt ja den Herrn ihre Wortklaubereyen; warum wollen sie uns nicht fühlen lassen?

d[en] 16. So eben erhalte ich das 3te H[e]ft des Museums. Ich schließe in Eile, damit dieses morgenfrüh wegkomme.

B v F.

36. Dorothea Campe, Braunschweig

Görslow den 26 Sep[tember] 1810

Ihre werthe Zuschrift vom 13 dieses habe ich erst den 22 erhalten; ich danke zuförderst von Herzen für die gute Besorgung aller meiner Aufträge, und schreite dann zur Erwiederung – Die Bereitwilligkeit des H[er]rn Hofrath Eschenberg hat mich mit Freude erfüllt, und Sie finden demnach hiebey ein Verzeichniß derjenigen Werke, die ich vorzüglich zu benützen wünsche, und die ich seit verschiedenen Jahren auf den Auktionen vergebens zu erhalten suchte. Ich verlange sie nicht alle auf einmahl, sondern nach und nach; Ihre Buchhandlung übernimmt wohl die Emballage und Versendung p[er] fahrender Post, deren Kosten ich gerne vergüten werde, so wie auch des nöthigen Wachstüches, um alles naßwerden vorzubeugen.

Wenn es nicht zu unbescheiden ist, so bitte ich um eine baldige erste Sendung, um das immer mehr abnehmende Tageslicht noch zu benützen.

Die Spanische Litteratur des 17t[en] Jahrhunderts ist mir noch immer sehr lieb, nur gebricht es mir an Materialien, da leider meine große und auserlesene Bücher Sammlung von mehreren Tausend Bänden sich noch immer in Cadiz befindet. Analecta habe ich viele, allein man muß die Poesie kennen, um sich daran zu ergötzen; die Uebersetzer Talente eines Schlegels hat mir die Natur nicht verliehen, sonst würde vielleicht manches an das Licht getreten seyn.

Ich sehe ein, daß sich der Abbé Lequeue nicht zum Hauslehrer eignet, begreife nur nicht wie ein Baron Schultz (den ich nie habe nennen hören) davon unterrichtet seyn kann. Warum ich so sehr auf einem katholischen Geistlichen bestehe, ist weil ich die Absicht habe, daß er bey der Vereinigung mit meiner Familie zugleich dem katholischen Theil derselben die Meße lesen soll, wozu ich in meinem Hause alsdann eine Kapelle einrichten würde. Sie werden selbst einsehen, wie angenehm und fast nothwendig dieses auf dem Lande sey. Ich werde gerne erfahren, was Sie über den andern katholischen Geistlichen hören werden. Es ist jetzt sehr wahrscheinlich, daß meine Familie hier zu mir kommen werde, sobald sie es möglich machen kann; die Unruhen die jetzt in Spanien herrschen haben ihnen das Land gänzlich verleidet. Wenn sich dieses mit einer Aufhebung meiner Handlungsverhältniße verbinden ließe, so würden alle meine Wünsche erfüllt.

Zu derselben Zeit ungefähr, daß Sie sich mit der Frau über Nicolas Schuback unterhalten haben, habe ich es mit dem Bruder gethan, der mit seiner Familie zwey Tage bey mir zugebracht hat. Dieser Nicolas ist wirklich ein psychologisches Phänomen, und die Plage seiner ganzen Familie; er ist von einer merkantilischen Wuth ergriffen, die ihn nicht allein verleitet hat 300 000 Thaler die er von seinem Vater erhalten hatte zu verhandeln sondern noch 400 000 Thaler obendrein, die der Vater zur Ehre seines Nahmens in Paris für ihn hat nachbezahlen müssen. Dabey hat er sich allen Lebensgenuß versagt nur das nothdürftige zur Fristung des Lebens genoßen und sich beständig am Schreibepult geschmiedet. Jetzt wird ihm Ruhe und alle Bequemlichkeit bey seinem Bruder aus Witmold angeboten, ja sein Vater will ihm noch ein eigenes Gut kaufen, nur mit der Bedingung der Handlung zu entsagen, allein darauf will er nicht hören, sondern besteht darauf wieder nach Paris zu gehen, um das Verlorene wieder zu erwerben. Von einem solchen Menschen ist es auch nicht zu verwundern, daß er eine früheren Verhältniße außer Acht läßt. Seine Frau kenne ich nicht, habe aber schon lange ihre Lage bedauert.

Auf der Retour Reise von Carlsbad ist Aug[ust] Campes Frau mit ihrem Vater bey mir gewesen, und ich habe von ihr vieles von Vaters Aufenthalt in Carlsbad gehört; innigst bedaure ich es, daß das Bad diesesmahl keine Wirkung gehabt hat. Die guten Nachrichten von Viewegs habe ich gerne gelesen, so wie auch daß Sie selbst, beste Pflege Mutter wohl und munter sind welches ich Ihnen bis im hohen Alter von Herzen wünsche und damit verbleibe Ihr PflegeSohn

J. N. Bohl

Obwohl ich weit entfernt von Reichtum bin, so trage ich gerne ein Schapflein zur Linderung fremder Noth bey, und werde bey der ersten Retour Sendung von Büchern, etwas für Ihre Wittwen beylegen.

– Ich danke für den neuen Froschmäusler, der schon bey dem Buchbinder ist –

37. *Nikolas Heinrich Julius, Hamburg*

Görslow, den 13 October 1810

Ihr liebes Schreiben vom 25 Sep[tember] ist wegen einer Abwesenheit und häufiger Besuche so lange von mir unbeantwortet geblieben – Gerade weil in dem Wunderhorn so viel vorzüglich ist, scheint mir es schwer solches nicht zu benutzen. Unsere Absicht ist ja dem rechten Geschmack zu beleben und den Nicht Litteratoren für wenig Geld, das Beste darzulegen, was bis jetzt an Ausbeute gewonnen ist. Wie mancher käuft das Wunderhorn wegen des hohen Preises nicht! – Sie ärgern sich über die Verfälschungen,[1] ich noch mehr über die ständlichen burlesken Titel, die Voß[2] nicht besser hätte ausdenken können, um den guten Eindruck zu stören. – Aus Docen dürfen wir N[ummer] 6 und 20 wegen der Zweideutigkeit absolut nicht aufnehmen, obwohl mir letztens besonders lieb ist – Ihre Erklärung von Minneliedern und Buhlliedern genügt mir völlig, und dürfte die letzte Klasse sehr arm ausfallen, da unser Zeitalter keine freie Ansicht der sinnlichen Liebe erlaubt, daher ich auch das Bräutlein seiner Naivität ohngeachtet, nicht für unsere Sammlung genehmigen kann. – Ich bemerke Ihre Erläuterungen über das Kommenlassen der Bücher; wahrscheinlich erhalte ich nächstens aus Eschenbergs Sammlung vieles wichtige worüber dann ein mehreres – Gottschalds Lieder Remarquen[3] habe ich jetzt doppelt; das eine Exemplar kostet nur 4 Groschen wofür Sie sie von mir erhalten können, ist aber auch nicht mehr werth – Von Kempii Madr[igalen] sind sehr mittelmäßig und nur litterarisch merkwürdig; Anton Ulrichs Lieder sehr matt. Angeli Hirtenlieder aber sehr schön so wie der Wandersmann welches Geistlich-mystische Sinngedichte sind, die ich mitbringen werde.

Die Briefe über das Theater sollen sobald möglich erfolgen; unterdessen sende ich Ihnen hiebey meinen nothwendigen Nachtrag zu Bouterweks Geschichte der englischen Poesie,[4] den ich wirklich aus Drang aufgesetzt habe, da ich so eben den letzten Theil des genannten Werkes erhalten hatte. Sehen Sie zu diesen Aufsatz irgendwo anzubringen, allenfalls in den Heidelberger Jahrbüchern; die Korrektur und Abründung bleibt Ihnen unbedingt überlassen

Ich freue mich sehr daß Sie von Görres[5] und anderen so viele Aufsätze für das Museum erhalten. Im 3 Hefte ist die gedrungene Darstellung des Karl Gustav v[on]

Bülow recht interessant; Ihre Betrachtungen sind mir sehr lieb auch ohne den Schmuck der schönen Sprache; ich habe einige Verwandschaft mit den Schubertschen Ideen mehr darin gefühlt, als ich es nachzuweisen wüßte – Der Aufsatz v[on] Villers ist ganz an seiner Stelle und ich freue mich ihn aus dem unbedeutenden Tagebuche wo er stand gerettet und wills Gott, vereinigt zu sehen – Der 4te Aufsatz habe ich noch nicht gelesen. Im 4ten Heft kann ich Ihnen nur von dem Br[ief] über Gripsholm und die Gedichte reden. Der Brief ist ein äußerst geistreiches Produkt und wird gewiß allgemein gefallen. Das Gedicht von Stollberg ist recht schön, erinnert nur zu sehr an Klopstocks Frühlingsfyer die doch höhere Begeisterung noch athmet, der Todtenkopf ist herrlich und des Verf[assers] vollkommen würdig.[6]

Von Adelung habe ich das Verzeichniß der vatikanischen Bibliothek, die aus Heidelberg dabei gekommen sind, aber keine Heidelberger. Sollte sich indessen von Lieder Sammlungen aus dem 16 und 17ten Jahrhundert mit oder ohne Musik daselbst etwas finden so würde ich gerne die Kosten des Abschreibens daran wenden. Neulich erhielt ich Draudii[7] Bibl[ia] Librer[ae] German[ica] Classica Frankfurt 1611 und finde darin nicht weniger als 276 musikalische Werke aus dem Ende des 16ten und Anfang des 17ten Jahrh[undert]s verzeichnet. Wo sind sie alle geblieben?

Ich bin neugierig auf Meisters Wanderjahre;[8] auf Schubarts Schriften[9] unterzeichne ich gerne, besonders wenn seine musikalischen Komposition[en] dabey seyn sollten – Auf dem spanischen Romancero von 1555[10] bey Hitzig[11] unterschreibe ich 6 Exemplare, ob ich gleich das kleine Format haße und lieber einen guten 8 Band dafür erhielte – Wenn meine spanische Bibl[iothek] einmahl herüberkommt wollen wir noch manches veranstalten – Das Schicksal des Dr. Norwich[12] vernehme ich ungern, doch bin ich mit dem Druck seines Theaters nicht zufrieden: bey kurzen Reihen muß man absolut gespaltene Kolumnen machen, um das Papier gehörig auszufüllen.

D[en] 14 früh – Diesen Morgen habe ich noch Claudius seinen Aufsatz gelesen: er ist mir ächt mystich und kann manche dürftige Seele, die mit den Feßeln der Zukunft ringt, auf halbem Wege entgegen kommen. Wird diese Sinnesart gut aufkommen, so kann sie den Weg zu noch herrlicheren Sachen bahnen, wozu ein Auszug aus der Teutschen Theologie gehören müßte – Ich schließe für heute

Ganz der Ihrige

B. v: F.

P. S. Zu der dortigen Auktion vom 22 Oct[obe]r im Einbeckschen Hause habe ich N[ummern] 5. 6.11.22.23. und 83 anderweitig aufgegeben. Wenn Sie hingehen und die Holzschnitte sind gut, so mögte ich sie wohl haben, so wie auch S[eite] 22. N[ummern] 50. 51. Thiess Gelehrtengeschichte.[12]

38. Nikolas Heinrich Julius, Hamburg

Görslow den 8 Nov[ember] [1810]

Bester Freund

Ich habe lange nichts mehr von mir hören lassen; das macht ich bin so sehr beschäftigt gewesen. Aus der Bützower Auktion habe ich neulich wieder 300 Bände zu Spottpreise erhalten; das ganze für 40 Thaler und frey von Fracht, da ich es selbst habe abholen lassen. Ich habe 14 Tage völlig gehabt, um eine Art raisoniertes Verzeichniß zu machen, welches 9 Bogen beträgt; das meiste sind rara und rarißima, nur leider wenig poetisches in unserem Sinn. Es zeichnen sich aus 10 alte Chroniken einige alten Kräuter und Naturbücher, ein alter Cardan,[1] die meisten Werke v. Weigels,[2] einige sehr rare Sociniana und Jesuitica, einige Inkunnabeln v[on] 1509/1512 Kuhlmanns Kühlpsalter,[3] eine duodez Ausgabe des Moscherosch[4] in 8 Bänden, viele Chymica und Alchymica etc. Zugleicher Zeit habe ich (was für uns noch wichtiger ist) eine Sendung von Eschenberg erhalten, woraus ich Ihnen pour la bonne bouche beygehendes Poetisches Lustgärtlein[5] mittheile, welches Sie behalten können biß es Ihnen selbst wieder abfordere; ich mögte indessen nicht daß jemand anders wüßte daß es aus des Pr[ofessor] Eschenbergs Bibl[iothek] ist. Zu Ihrer Nachricht dient daß ich alle Dachiana und Roberthiniana und Albert: die sich durch die Initialien auszeichnen selbst besitze und daß ich noch überdem 24 Stück für mich abgeschrieben habe, nemlich p. 80, 112, 149, 183, 119, 104, 109, 162, 179, 140, 142, 157, 31, 129, 59, 62, 73, 78, 188, 48, 114, 168, 189, 192. Dieses wird Ihre Excerpta sehr erleichtern. Ueber den Werth dieser mir bißjetzt ganz unbekanten Sammlung mündlich – Ich habe auch den Band erhalten, woraus Büsching verschiedenes in seiner Sammlung gegeben hat; mit der Nachlese bin ich jetzt beschäftiget: Sie sollen ihn auch zu sehen kriegen – ferner die fol[io] Ausgabe von Alberts Arien, den Dach (der nichts interessantes sondern nur Gelegenheits Gedichte, und kein einziges seiner schönen Lieder enthält) den Schwieger,[6] Lund,[7] Siebert[8] et alia wovon alles mündlich – Sie sehen also wohl daß mir die Zeit knapp werden muß, da ich leider die langen Abende nicht zu Hülfe nehmen kann –

Ihre Zeilen vom 13 8ten habe ich wohl erhalten. Der kleine Romancero aus Stuttgard ist lange das Geld nicht werth; ich werde mich künftig für illimitirte Aufträge hüten. Es sind einige artige mir sonsten ganz unbekante Rom[ances] zwischen mehreren bekanten von Lope de Vega,[9] Gongora[10] etc darin. Aus Göttingen haben Sie schöne Sachen erhalten: auf dem Schoch[11] und Kongehl,[12] die ich gar nicht kenne, freue ich mich. Aber der Hans Sachs[13] für 12 Mark das nenne ich Glück! So wie ich im addvertissement Blatt die Anzeige fand, trug ich es gleich auf, allein es war zu spät: Sie sind indessen der Einzige dem ich es gönne – An Perthes trage ich auf nichts mehr für mich abzusenden; meine Reise kann ich indessen noch nicht fortsetzen. Wahrscheinlich wird es sich wohl biß Anfang Dec[ember] hinziehen.

Bis dahin wie bekant
aufrichtigst der Ihrige
B. v: F.

39. Nikolas Heinrich Julius, Hamburg

Görslow den 28 Nov 1810

Ich würde Ihr Liebes vom 17 dieses lieber mündlich beantworten; allein ich kann noch nicht abkommen – die angezeigten Stellen habe ich in Maness[ischen][1] nachgelesen; auch die Zeile 'Starke Liebe heißet Meine' könnte als Epigraph unserer Minnelieder dienen

Wenn Sie dem Beytrag zum Bouterw[ek] wienerwärths[2] hinsenden, so mögte ich daß nur ein B darunter stünde. Es freut mich sehr daß er Ihnen gefallen hat; ich glaube daß ich das Rechte fühle, allein der Ausdruck steht mir nicht zu Gebot: meine ganze Natur ist überhaupt mehr passiv und haben die Seelen ein Geschlecht, so ist die meine sicherlich weiblich, weil sie sich nie glücklicher fühlt, als wenn sie den Willen eines geliebten Gegenstandes zu dem ihrigen machen kann.

Die 8°° Ausgabe von Moscherosch ist ansehnlich vermehrt und verbessert nur durch die Zesianische Rechtschreibung[3] verunziert. Die frühere 12 Ausgabe hat diese nicht. Was über den 14 Gesichter der 8°° Ausgabe ist hat M[oscherosch] selbst verworfen und dem ersten Ueberblick nach, sind alle diese Fortsetzungen auch nichts besseres werth.

Die Lieder Remarquen sollen Sie erhalten: Wetzels Analecta entbehre ich noch immer.

Ich bin gar nicht damit zufrieden, daß Sie in dem Poet[ischen] Lustg[ärtlein] so abweichend von mir angezeichnet haben; vielleicht aber sind es Dachs und Roberthins Sachen die ich schon aus Alberts Arien notirt hatte. Alles von Roberthin ist mir sehr lieb; Schade daß es so wenig ist.

Ueber Dach folgendes:

Neumeister sagt: Specimen autem venae Dachianae qui desiderat Hennr. Alberti Lustwäldlein. Ano regni item poetisches Lustgärtigen Chr Caldenbachii poeticon evolvat[4] – Ersteres sind wahrscheinlich die Arien, die vielleicht früher unter diesem Titel erschienen sind; wegen der verschiedenen Auflagen dieser Arien verweisen Gottsched und Jördens auf v. Baczko Preußische Geschichte,[5] welches ich nicht besitze.

Die zweite Quelle ist nun unser Poetisches Lustgärtigen welches aber wie Sie sehen schon Neumeister als anonym anführt; im Placcius und Mylius[6] habe ich vergebens danach gesucht. Ich halte den Verf[asser] des Anhanges für den

Herausgeber; ich hoffe daß Sie aus diesem Anhange nichts werden angezeichnet haben, denn mir ist er durchaus schlecht vorgekommen.

Im Büchersaal[7] steht zwar eine Alfabetische Liste aller Gedichte Dachs nach dem Vorrathe des Breslauer Arlet[8] sonst aber keine Werke vom ihm als die bekannten. Die Churbrandenb[urgische] Rose[9] hat in Hinsicht von Liedern keinen Werth.

Das 5te Heft des Vat[erländischen] Mus[eums] habe ich durch Güte eines Freundes gelesen. Der Aufsatz von Stollb[erg] hat meine gespanntesten Erwartung übertroffen; er ist herrlich durch und durch, und macht daß man seiner <u>Deutschheit</u> einmahl wider froh wird. Der Aufsatz von Meyer ist sehr interessant und brav geschrieben, der von Sartorius hat mich nicht sehr angesprochen, ich sehe aber daß ihn die Beziehungen wichtig machen. Von Fr[iedrich] Schlegel hätte ich mehr erwartet. Der Klopst[ock] Nachlaß ist herrlich, sowohl der Brief, als der schöne mystische Aufsatz, als auch die karaktisierenden Noten (von Ihnen oder von Perthes selbst?) – Unter den Gedichten hat mir das von Hegener am besten Gefallen[10] – Die Kinderlieder von Horstig[11] haben Sie wohl aus einer der letzten Auktion; ich hatte auch darauf bieten lassen, weil mir die kleinen Aufsätze von Horstig im Morgenblatt so wohl gefallen –

Die Beyträge von Orelli[12] habe ich Perthes zurückgeschickt, weil ich das Ital[ienische] nicht kundig bin und noch so viel durch zu arbeiten habe.

Mit dem Schwieger bin ich nun durch: Eschenberg hat ganz recht, daß die Geharnschte Venus sein vorzüglichstes Werk ist, und in den übrigen sein Geist sich nur sparsam zeigt. Auch Lund und Sieber die mir wenig Ausbeute gegeben haben. Merkwürdig ist Greflinger;[13] am merkwürdigsten aber das alte Weckherlin den ich am meisten bedaure nicht selbst zu besitzen, da sich doch nicht alles abschreiben läßt.

Uebrigens drängt sich mir immer mehr die Ueberzeugung auf daß die sogenannten Klaßischen Dichter die ächte und wahre Poesie immer auf eine Zeitlang unterdrückt haben. So thaten es Opitz und seine Schüler im 17. und Haller[14] und Hagedorn[15] im 18. Jahrhundert. Doch dieses verdient eine weitläufigteren Aufklärung.

Zu der Liedersammlung habe ich auch <u>für jetzt</u> den Muth verloren; es ist nun einmal diese deutsche Art, das wir gerne etwas vollständiges, womöglich erschöpfendes liefern, und dazu fehlt uns noch so viel. Wie wäre es das Andenken einzelner Dichter durch Auszüge zu erneuern im Vaterl[ändischen] Mus[eum], wie es im Deutschen Mus[eum][16] damals mit Weckherlin, Murner,[17] Andrea,[18] Rosenplut,[19] Balde,[20] v. Zesen etc geschehen ist. Es könnten vors erste sage, Dach, Roberthin, Greflinger, v. Abschatz.

Und nun auch genug geplaudert.
Der Ihrige
B v F

40. Elise Campe, Hamburg

Görslow den 20 Märtz 1811

Ich habe einige Zeilen von Dr Julius erhalten, worin er sich nach mir erkundiget und auch erwähnt, daß Sie sich gütigst über mein Stillschweigen beunruhigt hätten. Es giebt Lagen die alle Mittheilung hemmen, weil sie alle Kraft in Anspruch nehmen, und die Meinige fängt an in diese Klasse zu treten; meine Verhältniße jeder Art haben sich so schrecklich verwickelt, daß ich weder aus noch ein weiß, und eben diese Unbestimmtheit ist peinlicher, als der wirkliche Schlag des Unglücks. Meine ganze Zeit ist getheilt zwischen diesem weltlichen Drang, und der stärksten Wendung zu dem Ewigen, und nur nach der Entscheidung meines irdischen Schicksals, werde ich meinen Freunden wieder etwas sagen können. Ich bitte dieses dem Dr Julius mitzutheilen, damit er mich nicht verkenne. Uebrigens bin ich weder mürrisch noch mißmüthig; ich preise dem guten Gott, daß er mich auf diesem Wege führt, denn nur der Unglückliche kann faßen was es ist: der süße Trost im Herzen den Gott sendet.

Meine Lieder Freude hat mich nicht verlassen: ich spiele und singe mich alle Abende in sanfte Rührung; die meisten sind zwar geistlichen Inhalts, doch klingen auch weltliche mit ein, besonders wenn mein Juan zuhört. Dieser ist Gottlob immer gesund und froh, und tröstet mich über manches Ungemach.

Leben Sie gesund und so froh als es die trüben Zeitläufte erlauben, und mögen wir alle das beste Theil erwählt haben.

Ihr ergebenster
Böhl v: Faber

41. Nikolas Heinrich Julius, Hamburg

Görslow den 3 April 1811

Ihre Zeilen vom 8 Märtz erhielt ich verspätet: ich schloß daraus, daß Sie Mad[ame] Campe öfters sähen, und trug ihr auf Ihnen meine Antwort mitzutheilen; jetzt empfange Ihren Brief vom 26 d[it]o woraus ich sehe, daß mein Auftrag an Mad[ame] Campe nicht in Erfüllung gegangen ist, und Sie daher mit Recht über mein langes Stillschweigen staunen – Ich habe aber mit Fleiß geschwiegen, weil mein Herz zu voll ist und ich mich doch nicht mittheilen darf, weil meine halbe Thätigkeit nothgedrungen sich mit niedrigen Geld und Gut Sachen erschöpft, und mir meine Muße fast einzig auf das Einige gerichtet ist. Ich harre auf die Entscheidung meines irdischen Schicksals; biß dahin hatte ich es aufgeschoben Ihnen zu schreiben; nach Ihrer doppelten Anforderung kann ich Sie jedoch nicht länger in Ungewißheit lassen.

Gesund bin ich Gottlob gewesen, und bin es noch; auch fehlt es mir nicht an Muth, wohl aber an Unbefangenheit. Ich habe dennoch nichts für unsere Sammlung thun können, sehe auch noch nicht den Zeitpunkt ab daß es geschehen wird. Ich habe auch nichts neues weder erhalten noch gelesen, auch keinen Wunsch darauf verspürt. Desto fleißiger bin ich bey Stollbergs Religionsgeschichte[1] gewesen, und jetzt in der zweiten Hälfte des 5ten Bandes; ich bin doch <u>nicht ganz</u> damit zufrieden; ich finde zuviel profane Geschichte eingemischt; der erste und fünfte Band sind mir die liebsten; die Erklärung des Vater Unsers ist vortrefflich – Dabey Pascal;[2] einzig in seiner Art: quot verba, tot pondera. Das Buch ist mir lieb geworden – Auch herrliche Kirchengesänge habe ich gefunden, komponiert, und gesungen: den Paul Gerhard[3] gewinne ich immer lieber; sollten Ihnen seine so wohl gedruckten Lieder vorkommen (da Sie doch mehr Auktions Verzeichniße sehen) so schaffen Sie sie doch für mich an, so wie auch Olearius Evangelischer Liederschatz[4] den ich schon lange suche – Der Hannöversche Catalogus hat für mich nur einige alte französische Sachen enthalten; auf den Brandenburg[ischen] Ulyßes[5] habe ich nicht reflektirt: die alten Reisen lohnen wirklich die Mühe des Lesens nicht.

Dagegen erhielt ich ein Bremer Verzeichniß direkt auch auf d[en] 1 April, wo herrliche Sachen in waren besonders lateinische und italiensische; überhaupt pflegen die Bremer Verzeichniße reich an alten Sachen zu seyn. Ich habe jedoch nur einiges komittiren können, hauptsächlich eine deutsche Biblia pentapla, und Harsdorffer seine Gesprächspiele.[6]

Wenn Sie mir Auktions Verzeichniße zusenden können so geschieht mir immer ein Dienst; Perthes hat keine Zeit auf dergleichen zu paßen.

Ich lade Sie nicht zu mir ein, weil ich auf dem Punkt stehe das Gut zu verkaufen; geschähe dieses (so wie ich es den Umständen nach wünschen <u>muß</u>) so würde ich Ihnen näher rücken: doch darüber das eigentliche sobald es seyn kann.

Sehen Sie Speckter[7] so grüßen Sie ihn bestens von mir.
Der Ihrige
B. v. F.

42. *Nikolas Heinrich Julius, Hamburg*

Görslow, den 5 May 1811

Ich beantworte Ihre liebe Zuschrift vom 26 April. Schade daß Sie nicht abkommen können! Es würde heilsam für Sie und mich seyn, und an schöner grüner Waldung ist hier kein Mangel, mit Wasser oberdrein – denn sollten Sie auch mehr Lieder sehen und hören. Ich könnte leicht andere 24 in demselben Sinn und Geschmack liefern, allein ich muß warten biß Mohr und Zimmer[1] sie haben wollen, und jetzt da alles in den französischen Listen gezwungen wird, werden die Theilnehmer immer weniger werden.

Die Weisheit aus den Gassen habe ich von Hamburg mitgebracht und mich sehr daran gefreut: die Genoveve als Buch für Kinder und Grimm über die Meistersänger[2] (vermuthlich in Antwort Docens in dem Museum) habe ich noch nicht gesehen und bitte an Perthes zu sagen sie mir gelegentlich zuzusenden – Von den Blumen die Sie aus Luthers Schriften lesen werden habe ich keine günstige Meinung: es ist aber an meiner Seite Vorurtheil, weil ich keine seiner Schriften gelesen und nur in den Tischreden geblättert habe. Von dem verbotenen Gesangbuchs Liedern hatte schon gehört: ich glaube es nicht, wir sind aber auf dem Wege der dahin führt. Bey der schrecklichen Mishandlung Villers in einem der letzten Korrespond[enz Nachrichten] habe ich gebebt vor Unwillen.

Von Bremen habe ich noch keine Nachricht: die Auktionärs sind recht saumselige Leute: den Aldrete[3] habe ich mit kommittirt, und so hört er Ihnen mit, wenn ich ihn erhalte. Die Auktion des bekannten Beireis[4] in Helmstädt ist angekündigt: sehen Sie doch zu Verzeichniße zu erhalten für Sie und für mich – Von der Altonaer Schütze Auktion hätte ich mir mehr vorgestellt: es ist doch eigentlich eine elende Sammlung für einen Gelehrten. Meine Wünsche finden Sie beygehend aufgezeichnet: da wir wohl auf verschiedenes zusammentreffen werden, so können wir nachher darum loosen oder uns auf anderer Weise vergleichen; es freut mich daß Sie selbst hingehen wollen.

Wie gerne würde ich der Dem[oiselle] Hermes eine Stelle verschaffen, allein meiner Familie ist jetzt keine Vakanz und in Mecklenburg kenne ich so wenig Leute! Im Gedächtniße behalte ich es gewiß und benutze sicherlich jede Gelegenheit sie zu empfehlen.

Sie schreiben mir daß Luise Reichhardt[5] die original Komposition der _____ Lieder durchgeht; das Wort vor Lieder ist mir aber unmöglich geworden zu entziffern und doch bin ich neugierig es zu wissen; da ich in dem Worte keine Selbstlaute entdecken kann, so sind es wohl polnische oder rußische.

Meine Lage ist dieselbe: man gewöhnt sich aber an alles und so bin ich mir fast ganz wiedergegeben. Das Trost von oben hat auch das seinige gethan – da ich den größten Theil meiner englischen Bücher zu veräußern denke, so lese ich jetzt zum Abschied viel Englisch, alles sehr vernünftig, zum Theil auch verständig, aber wenig gefühltes. Wir Deutsche bleiben doch das Herz der Jungfer Europa, die Franzosen ihr Verstand, die Engländer ihre Vernunft und die Südländer ihre Fantasie.

Der May ist schön: seitdem ich aber den geoffenbarten Gott mehr kennen gelernt habe, ist mir die Natur nicht mehr was sie war. Unsere Naturliebe ist wahrlich nur Täuschung – denn unfühlend ist die Natur; es leuchtet die Sonne über Bös' und Güte, und dem Verbrecher glänzen wie dem besten der Mond und die Sterne.[6]

Seit Ostern habe ich leider Einquartierung und das Italienische: unleidlichere, mehr verschloßene und gänzlich ungehobelterte Menschen sind mir nie vorgekommen. Es ist eine wahre Quaal mit solchen Unholden zu Tisch sitzen zu müssen; allgemein will man lieber Franzosen. Der Himmel erlöse uns bald von dieser eben so lästigen als bey jetzigen Zeiten kostbaren Beköstigung.

Was haben Sie auf den Sommer vor?

Der Ihrige

B.

Wie erhalte ich doch wohl die 5½ Thaler aus Leipzig die mir Weigel noch für den Theuerdank schuldig ist – kann Perthes sie nicht einkassiren lassen?

43. Elise Campe, Hamburg

Görslow, den 19 May 1811

Ihr lieber Brief vom vorigen Monath ist mir so recht erquickend gewesen, wie ein milder Schauer dem ausgedörrten Boden; denn obgleich man sich manches und das meiste und ungunstlichste selbst sagt, so macht dieses selber, doch durch ein fremdes Organ auch einen anderen Eindruck. Ich weiß nicht wer sagt 'daß die angenehmste Unterhaltung immer diejenige sey in welcher man hört was man weiß und fühlt, und sagt was eben die anderen auch wissen und fühlen' Es ist sicher wohl das härteste in der Widerwärtigkeit, wenn man so allein stehen muß, aber wem geht es anders? Wie selten sind die Uebereinstimmungen des Gefühls, auch in den achtbarsten und edelsten Verhältnißen? Hieneiden ist für feiner fühlende Menschen nichts als Mislaut; selbst was wir schöne Natur nennen, ist nur Täuschung. Mit dem Frühlinge erwacht der allgemeine Krieg; die stillen bescheidenen Pflanzen werden gefreßen von kleinen Thieren; diese kleinen Räuber dienen größeren zur Nahrung, und am Ende verschlingt das unersättliche Menschen Thier die Gräber so vieler Gräber, um im Schooße des großen Mutter Ungeheuers (der Erde) den Pflanzen den ersten Raub wieder zu erstatten. Gottlob daß wir einen geoffenbarten Gott haben, der unseren besten Theil aus dieser Verbannung erlösen wird, wenn wir an Ihn glauben Ihn lieben, und auf Ihn hoffen wollen.

In meiner Lage ist noch immer keine Entscheidung eingetreten; allein ich habe gefunden daß man auch diese Ungewißheit gewohnt werden kann, ich danke Gott für jeden ruhigen Tag mehr, und stelle Ihm die Zukunft gänzlich anheim. Vierzehn Tage Einquartirung fremder Truppen habe ich überstanden, und bin jetzt Gottlob wieder frey; ich genieße es, so lange es währt.

Seit ungefähr 12 Tagen haben wir hier strengen Sommer, und vermuthlich Sie nicht weniger als wir. Ich wage mich nicht weiter als die Schatten meines Gartens, und auch aus diesen werde ich bald von den Legionen blutgieriger Mücken verjagt. Ich stelle mir vor, daß Sie es recht genießen, und lasse es mir daher gefallen. Meine letzte Lesung war Miltons Paradise Lost,[1] welches mir, ganz gegen Erwarten, viel besser, als in früheren Zeiten gefallen hat; es hat mich fast mit der epischen Dichtungsart versöhnt.

In der letzten Ausgabe der Geschichte von Hagedorn durch Eschenburg[2] finde ich folgende Note: 'In Ansehung der älteren und mittleren Geschichte der deutschen lyrischen Poesie hat die Gottschedin[3] eine handschriftliche Sammlung von Materialien hinterlassen, die H[er]r Prof[essor] Ebeling[4] in Hamburg besitzt' – Wäre es nicht möglich durch Ihren guten Bekannten den Dr Ebeling eine Ansicht dieser Materialien zu erhalten; wenn der alte Fanatiker sie nur nicht verbrannt hat!

Bitten Sie doch Campe mir ein AuktionsVerzeichniß der Schlötzerschen Bibliothek[5] zuzusenden (welches Ruprecht haben soll) und das sobald möglich – Ich erhalte auch gerne den Leipziger Meßkatalog; geht Campe noch nach Leipzig? Gehen Sie mit, oder was haben Sie vor Entwurfe auf den Sommer? Campe wollte schon lange einmahl nach Schwerin kommen; dann kämen Sie mit, und ließen sich hier in Görslow von der Sonne braten, während Campe seine Geschäfte abmachte; nebenher trieben wir dann Poesie und Gesang. Den Dr Julius will ich dazu einladen.

Ganz der Ihrige
Böhl v: Faber

44. Nikolas Heinrich Julius, Hamburg

Görslow, den 27 May 1811

Ich danke für Ihren langen Brief vom 22. Die Eintheilung der Auktions Bücher von Schütze lasse ich mir gerne gefallen; in gleichen Fällen soll Ihnen die Eintheilung immer überlassen bleiben. Dieses zur Aufmunterung, damit Sie nicht unterlassen mir Auktions Katalogen zuzusenden, wenn sie Ihnen vorkommen. Der von Beyreis ist zu spät gekommen: ich habe jedoch auf gutes Glück noch einiges kommittirt. Viel war auch für mich nicht darin. –

N[ummer] 456 od[er] Memel lustige Gesellschaft[1] ist bey weiten das beste Buch dieser Art, welches mir vorgekommen ist: Koch[2] erwähnt es nicht. Ich besitze es, aber in schlechtem Zustand und etwas defekt; der poetische Theil ist besonders interessant, vieles aus dem Logau – Ob Sie etwas gutes in der Schaubühne[3] und den plattdeutschen Liedern gefunden haben, erwarte ich gelegentlich zu vernehmen.

Wenn ich nicht irre, so sind Sie mir noch von der Schweriner Auktion 9 Mark 8 Schilling und von der Kieler 4 Mark 12 Schilling schuldig, zusammen 14 Mark 4 Schilling wovon um die 9 Mark 8 abgerechnet, mir noch 4 Mark 12 Schilling bey Ihnen zu Gute bleiben. Der Belauf des Theuerdanks war 5½ Thaler und nicht 3½ wie Sie schreiben. Kommen in Leipzig wieder Auktionen, so lassen Sie mir doch die Verzeichniße zukommen.

Daß ich der Uebersetzung des Baco[4] entgangen bin ist mir wahres Glück, welches ich Ihrer Aufmerksamkeit verdanke – Von der Schelmenzunft[5] habe ich den neueren Druck vom 1788, und hatte deswegen keinen hohen Preis darauf gesetzt. Wenn es noch Zeit ist, so nehmen Sie den Gottsched wieder zurück, den ich auch schon doppelt besitze; aber erst neulich habe ich aus Bremen den 2ten Theil erhalten, welcher viel seltener vorkommt, und durch die abgedruckten alten Sachen viel interessanter ist. Den Segens nehme ich mit dank an. Zu Fr[iedrich] Schlegels Historische Vorlesungen[6] freue ich mich recht – Joh[annes] Müller[7] aber ist nicht mein Mann, Sie mögen ihn herausstreichen, so viel Sie wollen. Ich habe für ihn eine estime raisonnée, aber auch weiter nichts.

Was ich von den Liedern erwähnte, ist bloß in musikalischer Hinsicht, und in der Ueberzeugung, daß M[ohr] und Z[immer] nicht in Versuchung kommen werden mehrere streichen zu lassen. Unseren Plan habe ich keinesweges vergessen; ich kann mich nur als ein ächter deutscher Bücherwurm die Idee der Vollständigkeit nicht ausschlagen, und so scheint es mir, daß wir noch lange zu sammeln haben – Ich revidire jetzt zum letztenmahl einen großen Theil meiner englischen Bücher und ziehe einige Noten daraus: Sie werden sich wundern warum, weil ich nemlich muß zu verkaufen suchen, um dringende Bedürfniße zu decken (dieses unter uns) Ich bin mir noch nicht einig, ob ich sie dorthen in Auktion gebe oder unter der Hand zu verkaufen suche: es sind alles ausgesuchte Ausgaben vortrefflich gebunden und konditionnert, und begreifen hauptsächlich Geschichte, Poesie, Ackerbau und Naturgeschichte. Sie kosten mir in London c[irc]a 1000 Thaler; ich würde aber mit 500 Thaler zufrieden seyn; sagen Sie mir doch Ihre Meinung darüber.

Es ist jetzt wahrscheinlich, daß ich vors erste noch in Mecklenburg und zwar auf Görslow bleibe; können Sie also eine Tour kombiniren, so treffen Sie mich. Der Monath Juny werde ich größtentheils von Verwandten umringt seyn; später aber finden Sie mich allein, und die ländliche Kost die ich meinen Freunden vorsetze, verursacht mir keine Auslagen. Brächten Sie Speckter mit würde es mir noch lieber seyn.

Das allerliebste Nach Sevilla gehört zu meinen Lieblingsliedern so wie das Ich wollt ein Sträußlein binden in derselben Sammlung. Meine Unterschrift zu Luthers Liedern bestätige ich gern: aber von Vandalen umgeben, wem soll ich weiter ansprechen? Die Wahl von Luthers Liedern billige ich nicht: Paul Gerhard ist viel mehr Dichter, auch andere genannte und ungenannte in den gewöhnlichen alten Gesangbüchern.

Von deutschen Sprichwörter Sammlungen habe ich den Agricola[8] Frank[9] und Lehman[10] und Blum:[11] auch in andrer Sprache mehrere, deren Titel ich aber nicht zur Hand habe: am besten ist Sie kommen und machen sich Auszüge – Übrigens liegen der eigentliche Ernst und der eigentliche Spaß nah bey einander – Denken

Sie an die Spanier und deren Graziosos und Entremeses. – Doch dieses ist ein weites Feld, ebenso wie die Ansicht der Natur. Ich bleibe dabey, daß der Gott den ich im und aus der Natur erkennen kann nicht der geoffenbarte Gott ist; er ist mächtig und groß hat aber <u>kein Ohr</u> zu <u>hören meiner</u> Klag, <u>kein Herz</u> wie <u>eines sich der Bedrängten</u> zu <u>erbarmen</u> – das hat nur Christus des Menschen Sohn und Gottes Sohn.[12]

Von Bremen habe an wichtigen Sachen erhalten: Biblia Pentapla,[13] Harsdorfer Gesprächspiele, und Wahlenbergs Deutsche Florus.[14] Die Gesprächspiele machen mir viele Freude; es sind eigentliche Spiele voller Lieder, Musik, Sinnbilder, Kupfer, und allein Ihr Reise Werth. Ein eigentlicher Dichter ist H[arsdorfer] nicht, aber ein heiterer alles umfaßender Geist, und der wahre Typus der damahligen gesellschaftlichen Bildung. In Markheim erhielt ich es damals nicht für 10 Thaler und habe es nun für 1 Thaler 12 Schilling erhalten, schön in Pergament gebunden – Der Deutsche Florus ist die gleichzeitige Erzählung der 30en Krieges von <u>Katholischer</u> Feder mit vielen 64 Bildniße sehr rar für 2 Schilling – Die fünffache deutsche Uebers[etzung] der Bibel 3 Quartbände 36 Schilling – In der Hoffnung Sie bald hier zu sehen, bin ich beständig

Ganz der Ihrige

45. Nikolas Heinrich Julius, Hamburg

Görslow, den 13 Juny 1811

Der Auftrag der mir Ihr Liebes vom 7 dieses überbracht hat, ist nach Rostock befördert; meinen Katalogus habe ich aber in dem Paket von Perthes nicht vorgefunden. Jetzt können Sie nur ganz behalten, da ich mir einen anderen verschafft habe – Einen alten Josephus mit treflichen Holzschnitten von Tobias Stimmer[1] besitze ich schon. Den Kranz habe ich noch nachkommittirt. Den Hammelman[2] suche ich wegen der Kupfer, und wegen seiner Seltenheit – Der satyrische Komponist ist nicht die Sing Klang und Spielkunst sondern ein andres Werk desselben Verfaßers[3] – S[eite] 8 N[ummer] 130 habe ich noch zu verschreiben. S[eite] 9 N[ummer]167 ist doch nach Clement[4] so selten nicht; 12 Schilling habe ich indessen darauf bieten lassen – N[ummer] 18 S[eite]14. welches Sie mir zu kaufen rathen findet sich auf solcher Seite gar nicht – Den Soldaten in Fol[io] v[on] Fleming[5] habe ich gar nicht kommittirt, da er das Portho nicht werth seyn mögte; vielleicht ist von einem Herr von Fleming der im Anfang des vorigen Jahrhunderts den <u>vollkommenen Jäger</u>[6] in 2 Fol[io] Bände herausgab, den ich besitze, der aber von Jöcher[7] und Dunkel[8] mit Stillschweigen übergangen wird – die Burlesken habe ich kommittirt –

Von dem Petro de Memel habe ich nirgends etwas ausfinden können; es war unter der Würde der Gelehrten sich mit solchen Lustigmachern zu beschäftigen.

Dagegen habe ich Ihren C[arl] M[elchior] Grodnitz von Grodnau[9] leicht in Neumarks Palmbaum[10] p. 390 und 456 gefunden; seine Uebers[etzung] des Tacitas kommt in Schemels[11] Uebers[etzungs] Bibliothek p. 267 schlecht weg. Im Placcius p. 341 werden Observationes politicas hiper nuperis Galliae motibus 1649 [illeg.] Carolo a Grotniz Nobili Pomerano[12] zugeschrieben, und dieses Buch sehr gelobt; vielleicht ist es dieselbe Person. Von Jöcher und Dunkel ist nichts von ihm zu finden; den Jöcher habe ich recht zum Aerger, da ich nie darin finde, was ich eben suche. Gottscheds Beyträge 1er Th[eil] p. 42 können Sie auch nachschlagen. Der Geschichts Saulen habe ich aber noch nirgends erwähnt gefunden.

Ich bemerke daß ich Ihnen noch 8 Schilling schuldig bleibe, um sie bey der Rostocker Auktion abzurechnen. Ihr Brief vom 30 May vorigen Jahres, den ich vor mir liegen habe, führt den Theuerdank p. 308, N[ummer] 5475 mit 5 Thaler 12 Groschen an; anders kommen auch die 14 Thaler die ich damals bezahlte nicht heraus – Wenn Sie mir einmahl wieder einen Leipziger Auktions Katalogus schickten, so ließe es sich leicht abtragen; aber ich erhalte jetzt auch keinen, weder von Ihnen noch von Perthes noch von Campe. Neulich blätterte ich bey meinem Brüder im Morgenblatt: was für herrliche Auktionen sind im Anfange und Frühling dieses Jahres gewesen, in Basel, Frankfurt, Heidelberg etc. Das geht uns alles aus der Nase! – Haben Sie gar nichts von Mozler aus Freysingen erhalten, und ist von der Wiener Auktion in Januar uns nicht das gerringste zu Theil geworden? – Ich fand auch im Morgenblatt einen Aufsatz unterschrieben Julius[13] gegen die Romantiker, doch hoffentlich nicht von Ihnen? –

Den Wagenseil[14] habe ich noch nicht und erhalte ihn gerne für das was er Ihnen gekostet hat; dann senden Sie mir auch wohl Les abus du monde Paris 1504[15] mit, welches Sie im Winter von den Büchern die für mich von Helmstädt kamen behielten. Von derselben Sendung fehlen mir Neußens Geistliche Lieder 1692;[16] sollten sie allenfalls in Ihre Hände gekommen seyn?

Hiebey erfolgt das Verzeichniß derjeniger englischer Bücher die ich gerne Verkaufen würde; alles was sich auf Schottische Lieder Balladen etc. bezieht habe ich natürlich zurückbehalten; auch einiges andere. Ich glaube daß meine Forderung sehr billig ist; ich erwarte gelegentlich P[erthes] seiner Meinung.

Ich freue mich sehr daß L[uise] R[eichardt] weltliche Lieder komponirt. – Die Vorlesungen von Fr[iedrich] Schlegel sind vortrefflich im einzelnen, dennoch ermüde ich im ganzen dabey, ich weiß nicht warum. Das zu Allgemeine ist immer etwas kalt; es ist mir als wäre der Verf[asser] um nicht selbst zu bestimmen überhaupt, nicht ganz bestimmt. Die durchschneinende Vorliebe für die Oesterr[eichische] Monarchie ist der Natur seiner Lage angemeßen: der rothe Faden französischer Abneigung wird dem Buche viele Freunde machen, aber es auch in die Proskriptions Liste bringen; eine schöne Erscheinung bleibt es in allen Fällen – Hackerts Leben[17] ist doch gar zu leicht; ich habe keine Versuchung es zu behalten und begnüge mich an der Durchblätterung, ohne es aufzuschneiden –

Grims Lieder[18] muß ich behalten obwohl es für 10 Mark entsetzlich Theuer ist. In dem Meß Katal[alog] stehen sonst noch schöne Sachen von v. d[e]r Hagen etc. die aber wohl nur noch proyektirt sind –

Die Sachen aus der Altonaer Autkion habe ich nun erhalten; an dem schönen Reynicke Voß fehlen leider etliche Blätter in der Mitte. Der Esmarck[19] ist ein vorzüglicher Dichter, und glücklicherweise war sein Helicon oder weltliche Ged[ichte], dem Sion angebunden; meiner Ahnung in Hinsicht seiner hat mich nicht betrogen: seine Epigr[amme] kommen den Logauschen nahe; Schade daß es so wenige sind –

Sehr leid thut es mir, daß Sie nicht kommen können. Ich glaube ich würde Ihnen hier mehr sagen können, als in Hamburg; wenigstens würden wir sicherlich in unserer gemeinschaftlichen Liebhaberey durch einander weiter kommen: in der Stadt ist mir alles doch immer wie zerstückt, und ich höre mir selbst nie ganz an.

Ganz der Ihrige

B v F

46. Elise Campe, Hamburg

G[örslow] den 17 July 1811

Ich weiß wirklich nicht, ob ich Ihre angenehme Zuschrift vom 27 May beantwortet habe; ist es geschehen, so werden Sie sich gütigst einige Wiederholungen gefallen lassen. Ich schreibe recht gerne, nur keine Geschäftsbriefe; Sie brauchen mir also für meine gar nicht dankbar zu seyn, da mir Gottlob keine andere Geschäfte als Tauschhandel von Gedanken und Gefühlen zu treiben brauchen – Wissen Sie denn nicht, das alle Nazionen unter den Fahnen des großen Helden zu dienen die Ehre haben?; daher meine unaustehlichen Piemontschen. Jetzt beherbergt Schwerin zusammengeraffte Ungarn Polaken und Deutsche, die Lanciers heißen, und gar unausstehlich sind – Ich wünsche Glück zu Ihrer Villa und wünsche sie möge Ihnen ein Sorgenfrey seyn; doch das wäre zu viel hienieden . . . also nur ein Sorgenvergeß! – Ich hoffe daß Ihr guter Vater ganz wiederhergestellt ist, Ihren Gründen für das Zuhausebleibens kann ich nur Geschäfte entgegensetzen, und die gelten nicht wenn die Vernunft befiehlt – Von Mutter Campen habe ich einen Brief vom 10 Juny gehabt der aber nichts merkwürdiges enthält; die Vieweg und das letzte Kind hatten gekränkelt waren aber in der Besserung – Den Hackert von Göthe habe ich unaufgeschnitten gelesen und zurückgesandt; ich hoffe daß er aus den gesammelten Werken wegbleiben wird; es ist doch gar zu leichte Speise! – Fr[iedrich] Schlegel seine Vorlesungen sind sehr schön; ich bin aber jetzt zu sehr in meiner alten Litteratur befangen, um sie so ganz zu genießen, und habe sie biß zu mehrerer Geistesfreyheit zurückgelegt. – Ein allerliebstes fantastisches Ding hat mir Campe neulich gesandt: die Jahreszeiten von Fouqué;¹ Sie müssen es lesen, und sich darüber freuen. Der Kühleborn² hat mir unendlich gefallen. Das ist die rechte Art Märchen, fast mögte ich sagen das wahre Märchen, aber was darin liegt ist nicht für alle, wohl aber die heitere Darstellung und so vieles einzelne zart gefühlte – die beyden ersten Melodien von Stilling³ verdienen dabey ihre Stelle.

Ich schätze die gute S- von Grund meiner Seele so wie Sie es thun, allein innigen Umgang könnte ich nicht mit ihr haben. Ich bin der Meynung daß der ganze R-Zirkel antikristlich denkt und fühlt; es sind eigentliche Vernunft Menschen, also auch allgemein, kalt ja strenge wie es eine ewige unabänderliche Gesetzesform mit sich bringt. Ganz entgegengesetzt ist die politische Sinnesart die einen Beruf annimmt, oder eine von Gott ausgehende Richtung des Herzens, die also auch weder von dem Rosenstrauch Früchte noch von dem Früchtbarem Rosen heischt, sondern neben Martham auch Mariam anerkennt, und sich ebensowohl durch den thätigen Petrus als durch den betrachtenden Johannes zu verherrlichen weiß – Letztere Ansicht hängt genau mit dem politischen Gefühl zusammen, und ist also den meisten Mitgliedern des erwähnten Zirkels fremden Sie mögen es nun gestehen oder läugnen.

Nun ich denke Sie haben sich nicht (die vorige Woche etwa ausgenommen) über Mangel an Sonne zu beklagen gehabt; ich habe mich wenig auswagen können, destomehr dagegen in alten Büchern gelesen. Die Besuche meiner Fr[eunde] sind sparsam ausgefallen; meine Mutter war unterwegens, mußte aber wieder umkehren um ihren kranken Mann zu pflegen. Einen angenehmen Tag haben mir Patrick Peale⁴ und seine Frau gemacht; er hat viel nachgedacht und nichts ist ihm fremd.

Ich hätte gerne einen Besuch des Dr Ebeling erhalten, wenn er in hiesiger Gegend gekommen ist, um womöglich einen Theil der Schätze entzaubern die der alte Drache bewacht.

Nun wird Mad[ame] Siebung auch wohl nicht zu mir kommen da Sie es aufgegeben haben; ich höre von Thurow daß sie sich diesen Sommer ganz wohlbefindet, welches mir von Herzen lieb ist.

Erinnern Sie Ihren lieben Campe gelegentlich daran, daß er mir Ende December eine gewiße JahresRath hätte zustellen sollen, und daß wir jetzt schon in der zweiten Hälfte des J[ahres] sind.

ergebenst

B. v. F.

47. Elise Campe [Hamburg]

Görslow den 11 Sept[ember] 1811

Ich danke Ihnen für Ihren liebenswürdigen Brief vom 12. Aug[ust]. So sehr ich mich für die gute Luise R[eichardt] interessiere, so wenig ausgedehnt ist meine hiesige Bekanntschaft: sechs Exemplare denke ich indem zu vertheilen, und bitte mich für soviele in Ihrer Liste zu setzen – Das 4te Heft von Göthes Lieder[1] habe ich von Perthes e̲r̲halten und be̲halten – Schillers Ged[ichte][2] haben mir nie musikalisch geschienen – Die Sonnette habe ich richtig durchgesehen, aber da ich des Ital[ienischen] nicht mächtig bin, haben sie mich nicht angesprochen – Im Winter kann ich es noch bey Ihnen nachholen. Gewiß werden sie mir gefallen wenn Luise sie singt – Ich freue mich des Glückes ihres Vaters, weiß aber nicht genug von seiner Individualität um zu verstehen, in wiefern er es n̲i̲c̲h̲t̲ zu würdigen versteht; das erklären Sie mir wohl alles nächsten Winter – Ueber den schönen t̲r̲o̲c̲k̲e̲n̲e̲n̲ Sommer möchten wir armen Landleute weinen, damit die Erde doch etwas befeuchtet würde; das Vieh ernährt sich durch ein Wunder. Die Erndte ist schlecht [illeg.] kaum die Hälfte der vorigjährigen, und jetzt da man säen soll weigert sich die harte Erde das Korn in ihren Schoß aufzunehmen – Traurig ist was Sie mir von W. Sievkings Krankheit melden . . . indessen traurig ist alles, nur die Gemüthswelt nicht und der Blick auf Gott und seine unendliche Liebe die uns alles dieses zu unserm Besten auflegt! – Recht sehr freut es mich daß Sie bey der Undine gefühlt haben, so wie ich: Ihrem Campe wollen wir es eintreiben daß er ein Romantiker geworden ist – Die Briefe der Frauenz[immer] aus dem xv Jahr[undert][3] kenne ich recht gut und mag sie wohl leiden. – Den Benv[enuto] Cellini[4] habe ich nie gelesen – aufrichtig gesagt bin ich mit Fr[iedrich] Schlegels Vorlesungen auch nicht zu Ende gekommen, oder vielmehr zu Anfang, denn ich fing hinten an; sie gehören zu den k̲a̲l̲t̲e̲n̲ ̲S̲c̲h̲ö̲n̲h̲e̲i̲t̲e̲n̲ die man grüßt, gähnt, und vorüber geht (dieses doch unter uns, um meinem Kenner Ruf keinen Eintrag zu thun) – Die Neue Heloise[5] kann dem J̲ü̲n̲g̲l̲i̲n̲g̲e̲ gefallen aber der M̲a̲n̲n̲ muß sie verwerfen; was Sie darüber bemerken, unterschreibe ich alles – Ich habe leider einige Wochen gar nicht g̲e̲l̲e̲b̲t̲: meine Augen oder vielmehr Augenlieder waren so schlimm, daß ich weder lesen noch schreiben durfte: ich flüchtete mich nach meiner Schwester in Thurow und habe da 14 Tage vegetiert. Unterdessen ist die Verlobung meines Bruders mit Dem[ioselle] Stockfleth zu Stande gekommen, und nächste Woche werden wir wohl die Heirath auf seinem Gute Cramon feiern. Dabey werde ich sehr lustig scheinen, ohne es zu seyn: eine Heirath hat für mich immer mehr ängstliches als munteres (dieses wieder unter uns) – Einige herrliche alte Uebersetzungen von Klaßikern aus dem xvi Jahrh[undert] habe ich kürzlich von Rostock erhalten, mit trefflichen Holzschnitten – In den Hamburger Versteigerungen werden die alten Sachen noch immer verhältnismäßig theuer bezahlt – Haben Sie noch den T̲o̲d̲e̲s̲b̲u̲n̲d̲[7] (den am Ende der Undine angezeigten Roman desselben

Verfaßers) nicht erhalten? – Die <u>Altdänischen Lieder</u> von Grimm übersetzt, kann ich Ihnen zum Durchblättern empfehlen – Sonsten sind die Einschränkungen des Buchhandels dorten von der Art, daß man sich an jemand in Berlin wird wenden müssen, wenn man etwas haben will. Haben Sie einen persönlichen Bekannten unter den Berliner Buchhändlern, den Sie mir empfehlen können – Dr Julius hat meiner in jeder Hinsicht ganz vergeßen; ich bin recht böse, auch weil er mir gewiß heimlich die alten Bücher in den dortigen Versteigerungen eingekapert – Den Dr. Eberhard haben Sie wohl gar nicht wieder gesehen – Ich hätte Sie wohl in Ihrem Sorgenfrey überraschen mögen, so an einem mondhellen Abend! – Von meiner Familie nicht die gewünschte Nachricht, und so hängt noch immer über meiner Zukunft die alte dunkle Wolke. Ich singe indessen mit Paul Gerhard: Der beste Will ist Gottes Will, auf diesen ruht man sanft und still; da gib dich allzeit frisch hinein, begehre nichts als nur allein, was Gott gefällt![8] – Verzeihen Sie diesen fragmentarischen in großer Eile hingeworfenen Wisch! – Schneiden Sie das andere Blatt für Ihren lieben Romantiker ab und erfreuen Sie mich bald wieder mit einer Zuschrift

aufrichtigst und ergebenst B v F

48. *Nikolas Heinrich Julius, Hamburg*

Görslow, den 2 October 1811

Endlich, endlich, habe ich wieder Ihre Handschrift erblickt; ich war schon auf dem Punkt Ihnen wieder zu schreiben, um mein englisches Verzeichniß zurück zu erbitten. Wären die neuen Verhältniße nicht eingetreten, so hätte es sich vielleicht mit P[erthes] machen lassen, so daß ich nach und nach statt Geld Bücher in Bezahlung genommen hätte. Jetzt aber ist nicht daran zu denken, und so erbitte ich mir mein Verzeichniß zurück, nebst einige Zeilen an Hitzig, dem ich selbst darüber schreiben will. Können Sie mir diesen Hitzig auch sonst als reellen und genauen Geschäftsmann empfehlen? Das wenige was ich noch von neuen Sachen nehme, denke ich künftig von Berlin zu beziehen –

Könnten Sie Ihre Bücher von Lüneburg nach Schwerin schicken lassen, so würde ich sie Ihnen gelegentlich mitbringen, oder mitsenden können, wenn es nemlich keine Fol[io] sind – Auch aus den Leipziger Auktionen könnten die Bücher wohl direkt nach Schwerin kommen, ohne die französ[ische] Grenze zu berühren – das Verzeichniß der letzten dortigen Auktion hatte mir Campe gesandt; wir haben auf die <u>gepflückten Finken</u>[1] und den <u>Olearius</u> konkuriert. Auf ersteres hatte ich 12 Schilling gesetzt und auf letzteres 24 Schilling. Dann hatte ich noch ein paar alte Bibeln der Fama Fraternatatis[2] und die Uebers[etzung] der Argenis von Opitz[3] kommittirt; ich habe aber noch keine Nachricht von Campe ob ich etwas erhalten.

Das neue Heldenbuch[4] habe ich behalten, weil ich das alte leider nicht habe; was darin gelesen aber habe ich noch nicht, weil mich der Geist noch nicht dazu getrieben. Ueber das Narrenbuch denke ich gerade wie Sie; manches läßt sich in dem alten Drucke mit den alten gothischen Lettern ertragen, was einem in moderner Form anekelt. Bey den Markolten (die ich gar nicht kannte) habe ich jedoch manchmahl lachen müssen.

Den Sieveking Katalogus habe ich schon; es ist gar nichts für mich darin, außer allenfalls Denis Anleitung zur Bücherkunde[5] – Mein abus du monde behalten nun biß auf Ansicht, denn wahrscheinlicherweise komme ich doch wohl gegen Ende November zur Stadt, weil mich meine Mutter gerne haben will und weil mir auch bey meiner Unfähigkeiten im künstlichen Lichte zu lesen und zu schreiben, die Abende lang werden, die ich am liebsten im Schauspielhause zubringe – Uebrigens habe ich von der alma mater nicht Ihr vages Mitgefühl erhalten, welches ich besonders vorig Jahr, bey der ersten Nachricht der französ[ischen] Besitzergreifung, inne ward. Vielleicht trägt dazu bey, daß ich in meinen besonderen Verhältniße alles dasjenige früher erfahren habe, was jetzt im Großen über Hamburg ausbricht, und daß da ich mich selbst nie bedauert habe, ich auch andere nicht bedauern kann. Damit verbindet sich noch das Gefühl unserer tiefen Hinderniß, und daß wir in allgemeinen nichts anderes werth sind, und daß nur Druck und Noth uns aus unserer weltlich-sinnlichen Beschränkung heraustreiben vermögen . . . Und was haben Sie denn <u>für sich</u> zu trauern? Ihre Kentniße sichern Ihnen allenthalben das tägliche Brod, und mehr muß man, besonders jetzt, nicht haben wollen – Hätten Sie Kinder, so wie mancher andere, Knaben weichherzig und mild die kein Lamm können bluten sehen, Mädchen deren man ihre letzte Zuflucht die Klöster geraubt hat . . . Ja dann . . . aber auch das läßt sich <u>mit Gottes Beistand</u> tragen – dabey kann ich Ihnen melden, daß meine Familie glücklich in E——— angekommen ist und nun also wohl bald mit mir vereinigt werden wird; meine Verhältniße sind von der Art, daß ich nicht bestimmt sagen kann, daß ich mich darüber freue. Vielleicht werde ich mich dann eben entfernen müssen, wenn sie endlich bey mir eingetroffen ist.

Ich mögte Sie hätten die vorige Woche bey mir seyn können, nach den (traurigen) Hochzeits Festen (es klang mir nur 'Komm raus komm raus Du schöne Braut' in den Ohren) und nachdem sich die rauschenden Stadtgäste verloren hatten, bleib ein enger Ausschluß bestehend aus der Ihnen bekannten Dem[oiselle] Haack, meiner Nichte und Tochter bey mir zurück, alles durstige und für das Höhere empfängliche Seelen, die sich geschwingt hatten unter den, Saus und Braus, und nun die Fittige wieder frey bewegen durften. Wir haben gearbeitet, gelesen, vorgelesen und gesprochen: Guitarre, Stimme und Klavier wechselten ab; auch blinde Kuh und Poch mit den kleinen Kindern – Die Woche zerfloß wie ein Tag, und ich müßte mich sehr trügen wenn wir nicht alle besser, doch gewiß liebevoller voneinander geschieden sind.

Ich hoffe, daß Sie in Ihrer neuen Wohnung mehr Platz für Ihre Bücher haben werden, damit nicht ein Theil auf der Erde und auf den Fenstern kampiren müße, welches nicht ohne Wunden und Flecken abgeht – Die kleinen Erzählungen der Baronin M[otte] Fouqué[6] sind wohl nur leichte Waare, wenn sie den früheren Romanen dieser dann ähnlich sind; dagegen sollte man seine herrlichen Erzählungen sammlen, wovon 2 in dem Pantheon[7] stehen und eine dritte Undine neulich in den Jahreszeiten erschienen ist. Das nenne ich ächt-romantisch –

Von Rostock habe ich schöne Sachen erhalten. Einige der Uebers[etzungen] der alten Klaßiker zeichnen sich durch herrliche Holzschnitte aus, besonders der Cicero von Schwarzenberg[8] der davon 103 hat und der Plutarch mit nur wenigen aber sehr schönen von H[ans] Schäufelein[9] – Besard Unterricht über die Laute,[10] habe ich im Notenbuch für die Laute angehängt gefunden von 1615, worin auch die Melod[ien] folgender alter Lieder 'Ach Fräulein [illeg.]' 'Ich habs gemagt' 'Ein alter Greis' 'Ich dank Dir lieber Herr' 'So wünsch ich ihr eine gute Nacht'. Ich kenne nur das letzte: mehr als diese ersten Worte stehen nicht dabey. Der Tabulatur weicht aber ganz von den gewöhnlichen Noten ab, und es wird Kunst kosten sie herauszufinden – Matthison seine Schriften sind interessant und dazu jetzt schon rar. – Unter den 33 Bänden Bücherverzeichnissen sind nur wenige interessant gewesen: als Bibl[iothecae] Salthen[11] – Vogt[12] – P[eter] v. Mastricht,[13] doch ist das Ganze von 8 Fol[io] 13 quart[al] und 49 Octanten für 6 Thaler 22 Schilling gefunden – Von unseren älteren Aufträgen nach Wien etc. ist wohl nichts zu erwarten; auch ertheilte ich damals an Perthes einen kleinen Auftrag zu der Auktion von Beireis, wonach sich gelegentlich zu erkündigen bitte.

Ich lege Ihnen ein geistliches Lied bey, welches in der erwähnten Woche ein Leibgesang geworden ist; es ist eines von den vielen denen ich nach meiner Weise Noten untergelegt habe, ohne auf Erfindung Anspruch zu machen; vielleicht gefällt es Ihnen, wie dem weiblichen Häuflein. Der Text ist von meinem trefflichen Paul Gerhard nach dessen gesammelten Lieder ich noch immer vergebens seufze – Schreiben Sie bald wieder.

Ganz der Ihrige

B v F

Kennen Sie den Julius der sich im Morgenblatt gegen die romantische Poesie erklärt hat? Kennen Sie den Julius der für das Hamburgische Morgenblatt[14] (dessen erste Nummer sich durch den antikristlichen Brief des Chinesischen Kaisers auszeichneten) der Ankündigung zufolge arbeiten wollte? – es ist doch wohl nicht ein und dieselbe Person! –

49. Nikolas Heinrich Julius, Hamburg

G[örslow], den 1 Nov[ember] 1811

Mit Sehnsucht habe ich jeden Posttag das zurück verlangte Verzeichniß meiner englischen Bücher erwartet, aber vergebens; vermuthlich ist es von abhänden gekommen und ich muß wohl in den sauren Apfel beißen ein neues zu machen.

Mein guter Campe (der noch manchmahl an den Abwesenden denkt) hat mir ein paar Auktions Verzeichniße zugesandt; ich habe daraus unterstehendes notirt und bitte es für mich zu besorgen oder besorgen zu lassen. Der Nachtrag im Magdal[enen] Kirchhof ist sehr reich an alten und raren Sachen, allein mir fehlen jetzt die Mittel.

Ich habe diese letzte Zeit mehr gelesen als geschrieben oder studirt, weil die Begebenheiten zu unfreundlich auf mich eingestürmt haben; ich habe gelesen den spanischen Don Quixote,[1] den spanischen Calderon von Norwich, Klopstocks Messias,[2] den Young,[3] Göthes Faust Werther und Meister;[4] Sie sollen aber nichts darüber von mir hören, weil auch Sie mich unfreundlich behandeln – In 3 Wochen denke ich nach dorten zu kommen. Was Sie für mich erhalten sollten, legen Sie bey sich nieder.

B. v. F.

50. Nikolas Heinrich Julius, Hamburg

Görslow, den 14 Nov[ember] 1811

Das Ihrige vom 25 8er ist mir sehr spät zu Händen gekommen; Gott weiß wo es gesteckt hat. Jetzt erhalte ich noch dasjenige von 7 dieses und beantworte nun beyde zugleich. Die Einlage für H[er]rn Hitzig habe ich erhalten und ist dieselbe schon nebst dem Verzeichniße der englischen Bücher nach Berlin unterwegens. Ihr Brief aber kam zu spät, als daß ich hier noch die Antwort darauf hätte erhalten können, und so hat es mit der Verschreibung der neueren Schriften unterbleiben müssen.

Ich freue mich, daß mein kleiner Auftrag zu der Versteigerung des Dr. Rosenberger noch zeitig genug gekommen ist; viele der darin vorkommenden mystischen Schriften besitze ich schon – Ich hoffe daß Sie den Amadis[1] erhalten werden, um wenigstens des Anblicks zu genießen; wenn er so großen Werth hat so sind vermuthlich Druck und Holzschnitte sehr schön.

Ihre Bemerkung über den zerfleischenden Zeitgeist ist tief und wahr; sie paßt indeß nicht völlig auf meine Familien Verhältniße; bey der Aurelie im Meister[2] erkannte ich nahe verwandte Züge, und das Wort: <u>sie war nicht liebenswürdig, wenn sie liebte</u> enthält den Schlüssel meiner Herzensangelegenheiten.

Morgen reise ich ab, halte mich einige Tage in Cramon und in Thurow auf und denke den Montag nach St. Clemens die Stadt zu erreichen. Ich suche Sie dann in Pastorenstraße No.142 auf.

Ihr Wiederzeile ist nicht übel; wir haben aber das alte deutsche Ringelreim, welches ich vorziehe.

Ich danke für das schöne Volkslied und habe es meiner Sammlung mit Vergnügen einverleibt.

Ein Exemplar der alten Lieder[3] werde ich für Sie mitbringen, und ein Manuscript von 24 anderen gleichfalls für Sie, die ich seit dem Empfang Ihres Briefes aus meiner musikalischen Kladde abgeschrieben habe.

In Hinsicht der bedrängten Familie, der ich so gerne wie Sie beyspringen würde, verlangen Sie etwas ganz unmögliches. Gutsbesitzer können natürlich kaum junge Leute zur Landwirtschaft anführen: es müssen also Pächter seyn, ein Pächter aber thut dieses nur aus Interesse oder fürs Geld. Wer also nicht ein paar Hundert Thaler Pension bezahlen kann, oder von einem Verwandten aus Pflicht aufgenommen wird muß sich die Gedanken an Landwirtschaft hier zu Lande wenigstens vergehen lassen – doch hierüber so wie über vieles andere mündlich das Mehrere.

Der Ihrige

B. v. F.

51. Dorothea Campe, Braunschweig

Hamburg, den 10 Dec[ember] 1811

Ihre werthe Zuschrift vom 21 Nov[ember] ist mir hieher nachgesandt worden, wo ich in meiner Mutter Hause die kürzesten Tage des Jahres zu verleben pflege. Es ist eine Eigenheit meines Schicksals, daß es andere mehr bekümmert als mich; so quält sich meine gute Mutter seit einigen Jahren über alles was mir künftig noch begegnen köne, und so blickt auch aus Ihren freundschaftlichen Briefen eine Unruhe die ich weit entfernt bin zu theilen. Daß ich mich keiner schlaffen Unthätigkeit hingeben werde, dafür muß Ihnen mein Pflicht und Ehrgefühl bürgen; man kann nur dann ruhig seyn wenn man sich bewußt ist das Seinige redlich gethan zu haben, aber ich kann meine Thätigkeit nicht in der Administrazion meines Gutes beweisen. Wenn man bey einem Ertrage von c[irc]a 2000 Thaler, 3000 Thaler zu bezahlen hat, so ist dieses ohne anderweitige Hilfsquellen nicht möglich zu machen, und da die jetzigen Zeitläufte einen Verkauf fast gar nicht zulassen, so werde ich in einigen Monathen das Gut meinen Gläubigern überlassen müssen. Unterdessen bewerbe ich mich um eine kleine Stelle im diplomatischen oder administrativen Fach; mit 600 Thaler werde ich jetzt in einer kleinen Stadt auskommen können.

Die kostbarsten meiner Bücher sind schon auf Reisen um Liebhaber zu suchen, andere werden statt Bezahlung an gute Freunde überlassen. Ich werde nur das

Fach der älteren deutschen Litteratur (welches nur einen eingebildeten Werth hat) und das geistliche Religionsfach behalten, und meine Bibliothek wird künftig nicht mehr aus Tausenden sondern aus Hunderten bestehen. Sie sehen daß ich mich einzuschränken weiß; von fremdartigen Gaumesgenüßen ist schon lange bey mir nicht mehr die Rede.

Gegen Mitte Januar denke ich wieder auf dem Gute zu seyn: sollte sich Vater alsdann zu einem Besuche entschließen können, so würde mir natürlich dadurch eine große Freude erwachsen, umsomehr wenn Sie ihn begleiten können.

Meine Familie wird wohl den Winter in England zubringen; ich bin überzeugt, daß die äußere Noth einen heilsamen Einfluß auf unsere inneren Verhältniße haben wird, und erkennen auch darin die weisen Wege der Vorsehung. Mit herzlichster Ergebenheit
 der Ihrige
 J. N. Böhl

52. *Elise Campe, Hamburg*

[Hamburg], den 16 Jan[uar] 1812

Diese Zeilen können nicht besser anfangen als wie Ihre gestrigen 'der Mensch denkt, Gott lenkt' – demzufolge muß ich heute gleich nach Tische mit meinem Schwager abreisen, und habe den Vormittag so viel in Ordnung zu bringen, daß ich schwerlich werde zu Ihnen kommen können – Ich tröste mich damit, daß in der bevorstehenden Entfernung sich unsere Seelen näher seyn werden, als sie es waren, weil wir einen gemeinschaftlichen Mittelpunkt unseres Strebens in unserem Heilande Jesus Christus haben.

Meine besten Grüße an Ihren Campe und er solle mir nichts nach Mecklenburg senden, auch keine Auktionsverzeichniße, biß er weiter von mir hört.

Meine freundschaftlichste Achtung bleibt Ihnen stets gewidmet.
 Böhl v: Faber

53. *Elise Campe, Hamburg*

Heute den 13 Juny 1812 um 5 Uhr Nachmittags fange ich an Ihre lieben Briefe vom 26 Oct[o]b[e]r 1811 und 13 April dieses Jahres der Form und Regel nach zu beantworten. Kaum scheint es möglich, daß man sich im Raume so nahe und in der Zeit so ferne seyn kann! Ueber manches haben wir seitdem gesprochen, und können es, biß zu einer neuen Anregung, als abgethan ansehen – Wie haben Sie aber von Ihrem letzten Briefe so unglimpflich reden können? Es ist mir einer der liebsten, eben weil er mit der so gefälligen Hingebung der Zutraulichkeit aus der Feder gefloßen ist – Ueber die herrliche Rezension Fr[iedrich] Schlegels im Wiener d[eutsches] Museum¹ sind wir völlig eins; wenn Sie sie zum zweitenmal lesen wollen, so bleibt Ihnen gewiß nichts darin dunkel – Auch A[ugust] W[ilhelm] Schlegels Aufsatz über die Nibelungen² hat mir sehr gefallen.

Die Bekehrung, welche den wahrscheinlichen Verlag des Poetischen Almanachs³ zur Folge haben wird, hat mich so gerührt, daß ich mich recht angreifen werde, ihn nach besten Kräften auszustatten; und da ich seit ohngefähr 14 Tagen aus dem Reiche der Participia und Zeitformen glücklich und mit unverwelktem Sinn zu Hause gekommen bin, so liegen jetzt schon für den Poetischen Almanach fix und fertig neben mir: 1) Madrigalische Blumenlese aus deutschen Dichtern des 17 Jahrhunderts, enthält 52 kleine Gedichte, meistens völlig unbekannt. Kein eigentliches Lied, weil ich eine besondere Liedersammlung mit Dr Julius zu liefern, noch immer im Kopfe trage. 2) Sechs Gedichte aus dem englischen des Wordsworth,⁴ den Sie aus meinem Aufsatz in dem letzten Stücke des dortigen Vaterländischen Museums kennen werden 3) Bruchstücke von Volksliedern aus dem Spanischen, bis jetzt 9 die sich aber noch vermehren werden; beträgt schon 8 Bogen – Ich schicke sie darum nicht mit der Post weil es zu viel kosten würde, und da es ja nicht damit eilt, so denke ich sie meiner Mutter mitzugeben, die mich wohl in wenigen Wochen besuchen wird – Nun hoffe ich werden Sie mich recht loben. Ich las damals in Ihren Augen den leisen Vorwurf wohl, da mich die Participia in ihren Kreis gebannt zu haben schienen; allein die Quelle war erfreudig. Es galt einen Erwerb; daß es sich aber (ohne mein Zuthun) zerschlagen hat, thut meinem Herzen eben so wohl, als es meinem Verstand kränkt. Wahrlich lieber esse ich Wasser und Brod im Umkreis der deutschen Sprache (denn Deutschland giebt es ja nicht mehr) als Pasteten in Paris – Uebrigens rückt die von mir so sehnlich gewünschte, von meinen Verwandten so sehr gefürchtete, Stunde der Lösung meines irdischen Schiksals immer näher. Ich werde fallen, aber mit Ehre, und die Zukunft wird beweisen, daß ich nicht auf Unkosten meiner Gläubiger leben will – Mit meiner Familie bleibt es noch beim Alten, und Gott weiß ob sie je wird überkommen können.

Doch wieder zu angenehmeren Dingen – den poetischen Almanach habe ich damals nicht beachtet wie er es verdient. Hitzig hat ihn mir von Berlin zugesandt und ich behalte ihn gerne. Fouqué seine Sachen sind treflich, besonders am Ende des Schlachtabendtheuers. V. Loebens kleiner Beitrag ist allerliebst, und von Kerners selbst sind 43. 85. 94. 115 und 121 sehr schön. S[eite]129 steht ein herrliches Lied im Volkssinn, worauf ich den Dr Julius aufmerksam zu machen bitte.⁵

Nun was macht denn Ihr lieber Campe? Was bringt er von Nachrichten von Braunschweig, von woher ich schon lange nichts gehört habe. Hat er meine kleine Anweisung auf Weigel in Leipzig einkassirt? Hat er die Kritik der Partizipien⁶ mitgebracht, und Radloffs Werke⁷ über die deutsche Sprache? – So wie sich der Sommer bisjetzt anläßt haben Sie wenig Ursache Ihr Sorgenfrey zu vermissen; diese letzte Woche war besonders rauh und stürmisch. Ich habe den Fuß bis auf heute die ganze Woche durch, nicht aus dem Hause gesetzt: die Nachtigallen sind verstummt, statt deren haben wir Maykäfer Gesang gehabt – da lebe ich lieber in dem ewigen Frühling der Dichtkunst, und habe mich die letzte Zeit durch meinen alten Bekannten die Iberier besonders angezogen gefühlt. Dabey ist mir folgende Stelle eines geistreichen Schriftstellers recht klar geworden 'Es ist klar, daß ich durch eine Erlernung der Sprache und durch ein Studium der poetischen Kunstwerke einer jeder Nazion, eigentlich zum Mitgliede dieser Nazion selbst werde – ich durchlebe mit ihr die ganze Dauer ihrer Existenz, auch wenn sie viele Jahrhunderte begreift, und vereinige die meisten Streben der Bildung derselben mit mir; es ist das ewige Leben in der Vergangenheit, was ich gewinne'[8] – Bey einer solchen Ansicht verlieren die Uebersetzungen nur gar zu sehr, selbst die besten, wenn man etwas anderes als eine bloße Ähnlichkeit des dargestellten dadurch bezwecken will.

Noch bleibt mir ein Punkt Ihres Briefes zu beantworten übrig, nemlich einen Unterstand (sujet) od[e]r Stoff zu einer Oper für unsere gute L[uise] R[eichardt] auszumitteln. Da L[uise] doch Novalis kennt und glaube ich auch liebt, so fiel mir gleich das Märchen von Rosenblüthe und Hyazinth 2er Theil p. 196 bei.[9] Erstlich die unschuldige und glückliche Liebe der beiden, dann der Weise, der durch das Buch dem Hyazinth tiefsinnig macht, dann die Sybille im Walde die das Buch verbrennt, und den Hyazinth den Tempel des Isis aufsuchen frißt, dann einige Reisebeschwerden, Unruhen, Ermattungen endlich der Tempel, die verhüllte Statue, die Rosenblütchen selbst ist – Nur wäre vielleicht alles lieblichästhetische, alles tiefgedachte und gefühlte was diese Mythe enthält für ein größeres und grobes Publikum nur gemeiner Dunst ... Ich will dannach mich noch weiter umsehen und bitte mir nur gelegentlich zu melden ob die Oper groß oder klein, in einem oder mehreren Aufzügen, recht romantisch, oder komisch seyn soll?

Was sagen Sie zu diesem Brief in klein Folio? Sieht er nicht gewaltig gelehrt auch? Es ist aber, wie Sie sehen, ganz unschuldig, und zeigt sich nur aus leidiger zwungender Oekonomie, auf wohlfeilen Landespapier, so weit ist es mit uns Gutsbesitzern gekommen – Indessen: Wer uns hat ohne uns gebracht in dieses Leben, der wird auch ohne uns uns unser Nothdurft geben[10] – Mit diesem Kraft- und Trostspruch des alten Logau beschließe ich diese lange Epistel, und halte mich Ihrer beiden freundschaftlichen Andenken befohlen.

Böhl v: Faber

54. Elise Campe, Hamburg

Görslow, den 26 Aug[ust] 1812

Kurz vor meiner Abreise nach Osnabrück um meine endlich übergekommene Familie in Empfang zu nehmen, erhielt ich Ihr liebes Schrieben vom 22/31 July, welches mir in jeder Hinsicht sehr angenehm gewesen ist. Ja wohl ist es ein Trost bei jetzigen Zeiten in gleichgesinnten Gemüthern zu lesen, und Beweise über das allgemeine Unglück einzuholen um nicht an seinem Schiksal irre zu werden. In dem ersten Freudenrausch des Wiedersehens war meine Seele betäubt, jetzt aber fühlt sie die verdoppelten Sorgen für den Unterhalt einer zahlreichen an Entbehrungen noch wenig gewohnten Familie um desto schmerzlicher; da nun auch meine jetzigen Pflichten als Lehrer und Vorsteher dem süßen Versinken und Selbstvergeßen in irgend eine Geistesbeschäftigung Eintrag thun, so fühle ich mich unglücklicher als vorher, denn das Bewußtsein erfüllter Pflicht will nicht immer auslangen – Ist es nicht sonderbar daß uns der vergangene Zustand immer besser als der gegenwärtige scheint? Dieses Hängen an die Vergangenheit mit dem Schauen nach der Zukunft in Uebereinstimmung zu bringen zu bringen, ist eine schwere Aufgabe. Ich helfe mir durch eine poetische Ansicht heraus; Zeit und Raum nemlich sind Täuschungen welche Poesie zu vertilgen strebt, Zeit durch den Rythmus, Raum durch die Metapher oder Uebertragung welche alle poetischen Ideen zum Grunde liegt. Poesie ist Ahnung des künftigen vollkommeneren Zustands. So wäre demnach vielleicht nichts unwiederbringlich verloren, des Vergangenen und des Zukünftigen könnten dereinst zusammenfallen, Himmel und Erde eins werden, und was sich darüber weiter noch Schönes fortträumen läßt . . .

Von dem liebenswürdigen Fouqué habe ich nur das zweite Stück der Jahreszeiten gelesen, welches wiewohl schön, doch auch in meiner Ansicht der reizenden Undine nachsteht. Den Zauberring[1] und die Romanenbibliothek[2] will ich mir zu verschaffen suchen; ich freue mich, daß Sie diesesmal so gut mit Neuigkeiten versorgt gewesen sind – Von früheren Sachen unter dem Namen Pellegrin[3] kenne ich noch etwas dramatische Spiele betitelt; dem stehen aber noch in dem Pantheon zwei vorzüglich schöne Mährchen unter dem Namen Fouqué. Ihres lieben Campes Bekehrung ist denn so wie die meisten Bekehrungen: allerlei äußere Gründe können eine Stellung hervorbringen, wodurch man nicht allein andere sondern auch sich selbst täuschen kann; am Ende aber kehrt man zu <u>seiner Natur</u> zurück, zu diesem unveränderlichen, in sich begründeten, tiefen eigentlichen Kern unseres Wesens, der wie der Fels im Meere wohl periodisch von den Wellen bedeckt, aber nie verrückt werden kann. – Eigentlich aber möchte ich nun wohl noch wissen 1) ob Campe jetzt bei Ihnen ist 2) ob er dem poetischen Almanach verlegen wird 3) ob ihm mit der altdeutschen Madrigalen Anthologie gedient ist oder nicht, ohne Fürcht daß ich die Ablehnung übel nehmen werde.

Stellen Sie sich vor, daß ich d[en] 12 dieses um 8 Uhr Abends bei der Pauli in Rückeberg war, und daselbst den braven Vogt traf, der nach Flottbek eilte; dadurch wird der dasige Zirkel ein vermehrtes Interesse gewinnen: vielleicht haben Sie schon davon genoßen. V[ogt] bleibt trotz seiner Eitelkeit ein belohnender und unterhaltender Gesellschafter und seine letzte Reise giebt Stoff zu den interessantesten Gesprächen.

Vielen Dank für die Nachrichten von dem Siev[ekingschen] Zirkel, von dem ich sonst nichts höre. Der liebe Gott wird auch da so lenken wie es ziemlich ist, obwohl wir es nicht verstehen.

Ergebenst der Ihrige
Böhl v: Faber

55. Elise Campe, Hamburg

Sontag um 2

Vielen Dank für den mitgetheilten Brief der einliegend zurück erfolgt. Dem Schluße stimme ich andächtig bey; Eija, wären wir da! – Unterdessen schlägt man sich mit besten Kräften durch, und lebt so viel möglich im Reich des Geistes und der Fantasie. Ich verspreche Ihnen wenigstens, das weder die Participia noch die Tempora verborum mich abhalten sollen, einige altdeutsche Blumen zu dem P[oetischen] Alm[anach] hervorzusuchen. Gebe der Himmel nur auch altdeutsche Nasen sie zu genießen.

ergebenst
Böhl v: Faber.

56. Nikolas Heinrich Julius, Hamburg

Görslow d[en] 28 Febr[uar] 1813

Eigentlich ist es zwar häßlich von mir, daß ich Ihnen gar nicht geschrieben habe; wenn ich aber bedenke daß es Ihnen nicht mehr und nicht weniger Zeit Papier und Dinte gekostet haben würde, so tröste ich mich, und so wollen wir es denn auch gegen einander aufgehen lassen. Daß ich seit 6 Monathen meine Familie mit mir vereinigt habe, wissen Sie; daß der dadurch erwachsene Zufluß von Freuden, durch leibliche und geistige Sorgen aufgewogen wird, können Sie schließen; daß mein Vermögen in Spanien so gut als verloren ist, habe ich leider der halben Stadt Hamburg verkündigen müssen; daß ich das Gut G[örslow] nur in Folge unserer langwierigen Prozeßformen noch bewohne, folgt aus dem Vorigen; daß ich demungeachtet ein leidliches Leben führe, und mich auf keine Weise der Muthlosigkeit hingebe, dafür ist Ihnen mein bekannter Karakter und mein christlicher Sinn Bürge – Meine kostbarsten Bücher habe ich in Berlin versteigern lassen und mehr Geld dafür erhalten als ich glaubte; es waren meist englische. Jetzt sind auch die französichen dahin unterwegens. Ich habe mich auf drei Fächer beschränkt: Christenthum, ältere deutsche Litteratur, und Sprachkunde; immer noch Stoff genug zur Beschäftigung, besonders wenn die Stunden der Muße abnehmen. Ich treibe nemlich seit 6 Monden das Lehramt bei meinen Kindern in vollem Ernst, des Morgens von 9 bis 1 und des Abends von 6 bis 8; es bleibt mir also nur eine Morgenstunde und einige Nachmittagsstunden – Daß durch den Umgang einer solchen Erzspanierin als meine Frau ist, meine Studien wieder eine spanische Wendung genommen haben, werden Sie natürlich finden. Meine Kollektaneen zu einem spanischen Parnaß[1] habe ich durch die Benutzung der Bibliothek des Prof[essor] Tychsen in Rostock[2] ansehnlich vermehrt, und es fehlt nur wenig an die völlige Anordnung eines ersten Theils, den ich auf Subskription herauszugeben denke. Das <u>Fehlende</u> ist die Benutzung eines Garcilaso de la Vega,[3] eines Boscan[4] und eines Diego de Mendoza[5] die Tychsen leider nicht hat. Jetzt also ergeht mein Ersuch an Sie, mich aus dieser Noth zu helfen. Vielleicht haben Sie diese Bücher selbst; vielleicht können Sie solche von einem Freunde erhalten. Wenn ich auch nur vors erste den Garcilaso erhalte, so machen Sie mich glücklich; man wird auf der Post keine Schwierigkeiten machen, ein paar Bücher paßiren zu lassen – Ich werde daraus schließen wie Sie gegen mich gesinnt sind; in einigen Wochen erhalten Sie das Buch oder die Bücher ohne Verletzung zurück! –

Wie haben Sie denn gelebt? Wie geht es mit der Praxis? Haben Sie auch Ihren altdeutschen Schatz vermehrt? – Es war vorigen Herbst in Regensburg eine Palmsche Auktion, ach! wie voll herrlicher alter Ritterbücher, und welche schöne spanische Sachen! – Nur in solchen Augenblicken drückt mich die Armuth.

Meine schöne Sammlung in C[adiz] ist durch beispiellose Verrätherei zu Spottpreisen verschleudert worden! – Doch weg mit solchen Erinnerungen! – Vielleicht verlasse ich Deutschland bald; dann würde ich auch meine mystichen und altdeutschen Sachen verkaufen, wenn ich einen Liebhaber en bloc fände. Ihre und meine Sammlung zusammen, wären schon etwas werth, nemlich für den Liebhaber. Von Opitz allein habe ich 7 Ausgaben und gerade die besten und seltensten. Oder wollen Sie mir Ihre spanischen Sachen gegen altdeutsche eintauschen; dann senden Sie mir ein Verzeichniß Ihrer Spanier das ich mit einem Verz[eichniss] m[einer] altdeutschen erwiedern werde; eigentlich glaube ich daß ich Ihnen darin nur den Hans Sachs und den Amadis zu beneiden brauche; dagegen meine erste Ausg[abe] des Opitz, der Logau, die Alberts Arien, und des Harsdörfer Gesprächsspiele zu den rarissimi gehören – Wir sehen hier täglich unserer Erlösung entgegen; vermuthlich thun andere gute Freunde dasselbe – Unverändert
Ganz der Ihrige
B. v. F.

57. Nikolas Heinrich Julius, Güstrow

Görslow, den 9 Aug[ust] 1813

Endlich, bester Freund, hat die hehre Stunde meines Lebewohls geschlagen, und ich muß meinem Vaterlande in demselben Augenblick den Rücken kehren, da sich ihm eine herrliche Zukunft eröffnet. Doch mit Gott im Himmel hadere nicht . . . ich folge dem Gebote der Pflicht, und so hoffe ich den Lohn so vieler schweren Opfern zu ärndten, sei es äußerlich oder innerlich. Solbald ich irgendwo festen Fuß faße, lasse ich Ihnen von mir wissen; vor Ende des Jahres sehe ich (im Geiste) freien Handel und Wandel allerwärts hergestellt, und dann wird man sich wenigstens brieflich unterhalten können.

Sonderbar daß Sie sich nie recht mit mir über christliche Gegenstände haben einlassen wollen. Daß Sie Christ sein müßten, fühlte ich Ihnen bald ab, aber von welchem Bekenntniß war mir nie klar. Sind Sie katholisch, so werden Sie sich freuen, wenn ich Ihnen hiemit anzeige, daß ich vor einigen Tagen mein öffentliches Glaubenskenntniß nach dem trident[ischen] Conc[ordat] abgelegt habe und demnach ein Mitglied der allgemeinen Kirche geworden bin. Ich finde mich seitdem innerlich einig und beruhigt und rathe jeder liebenden und suchenden Seele ein Gleiches zu thun. Hätte ich Zeit wie viel Wunderbares würde ich Ihnen über diese Bekehrung mittheilen können! Daß sie <u>aus dem Herzen</u> kommt brauche ich Ihnen der mich kennt, wohl nicht noch besonders zu versichern. – Sind Sie Protestant so nehmen Sie sich die Mühe den Katholizismus aus seinen Quellen kennen zu lernen und nicht aus den falschen Aussagen und Verdrehungen der Irrlehrer; dann werden Sie bald meinem Beispiele folgen.

Wo mich der Himmel auch hinführen wird, werde ich Ihrer, Deutschlands, unserer alten Lieder und besonders der Hamburger Patrioten eingedenk sein. Vielleicht sehen Sie Perthes über kurz oder lang; dann sagen Sie ihm meinen Abschied und meine besten und heißesten Wünsche für sein und aller Patrioten Wohlergehen. Und damit Gott befohlen! –

Der Ihrige von Herzen
Böhl v: Faber

58. Friedrich Perthes, Hamburg

Cadiz, den 22 Märtz 1815

Obgleich ich geradezu seit meiner Abreise nichts von Ihnen gehört, und wenngleich verschiedene meiner Briefe an Sie unbeantwortet geblieben sind, so leben Sie dennoch in meiner Erinnerung, und aus Ihrer Fahrläßigkeit ist kein anderer Nachtheil erwachsen, als daß meine Ergießungen über die hiesigen Angelegenheiten eine andere Richtung genommen haben – Ueber die deutsche

Sachen wäre ich gänzlich im Dunkeln geblieben hätte mich mein ehrlicher Schwager Berckemeyer nicht meiner erbarmt und mir im Sommer ein kleines Packet Flugschriften übersandt. Jetzt ist das Interesse daran vorüber, und ich verlange nichts weiter über Politik zu sehen, als allenfalls eine pragmatisch[e] authentische Darstellung der Kongreßverhandlungen wenn solche nach völliger Beendigung erscheinen sollte.

Ich sehe mich genöthiget meinen Knaben wieder auf einige Jahre nach Deutschland zurückzusenden, da der Unterrricht hier nur mittelmäßig bestellt ist und ich selbst keine Muße habe ihn fortzusetzten. Diese Gelegenheit benutze ich um Ihnen einen Koffer spanischer Bücher zuzusenden, davon Verzeichniß hiebei erfolgt, und welche ich irgend einer Bücherversteigerung anzufügen bitte, damit solche bestmöglichst verkauft werden. Es sind Doubletten der Trümmer meiner spanischen Büchersammlung; ex unque leonem: seit meiner Rückkunft habe ich indessen schon fleißig wieder gesammelt und mein poetisches Fach ist fast schon wieder komplet. Meine Liebhaberei dafür nimmt (Gottlob) nicht ab, und so behalte ich ein eigentliches Solatium für die wenigen Stunden die nicht von dem Brodterwerben verschlungen werden.

Sie werden gleichfalls einige Kupferstiche erhalten nach dem gleichfalls beiliegenden Verzeichniß. Da es alle spanische Kupferstiche folglich dorten rar sind, so bietet man Ihnen vielleicht im Ganzen dafür; den Band von Dürer[1] könnte man allenfalls durch die Zeitungen ausbieten lassen. Wenn Ihnen ein ordentliches Bot dafür gemacht wird, so schreiben Sie es mir p[er] Post damit ich darüber beschließe.

Ich bin noch immer im Ganzen mit meiner Lage zufrieden, wenngleich mir oftmals die Nahrungssorgen nahe auf den Hals rücken. Dagegen werden mir die Eigenthümlichkeiten der hiesigen altgewohnten Lebensart immer lieber; in Hinsicht meines Geistes stehe ich zwar allein, doch dieses war in Görslow auch der Fall, und hier habe ich überdem <u>Seelenverwandte</u>, die mit mir das Ueberirdische suchen.

Ich wünsche von Herzen daß Sie sich von Ihnen harten Verlüsten mögen erholt haben und in Gesellschaft der lieben Ihrigen die Segnungen des Friedens und der Freiheit genießen, zu deren Herbeiführung Sie so redlich das Ihrige beitragen.

ergebenst
Bohl v: Faber.

59. August Campe, Hamburg

Cadiz, den 6 May 1815

Es hat sich so sonderbar gefügt daß ich Ihre freundschaftliche Zuschrift vom 30 July mit den 4 Büchern erst ehegestern durch H[er]rn Grund erhalten habe. Ich ersehe daraus daß Sie sich meiner schon früher errinert haben und bin Ihnen dafür dankbar. Was müssen Sie während der schrecklichen Belagerung ausgestanden haben! und wie hat Ihre liebe Frau so mannigfaltigen Drangsalen wiederstehen können? Wie gerne unterhielte ich mich mit Ihnen darüber mündlich! Doch diese Lust muß ich mir mit so manchen Anderen vergehen lassen.

Der scheinbaren Zweck meiner Reise ist nicht erreicht, und ich wußte auch recht wohl daß er nicht zu erreichen war. Das Handlungshaus ist total ruinirt und nichts für mich zu retten. Dagegen aber sind mir meine Freunde zur Errichtung einer Assurantz Comp[anie] behülflich gewesen, deren Besoldung so eben vor Verhungern sichert und da nebenher noch andere kleine Verdienste aus Commisionen und Spedizionen entspringen, so war ich sehr zufrieden, bis die Wiedererscheinung des Höllenfreundes Alles wieder ins Stocken gebracht hat – Meine Empfindungen über diesen Gegenstand können Sie aus meinen früheren Expektorazionen schließen; jetzt ist die Sprache für meinen Unwillen zu arm und ich glühe mehr wie je von Begierde ihn durch Thaten zu verwirklichen. Fühlten nur hundert Tausend Deutsche so wie ich, so ist es mit Frankreich vorbei; der neue Wahlspruch kann nur delendum sein! –

Vielen Dank für die Bücher – Von altdeutschen Sachen aber müssen Sie mir nichts senden; alles darauf Bezug habende ist in Deutschland geblieben und ich habe diesen Litteratur Zweig vors erste an den Nagel gehangen – Also nur die vorzüglichsten Sachen in der schönen Litteratur, Religion und Politik – Der 3te Theil von Göthes Leben[1] hat mich ungemein besagt, wenngleich eine feine Ader von Ruchlosigkeit selbst da durchscheint, wo es am Ernsten aussieht. Die Karakteristik berühmter Männ[er] ist sehr unterhaltend, und die eingestreuten Bemerkungen ein wahrer Schatz von Lebensweisheit – Niemand heitert mich so auf als Göthe; durch wenige schlichte Worte macht er mir die verwickelsten inneren und äußern Verhältniße klar; ich fühle mich selbst doppelt nachdem ich ihn gelesen; ich werde zufrieden mit mir selbst weil ich mich besser kenne und meine Eigenthümlichkeit mehr zu ehren lerne. Ich merke wohl daß sich hiebei leicht etwas unmoralisches einschleichen kann; dieses ist aber eine Klippe woran alle tiefere Untersuchungen über Willkühr und Nothwendigkeit stoßen müssen und wobei nur das innere Bewußtsein entscheiden kann – Das Werkchen Wahrheit und Liebe ist recht gut, wenngleich etwas breit.

Ich würde Sie geradezu darum bitten mir ferner das Wichtige zu senden, wenn ich nicht fürchtete daß es sich mit Sendungen von Perthes kreuzen und verdoppeln könnte. Perthes vernachläßigt mich außerordentlich und hat mir außer einige Flugschriften von London aus noch nichts gesandt. Wenn es Ihre Verhältniße daher erlauben Perthes in meinem Namen zu sagen, daß in Hinsicht seiner vielen Geschäfte ich ihm meine geistige Vorsorgung abzunehmen und sie Ihnen übertragen wolle, so wird es mir völlig recht sein – Ich wünsche dann die Bücher in feiner Pappe gebunden zu erhalten; jedes Buch besonders in einem Umschlag mit addresse die mein alter Freund Lohmann (und wo nicht sein Sohn Pieter) zur

Behändigung an die auf hier fahrende Schiffe wohl übernehmen wird – Von der neuen Auflage von Tiecks Phantaus habe ich zwei Theile und erhielte gern die folgenden. Auch hat mir Frau Sieburg von einem schönen Werke Fouques geschrieben. Kurz Sie kennen meinen Geschmack und noch besser kennt ihn Ihre liebe Frau. Was diese für mich aussucht das senden Sie ohne Widerrede. Aber nur das <u>Beste</u>! Kein Mittelgut; auch nichts dramatisches. Auf ein halb Dutzend Bände p[er] Messe nehme ich nur – Vor Ansicht dieses haben Sie wahrscheinlich meinen Juan gesehen, der einige Jahre dorten noch zulernen soll. Die Trennung ist mir sehr sauer geworden, allein es war nothwendig, und alles ist ja am Ende hieneiden Entbehrung und Aufopferung.

B. v. F.

60. *Friedrich Perthes, Hamburg*

Cadiz, den 20 Juny 1815

Wenn es auf Beförderung der guten Sache ankommt, so muß man alle privat Beschwerden vergeßen; demnach finden Sie einliegend einen flüchtig übersetzten Auszug eines Briefes von Margarita[1] der die ersten Verrichtungen unserer im Februar ausgegangenen Expedizion enthällt. Ich bitte demselben die möglichste Publizität zu geben. Es haben sich Hölle und Teufel verschworen die jetzige spanische Regierung verhaßt zu machen, um das vorige Chaos wiederherzustellen, und da der Spanier seine eigenthümliche Beschwerlichkeit auch leider im Bösen behauptet, so sind die hiesigen Aufklärer (liberales) jetzt Anhänger Bonapartes und Vertheidiger der [illeg.] Republikaner in Amerika geworden, so daß es nöthig ist darüber <u>getreue</u> Berichte in Umlauf zu bringen.

Ich hoffe Sie werden die spanischen Bücher und Kupferstiche wohl erhalten haben und einen guten Markt damit treffen – Woran es liegt das ich weder von Ihnen noch von Bokelmann eine Zeile erblicke, gehört zu den Verhängnißen die sich nicht erklären lassen. An Zeit kann es in so langer Zeit nicht gefehlt haben; an Willen hoffe ich eben so wenig! Also nur Fatalität –

ergebenst
Bohl v: Faber

61. *Friedrich Perthes, Hamburg*

Cadiz, den 6 October 1815

Vor einiger Zeit erhielt ich Ihre Zeilen vom 12 May über Lissabon sehr verspätet. Sie beziehen sich darin auf frühere Briefe mit Bücher ordres die ich aber nicht erhalten habe; die 3 Exempl[are] von Calderon, 2 Dicc[ionarios] de la Academia[1] und 1 obras de Sta Teresa werde ich besorgen, sobald sich ein Schiffsgelegenheit nach dorten findet. Während der Revoluzion sind außer politischen Flugschriften nichts gedruckt, und da die meisten schönen Geister die französische Parthei damals ergriffen und jetzt in Verbannung leben, da die Regierung keine Mittel hat die Herausgeber wichtiger Werke zu unterstützen, so kann man auch vors erste nichts Wichtiges erwarten. Man spricht von der Sammlung der Briefe des Filosofo rancio[2] die einzeln während der Revoluz[ion] erschienen und sich durch gediegenen Gehalt und trefflicher Darstellung auszeichnen: diese sende ich Ihnen, wenn sie zu Stande kommt – daß ich so wenig von Ihnen und Litteratur höre ist mir sehr empfindlich. Die Campen schickte mir neulich den Dichterwald,[3] Fouqués Thiodolf,[4] und den 3. Theil von Göthes Leben – Gerne erhielte ich die Forts[etzung] von Tiecks Phantasus wovon ich nur den 1 und 2ten Theil besitze, Fouques gesammelte Erzählungen,[5] desselben Jahreszeiten, Schuberts Ahnungen und Ansichten,[6] die Uebers[etzung] von St Martins Wesen der Dinge,[7] und sonst das Vorzügliche in diesem Geschmack, aber nichts altdeutsche da ich dieses Studium hier habe aufgeben müssen – Von meiner Sendung spanischer Bücher und Kupferstiche habe ich noch kein Wort erfahren –

ergebenst,
J. N. Bohl

Die Bücher die Sie mir senden, erwarte ich alle eingebunden in feiner Pappe.

62. *Friedrich Perthes, Hamburg*

Cadiz, den 22 Dec[ember] 1815

Ihre Zuschriften vom 16 Sep[tember] und 20 Nov[ember] habe ich ungefähr zu gleicher Zeit erhalten; was Sie zur Entschuldigung Ihres Stillschweigens sagen soll gelten ob ich gleich mit dem christlichen pater peccari noch zufriedener geblieben wäre. Wer hat Ihnen aber den Unsinn in dem Kopf gesetzt, daß es gefährlich sei frei hieher zu schreiben? Hätte mir die Aufklärerei noch verhaßter werden können, so wäre sie es durch den ungeheuren Nebel von Lug und Trug geworden, den sie über die spanischen Sachen geworfen hat. Alles was darüber in allen fremden Zeitungen steht ist grundfalsch: die spanischen Finanzen sind zerrüttet weil der Zufluß aus Amerika mangelt; niemand im Dienste der Regierung wird bezahlt und dadurch vermehren sich Unterschleif und Diebereien. Was hat dieses aber mit Monarchie und cortes gemein? – Die Inquisizion oder vielmehr ein Schein von Inquisizion ist da ohne Kraft ohne Muth ohne Eifer, ein mildes freundliches Konsistorium, welches seine Existenz nur durch das Verbot der jakobinischen cortes Schriften dargethan hat, so elend daß ich mich darüber in einer Fromme ergoß, die von einem Inquisitor selbst als Ernst verstanden wurde. Also (wenn Ihnen daran gelegen ist) auch nicht die entfernteste Hoffnung zur Auferstehung des altchristlichen Eifers; ich kenne viele herrliche Priester aber es sind alle Johannes, kein Petrus darunter; ich der Norddeutsche, bin der einzige Fackelträger in meiner Umgebung, der Einzige der glühend haßt, wie er glühend liebt der Einzige der das verderbte Glied will abgehauen wissen ehe es den ganzen Körper ansteckt – Ueber das <u>Festhalten Wollen</u> kann ich nicht mit Ihnen einig sein; ich finde daß Einige dazu bestimmt sind, wie Andere zum Zerrütten. Ob es gelingen werde oder nicht ist keine Frage. Was ich als einzig heilig ehrwürdig und fördernd anerkenne lasse ich mir nicht nur nicht nehmen, sondern verbreite es nach besten Kräften. Grade diese willkührliche Beschränkung bei einer unbeschränkten Bildsamkeit ist mir Heil; in dieser Demuth liegt der eigentliche christliche Geist der anstatt keck herumzuflattern sich im Schooße der Mutter verhällt bis er in Liebe genährt und durch Liebe gestärkt dereinst aufsteigen wird zur Quelle des Lichtes – Die Sammlung von Durer und die übrigen Kupfer und Bücher bitte bestmöglichst zu verkaufen. Sobald Cap[itain] Schmidt ankommt, werde ich Ihnen meine Meinung über die gesandten Bücher sagen; auch Ihre Comission mit dem ersten Sch[iff] nach dorten ausrichten – Ich hätte gerne einiges von Ihnen über die letzten Augenblicke Ihres guten christlichen Schwiegervaters[1] gehört – Nächstens weitläuftiger.

Der Ihrige B. v. F.

63. Friedrich Perthes, Hamburg

Cadiz, den 5 April 1816

Ihre Briefe vom 16 Sep[tember] und 20 Nov[ember] vorigen Jahres habe ich wohl erhalten, und muß darin finden daß unsere Mittheilungen nur fragmentarisch sind und sein können; nur kann ich Ihren Grund von <u>Briefen die in unrechten Händen kommen könnten</u> nicht gelten lassen. Dieses hört mit zu dem Lügengewebe welches von den Aufklärern verbreitet wird um den Katholizismus und indirekt das ganze kristliche Sistem verhaßt zu machen. Kein Brief wird jetzt in Spanien geöffnet; ein Jeder sagt frei was er denkt und gegen einen Vertheidiger des herrschenden Sistems finden sich hundert Ankläger; es gehört zum guten Ton auf den König und die Geistlichkeit zu schimpfen und einer meines Schlages ist rara avis. Alle Häuser wimmeln von verbotenen Büchern, aber noch keins ist von der Inq[uisizion] weggenommen. Alles was von den tyrannischen Machtsprüchen von Festsetzungen und von Tortur in Madrid verbreitet wird sind Märchen, die nur beweisen wie tief der Haß gegen Monarchie und Religion gewurzelt hat – Wenn man <u>das Alte</u> so herzlich liebt als Novalis so ist es schwer nicht nur dessen Rückkehr zu wünschen sondern auch zu diesem Zweck nach besten Kräften mitzuwirken. Man sieht zwar ein daß es nicht ganz und völlig <u>das Alte</u> wieder sein kann, allein man möchte doch gerne etwas Ähnliches. Wenn ich selbst durch das Neue zum Alten geführt bin, warum nicht auch die Andern? Daß das Christenthum zeitgemäß sein kann und darf gebe ich gerne zu; auch lassen die Gränzen des Katholizismus einen sehr großen Spielraum – Gott gebe daß die deutschen Bestrebungen zu etwas Gutem führen mögen. Ich vernehme daß bisjetzt sich noch wenig von Früchten spüren läßt, und daß es wohl nach deutscher Weise auch diesmal bei Idealen bleiben wird.

Von den Büchern die Cap[itain] Schmidt bringen sollte ist nichts erschienen und dieser Cap[itain] behauptet keine Bücher empfangen zu haben; die Unkosten des an Bord Schickens sind dabei verloren gegangen. Da Sie in diesen Schiffsachen wenig bewandert scheinen, so würde unser Freund J[ohann] D[aniel] Runge[1] es gewiß übernehmen mir die Packete zu befördern, wenn Sie ihm solche einhändigten. Die einfältige Furcht dieser Menschen wird ja wohl der Erfahrung weichen.

Cap[itain] Voß überbringt Ihnen eine Sendung von 35 Kisten Bücher meist spanischen, die Bibliothek eines verstorbenen Liebhabers die hier nicht im Ganzen anzubringen ist, und die dorten in Aukzion verkauft werden muß. Einen genauen von mir selbst verfertigten Katalogus erhalten Sie p[er] Post. Es wird also nur nöthig sein die Bücher aufzustellen, sie mit N[ummern] zu versehen, die Verzeichniße drucken zu lassen, den Aukzionstag etwas enfernt festzusetzen damit ordres einlaufen können und dann den Belauf entgegen zu nehmen. Ich selbst werde Ihnen auch einen Auftrag machen. Sollte von den vorig Jahr gesandten Büchern noch etwas nach sein, so könnten Sie als als Anhang beifügen – Die Kupferstiche verkaufen Sie nur bestmöglichst, da bei dem längeren Warten doch kein Vortheil sein wird – die verlangten spanischen Bücher finden sich in der obigen Sammlung, woraus Sie solche wohlfeiler als neu werden erstehen können.

Auch bringt Ihnen Cap[itain] Voß ein kleines Packet 30 Abdrücken eines anatomischen Phänomens nebst Beschreibung, um es in den Anzeigen bekannt machen zu lassen und den Verkauf zu besorgen. Der Preis ist hier 1 piaster; finden Sie es aber zu theuer so können es auch wohlfeiler aufsetzen.

Von wissenschaftlichen Sachen wird hier in Spanien jetzt gar nichts gedruckt; einige Geschichten Bonapartes, etwas gegen Freimaurer und geheime Gesellschaften, und eine berichtigte Uebersetzung von Labordes Itineraire[2] sind die einzigen Früchte der Presse in der letzten Zeit. Von den Revoluzionsschriften sind die Meisten verboten, weshalb eine sehr vollständige Sammlung dieser Art welche bei den Büchern befindlich ist wahrscheinlich dorten Liebhaber finden wird. Das Hauptwerk zu Gunsten der alten Grundsätze betitelt (cartas del filosofo rancio) welche damals einzeln erscheinen sollten vermehrt geordnet und zusammen neugedruckt werden, wozu es aber noch nicht gekommen ist. Die gänzliche Zerrüttung der Finanzen bringt eine Stockung in den ganzen gesellschaftlichen Getriebe hervor, die sich auf alle Zweige des Verkehrs erstreckt, und dennoch ißt die ganze Schaar der königlichen Diener ohne auch nur einen Heller Besoldung einzunehmen. Wie sich das Ganze noch so zusammenhält ist unerklärlich; dennoch scheint ein Umsturz unvermeidlich, nicht aus falschen Grundsätzen sondern aus Noth, der aber darum nicht weniger eine Regierung des Pöbels nach sich ziehen wird – Die Aussichten sind sehr trübe; nur die Allmacht Gottes kann aus dieser Gährung das Gute entwickeln.

Stets der Ihrige
Böhl v: Faber

64. Elise Campe, Hamburg

Cadiz, den 6 April 1816

Unglaublich scheint es mir daß Ihr lieber Brief vom 25 May schon fast jährig ist, und daß ich bisjetzt nichts darauf erwiedert habe. Aber die Welt in welcher ich lebe ist von der dortigen so verschieden, und meine Empfänglichkeit für alle Arten von Existenz so lebhaft, daß ich mich ordentlich zusammennehmen muß um zu glauben, der Görslower Filosof und der spanische Geschäftsmann seien eine und dieselbe Person. Nur in der Poesie finde ich mich wieder; den alten Liedern bleibe ich getreu, und bedaure jetzt sehr, daß ich meinen gesammelten Vorrath in der Verwahrung meines Bruders gelassen habe. Um desto eifriger vermehre ich meine spanische Sammlung alter Poesie und arbeite auch unterweilen an dem lange entworfenen Werke darüber. Je mehr ich diese Dichter studire desto klarer fühle ich die Uebereinstimmung der altromantischen Sinnesart mit der Meinigen, aber auch den Kontrast mit der Allgemeinen, und dem bleibt nur die Ertödtung des Nachdenkens, und das Ergreifen des flüchtigen Genußes den Zeit und Umstände darbieten – Mit der Erinnerung an unserer letzten Zusammenkunft geht es mir gerade wie Ihnen; Sie entwickeln Ihre Gefühle darüber so schön, daß ich mich darin mir selbst verdeutlicht wieder finde. Am Ende aber ist es die Elegie worauf Alles in der jetzigen Zeit hinausläuft, und man muß sich selbst betäuben wenn man nicht an der Menschheit verzweifeln will – Ich versetzte mich ganz in Ihre ruhige harmlose gleichförmige Lebensweise und beneide Sie zuweilen, wenn zu viele Ansprüche an meine Geschäftskunde gemacht werden. Wenn ich mich aber in den Mußestunden meiner brausenden Fantasie überlassen kann, wenn ich angehört werde von Einigen die mich verstehen, wenn ich hier Ueberirdische und Irdische Gegenstände für die Bedurfniße meines Herzens finde, dann freue ich mich dem erkältenden nordischen Dunstkreise entgangen zu sein – der leblosen Natur so zugethan zu sein wie Sie, ist eigentlich eine nordische Unart, die den verzogenen Kindern schwer abzugewöhnen ist; demnach bedaure ich in Ihrer Seele den Untergang so vieler grünenden Freunde und verfluche in Meiner die verruchten Hände die so absichtlich ohne eigene Nutzen, Wahr thaten.

Alles was Sie mir über unsere gemeinschaftlichen Bekannte schreiben hat mich sehr interessiert, hauptsächlich die sich nähernde poetische Bekehrung unseres lieben Campe. Vielleicht entschließt er sich wohl, den 2ten Theil der von mir gesammelten deutschen Volkslieder mit Melodien[1] (den ich dem Dr Julius handschriftlich hinterließ) herauszugeben, und in diesem Falle würden mir einige Exemplare sehr willkommen sein. Jedesmal das ich mir diese alten Dinger im Kopfe wiederhole drücken sie sich mir tiefer ein.

Die gesandten Bücher haben mir viele Freude gemacht, aber mitunter auch Wehmuth. Alles was so schön im Werden ließ, verliert seinen Zauber sobald es fertig da steht. Ach! über die Eitelkeit aller menschlichen Bestrebungen! Und doch werden wir es nicht müde dieses beständige Streben –

Meine weltliche Lage ist wie sie von der Zeit zu erwarten steht; mit einiger Anstrengung aber in beständiger Angst zu versinken, weicht sie gerade das Nöthige ab, und dieses ist in Cadiz für eine Familie 10 [illeg.]. Meine Frau ist glücklich in ihrem Vaterland und begnügt sich mit dem Nöthigen; meine älteste Cecilia verheirathet sich mit einem schönen Grenadier Cap[itain] von 28 Jahren, der ein kleiner Majorat zu erben hat und geht mit ihm nach Puerto Rico auf drei Jahren;[2] meine zweite Aurora ist ein gutes liebevolles Mädchen, ist aber von zarter Leibesbeschaffenheit woraus Sorgen für uns erwachsen. Meine dritte[3] leidet noch immer an der Hüfte und hinkt sehr stark; auch eben kein Trost. Von Juan habe ich fortwährend angenehme Nachrichten, und wünsche fast daß er seinen Beruf bei der Landwirtschaft finden möge da es für den Kaufmannstand so höchst betrübt aussieht – Von der guten Sieburgen schreiben Sie mir nichts; ich hoffe daß sie nach überstandenem Schmerze als Tochter, jetzt einer ungetrübten Existenz genießen werde; auch stelle ich mir vor daß es Ihnen nicht an Einladungen nach Mindorff wird gemangelt haben und daß Sie diese Zeilen vielleicht Pfingsten daselbst lesen werden. Dann denken Sie in der Solitude des Menschen doppelt, daß ein Herz kalt gegen Frühling und Natur um desto wärmer für schöne Seelen gleich der Ihrigen und der Sieb[urg] schlägt und beständig schlagen wird.

Böhl v: Faber

65. Friedrich Perthes, Hamburg

Cadiz, den 16 July 1816

Ihre Zuschrift vom 13 passto habe ich erhalten, und daraus gerne ersehen, daß die 35 Kisten Bücher glücklich zu Händen gekommen sind. Ihre dispositionen in dieser Hinsicht so wie auch was meine Bücher und Kupferstiche betrifft genehmige ich vollkommen und bemerke daß ich c[irc]a 500 Mark bei Ihnen zu Gute habe. Ich hoffe daß Cap[itain] Köster mit dem Verzeichniß der Bücher wird geschwinder überkommen sein als Cap[itain] Voß, damit keine Zeit verloren gehe.

Um künftig alle Schwierigkeiten bei dem Abschiffen der Bücher zu beseitigen, so lassen Sie solche in ein Kistel packen, versehe es mit Mark und N[ummer], geben es für Proviant aus damit der Cap[itain] es in der Kajüte nehme, lassen ihm ein Recief darüber zeichnen und es auch ein Manifesto setzen; ich werde dann für das Uebrige sorgen. Was die Auswahl anlangt so muß es nur das Gewichtige sein, und ich fürchte daß wenn die vorjährige Sendung zu Händen kommt ich Manches zu leicht befinden werde.

Von Politik mag ich nichts mehr sehen noch hören; Poesie sehe ich jetzt mehr als Studium an und habe meine ganze Aufmerksamkeit dem technischen Theile zugewandt; meine Arbeit über die alten Spanier rückt daher fort. Ein Werk welches mir abgeht und welches ich absolut in Spanien nicht auftreiben kann ist: Joannis Caramuelis (Lobkowitz) primi Calami Tomus Secundus Rhythmica appelatus Sanctangelii 1665. oder besser und vermehrt Campaniae 1668.[1] Vielleicht gelingt es Ihnen mir dieses Werk auf Ihren Reisen Wienerwärths aufzuspüren, wofür ich Ihnen sehr dankbar würde; da es in Italien gedruckt ist kann es sich leichter im südlichen Deutschland finden lassen – Was ich sonst noch wünsche finden Sie ueberstehend verzeichnet, wobei ich wiederhole daß Alles in feiner Pappe eingebunden sein muß.

Für heute gebietet die Zeit zu schließen; ich fühle so halb und halb daß wir einig sind ob ich gleich nicht recht begreife Wie? Ich werde immer unduldsamer und bin sehr unzufrieden daß die Machthaber nicht mehr hängen und köpfen; der Abscheu gegen Unrecht und Laster scheint mir bei weitem noch nicht genug aufgeregt, und Bonaparte ist vielleicht noch zu früh abgetreten.
Der Ihrige
J. N. Bohl.

66. Friedrich Perthes, Hamburg

Cadiz, den 10 Sep[tember] 1816

Seit einigen Wochen besitze ich endlich die so lange erwarteten Bücher und obwohl ich bisjetzt nur habe darin blättern können, kann ich ihnen doch sagen daß ich mit der Auswahl im Ganzen sehr zufrieden bin. Blos die Kieler Blätter[1] haben kein Interesse für mich, und auch die dramatischen Sachen werde ich schwerlich anbeißen. Von der ersten factura vermiße ich Humboldts Reise[2] und Mullners Schuld[3] welches Sie mir sehr anpreisen.

Schuberts Symbolik des Traumes[4] hat mich am meisten ergriffen; alle ferneren Schriften dieses Verfaßers bitte ich mir aus – die Fantasiestücke[5] entsprechen dem Titel; man wird dabei schwindeln; alles ist hinreißend, einiges zu gräslich – Fausts Versöhnung,[6] dencke ich, wird mich nach den Schlußstrophen zu urtheilen ansprechen – v. Baaders Schriften[7] bitte ich das Nächstemal mitzusenden; auch Schlegels Comparaison des deux Phedres in franz[ösischer] Sprache.[8]

Ich hoffe daß Cap[itain] Köster das Bücherverzeichniß wird wohl eingehändiget haben – die alten spanischen Bücher, besonders Dichter, werden hier immer seltener. Für einige mir abgehende habe ich neulich in Madrid 12 a 16 piaster p[er] Stück bezahlen müssen.

Der Eigenthümerin der Bücher haben Sie noch nicht geschrieben, wiewohl ich Sie darum ersucht hatte; auch melden Sie mir doch ob die anatomischen Kupfer Interesse erweckt und Liebhaber gefunden haben? –

Wenn beigehend notirte alte Sachen zu finden wären so bitte sie für mich anzuschaffen und abzusenden – daß die meisten Bücher gebunden waren ist mir sehr willkommen gewesen, und bitte damit fortzufahren.

D[en] 21 Sep[tember]

Den dorten gedruckten Bogen des Catalogus habe ich erhalten und so ziemlich fehlerfrei gefunden. Auch ist Ihr Brief für Mrs Grant[9] eingetroffen welches mir sehr lieb ist.

Jovellanos Schriften[10] sind noch nicht zusammengedruckt; man beschäftigt sich jetzt damit und werde Ihnen einen Abdruck senden sobald sie heraus sind.

Ergeb[en]st
B. v. Faber

67. Friedrich Perthes, Hamburg

Cadiz, den 3 Jan[uar] 1817

Ihr werthes vom 15 Oct[ober] habe ich wohl erhalten und Cap[itain] Köster hat mir die verzeichneten Bücher richtig überliefert. Von Uebersetzungen von Calderon habe ich genug; Kanne Sämundi[1] hat mir vielen Genuß gewährt; die Kieler Blätter interessiren mich ganz und gar nicht – Humboldts ReiseErzählung wünsche ich sehr zu erhalten, so wie Baaders Schriften, auch Alles wird Neu eine Schrift[2] welche mehrmal von Kanne angeführt wird.

Der Hauptzweck des Gegenwärtigen ist Ihnen meinen veränderten Auftrag zur Versteigerung des 10 Febr[uar] zu behändigen; eigentlich ist mir nur an N[ummer] 569 gelegen; sollten indessen die übrigen zu den limitirten Preisen zu erhalten sein so bin ich sicher sie hier mit Vortheil wieder verkaufen zu können. Es wird mir Vergnügen machen den Ausgang der Versteigerung speziell zu erfahren d.h. die Preise nach den N[ummern].

Suchen Sie doch auch die anatomischen Kupfer bestens loos zu werden, und melden Sie mir wieviel Sie mir dafür vergütet haben.

Meine besten Grüße an Dr Julius, und daß ich das verlangte medizinische Buch noch immer vergebens von Madrid erwarte; sobald ich es erhalte übersende es ihm und beantworte alsdann ausführlich seinen Brief.

Ich vermiße Weinmanns großes botanisches Werk[3] in dem Verzeichniß, und bin doch sicher daß es mit bei den Büchern war; wahrscheinlich hat der Kopist des Verzeichnißes aus Mangel an Kunde der Sprache es ausgelassen.

Den Ihnen aufgetragenen Caramuel Rhythmica bin ich so glücklich gewesen neulich in Valencia aufzutreiben, so daß ich diesen Auftrag zu streichen bitte.

Die Ausgabe der gesammelten Werke von Jovellanos wird noch immer erwartet so wie auch der vortreflichen Briefe des Filosofo rancio. Der drückende Mangel scheint alles litterarische Leben erstickt zu haben; außer einigen Schulbüchern sind im vergangenen Jahr nur die beiden letzten Theile der 8°° Ausgabe der Werke des Fr[ay] Luis de Leon[4] und neue vermehrte Ausgaben der Gedichte des Conde de Noroña[5] und des Cienfuegos[6] herausgekommen; die ökonomischen Gesellschaften rühren sich und schreiben ganz schöne Memorias aber ganz ohne Erfolg –

ergebenst
Böhl v: Faber

Die Eignerin der Bücher Mrs Grant ist nach England zurückgekehrt; ich weiß aber ihre addresse nicht; vermuthlich hat sie Ihnen wohl schon aus England geschrieben.

68. Nikolas Heinrich Julius, Hamburg

Cadiz, den 28 Febr[uar] 1817

Ich erhielt, theurer Freund, seiner Zeit Ihre liebe Zuschrift vom 6 Aug[ust] mit der wenngleich kurzem doch lebhaft anschaulichen Beschreibung Ihres Pariser Aufenthalts um den ich Sie wahrlich beneide. Daß Sie jetzt wieder in Ihre bürgerlichen Verhältniße als Artzt zurückgetreten sind ist völlig in der Ordnung, und hoffe ich daß Sie des nöthigen Wirkungskreises nie entbehren werden. Der größte Theil meines Lebens ist leider an das undankbare Handlungsgewerbe verschleudert geworden, welches nachdem ich mein ganzes Vermögen dabei zugesetzt habe, mich nun auch nicht einmal als Handlanger nähren will. Mit dem Rufe eines einsichtsvollen Kaufmanns, mit der Kenntniß von vier lebendigen Sprachen, fähiger Buchhalter, gewandter Rechner, von vielen Freunden beschützt, finde ich keine Beschäftigung, weil wirklich keine Beschäftigung vorhanden ist. Hätte mich mein Vater studieren lassen, wie es meine Neigung war, wie ganz anders wäre mein Schicksal gewesen! Doch dieser hörte nun einmal in den Plan der Vorsehung, und dient sicherlich meiner Seele zum Heil, wenngleich die beständige Sorge für das tägliche Brodt das Leben sauer und widrig macht.

Der Besitzer der jetzt wahrscheinlich schon veräußerten Büchersammlung war ein Schottländer Nahmens Campbell,[1] der kurz nach meiner Rückkehr im Jahr 1813 am gelben Fieber starb; ich habe ihn daher nicht gekannt, weiß aber daß er ein interessanter Mann war. Er hat auch eine artige Gemälde Sammlung hinterlassen, die seine Schwester mit nach England genommen hat. Gemälde sind hier jetzt umsonst zu haben; eine andere Sammlung die 4000 piaster taxirt war, ist neulich für 600 verkauft, und eine noch größere nebst einer auserlesenen und (wie man mir sagt) vollständigen Münzen Sammlung steht feil, ohne daß man auch nur einen Heller dafür böte. Dieses ist aber nicht aus Mangel an Gelde, sondern weil sich das Geld jetzt in Händen gemeiner, roher, völlig ungebildeter Menschen befindet, die es weder zu geistigen noch zu sinnlichen Genüßen verwenden, sondern es in Kasten verschließen und sich in dem Bewußtsein genügen reich zu sein. Wie dieses hier gekommen ist wäre leicht zu erklären, wenn es sich der Mühe verlohnte.

Aber mein lieber Freund wenn Sie sich über diese Sammlung spanischer Bücher freuen, was würden Sie zu meiner sagen? Im Fach der alten spanischen Litteratur und hauptsächlich der Poesie ist jene nur ein unbedeutendes Fragment der Meinigen. Durch unermüdeten Fleiß, durch Tausch und durch soviel Aufwand als meine Lage es mir gestattet habe ich zusammengebracht was vielleicht kein Privat Mann in dem poetischen Fache vereinigt, und keiner schwerlich wieder vereinigen wird, weil durch das Aufkaufen der Engländer und durch die Zerstörung der Franzosen, es gar keine kursirende Bücher dieser Art mehr giebt. Alles dieses sind Materialien zu dem Parnaso Espanol, den ich im Kopfe trage und dessen Einleitungen größtentheils schon bearbeitet sind, hauptsächlich eine <u>ganz neue Metrik</u> der alten spanischen Poesie worüber Sie sich freuen werden. Daneben ist im Geiste fertig ein <u>altspanisches Theater,</u> welches nur Stücke enthält die vor Lope de Vega, also am Ende des 15ten und in der ersten Hälfte des 16ten Jahrhunderts geschrieben wurden, so gut wie unbekannt; dann eine Romanzensammlung aus fliegenden Blättern, kurz, giebt nur die Vorsehung noch einmal Brodt und Weile, so hoffe ich in einigen Bänden den Kern der alten spanischen Poesie ans Licht zu fördern, und dadurch ein Denkmal meiner irdischen Laufbahn zu hinterlassen, woran sich alle poetische Gemüther freuen sollen.

Da ich wegen dieser alten Sachen in beständiger Korrespondenz mit einer Madriter Buchhändler bin, so verschrieb ich <u>Cavanellas[2] über die Post</u> für Sie, nachdem ich es hier vergebens gesucht hatte. Aber vergebens habe ich dieses Gesuch verschiedenemal wiederholt, mich darauf an einen Anderen mit derselben Bitte ebenso vergebens gewendet und jetzt ist der Dritte von mir deshalb in requisition gesetzt. Die Apathie der hiesigen Buchhändler übersteigt alle Begriffe. Morgen geht Cap[itain] Köster nach Hamburg mit dem ich es Ihnen senden wollte und deshalb meine Antwort so lange verschoben hatte. Sie sehen aber daß es nicht sein soll, da ich keine Mühe erspart habe, um den Endzweck zu erreichen.

Dagegen hatte ich mir Folgendes von Ihnen erbitten wollen. Ich hinterließ Ihnen einen zweiten Theil von deutschen Volksliedern mit Melodien, nach denen ich mich jetzt sehne; ich bitte um eine Abschrift derselben die Melodien mit einbegriffen.

Es ist ein Glück für mich daß die spanische Poesie meine Aufmerksamkeit so sehr verschlingt daß für sonstige Litteratur kein Platz bleibt; ich würde sonst vermißen nicht au courant zu sein. Jetzt bin ich zufrieden von Zeit zu Zeit das <u>Vorzüglichste</u> im poet[ischen] und relig[iösen] Fach zu erhalten; Schubarts Schriften sind mir sehr wichtig; auch Kanne spricht mir zu; Fouque ist weich und sinnig, aber Niemand ersetzt <u>mir</u> Tieck, dessen Fortsetzung des Phantasus ich schmerzlich vermiße – billig ist es daß ich Ihnen noch zuletzt sage, daß der alte katholische Glaube Stich hält, daß ich mich täglich mehr durch ihn gestärkt und getröstet fühle, und daß ich mich über diesen Gegenstand den Drang fühle Manches auszugießen, wenn mich die Nahrungssorgen nur zu Athem kommen ließen. Denken Sie meiner in brüderlicher Liebe so wie ich Ihrer und und auch vor Gott wie ich es thue.

Der Ihrige
B.v.F.

69. Friedrich Perthes, *Hamburg*

Cadiz den 1 Märtz 1817

Ich hoffe daß die im vorigen Monath stattgehabte Versteigerung der Büchersammlung der Mrs Grant gut ausgefallen sein wird; wahrscheinlich wird Ihnen diese Dame von England aus ihre Disposizionen ertheilt haben.

Hiemit erhalten Sie ein Packet mit 50 spanischen Schauspielen, um solche gelegentlich zu versilbern; der hiesige Preis ist 3 reales od[er] c[irc]a 8 Schilling court, wenn Sie mir diese dafür vergüten so bin ich zufrieden; wonicht verkaufen Sie solche für meine Rech[nun]g Ich denke einzeln müssen sie dorten 12 Schilling werth sein. Die alten abgenutzten sind die besten; besondere Aufmerksamkeit verdienen die ziemlich raren Stücke des Tirso de Molina[1] und des Alarcon.[2]

Von den verschriebenen Sachen vermiße ich noch immer: Humboldts Reisebeschreibung, Sismondi Litterature du midi,[3] und Wordsworth Excursion[4] in 8°°.

ergebenst
Böhl v: Faber

70. Friedrich Perthes, Hamburg

Cadiz, den 3 Juny 1817

Leider ist wieder eine lange Ebbe in Ihren Mittheilungen an mich eingetreten, und vier Schiffe von dorten sind angekommen ohne weder Briefe noch Bücher für mich zu überbringen. Ich habe es zwar aufgegeben au courant der deutschen Litteratur zu bleiben, allein gewiße Hauptwerke kann ich doch nicht entbehren, und es sind daran Mehrere die ich ausdrücklich gefordert habe, ohne daß sie mir bisjetzt geworden sind. Ich muß daher Ihr Gedächtniß mit deren nochmaligen Aufzählung erfrischen:

1) Die eigentliche Reisebeschreibung Humboldts, die schon in mehreren Sprachen übersetzt ist
2) Sismondi Litterature du midi de l'Europe
3) Poems by William Wordsworth und with additional poems a new preface and a supplementary essay 2 vol[umes], 8°°
4) Desselben The Excursion, wenn nemlich nach ersten Ausgabe in 4. eine andere in 8 od[er] 12 erschienen ist.
5) The Edinburgh Review:[1] die letzt erhaltene ist N[ummer] 52

Ich habe auch eine englische Uebersetz[ung] eines Werkes von Gneisenau über den Feldzug der Deutschen nach Frankreich[2] angezeigt gefunden, und bemerke dabei, daß Sie mir noch nichts über diesen Gegenstand gesandt haben. Natürlich kann mich nur eine echtdeutsche, patriotische geistreiche Darstellung interessiren; nichts von Strategie und allgemeine Politik, sondern ein lebendiges Ergreifen des Selbsterlebten. Ist in dieser Art etwas erschienen, so werde ich es gerne lesen – Auch sehne ich mich noch immer nach der Fortsetzung von Tieks Phantasus. Fr[iedrich] Schlegels Vorlesungen über Litteratur[3] (die ich erst kürzlich habe lesen können) haben mir einen großen Genuß gewährt. Sonst bleibt meine ganze Muße dem Studium der spanischen alten Poesie gewidmet und mein schon so lange entworfener spanischer Parnaß rückt seiner Vollendung immer näher.

Bei dieser Gelegenheit habe ich entdeckt daß ein Spanier Don Ignacio de Asso[4] in den Jahren 1781/1783 in Amsterdam bei Sommers Erben und Co verschiedene altspanische Poesien hat drucken lassen. Da dieser Zeitpunkt noch nicht sehr entfernt ist, so finden sich vielleicht noch Exemplare dieser Werke in der besagten Buchhandlung. Es ergeht daher meine Bitte an Sie ohne Zeitverlust (damit es nicht auf die lange Bank liegen bleibe) nach Amsterdam zu schreiben und für mich ein Exemplar jedes dieser Werke kommen zu lassen, um solche <u>eingebunden</u> mir zuzusenden.

Nach und nach könnte ich auch wohl Nachrichten über den Ausgang der Auktion erwarten; durch Mrs Grant habe ich erfahren, daß sie verschoben worden. Sobald ich vernehme, welche Bücher Sie für mich erstanden haben, werde ich darüber verfügen.

Ich könnte Manches über Spanien und über die schändliche Verdrohungen und Verfälschungen des Polit[ischen] Journal etc sagen, allein ohne Aufmunterung und gegenseitige Mittheilung bleibt es liegen; auch bin ich es fast müde länger gegen den bösen Geist anzufechten. So viel ich vernehme ist das <u>Allgemeine</u> in Deutschland nicht weniger verkehrt, und träumt von Verfaßungen, Fabriken, Handlungssperren und Bilanzen, völlig enzyklopädisch-ökonomisch, anstatt Jeder in seinem Beruf redlich treu und fromm zu wandeln und so das Reich Gottes auf die rechte Weise, von unter an, zu begründen.

Der Ihrige Böhl v: Faber

P. S. Sollte von ungefähr N[ummer] 554 (Lusiada traducida p[or] Garces[5]) in Händen eines Spekulanten gefallen sein, so sagen Sie mir zu welchem Preise er es wieder abstehen würde –

Sollten Sie es vorräthig haben, so senden Sie mir das schöne Kupfer des heiligen Johannes nach dem Dominicatio gestochen, und damit es nicht gekrunkelt werde unter Glas und Rahmen. Cap[itain] Köster oder Voß nehmen es gerne für mich mit. Ich bitte um Beförderung der Einlage.

Derselbe.

71. *Nikolas Heinrich Julius, Hamburg*

Cadiz, den 15 July 1817

Es ist fast ein Jahr daß Ihr letzter lieber Brief an mich geschrieben ist, so ersehe ich mit Verwunderung aus dessem Datum von 4 Aug[ust] 1816. Schnell vergeht die Zeit und besonders schnell hier wo bei äußerer Einförmigkeit eine so vage Abwechslung herrscht. Auf solche Weise gleitet man am gelindesten den Lebensstrom hinab, und überläßt sich den Nahrungssorgen nur, wenn das Wasser an der Kehle steht. Sei es Religion, sei es der heitere Himmel, sei es Vernunft oder alle drei zusammen, so viel ist gewiß, daß ich mich nie inniger über die Zukunft gequält habe, als seitdem ich mit keiner bestimmten Einnahme rechnen kann und lediglich von der Vorsehung lebe. Der alte Logau hat wohl recht wenn er singt

> Hat Gott mich <u>ohne mich</u> gebracht
> in dieses Leben
> wird Gott das was mir fehlt mir
> <u>ohne mich</u> auch geben.[1]

Desto unbedeutender die Äußerlichkeiten, desto lebhafter gestaltet sich die innere Welt. Daß ich hier, wie allenthalben, mit der herrschenden Ansicht in Widerspruch stehe versteht sich von selbst. Daraus werden Sie schließen, daß es hier geht wie Göthe einstmals von Wien sagte: Während die neuen Katholiken hineindrängen, drängen die Alten heraus. Alles was hier Sitz und Stimme hat, alles was lesen und schreiben kann und nicht zu den Wächtern Zions gehört, alles ist anti-katholisch und anti-monarchisch gesinnt. Ich habe nie an geheime Gesellschaften zur Beförderung solche Zwecke geglaubt, wenn ich indessen jetzt die wunderbare Übereinstimmung aller Sprechenden und Schreibenden betrachte, wenn ich bedenke wie im Lande selbst die handgreiflichsten Lügen zur Herabwürdigung des Throns und des Altars umlaufen, wenn ich sehe wie alle fremde Zeitungen und Journale an diese Rotte verkauft sind, so weiß ich nicht mehr was ich darüber denken soll. Man hat mich hier zu einem Mitgliede einer ökonomischen (eigentlich <u>aufklärenden</u>) Gesellschaft gemacht, mit der alle meine Ansichten in Widerspruch stehen; ich darf sie aber nicht laut werden lassen, um nicht den Haß derjenigen Menschen auf mich zu laden, von denen mein Lebensunterhalt abhängt. Ich vertraue hier dem Papiere allein und der Diskretion einiger Wenigen des alten Schlages. Zwanzig Aufsätze dieser Art zählte ich jüngst zwischen meinen Papieren. Ich zweifle, daß man hier den Druck erlauben würde, weil sie zu heftig gegen Aufklärung, französ[ische] Filosofie und enzyklopedische Oekonomie sind, auch die alte Religion, ihre Stütze die Inquisition und das unabhängige Königthum zu sehr in Schutz nehmen. Sollte es indessen auch gedruckt werden können, so würde es hier niemand kaufen. – Während der Revolutionszeit trat ein mächtiger Kämpfer für die alte Sache auf, und donnerte unter dem Namen des Filosofo rancio die Aufklärer nieder, und zermalmete ihre Sofistereien mit seiner geistigen Logik. Keiner wagte es gegen ihn aufzutreten und es blieb nichts übrig, als das Verschmieren welches dann auch mit so gutem Erfolge ins Werk gerichtet wurde, daß es noch zur Stunde eine Schande ist, dieses Buch zu besitzen, und eine unverzeihliche Sünde es zu loben. Wenn man in Deutschland auf ein spanisches Publikum rechnen könnte, so würden Auszüge aus diesem Werke Glück machen. Da es aus 43 zu verschiedenen Zeiten und an verschiedenen Orten gedruckten Briefen besteht, so sind vollständige Exemplare sehr rar geworden. –

Dieser Brief ward eigentlich für unsere liebe Freundin Elise Campen angefangen; allein ich verlief mich zu sehr in Allgemeinheiten und so wurde es Ihrer, der mein litterarischer Mitfühler waren und hoffentlich noch sind.

Stein und Bein muß ich über Perthes klagen; noch kein Wort habe ich von der spanischen Bücherversteigerung erfahren – Keine Sendung von verschiedenen Büchern die ich gefordert habe und doch sind kürzlich wieder 3 Schiffe von dorten angekommen – Keine Nachricht und Beendigung der so sehr ans Herz gelegten chirurgischen Kupfer! – Treiben Sie bester Freund dahinter an; wie kann doch Freund Perthes so ganz vergeßen, die <u>Länge</u> des Wissens und die <u>Kürze</u> des

Lebens? – Auch tragen Sie auf mir lithographische Probeblätter und eine genaue Beschreibung des lithographischen Prozeßes einzusenden. Es heißt mein guter Freund Cap[itain] Voß kommt wieder mit hier: Dieser wird gerne alle Kleinigkeiten für mich mitnehmen, und auch den geforderten heil[igen] Johannes mit Rahmen und Glas. – Ihnen bringe ich die geforderte Abschrift des zweiten Theils der Volkslieder wieder in Erinnerung. Sie sollen dagegen einige allerliebste spanische Volkslieder haben, wenn Ihnen damit gedient ist.

72. Friedrich Perthes, Hamburg

Cadiz, den 19 October 1817

Ich beantworte heute vorläufig das Ihrige vom 5 Sep[tember] Wenn Sie sich bessern wollen, so soll Alles Vergangene vergeßen sein; ich bin so genugsam, daß ich zufrieden sein will, wenn Sie mir nur einmal im NachJahre eine kleine Sendung machen, und zweimal im Jahre einige litterarische Nachrichten ertheilen.

Meine Kunde der Handlungsweise der spanischen Regierung erstreckt sich über Spanien und insbesondere Cadiz, demzufolge ich Ihnen abermals versichere, daß die Inquisizion nur dem Namen nach existirt, daß die meisten Inquisid[ores] Liberales sind und sich ihres Amtes scheuen, daß alle verbotenen Bücher von Jedermann beseßen und gelesen werden, daß alle Reden in Gesellschaft ertragen werden nur nicht Vertheidigung von Mönche, Inquisizion, Rosenkreuz etc, kurz daß die allgemeine Tendenz zur Aufklärerei so entschieden ist, daß die wenigen Anhänger des Alten schweigen und sich verstecken müssen. Es steht Ihnen natürlich frei dem politischen Journale zu glauben, welches das Gegentheil sagt, oder den Schiffscaptaine, wenn sie sich durch eine Lüge von einer Beschwerde lossagen die ihnen nichts einbringt. Auch können Sie dem dortigen spanischen Konsul, der gerne viele Zertifikate a 3 Mark 8 Schilling geben will, hohe politische Zwecke unterlegen, wenn er sein Raubgier zu beschönigen, lächerliche Eide verlangt. Alles dieses fährdet meine Wahrhaftigkeit nicht. Gottlob daß Cap[itain] Voß mein Freund ist und sich der Bücher Beschwerde unterziehen will; so lange er in der Fahrt bleibt, brauchen Sie keines anderen Schiffer Gunst zu erflehen.

So eben fällt mir ein, daß die Inquis[izion] sich doch wirklich vor einigen Monathen gezeigt hat. Kaum hatte ein französisches Schiff von Marseille die Anker geworfen, als man den Inquis[idores] angab, daß sich eine Kiste so und so markirt an solcher Stelle des Schiffes befinde die mit gewissen schändlichen Werkzeugen der Wollust angefüllt sei, deren Beschreibung jedes rechtliche Gemuth empört ... Was geschah? Legte man etwa Beschlag auf Schiff und Ladung: Setzte man den Cap[itain] fort? Verhörte man die Mannschaft? – Nichts von Alledem? Der Alguazil der Inquis[izion][1] ging mit zwei verkleideten Soldaten ganz in der Stille an Bord, lies sich die Kiste auskiefern, und theilte sodann den Verlauf dem französ[ischen] Konsul mit – dieser dankte dem Inquis[idor] für sein kluges Benehmen, und daß er seiner Nazion die Schande einer Untersuchung solcher Schändlichkeiten erspart habe, und seitdem sind der Inquis[idor] und der franz[ösische] Konsul die besten Freunde –

Ich verspreche mir viel Genuß von den Büchern per Cap[itain] Voß; das dem Wordsworth getroffenen Unglück[2] ist mir empfindlich, denn ich gestehe daß dieser Dichter noch immer bei mir oben an steht. Ich dancke für die gehabte Mühe in Amsterdam – den Einschluß über Paris habe ich <u>nicht</u> erhalten und bleibe dennoch noch immer über den Ausfall der Aukzion in Ungewißheit. Ich sehe gerne, daß Sie für mich grade die Comöd[ien] Sammlung erhalten haben an der mir gelegen war und das sehr billig – Ihre große Bücher ordre hat mich in Verwunderung gesetzt, da grade so viele Bücher darunter sind die in der Grantischen Sammlung befindlich waren. Ich habe darüber folgendes beschloßen: Ich sende eine Abschrift der nota nach Madrid und lasse die Preise beisetzen; dann sende ich Ihnen diese nota, damit nach Ansicht der Preise die ordre bestätiget oder wiederrufen werde. Da vor dem Frühjahr kein Schiff nach Hamburg abgehen wird so ist zu Allem Zeit. Die span[ischen] Bücher sind sehr theuer und gewöhnlich in Leder gebunden welches sie noch vertheuert. Dieses weiß vielleicht der Kommittant nicht. Ich meine, daß die Meisten zu haben sein werden, nur nicht die aus den 16. und 17. Jahrh[undert] welche höchst selten vorkommen. Ich nehme sie lieber in Madrid um zu besparen, weil die hiesigen Buchhändler wenigstens 20% aufschlagen, und keine komplete Sortiment haben.

Nachdem ich den heil[igen] Johannes werde empfangen haben, entschließe ich mich vielleicht zu der Madonna, und werde wenigstens bei Gelegenheit dieses schönes Stiches Gelegenheit haben einigen Liebhabern die erwähnte Madonna anzutragen welche nur leider sehr theuer ist.

Die Madriter Gelehrten klagen Stein und Bein über die Buchhändler, und sagen daß in früheren Zeiten (hauptsächlich die berühmten Sanchas[3]) sich auf Unkosten der Autoren bereichert hätten. Der Buchhändler übernimmt den Verlag gewöhnlich, mit der Bedingung daß das Produkt eine gewiße Anzahl zu verkaufender Exemplare für die Kosten gerechnet werden soll, und was z B. über 500 Ex[emplare] verkauft wird ist für den Autor nach Abzug der Comiss[ion] des Buchhändlers; nun aber, sagen die Autoren, richtet der Buchhändler es so ein, daß die ersten 500 Ex[emplare] nie als abgesetzt erscheinen, er mag auch tausende verkaufen. Daher denn auch das Wenige was noch gedruckt wird nun auf Unkosten des Verfaßers ist; dieses ist aber ungeheuer kostspielig, daher meine Idee in Hinsicht meiner Parnaßo ist, den Erlaubniß eines auswärtigen Druckes nachzusuchen, dann den Druck in Deutschland besorgen zu lassen, und die Hälfte der Abdrücke hier einzuführen – Leider ist meine Zeit jetzt aufs Neue durch Berufsarbeiten auf zwei Tage in der Woche beschränkt, und diese zwei Tage noch durch unendliche Nebenvorfälle so stark besetzt daß ich nur auf Sonntag und Festtage rechnen kann, so daß wenn mir der Himmel nicht durch anderweitige Einnahmen (als mein nochgesuchtes Konsulatgehalt und andere Agenzien) unterstützt, die Sache aufgeschoben bleiben muß. Der erste Theil Lira Española antigua nebst allen Prologomena, ist bis auf einigen Auszügen in der Kladde fertig; er begreift nur Gedichte in den nacional Metern; der 2te Theil der Lira soll die Ged[ichte] in ital[ienischen] Metern enthalten. Dann folgt Drama Español antiguo 1. Th[eil] Theater vor Lope de Vega (höchst interessant und so gut wie gänzlich neu) 2er Th[eil] Zeitalter der Lope und Calderon. Endlich Epos Espan[ol] ant[igu]o Räsonirte Auszüge aus 100 spanischen Epopeen.

Wie ist es mit den Heidelberger Jahrbücher gegangen? – Eine gute kritische Uebersicht der deutschen schönen Litteratur wäre mir sehr willkommen wenn sie mit poetischem Sinn geschrieben und nicht zu weitläuftig wäre. Ich würde darnach vielleicht Manches verschreiben können. Vorzügliche Sachen in franz[ösischer] Spr[ache] sind mir für m[eine] Frau immer willkommen, als die posthume der Fr[au] von Stael,[4] Bonalds Werke etc[5] – Sind die Schlegel so ganz müßig? – Wie freue ich mich auf den 3 Th[eil] von Tieck! –

Ich erwarte die versprochene Abschluß unter Rech[nun]g und bin beständig
Ganz der Ihrige Böhl v: Faber

73. Nikolas Heinrich Julius, Hamburg

Cadiz, den 19 October 1817

Endlich, endlich, endlich erhielt ich vor einigen Posttagen Ihr Schreiben vom 5 Sept[em]b[e]r; über und von Paris ist mir bestimmt Nichts weder von Ihnen noch von Perthes zugekommen, und doch ist mein Name hier bekannt genug um mich nicht zu verfehlen. Der Brief ist also bestimmt nicht auf die Post gekommen, und haben Sie mir darin einige Aufträge gegeben so müssen Sie mir solche wiederholen – Ich danke für die Deutlichkeit dieser Epistel, die ich mir ohne Anstoß habe aneignen können, und freue mich daß wir noch immer konvergiren. Die gute Sache gebe ich hier immer mehr auf, da sich die filosofische Parthei täglich stärkt, und den wohlmeinenden (leider aber kurzsichtigen) König völlig umstrickt hat. Durch die feindliche Verwaltung der neuen Kontribuzionsgelder haben die Wohlmeinenden allen Muth verloren, und so kann es nicht lange mehr bleiben – Ich freue mich auf die Sendung p[er] Cap[itain] Voß und werde Ihnen seiner Zeit mein Urtheil melden. Ich vermiße die geistliche Anthologie, wovon Sie mir in Ihrem Briefe reden, und bitte sie der ersten Sendung beizufügen. Altdeutsche Sachen die ein Studium erfordern können mir jetzt nicht dienen, aber für Volkslieder und sonstige alte lyrische Ergüße hege ich noch immer das lebhafteste Interesse – Die 2 Bände von Gries Calderon[1] habe ich erhalten und gerne gelesen, doch habe ich zu wenig Geld um solches in Übersetzungen anzulegen, die ich mir

deshalb verbitte. Calderons Autos stehen in meiner Ansicht noch höher als seine Comed[ias] sind aber wohl auch noch schwerer zu übersetzen, und können nur einen durchaus katholischen Sinn ansprechen – Gegen meine deutschen Lieder sollen Sie bestimmt p[er] retour von Cap[itain] Voß 6 original spanische Volkslieder, Melodie und Text, erhalten, die merkwürdigsten die seit meiner Rückkunft sich erzeugt haben, und die ich nicht müde werde zu spielen und zu hören – Meine alten deutschen Bücher stehen in einer großen Kiste verpackt bei meinem Bruder auf Cramon, der eben kein großer Litterator ist, und sind daher bei ihm so gut als unzugänglich; ich glaube indessen, daß ich weniges besitze, was auch Sie nicht haben. Das Wichtigste was ich im lyrischen Fache kenne ist Eschenburgs Sammlung in Braunschweig; wahrscheinlich ist er wohl schon gestorben, und seine Sammlung nach Wolfenbüttel[2] gekommen – Von den drei musikalischen Werken die Ihr Freund P[erthes] zu haben wünscht, besitze ich den Salinas[3] seit vorigem Jahr, nachdem ich in ganz Spanien drei Jahre danach hatte suchen lassen; wie merkwürdig er ist, weist Burney[4] aus: ich würde 100 Thaler dafür ausschlagen. Die andern beiden Werke habe ich nie gesehen und es ist ganz vergeblich bei den Buchhändlern darnach zu fragen; ich werde sie mir aber notiren, um sie in Beschlag zu nehmen sollte sie mir ein glücklicher Zufall vorführen. – Was Sie für sich von Romanz[en] wollen weiß ich nicht, da Ihr Brief verloren gegangen ist – den Filosofo rancio (den die liberales auf alle Weisen zu verwüsten suchen) hoffe ich Ihnen zu verschaffen. Von Ihrer Bibliothek germanica habe ich keinen Begriff und wünsche sehr sie zu sehen – Gebe der Himmel daß Ihnen die Bibliothekarstelle dorten möge zu Theil werden! Wär ich in Hamburg würde ich mich vielleicht zum Kompetenten aufwerfen; nichts würde ich mehr con amore treiben! Würden Sie Biblioth[ekar] so schenkte ich meine altdeutschen Sachen vielleicht der dortigen Bibliothek – Ich bemerke die dortige Liebhaberei für KunstSachen, und werde hiesige Verkäufer darauf aufmerksam machen; solche Sachen werden hier täglich werthloser – bald mehreres
 von Ihrem ergebensten B.v F

74. Nikolas Heinrich Julius, Hamburg

Cadiz den 13 Febr[uar] 1818

Ich schrieb Ihnen zuletzt d[en] 19 Oct[ober] und erhielt kurz darauf Ihr (Gott weiß wo zurückgehaltenes) Schreiben vom 18 April – Daß Ihnen gegenwärtiges Briefporto kostet ist abermahls der unverzeihlichen Fahrläßigkeit von Perthes zuzuschreiben. Ich rechne jetzt ernstlich auf Ihre Mitwirkung damit meine Kaufeignung gerettet werde, die aufs Spiel steht 1) bombardirt mich Mrs. Grant mit Briefen und Klagen daß sie weder die Komision für die letzte ½ der verkauften Bücher erhält, noch irgend eine Zeile Antwort aus 3 Briefen 2) quält mich der Buchhändler in Madrid ob die zum Theil mühsam zusammengesuchten Bücher beliebt sind oder nicht 3) seufzt der Dilettant dessen Sammlung ich angeboten habe nach irgend einem Bericht, um darnach seine Maasregeln zu treffen – Auf alle 3 Punkte erwarte ich umgehend p[er] Post Auskunft von Ihnen und flehe darum im Namen unserer Freundschaft. Mit Perthes will ich in Hinsicht von Geschäften nichts mehr zu thun haben; die Hoffnung meine Abrechnung zu erhalten habe ich lange aufgegeben – Jetzt zu etwas Angenehmeren: die Sendung p[er] Cap[itain] Voß hat mir im Ganzen vielen Genuß gewährt. Sismondi ist ein würdiger Nachtreter der Fr[au] v. Stael; es fehlt ihm aber sowohl die Kenntniß der span[ischen] port[ugiesischen] Litterat[ur] als auch der wahre Verstand der Sprache – Humboldts Reise ist vortrefflich, und es ist eine Schande daß schon mehrere Theile davon in Franz[ösisch] und Engl[isch] heraus sind, und in Deutsch nur der erste Theil – Die Kriegeswerke sind nicht was ich eigentlich suchte; ich wollte eine lebendige Schilderung des deutschen Triumphzuges nach Paris, französischer Erniedrigung und deutschen Trotzes, im Styl von Blücher[1] und Gneisenau. Wahrscheinlich ist nichts dieser Art erschienen – Tiecks Phantasus 3ter Theil hat meiner Erwartung nicht entsprochen; der 4te. wird hoffentlich um desto interessanter ausfallen – Mit der Schuld bin ich sehr zufrieden; König Tugends Machtlosigkeit hat mich bis jetzt geschreckt – Görres seine altdeutsche Lieder sind brav und die Vorrede noch braver.[2] Welch ein Abstand aber gegen das Altspanische! – Und wie hat sich der dichterische Görres so in demokratischen Unsinn und fabricken Wuth verlieren können, als es (laut englischen Berichten) im Rheinischen Merkur[3] geschehen ist? – Der ungarische Codex[4] interessiert mich nicht, aus Mangel an Zeit die Abweichungen der Sprache zu studiren. Daher nichts altdeutsches, als nur Volkslieder in gang und gäber Sprache – Göthes Italien[5] ist ganz angenehm zu durchlaufen aber die neuen und scharfen Ansichten darin lassen sich auf ein Paar Blätter zusammendrängen. Grimm seine Rom[ances] viejos[6] sind mir sogleich entrißen und der Span[ischen] Acad[emia] in Madrid zugesandt – ich bitte um andere zwei Exemplare gebunden – Die Vereinigung zweier Zeilen in einer wodurch die Assonanz am Ende einer jeden Reihe erscheint hat meinen völligen Beifall und ist dem metrum vollkommen angemeßen – Schuberts Altes und Neues[7] hat in dem Packet gefehlt und ist wahrscheinlich zurückgeblieben; ich erwarte es mit der ersten Sendung. – Schloßer sein Fievee[8] spricht meine ganze Sinnesart aus; ich sehne mich nach dem zweiten Theil, so wie überhaupt nach anderen räsonnirenden Werkes dieses gemüthlichen Schriftstellers, der meines Erachtens nach, das eigentlich Bedürfniß der Zeit ausspricht – In der Anordnung Ihrer Bibl[iothek] kann ich mich noch nicht recht finden, obwohl ich keine bessere ausdenken kann – Ein Verzeichniß meiner altspanischen Sachen sollen Sie p[er] Cap[itain] Voß erhalten – Von den 400 Preguntas giebt Southey in seiner Omniana Nachricht;[9] dieses Buch hat wenig poetisches Interesse aber ist ein reicher Beitrag zur Kenntniß der Meinungen und Sitten damaliger Zeit – Daß man Calderon dorten auf die

Schau Bühne gebracht und gerne gesehen hat ist mir sehr erfreulich gewesen; ich bitte um fernere genaue Nachricht, welche Stücke von ihm, auf welchen Bühnen, und wievielmal man sie gegeben hat und sonstige Umstände von Beifall etc –

Meinen besten Dank für die Abschrift der Volkslieder, die mir meine sonderbar isolirte jetzt traumähnliche Existenz auf Görslow lebendig zurückgerufen haben; ich finde noch immer großes Behagen daran sowohl Text als Musik. Rechnen Sie dagegen auf die spanischen p[er] Cap[itain] Voß zwar nicht zahlreich aber gewichtig und ächt – mein Parnasso Esp[añol] ist bei meinen anhaltenden Beschäftigungen zur Erwerbung des täglichen Brodtes jetzt wieder etwas im Hintergrund getreten; doch kommt, wills Gott, dereinst die Sonne die ihn ans Licht locken wird – Von den alten Ritter Romanen habe ich nur den Amadis; sie sind höchst kostbar und doch fast unmöglich zu kompletiren – Ihren Entschluß die Geschichte des span[ischen] Befreiungskrieges zu schreiben billige ich sehr; allein die Sammlung der Karoling[ischen] Schriften ist ein Mare magnum;[10] Mehreres darüber p[er] Cap[itain] Voß – Das unbedeutende Werkchen von Cabanells[11] müssen Sie mit den Comed[ias] erhalten haben; der Werth den Sie darauf legen muß auf einen Mißverständniß beruhen. – Den Romancero Canc[ionero] de Anv[ers] von 1558 habe ich nie in Spanien gesehen: er ist von der allerhöchsten Seltenheit und hätte ich nicht eine Abschrift durch Hitzig in Berlin erhalten, so müßte auch ich seiner entbehren.– Dagegen sollen Sie den kleinen Romancero des Cid[12] p[er] Cap[itain] Voß erhalten, da ich ihn glücklicherweise doppelt besitze – Cervantes seine Entrem[eses][13] sind neugedruckt wohlfeil zu haben – Hoffentlich treibe ich Ihnen ein wohlfeiles Ex[emplar] von Calderon auf; mit Lope de Vegas Theater aber müssen Sie resigniren. – Ich selbst habe es nicht, lege aber auch keinen großen Werth darauf, da selbst die 25 gedruckten Bände seiner Schauspiele doch nur ein Fragment seines Theaters sind, und man an einzeln gedruckte Stücke leicht genug auftreiben kann um sich einen genauen Begriff davon zu machen – Den Conde Lucanor[14] kann ich Ihnen zu 1 ½ Schilling verschaffen; es giebt nur die beiden Auflagen davon und beide rar; es ist ein höchst merkwürdiges Buch. Sowohl für Sprache als Inhalt – Eine Trutz Nachtigall[15] der neuen Ausgabe erwarte ich mit der ersten Sendung, so wie auch die geistliche Anthologie, die Sie mir unbegreiflicherweise vorenthalten haben – In öffentlicher Hinsicht ist es leider schlecht mit mir bestellt; die besten Pläne werden zu Wasser, da die Administrazion in feilen Händen ist und bleibt; ich sehe nicht ab, wo es hinaus soll – Unsere Handlung ist ein für allemal ruinirt, und sollte auch der puerto franco zu Stande kommen, so kann es nichts helfen. – Ich schlage mich so durch, muß aber tapfer arbeiten, so daß mir wenig Zeit zum studiren übrig bleibt; dabei aber Gottlob heiter und gesund und stark und glücklich im Glauben – Wie ist es weiter mit Ihrer Bibliothekar Stelle gegangen? Ich muß schließen. Sehen Sie die gute Campen, so rufen Sie mich in ihr Andenken zurück – Mit Cap[itain] Voß schreibe ich (wills

Gott) ausführlicher – Ich empfehle nochmals die bestimmte und promte Antwort auf N[ummer] 1. 2. und 3.
   Von Herzen Ihr treuer Freund
   J. N. Böhl v: Faber

75. *Nikolas Heinrich Julius, Hamburg*

Cadiz, den 30 April 1818

Der Himmel verleihe mir Muße um Ihnen lieber Freund wenigstens einen großen Bogen voll zu schreiben, ohne Furcht vor das leidige Porto, indem Cap[itain] Voß der Ueberbringer sein wird – Von Perthes dem ich d[en] 24. dieses facturo der spanischen Bücher übersandte werden Sie vernommen haben daß in der Kiste N[ummer] 4 folgendes für Sie befindlich ist:

4 Theile der Collecc[ion] alter Gedichte von Sanchez Rom[ancer]o[1]	80 –
Diese habe ich so wohlfeil erhalten können weil der Band etwas von Würmern angefreßen ist, das Buch selbst aber wie neu	
9 Theile eines vollständigen Calderon	135 –
Diese erste alte Ausgabe enthält gerade dassselbe was die zweite von Apontes[2] in sogenannten 11 Bänden enthält; nur sind die Stücke anders geordnet, in beiden Ausgaben ohne Sinn noch Verstand; sie ist sehr wohlfeil.	
1 Conde Lucanor in sehr gutem Zustande.	30.
ein unschätzbares Buch an Inhalt und Stil	
1 Romances de Germania Franzband[3]	22
1 Entrem[ese]s de Cervantes	10
Neue hier gedruckte Auflage, mit einer guthgemeinten Vorrede, doch voller literarischer Böcke	
	R[eales] 277
	Oder 39 Thaler

    Als Zugabe oder Angebinde:

Der Romancero del Cid, der hier nicht in derselben Achtung steht als in Deutschland, und la Florida del Inca[4] ein höchst interessantes altes Buch (erste Ausgabe Lisboa 1605) welches Ihnen gewiß Freude machen wird, und eine innere Wahrheit hat die alle äußeren Zeugniße aufwiegt. Das noch wunderbarere Werk Naufragios de Cabeza de Vaca 1555,[5] worauf sich die Florida bezieht, gehört zu den seltensten Stücken meiner Sammlung. – Dem Dichter Southey verdanke ich die Aufmerksamkeit auf diese Werke die ich lange besaß, ohne sie zu schätzen

Diesen Brief begleiten ferner:

1) Die vorzüglichsten Volkslieder die seit meiner Wiederkunft gang und gabe gewesen sind. Das erste rührt noch aus der französischen Belagerung her: die übrigen haben keine politische Beziehung mehr. Die Melodien sind für mich höchst reizend, müssen aber (wie alles volksmäßige) erst noch eingehört werden. Die Wörter sind so flüchtig daß ein jeder Sänger abnimmt oder zuthut und haben lokale Beziehung die in der Fremde unverständlich bleiben müssen. Ich hätte Ihnen hundert artige Liederchen kaufen können die von den modischen Damen am Klavier gesungen werden, aber diese Volksweisen habe ich selbst mühsam aufschreiben müssen, und in einigen Jahren werden sie verschwunden sein, wie so viele ältere Weisen die man nur dem Namen nach kennt.

2) Drei literarische Streitschriften, die uns die letzten Monathe durch unterhalten haben. Obwohl das Meiste für Sie unverständlich bleiben wird, so sende ich sie Ihnen a) damit Sie sehen, daß es noch gute Meister giebt die die Sprache zu handhaben wissen b) damit man sich dorten überzeuge, daß die Preßfreiheit eben nicht sehr eingeschränkt sei, wenn man solche Schwänke über die Mönche als N[ummer] 3. pag. 8 paßiren läßt.

3) Zwei Nummern des hiesigen Diario[6] mit kleinen Aufsätzen von mir. Zu demselben Endzweck bitte ich es ja nicht zu unterlassen mir alles was auf spanische Litteratur Bezug hat genau zu melden, welche spanische Bücher dorten gedruckt werden, welche Uebersetzungen aus dem Spanischen, besonders aber ob die übersetzten spanischen Schauspiele gegeben, wo, wie oft und mit welcher Aufnahme. Das Porto für einen Brief mit dergleichen Nachrichten werde ich willig erlegen. Da die verruchte französische Parthei (die allein das Wort führt) so sehr darauf hinarbeitet, alles ächt Spanische zu verdrängen, so ist ein jeder Beweis von Achtung fremder Nazionen dafür, mir höchst willkommen.

4) Zwei Comödien die ich vorzüglich gerne übersetzt sähe und die ich zu diesem Endzwecke H[er]rn Gries zu übersenden bitte. El Desden con el Desden von Moreto,[7] ein Stück welches keine Neuerer, keine Kritikaster von dem Theater haben verdrängen können, woselbst es jährlich verjüngt auftritt und die Welt erfreut. Es spreche von sich selbst! Moliere Princesse d'Elide soll eine erbärmliche Nachahmung davon sein; auch in Ital[ien] ist es öfters und mit Beifall nachgeahmt. El Diablo Predicador[8] ein Stück aus der Mitte des vorigen Jahrhunderts dessen Verfaßer ein geistreicher Mönch ist Fr[ay] Damian Cornasto, öfters verboten und wieder erlaubt, stets aber die Theater Kassen anfüllend. Es ist ein ächtromantisches Stück, wo das höchste Pathos den lustigsten Parteien gegenübersteht.

5) 17 Auszüge von spanischen Epopöen, womit sich meine Frau die Zeit vertrieben hat und die Sie Ihnen zum beliebigen Gebrauch übermacht: es ist wirklich ein sauer Stück Arbeit sich durch tausende von Oktaven durch zu arbeiten und die spärlichen poetischen Brocken so mancher Reimer herauszuklauben. Die Epik ist bestimmt die schwache Seite der spanischen Poesie; von den 104 Epopöen die ich besitze habe ich kaum eine halb Dutzend gelesen und die übrigens nur oberflächlich durchgeblättert; indessen müßte ein programatischer Auszug in literarischer Hinsicht anders sein, das weiß ich. So wie diese gesammelten Blumen indes sind werden sie Jedem der Spanisch versteht angenehm sein, und ich brauche es Ihnen nicht zu sagen, daß einige artige Zeilen die einzige Erwiederung ist, die bezweckt und erwartet wird.

Gerade ist es mein immer tieferes Eindringen und genauere Bekanntschaft mit der spanischen Poesie die das Hervortreten meines Parnasos verzögert – Ich sehe immer mehr ein daß ich ohne Benutzung der Königlichen Bibliothek in Madrid nichts Vollständiges werde liefern können, obwohl ich in meiner eigenen Sammlung Materialien zu vielen Theilen besitze. Um indessen wenigstens einen Theil meines mühsam Gesammelten für die Nachwelt zu retten, bin ich jetzt darauf bedacht ein Museo de Poesia antigua Castellana in Heften von 6 Bogen herauszugeben, und sollte das erste Heft die Druckkosten bestreiten, so denke ich 12 Hefte zu liefern welche 3 Oktavo Bände ausmachen sollen. Es sollen in diesem Museo nur solche Stücke erscheinen, die weder in den neuen Auflagen alter Dichter, noch auch in irgend einer neuen Sammlung Parnaso Colecc[ion] etc. aufgenommen worden. Ein Theil aus alten Handschriften niemals gedruckt, ein Theil aus fliegenden Blättern. Dieses sollen lauter Sachen aus der völlig ausgebildeten Poesie von 1550–1650 sein, da der Geschmack für das Frühere, Einfache, noch lange nicht genug gebildet ist. Die alten Romanzen so wie auch die Auszüge der Canc[ioner]o[s] bleiben davon ausgeschloßen und müssen einen günstigeren Zeitpunkt abwarten. Dieses ist auch der Fall mit dem ersten spanischen Theater von 1490/1560, dessen aristophanische Derbheit und groteske Anordnung ein gebildetes oder verbildetes Publikum nicht vertragen kann. Das ich übrigens bei meinen Berufsarbeiten, Zeit genug zu diesem allen abmüßigen kann ist eine Art Wunder, und kann nur durch rastlose Thätigkeit erzwungen werden die von Tages Anbruch bis in die Nacht sich erstreckt, wobei ich aber vollkommen heiter und wohlgemuth bin, und ohne Ziererei sagen kann daß ich mich nie glücklicher gefühlt habe. Eine vorgeschriebene Arbeit für fremde Rechnung die mich nur während ihrer Dauer beschäftigt ist meiner Natur angemeßen und läßt meinem Geiste seine Freiheit; nie ist derselbe produktiver gewesen als gerade jetzt und Muse und Poesie, Ernst und Spaß drängen sich mir aus der Feder.

Alle Ihre Aufträge denke ich sind hiermit erfüllt, bis auf <u>Einen</u>, nämlich die Revolutionsschriften: die Zahl derselben ist so ungeheuer, die Meisten sind so aufgeklärt voltärisch, die besten sind so persönlich, daß ich weder Muth noch Lust habe mich damit zu befaßen. Eine in Madrid gemachte Sammlung der früheren und besten Schriften ist mir versprochen, und sollen Ihre werden wenn ich sie erhalte, aber alles was hier zur Zeit der Cortes gedruckt ist verdient wahrlich keine Aufmerksamkeit und gereicht der Nation zur Schande und nicht zur Ehre. Ihre Uebersetzung von Escog[inez] und Cev[alles][9] schickte ich damahls nach Madrid; ich besinne mich indeß, daß mir die Vorrede sehr wohl gefiel: beide sind jetzt vom Hofe entfernt. Unser armer König, von dem besten Willen beseelt aber schwach im Kopf, ist das Spiel der Schmeichler und Intriganten; aus Rechtlichkeitstrieb hört er Alle an und der Letzte behält Recht. Den Einfluß verabscheuend den der Friedensfürst[10] auf seine Eltern übte, will er sich von solchem Einfluß frei erhalten und ein Höfling braucht ihm nur zu sagen, daß man meine, ein solcher Minister oder Favorit oder Beichtvater beherrsche ihn, um dessen Entfernung zu bewirken. Auf solche Weise hat man seine besten Freunde Cevalles,[11] Escoginez,[12] Bandizabal,[13] Infantado[14] etc. von ihm entfernt und es ist ein Rätsel wie Garay[15] sich so lange erhält. Doch da fällt mir ein daß Garay zu den liberales gehört, und also keinen Feinde zwischen den Schurken und Spitzbuben haben kann. – Ich komme immer wieder darauf zurück, Spanien ist von den Filosofen und Aufklärern vollkommen umstrickt und die Revoluzion kann nicht lange mehr ausbleiben; das Volk wird zwar keinen Antheil daran nehmen, doch wird es machen lassen da man im Anfange die Religion <u>dem Namen nach</u> respektiren wird. Ich hoffe jedoch daß zu eben dieser Zeit die alte katholische Kirche ihr Haupt in England und Norddeutschland erheben werde, das ich mich werde anschließen können, sollte der Druck hier zu heftig werden. Wie wahr sagt der treffliche Schloßer in seinem Fiévée p. 248, Man hat Aberglaube gerufen, und ruft noch Aberglaube, während man Unglaube rufen müßte. Man hat Fanatismus gerufen, und erneut sich sehr bedenklich die albernsten Mährchen über ihn daß während man Indifferenz und Auflösung aller Positionen zu rufen hätte' – Dabei muß ich seufzen und sagen: welches schlimme Zeichen der deutschen Zeit, daß von einem solchen Buche der versprochene zweite Theil nicht hat erscheinen können! –

Jetzt zur Beantwortung Ihres Briefes vom 13 Märtz, mit der Einlage von P[erthes] – Ich würde seine Beschwerde gegen mich völlig begründet finden hätte ich Erkundigung nach den Sachen der Mad[ame] Grant einem Kaufmann übertragen, aber <u>Sie</u> (einen Literatus) darum zu ersuchen, was ja deutlich erklärt, daß kein Mistrauen im Spiel sei und daß ich nur die leidige Saumseligkeit sparen wollte. Die alte Frau bombardirte mich mit Briefen deren theueres Porto nicht wenig dazu beitrug mir den Kopf warm zu machen. Gottlob daß sie jetzt zufrieden ist! – Ebenso quälte mich der Madriter Buchhändler, welches jetzt auch abgemacht ist, ohne daß dazu der förmliche Kredit nothwendig gewesen ist – Der Eigner der Münzen, Kupferstiche, Kunstsachen und Bücher hat (wie es scheint) den

Gedanken aufgegeben, sie nach dorten zu senden: wenigstens hat er, nach den unbestimmten Berichten, die ich ihm zufließen ließ, sich nicht weiter bei mir sehen lassen. –

Was Sie mir über meinen Juan sagen ist mir sehr angenehm: ich kann diese Trennung bis jetzt noch nicht gerade ins Gesicht faßen, und muß sie mir aus dem Sinn schlagen. Es ist das härteste Opfer gewesen welches ich der Pflicht gebracht habe. Gottlob daß mir diese Aufopferung allem Anschein nach guten Lohn bringen wird. Ich möchte nur, daß der gute Juan etwas mehr Fähigkeit hätte, um auf Universitäten tüchtige Erkenntniße zu erwerben, die sein Leben sichern und verschönern würden! – Der alte Hoffman war weise und ich sage immer mit unserem Logau

Ist ein Frommer wo verschieden
<u>Freu dich</u>, denn er ist im Frieden[16]

vielleicht wird dieses einen günstigen Einfluß auf die Thätigkeit seines Schwiegersohns haben, welches ich von Herzen wünsche – Meine besten Grüße an seine liebe Frau und daß die Last der Geschichte die mir obliegen mir fast alle Privat Korrespondenz verbietet –

In meiner Ansicht (die in der Einleitung zu meinem Parnaso gehörig ausgeführt erscheint) ist die Hauptbestimmung des Reimes eine metrische Reihe scharf zu begränzen und demnach der Reim in der Mitte der Reihe eine Künstelei die erst spät in der spanischen Poesie erschienen ist, und auch dann nicht den End Reim aufgehoben hat – Der Einschnitt findet sich sehr früh in der spanischen Poesie, sowohl in den jambischen, als den trokäischen Silbenmaaßen; meistens finden sich in den älteren Handschriften die zwei Hälften der Reihe in <u>eine</u> geschrieben, wie in Sanchez und Grimm: einige Beispiele aber auch giebt es wo die zwei Hälften der Reihe in zwei Zeilen geschrieben sind. Auf der ersten Weise findet sich am Ende jeder Reihe ein Reim, welcher sich später in Assonanz verwandelte; nach der andern Art (welche ohne Zweifel der Bequemlichkeit zu Liebe, und um gleiche Form mit den Redondillas zu erhalten, die gewöhnliche geworden ist) erfolgt der Reim oder Assonanz nur am Ende jeder geraden Zeile, weil der Einschnitt keinen Reim hat, wenn in Romance geschrieben wird, welches der Natur dieser Gattung völlig angemeßen ist, die eben weil <u>derselbe</u> Reim oder Assonanz durchstehend ist, keine so häufige Wiederholung desselben braucht, als die Redondilla und alle ihre Gattungen – Ich theile übrigens nicht mit Ihnen Ihre Parteilichkeit für die Romanzen; mir besagen nur die alten gereimten der Cancioneros; die späteren mit assonancias, die den Haupt Inhalt der Romanceros ausmachen, sind mir leichte Speise die weder Herz noch Geist erquicken, besonders wenn verliebte Schäfer erscheinen –

Ich freue mich der Sachen, die Sie schon für mich bestimmt haben, und bin ganz besonders neugierig auf Depping Romances Españoles,[17] welche mir in der Form eines Briefes mit dem ersten Sch[iff] zuzusenden bitte. Was ich übrigens noch von Büchern wünsche, gebe ich an Perthes auf. Versuchen Sie es doch ob nicht ein früher abgehender Schiffer ein Paket Bücher nehmen will, da es mit Voß seiner Retour auf hier wohl bis in den Herbst zögern wird. Laß ihm dafür eine Fracht einsetzen, und wenn sie mir sein Recief p[er] Post einsenden so kann der Schiffer darauf rechnen, daß 24 Stunden nach seiner Ankunft die Bücher abgeholt werden und ihm seine Fracht an Land bezahlt wird. Er muß das Paket natürlich in der Kajüte nehmen, um es bei der Hand zu haben –

Nun endlich noch ein Riß meines Bücherverzeichnißes, woraus Sie sehen werden daß die eigentliche Abschrift mehr Zeit erfordern würde als ich absparen kann; sollte Ihnen aber in litterar[ischer] Hinsicht daran gelegen sein so kann die Abschrift veranstaltet werden.

Nun denke ich, werden Sie mit mir zufrieden sein! – Gott verleihe dem Sch[iff] Voß eine geschwinde Reise! und Ihnen Muße Alles übersandte zu genießen – Meine alten teutschen Lieder spiel und brumm ich bis mir die Augen naß, und ich danke Ihnen nochmahls für die Abschrift. Sehr vermiße ich die Geistlichen, denen ich auf ähnliche Art Melodien angepaßt hatte, und die wohl in der Kiste auf Cramon vergraben bleiben werden.

Ich überlasse es Ihnen, mir den Oesterreichischen Beobachter[18] und die Heidelberger Jahrbücher zu senden, je nach dem Sie finden daß solche meiner Sinnesart entsprechen. Laß Göthe und die Weltkinder über den poetischen Katholizismus und die katholisch-mystische Poesie spotten; mich hat sie zum Heil geführt und ich halte darauf und daran. In meiner Ansicht ist ein Katholik ohne Poesie ein Jansenist alias ein verkappter Kalvinist, ein Prediger der Nothwendigkeit, ein Rigorist der zur Verzweiflung führt, und ein Poet ohne Kristenthum nichts mehr als ein sinnlicher Reimer – Ich habe manche Aufsätze über Katholizismus in meinen Papieren aber für das hiesige Publikum sind sie viel zu katholisch; wären sie deutsch, so würde ich sie Ihnen übersenden.

Da noch Platz bleibt, füge ich einiges über die 3 Streitschriften bei: N[ummer] 1 ist von Vargas[19] einem Veteran der spanischen Litteratur, Mitglied aller gelehrten Gesellschaften Spaniens, der als er vorigen Sommer nach Cadiz kam, zum Ehren-Mitglied uns[erer] patriotischen Gesellschaft gemacht wurde. Seine Haupt Absicht war die Errichtung einer großen Erziehungs Anstalt für diese Provinz, die anfänglich von der Gesellsch[aft] begünstigt, bald darauf aber durch Intriguen und niedrige Künste verworfen und vereitelt wurde; statt dessen beschäftigte man sich mit Spielereien von Gas Erleuchtung: darauf erfolgte N[ummer] 1. – N[ummer] 2. ist von einem jungen Artillerie Offizier Navarro[20] redactirt und hat einen sehr guten Stil, ist aber langweilig und unter der anscheinenden Mäßigkeit sehr boshaft. – N[ummer] 3. ist die Erwiederung des Vargas, die in Erfüllung bringt, was die erste versprach Efficiam post hac ne quemquam voce lascescas; er hat seine Gegner so lächerlich gemacht, daß keiner etwas mehr zu Kauf hat, und ihre defaite unter einer vornehmen Verachtung verbergen. Da indessen einige starke Anzüglichkeiten auf die Person eines angesehenen Richters p. 5 befindlich sind, welcher Peña[21] heißt, so ist die Zirkulation dieser N[ummer] 3. untersagt worden. Von p. 24 an ist der Traum ein Meisterstück launiger Schreibart mit lebendiger Schilderung des hiesigen Treibens und verdient dem besten von Quevedo[22] zur Seite gestellt zu werden.–

Ich habe nichts weiter vom dem Bibliothekariat gehört, vermuthlich haben also wohl unlitterarische Einflüße mehr Kraft gehabt, als litterarische Verdienste und die Muse versprechen – Paciencia y berasar. Ihre Bibliothek hat mir Manches Interessante nachgewiesen. In die Anordnung kann ich mich nicht recht finden, aber ich sehe deren Schwierigkeit ein.

Und damit ist dann dieser zweite Bogen heute 10 May PfingstSontag beendiget – Ich empfehle nochmals die Novitäten über spanische Literat[ur] sowohl in Deutschland als anderen Ländern und brauche nach dieser Epistel kaum zu wiederholen daß ich Ihr Freund bin und bleiben werde –

Böhl v: Faber

76. *Nikolas Heinrich Julius, Hamburg*

Cadiz, den 15 May 1818

Mein Brief vom 24 Apr[il] an Perthes enthielt für Sie die Nachricht daß in der p[er] Cap[itain] Voß verladenen Kiste N[ummer] 4 für Sie befindlich wären Sanchez Col[eccion] 4 Th[eile] 80 Reales, Calderon 9 Th[eile] 135 –, Conde Lucanor 30 –, Rom[ances] de Germ[ani]a 22 –, Entr[e]m[ese]s de Cervantes 10 –, zusammen 277 Reales oder 39 Thaler – die ich heute auf Sie 8 Tage Sicht ordre Schwartz angewiesen habe; ferner als Geschenk Roman[cero] del Cid, und la Florida del Inca – Jetzt füge ich hinzu, daß ich H[er]r Wibel (der mit Cap[itain] Voß reist) ein Paket für Sie mitgegeben habe enthaltend Volkslieder, gedruckte Sachen und Handschriften unter Begleitung eines 9 folio Seiten langen Briefes mit Einlage für Perthes, so daß ich denke Sie mit mir zufrieden sein werden.

Seitdem habe ich Ihren Brief vom 14 Apr[il] mit dem Kredit Brief auf [illeg.] erhalten, der jetzt unnütz ist und den ich Ihnen mit Cap[itain] Voß zurücksenden werde. Die darin enthaltenen litterar[ischen] Nachrichten sind immer höchst interessant für mich, und bitte besonders auf Alles aufmerksam zu sein was die span[ische] Litter[atur] und die Aufführung der aus dem Span[ischen] übersetzten Stücke betrifft; die neuliche Bearbeitung des Lebens ist ein Traum[1] sind vermuthlich Opern? – Wie vielmal ist es wohl in Hamburg gegeben? und einmal daß es gefallen hat warum hat man nicht die andern übersetzten Stücke des Calderon auch hervorgeholt? – Von den angezeigten Sachen paßen sich für meine jetzigen Bedürfniße nur Görres Vergangenheit[2] etc (im Fall nämlich keine demokratische od[er] bonapartische Ideen darin herrschen) und Tiecks Briefe über England,[3] auf die ich sehr neugierig bin – Habe ich über den Fortunat[4] unglimpflich gesprochen, so bitte es ab, nachdem ich ihn jetzt gelesen; dennoch ziehe ich die Erzählungen des ersten Theiles den dramatisch[en] Märchen vor –

Könnten Sie mir von dem Meß Katal[og] Folgendes detailliren, so würde ich es dem hiesigen Publikum mittheilen: – wieviel Seiten? – wieviel Werke in jedem Fache? – Das Hautptsächlichste in jedem Fache haupts[ächlich] in schöner Litteratur. Ich wiederhole, daß ich kein Porto lieber bezahle als für litterar[ische] Notizen besonders wenn sie die günstigen Schicksale der span[ischen] Litter[atur] dorten betreffen. – Ich bemerke was es jetzt mit der Biblioth[ekar] Stelle für eine Bewandtniß hat und daß Sie nicht mehr darauf rechnen, welches ich bedaure. – Für das einzige mir bekannte Exemplar des Filosofo rancio wird 20 piaster gefordert; Sie müssen sich also dieses Gelüste vergehen lassen –

Der Ihrige B.v: F.

77. *Nikolas Heinrich Julius, Hamburg*

Cadiz, den 30 Juny 1818

Ich hoffe, werther Freund, daß Sie diesen Augenblick im Besitz der litterarischen Schätze sind die Ihnen Cap[itain] Voß von mir überbracht hatt. Diese Zeilen schreibe ich, um Ihnen die seitdem erschienene N[umer]os meiner Verteidigung des spanischen Theaters und Calderons insbesondere vor der gegen die im französischen Sinn geschriebenen Madriter Cronica zu übersenden. Dieser Streit hat mehr Aufsehen gemacht als ich es erwartete; in Hinsicht des Gegenstandes sind die Stimmen getheilt, was aber die Führung des Streites betrifft so sind alle Stimmen für mich, da sich mein Gegner höchst ungeschickt benommen und durch seinen Haß gegen mich und Schlegel verleitet das unsinnigste Zeug von der Welt ans Licht gefördert hat. Da er jetzt gegen die Maße von Zeugnißen die ich ihm entgegen gestellt habe nichts zu erwiedern weiß, so hat er den letzten Winkelzug gemacht und nachdem er mir die Absicht aufgebürdet seine Cronica herabzusetzen (in welcher viele gute Aufsätze von zientifischen Mitarbeitern sind) so will er künftig aus Verachtung eines so schwachen Feindes meine Verläumdungen mit einem tiefen Stillschweigen beantworten.

Ich glaubte nicht den Sieg so leicht zu erringen, und möchte nur daß Schlegel den ganzen Vorgang erführe, und sich darüber <u>irgendwo</u> vernehmen ließe, obwohl es auf der andern Seite zu viel Ehre für einen so unverwüstlichen Kläffer sein würde, daß ein Schlegel von ihm Notiz nähme, und sich demnach mein Wunsch billiger darauf beschränken müßte eine direkte schriftliche Billigung meiner

Bemühungen von Schlegel zu erhalten. Sehen Sie ob Sie dies ohne große Beschwerde einleiten können, zu welchem Endzweck ich Ihnen noch einen Abdruck des ersten Ursprunges dieses Streites[1] beilege.

Ferner finden Sie eingeschloßen die Beschreibung einer sonderbaren Misgeburt, die ich lebend gesehen habe: der Anblick einer solchen Doppelexistenz hat etwas überaus angreifendes, besonders da das weibliche Geschöpf einen höchst ausdrucksvollen Blick hatte, das männliche hingegen wie in Lethargie versunken war.

Seien Sie so fleißig mich zu versorgen als ich Sie versorge. Unwandelbar
Der Ihrige
Böhl v: Faber

78. Nikolas Heinrich Julius, Hamburg

Cadiz, den 18 July 1818.

Einliegend finden Sie N[ummer] 12 (wahrscheinlich letztes für jetzt) der Vertheidigung Calderons; es fehlt nur noch ein Anfang und Epilogus, der nächsten Sontag erscheinen wird – Bei den Auszügen aus Humboldt vermiße ich schmerzlich die folgenden Theile, da ich nur den ersten der Reise Erzählung besitze; unterlassen Sie ja nicht mir die folgenden zu senden; im Englischen sind schon 3 Theile heraus –

Es äußern sich schon einige Wünsche Schlegels dramatische Vorlesungen ins Spanische übersetzt zu sehen; sollte allenfalls eine zweite vermehrte od[er] veränderte Auflage davon erschienen sein, so erwarte ich sie; auch bitte mir die französische Uebersetzung[1] baldmöglichst zu senden – Ich empfehle mehr neue p[er] Post alle litterarische Nachrichten die Bezug auf Spanien haben oder sonst interessant sind.

Wenn die Edinb[urgh] Review nicht abgegangen ist, so bestellen Sie solche ab, da ich sie hier ohnedem lesen kann und mir jetzt die Quarterly[2] viel wichtiger ist –
Ihr wahrer Freund
Böhl v: Faber

79. Nikolas Heinrich Julius, Hamburg

Cadiz, den 7 October 1818

Vor einigen Wochen erschien endlich die so lange ersehnte Antwort auf meinen langen Episteln p[er] Cap[itain] Voß, allein welche ein Augenquäler für meine fast 50jährigen jetzt so hart mitgenommenen Augen! Wie gerne hätte ich denselben Inhalt auf zwei Bogen gedehnt gelesen und das doppelte Porto dafür bezahlt! – Jetzt kann ich ihn nur fragmentarisch genießen da alle Zeilen in einander gehen.

Allein auch so meinen besten Dank. – Calderon ist natürlich für einen Fremden sehr schwer, und die Graziosos müssen oft ganz unverständlich sein, allein wenn Schlegel und Gries ohne andere Hilfsmittel als dortige Wörterbücher übersetzt haben, so müssen auch Sie nicht verzweifeln – Die neue Auflage der Entrem[eses] von Cervantes ist leider keine Folge von Beliebtheit, sondern die Frucht der Vorliebe eines Einzelnen; der größte Theil der Abdrucke ist wie Blei liegen geblieben. Diese Auflage enthält nur die Entrem[eses] und nicht die 8 Comedias die den größten Theil der 2 Q[uartal]bände von 1749 ausmachen; allein gerade diese Comedias werden von den Liebhabern gar nicht geschätzt – das Ensayo cronologico de la Florida hat vielleicht einen historischen Werth ist sonst aber höchst unbedeutend und ganz ohne Zusammenhang mit dem romantischen Feldzuge den der Inca beschreibt. – die Rom[ances] des Tortosada[1] sind hier sehr bekannt und grostentheils aus den alten Canc[ione]ro de Romances genommen – Es soll mich freuen wenn Sie etwas von den spanischen Drucken des Konsuls Asso in Amsterdam auftreiben können; es ist dieses derselbe Rechtsgelehrte welcher so vieles in diesem Fache hat drucken lassen. – Ich bin neugierig auf den englischen Essay des Anaya;[2] sein Teatro Esp[añol] escogido hoffe ich von England zu erhalten – Mit dem größten Schrecken habe ich gelesen was Sie von dem alten weisen ExempelSpruch[3] schreiben: ich bin der Meinung daß ich alle meine sich auf altdeutsche Litteratur beziehenden Bücher in einer großen Kiste besonders verpackt bei meinem Bruder auf Cramon stehen habe und kann nicht begreifen, wie sich dieses kann verirrt haben. Um für den Augenblick das Mögliche zur Rettung dieses Schiffbruches zu thun, finden Sie einliegend ordre Brief an meinen Bruder, der dazu dienen wird um die zerstreuten Stücke dieser Art sogleich für mich einzuziehen und zu meiner Verfügung aufzubewahren. Weiterhin werde ich über den Rest disponiren und in Ihre Hände bringen. – Sie haben sehr wohl gethan mir die Schriften über den Harmsschen Religionsstreit[4] nicht zu senden da ihrer so viele sind. Der Kampf zwischen die Verstandes Menschen und die Anhänger des Herzens muß lang und herbe sein; unterliegen die Letzten so wird es wenig behaglich für Unsereinen hienieden sein und die Lust des Abscheidens wird wachsen. Monaco ist das Italiänische Städtchen; München wird von den Spaniern Munich genannt mit den Franzosen.– Es ist nicht der Mühe werth daß Sie die elende Reimerei des Selva Danica[5] in Kopenhagen suchen; ich habe die prächtige Antwerper Auflage des Rebolledo,[6] finde aber nur einiges aus seine Ocios erträglich – Ich wundere mich nicht daß man am Ende bei der Hamburger Armen Anstalt auf das Resultat des Malthus[7] gestoßen ist; daß eine jede solche Anstalt das Uebel vermehrt anstatt zu vermindern – Die Sapho[8] wünsche ich baldmöglichst zu erhalten da sie in dem Streite mit den Madritern als ein Muster des klaßischen Geschmacks angeführt ist, und da gesagt wird daß der Verfaßer früher schlechte Sachen im romantischen Geschmack geschrieben habe – Was sind denn eigentlich diese Bearbeitungen der Wert? Sind es Umgestaltungen oder was ist es?

Senden Sie mir solche. Es ist mir interessant zu wissen ob die Stücke (spanischen) nach den wörtlichen Uebersetzungen des Schlegel und Calderon gegeben werden, oder umgearbeitet. Das D[onn]a Diana des Moreto[9] ist vermutlich el Desden con el desden, ein auch hier noch beliebtes Stück! – Warum diese Namensverfälschung! – Senden Sie mir auch Carl der Große von einem Biergang[10] in Aachen, worüber sich gleichfalls die Madriter (Nachbeter der französischen Kritiker) lustig machen – Gerne vernehme ich die guten Nachrichten über unsere gute Freundin Elise Campe. Während dieses heißen und heiteren Sommers habe ich recht oft an sie gedacht, und daß sie (wie die Fliegen am Ofen) so recht aufgegangen und aufgelebt ist. Ich freue mich auf ihr Paket – Also Lebewohl der Bibliothekar Stelle! – Frisch auf und auf etwas Anderes die Augen geheftet! – Während dem spinnt die Parze leise fort und die Hoffnung führt angenehmer zum Ziele als der Genuß – Die Erdkunde werde ich gerne erhalten: Alles Gediegene in seiner Art ist interessant – Bei der ungeheuren Geschäftslast die mir jetzt obliegt ist mein Parnaso oder Museo wieder in den Hintergrund gerückt, jedoch sind mir die Berechnungen des Druckes sehr willkommen gewesen – Wir haben eine sehr schöne spanische Uebersetzung der Bibel von Scio[11] mit Noten in 8 folio oder 16 quart[al] Bänden, in dem letzten docennien erschienen; sie ist aber sehr kostbar: ich glaube nicht daß eine andere existirt. – Ueber Kotzebues Menschenhaß und Reue[12] erschien zu seiner Zeit eine sehr artige dramatische Satire unter dem Titel el gusto del dia; sonsten ist mir von einer Vertheidigung eines Bischofes nichts zu Ohren gekommen.

So weit die Beantwortung Ihres Briefes – Mit diesem Briefe erfolgen:

1) 50 Abdrücke eines Pasatiempo critico gegen das Madriter Gesindel und zur Ehren Rettung Calderons und der deutschen Kritik; die meisten Aufsätze sind von mir; 2 gezeichnet C_a von meiner Frau[13] und einige des Anhanges von einem andern Freund.[14] Im Ganzen hat es wenig Aufmerksamkeit erregt, so wie alles Litterarische, weil die Meisten durch Nahrungssorgen und Intrigen beschäftigt sind, und es sind kaum 100 Abdrücke in Umlauf gekommen; im Einzelnen dagegen hat es den größten Eindruck gemacht, und mir von den angesehensten Litteratoren und Staatsmännern die schmeichelhaftesten Briefe erworben. Der wenige Kredit den die Cronica hatte ist völlig vernichtet und in ohnmächtiger Wuth rühen sich die Herausgeber durch handschriftliche Libellen auf frühere persönliche Verhältniße. – So weit hat es jedoch meinen Zweck befördert daß die Cronica alle Ungebührlichkeiten gegen Calderon und die deutsche Nazion eingestellt hat und sich mit vaguen Sticheleien auf die Romantiker und den oscuro folletista Germano Gaditano beschränkt – Ein paar Deutsche die gerade hier waren Baron d'Alton und Dr Pander[15] (ein Rigaer) haben mit Antheil an diesem Streite genommen und Exemplare nach Deutschland befördern wollen. Sie sind jetzt in Granada; wir erwarten sie aber zurück und dann haben wir ihnen im Schauspiel ein Stück von Calderon vorbereitet, damit sie doch nicht Spanien verließen ohne etwas von diesem

großen Meister hier auf der Bühne gesehen zu haben, bei welcher Gelegenheit eine neue Satire gegen die Madriter vertheilt werden wird. Sagen Sie mir etwas von diesen Deutschen; der Baron ist ein interessanter wohl unterrichteter Mann, der aber Niemand zu Worte kommen läßt, und scheint mit Perthes in Verbindung zu stehen; der Dr ist bescheiden und hat eine brennende Wißbegierde, und scheint mir manches Neue in naturhistorischer Hinsicht aufgefunden zu haben – Sie können diese Pasatiempos <u>umsonst</u> unter die Freunde der spanischen Litteratur vertheilen und ich wünsche sehr daß er Schlegel zu Gesicht käme, wie schon gemeldet. – Die Diarios de Cadiz die von dieser Materie handeln haben Sie alle erhalten. N[ummer] 703 war das letzte N[ummer] – der elende Herausgeber dieser Diario von den Madritern bestochen hat nichts mehr gegen die französische Sinnesart darin aufnehmen wollen.

2) eine Sammlung von Papieren aus der spanischen Revoluzionszeit in 4 Theilen, die sehr gute Sachen enthält
3) die Origines de la lengua Española von Mayans[16]
4) Servicios de Cadiz[17] kostet 1 piaster zur Probe; sollten dorten Exemplare abzusetzen sein, so können Sie erhalten so viele Sie wollen
5) ein Kistel und ein klein rundes Packet, welche nebst den beigehenden Briefen meiner Mutter einzuhändigen bitte

Ich freue mich auf die Ankunft des Cap[itain] Voßes und aller schönen Sachen die er uns bringen wird – Ueber mein äußeres Schicksal kann ich nicht klagen; meine Lage hat sich etwas verbessert, auf Kosten meiner Muße. Gott gebe nur daß die alten Augen es aushalten. Mein Gemüth bleibt jung und ich nehme immer das lebhafteste Interesse an <u>Allem</u> vom Ysop bis zur Zeder aus Libanon; für diese Beweglichkeit und Empfänglichkeit der Fantasie kann ich dem Himmel nicht genug danken; auch bleibt mir der alte katholische Glaube und die Zuversicht auf die Fürbitte der heiligen Jungfrau Maria ein fester Beruhigungsgrund in allen Anfällen von Kleinmuth und so harre des <u>Lebens letzte Stufen</u> – bitte sehr um <u>größere</u> Schrift.
   Ihr treu ergebener
   Böhl v. Faber

P. S. Nach weiterer Ueberlegung bitte ich in der Einlage meinem Bruder Ihnen alle meine altdeutsche Bücher zuzusenden; wahrscheinlich ist ein Verzeichniß dabei. Nachdem Sie dieselben erhalten und untersucht haben bitte mir Ihre Meinung über den Werth und Zustand zu sagen, und dann werde ich beschließen was zu thun ist – Indem Sie diese Einlage meinem Bruder zusenden, melden Sie ihm daß Sie von mir den Auftrag hätten meinen altd[eutschen] Bücher zu empfangen und zu verkaufen.

80. Friedrich Perthes, Hamburg

Cadiz, den 16 Oct[ober] 1818

Ihre werthe Zuschrift vom 18 des vorgegangenen Monathes habe ich richtig erhalten und darin das Recief über ein Päckel Bücher p[er] Cap[itain] Volmers vorgefunden welcher hoffentlich bald erscheinen wird. Die Bücher sind ganz verzweifelt Theuer; ich tröste mich jedoch wenn ich bedenke daß ich bei Ihnen Kredit habe.

Einliegend Empfang Schein über ein Kistel und einen dicken Brief für Sie oder eigentlich für unseren Freund Dr Julius p[er] Cap[itain] Paulson der schon seit einigen Tagen unterwegens ist, und welches der Cap[itain] versprochen hat franco Fracht abzuliefern.

Wir besitzen hier jetzt ein paar interessante Deutsche den Baron d'Alton und den Dr Pander die in wissenschaftlicher Hinsicht Spanien bereisen und hier manches interessante aufgefunden haben. Als Liebhaber der Poesie und Bekante von Schlegel haben sie sich sehr für unseren Streit mit den Madriter französirenden Kritikern interessirt, der, wie es zu gehen pflegt, von der Madriter Seite in platte Persönlichkeiten ausgeartet ist weil sie uns keine Gründe haben entgegen setzen können. Im Ganzen interessirt sich nur ein sehr kleiner Theil des Publikums für diese Sache; wir haben es jedoch so weit gebracht daß am 17 ein prächtiges Trauerspiel von Calderon (a secreto agravio secreta venganza) mit einigen Auslaßungen, den Reisenden zu Ehre hier aufgeführt ist, und das Publikum hat uns die Höflichkeit erwiesen es geduldig anzuhören und nicht auszupfeifen. Eine kleine Schrift der denselben Tag ausgegeben wurde giebt den gehörigen Aufschluß zur Schande der Madriter und Ehre des Deutschen und Kadixer.[1] Den Baron hat die Sache sehr interessirt und ich hoffe daß seine Berichte darüber in deutschen Tageblättern figuriren werden.[2] Von der Schrift werde ich Ihnen mit erster Sch[iffs]gelegenheit einige Abdrücke zusenden, so wie auch von dem Trauerspiel, so wie es hier gegeben ist.

Ich hoffe daß mir Cap[itain] Voß die noch fehlenden Bücher von den verschriebenen überbringen wird, hauptsächlich die französische Uebersetzung von Schlegels Dramatischen Vorlesungen und die Wiener Poetische Zeitschrift[3] nach Art der vierteljärigen Englischen.

Eine kurze Uebersicht der Messneuigkeiten so wie solche in der Zeitung für die eleg[ante] Welt ehemals gegeben wurde, Zahl der Werke, wieviel in jedem Fache, und das Merkwürdigste herausgehoben, würde mir besonders willkommen sein für eine Spanische [damage] Minerva dessen Verfaßer[4] (obwohl nach der franzö[sischen] Seite hinkend) doch offene Augen und Ohren hat, mit dem ich jetzt in Korrespondenz stehe und der schon etwas von Schlegel aufgenommen hat. Wenn es <u>ein</u> oder <u>zwei</u> Bogen sind, so wende ich gerne das Porto daran und bitte mir dieselben p[er] Post zuzuschicken.

Ueber die hiesigen inneren Verhältniße kann ich Ihnen leider nichts Tröstliches sagen; es ist ein wahres Wunder wie das Gebäude noch zusammenhält, und wie bei dem gänzlichen Mangel an Besoldungen den Truppen der Geduldsfaden nicht bricht. Der König wird am Ende nothgedrungen thun müssen, was er anfänglich hätte thun sollen, und unter einer anderen Form wird man willig die Opfer bringen, gegen die sich jetzt jeder Aufgeklärter (nicht das Volk) empört – Den Schreiern und Leitern ist nun einmal die Aufklärung inokulirt und die Krankheit muß ihre Stufen durchlaufen. Ob der Kranke daran sterben oder wieder genesen werde bleibt die Frage! – Meine besten Grüße an den ganzen Perthschen Zirkel und sonstige Freunde.

Ihr Freund der Ihrige

Böhl v: Faber

81. Nikolas Heinrich Julius, Hamburg

Wir haben hier jetzt einen preußischen Agenten Pütter, das gerade Widerspiel des gemüthvollen d'Alton, an dem ich mich fürchterlich ärgere; ein Aufklärer wie ich glaubte daß solche längst verblichen wären. Weh Preußen wenn solche die allgemeine Stimmung ist.

Cadiz, den 16 Febr[uar] 1819

Endlich finde ich ein Stündchen um Ihre lieben Briefe vom 18 Aug[ust] 30 Sep[tember] und 13 Dec[ember] vorläufig zu beantworten und den Empfang der Bücher p[er] Cap[itain] Voß und Vollmers anzuzeigen. Der letztere hatte das Packet verlegt und ich besitze es erst seit 8 Tagen. Zuerst meinen herzlichen Dank für Alles für die köstlichen Notizen und Auszüge, für die allerliebsten Steindrucke für den Cavallo[1] und für die große Auswahl der nicht geforderten Bücher. Ich habe bisjetzt nur darin blättern können bin jedoch völlig befriedigt durch die Wiener Jahrbücher (wie haben Sie es unterlassen mir die darin so vortheilhaft beurtheilte Sängerfahrt[2] zu senden?) Quarterly Reviews (deren frühere N[umer]os ich vors erste nicht haben will, und sollten Sie verschrieben sein bei sich liegen zu lassen bitte) die deutschen Lieder für Jung und Alt[3] (in denen ich einige der meinigen mit den Begleitungen begrüßt habe) Ancillon[4] (mitten in seiner Oberflächlichkeit ein nothwendiges Verbindungsglied für Nicht Deutsche) Schubert Altes und Neues (unübertrefflich schön wenn er seine Gefühle schildert und seine Gedanken mahlt aber zu breit in vielen trivialen Erzählungen) Wordsworth (immer noch der Dichter der mich am tiefsten ergreift und nebst Göthen mich mir selbst am meisten aufgeklärt haben) und die beiden Romanzen Sammlungen. Hingegen hat der englische Abdruck mit der Uebers[etzung] (Hist[ory] of Charles the Great)[5] keinen Werth für mich, da das original in 1764 gedruckt gar kein rares Buch ist und ich es doppelt besitze. Da das Werk nun überdem alt, verlegen, gebraucht und sehr schmutzig ist so glaube ich für die ½ des ausgesetzten Preises von 21 Mark sehr gut zu bezahlen. – Harms seine Thesen haben mir sehr gefallen: Das übrige habe ich noch nicht angesehen. Die Armen Anstalt ist jetzt nicht bei mir an der Tagesordnung, wird aber schon kommen –

Der Steindruck für m[eine] Fr[au] ist übergeben und dankbar entgegen genommen; einige Zeilen dabei sind vermißt.

Nach der hier erschienenen Geschichte des Krieges mit Bonaparte[6] ist es wie gewöhnlich gegangen daß nämlich die Ausländer uns auf das einheimische Gute aufmerksam machen müssen. Ich habe den ersten Theil mit vielem Interesse gelesen, und Sie werden ihn erhalten: ich sehe aber nicht ein daß es früher als p[er] Cap[itain] Voß (der Ende nächsten Monathes absegeln will) wird sein können. Dieser Theil enthält nur eine allgemeine Uebersicht der Geschichte Bonapartes und der spanischen Angelegenheiten bis zum 2 May, nach meiner Ansicht edel erhaben freimüthig und gediegen, zu Ihrem Zwecke aber wenig dienlich. Zu einer Fortsetzung ist wenig Hoffnung da, indem hier in dem lesenden oder aufgeklärten Publikum die größte Launigkeit herrscht, wozu Mangel und Noth das ihrige beitragen. Ueber alte und neue cortes giebt es einen solchen Wust von Schriften daß darin um so weniger möglich etwas zu sammeln da die meisten verboten. Das beste darüber sollen die Schriften von Martinez Marina[7] sein, die man mir versprochen hat; erhalte ich sie so erfolgen sie mit Cap[itain] Voß – Den Conde Lucanor werden Sie, wegen der vielen veralteten Wörter schwerer finden als Calderon: es sind aber so herrliche und zum Theil so originale Erzählungen darin daß es der Mühe werth ist sie zu studiren; einige alte Wörter sind im Anhange erklärt – Die neue Aufl[age] der Entrem[ese]s de Cervantes enthält alle 8 Entrem[ese]s aber nicht die 8 Komöd[ien] woran Sie nichts verlieren, da sie äußerst elend sind – Der Ensayo cronol[ogico] de la Florida hat gar keinen Werth. In seiner Anmerk[ungen] zu dem Gedichte vision of Rodrigo[8] macht Southey auf die Florida des Inca aufmerksam, und dieser auf die Naufr[agio] des Caveza de Vaca die ich jetzt besitze und zu den größten Seltenheiten meiner Sammlung rechne – Anstatt einer schriftlichen Ergänzung sende ich Ihnen einen neuen Abdruck des Rom[ancer]o des Cid, ein wahres Wunder in dieser profanischen Zeit – Deppings Sammlung hat mir verschiedenes <u>Neues</u> kennen gelernt, zum Theil allerliebst und wahrscheinlich aus den kleinen Cancion[ero]s von Barcelona und Zaragoza genommen; es ist ein Fehler dieser Sammlung daß die Quellen eines jeden Liedes nicht besonders benannt sind – Der Jurist Asso und der Amsterd[amer] Konsul ist dieselbe Person: es wäre doch eine Schande wenn sich in Amsterd[am] die Gedicht Sammlungen nicht auftreiben ließen! – Anaya in London ist ein elender Held, an dem man nur die guten Willen preisen kann – Monaco ist das italiänische Städtchen; München nennen die alten und neuen Spanier Munich – Die Beiträge zur romantischen Poesie von Schmid[9] haben sich nicht angefunden – Die neue Erdkunde von Karl Ritter[10] unterlassen Sie ja nicht mir zu senden – Es giebt keine spanische Bibelübers[etzung] von Escoinquez, aber eine von Pater Scio die sehr gelobt und viel gelesen wird, obwohl solche in vielen Bänden und kostbar ist – Ich entsinne mich einiger Streitigkeiten über Kotzebues Menschenhaß und Reue in den Diarios die lange vergeßen sind. Das Beste war ein kleines Schauspiel el gusto del dia, welches die Sentimentalität des Publikums lächerlich machte; ich habe es aber nicht konservirt. Den Cancionero des Baena[11] habe ich lange aufs Korn gefaßt; es giebt aber nur ein einziges schöngeschriebenes Orig[inal] davon in der Escorial Bibliothek; kaum Hoffnung zum Druck, und wegen der alten Schrift sehr schwer abzuschreiben: seit Jahren schon suche ich dahinter zu kommen. Unterdessen giebt ein sehr weitläuftiger Auszug in der Bibliotheca Española des Castro[12] einen genügsamen Begriff davon; die Ausbeute an eigentlicher Poesie darin ist höchst geringe; desto größer die Aufschlüße über die allmähliche Ausbildung der Sprache, und für mich an allerinteressantesten die Künstlichkeit des meter den Minnesingern nicht unähnlich – Ich wußte daß die 400 preg[untas] von Southey in den Omniana beleuchtet waren, welches die Veranlaßung zur Verurtheilung dieses Büchleins wurde, so mich nicht gereut hat; den 2te Theil dieser preg[untas] habe ich ja weder gelesen noch auftreiben können: er soll jedoch dem ersten weit nachstehen – Okens Isis[13] werde ich gerne erhalten, wenn sie in unserem Sinne geschrieben ist, so wie auch die neue Quartal Schrift Hermes:[14] fröhnen sie aber der Vernünftelei und der Aufklärung so unterbleibe es – Die Geschichte der aufgefundenen Novela des Cervantes La tia fingida[15] finden sie in der Vorrede des Entrem[ese]s desselben, deren Verfaßer sie aber (aus dem moral[ischen] Gesichtspunkte) sehr unglimpflich behandelt – Die neue Ausgabe in 3 Quartbänden der Partidos ist sehr schön kostet aber 6½ piaster – Eine Sammlung meiner Notic[ia]s liter[aria]s[16] werden Sie p[er] Cap[itain] Voß erhalten – Von der durch [illeg.] verkauften Gemälde Sammlung habe ich nichts in Erfahrung bringen können – Die aufgetragenen Bücher habe ich notirt, um gelegentlich wohlfeil anzukommen – Das Verz[eichniß] der alten span[ischen] Sprache sollen Sie nach besten Kräften berichtigt p[er] Cap[itain] Voß zurück erhalten – Quintana[17] hat von alten Sachen nur seine 3 Th[eile] Coleccion herausgegeben: sehr mittelmäßig meistens das bekannte und ganz gewöhnliche Urtheile – Mad[ame] de Stael Consid[erations][18] habe ich noch nicht gelesen: nach dem aber was ich von m[einer] Frau gehört, sehe ich es an als einen Versuch sich mit den Franzosen wieder auszusöhnen; ich bin daher dagegen eingenommen, und wünsche sehr Bonalds seine Anmerk[ungen][19] darüber zu lesen. Wie kommt es daß Sie mir von diesem großen Geiste nichts senden, besonders sein Considerations sur etc de la morale? – Volksbücher giebt es im Span[ischen] nicht: nur fliegende Blätter Romances und Relaciones die sich auch mehr und mehr verlieren und woran nicht viel verloren ist daß es entweder Räuber und Diebsgeschichten oder Stücke aus bekannten Schauspielen sind. – Ihr Zuruf und Aufmunterung in Hinsicht meines Parnaso soll nicht in Sand geschrieben sein, sondern in großen Buchstaben an der Wand meines Kabinettes paradiren: doch Muße will es haben, die mir jetzt nicht zu

Gebote steht – Gerne habe ich gelesen was Sie mir über d'Alton und Pander schreiben; ich halte mich überzeugt daß diese in gewandterem Stil alles Nöthige über unsern Kalderonischen Streit dorten bekannt machen werden. P[er] Voß erhalten Sie einen zweiten Pasatiempo, der den ersten sowohl an Gediegenheit des Inhaltes als auch an Stil übertreffen soll. Ueber Calderon und alte span[ische] Literatur habe ich die Gegner zum Schweigen gebracht, und jetzt sucht sich der Sudler durch Sticheln auf die Deutschen zu rächen. –

Die Rambachische Anthol[ogie][20] hat mir viele Freude gemacht, sowohl die ehrlichen latein[ischen] Hymnen (die auch hier so geläufig sind) als auch die deutschen Minne liebsten Lieder von Dach Pappus[21] Roberthins etc habe ich darin gefunden: ich sehne mich nach dem 3ten Theile – In Hinsicht meiner alten deutschen poet[ischen] Sachen bleibe ich ungewiß, da das übers[andte] Verz[eichniß] nichts eigentlich poetische enthält, und auch die mystischen Sachen ein besonderer Zweig war. Ich hoffe noch daß Sie diesen alten Schatz von meinem Bruder erhalten werden, und dann melden Sie mir (sollte ein Bot geschehen), ehe Sie solche angeschlagen. – Ueber das mir gesandte Verzeichniß werde ich mich p[er] Voß erklären – Und jetzt geht das Papier zu Ende. Meine besten Grüße an Perthes und andere Freunde. Auch die Elise Campen, deren liebe Br[iefe] ich ohne Fehl mit Voß beantworte, sowie auch dann an Perthes schreiben werde.

Ganz der Ihre
Böhl v. Faber

Da ich mir eine Brille zugelegt, so brauchen Sie künftig weniger Sorgfalt auf große Buchstaben zu verwenden, der Deutlichkeit unbeschadet. – Die Idee des Briefes des Pascha von Egypten werde ich benutzen. –

82. *Nikolas Heinrich Julius, Hamburg*

Cadiz, den 30 Martz 1819.

Unter d[en] 16 Febr[uar] beantwortete ich vorläufig Ihre Briefe p[er] Voß und Vollmers. Seitdem habe ich einen Brief meines Bruders erhalten und daraus besonders gerne ersehen daß die Kiste mit meinen deutschen altpoetischen Sachen unangerührt war und Ihnen eingeliefert werden sollte. Ich wiederhole dabei meinen Auftrag daß ich nur in dem Fall diese Sammlung wegschlagen würde wenn ein Both <u>im Ganzen</u> dafür gethan würde; unterdessen (versteht es sich) daß Sie nun von mir autorisirt sind die Bücher nach Willkühr zu benutzen.

Wegen der herrlichen Geschichte des Krieges der Spanier gegen Napoleon muß ich Ihnen leider sagen, daß es mit dem ersten Theile sein Bewenden haben wird. Es sind so viele Klagen von Frankreich gekommen, daß die schwache Regierung es aufgegeben hat und vielleicht erleben wir noch daß der herausgekommene Theil verboten wird – Die Verkehrtheit die jetzt im Ganzen herrscht macht einem das

Leben, als Mitglied der menschlichen Gesellschaft, wirklich sauer. Was hilft es die offene Gewalt des Bösen gebrochen zu haben, wenn wohlmeinende Machthaber im Spiel der schleichenden Giftmischer bleiben und in ihrer Einfalt die Hände zur Untergrabung alles Guten bieten! Ich kann dieses auch in Bezug meines Kampfes für Calderon und die alte Spanische Poesie sagen. Mein zweiter Pasatiempo, der die elenden Herausgeber der Madriter Cronica in ihrer ganzen Ärmlichkeit darstellt, hat diese Menschen auf das ärgste erbittert, bis dahin natürlich; daß aber diese Menschen die Madriter Censores dahin bringen können alle ihre falschen Grundsätze, alle ihre Verläumdungen der Deutschen, alle ihre niedrigen Ausfälle auf meine Persönlichkeit gutzuheißen und den Verkauf <u>meines</u> Pasatiempos nicht zu erlauben, ist solches glaublich? – Noch mehr; seit einigen Wochen erscheinen in der Madriter Hofzeitung[1] Artikel ganz in demselben Sinn der Cronica, welche es höchst wahrscheinlich machen daß die schändlichen Menschen durch Intriguen und <u>Brüderhaß</u> Einfluß auf die Redakzion erworben haben. Hier haben Sie die hauptsächlichsten:

N[ummer] 24. Jueves 25 de febre[ro] 1819 – Stockolmo 2 de Enero. – La mayor parte des las obras dramaticas que se representan son francesas, porque los suecos prefieren estas a las Inglesas y las Alemanas, a pesar de los esfuerzos de una <u>secta</u> nueva literaria que ha querido poner en moda el género llamado <u>germanico-romancesco</u>. Nuestros mejores escritores se han opuesto a la invasion, y continuan sosteniendo la literatura francesca, q[ue] mucho tiempo hace es clasica entre nosotros.

N[ummer] 33. Jueves 18 de Marzo 1819 – Paris 24 de febr[er]o – Se ha reparado que muchos de los periodicos alemanas pertenecen a <u>judios</u>, ya como empresarios ò como redactores: de este numero son etc

N[ummer] 35. Martes 23 de marzo 1819 – Francfort 22 de febr[er]o – Bei Gelegenheit einer famosa memoria von Mr. de Stourdza[2] wird gesagt: este consejero no ha hecho mas que traducir al frances ciertos pasages en los quales se reconoce el estilo de <u>los misticos Alemanes</u>, <u>secta extravagante</u>, que se entremete en cuestiones de filosofia de politica y de religion, sin entender ella misma que opina – Ich glaube gern daß dieses aus französischen Zeitungen übersetzt ist, allein muß eine bedächtige ernste Hofzeitung dergleichen Zeug aufnehmen? –

Bei den wenigen ächten und gelehrten Spaniern gewinne ich natürlich um desto mehr, so daß sich sogar einige Hoffnung habe in der so sehr geschätzten Real Academia Española[3] aufgenommen zu werden. Kommt dieses zu Stande so platzen meine Gegner für Neid. Um es zu erleichtern, ist es immer dienlich einige andere Titel aufweisen zu können. Ich habe ein Diplom als Mitglied der Mecklenb[ur]g[ischen] ökonomischen Gesellschaft und das der hiesigen patriotischen Gesellschaft; nun möchte ich noch gerne den Titel als korrespondierendes oder Ehren Mitglied der dortigen patriotischen Gesellschaft aufweisen können. Sehen Sie zu ob dieses nicht einzurichten ist; ein paar Zeilen von dem Sekretär der

Gesellschaft sind zu meinem Zweck hinreichend, und würde ich auch einige mäßige Beiträge (wären solche erforderlich) nicht scheuen – An meinem Patriotismus zweifeln meine dortigen Freunde und Bekannten sicherlich nicht; es ist schon kein kleines Opfer daß ich das Hamburgische Konsulat jetzt ganz umsonst verwalte –

Wahrscheinlich wird meine Tochter die Wittwe mit Cap[itain] Voß im M[ona]th May sich nach dorten einschiffen um den Sommer mit ihrer Großmutter und Verwandten zuzubringen. Sie wird dann die Ueberbringerin Ihrer verschiedenen Aufträge sein. Unterdessen bitte gelegentlich von England kommen zu lassen: 1) New Monthly Magazine[4] for February 1819 with a likeness of W[illia]m Wordsworth, bloß dieses Bildnißes wegen 2) Crabbe's Poetry.[5] Dieser Dichter im Geschmack des Wordsworth wird oft angeführt; ich habe aber nie den Titel seiner Gedichte gesehen.

Ich bin so in die Spanischen Dramatiker vertieft daß ich kaum mir Zeit nehme etwas anderes zu lesen, nicht einmal die interessanten Consider[ations] der Mad[ame] de Stael. Ich kann Ihnen sagen daß unsere Academia von politischem Elende umgeben, sehr fleißig ist und in kurzem mehrere neue Auflagen alter Dichter herausgeben wird Garcilaso, Valbuena[6] und Ercilla[7] werden die ersten sein. Eine neue Ausgabe des D[on] Quixote ist unter der Preße, mit einem neuen Leben des Cervantes welches vieles Unbekannte enthalten wird; darauf sollen die übrigen Werke des Cervantes[8] gleichförmig folgen. Von der 4. Aufl[age] des Wörterbuches sind 4000 Abdrucke verkauft, und man denkt schon an eine fünfte die ich bereichern werde.

Meine Spanische Sammlung Dichter habe ich kürzlich mit einem halben Dutzend Raritäten aus Valencia vermehrt, die mir jedoch 30 piaster kosten. Wo das Geld herkömmt weiß ich selbst nicht. Es ist dorten mehreres feil aber zu welchen Preisen!! – Jeder Band alte Rittergeschichten 16 a 20 piaster, historische Handschriften 50–60 piaster, Celestina[9] und kleine Cancioneros a 12 a 15 piaster p[er] Stück.

Und damit für heute Gott befohlen – Antworten Sie mir baldmöglichst, und kehren sich nicht an Porto. Meine besten Grüße an Perthes und alle Freunde –
Ergebenst
Böhl v: Faber

83. *Nikolas Heinrich Julius, Hamburg*

Cadiz, den 20 May 1819

Ich schrieb Ihnen zuletzt p[er] Post den 30 Märtz. In meiner litterarischen Streitsache hat sich seitdem zugetragen, daß der schändliche Mora (Herausgeber der Madriter Cronica) plötzlich nach Italien verreist ist, einige sagen von der

Regierung in Bezug auf eine erwartete hohe Person dahin gesandt andere in privat Angelegenheiten. Die Folge ist, daß seitdem weder in der Cronica noch in der Madriter Zeitung Anzüglichkeiten von der gerügten Art erschienen sind, und ich daher auf Ruhe bis zu seiner Rückkunft rechnen kann. – Diese Tage hat mir ein Bekannter den Conservateur[1] geliehen, welcher für mich der Vereinigungspunkt der Gutgesinnten ist. So arg hätte ich mir die Macht der Gegner doch nicht vorgestellt! Ich wundere mich jetzt nicht mehr über die Verblendung der hiesigen Regierung, da sich ein Ludwig XVIII so bethören läßt! – Was soll daraus werden! Man möchte aus der Haut fahren solche Verkehrtheit zu erleben, nachdem man Jakobiner und Bonaparte erprobt hat – Dieser Bekannte erwartet auch andere französische Tagesschriften, so daß ich davon nichts mehr von Perthes haben will. Ich habe so eben die Nachricht einer Sendung p[er] Cap[itain] Bandix von Perthes erhalten, worunter endlich 3 Werke von Fiévée[2] sind, die aber leider 54 Mark kosten. Zu diesen Preisen will ich keine Politik auch die beste nicht. Perthes sagt mir, daß Sie alles dieses ausgesucht haben und ich bemerke Ihnen daher Folgendes:

Von den Oesterr[eichischen] Jahrbüchern[3] erfolgt leider der 4te Band ohne daß ich den 3ten erhalten hätte. Diese Uebersicht ist für mich sehr empfindlich, da wahrscheinlich im 3ten die Beendigung des trefflichen Aufsatzes über die Preß Freiheit enthalten ist, auf die ich brenne. Die Fantasiestücke in Callots Manier die 1814 herauskamen haben Sie mir schon vor Jahren gesandt. Almanache (sei es welcher Art es wolle) habe ich mir verbothen, da ich mich mit dem kleinen Formate nicht vertragen kann – dagegen fehlt die bestellte <u>Sängerfahrt</u> – Es scheint als wenn dieses Alles geheftet kommt, da ich so öfters geschrieben habe daß <u>alles</u> (kleine Flugschriften ausgenommen) <u>in feinem Papiere gebunden kommen muß</u>, indem das Binden hier so ungeheuer kostbar ist – Ein Mehreres wenn mir das Packet wird zu Händen gekomen sein.

Von meinem Bruder habe ich sehre gerne erfahren, daß meine Kiste altdeutscher Sachen unangerührt bei ihm stand, und daß er Ihnen dieselbe nebst dem Verzeichniße zusenden würde – Ich bestätige meine Idee die Sammlung nicht zu vereinzeln sondern sie einem Liebhaber im Ganzen anzustellen, und meine Genehmigung eines etwaigen Botes einzuholen. Hiebei erfolgt nun auch das Verzeichniß der Bücher mit Dr. Wehbers Bot zurück, welche (die vier bekreuzten ausgenommen) für die gebotenen 148 Mark wegzuschlagen bitte, welche Summe Sie an Perthes gütigst für mich einhändigen werden. Von den bekreuzigten fügen Sie die beiden deutschen der Sammlung bei, und übersenden mir die beiden lateinischen gelegentlich.

Sie finden hiebei:

1) Historia de la guerra contra Europa.[4] Von Madrid aus macht man mir Hoffnung, daß der zweite Theil alles Widerspruches zum Trotz bald erscheinen wird. Nicht nur die Franzosen intriguiren gegen dieses Werk, sondern mehrere schlechte Spanier die sich für die Enthüllung ihres zweideutigen Benehmens

fürchten 2) Das neue Abdruck des Romancero del Cid;[5] kosten zusammen 7 Mark, die mit den 18 der vorigen Sendung, gleichfalls an Perthes für mich zu bezahlen bitte 3) Meine Notic[ia]s liter[aria]s del Diario de Cadiz zusammen geheftet; eine neue verbesserte Auflage wird einen Theil des 3ten Pasatiempos ausmachen das auf dem Stapel liegt und nur eine Kassenflut abwartet um zu erscheinen. 4) Abdrucke des zweiten Pasatiempos das von den wenigen die es verstehen noch mehr gelobt ist als das erste, und sicherlich in Hinsicht des Stiles unverkennbare Vorzüge hat.

Das Verzeichnis der alten spanischen Sachen erfolgt noch nicht, weil ich verschiedene Berichtigungen von Madrid erwarte, um womöglich die Bibliografie des Canconiero und Romanceros aufzuklären – Man hat jetzt Mail coaches von Madrid nach Sevilla errichtet und von hier dahin giebt es ein Dampfboot, so daß sich die Reise jetzt geschwinder und wohlfeiler machen läßt. Für hundert piaster kann man jetzt hin und her kommen so daß ich stark darauf bedacht bin einen Abstecher zu machen und acht Tage der Königl[ichen] Bibliothek zu widmen, welches meinen Parnaso am sichersten fördern würde. Bitten Sie zu Apoll und den neun Musen daß sie sich bei Fortuna verwenden mir einen kleinen Glückszettel in der Lotterie zuzuschanzen, denn ohnedem weis ich das Geld nicht aufzutreiben. Bis zum Herbste wird es auf alle Fälle verschoben bleiben da ich meinen Juan zum Besuch erwarte, ehe er unter Leitung meines trefflichen Stiefvaters Faber,[6] seine akademische Laufbahn antritt.

Ich habe mich angegriffen unsere Freundinnen Campe und Sieburg nicht ohne Erwiederung ihrer freundschaftlichen Mitteilungen zu lassen, und an <u>Sie</u> über das Nähere meiner litterarischen Fehde verwiesen. Füllen Sie diese Lücke bestens aus, da Sie von Allem unterrichtet sind. Von unserm Baron d'Alton, und Dr Pander haben wir nichts weiter gehört. Wissen Sie etwas von ihnen? –

Man sagt die jüngste Nichte des Königes von Sachsen[7] soll Königin von Spanien werden. Sagen Sie mir etwas von der Bildung, Sinnesart und sonstigen Umständen dieser Prinzeßinnen? – Wären sie von ungefähr durch Schlegel mit dem spanischen Theater bekannt, so könnten wir einen großen Triumph erleben.

Giebt es Verzeichniße von dort (in Deutschland) gedruckten lateinischen Autoren, so erwarte ich dieselben mit erster Gelegenheit für einen hiesigen Buchhändler.

Und hiemit Gott befohlen.
Ganz der Ihrige
Böhl v. Faber

Ich lege annoch bei:

Die schöne oda unseres Arriaza auf dem Tod der Königin[8] eine alte von mir angepaßte oda auf d[it]o Yo solo,[9] eine Flugschrift und mehreres andere aus dem

Streit über Calderon und die Pasatiempos bezug habende Flugschriften. – Auch bitte um Bestellung der Einlagen.

P. S. Gestern ward das Leben ein Traum mit der größten Pracht und vor einem vollen Hause mit Beifall gegeben. Die Stimmung hat sich gebessert, und so haben im Stillen die Pasatiempos, gegen Erwartung gewirkt.

84. Elise Campe, Hamburg

Cadiz, den 20 May 1819

Wenn nicht in höheren Verhältnißen das Geben und Nehmen beinahe einerlei wären, so müßte ich mich wahrlich schämen auf meiner Seite so lange unthätig gegen Sie, beste Freundin, gewesen zu sein. Ihre höchst interessante Mittheilung aus Ottensen (die über ein halbes Jahr unterwegens gewesen ist) erheischt jedoch wenigstens einen Empfangsschein, der (ist die Feder nur einmal recht angesetzt) aller Beschäftigungen zum Trotz, eine schicklichen Bogen erfüllen wird. Während der mehrmaligen Lesung Ihres so ganz natürlichen Briefes, habe ich mich so in Ihrer Umgebung versetzt gefühlt, daß die Beendigung einem Erwachen glich, wo die Gegenstände des Gesichts schwanken, bis sich das Bewußtsein wieder mit der Wirklichkeit verknüpft hat. Ich wende mich ab von dem Sterbenbette des Verklärten, und hafte meinen Blick auf Ihr liebes Lisel, da ich so ganz gefühlt habe und noch fühlen kann, welchen unendlichen Reiz unentwickelte Anlagen und Andeutungen für die Fantasie haben, und wie viel mehr uns eine grenzlose Bildsamkeit, als die hieneiden mögliche Ausbildung ergreift. Auch freue ich mich Ihrer Freude an der naturlichen Natur, obwohl ich mich nun schon seit beinahe 6 Jahren auf den öden Kadizer Felsen ganz wohl ohne Schatten nach Quellen behelfe, und nur der poetischen Natur huldige.

Sie errathen es, daß ich bei einer äußeren Einförmigkeit und in ziemlich beschränkten Umständen, ein höchst reiches inneres Leben führe und daß mir die den Berufsgeschäften abgenommenen Stunden doppelt genußreich verfließen. Meine Thätigkeit ist lebendiger als sie es je gewesen ist; einiges ist schon gedruckt und manches Wichtigere nähert sich der Vollendung. Ich brauche darüber nicht weitläufig zu sein, indem ich darauf rechne, daß der Dr Julius Sie von meinen litterarischen Fehden wird unterrichtet haben. Ich bin dadurch mit der altspanischen Litteratur noch bekannter geworden als ich es war, und finde immer mehr Nahrung für Geist und Herz in diese durch die Afteraufklärung so ganz verdunkelten Helden der Poesie. Jammervoll ist dagegen der Gemuthszustand der jetzigen Spanier. Von dem französischen Witze geblendet und von der französischen Vernünftelei bestochen, zwingen sie sich alle wahre Poesie zu verachten, und der unglückliche Hang gelten, zu wollen aufgeklärt zu scheinen, sich über das Gewöhnliche und Gemeine zu erheben, hat sich in den Städten unter alle Klassen verbreitet, und einen bis an Haß gränzenden Widerwillen gegen alles Nazionale erzeugt, der die Empfindung des unbefangenen Zuschauers auf das Peinlichste quält. Von dem jetzigen Geschlechte ist in dieser Hinsicht keine Besserung zu erwarten, da der Spanier nicht weniger hartnäckig auf Irrthümer besteht als er im Rechten beharrlich ist, und ich arbeite daher im eigentlichen Sinne für die Nachwelt, darum aber nicht weniger eifrig. Jede wahre, der inneren Natur angemeßenen, und aus der Tiefe des Wesens entsprungene Bestrebung, pflegt sich auch schicklich zu gestalten und in einer verhältnißmäßige vollendeten Form, unser Ich zu verdoppeln. Diese Verdoppelung ist ein von allem Beifall unabhängigen Genuß, das Fantom einer irdischen Unsterblichkeit, die Ahnung einer geistigen Berührung mit allem Edlen was ist und sein wird, kurz eine Erscheinung die alle Anfeindungen und Mißverständniße versüßt und mit der Hoffnung schmeichelt nicht spurlos in das Meer der Zeiten zu versinken – Sie sehen ich bin der alte Schwärmer, obwohl der Kopf greist und ich bald ein halbes Jahrhundert hinter mir haben werde; für mich aber ward gesagt:

Setz die Perücken auf von Millionen Locken
Setz deinen Fuß auf ellenhohen Socken
Du bleibst doch immer was du bist[1]

Die Gegenstände mögen wechseln, die Glut bleibt dieselbe. Und sonderbar daß diese Glut die eigentliche Vereinigung bezweckt jetzt so ganz auf Vereinzelung oder Karakteristik, als eigenthümliche Poesie und Nazionalität gerichtet ist! – Es ist sicherlich weil ich fühle, daß das von der Filosofie beabsichtige Ein und All, ein todtes Meer ist, ein grauer nebligter Kirchhof, eine stumme lichtlose Halle. Ich will dagegen lebendige scharfbegränzte Körper deren Anziehen und Abstoßen die Beweglichkeit unterhält, ohne welche gewöhnliche Naturen, dem stehenden Wasser gleich, faulen. Dieses ist nicht Krieg, den angreifender Krieg ist nur ein Werkzeug der filosophischen Nivellirung und ein zur Vernichtung führender scheuslicher Zwang; es ist ein freies Spiel der so wunderbar verschiedenen Naturgaben in Bezug auf gesellschaftliche Verhältniße ohne daß Dreßur (alias Erziehung), Nützlichkeit (alias Moral), Verkehrtheit (alias Aufklärung) diese schönen Anlagen verhungern und die sinnvolle Selbstständigkeit in ein gleichförmiges Uhrwerk verwandeln. Werden wir nur inne, daß uns verschiedenen Tönen die eigentliche Harmonie entspringt und sehr verschiedene Instrumente die prachtvolle Simfonie hervorbringen, so ist das Räthsel in soweit gelöst, als es ein Empfangsschein zuläßt.

Meine Äußerlichkeiten haben sich wenig verändert; ich schlage mich so durch und lebe von Hand zu Mund. Außer meiner Jüngsten, die von dem Hinken nicht ganz geheilt ist, genießen die Anderen einer guten Gesundheit und machen uns Freude. Die junge Wittwe werden Sie nächsten Winter dorten sehen. Juan (hoffe

ich) ist jetzt unterwegens, um uns einen Besuch zu machen, ehe er seiner Universität bezieht; nur wird die Freude des Wiedersehens durch die bevorstehende frische Trennung getrübt werden – Meine freundschaftliche Erinnerung Ihrem lieben Mann und einen Kuß dem Pflegetöchterlein, der ich gerne Mährchen erzählen, und alte Lieder vorspielen würde, um den Sinn (der über alle Vernunft ist) zu nähren und bilden – Meine herzliche Anhänglichkeit bleibt Ihnen und den lieben Ihrigen stets gewidmet.
B. v: F.

85. Nikolas Heinrich Julius, Hamburg

Cadiz, den 30 May 1819

Da Cap[itain] Voß seiner Natur gemäß noch immer zögert, so erfolgt einliegend als Nachtrag:

– eine prächtige Ode auf die bevorstehende Unternehmung nach
Buenos Ayres von einem jungen Dichter, der die
altspanischen Autos studirt hat
– ein paar Briefe über Theater im guten Sinne, obwohl für
Sie nur halbverständlich der vielen lokalen Anspielungen
halber.

Dann melde Ihnen wie wir endlich Nachrichten von dem Baron d'Alton und Dr. Pander erhalten haben, und daß der erste mir sagen läßt „daß nächstens Hülfstruppen aus Deutschland in Spanien anlangen werden, womit den Madritern eine Diversion im Rücken gemacht werden soll, die den vollständigsten Sieg nicht lange zweifelhaft lassen wird" – Sollte Ihnen etwas davon zu Händen kommen, so erwarte ich es [na]türlich mit erster Gelegenheit, und in Form eines großen [Br]iefes wird kein Capitän Anstand nehmen, es mitzubringen.

Noch sage ich Ihnen, daß mir ein ganz vortreffliches Werk: de la Mennais ou l'indifference en matiere de Rèlègion[1] zu Händen gekommen ist, und das (zu meinem Erstaunen) eine vierte Auflage des ersten Theiles. Eine solche Empfänglichkeit für dergleichen, hätte ich in der französischen Zunge nicht vermuthet und ich gestehe daß ich aus diesem Grunde die Franzosen jetzt weniger haße und verachte. Sie brauchen mir demnach dieses Werk nicht zu schicken. Ich habe daran nur die Weitläufigkeit der Polemik gegen einzelne Sätze zu tadeln –

Cap[itain] Bandix ist noch nicht erschienen. Cap[itain] Nielsen hat die Reise in 18 Tagen gemacht.

Der Ihrige
Böhl v. Faber

86. Friedrich Perthes, Hamburg

Cadiz, den 16 Aug[ust] 1819

Seiner Zeit habe ich Ihre werthe Zuschrift vom 16 April erhalten, so wie später die Bücher p[er] Cap[itain] Bandix über welche ich an Dr Julius ausführlich schreibe. Ich danke Ihnen für Ihre Bemerkungen über Kotzebues Ermordung;[1] ich kann darüber keine eigene Ansicht haben, da mir die antecedentes zu ferne liegen. – Den Briefwechsel über den Adel[2] habe ich gerne gelesen; mein Gefühl neigt sich nach Fouqués Seite, obgleich Ihre Gründe gewichtig sind. Es ist nicht abzusehen was noch aus dieser Gährung endlich hervorgehen werde. Ich bin es von Herzen müde gegen den Zeitgeist anzukämpfen und möchte mich verschließen für alle Weltkunde, und nur in alten Büchern leben. In meinen Augen ist die beliebte vernünftelnde Aufklärerei ein wahrer Greuel und der Tod der Poesie, des Enthusiasmus, und [aller] schönen Gefühle in denen ich lebe und webe. Mit dem innigsten Behagen habe ich kürzlich Ihres trefflichen Schwiegervaters Claudius Sämtliche Werke[3] von Anfang bis zu Ende (6 Bände) wieder durchgelesen, und darin allerwärts die Andeutungen jener belebenden Sinnesart gefunden, die sich späterhin so vorzüglich entwickelt hat, leider aber immer Minorität geblieben ist – Ueber meine litterarischen Bedürfniße wird Ihnen Dr. Julius das Nöthige mittheilen – Meine aufrichtige Freundschaft und Liebe bleibt Ihnen und dem Zirkel unserer gemeinsamen Freunde stets gewidmet.

Böhl v. Faber

87. Nikolas Heinrich Julius, Hamburg

Cadiz, den 18 Aug[ust] 1819

Ich beantworte Ihre Briefe und Sendung p[er] Cap[itain] Bandix. Zuerst eine Klage über den Mangel an Einband, der mir einen großen Theil des Genußes geraubt hat. Alles was nicht Zeitschriften oder Flugschriften sind wünsche ich immer in feiner Pappe gebunden zu erhalten, auch Fortsetzungen mit eingeschloßen – Ich wiederhole daß mir der 3te Band der Oesterr[eichischen] Jahrb[ücher] fehlt: den 4 und 5 habe ich nicht so interessant als die ersten gefunden. Sonderbar daß man in Deutschland den Ton der Englischen Quartalschr[iften] nicht treffen kann, daß man es nicht versteht nur <u>allgemein</u> interessante Werke hervorzuheben, und an deren Kritik allgemeine Uebersichten anzuknüpfen, wodurch sich die Edinb[urgh] Rev[iew] so sehr auszeichnet – Großen Genuß hat mir Humbolds 2. Theil gewährt: Fiévée hat mich und besonders meine Frau besser unterhalten als wir glaubten. An Ritters Erdkunde werde ich mich sobald nicht machen, da ich das schlechte Papier mühsam aufschneiden muß – Die Fantasiestücke hatte ich schon früher erhalten, und machten sie mir viele Freude. Gerne werde ich die späteren Werke des

Verf[assers] erhalten <u>versteht sich gebunden</u> und sind die Theile nicht stark zwei in einem Band. – Die Vorrede des Calderon von Malsburg[1] ist herrlich – Schlegels Observ[ations][2] und Göthes 3te Theil haben mich sehr befriediget, aber bei weitem mehr als ich erwartete habe ich in de Bonalds recherches[3] gefunden, und begreife nicht wie Sie mir dieses wichtige Werk nicht von selbst geschickt haben. Gelegentlich wünsche von demselben Verf[asser] zu erhalten: Pensées diverses und opinions politiques 2 vol[umes] Melanges litteraires, politiq[ues] und philosoph[iques] 2 vol[umes] <u>versteht sich gebunden</u>. – Sommers Ansichten der Kirche[4] sind auch mir vortrefflich vorgekommen – Schmidts Vorarbeit über Calderon[5] hat mich natürlich sehr interessirt; nur möchte ich den Verf[asser] warnen ja nicht alles für von Calderon zu halten was unter dessen Namen gedruckt ist. In der alten Ausgabe sowohl als in Huerta Teatro Espanol[6] findet sich eine von Calderon selbst ausgefertigte Liste seiner Schauspiele, die jeder Forscher als Grund legen muß. In dem Catal[ogo] del Teatro Espanol als suplemento des Huerta finden sich allein 91 Stücke unter dem Namen Calderons, die nicht in seinen Werken stehen und wahrscheinlich nicht von ihm sind. Da die ächte Sammlung so reich ist, so scheint es mir Uebermuth sich nach zweifelhaften Stücken umzusehen. Ich könnte vielleicht ein Dutzend in meiner Sammlung auftreiben, aber ich halte es nicht der Mühe werth sie zu studiren. Dahingegen kann ich mit der Abschrift von 6 Entremeses von Calderon aufwarten die allerliebst sind, wenngleich es auffallend ist daß zwischen den 400 woraus meine Sammlung besteht nur so wenige dem Calderon namentlich zugeschrieben sind – Das Stück Yo me entiendo y Dios me entiende[7] ist bestimmt nicht von Calderon sondern von Cañizares – Calderon sein Bild müßte man aus der Colecc[ion] de Espan[ole]s ilustres[8] nehmen (18 Hefte in groß folio) welche alle nach original Gemälden gestochen sind – Die Aufsätze über Moretos Desden in den Originalien[9] haben mir sehr wohl gefallen. Ihre Ausgleichung der Ital[ischen] Epick mit der Span[ischen] Dramat[ick] ist sehr artig: auch stimme Ihrer Würdigung Moretos völlig bei: nur fehlen in Ihrer Anführung der vorzüglichen Stücke des Dichters mehrere die wir hier besonders schätzen, als: el parecedo en la corte (welches noch neuerdings mit Beifall hier gegeben und mich in ein ununterbrochenes Gelächter erhält) la tia y la sobrina, ein vollkommenes Lustspiel und vortrefflich geschrieben, el lindo don Diego ein unverbesserliches höchst komisches Stück und lebendiges Bild der damaligen süßen Herren, el rico hombre de Alcalá,[10] welches bestimmt das Moreto auch den heroischen Geist zu beschwören vermochte etc – Vielen Dank für die Zeitung mit Pr[inz] Gustav und Gr[af] Stolb[erg] Briefen,[11] hier ist dieses nicht a l'ordre du jour und das Gegentheil würde mehr Interesse erwecken. – Leid thut es mir der herrlichen Stolberg Werke[12] (ihrer Bänderzahl halben) vor's erste entbehren zu müssen; gerne aber werde ich das Inhaltsverzeichnis erhalten. – Das Heft mit der Misgeburt ist von dem ärtzlichen Verein hier mit Dank angenommen: sollte dorten eine Mediz[inische] Zeitschr[ift] im Latein[ischen] erscheinen so melden Sie es mir –

Die Sängerfahrt die in den Wiener Jahrb[üchern] gelobt ist und ich gefordert habe ist nicht von Fouqué, sondern gesammelt von Fr[iedrich] Förster, Berlin 1818 in der Maurersch[en] Buchhandl[ung] mit Beiträgen von Tieck und Novellen von Arnim und Brentano, und erwarte solche demnach mit erster Sendung – Den deutschen wohlfeilen Abdruck von Lord Byron[13] werde gerne erhalten versteht sich gebunden: meine Fr[au] bewundert diesen Dichter, so wie Scott,[14] mehr als ich es vermag. Meiner Sinnesart spricht Wordsworth mehr an, und vermutlich Crabbe (tales of the hall)[15] wenn Sie mir solchen verschaffen können.

Die Sammlung alter Kirchen Musik sende ich zurück, da sie weder mir noch den Meinigen dienen kann. Von Musik können mir nur schlichte Volkslieder dienen – Die latein[ische] Disert[ation] über Calderon[16] hat hier das größte Vergnügen gemacht, und sind sie zur Hand so können Sie mir noch ein paar Abdrücke zusenden: diese geheftet – Die Morgenblätter[17] die des hiesigen Calderon[ischen] Streites erwähnen hatte ich gerne erhalten: nichts haben Sie mir darüber geschrieben. Erscheint die Reise des Baron d'Alton so erwarte ich solche ohne Fehl. – Von dem Fuero juzgo[18] (nicht dem viejo) erhalten Sie die schöne neue Ausgabe, so wie auch 2 Entrem[eses] de Cervantes; ersteres kostet 70 Reales die andern beiden 24 Reales. Die Roman[cer]os sind von Madrid verschrieben. Einen Moreto habe ich nie selbst verschaffen können und besitze nur gesammelte einzelne Abdrücke. Die gewünschte Sammlung alte Schauspiele ist ein opus magnum, und wird immer schwerer da jetzt die alten Stücke nicht mehr neu aufgelegt werden. Eine Sammlung dieser Art in 50 Bänden hat mir jahrelanges Suchen Anstrengung Korrespondenz und Aufwand an Geld und Zeit gekostet. Von meinen Doubletten ließe sich jedoch eine artige Sammlung aufstützen, die Ihren werden soll, wenn der Himmel mir ja Muße giebt diese Stücke zu mustern und zu ordnen –

Ich beneide Sie um Ihre frühe Frühjahrsreise und die interessanten Leipziger Bekanntschaften. Wie kann aber Calderon in 8 duodez Bänden hereingezwängt werden? – Also nur eine Auswahl vermuthlich – Abermals eine kleine Unmöglichkeit die Erklärung der span[ischen] Volkslieder, die ich von einem poetischen Sinn nicht erwartet hätte! Gerade in der Unbestimmtheit der Wörter cactucha, alelillo, duendito, liegt das Komische od[er] Schalkhafte od[er] Empfindsame dieser Lieder, je nachdem man es auffaßt. Da meine Tochter jedoch den Winter dorten zubringen wird, so kann sie Ihnen vielleicht mehreres darüber andeuten; auch singt sie einige herrliche wirksamste Lieder, die Sie müssen auszuforschen suchen. – Mir ist nichts mehr von Volksliedern vorgekommen und geht auch dieser Nazionalzug immer mehr verloren, wenigstens in Cadiz, wo kleine italienisch[en] Lieder immer mehr die eingeborenen verdrängen – Was hier erscheinende Bücher betrifft, die treu in der Gazeta de Madrid[19] angezeigt werden, kann ich Ihnen nur sagen daß nichts gar nichts originales gedruckt wird was irgend von Belang wäre. Die Anzeigen sind nur Wiederholungen schon lange gedruckter Bücher, oder Uebers[etzungen] medizinischer und ökonomischer

Schriften und Romane, oder auch neue Auflagen von Andachtsübungen. Es existirt gar kein Interesse mehr für Litteratur und wo noch etwas Geist sich regt ist es nur für die vermaledeite Politik die den Menschen hier völlig den Kopf verrückt hat. Durch eine besondere Vorsehung ist hier kürzlich ein unsinnigen Revoluzionsplan gerade in dem Moment des Ausbruchs erstickt. Wenn indessen 99/100 der lesenden und schreibenden Maße eine Veränderung wollen, wenn die Offiziere der Armee fast ohne Ausnahme dasselbe bezwecken und wenn das Volk gleichgültig ist so muß diese Veränderung endlich erfolgen. Ich habe daher die gute Sache <u>hier</u> völlig aufgegeben, und würde jetzt gerne nach Deutschland zurückkehren wenn es von meiner Willkühr abhinge. Mein Streit mit der Cronica ist eingeschlafen: sie haben das letzte Wort behalten, weil mein dritter Pasatiempo aus Mangel an Geld noch ungedruckt ist. Ich hoffe jedoch durch Einsendung einiger die span[ische] Sprache betreffender Arbeiten (denen nur die letzte Hand mangelt) die Ernennung als Akademiker nicht zu verfehlen. Die anhaltende Hitze hat meine gewöhnliche Thätigkeit etwas gelähmt; auch widme ich natürlich meinem Juan einen Theil meiner Freistunden. Er ist ein braver Junge, dessen Herzensgaben den Mangel an Umfang und Energie des Geistes ersetzen. Die ziemlich beschwerliche Hitze ist hier seit c[irc]a 6 Wochen 21 ½ Grad Reaum: mehrere Tage 22° und Mitte July 23° und dorten haben Sie laut der Zeitung 30° gehabt! –

Wenige Hoffnung habe ich Ihnen Handschriften berühmter Männer verschaffen zu können. Hier ist nicht daran zu denken dergleichen aufzufinden; nach Madrid habe ich geschrieben, befinde mich jedoch bis jetzt noch ohne Antwort – Hiebei die Liste die unter Calderons Namen in meiner Sammlung befindlich sind, und zwei einzelne Stücke wenn die Sie dem Pat[er] Schmidt in meinem Namen übersenden können – P. S. So eben klaube ich aus einem alten Bande geschriebener Sachen einen Brief des berühmten Padre Yslas,[20] Verfaßer des Gerundio und Uebers[etzer] des Gil Blas heraus, den Sie wenigstens als einen Beweis meines guten Willens Ihren Freunden zusenden können – Das erste Blatt nach dem Titel im Rom[ancero] del Cid enthält nur eine aprobacion, suma de la licencia, fe del corrector und ein schlechtes Sonnett al autor, alles Sachen die wahrlich nicht verdienen abgeschrieben zu werden.

Wie wäre es wenn Sie in den Zeitungen setzen ließen, daß eine Sammlung von soviel Bänden alter deutscher Poesie im Rummel verkäuflich sei, deren Verzeichniß bei Ihnen zur Einsicht läge? Ich dächte, daß Sie im Durchschnitt doch 1 Thaler p[er] Band werth sein müßten! – 400 Mark ist doch gar zu wenig.

Gerne würde ich der alten Räthin Campe[21] schreiben, da ich ihrer mütterlichen Liebe stets eingedenk bin; allein Sie wissen wie weit meine Sinnesart von der damaligen filantropischen entfernt ist, und wie sehr ich mich daher zieren müßte um die alten Verhältniße nicht unsanft zu berühren. Tragen Sie es unserer lieben Elise Campe auf von abseiten meiner etwas recht Freundschaftliches an die alte

Räthin zu sagen, und den Mangel an eigener Darstellung meiner Gefühle auf meine gehäuften Geschäfte und Nahrungssorgen zu schieben.

Cap[itain] Voßens endliche Ankunft haben wir kürzlich erfahren; wenn Sie mir aber im Frühjahr etwas zu senden haben so geben Sie es lieber an Cap[itain] Bandix der gerne alles für mich nehmen wird.

Beim Durchsehen dieses Briefes finde daß Sie glauben könnten ich wäre ungerecht gegen einige herrliche Rezens[ionen] der Wiener Jahrbücher deswegen hole ich nach daß mir besonders gefallen haben im 4 J[ahr]b[uch] die Beurtheilung des Lotosblattes und Grävells Mensch und im 5ten die Zurechtweisung des elenden aufgeblasenen Merkels des noch elenderen und verächtlichen Stadts, die Bemerkungen über Gall und Sporzheim und die sehr würdige Revision der Turnkunst – Aber was soll mir 87 Seiten zum Fried[rich] II Staatseinrichtung in Sicilien; dann wieder 18 S[eiten] österreicher Lohn Recht und 36 S[eiten] über ein (meiner Ansicht nach) unbedeutendes Gedicht, und im 5. Bande 35 S[eiten] Noten über die bairische Geschichte, und eine kirchliche Topogr[aphie] Oest[e]r[eichs] und das lächerliche Ital[ienische] Ged[icht] über Don Quichote? –[22]

Mir fehlt Schlegels Deutsches Museum[23] welches versteht sich in f[einer] Pappe gebunden zu erhalten wünsche. Wahrscheinlich ist es in Stocken gerathen und doch muß es (nach den Hinweisungen zu urtheilen) voll von interessanten Aufsätzen sein –

Giebt es jetzt ein sistematisches Handbuch der neueren Ästhethik? Nemlich nach Kants Schillers und Schlegels Ideen. Senden Sie mir ein solches versteht sich eingebunden in feiner Pappe, wenn es nemlich vorzüglich ist –

Hiebei vier geheftete Bücher um solche binden zu lassen laut Aufschrift. Ich hoffe daß Sie mir solche auf das Frühjahr mit den gleichfalls gebundenen Fortsetzungen werden zusenden können. Es sind:

Bouterweck[24] 10r Theil
Phantasus 3r Theil
Rambachs (recht brave) Anthologie 3r Th[eil]
Humboldts Reise 2r Th[eil]

Die neue Auflage Paul Gerhards fügen Sie der ersten Sendung bei, versteht sich in f[einer] P[appe] gebunden.

Und damit für heute Gott befohlen und schließen Sie mich in Ihrem Gebete ein, wie Sie in dem Meinigen stets begriffen sind. Alles ist doch Tand außer der Ewigkeit! Eya, wären wir da! – Die Herberg' ist zu böse, des Jammers ist zu viel!
Der Ihrige
B.v.F.

D[en] 20 Aug[ust] Noch so eben erhalte ich beigehendes Florez Medallas,[25] welches anfängt rar zu werden da so viele Abdrücke nach England gehen.

Die Heirath mit der sächsischen Prinzeßin ist nun gewiß: was Sie mir über Charakter Figur und Eigenschaften der Prinzeßin sagen können, wird mir sehr interessant sein, und sollte ihr Konterfei in klein Format dorten Käuflich sein, so senden Sie es mir p[er] Post –

Derselbe

88. Nikolas Heinrich Julius, Hamburg

Cadiz, den 24 September 1819.

– Schon lange entbehre ich Ihrer Nachrichten und der Beantwortung meiner Mittheilungen p[er] Cap[itain] Voß, und doch hat es nicht an Schiffsgelegenheit gemangelt; auch wissen Sie, daß ich das Briefporto p[er] Post nicht scheue. Besonders gerne hätte ich eine Karakteristik und allenfalls das Brustbild in Kupfer unserer künftigen Königin erhalten – Meine Kinder sind seit d[em] 3 dieses in See und jetzt hoffentlich nicht weit von der Elbe mehr. Wenn man das Schiff nach dorten zuläßt und nicht nach Norwegen zur quarantaine sendet! – Hier hat seit 14 Tagen das gelbe Fiebe ziemlich um sich gegriffen und es sterben täglich 50 a 60 Menschen daran. Es bestätigt sich, daß man hier nicht zum zweitenmal davon befallen wird; ich habe indessen meine jüngste Tochter und zwei Bedienten denen es noch bevorsteht, so daß man sich der Ängstlichkeit nicht entschlagen kann – Man läßt hier jetzt keine Schiffe ausgehen wodurch der nach dorten bestimmte Cap[itain] Nordberg aufgehalten wird; mit demselben werde ich Ihnen verschiedenes zusenden. Vergelten Sie meine Aufmerksamkeit und lassen mich künftig nicht so lange ohne Berichte. Ich brenne auf des Baron D'Altons Beschreibung seiner spanischen Reise – Ich war 3 Tage in Sevilla als ich meine Kinder dahinbrachte. Cap[itain] Nordberg wird Ihnen meinen Aufsatz[1] über diesen sehr interessanten Flug mitbringen. Anstatt daß das Alter mich abstumpfen sollte wird mein Gemüth allen schönen Eindrücken stets offener. Diese Fertigkeit auch aus dem Gemeinsten das Edle abzuziehen verdanke ich Wordsworth und Göthe –

Der Ihrige B.v.F

89. Nikolas Heinrich Julius, Hamburg

Cadiz, den 2 October 1819

Hieneben einige Abdrücke der zweiten Ausgabe derjenigen Flugaufsätze die den Pasatiempos vorangingen. Dieses mit den Pasatiempos vereiniget (deren dritter jetzt gedruckt wird) wird einen mäßigen Band unter dem gemeinschaftlichen Titel Vindicaciones de Calderon[1] machen.–

Ich hätte Ihnen gerne die Beschreibung meiner Flucht nach Sevilla gesandt, allein ich habe keine Zeit gehabt sie aus der Kladde abzuschreiben. Vielleicht sende ich sie Ihnen p[er] Post da ich denke es aus zwei Bogen zusammendrängen zu können. Vielleicht eignet sie sich für eine Zeitschrift.

Hiebei die Anzeige des einzigen wichtigen Werkes welches seit langer Zeit erschienen ist; ich habe es noch nicht gesehen.

Das gelbe Fieber dauert fort; seine Periode pflegt 3 Monath zu sein, wovon nur der erste vorüber ist. Es sind daran c[irc]a 1200 Menschen verstorben ¾ männlichen und nur ¼ weiblichen Geschlechts. Es fährt fort die eigentliche Lebenskraft zu befeinden, und den stärksten und blühendsten jungen Männern am gefährlichsten zu sein. Beförderung der Leibesöffnung und des Schweißes, nebst mäßigen Dosen von Oel innerlich und äußerlich, pflegen am besten anzuschlagen. Da die meisten Aertzte jetzt völlig vor Ansteckung gesichert sind, so werden ihre Beobachtungen dieses Mal die Kenntniß des Uebels befördern. Von Lazo erwarte ich etwas sehr durchdachtes und erprobtes darüber.

In trüben Zeiten greife ich zu Romanen und habe manches alte durchgelesen. Der <u>Lebenslauf</u>[2] haben mich (außer den interminablen Einlagen und Lehrbriefen) sehr interessirt. Die <u>Fisonomischen Reisen von Musäus</u>[3] sind der geflickten Sprache zum Trotz, ein Meisterstück von gesunder Filosofie und Laune. <u>Die Kinder Märchen von Grimm</u>[4] sind ganz allerliebst. – <u>v. Arnims Kronenwächter</u>[5] höchst fantastisch mit der Eigenheit daß die Prosa öfters poetisch und die Verse gewöhnlich matte gereimte Prosa. Begierig bin ich indessen auf die Fortsetzung.

Ich habe das Fieber im Hause zwischen den Bedienten und meine jüngste Tochter hat es noch nicht gehabt. Indessen als Christ

„nicht widerstreben
Gottes Willen thu ich mich ergeben"

Der Ihrige
Böhl v: Faber

90. Nikolas Heinrich Julius, Hamburg

Cadiz, den 15 October 1819

Meine erste Absicht war Ihnen den Inhalt p[er] Cap[itain] Nordberg zuzusenden. Da es aber leicht möglich ist daß man diesen Schiffer zur quarantain nach Norwegen sende, so habe ich beschloßen das Porto daran zu wenden und bitte an Perthes zu sagen daß er mir solches in Rechnung belaste. Ich denke den Aufsatz qualifizirt sich für irgend eine Zeitschrift: zum Ausfeilen habe ich keine Zeit gehabt, und ich bitte allenfalls entschlüpfte Nachläßigkeiten zu verbessern. Für das dortige Publikum ist die Tendenz wohl zu poetisch und zu katholisch. Indessen Sie schalten damit nach Willkühr; lassen Sie es drucken so reserviren Sie mir ein halb Dutzend Abdrücke, die Sie der ersten Sendung für mich beifügen, und senden auch <u>in meinem Namen</u> Abdrücke an Fr[au] Elise Campe, Fr[au] Sieburg, Fräulein Staack auf Thurow, Fr[au] Henriette Schwarz (die Frau des spanischen Konsuls) meiner Tochter Cecilia, Perthes, Bokelman und Poels.

Unsere sächsische Prinzeßin ist diesen Augenblick schon in Madrid, ohne daß ich von Ihnen die so sehr erwünschte Nachricht über ihre Figur Karakter und Bildung erhalten hätte. Ihr Bild besitzen wir nun schon; sonstige Nachrichten werden aber immer noch willkommen sein.

Das gelbe Fieber wüthet bei der anhaltenden Temperatur von 19 a 20 Reaum mit trocknen Ostwinden heftig und nimmt an Bösartigkeit zu. Man nimmt an, daß wenigstens 20000 Menschen es zu überstehen haben. 4 a 5000 sind glücklich durchgekommen, 11000 liegen darnieder; über 2000 sind schon begraben. Gottlob daß es sich nicht zum zweitenmal einstellt! Unsere jüngste Tochter hat es noch zu überstehen: ein Dienstmädchen in unserm Hause lag arg daran nieder, ist aber in der Besserung – Gegen 5 Männer stirbt nur 1 Frau und 1 Kind. – In der Mitte dieses Trübsals haben wir den Trost, daß es keinem Kranken an etwas gebricht. Die Wohlthätigkeit der hiesigen Einwohner kennt keine Gränzen. Nachdem sie die umliegenden Ortschaften, besonders S[an] Fernando, auf das Reichlichste unterstützt haben, vertheilen sie jetzt tausende täglich hier. Artz und Apotheker laben alle Armen umsonst. Unser würdiger Bischof, ein Engel des Friedens, den wir erst seit dem Ausbruch der Krankheit besitzen, spendet persönlich die geistigen Tröstungen, und setzt sich für die Armen in Schulden – Ich bin Gottlob gleichmüthig, und auf alles gefaßt. Auch ohne eine solche Heimsuchung war ich von dem Nichtigen alles Irdischen hinreichend überzeugt, und daß wir nur Gäste auf Erden sind. Es sterben jetzt über 100 täglich.

Ihr wahrer Freund etc.
Böhl v: Faber

91. *Nikolas Heinrich Julius, Hamburg*

Cadiz, den 17 Dec[ember] 1819

Perthes wird Ihnen wahrscheinlich meinen heutigen Brief an ihn mittheilen und Sie werden daraus den Ernst Ihres früheren Aufrufes an meine Thätigkeit vernehmen. Zwei Umstände haben in Verbindung mit der ungewöhnlichen Muße, die Sache befördert: 1) die Aufgebung der sistematischen Bearbeitung 2) die mir selbst vorgeschriebene Beschränkung auf ein Alphabet und die Berechnung der Zeilen um besonders bei den kurzen Gedichten das Umschlagen vorzubeugen: meinen

Fleiß bei dieser Berechnung werden Sie bei Ansicht der Handschrift bewundern –
Was sagen Sie zu 380 fast alle unbekannten Gedichte? die die spanische Poesie von
einer ganz neuen Seite zeigen, die fast alle das Gefühl ansprechen und deren viele
eine Zärtlichkeit athmen die man sonst an der erhabenen Kastilischen Muse
vermißt? Die Numerirung scheint mir sehr glücklich, und weiterhin können Sie mir
und ich Ihnen nach den Nummern unsere Bemerkungen mittheilen. Ob ich ein
paar Bogen Anhang mit <u>deutschen</u> Noten nach den Nummern, zufügen werde, ist
noch unbestimmt. Jetzt kommt es darauf an ob unser Perthes den Muth haben
wird den Verlag zu übernehmen: in diesem Falle rechne ich auf Sie als Korrektor.
– Ihre lieben Grüße vom 7 Sept[ember] und 19 Nov[ember] sind in meinen
Händen. Heute jedoch müssen Sie sich mit dieser Anzeige begnügen. Es freut mich
daß Ihnen mein Aufsatz über Sevilla gefallen hat und sehe seiner Zeit die denselben
enthaltenden Morgenblätter entgegen – Ihre Aeußerungen über meine Kinder sind
mir sehr erfreulich; in Hinsicht des Textes der spanischen Volkslieder verweise ich
Sie nochmals an meine Tochter, ohne jedoch Ihnen die verlangte Uebersetzung zu
verweigern.

    Ich hoffe Sie werden sich mit Dr Wehber über die alten Bücher verstanden
haben: mit meinen altdeutschen Sachen hat es keine Eile und nimmt die Liebhaberei zu so verliere ich nichts mit Warten – Sie vergeßen doch die zum Binden
gesandten Bücher nicht? –

    Ihr aufrichtig ergebener
    Böhl v: Faber

92. Friedrich Perthes, Hamburg

Cadiz, den 17 December 1819

Ihre Zeilen vom 22 Sep[tember] mit dem Recief über ein Packet Bücher p[er]
Cap[itain] Voß habe ich wohl erhalten, auch bemerkt daß Ihnen H[er]r v. Faber 82
Mark für mich bezahlt hat. Sie erwähnen nicht 25 Mark – die mir Dr Julius
schreibt Ihnen für meine Rech[nun]g eingehändigt zu haben. Dieser Freund hat mir
kürzlich Ihre Erklärung gegen Voß[1] in Hinsicht unseres lieben edlen Claudius
übersandt. Bei einer solchen Begebenheit kann man nur <u>staunen</u> und sich in dem
Glauben halten, daß die Pforten der Hölle das Reich Christi doch nicht überwältigen werden. Ist es möglich bei solchen grauen Sündern irgend einen anderen als
den noch rein teuflischen Zweck der Entzweiung auszudenken? Ist das Schandbuch nicht schon unterwegs, so will ich es lieber gar nicht sehen.

    Das gelbe Fieber ist überstanden und meine jüngste Tochter davon verschont
geblieben, wenngleich zwei Bediente es in meinem Hause gehabt haben. Wir
denken jetzt kaum mehr daran, und wünschen nur freies Verkehr um das
Versäumte nachzuholen. Ich habe während desselben einer ungewohnten Muße

genoßen, und dieselbe benutzt um den ersten Theil meiner so lange vorbereiteten Sammlung altspanischer Gedichte anzuordnen und für den Druck abzuschreiben. Zwei Drittel ist schon vollendet und auf eine Weise die dem etwaigen Setzer viel Mühe ersparen wird. Die Sammlung ist auf ein Alphabet oder 384 Seiten in 8^{oo} berechnet; jede Seite auf 36 Zeilen und alle kurzen oder achtsilbigen Verse in zwei Kolonnen, so daß die Sammlung über 20 000 Verse enthält. Die Abschrift ist von der Art daß der Druck, derselben Seite für Seite entsprechen muß. Der Titel ist Floresta Española de rimas antiguas. Sie enthält 380 N[umer]os in vier Abtheilungen von Rimas sacras, Rimas doctrinales, Rimas amorosas und Rimas festivas, das älteste jedesmal an der Spitze. Hintenan nach den Nummern die Quellen Verfaßer und kurze Bemerkungen wo es nöthig scheint. Diese ansehnliche Sammlung enthält (mit Ausnahme einiger Romanzen) nichts, was in den 9 Th[eilen] des Parnaso Español[2] den 19 Th[eilen] des Ramon Fernandez und den 3 Th[eilen] des Quintana[3] abgedruckt steht und kann also als ein Ergänzungsband für die Besitzer dieser Sammlungen dienen. Fast alle bekannten Dichter sind ausgeschloßen, als Garcilaso, Herrera,[4] Quevedo, Jauregui,[5] Cervantes, Lope de Vega, Argensolas,[6] Rioja,[7] Leon, Castillejo,[8] Burguillos[9] etc. Ferner sind ausgeschloßen, alle eigentliche Satiren, alle <u>historischen</u> Romanzen und alle Sonnette, und dennoch (wenn mich mein Gefühl nicht trügt) ist in dieser Sammlung mehr ächte Poesie als in allen vorhergegangenen. Schwer war es bei den ganz alten, das Metafisische ganz zu umgehen, schwer bei den späteren Wortschwall und Bombast. Ich hoffe daß ich beide Klippen vermieden habe; aber auch wie viel Gereime habe ich durchklauben müssen um diese Ausbeute zu gewinnen! – Dennoch unterfange ich mich einen gleich starken Band zu liefern, wenn ich neben meinem übrigen Vorrath auch das beste der bekannteren Dichter in Anspruch nehme. Dann würden die beiden Bände eine lirische Blumenlese enthalten, die sowohl an Vollständigkeit als an innerem Werth sich schwerlich übertreffen ließe. Einen gleich starken Band würde ich später liefern können mit dem spanischen Theater <u>vor</u> Lope de Vega, und ein vierter könnte den Beschluß machen, dem spanischen Epos gewidmet – Ich füge noch hinzu, daß meine Sammlung mehreres aus alten Handschriften enthält, was nie gedruckt ist. Ich glaube daß wer genug Spanisch versteht um in den Sinn der Sache einzudringen und dem es nicht an poetischem Geiste mangelt, dieser Sammlung seinen Beifall nicht versagen wird. Alle Seiten des menschlichen Gemüths werden darin berührt: von der erhabensten religiösen Ansicht steigen wir zu den praktischen Vernunftregeln herab, vernehmen dann die Sprache der irdischen Liebe in ihren so mannigfaltigen Tönen, berühren die sonstigen Lebensgenüße, lachen über unsere und anderer Thorheiten und endigen mit Poßen.

Dulce est desipere in loco.

So weit der Dichter [damage] Geschäftsmann und hier hapert es. Ich habe keine Mittel für meine Rechnung den Druck zu veranstalten, und findet sich kein Verleger so bleibt die Sache liegen. Honorar verlange ich nicht, dagegen aber eine

Anzahl Abdrücke. Auf Absatz in Spanien ist nicht zu rechnen; auch würde das Einbringen einer Menge Abdrücke schwer und kostbar, und am Ende der öffentliche Verkauf nicht thunlich sein, da alle spanische in der Fremde gedruckte Bücher einzuführen verboten sind – Sehn Sie was dabei zu thun ist. Einen reinlichen Druck und gutes Papier wünsche ich natürlich und ein in Stein gestochenes Titelblatt mit altgothischen Verzierungen und den Titel mit gothischen Buchstaben. Vorrede Register und Bemerkungen werden (meine ich) drei Bogen anfüllen. Dr. Julius würde hoffentlich die Korrektur übernehmen – Auf alle Weise anfolgt die Handschrift, wo nicht früher, mit H[er]r Färber der nächstes Frühjahr nach dorten zurückgeht. Sollten Sie also eine vorläufige Anzeige machen wollen, so können Sie es <u>sicher</u> thun. Ob in Ihrem oder in meinem Namen ist mir gleich, auf alle Fälle aber wünsche ich als Sammler genannt zu werden mit Vor und Zunamen nemlich Böhl von Faber, da ich Ehre und Beifall dorten einzuärndten hoffe.

Unsere junge Königin verherrlicht ihre deutsche Abkunft: sie ist das Muster aller Tugenden. Ihre Bescheidenheit und strenge Zucht wird von allen Graubärten eben so hoch gepriesen als von den Hofdamen verschrieen. Bei den spanischen Tänzen, die der König sehr liebt, sitzt sie mit niedergeschlagenen Augen: auch will sie den Stiergefechten nicht beiwohnen. Die Geistlichen erheben sie bis in den Himmel. Gott verleihe ihr Beharrlichkeit und gebe ihr bald einen männlichen Erben um ihren Einfluß zu vermehren.

Gratuliren Sie Bokelman zu seiner Verehlichung, grüßen Sie den Sievekingschen Zirkel und glauben mich stets Ihren Freund und Diener:

B. v. Faber.

93. Nikolas Heinrich Julius, Hamburg

Cadiz, den 19 Februar 1820.

H[er]r Färber (der diesen Brief mitnimmt) hat die Güte gehabt die 108 Bogen enthaltende Handschrift meiner Floresta (an Perthes addressirt) seinen Sachen beizulegen, und da er in großer Eile reiset giebt er mir Hoffnung binnen vier a fünf Wochen an Ort und Stelle zu sein. Drei deutsch geschriebene Bogen sind für Sie als Korrektor, im Fall P[erthes] den Verlag übernehmen würde. Sie können auf alle Fälle als Wegweiser beim Lesen dienen. Bei Ansicht der Handschrift werden Sie meinen Fleiß loben, und nach bedächtiger Lesung die Spanische Poesie noch höher schätzen, als Sie es jetzt thun – Da ich fortwährend Muße habe und jetzt in Schuß bin, so habe ich den Ueberschlag meines alt[en] dramatischen Vorrathes gemacht, und sehe daß ich gerade ein Alfabet, wie die Floresta (von 36 Z[eilen] durchaus in zwei Kolonnen also c[irc]a 26 000 Verse) liefern kann, welcher 32 Dramas aus dem Ende des 15. und der ersten Hälfte des 16. Jahrhunderts enthält. Alle diese sind gereimt, und die prosaischen Stücke aus derselben Zeit müssen (insofern es überhaupt gerathen ist sie auf's Neue zu publiziren) einer andern Sammlung aufbehalten bleiben. Der Erfinder des spanischen Drama ist sonder Zweifel Juan del Encina.[1] Sein Nebenbuhler war der Portugiese Gil Vicente[2] der ihn weit übertraf. Schade daß dieser so weniges Spanische hat: was er Spanisch schrieb ist unübertrefflich und wird diese Sammlung zieren. Seine meisten Stücke sind Portug[iesisch] und Spanisch durcheinander, die ich nicht aufnehmen kann, weil ich entschloßen bin mich auf das Spanische zu beschränken. Dann kömmt der herrliche Torres Naharro:[3] von seine 8 Stücken denke ich 6 zu geben dann 4 uralte grobe (aber kräftige) Farzas, die ersten alten einfachen Autos und einige alte Schäfergespräche. Jetzt kommt es uns darauf an, ob Sie mich dazu aufmuntern wollen und können: ich habe meine Kräfte und Augen jetzt erprobt und übernehme es in 3 Monathen die Handschrift auszuarbeiten.

Ich überlaufe jetzt nochmal Ihren letzten Brief vom 19 Nov[ember]. Wegen Moreto glaube ich Ihnen schon gemeldet zu haben daß er hier ganz unauftreibbar ist. Den Katalog des spanischen Theils [der] Ebelingschen Bibliothek hätten Sie mir wohl senden können, da vielleicht einige daraus meine wenigen Lücken ausgefüllt hätten. Künftig, fallen Ihnen spanische Versteigerung in die Hände, so schneiden Sie die Blätter aus und senden Sie mir p[er] Post, wenn nemlich ein Auftrag a retour von Post noch in Zeiten kommen würde, So hätten Sie mit der Brentanoschen machen sollen, wo mir vielleicht Manches entgangen ist. Ich lege eine Liste derjenigen Bücher bei, woran mir am Meisten gelegen ist, mit Bestimmung der Preise. Sie werden sich wundern wie hoch ich bei einigen gehen würde, da ich doch eben kein Geld übrig habe. Doch nein! Sie sind ja auch ein Sammler und fühlen (wie ich) daß man acht Tage hungern kann, um eine alte Romanze zu erhaschen.

Von Valencia hat man mir geschrieben daß der treffliche Graf Fr[iedrich] v. Stollberg[4] gestorben ist – Die Cronica hat selbst berichtet, daß in der Revue encyclopedique[5] zu Paris eine sehr falsche Darstellung des Streites über Calderon enthalten sei, aus deutschen Zeitungen entlehnt. Das Wort falsch beweist das Gegentheil. Dieses (meine ich) wird von dem Baron D'Alton veranstaltet sein und sind wohl die versprochenen Hülfstruppen. Ein dritter Pasatiempo der weniger Polemik und mehr über den Geist und Eigenthümlichkeit des Spanischen Theaters enthält ist jetzt gedruckt, und wird mir hoffentlich (nebst andern schriftlichen Abhandlungen über Metrik, Geschichte der Poesie, Grammatik) den Weg zu der Real Academia Española bahnen – Meine Tochter schreibt mir unter d[en] 4 Jan[uar] etwas von Erwähnung meiner bei dortigen patriotischen Gesellschaft: da ich aber nichts von Ihnen direkt darüber höre, bleibe ich in Ungewißheit. Zugleich sagt sie mir, daß ich mit meinen Meinungen in dortigen Zirkeln übel anlaufen würde, weil Alle fanatische Apostel der Aufklärung wären. Ich dächte doch Sie wenigstens, unsere liebe Elise Campe, und Perthes (in mancher Hinsicht) machten doch wohl Ausnahmen! Daß unser geistiger Verein klein ist und nirgends kleiner als in Hamburg gebe ich gerne zu. Ich möchte jedoch nicht gerne den Glauben aufgeben, daß (wenngleich dünn gesäet) über ganz Deutschland eine stille Bruderschaft verbreitet ist, die in Demuth und Liebe leben und weben, die an <u>alten Glauben</u>, an <u>alte Treue</u> und an <u>alte Lieder</u> hängen und einen unüberwindlichen Ekel vor der Absprecherei und Dünkel der tollgewordenen Vernunft hegen. Bei meinen glühenden Gefühlen artet dieser (ich sehe es wohl ein, ohne mich darüber zu grämen) in Schwärmerei und Intoleranz aus: allein, wie kann man das Gute heftig lieben, ohne sein Widerspiel eben so heftig zu haßen? Stellen Sie sich demnach vor, was ich jetzt auszustehen habe, da zwei Meilen von hier in San Fernando die Hidra ihr fürchterlichstes Haupt kühn erhoben hat, und das ausgedroschene Stroh der französischen Aufklärerei von hundert Schöpfen wiedergekaut wird. Als Herausgeber des dort gedruckten Sudelblattes nennt sich S[eñor] Alcala Galiano,[6] der mich wegen meiner Lobrednerei Calderons so giftig angefochten hatte. Schade daß sein Spießgeselle Mora nicht auch in dieser Provinz war, um denselben Beweis seiner Tugend und Moral abzulegen! – Eines ihrer Blätter ist gegen ein Pastoral unseres trefflichen Bischofs gerichtet, dem sie auf den Kopf zusagen daß er falsch zitire, die Bibel falsch auslege, seine Pflichten verkenne etc warum? weil er die alte christliche Lehre des Gehorsams gegen die rechtmäßige Obrigkeit eingeschränkt hat! Und doch behaupten die Aufklärer daß kein Zusammenhang zwischen Politik, Religion und Poesie statt finde! – Daß ich dieses in den Pasatiempos so handgreiflich (wenngleich verdeckt) dargethan habe, ist gerade die Ursache ihres Haßes und nicht Calderon – Das Gesindel ist zwar von königlichen Truppen eingeschloßen, allein da es den königlichen Generalen zur Pflicht gemacht ist, nur im äußersten Fall Blut zu vergießen, so kann noch Zeit verstreichen ehe die Noth sie zwingt sich zu ergeben. Die andere Hälfte des aufrührerischen Haufens befindet sich in Algeciras in einer ähnlichen Lage. Es bleibt indessen höchst traurig, daß sich über 4 000 gemeine Soldaten von ihren Offizieren zu dieser Meuterei haben verleiten lassen, und beweist wie weit sich durch den letzten Prinz die französischen Ansichten verbreitet haben.

Görres Schrift Teutschland und die Revoluzion würde ich gerne erhalten: sein Persisches Heldenbuch[7] aber verbitte ich mir, so wie alles Orientalische und Alt Deutsche. Ich muß mich absolut beschränken auf das <u>Vorzüglichste</u> der schönen Litteratur. Ich zweifle daß mir des unheiligen Göthes Divan[8] gefallen werde: hat es eine politische Tendenz so protestire dagegen, ohne es noch gesehen zu haben.

Ich hoffe daß Sie sich der Spanischen Volkslieder wegen mit meiner Tochter werden verstanden haben – Das zweite Blatt des alten Romancero del Cid erfolgt hieneben wörtlich abgeschrieben und Zeile vor Zeile: dorten können Sie es nach der Größe ihres Originals einrichten – Ueber die Epidemie arbeitet unser Lazo[9] etwas aus welches vorzüglich sein wird: er wünscht es dort gedruckt zu wissen, und da es nicht lang sein soll, so sende ich Ihnen die Handschrift zu sobald er sie mir giebt, damit Sie es übersetzt in einer bekannten Zeitschrift einrücken lassen.

Die franz[ösischen] Aertzte Pariset und Maret[10] haben sich hier ein paar Monathe aufgehalten um Nachrichten einzuziehen und jetzt auf der Rückreise begriffen – Cap[itain] Nordberg hatte für Sie nur einiges Gedruckte in meiner Streitsache und einen nicht eben wichtigen Brief – Ich erwarte Fr[iedrich] Schl[egels] Deutsches Museum, und Meyers Leben Schröders:[11] letzteres wird mir meine Kinderjahre vergegenwärtigen und die ersten Eindrücke des Theaters – Ich gratulire zu Ihrer neuen angenehmen Wohnung. Mit der Berichtigung der Canc[ionero]s und Roman[cero]s kann ich nicht in Ordnung kommen, da ich alles Schreibens ungeachtet nichts von Madrid erlangen kann. – Ich stimme Ihnen bei daß es am besten sein wird meine altdeutschen Sachen nach Berlin zur Versteigerung zu senden: ist Hitzig noch in Wirksamkeit so wäre er zu erwählen, da ich in 1812 mit seiner Bedienung bei dem Verkauf meiner englischen Bücher wohl zufrieden war – Haben Sie die 100 und so viel Mark von Dr Wehber noch nicht erhalten? – Stollbergs Beherzigungen und Betrachtungen der heil[igen] Schrift[12] werde ich gerne erhalten: alles (versteht sich) in f[einer] P[appe] gebunden. Dabei denke ich an meine zum Binden übersandten Bände die nicht zu vergeßen bitte – Ich muß noch immer auf der <u>Sängerfahrt</u> bestehen, nicht von Fouqué, sondern von Tiek, Schütz, Brentano, v. Arnim etc. wie Sie sich eines breiteren im 2ten Bande der Wiener Jahrbücher pag. 201 belehren können – Daß Ihnen ein so merkwürdiges Produkt so ganz unbekannt geblieben, ist sonderbar!

Im N[ummer] 63 der Edinb[urgh] Review steht eine Rezension der letzten Gedichte des Crabbe die schöne Sachen enthält.[13] Die Kritik von Gedichten ist mir zwar im Ganzen verhaßt, weil es eine unausstehliche Anmaßung ist, den Leisten des eigenen Sinnes für Normal und Regulativ des allgemeinen Sinnes zu halten. Ich lache daher auch über den scharfsinnigen Schotten wenn er tadelt was seiner Bildung nicht zusagt, finde aber in seinen Betrachtungen vieles Dunkle schön entwickelt. So sieht er hier in der Satire od[er] Unzufriedenheit mit der Welt nur die erste Bildungsstufe des Dichters. Genauere Beobachtung und tieferes Nachdenken leitet ihn zu der Entdeckung, daß es in den niedern unsichtlichen Regionen des Lebens eine Welt von unbewußten Regungen giebt die von dem göttlichen Ursprung der Seele zeugen und allen Glitter und Tand der großen Welt aufwägen und ersetzen – Dieses nun (meinen wir) müßte gerade zu der Anerkennung der großen Verdienste des Wordsworth und Crabbe führen. Mit nichten! Wordsworth wird gar nicht erwähnt, und Crabbe das Lob nur sparsam zugemeßen. Crabbe (sagt uns der Rezensent) ist der größte <u>Manierist</u> (bei anderen Gelegenheiten hatte er von der <u>Affektazion</u> von Wordsworth viele Worte gemacht) <u>Manier</u> nannten vormals unpoetische Gemüther eine gewiße bunte Zierlichkeit die <u>ihnen</u> unnatürlich vorkam, und jetzt nennen dieselbe Art Menschen gerade das Gegentheil <u>Manier</u>, nemlich eine Natürlichkeit die ihrem Ideal von der nothwendigen Zierlichkeit und Prunk nicht angemeßen ist. Ueber den Geist eines Gedichtes sollte ein Kunstrichter nichts anderes sagen als: er sagt mir zu od[er] obgleich er <u>mir</u>

nicht zusagt wird er sein Publikum finden oder sein Publikum machen, wenn es ein ächtes Erzeugnis des Genius ist. Ueber den äußeren oder technischen Theil möge sich darauf der Kritiker nach Belieben verbreiten – Crabbe so viel ich ihn aus den Proben der Review beurtheilen kann ist mir ein wahrer Dichter, der das Interessante an dem Gemeinsten und Kleinen genau auffaßt und lebendig darstellt, allein er verknüpft es nur selten mit dem Höheren wie der treffliche Wordsworth. Crabbe scheint mir daher in demselben Verhältniß zu Wordsworth zu stehen, wie Gerhard Dorn[14] zu Raphael – Verschiedene der Bruchstücke in der Review laufen auf eine seelenlose Anatomie aus. – Wenn Crabbes Tales of the hall nicht zwischen den für mich abgesandten Werken sind, so bitte ich sie mir gelegentlich aus.

Hiebei der dritte Pasat[iem]po der weniger polemisches und mehr litterarisches enthält: mit nächstem Schiff erfolgen mehrere Abdrücke. A[ugust] W[ilhelm] Schlegel ist wohl in seinem Sanskrit so vergraben, daß die spanische Litteratur das Interesse für ihn verloren hat. Sonst hätte er mir wohl den Empfang der Pasatiempos mit ein Paar Zeilen anzeigen können.

Ihr treuer Freund
Böhl v. Faber

94. *Friedrich Perthes, Hamburg*

Cadiz, den 4 April 1820

Es ist mir eigentlich nicht recht, daß Sie (wahrscheinlich um mir das Briefporto zu ersparen) meinen Brief vom 17 Dec[ember] bisjetzt unbeantwortet gelassen haben. Hoffentlich ist die Handschrift meiner Floresta zur Stunde das ich dieses schreibe in Ihren Händen, und halte ich mich überzeugt daß sollte es Ihnen nicht paßlich gewesen sein den Verlag selbst zu übernehmen, Sie nicht unterlassen haben werden sich nach einem anderen Verleger umzusehen.

Der Zweck des Gegenwärtigen ist Ihnen die Beförderung der Einlage dringend anzuempfehlen. Sollten Sie es möglich machen können die Einhändigung durch einen kaufmännischen Agenten zu lassen der die Antwort einfordern und Ihnen zusenden müßte, so wäre es freilich das Beste. Diese Antwort würden Sie mir dann ungesäumt zusenden und mir die Kosten belasten. Ist aber in Plock kein Korrespondent aufzutreiben, so bleibt nichts übrig als den Brief der Post anzuvertrauen.

Ist dorten das Arabische Lexicon von Golius[1] aufzutreiben, ferner eine Arabische Bibel mit oder ohne Lateinischer Uebersetzung, und zu welchen Preisen? Ein Verzeichniß von verkäuflichen Büchern die sich auf das Studium der Griechischen Arabischen und Hebräischen Sprachen beziehen nebst Preisen, würde sehr willkommen sein.

Sie werden natürlich erwarten daß ich Ihnen etwas über unsere neue Staatsumwälzungen sage. Wäre ich gestimmt wie die Weisen dieser Welt, so würde ich lauter Unheil profizeien, weil es in Frankreich damit so übel ablief, weil die Jakobinerbrut auch hier im Finstern schleicht, weil das Volk so gar unreif ist und aus hundert anderen Gründen. Ich erinnere mich aber wie sich die Weisen, besonders in Hinsicht von Spanien stets so arg verrechnet haben und nehme also grade das Gegentheil an. Eben weil die Franzosen die Freiheit gemißbraucht haben glaube ich daß die Spanier die Gränzen der Mäßigung im Ganzen nicht überschreiten werden. Eben weil man in Frankreich die Jakobiner angestaunt und bewundert hat, wird man sie hier verachten und haßen sobald sie sich in ihrer wahren Gestalt zeigen. Eben weil das Volk in politischer Hinsicht so gar roh ist, wird es nicht diesen Regierungstrieb fühlen, der alle Regierungen vernichtet. Es ist unglaublich welche Sinnlosigkeit für bürgerliche Freiheit, sogar bei den Aufgeklärt-sein-wollenden herrscht. Unter Konstituzion versteht ein Jeder die Befreiung von dem was ihn bisjetzt belästigte; mit eigenen Ohren habe ich gehört wie der eine meinte er brauchte nun nicht mehr zu fasten, der andere er könne jetzt umsonst Taback rauchen, der dritte es würde nun die alten Silberflotten wieder ankommen. Was die Preßen jetzt täglich Bogen über Bogen ans Luft fördern ist das elendeste seichste Gerätsche, ein Schwall tönender Worte ohne bestimmten Sinn, doch ohne Ruchlosigkeit und mit der ausgezeichnetesten Achtung für den Karakter und Person des Königes. Dieser so stündlich verläumdete Monarch hat den gekrönten Häuptern ein schönes Beispiel gegeben. Sobald er sich überzeugte, daß der größte Theil der Nazion wirklich die Konstituzion wünsche, hat er anstatt zu flüchten oder an seinen Truppen zu appelliren, die Konstituzion beschworen und von Herzen angenommen. Seitdem beräth er sich nur mit den Männern die ihre Anhänglichkeit daran bewährt hatten, und so geht Alles rasch und ungehindert die neue Bahn. Die Monarchischen fügen sich jetzt willig in die Konstituzion da ihr geliebter König sie angenommen und beschworen hat, und die Liberalen lieben den König jetzt herzlich, weil er ihnen ihr Schooßkind wiedergegeben. Die Jakobiner bleiben wills Gott die kleine Minderzahl. Der König hat ihnen durch Annahme der Konstituzion einen Strich durch die Rechnung gemacht. Ich fürchte einzig für den alten katholischen Glauben und besorge die Einführung einer Art Kirche mit Gallischen Freiheiten. Die Abschaffung der jetzt so milde Inquisizion ist mir nicht recht, und schwerlich werden sich die Kloster behaupten. Dieses wird sich in den nächsten cortes ausweisen. Unterdessen genießen wir der vollkommensten Sicherheit und Ruhe.

   Meine besten Grüße dem Dr Julius und übrigen Freunde.

Von Herzen der Ihrige,

Böhl v: Faber

95. Nikolas Heinrich Julius, Hamburg

Cadiz, den 11 May 1820

Ich kann mir keine andere Entschuldigung Ihres langes Schweigens ausdenken, als daß Sie dabei geblieben sind Ihre Briefe an Bord von Cap[itain] Voß zu senden, den wir nun schon 8 Monathe lang erwarten. Mein Brief vom 17 Dec[ember] ist noch immer von Ihnen unbeantwortet. Wir wissen seit mehreren Wochen, daß H[er]r Färber in Hamburg ist und Sie also die Handschrift meiner Floresta in Händen haben und keine Zeile über den Empfang dieses für mich so wichtigen Werkes! – Wie wenig wir uns doch in anderer Menschen Lage zu versetzen wissen! Um mir einen halben Thaler porto zu besparen, verursachen Sie mir einen Aufwand von hundert Thalern an Geduld! –

Diese Zeilen gehen mit Cap[itain] Eeden, der ein Packet an H[er]rn Perthes überbringt: außer den zwei Folianten des fuero juzgo ist alles übrige für Sie. 1) 24 Abdrücke des 3ten Pasatiempo um unter Freunde und Kenner zu vertheilen 2) Die Declamacion und verschiedene Hefte Gedichte, von meinem Freund Vargas[1] als Geschenk für Sie; dieser Freund ist ein guter Litterator, aber nur ein schaaler Reimer welches er leider nicht merkt 3) Mehrere Entwürfe einer medizinischen Zeitschrift, um solche in Deutschland zu verbreiten 4) Drei sogenannte patriotische Lieder und das Bildnis von Riego, um solche meiner Tochter einzuhändigen. Nur die Cancion de Riego[2] ist zum Gaßenhauer geworden und wird hier jetzt von jung und alt gequickt, wobei sich das Wort patria im Munde der Wollust athmenden Gaditanos gar sonderbar ausnimmt – Bei dieser Gelegenheit mache ich Sie auf die Erscheinung aufmerksam, daß die Cadizer Frauen größtentheils einen Enthusiasmus für die Konstituzion erwiesen haben, welcher (nach des großen Quiroga[3] Ausspruch) den Sieg der guten Sache in Cadiz entschieden hat. Alle meine Weltkenntnis und Erfahrung ist an diesem Phänomen gescheitert. Ich habe liebliche Mädchen in der ersten Jugendblüthe gesehen, die bachantengleich die königlich gesinnten Anführer zerreißen wollten, und den bärtigen Männern ihre Apathie und Feigheit vorwarfen! Ich habe sittige Hausfrauen ausrufen hören: Wer doch die Befreier des Vaterlandes mit einer gefälligen Nacht lohnen könnte! – Bei den ersten öffentlichen Erscheinungen der Helden hier zeichneten sich allemal die Frauen durch ungestümes Drängen, Rufen und Tüchschwenken aus. Dagegen ist der kleinere edlere und besonnenere Theil dieses Geschlechtes (mit mehr Zurückhaltung) innerlich mit gleicher Heftigkeit königlich gesinnt. Bei den meisten Männern dieser Denkungsart hat des Königes Genehmigung der Konstituzion wenigstens eine äußerliche Einstimmung hevorgebracht: alle Frauen aber behaupten der König sei gezwungen worden sie zu beschwören und können sich nicht darein fügen. Sollte sich demnach ein bürgerlicher Krieg entspinnen so wird er zwischen den Frauen sein und nicht zwischen den Männern.

Im Anfang April sandte ich endlich die Abschrift meiner Floresta nebst mehreren Abhandlungen über metrum, Reime, Geschichte der Formen und Sprache mit Empfehlungen meines Freundes Vargas an die Real Academia Espanola und schon am 20ten ernannte man mich zum Academico honorario (wer nicht in Madrid wohnt kann nichts anderes sein) mit einem schmeichelhaften Schreiben dessen Abschrift ich beilege. Ich hätte nicht geglaubt, daß es so schnell gehen würde, und habe mich desto mehr darüber gefreut. Ich halte mich jetzt für alle meine Anstrengungen belohnt, und meine Gegner auf das Empfindlichste bestraft. Meine Anzeige[4] darüber in dem hiesigen Diario lege ich gleichfalls bei und überlasse es Ihnen auf welche Weise Sie es dortigen Zeitungen bekannt machen wollen. Der dritte Pasat[iem]po (den ich unter den Mitgliedern der Academia vertheilen ließ) mag auch dazu beigetragen haben. Er enthält weniger Polemik und mehr über Poesie und das Spanische Drama. Senden Sie ein paar Abdrücke davon an den Baron d'Alton mit der Einlage und bitte den einen an A[ugust] W[ilhelm] Schlegel einzuhändigen, sollten beide noch in Bonn sein.

Wenn ich daran denke wie Sie mich vernachläßigen so fällt mir die Feder aus der Hand, obwohl ich nicht unterlassen kann Ihr guter Freund zu verbleiben dem zu Trotze.

Böhl v: Faber

96. Friedrich Perthes, Hamburg

Cadiz, den 12 May 1820

Den 4 dieses schrieb ich Ihnen p[er] Post mit einer Einlage für Plock. Seitdem haben wir vernommen, daß der Jesuiten General an den dieses Schreiben gerichtet war gestorben ist. Demnach bitte ich es mir gelegentlich p[er] Post zurück.

Hiebei ergeht ein Packet in Wachstuch worin zwei Abdrücke des Fuero juzgo für Sie befindlich sind, wofür ich Sie 24 Mark belaste. Die anderen beiden Abdrücke für Sie erwarte ich noch von Madrid, wo man mir die lateinischen Werke des Finistres[1] bisjetzt noch nicht hat auftreiben können. Die übrigen in dem Pakete befindlichen Sachen werden Sie gütigst dem Dr Julius einhändigen.

Es ist mir auf Zusendung meiner Floresta und anderer auf Spanisch und Poesie Bezug habenden Abhandlungen die Auszeichnung geworden von der Real Academia Española zum Ehrenmitglied ernannt zu werden. Die Abschrift der Kundmachung wird Ihnen Dr Julius mittheilen. Ein Fremder kann sich auf keine Weise mehr geschmeichelt fühlen, besonders da die Academia Española sehr sparsam mit ihren Gunstbezeugungen ist. Meinen spanischen Gegnern ist dieses die empfindlichste Strafe. Sollte es einmal mit der Floresta zum Drucke kommen, so folgt jetzt meinem Namen de la Real Academia Española, welches dem Werke zur Empfehlung gereichen wird.

Ist es nicht schon geschehen so bitte ich der ersten Sendung beizufügen: Schröders Leben von Prof[essor] Meyer und die späteren Werke des geistreichen Hoffmann von dem ich nur die Fantasien in Callots Manier besitzte. Auch würde ich einen wohfeilen deutschen Druck von Burkes politischen Schriften[2] – Englische Bücher senden Sie mir keine mehr, auch nicht die Reviews da ich jetzt Gelegenheit habe solche direkt zu beziehen.
ergebenst
Böhl v: Faber

NB. in feiner Pappe gebunden.

97. *Nikolas Heinrich Julius, Hamburg*

Cadiz, den 2 Juny 1820.

Endlich hat mich gestern Ihr Schreiben vom 6 May aus meiner langen und peinlichen Ungewißheit gezogen. Einige Tage zuvor hatte mir Cap[itain] Voß dasjenige vom Grünen Donnerstag nebst Büchern und Schriften überbracht. Zuförderst demnach die Bezeugung meines herzlichen Antheils an Ihrer Genesung. Der Himmel erhalte Sie ferner gesund für sich und für Ihre Freunde und für den kleinen Kern der Gläubigen. Die trefflichen Noten zu dem Aufsatz über die NordAmerikaner stempeln Sie zu einem ächten Spiritualisten! –

Die Druckprobe der Floresta habe ich natürlich mit der reinsten Wonne entgegen genommen. Gerade so hatte ich es gewünscht und mir eingebildet. Ich stimme gleichfalls für das größere Papier wenngleich nicht so fein. Meine Korrekturen erfolgen hiebei: bei den späteren Gedichten wird nicht so viel Schwieriges vorkommen. Es wäre natürlich zu wünschen, daß ich Alles nachkorrigiren könnte, allein dieses ist leider unmöglich, und so müssen Sie Ihr Bestes thun und die Leser so vorliebnehmen. Ich billige vollkommen die Streichung des Semikolons. – An einem feinen Stich für das Titelblatt ist mir gar nicht gelegen. Ich habe den Steindruck vorgeschlagen, weil ich ihn für wohlfeiler halte. Ich bleibe bei der Idee eines gothischen Porthals oder Kapelle: unten ein Grabmal oder Altar, zur Seite allenfalls ein knieender Ritter. Können Sie von einem Zeichner einige verkleinerte Umriße vorfertigen lassen und sie mir zur Auswahl zusenden, so wende ich gerne das Porto daran. – In Hinsicht der Anmerkungen sage ich Ja und Nein. Ja insofern ich sie erweitern will, Nein zu der Uebersetzung in das Spanische, und das weil sie sich nicht allein gar nicht übersetzen lassen, sondern auch weil sie für Spanier (d.h. für heutige Spanier) lächerlich sein würden. Da es (auch bei einiger Erweiterung) doch nur Fingerzeige bleiben sollen, so werden sie sich auf wenige Bogen zusammenpreßen lassen und eben keinen Uebelstand hervorbringen. Meine Abhandlungen die jetzt gewißermaßen von der Academia Española gebilligt sind sollen Sie erhalten, um damit nach Belieben zu schalten – Einige Aufsätze des

Pasatiempos bleiben wohl am füglichsten für den dramatischen Theil des Werkes liegen – Worterklärungen scheinen mir nur dann nöthig wenn ein Wort nicht im Dicc[ionari]o de la Academia steht. Wo wäre sonst die Gränze zwischen schwer und leicht? – Für etimologische Nachweisungen besitze ich die erforderliche Gelehrsamkeit – Ich glaube nicht daß sobald wieder ein Sch[iff] nach Hamburg ausgeht: ich denke Ihnen demnach die Abhandlungen über England zuzusenden, und die <u>Fingerzeige</u> p[er] Post – Die alten Volkslieder sind unwiederbringlich verloren, wie so manche Deutsche die als Gesangbeweise für geistliche Lieder angeführt sind – Macias[1] seine wenigen Gedichte sind in der Galizischen Mundart die dem Portug[iesischen] näher liegt als dem Kastill[ianischen] – Ich protestire gegen den beabsichtigten 2ten Theil der Floresta als rimas <u>modernas</u>: ein 2ter Theil der Floresta soll (wenn er verlangt wird) diejenigen vorzüglichen lirischen Gedichte enthalten, die schon im Parnaso Español, Ramon Fernandez und andern gedruckt sind, damit in meinen zwei Bänden <u>alles</u> vorzügliche lirische der <u>alten</u> spanischen Dichter enthalten sei, verbunden damit noch mehreres Unbekannte welches im ersten Theil keinen Platz fand, nebst Auszügen aus den mir fehlenden lirischen Sammlungen, sollte das Glück mir einige in die Hand spielen – Den dramatischen Theil könnten wir nicht wohl Floresta nennen, weil es keine Auswahl ist, sondern fast alles was aus der Zeit <u>vor</u> Lope in Versen vorhanden ist: also Teatro Español anterior á Lope oder Primer teatro Español. Diesen könnte ich am ersten ausarbeiten da ich fast alles besitze und nur ausschreiben aufklären und anordnen müßte, und kommt im Herbst irgend ein farbiges Fieber zum Vorschein, das uns von der sonstigen Welt isolirt, so lege ich wohl Hand ans Werk, besonders wenn Sie und Perthes fortfahren mich aufzumuntern. Zu der Floresta von epicas finde ich mich am wenigsten aufgelegt: auch hört gerade dazu die meiste Muße und so spare ich sie auf zu dem Abend meines Lebens, den ich noch immer in Deutschland zu feiern beabsichtige – Von dem Cancionero de Baena existirt nur ein einzelnes Manuscript in Madrid und dieses nicht komplet und in alter schwer zu lesender Schrift. Alle Bemühungen Abschriften von daher zu erhalten sind bis jetzt gescheitert, aus Mangel an Skribenten. Uebrigens haben wir eine genaue Beschreibung und Auszüge daraus in der Biblioteca von Castro die zwar in Hinsicht von Sprache und Form der Gedichte sehr merkwürdig sind, aber wenig <u>poetische</u> Ausbeute versprechen – In Hinsicht der Handschrift von Lazo hapert es gleichfalls wegen Mangel eines Abschreibers – Ihr Verzeichniß der Roman[cer]os und Canc[ioner]os soll so viel möglich berichtiget mit den Abhandlungen über England erfolgen – Schicken Sie meine altdeutschen Bücher in Gottes Namen an Reimer[2] in Berlin zum Verkauf: das von mir angefertigte Verzeichniß wird Ihnen nützlich sein – Den Dr Wehber wollen wir nicht ferner mahnen, da er jetzt meinem Sohn privat Stunden giebt und auf solche Art die Rechnung saldirt – Ihre Aufträge sind notirt – Pergament <u>Druck</u> habe ich nie in Spanien gesehen: ich werde darüber nach Madrid anfragen – Die erhaltenen Bücher habe ich nur eben flüchtig durchlaufen können. Crabbe behalte ich gerne, wiewohl er nicht verdient Wordsworth die Schuhriemen zu lösen – Der Divan will mir gar nicht munden: kommt mehr dergleichen so verbitte ich es mir ausdrücklich, trage es immer den Namen Göthe an der Stirn – Grimms Grammatik[3] ist mir zu gelehrt – Die ersteren Volkslieder sind allerliebst; am meisten aber habe ich mich an A[dam] Müllers kleinere Schrift über die theolog[ische] Grundl[age] des Staates[4] gefreut. Ich war gegen diesen Schriftsteller (ich weiß nicht mehr warum) eingenommen: er oder ich haben uns gebessert – Die Bestellung der patr[iotischen] Gesellsch[aft] und das sehr artige Schreiben H[er]rn Dr Meyer[s] habe ich dankbarlich erhalten: mit erster Schiffsgelegenheit erfolgt die Beantwortung und vielleicht etwas Zweckdienliches für die Gesellschaft. Meine Gesellung zu der R[ea]l Acad[emia] Esp[añol]a hat mir hier viele Wichtigkeit gegeben. Setze ich meine übrigen Titel zu meinem Namen auf der Floresta oder nicht? – So viel für heute.

Der Ihrige B.v.F.

N. B. Das einzelne a hat immer den Akz[ent]

Meine völlige Titelatur wäre:

Consul de las cuid[ade]s anseat[ica]s en Cadiz y por
el reino de Sevilla, de la Real Acad[emia] Espan[ol]a,
de la sociedad patriotica de Cadiz, de la economica
de Mecklenburg y la artistica de Hamburgo.
Letztere Uebers[etzung] ist zweideutig, welches
hier kein Uebelstand ist. – Mir scheint am
besten bloß de la Real Academia Española
dem Namen folgen zu lassen –

98. *Nikolas Heinrich Julius, Hamburg*

Cadiz, den 7 July 1820

Den 2 Juny schrieb ich Ihnen zuletzt, und habe seitdem keine Nachricht von Ihnen erhalten. Cap[itain] Bandix scheint Cap[itain] Voß nachmachen zu wollen und läßt sich nicht blicken. Letzterer will Ende dieses Monaths nach dorten zurückkehren, worauf aber schwerlich zu nehmen ist.

Dieses hat nur zum Zweck Ihnen einliegend die Umarbeitung der Fingerzeige für die Floresta zu begleiten, da das Ganze so wenig Platz einnimmt so ist es kein Uebelstand daß es in deutscher sprache ist. So oder gar nicht. Ich bestätige daß eine spanische Uebers[etzung] nicht nur unmöglich sondern auch zweckwidrig sein würde. Ausführlicher habe ich nicht sein können 1) weil mir die Zeit mangelt 2) weil ich kein Abschrift der Floresta habe, und also nur aus dem Gedächtniß nachholen konnte. – Die Sammlung ist mir bei dieser Uebersicht noch herrlicher vorgekommen. Gebe der Himmel daß ich mich nicht täusche! Ich bitte ja mir kein Urtheil eines Kenners vorzuenthalten –

Sie wissen schon daß meine äußere Lage sich gebessert hat, allein auch meine Hauptgeschäfte haben sich gehäuft und nur wenige Stunden bleiben für Litteratur. Auch kann man nicht unterlassen der Geschäfte des Tages einige Zeitopfer zu bringen. Wie gerne schriebe ich etwas darüber für Sie! – Ich würde zwar Hohn dafür bei dortigen Aufklärern ärndten, allein Wahrheit bleibt Wahrheit. Es geht mit Riesenschritten auf den Jakobinismus loos, und wäre das Volk nicht so schlicht und wohl so würde es schon an allen Ecken brennen. – Ein Berner Haller[1] hat gegen die span[ische] Konst[ituzion] geschrieben können Sie dieses habhaft werden, so senden Sie es mir mit erster Gelegenheit

Meine Familie ist auf dem Lande: es kränkelt immer die einen od[er] die anderen, und so wird man seines Lebens nie ganz froh.

Von meiner Sevilla Flug Reise habe ich nichts weiter vernommen. Vermuthlich ist sie den dortigen Journalisten zu katholisch vorgekommen. Am Ende werden wir armen Christen nur noch verkriechen müssen um nicht angespien zu werden demohngeachtet, denke ich, beharren wir wohl und begnügen uns mit dem Frieden Gottes der über allen Verstand ist.

Ihr treuer Freund und Diener
Böhl v: Faber

P. S. den 7 July. Ich habe verschiedene N[ummer] der Quarterly Review mit dem grössten Interesse gelesen und danke Ihnen für die Anempfehlung – Gerne hätte ich das ganze Werk: sollte es sich zwischen Perthes Vorrath befinden – das beste Mittel mir solches mit den übrigen für mich bestimmten Schriften zukommen zu lassen ist folgendes: Sie nehmen ein Fässel, legen die Bücher unten wohlverpackt ein und füllen das Fässel mit Kartoffeln, senden es dann an Bord als ein Fässel Kartoffel ohne dass der Capitän mehr davon weiss. Bloss mit der Bitte es in die Kajüte zu nehmen weil man es gleich nach seiner Ankunft abholen würde, und den Empfangsschein senden Sie mir p[er] Post – Die Bücher alle eingebunden, sollten es auch Fortsetzungen sein, in feiner Pappe –

Hier noch meine Erwiederung auf einen fürchterlichen Ausfall der Madriter, gegen den Deutschen in Cadiz der einen neuen Geschmack einführen will –

Der Ihrige
B.v.F

99. *Nikolas Heinrich Julius, Hamburg*

Cadiz, den 1 August 1820

Mit Cap[itain] Voß dem Ueberbringer dieses erhalten Sie eine Kiste Bücher, worüber anbei original Rechn[un]g betragen Reales 1041 od[er] 139 Thaler. In demselben Kistel befinden sich 2 Fueros juzgos, den ich dem Herrn Fr[iedri]ch Perthes verabfolgen zu lassen bitte, das 2te Stück der Cecilie[1] welches mir nicht dienen kann, das Stück der Kieler Blätter mit Ihrem Aufsatze über NordAmerika[2] und Brentanos Katalog, den ich mit Interesse durchgeblättert habe. Für mich ist darin eigentlich nur der Cancionero general Anvers 1573[3] merkwürdig, für den ich gerne 20 Thaler gegeben hätte. Wenn es Ihnen denn gelingt mir ein genaues Inhaltsverzeichnis derselben zu verschaffen, so werde ich den Verlust verschmerzen. Um dieses zu erleichtern finden Sie hieneben die Abschrift des Inhaltsverzeichnißes meiner Antwerper Ausgabe von 1557.[4] Wahrscheinlich enthält die Ausgabe von 1573 alles dieses in derselben Ordnung und obendrein eine Zugabe. Nur von dieser ist mir eine Abschrift wichtig –

Ferner finden Sie Ihr Spanisches Bücher Verzeichnis zurück, und was ich zu dessen Vervollkommnung liefern kann, nemlich die genauen Titel der Werke die ich selbst besitze. Ueber die Cancionieros und Romanceros habe ich hinzugefügt was ich weiß.

Ferner finden Sie einige Kapitel unseres Lazo aus dem trefflichen Werke welches die hiesige Medizinische Gesellschaft jetzt ausarbeitet. Meine Frau hat sich der Mühe unterzogen die Abschrift zu machen. Sonsten würden Sie solche schwerlich erhalten. Mir scheinen sie höchst interessant.

Eine andere Abschrift ist nach Paris gegangen und das über Land so daß wahrscheinlich die französische Uebersetzung eher erscheinen wird: doch dieses war nicht zu ändern, wollte man nicht mehrere Thaler als Briefporto aufopfern.

Ferner sende ich Ihnen das erste Stück der angekündigten Medizinischen Zeitschrift, die Ihnen sicherlich gefallen wird. Ich mache Sie aufmerksam auf Seite 83 und die Nekrologie der drei ersten Monathe des Jahres um daraus die Zahl der am 10. Märtz Getödteten zu vermitteln. Es sind einige dreißig so wie ich in meinem Bericht vom 14 Märtz an dortige Freunde angab. Es war aber das Interesse der Konstituzionellen Parthei dieser parziellen Meuterei den Anstrich einer Bartholomäus Nacht zu geben.

Die Bücher p[er] Cap[itain] Bandix habe ich wohl erhalten und lese solche jetzt mit großem Interesse. – Die Abscheulichkeit des Voßischen Angriffes übersteigt allen Begriff! Schade um die darin vergeudete so gediegene deutsche Darstellung!– Stollbergs Antwort[5] ist seiner würdig. Der Anfang des Buches von der Liebe hat mich entzückt: es ganz zu lesen hat die Zeit noch nicht gestattet. Auch bin ich überzeugt daß mir die Betrachtungen über die heil[i]g[en] Schrift genügen werden – Die Wiener Jahrb[ücher] haben treffliche Aufsätze, wie der über Schlegels Vorlesungen[6] (worin auch meiner gedacht wird) Wie viele Menschen kann aber Persiens Geographie interessieren, um damit über 200 Seiten auszufüllen?

Hofmann's Serapions Brüder[7] sind interessant, doch (so weit ich darin gekommen) nicht mit den Fantasie Stücken zu vergleichen – Crabbe seine nähere Bekanntschaft hat mir viel Vergnügen gewährt: er ist mehr ein geistreicher

Beobachter und tiefer Kenner des menschlichen Herzens als eigentlicher Dichter und dennoch trifft er mit seiner trockenen Manier öfters die innersten Seiten des Gefühls – Wordsworth ist sich nicht immer gleich: seine ältern Stücke bleiben mir die liebsten – Bouterwek scheint sich in seinem letzten Theil[8] absichtlich Preis geben zu wollen. Die deutsche Dichtkunst kommt am Schlimmsten in seinem Werke weg – Die Zwickauer Kleinen Ausgaben sind allerliebst: nächsten[s] denke ich mehrere zu bestellen. In Schlegels Museum werde ich gewiß vieles nach meinem Geschmack finden. Der agronomischen Briefe Müllers[9] erinnere ich mich und wie sehr sie schon damals meine innere Empfindung aussprachen. Doch fürchte ich kämpfen wir vergebens. Das Prinzip des Schützens und der Tauglichkeit hat sich zu fest eingenistet, stimmt zu sehr mit der breiten Mittelmäßigkeit überein verdunkelt zu vollkommen allen Adel der Seele, um nicht das Schiboleth aller Filister zu bleiben. Hier wird es uns jetzt auf allen Ecken und Enden eingetrichtert. Unser Perthes verlangt für den trefflichen Rehberg[10] eine Sammlung der seit der Preß Freiheit erschienenen Flugschriften. Wie würde die laffe Speise ihn anekeln, wäre er verdammt die alle zu kosten! Alles ist über einen Leisten geschlagen, und läuft auf Gemeinplätze gegen Gewalthaber und Geistliche aus. Nur einzeln hat sich ein Oppositionsblatt gezeigt und ist sogleich unterdrückt. Hier haben sich die Urheber der Empörung in der Armee weidlich miteinander gezankt und in den gewechselten Schriften ist dem ganzen Vorgange die patriotische Maske abgezogen und er steht in seiner Erbärmlichkeit da. Doch darüber vielleicht etwas in meinem Fluge nach Arcos (24/26 July) wo sich meine Familie um die Bergluft zu genießen einige Wochen aufgehalten hat. Ich sollte zwar nach der wenigen Aufmerksamkeit die mein vorjähriger Flug nach Sevilla verdient hat unlustig sein neue Ansichten mitzutheilen, doch wenn der Geist treibt fallen dergleichen Rücksichten weg. Ueberhaupt muß sich wer zu weit voraus ist darauf gefaßt machen wenige Gleichgesinnte zwischen den Mitlebenden zu finden.

Ich bitte um Behändigung der Einlagen für H[err]n Dr. Meyer und Aug[ust] Campe und verbleibe unwandelbar
Ganz der Ihrige
Böhl v: Faber

100. Nikolas Heinrich Julius, Hamburg

Cadiz, den 11 Aug[ust] 1820

Unser Cap[itain] Voß scheint seine dortige Unthätigkeit wieder gut machen zu wollen, und steht auf dem Sprunge mit einer schönen Ladung nach dorten abzugehen. Sie erhalten mit ihm laut beigehendem Rezief ein Kistel Bücher enthaltend Calderon Comed[i]a 11 Th[eile] und Autos 6 Th[eile] ein sehr schönes wohlgebundenes nagelneues Exemplar Reales 400.

die 21 Bände von Hervas[1] für die Göttinger Bibliothek   560.
2 Abdrücke Cervantes Entrem[ese]s und 3 Rom[ancer]o   57.
del Cid. 33
    Kiste und an Bord bringen   <u>24</u>
                                             R[eales] <u>1041</u>
                                           oder Thaler <u>139.8</u>

welche ich an die ordre meiner Tochter auf Sie angewiesen habe. In der Kiste sind ferner befindlich 2 Fueros juzgos für Perthes, ein H[e]ft Kieler Blätter, Brentanos Katalog und ein St[üc]k Musik. In dem Packete: die spanischen Bücherverzeichniße, Lazos Handschrift über das gelbe Fieber, d[it]o mediz[inische] Zeitschrift, Briefe für Dr Meyer und Aug[ust] Campe. Zu meinem langen Briefe in demselben Packet habe ich jetzt wenig hinzuzusetzen. Ich habe die neue Ausgabe des Don Quijote (die vierte die von der Academia veranstaltet ist) jetzt in Händen. Es sind 5 Bände in 8ºº schön gedruckt mit 20 neuen nur mittelmäßigen Kupfern und kostet gebunden 6 piaster. Der eine und dickste Band ist dem neuen Leben des Cervantes gewidmet und wird besonders verkauft. Es ist sehr interessant und sorgfältig schön geschrieben und zeugt ebensosehr von der Trefflichkeit des Cervantes als Mensch, als von der Empfänglichkeit des Beschreibers[2] für Seelengröße. Die Academia verspricht die übrigen Werke des Cervantes in demselben Format, nebst andern klaßischen Schriftstellern, Garcilaso, Valbuena, F[rancisc]o de la Torre,[3] Ercilla, Mendoza und Rivadeneira[4] doch fürchte ich wir werden darüber wegsterben, so langsam schreitet es damit fort – Valcarcel[5] und die Flora Chilensis[6] habe ich von Madrid verschreiben müssen. Des Berner Hallers Schrift sehe ich mit Ungeduld entgegen. Mit Ad[am] Müller bin ich jetzt völlig ausgesöhnt. Hier schiebt man den Karren immer tiefer im Dreck: von keiner Seite ist Heil zu erwarten und ich sehe nicht wie einem totalen Zusammensturz des gesellsch[aftlichen] Gebäudes zuvorzukommen ist
  Der Ihrige B.v.F.

101. Friedrich Perthes, Hamburg

Cadiz, den 11 August 1820

Ihre werthe Zuschrift von 16 Juny mit Factura über die Bücher p[er] Cap[itain] Bandix habe ich seiner Zeit wohl erhalten; auch hat Cap[itain] Bandix die Bücher wohl überliefert und es ist mir dadurch ein vielfacher Genuß geworden. Ich habe zu bemerken daß Sie mir von Ramb[achs] Anthol[ogie] 3ter Th[eil] – Humboldts Reise 2ter Th[eil] – Tieks Phantasus 3ter Th[eil] – Bouterw[eks] Geschichte 10ter Th[eil] – nur den Einband zu belasten haben. Die englischen Drucke sind gar zu theuer, die Zwickauer Nachdrucke dagegen sehr artig nur voller Fehler – Wie sehr mich Voßens unwürdiger Angriff Stollbergs und seiner Freunde empört hat, können Sie sich bei meiner Anhänglichkeit an der Religion des Gefühls vorstellen. Desto beschwichtigender und labender waren mir des Seligen letzten Schriften. – Den Golius giebt der Liebhaber auf. In Hinsicht der politischen Flugschriften die unser verehrter Rehberg zu enthalten wünscht setzen Sie mich in großer Verlegenheit. Ihr Zahl ist Legion meistens Tageblätter die sich nur auf Lokalitäten und Neuigkeiten beziehen, tüchtig auf Mönche und Serviles schimpfen, sich aber sonsten auf keine Erörterungen einlassen. In Cadiz erscheinen viel mehr Flugschriften als Tageblätter: sie beziehen sich aber fast alle auf Personalitäten die nur für die Zeugen der Begebenheiten Interesse haben können. Oppositionsblätter duken selten auf und werden sogleich vertuscht. Hätte ich Ihren Auftrag früher erhalten, so würde ich eine Sammlung angelegt haben. Jetzt ist es zu spät: etwas jedoch und nicht das minder Wichtige sollen Sie erhalten –

Für die 2 Fueros juzgos die Ihnen Dr Julius einhändigen wird, belaste ich Sie abermals 24 Mark – den Brief nach Plock erbitte ich p[er] Schiffsgelegenheit zurück – Alte Bücher über den Adel einzelner Provinzen kenne ich, aber keine neue allgemeine. Ich werde darüber nach Madrid schreiben –

ergebenst
Böhl v: Faber

Nota

N[ummer]1. Der Verfaßer dieser Zeitung ist Ant[oni]o Alcalá Galiano der Sohn eines verdienten Seeoffiziers. Es hat Verstand, Kentniße und schreibt seine Sprache richtig und schön; sonsten ein Ausbund aller Laster mit dem Abscheu jedes rechtlichen Menschen gebrandmarkt – Diese Zeitung ist natürlich partheiisch übrigens aber zum Verständniß der Ganzen unentbehrlich. In nuce liegt darin die völlige Auflösung der Gesellschaft die wir zu erwarten haben, wenn diese Parthei oben blüht.

N[ummer] 2.3.4.5. beziehen sich auf die Heldenthaten des Riego und beweisen wie wenig Antheil die <u>Nazion</u> daran genommen hat und wie der Held so eben die Sache aufgegeben hatte als die Königliche Genehmiging sie wieder ins Leben rief.

N[ummer] 6.7.8.9. beziehen sich auf den verunglückten Plan des Rotaldo[1] Cadiz d[en] 24 Januar den Patrioten zu überliefern. Rotaldo ist ein anerkannter Schurke, ohne Geist und ohne Kentniße der nur durch seine unvergleichliche Unverschämtheit je eine Rolle spielen kann. Er hat indessen manches Geheimniß der sauberen Rotte enthüllt nachdem er sich mit derselben überworfen.

N[ummer] 10.11.12. über den 10 Märtz: Freyre[2] ist ein schlaffer nichtswürdiger Mensch, der durch seinen Wankelmuth und seinen Wunsch es mit keiner Parthei zu verderben die Greuel Szenen des 10 Märtz veranlaßt hat. Die Königlichen werden es ihm nie vergeben daß er das Ungeheuer nicht in seiner Wiege erstickt hat, wie er es so leicht gekonnt hätte. N[ummer] 12 halte ich für die einzige wahre Darstellung dieses Unglücks: es wird mit dem größten [illeg.] unterdrückt und ist sehr rar.

N[ummer]13. Zwei Briefe des berühmten Odonel od[er] Abisbal,[3] der den Haß den beide Partheien gegen ihn hegen womöglich noch vermehrt haben. Dieses sind die <u>aufgeklärten</u> Spanier.

N[ummer] 14. Ein bescheidenes Opposizionsblatt aus Sevilla besser gemeint als ausgeführt, welches den allgemeinen Unwillen der sonstigen Skribler erregt hat.

N[ummer]15. In demselben Sinn viel geistreicher: man hat sehr kläglich kein Notiz davon genommen.

N[ummer]16. Auch gut: ist kaum bekannt geworden.

Cadiz d[en] 17 Aug[ust] 1820

    B. v. F.

Hier einiges Politisch.	Meine Bemerkungen sind natürlich Sub rosa. Nachstens mehr. Die Kosten sind Reales 82.

102. Nikolas Heinrich Julius, Hamburg

Cadiz, den 31 Oct[ober] 1820

Den 20 dieses traf meine Tochter glücklich mit Cap[itain] Doorman von dorten ein, und seitdem haben ihre lebhaften Darstellungen des nordischen Lebens und Webens manche Sehnsucht in mir angefrischt, besonders da hier jetzt alles was mir und Ihnen lieb und werth ist so bitter und hämisch angefochten wird. Ich habe besonders gerne vernommen, daß Sie ein ächter und wahrer Servil sind, eine Menschenart die immer mehr ausgeht. Ich werde Ihnen daher von nun an frei über Politik schreiben können. Für heute aber (und p[er] Post) nur daß wir mit Riesenschritten dem Verderben entgegenrennen und daß kein Ausweg bleibt zwischen dem Abfall von der Römischen Kirche und einer fürchterlichen Reakzion deren Folgen nicht zu berechnen sind.

  Ihr lieber Brief vom 11 Sep[tember] in 4 Nummern hat mir viele Freude gemacht. Die Antwort summereich. Die Büchersendung ist wirklich höchst interessant. Von den Oelzweigen[1] fehlt mir noch das erste Heft. Den Angelus kannte ich sehr wohl und glaubte seine <u>Wandersmann</u> zwischen meinen altdeutschen

Büchern zu haben. Doch noch viel mehr hat mich Fr[iedrich] Schl[egel]s Concordia[2] angesprochen: dieses ist wohl das Tiefste und Klarste zugleich was sich zum Verständnis der Zeit sagen läßt. Beide Leibnitz[3] und Dallas[4] sind Nothanker im Schiffbruch.

Mit dem Druck der 4 Bogen der Floresta bin ich sehr zufrieden einliegend eine nota der Druckfehler, deren verhältnismäßig wirklich wenige sind und auch von diesen nur die wenigsten den Sinn entstellen. Schade daß nicht alle Glosas den glosirten Fuß kursiv gedruckt haben wie N[ummer] 33 – Im Wörterbuch der Akad[emie] fehlt nur merletes N[ummer]13, worüber ich aber auch nicht einmal eine Vermuthung ausbrüten kann, obwohl es sich rathen läßt daß es etwas spitziges dornartiges bedeutet. albedrio steht im Nachtrag des Wörterb[uches] – Das andere Wort mont _ kann ich nicht lesen. Es freut mich daß Sie immer mehr in den Sinn der Gedichte eindringen: ich bin fest überzeugt, daß keine spanische Krestomathie auch nur entfernt mit dieser die Vergleichung aushält. Dem guten Setzer bitte ich die angeschafften Bücher für meine Rech[nun]g zu bezahlen.

Ich werde besonders gerne die folgenden Bogen nach und nach p[er] Sch[iff] erhalten und ist es in Briefesform so erreichen sie mich desto sicherer – Die Hallersche Schrift über die cortes[5] habe ich mit Heißhunger verschlungen und mich über deren Geist gefreut. Das größere Werk deßelben Verf[aßers] erwarte ich mit der nächsten Sendung, so wie auch die Gedichte des Lamartine[6] – Jacobsens Schrift[7] ist mir wegen der Bilder und Auszüge ganz recht gewesen – Ich billige alles was Sie in Hinsicht meiner altdeutschen Sachen beschloßen haben, nur nicht den Verkauf an H[er]rn Pastores für 9 Mark, da die geistliche Kurzweil[8] eines der rarsten Bücher der ganzen Sammlung sind. Doch á lo hecho pecho, d.h. was geschehen ist, bleibt geschehen und von mir bestätiget – Roscoes Sonnet[9] ist sehr schön – Das Recief von Voß haben Sie hoffentlich später durch meine Tochter erhalten – Für die nota des Cancionero danke – Wer die Wahl hat, hat die Qual: so ist es uns mit den gezeichneten Titeln gegangen. Beide sind allerliebst besonders der Santiago,[10] aber nach reiflicher Ueberlegung paßt eigentlich keiner, gerade weil sowohl die Romanzen vom Cid als alle maurische Romanzen ganz von der Sammlung ausgeschloßen sind, und die Architektur beider nun maurisch ist. Ich ziehe daher als Titelblatt den Titel in großen Fraktur Buchstaben vor, allenfalls mit einer Einfaßung von Arabesken verziert. Die Zeichnungen erfolgen mit erstem Sch[iff] zurück, so wie Schlegels Indisches Magazin[11] und mehrere der bestellten Bücher. Die Flora von Pavon habe ich endlich aus Madrid erhalten: es sind 4 große folio Bände die 1200 Reales kosten, da es meist Kupfer sind. Die Quinologia etc sind nicht aufzutreiben. Die neue Auflage des D[on] Quichote erhalten Sie auch und nebenher 2 Leben des Cervantes. Den Fuero juzgo werde ich aber von Madrid verschreiben müssen – Die erste Abtheilung einer kleinen Sammlung bedeutender Flugschriften wird Perthes für R[ehberg] mit Cap[itain] Voß erhalten haben. Eine zweite wird für denselben mit dem nächsten Sch[iff] erfolgen. Für Sie und mich ist durchaus nichts darunter (einige wenige Oppositionsblätter ausgenommen) was anders als Ekel und Abscheu erregen kann. Wir besitzen jetzt einen verlaufenen Mönch der sich Clararosa schreibt (sein wirklicher Name ist Olabarrieta[12]). Er ist von der Inquisicion in Mexico wegen verruchter Schriften und grober Schändlichkeiten gestraft und seines Priesteramtes entsetzt geworden. Die Preßfreiheit hat ihm nun verstattet, sich seiner Galle zu entladen und sein Gift und Geifer über alles Heilige und Rechte auszugießen. Unter dem gewöhnlichen Vorwande Mißbräuche abzustellen, verbreitet er die abgedroschenen Klatschereien Voltaires,[13] Volneys,[14] Paines[15] etc. über Geistlichkeit Sakramente und Rom, belehrt unsern König, beschimpft den Rußischen Kaiser und die heilige Allianz und verläumdet unsern trefflichen Bischof, alles in seinem Tageblatte. Es sind zwar sehr gute Gegenschriften erschienen, da sie aber gründlich und gelehrt sind, so lesen sie nur wenige, und der große Haufen staunt diesen verruchten Bösewicht als einen neuen Apostel an. Sie können sich vorstellen was ich und m[eine] Frau dabei leiden! –

Wie können Sie doch ignorieren daß seit d[em] 1 July in Madrid ein Gazeta de gobierno[16] erscheint wo alle Sitzungen der cortes in epitourirt werden? Nebendem wird auch besonders im Diario de las cortes[17] gedruckt wovon schon mehrere Bände erschienen sind. Was ich von letzteren erhalten kann soll mit erstem Sch[iff] für Sie erfolgen.

Lord Byron ist nie mein Liebling gewesen: seine Gedichte habe ich bewundert, ohne sie zu Ende bringen zu können. Wer Bonaparte auf Unkosten seines Vaterlandes loben konnte mußte im tiefsten Grunde verderbt sein! Sein D[on] Juan[18] hat es ausgewiesen. Vergleichen Sie damit Wordsworths Peter Bell[19] und einige Sonette seines River Duddon![20] – Kein Dichter spricht mein Innerstes aus wie dieser! –

Wie arm ist Perthes halbjähriger Katalog! – Sind alle Meister schlafen gegangen? – Wozu haben Sie mir den ersten Theil von Göthes Leben in einer neuen Auflage gesandt? – Hoffmans Werke wenngleich ungemein anziehend scheinen mir doch im Ganzen frivoler als die Fantasiestücke. Und damit für heute Gott befohlen.

Der bewußte Ihrige

Das gelbe Fieber ist dieses Jahr sehr milde gewesen. Für September sind in allem 233 Leiber begraben und in October wird es nicht an 300 kommen. Da nun unsere gewöhnliche Sterblichkeit auf 6 p[er] Tag anzuschlagen ist, so können Sie selbst urtheilen. Die Zahl der epidemisch Kranken ward d[en] 20 Oct[ober] 169 angegeben: dieses war das climax; jetzt sollen nur 19 noch da sein. Jerez ist härter mitgenommen und da Puerto so zwischen beiden liegt hat nur einzelne Fälle erlebt. Der Aderlaß hat hier dieses Jahr den besten Erfolg gehabt und in Jerez das Gegentheil. Es bleibt alles bei dieser verzweifelten Krankheit rätselhaft!

103. Nikolas Heinrich Julius, Hamburg

Cadiz, den 16 Feb[uar] 1821

Zu lange schon habe ich aufgeschoben oder vielmehr es aufschieben müssen Ihnen, werther Freund, das anhängende Verzeichniß der Druckfehler der Bogen 5 a 10 der Floresta einzuhändigen. Es bleibt Ihnen überlassen ob Sie die vernachläßigten Kommas mit anführen wollen oder nicht. Im Ganzen sind der Fehler doch nicht viele, und der sinnentstellenden gar wenig. Der Druck ist sehr hübsch und die Gedichte gefallen mir in dieser Form noch mehr als vorher. Entweder bin ich ein Esel, oder diese Sammlung muß allen Kennern der spanischen Sprache höchst erfreulich sein – Ich habe mich seit einiger Zeit nach reiflicher Ueberlegung entschloßen diese Abtheilung der Floresta erst ganz auszuarbeiten, und den dramatischen Theil später vorzunehmen. Dazu sind noch zwei gleich starke Theile jeder von 24 Bogen erforderlich. Der zweite ist schon im Entwurf fertig und beinahe die Hälfte ausgearbeitet. Es ist damit nicht auf einen privaten Druck abgesehen. Wir müssen erst warten wie es mit dem Absatz des ersten Theiles gehen wird. Auf ein gestochenes Titelblatt kommt es am Ende auch nicht an. Nicht übel würde sich der Titel mit großer deutscher Schrift <u>rothgedruckt</u> ausnehmen Floresta de rimas antiguas castellanas. Das übrige schwarz mit lateinischen Lettern.

Ich beantworte heute keinen Ihrer Briefe. Nur so viel daß die von Madrid verschriebenen Bücher noch nicht angekommen sind. Auf alle Fälle überbringt Ihnen Cap[itain] Doorman eine Kiste mit dem Pavon und was sonst hier aufzutreiben war.

Die kleine Sendung p[er] Cap[itain] Voß war mir sehr angenehm. Für den Golius habe ich einen Liebhaber gefunden und so bleibt er für meine Rechnung. Für die Bibl[ioteca] Española von Bayona suche ich einen. Die Auswahl ist elend und nur die Vorrede hat einige interessante Stellen. Für den 1. Theil des Hallerschen großen Werkes[1] kann ich nicht genug danken. In welcher unglaublichen Verblendung lebten wir alle, und wie wenige <u>wollen</u> noch jetzt die Augen öffnen! – Der 2te Theil der De Mennais ist herrlich, und der Dichter la Martine überaus lieblich und überraschend. Mit erster Gelegenheit senden Sie mir noch zwei Abdrücke seiner Gedichte.

Nichts von hiesiger Politik. Der Ekel den diese hölzernen Nachbeterei aller erdenklichen Gottlosigkeit, dieses schale Gerätsch über alles was sich von selbst versteht, dieses elende Gewäsch über Rechte nach die niemand frägt, der Ekel (sage ich) den alles dieses einflößt ist zu groß um sich dabei zu verweilen. Die Scharteken die ich p[er] Doorman an Perthes zur Erleuchtung der dortigen Finsterniß schicken werde, sollen für sich reden. Uebrigens fängt der gedrückte Theil an sich zu rühren, und blutige Auftritte sind hauptsächlich zwischen den Truppen zu befürchten. Gottlob das meines Bleibens allhier nicht lange mehr sein kann! Mit diesem Geschlecht habe ich nichts gemein und nur die Hütten der Altväter reizen mich.

Meine Familie seit 10 Wochen in Puerto und alle wohl.
Der Ihrige in Eile
B.v.F.

104. Nikolas Heinrich Julius, Hamburg [appended to a letter from Francisca]

Cadiz, den 14 Märtz [1821].

Cap[itain] Doorman überbringt eine blecherne Dose an Perthes mit Flugschriften der Rev[oluzion] betreffend, und auch 2 Packete für Sie, eines medizinisch und ein anderes mit einem gebundenen Abdruck meiner Pasatiempos als ein Andenken.

Daß ich mit dem vorstehenden einstimme wissen Sie, allein Sie wissen nicht wie hier stets mehr die Filosofie an der Tagesordnung ist und wie es einem widert so etwas ansehen zu müssen. Keine Hoffnung mehr für das unglückliche Spanien! Der Geist des Truges singt: Religion und Elan muß flüchtig werden. Nord Amerika ist das Vorbild, dem man noch nachzuahmen trachtet, und welch ein Vorbild!–

Bis p[er] Post in großer Eile
Böhl v: Faber

105. Friedrich Perthes, Hamburg

Cadiz, den 18 May 1821

Ihre werthe Zuschrift vom 30 Märtz erhielt ich seiner Zeit. Den 4 dieses traf Cap[itain] Lorenzen glücklich ein und ein paar Tage darauf waren die 10 Ex[emplare] der Floresta in meinen Händen. Zuförderst meinen herzlichen Dank für alles was Sie für das Werk gethan haben. Der gestochene Titel ist allerliebst, Druck und Papier sehr sauber und in Hinsicht der Druckfehler waren eine Menge unvermeidlich, besonders was die Akzente betrifft, wo vieles selbst bei der Academia noch schwankend ist, und sich die Ortografía und der Dicc[ionari]o zuweilen widersprechen. Gehäufte Geschäfte haben einliegende Liste verspätet. Ich bin die letzte Bogen nochmal durchgegangen: vielleicht ist darin etwas wiederholt, doch das thut nichts da vermuthlich noch nichts davon gedruckt ist. Es mag Sie trösten daß in dieser Legion nur sehr wenige Druckfehler sind, die den Sinn entstellen oder bei der Lesung stören.

Höchst fatal ist es daß die Einfuhr aller Bücher erlaubt ist mit Ausnahme der spanischen. Wir müssen also die Floresta einschwärzen, welches sie vertheuern wird. Senden Sie mir vors erste 96 Abdrücke in Packeten von 12 und die 8 Packete wieder zusammengepackt in ein großes. Ferner 4 Abdrücke besonders im besten [illeg.]band gebunden, zum verschenken. Der cours verstattet mir Ihnen diese Abdrücke mit 6 Mark zu bezahlen und hier werde ich 45 Reales dafür erhalten. Diese 600 Mark übermache ich Ihnen nächstens.

Ich bitte besonders aufmerksam zu sein auf was die kritischen Anstalten von der Floresta sagen werden. An die vorzüglichen Kenner Schlegel, Gries, Keil[1] etc möchte ich wohl daß Sie Abdrücke für meine Rechnung einhändigen ließen, und sich ihr Urtheil erböten. Für jede Beurtheilung gedruckt od[er] geschrieben, werde ich das Porto p[er] Post sehr willig bezahlen. Sollten Sie (wie ich hoffe) bei der Unternehmung bestehen, so liegt der 2te Theil in gleicher Bogenzahl völlig ausgearbeitet fertig.

Die Zeit erlaubt mir heute nicht ein Blatt für unseren guten Julius beizulegen. Was ich von seinen Aufträgen habe habhaft werden können überbringt Cap[itain] Voß. Auch ihm meinen besten Dank für die Pflege der Floresta, die ich hoffe ein Liebling aller poetischen Gemüther werden wird.

Ergebenst Böhl v: Faber

Cap[itain] Lorenzen hat mir Dr Paßavant herrliches Buch über den Magnetismus[2] gebracht.

106. *Nikolas Heinrich Julius, Hamburg*

Cadiz, den 25 May 1821

Es war mir unmöglich meinem letzten Brief an Perthes ein Blättchen für Sie, bester Freund, beizulegen. Sie hadern mit mir ohne daß ich mich schuldig finde. Was ich aus mir selbst beantworten kann oder selbst ausrichten kann damit säume ich nie. Muß ich aber nach Madrid schreiben so rechnen Sie auf nichts. Wegen Ihres letzten Auftrages habe ich mich mit meinem Buchhändler Orea überworfen, und jetzt hat einer Sanchez den Auftrag der nicht weniger saumselig scheint. Was ist dabei anzufangen? Man möchte sich krank ärgern, könnte es nur fruchten.

Sie wissen schon wie zufrieden ich mit der Floresta bin. Ich mache Ihnen keine besondere Danksagung da ich weiß daß die Liebe zur Sache Ihnen die Mühe versüßt haben wird. Auch hoffe wird der Beifall der Kenner uns beide lohnen. Die Wenigen die das Werk hier beurtheilen können loben es über die Maaßen, so daß ich wünsche daß die Absendung der geforderten 100 Abdrucke so viel möglich beschleunigt werde. Auch Ihnen trage ich auf mir ja keine Beurtheilung zurückzuhalten und mir die ausgeschnittenen Blätter p[er] Post unverzüglich zuzusenden. – Die Vorstellung des [illeg] ist zwischen denen an P[erthes] gesandten Flugschriften. Dem Prof[essor] Reuß[2] bin ich für das übersandte Inh[alts] Verz[eichniß] der Canc[ioner]o von 1573 besonders verpflichtet, doch wäre die Bleistiftbezeichnung in der von mir übersandten tabla hinlänglich gewesen, nunmal doch diese Ausgabe keine vermehrte sondern eine verminderte ist – Auf Absatz vom dem dort gedruckten Calderon ist hier nicht zu rechnen da die Apontische Ausgabe[2] noch in den meisten Buchhandlungen gefunden wird – In dem Seckendorfschen Verz[eichniss] kann ich nur wenige Wörter selbst erklären: ich werde einige andere Freunde zu Rathe ziehen und es dann nach Madrid an Navarrete senden – Mit Voß erhalten Sie die letzten Theile der Period[ic]o medico, den Pavon, D[on] Quichote, Marina, und was ich noch von Madrid erwarte die Aufträge vom 30. Jan[uar] mit eingeschloßen – Ich habe nie eine Ausgabe der guerras de Granada mit Holzschn[itten] gesehen, auch überhaupt keine alte Ausgabe dieses in der ersten Hälfte des vorigen Jahrh[underts] so häufig nachgedruckten Buches. Die erste Ausgabe die [illeg.] anführt ist Alcalá 1604. – Lazo sagt mir daß er Parisets elendes Werk rezensirt hat, und daß diese Rez[ension] in seiner Zeitschrift erscheinen wird. Hier hat man ihn nie für einen Helden gehalten – Lazo ist der Meinung zugethan daß das gelbe Fieber nicht epidemisch ist sondern immer aufs neue eingeführt wird. Ich glaube das Gegentheil – die Meinung der Aerzte darüber ist getheilt. In dem Period[ic]o medico werden Sie manches darüber finden – Von d'Alton haben wir nichts weiter vernommen. Für sein Alter scheint er etwas windig zu sein. Durch Pander erhalten wir vielleicht manches interessante über China. – Dr. Passavants Werk über Magnetismus hat mich sehr erfreut. Auch habe ich Göthes Divan mehr Geschmack abgewonnen. Senden Sie mir Dr Spikers Reise in England,[3] zwei Abdrucke von Lamartines Gedichten und Le Solitaire de Arlincourt,[4] alle gebunden in feiner Pappe – Der 2. Theil der Floresta ist in ganz gleicher Bogenzahl hiebey: es prangen darin 116 Sonettos Auswahl aus mehreren tausenden. Ein 3. Theil beschließt die Auswahl aller kürzeren Gedichte, dann könnte das altspanische Theater folgen und endlich die epischen Auszüge. –

Kein Wort über die verhaßte Politik. Bankerott und Bürgerkrieg sind unvermeidlich. Wer aber oben bleiben wird das weiß Gott

Ihr stets ergebener

Alles was die Samml[ung] von Fernandez aus den Canc[ioneros] und Rom[anceros] enthält steht in den Bänden 16. und 17. die Sie von mir erhalten haben. Die Bände waren in bunt Papier geheftet. Der Dicc[ionario] de la Acad[emi]a kostet gebunden 160 Reales, die drei Quartbände der nota partida 130 Reales.

107. Nikolas Heinrich Julius, Hamburg

Cadiz, den 21 Juny 1821

Ich sandte Ihnen ehegestern p[er] Post die factura der bestellten Bücher p[er] Cap[itain] Voß. Hiebei erfolgt noch das erste diesjährige Stück des Periodico medico: das zweite ist noch nicht heraus, wird aber in Hinsicht des gelben Fiebers viel interessanter ausfallen.

Zugleich finden Sie eine kürzlich erschienene Satire auf den berühmten spanischen Gesetzgeber, die viel Aufsehen macht. Sie ist sehr wohl geschrieben, höchst komisch und treffend, scheint aber keinen politischen Zweck zu haben, sondern huldigt schlechtweg dem Geist des Zeitalters der Spottsucht. Sie hat nicht verboten werden können, da der Verfaßer binnen den Grenzen der jetzigen Druckfreiheit geblieben ist.

Ich muß Sie über meine Kürze schmollen lassen, ohne es helfen zu können. Meine Töchter warten auf mich um uns nach Puerto einzuschiffen wo sie das Frohnleichnamsfest sehen wollen. Allerwärts ist mehr Andacht als in Cadiz dem Sitz hoher republikanischer Gesinnung die über dergleichen weg ist.

Ganz der Ihrige

Böhl v: Faber

108. Friedrich Perthes, Hamburg

Cadiz, den 21 Sep[tember] 1821

Mein Brief vom 19 Juny mit Bücherfactor und 600 Mark [illeg.] gegen 100 Abdrücke der Floresta ist bisjetzt unbeantwortet geblieben. Ich will jedoch nicht länger anstehen Ihnen den richtigen Empfang Ihrer Briefe vom 10 und 24 desselben Monathes und der darin erwünschten Bücher p[er] Cap[itain] Bandix und Nielsen anzuzeigen. Mein Urtheil darüber wird Ihnen Dr Julius mittheilen, so wie auch wie es mit der Floresta hier gegangen. Wenn Sie in England einen Abdruck an den Herausgeber von Blackwoods Magazin[1] gelangen ließen, so würde dieser vielleicht ehrenvolle Erwähnung davon machen. Dieses herrliche Magazin hat mir den größten litterarischen Genuß gewährt, nemlich die völlige Entwicklung eigener früherer Andeutungen die gewöhnlich unverstanden bleiben, manchmal aber auch misverstanden werden. Daß der deutsche Geist in Schottland so herrliche Früchte trage hätte ich nie geglaubt. So näheren sich die vorzüglichen Geister aller Völker immer mehr und wirken harmonisch zur Aufrechterhaltung des Unsterblichen in uns, während sich alles Gemeine zum Triumph des Materiellen zusammenrottet. Hier zeigt sich der öffentliche Geist immer mehr in der allerwidrigsten Armseligkeit. Ich mag weder davon schreiben noch daran denken. Gottlob daß es mir vergönnt ist mich an die altspanischen Geistesprodukte zu laben und nicht weniger Verwandte in so vielen treflichen neuen deutschen englischen und französischen Schriftstellern zu finden.

Des großen Goethe Äußerungen über die Floresta[2] sind für mich höchst wichtig und erfreulich, und kommt es zum Drucke des zweiten Theiles so sollen die Fingerzeige erweitert werden. Die Floresta fürchte ich jedoch wird das Schiksal der Wordworthschen Gedichte theilen. Nur wenige werden sie liebgewinnen, aber wer sie liebt wird sie aus ganzer Seele lieben. Die wenigen Kenner hier sind über alle Maaßen für sie eingenommen: es sind grade 4 aus 60.000.

Das Geld aus der Berliner Versteigerung ist für Sie zur Abtragung meiner Bücherschuld bestimmt. Senden Sie mir gelegentlich ein Conto Court aber ohne Wiederholung der einzelnen Titel jeder Sendung.

Ihr aufrichtigst ergebener
Böhl v: Faber

109. *Nikolas Heinrich Julius, Hamburg*

Cadiz, den 22 September 1821.

Seit geraumer Zeit warte ich schon auf Berichte von dorten, die mir den Empfang meiner Ramassen an Perthes und die Ankunft von Cap[itain] Voß anzeigen sollten. Da es aber zu lange damit zögert, so kann ich Sie nicht länger ohne Nachrichten von mir lassen – Die Sendungen p[er] Cap[itain] Bandix und Nielsen sind mir wohl zu Händen gekomen. Der Verkauf der Floresta hier ist durch einen böshaften liberal,[1] dem die geistlichen Gedichte misfielen, hintertrieben. Spanische Bücher im Auslande gedruckt sind einzuführen verboten: darauf gründete er seinen Antrag zur Konfiszirung der Bücher und Bestrafung des hiesigen Buchhändlers der sie feil bot. Die Regierung hat kaum Notiz davon genommen: dennoch durfte man sie nicht durch öffentliches Feilbieten trotzen. Der Buchhändler hat jetzt die meisten Exemplare nach Madrid gesandt wo er sich einen besseren Absatz verspricht. Ich glaube jedoch nicht, daß er seinen Vorrath so bald versilbern wird. Die Gleichgültigkeit gegen Alles was nicht politische Kannengießerei ist, übersteigt allen Begriff. Nie hätte ich geglaubt, daß die seichten französischen Ansichten den litterarischen Theil der Nazion so total hätten entnerven und umkehren können. Kein Heil ist hier zu erwarten! Das alte ächte Spanien existirt nur noch in einem Theil des Volkes und in weitsichtigen deutschen und englischen Gemüthern.

Mit den Wiener Jahrbüchern bin ich nicht zufrieden. Gegen einen allgemein interessanten Aufsatz sind wenigstens immer vier nur gelehrte da. Ist es zum Beispiel möglich mit der Topographie Persiens hunderte von Seiten anzufüllen? Weiter als für dieses Jahr 1821 wünsche ich sie nicht zu erhalten. Wie hoch (in Bezug auf die Bedürfniße des gebildeten Mannes aus allen Ständen) steht die Quarterly Review über alles mir sonst bekannte. Ich habe mir kürzlich die ganze Sammlung dieses herrlichen Werkes angeschafft. Welch ein tiefer herrlicher klarer und durchdringender Verstand! Welch eine überzeugende Entlarvung aller filosofischen und liberalen Marktschreierei! Nur die poetischen Ansichten sind nicht ganz die rechten – Zugleich habe ich Blackwoods herrliches Magazine (nicht die ganze Sammlung) erhalten und möchte aus der Haut fahren, daß ein solches Werk seit mehreren Jahren ohne meine Kenntnis davon existiren konnte. Alle meine

Ahnungen und Andeutungen finden sich darin entwickelt. Ich gestehe daß ich nie einen litterarischen Genuß gehabt habe der diesem zu vergleichen wäre! – Erstlich die völlige Anerkennung meines herrlichen Wordsworth, den Blackwood nie müde wird zu erheben und zu loben. Zweitens die tiefen deutschen Ansichten von Geschichte Kunst Poesie und Kritik die unter dem Namen von Lauerwinckel und Kempfershausen[2] diese Zeitschrift zieren. Drittens die einzige unnachahmliche Laune womit Tickler[3] die Verfaßer der Edinburgh Review abstraft. Viertens die Kenntnis der deutschen und dänischen Litteratur und die Vorliebe für dieselben. – Sollten Sie diese Zeitschrift nicht haben, so schaffen Sie solche an es koste was es wolle. Die ersten Theile sind etwas matt, desto weiter aber um desto trefflicher.

Die Oehlzweige sind ein allerliebstes Werk und gewiße Aufsätze ganz vorzüglich: auch Schuberts nächster Theil sehr interessant. Ebenso Hallers Zweiter Band, dessen Erklärung seines Uebertrittes zur Mutterkirche ich mit Ungeduld erwarte. Die Concordia spricht mich sehr an: mit Hamanns Werken[4] bin ich gleichfalls zufrieden. Zimmermanns dramaturgische Blätter[5] gefallen mir sehr und werde die Fortsetzung gerne erhalten – Noch muß ich Sie auf die englische Retrospective Review[6] aufmerksam machen wovon ich drei Theile besitze. Es sind Auszüge aus alten merkwürdigen Büchern mit mancherlei Nutzanwendungen auf die Gegenwart. Gerade so möchte ich die Ausbeute meiner alten Spanier ans Licht fördern, der Prosaiker nemlich, und allenfalls der Epiker. Aber wo soll die Zeit herkommen? – Nächstes Jahr gewinne ich wahrscheinlich mehr Muße, indem die Weinhandlung der ich vorstehe nach Puerto verlegt wird. Dann bespare ich die vielen Reisen und die tägliche Korrespondenz mit dem Kellermeister. Zuerst mache ich mich dann an die Ausarbeitung des 3. und letzten Theils der Floresta. Mein Gehalt ist ansehnlich erhöht, so daß ich sorgenfrei leben kann: dabei genieße ich das Glück unsere Weinhandlung immer wachsen zu sehen und zu erleben daß dieser <u>einzige</u> Handlungszweig blüht, während alles andere zu Grunde geht.

Hier reift übrigens alles dem Partheien Kriege entgegen und selbst die eifrigsten Konstituzionsfreunde verzweifeln. Was aber dem Falle des K[önigs] folgen wird, das läßt sich nicht errathen. Ich erwarte vors Erste nichts Gutes. Meiner Frau habe ich Ihren Brief vorenthalten müssen. Sie ist so überspannt, daß es mir Mühe genug macht sie in den Gränzen der Klugheit zu halten – Mit dem ersten Schiffe sollen Sie verschiedene Fortsetzungen erhalten. – Ich danke für die Abschrift der Anzeige der Pasat[iem]pos in den Göttinger Anzeigen[7] – Was Sie für den Verkauf der altdeutschen Bücher erhalten, bitte an Perthes für mich auszuzahlen – Ich wünsche den Griechen den besten Fortgang und ist es mir ärgerlich daß der Rußische Kaiser so lange säumt loszuschlagen.

In Puerto haben wir das gelbe Fieber schon wieder: es greift aber wenig um. Der Sommer ist brütend heiß gewesen und ist mir sehr beschwerlich gefallen. Die Füße sind mir geschwollen, welches in Hinsicht des Anziehens von Schuh und Strümpfe sehr beschwerlich ist. Folgen des Alters und der sitzenden Lebensart – Das Haus wird nach und nach morsch wie Alcazar[8] es so lieblich in der Floresta N[ummer] 351 darstellt. Die Liberalen werden uns den Ausgang erleichtern, denn in ihrer werthen Gesellschaft hat das Leben wahrlich wenig Reitz. Ich bedaure nur meine Kinder die ich zwischen seelenlosen Geschöpfen zurücklassen müßte. Cecile ist auf dem Punkte sich zum zweitenmal zu vermählen und leider mit einem liberal wenngleich von der besten Art.[9] Ich denke sie bekehrt ihren Mann noch wohl.

Mit diesem Briefe werden Sie hoffentlich zufrieden sein; er geht zu Lande weil das nächste Sch[iff] von hier dorten wohl nicht angenommen wird sondern in Norwegen überwintern muß – Unverändert Ihr wahrhaft ergebener
Böhl v: Faber

110. Nikolas Heinrich Julius, Hamburg

Cadiz, den 13 Oct[o]b[e]r 1821

Da der holländische Schiffer Ueberbringer des Gegenwärtigen wahrscheinlich zur Quarantaine nach Norwegen wird verwiesen werden, so will ich was ich für Sie und Perthes liegen habe bis zu einer andern Gelegenheit aufsparen. Das gelbe Fieber ist zwar nicht in unserer Stadt ausgebrochen aber gegenüber im Puerto wüthet es wie gewöhnlich zwischen den Neuangekommenen, und da die dortigen Aertzte bei der erregenden Quina Kur beharren so kommen wenige durch. Gestern hat es endlich angefangen etwas zu regnen und so sehen wir einer kühleren und gesunderen Periode entgegen.

Einliegend die feindliche Erklärung gegen die Floresta welche deren Verkauf hier hintertrieben hat. Von Madrid habe ich noch keine Nachricht der Ankunft der für dort bestimmten 50 Abdrücke. Indessen ist nicht zu erwarten daß irgend etwas poetisches jetzt Aufmerksamkeit erregen könne. Wo der große Theil des lesenden Publikums sich nur mit politischen Klatschereien beschäftiget, wo der Sinn für alles Geistige völlig ausgegangen ist, da muß man auf Poesie Verzicht leisten. Ich bleibe der Meinung daß Blackwood die Floresta zu würdigen wissen wird. Sein Magazin wovon ich nun die 8 Baende (mit Nachtheil meiner Augen) verschlungen ist ein Kommentar der Pasatiempos was Literatur betrifft, und seine Politik zermalmet die elenden Whigs und Liberales wie sie es verdienen.

Stets der Ihrige
Böhl v Faber

111. Nikolas Heinrich Julius, Hamburg

Cadiz, d[en] 23 Dec[ember] 1821

Die Verlegung der Weinhandlung der ich vorstehe nach Puerto a S[an]ta M[arí]a, die eine doppelte Umhausung nach sich zieht, nimmt meine Zeit so gänzlich in Beschlag, daß ich seit mehreren Wochen vergeblich bemüht gewesen bin ein paar Stunden zur Beantwortung Ihrer lieben Briefe vom 19 Oct[ober] und 9 Nov[ember] (Norberg) (11 Dec[ember]) zu gewinnen – Einmal aber in Puerto ansäßig werde ich nicht nur Muße zu einem ordentlichen Briefwechsel sondern auch zur Erneuerung meiner litterarischen Thätigkeit erübrigen. Meine spanischen Bücher sind schon im Puerto in einem günstigeren Lokal aufgestellt als meine Cadizer Wohnung erlaubte so daß ich sie noch mit mehr Liebe werde benutzen können. – Die Abdrücke der Floresta haben bis jetzt Madrid noch nicht erreicht: sie ruhen wahrscheinlich am Kordon oder Gesundheit Linie, so daß ich nicht wissen kann wie es mit dem Absatze dort gehen wird. Ehe ich dieses nicht erfahre mag ich Ihnen den zweiten Theil nicht auf den Hals schicken – Seitdem das Wetter frischer geworden ist und ich habe Bewegung machen können hat sich das Geschwulst an den Füßen gelegt. Ich bin nichtsdestoweniger dankbar für Ihren so freundschaftlichen Antheil an dieser Unbequemlichkeit und habe Ihren guten Rath und das Rezept sorgfältig notirt. Wollen Sie glauben daß es sich nicht hat fügen wollen mit Lazo darüber zu konferiren? Unsere Wirbel haben keine Berührungspunkte und expresse Berathschlagungen mag man über Kleinigkeiten nicht anstellen. – Es freut mich daß der Dr. Pfeilschütze meiner in Ehren gedacht hat. Da nun das Fieber vorbei ist so glaube ich daß er auch herkommen wird. Seine Korrespondenz mit einem meiner Bekannten läßt nicht viel erwarten. Ihre Anzeige der Floresta in den Originalien[1] kann mir nicht anders als sehr behagen da sie con amore verfaßt ist. Die Vergleichung der Fingerzeige mit Göthes Bemerkungen über das Wunderbare läßt sich nur als persönliche Vorliebe rechtfertigen. Die Anzeige in den Göttinger Blättern werde ich gerne erhalten. Was mich verdrießt ist daß von A[ugust] W[ilhelm] Schlegel keine Würdigung dieser Sammlung, sei es auch nur als privat Schreiben, zu erhalten ist. Er und Gries sind die Einzigen deren Stimme für mich Gewicht haben kann – Ich danke Ihnen für die Nachrichten über Blackwoods Mitarbeiter. Ich habe neulich wieder 6 Hefte erhalten, die sich immer treu bleiben. In dem einen wird der alte Tollhäusler Jeremias Bentham[2] auf das herrlichste bearbeitet – Des <u>großen Ungenannten</u> Roman besitze ich nicht und habe auch nur den ersten gelesen. Für Romane auch wenn sie noch so trefflich sind gebe ich nicht gerne Geld aus.

Ihre zusammengezogene Bestellung auf Bücher ist nach Madrid gesandt und es wird sich zeigen was man davon wird auftreiben können. Von Conde's Arabes[3] habe ich schon den 2 und 3t letzten Theil für Sie liegen. Die Diarios der alten cortes[4] von 1811/13 sind <u>komplet</u> sehr selten und werden mit 100 piaster bezahlt. Die letzten Theile wurden 1814 aufgegriffen und vernichtet. Die 21 ersten Theile sind um ein Geringes zu haben. Ohne Ihre expresse order kann ich mich nicht entschließen 200 piaster für diese Sammlung von Unrath wegzuschmeißen. Haben Sie den tom[os] XVI. und XVII. von R[amón] Fernandez nicht erhalten so ist es Perthes gewesen dem ich sie in bunt Papier geheftet und etwas wurmstichig zum Verkauf nebst andern Doubletten gesandt habe.

Es ist nicht zu läugnen daß Ihre Briefe Augenpulver sind und ohne Brille gar nicht zu lesen wären. Der Gebrauch der Brille ist meinen Augen wohlthätig gewesen und ich kann ihnen jetzt mehr anmuthen als je.

Der Stollberger Werke sind mir sehr angenehm gewesen. An Göthes M[eisters] Wanderungen[5] habe ich mich wenig erbaut – Die heilige Familie scheint mir flach und geistlos: das pädagogische Land eine langweilige utopische Fratze: die interessanten Liebschaften des 50Jährigen bleiben leider Fragment: die Verwechslung der Schwestern am Schluß ist sehr gewöhnlich. Kurz nur das Mährchen und die eingestreuten Bemerkungen über Menschen und Dinge haben meinen unbedingten Beifall. Und doch ziehe ich Hoffmans Mährchen im 4t[en] Serapion noch vor: eine solche Laune ist mehr als Hamilton.[6] Hoffman sollte sich auf dieses Fach legen: seine ernsten Sachen sind zu grell, wie die Leichenfreßerin in diesem Bande – Silberts Dom heiliger Sänger[7] hat mir viel Freude gemacht: Sie werden darin Bekannte aus der Floresta gefunden haben – Die Medit[ations] poet[iques] gewinne ich immer lieber – Hallers Brief[8] ist edel und schön – Ich bemerke daß unsere Geldangelegenheiten berechtiget sind – Ich freue mich zu Keils Anzeige der Floresta[9] – Über spanische Mundarten kenne ich absolut nichts – Das Vascuense ist eine eigene Sprache so wie das Catalan und Valenciano Abarten des Provencal. Der Galizische Dialekt ist genau mit dem Portugies[ischen] verwandt. Alles übrige in Spanien ist Castellano und die Provinzialismen beschränken sich auf einzelne Wörter.

Nichts über Politik: sie ekelt mich an. Rußlands Zaudern hat mich vergrimmt. Oesterreichs Benehmen ist erbärmlich. Am Ende werden die Perser dem Türken mehr Abbruch thun als diese engherzigen Kristen die ihre Brüder gelassen durch die Mordsünde morden und sengen lassen. Solche Maulkristen verdienen daß der gerechte Gott den Ungläubigen Wien und Moskau zu Händen liefert – Halten Sie wenn es Zeit ist den Oestlichen Rosen[10] zurück. Ich bin nicht morgenländisch gestimmt und tausche mit Ihnen Göthes Divan für einen Spruch des cherubinischen Wandersmannes.

Das gelbe Fieber ist diesesmal eigensinniger als je gewesen. In Puerto hat es sich verbreitet und in Cadiz nicht obwohl der Zusammenhang nicht gefehlt hat. Es hat diesesmal die weibliche Jugend sehr mitgenommen die sonst verschont blieb. Ich werde suchen Ihnen die genausten Todtenlisten zu verschaffen sobald ich im Puerto ansäßig bin – Ihre Briefe addressiren Sie künftig: A D[on] G[uiller]mo Duff Gordon,[11] Puerto, Andalucia ohne Beifügung meines Namens.

Der Ihrige

B. v: F.

112. Nikolas Heinrich Julius, Hamburg

Puerto, den 14 July 1822

Cap[itain] Norberg ist vor wenigen Tagen nach dorten unter Segel gegangen, und obwohl ich ernsthaft darauf bedacht gewesen bin einen Tag abzusparen um von Cadiz die Verschiffung Ihrer Bücher zu besorgen, habe ich es dennoch nicht möglich machen können. Sie erhalten also nur die seit kurzem in Madrid angekommene letzte Kiste wovon eingehend Rezief, so wie auch die nota des Inhaltes. Die Kosten an Bord sind 747 Reales die ich einstweil zu Ihren Lasten notire, bis sich Gelegenheit findet zum trassiren. Von dem Umfang der Geschäfte die mir jetzt obliegen werden Sie sich einen Begriff machen wenn ich Ihnen sage daß ich für das Haus dem ich vorstehe dieses Jahr schon 20000 £ Werth an Wein verschifft habe und daß nun jede Pipe dieses Weines unter meiner unmittelbaren Aufsicht zubereitet worden. Wer hätte mir in den ersten Jahren auf Görslau vorgesungen daß ich auf meinen alten Tagen noch ein Weinbrauer sein würde! und wer unter meinen Freunden hätte geahnet, daß ich auch dieser Beschäftigung eine interessante Seite abgewonnen habe und solche jetzt mit Vorliebe treibe! und wer unter den Gegnern meiner (poetischen) Sinnesart hätte sich geträumt daß ich in diesem praktischen Fache alle meine Gesellen aus dem Felde schlagen würde! In anderthalb Jahren daß ich an der Spitze dieses Hauses bin haben sich dessen Geschäfte wahrlich verdoppelt und sind noch im Zunehmen. Mein Premium dabei ist 8 000 Reales, freie Wohnung, freien Wein etc. welches jedoch in einem großen Hause mit einem Schaaren alter invalider Diener, mit der antiökonomischen Natur meiner Frau und mit einer stets offenen Boise für alle Bedürftige nicht ausreicht. Doch wird mir der nötige Zuschuß von dem Eigner des Hauses bei seinem ansehnlichem Gewinn nicht fehlen.

Mitte May hatte ich das Vergnügen meinen Neffen Eduard Berckemeyer[1] zu bewillkommen der mir Ihre lieben Briefe vom 5 und 6 April mit einem Päckchen Bücher, der Oper von Weber,[2] dem Bilde für Cecilia etc überbrachte. Nur wenig davon habe ich bis jetzt lesen können. So viel für künftige Sendungen vorläufig. Nichts über die Hellenen, die mich nicht interessieren. Keine französischen Bücher mehr, da ich jetzt solche direkt von Marseille erhalte. Ueberhaupt nur das Gediegene im Fache der Religion Poesie und Kritik, da meine Zeit jetzt so sehr beschränkt ist. De Maistre[3] ist ein herrlicher Geist der deutschen Tiefsinn mit französischem Witze verbindet. Leider liegen seine übrigen Werke für mich schon seit 6 Monathen im hiesigen Zollen unter embargo, durch eine Verkettung sonderbarer Umstände, deren Entwicklung täglich versprochen wird. – Am meisten Genuß hat mir der Klavierauszug des Freischützen[4] (er sollte heißen die Freikugeln) gewährt. Wenn ich schildern wollte was ich dabei fühle so sollten Sie sehen daß die Poesie in mir nicht ausgegangen ist! Das erste Duett im zweiten Akt hat mich zum sterben in Aenchen verliebt gemacht. Die herrlichen Jäger bewegen das innerste Leben auf. Zimmermanns Beurtheilung ist sehr brav: ich erwartete sie so nicht, da er den mehr poetischen Houwald[5] so hart behandelt. Kurz und gut, Freund! seit der Ankunft meines Neffen (der sich als tüchtiger und gewandter Comptoir Gehülfe verweist) denke ich an einen Besuch in Hamburg nächsten Sommer. Die erste Triebfeder ist natürlich mit meiner alten guten Mutter noch ein paar Monathe zu verleben, der zweite, Sie und meine sonstigen dortigen Freunde und Verwandte lang und breit zu besuchen um die Modifikazionen des Ichs auszutauschen und sich fester aneinander zu schließen wenn sich solche in kommerzierenden Linien offenbaren, wie ich fest überzeugt bin daß es zwischen uns beiden der Fall ist. Ihr Haß der span[ischen] Revoluzion bürgt mir dafür – die dritte Triebfeder wäre die deutsche Oper, der Freischütz Mozart und die Uebersetzung Calderons. Dies alles sub rosa.

Die Floresta erreichte Madrid im May: seitdem ist nichts über sie laut geworden. Wie kann es auch anders sein! – Die englische Kritik des Monthly ist schmeichelhafter als ich sie erwarten konnte. Das Jan[uar] Stück von Blackwood habe ich leider noch nicht erhalten. Eine gründliche deutsche Rezension wird ja wohl endlich irgendwo erscheinen! – Hätte ich nach Cadiz gehen können, so wäre mit Cap[itain] Norberg der zweite Theil erfolgt. Jetzt bleibt er hier zum nächsten Schiffe. Er liegt völlig fertig.

Einen wohlfeilen Nachdruck der Scottschen Romane erhalte ich gerne, wenn die Schrift nur nicht zu klein ist: es müßte auch ein wohlfeiler Einband sein, wie ich bei Schillers wohlfeiler Ausgabe gesehen habe: gewöhnliche Pappe, beschnitten und schwarze Titel – Den Kleist hatte ich schon gebunden erhalten und send Ihnen das ungebundene Exemplar nächstens zurück – Sicher ist castellano richtiger als español. War dem Verfaßer die Autorität der Acad[emia] nicht hinreichend? – Auch bei mehrer Muße wäre es mir unmöglich diejenigen Wörter zu erklären die im großen D[iccionario] de la Ac[ademia] fehlen. Wenn man selbst dergleichen in alten Büchern auffindet, so erklärt man sie aus dem Zusammenhange – Auch kein einziges dieser Wörter habe ich aus eigener Kenntniß erklären können. Bei nächster Sendung erfolgen demnach diese Bogen zurück – Für Blüchers Brief danke. Schon jetzt fangen die damaligen Begebenheiten an fabelhaft zu scheinen. Wir werden immer kleiner! Dank der neuen Politik und der Aufklärungs-Filosofie!

Ich will sehen was ich in Ihren Quina Aufträgen ausrichten kann sobald es mir möglich ist einen Tag für Cadiz abzusparen – Von dem rekapitulirten Bücherauftrag werde ich tilgen was Sie mit Norberg erhalten, und den Rest nochmals in Madrid bestellen – An Lazo habe ich die medizinische Sachen einhändigen lassen wofür er dankbar: die Forts[etzung] seines Periodico liegt bei mir bis zur nächsten Sendung. Ihre mediz[inische] Zeitschrift habe ich mit Interesse durchblättert. Wie konnten Sie aber die Abscheulichkeit über Ausschneidung der clitoris abdrucken lassen! –

Da die großen viertel-elligen Cigarren hier gar nicht beliebt sind so stehen sie auch nicht feil. Was davon auf den Straßen ausgeboten wird ist [illeg.]. Nur direkt von der Havana können Sie solche erlangen. Ihren politischen Brief habe ich meiner Frau (die schon überspannt genug ist) nicht übergeben können. Hingegen werde ich einige Zeilen von Ihrer Hand über ihre eigenen Aufsätze (die Sie lange müssen erhalten haben) gerne überreichen, da sie mehreremal gefragt hat ob Sie diese Aufsätze erhalten.

Wir brüten hier seit mehreren Wochen in einer Atmosphäre von 21 a 24°. Die Nächte erfrischen nicht. Alle Quellen vertrocknen. Die Erndte ist knapp gewesen, welches bei den großen Vorräthen wenig zu bedeuten hat: jetzt schrumpfen schon die Trauben ein. Aller Appetit ist verschwunden, und man hat nur Lust zu trinken und zu Früchten. Was würden wir um 8 Tage dortigen Herbstwetter geben.

Die öffentliche Gesundheit ist bis jetzt gut – Lazo und seine Gehülfen bleiben dem Ansteckungs-System getreu und es ist daher viel von Quarantaine etc. die Rede – Vom Geschwulst an den Füßen hat sich bis jetzt wenig bei mir eingestellt, welches ich wahrscheinlich einer größeren körperlichen Thätigkeit zu danken habe. Hätte die Hitze nicht das so sehr unbequeme und unausstehliche Schwitzen zur Folge, würde ich mich nicht übel mit ihr vertragen. Ich muß jetzt öfters in der ärgsten Hitze 2 M[eilen] nach Jerez fahren und dort in den breiten schattenlosen Straßen stundenlang herumwandern, hunderte von Pipen Wein probiren, aus Durst viel Wein trinken (da das Wasser in Jerez schlecht ist) ohne je ein Kopfweh verspürt zu haben.

Gottlob daß ich heute Sonntag ohne Unterbrechung so weit gekommen bin und damit Gott befohlen.

B.v:F.

113. Nikolas Heinrich Julius, Hamburg

Puerto, den 6 Aug[ust] 1822

Bester Freund – Mein Brief vom 14 July wird Ihnen mein langes Stillschweigen aufgeklärt haben. Anstatt der erwarteten Muße sind mir gehäufte Geschäfte geworden: indessen wird auch darin eine Ebbe eintreten und dann sollen Sie fleißiger von mir hören. Von Madrid ist schon eine neue Sendung für Sie unterwegens. Mein Korresp[ondent] schreibt mir wegen der Quina Liste: Ruiz y ademas Pabon me han dicho, que los mismos nombres se usan en España q[ue] en America y que ni tienen ni pueden darles otros, que estan haciendo un tratado de la quina en el que va un catalogo gén[eral]. Die Liste sende ich mit erster Gelegenheit zurück. Die Muster werden in Cadiz bestmöglichst besorgt – Die Schriften über das gelbe Fieber gebe ich nächstens nach Madrid auf – Jetzt Dank für Ihre Erinnerung der 2 Rom[ancero]s aus Eschenburgs Verlassenschaft. Beide habe ich und aus beiden stehen 8 N[umer]os in der Floresta. Die Primavera[1] ist die beste. Sonst ist mir eine jede alte Rom[anzen] Sammlung die ich nicht besitze von sehr hohem Werth. Depping hat aus Quellen geschöpft die ich nicht habe – Also ist der herrliche Hoffmann[2] sobald abgetreten! Ich bitte um eine Notiz aller seiner Schriften – Ganz kürzlich erst habe ich die 4 Bändchen die mit Meisters Wanderjahre[3] anfangen gelesen und mit steigendem Interesse. Wer ist dieser neue Stern? – Seine Kritik Göthes ist sehr richtig so lange sie gegen dessen Gottlosigkeit kämpft. Mir hat sie jedoch eines meiner Lieblingswerke des großen Dichters verleidet. Auch Shakesp[eare] stellte die Menschen dar wie sie <u>sind</u>, nicht wie <u>sein sollten</u>. Die Urtheile über Werther und Bar[on] Eduard[4] sind höchst einseitig. Die letzten Theile von W[ilhelm] Meister haben mir nie gefallen. Faust bleibt ein hohes gewinnliches Produkt und eine hohe Zierde unserer sonst so rauhen Sprache. – Was sagt der alte Göthe zu diesen Anfechtungen? – In dem Tagebuche W[ilhelm] M[eisters][5] habe ich mich ganz wiedergefunden: Sie sind öfters ein Kommentar meiner Pasatiempos – Die fromme Gräfin[6] ist das herrlichste was ich in dieser Gattung kenne – Das Werk über Spanien ist soviel ich und andere es haben prüfen können höchst genau und sehr unpartheiisch und damit für heute Gott befohlen –

Ihr ergeb[ene]r B. v. F.

114. *Nikolas Heinrich Julius, Hamburg*

Puerto, den 1 Nov[ember] 1822

Nur durch ein Ohngefähr erhielt ich vor einigen Tagen durch Cap[itain] Lolli zwei kleine Packete Bücher und Ihren Brief vom 9 Aug[ust] – Der Cap[itain] war auf dem Punkte mit den Packeten wieder zu versegeln als wir in Cadiz aufeinander stießen. Dieses wäre vermieden hätten Sie den Brief separat dem Cap[itain] mitgegeben und darauf verzeichnet <u>mit einem Packet Bücher</u> so und so. Ueber die Bücher kann ich Ihnen noch wenig sagen. Von den Nachdrücken der Scottschen Romane behalte ich die größere und sende die kleine zurück.

Ich würde mich recht freuen wenn Sie den Alcalde de Zalamea[1] zur Vorstellung bringen könnten, gerade aus eben den Gründen die Sie anführen. Ich gestehe indessen aufrichtig daß ich mich noch in keine deutsche Uebersetzung des Calderon habe hinein hören können, weil mir die deutschen Trochäen misklingen. Vielleicht ist dieses ein Wahn den eine gute dortige Darstellung heilen würde. Zimmermanns dramatische Blätter lese ich mit dem größten Interesse wenngleich (wie <u>Sie</u> es fühlen werden) manches Einzelne mich abstoßen muß, wie z.B. das alberne Gewäsche über <u>weibliche Tartüffe</u> p. 232 welches schon seit einem halben Jahrhundert aller Unterlage mangelt. Ein läppisches Geschrei nach Wasser zum Löschen, wo auch keine Spur von Feuer vorhanden ist. Wie kann der geistreiche Zimmermann eine solche Blöße geben! – Wie freut mich dagegen die Anerkennung des Werthes der Wiener Opern (Donauweibchen, Sonntagskind etc[2]) die ich in früheren Zeiten einzig und allein zwischen den dortigen sich gebildet dünkenden vertheidigen mußte!

Ich lese immer mit Interesse was Sie selbst über das gelbe Fieber sagen, weil ich a priori von Ihrer Ansicht überzeugt bin. Die Ärtzte hier bleiben bei Ihrer Kontagionsroutine. In den beiden Kisten die Gegenwärtiges begleiten finden Sie manches über diesen Gegenstand. Diesen Herbst sollen sich hier einige Fieberkranke gezeigt haben: die Cadixer Ärtzte kamen herüber und erklärten es sei das gelbe Fieber. Puerto wurde mit hartem Interdikt belegt: nichts sollte aus noch ein und man schoß mit Kugeln auf unsere Fahrzeuge die sich dem Cadixer Ufer näherten. Man bloquirte sogar unsern Fluß. Man erschrak vermuthlich das Fieber und da sich in 14 Tagen kein einziger Fall von Fieber zutrug so wurden wir von der Sperre erlöst und es heißt nun daß die kräftigen Maasregeln der Regierung die Krankheit im Keime erstickt hätten.

Was der Staatsmann von Galiano in seinem 1. Stück[3] liefert ist nicht eben sehr erbaulich: ich hätte wenigstens noten erwartet um darzuthun wie wenig [illeg.] oder volksmäßiges in dem ganzen Unternehmen aufzuweisen sei. Hiebei erhalten Sie (durch meine Frau) die sehr seltene gewichtliche Vertheidigung des so schaamlos verwendeten Elios,[4] die sich (wenigstens auszugsweise) besonders für eine Zeitschrift wie sie sein muß, eignet.

Ein lockerer Kauz muß der Uebersetzer der Briefe des Holgazan[5] für das katholische Deutschland sein! Genug meinerseits um ihn für einen ächten Ordensbruder der Verbündeten gegen Altar und Thron zu halten, die ihren Hauptsitz jetzt in dem unglücklichen Spanien haben.

Nichts habe ich bisjetzt von Navarrete noch einem andern Cadizer Sprachkundigen für Seckendorf erhalten können. Schreiben Sie mir ob ich Ihnen die Hefte zurücksenden soll oder ob ich sie behalten kann in der Hoffnung bei mehrerer Muße noch selbst etwas herauszuklauben. Wozu Sie nur die vielen Ankündigungen des Wörterbuches schicken weiß ich nicht. Wie viele Menschen mag es überhaupt in Spanien geben die beide Sprachen verstehen? Gewiß nicht so viele als die Zahl der gesandten Ankündigungen. Daß ich selbst einen Abdruck gerne erhalten werde versteht sich.

Daß über die Quina Namen von Madrid mitgetheilt haben Sie ebenso verstanden wie ich. Auf die Erscheinung des Werkes darüber werde ich aufmerksam bleiben um es Ihnen seiner Zeit zu senden. Mit den Mustern in Cadiz hapert es auch: von der Gleichgültigkeit der Kadixer für alles was nicht Geschichte (vordem) und Politik (jetzt) ist haben Sie gar keinen Begriff. Interesse am reinen Wissen nehmen (glaube ich) eigentlich nur Deutsche! –

Ich möchte daß ich nichts über Hoffmann gefragt hätte! Die Frankfurter Anekdote benimmt seiner dichterischen Erscheinung allen nimbus. Ein poetisches Gemüth und ein Staatsumwälzer! – Welch ein Widerspruch! – Den zweiten Theil des Kater Murr⁶ wünsche ich zu erhalten: die Prinzeßin Brambilla⁷ nur wenn sie Ihnen zugesagt hat. Alles übrige von ihm besitze ich.

Ich danke für die Nachrichten über Pustkuchen. Die Gedanken der frommen Gräfin sind doch mehr als [illeg.] Den 3. Th[eil] der Wanderungen habe ich noch nicht gelesen. Es ist doch sonderbar, daß es niemals in Deutschland zu einem eigentlich litterarischen Journal kommt, einer wirklichen Litteratur Zeitung aber ohne förmliche Rezensionen und in mäßigen wöchentlichen oder monathlichen Heften, mit Nachrichten über Bücher, Verfaßer, Nekrologien, Aukzionen etc kurz alles was den bloßen Litteraten interessirt.

Ich bin gewiß daß Göthen Champagna⁸ mir sehr gefallen wird: schon die ersten Seiten verrathen den Meister in der Kunst lebendig darzustellen.

Ich habe des spanischen Getreibes in der Politik so satt daß mich jedes Blatt darüber anekelt. Durch einige Freunde weiß ich indessen daß absolut nichts gedruckt wird was auf allgemeine (schiefe oder gerade) Grundsätze bezug hätte sondern sich alles Geschreibe um die allerkleinlichsten Personalitäten dreht die für Niemand außer dem engen Zirkel des Schreibers Interesse haben können. Dergleichen nun kann ich mich nicht entschließen aufkaufen zu lassen und der mir sehr schätzbare Syndicus Sieveking⁹ wird es mir sicherlich Dank wissen seine schöne Zeit nicht durch dergleichen zu verderben. Von politischen in Amerika gedruckten Schriften ist mir (außer Murillos Vertheidigung¹⁰) noch keine je zu Gesicht gekommen.

Die Göttingische Beurtheilung der Floresta ist wirklich günstiger als sie aus dem Verstandesquartier zu erwarten war. Ich hätte einige Seitenhiebe auf katholischen Aberglauben erwartet, den man unter dem Mantel der Poesie neuerdings einzuschwärzen suche. Ein Unglück ist es daß Schlegel sich im Orient verloren hat: von ihm wäre eine Anzeige con amore zu erwarten gewesen – Schm[idts] Aufsatz über Calderon¹¹ hat mich sehr interessirt – Eine kleine Abhandlung von Calderon über Mahlerei¹² findet sich in einem alten Buche welches ich haben muß die ich Ihnen werde abschreiben lassen.

Endlich erfolgt nun auch der 2t[e] Band der Floresta in genauer Bogenzahl und Anordnung dem ersten völlig gleich. Für gründliche Kenner der sp[anischen] Poesie wird dieser Theil vieles bekannte liefern und daher wenig Genuß gewähren: für andere aber muß das anerkannt vortrefflichste so großer Dichter noch mehr Reitz haben – Die prächtigen Sonette müssen Jeden entzücken. Ich kann Ihnen zugleich anzeigen, daß der Entwurf und Auswahl des dritten und letzten Theiles fertig daliegt, und so Gott mir Gesundheit und Gesicht verleiht diesen Winter über ins Reine gebracht werden soll. Die Bogenzahl ist wieder gleich und die Gesamtzahl der Gedichte beläuft sich auf 1000. Sobald ich damit zu Stande bin sollen meine persönlichen Ansichten folgen. Diese denke ich jetzt in Spatziergänge durch die Floresta einzukleiden. Ich bin mit mir selbst darüber noch nicht recht ins Reine, fühle aber daß sich an einem solchen Faden vieles reihen läßt. Ach! hätte ich doch nur Muße!

Was ich nun aber sehr wünsche ist, daß die Perthessche Handlung bei dem Drucke nichts zusetze! So angenehm es mir natürlich ist die Frucht meines langjährigen Sammlens geborgen zu sehen und einzelne poetische Gemüther dadurch zu erquicken, so kann ich mich dennoch nicht mit dem Bewußtsein versöhnen daß dieses auf Kosten der genannten Handlung geschehe. Viel lieber mag der Druck unterbleiben bis ich ihn auf meine Kosten veranstalten kann. Von den 100 Exemplaren die auf hier gekommen sind ist knapp ein Drittel abgesetzt. Ich kann mich daher nur für 50 für den 2t[en] Band verbindlich machen. Alles dieses werden Sie mit genanntem Freunde überlegen. Ein geätzter Titel von demselben Geschmack des ersten Bandes wäre natürlich eine große Zierde, doch habe nichts dagegen wenn dasselbe unterbleibt, wenn es zur Beförderung des Interesse des Verlegers dienlich ist.

Ihren Brief in Blackwoods Januar Stück[13] habe ich gerne gesehen: von dem Monthly Review haben Sie mir aber ein unrechtes N[ummer] aufgegeben, in welchem nichts von der Floresta steht. Sollten Sie das rechte N[ummer] dorten haben oder kaufen können, so fügen Sie es wohl der nächsten Sendung bei.

Blackwood hat neuerdings wieder einen schönen Schwung genommen. Coleridge hatte den Anfang einer Nachahmung von Hoffmanns goldenem Topf geliefert,[14] die sehr interessant ist. Lord Byron fällt immer mehr durch, wie ich es lange prophezeit habe und Wordsworth steigt fortwährend in der öffentlichen Meinung, wie ich es noch früher ahnte.

Von der Cadixer Ausgabe der Entremeses des Cervantes[15] soll der nächsten Sendung ein Abdruck beigelegt werden. Alle Werke des Lope des Vega (sein Theater ausgenommen) sind in den 70 Jahren des vorigen Jahrhunderts bei Sanchez[16] schön gedruckt in 21 Bänden 4°° wieder aufgelegt, und kosten eingebunden ungefähr 600 Reales. Sein Theater ist nie wieder aufgelegt und die 25 Bände woraus es besteht sind <u>komplet</u> eine litterarische Seltenheit. Einzelne Bände finden sich manchmal. Ich habe davon 17. Mehr als Lord Holland![17] Vor wenigen Jahren bezahlte ein Freund für 14 od[er] 15 Bände 3000 Reales.

Ich fing in dem ersten Jahr der sogenannten Freiheit (1820) an Ihnen die markanten Flugschriften zu senden. Sie haben damals alles erhalten was auf der einen Seite den erbärmlichen Ursprung der Sache klar darlegten und auf der andern die <u>gottlosen</u> Absichten der Rädelsführer bewies. Alles übrige seitdem sind nur Folgen dieser Grundlage gewesen. Seit dem Tode des Höllenbrandes Clararosa wird die Religion zwar nicht so geradezu angegriffen, aber des Schimpfens auf Mönche und Klerisei als Urheber aller politischen Uebel nimmt kein Ende, und alle Klöster und geistliche Stiftungen werden nach der Reihe eingezogen und ihre Güter veräußert. Die Nonnenklöster nur stehen bis jetzt noch, erwarten aber mit Beben ihren Untergang. Es geht alles den französischen Gang, nur etwas bedächtiger und mit mehr Rücksicht auf den Skandal. Die Zwecke sind aber dieselben.

Hiebei factura von den 2 Kisten mit Büchern die Ihnen Cap[itain] Lorentzen (der morgen segeln will) mitnimmt. Der Belauf dieser factura ist 3297 Reales. Die vorige belief sich auf 1407 Reales, zusammen 4704 Reales die ich uso ordre J[ohann] H[einrich] Berckemeyer auf Sie entnommen habe. Gott gebe dem Cap[itain] eine geschwinde und glückliche Reise – Von Madrid sind von der letzten großen ordre drei Kisten unterwegens die leider nicht zeitig genug für Cap[itain] Lorentzen kommen und vermuthlich wohl bis Frühjahr werden liegen müssen.

H[er]r Berckemeyer hat die ordre Ihnen ein Fäßel von 2 @ oder c[irc]a 40 Bout[eille]s Besten Jerez Wein zu überliefern. Sind Perthes und Besser[18] Kenner dieses Artikels so bitte ich ihnen ein Dutzend Bout[eille]s in meinem Namen davon zukommen zu lassen.

Dieser ist einmal ein tüchtiger Brief. Dem Feste haben Sie zu danken, daß er so lang hat werden können. – Unveränderlich Ihr wahrer Freund
J. N. Böhl v: Faber

115. Nikolas Heinrich Julius, Hamburg

Puerto, den 8 Nov[ember] 1822

Cap[itain] Lorentzen führend das Sch[iff] Delas ist am 4 dieses nach dorten unter Segel gegangen und bringt Ihnen laut einlieg[endem] 2 Kisten Bücher J. N. B. Die factura befinden sich an Bord desselben Schiffes mit einem langen Brief an Sie. Der Belauf ist (die vorige Sendung eingeschloßen) die ich heute a 1½ uso auf Sie entnehmen ordre J[ohann] H[einrich] Berckemeyer womit dieser Gegenstand schließt. Auch wird Ihnen H[er]r Berckemeyer ein Fäßel besten Jerez Weins von meinetwegen einhändigen, welches (in Theilnahme mit H[e]rrn Perthes und Besser) auf meine Gesundheit zu verzehren bitte.

In einer dieser Kisten werden Sie die Handschrift des 2t[en] Theiles der Floresta finden, worüber ausführlich in dem Briefe p[er] Cap[itain] Lorentzen. Der dritte und letzte ist gänzlich im Entwurfe vollendet und die Ausarbeitung schon begonnen. Es werden gerade 1000 und manches herrliche unbekannte erscheint in dieser letzten Abtheilung – Dann käme das alte vor Lope de Vega'sche Theater an der Reihe, welches als mehr an der Tagesordnung vielleicht auch mehr Interesse erregen würde. Auch ist es wahrscheinlich daß ich nächstes Jahr mehr Muße haben werde. Doch ist es thörigt zu weit in die Zukunft einzugreifen. Ist die Handschrift der Floresta einmal <u>ganz</u> ausgearbeitet, dann wollen wir das weitere überlegen – Ein Engländer Namens Bowring[1] der mich dieses Frühjahr besuchte und ein Kenner der Spanischen Litteratur ist, auch Mitarbeiter an englischen Zeitschriften, quält mich um Abschriften für ein Teatro Español welches er herauszugeben denkt.

Spätere Stücke die ich doppelt besitze schicke ich ihm vielleicht: die früheren, die ich für mein Teatro bestimme natürlich nicht.

Gott gebe dem Cap[itain] Lorentzen eine baldige Ueberkunft! – Der ich unwandelbar verharre.

Ganz der Ihrige

B.v.F.

116. Nikolas Heinrich Julius, Hamburg

Puerto, den 21 Jan[uar] 1823

Werther Freund

Ich beantworte Ihre lieben Briefe vom 2 und 9 Nov[ember] und 10 Dec[ember] der erste mit Cap[itain] Grote der die mitgegebenen Bücher wohl überliefert hat. Die kleinen Ausgaben von Scotts Romanen konveniren mir nicht, sondern die andere in 12 wovon ich bisjetzt nur den Pirate, Monastery und Abbot[1] erhalten habe. Der Pirate hat mir am besten gefallen, Magnus Troil mit seiner Familie werde ich sobald nicht vergeßen. Die weiße Frau mit der Bibel kann ich in meiner Fantasie nicht paaren. Der sogenannte Abbot ist besser, sollte aber Marias Befreiung heißen. Llorente[2] über Gil Blas hat für mich wenig Interesse. Auch Moores Lalla Rooke[3] hätte ich entbehren können. Erskines Letter[4] habe ich nicht weitergelesen als bis zu seiner Misbilligung der Behandlung Neapels. Halten Sie mich für einen Radikal Freund, daß Sie mir solches Zeug aufseilen – Bei meinen vielfachen Beschäftigungen behalte ich nur Zeit zur Lesung von Kernsachen, weshalb Ihre Auswahl fernerhin beschränkt sein muß – H[er]r v. Rumohr[5] kenne ich dem Rufe nach und bin überzeugt daß ich mich in seiner Gesellschaft sehr wohl befinden würde. Seinen „Geist der Kochkunst" erwarte ich mit erster Gelegenheit, so wie auch von Ihrer Freundschaft die beiden zusammengebundenen Romanceros, die ich nicht besitze und nur dem Titel nach kenne. Ich werde daraus entnehmen was mir dient und sie Ihnen dann mit Dank zurücksenden. Die 4 Pfund alten Schnupftoback folgen mit ersten Frühjahrssch[iff].

Es ist sicher daß bei der Zerstörung so vieler Klöster und Kirchen jetzt manches schöne Gemälde unter der Hand wohlfeil verkauft wird, allein um sie habhaft zu werden muß man nicht nur Kenntniße haben die mir mangeln sondern auch herumwandern können. Ich kann Ihnen und Ihren Freunden daher in dieser Hinsicht nicht behilflich sein. Eben so steht [es] mit den Barcelona Flugschriften über das gelbe Fieber. Der Buchhändler in Madrid schickt sie mir nicht, obgleich ich sie wiederholtemal gefordert habe: er sagt sie sind nicht zu finden. Sie müssen Sie direkt von Barcelona verschreiben sonsten erhalten Sie solche schwerlich – Die sonstigen Werke die nicht in den 3 Kisten enthalten sind die bei mir das erste Frühjahrsschiff abwarten werde ich verschreiben – Wenn das Dicc[ionari]o anfängt selten zu werden so erhöhen die Buchhändler den Preis – So eben ist die 6te Auflage erschienen, die ich noch nicht gesehen habe.

Ich möchte wissen wie eine Rezension der Floresta aussehen muß die Ihnen Genüge leistet! – Die Leipziger[6] hat den Fehler daß sie das Günstige übertreibt, sonsten geht sie ganz von dem rechten Gesichtspunkt aus.

Sehr schmeichelhaft für mich ist Ihr wiederholt geäußerter Wunsch und Aufforderung zur Verwirklichung meines beabsichtigten Sommerbesuches. Allein die Geschäfte des mir anvertrauten Hauses haben nun solche Ausdehnung gewonnen, daß ich ihrer besonnenen und nachhaltigen Leitung alle meine Zeit und alle meine Kräfte widmen muß. Es ist indessen wahrscheinlich daß der Zeitpunkt nicht fern ist wo die Ueberfüllung des Londoner Marktes die Frage nach unseren Weinen vermindern wird und dann wird es nicht schwer sein abzukommen. So lange ich aber monathlich an 100 Pipen Wein abzuschiffen habe solange auch bin ich unerläßlich an diesen Beruf gebunden.

Mit Freude erhielt ich durch Ihren letzten Brief die erste Nachricht der Ankunft von Cap[itain] Lorentzen mit den Büchern, dem Wein und der Floresta. Von Calderon kenne ich noch einige Romanzen die mir aber nicht ausgezeichnet scheinen. Das (Cadiz 1821) braucht nicht gedruckt zu werden, sondern anstatt dessen Hamburgo 1823. Die Fingerzeige sind von meinem Neffen abgeschrieben und billige ich völlig was Sie über deren Druck bemerken – Daß Burguillos von Cean Bermudez[7] angeführt wird ist mir neu, doch wird der Streitpunkt dadurch nicht entschieden, denn es könnte ja Lope seinen Namen geliehen haben – Ich danke dem guten Hitzig daß er sich meiner erinnert: seine Empfehlung würde ich bestens geachtet haben. Hoffmanns Lebensbeschreibung[8] werde ich gerne erhalten. Sein Meister Floh[9] hat mir sehr behagt – Wenn Sie das hiesige Revoluzionswesen besser kennten, so würden Sie mir nicht anmuthen sein in solchem Schmutz zu wühlen. Ich wiederhole es zum drittenmal daß gar nichts über <u>Grundsätze</u> verhandelt wird, sondern daß alle Flugschriften sich auf persönliche Anfeindungen beziehen die weder Sinn noch Interesse für Fremde haben können. Jetzt wundert sich alles darum, wer Communero und wer Mason ist, die sich gegenseitig mit Vorwürfen überhäufen und sich selbst als die einzigen Freunde der Konstituzion ausgeben. In welchen Grundsätzen diese Herren voneinander abweichen, das weiß niemand – Die Verfaßer des Censor[10] verstanden wenigstens ihre Muttersprache: es waren Leute von Geist, Minaño (Verf[asser] der Br[iefe] der Holgazan) ein abtrünniger Kanonikus, Lista[11] ein ziemlicher Dichter und noch ein dritter Advokat dessen Namen mir nicht beifällt. Sie sind alle afrancesados und waren erst kürzlich zurückgekehrt. Weder ächte noch unächte Spanier haben sich je mit dieser Kaste befreunden können. Von allen werden sie gehaßt: ich finde darin den sichtbaren Finger Gottes – Um die Spatziergänge zu Papier zu bringen, müssen die 3 Theile der Floresta vollendet sein, und mir dann ein Paar Monathe Muße werden

– Das altspanische Theater datirt nur vom Ende des 15t[en] Jahrhunderts und doch ist es so gut wie unbekannt – Und damit für heute Gott befohlen.

P. S. Sollte mein Juan Sie um einige katholische Erbauungsbücher bitten, so suchen Sie ihm ein halb Dutzend Bände der besten für meine Rechn[ung] aus, als Stollbergs kleine Schriften, Sailer[12] od[er] was Sie sonst für orthodox erbaulich anerkennen.

Der Ihrige
Böhl v: Faber

P. S. Mit Mr Bowring kann ich trotz seines ausgezeichneten Talentes nicht harmoniren. Wir kamen in unserer einzigen Unterredung gleich aneinander weil er behaupten wollte nur das maurische in der spanischen Poesie sei original und achtungswerth. Ich schickte ihm darauf die Floresta und er schrieb diese zeuge für seine Meinung – die ganze Floresta athmet der katholisch-christliche Geist der alle ächte spanische Poesie karakterisirt – Hernach sprach er schlecht von Blackwoods Magazine: Kurz er stieß mich in jeder Hinsicht ab und ist sicherlich ein Freigeist und Radikal – Dabei fällt mir ein Ihnen Hoggs Winter Evening Tales[13] zu empfehlen, wenn Sie zugleich lachen, weinen und schaudern wollen. Die Macht und Lebendigkeit der Darstellung ist noch über Scott.

B.

117. *Nikolas Heinrich Julius, Hamburg*

Puerto, den 21 Febr[uar]1823

Aus Ihrer Zuschrift vom 3 Jan[uar] habe ich, bester Freund, mit Vergnügen ersehen daß wir in Hinsicht des Geschmacks unserer Zungen ebenso gut harmonisiren als in unseren poetischen Ansichten. Mit erster Gelegenheit soll noch ein Fäßel derselben Art folgen. In England bezahlt man uns diese Gattung £50. – Mit Cap[itain] Dirks der Ende Märtz nach dorten zurücksegelt empfangen Sie wahrscheinlich 4 Kisten Bücher, die 3 die ich schon seit mehreren Monaten in Besitz habe und die 4te mit den letzten Aufträgen die ich täglich erwarte. Auch ein Packet meiner Doubletten einige von Werth und andere sonder Werth. Den Romancero von Rumohr erwarte ich mit Ungeduld. Die von Eschenburg erstandenen besitze ich, wenn mein Gedächtnis mich nicht trügt. Alle die ich besitze sind in den Quellen des 1. Bandes der Floresta angeführt. Wenn Sie solche da nicht finden, so bitte ich sie mir aus, zur Durchsicht und Exzerpten. – Kürzlich erst habe ich den Einsiedler od[er] Fragmente über Sittenlehre Staatsrecht und Politik. Cotta 1822[1] aufmerksam angesehen und sehne mich nach der Forsetzung ohne sie zu erwarten. Wenn ich daran denke daß Schloßers Fievée, Schlegels Konkordia und Tieks Phantasus ohne Fortsetzungen bleiben, so wäre ich geneigt an dem Fortgang der guten Sache in Deutschland zu zweifeln. Dann aber kommt mir der wohlbeliebte

Haller in den Sinn dessen vier wenngleich treffliche doch sehr schwerfällige Bände schon eine zweite Auflage erlebten und ich tröste mich. Daß Sie mir die franz[ösische] Uebers[etzung] der Hallerschen Schrift gegen den Sp[anischen] K[ortes] nicht gesandt haben ist eine arge Uebersicht. Diesen Augenblick wäre sie schon in spanisch übers[etzt] und thäte sicherlich Wirkung. Seit der Rede des K[önigs] von Fr[ankreich] tragen wir den Kopf hoch und meinen daß die Ratze jetzt aus ihrem letzten Loche pfeift. In Cadiz fahren die Partheien fort sich zu befeinden und scheinen keine Gefahr für den hochheiligen Kodex zu ahnen – Dieses a conto eines längeren

P[er] Cap[itain] Dirks

Ihr ergebenster

Hat der treffliche La Martine
nichts weiter von sich hören lassen?

Das geheftete Exemplar von Conde kann nur 135 Reales kosten: die 55 Reales die an 190 Reales fehlen sollen Ihnen von der nächsten Factura vergütet werden – Von dem Viage á las Iglesias a España[2] sind 8 Th[eile] heraus und kosten 144 Reales. Von den Flugschriften über das gelbe Fieber habe ich immer weniger Hoffnung etwas aufzutreiben. Von der spanischen Gleichgültigkeit gegen alles wissenschaftliche haben Sie keinen Begriff, besonders seitdem sie Politiker geworden.

118. *Nikolas Heinrich Julius, Hamburg*

Puerto, den 18 Märtz 1823

Diesesmal, bester Freund, schreibe ich ohne Schuldigkeit der Beantwortung. Sie sind mir im Gegentheil noch Antwort auf die meinigen vom 21 Jan[uar] und 21 Febr[uar] schuldig die ich seiner Zeit erwarte.

Da Cap[itain] Dirksen führend die Frau Maria sich zur Absegelung nach dorten fertig macht, so habe ich ihm laut beigehendem Konnassement 4 Kisten Bücher für Sie an Bord gesandt so wie auch ein Fäßel des Weins der Ihnen gefallen hat. Die Bücher belaufen nach beigehenden Rechnungen 4284 Reales [illeg.] die ich a 1½ uso auf Sie ordre Robert White Sons entnehme. Ich bitte den einliegenden prima dieser Tratta angenommen an H[er]rn J[ohann] H[einrich] Berckemeyer zuzustellen um selben zur Disposizion das secunda zu halten. In der Kiste N[ummer] 4 (die ich habe vergrößern lassen müssen) finden Sie eine blecherne Dose Schnupftoback für H[er]rn v. Rumohr, ein klein Packet im Hause H[er]rn Geheim Rath v. Faber abzuliefern, 32 alte spanische Bücher und mehrere alte Schauspiele, wovon die Liste der Schiffer überbringen wird mit meinen Bemerkungen darüber.

Ich sehe hiemit Ihre Bücher Kommißion (bis auf die unauftreibbaren gelben Fieber Schriften) als abgethan an. Wenigstens erwarte ich (sollte etwas fehlen) eine neue Liste, groß und deutlich geschrieben und jeder Titel abgesetzt. Was mir dieses an Porto mehr kosten kann, erspare ich an Vergrößerungsgläsern, denn eine gewöhnliche Brille ist zur Entzifferung öfters nicht hinreichend. Es sind auch mehrere politischen Flugschriften in der Kiste die meine Frau Ihnen sendet und die Sie an Sind[icus] Sieveking indeßiren können. Für mich bleibt es eine reine Unmöglichkeit mich damit zu befaßen. Der mit Unwillen vermischte Ekel den das Treiben dieser Menschen in mich erweckt ist ein Gegengewicht der vielen Annehmlichkeiten meiner jetzigen Lage. Sie können kühn behaupten, daß so schlecht man sich die jetzigen Führer der öffentlichen Angelegenheiten denken mag, man sich dennoch nie einen anschaulichen Begriff einer so totalen Nichtswürdigkeit machen wird. Tief hat es mich verletzt, daß Liverpool und Canning[1] von einer solchen Verblendung mit ergriffen sind und daß sie wahrscheinlich das Schwerdt der Gerechtigkeit in der Scheide werden zurückhalten. Käme es dann nur bald zu einer Schreckens Regierung, so würde auch die Rettung nahe sein, allein gerade die Rechtlichkeit des Volkes und sein weniges Interesse an politischen Fragen wird den Ausbruch der gemeinen blutgierigen Demagogie verhindern und den Rädelsführern desto mehr Zeit lassen nach und nach ohne Lärm alles Gute zu untergraben und zu vertilgen.

Aufgemuntert haben mich in etwas die trefflichen Schriften des Großen Le Maistre, die ich diese letzten Wochen erst habe lesen können. Alles was er über die so gepriesene gallicanische Kirche sagt, habe ich lange deutlich gefühlt. Bossuet ist mir nie völlig recht gewesen. Die Jansenisten (Pascal mit eingerechnet) haben der katholischen Kirche mehr geschadet, als Voltaire und sein ganzer Anhang. Die Spötter und Materialisten können auf der Länge nur Alltagsmenschen schaden: die Jansenisten vergiften dagegen nur vorzügliche Köpfe. Die Conversations de St Peter[sbourg][2] haben mich entzückt. Wann sah ein Nichtdeutscher so weit? – Es ist viel mehr darin angedeutet als ausgeführt. Ich erwarte viel von der Wirkung dieses Buches, weil es französisch geschrieben ist. Es muß dem Verstande eine neue weit bessere Richtung geben und dasjenige im Gebiete des Nachdenkens bewirken was La Martine im Fache des Gefühls geleistet hat.

Wenngleich die Geschäfte des Hauses von Duff Gordon noch immer im Steigen sind, so weiß ich dennoch die Nebenstunden so gut zu nützen, daß von dem 3t[en] Theil der Floresta schon über die Hälfte ins Reine ist. Ich eile damit nicht wegen des Druckes, sondern weil ich das ganze Werk vor mir haben muß, um die bezweckten Spatziergänge auszuarbeiten. Ich denke darin meine Ansichten über Manches darzulegen, da sich in unserer Faßungsweise Alles an Poesie knüpfen läßt. Wäre es nicht gar zu schwer, so kleidete ich es in Gespräche ein, zwischen dem Poetischen, dem Verständigen und dem Vernünftigen (a la Tiek). Wir wollen sehen was der Genius des Augenblicks mir eingeben wird!

Wir sind Gottlob alle wohl. Mit meiner fisischen Behaglichkeit geht es auf die Neige seitdem wir wieder 14 a 15° Wärme haben: übrigens aber habe ich erfahren,

daß mir das starke Schwitzen heilsam ist und so unterwerfe ich mich in Geduld. Unwandelbar Ihr ergebenster
J. N. Böhl v: Faber

119. Nikolas Heinrich Julius, Hamburg

Puerto, den 25 Märtz 1823

Einliegend finden Sie, werther Freund, ein Duplikat des Konassements der 4 Kisten Bücher und 1 Fäßel Wein welches ich Ihnen d[en] 18 dieses p[er] Post sandte. Auch erfolgt die Liste der in demselben Briefe erwähnten Doubletten aus meiner Sammlung. Sollte sich dieser Brief verloren haben so bestätige ich zum Überfluß meine Tratta auf Sie von 1153.2 Reales de uso ordre Robert White Sons gegen den Belauf der kommittirten Bücher, deren prima zur Annahme und Einlieferung an H[er]rn J[ohann] H[einrich] Berckemeyer in diesem Briefe enthalten war. Sollte sie nicht erschienen sein, so werden Sie gütigst die Secunda annehmen.

Da Cap[itain] Dirksen auf den Stutz ausgehen will, so kann ich nur noch hinzufügen, daß ich morgen nach Sevilla gehe um daselbst die Festtage zuzubringen und unabänderlich verbleibe
Ihr ergebener
J. N. Böhl v: Faber

PS. In diesem Augenblick erhalte ich die Einlage von Lazo, die einige Hoffnung giebt die Barcelona gelben Fieber Schriften zu erhalten – Auch lege ich das eben erschienene 3. Heft der medizinischen Zeitschrift bei – Die Auferstehung des Aussatzes in Rens ist schrecklicher als alles gelbe Fieber.
Derselbe

120. Nikolas Heinrich Julius, Hamburg

Puerto, den 22 Juny 1823

Vor einigen Tagen habe ich das Bücherpacket mit Cap[itain] Bandix samt Ihren Brief vom 27 April wohl erhalten welches ich heute vorläufig in ziemlicher Eile beantworte. Wenn ich Ihnen sage daß wir jeden Augenblick unsere Retter die Franzosen hier erwarten, daß dann Cadiz sich verschließen wird und daß dieser Brief über Cadiz mit der Amphitrite nach dorten gehen soll so ist alles erklärt.

Gottlob, Freund! daß die Redlichen endlich wieder frei athmen! Seit ehegestern daß sich alle Häupter der Liberales vom panischen Schrecken ergriffen nach Cadiz geflüchtet haben, glauben wir uns in das vormalige biedere Spanien versetzt. Ganz ohne Truppen, ohne Bürgerwache (man nahm ihnen vor der Flucht die Waffen ab) nur unter der Obhut einiger Dutzend Hausväter, die einen Geistlichen an der

Spitze während der Nacht die Straßen durchwandern, genießen wir der vollkommensten Ruhe. Alles anführerische Geschrei, alle mordlustigen Gesänge, alle Lästerungen, alle Schimpfreden scheinen mit dem Gesindel davon gezogen zu sein.

Was eigentlich in dem übrigen Spanien vorgeht wissen wir nicht. Das Lügengewebe welches die liberalen Papiere auftischen, hat nur diejenigen getäuscht die getäuscht sein wollten. Aus einigen durchgeschlüpften Privatbriefen wußte man indeß daß die Franzosen ohne Widerstand fortrückten und in den großen Städten (wie natürlich) mit Jubel aufgenommen wurden. Den 12 fiel es plötzlich der Regierung in Sevilla ein davon zu laufen. Um die Sache zu erleichtern, ward der König in Geschwindigkeit abgesetzt und als Gefangener mit fort geführt. Den 14. um 1 ½ Uhr Nachts ward er hier eingebracht und erreichte den 15. um 6 ½ das unentweichte Heiligthum der spanischen Freiheit, das Bollwerk der heiligsten Menschenrechte, die weiland große Handelsstadt Cadiz. Zwanzig tausend hungrige Menschen sind im Gefolge der Regierung mit herum gestürtzt und müssen einquartirt werden. Von der Seeseite schneidet der französische escadre alle Zufuhr ab: in wenigen Tagen wird die Landseite umzingelt sein. Die Cadizer Liberales sind in mehreren Partheien getheilt. Die Reichen sehen ein daß die Unterhaltung des ganzen Troßes allen auf sie fallen wird. Das Volk murrt <u>jetzt</u> schon daß es von den Regierern verkauft und betrogen ist. Es läßt sich also mit ziemlicher Sicherheit schließen, es werde das <u>Bollwerk</u> diesesmal bald kapituliren. Ueber die kunstvollen Retiraden mit Zurücklassung von Artillerie und Bagage <u>ohne den Feind gesehen zu haben</u>, ließe sich eine neue liberale Taktik schreiben. Aus dem Zerstäuben der Regimenter <u>ohne geschlagen zu sein</u>, könnte man die gränzenlose Anhänglichkeit der Spanier an ihre makellose Konstituzion auf eine liberale Art beweisen und aus dem Jubel der besetzten Städte wäre es leicht darzuthun wie sehr die Bewohner, die <u>Horden des Principe tonto</u>[1] (so wird der Neffe des edlen Ludwig XVIII nach einem bekannten spanischen Lustspiel von den geistreichen Cadizer Zeitungsschreibern genannt) haßen.

Ob es nach diesen handgreiflichen Beweisen noch freche Schreiber geben wird, die von der span[ischen] Kunst als einer Angelegenheit der Nazion sprechen werden! – Sollte dieser Brief geschwind überkommen, so ändern Sie nach Belieben und geben ihm die möglichste Publizität. Gerne sagte ich mehr, wenn es die Zeit erlaubte.

Die 11 Bogen der Floresta habe gerne erhalten. Obenhin angesehen scheinen sie mir sehr korrekt. Da Cap[itain] Voß wahrscheinlich nach dorten zurückgeht, so hoffe ich die Korrektur mit ihm zu übersenden. Doch wo denke ich hin? In einigen Tagen ist wahrscheinlich der direkte Weg wieder eröffnet, und dann ein mehreres.

Die beiden Romanceros habe ich gerne erhalten und schon entdeckt daß dieselben (mit wenigen Auslassungen) in dem Roman[cer]o general wieder abgedruckt sind. Dieses ist eine interessante litterar[ische] Notiz. Jetzt werde ich in wenigen Wochen den 3 und letzten Theil der Floresta ausgefertiget haben, und dann soll sogleich Hand an die Spatziergänge gelegt werden.

Der französ[ische] Haller ist sehr willkommen gewesen. Rumohrs Buch hat mir (so viel ich hineingesehen) sehr wohl gefallen, so wie auch Gagern Schriften.[2]

Ihre Briefe mit der Preisaufgabe ruhen diesen Augenblick bei mir bis die politische Komödie ausgespielt ist. – Ebenso geschieht mit der Liste der aufs neue verlangten Bücher. –

Cecilie ist jetzt bei uns und grüßt Sie herzlich und schämt sich noch nicht für den schönen Erzengel gedankt zu haben – Ihr Mann und seine Brüder haben sich nach Cadiz flüchten müssen, da sie (wenngleich herzensgute Menschen) von dem liberalen Schwindel angesteckt waren und wichtige Stellen bekleideten – Dem verächtlichen Liaño habe ich nie geantwortet –

Vielen Dank für Ihre sonstigen litter[arischen] Nachrichten. Senden Sie ja alles was im rechten Geist über den spanischen Krieg erscheinen möchte. Chateaubriands treffliche Reden darüber,[3] kennen wir nur durch entstellte Auszüge. Ich danke Perthes für den herzlichen Brief. Die Antwort nächstens.

Stets der Ihrige B.v. F.

121. Nikolas Heinrich Julius, Hamburg

[no date]

Hiebei befinden Sie die Beantwortung der Fragen über das gelbe Fieber von zwei französ[ischen] Aertzen. Die erstere von Dupny dem Staabs-Artzt in Cadiz und die andere von dem Regimentschirurgen des hier stationierten 13. Kavallerie Regiments – Die spanischen Aertzte haben die Sache fallen lassen. Lazo ist bestimmt für die Einführung von America und Ansteckung, und daß dem strengen quarantainen System der Franzosen die Nichterscheinung des gelben Fiebers allein zuzuschreiben ist.

Es ist unglaublich, dass so viele Abdrucke des Calderons Abnahme finden. In dem aber die Ausgabe von Keil von der ich drei dicke 12^{oo} Bände besitze in Stocken gerathen?– Ich will weder die eine noch die andere, werde indessen gerne hören daß die Ausgabe in den 4 großen Bänden zu Stande kommt, und auch was Sie dann kosten wird.

Das letzte Bücherpacket mit meistens Fortsetzungen habe ich erhalten und das beigeschloßenen Packet ist nach Gibraltar spedirt. Die kleinen Schriften von Görres hatten Sie mir schon früher gesandt. Neanders Geschichte der Religion[1] konvenirt mir um so weniger, da ich die früheren Teile nicht habe. Nur etwas ganz vorzügliches müssen Sie mir schicken, wenn es nicht von mir beordert ist. Wann wird endlich einmal eine kritische deutsche Zeitschrift erscheinen, die den englischen an der Seite zu setzen ist? Die Wiener Jahrb[ücher] sind recht brav, aber

kaum ⅓ der Aufsätze sind <u>allgemein</u> interessant. Das rein wissentschaftlich muß ausgeschloßen bleiben, wenn man für die höhere Klasse der Gebildeten schreibt. Die englischen lese ich von Anfang zu Ende.
    Der Ihrige B.v.F.

122. *Nikolas Heinrich Julius, Hamburg*

Puerto, den 12 Aug[ust] 1823

Durch einen glücklichen Zufall habe ich Ihre Briefe und Packete von May p[er] Cap[itain] Voß (welche dieser Esel erst bei seiner Abreise und nach völliger Sperrung der Verbindungen ablieferte) erhalten – Hoffmanns Leben hat mich interessirt ohne mich zu befriedigen. Seine jugendliche Korrespondenz verdiente nicht gedruckt zu werden. Diese so gewöhnliche Unzufriedenheit mit den gesellschaftlichen Verhältnißen ist sehr langweilig wenn sie sich nicht wie Göthes Werther ausspricht. Hoffmann hatte viel von Rousseau und muß im gewöhnlichen Leben unausstehlich gewesen sein. Sollte etwas von seiner Musik gedruckt od[er] gestochen werden, so senden Sie mir es wohl, so wie auch wenn etwas von seinen Zeichnungen und Karikaturen ans Publikum käme. Die Skizze des Sandmann[1] hat mich ungemein ergötzt. Wenngleich mich diese grausliche Erscheinung jedesmal verstimmt, kann ich doch nicht umhin sie oft zu lesen – Die Antikritik Grimms[2] hat mich sehr interessirt obwohl ich in der Hauptsache mit dem Rez[enzent] einig bin, daß nämlich diese Ritter Romanzen am häufigsten wieder gedruckt sind – Das Volkslied sollen Sie verbessert mit erstem Sch[iff] zurückerhalten: es ist ganz modern d.h. taugt nichts, wie es von den Herausgebern des Morgenblattes nicht anders zu erwarten war.
    Des Königes rein fr[an]z[ösicher] Flugschrift hat mir viel Freude gemacht, aber auch nur <u>mir</u>. Für gewiße Feinheiten und leisen Anklängen schöner Menschlichkeit haben nur wenig Menschen Sinn.
    Ihre Briefe mit der Preisfrage sind gerade zu dem unglücklichsten Zeitpunkt eingetroffen, und wir müssen die finale Beruhigung abwarten ehe an die Behändigung zu denken ist.
    Die 11 Bogen des 2t[en] Bandes der Floresta habe ich mit Interesse durchgesehen. Die Druckfehler sind nicht zahlreich, wie Sie aus beigehender Liste ersehen werden. Einige fehlende oder versetzte Kommas habe ich mit Fleiß nicht berichtigt, da sie den Sinn nicht stören. Häßlich ist es aber für das Auge wenn die Kolonnen ungleich sind wie p. 28.30. Mitte von 31. Bei den Sonetten hätte der unterste Strich niedriger stehen sollen. Das Wort opuesto was p. 126 fehlt hatte ich selbst in der Handschrift ausgelassen. Ein litographisch gezeichneter Titel wäre mir auch für den 2t[en] Band angenehm sein und da ich annehme daß er nicht über 20 Reales kosten kann so bitte ich denselben für meine Rechnung besorgen zu lassen.

Es muß wieder eine neu gotische Verzierung sein, denn nicht andres ist paßlich: etwas architektonisches: Figuren sind entbehrlich – Der 3t[e] und letzte Band der Floresta ist nun auch völlig ausgearbeitet und Sie erhalten ihn im Herbst. Er hat mir die meiste Mühe gemacht wegen Lope de Vega und Quevedo die ich aufs Neue ganz habe durchgehen müssen. Jetzt aber glaube ich kühn behaupten zu können daß es kein <u>schönes</u> lirisches Stück in der alten Spanischen Poesie giebt welches nicht in der Floresta enthalten wäre. Nun kommt die Reihe an die <u>Spatziergänge</u> und finde ich nur den rechten Faden so soll das Abspinnen nicht schwer werden, da mein Kopf voll ist – Von einem prächtigen Steindruck eines Kopfes (vermuthlich Blüchers) der die letzten Sachen begleitet hat, erwähnen Sie nichts.

Hoffentlich haben Sie meinen Brief vom 22 Juni p[er] Cap[itain] Djörkman erhalten. Den Tag darauf hatten wir das unbeschreibliche Vergnügen den ersten Franzosen einrücken zu sehen. Wir hofften damals daß Cadiz sich kaum einen Monath würde halten können haben uns aber leider verrechnet. Es ist nemlich nicht möglich die Zufuhr durch Santi Petri den kleinen Küstenfahrern zu verschließen, so daß so lange als Geld da ist es nicht an Korn mangeln wird. Wenngleich also auch alles theuer ist so fehlt weder Brodt noch Fleisch und ohne einen ernsthaften Angriff kann es noch lange zögern. Um diesen zu machen haben aber die Franzosen noch keine Mannschaft genug. Ganz Spanien zu besetzen ist keine Kleinigkeit! Nun aber daß nach Murillo auch Ballesteros[3] kapitulirt hat werden sich hier 20 Tausend Mann versammeln und der Herzog von Angouleme[4] selbst wird in wenigen Tagen erwartet. Unterdessen sind auch einige 20 Bombardisten in Ordnung gebracht, so daß man dem <u>Bollwerk der Freiheit</u> von allen Seiten zusetzen wird. Die unglücklichen Einwohner von Cadiz seufzen unter dem Joch der Demagogen, die durch die allerfrechsten und ungereimtesten Siegesnachrichten ihrer Armeen, den öffentlichen Geist suchen aufrecht zu erhalten, nebenher aber Kontribuzion über Kontribuzion ausklopfen.

An Einquartirung mangelt es natürlich nicht, und obwohl die Franzosen sehr artig sind so leidet doch die häusliche Bequemlichkeit stark. Ich bin auf einen kleine beklommene Stube beschränkt die in den Hundestagen doppelt unangenehm ist: mir sind daher diese Sommermonathe noch drückender wie gewöhnlich gewesen und ich esse und schlafe weit weniger wie sonst. Gottlob daß mit diesem Monath das Aergste vorüber ist – Die Damen sind in high spirits, da sie alle Abend von einem Dutzend liebenswürdiger, hochadliger, ächter ultras umgeben sind, die Konstituzion und Riego auf das Innigste verabscheuen. Unbegreiflich ist es wie man den Soldaten dieselben Gesinnungen eingeflößt hat, und wie sie alle darauf brennen mit den sogenannten negros handgemein zu werden. Es sind übrigens prächtige Menschen, still, freundlich, guthmütig und allerwärts in dem besten Vernehmen mit ihren Wirthen. Von Religion lassen sie leider wenig Spuren blicken, obwohl sie ordnungsmäßig Meße hören. Ist ihr gutes Benehmen nur der militärischen Disziplin zuzuschreiben? oder sind die Franzosen von Natur moralischer als andere Völker?

Zwischen den Offizieren herrscht mehr Verschiedenheit. Die Leichtigkeit des Nazional Karakters, das Absprechen über jeden Gegenstand, das Herabsehen auf alles Nichtfranzösische verläugnet sich zwar bei keinem gänzlich. Es giebt aber Mehrere die durch Kenntniß fremder Sprachen ihren Gesichtskreis erweitert haben und dadurch sehr geistreich erscheinen. Eigentliches Gemüth und warmes Gefühl habe ich bisjetzt nur an einem entdeckt, dem Comte de Villeneuve[5] der daher auch am häufigsten im Hause erscheint. Taylor Mitherausgeber einer mahlerischen Reise durch das alte Frankreich[6] scheint mir viele Kenntniße zu besitzen.

Mit dem ersten Sch[iff] erhalten Sie die neue offizielle Madriter Zeitung,[7] woraus zu ersehen daß alle Städte das Alte (absolutismo e inquisicion) wieder haben wollen und daß sie jeden Gedanken von cameras oder representacion zurückweisen. Die Franzosen scheinen hingegen ein billiges repräsentatives System zu bezwecken. Was wird nun der König nach seiner Befreiung thun? Es ist eine verzweifelte Lage! Soll Spanien ruhig bleiben so muß das Unheil bis auf die Wurzel vertilgt werden, und alle die ansehnliche Stellen bekleidet haben müssen den spanischen Boden räumen, alle Freimaurerei muß mit Todesstrafe belegt werden und alle Verbreitung liberaler Ideen muß man strenge hemmen. Der Sinn der französ[ischen] Regierung scheint auf eine Versöhnung oder [illeg.] gerichtet zu sein die unmöglich ist. Jede Parthei würde nur zum Schein etwas einräumen. Der Zwiespalt ist zu groß: sie können nicht mehr neben einander existiren. Eine muß das Feld räumen, oder sie werden sich würgen bis zur Vernichtung. Traurige Zukunft für dieses unglückliche Land.

Ihr aufrichtigst ergebener
B.v: F.

123. Nikolas Heinrich Julius, Hamburg

Puerto, den 2 Sept[ember] 1823

Als der Herzog von Angouleme hier den 16 vorigen Monathes seinen Truppen zuvoreilend ankam, glaubten wir alle, daß unter der Hand alles abgemacht sei und daß er nur käme um unseren befreiten König in Triumph nach seiner Hauptstadt zurückzuführen. Wir haben uns alle geirrt. Wahrscheinlich sind die Vorschläge der Franzosen mit Spott von den Kadixer Demagogen zurückgewiesen. Nun mußte man endlich Ernst machen. Nun mußte man einsehen, was wir nicht müde geworden sind zu predigen daß dergleichen Gesindel nur der Gewalt weicht. Nach vielen (meiner Ansicht nach ganz überflüßigen) Maasregeln ward endlich in der Nacht vom 30. Aug[ust] die hinter einem Kanal aufgeworfene, mit 32 vierundzwanzig Pfündern besetzte Batterie der trocaderos von 500 Mann der Garde und einigen Comp[anien] Schweitzern in 10 Minuten mit Verlust von 12 Mann erstürmt. Mit Tagesanbruch ward der Feind weiter verfolgt und gänzlich von dem trocadero vertrieben. Von 2000 Mann die diesen interessanten Punkt besetzten, sind 500–600 getödtet c[irc]a 1100 gefangen und einige hundert haben sich mit Mühe auf den Kanonenböten gerettet. Die Franzosen behaupten, daß sie keine 100 Mann verloren haben. Das Resultat ist 54 Kanonen, gerade was den Franzosen mangelte, vielen Mundsvorrath, Munizion und Montirung und die Besetzung eines Punktes der die Verbindung zur See zwischen Cadiz und der Insel abschneidet und die Operazion des Bombardements sehr erleichtert. Noch denselben Tag haben die Kadixer Zeitungen von der Unüberwindlichkeit dieses Punktes geschwatzt und sich über die Schrecken lustig gemacht den diese prächtige Batterie den erstaunten Pariser Herrn einflößten.

Das Bombardement soll nun in einigen Tagen vor sich gehen und es wird ernsthaft sein. Die unglücklichen Einwohner von Cadiz hat man überredet es sei unmöglich und man werde die königliche Familie respektiren. Doch was haben diese Leute nicht der Welt aufgebürdet. Die Franzosen hatten einen gewaltigen Begriff von ihrer Kraft und Muth und die 200 Meilen die sie vor ihnen geflohen sind haben sie noch nicht entzaubern können. Der trocadero hätte von Anfang an auf dieselbe Art genommen werden können und Cadiz wäre lange bombardirt, könnte man die Franzosen nur von der absoluten Nichtigkeit und elenden Zaghaftigkeit des liberalen Gesindels überzeugen. Leider auch giebt manches Anlaß zu glauben daß mehere der chefs die Vertilgung und gänzliche Unterdrückung der Liberales <u>nicht</u> wollen. Dieses ist höchst traurig, um so mehr da die Serviles die solches merken, schon anfangen die Franzosen mit übelen Augen anzusehen, wozu das berühmte Dekret von Andujar den meisten Anlaß gegeben hat. Die Serviles wollen keine Kommune und keine Charta, sondern einen unabhängigen König und die Inquisizion und wollen die Franzosen eine wenngleich gemilderte Konstituzion einführen, so werden sich die Serviles mit ihnen schlagen.

Wir haben jetzt einen interessanten Rußen den Obersten Boutourtin hier den wir häufig sehen da er mir in Hinsicht von GeldSachen empfohlen ist. Ueberhaupt fügt es sich so daß ich unbedeutender Privatmann als verbindendes Glied die geheimen Triebfedern des wichtigen hier jetzt sich seiner Auflösung nähernden Ereignißes beobachten kann. Das Resultat einer solchen Anschauung ist natürlich kein anderes als daß manches Große sich in der Nähe verkleinert, doch kann ich auch Gottlob hinzufügen, daß manches Herrliche der gewöhnlichen oder allgemeinen Ansicht entzogen bleibt. Was könnte ich Ihnen nicht für edle Züge französischer Soldaten bei dem letzten Angriff erzählen! Die Schweitzer sind weniger gutherzig gewesen und es hat Mühe gekostet ihre Mordlust zu bändigen. Diesen Morgen hat der Herzog den versammelten Truppen die Ehrenzeichen vertheilt: es soll höchst rührend gewesen sein. Ganz vorzüglich hat sich der Prinz von Carignan[1] ausgezeichnet. Beim Waden durch das 4 a 5 Fuß hohe Wasser hat er einen Stiefel verloren. Auch unser Villeneuve ist einer der ersten auf der Schanze gewesen. – Die Kadixer Schurken werden natürlich sagen es sei eine Verrätherei gewesen oder eine Bestechung durch französisches Geld. – Den Herzog habe ich in der Muße am Tage St Louis gesehen: seine Figur gefällt mir sehr wohl, obgleich sie nicht ausgezeichnet ist. Sie verräth Gutmüthigkeit und Geradheit: seine Andacht ist erbaulich.

Es ist spät und ich muß schließen. Sehen Sie meine Mutter so sagen sie ihr daß Sie von mir wissen und daß wir alle wohl sind. Nur leide ich unbeschreiblich an Hitze die zuletzt gerade 22–23° war und noch ist. Gottlob das wir auch nicht eine Spur des gelben Fiebers haben.

Ganz der Ihrige
Böhl v. Faber

124. Nikolas Heinrich Julius, Hamburg

Puerto, den 3 Oct[ober] 1823

Es kann nicht fehlen daß Sie schon früher durch Eilboten von der großen Begebenheit unterrichtet sind, die den 1 October allen Freunden der Ordnung und Tugend unvergeßlich machen wird. Ja, Freund, am Mittag dieses Tages (gerade 100 Tage nachdem die Franzosen hier am 23 Juny erschienen waren) hatten wir die unbeschreibliche Wonne unseren guten König mit seiner ganzen Familie wohlbehalten bei uns landen zu sehen, wo Ihn der treffliche Herzog von Angouleme an der Spitze eines zahlreichen Gefolges erwartete. So wie der König die Treppe des Landungsplatzes erstiegen hatte wollte der Herzog ihm die Hand küßen welches der König nicht verstattete sondern ihn an sein Herz drückte. Die junge engelschöne Königin war so bewegt, daß sie kaum athmen konnte. Eine der Prinzeßinnen neigte sich nieder um den Boden zu küßen. Die Rührung war so groß daß wenige Augen trocken blieben und der ganzen Szene einen unerwareteten Grad von Feierlichkeit gaben der alles lärmende Jauchzen in Schranken hielt. Von beiden Seiten war alles im höchsten Putz. Der König hat sich mit einer liebreichen Würde benommen die den Franzosen besonders gefallen hat. Die Königin wird wie eine Erscheinung höherer Art von Allen verehrt. Von den liebenswürdigen und sehr hübschen Infantas sind sie bezaubert. Kurz wenn man es mit Augen sieht welche Familie das Stichblatt der Jakobiner Frechheit seit mehreren Jahren gewesen ist, so zittert man über den Abgrund von Bosheit zu welchem die gepriesenen liberalen Gesinnungen führen können.

Gestern ward ein feierliches Te Deum in der Priorial Kirche gesungen, dem die ganze königliche Familie, der Herzog von Angouleme und viele der vornehmen Spanier und Franzosen beiwohnten. Von der ganzen Familie und dem Herzoge ward es kniend angehört. Um 4 setzten sie ihre Reise nach Madrid fort. Jetzt bleibt nur noch die Besetzung des Isla und Cadiz durch französische Truppen übrig.

Die wichtigsten Ereigniße seit der Stürmung des trocadero waren am 20 Sep[tember] die Einnahme des Schloßes Santi Petri von der französischen escadre nach einer mehrstündigen heftigen Kanonade, wodurch der Uebergang des Meeresarm der den Isla von dem festen Lande trennt sehr erleichtert wird. Am 23 von 8 bis 10 ward Cadiz bombadirt. In den Gebäuden sind 55 Bomben und 87 Kugeln gefallen die zwar vielen Schaden gethan, jedoch glücklicherweise nur wenige Menschen verwundet haben. In den letzten Wochen hat man die Franzosen mit Unterhandlungen genarrt und es war alles zur Stürmung der Insel in Verbindung mit einer Landung von 4000 Mann unter dem General Bourmont[1] durch die Eskadron bereit, als plötzlich sich das Blatt wendete und ein königlicher Kammerherr die Ankunft des Königes mit seiner Familie meldete. Die geheimen Triebfedern dieser so plötzlichen Veränderung sind bis jetzt nicht bekannt. Ich der so gerne an Wunder glaube, halte es für ein Wunder desjenigen der alle Herzen lenkt. Man hat die ganze Familie aus Cadiz in größter Ruhe abziehen lassen, und der berühmte Cayetano Valdes[2] führte (als Admiral) selbst das Steuerruder des prächtigen Fahrzeuges welches den Liberales ihre letzte Hoffnung raubte.

Nun werden wir auch wills Gott unsere Einquartirung bald loos werden: seit dem 24 haben wir den französ[ischen] Gesandten Marquis de Lalarn mit mehreren Sekretären und einem Troß unverschämter Bedienten, die uns das Leben sauer machen.

Ueber Gibraltar habe ich bei Gelegenheit der Reise meines Neffen ein kleines Packet von Ihnen erhalten welches Cap[itain] Wallis anvertraut war; darin die ferneren Probebogen der Floresta einige Bücher und ein sehr interessanter Brief der lieben Campen den ich mit erstem Sch[iff] beantworte.

So eben erhalte noch das Ihrige vom 9 Sep[tember] dessen Beantwortung ich nothwendigerweise aufschieben muß, wenn dieser Brief mit der heutigen Post wegsoll. Theilen Sie ihn und meine Freude, meiner guten Mutter mit.

Ganz der Ihrige

Böhl v: Faber

PS. Aus ziemlich glaubwürdigen Quellen vernehme ich daß Valdes als er sich überzeugt daß die schändliche Comuneros dem König mit seiner Familie ermorden wollten, plötzlich in sich ging und obwohl ein eifriger Constitucional, die Befreiiung des Königes und vermuthlich der Constitucion dieser ungeheuren Mißethat vorzog. Ist dieses so, so verdient Valdes alles Lob.

B.

125. Nikolas Heinrich Julius, Hamburg

Puerto, den 15 Oct[ober] 1823

Cap[itain] Voß, der mir unbewußt während der ganzen Belagerung in Cadiz gelegen hat, entschließt sich plötzlich zur Abreise nach dorten und läßt mir nur eben Zeit ihm etwas Wein an Bord zu schicken. Darunter ist ein Fäßel D[r] J[ulius] für Sie bestimmt, diesesmal von 80 Bout[eilles] damit Sie den Freunden Perthes und Besser die Hälfte überlassen können. Das Recief erfolgt p[er] Post. Zugleich begleiten den jetzt schon warmen Redactor von Cadiz[1] während der Belagerung, als das Non plus ultra [damage] Truges, und der Mittel die angewendet worden den Geist des Volkes aufrecht zu erhalten. Dann eine gefüllte Epistel unseres trefflichen Arriaza, die er meiner Frau während der Belagerung zuschrieb – Der letzte Theil der Floresta kann diesesmal nicht gehen weil die Register noch nicht in Ordnung sind. Doch hat es damit auch keine Eile – Die politischen Sachen hier ordnen sich jetzt besser, als ich erwartete, doch bis der König in Madrid ist läßt sich nichts bestimmtes urtheilen.

Mit unwandelbarer Liebe der Ihrige
Böhl v: Faber

126. Nikolas Heinrich Julius, Hamburg

Puerto, den 10 Febr[uar] 1824

Werther Freund

Seit Anfang December da ich von Perthes factura und Conaiss[emen]t über eine Sendung Florestas und Bücher p[er] Cap[itain] Kirchhoff erhielt habe ich vergebens sowohl nach diesem Schiffer als nach sonstigen Nachrichten von Ihnen ausgesehen. Die Geschäfte haben sich dabei so sehr für mich gehäuft, daß einiger halbstündiger kursorischer Leserei ausgenommen, alle litterarische Beschäftigungen am Nagel gehangen sind. Eine schlimme Folge davon ist daß ich meiner idealischen Welt entrißen in einen zerrißenen Gemüthszustand verfallen bin, die Geschäfte interessiren mich nicht genug um mich ihnen ganz hinzugeben und beschäftigen mich doch zu viel um meine Geistesfreiheit zu behaupten. Daraus entspringt etwas Halbes, welches mißmüthig und gar zuweilen trübsinnig macht. Ich ernte dabei nicht die Anerkennung von dem Londoner Hause ein, welche dem Resultat meiner Anstrengungen angemeßen ist. Es muß in diesen gedrückten Zeiten zu den seltenen Fällen gerechnet werden in 3 Jahren (1821, 22 und 23) mit knappen Mitteln und schwankendem Kredit bei einer Weinhandlung 300.000 Thaler zu erübrigen, und dieses ist wahrlich keine Uebertreibung!

Von Einquartirung bin ich Gottlob seit October frei obwohl noch immer französische Truppen bei uns kantoniren. Diese habe ich meinem sonst sehr unbedeutenden Konsulat zu verdanken. Uebrigens aber sind meine häuslichen Verhältniße nicht sehr equickend. Meine Frau die so lange in Ueberspannungen aller Art gelebt hatte, ist aus Mangel an Reiz in Abspannung verfallen. Die Damen nennen solches Nervenschwäche und die daraus entspringen Erscheinungen sind gar nicht behaglich. Cecilia ist seit einem Monate mit ihrem Mann in der Landwohnung Dos Hermanas. Meine herzensgute Aurora empfindet doppelt und dreifach alle Beschwerden ihrer Mutter. Sie darf mir das nicht sein was sie mir sein könnte, aus Gründen die sich nicht sagen lassen. Meine jüngste Angela ist jetzt Gottlob von Gesundheit ziemlich wohl und trotz ihres kurzen Beines ein bildschönes Mädchen. Durch ihren Gesang vertreibt sie mir manche Grille und sänge sie unsere Volkslieder wie Rossinis Arien[1] so würde ich keine Opern vermißen.

Nächst dem Drang mich mit Ihnen zu unterhalten, schreibe ich diesen Brief um mir eine Abschrift Ihrer noch rückständigen Bestellungen auf spanische Bücher auszubitten. Zu Ende des Jahres (wo man seine Kopien gewöhnlich durchsieht) habe ich vergebens danach gesucht. Gott weiß wo sie steckt – Die Druckfehler der Floresta habe ich nicht gesandt, weil mir die letzten Bogen noch abgehen und Ihnen ein Theil zu nichts nütze ist. Daß die Handschrift des dritten Theils der Floresta beendiget ist glaube ich Ihnen geschrieben zu haben. Allein an die Spatziergänge ist noch keine Feder gesetzt. Ich muß eine andere Inspirazion abwarten. Ich habe den Londonern meinen Plan vorgelegt der mich des materiellen Theils meiner Arbeit entlediget. Ich kann so nicht fortfahren ohne meine Gesundheit und Ruhe aufs Spiel zu setzen. Wird er angenommen so gewinne ich wieder die gehörige Muße und entledige mich einer drückenden Verantwortlichkeit. Dann auch ziehen die Musen (ich fühle es) wieder bei mir ein und der alte Baum gibt noch wohl einige Früchte ehe er verdorrt.

Frappirt hat mich in den allerliebsten Balsaminen[2] die Erzählung von dem Bilde Marias in Nummern: sicherlich von dem Verfaßer mehrerer gleichartigen in den Oelzweigen. Sollten diese vorzüglichen Erzählungen je besonders gedruckt werden (so wie sie es verdienen) so säumen Sie nicht sie mir zu senden. Ist der Verfaßer bekannt?

Von Politik kann ich Ihnen nichts sagen. Daß alle unzufrieden sind versteht sich von selbst, denn nur sehr unterrichtete Menschen wissen daß ein wiedereingesetzter König weder alle seine Treuen belohnen noch alle seine Gegner bestrafen kann noch darf und daß gerade dieses die gräßlichste Folge aller Revoluzionen ist. Trefflich sagte dieses die Quarterly Review N[ummer] 57 p. 177 etc. So lange die Franzosen im Lande sind werden die Schurken nicht mucken, aber weiterhin? – Antworten Sie bald Ihrem treu ergebenen

Böhl v: Faber

127. Nikolas Heinrich Julius, Hamburg

Puerto, den 26 Märtz 1824

Endlich, werther Freund, ist die Flora mit der Sendung von November erschienen, begleitet von Ihrer Zuschrift vom 4.d[it]o – Das Quarterly Rev[iew] lese ich immer mit Vergnügen: N[ummer] 57 ist trefflich: auch in 58. ist ein geistreicher Aufsatz über die franz[ösische] Comödie.[1] – Die Vorrede zu Tiecks Vorschule[2] ist gediegen schön, in seiner besten Manier, die Novelle hinreißend, doch hätte ich lieber einen neuen Band des Phantasus gesehen.

Das Verzeichnis der hauptsächlichsten Druckfehler im 2. Bande der Floresta geht heute an Perthes mit Remise für den Belauf der 50 Abdrücke. Es sind verhältnismäßig nicht viele. Mit dem ersten Sch[iff] erfolgt die Handschrift des dritten Bandes. Blackw[ood's] (der mir im Sinken zu sein scheint) hat nichts weiter über die Floresta gesagt, wohl aber die Edinb[urgh] Rev[iew][3] in seinem letzten Januar Nummer, keine eigentliche Kritik sondern nur Aushängeschild um über die alte span[ische] Poesie zu dissertiren. Der Aufsatz ist gewiß von Jeffrey[4] selbst, schön geschrieben, mit einigen hellen Ideen, aber im Einzelnen unwissend, ungerecht und unpoetisch. Die preisenden Lobeserhebungen meiner Vorrede werden persiflirt, die religiösen Kindlichkeiten verlacht, dennoch wird die Sammlung excellent genannt. Mehr konnte ich von den Verächtern Wordsworth's und Coleridge nicht erwarten.

Wenn Sie die alten span[ischen] Bücher als eine Art Ersatz für die Hebammen Dienste bei der Floresta annehmen wollen, so bin ich damit zufrieden – Ihre Uebersetzung und Bearbeitung des Dr. Cheine[5] enthält für mich nichts Neues, als das Paradoxon über den Thee. Solche allgemeinen Regeln werden den Aertzten wenig Abbruch thun. Rumohrs Novellen werde ich mit Vergnügen lesen – Unsere Wein Geschäfte sind in Hinsicht der Federarbeit so geringe, daß ich nur aus Mildthätigkeit die zwei Personen die mir halfen nicht auf eine reduzirt habe – Wenn H[er]r G. D. Liborius mir aus Stettin berichten will, welche Qualität Jerez Wein dorten zu verkaufen wäre zu welchem Preis und auf welchem Weg sie hinzusenden sind, so werde ich vielleicht einen Versuch machen –

Meine Geschäfte als Weinversender sind noch immer im Wachsen, daher auch die Zeit zum Studiren immer beschränkter. An die Spatziergänge ist noch keine Hand gelegt. Ich bin aber Gottlob dabei gesund und munter. Meine Frau leidet viel an Nerven und ist in allerlei unfruchtbaren Grübeleien versunken. Cecilia mit ihrem Manne wohl, an ihrem vorigen Wohnort: auch die andern Töchter sind gesund.

Dieses p[er] Post in Eile. Mit dem ersten Schiffe länger

Der Ihrige

128. Nikolas Heinrich Julius, Hamburg

Puerto, den 11 April [18]24

Es ist mir angesagt daß in wenigen Tagen Cap[itain] Meyer nach Hamburg abgeht. Ich hätte gerne die fertige Handschrift des dritten Theils der Floresta mitgesandt, allein es fehlt noch ein Register der Verfaßer aller drei Theile. Das allgemeine Register der 1000 Dichtungen nach dem Alphabet ist beendiget. Meine Zeit ist noch immer sehr beschränkt da die Geschäfte dieses Hauses beständig im Wachsen sind. Indessen pflegen manchmal unerwartete Pausen einzutreten, die ich in solchem Fall eifrig zu benutzen denke.

Hiebei ein Brief von Lazo woraus Sie ersehen werden daß er mit dem Verschreiben von Barcelona nicht glücklicher gewesen ist als ich. Dabei die letzten Stücke seines Periodico. Die Herrn kämpfen noch immer tapfer <u>für</u> die ansteckende Eigenschaft des gelben Fiebers. Die französische Wachsamkeit während der Blockade ist ein Trugbild. Ein Schiff von der Havana wurde aufgebracht und in St Lucar ohne weitere Umstände zugelassen. Ich schmeichle mir daß die Periode des Fiebers hier vorüber ist, und daß es vors erste nicht wieder erscheinen wird. Solche periodischen Heimsuchungen gewißer Krankheiten sind, glaube ich, in der Geschichte der Arzneykunde schon bemerkt.

Ich benutze diese Gelegenheit Ihnen das interessante Werkchen über Hoffmann zurückzusenden.

Allen Verläumdern zum Trotze gehen die Sachen hier so ziemlich und besser als zu erwarten war. Hätte die Regierung nur die <u>Einsicht und den Muth</u> die Souveraineté über America aufzugeben und sich mit Handelstraktaten zu begnügen! – Dann könnte sie alle ihre Kräfte an die Organisirung des Mutterlandes wenden und besonders eine neue oder vielmehr <u>ausgesuchte</u> Armee einrichten und unterhalten. Den Feinden der katholischen Religion können Sie die gute Nachricht geben daß die Mannesklöster hier nach und nach von selbst aufhören werden da die Anzahl der Novizen gering ist. Bei den Nonnen hingegen ist starker Zudrang. Wer kann die weibliche Natur ergründen! Oder vielmehr wer hat irgend etwas <u>hier</u> ergründet. Mir wenigstens wird alles rätselhafter desto länger ich lebe. Um desto fester hänge ich an meinem <u>Glauben</u> der von oben <u>gegeben ist</u> und ohne welchen kein redliches Gemüth in Frieden bestehen kann.

Ihr aufrichtig ergebener
Böhl v: Faber

129. Nikolas Heinrich Julius, Hamburg

Puerto d[en] 28 May 1824

Ich schrieb Ihnen den 4 April mit einem Päckel welches meine Freunde Herrn Brerterfeldt über See nach dorten mitgenommen haben. Der Name des Schiffes und Schiffers ist mir aber leider entfallen.

Kürzlich ist mir einliegendes Recief in die Hände gefallen welches ich unterlassen habe Ihnen seiner Zeit einzusenden. Auch erinnere ich mich nicht, daß Sie mir eine bestimmte Anzeige des Empfanges dieses Fäßels gemacht haben. Kann das Rezief dienen, gut: haben Sie den Inhalt aber richtig erhalten so zerreißen Sie es nur.

Vor 14 Tagen erhielt ich unverhofft das Päckel mit der Wilhelmina und Ihre Zeilen vom 31 Märtz mit der interessanten Göth[e] Rez[ension] der spanischen Rom[ances][1] und mit letzter Post ist Ihr Brief vom 30 April erschienen und einer von Perthes vom 2 April. Ihr Brief vom 5 Märtz aber fehlt noch und ist wahrscheinlich verloren. In Hinsicht der Sendungen wiederhole 1) keine französ[ischen] Bücher die ich direkt erhalte 2) keine Duplikate: Hoffmann seine 20 Gedichte und Merle[2] sein unbedeutender Sermon sind doppelt erschienen 3) Flugschriften von wenigen Bogen sind der Kosten des Einbandes nicht werth – Schuberts Wanderbüchlein[3] ist eine der interessantesten Erscheinungen in unserer jetzt so matten deutschen Literatur. Die Oelzweige immer besser. Warum schließen sie mit dem 5t[en] Band? – Hoffentlich doch wohl nicht aus Mangel an Absatz? – Die Staatsmann immer trefflicher;[4] auch haben mich die letzten Stücke der Wiener Jahrbücher mehr als die früheren interessirt. Im Ganzen jedoch stehen wir weit gegen die jetzt so glänzende britannische Literatur zurück, mit der kaum Schritt zu halten ist hätte man auch Geld genug um alles lesenswerthe kommen zu lassen. Blackwood liefert immer noch neben den nicht nachlassenden so wohl verdienten Züchtigungen der Whigs, höchstliebliche innigst gefühlte Skizzen mancher Art. Nur das katholische Spanien und dessen bedauernswerther König wird von ihm ganz falsch beurtheilt, obwohl er darum die liberales nicht weniger durchhechelt.

Freund! Wenn der Nachtrag zur Bücher Kommißion 68 N[umme]r beträgt, wie hoch mag sich der Auftrag selbst belaufen haben! Es waltet ein unglücklicher Stern darüber. Gerade der Brief vom 5 Märtz der sie enthielt ist nie erschienen.

Ich beneide Sie um Ihren Besuch bei H[er]rn v. Rumohr. Seine italiänischen Novellen[5] haben mir viel Vergnügen gemacht. Von seinen tomos sueltos des Lope de Vega müssen Sie mir gelegentlich die Nummern und Inhalts Verzeichniß übersenden – Die liebenswürdige und innigst von mir geschätzte Frau von Rodde bitte ich meines lebhaften Andenkens zu versichern, auch sie zu ersuchen, sie möge die Güte haben ihren werthen Eltern meine dankbaren Erinnungen der Jahre 1806 bis 1813 mitzutheilen. Nicht weniger wünsche ich ihrem lieben Manne mein Gedächtnis und die Zusicherung meiner aufrichtigen Ergebenheit zu erneuern.

An den Geschäften bin ich gebundener als je, doch mit ziemlicher Lust da alles mir fortwährend gelingt und ich immer mehr Einsicht in die wirklich kunstvolle Behandlung der Weine erlange. Das Weinlager hat sich durch Zuziehung angränzender Gebäude und Plätze nicht allein vergrößert sondern ist auch ein angenehmer und fast romantischer Aufenthalt geworden. Mehrere Höfe sind mit Orange Bäumen und Granatäpfeln besetzt und einer mit Weinreben überzogen und beschattet. Durch die hohen vergitterten immer offenen Fenster spielen die Lüfte auf allen Seiten: auch fehlt es nicht an gefiederten Sängern. Dazu kommt das aus 150 eingebildeten Gründen meine Frau mit ihren Töchtern landwärtsein seit Ende vorigen Monathes eine Gesundheit sucht die sie nie verloren hat und eine Zufriedenheit die nur im Grunde des Herzens zu finden ist. Für mich ist daraus eine liebe klösterliche Einsamkeit entsprungen die ich seit Görslow entbehrt hatte und obwohl ich den größten Theil des Tages in der bodega mit den Arbeitern zubringe, so halte ich doch meine Mahle in tiefer Ruhe, kann um 9 Uhr die Hausthür schließen und mich um 10 niederlegen, in der Gewißheit nicht durch lärmende tertulianos aufgescheucht zu werden – In meinem Alter ist so etwas ein wahrer Genuß.

Wir werden von einer unerhörten Dürre geplagt und von stürmischen Ostwinden, die alles in Staub verwandeln, alles Laub verwittern und die Saaten schon jetzt zu Stroh machen. Die Quellen vertrocknen, die Thiere verschmachten und der Mensch sieht ängstlich einer trostlosen Zukunft entgegen. Der Preis des Weizens hat sich verdoppelt: Oel ist um die Hälfte gestiegen und Wein um ein Drittel. Manch möchte es wäre Schlafenszeit!!! –

Ihr getreuer B. v. F.

Mit dem ersten Sch[iff] nach Hamburg werde ich Ihnen die Weinproben für H[er]rn Liborius in Stettin schicken. Jetzt ist keines in Ladung.

130. Nikolas Heinrich Julius, Hamburg

Puerto, den 25 July 1824

Da man mir gemeldet hat, daß Cap[itain] D. H. Beuße führend das Sch[iff] Wilhelmine Ende dieses Monathes von Sevilla nach dorten unter Segel gehen wird so benutze ich die Gelegenheit Ihnen ein Kistel folgenden Inhaltes zuzusenden:

1) Die Handschrift des 3t[en] und letzten Theiles der Floresta, mit einem Register über die 3 Bände
2) 11 Hefte und 5 Bogen über das gelbe Fieber die endlich von Barcelona durch Vermittlung von Lazo erlangt geworden
3) Drei Hefte des Cadizer Periodico
4) 18 Pasatiempos von jedem 6 H[e]ft

5) Zwei Packete mit Bücher für meinen Sohn Juan, deren Uebersendung H[err] Berckemeyer wohl übernehmen wird
6) Ein Brief für H[er]r[n] Berckemeyer und
7) Ein schönes Gedicht des einzigen noch lebenden spanischen Dichters Arriaza.

Hiebei noch eine Einlage von Barcelona und eine andere von Lazo.
    Die Herrn in Barcelona haben keine Rechnung der Bücher schicken wollen.
    In gewöhnlicher Eile und Drang
    Ihr ergebenster
    Böhl v: Faber

131. *Nikolas Heinrich Julius, Hamburg*

Puerto, den 19 Nov[ember] 1824

Sie, bis jetzt ein so ordentlicher Korrespondent, haben mich, bester Freund, diesen Herbst gänzlich vergeßen. Die Ankunft des Cap[itain]s Beuße von Sevilla mit dem Kistel welches den 3t[en] Theil der Floresta und sonstige Sachen enthielt, weiß ich nur durch die erhaltene Antwort auf mehrere Briefe die ich mit ihm an andere Freunde geschrieben hatte – Dieses hat mich indessen nicht verhindert mich mit Ihren Bücheraufträgen zu beschäftigen und endlich ist es mir geglückt eine Kiste von Madrid zu erhalten die ich laut einliegendem Recief mit Cap[itain] Dirksen führend die Frau Maria an Sie abgeladen habe. Die zweite Auflage der Flora Peruana (schreibt mir Sanchez) ist nie erschienen und nach den übrigen Büchern Ihrer Liste hat er vergebens gesucht. Jetzt ist das Verzeichniß der noch fehlenden Bücher in Sevilla. Was aufzutreiben ist soll aufgetrieben werden. Die original factura der Bücher erfolgt hiebei und beläuft sich mit hiesigen Unkosten auf 457 Mark welche Sie nach Bequemlichkeit an dortigen H[er]n J[ohann] H[einrich] Berckemeyer für mich entrichten wollen. Cap[itain] Dirksen ist schon seit mehreren Tagen auf der Reise begriffen.

  In dem Recief ist ein Fäßel Wein begriffen welches mit den Verlegern der Floresta zu theilen bitte. Dieses ist von dem ältesten den wir besitzen und steht noch um einige Stufen höher als der vorige.

  Ihrem Freunde H[er]rn Liborius in Stettin schreibe ich nicht selbst um porto zu ersparen. Das Resultat seiner Berichte ist, daß der Stettiner Preis von 56 Thaler ungefähr <u>ein Drittel</u> des Preises ist den uns die Engländer für die ordinairste Sorte unseres Jerez Wein zahlen. Es ist demnach darüber weiter kein Wort zu verlieren. Eine Both des Weines den Sie mit C[apitain] Dirksen erhalten setzen wir den Engländern zu £80 an.

Ich finde daß noch ein Brieflein von Ihnen d[en] 27 May datirt unbeantwortet vor mir liegt. Die Oldenburger [illeg.] habe ich in mehreren spanischen Zeitschriften angezeigt gefunden, ich weiß aber nicht ob einige spanische Aertzte an deren Beantwortung denken – Die nachgetragenen Bücheraufträge sind der größeren Liste hinzugefügt.

Schade daß die neue Spanische Sprachlehre dänisch ist:[1] sie würde mich sonsten sehr interessirt haben.

Hier haben wir von dem fleißigen Navarrete den Prospektteil einer Sammlung der original Reisen spanischer Entdecker und Eroberer Americas,[2] ferner den langerwünschten neuen Druck des Cartas des filósofo rancio mit mehreren bis jetzt ungedruckten vermehrt und eine Coleccion eclesiastica española[3] die alles begreift was von spanischen Geistlichen zur Vertheidigung ihrer und der Kirche Rechte geschrieben ist. Letztere wird sehr gelobt und die erste Auflage ist vergriffen. Ich habe sie noch nicht gesehen. Die weitläufigen Geschäfte denen ich voranstehe, lassen mir nur Zeit zur leichten erholenden Leserei. Von Hamann habe ich gerade etwas gelesen, allein obgleich ich seinen Tiefsinn bewundere, kann ich mich doch nicht mit seiner Manier befreunden. Ich ermüde bald dabei, wie es mir vormals mit Jean Pauls Schriften ging. Meine Art Einbildungskraft eignet sich nicht zu so gewaltigen Sprüngen.

Die Engländer unterhalten mich noch immer am besten. Schade daß ihre Bücher so theuer sind. Sagen Sie mir, ob Sie dorten die wohlfeilen Drucke der besten englischen Werke haben, die Galigniani[4] in Paris besorgt. Auf alle Fälle lassen Sie Besser für mich verschreiben:

> Galignianis Magazine und Paris Monthly Review: so viele Stücke davon erschienen sind
>
> desselben Washington Irvin[g] Bracebridge Hall und Tales of a traveller[5]
>
> desselben Conversations of Lord Byron.[6]

In dem Magazine ist von der Floresta die Rede, ein Grund mehr um zu wünschen es sobald möglich zu erhalten.

Meine Tochter Cecilia lebt zufrieden mit ihrem Manne in Sevilla. Ich werde sie mit ihren Schwestern nächstens auf ein paar Tage besuchen und das Fest der heil[igen] Cecilia mit ihr feiern. Meine Frau kränkelt leider immer und lebt sich selbst und andern zur Last. Sie kann sich absolut nicht der Anbetung entwöhnen, die nur der Jugend und Reichthum gezahlt wird. Betrübte Leere! –

Unveränderlich der Ihre von Herzen

J. N. B.

132. Nikolas Heinrich Julius, Hamburg

Puerto, den 8 Märtz 1825

Daß Sie, werther Freund, meinen Brief vom 19 Nov[ember] so lange unbeantwortet gelassen haben wäre mir in allen Fällen verdrießlich gewesen. Nun aber ist Cap[itain] Dirksen mit den Büchern verunglückt und keine Zeile von Ihnen! Später schrieb mir J[ohann] H[einrich] Berckemeyer die ganze Ladung wäre gerettet und kein Wort abseiten Ihrer, so daß ich beständig in der unangenehmsten Ungewißheit in Hinsicht der Bücherkiste schwebe.

Zu meinem Trost erschien vor kurzem der Schwede der mir die Sendung vom 10. Nov[ember] und einen langen wenngleich sehr verspäteten Brief von Ihnen überbrachte. Ich ersehe daraus daß der letzte Band der Floresta in Leipzig gedruckt wird. Jede Individualität begründet natürlich Abstufungen in dem was minder oder mehr anspricht. Was mich am meisten ergreift habe ich im ersten Theil gegeben: ich habe immer geglaubt, daß der zweite Th[eil] (als sich dem Hergebrachten und Geregelten mehr nähernd) auch allgemeiner gefallen würde: der dritte Theil hat mehr sonderbares und ungewöhnliches. Das Ganze aber (glaube ich) ist ein treuer Spiegel spanischer Eigenthümlichkeit in allen ihren Richtungen. Die Spaziergänge sind nicht zu Stande gekomen: Sie wissen daß man sich zu so etwas nicht zwingen kann. Mein Geist ist nicht frei genug gewesen, weil ein böser Dämon meinen häuslichen Frieden untergraben hat. Meine Frau leidet seit 16 Monaten an einer Art Geistesverwirrung die dem Wahnsinn nahe verwandt ist und wodurch meine armen Töchter mehr gequält werden als ich. Nicht einmal das Mitleid kann eine solche Lage versüßen, weil dieser Zustand so sehr von ihrer Willkür abhängt daß er Fremden sehr selten bemerklich ist, ebendaher aber auch den Hausgenoßen doppelt hart fällt. Dieses unter uns.

Arejula[1] ist ein sehr bejahrter Mann, Erz-Jakobiner und Atheist den ich für fähig halte mit kaltem Blute den Kopf eines Königs oder Priesters abzusägen. Auch in Gibraltar hätte man ihn nicht gelitten: er ist entweder in Tanger oder NordAmerika.

Mit dem was die Edinb[urgh] Rev[iew] über spanische Dichtung sagt bin ich nicht ganz zufrieden, wegen der Beimischung von Politik. Ich glaube der Verfaßer ist Bowring: die Uebersetzungen aber sind sehr gelungen.

Es ist mir (in Hinsicht Ihrer selbst) gar nicht Recht, daß Sie Ihre alten Bücher verkaufen. Um so etwas zu thun muß man entweder den Geschmack dessen verloren haben, oder auch das Geld nötig haben, und beides sind Lagen in welchen man seinen Freund nicht sehen möchte. Wann indessen eine angenehme und zugleich litterarische Ausbeute gewährende Reise darauf begründet ist, so mag es sein.

Ich danke Ihnen für die Nachrichten aus den Ocios de Esp[añoles] emigr[ados][2] von denen mir wirklich der größte Theil völlig neu ist.

Was von Ihren Aufträgen aufzutreiben ist, soll mit der nächsten Sendung erfolgen. Von Madrid ist noch einiges nachgesandt. Ich dachte Sie würden mir nach dem Empfang der Kiste p[er] Cap[itain] Dirksen ein neues Verzeichniß des Fehlenden gesandt haben. Die neue Uebers[etzung] der Bibel von Amat[3] ist noch nicht ganz heraus: es fehlen noch einige Bücher des alten Testamentes. Von Escoiguez seiner Bibelübersetzung habe ich nie gehört.

Ihre Briefe über Paris sind nie erschienen.

Die Jahrgänge von Blackwood werde ich Ihnen um desto lieber schicken, weil sie bei dieser Gelegenheit dorten können eingebunden werden. Er liefert noch immer vortreffliche Aufsätze: mitunter aber auch muß man sich über seine protestantische Bigotterie ärgern.

Das Verzeichniß der hauptsächlichsten mir noch abgehenden alten spanischen Dichterwerke, sende ich Ihnen nächstens. Wiffen seinen Garcilaso[4] kenne ich aus dem Quarterly und das ist mir genug.

Das einzige rare Werk in der Bibliothek meines seel[igen] Onkels[5] (der sie von meinem Vater hatte) war ein Moreto in 3 Theilen.

Die letzte Sendung ist sehr gut. Die Geschichte der Hohenstaufen[6] cheint mir beim Durchblättern sehr brav, ist aber auch theuer und fürchte mich am Ende bei Perthes zu tief in Schuld zu gerathen. Spornen Sie ihn doch an, daß er mir ein conto court schickt, damit ich wenigstens weiß wie viel ich schuldig bin. Die 1001 Nacht[7] erfreuen mich sehr: daß Tiek seine schönen Mährchen so versplittert ist recht fatal: späterhin wird man sie in der Sammlung zum zweitenmal bezahlen müssen. Der Staatsmann immer kühn und tapfer. Collin über Stolberg vortrefflich![8]

Die Einlage an Lazo und nach Barcelona ist befördert: vom ersteren habe ich schon Antwort für Sie, mit einer Schrift über das gelbe Fieber in Pasages. Gebe der Himmel nur daß es nicht an Schiffsgelegenheit nach dorten mangele – Vielen Dank für die abgeschriebenen Lieder die sehr schön sind –

In der fisischen Natur scheint sich das Gleichgewicht verloren zu haben so wie in den moralischen. Dorten Ueberschwemmungen und hier schon ein zweiter Winter von einer solchen Dürre daß es zum Verzweifeln ist. Meine Reisepläne können sich nicht verwirklichen so lange nicht außerordentliche Umstände eintreten: für jetzt ist es wahrscheinlich daß ich meine Tage als Weinhändler beschließen werde – So aber oder anders bleibe ich Ihr wahrer Freund

B.

Da p. 384 gerade die letzte Seite ist so haben Sie auch die Liste aller Druckfehler die ich habe finden können.

133. Nikolas Heinrich Julius, London

Meinen Brief vom 8 Märtz werden Sie schwerlich noch in Hamburg erhalten haben.

Puerto, den 16 April 1825

Ihren Brief vom 4 Märtz habe ich, bester Freund, erst mit letzter Post erhalten. Es waltet ein Unstern seit einiger Zeit ueber unsern Mittheilungen und der so schwer zu ersetzende Verlust oder Verderb der Bücher p[er] Cap[itain] Dirksen ist eine Folge desselben. Es hat mich um so mehr gekränkt, da ich mir wenige Fahrläßigkeit in Hinsicht meines verspäteten advis vorzuwerfen habe. Es ist daher billig daß ich wenigstens einen Teil des Verlustes trage, und ich ersuche Sie demnach daher die 105 Mark Nachschuß von der 457 Mark (Belauf der factura) abzuziehen und nur 352 Mark an J[ohann] H[einrich] Berckemeyer für mich abzuschreiben. Recht ärgerlich sind auch die Defekte, wegen der Mühe und Zeit die es kosten wird sie von Madrid zu erhalten. Was Sie sonsten noch wünschen ist notirt und erfolgt mit erster Gelegenheit. Die Regierung ist am Ende auf die Ausfuhr der alten spanischen Buecher aufmerksam geworden und ein Verbot derselben ist schon erschienen oder wenigstens auf dem Stapel.

Der Druck der letzten Floresta ist recht sauber nur sind die Buchstaben weniger rund und daher nicht so angenehm für das Gesicht. In dem gesandten Blatte habe ich keinen Druckfehler gefunden.

Ich sende Ihnen diesen Brief nach London an der aufgegebenen addresse: in Edinburgh würde er Sie nicht mehr treffen. Seit dem Tode des Herrn Duff Gordon habe ich in England kaum persönliche Bekannte mehr und stehe daher auch in keiner andern Verbindungen, als pur merkantilische. Briefe an Londoner Kaufleute würden höchstens nur ein steifes Erben zu wege bringen, woran Ihnen nichts gelegen ist. Ich habe nie Gelegenheit gehabt in einen litterarischen Verkehr mit den trefflichen Wordsworth, Southey oder Coleridge zu treten; könnte ich jedoch England je besuchen so würde ich mich ohne besondere Empfehlungen die beiden ersten in dem romantischen Cumberland aufsuchen.

Ich sende Ihnen keine Liste altspanischer Buecher, erstlich weil mein Eifer in dieser Sache etwas erkaltet ist, zweitens weil, sollte sich dorten etwas auftreiben lassen, es mir gar zu theuer kommen würde. Im lyrischen Fach fehlt mir überdem nur weniges, und das sind gerade die fast verschwundenen kleineren Cancioneros und Romanceros des 16t[en] Jahrhunderts.

Ich hoffe Sie werden etwas über die Mitarbeiter von Blackwoods Magazine erfahren und wer die Leute sind die sich hinter den Namen von Chr[istopher] North,[1] Thomas Tickler, O'Doherty[2] und Y. Y. Y.[3] verbergen. Die drei ersten Stücke dieses Jahres die ich kürzlich erhalten sind prächtig. Ich nehme natürlich die höchstunwürdige Ansicht unsers katholischen Glaubens aus, welche die sonst so trefflichen Aufsätze des Y. Y. Y. entstellt – Auch wünschte wohl zu erfahren, wer die allerliebsten Lights und Shadows of Scotch Life[4] und die noch trefflicheren Trials of Margaret Lindsay[5] geschrieben hat – Jetzt lese ich mit großem Behagen die geistreichen Sayings und Doings[6] (die einem Theodore Hook zugeschrieben werden) – O! wie weit steht unsere Litteratur jetzt gegen die englische im Schatten! –

Gorostiza[7] zeigte einiges Talent in seinen ersten dramatischen Versuchen: der Liberalismus verwandelte ihn in einen elenden politischen Schmierer und seine jugendliche Heiterkeit in Gift und Galle.

Gerne höre ich was Sie mir von unseren dortigen Freunden sagen. Dortiges Klima ist sicher nicht reizend; allein Baron Voght und der Geheimrath v. Faber sind Zeugen daß es einen rüstigen Alter nicht zuwider ist.

Von Herzen wünsche ich, daß Sie den Zweck Ihrer Reise vollkommen erreichen mögen. Ich meines Theils bin jetzt schon zu eingewurzelt in meinen Berufsgeschäften um an Reisen denken zu können, es müßte denn sein daß mich meine Patronin für geleistete Dienste in Ruhestand zu versetzen geneigt werden möge –

Von Herzen der Ihrige

B:v: F.

134. Nikolas Heinrich Julius, Hamburg

Puerto, den 29 Aug[ust] 1825

Werther Freund

Ich erfuhr vor ein Paar Tagen daß das Schiff Wilhelmina Cap[itain] Beuße von Sevilla nach dorten segelnd sich in St Lucar einen Tag aufhalten werde. In Folge dessen habe ich zusammengepackt was ich für Sie vorräthig hatte und es erfolgt hinneben in Kiste [illeg.] J. N. B. Viele Mühe hat es gekostet diese Kiste an Bord zu schaffen, weil man jetzt (nach allbeliebter verkehrter Art) hier noch strenger über die Ausfuhr als die Einfuhr von Bücher wacht. Von Madrid habe ich die verschiedenen Defekte verschrieben allein nicht einmal eine Antwort erhalten. Es ist eine wahre Qual mit einer solchen Art von Menschen Geschäfte zu haben und es ist nur unsere alte Freundschaft die mich bewegen kann, mich noch ferner mit Kommißionen auf spanische Bücher zu befaßen.

Ich denke dieser Brief wird Sie in guter Gesundheit in unserer Vaterstadt antreffen und mit einer reichen Ausbeute Ihrer Reise in Groß Britannien. Der Sommer ist für mich sehr reich an Begebenheiten gewesen. Meine beiden Töchter haben gute ansehnliche Freier gefunden und vor Ende des Jahres werde ich mich in einer sehr willkommenen Abgeschiedenheit befinden die mir die Görslower Jahre ins Gedächtnis bringen wird. An litterarische Muße aber ist noch nicht zu denken. Die Weingeschäfte des Hauses nehmen noch immer zu und ich arbeite jetzt mit verdoppeltem Eifer, da es darauf abgesehen mir ein Fixes lebenslänglich zu sichern – Die Heirathen verursachen natürlich viele extra Unkosten. Ich muß mich daher einschränken und will also auch keine Bücher mehr von dorten haben bis ich wieder au courant bin. Von Perthes remittire [damage] 546 Mark – Davon 300 für 50 Hefte der letzten Floresta und der Rest a conto. Suchen Sie mir Abrechnung von ihm zu erhalten. Die Geschichte der Hohenstaufen sende ich zurück: theils habe ich keine Zeit sie zu lesen: theils ist sie zu kostbar.

Einliegend der Inhalt der Kiste. Wenn Sie die spanischen Bücher für sich behalten so ist es nicht nötig die Preise anzusetzen.

Unser Sommer hat seine gewöhnliche Hitze mit sich gebracht, indessen sind die Winde wenigstens kühl gewesen. Da ich nun in Paris und London von 27 a 28 Reaumur gelesen habe, so können wir uns über 22 a 23° nicht beklagen. Einige frühe Regenschauer haben uns bis 19 a 20 abgekühlt. Die Korn Erndte ist indessen knapp gewesen und die Weinlese wird auch nicht besonders ausfallen, obwohl reichlicher als im vorigen.

In Erwartung baldiger Nachrichten
Ihr aufrichtig ergebener
Bohl v: Faber

135. Nikolas Heinrich Julius, Hamburg

Puerto, den 20 Januar 1826

Ich war wirklich von Herzen etwas ungehalten auf Sie werther Freund, weil ich seit der englischen Reise keine Zeile mehr von Ihnen gesehen hatte, als ich vor wenigen Tagen zu derselben Stunde Ihren Brief p[er] Post vom 25 Nov[ember] und ein Packet p[er] Cap[itain] Lorenzen erhielt, in welchem sich Ihr interessanter Brief über England befand. Das Packet habe ich nur durch den sonderbarsten Zufall empfangen, weil versäumt war dem Cap[itain] einen separaten Brief mitzugeben, der von der Abladung Bericht ertheilte.

Wie freue ich mich, daß Ihre Reise so schön und glücklich ausgefallen ist, und Ihnen Genüße aller Art gewährt hat! Es fehlt darin nur Cumberland mit seinen Seen und Bergen, und die Bekanntschaft des ehrwürdigen Wordsworth, der für meine Sinnesart noch immer der erste aller Dichter ist, gerade weil er das Gewöhnliche mit dem Allerhöchsten zu verknüpfen weiß. In seinen Fußstapfen tritt der Verfaßer der trefflichen Romane Light und Shadows, Margaret Lindsay, und The Foresters, meinen Nachrichten zufolge Allan Cunningham[1] und nicht Wilson. Wie gerne hätte ich Sie auf dieser herrlichen Reise begleitet, allein die Zeit der Lustreisen ist für mich verstrichen. In meinem Alter muß Ruhe und Abgezogenheit der Zweck aller den Bestrebungen sein. Sehr angenehm ist es mir, daß Sie die Hauptabsicht der Reise durch die Liberalität H[er]rn Peele[2] so vollkommen erreicht haben, und hoffe daher auch recht bald die Wirkungen davon in denen dort nun aufzuführenden Gebäuden ans Licht treten zu sehen.

Ich bemerke daß Sie mich von aller Vergütung in Hinsicht der beschädigten Bücher frei sprechen, welches mir in meiner jetzigen Lage gut zu Statten kommt. Dagegen soll Ihnen der Lope de Vega in 21 Bänden nicht entgehen. Zu einigen Bänden des alten Theaters kann ich Ihnen wenig Hoffnung machen: doch bleibt es in petto angeschrieben.

Sobald ich den 3t[en] Band der Floresta erhalte, übersende ich die Druckfehler. Habe ich das ganze Werk erst vor mir liegen, so ermanne ich mich vielleicht zu den Spatziergängen. Einige neue Anregung habe ich kürzlich empfunden. Bowring hat in seinen Ancient poetry and romances of Spain (sie stehen in Perthes seinem letzten Verz[eichnis] fremder Bücher) von 193 Stücke die sein Werk enthält 158 aus den Florestas entlehnt. Sie sind sehr wohl gewählt und größtentheils trefflich übersetzt. Auffallend ist es daß ein solcher Radikal, so einen feinen Sinn für das einfach weise und sogar eigentümlich Katholische haben kann!– In Paris erklärt sich die Zeitschrift Globe[3] immer mehr für die neue liberale allseitige Kritik. In N[ummer] 1 des III Theils (25 Dez[ember] 1825) ist ein Aufsatz über die unités, der aus den Pasatiempos übersetzt zu sein scheint. Schade nur daß leider auch diese Zeitschrift eine falsche politische Tendenz hat. Es bleibt indessen angenehm frühere weniger beachtete Ansichten durchdrängen zu sehen und ich habe deshalb die Pasatiempos kürzlich mit erneuerter Billigung wieder durchgelesen. Mein elender Gegner Mora ist jetzt auch in London und schreibt Lobreden auf die heroischen Häupter der amerikanischen Insurgenten.

Ich kenne die Sammlung die von Sevilla nach dorten zum Verkauf geschickt ist: für mich enthält sie nichts; für Sie vielleicht einiges Historische.

Von Navarrete weiß ich daß nächstens der Oviedo als erster Theil der spanischen Geschichtsbücher über Amerika erscheinen wird, so wie auch der 7. Theil der Memor[ia]s de la Acad[emi]a.[4]

Die Defekte in der Paleografia Española[5] sind von mir sorgfältig verzeichnet und dem Madriter Kommißioner eingesandt. – Die Sachen von Cadiz sollen mit erster Gelegenheit erfolgen.

Es ist wohl daß Perthes mir für die überlieferten Spanischen Bücher 40 Mark vergütet haben. Von der Colecc[ion] eccl[esiastica] ist nichts weiter erschienen und schon der letzte Band war ein Supplementband.

Ich muß jetzt wiederholen daß ich meine Ausgaben auch in Büchern beschränken muß und Sie mir also vors erste nichts senden müssen, als was ich ausdrücklich auftrage. Die Fortsetz[ung] und Schluß der 1001 Nacht so wie auch des Staatsmannes habe ich gerne erhalten, aber M[aler] Müllers Werke[6] und Grillparzer Ottokar[7] sind ein Ueberfluß: auch will ich die Wiener Jahrbücher nicht fortsetzen. Den Blackwood lassen Sie bei sich liegen biß ich in fordere. Seitdem er sich so wüthend gegen die Katholiken erklaert hat ist er in meiner Gunst gesunken.

Als Engländer (d.h. reformirter Engländer) bin ich auch gegen die völlige Gleichstellung der Katholiken, weil der eifrige katholische Geist den verschlafften gleichgültigen Protestantismus <u>nach und nach</u> sicherlich ganz verdrängen würde, allein darum muß man den katholischen Glauben nicht verläumden und verunglimpfen.

Von meiner Familie nichts als Gutes. Cecilia wieder in Sevilla, nachdem sie die Schwestern unter der Haube gesehen hat. Wollen Sie ihr etwas angenehmes senden, so seien es Houwald's dramatische Arbeiten[8] welche ihr besonders gefallen. Aurora lebt mit ihrem Mann in Cadiz in höchstem Ueberfluß und geliebt und geschätzt wie sie es verdient. Angela ist mit ihrem Mann noch bei uns, wird uns aber Mitte Märtz verlassen und 4 Wochen in Chiclana zubringen – Ich immer bis über den Ohren in den Weingeschäften, und daher für alles Geistige gleichgültiger als ich sein sollte. Ich fühle mich jedoch gedrungen meine ganze Thätigkeit dem Wirkungskreise zu widmen welchen mir die göttliche Vorsehung so bestimmt angewiesen hat. Mein letzter Endzweck bleibt immer eine sorgenfreie Ruhe dorten. Das <u>Wann</u> ist oben verzeichnet! Ganz der Ihrige

B.v.F.

136. *Nikolas Heinrich Julius, Hamburg*

Puerto, den 17 Febr[uar] 1826

Werther Freund

Ihr lieber Brief vom 13 Dec[ember] ist beinahe zwei Monathe unterwegens gewesen. Ich vermuthe daß Sie und Perthes um mir Porto zu sparen Ihre Briefe mit Fracht nach Paris senden. Deswegen sind vielleicht einige verloren gegangen und andere so spät angekommen. Ich erbitte mir daher jede interessante Mittheilung p[er] Post von dorten direkt.

Was Sie mir über eine neue Auflage des ersten Bandes der Floresta sagen ist mir in jeder Hinsicht angenehm. Ich freue mich, daß die allgemeine Stimme meinen Geschmack bestätigt. Ich freue mich daß der religiöse Sinn (ohne den man die Floresta weder verstehen noch genießen kann) so viel mehr verbreitet ist als ich es zu ahnen wagte. Ich freue mich daß P[erthes] und B[esser] für ihre grosmuthige Uebernahme des ersten Druckes nunmehr entschädigt werden.

Einige Aenderungen auf der letzten Seite.

Gestern Abend habe ich endlich die 36 Abdrücke des dritten Theils erhalten, und zwar nur durch einen Zusammenfluß günstigen Umstände. Zuförderst war Cap[itain] Beuße nach Sevilla bestimmt und nicht nach Cadiz. In Sevilla ward es für ganz unmöglich erklärt die Bücher ans Land zu bringen. Eine gute Seele (die ich noch nicht ausgekundschaftet habe) transportirte die Packete nach St Fernando und von daher habe ich die <u>unter französischem Schutz</u> empfangen. Ich werde ihn jetzt genau durchgehen und die Liste der Druckfehler soll nicht lange ausbleiben. Die form der Buchstaben ist nicht angenehm und ermüdet weit mehr als die anderen Theile, wegen Mangel an Ründung.

Cap[itain] Beuße hat für Sie ein kleines Packet an Bord mit dem fehlenden N[umer]o des Periodico medico de Cadiz und den einzelnen Abdrücken so wie auch zwei Abdrücke des Romancero del Cid. Erhalte ich die von Madrid verschriebenen Defekten so erfolgen sie mit derselben Gelegenheit.

Es erschien bei mir vor Kurzem ein Graf Panin, bei der Rußischen Gesandtschaft in Madrid angestellt. Nie habe ich einen so vielseitig gelehrten und gebildeten Mann von seinem sehr jugendlichen Alter getroffen. Er ist enthusiastisch für alles nazionale, also auch für spanisches Theater und Dichtkunst. Die Florestas interessiren ihn daher sehr. Er hat einen Briefwechsel mit mir begonnen, den ich gerne fortführe.

Stets Ihr treuergebener
J. N. Böhl v: Faber

Wieviele Abdrücke wurden von dem 1ten Band der Floresta gezogen? –

137. Nikolas Heinrich Julius, Hamburg

Puerto, den 17 Märtz 1826

Versprochenermaßen erfolgt hiemit, bester Freund, die Anzeige der Druckfehler der dritten Floresta, die leider in größerer Anzahl vorhanden sind, als in den vorigen. Finden Sie es schicklich, so mag die Anzeige der fehlenden Kommas wegbleiben. Bei genauer Durchgehung dieser Sammlung habe ich mich aufs Neue von deren Trefflichkeit überzeugt. Der matten Stellen giebt es nur wenige. Die wenigen Kenner in meiner Umgebung loben diesen Band noch mehr als seine Brüder. Einer wünscht in der neuen Ausgabe die Gedichte mit Ueberschriften versehen zu erblicken. Bei den größeren Stücken ginge dieses wohl an: bei den kurzen würde ich es störend finden. Dann auch würde die Oekonomie der Anordnung gestört werden, auf der ich mehr Fleiß verwandt habe als sichtbar ist.

Cap[itain] Beuße ist leider so schnell wieder nach dorten zurückgesegelt, daß mein kleines Packet für Sie mit den in Cadiz gedruckten Sachen mir wieder von Sevilla zurückgesandt ist und jetzt eine andere Gelegenheit abwarten muß. Von Madrid habe ich noch keine Antwort in Hinsicht der Defekte erhalten, obwohl ich meine Anforderung erneuert habe.

Hiebey ein an Perthes und Besser endoßirter Wechsel von 269 Mark mit Bitte, ihn einzukaßiren und mir in Rechnung zu vergüten.

Ich bin jetzt aufs Neue für die alte spanische Poesie belebt geworden, und wenn (wie es scheint) diesen Sommer unsere Verschiffungen nach England minder lebhaft sein werden, so findet sich wohl Zeit zu einer Ausarbeitung des spanischen Theaters.

Meine Familie ist wohl. Die ältesten mit ihren Männern in Sev[illa] und Cadiz; die jüngste mit ihrem Manne noch immer bei uns. Nächsten Monath jedoch wird das Regiment nach Chiclana verlegt.

Treu ergebenst der Ihrige

Böhl v: Faber

Mit N[ummer] 809[1] (welche ich auswending weiß) beschwichtige ich manche schlaflose halbe Stunde.

138. Nikolas Heinrich Julius, Hamburg

Puerto, den 5 July 1826

Endlich, bester Freund, hat sich eine Schiffsgelegenheit nach dorten angefunden und Cap[itain] Meinerts führend die Cristina Elisabeth hat, neben diesem Brief, eine Kiste Bücher fuer Sie mit D[r] J[ulius], welche Ihnen H[er]r J[ohann] H[einrich] Berckemeyer gegen Entrichtung von Fracht und Spesen wird verabfolgen. Solche enthält

1) 4 Exemplare der neuen Coleccion de viajes von Navarrete die mich sehr interessirt haben. Es ergiebt sich daraus, daß Colon wenngleich ein großer Mann doch die Indianer hart und grausam behandelte und demnach mit Recht von den katholischen Herrschern bestraft wurde. 340 Reales –
2) Der fuenfte Theil des Filosofo rancio 20 Reales, zusammen 360 Reales – oder 60 Mark die Sie gelegentlich an Perthes fuer mich zahlen werden
3) Ein anderes Exemplar des Filósofo rancio
4) Von englischen Büchern: Galignanis Magazine, Points of humour,[1] Points of misery,[2] The Liberal N[ummer] 1–4.[3] The last man 3 Th[eile][4] – Margravine of Anspach 2 Th[eile][5] – Letztere sind verächtlich: the last man mit großer Kraft geschrieben allein so gräslich daß ich es den Augen meiner weiblichen Familie entziehen muß
5) Von deutschen Buechern: Hamann Werke, mit dessen Darstellungsweise ich mich nicht befreunden kann obwohl ich seinen Tiefsinn verehre. Verschiedenes von Grillparzer, Görres, den Griechen und Landt[6] –

Alles dieses um nachdem Sie es nach Belieben benutzt haben, gelegentlich einer Bücherversteigerung beizufügen und das Produkt an Perthes einzuhändigen – Das frueher zubereitete kleine Packet mit dem Romanc[er]o del Cid und periodica de medicina ist gleichfalls in der Kiste befindlich.

Wollen Sie wohl glauben, daß ich bis jetzt noch keine Antwort von Madrid über die defecta habe erhalten können! – Man muß wirklich allen litterarischen Verkehr mit Spanien aufgeben.

Jetzt beantworte ich Ihr liebes vom 12 May woraus ich den begonnenen zweiten Abdruck der ersten Floresta gerne ansehe. Ein Dutzend davon bitte mir seiner Zeit zukommen zu lassen, so wie auch noch einige des dritten Theils. Wenn auch die eigentliche Volksdichtung zu Grabe geht, (weil die liebe Aufklärung alles volksthümliche vernichtet) so finde ich dagegen, daß der Sinn für solche bei den eigentlich Gebildeten immer lebendiger wird. Die Sammlungen die Sie anführen beweisen dieses. Wenigstens wird sich erhalten was bisjetzt zu retten war. Ob ich etwas weiter für die Spanische Poesie thun werde bleibt unbestimmt. Die Verlegung meiner Wohnung nach den bodegas (der in einigen Monathen vor sich gehen wird) kann möglicherweise ein Anstoß dazu werden. Ich werde alles mehr zur Hand haben und nicht so viele Zeit mit hin und her Kreuzen zwischen bodegas, comptoir und Wohnstube verlieren.

Ich habe die Rezension des englischen Werkes über die Minnesinger[7] mit Vergnügen gelesen. Ich ziehe mit Ihnen Bowrings Uebers[etzungen] aus dem Spanischen denen des Lockhart[8] weit vor. Letztere sind parafrastisch, welches bei schlichten alten Liedern und Balladen besonders übel angebracht ist.

Weder Mayans Origenes noch Guzman de Alfarache sind in Cadiz verkäuflich! – Es fehlt nur noch daß auch der D[on] Quijote ausgeht.

Ich würde Calderons Schauspiele nach Fächern ordnen: 1) Comedias heróicas 2) de capa y espada (Intrigenstück) 3) Tragedias 4) históricas 5) mitológicas 6) eigentliche Lustspiele

Mit dem braven Vial stehe ich leider in einem etwas unbequemen Verhältniß. Er war so edelmüthig meiner Frau in ihrer ehemaligen verlassenen Lage £60 – vorzustrecken, welche noch nicht bezahlt sind. Leider habe ich solche seitdem noch nicht erübrigen können.

Woodstock[9] habe ich mit großer Freude in einer französischen Uebersetzung gelesen. Ich finde nur die Fantasmagorie in dem Schloße darin auszusetzen: sonsten halte ich es für eines der gelungesten Werke dieses großen Geistes. Der Kavalier ist herrlich von Anfang an bis zu dem rührenden Ende. Der König ist brav und Cromwell sehr gelungen.

Ich wußte nicht daß die gute alte Räthin ihrem Manne gefolgt sei.[10] Wahrlich ein edles deutsches Herz von altem Schrot und Korn. Wie kommt Vieweg fort?

Butlers Book of the Catholic Church[11] habe ich, so wie auch die Vertheidigung. Die unwandelbare Gleichmüthigkeit dieser trefflichen Kämpen unserer Kirche hat sicherlich nicht ihresgleichen in den Annalen der Polemik. Wie sticht sie ab gegen die bittere Lieblosigkeit des abtrünnigen Blanco White![12] der alle katholischen Geistlichen Spaniens für Atheisten erklärt! – Ecksteins le Catholique[13] der in Paris erscheint, macht viel Aufsehen und ich hoffe ihn bald direkt zu erhalten.

Allem diesen zu Trotz ist unser Wissen Stückwerk und die Stunde der Erlösung und endlichen Aufklärung dieses großen Räthsels a consummation devoutly to be wished. Ich bin <u>zeitlich</u> beglückt so wie Wenige: dennoch jauchze ich innerlich jedesmal daß ich danke wie wenig Zeit mir noch zur Vollendung fehlt.

Ihr treu ergebener B:v: F:

139. Friedrich Perthes, Hamburg

Puerto, den 30 Märtz 1827

Ich habe, werthster Freund, Ihre beiden Mittheilungen vom 16 Märtz und 26 Dec[ember] mit dem größten Interesse gelesen. Daß Ihnen bei Ihrer Sinnesart häusliche Liebe und Pflege ein Bedürfniß ist, begreift gewiß niemand besser als ich und so billige ich vollkommen ihre zweite Verbindung. Aus dem Reiche der <u>allgemeinen</u> Liebe sehen die Seligen gewiß mit Freude auf jeden neuen Bund dieser Art nieder.

Der frühseitigen Tod des guten Bessers ist mir sehr nahe gegangen. Doch was wissen wir von Gottes Wegen? Für Sie entspringt daraus die Nothwendigkeit einer verdoppelten Thätigkeit, wozu ich Ihnen von Herzen Kraft und Gesundheit wünsche. Ich begreife jetzt woran es lag daß unsere Rechnung so lange unberichtiget geblieben.

Ich bemerke was Sie mir über die Floresta melden. Ich zweifele nicht daß in spanischen Amerika Begehr darnach sein werde: die spanischen Zeitschriften in London sollen viel zu ihrem lob gesagt haben. Auch hier fängt man an darnach zu fragen. Ich stehe aber kein Exemplar ab (weil ich sie nur an <u>Würdige</u> verschenke) und verweise immer an die Verleger dorten.

Das Connais[sement] über Bücher p[er] Cap[itain] Ebbesen habe ich erhalten. Dieses Sch[iff] ist noch nicht erschienen. Vergeßen Sie übrigens nicht, daß ich außer den Fortsetzungen nur das ganz <u>vorzügliche</u> zu erhalten wünsche, woran leider seit mehreren Jahren ein arger Mangel in Deutschland ist.

140. Nikolas Heinrich Julius, Hamburg

Puerto, den 1 Juny 1827

Seiner Zeit erhielt ich, werther Freund, das Ihrige vom 16 Dec[ember] sehr verspätet; ich bemerke Ihre Anzeichnungen und bin mit Perthes in unserer Rechnung akkord.

Ich freue mich daß Ihnen Navarretes Sammlung gefallen hat: der 3t[e] Theil soll diesen Sommer erscheinen. In N[ummer] 70 des Quarterly Review[1] wird das Buch wegen serviler Tendenz hart mitgenommen, dahingegen gewiße Notic[ia]s Secretas über America (angeblich von Ulloa und Jorge Juan)² sehr gepriesen. Ich zweifle an der autenticität dieser Notic[ias] secretas.

Ihre Bücher order ist bemerkt und wird mit erstem Sch[iff] erfolgen, allein von Madrid her ist es mir noch nicht gelungen eine Antwort zu erpreßen und ich fürchte wir werden die Hoffnung die Defekte je zu erhalten aufgeben müssen.

Die Irländischen Fairy Tales³ haben mir viel Freude gemacht, besonders die komischen – Wie wäre es möglich daß Ihre edle warmherzige kleine englische Schrift Anlaß zu Tadel geben könne! – Aufrichtig gesagt war ich und bin auch jetzt noch nicht in der Stimmung christlich – erhabene Ansichten dieser Art nach Würden zu schätzen. In meinen religiösen Gefühlen ist eine Ebbe eingetreten die mich innerlich verdorrt und verhärtet. Gott gebe daß eine neue Fluth mich bald wieder erquicken möge.

Kein Wort wird hier über Portugal weder gedruckt noch auch gewechselt und die Sachen dorten verdienen es auch wahrlich nicht, daß man sich damit beschäftige.

Unser voriger Sommer war ein gewöhnlicher hier, trocken und warm, doch nicht übermäßig. Der Winter mehr Regen als die vorigen und daher dem Lande günstiger. April und May besonders frisch und angenehm – Sonst alle Meinigen wohl. Den 31 Dec[ember] wurde ich durch meine Tochter Aurora Großvater eines allerliebsten Mädchens Maria Manuela Rafaela getauft – Ach! Freund! wie hart ist das Schicksal daß es uns Gleichgesinnte so entfernt von einander hält! –

Unwandelbar ganz der Ihrige B:v: F:

141. Friedrich Perthes, Hamburg

[Puerto], den 1 Juny 1827.

Durch mehrere Zufälligkeiten hauptsächlich eine Umhausung, ist dieser Brief bis heute liegen geblieben, welches mich in den Stand setzt Ihnen den Empfang des Packetes mit Cap[itain] Ebbesen anzuzeigen. Für das schöne gebundene Exemplar der Stolbergschen Werke empfangen Sie meinen besten Dank: da Sie es mir nicht in der Rechnung belasten muß ich es als ein Angebinde ansehen, und kein paßenderes kann es für mich geben als die Ergöße dieser herrlichen Geister die der so gesunkenen Menschheit überhaupt und uns Deutschen insbesondere so viele Ehre machen. Ueber die Rechnung habe ich nur zu bemerken daß Sie mir die zwei Theile von Seckendorfs Wörterbuch und ich weiß nicht wieviel Abdrücke der Floresta schuldig bleiben, wogegen ich mich gleichförmig in <u>486.4 Mark</u> Ihr Schuldner erkläre.

Aus den Wiener Jahrbüchern lerne ich einen originellen Dichter H[einrich] Heine¹ kennen, dessen Werke ich zu erhalten wünsche. Senden Sie mir auch gelegentlich Houwalds Schriften, sowohl sein Theater, als seine vermischte Schriften; auch Tieks Dramaturgische Blätter[2] alles in Pappe gebunden. Auch die neue Auflage von Musäus Volksmährchen.[3]

In meiner äußeren Existenz bleibt mir wenig zu wünschen übrig. Wenn auch die verheiratheten Töchter jede ihr kleines heimliches Kreuz zu tragen haben, so liegt das an der Gebrechlichkeit die uns allen anklebt. In der Hauptsache ist es bei allen richtig. Nur eine hat mich bis jetzt Großvater gemacht, womit ich ganz zufrieden bin. Ich finde das Leben nicht so reizend um mich über eine jede Geburt so sehr zu freuen. Ich sage vielmehr täglich mit dem trefflichen La Martine:

Je ne veux pas d'un monde ou tout change ou tout passe
Ou, jusqu'au souvenir tout s'use et tout s'efface:
Ou tout est fugitif, perusable, incertain
Ou le jour du bonheur n'a point de lendemain[4]

Der zweite Theil seiner Meditations hat mich noch mehr angesprochen als der erste. Niemals hätte ich geglaubt daß ein <u>französisches</u> Gemuth so fühlen und <u>französische</u> Worte solche Gefühle ausdrücken könnten.

Ueber mein <u>Inneres</u> habe ich mehr Klagen zu führen. Periodische Launigkeiten sind zwar die Quaal aller suchenden Seelen: allein im reifen Alter leidenschaftliche Anfechtungen, die ganz von Gott abwenden, und denen man nicht widersteht weil der rechte Wille zum widerstehen mangelt, dieses erniedriget um so tiefer, wenn man in früheren Zeiten ganz anders war. Und doch bleibt nichts anders übrig als von der <u>Zeit</u> die Beschwichtigung des Sturmes zu erwarten – Und wenn während dem der Baum fiele!!! – Um den inneren Frieden ist es geschehen, so lange das Harren dauert. Meine Gesundheit hatte darunter gelitten: ich erhole mich aber jetzt da die Raserei des Gefühls im Sinken ist. Halten Sie mir, werther Freund, diese kleine Ausschüttung zu gute: nur einem gleichgesinnten, liebevollen und weltkundigen Manne läßt sich so etwas sub rosa sagen.

Mit treuer Anhänglichkeit verbleibe ich stets
Ihr ergebenster
J. N. Böhl v: Faber

Von der neuen Ausgabe Göthes[5] will ich nichts bis sie vollendet ist.

142. *Nikolas Heinrich Julius, Hamburg*

Puerto, den 19 Oct[ober] 1827

– Ihre Briefe, werther Freund, versetzen mich immer in eine andere und geistig bessere Welt als die in welcher ich zu hausen bestimmt bin. Welche edle Zwecke die Ihrige und wie selbstich im Vergleich die meinige! Doch wenn Sie mich gleich beschämen, so liebe ich Sie darum nicht minder. Cecilia wird von der Landstelle wo sie jetzt hauset die kleine Schrift und Zueignung beantworten – Ich danke für die lieben herzlichen Bücher des guten Heise[1] – Das letzte Sch[iff] nach Hamburg ist mir bei meiner Entfernung von Cadiz leider entgangen. Jetzt soll das Nächste die bestellten neueren Sachen (die lange in meinen Händen sind) unfehlbar für Sie mitnehmen – Mir hätte ein Abdruck der Romancero general viel interessanter geschienen als der so sehr vervielfältigte des Cid. Da er aus 13 partes besteht, so könnte er parteweise erscheinen – Mit dem neuen Schauspielhause und dem neuen Jungfernstieg machen Sie mir den Mund wässern, allein ich bin nun einmal an die Weingaleere geschmiedet und muß verharren bis zum ausspannen. – Von dem letzten Packet von Perthes haben mich die Schriften des ruchlosen Heine außerordentlich interessirt. Ich ärgere mich blau und blaß an ihm und werde nicht müde ihn zu lesen. Die Nordsee[2] sind ganz originale Gedichte und der darin waltende humour spricht mich recht eigentlich an. Wenn er aber den kleinen Byron spielt und seiner abgeschmackten Vergötterung Bonapartes die Zügel schießen läßt, dann ist er um so widerlicher da man es bei seinem Geiste nur als eine bezweckte Verhöhnung des Publikums ansehen kann, gleichsam als wolle er sehen wieviel sich die deutschen Leser bieten lassen. Die Wiener Jahrbücher haben ihn viel zu gelinde behandelt. Demohngeachtet brenne ich auf den dritten Theil der Reisebilder,[3] oder irgend etwas von ihm. Das originelle ist so rar, daß man es auch übersalzen und überpfeffert verschlingt. Von den kürzeren Liedern weiß ich ein halb Dutzend auswendig ohne es beabsichtiget zu haben – Nächstens ein Mehreres.

Ganz der Ihrige Böhl v: Faber

143. Nikolas Heinrich Julius, Hamburg

Puerto, den 28 Maertz 1828

Bester Freund

Ihr lieber Brief vom 21 Nov[ember] ist leider so lange unbeantwortet geblieben, weil man mich in Cadiz immer mit einer Schiffsgelegenheit vertröstete, die aber bis jetzt unerfüllt bleibt. Von Sevilla geht ein Cap[itain] Bückman nach dorten: es ist aber fuer alles wegen den Zöllnern und Mauthvorstehern so weitläuftig daß ich es habe aufgeben Bücher für Sie über Sevilla abzusenden. Was ich übrigens für Sie habe sind nur die neugedruckten Werke: alle Hoffnung etwas Altes und Seltenes in Spanien aufzutreiben muß gänzlich aufgegeben werden und ich bin überzeugt daß sich nur in London noch etwas dergleichen auftreiben läßt.

Wenig dachten wir daran, als wir uns mit Plänen über meine Reise unterhielten, daß meine gute Mutter ihrem Manne so bald folgen würde![1] Ich habe sie von

Herzen beweint, bin aber sehr ruhig wenn ich an ihr hohes Alter und sanftes Ende denke. Ich danke Gott daß sie einen Brief von mir nicht mehr erhalten worin ich die Unmöglichkeit meiner Reise für dieses Jahr zu erklären gezwungen ward. Es sind so viele Angelegenheiten meiner besten Freunde in meinem hiesigen Wirkungskreis verwebt, daß ich wahrlich nicht weiß wie eine Abwesenheit von 4 od[er] 5 Monathen möglich zu machen ist. Daß ich auch, ohne den Zweck meine gute Mutter zu umarmen, mächtige Antriebe zu einem Besuch der Vaterstadt habe, kann Ihnen nicht entgehen. Wie gerne wäre ich nicht Zeuge der Niederlassung und Heirath meines einzigen so geliebten Sohnes, die wahrscheinlich diesen Sommer Statt finden wird! Wie würde ich mich freuen Schwester Bruder und Nichten, Sie, Campens, Perthes und sonstige Freunde wieder zu sehen. Wie sehr würden mich die Verschönerungen Hamburgs, das neue Schauspielhaus und Webers Opern ergötzen! Ich gebe also den Plan keinesweges auf, aber den Zeitpunkt kann ich nicht bestimmen.

Sie haben Recht, daß der Abdruck des ganzen Romancero ein starkes Unternehmen ist und schwerlich den Verlegern lohnen würde. Ueberdem bin selbst ich noch immer im Zweifel ob die Romanceros von Madrigal und Flores[2] dieselben sind oder nicht, da ich keinen je zu Gesicht bekommen habe. Der Meinige von 1604 ist von Juan de la Cuesta,[3] vendese en casa de F[ederi]co Lopez. Und die Secunda parte recopilada p[or] Mig[ue]l de Madrigal. 1605 Valladolid p[or] Luis Sanchez. Giebt es nun aber ein primera parte von Mig[ue]l de Madrigal? Und was enthalten die von Flores?

Die Edinb[urgh] Review halte ich nicht und habe daher den Aufsatz über Richter[4] nicht gelesen, weiß jedoch daß Carlyle[5] ein trefflicher Kritiker ist der jetzt an der Foreign Review[6] arbeitet die ich von London erwarte.

Heine ein politischer Schriftsteller ist el diablo predicador! Es macht dem deutschen Buchhandel keine Ehre, daß der angesehene Cotta die Hand zu einem solchen Unternehmen bieten kann, welches nichts anderes als die Herabziehung alles Ehrwürdigen und Legitimen bezwecken kann.

144. Nikolas Heinrich Julius, Hamburg

Puerto, den 27 Mai 1828

Werther Freund

Ich hoffe daß Cap[itain] Bückman von Sevilla dorten wird glücklich eingetroffen sein, und daß er Ihnen meinen Brief vom 28 Märtz übergeben hat. Mit Abschiffungen von Cadiz nach dorten scheint es gänzlich vorbei zu sein. Ich habe mich also nach Sevilla gewandt und mit vieler Mühe einige der gangbarsten von den bestellten Büchern erhalten (wovon umstehend das Verzeichniß) welche in einem Kistel verpackt Ende dieses Monathes von Sevilla mit diesem Briefe abgehen werden. Ich wünsche jetzt, daß Sie mir eine neue Liste aller Bücher senden mögen, die Sie von hier noch zu erhalten wünschen, in der Voraussetzung daß weder auf ältere Drucke noch auf Flugschriften zu rechnen ist. Ich bin überzeugt daß alte spanische Bücher jetzt günstiger und wohlfeiler in England zu haben sind als hier. Sollten Sie einen litterarischen Korrespondenten in London haben, so senden Sie ihm die einliegende Liste mit den Preisen die ich geben würde, wenn etwas davon in den gedruckten Ausbietungen von Bowring und andern vorkäme.

Die Uebersetzung von Bouterwecks Geschichte der spanischen Poesie[1] etc wird nun wirklich gedruckt, und ich habe die ersten Bogen jetzt vor mir. Den für uns interessantesten Theil werden die Noten enthalten, von denen ich aber nichts gesehen habe, da sie hintenangefügt werden. Es ist dieses in der bedrückten Lage Spaniens ein gewagtes Unternehmen und zweifle ich, daß die Kosten des Druckes herauskommen werden.

In meinen häuslichen Verhältnißen ist Gottlob kaum Veränderung. Die drei Ehepaare sind jetzt wieder zum Besuch hier vereint. Cecilia hat ein schleifendes Nervenfieber glücklich überwunden.

Mit der aufrichtigsten Anhaenglichkeit
Ihr treu ergebener
J. N. Böhl v: Faber

145. Nikolas Heinrich Julius, Hamburg

Puerto, den 6 Febr[uar] 1829

Seit einigen Tagen bin ich, bester Freund, in Besitz Ihres Briefes und Packets p[er] Wilhelmina Cap[itain] Beuße. Nach einem so langen Zwischenraum war es mir eine wahre Freude etwas von Ihrer Hand zu lesen. Ich beantworte jedoch den Brief heute nur vorläufig, weil ich ihn an meine Tochter Cecilia nach Sevilla gesandt habe. Ich erkenne und vernehme Ihre jetzigen dem Wohl des verwahrlosesten Theils der Menschheit gewidmeten Bestrebungen. Die flüchtige Uebersicht Ihres Werkes zeugt von eisernem Fleiß und die edelsten Gefühle bieten sich in jeder Zeile dar. Gott segne einen so edlen Zweck! – Der kleine Romancero ist allerliebst und die Poesie hat (den Druckfehler zum Trotz) den Beifall aller Liebhaber erworben – Was Sie mir über meine künftige Schwiegertochter[1] sagen hat mich sehr erfreut und meinem Wunsch sie kennen zu lernen angefacht. Vielleicht, vielleicht ... doch ich will keine Hoffnungen rege machen ehe die Erfüllung wahrscheinlicher ist – Auch mir ist Moreto vorzüglich lieb. Die erstandenen 3 Bände waren in der Biblioth[ek] meines seel[igen] Oheims, nicht in Fabers. Mit 5 od[er] 6 Stücke die Ihnen fehlen werde ich aufwarten. Moreto ist ganz kürzlich in der Gazeta de Bayona nach Würden hervorgehoben und gelobt. In Madrid hat sich ein neuer

Verfechter des altspanischen Theaters und des Romantischen überhaupt hervorgethan: A[gustín] Duran.[2] Sie erhalten sein erstes Heft mit nächstem Schiff. An einem groben Klaßiker der á la Mora mit Knüppeln über ihn hergefallen ist hat es nicht ermangelt. Die englischen Foreign Reviews sind vortrefflich. Ueber spanische Poesie haben sie entgegensetzte Ansichten:[3] der von Treuttel und Wurtz die ächte unsere: der von Young die magere französirende von Moratin.[4] Letzterer hat dagegen Ansichten über deutsche Litteratur (besonders Göthe) die alles schlagen was ich je gelesen habe. Ich vermuthe sie sind von Carlisle und müssen den alten Göthe verjüngern, sollte ihm eine Verjüngung noch sein – Die Wiener Jahrbücher sind auch recht brav, nur daß sie weder Maaß noch Ziel kennen und zu wenig darauf bedacht sind, sich an das <u>allgemein</u> interessierende zu halten. – Ein Briefwechsel mit Duran hat meine Lust zur Anordnung des altspanischen Theaters von neuem belebt da er mich mit mehrerem auszuhelfen verspricht das mir abgeht. Seine Sammlung muß trefflich sein. Veremos. Ein mehreres p[er] Sch[iff] so wie auch die Beantwortung eines herrlichen Briefes den ich von Fr[iedrich] Perthes erhalten –

Ihr ergebenster B. v. F.

146. Nikolas Heinrich Julius, Hamburg

Puerto, den 12 April 1829

Diese Zeilen schreibe ich Ihnen, werther Freund, mit Cap[itain] Sundberg, Schiff Mercurius, der Ihnen in einem kleinen Packet mit addresse an Perthes die Schrift von [illeg.] über das gelbe Fieber von Pasages und alle Diarios von Cadiz überbringt die von dem letzten gelben Fieber in Gibraltar handeln. Die Meinungen über contagio und noncontagio bleiben noch immer getheilt: ich war sehr für die letzte, gestehe aber daß die letzten Erfahrungen in Gibraltar mich zu der ersten neigen machen.

Hiebei erhalten Sie:

1) Die kleine Schrift von Duran zu Günsten des altspanischen Theaters.
2) Der Diario N[úmero] 4503 mit einer Epistola bei Gelegenheit dieser Schrift zu meiner Ehre.
3) N[úmeros] 34 und 37 der Gazeta von Bayona mit einigen artigen Sachen über Moreto und Calderon
4) N[úmero] 52. derselben Zeitung, mit der ungeheuren Eselei des Erzbischofes von Valencia der 189 Theaterstücke (alt und neu durcheinander) verbietet. Die Bemerkungen des Herausgebers darüber sind sehr gut.

Die übrigen bestellten Bücher habe ich noch nicht alle zusammen. Hält sich der Cap[itain] noch einige Tage auf so nimmt er sie mit; wonicht das nächste Schiff, welches nicht lange zögern wird.

Der erste Band der spanischen Uebersetzung des Bouterwek ist heraus, aber in Cadiz noch nicht angekommen, wegen des langen beschwerlichen Landtransportes. Ich brenne darauf ihn zu sehen wegen der Noten und Erläuterungen.

In Madrid soll das von Moratin hinterlassenen Werk über das altspanische Theater[1] auf Kosten des Königes gedruckt werden. Da es Privateigenthum des Königes ist, so habe ich keine Abschrift erhalten können. Obwohl ich vorhersehe daß der Inhalt mir ärgerlich sein wird, so kann ich doch mein beabsichtiges altes Theater nicht anordnen bevor ich Moratins Werk nicht gesehen habe. Duran hat mir eine Abschrift vier alter Farzas machen lassen die sehr in meinem Kram dienen.

Die englischen Foreign Reviews fahren in Trefflichkeit fort. N[ummer] 4 und 5 des von Black Young und Young haben Artikel über das Leben Heyns des Filologen[2] und über die Dramatiker Grillparzer, Klingmann[3] und Müllner die ich für das Höchste der wahren Kritik halte und gewiß dem einzigen Carlisle zum Verfaßer haben.

Sobald der Puerto Franco in Ordnung ist (welches nicht lange mehr dauern wird) werde ich eine kleine Bestellung von Büchern machen.

Unwandelbar
Der Ihrige
Böhl v: Faber

147. Friedrich Perthes, Hamburg

Puerto, den 12 April 1829

Ihre werthe Zuschrift aus Gotha vom 30 May des vorigen Jahres hat sehr beunruhigend auf mich eingewirkt. Die Wellen der Leidenschaft hatten sich damals schon sehr gelegt, aber grade wird dann das Gefühl der Reue doppelt peinlich, wenn einem bei erwachter Besonnenheit das gewöhnliche Leben so sehr anekelt, daß man sich fast in den leidenschaftlichen Zustand zurücksehnt. Dann sind Betrachtungen wie die Ihrigen eine wahre Aerznei. Meine innere Ruhe ist jetzt so ziemlich ungestört, allein ist mir eine Lauheit geblieben von der ich mich noch nicht erholen kann, und ich kann mir nicht verheimlichen daß mein Friede mehr filosofisch als kristlich ist. Ich harre indessen in Geduld auf einen Hauch der göttlichen Linde der einzig unser Trachten erwärmen und beleben kann und erfülle unterdessen auch ohne wahre Andacht die Gottesverehrungen die uns unser Glaube auferlegt.

Mein seliger Stiefvater hat mir seine Handschriften hinterlassen unter Bedingung nichts davon drucken zu lassen. Wahrscheinlich werden es systematisch geordnete Gründe gegen die Möglichkeit des Christenthums sein. Ich habe daher keine große Neugierde sie zu sehen und vor's erste sollen sie dorten ruhen, biß ich einmal selbst herüberreise. Ich hatte geglaubt diesen Sommer meine so lange beabsichtigte Reise verwirklichen zu können, um ein Zeuge der Heirath meines Sohnes mit der (wie ich von allen Seiten vernehme) sehr liebenswürdigen Betsy Berckemeyer zu sein, allein es hat sich nicht fügen wollen. Jetzt setzte ich meine Hoffnung auf den Sommer von 1830, wo der GelehrtenVerein in Hamburg die Anziehungen vermehrt. Doch bin ich zum voraus gefaßt auch die Vereitlung dieses Planes in Geduld zu erleben.

Ich danke für die litterarischen Nachrichten die Sie mir mittheilen. Sobald die Wirklichkeit des Puerto Franco in Cadiz eingetreten ist, werde ich einiges von Ihrer Handlung für mich verschreiben.

Ich stimme völlig mit demjenigen ein was Ihnen Ihr Freund H[er]r Mentzel über die Lage des Christenthums schreibt. Auf dem Wege Rechtens d.h. durch die Römisch Katholische Kirche muß in einer allgemeinen Kirchensammlung eine modifizierte Kirchenform eingeführt werden, die ebensoweit von der albernen VernunftReligion der Neologen[1] als von der geistigen Hoffarth weltgesinnter Fürsten der Kirche abstehen wird. Leibnitz hinterlassene Handschrift wäre ein prächtiger Grundstein zu diesem erneuerten Tempel. Sind die Katholischen Magnaten und Wortführer zu dieser Erneuerung noch nicht reif (welches mehr als wahrscheinlich ist) so werden sie so lange durch die Verfolgungen der [illeg.] heimgesucht werden, bis sie sich alle Rücksicht auf geistliche Vorschriften entschlagen und im ächten Geiste Gottes ihre Kräfte zur Erneuereung vereinigen.

Hierbei ein ordre auf Vorzeige von welcher H[er]r J[ohann] H[einrich] Berckemeyer ein Fäßel von alten Jerez Weins abliefern wird mit dem ich es wie folgt zu halten bitte. Das Fäßel muß 90 und etliche Bout[eilles] enthalten. Sie lassen es abzapfen und behalten davon so viele Bout[eilles] Sie wollen und vergüten mir für jede Bout[eilles] 12 Schilling court in Rechnung und wollen Sie solche alle behalten gleich gut und wo nicht werde ich über die restirenden disponiren. Auf diese Weise hoffe ich Ihrem Zartgefühl nicht zu nahe zu treten.

Ich sehe daß Sie an der Spitze einer zahlreichen Nachkommenschaft stehen, für die unser Vater im Himmel sorgen wird, wie er für den [illeg.] sorgt. Ich bleibe bisjetzt der Großvater einer einzigen Enkelin und wenn meine neue Tochter dorten nicht fruchtbarer ist als meine hiesigen, so werde ich mich schwerlich je mit Ihnen in der Patriarchenwürde meßen können –

Mit wahrer Anhänglichkeit und Freundschaft
Ihr ergebenster
J. N. Böhl v: Faber

148. Nicolas Heinrich Julius, Berlin

Puerto S[an]ta M[arí]a, den 17 Nov[ember] 1829

Vor einiger Zeit erhielt ich, bester Freund, Ihre Zeilen vom 10 July aus Berlin durch Perthes mit einigen Fortsetzungen. Lista hat einen Theil gesammelter Gedichte[1] die ich Ihnen schicken werde. Duran ist ein Liebhaber der in Madrid lebt. Sein zweiter Romancero[2] ist nun auch heraus und er verspricht binnen Kurzem den dritten mit einer kritischen Einleitung. Sie sollen sie sämtlich erhalten – die 3 Th[eile] des Calderon von Keil[3] habe ich gerne erhalten. Gebe der Himmel das der 4te Theil nicht ausbleibe! In meinen Augen (und meherer Freunde) ist der schöne Druck durch die großen Anfangsbuchstaben der Zeilen sehr entstellt und der Verständlichkeit dadurch Eintrug geschehen – Vielen Dank für Ihre Beiträge zur Gefängnißkunde und Verbesserung. Wie sehr ich indessen auch dergleichen Bestrebungen ehre kann ich, werther Freund, nicht damit simpatisiren. Sollte indessen gerade diese Kunde Sie in unseren Winkel Europas führen, so werde ich sie segnen. Ich zweifle sehr daran: es kostet viel sich zu einer langen Reise zu entschließen, besonders wenn man die 50te im Rücken hat.

Cap[itain] Krützen Sch[iff] Margaretha Ulrica (die schon unterwegens ist) hat eine Kiste Bücher an D[r] J[ulius] oder Perthes und Besser für Sie mit, worüber Sie bei diesen Herrn disponieren werden. Der Kosten ist nach Rechnung nota 790 Reales od[er] 110.7 Thaler die Sie an Perthes zu vergüten haben. Dieses war alles was diesesmal aufzufinden war. Ist noch etwas von früheren Aufträgen zurück so müssen Sie es mir wiederholen. Allen alten Sachen und Flugschriften müssen Sie entsagen – Der Period[ico] med[ico] quirurg[ico] hat eine andere Form erhalten, die Sie mit einigen anderen Kleinigkeiten unter den Büchern finden werden –

In litterarischer Hinsicht bin ich nicht müßig, doch kann ich noch nicht bestimmt sagen, ob meine Art Kommentar über die Floresta oder das alte Theater zuerst in Ordnung kommen wird. Moratin sein Origenes sollen größtentheils gedruckt sein allein sie werden noch nicht ausgegeben. Die Uebers[etzung] von Bouterw[ek] gerieth wahrscheinlich in Stocken: die seichten weitschweifigen und doch unvollkommenen Noten haben wenig Glück gemacht und verdienen nichts anderes.

Stets der Ihrige B. v: F.

149. Nikolas Heinrich Julius, Hamburg

Puerto, den 8 Sept[em]b[e]r 1830

Mit großer Freude habe ich, werther Freund, diesen Tagen Ihren lieben Brief von July aus Berlin erhalten und gelesen. Gottlob daß Sie heiter und unermüdet den Lebensstrom herabschiffen! Möchte uns der Himmel wollen, daß sich der Ihrige nach Süden oder der meinige nach Norden wenden thäte. Ein paar Stunden mündlicher Mittheilung würde uns mehr früchten als der fleißigste Briefwechsel.

Ich freue mich daß Sie mir den 4ten Theil des Keilschen Calderon als gewiß versprechen. Ist das Werk recht Komplet so gelingt es mir vielleicht einige Exemplare hier anzusetzen. Auf den poetischen Ausdruck von Dr. Huber[1] bin ich neugierig und obwohl ich sonst mich entschloßen kein Werk vor dessen Beendigung zu nehmen, will ich mit dieser Sammlung eine Ausnahme machen.

Die unglückliche Verzögerung der schon so lange versprochenen Ausgabe der Geschichte des span[ischen] Theaters von Moratin in Madrid verhindert mich noch immer meinen Vorrath des Altspanischen Theaters zu ordnen. Die Werke des Lope de Rueda[2] besitze ich lange in einer schönen Handschrift, neulich seine vier Comedias, Eufemia, Armelina, Los Engaños und Medora und seine Dos Coloquios pastoriles Camila und Timbrea. Es fehlt mir nur El Deleitoso ein kleines Bändchen komischer Zwischenspiele oder Szenen, deren Abschrift ich gerne bezahlen würde. Da diese Stücke nicht in Versen sind so verlieren sie (in meinen Augen) viel und ich bin noch nicht entschloßen ob ich sie meinem Theater einverleiben werde oder nicht. Viel interessanter in schönen Versen und auch älter sind die 8 Stücke des Barth[olomé] de Torres Naharro, wovon ich die erste ganz unbekannte Ausgabe Napoles 1517 besitze die 6 Stücke enthält. Die folgenden Ausgaben Sev[ill]a 1520 und 1533 habe ich nie ausfinden können. Auch giebt es eine von Amberes die ein Freund von mir gesehen hat. Die letzte Madrid 1573 (die von Zeit zu Zeit vorkommt) ist sehr verstümmelt. Eine der mittleren Ausgaben ist mir unentbehrlich um die 2 Stücke die in der ersten fehlen unverstümmelt liefern zu können.

Göthes Äußerung über den standhaften Prinzen[3] ist sicherlich das Höchste was sich sagen läßt und werde ich sie zu verbreiten suchen – Duran hat seit seinem zweiten Romancero nichts weiter drucken lassen, außer einigen Gelegenheitsgedichten[4] die heibei erfolgen – Auch lege ich einige Cadizer Diarios bei, die kleine Aufsätze von mir enthalten,[5] die ich Ihnen, denke ich, nicht nachzuweisen brauche. Es ist immer dieselbe Tendenz, nemlich das Reich der Poesie zu erweitern und sich über jeden Neugläubigen zu freuen. Die Revue de Paris[6] hat der französischen kleinen Welt ein Stück der wahren großen Geisteswelt geöffnet. Es ist zwar nicht alles darin Gold, allein wo hat man zuvor in französischer Sprache den <u>großen Dichter</u> richtiger gewürdiget?

Ich habe die neue Aufgabe der Sammlung von Quintana[7] nicht gesehen, allein gehört, daß das <u>gute</u> Alte um nichts vermehrt ist, das mittelmäßige Neue um vieles. Als Blumenlese ist sie äußerst elend, und nur die Einleitung und Würdigung der einzelnen Dichter (so weit sie geht) zu loben. Es ist ein spanisches <u>Großthun</u> solcher Dichterlinge sich um fremde Arbeiten in demselben Fach gar nicht zu bekümmern. Hätte Quintana den Florestas zur Hand genommen so würde er gefunden haben daß er so vorzügliche alte Dichter als Aldana[8] Medrano[9] und Virues[10] ganz übergangen hat, und hätte er den richtigen Sinn für das Erhabene und Schöne so wäre seine Auswahl ganz anders ausgefallen. Zwei dritel seiner Sammlung sind in dieser Hinsicht verwerflich, wie ich es in dem Coment[ari]o über die Floresta (kommen sie je zu Stande) darthun werde.

Ich sende Ihnen sechs Abdrücke (zur beliebigen Vertheilung) einer Flugschrift des beruhmten Gallardo,[11] der in einer kleinen Landstadt verwiesen sein satirisches Talent nicht unterdrücken kann. Wenngleich der Gegenstand selbst schon kein großes Interesse hat, so verdienen doch die Bemerkungen über die Sprache alle Aufmerksamkeit, hauptsächlich die Cuestion logosófica im Anfange, die einen sehr schwierigen Punkt der span[ischen] Grammatik sehr glücklich löset. Nebenbei ist der Stil einzig: um Gallardo kann so ganz eigenthümlich der Stil der goldenen Zeit der span[ischen] Literatur nachbilden.

Ueber die visita de carceles will ich nach Madrid schrieben und sollte das Buch in den öffentlichen Bibliotheken sein, eine Abschrift zu erhalten suchen. Sonst ist nicht daran zu denken es käuflich irgendwo zu erstehen.

Ein Bekannter ist gerade auf dem Sprunge nach dorten sich einzuschiffen: ich kann daher nur noch die gerade bei der Hand habenden Romanceros des Duran beilegen. Was ich von den anderen Bücher habhaft werden kann, bleibt bis zu nächster Gelegenheit.

Mein Bein ist krumm und verkürzt geblieben und ich kann ohne Krücken keine ansehnliche Strecke zurücklegen. Dieser scheint mir Fingerzeig der Versehung alle Reisegedanken aufzugeben. Uebrigens bin ich sehr wohl und mein innerer Friede ist nicht nur derselbe, sondern ich finde mich auf immer mehr aufgelegt alles von der besten Seite anzusehen. Dieses paßt um desto besser da meine Frau mit dem Alter immer trübsinniger wird und nichts thut als seufzen und beten, auch mir meine Heiterkeit als meine arge Verstockung auslegt – Cecilia haben wir diesen Sommer zwei Monathe lang mit uns gehabt: sie ist sehr wohl und immer empfänglich für alles Schöne und Gute. Ich werde ihr Ihre Grüße mittheilen – Aurora hat gegen vorzeitige Niederkunft zu kämpfen. Durch mehr Vorsorge hat sie jetzt den 5ten Monath erreicht. Ihr kleines Mädchen ist allerliebst und ganz Geist und Leben – Die Französin erwarten wir jetzt mit ihrem Mann zum Besuch, da in gegenwärtigen Umständen wenig Ehre daselbst (in Frankreich) zu erwerben ist. Ich hoffe jedoch daß alles ohne Krieg (äußeren Krieg wenigstens) abgehen wird – Hier ist alles ruhig, die Zeitungen mögen lügen was sie wollen. Unwandelbar Ihr treuster Freund

J. N. Böhl v: Faber

150. Nikolas Heinrich Julius, Berlin

Puerto, den 26 Jan[uar] 1831

Werther Freund

Die (wie mir Perthes schreiben) mit Ihrer Hülfe gemachten Bücherauswahl, welche ich vor kurzem erhalten habe, reiset größtentheils zurück 1) weil ich überhaupt keine Bücher mehr ohne Auftrag von mir haben will 2) weil gerade Geschichte und Religion, wovon die meisten dieser Bücher handeln, für mich abgeschloßenen Kapitel sind 3) weil mir der deutsche Ideengang fremd geworden ist und ich mehr Freude an den praktischen Anwendungen der Engländer finde als an den zwecklosen Grübeleien der Deutschen. Ich habe 3 B[ände] Solgers Vorlesungen behalten,[1] aber schon mehreremal ans Feuer werfen wollen. 'Der Untergang der Idee als Existenz ist ihre Offenbarung als Idee' das soll den [illeg.] Eindruck der Tragödie erklären! Dieses finde ich gerade indem ich das Buch aufschlage. Und dieser Kunstrichter meistert A[ugust] W[ilhelm] Schlegel bei dem alles verständlich und befriedigend ist (wenigstens in seinen dramatischen Vorles[ungen]) Einige Sachen von Rochlitz[2] haben mir dagegen sehr gefallen. Hubers Skizzen von Spanien sind recht gut: man spürt sogleich daß der Mann wirklich in Spanien gewesen ist. Nur verdirbt er es mit seinen liberalen Anstrich, besonders bei den weiblichen Karakteren. Die Reize einer Spanierin sind unvereinbar mit Konstituzions Ideen. Ich habe keine spanische Patriotin gekannt die nicht gemein, aufgeblasen, eitel, zank und heiratsüchtig gewesen wäre – Posgaru Liebesgeschichten[3] sind sehr schön bis auf die Lobeserhebungen der verächtlichen Mutter Morgan die eine schneidende Dißonanz bilden. Ich glaube immer mehr, daß es in den meisten deutschen Köpfen nicht recht richtig ist, wenigstens unter den schreibenden.

Vor kurzem ist es mir geglückt einen Abdruck der noch nicht ausgegebenen Origines del teatro español von Moratin zu erhalten, wodurch ich endlich soweit gekommen bin den Entwurf meines Altspanischen Theaters fixieren zu können. Jetzt fehlt nur das Abschreiben und einiges aus der Ferne. Ich denke jedoch in einigen Monathen die Handschrift nach Hamburg senden zu können, welches ich heute an P[erthes] und B[esser] schreibe. Ich addressire sie natürlich Ihnen und sollten P[erthes] und B[esser] den Verlag übernehmen wollen so sind sie vorzuziehen. Sie wissen schon daß ich für mich nur ein paar Dutzend Abdrücke verlange.

Moratin liefert einen Prologo und einen Discurso histórico der nur 56 großgedruckte Oktavoseiten einnimmt, welche unberührt sollen wiedergedruckt werden. Diesem Discurso folgen 54 kleingedruckte Seiten notas die ich auslassen werde, da sie nur bekannte Sachen aus Sanchez, Mayans etc. enthalten. Dem folgt ein Catálogo histórico y crítico de piezas dramaticas anteriores á Lope de Vega auf 189 kleingedruckten Seiten. Dieses ist das Beste des Buches und muß größtentheils wiedergedruckt werden. Dann kommt ein Nachtrag dazu von mir. Moratin beschließt sein Werk mit einer Beispielsammlung von 18 Stücken, die groß und weitläuftig gedruckt 444 Seiten einnehmen. Dieses ist seine schwache Seite. Von den 18 werde ich nur 12 beibehalten und wenigstens 30 mehr hinzufügen, die auf die Weise der Floresta in zwei Kolonnen gedruckt in einem Bande Platz finden werden, da die meisten der alten Stücke nur kurz sind. Vielleicht füge ich den Stücken einige kurze deutsche Noten bei. Alles andere ist spanisch, wie in der Floresta. Der Titel soll sein:

Orígenes del teatro español. Obra pósthuma de D[on] L[eonardo] F[ernández] Moratin con una coleccion de piezas dramáticas anteriores á Lope de Vega co-ordinadas p[or] D[on] J[uan] N[icolas] B[ohl] de F[aber]. Der Name von Moratin wird wahrscheinlich dem Buche mehreren Liebhaber zuführen. Für mich ist sein Discurso ein altes abgeleiertes Lied, und die meisten Kritiken seines Catalogus ausgedroschenes Stroh; doch nur so (meine ich) lassen sich die alten derben kraftvollen ächtspanischen Poßen einschwärzen an dem es mir eigentlich gelegen ist.

Wenn ich bedenke, werther Freund, welche verschiedene Richtung Ihre Thätigkeit seit mehreren Jahren genommen hat, so zweifle ich fast das Sie sich noch lebhaft für den alten poetischen Plunder interessiren können. So schätzbar Ihre gegenwärtigen Bestrebungen mir auch sind, so kann ich doch nicht umhin darin etwas Untergeordnetes zu finden, ein schönes Feld für glebae-adscritpi, erdgebundenen Geister; aber welche Beschränkung für eine Seele die wie die Ihrige sich mit himmlischen Geistern zu tummeln gewohnt ist! Doch vielleicht wissen sie [sic] beides zu vereinigen, wie ich mein Wein-Handlung mit der Floresta.

In meiner Familie ist alles so ziemlich beim Alten. Man hätte mit Ihnen dorten dem Gelehrtenverein beigewohnt! Allein meine rührigen Tage sind vorbei.

Gott befohlen. J. N. B:

151. Elise Campe, Hamburg

Puerto S[an]ta M[arí]a, den 2 Juny 1831

Ich würde mich, beste Freundin, vergebens bemühen den Eindruck Ihres lieben Briefes vom 19 Märtz (durch Herrn Landvoigt eingehändiget) lebendiger darzustellen, als mit den Versen unseres einzigen Göthe:

> Ihr bringt mit auch die Bilder froher Tage,
> Und manche liebe Schatten steigen auf;
> Gleich einer alten halbverklungenen Sage
> Kommt alte Liebe und Freundschaft mitherauf.[1]

Meine Umgebungen sind seitdem so ganz verschieden gewesen, meine Wirklichkeit der damaligen so sehr entgegengesetzt, meine Bestimmung so sehr das Widerspiel der filosofischen Abgeschiedenheit auf Görslow, daß ich mir manchmal eine Doppelte Persönlichkeit anzueignen geneigt fühle, besonders da diese Kontraste meinem inneren Frieden auf keine Weise beeinträchtiget haben, und mich eben so heitere Fantasien bei der Rechenstafel und im Weinkeller umschweben, als damals am schönen Schweriner See im Sommer und dem mir so lieben Hamburger Stadttheater im Winter. Auch bin ich überzeugt, daß die flüchtigen Genüße unserer irdischen Pilgerschaft weder an bestimmten Oertern noch an gewissen Personen gebunden sind. Jeder ächte Seelengenuß ist ein freies Geschenk des Himmels, das kommt und geht niemand weiß wie und dennoch tiefe Spuren in der Erinnerung läßt. Dann sind mir mehrere aus unseren winterlichen Zusammenkünfte in Hamburg geblieben, und darunter auch unser gute Kampf für die Romantiker, den ich (wie Sie wissen) durch besonderen Umständen veranlaßt wurde in Spanien fortzuführen, der die Bekanntmachung meiner spanischen Floresta veranlaßte und mir dadurch die Thore der spanischen Academia eröffnete. So hängen die Dinge zusammen! Was aber unsere Spurkraft noch mehr Ehre macht ist, daß seit einigen Jahren gerade die Gebildesten unter Engländern und Franzosen das <u>eigenthümliche poetische</u> der deutschen Romantiker anerkennen, daß Göthe, Jean Paul und Tiek viele Verehrer daselbst haben und sogar die grellsten Erzählungen unseres Hoffmann in den besten englischen und französischen Zeitschriften prangen. Daraus entspringt nun wieder daß die Hyperklugen unter den Deutschen (wie in N[ummer] 36 der mir übersandten Kritischen Blätter[2]) die Romantiker von neuem bekritteln müssen, wie die kalte Beurtheilung der Fata Morgana von Fouque[3] darthut. Jetzt da sich die großartige liberale Kritik der Schlegel noch so langen Kämpfen in England und Frankreich zu entwicklen anfängt, wollen gerade die Neudeutschen wieder alles über einen Leisten schlagen, und weil Fouqué seiner Manier den Kritiker nicht anspricht, muß Fouqués Manier nichts taugen. Glücklicherweise giebt er Auszüge die jeden sinnvollen Leser bewegen werden sich das Werkchen zu verstehen.

Im Frühjahr 1830 war ich auf den Sprung meine Reise zu unternhemen, hauptsächlich um meine Kinder und Schmachtlingen zu besuchen, nebenher meine wenigen übriggebliebenen Freunde zu sehen, die Verschönerungen meiner guten Vaterstadt zu genießen und mich des frischen und naßen Dunstkreises, nach so langer Röstung in der Sonne, zu freuen. Es kam etwas dazwischen und im Juny hatte ich das Unglück auf einer Treppe auszugleiten und mir das rechte Bein zu verletzen. Es war weder Bruch noch Verrenckung sondern was die Wundärtzte für Subluxatio nennen: der Tibia ist ein wenig aus seiner vertikalen Stelle gewichen, die stark verletzten Sehnen haben sich zusammengezogen geheilt, das Bein hat sich nicht allein ein paar Zoll verkürzt, sondern bildet auch einen Bogen nach außen, so daß sich die Knien in stehender Stellung nicht berühren können. Ich kann also natürlich ohne Krücken keine drei Schritte zurücklegen und da das ganze Gewicht des Körpers immer auf dieselbe Seite fällt, so ermüdet mich das Gehen sehr und ich gehe nicht mehr als was die höchste Nothdurft erfordert. Ich gehe so ins Einzelne um Ihnen zu beweisen, daß an Heilung jetzt nicht mehr zu denken ist, wenngleich vielleicht anfänglich ein geschickter Wundartzt alles wieder hätte ins rechte Gleis bringen können – Sollte ich nun also auch die Geschäfte 6 Monathe lang am Nagel hängen können (welches auch viele Schwierigkeiten hat) was wäre mit mir dorten aufzustellen und würde nicht mein ganzer Genuß sich auf dem Empfang der Besuche meiner Freunde beschränken müssen? – Es ist klar, liebe Freundin, daß die göttliche Vorsehung eine Versetzung aus meiner Lage nicht für gerathen hält, sondern mir den hiesigen Kirchhof zum Ruheplatz des Leibes bestimmt hat, wogegen ich auch nichts anzuwenden habe – Noch andere zwei Betrachtungen machen mir die Scheiterung meines Reiseplans erträglich. Erstlich der unvermeidliche Abschied nach Verlauf weniger Monathe bis zum Wiedersehen in jener Welt. Zweitens der Schrecken alle meine Freunde (nach 18 jähriger Abwesenheit) so alt vorzufinden und die Unlust selbst ihnen als ein abgelabter Krüppel zu erscheinen. Lange Abwesenheiten sind der Tod aller kleineren Verhältniße und Beziehungen, in denen die eigentliche Annehmlichkeit eines vertrauten Umganges liegt. Man muß zusammen altern, um sich im Alter erträglich zu finden, denn wenngleich die Seele immer dieselbe ist so sträubt sich der Körper gegen diese Annerkennung.

Meiner Tochter Cecilia habe ich Ihren Brief nach Sevilla gesandt: sie hat ihn mit dem größten Vergnügen gelesen, und fühlt darüber wie Göthe und wir. Ihre Jugend in Deutschland wird ihr eine Feenwelt bleiben. Aurora lebt sehr glücklich in Cadiz mit einem trefflichen Mann und einer lieblichen Tochter von 4 Jahren. Sie hat keine ander Herzeleid als ihre öffteren Umschläge, seit der ersten glücklichen Geburt. Angela lebte in Frankreich sehr angenehm mit ihrem Manne und ihre Gesundheit hatte sich daselbst gestärkt. Bei der politischen Umwälzungen von July ward ihr Mann von seinen Unteroffiziren abgesetzt, und ist jetzt in Paris mit der Aussicht anderwärths angestellt zu werden: seine Frau ist jetzt mit uns bis sich das Schiksal des Obersten entscheidet.

Wie freue ich mich in Ihrer Seele über Ihren schönen Reisegenuß und des herrlichen Abends bei Tieck! Das Gedicht an Göthe[4] habe ich natürlich mit großem Interesse gelesen. Herzlich dankbar bin ich für die Nachrichten über unsere Freunde, von denen ich so lange nichts wußte. Bokelmann haben Sie vergeßen, auch Prof[essor] Meyer, Verfas[s]er jenes erhabenen orientalischen Dramas![5] – Gottlob daß die gute Sieveking noch so heiter ist und daß der trefliche Baron Voght (dessen sowohl ich als meine Frau uns mit großem Interesse erinnern) noch immer für alles Schöne lebt und webt – Beruhigend ist was Sie mir von den letzten Tagen unseres guten Sieburg melden. So mögen wir alle sanft hinüberschlafen! –

Nur eine schattenartige Erinnerung habe ich von Ihrer Pflegemutter. Die Idee indessen, wie ein Sechziger einem 20 jährigen Kinde Mährchen erzählt, ist ächt romantisch und begeisternd und für den Augenblick schwindet die Krücke und die 18° Breite die uns trennen – Nochmals Dank für Ihr gütiges Andenken: ich habe nicht alles geschrieben was ich fühle, aus Furcht der Ferula unseres Anti-Romantikers.

Der Ihrige

B. v. F.

152. Nikolas Heinrich Julius, Berlin

Puerto, den 26 July 1831

Ich sehe besonders gerne, bester Freund, daß wenngleich längere Zwischenräume zwischen unseren Mittheilungen verstreichen, unsere Simpathie dadurch auf keine Weise leidet. Unsere Seelen altern Gottlob nicht, wenngleich der Körper dem Weg alles Fleischiges geht. Ich bemerke keine Abnahme in der Intensität meiner Gefühle, und obwohl manche Gegenstände früherer Genüße mir jetzt fern sind und fern sein müssen, so ersetzt mir dieses das Bewußtsein meiner Fähigkeit zu genießen, welche ich als unsterbliches Wesen nie verlieren kann, und durch welche ich selbst bei den Unterirdischen etwas zu lieben finden würde. Dieses sage ich in Ansicht Ihres Briefes vom 5 May und in bezug auf Ihre Freude an dem altspanischen Theater, dessen Handschrift d[en] 18 Juny mit dem spanischen Sch[iff] Maria Ana nach Hamburg abgegangen ist. Jetzt begleite ich Titel, Prólogo, Worterklärung, tabla und einige Anmerkungen für deutsche Leser. Sie werden daraus ersehen daß ich die Materialien habe in zwei Theile spalten müssen erstlich weil ein einziger Band zu unbehülflich geworden sein würde, zweitens aber und hauptsächlich weil mir noch einiges abgeht (besonders der Deleitoso) wovon ich Hoffnung habe Abschriften zu erhalten. Die bestimmte Meinung meiner spanischer Freunde war, nichts von Moratin abdrucken zu lassen, theils weil es ihnen undelikat scheint theils weil sie es nicht des Nachdrucks werth halten. So wie das Theater jetzt erscheint ist es ganz der Floresta gleich: möglichst treue Ueberlieferung der besten originale, als Anfang oder Ergänzung jeder Geschichte der Litteratur. Dem urtheile ein Jeder nach belieben! – Was ich in den deutschen Andeutungen zum Lobe dieser alten Herrlichkeiten sage, hätte ich nie im spanischen gewagt. Sie haben mir aber einmal gesagt daß manche Deutschen es lieben mit der Nase auf das Vorzügliche gestoßen zu werden. Dieses hat mich ermuthiget. Ich habe mich indessen sehr gezügelt, weil ich weiß daß man eine unbillige Vorliebe für die Sachen erwirbt mit denen man sich lange beschäftigt. Vieles bleibt mir noch auf dem Herzen, besonders über die unvergleichliche Dikzion des Torres

Naharro und die so ganz idiomatische Sprache des einzigen Lope de Rueda doch wie Wenige können dieses ganz beurtheilen!

Perthes seinen Brief habe ich gerne gelesen bis auf den Punkt des so wenig lohnenden Absatzes der Floresta. Und doch ist das Buch bekannt genug, denn kein Kritiker spricht jetzt über spanische Poesie ohne die Floresta zu erwähnen. Den eigentlichen Werth der Sammlung hat jedoch bis jetzt niemand gefaßt und gleich seicht ist was mir darüber, sei es Lob oder Tadel, zu Gesicht gekommen. Jeder lobt nur was sein Sinnesart anspricht und tadelt was dagegen anstößt. Sind denn Sie und ich und noch ein halb Dutzend Käutze die einzigen Vielseitigen auf der Welt? Ist es denn so unerhört, daß derselbe Mensch des Morgens betet, zu Mittag räsonnirt, um Vesperzeit seine Geliebte besucht und am Abend Poßen treibt? – Ich bleibe der Meinung daß (einige Lückenbüßer ausgenommen) jedes Stück dieser ansehnlichen Sammlung einen eigenthümlichen Werth hat, und daß wenn nicht das ganze gesellschaftliche Gebäude zu Grunde geht die Zeit nicht ferne sein kann wo die Floresta als das einzige treue und umfaßende Handbuch der spanischen Poesie gelten wird.

Daß ich Ihre mühsamen Arbeiten über die Verbesserung der Gefängniße innigst schätze und ehre, brauche ich Ihnen schwerlich zu wiederholen. Daß man deren Wichtigkeit überall annerkennt muß Ihnen erfreulich sein, aber noch mehr was Sie mir über die Frucht dieser Bemühungen in Hinsicht von Preußen melden. Dieses wird Ihnen einmal, wenn es zum Abscheiden kommt, ein sanftes Kopfkißen sein.

Nichts will ich mehr von Politik und Geschichte wissen. An Perthes habe ich alles geschichtliche, und religiöse zurückgesandt und mir dagegen die Insel Felsenburg,[1] die Volksmärchen von Grimm und Busching, Schillers Theater und Rochlitz Romane kommen lassen. Ich hoffe mit allem was Ernst ist aufs Reine zu sein und will mich in meinen Mußestunden nur durch die Fantasie unterhalten lassen.

Wegen [illeg.] visita de carceles habe ich ausdrücklich nach Valencia geschrieben, bis jetzt aber nichts erhalten können. Den dritten Romancero von Duran erhalten Sie mit erstem Schiffe womöglich die Matilda und damit auch eine Abschrift des Discurso von Moratin der für das Teatro bestimmt war. Mit diesem können Sie nach belieben schalten, nur soll er nicht dem Teatro einverleibt werden. Zu Bouterw[eks] Uebers[etzung] ist nichts weiter erschienen: die Uebers[etzer] haben sich durch ihre Arroganz viele Feinde gemacht. Der vierte und letzte Romancero des Duran[2] (ganz geschichtlich) ist unter die Preße – Etwas unter Ladenpreis zu finden ist hier eine Seltenheit und Huerta sein Teatro ist den hohen Ladenpreis auf keiner Weise werth. Ich behalte Ihren Auftrag indessen in Andenken. – Ich bleibe, meiner Krücke zum Trotz, munter und bin übrigens vollkommen wohl. Für die cholera habe ich keine Furcht, obwohl ich sie erwarte. Meine Töchter sind jetzt bei uns. Der Oberst hat in den ersten Unruhen sein Regiment verloren und sucht jetzt bei den Remonten angestellt zu werden – Wir erwarten ihn nächsten Monath – Wir schmoren jetzt: seit fast drei Monathen keine Wolke! Wer gäbe uns Nebel und Regen! –

Die vier halben Bogen zum alten Theater gehörend gehen an Perthes in Hamburg mit der Bedingung sie Ihnen vor dem Drucke zur Revision zu übersenden. In den Andeutungen haben Sie meine Vollmacht zu verbessern, zu runden und zu polieren wo es erforderlich ist – Ich schreibe an Perthes auch, daß ich meine Freiabdrücke auf 12 beschränke und bestelle 18 für meine Rechnung –

Cecilia läßt Sie bestens grüßen. Sie hatte die Absicht einige Zeilen beizulegen, allein ihre Geschäfte haben es nicht verstattet. Sie wissen wohl daß die lieben Damen nie Zeit haben.

Derselbe

153. August Campe, Hamburg

Puerto, den 28 April 1833

Werther Freund

Da sich endlich wieder einmal eine Schiffsgelegenheit nach dorten darbietet, habe ich ausgefunden, daß ich Ihnen lange eine Antwort auf Ihr freundliches Schreiben vom 8 Sep[tember] 31 schuldig bin, welches ich mit den Kritischen Blättern und den Gedichten von Chamisso[1] seiner Zeit erhielt. Letztere haben mir wohl gefallen, und von den Kritischen Blättern werde ich gelegentlich gerne die Fortsetzung erhalten. Bis N[ummer] 62 inclusive haben Sie mir gesandt.

Ich freue mich daß Sie durch den Herrn Landvoigt umständliche Nachrichten über unser Leben und Weben erhalten. In einer halben Stunde läßt sich mehr plaudern als in einem halben Jahr schreiben. Der Schaden an meinem Bein ist Gottlob nicht von der Art dem Lebensgenuß eines bejahrten Mannes Eintrag zu thun. Da ich keine Schmerzen daran leide, so bleibt mein Geist frei und kann sich einer beliebigen Thätigkeit überlassen. Nichts reicht mich Haus Hof und Weinlager ja den Rücken zu wenden und auch ohne gelähmt zu sein würde ich jetzt keine andere Lebensart führen, daß ich den Gedancken Deutschland noch einmal zu besuchen aufgeben muß, ist die schlimmste Seite meiner Unbehülflichkeit: meine wenigen alten Freunde und Verwandte wieder zu sehen und die Familie meines Sohnes kennen zu lernen waren mächtige Magnete! Doch ist es überwunden.

Was mir sonsten beigefallen ist werden Sie aus der Einlage an Ihre liebe Frau sehen. Ich stimme ihr ganz darin bei daß einige Zeilen von Zeit zu Zeit hinreichend sind das geistige Band zwischen Gleichgesinnten aufrecht zu erhalten. Daran wollen wir es nicht fehlen lassen.

Ganz der Ihrige J. N. Bohl

Johann Nikolas Böhl von Faber (1770-1836): A German Romantic in Spain

154. Elise Campe, Hamburg

Puerto, den 28 April 1833

Kaum kann ich es, beste Freundin, glauben daß Ihr Brief vom 9 Sep[tember] 1831 über ein Jahr lang in meinem Pulte unbeantwortet gelegen hat. Bergab geht es viel reißender als bergauf, und dieses vereint mit der Einförmigkeit meiner Lebensart verschlingt die Zeit auf eine sehr behaglicher Weise. Den vorigen Sommer ging zwar mein schlimmes Bein offen und ich mußte mich mehreren Monathe mit einem bösen Geschwur plagen. Dieses heilte jedoch durch den Gebrauch der kalten Schwefelbäder in Chiclana (drei Meilen von hier) und seitdem genieße ich der besten Gesundheit und habe nur die Unbequemlichkeit nicht ohne Krücken gehen zu können. Appetit und Schlaf sind gut und die Stimmung (bei einer gedeihlichen Thätigkeit, der mein verkürztes Bein keinen Eintrag thut) noch besser, und da mir Muße genug bleibt mehrere Stunden täglich den Musen zu weihen, so halte ich mich für eines der glücklichsten Menschenkinder. Meine nächste Umgebung ist mit ihrem Schiksal weniger zufrieden; die natürlichen Schwächen des Alters scheinen ihr unerhört und die Annäherung des Todes schrecklich. Ich schiebe dieses auf ein Mißverständniß der geistlichen Ansicht. Schon unser alter Logau sagte:

'Wenn wir aus dieser Welt durch
sterben und begraben,
So lassen wir den <u>Ort</u> wir lassen
nicht das Leben.'[1]

Und da wir nun schon auf dieser Erde so weit kommen, daß uns an dem <u>Orte</u> wenig oder nichts gelegen ist, so lange der Geist geregelt und für alles Schöne und Gute empfänglich bleibt, so ist das Böse oder Gute was von einem anderen <u>Ort</u> erwartet wird, eine bloße Täuschung, und die Hölle ist mir eben so wenig ein Ort wo nur körperliche Quaalen walten, als der Himmel ein Konzertsaal wo Ohren und Augen erquickt werden. Wer in der Liebe ist und lebt der hat Himmel hier und dort und allerwärths: wer sich dem Haß und Neid freigiebt fühlt sich in der Hölle hier und dort. Bei dieser Ansicht, bei dieser inneren Ueberzeugung <u>nirgends</u> auf die Dauer unglücklich sein zu können, bei der Wahrscheinlichkeit, durch die nächste Seelenwanderung einen vollkommeneren dem Geiste folgsameren Körper zu gewinnen, bei der Herrlichkeit des Gefühls wovon Poesie und Musik nur schwacher Abglanz ist, endlich bei dem Bewußtsein, der Empfänglichkeit für die kaum zu ahnende Geheimniße der höchsten Liebe . . . kann das <u>Jenseits</u> sich uns als erfreulich darstellen.

Was Sie mir von dem treflichen Pr[ofessor] Meyer sagen tönt mir wie <u>alte halbverklungenen Sagen</u>. Es ist ein geistreicher Mann dessen Schröders Leben ich mit vielem Interesse gelesen habe und dessen kritischen Ansichten ich größtentheils beistimme.

Ihre Nachrichten über die Familie Bokelman haben mich sehr interessirt; das nächste Mal sagen Sie mir etwas von der guten Sieveking, Poehl und Baron Vogt. <u>Mein</u> Hamburg stirbt immer mehr aus; kaum kann ich ein halb Dutzend Freunde mehr aufzählen.

Der Cholera morbus hat Sie sehr gelinde behandelt, wofür ich Gott danke. Hier fährt die Regierung in ihrer ängstlichen Verkehrungen fort, besonders seitdem man von einigen verdächtigen Fällen in Portugal spricht. Ich bleibe dabei daß eine gesunde Ansicht die allen Verkehr lähmenden Vorsichtsmaasregeln viel schrecklicher sind, als die Vertilgung einiger meist elenden sich selbst und anderen zu Last fallenden Menschen.

Ich fühle mit Ihnen das Unbehagliche der allgemeinen Empörung gegen alles als hergebracht Bestehende. Es ist unnütz gegen eine solche Mehrheit zu kämpfen. Sie wird siegen wenn nicht <u>überirrdische</u> Hülfe erscheint. Bis dahin ziehen wir uns in den engsten Zirkel zurück, zufrieden wenn noch hin und wieder ein unverfälschter Sinn mit uns fühlt, daß unser inneres und wahres Glück ganz unabhängig von allen Regierungsformen und Freiheitsanstalten nur auf <u>Liebe</u> <u>Glauben</u> und <u>Hoffnung</u> gegründet sein kann. Unveränderlich der Ihrige,
J. N. Bohl

155. Nikolas Heinrich Julius [Berlin]

Puerto, den 28 April 1833

Bester Freund

Aus Mangel an Schiffsgelegenheit ist Ihr Werthes vom 27 July so lange unbeantwortet geblieben.

Nach einer langen Reise sind meine Abdrücke des Teatro antiguo endlich erschienen, und haben in Hinsicht der Richtigkeit des Druckes meine Erwartungen übertroffen.[1] Meine spanischen Freunde können sich nicht genug über die wenigen Druckfehler wundern. Warum die kurzen <u>deutschen</u> Nachweisungen nicht mitabgedruckt sind, kann ich icht begreifen. – Ich hatte die Perthesche Handlung ersucht mir die Anzeigen und Rezensionen des Teatro (sollten sie in Blättern erschienen sein) gleich p[er] Post einzusenden, allein entweder hat niemand davon Notiz genommen oder auch Herrn Perthes haben mir das Porto ersparen wollen, welches ich ihnen keineswegs danke. In Madrid hat man dem Teatro etwas mehr Aufmerksamkeit geschenkt als der Floresta. Da Ihre Thätigkeit jetzt so vielseitig in Anspruch genommen ist, so kann ich nicht von Ihnen erwarten die Stimmen der

Kritiker über das Teatro für mich zu sammeln. Ich will mich also mit Wordsworth begnügen zu glauben, daß einige gleichgesinnte Gemüther

>(and such there needs must be)
>Shall find solace there as I have found.[2]

Sollte der liebenswürdige Dr. Dietz[3] etwas über seine Reise in Spanien herausgegeben haben, so müssen Sie Perthes sogleich auftragen es mir zu senden. Der Falk über Göthe[4] ist noch nicht erschienen – Ihr Sonnett ist recht brav: die schriftlichen Anklänge erfreuen immer die so gutes Willens sind.

Mit großem Interesse habe ich gelesen was Sie mir von meiner langjährigen Freundin Doris Bokelmann melden. Ich schließe daraus, daß sie verhältnißmäßig jetzt eine ungetrübte Existenz genießt, davon sie so werth ist. Wir haben einige Lebensperioden miteinander durchlebt, die der Erinnerung reichen Stoff aller Art darbieten, doch nichts davon, damit mich das längst entwöhnte Sehnen nicht ergreife, und das strenge Herz sich milder und weicher fühle als billig ist – Ich schrieb sogleich an Uthoff über die Angelegenheiten unserer Freundin, und lege Ihnen die Antwort deselben original bei. Es thut mir leid daß ich hinzufügen muß, daß nicht die geringste Wahrscheinlichkeit vorhanden ist etwas von dem Schiffbruch des Simonschen Hauses zu retten, und das Cadiz überhaupt immer mehr verarmt und immer tiefer sinkt. Die beiden Uthoffs haben fallirt und schlagen sich mühsem durch. Beide sind reichlich mit Kindern gesegnet: der ältere hat zwei liebenswürdige Töchter deren schönsten Jahren verfließen ohne daß sich Gelegenheiten zu konvenablen Verbindungen darbieten. Die schöne lebendige Leidenschaft die in meiner Jugendzeit so viele uninteressirten Heirathen erzeugt fehlt der jetzigen Generazion und es ist ein rechter Jammer so viele liebliche Jungfrauen verwelken zu sehen.

Sie werden hiemit durch Perthes erhalten was ich für Sie habe auftreiben können, nemlich die 7te Auflage des Dicc[ionari]o de la Academia, die nicht nur keinen Vorzug über die 6te hat sondern auf schlechterem Papier gedruckt ist. Es ist schändlich, daß dieses Wörterbuch zu einer bloßen Spekulation herabgesunken ist. Ferner die Schrift von Benoît über den Cholera-morbus[5] nebst mehreren kleinen Schriften von spanischen Ärzten über denselben Gegenstand. Endlich den ersten Theil einer neuen Ausgabe des D[on] Quijote mit einem prächtigen für Litteratur und Sprache höchst anziehenden Kommentar von Clemencín.[6] Da sich indessen der spanische Starrkopf in allem zeigen muß, so giebt uns hier ein Akademikus das Skandal die ihm allein eigenthümliche Akzentuirung unter den Augen der Akademia der lesenden Welt aufzutischen. Der Prolog ist sehr brav, obwohl in Hinsicht der Theorien die alten Schackeln noch manchen abgedruckten Gemeinplatz hervorgerufen haben. Die freie Anerkennung der Fehler und Flüchtigkeiten des Cervantes hat mir sehr gefallen: sie ist indessen schon in der

Gaceta de Madrid zwar leise aber doch gewürgt worden. Die afrancesados, die mit St. Evremont[7] dafür halten, daß die spanische Lit[eratur] nur ein gutes Buch (nemlich don Quijote) aufzuweisen hat fechten für die Makellosigkeit dieses Phenix. Es sind beschränkte Eselsköpfe, so wie die französ[ischen] industriels und die englischen utilitarians, die alle Poesie vernichten möchten. In welchem elenden Zeitalter leben wir! – Gottlob daß sich die Zeit selbst verzehrt und diese Welt nicht immer währt (Logau[8]) Die Bücher bitte ich als einen kleinen Ersatz anzunehmen.
   Unveränderlich der Ihrige
   J. N. Böhl v: Faber

156. Friedrich Perthes, Gotha

Puerto, den 30 April 1833

Erst vor wenigen Monathen habe ich, werther Freund, die für mich bestimmten Abdrücke der Teatro español anterior a Lope de Vega erhalten und den Druck fehlerfreier gefunden als ich es je hätte hoffen können. Auch bin ich mit den Lettern und sonstiger Ausstattung sehr wohl zufrieden und vermiße nur den Anfang der kurzen deutschen Noten. Ich entsinne mich daß bei dem Drucke der Floresta Dr Julius die Fingerzeige für das deutsche Publikum sehr paßlich fand. Ich hatte Ihr Hamburger Haus ersucht mir die in Zeitschriften erscheinenden Beurtheilungen dieses Teatro ausgeschnitten p[er] Post einzusenden, allein entweder hat sich keine Stimme öffentlich darüber vernehmen lassen, oder H[er]rn P[erthes] und B[esser] haben gefürchtet einem brutal durch das Porto Eintrag zu thun, welches mir gar nicht recht ist. In Madrid hat man dem Teatro mehr Aufmerksamkeit geschenkt als der Floresta. Dennoch kann der spanische Stolz sich nicht zu dem unumwundenen Geständniß entschließen daß ein Fremder mehr zur Anerkennung ihrer alten Litteratur gethan hat als die Hände der Nazionalen und daß dieser dramatische Band eben so hoch über Moratin seine magere Sammlung steht, als die Floresta über die planlose einseitige Coleccion des Quintana im lyrischen Fach.

   Ich kann Ihnen meinen Dank für Ihre so ganz uninteressirte Vermittlung bei dieser Bekantmachung nicht anders als durch ein Produckt der hiesigen Preße darthun, welche bekanntermaßen sich mehr mit Trauben als mit Lettern beschäftiget. H[er]rn P[erthes] und B[esser] erhalten mit diesem Brief für Sie ein Fäßel eines alter Rabensaftes, der Herbstnebel zertheilen und Winternis auflösen kann, und hoffentlich Ihnen und den lieben Ihrigen willkommen sein wird.
   Mit Achtung und Ergebenheit unveränderlich der Ihrige.
   J. N. Böhl v: Faber.

157. Nikolas Heinrich Julius, Berlin

Puerto, den 30 Märtz 1834

6 April

Bester Freund

Sieben Monath nach seinem datum vom 11 July erhielt ich Ihren Brief mit der Post von Madrid, ohne von den spanischen Aerzten die dorten den Choleramorbus studirt haben, etwas weiteres vernommen zu haben. Die Studien dieser Herren haben indessen wenig Einfluß auf die Maasregeln der Regierung gehabt, die bei den Ausbrüchen der Krankheit im vorigen Herbst in dieser Provinz, keinen Fingerbreit von dem Schlandrian des Einschließens und Isolierens abgewiesen ist.

Die Krankheit hat sich auch hier sehr rätselhaft erwiesen. Aus den beiliegenden Diarios von Cadiz werden Sie ersehen, daß sie als da sich mit Milde geäußert hat. Von 6000 Befallenen sind ungefähr 900 gestorben. Ganz anders wirthschaftete das gelbe Fieber. Hier im Puerto haben wir nur einzelne Fälle und das in ganz verschiedenen Ecken und Enden der Stadt gehabt: da man aber durch das unsinnige Einschließen allen see- und landfahrenden Menschen das Brot nahm, so entstand ein schreckliches Elend welches nur durch große Aufopferungen der Begüterten sich nicht in Aufruhr und Pest verwandelte. In Sevilla und besonders in dessen Vorstadt Triana ist die Krankheit dagegen sehr mörderisch gewesen. In Malaga weder so milde wie in Cadiz, noch so arg wie in Sevilla. In Granada wieder unbedeutend. Sie schleicht so im Dunkeln fort, viele Ortschaften ganz überspringend. Hoffentlich erscheint sie diesen Sommer in Madrid, der einzige Weg um das [illeg.] über den Haufen zu werfen

Von Anzeigen und Beurtheilungen des Teatro antiguo habe ich bisjetzt noch nichts erhalten. Eine englische Anzeige habe ich gelesen: auch in der Revue de Paris[1] ist mit Lob die Rede davon, obwohl nur in einer nota. Ich bin im Ganzen (so wie Sie) etwas in dieser Hinsicht abgekühlt nur leider kann ich meine Launigkeit nicht einer so schönen Ursache zuschreiben, als Sie es durch Ihre Arbeiten über Gefängniße und BesserungsAnstalten zu thun berechtigt sind. Ich fühle vielmehr etwas mehr weltlich oder epikuränisch im guten Sinne. Ich neige mich immer mehr zum paßiren, zum sich dem Strom des Lebens heruntertreiben lassen ohne sich viel um das Allgemeine zu kümmern; dieses macht mich sehr tolerant, sehr geduldig und so glücklich als es derjenige sein kann, dem nur Ruhe und ein sanftes Hinüberschlummern mehr wichtig ist.

Für unsere gute Freundin Doris Bokelman erfolgt die versprochenen Einlage von Uhthoff, die unmöglich etwas anders als eine totale Entsagung aller Hoffnung enthalten kann. Zur Bestätigung dieser Ansicht dient, daß weder Mister noch ich (die so viele hundertausend von spanischen Schuldnern zu reklamiren haben) keinen Heller zu bekommen wissen. Aber wo nichts ist, gelten keine Rechte – Die Einlage dieser Freundin, deren Sie erwähnen, ist mir nicht zu Händen gekommen.

Duran hat auch etwas altdramatisches[3] versprochen welches mit seinem letzten Romancero nächsten erfolgen soll – Unsern politischen Verhältniße sind verwickelt: ich hoffe indessen die Parthei der Königin (zu welche ich mich rechne) werde die Oberhand behaupten. Die Liberales sind älter geworden und scheinen bisjetzt mit derjenigen Müßigkeit zu Werke zu gehen die einzig diesem unglücklichen Lande einige Erleichterung erschaffen kann. Die Gegenparthei macht sich durch die beschaulichsten Grausamkeiten und gänzliche Rücklosigkeit auf dem veränderten Zeitgeist stets verhaßter. Dennoch wäre das Einrücken von fremden Truppen sehr zu wünschen um dem schrecklichen Blutvergießen in nördlichen Spanien Einhalt zu thun.

Ich genieße im Ganzen der besten Gesundheit: mein krummes Bein macht mir keine Schmerzen und Leibesbewegung ist in meinem Alter nicht mehr nothwendig. Ich habe nur über häufigen Durchfall zu klagen. Dieses scheint nicht aus einer Schwäche des Magens zu entspringen weil ich guten Appetit habe, nie Schwere im Magen, noch Säure, noch üblen Geschmack noch Trockenheit im Munde verspüre. Es muß in den Gedärmen liegen oder in dem Organ der Absonderung des flüßigen Theils der Nahrungsmittel. Auffallend ist es, daß in London wo so viel nectrum gegen alle Arten Beschwerden feil geboten werden, ich nie etwas gegen looseness of the bowels gefunden habe nur Bücher die gegen [illeg.] ein Dutzend Rezepte zum Besten geben, übergehen aber den entgegengesetzten Zustand mit Stillschweigen. Mehr noch, keinen Artzt kann ich bringen mir etwas zur Verringerung dieser Ausleerungen zu verschreiben. Ich wende mich daher an Sie als Artzt, damit Sie mir Rezepte gegen dieses Uebel p[er] Post einsenden: eines gelinde, ein anderes kräftiger, und ein drittes für den Fall daß die ersten nicht wirken sollten. Ich hoffe Sie werden darin den laudenam nich sparen, welcher mir in früheren Magenbeschwerden wohl bekommen ist.

Von Kindern und Kinderskindern gewöhnlich umgeben und an der Spitze einer blühenden Handlung, mit Muße zum Lesen und Träumen habe ich niemand zu beneiden. Ich wünsche Ihnen und meinen sonstigen Freunde ein ähnliches Alter.

Ihr
J. N. Böhl.

158. Elise Campe, Hamburg

Puerto, den 24 Märtz 1836

Werden Sie es, beste Freundin glauben daß ich Ihren Brief vom 10 Oct[ober] 1834 gerade vor vier Tagen erhalten habe welches darthut, daß er 526 Tage auf der Reise gewesen ist? Dieses hat indessen dem Interesse der er in mir erweckt keinen

Eintrag getan und ich bin dafür so dankbar als wäre er nur einen Monath alt. Auch sind was Sie mir darin melden alles Neuigkeiten für mich gewesen, da meine Korrespondenz dorten sich auf die Familie meines Sohnes beschränkt die sich nur mit ihrer nächsten Umgebung beschäftiget, übrigens aber in dieser Beschränkung so glücklich lebt als es uns auf diesem Erdenkloos Verbannten möglich ist.

Ihre so schön ausgedrückten melankolischen Gefühle bei dem Hinscheiden der gewohnten Umgebung berühren harmonsiche Saiten auch in meiner Seele. Nur finde ich mich leider nicht so vollkommen resignirt als Sie es sind. Ich fühle mich immer gedrungen mit unserem Klopstock auszurufen: Warum muß gerade ich so lange zurückbleiben? Warum vielleicht der Letzte sein?[1] – Es wäre indessen undankbar zu verkennen, daß mir die periodische Umgebung von Kindern und Kindeskindern, ein schöner Ersatz für den Abgang der Zeitgenoßen ist, und daß meine Niedergeschlagenheit mehr leiblich als geistlich ist. Der Zustand meiner Beine hat sich leider seit 6 Monathen sehr verschlimmt. Ich habe mehrere offene Wunden, die beim Verbinden sehr schmerzhaft sind und mir den so nöthigen Schlaf rauben, Magen und Kopf ist jedoch bisjetzt gut, und wenn es Gott gefällt und mir dienlich ist, wird er mir die letzten Lebensjahre mildern.

Auch ich habe seit seiner Abreise nach America nichts weiter von unserem guten Dr Julius vernommen. Die Gesellschaft der gelehrten und geschraubten Miss Martineau[2] gönne ich ihm lieber wie mir. Ich wünsche mit Ihnen, daß er als Direktor irgend einer Versorgungsanstalt endlich einmal seinen Haven und Ruhepunkt finden möge.

Alles was Sie mir von der Fam[ilie] Sieveking und Poel sagen hat mich sehr interessirt. Des armen Bokelmann Schiksal geht mir sehr zu Herzen. Ich hoffe Sie werden mir das nächstemal darüber etwas mehr Beruhigendes sagen können. Die Lebendigkeit des betagten Baron Vogts ist zu bewundern und zu beneiden! Er besitzt etwas der allumfaßenden Natur des Stolzes unserer Nazion Göthe! – Mein Interesse an die deutsche Litteratur stirbt immer mehr ab. Meine Reife trifft mit den schönen Jahren von Göthe Schiller und Tieck zusammen. Was seitdem erschienen ist stellt sich mir als matter Abglanz dar und der neusten Tendenz kann ich kein Interesse abgewinnen. Die H[er]rn Heine und Börne[3] sind witzig genug allein solche Ruchlosigkeit kann durch keine Blume gedeckt werden.

Im Anfange gefiel mir die sogenannte romantische Litteratur der Franzosen und es wird immer heilsam bleiben den lächerlichen Damm der akademischen [illeg.] in Paris zerstört zu haben. Sie haben aber kein Maas und Ziel gehalten, und es bleibt einer neuen Generazion aufbehalten das Romantische (insoweit es in französischer Sinnesart möglich ist) edel und anständig darzustellen.

Englisch lese ich am meisten, nicht nur die älteren Werke, sondern auch die stets interessanten vierteljährigen Reviews.

Unsere liebe Cecilia ist seit einem Jahr zum zweitenmal Wittwe;[4] der Tod ihres trefflichen Mannes hat ihre Gesundheit sehr heruntergebracht. Sie denkt bald eine

Reise zu machen und ihre Schwester die Generalin La Fosse nach Paris zu begleiten. Wie gerne würde ich diese Reise mitmachen.

Ich wünsche Ihnen ein warmeres Frühjahr als wir hier haben. Nie habe ich einen rauheren April gekannt; das Kaminfeuer brennt ohne Unterbrechung.

Unwandelbar Ihr warmer Freund

J. N. Bohl

159. August Campe, Hamburg

Puerto, den 30 April 1836

Wenngleich, werther Freund, unsere Briefe sich nicht häufig kreuzen, so thut dieses sicherlich dem inneren Andenken keinen Eintrag, und ich werde mich jederzeit mit Wehmuth meiner Hamburger Winter (die schon so weit hinter uns liegen) erinnern. Diese Rückblicke sind um so schmerzlicher wenn man sie mit der kahlen Gegenwart zusammenstellt. Uns bleibt nichts übrig als uns an diejenige Zukunft zu halten, die hinter dem Schleier unser Verwandlung verborgen liegt. O wäre sie uns doch schon nahe diese glückliche Stunde die uns der Last eines entfremdeten [illeg.] Körpers befreien wird, der allen Aufschwung lähmt, alle alten Gefühle unterdrückt und unser ganzes Dasein auf dem Erdenkloos beschränkt.

Ich danke Ihnen für die kritischen Blätter, allein ich wiederhole was ich Ihr lieben Frau schreibe, Ich bin der deutschen Litteratur total abgestorben, und kann nichts <u>modernes</u> Deutsche lesen. So lange ich so fühle will ich nichts von Deutschland erhalten.

Wie traurig ist was Sie mir von der Familie Vieweg schreiben! – Und doch wird sich am Ende alles so fügen und werden daß niemand leer ausgeht.

In Hinsicht von Familien Nachrichten beziehe ich mich auf die Einlage. Von unseren öffentlichen Angelegenheiten mag ich nicht reden. Beide Partheien habe so gänzlich Maaß und Ziel verloren daß man sich schämen muß um denselben anzuerkennen. Es ist kein Funke von Edelsinn mehr auf der einen noch der anderen Seite und nur der niedrigste Egoismus erhöht durch barbarischen Starrsinn und Rachsucht zeigt sich unverholen. Wenn die fremde Mächte sich nicht ins Mittel legen, so werden sie sich wie die tollen Hunde einander total aufreiben. O wer hätte geglaubt, daß man Bonaparte jetzt als einen Schutzengel ansehen würde um dieses Höllengesindel zu Paare zu treiben. – Gott erlöse uns und vereinige uns in friedvolleren Gefilden! –

Ihr treu ergebener J. N. Bohl

Editor's Notes

The letters presented here are held by the *Staats- und Universitätsbibliothek Hamburg* (SUBHH) and the *Staatsarchiv Hamburg* (SAHH). The source of each letter is indicated by a number which relates to the following, noting both location and catalogue reference:

1. SUBHH: Thes ep 57 (Julius correspondence).
2. SUBHH: CS1: Böhl von Faber (Campe correspondence).
3. SUBHH: CS25 Anh. 3: Böhl von Faber, J. N. (Campe correspondence).
4. SUBHH: LIT ARCH (L. A. Böhl v Faber) (Campe correspondence).
5. SAHH: Perthes Nachlass (Perthes correspondence).

Occasionally, the age of the material has led to some deterioration, making words illegible. The instances of this are relatively rare, but where it occurs, gaps are denoted with either [illeg.] or [damage]. Unless otherwise stated, original orthography and idiosyncrasies of expression have been respected throughout. Abbreviated words have been completed in [ ] and currencies given in full.

The notes provided are not intended to be exhaustive, but focus primarily on Böhl's literary activities. The aim has been to provide brief information on authors and texts to aid further study of the material. Personal acquaintances and historical events are elaborated upon only where their role is significant. Each letter is furnished with a précis to aid those without a reading knowledge of German.

Biographical details of the various correspondents and the nature of their relations with Böhl can be found in the first part of the volume and are not elaborated upon in detail here.

1. Joachim and Dorothea Campe, Trittow; Amsterdam, 23 July 1784; Source 2

Mostly personal with an outline of travel from Hamburg to Amsterdam.

1. Joachim Heinrich Campe (1746–1818), *Theophron oder der erfahrene Rathgeber für die unerfahrene Jugend* (1783).

2. Joachim and Dorothea Campe, Trittow; Andover, 7 October 1784; Source 3

Description of journey to Andover and of his tuition under Dr Tay. Expresses reservations about the English character, but satisfaction with the country and its customs. Reports seeing Lunardi's hot air balloons.

1. Karoline Rudolphi (1754–1811), poet and pedagogue, associate of Campe, and her brother Ludwig, B.'s piano teacher at Billwerder.
2. Charlotte Campe (1774–1834), Campe's only daughter.
3. Vincenzo Lunardi (1759–1806), undertook the first manned balloon flight at Moorfields in London in 1784.
4. Lorenz Andreas Noodt (1743–1809), director of the Hamburg *Johanneaum*.

3. Joachim Heinrich and Dorothea Campe, Trittow; Andover, 3 March 1785; Source 2

Mostly personal. Expresses affection for the Campes and sadness at his separation from them. Outlines future plans to travel to Cadiz via France.

4. Joachim Heinrich Campe, Trittow; Cadiz, 2 August 1785; Source 2

Congratulates Campe on his birthday. Outlines his journey from England to Cadiz by ship. Describes the monotony of mercantile duties and the routine of Spanish social life. Expresses disquiet at the religious bigotry of Spain.

5. Joachim Heinrich Campe, Braunschweig; Cadiz, 1 May 1790; Source 3

Thanks Campe for a parcel of books. Comments on Campe's experiences in Paris during the revolution and his probable dislike of Spain. Outlines his future mercantile plans and the desire to expand his intellectual horizons, as well as the need to fulfil his role in society. Reference to the Hamburg circle.

1. Campe's *Briefe aus Paris aus der Zeit der Revolution geschrieben* (1790).
2. Campe's *Robinson der Jüngere* (1779) translated into Spanish in 1790 by Tomás de Iriarte (1750–91).

6. Dorothea Campe; Cadiz, July 1790; Source 3

Expresses the desire to return to Germany, but his future is uncertain due to the political situation between Spain and England. Continued disaffection vis-à-vis Spain and first evidence of a crisis of self-confidence for which he seeks advice and support. Explains his desire to study and become a man of letters rather than a merchant, but also makes clear his limitations in creative terms.

1. *Braunschweigisches Journal*, periodical which focused on literature, philology and pedagogy, published by Campe and Trapp (see letter 8, note 3) from 1788 to 1793, and later became the *Schleswigisches Journal*.

7. *Joachim Heinrich and Dorothea Campe, Braunschweig; Cadiz, 31 May 1791; Source 3; appended to a letter from Anton Gottlieb Böhl*

Mostly personal, but with further evidence of a crisis of self-confidence.

8. *Joachim Heinrich and Dorothea Campe, Braunschweig; Cadiz, 27 April 1792; Source 3*

Reports on the visit of Professor Stuve. Mention of an eye problem. Requests further copies of the *Braunschweigisches Journal* and other recommended books, which can be smuggled in with relative ease despite restrictions.

1. Johann Stuve (1752–93), pedagogue, associate of Campe.
2. Nicolas Conrad Schuback (1769–1835), son of the prominent Hamburg merchant, fellow pupil of Campe.
3. Ernst Christian Trapp (1745–1818), pedagogue and educational scientist, associate of Campe.

9. *Joachim Heinrich and Dorothea Campe, Braunschweig; Cadiz, 27 August 1793; Source 3*

Reports a year-long trip to France to cure his eye problem. Comments on the situation in France, expressing support for the political system there. Expresses the desire openly to condemn the prevailing mood in Spain, something he can only achieve with a return to Germany. First evidence of doubts in matters of faith as he requests guidance whilst also expressing his confidence in the value of reason. Responds positively to request for a charitable donation, but feels any such help should be rehabilitative and practical, rather than charitable.

1. Johann Valentin Meyer (1772–1800), B.'s trading associate.
2. Adolph Freiherr von Knigge (1752–96), novelist and writer, well known for his guides to social behaviour, author of *Benjamin Noldmanns Geschichte der Aufklärung in Abyssinien* (1790).
3. Charitable establishment founded in Hamburg by the *Patriotischer Gesellschaft von 1765* (Patriotic Society of 1765).

10. Joachim Heinrich and Dorothea Campe, Braunschweig; Cadiz, 24 October 1794; Source 3; cosignatory: Anton Gottlieb Böhl

Gratitude for a parcel of books which provide much needed intellectual stimulation in an uncultured environment. Comments on the work of Rousseau, agreeing with his view of women as intellectually inferior. First reference to Riem. Outlines future plans for the company in Cadiz and possibility of purchasing an estate in Switzerland. Also, plans to travel to the United States with his brother, Fritz. Expresses concern at current situation in Germany, where reason seems to be losing its hold.

1. Jean Jacques Rousseau (1712–78), *Émile, ou l'education* (1762), translated into German in 1789–91 by Hamburg writer and translator, Carl Friedrich Cramer (1752–1807) and published by Campe.
2. See letter 6, note 1.
3. Andreas Riem (1749–1814), theologian, *Christus und die Vernunft oder Prüfung der Wahrheit und Göttlichkeit der Lehre Jesu Christi des christlichen Lehrbegriffs und der symbolischen Bücher* (1792).
4. Karl Philipp Funk (1752–1807), pedagogue and historian, author of *Praktische Geschichte der Menschen* (1793).
5. Christian Garve (1742–98), moral philosopher and writer, pre-empts some of the Classic–Romantic debate, translated Cicero's *De officiis* into German in 1783.
6. Johan Hinrich Ludendorff (1757–1829), member of the prominent Hamburg family.
7. Franz Jacob Schuback (1774–1830), member of the prominent Hamburg merchant family, private scholar, cousin of Nicolas Conrad.
8. Leopold Graf Berchtold (1759–1809), ancestor of the early twentieth-century Austro-Hungarian foreign minister of the same name.

11. Joachim Heinrich and Dorothea Campe, Braunschweig; Cadiz, 3 February 1795; Source 3

Discussion of plans for a joint trip to America with Campe. Reports postponement of trip to Switzerland until 1796. Refers to an inner struggle between reason and nature. First mention of plans to marry. Further reference to Riem and request for Campe's response to his writings. Reiteration of agreement with Rousseau on the status of women.

1. Andreas Riem, *Reines System der Religion für Vernünftige* (1793).

12. Joachim Heinrich Campe, Braunschweig; Morges, 21 January 1797; Source 3

Discussion of plans to purchase property in the vicinity of Braunschweig. Reports birth of first child, Cecilia. Outlines difficulties in educating Francisca due to her romantic leanings. Description of his mother-in-law and hope that the company of Dorothea and Lotte will have a positive influence on them both. Discussion of recent books which reveals a divergence of opinion with his mentor and an increasing reliance on emotion and feeling rather than reason, one which causes a degree of disquiet. Reference to tensions in the relationship of Goethe and Schiller and a positive appraisal of Schiller's *Die Horen*, in particular the *Aesthetic Letters* which manage to combine emotion and reason. Expresses concern at potential problems of trying to settle his family in Germany, in particular the climate and the language. Reports on his brothers' plans and activities.

1. Reference to a missing letter.
2. Johann Wolfgang von Goethe (1749–1832) and Friedrich Schiller (1759–1805), the most prominent German writers of their day, central to both the *Sturm und Drang* and Wiemar Classicism.
3. *Die Horen*, periodical published by Schiller from 1795 to 1798, which contained his *Ästhetische Briefe*.
4. Reference to Lotte's first son.
5. Andreas Georg Friedrich Rebmann (1768–1824), *Ludwig Wagehals. Ein Gemälde menschlicher Sitten, Vorurtheile, Thorheiten, Laster, etc, etc, in allen Himmelstrichen* (1795).

13. Joachim Heinrich and Dorothea Campe, Braunschweig; Morges, 28 March 1797; Source 3

Family news including further negotiations for the purchase of a property near Braunschweig. Description of his wife, her family and their courtship.

1. Matthias Claudius (1740–1815), writer, known as the *Wandsbeker Bothe*, Friedrich Perthes' father-in-law.

14. Joachim Heinrich and Dorothea Campe, Braunschweig; Chiclana, 8 February 1798; Source 2

Explains reasons for leaving Germany so suddenly and describes the journey back to Spain, including the trip through Catholic Westfalia, an area much maligned by Campe. Expresses satisfaction at having decided to return, explaining that his wife and mother-in-law were unhappy in Germany. Describes life in Spain in far more positive terms than previously, praising his work as a merchant and the pleasures of family life. Refers to the Campes' nephew, August, who has been asked to send him the latest books. Expresses continued affection for his foster parents.

1. Reference to Campe's nephew, Franz August Gottlieb Campe (1773–1836), bookseller and correspondent of Böhl.

15. Dorothea Campe, Braunschweig; Chiclana, 16 April 1798; Source 3

Personal matters including the sale of the property near Braunschweig. Reports on the political situation and its impact on trade.

16. Dorothea Campe, Braunschweig; Cadiz, 16 October 1798; Source 3

Personal matters including Francisca's second pregnancy. Appraisal of his travel journal and discussion of the impact of the Spanish climate on his mood. Reports the purchase of estates by both his brother, Fritz, and his brother-in-law, Berckemeyer, events which have reawakened his own desire to be a landowner.

1. Jean François Bourgoing (1748–1811), *Tableau d'Espagne moderne* (1789).
2. Campe's *Wörterbuch zur Erklärung und Verdeutschung der unserer Sprache aufgedrungenen fremden Ausdrücke*, 2 vols (1801).

17. Dorothea Campe, Braunschweig; Cadiz, 8 February 1799; Source 3

Personal matters, including the birth of a second daughter, Aurora. Reiteration of desire to become a landowner.

18. Joachim Heinrich and Dorothea Campe, Braunschweig; Cadiz, 15 August 1799; Source 3

Personal matters including a report of illness due to the summer heat. Expresses a desire to return to Germany, but is restricted by family and business commitments and the political situation. Hopes that shipping restrictions will soon be lifted in order to take delivery of books requested, including Goethe's *Propyläen*, the Schlegels' *Athenaeum* and Gentz's *Journal*. Reports progress in studies in various areas including mathematics and astronomy. Complains about married life and reports some friction in the family. Copes with these problems by retreating into his studies.

1. Reference to Campe's son-in-law, the publisher, Johann Friedrich Vieweg (1761–1835), who married Lotte in 1795.

2. Christoph Wilhelm Hufeland (1762–1836), physician, author of *Bemerkungen über die natürlichen und künstlichen Blattern zu Weimar im Jahr 1788* (1799), *Makrobiotik oder Die Kunst das menschliche Leben zu verlängern* (1796) and *Guter Rath an Mütter über die wichtigsten Puncte der physischen Erziehung der Kinder in den ersten Jahren* (1799).
3. Garve's *Einige Betrachtungen über die allgemeinsten Grundsätze der Sittenlehre* (1798).
4. *Propyläen*, periodical established by Goethe in 1798 in opposition to the Schlegel brothers' *Athenaeum*.
5. *Athenaeum*, literary journal edited by August Wilhelm (1767–1845) and Friedrich Schlegel (1772–1829), main organ of early Romantic theory from 1798 to 1800.
6. Friedrich von Gentz (1764–1832), editor of the anti-revolutionary *Historisches Journal* from 1799 to 1800.
7. Friedrich Jean Paul Richter (1763–1825), poet and writer associated with early Romanticism.

19. Dorothea Campe, Braunschweig; Cadiz, 5 November 1799; Source 3

Personal matters, including improved health. Complains that August has failed to respond to a request to publish some music by a Spanish acquaintance (details not provided). Emphasises importance of his quest for knowledge by covering a wide range of topics, including chemistry and geometry. Expresses the wish to enrol at university and then acquire an estate near the Campes. Reference to the unstable financial situation caused by political events.

1. Joseph Haydn (1732–1809), Austrian composer.
2. Antoine Laurent Lavoisier (1743–94), founder of modern chemistry.
3. Johann Heinrich Gottlieb Heusinger (1767–1837), *Handbuch der Aesthetik oder Grundsätze zur Bearbeitung und Beurtheilung der Werke einer jeden schönen Kunst* (1792).
4. Francesco Petrarca (1304–74), Italian poet and scholar.
5. Reference to Campe's *Der neue Froschmäusler: ein Heldengedicht in drei Büchern* (1796), of which only one volume appeared, based on the orginal *Froschmeusler* (1595) by Georg Rollenhagen (1542–1609).

20. Dorothea Campe, Braunschweig; Cadiz, 13 April 1802; Source 3

Personal matters, including Campe's illness and possible visit to Spain.

21. Dorothea Campe, Braunschweig; Cadiz, 19 August 1803; Source 3

Personal matters including reports on the Hamburg circle and the Catholic education of his children. Reference to Campe's most recent travelogue on England. Describes problems facing trade due to the war and reiterates desire to return to Germany which cannot be realised because of his mother-in-law. Reports his new enthusiasm for older Spanish literature and the temperament of the age. Refers to some essays on Spanish theatre, one of which has been published by a friend (publication untraced) and reports first dissemination of ideas of Kant and Schiller in his Cadiz circle. Expresses enthusiasm for the Spanish language, in particular its colour and wit, and bemoans the fact that it is not more widely known and appreciated. Makes a first reference to German patriotism.

1. Ernst Daniel August Bartels (1778–1838), physician.
2. Johannes Schuback (1766–1822), member of the prominent Hamburg merchant family, brother of Nicolas Conrad.
3. August Friedrich Ferdinand von Kotzebue (1761–1819), dramatist, critical of Romanticism, murdered in 1819.
4. Luciano Francisco Comella (1751–1812), prolific Spanish playwright.
5. Gaspar Zavala y Zamora (1762–1824), playwright and novelist, known for his sentimental comedies.
6. Antonio Valladares y Sotomayor (1740–1820), translator and playwright.
7. Reference to some early writings on theatre which have not been located.
8. Immanuel Kant (1724–1804), philosopher of the German Enlightenment, influential for German Romanticism.
9. B.'s friend and Danish consul in Cadiz in 1803.

22. August Campe, Hamburg; Görslow, 27 September 1806; Source 4

Book orders on topics relating to war.

1. *Kaiserlich priviligierter Reichsanzeiger* (1791–1806).
2. Freiherr Heinrich Dietrich von Bülow (1760–1807), Prussian soldier and military writer, author of *Der Feldzug 1801* (1801), *Der Feldzug 1805* (1806), *Blicke auf zukünftige Begebenheiten* (1806) and *Geist des neueren Kriegssystems* (1805).
3. Louis XIV (1638–1715), on the French throne from 1661 to 1715, his *Ouevres* were published in 1806.
4. Johann Philipp Palm (1766–1806), bookseller in Nuremberg, executed by Napoleonic troops following the publication of the anti-Napoleonic pamphlet *Deutschland in seiner tiefen Erniedrigung* (1806).
5. Friedrich Bouterwek (1766–1828), scholar and philosopher, author of the

influential 12 volume study of European literature, *Geschichte der Poesie und Beredsamkeit* (1801–19).

23. Dorothea Campe, Braunschweig; Hamburg, 22 January 1807; Source 3

Refers to the political situation and its impact on communication. Describes his new life in Germany as a rebirth and bemoans the fact that he may have to return to Spain to be reunited with his wife and children. Outlines requirements for a tutor for the children in the hope that Dorothea can recommend someone. Admits to escaping reality in his studies.

1. Reference to the prominent *Nationaltheater* in Hamburg whose dramaturgists included Gotthold Ephraim Lessing (1729–81).

24. Dorothea Campe, Braunschweig; Hamburg, 13 February 1807; Source 3

Describes his current world view as one focused on the inner self. Explains the impact of the war on business, but feels it is no worse than that of piracy in peace-time. Describes Francisca's current situation in Spain and praises her strength of character in the face of a loss of status. Reports on friends and family in Hamburg and complains of August's incompetence as a bookseller when compared to Perthes.

1. A fellow pupil under Campe, son of Polycarp Leisching (1730–93).
2. Reference to August Campe's wife, Elizabeth (Elise) Campe, née Hoffmann (1786–1873), daughter of the publisher, Benjamin Gottlob Hoffmann (1748–1818), and correspondent of B.
3. Friedrich Perthes (1772–1843), bookseller and publisher in Hamburg, then Gotha, correspondent of B.
4. Reference to a member of the prominent Hamburg patrician family.

25. Dorothea Campe, Braunschweig; Görslow, 20 June 1807; Source 3

Personal matters including the appointment of a tutor. Describes his interest in agriculture.

26. Dorothea Campe, Braunschweig; Görslow, 25 February 1810; Source 3

Apologises for a long silence and goes on to describe life as a father and a landowner. He outlines the new direction of his studies, in particular older

German literature and mysticism, with which he feels he cannot quite connect. The tone suggests a more Romantic world view and focuses on the inner aspect of his life. Expresses desire to have family reunited, in Germany if possible, but concedes he may have to return to Spain.

1. Unattributed quotation.

27. Dorothea Campe, Braunschweig; Görslow, 24 March 1810; Source 3

Personal matters including the education of his children. Reference to the reworking of Campe's *Froschmäusler* and also to his dictionary. Voices a first defence of Catholicism in discussing the Bavarian situation under Napoleon and presents a positive view of mysticism. Discusses Schelling's *Freiheitsschrift* and identifies the influence of mystics on Schelling and Fichte.

1. Johann Joachim Eschenburg (1743–1829), critic and literary historian.
2. Friedrich Wilhelm Joseph Schelling (1775–1854), *Über das Wesen der menschlichen Freiheit* (1809).
3. Johann Gottlieb Fichte (1762–1814), writer and philosopher of transcendental Idealism.
4. *Theologia Teutsch*, an anonymous volume containing the key teachings of the mystics, discovered and then published by Luther in 1516.

28. Nikolas Heinrich Julius, Hamburg; Görslow, 6 April 1810; Source 1

Clear declaration of a new Romantic world view, including a reference to Goethe's *Die Wahlverwandtschaften* as a key text in his 'conversion'. Further comments on Schelling and mysticism and the discussion of a number of theologians. Reference to the *Vaterländisches Museum* and an interest in *Volkslieder* and religious music. Reports on various auctions and comments on mystical works, including St Martin, Böhme, St Teresa and Chateaubriand. Further defence of Catholicism.

1. Goethe's experimental novel of 1809, *Die Wahlverwandtschaften*.
2. Aurelius Augustinius (354–430), St Augustine.
3. Jacques-Benigne Bossuet (1627–1704), French bishop and orator, theologian, advocate of Absolutism.
4. Cornelius Jansensius (1585–1638), theologian, Catholic bishop of Ypres and founder of Jansenism.
5. John Calvin (Jean Chauvin) (1509–64), Protestant theologian and founder of Calvinism.
6. Miguel de Molinos (1640–96), founder of Quietism.

7. Possibly a reference to Johann Daniel Wagener's German–Spanish dictionary, *Diccionario de faltiriquera, ó sea portatil, Español-Aleman y Aleman-Español* (1808–9).
8. Reference to the *Vaterländisches Museum*, edited by Julius and published by Perthes from 1810 to 1811.
9. Bernhard Joseph Docen (1782–1828), philologist and writer, on the periphery of the Romantic school.
10. Rudolph Wasserhun, seventeenth-century song-writer from Lower Saxony, of whom little is known.
11. Michael Schirmer (1623–87), song-writer.
12. Ernst Christoph Homburg (1605–81), writer and religious poet.
13. Christian Wernike (1661–1725), epigrammist and diplomat, author of *Überschriffte oder Epigrammata* (1697).
14. Pseudonym of Gottlieb Stolle (1673–1744), collector and publisher of popular poetry.
15. Johann Christoph Friedrich Haug (1761–1829) and Friedrich Christoph Weisser (1761–1836), editors of the ten-volume *Epigrammatische Anthologie* (1807–9).
16. Erdmann Neumeister (1671–1756), theologian, author of the dissertation *De poetis Germanicus hiuis saeculi praecipius* (1695).
17. Heinrich Albert (1604–51), baroque composer.
18. Simon Dach (1605–59), hymnist and poet.
19. Friedrich Christoph Oetinger (1702–82), theosophist, influenced by Böhme (see note 21), translator of Swedenborg (see letter 29, note 10).
20. Louis Claude de Saint-Martin (1743–1802), theosophist, author of *Des erreurs et de la Verité, par un Philosophe Inconnu* (1775) and *Oeuvres posthumes* (1807).
21. Jakob Böhme (1575–1624), shoemaker, German mystic, influential for Pietism and Romanticism, theosophy of God in Nature.
22. François-René Vicomte de Chateaubriand (1768–1848), writer, politician and diplomat, author of *Le Genie du christianisme* (1802).
23. Friedrich Heinrich Jakobi (1743–1819), merchant, civil servant, writer and philosopher.
24. Semi-autobiographical chivalric verse authored by Kaiser Maximilian I (1459–1519), published in 1517.
25. Johann August Gottlob Weigel (1773–1846), bookseller in Leipzig.
26. Johann Christoph Adelung (1732–1806), *Geschichte der menschlichen Narrheit, oder Lebensbeschreibungen berühmter Schwarz-künstler, Goldmacher, Teufelsbanner, Zeichen und Linien-deuter, Schwärmer, Wahrsager und anderer philosophischer Unholden* (1785–9).

27. St Teresa de Avila (1515–82), mystic poet and Carmelite nun, who, along with San Juan de la Cruz (1542–91), represents height of Spanish mysticism.

29. *Nikolas Heinrich Julius, Hamburg; Görslow, 18 April 1810; Source 1*

Reports on various book orders, including a number of mystical and early German texts.

1. Reference to the popular fable *Reinicke Fuchs* (*Reinke Voss* in Low German).
2. Reference to the German translation of *Guzmán de Alfarache* (1599) by Mateo Alemán (1547–c1615), *Der Landstörzer Gusman von Alfarache oder Picaro genandt* (1615) by Aegidius Albertinus (1560–1620).
3. Possible reference to the *Lieder nach dem Anakreon* (1766) by Johann Wilhelm Ludwig Gleim (1719–1803).
4. Johann Balthasar Schuppius (1610–61), satirst and religious poet.
5. Christian Ludwig Liscow (1701–60), satirist, *Die Vortrefflichkeit und Nothwendigkeit der elenden Scribenten gründlich erwiesen von ***** * (1734).
6. Johann Lauremberg (1590–1658), satirist, *De veer olde beromede Schertz-Gedichte* (1652).
7. Joachim Rachel (1618–69), satirist, *Neu-verbesserte Teutsche Satyrische Gedichte* (1694) which contains Lauremberg's text.
8. Reference to the Göttingen bookseller and publisher, Vandenhoeck und Ruprecht, established in 1735.
9. Abraham de Santa Clara (Johann Ulrich Megerle) (1644–1709), Catholic moralist and Augustinian friar.
10. Emanuel Swedenborg (1688–1772), theosophist and mystic.
11. Reference to Oetinger's *Swedenborg und anderer irdische himmlische Philosophie, zur Prüfung des Besten, ans Licht gestellt* (1765).

30. *Nikolas Heinrich Julius, Hamburg; Görslow, 24 May 1810; Source 1*

Reports on book orders and auctions. Seeks a good guide to Catholicism and explains that mysticism has enhanced his ability to reason, rather than clouding it. Also requires works by a number of Romantic writers, including Friedrich Schlegel, Tieck, Arnim and Fouqué, as well as several Spanish writers. Notable for B's first reference to August Wilhelm Schlegel's lectures.

1. Gottlieb Jacob Planck (1751–1833), author of a number of texts on the history of Christianity and Protestantism, including *Worte des Friedens an die katholische Kirche gegen ihre Vereinigung mit der protestantischen* (1809).
2. No reference to this author could be found.

3. Savinien Cyrano de Bergerac (1619–55), author of *L'autre Mond où les états et empires de la lune* (1657).
4. Reference to Johann Gustav Büsching (1783–1829) and Friedrich von der Hagen (1780–1856), *Buch der Liebe* (1809), based on the 1587 *Buch der Liebe* published in Leipzig by Sigmund Feyerabend (1528–1590).
5. Reference to the Hamburg periodical, *Nordische Miszellen*.
6. Carl Michael Bellman (1740–95), *Kämpe-visa ofver Segren vid Hogland* (1788).
7. Friedrich Heinrich Graf von Seckendorf (1673–1763), commander in chief for Charles VI, Holy Roman Emperor.
8. Friedrich Schlegel (1772–1829), poet, philosopher, philologist, early Romantic theorist.
9. Johann Ludwig Tieck (1773–1853), poet, writer, early Romantic thinker.
10. Friedrich August Kanne (1778–1833), composer and writer.
11. Christian Wilhelm von Schütz (1776–1847), author of *Romantische Wälder* (1808).
12. Ludwig Achim von Arnim (1781–1831), Romantic writer and associate of Clemens Brentano (1778–1842), author of *Armuth, Reichthum, Schuld und Buße der Gräfin Dolores* (1810).
13. Friedrich de la Motte Fouqué (1777–1843), Romantic writer, author of the *Nibelungen* trilogy *Der Held des Nordens* (1808–10) and *Sigurd der Schlangentöter, ein Heldenspiel* (1808).
14. Johann Peter Hebel (1760–1826), poet, famed for his *Kalendergeschichten*, author of *Schatzkästlein des rheinischen Hausfreundes* (1811).
15. Alexander von Humboldt (1769–1859), scientist and geographer, author of *Versuch über den politischen Zustand des Königreiches Neu-Spanien* (1809–14).
16. Friedrich von Matthison (1761–1831), poet and prose writer whose *Erinnerungen* were published in five volumes from 1810 to 1816.
17. *Morgenblatt für gebildete Stände*, leading cultural periodical which appeared from 1807 to 1865, initially published by Johann Friedrich Cotta von Cottendorff (1764–1832).
18. Friedrich Müller (1749–1825), artist and writer associated with the *Sturm und Drang*.
19. Ginés Pérez de Hita (c.1544–c.1619), *Historia de los bandos de los Zegríes y Abencerrages*, known as the *Guerras civiles de Granada* (part one, 1595; part two, 1619), a novel derived from *romances* and historical material.
20. Reference to the second volume of August Wilhelm Schlegel's *Vorlesungen über dramatische Literatur* (1811).
21. *Bragur*, periodical published by Friedrich David Gräter (1768–1830), the founder of Nordic studies in Germany.

22. Lazarus Ercker (1530–94), *Aula subterranea. Unterirdische Hofhaltung* (1672).
23. Philippe de Mornay (1549–1623), *Traité de la verité de la religion chrétienne contre les athées, épicuriens, payens, juifs, mahométans et autres infidèles* (1581).
24. Antione-François Prévost d'Exiles (1697–1763), *Mémoires et aventures d'un homme de qualité qui s'est retire du monde* (1732).
25. Traiano Boccalini (1556–1613), civil servant and scholar, *Ragguagli di Parnaso* (1612).
26. Johann Jacob Brucker (1696–1770), *Ehren-Tempel der deutschen Gelehrsamkeit* (1747).
27. *Der teutschen Sprache Stammbaum und Fortwachs, oder, Teutscher Sprachschatz worinnen alle und iede teutsche Wurzeln oder Stammwörter, so viel deren annoch bekant und ietzo im Gebrauch seyn ... samt einer hochteutschen Letterkunst, Nachschusz und teutschem Register durch unermhudeten Fleisz in vielen Jahren gesamlet von dem Spaten* (1691), published by Kaspar Stieler (1632–1707).
28. Coelius Secundus Curio (1503–69), *Pasquillorum Tomi duo* (1544).
29. Jeanne Marie Bouvier de la Moth Guyon (1647–1717), French Quietist author.
30. Possible reference to Pierre Poivre (1719–86), writer and traveller.
31. *Koddige en ernstige opschriften, op luyffels, wagens, glazen, uithangborden en andere tafereelen; van langerhand by een gezamelt en uitgeschreven, door een liefhebber der zelve* (1698), compiled by Hieronymus Sweerts (1627–96).
32. Michael Prätorius (1571–1621), composer of church music and musical scholar.
33. Possible reference to the fairytale *Die Gänsemagd*.
34. Possible reference to Adam Gottlieb Detlef Graf von Moltke (1765–1843), writer, estate Gut Noer.

31. Nikolas Heinrich Julius, Hamburg; Görslow, 4 June 1810; Source 1

Discusses plans for a visit by Julius to Görslow. Reports on book orders and auctions. Emphasis on *Lieder*, using *Wunderhorn* as a measure. Continues to collect older German and mystical works and has completed his collection of Böhme.

1. Medieval German legend of a knight who discovered the Venusberg, found in both Grimms' *Deutsche Sagen* and the *Wunderhorn*.
2. Achim von Arnim and Clemens Brentano, *Des Knaben Wunderhorn* (1808), first major ballad collection of the German Romantic period, compiled with the collaboration of the Brothers Grimm.

Editor's Notes

3. No reference to this text could be found.
4. Heinrich Kornmann (1579–1627), published a version of the *Tannhäuser* legend, *Mons veneris* (1614).
5. Reference to the ballad of the Pied Piper of Hamyln, which, contrary to B.'s assertion, does appear in the *Wunderhorn*.
6. Reference to *Ueber die Entstehung der altdeutschen Poesie und ihr Vehältniss zu der nordischen* (1808) by Wilhelm Grimm (1786–1859).
7. Refers to the following works by Böhme: *Apologien* (1624), *De Signatura Rerum* (1622) and *Weg zu Christo* (1623).
8. Sextus Julius Frontinus (30–103), Roman military writer, whose *Kriegsanschlege* appeared in 1542.
9. Giovanni Boccati or Giovanni di Piermatteo (c.1420–c.1480), Italian painter.
10. Johannes Angeli Silesii (1624–77), *Cherubinischer Wandersmann* (1675).
11. Gottfried Arnold (1666–1714), *Die Erste Liebe Christo* (1696).
12. Gerhard Tersteegen (1697–1769), *Lebensbeschreibungen heiliger Seelen* (1733–53).
13. Jean Chapelain (1595–1674), French writer, author of the verse epic, *La Pucelle d'Orléans* (1656).
14. Pierre Belon (1517–64), French naturalist, author of *Les Observations de plusieurs singularites et choses memorables trouvées en Grèce, Asie, Judié, Egypte, Arabie et autres pays étrangèrs* (1553).
15. *Seder 'Olam*, earliest post-exilic Hebrew chronicle, first appeared in 1514.
16. Johann Karl Dähnert (1719–85), *Svensk-tysk och tysk-svensk ordbok* (1796).
17. *Histoire de Louis XI* (1745) by Charles Pineau-Duclos (1704–72).
18. Pierre-Louis-Pascale Jullian (1769–????), French anti-revolutionary, author of various texts, would later publish *Précis historique des principaux evenements politiques et militaries qui ont amené la revolution en Espagne* (1821).
19. Chivalric poem *L'Orlando innamorato* (1495) by Italian poet, Matteo Maria Boiardo (1434–94).
20. Vincentius Placcius (1642–99), *De scriptis et scriptoribus anonymis atque pseudonymis syntagma* (1674).
21. Earliest complete version of the Bible in Spanish, printed in 1569, so-called because the image of a bear printed on the frontispiece.
22. *Wertheimer Bibel* (1735), controversial free translation of the first five Books of Moses.
23. Sebastian Münster (1488–1552), *Kosmographey* (1550).
24. Johann Ludwig Gottfried (1584–1633), *Archontologia cosmica* (1628), translation of the original by Pierre d'Avity (1573–1635).
25. Tommaso Garzoni (1549–89), *Piazza Universale oder Allgemeiner Schauplatz der Künste* (1619).

26. Published in 1622 by Théophile de Viau (1590–1626) in defence of free speech.
27. *Le moyen du Parvenir* (1610) by Béroalde de Verville (1556–1626).
28. No reference to this author and text could be found.

32. Nikolas Heinrich Julius, Hamburg; Görslow, 16 August 1810; Source 1

Praises a sermon by Pastor Geibel which he interprets in mystical terms. Expresses approval of the *Vaterländisches Museum* and voices explicit patriotic views. Hopes to see *Lieder* published in it, even if this will upset Classical taste. Refers again to his travelogue on Spain, but feels it to be unsuitable for publication. Reports on book orders and auctions, with an emphasis on mystical texts. Ambivalent response to the work of Schubert.

1. Johannes Geibel (1776–1853), polemicist and Protestant pastor in Lübeck, father of the poet Emanual Geibel (1815–84).
2. Reference to the Romantic nationalist periodical, *Vaterländisches Museum*, published by Perthes and edited by Julius. B. refers to the following texts: vol. 1, part 1, no. 2: 'Nachdämmerung für Deutschland', Jean Paul Richter (pp. 6–44); no. 3: 'Über das Verderbniß im deutschen Charakter, nachgewiesen am Verfall des nationalen Gewerbefleißes von Georgius' (pp. 45–72); no. 4: 'Einige Vorlesungen über den wahren Charakter eines protestantischen Geistlichen', Philipp Konrad Marheinecke (1780–1846), (pp. 73–113); 'Das Verlorene' poem by Fouqué (p. 119); vol. 1, part 2: 'Aufsatz von Heeren' refers to 'Ueber die Mittel zur Erhaltung der Nationalität besiegter Völker', Arnold Heeren (1760–1842), (pp. 129–53); 'Reflexionen von Orion' (pseudonym Görres; see letter 37, note 5), (pp. 154–71).
3. Gotthilf Heinrich von Schubert (1780–1860), leading natural philosopher of German Romanticism and author of the three-volume *Ahndungen einer allgemeinen Geschichte des Lebens* (1806–21).

33. Dorothea Campe, Braunschweig; Görslow, 1 September 1810; Source 3

Personal matters including the education of his children and the postponement of his return to Spain. Describes Francisca's situation in Spain where she finds herself restricted by the French occupation. Her patriotism continues to impress. Reports the end of his exploration of mysticism, which he finds requires too much emotional effort. His main interests are seventeenth-century German literature.

Editor's Notes

34. Nikolas Heinrich Julius, Hamburg; Görslow, 5 September 1810; Source 1

Discussion of content of *Nordische Miszellen* and the *Vaterländisches Museum*. Outlines plans for a collection of *Lieder* in collaboration with Julius. Reports on book orders and auctions, in particular seventeenth-century German literature. Refers to the *Heidelberger Jahrbücher* with the first detailed reference to August Wilhelm Schlegel's *Wiener Vorlesungen*.

1. Probable reference to Karl Ludwig Friedrich Joseph von Brandenstein (1760–1847), politician and philanthropist.
2. Reference to the author of 'Reflexion von Orion' in the *Vaterländisches Museum*, attributed to Görres (see letter 37, note 5).
3. Bishop Thomas Percy (1729–81), *Reliques of Ancient English Poetry*, published in three volumes in 1765.
4. Friedrich Wilhelm Zachariä (1726–77), writer, translator and editor.
5. Martin Opitz (1597–1639), poet and philologist, seen as the father of modern German poetry.
6. Paul Fleming (1609–40), spiritual poet.
7. Leonhard Meister (1741–1811), *Characteristik deutscher Dichter nach der Zeitordnung gereihet* (1789).
8. Michael Ignaz Schmidt (1736–94), historian, *Geschichte der Deutschen*, begun in 1778, but never completed.
9. Karl Heinrich Jördens (1757–1835), pedagogue and lexicographer, *Lexicon deutscher Dichter und Prosaisten* (1805–11).
10. *Rubella* (1631) by Paul Fleming.
11. Adam Olearius (1599–1671), published Fleming's work posthumously in 1641 and 1646.
12. Johann Albrecht von Mandelslo (1616–44), writer and associate of Fleming and Olearius.
13. Christian Weise (1642–1708), pseudonym Sigmund Gleichviel, pedagogue and writer, author of *Die zwey Haupt-Verderber in Teutschland* (1671) and *Die drey ärgsten Ertz-Narren* (1672).
14. Robert Roberthin (1600–48), Baroque poet and scholar.
15. *Das Picardische Gesangbuch* (1539).
16. Reference to Gottsched's acrimonious polemic on regulation in poetry with eminent scholars of the Zürich school, Johann Jakob Bodmer (1698–1783) and Johann Jakob Breitinger (1701–76).
17. Johann Christoph Gottsched (1700–66), reformed German stage along neo-Classical lines, editor of various periodicals, including *Das Neueste aus der anmuthigen Gelehrsamkeit* (1751–62).
18. Schubert's *Ansichten von der Nachtseite der Naturwissenschaft* (1808).

19. Gonzalo de Berceo (1196–1252), poet and religious theorist, *Loores de nuestra señora*.
20. Reference to the *Heidelberger Jahrbücher der Literatur*, established in 1810 and one of the key organs of German Romanticism. August Wilhelm Schlegel wrote a number of reviews for the periodical.
21. Germaine, Baroness de Staël (1766–1817), French writer and advocate of German Romanticism.

35. Nikolas Heinrich Julius, Hamburg; Görslow, 15 September 1810; Source 1

Discussion of genre definition in relation to *Lieder*, ballads and *romances*. Expresses a preference for *Volkslieder* over *Minnelieder*. Views *romances* as outbursts of individual emotion. Reveals a self-awareness as a transcultural scholar and demonstrates broad knowledge of older German works. Reports on book orders and auctions. Refers again to his travelogue on Spain and also his unpublished essays on Spanish theatre, of which he is critical. Ends with a defence of the Romantic ideal.

1. Augustus Buchner (1591–1661), poet and Classical philologist.
2. Andreas Tscherning (1611–59), poet.
3. Hans Aßmann (Johann Erasmus), Freiherr von Abschatz (1646–99), poet and translator.
4. Ernst Christoph Homburg (1607–81), poet.
5. Albert's *Musikalische Kürbishütte und Lieder von Tod und Liebe* (1645).
6. No reference to this text could be found.
7. Friedrich Freiherr von Logau (1604–55), Baroque poet.
8. Georg Rudolf Weckherlin (1584–1653), Baroque poet.
9. Johann Caspar Wetzel (1691–1755), hymnist and song writer.
10. Reference to a jointly bound copy of works by Johannes Tauler (1300–61), mystic, whose sermons first appeared in 1498, and Johann Geyler (see note 12).
11. Christian Weise published a number of dramatic works including *Baurischer Machiavellus* (1679) and *Der verfolgte Lateiner* (1696).
12. Johann Geyler von Kaisersberg (1445–1510), wrote a commentary on *Das Narrenschiff* (1494) by humanist, Sebastian Brant (1457–1521), which was published with the text in 1511.
13. Martin Kempe (1642–83), poet.
14. Heinrich Bredelo (dates unknown), poet.
15. Ernst Stockmann (1634–1712), theologian and poet.
16. Kaspar Ziegler (1621–90), religious poet whose treatise on the madrigal form was influential into the eighteenth century.

17. Anton Ulrich, Duke of Braunschweig (1633–1714), Catholic convert and poet.
18. Angelus Silesius's *Heilige Seelenkunst Oder Geistliche Hirtenlieder* (1657).
19. Bodmer promoted the appreciation of medieval literature and published an edition of Opitz' *Gedichte* in 1745.
20. Philipp von Zesen (1619–89), author of pastoral novels; published his *Deutscher Helicon* in 1640.
21. Andreas Gryphius (1616–64), poet and lawyer.
22. Johann Christian Hallmann (1640–1704), Catholic convert and dramatist.
23. Matthison's *Lyrische Anthologie* (1803–8).

36. *Dorothea Campe, Braunschweig; Görslow, 26 September 1810; Source 3*

Refers to gaining access to Eschenburg's library in Hamburg. Still interested in Spanish seventeenth-century literature, but most of his collection still in Cadiz. Expresses desire to mediate through translation, but feels he lacks the talent of someone like Schlegel. Seeks a Catholic priest for his household in anticipation of the eventual arrival of his wife and daughters. Reports on activities of the Hamburg circle and a visit from Elise Campe and her father, Hoffmann.

37. *Nikolas Heinrich Julius, Hamburg; Görslow, 13 October 1810; Source 1*

Continued discussions surrounding the planned *Lieder* collection which is intended to offer the layman the best at a lower price than the costly *Wunderhorn*. Appraisal of some book acquisitions which might provide material for the collection. Refers again to his essays on Spanish theatre and encloses his supplement to Bouterwek's *Geschichte der englischen Poesie und Beredsamkeit* for inclusion in the *Vaterländisches Museum*. Discussion of the content of the periodical includes praise for Schubert and Stolberg. Praise for Claudius.

1. Reference to Arnim and Brentano's editorial approach in compiling the *Wunderhorn* which involved altering and enhancing text.
2. Johann Heinrich Voß (1751–1826), member of the *Göttinger Dichterbund*.
3. Johann Jakob Gottschald (1688–1748), author of *Allerhand Lieder-Remarquen* (1737–48).
4. Reference to B.'s article on English poetry, intended to supplement Friedrich Bouterwek's *Geschichte der englischen Poesie und Beredsamkeit* (1809–10).
5. Johann Joseph von Görres (1776–1848), Catholic writer and publicist known for his staunch patriotism.
6. Reference to the *Vaterländisches Museum*, vol. 1, part 3: 'Darstellung' refers to 'Karl Gustav, König von Schweden, von dem verstorbenen Heinrich von

Bülow' (pp. 257–87); 'Ihre Betrachtungen' refers to 'Betrachtungen über Amerika' by Julius (pp. 288–98); 'Villers' refers to 'Von dem wesentlich verschiedenen Charakter der erotischen Poesie bey den Franzosen und Deutschen, nach Karl von Villers' by Charles François Dominique de Villers (1765–1815), Franco–German writer (pp. 299–342); part 4: 'Brief über Gripsholm', H von Pl, (pp. 462–511); 'Gedichte' refers to 'Die Himmel' by Friedrich Leopold Stolberg and 'Der Todtenkopf' by Fouqué (pp. 458–60).

7. Georg Draudius (1573–1635), clergyman and writer.
8. Reference to the planned publication in 1810–11 of the first two parts of Goethe's novel *Wilhelm Meisters Wanderjahre*. This did not come to fruition until 1821.
9. Christian Friedrich Daniel Schubart (1739–91), poet and musician. An edition of *Vermischte Schriften* appeared in 1812.
10. Reference to the *Cancionero de Amberes* which appeared in Antwerp in 1555.
11. Julius Eduard Hitzig (Isaak Elias Hitzig before conversion from Judaism to Lutheran faith) (1780–1849), writer, publisher and lawyer.
12. A. Norwich, *Teatro español* (1809–10), published in Bremen, only two volumes appeared.
13. Johann Otto Thiess (1762–1810), *Versuch einer Gelehrtengeschichte von Hamburg* (1783).

38. Nikolas Heinrich Julius, Hamburg; Görslow, 8 November 1810; Source 1

Reports on book orders and auctions, including both German and Spanish texts.

1. Geronimo Cardano (1501–76), Italian mathematician and natural scientist.
2. Valentin Weigel (1533–88), Protestant mystic.
3. Quirinius Kuhlmann (1651–89), poet and mystic, *Kühlpsalter* (1684–1686).
4. Johann Michael Moscherosch (1601–69), writer and satirist.
5. Johann Jacob Weidner (dates unknown), *Teutsches poetisches Lustgärtlein* (c.1620).
6. Jacob Schwieger (c.1630–64), writer.
7. Zacharias Lund (1608–67), poet.
8. Justus Sieber (1628–95), poet and clergyman.
9. Félix Lope de Vega Carpio (1562–1635), leading Golden Age dramatist.
10. Luis de Góngora y Argote (1561–1627), poet.
11. Johann Georg Schoch (1627–c.1690), poet.
12. Michael Kongehl (1646–1710), poet and dramatist.
13. Hans Sachs (1494–1576), master shoemaker, poet, composer of *Meisterlieder*.

39. Nikolas Heinrich Julius, Hamburg; Görslow, 28 November 1810; Source 1

Demonstrates self-awareness, describing his soul as feminine in nature, which in turn explains his inability to express himself clearly. Discussion of *Lieder*, in particular Dach. Appraisal of *Vaterländisches Museum* with particular praise for Stolberg. Ambivalent response to Friedrich Schlegel. Commentary on various acquisitions.

1. *Manesse Codex* or *Grosse Heidelberger Liederhandschrift* (1305–40).
2. Reference to the possibility of publishing in the leading Viennese journal of the day, the *Annalen der Oesterreichischen Literatur*.
3. Zesen was known for his experimentation with orthography.
4. B. quotes from Neumeister's *De poetis Germanicus* (p. 26).
5. Ludwig Franz Adolf Joseph von Baczko (1756–1823), historian and writer, author of *Geschichte Preussens* (1792).
6. Placcius and Christoph August Mylius (1681–1764), authors of *Theatrum anonymorum et pseudonymorum* (1711), expanded in 1740 by Mylius.
7. Gottsched's periodical *Neuer Büchersaal der schönen Wissenschaften und freyen Künste* (1745–1750).
8. Reference to the collection of Johann Caspar Arletius (1701–84), pedagogue and librarian in Breslau.
9. Reference to Dach's *Chur-Brandenburgische Rose, Adler, Löw und Scepter* (1685).
10. Reference to the *Vaterländisches Museum*, vol. 1, part 5: 'Ueber unsere Sprache' by Friedrich Leopold Stolberg (pp. 513–30); 'Rechtfertigung Philipps II gegen den Verdacht einer Giftmischerey' by Friedrich Ludwig Wilhelm Meyer (pp. 531–43); 'Fragment aus der von dem Institut Frankreichs im J. 1810 gekrönten Schrift über die Herrschaft der Gothen in Italien' by Georg Sartorius von Waltershausen (1765–1828), historian and economist (pp. 544–86); 'Das Zeitalter der Kreuzzüge' by Friedrich Schlegel (pp. 571–86); 'Noch einiges aus den Papieren von Klopstock' (pp. 587–602); 'Ode auf Bergeshöhe', Hegener (p. 598).
11. Karl Gottlieb Horstig (1763–1835), *Kinderlieder und Melodien* (1798).
12. Johann Casper von Orelli (1787–1849), Swiss classical scholar.
13. Georg Greflinger (pseudonym Celadon) (1618–80), poet and writer.
14. Albrecht von Haller (1708–77), physician, natural scientist and poet.
15. Friedrich von Hagedorn (1708–54), poet and writer of fables.
16. *Deutsches Museum*, published from 1776 to 1791 by Heinrich Christian Boie (1744–1806) and Christian Konrad Wilhelm von Dohm (1751–1820).
17. Thomas Murner (1475–1537), satirist and Franciscan friar.

18. Johann Valentin Andreae (1586–1654), clergyman and writer associated with Rosicrucianism.
19. Hans Rosenplüt (c.1400–60), poet.
20. Jacob Balde (1604–68), Jesuit historiographer and Latin poet.

40. Elise Campe, Hamburg; Görslow, 20 March 1811; Source 3

Expresses current disquiet with various crises relating to his faith, family and finances.

41. Nikolas Heinrich Julius, Hamburg; Görslow, 3 April 1811; Source 1

Expresses the difficulty he has in contacting his foster parents given his current state of mind. He is exhausted by the various worries he has. Impressed by Stolberg's writings and other theological works. Reports on auctions. On the verge of selling his estate.

1. Friedrich Leopold Graf zu Stolberg (1750–1819), *Geschichte der Religion Jesu Christi* (1806 to 1818).
2. Blaise Pascal (1623–62), French mathematician and philosopher.
3. Paul Gerhardt (1607–76), evangelical hymnist.
4. Johann Christoph Olearius (1668–1747), theologian and hymnist, *Evangelischer Lieder-Schatz* (1705–6).
5. Sigmund von Birken (1626–81), *Hochfürstlich Brandenburgische Ulysses* (1688), written in honour of Christian Ernst von Brandenburg-Bayreuth (1644–1712).
6. Georg Philipp Harsdorffer (1607–58), Baroque poet, author of *Frauenzimmer-Gesprächspiele* (1644).
7. A member of the prominent Hamburg family of artists and collectors.

42. Nikolas Heinrich Julius, Hamburg; Görslow, 5 May 1811; Source 1

Refers to his edition of *Lieder* from the *Wunderhorn*, also to Grimm and Luther whose impact seems to be rather limited. Mention is made of French censorship impeding his reading. Reports on auctions and book orders. Refers to Luise Reichardt who is part of Julius' Hamburg circle. Fears he will have to sell most of his English books. Makes explicit reference to discovery of a revealed God. Current political situation means he must suffer the imposition of quartering Italian soldiers.

1. Publishing house established by Christian Benjamin Mohr (1778–1854) and

theologian Johann Georg Zimmer (1776–1853), which published both the original *Wunderhorn* and B.'s musical selection.
2. Reference to Jacob Grimm's polemic with Docen on the *Minne* and *Meistersänger*; Grimm's views are expressed in his *Ueber den altdeutschen Meistergesang* (1811).
3. Bernardo José de Aldrete (1560–1641), historian and linguist, *Del origen y principio de la lengua castellana o romance que hoy se usa en España* (1606).
4. Gottfried Christoph Beireis (1730–1809), polyhistorian.
5. Luise Reichardt (1779–1826), singer, daughter of the composer Johann Friedrich Reichardt (1752–1814).
6. Quotation from Goethe's poem 'Das Göttliche' (1783).

43. Elise Campe, Hamburg; Görslow, 19 May 1811; Source 3

Affectionate tone which shows the nature of their friendship. Once again, he refers to the discovery of a revealed God and describes his current discomfort, both financial and in terms of the quartering of troops. Refers to Dr Ebeling of Hamburg as possessing a notable collection of older German poetry which he would like to see. Reading Milton with a positive response. Reports on auctions and book orders.

1. John Milton (1608–74), *Paradise Lost* (1667).
2. Reference to the prologue of Eschenburg's *Friedrichs von Hagedorn Poetische Werke* (1800).
3. Luise Adelgunde Victoria Gottsched (1713–62), writer and translator, wife of J. C. Gottsched.
4. Christoph Daniel Ebeling (1741–1817), librarian and scholar, taught at various institutions in Hamburg.
5. Possible reference to the sale of the library belonging to August Ludwig von Schlözer (1735–1809), historian and publicist of the German Enlightenment.

44. Nikolas Heinrich Julius, Hamburg; Görslow, 27 May 1811; Source 1

Reports on auctions and book orders. Refers to Friedrich Schlegel's *Ueber die neuere Geschichte* with enthusiasm. Further reference to the *Lieder* collection and his publishing venture with Mohr and Zimmer. Outlines plans to sell his English books. Refers again to his discovery of a revealed God.

1. Johannes Petrus de Memel, pseudonym of Johannes Praetorius (Hans Schulz) (1630–1680), *Lustige Gesellschaft* (1656).

2. Heinrich Christoph Koch (1749–1816), musician and composer, compiled the *Musikalisches Lexikon* (1802).
3. Erasmus Francisci (1627–94), *Die lustige Schaubühne* (1663).
4. Francis Bacon (Baron Baco de Verulam), (1561–1626), English philosopher and statesman, father of Empiricism.
5. Murner's *Der Schelmenzunft* (1512).
6. Friedrich Schlegel's *Ueber die neuere Geschichte* (1811).
7. Johannes Müller (1752–1809), Swiss historian.
8. Johannes Agricola (1494–1566), German Reformer, author of *Sybenhundert und fünfftzig Teütscher Sprichwörter* (1582).
9. Sebastian Franck (c.1500–42), *Spruchwörter* (1541).
10. Christoph Lehmann (1568–1638), *Florilegium politicum* (1630).
11. Joachim Christian Blum (1739–90), *Teutsches Sprichwörterbuch* (1781–2).
12. Quotation from Goethe's poem 'Prometheus' (1774).
13. *Biblia pentapla* (1710–12), which contained five translated versions of the Bible, including that by Luther.
14. Georg Göran Wahlenberg (1780–1851), Swedish botanist.

45. Nikolas Heinrich Julius, Hamburg; Görslow, 13 June 1811; Source 1

Reports on auctions and book orders. Refers to the sale of his English books, pointing out that he has kept anything relating to Scottish ballads. Refers again to Luise Reichardt and also to Friedrich Schlegel's lectures, which he admits to finding difficult, but which please in their rejection of France. Critical of Goethe's *Hackert*.

1. Tobias Stimmer (1539–84), Swiss painter and playwright.
2. Hermann Hammelmann (1526–95), German Lutheran theologian.
3. Wolfgang Caspar Printz (1641–1717), writer and composer, *Phrynis oder satirischer Componist, welcher die Fehler der ungelehrten Componisten höflich darstellet* (1676) and *Historische Beschreibung der edelen Sing- und Kling-Kunst* (1690).
4. Franz Joseph Clement (1780–1842), violinist and conductor.
5. Despite B.'s doubts, the works referred to are by Paul Fleming, *Loob eines Soldaten zu Fusse* and *Loob eines Soldaten zu Rosse*, both 1631.
6. *Der vollkommene teutsche Jäger* (1719–24), published by Hanns Friedrich von Fleming (????–1726).
7. Christian Gottlieb Jöcher (1694–1758), lexicographer and historian, *Allgemeines Gelehrten Lexikon* (1750).
8. Johann Gottlieb Wilhelm Dunkel (1720–59), theologian and philologist, *Historisch-kritische Nachrichten von verstorbenen Gelehrten und deren Schriften* (1753–60).

9. Karl Melchior Grodnitz von Grodnau (dates unknown), member of *Fruchtbringende Gesellschaft*, the main literary society of the Baroque period.
10. Georg Neumark (1621–81), member of the *Fruchtbringende Gesellschaft*, hymnist and composer, author of *Der Neu-Sprossende Teutsche Palmbaum* (1668).
11. Georg Christian Schemelii (1680–1762), hymnist and composer.
12. Grodnau's *Obervationes politicae, super nuperis Galiae motibus* (1649).
13. No reference to this figure could be located.
14. Georg Christoph Wagenseil (1715–77), Austrian composer.
15. Pierre Gringore (c.1475–c.1538), *Les Abus du Monde* (1509).
16. Heinrich Georg Neuss (1654–1716), *Heb-Opfer zum Bau der Hütten Gottes, das ist, geistliche Lieder welche zur Andacht, Aufmunterung und Erbauung unsers Christenthums in allerhand Fällen zu gebrauchen und daher in gewisse Zehen und Classen vertheilet, und mehrentheils mit eigenen und neuen Melodeyen versehen seynd* (1692).
17. Goethe's biography of the artist Phillip Hackert (1737–1807), *Philipp Hackert. Biographische Skizze. Meist nach dessen eigenen Aufsätzen entworfen* (1811).
18. Wilhelm Grimm, *Altdänische Heldenlieder, Balladen und Märchen* (1811), intended as a continuation of the *Wunderhorn*.
19. Christian Hieronymus Esmarck (1752–1820), poet and member of the *Göttinger Hain*.

46. Elise Campe, Hamburg; Görslow, 17 July 1811; Source 3

Personal matters including experiences and events relating to the war and activities of the Hamburg circle. Repeats the comments on Goethe and F. Schlegel from previous letter. Praise for Fouqué's *Undine*.

1. Periodical published by Fouqué in 1811, of which only one volume appeared.
2. A character in Fouqué's *Undine* (1811).
3. Johann Heinrich Jung-Stilling (1740–1817), physician and writer whose autobiography appeared in four volumes between 1777 and 1804. *Romances* from the first two volumes, *Heinrich Stillings Jugend* (1777) and *Jünglingsjahren* (1778), appeared with music in 1811 in Fouqué's *Jahreszeiten*.
4. Probable reference to the pseudonym of poet and writer, Gustav Anton von Seckendorff (1775–1823).

47. Elise Campe; Görslow, 11 September 1811; Source 3

Personal matters including the activities of the Hamburg circle. Comments on a number of texts including poetry by Schiller and Goethe. Criticism of F. Schlegel's lectures and Rousseau's *Nouvelle Héloïse*, but praise for *Undine* and W. Grimm's *Altedänische Lieder*.

1. Reference to *Göthes Gedichte oder dessen Lieder, Oden, Balladan und Romanzen* (1810), published as part four of *Neuestes Hamburger Liederbuch*.
2. Reference to *Sechs deutsche Gedichte von Schiller, Fouqué, Schmidt u.m. für eine Singstimme mit Begleitung des Pianoforte* (1810).
3. *Briefe eines Frauenzimmers aus dem XV Jahrhundert* (1793) by Paul von Stetten (1731–1808).
4. Reference to Goethe's translation of Benvenuto Cellini's biography of 1796–1803.
5. Reference to Rousseau's sentimental novel *Julie, où la nouvelle Héloïse* (1761).
6. Johann Friedrich (Fritz) Böhl (1773–1844) married Elizabeth Stockfleth (1790–1828).
7. The novel by Fouqué (1810).
8. Quotation from Paul Gerhardt's 'Was Gott gefällt, mein frommes Kind, nimm fröhlich an' (1653).

48. Nikolas Heinrich Julius, Hamburg; Görslow, 2 October 1811; Source 1

Discussion of the sale of his English book collection via Hitzig. Reports on book orders and auctions. Comment on the concerns caused by the political situation in relation to his family. Personal matters including a family wedding. Discussion of *Lieder*. Reference to another Julius writing for the *Morgenblatt* in opposition to Romanticism.

1. *Gepflückte Finken, oder Studenten-Confect* (1670), an anthology of anecdotes and other texts.
2. Reference to the Rosicrucian Brotherhood, whose biblical text, *Fama fraternitatus*, was the first key document of the Brotherhood.
3. Historical allegory of religious conflict in France under Henry III and IV by John Barclay (1582–1621), translated into German by Opitz in 1626.
4. *Das Heldenbuch mit synen Figuren* (1509), attributed to *Minnesänger*, Wolfram von Eschenbach and Heinrich von Ofterdingen.
5. Johann Nepomuk Cosmos Michael Denis (pseudonym Sined der Barde) (1729–1800), Jesuit bibliographer, author of *Einleitung in die Bücherkunde* (1777–8).
6. Caroline de la Motte Fouqué (1774–1831), writer, wife of Friedrich, co-editor

with Amalie von Helwig of the *Taschenbuch der Sagen und Legenden* (1812–17), to the forthcoming publication of which B. refers.
7. Georg Büsching's *Pantheon* (1810), which included Fouqué's *Eine Geschichte vom Galgenmännlein*.
8. Johann von Schwarzenberg (1463–1526), humanist and statesman, *Teutscher Cicero* (1534).
9. Hans Leonhard Schäufelein (1480–1540), north German Rennaissance painter, provided the woodcuts for *Plutarchus Teutsch* (1534) by Hieronymus Boner (c.1490–1556).
10. Jean Baptiste Besard (1567–1625), *Isagoge in artem testudinariam das ist: gründtlicher Unterricht über das künstliche Saitenspil der Lauten*.
11. Daniel Salthenius (1701–50), *Bibliothecae viri, cum viveret, summe reverendi, atque excellentissimi* (1751).
12. Valentin Vogt (c.1487–1558), poet.
13. Peter von Mastricht (1630–1706), reformed theologian.
14. *Orient oder Hamburgisches Morgenblatt* (1811–17).

49. Nikolas Heinrich Julius, Hamburg; Görslow, 1 November 1811; Source 1

Reports on auctions. Lists current reading material which includes *Don Quijote*, Calderón, Klopstock, Young and Goethe.

1. Miguel de Cervantes y Saavedra (1547–1616), *Don Quijote de la Mancha* (1605).
2. Epic masterpiece by Friedrich Gottlieb Klopstock (1724–1803), published from 1749 to 1773.
3. Probable reference to Edward Young (1683–1765), author of *The Complaint: or Night Thoughts on Life, Death and Immortality* (1742–5).
4. Reference to three key works by Goethe: *Faust* (1808), *Die Leiden des Jungen Werther* (1774) and *Wilhelm Meisters Lehrjahre* (1795–6).

50. Nikolas Heinrich Julius, Hamburg; Görslow, 14 November 1811; Source 1

Personal matters including allusion to marital problems. Reports on auctions and sale of own English books. Reference to *Lieder* set to music.

1. *Amadis de Gaula*, sixteenth-century Spanish epic first published in Zaragoza in 1508.
2. Reference to the character of Aurelie from the fourth book of *Wilhelm Meisters Lehrjahre*.
3. Reference to B.'s *Vier und Zwanzig Lieder aus dem Wunderhorn* (1810).

51. Dorothea Campe, Braunschweig; Hamburg, 10 December 1811; Source 3

Discussion of financial problems, the enforced sale of books and the restriction of his studies to older German literature and religious material. Reports the likely arrival of his family from Spain.

52. Elise Campe, Hamburg; [Hamburg] 16 January 1812; Source 3

Brief note to bid farewell before returning to Görslow.

53. Elise Campe, Hamburg; [Görslow], 13 June 1812; Source 3

Agreed approval of both F. and A. W. Schlegel's recent writings. Refers to the *Poetischer Almanach* and outlines the material he hopes to publish there. Mediatory role clear as he outlines dissemination of Spanish and English material. Praise for earlier issues of the periodical. Reports a renewed interest in Spanish literature. Discusses the possibility of providing material for an opera for Luise Reichardt, suggesting Novalis' 'Rosenblüthe und Hyazinth' as possible material.

1. Reference to Friedrich Schlegel's periodical, *Deutsches Museum*, published in Vienna from 1812 to 1813.
2. 'Aus einer noch ungedruckten historischen Untersuchung über das Lied der Nibelungen' which appeared in the second volume of Friedrich Schlegel's *Deutsches Museum*.
3. *Poetischer Almanach für das Jahr 1812*, published in 1811 by Swabian poet, Justinus Kerner (1786–1862), with a second volume planned in 1812 to which B. was to contribute.
4. William Wordsworth (1770–1850), Lake poet, English Romantic.
5. B. refers to the following texts from the *Poetischer Almanach*: Fouqué: 'Wehmut' (pp. 131–2), 'Sinnspruch' (p. 152), 'Tröstung', (p. 160), 'An Otto Heinrich, Grafen von Loeben. In ein spanisches Wörterbuch' (p. 172), 'Das Schlachtfeld. Eine nordische Abentheure' (pp. 258–88); Otto Heinrich, Graf von Loeben (1786–1825), pseudonym Isidorus Orientalis, minor Romantic poet: 'Moosröslein' (p. 9), 'Frühlingstrost' (p. 72), 'Winterlied' (pp. 80–1), 'Verlorene Liebe' (p. 133), 'Botschaft, an Florens' (pp. 170–1); Kerner: 'Das weiße Roß' (pp. 43–4), 'An Friedeburge' (pp. 85–6), 'Morgengefühl' (pp. 94–5), 'Das Kreuz auf der Höhe' (pp. 115–17), 'Der Pilger' (p. 121), 'H' and 'Musketierlied' (pp. 129–30).
6. No reference to this text could be found.
7. Johann Gottlieb Radlof (1775–1827), philologist and linguist associated with Jacob Grimm.

8. Unattributed quotation.
9. Pseudonym Friedrich von Hardenberg (1772–1801), poet and writer, early German Romantic, author of *Die Lehrlinge zu Saïs*, which includes 'Das Märchen von Rosenblüthe und Hyazinth'.
10. Paraphrase of a quotation from the poem 'Am 15 Sontage nach der heiligen Dreyfaltigkeit' by the poet, Friedrich von Logau (1604–55), a member of the *Fruchtbringende Gesellschaft*, who was active between 1637 and 1653. The same stanza is quoted accurately in letter 71.

54. Elise Campe, Hamburg; Görslow, 26 August 1812; Source 3

Reports the arrival of his family in Germany. Reiterates his Romantic world view and expresses an appreciation of shared beliefs. Enquires after the status of the *Almanach*. Reports on the Hamburg circle.

1. Fouqué's *Der Zauberring* appeared in 1813.
2. Reference to the series *Kleine Romanenbibliothek für Damen* which featured work by, amongst others, Caroline de la Motte Fouqué.
3. Pseudonym used by Fouqué during his early career, in particular his *Dramatische Spiele* which were edited by August Wilhelm Schlegel in 1804.

55. Elise Campe, Hamburg; [Görslow] [1812] Sunday, 2pm; Source 3

Promise of material for the *Almanach*. Expresses a desire for a like-minded readership.

56. Nikolas Heinrich Julius, Hamburg; Görslow, 28 February 1813; Source 1

Reports the arrival of his family and the poor state of his finances in Spain and in Germany. Outlines restrictions on his studies due to the sale of books, his work now limited to Christianity, older German literature and linguistic studies. Describes tutoring his children and the impact of Francisca on his studies with a shift towards Spanish material, enabled through the use of the Tyschen library in Rostock. First reference to a collection of Spanish poetry leads to a request for material by Garcilaso, Boscán and Diego de Mendoza. Reports the loss of his collection in Spain, which has been sold off to pay debts.

1. The first reference in his correspondence to the *Floresta*.
2. Oluf Gerhard Tychsen (1734–1815), orientalist, at the University of Rostock from 1778.

3. Garcilaso de la Vega (1503–36), poet and soldier, key figure of the Spanish Golden Age, who adapted an Italianate style to Castilian poetry.
4. Juan Boscán Almogáver (c.1490–1542), poet and associate of Garcilaso, who employed the Italianate style.
5. Diego Hurtado de Mendoza (1503–75), poet and diplomat, and follower of the Italianate style.

57. Nikolas Heinrich Julius, Güstrow; Görslow, 9 August 1813; Source 1

Final letter from Germany. Reports his conversion to Catholicism. Bids farewell to all the Hamburg patriots.

58. Friedrich Perthes, Hamburg; Cadiz, 22 March 1815; Source 5

Criticises Perthes for a lack of communication and requests to be sent no further political material other than a reliable description of the Congress of Vienna. Reports the return of his son, Juan, to Germany and renewed collecting of Spanish material to replace his lost collection. Expresses general satisfaction with his new life in Spain.

1. Albrecht Dürer (1471–1528), artist, engraver, mathematician, key figure of northern European Rennaissance.

59. August Campe, Hamburg; Cadiz, 6 May 1815; Source 3

Reports the collapse of the Spanish business and his new occupation in assurance and supply. Expresses his horror at the resurgence of Napoleon. Asks to receive no further books containing older German literature. Expresses some ambivalence towards Goethe, but acknowledges his work as a guiding thread in his life. Asks to receive only the best in new literature, in particular Tieck and Fouqué.

1. Reference to the third part of Goethe's autobiography *Dichtung und Wahrheit* which appeared in 1814.

60. Friedrich Perthes, Hamburg; Cadiz, 20 June 1815; Source 5

Discussion of the political climate and makes a first mention of the defence of 'die gute Sache' (the good cause).

1. Reference to the 1815 Spanish expedition to regain control of the colonies

Editor's Notes

which took the island of Margarita off the Venezualan coast resulting in large losses for the Spanish.

61. Friedrich Perthes, Hamburg; Cadiz, 6 October 1815; Source 5

Reports on book orders which continue the trend from the Görslow years. Refers to the exile of conservative writers and the lack of funds for publication as reason for the paucity of period. Praise for the *Filósofo rancio*.

1. Reference to the *Diccionario de la lengua española de la Real Academia Española*, first published in 1780 at the behest of Carlos III.
2. Pseudonym of Francisco Alvarado (1756–1814), monarchist and defender of the Inquisition.
3. Kerner's *Deutscher Dichterwald* (1813).
4. Fouqué's novel, *Die Fahrten Thiodolfs des Isländers* (1815).
5. Fouqué's *Kleine Romane, Märchen und Erzählungen* (1815–18).
6. Reference to two of Schubert's works, *Ahnungen einer allgemeinen Geschichte des Lebens* (1806) and *Ansichten von der Nachtseite der Naturwissenschaft* (1808).
7. Schubert's 1811 translation of Saint-Martin's *L'Esprit des choses* (1800), *Vom Geist und Wesen der Dinge*.

62. Friedrich Perthes, Hamburg; Cadiz, 22 December 1815; Source 5

Comments on the current Spanish situation in negative terms, criticising its misrepresentation abroad. Critical of the powerlessness of the Inquisition and the Liberal nature of the *cortes*. Sees himself as the only person willing to speak up for decent, conservative values and does so with evangelical zeal. Reports book orders.

1. Reference to the death of Perthes' father-in-law, Claudius, in 1815.

63. Friedrich Perthes, Hamburg; Cadiz, 5 April 1816; Source 5

Repeats much of the previous letter. Reference to Novalis' love of 'das Alte' (the old way) as his guiding light in the current Spanish situation. Cannot understand how others do not appreciate old values and faith.

1. Johann Daniel Runge (1767–1856), brother of Romantic artist, Phillipp Otto Runge (1777–1810).
2. Alexandre de Laborde (1774–1842), *Itinéraire descriptif de l'Espagne* (1807).

64. *Elise Campe, Hamburg; Cadiz, 6 April 1816; Source 3*

Highlights the split nature of his existence and points to poetry as his haven. Outlines plans for a collection of Spanish poetry. Refers to August Campe's poetical conversion and suggests he complete the *Wunderhorn* project. Personal matters including Francisca's satisfaction at being in her homeland.

1. Reference to the material for a second volume of the *Wunderhorn* selection.
2. Reference to Cecilia's first husband, Antonio Planells y Bardají (1788–1817), who died in Puerto Rico.
3. Reference to B.'s third daughter, Angela.

65. *Friedrich Perthes, Hamburg; Cadiz, 16 July 1816; Source 5*

Discusses the difficulties inherent in shipping books. Expresses his disgust with current politics and observes that the study of poetry is becoming ever more central, in particular the technical side. Expresses a desire to see more severe punishment of those responsible for political instability.

1. Juan Caramuel y Lobkowitz (1606–82), Spanish theologian, author of *Primus Calamus ob oculos ponens Rhytmicam* (1665–8).

66. *Friedrich Perthes, Hamburg; Cadiz, 10 September 1816; Source 5*

Reports on book orders including an enthusiastic response to Schubert's work on dreams and Hoffmann's *Fantasiestücke*. Requests A. W. Schlegel's work on *Phèdre*. Reports the forthcoming edition of Jovellanos' works.

1. *Kieler Blätter. Eine Zeitschrift zur Erhaltung und Erweiterung des vaterländischen Sinnes*, published from 1815 to 1817 by Friedrich Christoph Dahlmann (1785–1860).
2. Alexander von Humboldt (1769–1854), *Voyage aux regions äquinoctales du Nouveau Continent fait en 1799–1804* (1807–39), translated into German from 1815 to 1839 as *Reise in die aequinoctial-Gegenden des neuen Continents in den Jahren 1799, 1800, 1801, 1802, 1803 und 1804*.
3. Amandus Gottfried Adolf Müllner (1774–1829), author of the tragedy *Die Schuld* (1813, published 1816).
4. Schubert's *Symbolik des Traumes* (1814).
5. E. T. A. Hoffmann (1776–1822), *Fantasiestücke in Callots Manier*, four volumes (1814–15).
6. Eberhard von Groote (1789–1864), *Fausts Versöhnung mit dem Leben* (1816).

7. Benedikt Franz Xavier von Baader (1765–1841), Catholic philosopher, influential for Friedrich Schlegel and Schelling.
8. August Wilhelm Schlegel's *Comparaison entre la Phèdre de Racine et celle d'Euripide* (1807).
9. Sister of a Scotsman named Campbell who died in Cadiz and in the disposal of whose estate B. was involved.
10. Gaspar Melchor de Jovellanos (1744–1811), key thinker of the Spanish Enlightenment, playwright, poet and politician. His collected works did not appear until 1830, *Coleccion de varias obras en prosa y en verso* (1830–2).

67. Friedrich Perthes, Hamburg; Cadiz, 3 January 1817; Source 5

Reports on book orders including the desire to see Baader's work and Humboldt's travel writing. Makes reference to the current lack of publishing in Spain due to shortages. Still awaiting Jovellanos' work, as well as that of the *Filósofo rancio*. Recent publications of note are listed including the work of Fray Luis de León.

1. Johann Arnold Kanne (pseudonym Walter Bergius; Johannes Author) (1773–1824), mythologian and linguist associated with Schubert, author of the novel *Sämundis Führungen* (1816).
2. Possible reference to the anonymous *Es wird alles neu*, published from 1807 by Silbermann of Strassburg.
3. Johannes Wilhelm Weinmann (1683–1741), botanist and author of the hugely popular *Phytanthoza Iconographia* (1734–45).
4. Fray Luis de León (1538–91), Spanish poet and theologian.
5. Gaspar María de Nava Álvarez, Count of Noroña (1760–1815), soldier and pre-Romantic poet.
6. Nicasio Álvarez Cienfuegos (1764–1809), pre-Romantic Spanish poet.

68. Nikolas Heinrich Julius, Hamburg; Cadiz, 28 February 1817; Source 1

Comments on Julius' return to medical practice after his work as a garrison physician. Describes his own difficulties in finding employment due to the precarious financial situation and expresses his regret at not having been allowed to undertake formal study. Reports on the widespread, enforced sale of personal property which results in valuable artefacts entering unappreciative hands. Describes the extent of his collection of old Spanish books and outlines their role in his future plans for a collection of poetry and theatre, as well as his plans for a theoretical work on metre. This project is to make his name for posterity. Requests a copy of the old German *Lieder* which he left with Julius. Still interested in current German literature, in particular Tieck. Also reiterates his Catholic conviction which is his support in such hard times.

1. Mrs Grant's deceased brother (see letter 66; note 9).
2. Miquel Cabanellas i Clavera (1760–1830), epidemiologist.

69. Friedrich Perthes, Hamburg; Cadiz, 1 March 1817; Source 1

Reports on book orders and commissions, with reiterated requests for works by Sismondi and Wordsworth.

1. Pseudonym of Fray Gabrial Téllez (c.1584–1648), prolific Golden Age dramatist.
2. Juan de Alarcón (c.1395–c.1451), writer, known for didactic texts.
3. Jean Claude Léonard Simonde de Sismondi (1773–1842), author of the influential *De la littérature du Midi de l'Europe* (1813).
4. Wordsworth's poem 'The Excursion', published in 1814 as the second part of *The Recluse*.

70. Friedrich Perthes, Hamburg; Cadiz, 3 June 1817; Source 5

Reminder of various outstanding book orders. Expresses his continued patriotic love of Germany and requests an account of the recent wars which will accord with this. Voices approval for F. Schlegel's lectures on literature and reports progress with his collection of Spanish poetry. Reports on book orders and commissions. Highly critical of the Liberal mood in both Spain and Germany.

1. Founded in 1802 by Francis Jeffrey (1773–1850), Sydney Smith (1771–1845) and Henry Brougham (1778–1868), supported the Whig party, ceased publication in 1929.
2. August Graf Neidhardt von Gneisenau (1760–1831), Prussian field marshall, author of *Der Feldzug von 1813 bis zum Waffenstillstand* (1813).
3. Friedrich Schlegel's *Geschichte der alten und der neuen Literatur* (1815).
4. Ignacio Jordán Claudio de Asso y del Rio (1742–1814), naturalist and historian, published *Poesias selectas de Martín Miguel Navarro* (1781), the Aragonese poet (1600–44).
5. Reference to Ignacio Garcez Ferreira's 1731 edition of the *Lusiada, poema epico* by Luís de Camões (c.1524–80).

Editor's Notes

71. Nikolas Heinrich Julius, Hamburg; Cadiz, 15 July 1817; Source 1

Expresses his extreme disquiet at his current financial insecurity. Very preoccupied with the current political situation as Liberalism seems to be on the rise and with it a threat to both throne and altar. Refers to texts he has written in opposition to this which cannot be published (but may include the text sent to Runge; see chapter 6). Praise for the *Filósofo rancio*. Complains that Perthes has been letting him down.

1. Quotation from Logau's poem 'Am 15 Sontage nach der heiligen Dreyfaltigkeit'.

72. Friedrich Perthes, Hamburg; Cadiz, 19 October 1817; Source 5

Complains that the Inquisition has been weakened by Liberal involvement and criticises the political material being published as a result. Reports on book orders and commissions. Explains that Spanish books are very expensive to produce and buy which is why he is seeking a publisher in Hamburg for his collection, which he goes on to describe. This is the original plan which includes poetry, theatre, the epic and his theoretical texts. Enquires as to the current state of German letters, including the Schlegels.

1. A low-ranking official of the Inquisition.
2. Probable response to the death of two of Wordsworth's children in 1812.
3. Prominent Madrid publishing house, Sancha.
4. Reference to Madame de Staël's posthumous publication, *Considérations sur la revolution française* (1818).
5. Louis-Gabriel-Ambroise, Vicount de Bonald (1754–1840), royalist statesman and philosopher, published his *Pensées sur divers sujets* (1817).

73. Nikolas Heinrich Julius, Hamburg; Cadiz, 19 October 1817; Source 1.

Expresses his dismay at the political situation in Spain and at the weakness of the king. Comments on Calderón, suggesting that only a Catholic could translate his work well. Offers Julius the use of his German library which is stored on his brother's estate. Reports on book orders and commissions.

1. Johann Diederich Gries (1775–1842), Hamburg merchant and translator, published *P. Calderón de la Barca Schauspiele* (1815–19).
2. Reference to the *Herzog August Bibliothek* in Wolfenbüttel, established in 1572.

3. Francisco de Salinas (1513–90), musical theorist and mathematician, known for his interest in popular forms.
4. Possible reference to Charles Burney (1726–1814), organist and musical historian, author of *History of Music* (1776–89).

74. Nikolas Heinrich Julius, Hamburg; Cadiz, 13 February 1818; Source 1

Reports on book orders and commissions, complaining again of Perthes' inefficiency. Comments on recently received, long-awaited texts with approval for Sismondi and Humboldt and disappointment with Tieck and Görres. Claims that older German poetry is inferior to its Spanish equivalent. Voices an ambivalent response to Goethe's *Italienische Reise*. Reports that Grimm's *Silva* was immediately sent to the *Real Academia Española* so he must order extra copies. He expresses approval for Grimm's methodology in presenting the poems. Great praise for Schlosser's *Fiévée* and reference to Southey's *Omniana*. Impressed that Calderón is to be performed in Hamburg. Reports on book orders and commissions including having obtained a copy of the rare *Cancionero de Amberes* from Hitzig in Berlin.

1. Gebhard Leberecht Fürst Blücher von Wahlstatt (1742–1819), Prussian Field Marshall.
2. Görres' *Altteutsche Volks- und Meisterlieder* (1817).
3. Periodical established by Görres in 1814; the English reports referred to by B. may have been inaccurate as Görres adopts a view very much in accordance with his own, although Görres was an admirer of Napoleon.
4. Possible reference to the twelfth-century Hungarian *Codex Albensis*.
5. Goethe's *Italienische Reise* (1816–17).
6. Jacob Grimm, *Silva de romances viejos* (1815).
7. Schubert's *Altes und Neues aus dem Gebiet der inneren Seelenkunde* (1817).
8. Christian Friedrich Schlosser (1782–1829), translated the work of Joseph Fiévée (1767–1839), agent of Napoleon, and later moved from a conservative to a more liberal stance, *Ueber Staatsverfassung und Staatsverwaltung* (1816) (*Correspondance politique et administrative*, 1816).
9. Robert Southey (1774–1843), poet of the Lake School, mentions *Los Quatrocientas respuestas a otras tantas preguntas* (1550) by Luis de Escobar (????–1552) in vol. 2 of his *Omniana* (1812), published in collaboration with Samuel Taylor Coleridge (1772–1834).
10. Reference to Julius' unrealised plan to write a history of the Spanish War of Independence, alluding to the writings of Carlos IV.
11. No reference could be found to this text.

Editor's Notes

12. *El Cantar del mio Cid*, medieval epic written c.1200, the authorship of which is unsure, but which is regarded as the cornerstone of Spain's national literature.
13. Reference to a new edition of Cervantes' *Ocho comedias y ocho entremeses* (1615).
14. Juan Manuel (1282–c.1348), *El libro de los ejemplos del conde Lucanor y Patronio* (1335), a series of didactic tales framed in a dialogue.
15. Collection of religious poems by Jesuit theologian, Friedrich Spee von Langenfeld (1591–1635), published posthumously in 1649.

75. Nikolas Heinrich Julius, Hamburg; Cadiz, 30 April 1818; Source 1

Reports on book orders and commissions. Acknowledges the influence of Southey. Describes the content of an accompanying parcel which includes some popular Spanish folk songs, a selection of literary polemic documents, copies of his own recent essays on Spanish literature (from the Calderón polemic) and two plays, Moreto's *El desden con el desden* and *El diablo predicador*, which he recommends to Gries for translation, describing the latter as a truly Romantic text. There are also a series of excerpts from Spanish epics, copied out by Francisca, the content of which leads him to comment that this is the weaker side of Spanish literature. Outlines his plans for the *Floresta* and the *Teatro antiguo*. Passes comment on the king as a weak figure and describes the effect this has had on political stability. Expresses despair at the current situation in Spain and wishes that he might be able to return to northern Germany one day should Catholicism establish a hold there. He supports his views with a quotation from Schlosser. Comments on how difficult it has been to be separated from his son, Juan. Outlines his understanding of metre in *Romanceros* and *Cancioneros* and is very keen to see Depping's new collection. Goes on to draw parallels between true poetry and faith and makes mention of some essays he would like to publish, but which are too Catholic for north German taste.

1. Reference to Tomás Antonio Sánchez' four volume *Coleccion de poesias castellanas anteriores al siglo XV* (1779–90).
2. The firm of Juan Fernández de Apontes (dates unknown) published various editions of Calderón's work, including a major edition in 1759.
3. *Romances de Germanía de varios autores*, published by Sancha in 1779, including works by Quevedo.
4. Garcilaso Inca de la Vega (1539–1616), son of a conquistador, wrote *La Florida del Inca* (1605).
5. Alvar Nuñez Cabeza de Vaca (c.1490–c.1557), Spanish explorer of North America, described his experiences in the *Naufragios* (1542; 2nd edn., 1555).

6. Reference to B.'s polemic documents published in the *Diario Mercantil de Cádiz*.
7. Agustín Moreto y Cavana (1618–69), playwright, author of *El desden con el desden* (1654), the source for *La Princesse d'Elide* (1664) by Molière (Jean-Baptiste Poquelin) (1622–73), playwright and satirist.
8. Luís de Belmonte y Bermúdez (c.1598–c.1650), playwright and associate of Moreto and supposed author of *El diablo predicador y mayor contrario amigo* (undated); B. attributes the play to 'Fr. Damian Cornasto'.
9. See notes 11 and 12.
10. Reference to Manuel de Godoy (1767–1851), known as *El Príncipe de la Paz* (the prince of peace), lover of Queen Maria Louisa and Prime Minister of Spain from 1792 to 1797 and from 1801 to 1808.
11. Pedro Ceballos (1764–1840), monarchist politician.
12. Juan Escoiquiz (1762–1820), monarchist politician.
13. No reference was found to this figure.
14. Duque del Infantado, Pedro Alcántara de Toledo y Salm-Salm (1773–1841), supporter of Fernando VII.
15. Martín de Garay (1760–1823), politician and Liberal, but favoured by Fernando VII.
16. Quotation from Logau's poem 'Leid und Freude'.
17. Georg Bernhard Depping (1784–1853), *Sammlung der besten alten Spanischen Historischen, Ritter- und Maurischen Romanzen* (1817).
18. First published in 1810 at Metternich's request, editors included Gentz and Friedrich Schlegel.
19. Reference to B.'s associate in the polemic, José Vargas Ponce (1760–1821), who was a poet as well as an historian.
20. Probable reference to Felipe Benicio Navarro (dates unknown), Valencian artillery officer and Liberal conspirator in 1817.
21. Probable reference to Diego de la Peña y Santander (dates unknown), honorary magistrate in Seville from 1819 to 1823.
22. Francisco de Quevedo (1580–1645), Spanish Baroque poet and author of the picaresque novel, *El buscón* (1626).

76. Nikolas Heinrich Julius, Hamburg; Cadiz, 15 May 1818; Source 1

Enquires about performances of Calderón in Hamburg and requests texts by Tieck and Görres. Expresses continued interest in developments in German Hispanism.

1. Reference to C. A. Mämminger's free reworking of Calderón's *La vida es sueño* (1636), entitled *Das Horoskop* (1818), which was performed earlier in Hamburg in 1816.

2. Probable reference to Görres' *Teutschlands künftige Verfassung* (1816).
3. Reference to Tieck's *Dramaturgische Blätter. Nebst einem Anhange noch ungedruckter Aufsätze über das deutsche Theater und berichten über die englische Bühne, geschrieben auf einer Reise im Jahre 1817*, which were eventually published in 1826.
4. A dramatic fairytale, one of the texts included in Tieck's *Phantasus*.

77. Nikolas Heinrich Julius, Hamburg; Cadiz, 30 June 1818; Source 1

Provides an update on the Calderón polemic and expresses pleasure at the attention it has attracted and that he has found much support. Reports that Mora has capitulated into silence. He is keen for A. W. Schlegel to know of his success and asks Julius to mediate.

1. Reference to the 1814 translation of Schlegel which was the catalyst for the Calderón polemic.

78. Nikolas Heinrich Julius, Hamburg; Cadiz, 18 July 1818; Source 1

Further update on the polemic. Reports that there is interest in seeing Schlegel's lectures translated into Spanish with the inference that he might undertake the task. Expresses interest in English periodicals, especially the *Quarterly Review*.

1. August Wilhelm Schlegel, *Cours de literature dramatique*, first translated into French in 1813 by Albertine Necker de Saussure (1766–1841), cousin of Madame de Staël.
2. *Quarterly Review* (1809–1967), Tory periodical, established by the publishing house founded by John Murray (1745–93) as a rival to the Whig *Edinburgh Review*, later edited by John Gibson Lockhart (1794–1854), and which supported the Lake School.

79. Nikolas Heinrich Julius, Hamburg; Cadiz, 7 October 1818; Source 1

Comments on recent publications as well as Spanish publications in Amsterdam and London. Enquires as to the nature of current Calderón performances in Germany and requests a copy of Grillparzer's *Sapho* which has been cited by the opposition in the polemic. Accompanies the letter with fifty copies of the first *Pasatiempo* for distribution (making reference to the visit of D'Alton and Pander). Reports that his financial situation has improved.

1. No reference could be found to this text.

2. Ángel Anaya (dates unknown), *An essay on Spanish literature* (1818).
3. *Der alten Weisen Exempel Sprüch mit vil wunder schönen Beyspilen und Figuren erleüchtet* (1536).
4. *Das sind die 95 Thesen oder Streitsätze Dr Luthers theuren Andenkens* (1817), published by Claus Harms (1778–1835), Lutheran theologian, to commemorate Luther's publication in 1517, causing a polemic and contributing to the establishment of neo-Lutheranism.
5. No reference could be found to this text.
6. Bernardino de Rebolledo (1597–1676), poet, translator and diplomat, published his *Ocios* in 1656.
7. Thomas Robert Malthus (1766–1834), English demographer and political economist who predicted that population growth would exceed food supply.
8. Reference to the 1818 play, *Sappho*, by Franz Grillparzer (1791–1872), Austrian playwright, writer and poet.
9. *Donna Diana, Lustspiel* (1819) by Carl August West (1768–1832), based on Moreto's *El desdén con el desdén*.
10. No text or author of this name could be traced. It may be a play on words.
11. Felipe Scío y Riaza (1738–96), translated the Bible into Castilian from 1790 to 1793 at the behest of Carlos III.
12. Reference to Kotzebue's play, *Menschenhass und Reue* (1789), which gained an international reputation.
13. Reference to Francisca's pseudonym, 'Cymdocea'.
14. Reference to Vargas Ponce's intervention early in the polemic.
15. Eduard D'Alton (1772–1840), anatomist and archaeologist, professor at Bonn with August Wilhelm Schlegel; Christian Heinrich Pander (1794–1865), embryologist.
16. Gregorio Mayans (1699–1781), scholar, author of the *Orígenes de la lengua española* (1737).
17. Vargas Ponce's *Servicios de Cadiz desde MDCCCVII a MDCCCXVI* (1818).

80. Friedrich Perthes, Hamburg; Cadiz, 16 October 1818; Source 5

Reports the visit of D'Alton and Pander and the performance of Calderón's 'Á secreto agravio secreta venganza' put on for their benefit, an action which went against current public taste, but which was tolerated politely. He hopes to see D'Alton's report on the event on the German press. Reports on book orders and trade fairs. Refers to the inclusion of his piece on Schlegel in the *Minerva*. Expresses dismay at the current political situation in Spain.

1. Reference to the pamphlet *Discurso en razon de la tragedia Á secreto agravio, secreta venganza*, published to accompany the staging of Calderón's play by B.'s associate Juan Bautista Cavaleri Pazos (dates unknown).

2. D'Alton did publish an article entitled 'Theaternachrichten aus Kadix' in Oken's *Isis*, no. 11, 1818 (see letter 81, note 13).
3. Reference to the *Wiener Jahrbücher der Literatur* which were established in 1817.
4. Reference to the periodical, *Minerva*, edited by Pedro de Olive (dates unknown).

81. Nikolas Heinrich Julius, Hamburg; Cadiz, 16 February 1819; Source 1

Partially repeats his previous letter to Perthes. Thanks him for a recent parcel of books, expressing satisfaction with the *Wiener Jahrbücher*, the *Quarterly Review*, Ancillon, Schubert, Wordsworth and collections of songs and *romances*. Praise also for Harms. Comments on current political journalism and recent histories of the Napoleonic Wars. Appraisal of Southey and Depping as useful sources of material. Requests more material and promises to send copies of his 'Noticias literarias' and the second *Pasatiempo*. Negative appraisal of Quintana. Enquires about Bonald.

1. Tiberio Cavallo (1749–1809), Italian physician who worked on the use of electricity in medicine.
2. Friedrich Christoph Förster (1791–1868), poet and historian, *Die Sängerfahrt. Eine Neujahrsgabe für Freunde der Dichtkunst und Mahlerey* (1818).
3. Anton (1803–48) and Josepf Gersbach (1787–1830), *Deutsche Lieder für Jung und Alt* (1818).
4. Johann Peter Friedrich Ancillon (1766–1837), Prussian historian, *Mélanges de literature et de philosophie* (1811).
5. Thomas Rodd (1763–1822), *History of Charles the Great and Orlando* (1812).
6. Alberto Baldrich y de Viciana (1790–1864), *Historia de la Guerra contra Napoleon* (1818), of which only one volume appeared.
7. Francisco Javier Martínez Marina (1754–1833), director of the Royal Spanish Academy, historian and priest, *Teoria de las Cortes ó grandes juntas nacionales de los Reinos de Leon y Castilla: con algunos observaciones sobre la Lei fundamental de la monarquia Española de 1812* (1813).
8. Reference to Southey's narrative poem, *Roderick; the Last of the Goths* (1814).
9. Christoph von Schmid (1768–1854), author of moral tales for children.
10. Carl Ritter (1779–1859), founder of scientific geography.

11. *Romancero* copied by Juan Alfonso de Baena (c.1375–1434), c.1426 at the behest of Juan II, not published until 1851.
12. José Rodríguez de Castro (1739–89), *Biblioteca española* (1781–6).
13. Lorenz Oken (1779–1851), German naturalist, published the encyclopaedic periodical, *Isis* (1816–48).
14. Probable reference to the *Theologische Quartalschrift*, established in 1819 by Peter Aloys Gratz (1769–1849), friend and follower of Georg Hermes (1775–1831), Catholic theologian and founder of Hermesianism.
15. *La tia fingida*, one of the texts found in manuscript form by Porras de la Cámera (dates unkown) and attributed to Cervantes.
16. Reference to B.'s 'Noticias literarias', published in the *Diario Mercantil de Cádiz*.
17. Manuel José Quintana (1772–1857), Liberal poet, writer and politician.
18. De Staël's *Considérations sur les principaux événements de la revolution française* (1818).
19. De Bonald's *Observations sur le dernier ouvrage de Madame de la Baronne de Staël* (1818).
20. August Jakob Rambach (1777–1851), theologian and hymnist, *Anthologie Christlicher Gesänge aus allen Jahrhunderten* (1817–33).
21. Johann Pappus (1549–1610), hymnist and song writer.

82. Nikolas Heinrich Julius, Hamburg; Cadiz, 30 March 1819; Source 1

Comments on a recent history of the Peninsular War which is struggling for publication due to French influence. Compares this situation to the problems he faces in the polemic. Provides examples of recent articles in the *Crónica* which seek to undermine the image of German culture. Comments on the positive reception of his work in certain circles and mentions for the first time the possibility of entry to the Royal Spanish Academy, hoping that his membership of other societies and role as Hanseatic consul will help. Reports Cecilia's forthcoming trip to Hamburg and requests further material. Currently engrossed in his study of ancient Spanish theatre so that other things remain neglected, including de Staël's *Considerations*. Reports recent edition of Spanish poets and the forthcoming new edition of *Don Quijote* and a new biography of Cervantes, most likely that by Navarrete.

1. Probable reference to the *Diario de Madrid*.
2. Alexandre Stourdza (1791–1854), reference to Baader's *Ueber die Vierzahl des Lebens aus einem Schreiben an den kaiserlich russischen Herrn Kämmerer Grafen Alexander von Stourdza* (1818).

3. Established by Juan Manuel Fernández Pacheco, Marquis of Villena (1650–1725), under Felipe V.
4. *New Monthly Magazine* (1814–1884), founded by Henry Colburn (1784–1855) to oppose the Jacobin *Monthly Magazine*.
5. George Crabbe (1754–1832), writer known for his realistic depictions of rural life, published his *Tales in Verse* in 1812.
6. Bernardo de Balbuena (c.1563–1627), poet and bishop of Puerto Rico.
7. Alonso de Ercilla y Zuñiga (1533–94), Chilean poet and historian.
8. Martín Fernández de Navarrete (1765–1844), sailor and historian, author of *Vida de Miguel de Cervantes Saavedra* (1819) and associate of B.
9. Fernando de Rojas (c.1465–1541), playwright, author of *La Celestina* (1499).

83. Nikolas Heinrich Julius, Hamburg; Cadiz, 20 May 1819; Source 1

Reports that Mora has gone to Italy, thus silencing the polemic for now. Expresses concern, having gleaned information from French newspapers, at the political situation in France. Comments, at times critically, on a recent parcel sent by Perthes, the contents of which were chosen by Julius. Discusses the sale of his German book collection, currently with his brother. Reports on books orders and commissions. Refers to plans for a trip to the royal library in Madrid and his son's forthcoming visit. Enquires as to the plans for the marriage of the niece of the king of Saxony to the Spanish king. Also encloses an ode by Arriaza on the death of the queen and further polemic documents. Expresses hope that the polemic is achieving something following a well-received performance of *La vida es sueño*.

1. *Le Conservateur* (1818–20), periodical established by Chateaubriand.
2. Probably included Fiévée's *Correspondance politique et administrative* (1816).
3. Reference to the *Wiener Jahrbücher der Literatur*. The first volume (January to March 1818) contained a number of essays on press freedom in France (pp. 199–255). The theme was not revisited in later volumes.
4. Probable error, reference to *Historia de la guerra contra Napoleon* (see letter 81).
5. A new edition appeared in 1818, edited by Vicente González del Reguero (dates unknown).
6. Reference to B.'s stepfather, Martin Ritter und Elder von Faber (1752–1827), Protestant clergyman.
7. Maria Josepha von Sachsen (1803–29), married Fernando VII in 1819 as his third wife.
8. Juan Bautista Arriaza y Superviela (1770–1837), poet, journalist and friend of Francisca.
9. Reference to the pamphlet published by Zulueta, *Yo solo a uno de los mismos*.

84. *Elise Campe, Hamburg; Cadiz, 20 May 1819; Source 3*

Apologises for the break in correspondence. Describes the emotional impact of her letter which reminds him of northern nature. Expresses his discomfort with the current political situation in Spain and explains how ancient poetry provides him with a refuge. Juxtaposes reason and emotion and draws together poetry and nationalism in an attack on Enlightenment values. Provides an update on family news.

1. Quotation from Goethe's *Faust I* (1808), Mephistopholes addressing Faust in the 'Studierzimmer' scene.

85. *Nikolas Heinrich Julius, Hamburg; Cadiz, 30 May 1819; Source 1*

Addendum to letter 83 enclosing some literary curios and news from D'Alton and Pander who have promised to make Böhl's endeavours in Spain known in Germany. Comments positively on the discovery of de la Mennais' work.

1. Felicité Robert de la Mennais (1782–1854), French priest and philosopher, *Essai sur l'indifférence en matière de religion* (1817).

86. *Friedrich Perthes, Hamburg; Cadiz, 16 August 1819; Source 5*

Mentions Kotzebue's assassination. Comments on the debate between Perthes and Fouqué on the role of the nobility, taking the latter's pro-nobility stance. Expresses exhaustion at fighting against the tide of opinion and complains that Enlightenment and reason have undermined poetry, enthusiasm and all finer feelings. Reports re-reading Claudius' work and finding it a comfort.

1. Kotzebue was assassinated in Mannheim in 1819 by theology student, Karl Ludwig Sand.
2. Perthes and Fouqué's joint publication *Ueber den deutschen Adel, über Ritter-Sinn und Militair-Ehre* (1819).
3. Claudius collected works appeared from 1775 to 1812 under the title *Asmus omnia sua secum portans oder Sämtliche Werke des Wandsbecker Boten*.

87. *Nikolas Heinrich Julius, Hamburg; Cadiz, 18 August 1819; Source 1*

Comments on the content of a recent parcel of books. Complains that German periodicals lack the generality of the British, in particular the *Edinburgh Review*. Positive appraisals of Fiévée, Hoffmann, Malsburg's introduction to Calderón, Schlegel's *Observations* and the third part of Goethe's autobiography. De Bonald was of particular interest. No longer interested in church music, preferring instead simple folk songs. Some discussion of folk songs and complaints at the paucity of the period. Has given up the good cause in Spain now, as no one really seems interested with revolution inevitable. Comments on how far he has become removed from the ideals espoused by Campe and how this affects his communication with Dorothea. Requests Schlegels' *Deutsches Museum* and enquires after a systematic outline of the new aesthetic from Kant to Schlegel. Further enquiries about the Saxonian princess.

1. Ernst Friedrich Georg Otto von Malsburg (1786–1824), writer, translator and poet, published *Pedro Calderon de la Barca Schauspiele* (1819–25).
2. August Wilhelm Schlegel's *Observations sur la langue et la littérature provençales* (1818).
3. De Bonalds *Mélanges littéraires, politiques et philosophiques* (1819), *Pensées sur divers sujets* (1817) and *Recherches philosophiques* (1818).
4. Johann Friedrich Joseph Sommer (1793–1856), *Von der Kirche in dieser Zeit* (1819).
5. Friedrich Wilhelm Valentin Schmidt (1787–1831), translator of Calderón, reference to the preparation of the translation.
6. Vicente García de la Huerta (1734–87), poet and man of letters, *Teatro español* (1785), which contained a supplement entitled 'Catálogo del teatro español'.
7. José de Cañizares (1676–1750), dramatist, *Yo me entiendo y Dios me entiende* (1730).
8. *Coleccion de retratos de los españoles ilustres; con un epitome de sus vidas* (1791–9).
9. Reference to the literary section of *Originalien aus dem Gebiete der Wahrheit, Kunst, Laune und Phantasie*, which appeared thrice weekly, edited by Georg Lotz (dates unknown).
10. Reference to Moreto's plays *El lindo Don Diego* (1662), *El perecido en la corte, La tia y la sobrina* and *El rico hombre de Alcalá,* which appeared in one volume in 1654.
11. The textual reference here is unclear. However, Stolberg was highly critical of Gustav III's attempts to disempower the Swedish nobility and attacked his policies in an ode entitled 'Die Ruhe' in 1772.
12. *Gesammelte Werke der Brüder Christian und Friedrich Leopold Grafen zu Stolberg*, published by Perthes und Besser in twenty volumes from 1820 to 1825.
13. George Gordon, Lord Byron (1788–1824). An edition of *Manfred* appeared in German in 1819, translated by Adolf Wagner (1774–1835).
14. Sir Walter Scott (1771–1832), poet and novelist.
15. Crabbe's *Tales of the Hall* (1819).

16. *De poëeos dramaticae genere hispanico: praesertium de Petro Calderone de la Barca, prinicipe dramaticorum* (1817) by Johann Ludwig Heiberg (1791–1860).
17. Reference to D'Alton's article 'Theaternachrichten aus Kadix' which was reprinted in the *Morgenblatt für gebildete Stände* on 2 March 1819.
18. Seventh-century *Liber judicorum*, became known as the *Fuero juzgo* in the thirteenth century, German law code, the basis of Spanish civil society.
19. *Gaceta de Madrid*, longstanding Madrid periodical, published from 1697 to 1934.
20. José Francisco de Isla (1703–82), priest and satirist, *Historia del famoso predicador Fray Gerundio de Campazos* (1758) and *Aventuras de Gil Blas de Santillana*, published posthumously in 1790.
21. Reference to Dorothea Campe, now widowed since the death of Joachim Heinrich Campe in 1818.
22. *Wiener Jahrbücher der Literatur*, established in 1817, published until 1849. B. refers to vol. 4, pp. 154–87: 'Lotosblätter. Fragmente von Isidorus, Erster Theil, Zweyter Theil' and 'Der Mensch. Eine Untersuchung für gebildete Leser', Maximilian Karl Friedrich Wilhelm Grävell (1781–1860); vol. 5: pp. 76–96, 'Ueber Deutschland, wie ich es nach einer zehnjährigen Entfernung wider fand', Garlieb Merkel (1769–1850), critic of Romanticism; pp. 163–82, 'Examinations of the Objections made in Britain against the doctrines of Gall and Spurzheim', Stadt, on the work of physicians and psychologists, Franz Joseph Gall (1758–1828) and Johann Christoph Spurzheim (1776–1832); pp. 215–61, several essays on gymnastics, including one by Friedrich Ludwig Jahn (1778–1852), pedagogue and politican who promoted physical exercise and became known as 'Turnvater Jahn'.
23. Reference to Friedrich Schlegel's *Deutsches Museum* (1812–13).
24. Reference to the tenth volume of Bouterwek's monumental work, *Geschichte der deutschen Poesie und Beredsamkeit* (1817), the second volume to be dedicated to German literature.
25. Enrique Florez (1701–73), Spanish numismatist, historian and theologian, *Medallas de las Colonias* (1757–8).

88. Nikolas Heinrich Julius, Hamburg; Cadiz, 24 September 1819; Source 1

Requests an image of the future queen. Comments on family matters including the impact of an outbreak of yellow fever and the forthcoming arrival of Cecilia and Juan in Hamburg. Great anticipation at D'Alton's description of his travels in Spain and mention made of his own essay describing his trip to Seville. Notes that his enthusiasm for new things is not diminishing with age and that he thanks Goethe and Wordsworth for his ability to see the beauty in everything.

1. Reference to B.'s text, 'Korrespondenz Nachrichten aus Kadix', published in Cotta's *Morgenblatt für gebildete Stände* in January 1820.

89. Nikolas Heinrich Julius, Hamburg; Cadiz, 2 October 1819; Source 1

Sends the first polemic documents and makes a first reference to *Vindicaciones*. Suggests the publication of the description of his trip to Seville. Reports on the latest outbreak of yellow fever. Comments that he turns to reading novels in troubled times.

1. First reference to publication of B.'s collected polemic documents, *Vindicaciones de Calderon* (1820).
2. Reference to Jean Paul Richter, *Briefe und bevorstehender Lebenslauf* (1799–1800).
3. Johann Karl August Musäus (1735–87), writer, author of the satirical novel, *Physiognomische Reisen* (1778–9).
4. Grimms' *Kinder und Hausmärchen*, the second edition of which was published in three volumes from 1815 to 1819.
5. Arnim's unfinished novel *Die Kronenwächter* (1817).

90. Nikolas Heinrich Julius, Hamburg; Cadiz, 15 October 1819; Source 1

Refers again to his Seville piece, which he sends unaltered for Julius to rework, claiming it will be too Catholic for north German tastes. Reports on the arrival of future queen in Madrid and the continued outbreak of yellow fever.

91. Nikolas Heinrich Julius, Hamburg; Cadiz, 17 December 1819; Source 1

Outlines his progress with the *Floresta*, proudly announcing that he has collated almost 380 poems which he hopes will show Spanish poetry from another side. He is not yet sure whether to add German notes. Expresses hope that Perthes will take on the project and, if so, Julius should act as proof reader. Reference to the appearance of his Seville piece in the *Morgenblatt*.

92. Friedrich Perthes, Hamburg; Cadiz, 17 December 1819; Source 5

Refers to the Voss–Claudius polemic, refusing even to read Voss' attack. Reports on progress with the first volume of the *Floresta* and explains his preferred layout. Outlines how it compares with other collections and the difficulties faced in selecting the material. Outlines his plans for future volumes, including the *Teatro antiguo*. Explains that he requires no fee and that it will be difficult to bring copies into Spain itself due to current restrictions. Describes his preferred frontispiece. Keen to have his name in full for maximum recognition. Praises the new queen for her good deportment and morals.

1. Reference to Perthes' proceedings against Johann Heinrich Voss (1751–1826) in which he claimed that Voss had attacked Claudius' honour in his piece criticising Stolberg which appeared in *Sophronizon* in 1819.
2. Compiled in 1768 by Juan José López de Sedano (1729–1801).
3. Reference to Quintana's *Poesias escogidas de nuestros cancioneros y romanceros antiguos* (1796), published as part of the larger collection compiled by Pedro Estala (1757–1815) under the name of Ramón Fernández.
4. Fernando de Herrera (1534–97), acolyte of Garcilaso de la Vega.
5. Juan Martínez de Jauregui (1583–1659), poet, scholar and artist.
6. Brothers Bartolomé Leonardo (1562–1631) and Lupercio Leonardo de Argensola (1559–1613), scholars and poets.
7. Francisco de Rioja (1583–1659), canon and inquisitor.
8. Cristóbal de Castillejo (1491–1550), poet opposed to the Italianate style.
9. Tomé de Burguillos, pseudonym of Juan Sánchez Burguillos (c.1520–75), poet.

93. Nikolas Heinrich Julius, Hamburg; Cadiz, 19 February 1820; Source 1

Reports sending the final manuscript of the *Floresta* to Hamburg. Has begun to re-examine ancient theatre and concludes that Juan del Encina is the true creator of Spanish drama, his work equalled only by that of Gil Vicente. Requests information on the sale of Spanish material in Germany. Mention of the continued reception of the polemic, including the potential intervention of D'Alton in Germany. Describes the content of the third *Pasatiempo* and states explicitly that its more academic content should help his quest to become a member of the Royal Spanish Academy. Criticises contemporary views in Germany where, according to Cecilia, there is a growing tendency towards Liberalism. Goes on to describe the impact of the Liberal resurgence in Spain and the threat this presents to the Church and his own value system. Rejects once more literature with an oriental emphasis. Describes recent book orders and problems of availability. Discussion of English literature including criticism of the *Edinburgh Review*, in particular a review of Crabbe who Böhl defends as a true poet. Ends with a criticism of A. W. Schlegel for not having acknowledged receipt of the first two *Pasatiempos*.

1. Juan del Encina (c.1469–1533), dramatist, regarded as the father of Spanish drama.
2. Gil Vicente (c.1465–c.1536), Portuguese playwright, actor and director, wrote in both Portuguese and Spanish.

3. Bartolomé de Torres Naharro (c.1485–c.1530), poet and dramatist.
4. Reference to the death of Friedrich von Stolberg in December 1819.
5. *Revue encyclopédique*, July 1819, p. 186.
6. Antonio Alcalá Galiano (1789–1865), writer and politician, Mora's associate in the Calderón polemic.
7. Görres' *Teutschland und die Revolution* (1819) and *Firdudis Heldenbuch von Iran* (1820).
8. Goethe's *West-östlicher Diwan* (1819).
9. Francisco Javier Laso de la Vega y Orcajado (1785–1836), founder of the *Sociedad Medico-Quirurgica de Cádiz*.
10. Etienne Pariset (1770–1847), author, along with Mazet, of *Observations sur la fièvre jaune à Cadix* (1819).
11. Friedrich Ludwig Wilhelm Meyer (1758–1840), published *Friedrich Ludwig Schröder. Beitrag zur Kunde des Menschen und des Künstlers* (1819), biography of actor, director and Freemason, Friedrich Ludwig Schröder (1744–1816).
12. Friedrich von Stolberg's *Betrachtungen und Beherzigungen der Heiligen Schrift* (1819–21).
13. A review article entitled 'Tales of the Hall by the Reverend George Crabbe' appeared in the *Edinburgh Review*, 38 (July 1819), 118.
14. Gerhard Dorn (c.1530–84), Belgian physician, follower of Paracelsus (1493–1541).

94. Friedrich Perthes, Hamburg; Cadiz, 4 April 1820; Source 5

Impatient for news of his *Floresta* manuscript and publication progress. Requests material on Arabic and Hebrew. Appraisal of the political situation which highlights the influence of the French and the danger of anarchy should so-called freedom prevail. Criticises the press for its maltreatment of the king who he feels has called the Liberals' bluff by accepting the Constitution. Fears for the future of the Catholic faith and bemoans demise of the Inquisition.

1. Jacob Golius (1596–1667), *Lexicon Arabico-Latinum* (1653).

95. Nikolas Heinrich Julius, Hamburg; Cadiz, 11 May 1820; Source 1

Still impatient for news of his manuscript. Describes the content of an accompanying parcel including some poetry by Vargas of which Böhl is critical. He encloses copies of the third *Pasatiempo* for dissemination and copies of current popular songs including the 'Cancion de Riego'. Appraises the current political situation and is particularly critical of the behaviour of young women who fail to understand the subtleties of the situation. Reports sending a copy of the *Floresta* manuscript along with essays on metre, etc. to the Royal Spanish Academy and having been accepted into their ranks. He is sure the third *Pasatiempo* also played a role and asks for a copy to be sent to A. W. Schlegel.

1. Rafael de Riego y Flórez (1784–1823), prominent Liberal General, the so-called 'Himno de Riego' written in his honour was the anthem of Spain from 1820 to 1823.
2. Antonio Quiroga (1784–1841), Spanish sailor and supporter of Riego.
3. Reference to B.'s announcement in the *Diario de Cádiz* of his admittance into the Royal Spanish Academy.

96. Friedrich Perthes, Hamburg; Cadiz, 12 May 1820; Source 5

Mostly relates to book orders. Reports his election to the Royal Spanish Academy.

1. José Finestres y Monsalvo (1688–1777), author of a number of Latin texts on church institutions.
2. Edmund Burke (1729–97), Irish statesman and political theorist whose *Reflections on the Revolution in France* (1790) were translated into German by Gentz in 1793 as *Betrachtungen über die französische Revolution*.

97. Nikolas Heinrich Julius, Hamburg; Cadiz, 2 June 1820; Source 1

Discusses the proofs for the *Floresta* and also the design for the frontispiece for which he requests something gothic and religious. He refuses to have the notes translated into Spanish, but the comments made suggest he may incorporate the essays sent to the Royal Spanish Academy into a fuller commentary along with a section of the third *Pasatiempo*. Some discussion of classification of *romances* with a view to publishing future volumes. More concrete plans also outlined for the *Teatro antiguo*. A collection of epic poetry will be left for his retirement. General comments on the sale of books and new acquisitions, including praise for Adam Müller. Reports an increase in stature following election to the Academy.

1. Fifteenth-century Galician troubadour, known as *El Enamorado*.
2. Georg Andreas Reimer (1776–1842), prominent Berlin publisher.
3. Jacob Grimm's *Deutsche Grammatik* (1819–37).
4. Adam Heinrich Müller (1779–1829), publicist, literary critic and political theorist, *Von der Notwendigkeit einer theologischen Grundlage der gesamten Staatswissenschaft und der Staatswirtschaft* (1820).

Editor's Notes

98. Nikolas Heinrich Julius, Hamburg; Cadiz, 7 July 1820; Source 1

Comments on development of German notes for the *Floresta* with further insistence that they should not appear in Spanish. Mercantile duties are impeding his studies and the rise of Liberalism is a cause for concern. Keen to see Haller's critique of the Spanish Constitution. Refers to poor reception of his piece on Seville.

1. Karl Ludwig von Haller (1768–1854), Swiss political scientist, opponent of the French Revolution.

99. Nikolas Heinrich Julius, Hamburg; Cadiz, 1 August 1820; Source 1

Describes the contents of a chest of books including a number of medical reports. Comments on the Voss–Stolberg polemic and mentions a reference to himself in a review of A. W. Schlegel in the *Wiener Jahrbücher*. Ambivalent response to Hoffmann's *Serapionsbrüder*. Expresses preference for Wordsworth's earlier work and approval of Crabbe. Discussion of political writings in Spain since the lifting of censorship suggests little of value. Explains the best way to smuggle in a foreign book, hiding it in a barrel of potatoes.

1. Heinrich Wilhelm von Kleist (1777–1811), dramatist and writer, *Die heilige Cäcilie oder die Gewalt der Musik. Eine Legende* (1810).
2. Julius may have been the translator of 'Von der Unterrichtsweise und dem Zustande der Gelehrsamkeit in den Vereinigten Staaten von Amerika' which appeared in 1819 in the *Kieler Blätter* (II/1: 395–450), taken from an article in vol. 4 of *Blackwood's Edinburgh Magazine*.
3. First appeared in print in 1511, compiled by Hernando del Castillo (dates unknown), the last edition published in Antwerp in 1573.
4. Reference to the first of two Antwerp editions of the *Cancionero general*.
5. Voss attacked Stolberg for his conversion to Catholicism in *Wie ward Fritz Stolberg zum Unfreien?* (1819); Stolberg responded with *Kurze Abfertigung des langen Schmähschrifts des Hofrats Voss gegen ihn* (1820), which appeared posthumously.
6. Reference to a review of Schlegel's *Wiener Vorlesungen* by Karl Friedrich Ferdinand Solger (1780–1819), which appeared in the *Wiener Jahrbücher der Literatur*, 7 (1819), 80–155, with a reference to B., but not by name (p. 147).
7. E. T. A. Hoffmann's *Serapionsbrüder* (1819–21).
8. Volume eleven of Bouterwek's *Geschichte*, part three of the *Geschichte der deutschen Poesie und Beredsamkeit* (1819).
9. Müller's *Agronomische Briefe* (1812).

10. August Wilhelm Rehberg (1757–1836), publicist and civil servant, supporter of the nobility.

100. Nikolas Heinrich Julius, Hamburg; Cadiz, 11 August 1820; Source 1

Reports on book orders and on the publishing activities of the Royal Spanish Academy. Expresses concern at the prevailing political situation.

1. Lorenzo Hervás y Panduro (1735–1809), Jesuit philologist, a number of whose works, over twenty volumes, are held in the *Staats- und Universitätsbibliothek* in Göttingen, presumably having been supplied by B.
2. Reference to Navarrete. See letter 131, note 2.
3. Francisco de la Torre (c.1534–c.1594), Spanish Rennaissance poet.
4. Antonio Solís y Rivadeneira (1610–86), poet and historian.
5. Possible reference to Antonio Valcarcél Pío de Saboya y Maura (1748–1808), archaeologist and writer.
6. Hipólito Ruiz y López (1752–1816) and José Antonio Pavón y Jiménez (1754–1840), *Flora Peruviana et Chilensis* (1794–1802).

101. Friedrich Perthes, Hamburg; Cadiz, 11 August 1820; Source 5

Reports on book orders. Emotive response to Voss's attack on Stolberg. Description of current political pamphlets which he finds to be of limited worth. Adds a list of descriptions dated 17 August which outlines the contents of a parcel of political pamphlets sent at the request of Rehberg. This includes a description of Alcalá Galiano and that of various other Liberal commentators. There are also some pro-absolutist publications.

1. Nicolás Santiago y Rotalde (1784–1833) was accused of treason when he tried to take Cadiz in 1820. He was known for his irascible nature.
2. Manuel Alberto Freire Andrade Armijo (1797–1835), General under Fernando VII who sought a peaceful resolution during the early days of the Liberal uprising.
3. Henry Joseph O'Donnell, count of La Bisbal (1769–1834), General loyal to Fernando VII.

102. Nikolas Heinrich Julius, Hamburg; Cadiz, 31 October 1820; Source 1

Reports the safe return of Cecilia from Hamburg. Expresses concern that Spain is veering away from Catholicism. Comments on a recent parcel of books including a positive appraisal of F. Schlegel's *Concordia*. Discussion of a further set of *Floresta*

Editor's Notes

proofs. Praise for Haller's critique of the *cortes* and a request for more of his work. Explains his requirements for the frontispiece of the *Floresta*, rejecting anything of a Moorish nature. Refers to the parcel of political pamphlets sent to Perthes for Rehberg and promises to send more. Vehement criticism of Clararossa. Explains his ambivalence towards Byron who is poor in comparison with Wordsworth. Brief report on a new outbreak of yellow fever and the preferred treatments.

1. Johann Emanuel Veith (1787–1876), Austrian physician and clergyman, and Anton Passy (1788–1847), Austrian writer and clergyman, editors of the literary and religious periodical, *Oelzweige* (1819–23).
2. Friedrich Schlegel's periodical, *Concordia* (1820–3), key organ of the *Wiener Romantik*.
3. Gottfried Wilhelm Freiherr von Leibnitz (1646–1716), philosopher and theologian.
4. The reference is unclear.
5. Haller published his *Über die Constitution der spanischen Cortes* in 1821.
6. Alphonse de La Martine (1790–1869), politician and poet of early French Romanticism, *Les meditations poétiques* (1820).
7. Friedrich Johann Jacobsen (1774–1822), *Briefe an eine deutsche Edelfrau über die neuesten englischen Dichter* (1820).
8. Andreae's volume of sacred poems, *Der geistliche Kurzweil* (1619).
9. William Roscoe (1753–1831), English historian and minor poet, *Sonnet on Parting with his Books* (1816).
10. Reference to proposed illustrations for the frontispiece of the *Floresta*.
11. August Wilhelm Schlegel's *Indische Bibliothek* (1820–30).
12. Pseudonym of Juan Antonio de Olabarrieta (1763–1822), anti-clerical polemicist.
13. Pseudonym François-Marie Arouet (1694–1778), philosopher and writer, leader of the French Enlightenment.
14. Constantin François de Chasseboeuf, Count Volney (1757–1820), French scholar and religious sceptic.
15. Thomas Paine (1737–1809), English writer, advocate of American independence.
16. Liberal *Gaceta del Gobierno*, appeared in 1809 and again from 1820 to 1821.
17. *Diario de las actas y discusiones de las cortes* (1820–3), main political record of the Liberal Triennial.
18. Reference to Byron's poem *Don Juan* (1819–24).
19. Poem by Wordsworth, written in 1798 and published in 1819 with a dedication to Southey.
20. Wordsworth's series of thirty-four sonnets written from 1818 to 1819, published in volume two of the *Miscellaneous Poems* in 1820.

103. Nikolas Heinrich Julius, Hamburg; Cadiz, 16 February 1821; Source 1

Discusses the *Floresta* proofs and outlines revised plans for future volumes which will delay the *Teatro antiguo* project. Reports on a recently received parcel of books, with particular praise for De la Mennais, La Martine and Haller. Disgust at the current political situation.

1. Haller's *Restauration der Staatswissenschaft oder Theorie des natürlich-geselligen Zustandes, der Chimäre des künstlich-bürgerlichen entgegengesetzt* (1816–34).

104. Nikolas Heinrich Julius, Hamburg; Cadiz, 14 March [1821] [appended to letter from Francisca]; Source 1

Comments on the political situation, in particular the Liberal rejection of religion and the presence of North America as a paradigm.

105. Friedrich Perthes, Hamburg; Cadiz, 18 May 1821; Source 5

Reports the arrival of the first copies of the *Floresta* with which he is delighted. Describes the difficulties in disseminating the collection due to the ban on the import of books in Spanish published abroad. Asks to be kept informed of the reception of the *Floresta* in Germany, especially the views of A. W. Schlegel, Gries and Keil. Hopes to send manuscript of the second volume soon.

1. Johann Georg Keil (1781–1857), published an original version of *La vida es sueño* in Leipzig in 1819, followed by a series of other *comedias* by Calderón.
2. Johann Karl Passavant (1790–1857), *Untersuchungen über den Lebensmagnetismus und das Hellsehen* (1821).

106. Nikolas Heinrich Julius, Hamburg; Cadiz, 25 May 1821; Source 1

Reports on book orders and commissions. Expresses thanks for the work undertaken on the *Floresta* and requests news of its reception. Reports continued contact with Pander, but nothing from D'Alton. Encloses the manuscript of the second volume of the *Floresta*.

1. Jeremias David Reuss (1750–1837), head librarian at Göttingen.
2. Reference to the edition of Calderón's *Autos sacramentales, alegoricas y historiales*, published by Juan Fernández de Apontes in 1759.

3. Samuel Heinrich Spiker (1786–1858), translator and librarian to Friedrich III of Prussia, *Reise durch England, Wales und Schottland im Jahre 1816* (1818).
4. Charles Victor Prévôt (1789–1856), French novelist, *Le Solitaire* (1821).

107. Nikolas Heinrich Julius, Hamburg; Cadiz, 21 June 1821; Source 1

Sends a satire on the current political situation which has evaded the censors.

108. Friedrich Perthes, Hamburg; Cadiz, 21 September 1821; Source 5

Asks for a copy of the *Floresta* to be sent to *Blackwood's Magazine*, expressing approval for the publication as a vehicle of the true German intellect. Explains he is happy to seek refuge from the current political situation in his studies and is pleased to see similar ideas expressed in the work of new writers. Expresses delight at Goethe's positive response to the *Floresta* and compares the volume to Wordsworth's poems in finding a limited audience of enthusiasts.

1. *Blackwood's Edinburgh Magazine* (1817–1980), established as a Tory rival to the *Edinburgh Review*.
2. Reference to Goethe's positive remarks on the *Floresta* in his correspondence with Perthes, 12 May 1821. The letter is held in the *Perthes Nachlass* in the *Staatsarchiv Hamburg*.

109. Nikolas Heinrich Julius, Hamburg; Cadiz, 22 September 1821; Source 1

Reports that a complaint has been made about the *Floresta* by a Liberal offended by the spiritual content, but that it has come to nothing in the end. All the copies have been sent to Madrid for sale. Expresses the sense that the true Spain now only survives in a few souls and in the minds of foreign scholars. Criticism of the *Wiener Jahrbücher* for dwelling too long on uninteresting topics, rather than the more general and informative approach of the British periodicals, especially the *Quarterly Review* and *Blackwood's*, as well as the *Retrospective Review*. Assesses recently received texts and praises Haller, F. Schlegel, Hamann and Zimmermann. Reports a probable move to El Puerto and progress on third volume of the *Floresta*. Describes unrest following the departure of the king. Reports Francisca's nervous disposition and comments briefly on the situation in Greece and Russia. Family news including Cecilia's second marriage.

1. Reference to Liaño's complaint against the *Floresta*; see chapter 15, note 12.
2. Frederick, Baron von Lauerwinckel and Philip Kempfershausen, pseudonyms of writer and editor, John Gibson Lockhart, writing in *Blackwood's Magazine*.

3. Timothy Tickler, pseudonym attributed to both Lockhart and Maginn (see letter 133, note 2), authors of the 'Letters of Timothy Tickler' in *Blackwood's Magazine*.
4. Johann Georg Hamann (1730–88), religious philosopher, critical of the Enlightenment, influence on the *Sturm und Drang*, known as the 'Magus of the North'.
5. Friedrich Gottlieb Zimmermann (1782–1835), *Dramaturgische Blätter für Hamburg* (1821–2).
6. *The Retrospective Review* (1820–6), edited by Henry Southern (1799–1853) as an alternative to the *Edinburgh Review* and the *Quarterly Review*.
7. Julius published a letter in the *Göttinger Gelehrten Anzeigen* under the rubric 'Cadix' on 7 July 1821 which discussed the first and second *Pasatiempos*.
8. *Floresta*, I, no. 351, 'Deseais, Señor Sarmiento', Baltasar del Alcázar (1530–1606).
9. Cecilia married her second husband, Francisco Ruiz del Arco de Paula, later Marqués de Arco Hermoso, in 1822 (dates unknown).

110. Nikolas Heinrich Julius, Hamburg; Cadiz, 13 October 1821; Source 1

Reports logistical difficulties due to quarantine regulations and the latest yellow fever outbreak. Sends a copy of the complaint made against the *Floresta* and expresses doubts that sales of the volume in Madrid will come to anything as everyone is obsessed with the political situation. Compares *Blackwood's Magazine* to the *Pasatiempos*.

111. Nikolas Heinrich Julius, Hamburg; Cadiz, 23 December 1821; Source 1

Reports his move to El Puerto, which should afford him more free time. Copies of the *Floresta* are still on their way to Madrid, delayed by the *cordon sanitaire*. Discussion of the reception of the *Floresta* in Germany including the lack of response from A. W. Schlegel. Reports on book orders and commissions. Some criticism of Goethe's *Wilhelm Meisters Wanderjahre* and comments on other texts received. Comments on European politics including Russia, Austria and the war between Persia and Turkey.

1. Julius' first advertisement for the *Floresta* in volume five of the *Originalien aus dem Gebiete der Wahrheit, Kunst, Laune und Phantasie* in 1821 under the title 'Altspanische Gedichte'.
2. Jeremy Bentham (1748–1832), English philosopher and barrister, advocate of social ethics, liberal and pacifist.

3. José Antonio Conde (1766–1820), Spanish orientalist, *Historia de la dominacion de los Arabes en España* (1820–1).
4. *Diario de las sesiones y actas en las cortes* (1811–13), main political record of the first Liberal government.
5. Goethe's *Wilhelm Meisters Wanderjahre, oder die Entsagenden*, the first part of which was published in 1821.
6. Possible reference to *Antar, a Bedoueen Romance* (1819–20), translated by Terrick Hamilton (1781–1876), which was hugely popular.
7. Johann Peter Silbert (1777–1844), *Dom heiliger Sänger* (1820), with a foreword by Friedrich Schlegel.
8. Albrecht von Haller's *Briefe über die wichtigsten Wahrheiten der Offenbarung* (1772).
9. Keil's review of Grimm, Depping and B. which appeared in no. 206 of the *Leipziger Literatur-Zeitung* in 1822.
10. Friedrich Rückert (1788–1866), poet, translator and orientalist, *Oestliche Rosen* (1822).
11. Reference to the Scottish wine importers, Duff and Gordon, established in Cadiz in 1768, later part of Osborne and Co. (1872), B.'s employers from 1818.

112. Nikolas Heinrich Julius, Hamburg; Puerto, 14 July 1822; Source 1

Reports on book orders and commissions and on his activities as a wine merchant. Comments on recently received texts and points out he can now obtain French texts directly from Marseille. Praise for De Maistre and Weber. Outlines plans for a visit to Hamburg. Discussion of the reception of the *Floresta*. Nothing heard from Madrid despite the fact that the copies have now arrived, but praise from the *Monthly Review*. Comments that he cannot show Julius' letters of a political nature to his wife for fear that she will overreact, such is her nervous state. Reports a particularly harsh summer and its impact on his health.

1. Son of B.'s sister, Cecilia Böhl (1778–1852) and Bernhard Berckemeyer (1764–1816).
2. Carl Maria von Weber (1786–1826), Romantic composer of operas, chamber music and songs.
3. Joseph Marie Comte de Maistre (1753–1821), French political theorist and absolutist.
4. Reference to the opera by Weber, *Der Freischütz* (1821).
5. Ernst Houwald (1778–1845), poet and playwright.

113. Nikolas Heinrich Julius, Hamburg; Puerto, 6 August 1822; Source 1

Reports on book orders and commissions including *romanceros*. Notes that Depping had recourse to better sources than he has. Enquires about the author of the rival *Wanderjahre* and his battle with Goethe.

1. *Floresta*, I, no. 321, 'La primavera hermosa', anonymous, from the *Romancero general* (1604).
2. Reference to E. T. A. Hoffmann's death in 1822.
3. Johann Friedrich Wilhelm Pustkuchen (1793–1834), Protestant clergyman and writer, *Wilhelm Meisters Wanderjahre* (1821).
4. Baron Eduard, one of the central characters in Goethe's *Die Wahlverwandtschaften* (1809).
5. Pustkuchen's *Wilhelm Meisters Tagebuch* (1822).
6. Pustkuchen's *Gedanken einer frommen Gräfin* (1822).

114. Nikolas Heinrich Julius, Hamburg; Puerto, 1 November 1822; Source 1

Reports on book orders and commissions. Expresses approval for plans to stage Calderón in Hamburg and comments on the lack of a good German translation. Discussion of yellow fever and the current treatments. Reports on the activities of Alcalá Galiano. Further criticism of German periodicals. Reception of the *Floresta* by Bouterwek pleases Böhl, but there is annoyance at A. W. Schlegel's continued silence. About to send the second *Floresta* manuscript which contains more familiar pieces than the first. Now planning to compile the 'Spaziergänge'. Reports on poor sales of the *Floresta* in Spain. Praise for *Blackwood's*, Coleridge and Wordsworth. Reports on own collection of Lope de Vega which numbers more than that of Lord Holland. Describes current political debate which is less anti-clerical following the death of Clararrosa.

1. *El alcalde de Zalamea*, play by Calderón (1636).
2. Reference to popular operas, *Das Donauweibchen* (1798) by Karl Friedrich Hensler (1759–1825) and Ferdinand August Kauer (1751–1831) and *Das neue Sonntagskind* (1793) by Wenzel Müller (1759–1835).
3. Reference to Alcalá Galiano's 'Apuntes para servir á la historia del origen y alzamiento del ejército destinado á Ultramar' (1820), which appeared in German translation in 1823 in volume one of *Der Staatsmann* (pp. 17–50), 'Ueberlieferung zur Geschichte des Aufstandes der spanischen Expeditionsarmee'. See letter 129, note 4.
4. Francisco Javier Elío y Olándriz (1767–1822), reactionary General sentenced to death by the Liberals in Valencia.
5. 'El pobrecito Holgazan', pseudonym Sebastian de Miñano (1779–1845),

writer and historian, *Cartas de don Justo Balanza* and *Cartas del madrileño* (1820–2), appeared in *El Censor*.
6. Hoffmann's novel, *Lebensansichten des Katers Murr* (1819–21).
7. *Prinzessin Brambilla*, short prose work by Hoffmann from 1820.
8. Reference to Goethe's *Kampagne in Frankreich* (1822).
9. Karl Sieveking (1787–1847), member of the Hamburg patrician family, given the title 'Syndicus' in 1821.
10. No reference to this could be found.
11. Friedrich Wilhelm Valentin Schmidt's *Die Kirchentrennung von England. Schauspiel des Don Pedro Calderón de la Barca* (1819), critical analysis of Calderón's *La cisma de Inglaterra* (1627).
12. Reference to Calderón's 'Deposicíon en favour de los profesores de la pintura' (1677), reproduced by Antonio Palomino de Castro y Velasco (1655–1726), *El museo pictórico, y escala óptica* (1715) and Francisco Mariano Nipho (1719–1803), in his *Cajon de sastre literario* of 1781.
13. Julius' 'Letter from Hamburgh', signed Eremita Hamburgensis, which appeared in *Blackwood's Magazine*, 11 (1822), 67–73.
14. Reference to Coleridge's 'The Historie and Gests of Maxilian' which took Hoffmann's text as its source and appeared in *Blackwood's Magazine* in 1822.
15. Reference to the 1816 edition of Cervantes' text, published by José de Cavaleri Pazos, a possible relative of B.'s associate in the polemic.
16. Lope de Vega, *Colección de las obras sueltas* (1776–9), published by Sancha in Madrid.
17. Henry Richard Vassall-Fox, third Baron Holland (1773–1840), *Some account of the writings of Lope Felix de Vega Carpio* (1806, 1817).
18. Reference to the full name of Perthes' publishing firm, including that of Perthes' partner, Johann Heinrich Besser (1775–1826).

115. Nikolas Heinrich Julius, Hamburg; Puerto, 8 November 1822; Source 1

Reports on book orders. An accompanying crate contains the manuscript of the second volume of the *Floresta*. The third is almost complete. Reports a visit from Bowring who was seeking help with a volume of Spanish theatre.

1. Sir John Bowring (1792–1872), Hispanist, scholar and political economist, later fourth Governor of Hong Kong, *Ancient Poetry and Romances of Spain* (1824).

116. Nikolas Heinrich Julius, Hamburg; Puerto, 21 January 1823; Source 1

Some discussion of Scott, Moore and Erskine, the latter having offended B.'s political sensibilities. Reports that the destruction of convents and monasteries means that there is a lot of art work in circulation. Further discussion of the reception of the *Floresta*. Still plans to visit Hamburg, but mercantile duties are impeding this. Comments on current Spanish intellectual activity including Ceán Bermúdez and the editors of *El Censor* (Lista and Minaño), who he claims are unpopular with both political factions. Further comments on Bowring, who he feels is a radical, and disagreement with his preference for the Moorish element of Spanish poetry.

1. Scott's novels, *The Pirate* (1822), *The Monastary* (1820) and *The Abbott* (1820).
2. Juan Antonio Llorente (1756–1823), scholar and clergyman, *Observaciones críticas sobre el romance de Gil Blas de Santillana* (1822), on the text by Alain-René Lesage (1668–1747), *Histoire de Gil Blas de Santillane* (1715–35).
3. Thomas Moore (1779–1852), Irish poet, *Lalla Rookh: an Oriental Romance* (1817).
4. Thomas, Baron Erskine (1750–1823), Lord Chancellor, *A Letter by Thomas Erskine to 'An Elector of Westminster'* (1819).
5. Karl Friedrich von Rumohr (1785–1843), art historian and writer, *Geist der Kochkunst von Joseph König* (1822).
6. Review of the *Floresta* by Keil which appeared in no. 206 of the *Leipziger Literatur-Zeitung* in 1822.
7. Juan Agustín Ceán Bermúdez (1749–1829), painter and historian.
8. Hitzig's *Aus Hoffmanns Leben und Nachlaß* (1823).
9. A fairytale by Hoffmann, published posthumously in 1822.
10. Liberal periodical, *El Censor* (1820–2), editors included Alberto Lista (see note 11).
11. Alberto Rodríguez de Lista y Aragón (1775–1848), scholar, poet, literary critic and Liberal thinker.
12. Johann Michael Sailer (1751–1832), editor of *Das Buch von der Nachfolgung Christi. Neu übersetzt und mit einer Einleitung und kurzen Anmerkungen* (1794).
13. James Hogg (1770–1835), poet and writer, known as the 'Ettrick Shepherd', contributor to *Blackwood's Magazine*.

Editor's Notes

117. Nikolas Heinrich Julius, Hamburg; Puerto, 21 February 1823; Source 1

Reports on book orders and commissions. Bemoans the fate of the good cause in Germany now that Schlosser's *Fiévée*, F. Schlegel's *Concordia* and Tieck's *Phantasus* have all ceased. Finds solace in the work of Haller. Political situation about to change with promised intervention from France.

1. Hans Christoph Ernst von Gagern (1766–1852), *Der Einsiedler, oder Fragmente über Sittenlehre, Staatsrecht und Politik* (1822–7).
2. Joaquín Lorenzo Villanueva Estengo (1757–1837) and Jaime Villanueva (1765–1824), *Viage literario a las iglesias de España* (1803–52).

118. Nikolas Heinrich Julius, Hamburg; Puerto, 18 March 1823; Source 1

Reports book orders and commissions. Discussion of the emerging political situation with which he finds it difficult to cope, especially the various political tracts. Criticism of Liverpool and Canning for their lack of action. Given heart by the works of de Maistre and sure that the Catholic Church has been done more damage by the Jansenists than the Enlightenment. Reports progress with the third volume of the *Floresta* and plans for the 'Spaziergänge'.

1. Robert Banks Jenkinson, second Earl Liverpool (1770–1828), statesman and Prime Minister (1812–27); George Canning (1770–1827), Liverpool's Foreign Secretary and later Prime Minister.
2. Reference to de Maistre's *Entretiens sur le gouvernement temporal de la Providence ou les Soirées de Saint-Pétersbourg* (1821).

119. Nikolas Heinrich Julius, Hamburg; Puerto, 25 March 1823; Source 1

Reports on book orders and commissions.

120. Nikolas Heinrich Julius, Hamburg; Puerto, 22 June 1823; Source 1

Mostly describes political events surrounding the fall of the Liberal government, with a marked change in attitude towards the French and the hope that normal channels of communication will soon be re-opened. Reports on book orders with praise for Haller and Rumohr. Positive reference to Chateaubriand's work on the Peninsular War.

1. Francisco Leira Ramírez (1630–76), playwright, *Cuando no se aguarda y príncipe tonto* (1675).
2. Reference to von Gagern's *Nationalgeschichte der Deutschen* (1813–26).

3. Reference to Chateaubriand's speech to the *Chambres des deputées* in February 1823 on French intervention in Spain.

121. Nikolas Heinrich Julius, Hamburg; Puerto [no date]; Source 1

Comments on recent and forthcoming publications.

1. August Neander (1789–1850), *Denkwürdigkeiten aus der Geschichte des Christenthums* (1823–1824/5).

122. Nikolas Heinrich Julius, Hamburg; Puerto, 12 August 1823; Source 1

Comments on recently received texts including Hoffmann's biography and a positive appraisal of *Der Sandmann*. Criticism of the *Morgenblatt* for an attack on Grimm. Discussion of the proofs for the second *Floresta* volume. The manuscript of the third volume is now also complete and he is ready to begin the 'Spaziergänge'. Describes the events surrounding the fall of the Liberal government and the siege of Cadiz. Mentions having to quarter French troops and finds them well behaved, but lacking in religious sincerity. Delighted to report that popular opinion supports the return of the old system, but worried that the French will try to impose something more democratic. Speculates on the response of the king once he has been freed.

1. Hoffmann's *Der Sandmann*, from the *Nachtstücke* (1816–17).
2. Reference to Wilhelm Grimm's 'Antikritik gegen die Recenzion der altdänischen Lieder in den Heidelberger Jahrbücher, 1813' in *Drei altschottische Lieder* (1813).
3. Francisco Ballesteros (1770–1832), Spanish General.
4. Louis-Antoine de Bourbon, duc d'Angoulême (1775–1844), who led the French forces to reinstate Fernando VII.
5. Possible reference to Alexandre-Louis Ducrest de Villeneuve (1777–1852), French Admiral.
6. Isidore Justin Taylor (1789–1860) and Charles Nodier (1796–1844), *Voyages pittoresques et romantiques dans l'ancienne France* (1820–78).
7. *Diario de Madrid*, one of the few publications sanctioned under Fernando VII.

123. Nikolas Heinrich Julius, Hamburg; Puerto, 2 September 1823; Source 1

Describes in detail the taking of Cadiz by the Duke of Angoulême. Asks Julius to let his mother know they are all well despite the current turmoil.

Editor's Notes

1. Charles-Albert, Prince de Carignan, House of Savoy (1798–1849).

124. Nikolas Heinrich Julius, Hamburg; Puerto, 3 October 1823; Source 1

Continues the description of events surrounding the fall of Cadiz and the arrival in the city of the royal family. The image created is one of harmony between the French and Spanish. Soon to be rid of the quartered troops. Has been able to return the *Floresta* proofs via Gibraltar. Reports a plot to kill the royal family which was averted by Cayetano Valdés.

1. Louis Auguste Victor, Count de Ghaisnes de Bourmont (1773–1846), Marshall of France.
2. Cayetano Valdés y Flores (1767–1834), Minister of War during the Triennial.

125. Nikolas Heinrich Julius, Hamburg; Puerto, 15 October 1823; Source 1

Reports improvement of political situation and encloses a letter from Arriaza to his wife written during the siege, as well as a copy of the *Redactor de Cádiz* as an example of material published during the crisis.

1. *Redactor general de Cádiz*, the title of a series of periodicals, one of which ran from 1820 to 1823.

126. Nikolas Heinrich Julius, Hamburg; Puerto, 10 February 1824; Source 1

Excuses silence due to lack of shipping and excess duties at work. Reports continued problems with his wife's health and continued presence of French troops in the area. Is attempting to negotiate a change in his working practice as it is robbing him of too much spare time.

1. Gioacchino Antonio Rossini (1792–1868), Italian composer whose first opera was staged in 1810.
2. Veith's *Balsaminen. Ein Taschenbuch für das Jahr 1823*.
3. Reference to the review article 'A Visit to Spain; detailing the Transactions which occurred during a Residence in that Country in the latter Part of 1822 and the First Four Months of 1823: with an account of the Removal of the Court from Madrid to Seville, General Notices of the Manners, Customs, Costume and Music of the Country. By Michael J. Quinn, London, 1823', *Quarterly Review*, 29 (1823), 240–76. B. has noted the wrong page reference.

127. Nikolas Heinrich Julius, Hamburg; Puerto, 26 March 1824; Source 1

Comments on recently received texts including *The Quarterly Review* and Tieck's *Vorschule*. Promises to send the manuscript of the third volume of the *Floresta* with the next ship. Critical of the *Edinburgh Review* for its review of the *Floresta* which he feels has not grasped the nature of the collection. Duties are still impeding his studies.

1. *Quarterly Review*, 29 (April–July 1823), 414–39, a series of reviews of French comedies.
2. Reference to the first volume of Tieck's *Shakespear's Vorschule* (1823, 1829), which contained examples of early modern and Elizabethan theatre translated into German.
3. 'Early Narrative and Lyrical Poetry of Spain', *Edinburgh Review*, 38 (1824), 393–432, which also reviewed the collections by Grimm and Depping.
4. Jeffrey was co-founder of the *Edinburgh Review*.
5. No reference could be found for this text.

128. Nikolas Heinrich Julius, Hamburg; Puerto, 11 April 1824; Source 1

Still not quite finished the third volume of the *Floresta*. Sending some medical publications and a letter from Laso. Expresses approval for recent political developments under Fernando VII.

129. Nikolas Heinrich Julius, Hamburg; Puerto, 28 May 1824; Source 1

Reports on book orders and commissions. Praise for Schubert's *Wanderbüchlein* as one of few highlights of the current poor German literature which is far behind its British counterpart. Criticises *Blackwood's* for its misrepresentation of Spain and her king. Comments of the work of Rumohr. Describes his working environment and claims to have recaptured something of the monastic atmosphere of Görslow.

1. Reference to Goethe's 1823 review of Beauregard Pandin's *Spanische Romanzen* (1823). Beauregard Pandin was the pseudonym of Karl Ferdinand von Jariges (1773–1826), erstwhile neighbour of Goethe in Weimar
2. Jean Henri Merle, 'Aubigne' (1794–1872), Swiss Protestant clergyman and historian, *Sermons laissés a mes auditeurs comme un souvenir de mon affection* (1823).
3. Schubert's *Wanderbüchlein eines reisenden Gelehrten nach Salzburg, Tirol und der Lombardei* (1823).

4. *Der Staatsman. Zeitschrift für Politik und Tagesgeschichte* (1823–31) edited by Johann Baptiste von Pfeilschifter (1793–1874).
5. Rumohr's *Italienische Novellen von historischem Interesse* (1823).

130. Nikolas Heinrich Julius, Hamburg; Puerto, 25 July 1824; Source 1

Describes the contents of the parcel containing the manuscript of the third *Floresta* volume and a selection of other texts and letters.

131. Nikolas Heinrich Julius, Hamburg; Puerto, 19 November 1824; Source 1

Reports on book orders and commissions. Reports on recent publications including Navarrete's work on the discovery of the Americas. Ambivalent response to Hamann whose style provokes same sentiments as Jean Paul once did. Still prefers English writing including Washington Irving. Refers to reception of the *Floresta* in *Galigniani's Magazine*.

1. Possible reference to a new edition of the 1808 *Den Spanske tolk*.
2. Martín Fernández de Navarrete (1765–1844), sailor and historian, *Coleccion de los viages y descubrimientos que hicieron por mar los Españoles desde fines del siglo XV* (1825–37).
3. *Coleccion eclesiastica española* (1823), Juan Antonio Merino, Bishop of Menorca (1772–1844).
4. *Galignani's Magazine and Paris Quarterly Review*, English language newspaper published in Paris from 1814, established by Giovanni Antonio Galignani (1752–1821).
5. Washington Irving (1783–1859), American writer and diplomat, author of *Bracebridge Hall* (1822) and *Tales of a Traveller* (1824).
6. Thomas Charles Medwin (1776–1829), *Journal of the Conversations of Lord Byron* (1824).

132. Nikolas Heinrich Julius, Hamburg; Puerto, 8 March 1825; Source 1

Reports the loss of a consignment of books due to a shipwreck. Gives an overview of his view of the three *Floresta* volumes, preferring the first. Reports that he has not had the peace to complete the 'Spaziergänge' due to his wife's continued nervous state. Reference to Arejula as an opponent of the monarchy and the Church, criticism of the *Edinburgh Review* for drawing politics into an essay on Spanish poetry and notice taken of the *Ocios de españoles emigrados*. Reports on book orders and commissions.

1. Juan Manuel de Arejula (1755–1830), physician and Liberal, introduced Laviosier's work to Spain.
2. *Ocios de Españoles emigrados* (1824–7), main organ for the exiled Spanish Liberals in London, edited by exiled Valencian pubisher, Vicente Salvá y Pérez (1780–1849).
3. Feliz Torres Amat (1772–1847), Bishop of Astorga, published a translation of the Bible in 1825.
4. Jeremiah Holmes Wiffen (1792–1836), Quaker poet and translator, *The Works of Garcilasso de la Vega* (1823).
5. Johann Friedrich Böhl (1739–1819), longest surviving member of B.s father's generation.
6. Friedrich Ludwig Georg von Raumer (1781–1873), German historian, *Geschichte der Hohenstaufen und ihrer Zeit* (1823–5).
7. *The Book of the Thousand and One Nights*, medieval Middle Eastern epic.
8. Matthaus von Collin (1779–1824), editor of the *Wiener Jahrbücher*, writing in *Der Staatsman*.

133. Nikolas Heinrich Julius, London; Puerto, 16 April 1825; Source 1

Reports on book orders and commissions including the losses incurred due to a recent shipwreck. Export of older Spanish texts about to be outlawed. Mentions the lack of contacts in London since the death of Mr Duff Gordon. Expresses regret that he has never entered into a correspondence with key English literary figures such as Wordsworth, Southey or Coleridge. Reports a waning interest in older Spanish literature. Comments on *Blackwood's Magazine* in the hope that Julius will be able to find out more about the contributors. Censures their attitude to Catholicism, but praises the tone of essays by YYY. Delighted by texts including *Lights and Shadows of Scotch Life*. Comment on Gorostiza as a wasted talent, lost in Liberalism.

1. Christopher North, thought to be the pseudonym of John Wilson (1785–1854), Scottish writer who contributed under the alias to *Blackwood's Magazine*.
2. Ensign O'Doherty, *Blackwood's* pseudonym of William Maginn (1794–1842), Irish poet and journalist.
3. Signature of David Robinson, one of the contributors to *Blackwood's* of whom little is recorded.
4. *Lights and Shadows of Scotch Life*, Wilson's novel published in 1822.
5. *Trials of Margaret Lindsay*, Wilson's novel published in 1823.
6. *Sayings and Doings* (1823) by Theodore Hook (1788–1841).

7. Manuel Eduardo de Gorostiza (1789–1851), Mexican dramatist, spent much of his life in Madrid and then in exile as a Liberal in London.

134. Nikolas Heinrich Julius, Hamburg; Puerto, 29 August 1825; Source 1

Reports logistical difficulties in sending books due to new laws and the unreliable nature of Madrid booksellers. Reports the engagement of both younger daughters and lack of free time for study. Reports on book orders.

135. Nikolas Heinrich Julius, Hamburg; Puerto, 20 January 1826; Source 1

Thanks Julius for a report on his trip to England. Praises Wordsworth and the author of *Lights and Shadows* who he wrongly identifies as Alan Cunningham, not John Wilson. Approval for Julius' purpose and reference to his collaboration with Mr Peel. Comments on Bowring's translation of ancient Spanish verse which has revived his own interest in the 'Spaziergänge'. Claims that an essay in the *Globe* on the unities has been taken from the *Pasatiempos* and complains that the publication sadly has the wrong political views. Mentions that Mora is now in London writing essays in favour of American revolutionaries. Reports on book orders and commissions. Has now had enough of *Blackwood's* following an open attack on Catholicism. Family news.

1. Allan Cunningham (1784–1842), Scottish poet and writer, contributor to *Blackwood's Edinburgh Magazine*.
2. Julius may have had contact with Robert Peel (1788–1850), founder of the modern British police force.
3. *Le Globe*, literary and philosophical periodical published in Paris from 1824 to 1832.
4. Reference to the *Memorias de la Real Academia de la Historia*, published from 1796 to 1852; the Royal Spanish Academy did not publish *Memorias* until 1870.
5. Estebán de Terreros y Pando (1707–82), *Paleografía Española* (1758).
6. Friedrich Müller's *Werke* appeared in 1825.
7. Grillparzer's 1825 play *König Ottakers Glück und Ende*.
8. Houwald published four plays in 1821: *Das Bild, Der Leuchtturm, Die Heimkehr* and *Fluch und Segen*.

136. Nikolas Heinrich Julius, Hamburg; Puerto, 17 February 1826; Source 5 [recipient wrongly identified as Friedrich Perthes]

Pleased to hear of positive and suitably religious reception of the second edition of the *Floresta*. Reports on book orders.

137. Nikolas Heinrich Julius, Hamburg; Puerto, 17 March 1826; Source 1

Sends amendments to third volume of the *Floresta* and comments on positive reception in certain Spanish circles. Reports on book orders and confirms revived interest in Spanish literature and his hopes to begin work on the theatre.

1. *Floresta*, III, no. 809, 'Ay sombre alegre, noche venturosa!', anonymous, *Cancionero manuscrito*.

138. Nikolas Heinrich Julius, Hamburg; Puerto, 5 July 1826; Source: 1

Describes the contents of an accompanying parcel which includes copies of Navarrete's work on Columbus, excerpts from the *Filósofo rancio*, some minor English publications and a number of German works including Hamann. Reflects that the truly educated seem to have a growing sympathy for popular poetry and that this might save some vulnerable material. Agrees with Julius in preferring Bowring's translations of Spanish poetry to those of Lockhart. Suggests a categorisation of Calderón's plays and a critique of Scott's *Woodstock*. Brief allusion to death of both Campe and his wife. Negative reference to Blanco White in the context of current theological debate.

1. Published in 1823 by George Cruikshank (1792–1878), caricaturist and book illustrator.
2. Published in 1823 by Clarles Westmacott (1787–1868), illustrated by Robert Cruikshank (1789–1856).
3. Literary periodical published irregularly from 1822 to 1823 by Byron, Percy Bysshe Shelley (1792–1822) and Leigh Hunt (1784–1859).
4. *The Last Man*, novel published in 1826 by Mary Shelley (1797–1851).
5. Elizabeth, Baroness Craven (1750–1828), *Memoirs of the Margravine of Anspach, written by herself* (1826).
6. Jørgen Landt (1753–1804), Danish geographer, expert on the Faroe Isles.
7. *Lays of the Minnesingers or German Troubadors of the twelfth and thirteenth centuries* (1825), Edgar Taylor (1793–1839).
8. John Gibson Lockhart, *Ancient Spanish Ballads Historical and Romantic* (1823).

9. Reference to the novel by Sir Walter Scott, *Woodstock; or the Cavalier. A Tale of the Year 1651* (1826).
10. Reference to the deaths of Dorothea and Joachim Campe in 1826 and 1818 respectively.
11. Charles Butler (1776–1832), *Book of the Roman Catholic Church* (1825).
12. José María Blanco White (1775–1841), theologian, critic and poet, went into exile in London in 1810 and converted to Anglicanism, then Unitarianism.
13. *Le Catholique* (1826–1830), journal established by Ferdinand, baron d'Eckstein (1790–1861), publicist and philosopher of Danish origin.

139. Friedrich Perthes, Hamburg; Puerto, 30 March 1827; Source 5

Regrets sudden death of Perthes' partner, Besser. Discussion of possible interest in the *Floresta* in Spanish America and an allusion to the positive reception of the collection in the exile press in London.

140. Nikolas Heinrich Julius, Hamburg; Puerto, 1 June 1827; Source 1

Discussion of the reception of Navarrete's work in England. Reports on book orders including praise for a volume of Irish fairy tales. Reports the birth of his first grandchild.

1. Reference to a brief but savage review of Navarrete's *Coleccion de los Viages y Descubrimientos que hicieron por Mar los Españoles desde fines del Siglo XV* (1825) which appeared in the *Quarterly Review*, 40 (1826), 347–51.
2. Reference to a new edition of *Noticias secretas de America* (1735) by Jorge Juan y Santacilia (1713–73) and Antonio de Ulloa (1716–95) which appeared in 1826.
3. Jacob and Wilhelm Grimm, *Irische Elfenmärchen* (1826).

141. Friedrich Perthes, Hamburg; Puerto, 1 June 1827; Source 5
[continues from 139]

Correspondence interrupted due to moving house. Reports on book orders and commissions. Comments on Heine, asking to see more of his work, and requests works by Tieck, Musäus and Houwald. Quotes from La Martine and praises the second part of his *Meditations*, amazed that a Frenchman could produce such a sensitive work. Reports feeling ill at ease with himself and also a minor crisis of faith.

1. Heinrich Heine (1797–1856), poet and writer, in exile in Paris from 1831, converted to Protestantism from Judaism in 1825.
2. Tieck's *Dramaturgishe Blätter* (1826).
3. Musäus' *Volksmärchen der Deutschen* (1782–6).
4. Quotation from La Martine's twenty-first *Méditation*, entitled 'La foi'.
5. Reference to the sixty-volume edition of *Goethes Werke* begun in 1827 and completed in 1842.

142. Nikolas Heinrich Julius, Hamburg; Puerto, 19 October 1827; Source 1

Praise for Julius' selfless work for others. Reports book orders including receipt of work by Heise. Reference to developments in Hamburg which Böhl would like to see. Response to the work of Heine, positive in terms of poetic ability, but negative in terms of political stance, in particular his praise of Bonaparte.

1. The reference is unclear. Possibly Carl Christian Heise (1799–1848) of Hamburg, who translated *Die Lusiade* (1806–1807); also Carl Johann Heise (1787–1857), who published a number of translations of Plato including the *Symposium* in 1820.
2. Reference to the poems by Heine, the first cycle of which appeared in the *Reisebilder* (1826–7).
3. Heine's *Reisebilder I–IV* (1826–31).

143. Nikolas Heinrich Julius, Hamburg; Puerto, 28 March 1828; Source 1

Reports logistical problems in obtaining and transporting books. Refers to the death of his mother and stepfather. He is glad that she would never have received his letter cancelling his summer visit to Hamburg. He is still keen to come, in particular to attend his son's wedding. Some comments on possible new editions of *romanceros*, but these would be too expensive to produce. Praise for Thomas Carlyle and criticism of Cotta for publishing Heine.

1. Reference to the deaths of B.'s mother and stepfather, who died in 1828 and 1827 respectively.
2. Miguel de Madrigal (dates unknown), *Romancero general y flor de diversa poesia* (1605) and Pedro Espinosa (1578–1650), *Flores de poetas ilustres* (1605).
3. Publisher of the *Siglo de oro* who published Cervantes and Lope de Vega.
4. Review article by Carlyle, 'Jean Paul Friedrich Richter's Leben, nebst Characteristik seiner Werke; von Heinrich Döring', *Edinburgh Review*, 46 (1827), 176–96. (See note 5)

5. Thomas Carlyle (1795–1881), Scottish writer and scholar, translator of Goethe and author of *Life of Schiller* (1823–4).
6. *The Foreign Review and Continental Miscellany* (1828–30).

144. Nikolas Heinrich Julius, Hamburg; Puerto, 27 May 1828; Source 1

Reports on book orders and commissions. Reports forthcoming publication of a Spanish translation of Bouterwek with new notes.

1. Only one volume appeared in 1829, entitled *Historia de la literatura española*, translated by José Gómez de la Cortina and Nicolás Hugalde y Mollinedo.

145. Nikolas Heinrich Julius, Hamburg; Puerto, 6 February 1829; Source 1

Further praise for Julius' charitable work and joy at his positive appraisal of Böhl's new daughter-in-law. Positive comments on Moreto and a report on Durán's defence of Spanish theatre. Further comments on English periodicals. Reports that a correspondence with Durán has revived his interest in his Spanish theatre.

1. Betsy Berckemeyer (1801–73), niece of B.'s sister Cecilia.
2. Agustín Durán (1789–1862), writer and critic, author of *Discurso sobre le influjo que ha tenido la crítica moderna en la decadencia del teatro antiguo español y sobre el modo con que debe ser considerado para juzgar convenientemente de su mérito peculiar* (1828).
3. Reference to the competing *Foreign Review*, published by Treuttel & Würtz of Paris, and the *Foreign Quarterly Review*, published by Black, Black and Young of London.
4. Leandro Fernández de Moratín (1760–1828), neo-Classical playwright and scholar; an article on his work appears in the *Foreign Quarterly Review*, 2 (1828), 147–65.

146. Nikolas Heinrich Julius, Hamburg; Puerto, 12 April 1829; Source 1

Reports on book orders and commissions. Accompanies a parcel with copies of Durán's *Discurso* and a number of newspaper clippings. Reports the situation surrounding Moratín's anthology of Spanish theatre and his desire to see a copy before beginning his own. Further praise of the *Foreign Review* and Carlyle.

1. Reference to Moratín's *Orígenes del teatro español*, published posthumously as part of his collected works in 1830–1.

2. Serialisation of Carlyle's *The Life of Heyne* (1828), biography of Christian Gottlob Heyne (1729–1812), Classical philologist and librarian.
3. August Klingemann (1777–1831), journalist and playwright.

147. Friedrich Perthes, Hamburg; Puerto, 12 April 1829; Source 5

Still suffering a crisis of faith. Reports having been left his stepfather's papers which may not be published. His plans for a trip to Hamburg have been postponed once more. Some discussion of recent theological debate including an overt criticism of Neology.

1. Neology, a branch of the Protestant faith based on reason favoured by Campe.

148. Nikolas Heinrich Julius, Berlin; Puerto, 17 November 1829; Source 1

Provides information on Lista and Durán, mentioning the latter's second *Romancero*. Praise for Keil's edition of Calderón. Reports on book orders and commissions. Unsure whether he will work first on the 'Spaziergänge' or the *Teatro*. Reports negative reception of the first volume of the Spanish Bouterwek.

1. Lista's *Poesias* (1822).
2. Reference to Durán's *Romancero de romances doctrinales, amatorios, festivos, jocosos, satíricos y burlescos, sacados de varias colecciones generales y de las obras de diversos poetas de los siglos XV, XVI y XVII* (1829).
3. Keil's edition of *Las comedias de Don Pedro Calderón de la Barca* (1827–30).

149. Nikolas Heinrich Julius, Hamburg; Puerto, 8 September 1830; Source 1

Positive reference to Keil and Huber. Outlines the problems being caused by the delay in publishing Moratín's *Orígines*. He has all the material he needs apart from *El deleitoso*, but cannot proceed until the other anthology appears. Refers to Goethe's positive comments on Calderón's *El principe constante* and encloses some poems by Durán and some essays by Böhl himself which have appeared in local newspapers. Negative appraisal of Quintana's anthology of older Spanish poetry which seems to have ignored the *Floresta*. Also sends some pieces by Gallardo. Health means the trip to Hamburg looks unlikely. Begins to sound resigned to old age.

1. Victor Aimé Huber (1800–69), son of writer, Therese Huber (1764–1829), *Skizzen aus Spanien* (1828–33).

2. Lope de Rueda (1510–64), playwright, works published posthumously in 1567 by Juan de Timoneda in a collection entitled *El Deleitoso*.
3. Goethe's positive comments on Calderón's *El príncipe constante* are recorded in the notes for the year 1807 which appeared in the 'Tag- und Jahreshefte', vols 31 and 32 of *Goethes Werke. Vollständige Ausgabe*, published by Cotta beginning in 1827.
4. Durán published a series of *Trovas* from 1829 to 1830 to celebrate the marriage of Fernando VII to María Cristina and the birth of their daughter, Isabel.
5. It was not possible to trace these texts.
6. French literary periodical founded in 1829 by Louis Desiré Veron (1798–1867).
7. Quintana's *Poesias selectas castellanas desde el tiempo de Juan de Mena hasta nuestros dias* (1830).
8. Francisco de Aldana (1537–78), soldier and poet.
9. Francisco de Medrano (1570–1607), poet.
10. Cristóbal de Virues (1550–1614), dramatist and epic poet.
11. Bartolomé José Gallardo y Blanco (1776–1852), critic, writer and scholar, author of *Cuatro palmetazos bien plantados por el dómine Lúcas a los gazeteros de Bayona, por otros tantos puntos garrafales que se les han soltado contra el buen uso y reglas de la lengua y gramática castellana, en su famosa crítica de la Historia de la literatura española* (1830).

150. Nikolas Heinrich Julius, Hamburg; Puerto, 26 January 1831; Source 1

Comments negatively on the contents of a recent parcel, revealing his disaffection with German literature, religious texts and historical works. Particularly negative appraisal of Solger, especially in comparison with A. W. Schlegel. More positive response to Rochlitz and Huber, although the latter has given too positive a depiction of Spanish women. Reports having finally obtained a copy of Moratín's collection, the prologue of which he now intends to publish with his own additions. He proposes a title which acknowledges them both.

1. Karl Wilhelm Ferdinand Solger, *Vorlesungen über Ästhetik* (1829).
2. Johann Friedrich Rochlitz (1769–1842), writer and librettist, *Für ruhige Stunden* (1828).
3. Pseudonym of Karl Adolf Suckow (1802–47), *Die Liebesgeschichten* (1829).

151. Elise Campe, Hamburg; Puerto, 2 June 1831; Source 3

Recommences correspondence, quoting from Goethe. Describes his life over the last years, pointing to the discrepancy between his life as a scholar and as a merchant. Makes explicit reference to their relationship and his own endeavours as part of the battle for Romanticism which he feels has triumphed as German Romantic ideas are now accepted elsewhere. Bemoans the fact that now the Germans themselves seem to be giving up the good cause in favour of more Liberal ideas. Explains that his planned trip to Hamburg in 1830 had to be cancelled following an accident coming down stairs in the *bodega* which has left him partially immobile. To some extent he is glad not to have gone, fearful of his own response to changes in friends and environment. Recalls family matters and the Hamburg circle.

1. Quotation from the 'Zueignung' which precedes Goethe's *Faust* (1808).
2. *Kritische Blätter der Börsenhalle* (1830–4), edited and published in Hamburg by Christoph Friedrich Wurm (1803–59).
3. Fouqué's *Novelle Fata Morgana* (1830).
4. Reference to Tieck's poem 'Prolog zur Aufführung von Goethes Faust an Goethes Geburtstag' (1829).
5. Possible reference to theologian, scholar and senator, Johann Friedrich von Meyer (1772–1849).

152. Nikolas Heinrich Julius, Berlin; Puerto, 26 July 1831; Source 1

Rather melancholy tone continues. Reports sending the manuscript for the *Teatro* and outlines the contents. Confesses that his Spanish friends have dissuaded him from using Moratín's apparatus and so he has adopted the same format as the *Floresta*. Comments on the German notes he has provided, saying he would never have dared write them for a Spanish readership. Expresses disappointment at the poor sales of the *Floresta*, especially given the critical acclaim it has received. Expresses admiration for Julius' work on prison reform. Rejects all political and historical writing, admitting instead to an escapist tendency. Reports on current publications in Spain, including Durán's fourth *Romancero*. Promises to send the third along with Moratín's prologue. Gives Julius the authority to revise the *Teatro* as required once it reaches Perthes.

1. Johann Gottfried von Schnabel (1692–c.1752), *Wunderliche Fata einiger See-Fahrer* (1731–8), reworked by Tieck and published as *Insel Felsenburg* (1827).
2. Reference to Durán's *Romancero de romances caballerescos e históricos anteriores al siglo XVIII* (1832).

153. August Campe, Hamburg; Puerto, 28 April 1833; Source 3

Acknowledges receipt of a parcel including Chamisso's poems. Reports on his current health and mercantile activities. Refers August to the letter sent to his wife, which follows.

1. Adelbert von Chamisso (1781–1838), poet and botanist, associated with Madame de Staël.

154. Elise Campe, Hamburg; Puerto, 28 April 1833; Source 3

Describes his current health, with a quote from Logau. Again, rather melancholy. News about the Hamburg circle.

1. Quotation from Logau's poem, 'Der Todt'.

155. Nikolas Heinrich Julius, [Berlin]; Puerto, 28 April 1833; Source 1

Reports receipt of the *Teatro* and outlines the errors he has found. Disappointed that no German reviews have been forthcoming, but reports a better reception in Madrid. Reports a visit from Diez and the desire to hear if he publishes anything on his visit to Spain. News from the Hamburg circle. Reports on book orders and commissions including a defence of *Don Quijote* in the face of *afrancesado* criticism.

1. List of errata omitted here.
2. Quotation from Wordsworth's 'Nuns fret not at their Convent's narrow room' (1802).
3. Friedrich Diez (1794–1876), philologist credited with founding Romance Studies in Germany.
4. Johannes Daniel Falk (1768–1826), writer and pedagogue, pseudonym Johannes von der Ostsee, author of *Goethe aus näherem persönlichem Umgange dargestellt* (1832).
5. Charles Louis Benoît (dates unknown), *Essai sur le cholera-morbus de l'Inde* (1827).
6. Diego Clemencín (1765–1834) published a new edition of *Don Quijote* from 1832 to 1835.
7. Charles Margetel de Saint Denis (1610–1703), seventeenth-century French critic who heavily criticised the Spanish *comedia* in his 1677 *Sur nos Comédies, excepté celles de Moliere où l'on trouve le vrai esprit de la Comédie*, but was a great admirer of *Don Quijote*.

8. It was not possible to trace this quote from Logau, which may be a paraphrase.

156. Friedrich Perthes, Gotha; Puerto, 30 April 1833; Source 5

Expresses approval for the *Teatro* and reiterates his request for reviews. Feels Spaniards are still uncomfortable that a foreigner should show them how to appreciate their own culture. Parallel criticism of Moratín and Quintana.

157. Nikolas Heinrich Julius, Hamburg; Puerto, 30 March and 6 April 1834; Source 1

Reports on outbreak of cholera. Still waiting for reviews of the *Teatro*. Expresses a sense of fatigue, no longer enthusiastic about his studies or life in general. Reports that Durán has promised some work on the theatre. Describes the political situation in the early phases of the first Carlist War. Describes his current health and asks for advice on treating certain complaints.

1. Neither of these reviews could be located.
2. Durán's *Talia española* (1834).

158. Elise Campe, Hamburg; Puerto, 24 March 1836; Source 3

Again, melancholy in tone with a sense that death must now come, especially as other loved ones are disappearing and his health is deteriorating. Has not heard from Julius since he left for America in the company of Harriet Martineau. Recalls members of the Hamburg circle. Feels he has lost all interest in German literature, nostalgic for the heyday of Goethe, Schiller and Tieck and disappointed by new writers such as Heine and Börne. Was initially interested in emerging French Romanticism, but soon saw its true excessive nature. Still reading mostly English works.

1. B. paraphrases Klopstock's ode 'An Ebert' (1748): 'Stirbt dann auch Einer von uns, und bleibt nur Einer übrig;/Bin der Eine denn ich'.
2. Harriet Martineau (1802–76), writer and social reformer who travelled to the United States in 1834 to support the abolition of slavery.
3. Ludwig Börne (1786–1837), Jewish satirist and revolutionary republican.
4. Reference to the death of Cecilia's second husband and its devastating impact.

Editor's Notes

159. August Campe, Hamburg; Puerto, 30 April 1836; Source 3

Nostalgic and melancholy, wishing death might reunite them in a better place. Asks to receive nothing more from Germany as he has lost all interest. The political situation in Spain does little to lift his mood, bemoaning the fact that Bonaparte now almost seems like a guardian angel in comparison.

Select Bibliography

Alborg, J. L., *Historia de la literatura española IV: El Romanticismo* (Madrid: Gredos, 1980).

Alcalá Galiano, A., *An Introductory Lecture Delivered in the University of London on Saturday, November 15, 1828* (London: John Taylor, 1828).

—— 'Literature of the Nineteenth Century: Spain', *The Atheneaum*, 7 (1834), 290–5; 329–33; 370–4; 411–14; 450–4.

—— *Memorias de Don Antonio Alcalá Galiano publicadas por su hijo*, 2 vols (Madrid: Rubiños, 1886).

—— *Recuerdos de un anciano* (Madrid: Biblioteca clásica, 1907).

—— 'Prólogo' in Ángel Saavedra, Duque de Rivas, *El moro expósito*, A. Crespo (ed.), 2 vols (Madrid: Espasa-Calpe, 1982), I.

Anaya, A. (ed.), *El Teatro Español ó coleccion de dramas escogidos*, 3 vols (London: Smallfield, 1817).

Ancillon, F., *Essais philosophiques ou nouveau mélanges de litterature et de philosophie*, 2 vols (Paris: Paschoud, 1817).

Arnim, A. von and Brentano, C., *Des Knaben Wunderhorn. Alte deutsche Lieder gesammelt von Achim von Arnim und Clemens Brentano. Kommentierte Gesamtausgabe*, Heinz Rölleke (ed.), 3 vols (Stuttgart: Reclam, 1987).

Arriaza, J. B., *Ensayos poéticos* (Palma: [no publ.], 1811).

Ashton, R., *The German Idea in four English writers and the reception of German thought 1800–1860* (Cambridge: Cambridge University Press, 1980).

Barrera, C. A. de la, *Catálogo formado por D. Bartolomé José Gallardo en los principales artículos que componian la selecta librería de Don Juan Nicolas Bohl de Faber* (Madrid: Tipografía de la Revista de Archivos, 1923).

Bausinger, H., *Formen der 'Volkspoesie'* (Berlin: Erich Schmidt Verlag, 1968).

Becher, H., 'Pensamientos españoles de Da. Francisca de Larrea Böhl de Faber', *BBMP* (1931), 316–35; (1932), 1–45.

Becker, K., 'Andreas Riem als Theologe' in Welker, pp. 61–77.

Becker-Cantarino, B., 'Die "Schwarze Legende". Zum Spanienbild in der deutschen Literatur des 18. Jahrhunderts', *Zeitschrift für deutsche Philologie*, 94 (1975), 183–203.

Behler, E., 'The Reception of Calderón amongst the German Romantics', *Studies in Romanticism*, 20 (1981), 437–60.

—— *Die Zeitschriften der Brüder Schlegel* (Darmstadt: WBG, 1983).

Beiser, F. C., *German Idealism. The Struggle against Subjectivism 1781–1801* (Cambridge, Mass.: Harvard University Press, 2002).

Blanco White, J. M., 'Conclusion de esta obra', *El Español*, 8 (1814), 297–8.

Böhl von Faber, J. N., 'Reflexiones sobre la poesía', *Variedades de ciencias, literatura y artes*, 8.22 (1805), 247–52.

—— 'Auch etwas über Handels-Monopol und Handels-Bedrückung; bei Gelegenheit des im 58 und 59ten Stück der Hamb. Addr. Comp. Nachrichten abgedruckten Fragments aus den Dialogen über Krieg und Handel', *Nordische Miszellen*, 31 August 1806.

—— 'Ueber die spanische Literatur in Bezug auf die fragmentarischen Bemerkungen darüber in den Nordischen Miszellen von 7. und 14ten Februar 1808', *Nordische Miszellen*, 13 March 1808.

—— *Vier und Zwanzig deutsche Lieder aus des Knaben Wunderhorn mit bekannten meist älteren Weisen beim Klavier zu singen* (Heidelberg: Mohr und Zimmer, 1870).

—— 'Von der neuesten englischen Poesie', *Vaterländisches Museum*, 2.1 (1811), 101–6.

—— 'Korrespondenz-Nachrichten: Cadix', *Morgenblatt für gebildete Stände*, 10, 11 and 12 January 1820.

—— *Vindicaciones de Calderón* (Cádiz: [no publ.], 1820).

—— *Floresta de rimas antiguas castellanas ordenado por Don Juan Nicolas Böhl de Faber de la Real Academia Española*, 3 vols (Hamburg: Perthes und Besser, 1821–5).

—— *Teatro español anterior á Lope de Vega por el editor de la Floresta de rimas antiguas* (Hamburg: Perthes, 1832).

—— 'Creer y obrar', *Revista de ciencias, literatura y artes*, II (1856), 5–7.

Bouterwek, F., *Geschichte der Poesie und Beredsamkeit seit dem Ende des dreizehnten Jahrhunderts*, 12 vols (Göttingen: Johann Friedrich Röwer, 1801–19).

—— *Neues Museum der Philosophie und Literatur*, 1803–5.

Bowring, J., 'Spanish Romances', *London Magazine*, VII (1823), 405–10; 509–14; 605–15; VIII (1823), 47–56; 158–68; 485–92; 593–6.

—— *Ancient Poetry and Romances of Spain* (London: Taylor and Hessey, 1824).

Brüggemann, W., *Die Spanienberichte des 18. und 19. Jahrhunderts und ihre Bedeutung für die Formung und Wandlung des deutschen Spanienbildes* (Münster: Aschendorffsche Verlagsbuchhandlung, 1956).

—— *Spanisches Theater und deutsche Romantik* (Münster: Aschendorffsche Verlagsbuchhandlung, 1964).

Campe, E., *Johann Nikolas Böhl von Faber: Versuch einer Lebensskizze nach seinen eigenen Briefen* (Leipzig: [no publ.], 1858).

Campe, J. H., *Theophron oder der erfahrene Rathgeber für die unerfahrene Jugend* (Tübingen: Schramm und Balz, 1786 [1783]).

—— *Sämmtliche Kinder- und Jugendschriften von Joachim Heinrich Campe. Vierte Gesammtausgabe der letzten Hand*, 39 vols (Braunschweig: Verlag der Schulbuchhandlung, 1831–6).

—— *Briefe von und an Joachim Heinrich Campe*, Hanno Schmidt (ed.), (Wiesbaden: Harrasowitz, 1996–).

Carnero, G., *Los orígenes del romanticismo reaccionario español: el matrimonio Böhl de Faber* (Valencia: Universidad de Valencia, 1978).

—— 'Documentos relativos a Juan Nicolás Böhl de Faber en el Ministerio Español de Asuntos Exteriores', *Anales de Literatura Española*, 3 (1984), 159–86.

—— 'El teatro de Calderón como arma ideológico en el origin gaditano del romanticismo español', *Cuadernos de Teatro Clásico*, 5 (1990), 125–39.

Clavijo y Fajardo, J., *El Pensador*, 1762–3.

Davies, O., *The Rhineland Mystics. An Anthology* (London: SPCK, 1989).

Deghaye, P., 'Die Natur als Leib Gottes in Jacob Böhmes Theosophie' in J. Garewicz and A. M Haas (eds.), *Gott, Natur und Mensch in der Sicht Jacob Böhmes und seiner Rezeption* (Wiesbaden: Harrassowitz, 1994), pp. 71–111.

Depping, G. B., *Sammlung der besten alten Spanischen Historischen, Ritter- und Maurischen Romanzen* (Altenburg and Leipzig: Brockhaus, 1817).

—— *Coleccion de los mas célebres romances antiguos españoles, históricos y caballerescos publicada por C. B. Depping y ahora considerablemente enmendada por un español refujiado*, Vincente Salvá (ed.), 2 vols (London: Salvá, 1825).

—— *Romancero castellano ó coleccion de antiguas romances populares de los españoles publicada con una introduccion y notas por G. B. Depping. Nueva edicion, con las notas de Don Antonio Alcalá Galiano*, 2 vols (Leipzig: Brockhaus, 1844).

Derozier, A., *Manuel José Quintana y el nacimiento del liberalismo en España* (Madrid: Ediciones Turr, 1978).

Diez, F., *Altspanische Romanzen besonders vom Cid und Kaiser Karls Paladinen* (Berlin: Reimer, 1821).

—— *Friedrich Diez kleinere Arbeiten und Recensionen*, Hermann Breymann (ed.), (Munich: Oldenbourg, 1883).

Dieze, J. A., *Don Luis Joseph Velazquez Geschichte der Spanischen Dichtkunst. Aus dem Spanischen übersetzt und mit Anmerkungen erläutert von Johann Andreas Dieze* (Göttingen: Victorianus Bassiegel, 1769).

Dornhof, J., *Johann Nikolas Böhl von Faber: ein Vorkämpfer der Romantik in Spanien* (Hamburg: Seminar für romanische Sprachen und Kultur, 1925).

Durán, A., 'Discurso sobre el influjo que ha tenido la crítica moderna en la decadencia del teatro antiguo español y sobre el modo con que debe ser considerdao para juzgar convenientemente de su mérito peculiar', *Memorias de la Academia Española*, 1.2 (1870), 280–336.

—— *Romancero de romances moriscos, compuesto de todos los de esta clase que contiene el Romancero General impreso en 1614* (Madrid: Leon Amarita, 1828).

—— *Romancero de romances doctrinales, amatorias, festivos, jocosos, satíricos y burlescos: sacados de varias colecciones generales y de las obras de diversos poetas de los siglos XV, XVI y XVII* (Madrid: Leon Amarita, 1829).

—— *Cancionero y romancero de coplas y canciones de Arte Menor, letras, letrillas, romances cortos y glosas anteriores al siglo XVIII pertenicientes á los géneros Doctrinal, Amatorio, Jocoso, Satirico etc* (Madrid: Eusebio Aguado, 1829).

—— *Romancero de romances caballerescos é históricos anteriores al siglo XVIII, que contiene los de Amor, los de la Tabla Redonda, los de Carlo Magno, y las Doce Pares, los de Bernardo del Carpio, del Cid Campeador, de los Infantes de Lara, etc*, 2 vols (Madrid: Eusebio Aguado, 1832).

'Early Narrative and Lyrical Poetry of Spain', *Edinburgh Review*, 39 (1824), 393–432.

Eichhorn, J. G., *Allgemeine Geschichte der Cultur und Literatur des neueren Europa*, 2 vols (Göttingen: Rosenbusch, 1796).

Eichner, E. (ed.), *Romantic and Its Cognates/The European History of a Word* (Manchester: Manchester University Press, 1972).

Fernández Poza, M., *Frasquita Larrea y 'Fernán Caballero'. Mujer, revolución y romanticismo en España 1775–1870* (El Puerto de Santa María: Ayuntamiento de El Puerto de Santa María, 2001).

Flitter, D., *Spanish Romantic literary theory and criticism* (Cambridge: Cambridge University Press, 1992).
'Floresta de rimas antiguas castellanas', *Ocios de españoles emigrados*, 5 (May 1826), 449–68.
Fouqué, F., de la Motte and Perthes, F., *Ueber den deutschen Adel, über Ritter-Sinn und Militair-Ehre in Briefen* (Hamburg: Perthes und Besser, 1819).
Friemel, B., 'Zu Jacob Grimms Silva de Romances viejos', *Brüder-Grimm-Gedenken*, 9 (1990), 51–88.
Fröschle, H., *Goethes Verhältnis zur Romantik* (Würzburg: Königshausen und Neumann, 2002).
Gallardo, B., 'Anuncio literario', *El Criticón, papel volante de Literatura y Bellas-artes*, 4 (1836), 2.
García Barron, C., *La obra crítica y literaria de Don Antonio Alcalá Galiano* (Madrid: Gredos, 1970).
Gies, D. T., *Agustín Durán, A Biography and Literary Appreciation* (London: Tamesis, 1975).
—— ed., *The Cambridge History of Spanish Literature* (Cambridge: Cambridge University Press, 2004).
Ginger, A., *Political Revolution and Literary Experiment in the Spanish Romantic Period (1830–50)* (Lewiston, NY: Mellen, 1999).
Glendinning, N., *A Literary History of Spain: The Eighteenth Century* (London: Benn, 1972).
Goethe, J. W. von, *Goethe. Berliner Ausgabe*, Siegfried Seidel (ed.), 22 vols (Berlin: Aufbau, 1970–8).
—— *Johann Wolfgang von Goethe Sämtliche Werke, Briefe, Tagebücher und Gespräche*, Karl Eibl et al (eds.), 40 vols (Frankfurt am Main: Deutscher Klassiker Verlag, 1999).
Grimm, J., *Silva de romances viejos* (Vienna: Mayer, 1815).
—— *Jacob Grimm. Wilhelm Grimm. Schriften und Reden*, Ludwig Denecke (ed.), (Stuttgart: Reclam, 1985).
Hardenberg, F., von, pseudonym Novalis, *Novalis Schriften. Die Werke Friedrich von Hardenbergs*, P. Kluckhohn and R. Samuel (eds.), 2nd edn., 4 vols (Stuttgart: Kohlhammer, 1968).
Herder, J. G., *Herders Werke in fünf Bänden*, Wilhelm Dobbek (ed.) (Berlin/Weimar: Aufbau, 1969).
Herrero, J., *Fernán Caballero: un nuevo planteamiento* (Madrid: Gredos, 1963).
Hirsch, E. D., jr., *Wordsworth and Schelling. A Typological Study of Romanticism* (Hamden: Archon Books, 1971).
Humboldt, W., von, *Gesammelte Schriften*, 17 vols (Berlin: Behr, 1903–).
Iarocci, M., *Properties of Modernity. Romantic Spain, Modern Europe, and the Legacies of Empire* (Nashville, Tenn.; Vanderbilt, 2006).
Irving, P. (ed.), *The Life and Letters of Washington Irving*, 3 vols (London: Richard Bentley, 1862).
Irving, W., *Legends of the Conquest of Spain* (Philadelphia: Caray, Lea and Blanchard, 1835).
Jakšić, I., '"My King, my Country, my Faith": Washington Irving's Writings on the Rise and Fall of Spain', unpublished article.

Select Bibliography

Janner, H., 'Algunos datos nuevos acerca de J. N. Böhl de Faber', *Boletín de la Real Academia Española* (1945), 229–39.

Joshua, E., *Friedrich Leopold Graf zu Stolberg and the German Romantics*, British and Irish Studies in German Language and Literature 36 (Bern: Lang, 2005).

Juretschke, H., 'Die Deutung und Darstellung der deutschen Romantik durch Böhl in Spanien. Mit einem Anhang von Briefen an Martín Fernández de Navarrete', *Spanische Forschungen der Görresgesellschaft* (1956), 147–91.

—— 'La presencia del ideario romántico alemán en la estructura y evolución teórica del romanticismo español', *Romanticismo I. Atti del II congresso sul romanticismo spagnolo e ispanoamericano* (Genova: Biblioteca de Letterature, 1982), pp. 11–24.

—— *España y Europa. Estudios de Crítica Cultural. Obras completas de Hans Juretschke*, Miguel Ángel Cernuda (ed.), 3 vols (Madrid: Editorial Complutense, 2001).

Kant, I., *Immanuel Kant. Werke in sechs Bänden*, Wilhelm Weischedel (ed.), 6 vols (Darmstadt: Wissenschaftliche Buchgesellschaft, 1983).

Kerner, J., *Justinus Kerners Briefwechsel mit seinen Freunden*, Theobald Kerner (ed.), 2 vols (Stuttgart and Leipzig: Deutsche Verlags-Anstalt, 1897).

Kayser, W., *Die iberische Welt im Denken J. G. Herders* (Hamburg: Ibero-Amerikanisches Institut, 1945).

Koch, H., *Schiller und Spanien*, Münchener Romanistische Arbeiten 31 (Munich: Hueber, 1973).

Lichtenstein, E., 'Die Idee der Naturpoesie bei den Brüdern Grimm und ihr Verhältnis zu Herder', *DVJS*, 6 (1928), 513–47.

Leyser, J., *Joachim Heinrich Campe. Ein Lebensbild aus dem Zeitalter der Aufklärung*, 2 vols (Braunschweig: Vieweg, 1877).

Lindemann, M., *Patriots and Paupers. Hamburg 1712–1830* (Oxford and NY: Oxford University Press, 1990).

Littlejohns, R., 'Early Romanticism' in Mahoney (ed.), *The Literature of German Romanticism*, pp. 61–77.

Llorens Castillo, V., *El romanticismo español* (Madrid: Castalia, 1975).

—— *Liberales y románticos*, 2nd edn. (Valencia: Castalia, 1979).

Luzán, I., *La Poetica, ò reglas de la poesia general, y de sus principales especies* (Zaragoza: Francisco Revilla, 1737).

'Lyric Poetry of Spain', *Edinburgh Review*, 40 (1824), 443–76.

Mahoney, D. F. (ed.), *The Literature of German Romanticism*, Camden House History of German Literature 8 (Rochester, NY: Camden House, 2004).

Masiakowska, D., *Vielfalt und Einheit im Europabild August Wilhelm Schlegels* (Frankfurt am Main: Lang, 2002).

Meyer, E. L., and Tesdorpf, O., *Hamburgische Wappen und Genealogien* (Hamburg: Im Selbstverlag der Verfasser, 1890).

Monguió, L., *Don José Joaquín de Mora y el Perú del Ochocientos* (Madrid: Castalia, 1967).

Montesinos, J. F., *Fernán Caballero. Ensayo de justificación* (Mexico: El colegio de Mexico, 1961).

Montoto, S., *Fernán Caballero. Algo más que una biografía* (Seville: Gráficas del Sur, 1969).

Mora, J. J., *De Buonaparte y de los Borbones por F. A. de Chateaubriand. Traducido al castellano por José Joaquin de Mora* (Cádiz: Ramon Hovve, 1814).

—— *Nino II. Tragedia escrita en francés por Mr Brifaut, traducida al castellano por Don José Joaquin de Mora, y representada en el Teatro del Principe en la noche del 2 de junio de 1818* (Madrid: Repullés, 1818).

Murphy, M., *Blanco White. Self-banished Spaniard* (New Haven and London: Yale University Press, 1989).

Nasarre, Blas Antonio (ed.), *Comedias y entremeses de Miguel de Cervantes Saavedra, el autor de Don Quijote, divididas en dos tomos con una dissertacion, o prologo sobre las Comedias de España*, 2 vols (Madrid: Antonio Marin, 1749).

Navas Ruiz, R., *El romanticismo español. Historia y crítica* (Salamanca: Anaya, 1970).

Nemoianu, V., *The Triumph of Imperfection. The Silver Age of Sociocultural Moderation in Europe, 1815–1848* (Columbia: University of South Carolina Press, 2006).

Orozco Acuaviva, A., *La gaditana Frasquita Larrea, primera romántica española* (Jeréz de la Frontera: Gráficas del Exportador, 1977).

Par, A., *Shakespeare en la literatura española*, 2 vols (Madrid/Barcelona: Suárez/Balmes, 1935).

Penney, C. L., *Washington Irving's Diary Spain 1828–1829* (NY: Hispanic Society of America, 1926).

Perthes, C. (ed.), *Friedrich Perthes Leben*, 3 vols (Hamburg and Göttingen: Perthes, 1848–55).

Pérez Galdós, B., *Obras completas*, Federico Carlos Sainz de Robles (ed.), 6 vols (Madrid: Aguilar, 1950).

Pitollet, C., *La querelle caldéronienne de Johan Nikolas Böhl von Faber et José Joaquín de Mora reconstituée d'aprés les documents originaux* (Paris: Alcan, 1909).

—— 'Une lettre inédite de Böhl von Faber à l'éditeur Friedrich Perthes à Hambourg relative à la Floresta de rimas antiguas castellanas', *Revue germanique*, 5 (1909), 301–18.

Reyes Ponce, M. G., 'August Wilhelm Schlegel's Wiener Vorlesungen and Böhl von Faber's Sobre el teatro español', *Bulletin of the John Rylands University Library of Manchester*, 71 (1989), 105–24.

—— 'Spanish and German Antecedents to Agustín Durán's Coleccion de Romances Castellanos Anteriores al Siglo XVIII (1828–1832)', unpublished doctoral thesis, University of Manchester, 1991.

Richardson, A. (ed.), *A Dictionary of Christian Theology* (London: SCMP, 1969).

Rodríguez Moñino, A., *La polémica entre Gallardo y Cavalieri Pazos sobre el asonante (1824)* (Badajoz: Imprenta provincial, 1959).

Romero Tobar, L., 'Textos inéditos de Agustín Durán, Gallardo, Böhl, Quintana y Martínez de la Rosa', *Revista de archivos, bibliotecas y museos* (1975), 409–28.

Saglia, D., '"The True Essence of Romanticism": Romantic Theories of Spain and the Question of Spanish Romanticism', *Tessarae*, 3 (1997), 127–45.

Sainz Rodríguez, P., 'Documentos para la historia de la crítica en España. Un epistolario erudito del siglo XIX', *BBMP* (1921), 27–43; 87–101; 155–65; 251–62.

Schiller, F., *Friedrich Schiller, Sämtliche Werke*, Gerhard Fricke and Herbert G. Göpfert (eds.), 9th edn., 5 vols (Munich: Hanser, 1959 [1993]).

Schlegel, A. W., *Spanisches Theater*, 2 vols (Berlin: Julius Eduard Hitzig, 1803–1809).

―― *Blumensträusse. Italienischer, spanischer und portugiesischer Poesie* (Berlin: Realschulbuchhandlung, 1804).
―― *A Course of Lectures on Dramatic Art and Literature*, translated by John Black, revised by A. J. W. Morrison (London: Bohn, 1846).
―― *A. W. Schlegel, Kritische Schriften und Briefe*, E. Lohner (ed.), 7 vols. (Stuttgart: Kohlhammer, 1967).
Schlegel, F., *Europa. Eine Zeitschrift* (1803–1805).
―― *Kritische Friedrich-Schlegel-Ausgabe*, Ernst Behler et al (eds.), (Paderborn: Schönigh, 1961–).
―― *Literary Notebooks 1797–1801*, Hans Eichner (ed.), (London: Athlone, 1957).
―― *Kritische Schriften und Fragmente; Studienausgabe in sechs Bänden*, Ernst Behler and Hans Eichner (eds.), 6 vols (Paderborn: Schönigh, 1988).
Secondat, C., de, Baron de Montesquieu, *Lettres persanes*, 2 vols (Paris: Bure, 1824).
Seoane, M. C., *Historia del periodismo en España*, 3 vols (Madrid: Alianza, 1983).
Sharpe, L., *Schiller's Aesthetic Essays. Two Centuries of Criticism* (Rochester, NY: Camden House, 1995).
Shaw, D. L., *A Literary History of Spain: The Nineteenth Century* (London: Benn, 1972).
―― 'Time and History in Spanish Romantic Poetry' in *Romantic Poetry*, Angela Esterhammer (ed.), (Amsterdam/Philadelphia: John Benjamins, 2002), pp. 287–303.
Siebenmann, G., 'Johann Nikolaus Böhl von Faber (1770–1836): Ein deutscher Wahlspanier zwischen Selbst und Entfremdung', Thomas Bremer and Jochen Heymann (eds.), *Sehnsuchtsorte. Festschrift zum 60. Geburtstag von Titus Heydenreich* (Tübingen: Stauffenberg, 1999), pp. 119–34.
Silver, P. W., *Ruin and Restitution: Reinterpreting Spanish Romanticism* (Liverpool: Liverpool University Press, 1997).
Solis, R., *Historia del periodismo gaditano 1800–1850* (Cadiz: Instituto de Estudios gaditanos, 1971).
'Spain', *Blackwood's Edinburgh Magazine*, 14 (1823), 675–94.
Stoeffler, F. E., *German Pietism During the Eighteenth Century* (Leiden: Brill, 1973).
Stolberg, F., *Gesammelte Werke der Brüder Christian und Friedrich Leopold Grafen zu Stolberg*, 20 vols (Hamburg: Perthes, 1827).
Sullivan, H., *Calderón in the German Lands and Low Countries: his reception and influence* (Cambridge: Cambridge University Press, 1983).
Ticknor, G., *Geschichte der schönen Literatur in Spanien. Deutsch mit Zusätzen herausgegeben von Nikolaus Heinrich Julius*, 2 vols (Leipzig: Brockhaus, 1852).
Tully, C., *Creating a National Identity: A Comparative Study of German and Spanish Romanticism*, Stuttgarter Arbeiten zur Germanistik 347 (Stuttgart: Hans-Dieter Heinz, 1997).
Uhland, L., *Uhlands Briefwechsel*, Julius Hartmann (ed.), 4 vols (Stuttgart and Berlin: Cotta, 1916).
Weeks, A., *German Mysticism. From Hildegard of Bingen to Ludwig Wittgenstein. A Literary and Intellectual History* (NY: SUNY, 1993).
Welker, K. H. L. (ed.), *Andreas Riem. Ein Europäer aus der Pflaz*, Schriften der Siebenpfeiffer-Stiftung 6 (Stuttgart: Thorbecke, 1999).

Wolf, F., *Floresta de rimas modernas castellanas; ó poesias selectas castellanas desde el tiempo de Ignacio de Luzan hasta nuestros dias, con una introducción histórica, con noticias biograficas y críticas*, 2 vols (Paris: Rohrmann y Schweigerd, 1837).

—— 'Ein Beitrag zur Bibliographie der Cancioneros und zur Geschichte der spanischen Kunstlyrik am Hofe Kaiser Karls V', *Sitzungsberichte der philosophisch-historischen Classe der kaiserlichen Akademie der Wissenschaften*, X (1853), 153–204.

—— 'Zur Bibliographie der Romanceros', ibid., 484–516.

Wolf, T., *Pustkuchen und Goethe. Die Streitschrift als produktives Verwirrspiel* (Tübingen: Niemeyer, 1999).

Wordsworth. W., *William Wordsworth. A Critical Edition of the Major Works*, Stephen Gill (ed.), (Oxford: Oxford University Press, 1984).

—— *Lyrical Ballads*, Michael Mason (ed.), (London: Longman, 1992).

Ziolkowski, T., *German Romanticism and its institutions* (Princeton: Princeton University Press, 1990).

Index

References which appear in normal script are to the study of Böhl's Life and Work; references in italics are to the Literary Correspondence; references in parentheses are to the Editor's Notes. Works are referred to under the relevant author, except in the case of anonymous texts or periodicals which are listed by title. Indexed items for the Correspondence have been selected on the same basis as those deemed worthy of annotation in the Editor's Notes. The numbered headings describing each letter in the Correspondence and Editor's Notes have not been indexed.

Abschatz, Hans Aßmann, Freiherr von *318, 320, 322* (522)
Ackermann, Rudolf 169, 249n.
Addison, Joseph 12
Adelung, Johann Christoph *309, 325* (515)
Agricola, Johannes *334* (528)
Aheran y Malone, Francisca Javiera 40, 51, 101, *282, 284, 287, 298, 302, 306*
Alarcón, Juan de *364* (538)
Albert, Heinrich *308, 318, 321, 326, 327, 350* (515, 522)
Albertinus, Aegidius *309* (516)
Alcalá Galiano, Antonio 53, 106, 123, 142, 160–6, 169–71, 178, 251, 254, *410, 423, 441* (553, 556, 562)
Alcántara de Toledo y Salm-Salm, Pedro Duque del Infantado *377* (542)
Alcázar, Baltasar del *434* (560)
Aldana, Francisco de *487* (577)
Aldrete, Bernardo José de *331*
Alemán, Mateo (516)
Alfieri, Vittorio 131
Alvarado, Francisco (pseud. El Filósofo rancio) 175, *355, 357, 362, 367, 371, 381, 466, 475* (535, 539, 557, 572)
Álvarez, Rafael 158n.
Amadis de Gaula 343, 350, 373 (531)
Anaya, Ángel 159n., *383, 388* (544)
Ancillon, Johann Peter Friedrich 155–6, *387* (545)
Andreae, Johann Valentin *328, 425* (526, 557)
Andrés, Juan 214
Angeli Silesi, Johannes *313, 321, 324, 424, 436* (519, 523)
Annalen der Oesterreichischen Literatur 327 (525)
Anton Ulrich, Duke of Braunschweig *321, 324* (523)

Apontes, Juan Fernández *374, 430* (541, 558)
Arco Hermoso, Francsico Ruiz del Arco de Paula, Marqués de 183, *434, 452, 460, 502* (560, 580)
Arejula, Juan Manuel de *467* (569–70)
Argensola brothers 78, *407* (552)
Aristotle 113–14
Arletius, Johann Caspar *328* (525)
Arnim, Ludwig Achim von 11, 80–1, 83, 85, 105–6, 195, 205, 207, 218, 234, *311–13, 324, 400, 404, 411* (516–17, 518, 523, 551)
Arnold, Gottfried *313* (519)
Arriaza, Juan Bautista de 143, 158n., 185n., 240, *394, 459, 465* (547, 567)
Asso y del Rio, Ignacio Jordán Claudio de *365, 383, 388* (538)
Athenaeum 59, 62–63, 66, 77, 292
Augustinius, Aurelius (St Augustine) *307* (514)
Avila, Teresa de 78, 90, *309, 355* (514, 516)

Baader, Benedikt Franz Xavier von 193, *360, 361* (537, 546)
Bacon, Francis (Baron Baco de Verulam) *334* (528)
Baczko, Ludwig Franz Adolf Joseph von *327* (525)
Baena, Juan Alfonso de *389, 417* (546)
Balbuena, Bernardo de *392, 422* (547)
Balde, Jacob *328* (526)
Baldrich y de Viciana, Alberto *388, 393* (545, 547)
Ballesteros, Francisco *454* (566)
Bandizabal 377
Barclay, John (530)
Bartels, Ernst Daniel August *297* (512)
Basedow, Johann Bernhard 38n.

Index

Batteux, Charles 156
Becher, Hubert 55
Becker, Katharina 34
Beireis, Gottfried Christoph 331, 333, 342 (527)
Bellman, Carl Michael 310 (517)
Bell's Weekly Messenger 74
Belmonte y Bermúdez, Luís de 203n., 375 (542)
Belon, Pierre 313 (519)
Benoît, Charles Louis 498 (579)
Bentham, Jeremy 435 (560)
Berchtold, Leopold Graf 275 (508)
Berckemeyer, Bernhard Philip 20n., 42, 75, 289, 292, 312, 352 (510, 561)
Berckemeyer, Betsy (later Böhl von Faber) 482, 485 (575)
Berckemeyer, Eduard 281, 286, 437, 446, 458 (561)
Berckemeyer, Johann Heinrich 444, 448, 450, 465, 467, 469, 475, 485
Berceo, Gonzalo de 318 (522)
Bernhardi-Tieck, Sophie 71n.
Besard, Jean Baptiste 342 (531)
Besser, Johann Heinrich 444, 466, 473, 474, 477, 486, 489, 499 (563, 573)
Bible de l'Ours 313 (519)
Biblia pentapla 335 (528)
Birken, Sigmund von 330 (526)
Black, John 155
Black, Black and Young, publishers 483, 484
Blackwood's Edinburgh Magazine 199, 236, 431, 432–33, 434, 435, 438, 443, 447, 461, 463, 468, 469, 472 (555, 559–60, 562–3, 564, 568, 570, 571)
Blair, Hugh 126, 156
Blanco White, José María 103, 476 (572–3)
Blücher von Wahlstatt, Gebhard Leberecht, Fürst 372, 438, 454 (540)
Blum, Joachim Christoph 334 (528)
Boccalini, Traiano 311 (518)
Boccati, Giovanni (Giovanni di Permateo) 313 (519)
Bodmer, Johann Jakob 12, 318, 321 (521, 523)
Böhl, Anton Gottlieb 19n., 23, 24, 32, 33, 39n., 42, 45, 49, 57n., 268, 274, 277, 280, 282, 283, 285, 289, 290, 292, 296
Böhl, Carl Wilhelm 19n., 20n., 38n., 42, 57n.
Böhl, Cecilia (later Berckemeyer) 19n., 20n., 75, *315* (561, 575)
Böhl, Cecilia Isabel (née Lütkens) 19n., 23, 338, 341, 343, 458, 480 (574)
Böhl, Ferdinand 19n., 20n., 38n.
Böhl, Johann Friedrich 468, 482 (570)
Böhl, Johann Friedrich von (Fritz) 19n., 20n., 23, 42, 105, 273, 276, 280, 288, 289, 290, 292, 302 (510, 530)
Böhl, Johann Jacob 19n., 23, 38n., 259, 261
Böhl, Peter 19n., 20n., 38n.
Böhl von Faber, Angela 57n., 101, 179, 298, 359, 396, 403, 406, 460, 470, 473, 488, 492, 503 (536)
Böhl von Faber, Aurora 57n., 101, 179, 290, 291, 296, 359, 460, 470, 473, 478, 488, 492 (510)
Böhl von Faber, Cecilia (pseud. Fernán Caballero) 5, 6, 16, 41, 51, 54, 75, 128, 171, 171n., 180, 181, 183, 184n., 251, 254–5, 281, 283, 284, 286, 287, 289, 290, 291, 296, 305, 315, 359, 392, 396, 405, 406, 409, 410, 414, 424, 434, 437, 452, 460, 461, 466, 473, 480, 482, 488, 492, 495, 502 (508, 536, 546, 550, 556, 559–60)
Böhl von Faber, Johann Nikolas
  Works:
  'Auch eine Stimme über Bonaparte' 104–5
  'Auch etwas über Handels-Monopol' 73–4
  'Creer y obrar' 184n.
  Donde las dan, las toman 107, 123, 135–40
  Floresta de rimas antiguas castellanas 98, 167, 179–80, 194, 204, 208, 217, 218–24, 226, 227, 228–31, 234–44, 247–8, 249n., 350, 363, 365, 369, 373, 376, 384, 389, 394, 405–6, 407, 408, 412, 414, 415, 416, 417, 418, 425, 427, 428, 430, 431, 433, 434, 435, 436, 438, 440, 442, 443, 444, 446, 447, 449, 451–2, 453–4, 458, 459, 460, 462, 464, 465, 467, 469, 472, 473, 474, 476, 477, 486, 487, 488, 490, 497, 499 (533, 539, 541, 551, 552, 553, 554, 555, 556–7, 558, 559, 560, 561, 562, 563, 564, 565, 566, 567, 568, 569, 572, 573, 576, 578)
  'Korrespondenz Nachrichten. Cadix' 180, 403, 404, 406, 419 (551)

'Noticias literarias originales' 154–7, 162, 164, 187, 212–15, *389, 394* (545–6)
Pasatiempo crítico 107, 143–4, 146–8, 152, 158n., 165, 172n., *384* (543, 560)
'Peculiaridades de España' 46, *288, 314–15, 319, 322*
'Reflexiones sobre la poesía' 59, 76, 111, 120, 122, 146, 150–1, 224, 256
'Reflexiones de Schlegel sobre el teatro' 110–26, 128–40, 142, *381–2*
Segunda parte del pasatiempo crítico 107, 123, 152, 161, 164, 165–6, 172n., 188–90, *390, 391, 394* (545, 560)
Teatro antiguo anterior à Lope de Vega 180, 204, 218, 224–6, 227, 231–3, 236, 242–3, 244, *363, 370, 407, 408, 417, 444–45, 475, 486, 487, 489–90, 493, 494, 495, 497, 498, 499, 500* (541, 551, 554, 558, 576, 578, 579, 580)
Tercer parte del pasatiempo crítico 108, 156, 159n., 172n., 190–2, 206–7, 219, 227, 229–31, 254, *394, 401, 409, 412, 414* (552, 553, 554)
'Ueber die spanische Literatur' 76–80, 110, 227
Vier und Zwanzig Lieder aus des Knaben Wunderhorn 81–2, 218–19, 252, *330, 334, 344, 359, 364* (526, 531, 536)
Vindicaciones de Calderón 108, 115, 121, 135, 141n., 153, 156, 159n., 168, 201, *403* (551)
'Von der neuesten englischen Poesie' 83–7, 137, *324*
Böhl von Faber, Juan Jacobo 51, 76, 180, *305, 315, 329, 352, 354, 359, 378, 394, 396, 401, 447, 465, 481, 485, 495, 502* (534, 541, 550, 574)
Böhme, Jakob 90–91, *308, 310, 313* (514–15, 518, 519)
Boiardo, Matteo Maria *313* (519)
Boie, Heinrich Christian (525)
Boileau-Despréaux, Nicolas 131, 143, 156, 169
Bokelmann, W. *299, 354, 405, 408, 492, 497, 502*
Bonald, Louis-Gabriel-Ambroise, Vicomte de 148, *370, 389, 399* (539, 545, 546, 548–9)

Bonaparte, Napoleon 9, 51, 74, 75, 76, 104–5, 125, 148, 187, 197–8, *306, 308, 354, 357, 360, 388, 390, 393, 426, 480, 503* (514, 534, 540, 574, 581)
Boner, Hieronymus (531)
Book of Spiritual Poverty 93
Börne, Ludwig 184, *502* (580)
Boscán Almogáver, Juan 78, 222, *350* (534)
Bossuet, Jacques-Benigne 78, *307,* 449 (514)
Bourbon, Louis-Antoine de, duc d'Angoulême 178, *451, 454, 455, 456–7* (566)
Bourgoing, Jean François *289* (510)
Bourmont, Louis Auguste Victor, Count de Ghaisnes de *458* (567)
Bouterwek, Friedrich 13, 78–9, 81, 82, 83, 154, 155, 169, 196, 201, 234, 235, 236, 245, 247, 252, 253, *300,* 324, 327, *402, 421, 422, 482, 484, 486, 494* (512, 523, 550, 555, 562, 575, 576)
Bowring, John 172n., 181, 215–16, 237–8, 249n., 251, 444, 447, 467, 472, 476, *482* (563, 571, 572)
Brandenburg-Bayreuth, Christian Ernst von (526)
Brandenstein, Karl Ludwig Friedrich Joseph von *317* (521)
Brant, Sebastian (522)
Bredelo, Heinrich *321* (522)
Breitinger, Johann Jakob 12, *318* (521)
Brentano, Clemens 80–1, 83, 85, 89, 106, 118, 195, 205, 207, 218, 234, 256, *312–13, 324, 400, 409, 411, 422* (517, 518, 523)
Brifaut, Charles 151–2, 153, 162, 163, 172n.
Brougham, Henry (538)
Brucker, Johann Jacob *311* (518)
Brüggemann, Werner 18
Buchner, Augustus *320* (522)
Bülow, Heinrich Dietrich, Freiherr von *300, 324–5* (512, 524)
Bürger, Gottfried August 13
Burguillos, Juan Sánchez *407, 446* (552)
Burke, Edmund 30, *416* (554)
Burney, Charles *371* (540)
Burns, Robert 84, 137, 234
Büsch, Johan Georg 38n.
Büsching, Georg *342, 348* (531)
Büsching, Johann Gustav *310, 319, 326, 494* (517)
Butler, Charles *476* (573)

Index

Byron, George Gordon, Lord 4, 56, 58n., 137, 156, 197, 200, 234, *400, 426, 443, 466, 480* (549, 557, 572)

Caballero, Fernán *see* Böhl von Faber, Cecilia
Cabanells *373*
Cabanellas i Clavera, Miquel *363* (538)
Cabeza de Vaca, Alvar Nuñez *374, 388* (541)
Cabrera, Ramón 167, 172n.
Cadalso, José 126, 214
Cádiz, Fray Diego José de 98n.
Calderón de la Barca, Pedro 11, 12, 13, 14, 15, 55–6, 77, 79, 98, 106, 108, 110–26, 130–1, 134, 136, 137, 139, 143, 147, 149, 150, 153, 154, 156, 157, 161, 162, 163, 164, 165–6, 168, 170, 172n., 175, 192, 200, 201, 215, 233, 253, *343, 354, 361, 370, 371, 372, 373, 374, 380, 381, 383, 384, 386, 388, 390, 391, 395, 399, 400, 401, 403, 409, 410, 421, 430, 438, 440, 442, 446, 452, 476, 483, 486, 487* (531, 539, 540, 542, 543, 544, 547, 548–9, 558, 562–3, 572, 576–7)
Calvin, John *307* (514)
Camões, Luís de *366* (538, 574)
Campe family 8, 41, 57n., *480* (511)
Campe, August 74–75, 81, 82, 105–6, 183, 184, 184n., 185n., *286, 287, 288, 290, 293, 294–5, 297, 300, 302, 304, 306, 323, 333, 336, 337, 338, 339, 340, 344, 345, 346, 348, 355, 359, 378, 397, 421, 422* (510, 511, 513, 536, 579)
Campe, Charlotte (Lotte; later Vieweg) 37, 71n., *260, 262, 263, 265, 268, 269, 271, 275, 277, 286, 287, 290, 291, 296, 300, 305, 323, 337* (506, 509)
Campe, Dorothea 23, 49, *263, 265, 269, 304, 337, 401, 476* (509, 513, 549, 550, 572–3)
Campe, Elise (née Hoffmann) 16–17, 57n., 74–5, 82, 183, *249, 302, 323, 329, 353, 367, 373, 378, 384, 390, 394, 401, 404, 409, 458, 503* (513, 523, 579)
Campe, Joachim Heinrich 4, 5, 10, 23–38, 39n., 40, 42, 43–44, 45, 48, 49, 59, 61, 63, 73, 80, 88, 91, 95, 125, 158, 194, *256, 259, 261, 263, 264, 265, 267, 269, 272, 287, 290, 293, 296, 297, 304–5, 306, 316, 323, 324, 345, 476* (505, 506, 508, 509, 510, 511, 512, 514, 549, 550, 572–3, 576)
Campoamar, Ramón de 255
Cancionero de romances de Amberes 205, 209, 220, 244, *325, 373, 420* (524, 540, 555)
Cañizares, José de *399* (549)
Canning, George *449* (565)
Capmany, Antonio de 126, 176
Caramuel y Lobkowitz, Juan *360, 362* (536)
Cardano, Geronimo *326* (524)
Carignan, Charles Albert, Prince de *456* (567)
Carlos III 39n., 53, 98n. (535, 544)
Carlos IV *373* (540)
Carlyle, Thomas 200, *481, 483, 484* (574–5, 576)
Carnero, Guillermo 17, 19, 20n., 51, 71n., 98n., 107, 123, 127n., 136, 140n., 145, 158n., 161, 172n., 176, 230
Carrillo, José 15
Castillo, Hernando del (555)
Castillejo, Cristobal de 78, *407* (552)
Castro, José Rodríguez de *389, 417* (546)
Castro y Velasco, Antonio Palomino de (563)
Cavaleri Pazos, Juan Bautista 106, 152, 162–4, 165, 166, 172n., *386* (544, 563)
Cavallo, Tiberio *387* (545)
Ceán Bermúdez, Juan Agustín *446* (564)
Ceballos, Pedro *377* (542)
Cellini, Benvenuto *339* (530)
Cervantes y Saavedra, Miguel de 11, 13, 14, 77, 78–9, 146, 154, 157, 162, 172n., 221, *343, 373, 374, 380, 383, 388, 389, 392, 400, 402, 407, 422, 425, 430, 443, 476, 498, 499* (531, 541, 546, 563, 574, 579)
Chamisso, Adalbert von 82, *495* (579)
Chapelain, Jean *313* (519)
Chateaubriand, François-René Vicomte de 4, 11, 128, 139, 148, 153, 158n., 255, *308, 393, 452* (514–15, 547, 565–6)
Chatry de la Fosse, Baron 179, *470, 494*
Cheine, Dr. 461
Cienfuegos, Nicasio Álvarez *362* (537)
Claudius, Matthias 38n., *283, 325, 356, 398, 406* (509, 523, 535, 548, 551–2)

594

Index

Clavijo y Fajardo, José 12, 69, 157, 159n., 164
Clemencín, Diego 167, 172n., *498* (579)
Clement, Franz Joseph *335* (528)
Codex Albensis *372* (540)
Colburn, Henry (547)
Coleccion de retratos de los españoles ilustres *399* (549)
Coleridge, Samuel Taylor 4, 11, 85, 237, *443, 461, 469* (540, 562–3, 570)
Collin, Matthaus von *468* (570)
Colon, Cristóbal (Columbus) *475* (572)
Comella, Luciano Francisco *299* (512)
Conde, José Antonio *435, 448* (561)
Cotta von Cottendorff, Johann Friedrich 107, 180, *481* (517, 574, 577)
Cowper, William 83–4
Crabbe, George 200, *392, 400, 411–12, 417, 420* (547, 549, 552–3, 555)
Cramer, Carl Friedrich (508)
Craven, Elizabeth, Baroness *475* (572)
Crónica científica y literaria 107, 142–8, 153, 158n., 159n., 160, 162, 163–4, 165, *381, 391, 392–3, 401, 409* (546)
Cruikshank, George *475* (572)
Cruikshank, Robert *475* (572)
Cruz, San Juan de la (516)
Cruz, Sor Juana Ines de la 228
Cuesta, Juan de la *481*
Cunningham, Alan *471* (571)
Curio, Coelius Secundus *311* (518)
Cyrano de Bergerac, Savinien *310* (517)

Dach, Simon *308, 315, 318, 320, 326, 327, 328, 390* (515, 525)
Dahlmann, Friedrich Christoph (536)
Dähnert, Johann Karl *313* (519)
D'Alton, Eduard Baron 163, *384, 386, 387, 390, 394, 397, 400, 403, 409, 415, 430* (543, 544, 545, 548, 550, 552, 558)
D'Avity, Pierre (519)
Dante Alighieri 131, 156
Defoe, Daniel 24
De Maistre, Joseph Marie, Comte 11, *437, 449* (561, 565)
Denis, Johann Nepomuk Cosmos Michael *341* (530)
Depping, Georg Bernhard 14, 204, 209, 211–12, 213, 215, 217, 220, 223, 226, 234, 236, 237, 239, 248, 249, *379, 388, 440* (541–2, 545, 561, 568)
Der alten Weisen Exempel Sprüch *383* (544)
Der Vernünftler 38n.
Deutsches Museum (1776–91) *328* (525)
Diario de Cádiz 182
Diario de las actas y discusiones de las cortes *426* (557)
Diario de las sesiones y actas en las cortes *435* (561)
Diario de los literatos de España 157
Diario de Madrid *391, 455* (546, 566)
Diario mercantil de Cádiz 107, 142, 143, 153, 154, 158n., 159n., 160, 165, 167, 240, *375, 385, 394, 415* (546, 554)
Diez, Friedrich 14, 181, 211, 217n., 226, 234, 235, 238, 249, 251, *498* (579)
Dieze, Johann Andreas 13, 154, 214, 234, 247
Docen, Bernhard Joseph *307, 311, 319, 324, 331* (515, 527)
Dohm, Christian Konrad Wilhelm von (525)
Donoso Cortes, Juan 171, 255
Dorn, Gerhard *412* (553)
Dornhof, Johann 17, 243
Draudius, Georg *325* (524)
Duclos, Charles Pineau *313* (519)
Duff Gordon family 175, 183, *436, 449, 469* (561, 570)
Dunkel, Johann Gottlieb Wilhelm *335, 336* (528)
Durán, Agustín 6, 171, 181–2, 185n., 195, 209, 213, 216, 224–5, 226, 229, 240–2, 244–8, 249, 251, 255, *483, 486, 487, 488, 494, 501* (575, 576, 577, 578, 580)
Durán, Francisco 245
Dürer, Albrecht *352, 356* (534)

Ebeling, Christoph 38n., *333* (527)
Eckart, Meister 93
Eckermann, Johann Peter 67
Eckstein, Ferdinand, Baron d' *476* (573)
Edinburgh Review 155, 156, 159n., 199, 237–8, *365, 382, 398, 411, 416, 433, 467, 481* (543, 548, 552–3, 559–60, 568, 569, 574)
Eichendorff, Joseph von 7, 75
Eichhorn, Johann Gottfried 208

El Cantar del mio Cid 209, 217n., 239, *373, 374, 380, 388, 394, 401, 410, 422, 425, 474, 475, 480* (541)
El Europeo 171, 245, 254
Elió y Olándriz, Francisco Javier *441* (562)
Encina, Juan del 225–26, 232, *409* (552)
Erauso y Zavaleta, Tomás 15, 157
Ercilla y Zuñiga, Alonso de *392, 422* (547)
Ercker, Lazarus *311* (518)
Erskine, Thomas, Baron *445* (564)
Eschenbach, Wolfram von (530)
Eschenburg, Johann Joachim 80, *306, 316, 317, 322, 324, 326, 328, 333, 371, 439, 447* (514, 523, 527)
Escobar, Luis de (540)
Escoiquiz, Juan *377* (542)
Esmarck, Christian Hieronymus *337* (529)
Espinosa, Pedro *481* (574)
Espoz y Mina, Francisco 176
Esquilache, Francisco de Borja y Aragón, Prince of 78
Estala, Pedro (pseud. Ramón Fernández) 213, 221, 222, 239, *407, 417, 430, 436* (552)
Es wird alles neu 361 (537)
European Review 169, 461

Faber, Martin Jakob von 23, 58n., *338, 394, 406, 448, 470, 480, 482, 484* (547, 574)
Falk, Johannes Daniel *498* (579)
Fama fraternitatis 340 (530)
Felipe II 12, 118 (525)
Felipe V 156 (547)
Fernández de Moratín, Nicolás 162, 201
Fernández de Moratín, Leandro 137, 224–26, 243, 250n., *483, 484, 486, 487, 489, 490, 493, 494, 499* (575, 576, 577, 578, 580)
Fernández Pacheco, Juan Manuel (547)
Fernández Poza, Milagros 40, 54
Fernando VII 10, 51, 54, 102–3, 107, 109, 125, 134, 160, 171, 172n., 175, 176, 178, 182, 186, 194, 200, 255, *370, 377, 387, 408, 413, 414, 433, 451, 455, 457, 460, 463, 484* (541, 542, 547, 556, 566, 568, 577)
Feyerabend, Sigmund (517)

Fichte, Johann Gottlieb 61, 90, 93, 122, 124, *306* (514)
Fiévée, Joseph *393, 398, 447* (540, 547, 548)
Finestres y Montsalvo, José *415* (554)
Fischer, Christian August 47
Fleming, Hanns Friedrich von *335* (528)
Fleming, Paul *317, 320, 321, 335* (521, 528)
Flitter, Derek 5–6, 16, 18, 19, 122–4, 135, 145, 171, 254–5
Floranes, Rafael 213
Florez, Enrique *402* (550)
Foreign Quarterly Review 200, 483, *484* (575)
Foreign Review 483 (575)
Foreign Review and Continental Miscellany 481 (575)
Förster, Friedrich Christoph *387, 393, 400* (545)
Fouqué, Caroline de la Motte *342, 348* (530, 533)
Fouqué, Friedrich de la Motte 82, 83, 89, 177–8, 195, *311, 325, 337, 338, 342, 346, 348, 354, 355, 364, 398, 400, 411, 491* (516–17, 520, 524, 529, 531, 532, 533, 534, 535, 548, 578)
Francisci, Erasmus *333* (528)
Franck, Sebastian *334* (528)
Freire Andrade Armijo, Manuel Alberto *423* (556)
Friemel, Berthold 208
Frölich, publishers 71n.
Frontini, Sextus Julius *313* (519)
Fröschle, Helmut 89
Freysinger und Furth, booksellers 322
Fuero juzgo (Liber judicorum) 400, 414, 415, 420, 422, 423, 425 (550)
Funk, Karl Philipp *272* (508)

Gaceta de Bayona 482, 483
Gaceta del Gobierno 426 (557)
Gaceta de Madrid 400, 499 (550)
Gagern, Hans Christoph Ernst von *447, 452* (565)
Galiano *see* Alcalá Galiano
Galignani, Giovanni Antonio *466* (569)
Galignani's Magazine 238, *466, 475* (569)
Gall, Franz Joseph *402* (550)
Gallardo y Blanco, Bartolomé José 162, 182, 185n., 242, 251, *488* (576–7)
Garay, Martín de *377* (542)

Index

Garcez Ferreira, Ignacio 366 (538)
García Morente, Manuel 60
García de Arrieta, Agustín 157
García de la Huerta, Vicente 157, 162, *399*, *494* (549)
Garcilaso de la Vega, 78, 221, 222, *350*, *392*, *407*, *422*, *468* (534, 552)
Garcilaso de la Vega, 'El Inca' *374*, *380*, *383*, *388* (541, 567)
Garve, Christian 59, 60, 273, *292* (508, 511)
Garzoni, Tommaso *313* (519)
Geibel, Emanuel (520)
Geibel, Johannes 93, *314* (520)
Gentz, Friedrich von 59, 60, *292* (510, 511, 542, 554)
Gepflückte Finken *340* (530)
Gerhardt, Paul 91, *330*, *334*, *340*, *342*, *402* (526, 530)
Gersbach, Anton and Joseph 38 (545)
Geyler von Kaiserberg, Johann, *321* (522)
Gies, David 4–5, 245
Gil y Zarate, Antonio 255
Gil Polo, Gaspar 216
Gil Vicente 226, 232, *409* (552)
Ginger, Andrew 15, 126
Gleim, Johann Wilhelm Ludwig 205, 217n., *309* (516)
Gneisenau, August Graf Neidhardt von 365, *372* (538)
Godoy, Manuel de 136, *377* (542)
Goethe, Johann Wolfgang von 4, 5, 12, 14, 59, 60, 62, 67, 68, 80–1, 85, 89–90, 95, 105, 137, 180–1, 184, 194–6, 200, 234–5, 238, 249n., 252, 256, 279, *292*, *307*, *325*, *331*, *335*, *336*, *337*, *339*, *343*, *353*, *355*, *367*, *372*, *379*, *387*, *396*, *399*, *402*, *418*, *426*, *430*, *431*, *435*, *436*, *440*, *442*, *453*, *463*, *479*, *483*, *487*, *490*, *491*, *492*, *498*, *502* (509, 510, 511, 524, 527, 528, 529, 530, 531, 534, 540, 548, 550, 553, 559, 560–1, 562–3, 568, 574, 575, 576–7, 578, 580)
Golius, Jacob *412*, *423*, *427* (553)
Gómez de la Cortina, José (575)
Góngora y Argote, Luis de 13, 78, 208, 212, 216, 217n., 222, *326*, *410* (524)
González, Francisco Antonio 167, 172n.
González del Reguero, Vicente (547)
Gonzalo Morón, Fermín 255

Gorostiza, Manuel Eduardo de *470* (570–1)
Görres, Jacob 83, 91, 124, *313*, *317*, *324*, *372*, *381*, *410*, *452*, *475* (520, 521, 523, 540, 542–3, 553)
Gottfried, Johann Ludwig *313* (519)
Göttinger Gelehrten Anzeigen 235, *433*, *435*, *442* (560)
Gottschald, Johann Jakob *324*, *327* (523)
Gottsched, Johann Christoph 12, 130, *318*, *327*, *328*, *334*, *336* (521, 525, 527)
Gottsched, Luise *333* (527)
Goya, Francisco de 57n.
Gramondi 313
Granada, Fray Luis de 78
Gräter, Friedrich David *311* (517)
Gratz, Peter Aloys *389* (546)
Grävell, Maximilian Karl Friedrich Wilhelm *402* (550)
Greflinger, Georg (pseud. Celadon) *328* (525)
Gries, Johann Diederich *370*, *375*, *383*, *429*, *435* (539, 541, 558)
Grillparzer, Franz *383*, *472*, *475*, *484* (543–4, 571)
Grimm brothers 6, 13, 80, 195, 205, 207–8, 214, 226, 234, *404*, *478*, *494* (518, 551, 573)
Grimm, Jacob 13, 14, 154, 204, 207, 208–12, 213, 214, 215, 217, 217n., 226, 234, 236, 237, 247, 248, 252, 253, *331*, *372*, *378*, *418* (526–7, 532, 540, 554, 561, 568)
Grimm, Wilhelm 208, *313*, *337*, *340*, *453* (519, 529, 530, 566)
Gringore, Pierre *336*, *341* (529)
Grodnau, Karl Melchior Grodnitz von *336* (529)
Groote, Eberhard von *360* (536)
Gryphius, Andreas *321* (523)
Gustav III *399* (549)
Guyon, Jeanne Marie Bouvier de la Moth *311* (518)

Hackert, Phillip (529)
Hagedorn, Friedrich von 38n., *328*, *333* (525)
Hagen, Friedrich von der 80–1, *310*, *319*, *337* (517)
Hall, John Nadder 181
Haller, Albrecht von *328*, *436* (525, 561)

Index

Haller, Karl Ludwig von 65, 192, 196–7, 203n., *419, 422, 425, 427, 433, 448, 452 (555, 557, 558, 559, 565)*
Hallmann, Johann Christian *321 (523)*
Hamann, Johann Georg *433, 466, 475 (559–60, 569, 572)*
Hamburger Versorgungsanstalt 39n., 271
Hamilton, Terrick *436 (561)*
Hammelmann, Hermann *335 (528)*
Hardenberg, Friedrich von (pseud. Novalis) 8, 62, 66, 74, 86, 97, 118, 181, 194, *347, 356 (532–3, 535)*
Harms, Claus *383, 388 (544, 545)*
Harsdörffer, Georg Philipp *330, 335, 350 (526)*
Haug, Johann Christoph Friedrich *308 (515)*
Haydn, Joseph *295 (511)*
Hebel, Johann Peter *311 (517)*
Heeren, Arnold *314 (520)*
Hegener *328 (525)*
Heiberg, Johann Ludwig *400 (550)*
Heidelberger Jahrbücher 87n., *319, 324, 370, 379 (521, 522)*
Heine, Heinrich 184, 197–8, *478, 480, 481, 502 (573–4, 580)*
Heise, Carl Christian *480 (574)*
Heise, Carl Johann *480 (574)*
Helwig, Amelie von *(531)*
Henrich, Dieter 3
Hensler, Karl Friedrich *441 (562)*
Herder, Johann Gottfried Wilhelm 4, 13, 14, 16, 30, 60, 61, 68, 69–70, 77, 90, 108, 114, 121, 122, 124, 135, 139, 145, 176, 194–5, 196, 197, 204, 205–7, 208, 210, 211–12, 213, 215, 216, 217n., 226, 228, 236, 244, 247, 252, 253
Hermes, Georg *389 (546)*
Hermosilla, José 245, 246
Herrera, Fernando de 78, *407 (552)*
Herrero, Javier 17, 54
Hervás y Panduro, Lorenzo *422 (556)*
Heusinger, Johann Heinrich Gottlieb *296 (511)*
Heyne, Christian Gottlob *484 (576)*
Hitzig Julius Eduard 217n., 220, *325, 340, 343, 346, 373, 411, 446 (524, 530, 540, 564)*
Hobbes, Thomas 24
Hoffmann, Benjamin Gottlob *323, 339, 378 (513, 523)*

Hoffmann, E. T. A. 8, 13, 195, *360, 393, 398, 416, 420, 426, 436, 440, 441–2, 443, 446, 453, 462, 463, 491 (536, 548–9, 555, 562–3, 566)*
Hogg, James 200, *447 (564)*
Homburg, Ernst Christoph *308, 320 (515, 522)*
Homer 137
Hook, Theodore 201, *470 (570)*
Horace 161, 169
Horstig, Karl Gottlieb *328 (525)*
Houwald, Ernst *438, 473, 479 (561, 571, 573)*
Huber, Therese *(576)*
Huber, Victor Aimé 249, 250n., *487, 489 (576, 577)*
Hufeland, Christoph Wilhelm *292 (511)*
Hugalde y Mollinedo, Nicolás *(575)*
Humboldt, Alexander von *311, 360, 361, 364, 365, 372, 382, 398, 402, 422 (517, 536, 540)*
Humboldt, Wilhelm von 4, 6, 45–6, 57n., 75, 93
Hunt, Leigh *(572)*

Iarocci, Michael 18
Iriarte, Tomás de 126, *137 (506)*
Irving, Washington 181, 185n., 201–2, 251, *466 (569)*
Isabel II *(577)*
Isla, José Francisco de *401 (550)*

Jacobi, Johann Georg 205, 217n.
Jacobsen, Friedrich Johann *425 (557)*
Jahn, Friedrich Ludwig *(550)*
Jahrbücher für wissenschaftliche Kritik 235
Jakobi, Friedrich Heinrich *308 (515)*
Jakšić, Ivan 202, 203n.
Janner, Hans 172n.
Jansensius, Cornelius *307 (514)*
Jariges, Karl Ferdinand von (pseud. Beauregard Pandin) 235, 249n., *463 (568)*
Jauregui, Juan Martínez de 407
Jeffrey, Francis Lord *461 (538, 568)*
Jenaische Allgemeine Literaturzeitung 80
Jenkinson, Robert Banks, Earl Liverpool *449 (565)*
Jérica, Pablo de 143

Index

Jöcher, Christian Gottlieb 335, 336 (528)
Johnson, Samuel 156
Jördens, Karl Heinrich 317, 321, 327 (521)
Joshua, Eloema 94
Jovellanos, Gaspar Melchor de 126, 135, 166, 191, 361, 362 (536–7)
Juan II (546)
Juan y Santicilia, Jorge 477–8 (573)
Julius, Nikolas Heinrich 8, 16, 55, 57n., 58n., 75, 82, 87n., 93, 96, 180, 182, 200, 218–20, 228, 229, 234, 236, 237, 247, 249, 252, 328, 329, 333, 340, 346, 359, 361, 386, 395, 398, 406, 408, 413, 415, 423, 429, 431, 459, 475, 486, 499, 502 (515, 518, 520, 521, 524, 526, 530, 537, 539, 543, 547, 551, 555, 560, 571, 574, 575, 578, 580)
Jullian, Pierre-Louis-Pascale 313 (519)
Jung-Stilling, Johann Heinrich 338 (529)
Junta Patriótica de Cádiz 103
Juretschke, Hans 15, 17, 18, 19, 60, 71n., 121–4, 127n., 130, 146, 172n., 176, 216–17, 247, 249n.

Kanne, Friedrich August 311 (517)
Kanne, Johann Arnold 361, 364 (537)
Kant, Imanuel 34, 60–1, 63–4, 68, 69, 71n., 77, 85, 93, 111, 122, 148, 151, 245, 402 (512, 549)
Karl Gustav of Sweden 324 (523)
Kauer, Ferdinand August 441 (562)
Keil, Johann Georg 235, 251, 429, 436, 452, 486, 487 (558, 561, 564, 576)
Kempe, Martin 321, 324 (522)
Kerner, Justinus 5, 82, 87n., 98, 219, 252, 346, 348, 349, 355 (532, 535)
Kieler Blätter 360, 420, 422 (536, 555)
Kirkpatrick, Susan 18
Kleist, Heinrich von 76, 420, 438 (555)
Klingemann, August 484 (576)
Klopstock, Friedrich Gottlieb 38n., 183, 325, 328, 343, 502 (525, 531, 580)
Knigge, Adolf Freiherr von 270–1 (507)
Koch, Heinrich Christoph 333 (528)
Koch, Herbert 60
Kongehl, Michael 326 (524)
Kornmann, Heinrich 312 (519)

Kotzebue, August Friedrich Ferdinand von 137, 299, 384, 389, 398 (512, 544, 548)
Kritische Blätter der Börsenhalle 491, 495, 503 (578)
Kuhlmann, Quirinius 326 (524)

Laborde, Alexandre de 357 (535)
La Harpe, Jean-François de 156
La Martine, Alphonse de 193, 425, 427, 430, 436, 448, 449, 479 (557, 558, 573–4)
La Mennais, Felicité Robert de 184n., 397, 427 (548, 558)
La Metrie, Julien Offray de 191
Lancaster, John 147
Landt, Jørgen 475 (572)
Larra, Mariano José de 171, 254–5
Laso de la Vega y Orcajado, Francisco Javier 410, 417, 420, 422, 430, 438, 439, 450, 452, 462, 464, 465, 468 (553, 568)
Lauremberg, Johann 309 (516)
Lavoisier, Antoine Laurent 296 (511)
Lazarillo de Tormes 77
Le Globe 472 (571)
Lehmann, Christoph 334 (528)
Leibnitz, Gottfried Wilhelm Freiherr von 30, 425, 485 (557)
Leineke, Max 310 (516)
Leipziger Literatur Zeitung 209, 235, 446 (561, 564)
Leisching, August Polycarp 23 (513)
Leisching, Dietrich 23
Leisching, Hans 302, 303
León, Fray Luis de 78, 222, 362, 407
Lesage, Alain-René 401, 445 (564)
Lessing, Gotthold Ephraim 12–13, 14, 38n., 77 (513)
Leyser, Joachim 29–30
Liaño 217n., 240, 249n., 432, 452 (559)
Lichtenstein, E. 207
Liscow, Christian Ludwig 309 (516)
Lista y Aragón, Alberto Rodríguez de 172n., 245, 250n., 254, 446, 486 (564, 576)
Littlejohns, Richard 7
Llonín, Juan 163
Llorens, Vicente 15, 169
Llorente, Juan Antonio 445 (564)
Locke, John 24, 29

Lockhart, John Gibson (pseud. Lauerwinckel und Kempfershausen, Timothy Tickler) 238, *433, 469, 476* (543, 559–60, 572)
Loeben, Otto Heinrich Graf von 346 (532)
Logau, Friedrich Freiherr von *321, 333, 337, 347, 350, 366, 378, 496, 499* (522, 533, 539, 542, 579, 580)
London Magazine 238
Lope de Rueda, 225–6, 232, 247, *487, 493, 494* (576–7)
Lope de Vega Carpio, Félix 11, 12, 14, 154, 157, 162, 201, 212, 221, 222, 226, *326, 363, 370, 373, 407, 417, 443, 446, 454, 463, 472, 489* (562–3, 574)
López Soler, Ramón 245
Lotz, Georg (549)
Louis XIV *300* (512)
Louis XVIII 105, *393, 448, 451*
Ludendorff, Johan Hinrich *274, 277* (508)
Lunardi, Vincenzo *261* (506)
Lund, Zacharias *326, 328* (524)
Luther, Martin 29, 48, 93, *331, 334* (514, 526, 528, 544)
Lütkens, Nicolaus Gottlieb 19n.
Luzán, Ignacio de 11, 156–7, 213, 236

Macias *417* (554)
Macpherson, James (Ossian) 13, 59, 205–7
Madrigal, Miguel de *481* (574)
Magazin für Literatur des Auslandes 248
Maginn, William (pseud. Timothy Tickler, Ensign O'Doherty) *433, 469* (560, 570)
Mahoney, Dennis F. 19
Máiquez, Isidoro 151
Malsburg, Ernst Friedrich Georg Otto von *399* (548–9)
Malthus, Thomas Robert *383* (544)
Mämminger, C. A. (542)
Mandelslo, Johann Albrecht von *318* (521)
Manesse Codex 327 (525)
Manuel, Juan *373, 374, 380, 388* (541)
Marcos de Obregon, 77
Maret *411*
Marheinecke, Philipp Konrad (520)
María Cristina 171, *501* (577)
María Josepha von Sachsen *394, 403, 404, 408, 457* (547, 549)

Martineau, Harriet *502* (580)
Martínez de la Rosa, Francisco 245, 246
Martínez Marina, Francisco Javier *388, 430* (545)
Masdeu, Juan Francisco de 157
Massillon, Jean Baptiste 78
Mastricht, Peter von *342* (531)
Matthison, Friedrich von *311, 322, 342* (517, 523)
Maximilian I *308, 309, 332, 333, 336* (515)
Mayans, Gregorio 250n., *385, 476, 489* (544)
Medrano, Francisco de *487* (577)
Medwin, Thomas Charles *466* (569)
Meister, Leonhard *317* (521)
Meléndez Valdés, Juan 59, 214
Memel *see* Praetorius, Johannes
Mendoza, Diego Hurtado de 78, *350, 422* (534)
Menéndez y Pelayo, Marcelino 18
Mercurio gaditano 107, 110, 128, 129, 131
Merino, Juan Antonio *466, 472* (569)
Merkel, Garlieb *402* (550)
Merle, Jean Henri *463* (568)
Metternich, Klemens Wenzel Fürst von (542)
Meyer, Friedrich Ludwig Wilhelm *328, 411, 416, 418, 421, 422, 492, 497* (525, 553)
Meyer, Johann Friedrich von *492* (578)
Meyer, Johann Valentin 19n., 59, *270, 273, 275, 280* (507)
Meyer, Sophie Therese (later Böhl) 19n., 42, 285, 286, 290, 296
Milá y Fontanals, Manuel 255
Milton, John *333* (527)
Miñano, Sebastian de (pseud. El pobrecito Holgazán) *441, 446* (562, 564)
Minero 248, 250n.
Minerva 107, 142, 146, 158n., *386* (544, 545)
Mirabaud, Jean Baptiste (pseud. of Paul Henri Thiry Baron d'Holbach) 191
Mohr und Zimmer, publishers *330, 334* (526–7)
Molière (pseud. of Jean-Baptiste Poquelin) 11, *375* (542)
Molinos, Miguel de *307, 309, 321* (514)
Moltke, Adam Gottlieb Detlef, Graf von *312* (518)
Monguió, Luis 134, 140n., 170
Montalvo, Luis Gálvez 250n.
Monteggia, Luis 245

Montengón, Pedro   140n.
Montemayor, Jorge de   78
Montesquieu, Charles-Louis de Secondat, Baron de   11, 34
Monthly Magazine   (547)
Monthly Review   236, 438, 443 (561)
Montoto, Santiago   17, 57n., 98
Moore, Thomas   156, 234, 445 (564
Mora, José Joaquín de   71n., 106–7, 108–9, 112, 117–18, 121, 127n., 128–40, 140n., 142–56, 158, 158n., 159n., 160, 162, 163, 164, 165, 167, 169–71, 171n., 172n., 175, 178, 188, 249n., 251, 254, 392, 410, 472, 483 (543, 547, 553, 571)
Moratín *see* Fernández de Moratín
Moreto y Cavana, Agustín   375, 384, 399, 400, 409, 468, 482, 483 (541–2, 544, 549, 575)
Morgenblatt für gebildete Stände   180, 252, 311, 328, 336, 342, 400, 406, 453 (517, 530, 550, 551, 566)
Mornay, Philippe de   311 (518)
Moscherosch, Johann Michael   326, 327 (524)
Mozart, Wolfgang Amadeus   438
Müller, Adam Heinrich   11, 76, 192, 193, 418, 421, 422 (554, 555)
Müller, Friedrich (Maler)   311, 472 (517, 571)
Müller, Johannes   334 (528)
Müller, Wenzel   441 (562)
Müllner, Amandus Gottfried Adolf   360, 484 (536)
Münster, Sebastian   313 (519)
Murillo   442
Murner, Thomas   328 (525, 528)
Murray, John   (543)
Musäus, Johann Karl August   404, 479 (551, 573–4)
Mylius, Christoph August   327 (525)

Nasarre, Blas Antonio   11, 15, 157, 159n.
Nava Álvarez, Gaspar María de, Count of Noroña   362 (537)
Navarrete, Martin Fernández de   167, 172n., 182, 201, 218–20, 224–5, 240, 250n., 251, 392, 430, 441, 466, 472, 475, 477 (546–7, 556, 569, 572, 573)
Navarro, Felipe Benicio   379 (542)
Navas Ruiz, Ricardo   15, 18

Neander, August   452 (566)
Necker de Saussure, Albertine   (543)
Nemoianou, Virgil   10–11
Neumark, Georg   336 (529)
Neumeister, Erdmann   308, 318, 321, 327 (515, 525)
Neuss, Heinrich Georg   336 (529)
New Monthly Magazine   392 (547)
Nieto de Molina, Francisco   159n.
Nipho, Francisco Mariano   15, 135, 157, 158n., 164, 214, 255 (563)
Nodier, Charles   455 (566)
Noodt, Lorenz Andreas   25, 261 (506)
Nordische Miszellen   73, 76, 77, 252, 310, 316 (517, 521)
Norwich, A.   325, 343 (524)
Novalis *see* Hardenberg, Friedrich von

Ochoa, Eugenio de   243
O'Donnell, Henry Joseph, Conde de la Bisbal   423 (556)
Oelzweige   424, 433, 460, 463
Oesterreichischer Beobachter   379
Oetinger, Friedrich Christoph   91, 308, 310 (515, 516)
Ofterdingen, Heinrich von   (530)
Oken, Lorenz   389 (545–6)
Olabarrieta, Juan Antonio de (pseud. Clararossa)   202–3n., 426, 443 (557, 562)
Olearius, Adam   318 (521)
Olearius, Johann Christoph   330, 340 (526)
Olive, Pedro de   142, 146, 158n., 386 (545)
Opitz, Martin   317, 320, 321, 328, 340, 350 (521, 523, 530)
Orea, publisher   249n., 429
Orelli, Johann Caspar von   328 (525)
Orient, oder Hamburgisches Morgenblatt   342 (530, 531)
Originalien aus dem Gebiete der Wahrheit   234, 399, 435 (549, 560)
Orozco Acuaviva, Antonio   40, 54, 58n.
Osborne family   17, 57n., (561)
Osborne, Thomas   179, 470

Pabst, Walter   18
Paine, Thomas   426 (557)
Palm, Johann Philipp   74, 300 (512)

Index

Pander, Christian Heinrich 163, *384, 386, 390, 394, 430* (543–4, 548, 558)
Pappus, Johann *390* (546)
Par, Alfonso 146
Paracelsus (553)
Pariset, Etienne *411, 430* (553)
Pascal, Blaise *330, 449* (526)
Passavant, Johann Karl *429, 430* (558)
Passy, Anton (557)
Patriotische Gesellschaft (Hamburg) 39n.
Pavón y Jiménez, José Antonio *422, 425, 427, 430, 439* (556)
Peel, Robert *471* (571)
Pelayo 116
Peña y Santander, Diego de la *380* (542)
Percy, Bishop Thomas 13, 205, 243, *317* (521)
Pérez de Hita, Ginés 205, 232, *311, 430* (517)
Pérez Galdós, Benito 53
Perthes, Friedrich 5, 8, 75, 82, 177–8, 197, 217n., 220, 226, 233n., 236, 252, *302, 308, 310, 311, 313, 314, 317, 326, 328, 330, 331, 332, 335, 336, 339, 340, 342, 351, 353, 367, 370, 371, 372, 374, 377, 379, 380, 385, 390, 392, 394, 404, 405, 406, 408, 409, 414, 417, 419, 420, 421, 422, 425, 426, 427, 428, 429, 432, 433, 434, 436, 443, 444, 452, 459, 461, 463, 468, 471, 472, 473, 474, 475, 477, 480, 483, 486, 489, 494, 495, 497, 498, 499* (509, 513, 520, 534, 535, 539, 540, 545, 547, 548, 551–2, 557, 559, 573, 578)
Pestalozzi, Johan Heinrich 38n.
Petrarca, Franceso *296, 313* (511)
Pfeilschifter, Johann Baptiste von *463, 468, 472* (569)
Philosethus, Sylvander 312
Picardische Gesangbuch 318, 321 (521)
Pitollet, Camille 16, 17, 19, 57n., 71n., 87n., 121–2, 129, 140n., 146, 147, 153, 157–8, 158n., 159n., 162, 171n., 172n., 249n.
Pitt, William 51, 75
Placcius, Vincentius *313, 327, 336* (519, 525)
Planck, Gottlieb Jacob *310* (516)
Planels y Bardají, Antonio, *359* (536)
Poivre, Pierre *311, 313* (518)
Pope, Alexander 83
Porras de la Cámera (546)

Praetorius, Johannes (pseud. Memel) *333, 335* (527)
Prätorius, Michael *311, 312* (518)
Prévôt, Charles Victor *430* (559)
Prévôt d'Exiles, Antoine-François *311* (518)
Printz, Wolfgang Caspar *335* (528)
Pustkuchen, Johann Friedrich Wilhelm 196, *440, 442* (562)

Quarterly Review 199, *382, 387, 419, 432, 460, 461, 468, 477* (543, 545, 559–60, 567, 568, 573)
Quevedo, Francisco de 78, 212, 221, 222, *380, 407, 454* (541–2)
Quintana, Manuel José 59, 63, 70, 111, 117, 126, 135, 166, 169, 172n., 176, 213, 216, 221–4, 239, 240–2, 243–4, 245, 247, 254, *389, 407, 487, 499* (545–6, 552, 576–7, 580)
Quiroga, Antonio *414* (554)

Rachel, Joachim *309* (516)
Racine, Jean 11, 151
Radlof, Johann Gottlieb *346* (532)
Rambach, August Jakob *390, 402, 422* (546)
Ramírez, Francisco Leira (565)
Ramón Fernández *see* Estala
Rattenfänger 312 (519)
Raumer, Friedrich Ludwig Georg von *468* (570)
Real Academia Española 108, 138, 159n., 167–9, 172n., 218, 219, 224, 229–30, 233, 233n., 235, 250n., 252, *354, 372, 391, 392, 409, 415, 416, 418, 422, 438, 491, 498* (535, 540, 546, 552, 554)
Real Sociedad Económica de Cádiz 103–4
Rebmann, Andreas Georg Friedrich *281* (509)
Rebolledo, Bernardino de *383* (544)
Redactor general de Cádiz 459 (567)
Rehberg, August Wilhelm *421, 423, 425* (556, 557)
Reichardt, Friedrich (527)
Reichhardt, Luise *331, 336, 339, 347* (526–7, 528, 532)
Reichsanzeiger (Kaiserlich priviligierter) 300, 303 (512)
Reimer, Georg Andreas *417*

Index

Reinicke Fuchs 309, 311, 321, 337 (516)
Reinoso, Félix José 172n.
Repullés, publisher 151
Retrospective Review 199, 433 (559–60)
Reuss, Jeremias David 429 (558)
Revue de Paris 487, 500
Revue encyclopédique 409 (553)
Reyes Ponce, María Guadalupe 8, 17–18, 19, 110–12, 115, 118, 122–4, 140, 176, 210, 213–14, 216, 217n., 228, 255
Ribadeneira, Pedro de 78
Richter, Jean Paul 196, *294, 314, 404, 466, 481, 491* (511, 520, 551, 569)
Riego y Flórez, Rafael de 176, *414, 423, 454* (553–4)
Riem, Andreas 34–36, 40, 88, *272, 276* (508)
Rioja, Francisco de 78, *407*
Ritter, Carl *388, 398* (545)
Roberthin, Robert *318, 320, 326, 327, 390* (521)
Robinson, David (pseud. Y.Y.Y.) *469–70* (570)
Rochlitz, Johann Friedrich *489, 494* (577)
Rodd, Thomas *387* (545)
Rojas, Fernando de *392* (547)
Rollenhagen, Georg *306* (511)
Romances de Germania 374, 380 (541)
Romea y Tapia, Juan Cristóbal 15, 135, 157, 164
Roscoe, William *425* (557)
Rosenplüt, Hans *328* (526)
Rousseau, Jean Jacques 24, 28, 29, 40, 42–3, 74, 97, *272, 277, 301, 339, 453* (508, 530)
Rossini, Gioacchino Antonio *460* (567)
Rückert, Friedrich *436* (561)
Rudolphi, Karoline *260, 262, 263* (506)
Rudolphi, Ludwig *260, 262, 263* (506)
Ruiz de Larrea, Antonio 40
Ruiz de Larrea, Francisca 40–5, 51–6, 73, 94, 96, 101–4, 106, 107, 125, 128, 143, 148–9, 158–9n., 179, 183, 184, 236, 240, 252, 278, 282, 284, 286, 287, *288, 289, 290, 296, 299, 302, 306, 316, 350, 359, 370, 376, 384, 389, 398, 400, 420, 426, 433, 439, 449, 459, 461, 464, 466, 467* (509, 510, 513, 520, 533, 536, 541, 544, 561, 567, 569)
Ruiz y López, Hipólito *422, 425, 427, 430, 439* (556)

Rumohr, Karl Friedrich von *445, 447, 448, 452, 461, 463* (564, 565, 568–9)
Runge, Johann Daniel 104–5, *357* (535, 539)
Runge, Phillip Otto 104 (535)
Ruprecht *see* Vandenhoeck und Ruprecht (publishers)

Saavedra, Ángel, Duque de Rivas 170
Sachs, Hans *326, 350* (524)
Saglia, Diego 253–4
Sailer, Johann Michael *447* (564)
Saint-Chamand 158n.
Saint Denis, Charles Margetel de (pseud. St Evremont) *499* (579)
Saint Martin, Louis Claude de 90, *308, 355* (514–15, 535)
Salinas, Francisco de *371* (540)
Salvá y Pérez, Vicente 238–9, 244, *468* (569–70)
Salthenius, Daniel *342* (531)
Sand, Karl Ludwig (548)
San Miranda 78
Sancha, publisher *369* (539)
Sánchez, publisher 250n., *429, 443, 465*
Sánchez, Tomás Antonio 209, 213, *374, 378, 380, 489* (541)
Santa Clara, Abraham de (pseud. of Johann Ulrich Megerle) *310* (516)
Santiago y Rotaldo, Nicolás *423* (556)
Sarmiento, Martín 213
Sartorius von Waltershausen, Georg *328* (525)
Schäufelein, Hans Leonhard *342* (531)
Schemelii, Georg Christian *336* (529)
Schelling, Friedrich Joseph Wilhelm 11, 71n., 85, 90–4, 97, *306, 307, 310* (514, 537)
Schiller, Friedrich 12, 58n., 60–70, 71n., 76, 79, 85, 89–90, 111, 120, 122, 137, 146, 150–1, 184, 188, 200, 204, 224, 245, 252, 253, 256, *279, 339, 402, 438, 494, 502* (509, 512, 530, 580)
Schirmer, Michael *308, 320* (515)
Schleiermacher, Friedrich 62
Schlegel brothers 4, 5, 8, 13, 14, 18, 59, 62–3, 71n., 86, 97, 181, 247, 256, *292, 370, 491* (510, 511, 539)
Schlegel, August Wilhelm 13, 15, 19, 56, 60, 61, 68, 76–7, 79, 97, 107, 108, 110–26, 128–40, 140n., 142, 145, 147–51, 153, 154, 155, 156, 158n.,

Index

159n., 162, 163, 164, 165–6, 169, 171, 176, 181, 185n., 188–90, 194, 200, 203n., 204, 205, 215, 221, 226, 235, 236, 245–6, 248, 252, 253, *311, 319, 323, 346, 360, 381–2, 383, 384, 385, 386, 394, 399, 402, 412, 415, 420, 425, 429, 435, 442, 489* (511, 516, 517, 521, 522, 523, 532, 533, 536, 537, 543, 544, 548–9, 552, 554, 555, 557, 558, 560, 562, 577)

Schlegel, Dorothea 71n.
Schlegel, Friedrich 11, 13, 77, 79, 83, 91, 94, 114, 192–4, 195, 196, 205, 209, 216, 235, *311, 328, 334, 336, 337, 339, 345, 365, 402, 411, 421, 425, 433, 447* (511, 516–17, 525, 527, 528, 529, 530, 532, 537, 538, 542, 549–50, 556–7, 559, 561, 565)
Schlegel-Schelling, Caroline 71n.
Schlosser, Christian Friedrich 196, *372, 377, 447* (540, 541, 565)
Schlözer, August Ludwig von *333* (527)
Schmid, Christoph von *388* (545)
Schmidt, Friedrich Wilhelm Valentin *399, 401, 442* (549, 563)
Schmidt, Michael Ignaz *317* (521)
Schnabel, Johann Gottfried von (578)
Schoch, Johann Georg *326* (524)
Schröder, Friedrich Ludwig *411, 416, 497* (553)
Schuback, Franz Jacob *275* (508)
Schuback, Johannes 23, *298, 302, 303, 316* (512)
Schuback, Nicolas 23, *269, 270, 271, 298, 323* (507)
Schubart, Christian Friedrich Daniel *325, 364* (524)
Schubert, Gotthilf Heinrich 197, *314, 318, 325, 355, 360, 372, 387, 433, 463* (520, 521, 523, 535, 536, 540, 545, 568)
Schuppius, Johann Balthasar *309* (516)
Schütz, Christian Wilhelm von *311, 333, 411* (517)
Schwarzenberg, Johann von *342* (531)
Schwieger, Jacob *326, 328* (524)
Scío y Riaza, Felipe *384, 389* (544)
Scott, Walter 4, 76, 137, 200, 234, 255, *400, 438, 440, 445, 447, 476* (549, 564, 572–3)

Seckendorf, Friedrich Heinrich *311, 430* (517)
Seckendorff, Gustav Anton von (pseud. Patrick Peale) *338, 441, 478* (529)
Sedano, Juan José López de 213, 216, 221, 241, *407, 417* (552)
Seder 'Olam 313 (519)
Shakespeare, William 4, 68, 110–11, 112–13, 115, 128, 131, 137, 149–50, 155, 156, *440*
Sharpe, Lesley 67–8
Shaw, Donald 15–16
Shelley, Mary *475* (572)
Shelley, Percy Bysshe (572)
Siebenmann, Gustav 8, 20n.
Sieber, Justus *326, 328* (524)
Sieveking family 5, 75, *302, 339, 341, 349, 408, 442, 449, 492, 497, 502* (563)
Silbert, Johann Peter *436* (561)
Silesius, Angelus 91
Silver, Philip 15, 18
Sismondi, Jean Caude Léonard Simonde de 155, 159n., 245, 253, *364, 365, 372* (538, 540)
Smith, Sydney (538)
Solís y Rivadeneira, Antonio *422* (556)
Solger, Karl Friedrich Ferdinand *489* (555, 577)
Sommer, Johann Friedrich Joseph *399* (549)
Sorgenlügnerin *321* (522)
Southern, Henry (560)
Southey, Robert 11, 84, 137, 201, *372, 375, 388, 389, 469* (540, 541, 545, 557, 570)
Spalding, Johann Joachim 30–1
Spaten 311
Speckter family *330, 334* (526)
Spee von Langenfeld, Friedrich *373* (541)
Spiker, Samuel Heinrich *430* (559)
Spinoza, Benedikt de 191
Spurzheim, Johann Christoph *402* (550)
Staël, Germaine, Baroness de 139, 154, 155, 192, 245–6, 253, 255, *319, 370, 372, 389, 392* (522, 539, 543, 546, 579)
Stetten, Paul von *339* (530)
Stieler, Kaspar (518)
Stimmer, Tobias *335* (528)
Stockfleth, Elizabeth *339* (530)
Stockmann, Ernst *321* (522)
Stoeffler, F. Ernst 30

604

Stolberg, Friedrich Leopold 94–5, 193, 202n., *325*, *328*, *330*, *399*, *409*, *411*, *420*, *423*, *436*, *447*, *468*, *478* (*523*, *524*, *525*, *526*, *549*, *552*, *553*, *555*, *556*)
Stolle, Gottlieb (pseud. Leander) *308*, *320* (*515*)
Stourdza, Alexandre *391* (*546*)
Stuve, Johann 268–9, *271*, *275*, *276* (*507*)
Suckow, Karl Adolf (pseud. Posgaru) *489* (*577*)
Sullivan, Henry 12, 14
Sulzer, Johann Georg 154
Swedenborg, Emanuel *310* (*515*, *516*)
Sweerts, Hieronymus *311* (*518*)

Tap y Núñez, Nicolás 140n.
Tauler, Johannes *321* (*522*)
Tay, Dr. 25
Taylor, Edgar *476* (*572*)
Taylor, Isidore Justin *455* (*566*)
Terreros y Pando, Estebán de *472* (*571*)
Tersteegen, Gerhard *313* (*519*)
The Book of the Thousand and One Nights *468*, *472* (*570*)
The Liberal 475
Theologia Teutsch 93, *306*, *325* (*514*)
Thiess, Johann Otto *321*, *325* (*524*)
Ticknor, George 16, 140n., 236, 249
Tieck, Ludwig 4, 8, 13, 14, 71n., 77, 89, 98n., 105, 118, 137, 183, 195, 196, 205, 256, *311*, *354*, *355*, *364*, *365*, *370*, *372*, *381*, *400*, *402*, *411*, *422*, *447*, *449*, *461*, *468*, *479*, *491*, *494*, *502* (*516–17*, *534*, *538*, *540*, *542–3*, *565*, *568*, *573–4*, *578*, *580*)
Tiemann, Hermann 18
Timoneda, Joan *225* (*577*)
Tindall, Matthew 29
Torre, Francisco de la *422* (*556*)
Torres Amat, Félix *468* (*570*)
Torres Naharro, Bartolomé de 226, 232, *409*, *487*, *493–4* (*553*)
Tirso de Molina (pseud. of Fray Gabrial Tellez) *364* (*538*)
Trapp, Ernst Christian 269, *271*, *275*, *277*, *281*, *303*, *305*, *306* (*507*)
Treuttel and Würtz, publishers 483

Tscherning, Andreas *320* (*522*)
Tubino, Francisco María 18
Tychsen, Olaf Gerhard *350* (*533*)
Tychsen, Thomas Christian 13

Uhland, Ludwig 5, 82
Ulloa, Antonio de *477–8* (*573*)

Valcarcél Pío de Saboya y Maura, Antonio *422* (*556*)
Valdés y Flores, Cayetano *458* (*567*)
Valladares y Sotomayor, Antonio *299* (*512*)
Vandenhoeck und Ruprecht, publishers *309*, *333* (*516*)
Van Halen, Antonio 172n.
Vargas Ponce, José 106, 135, 141n., 160, 167, 172n., 213, *379*, *384*, *385*, *414*, *415* (*542*, *544*, *553*)
Vassall-Fox, Henry Richard, Lord Holland 154, *443* (*562–3*)
Vaterländisches Museum 75, 83, 93, 200, 233n., 252, *307*, *314*, *317*, *318*, *319*, *322*, *324*, *328*, *331* (*514*, *515*, *520*, *521*, *523*, *525*)
Veith, Johann Emanuel *460* (*557*)
Velázquez, Luis José 13, 214
Veron, Louis Desiré (*577*)
Verville, Béroalde *313* (*520*)
Viau, Théophile de *313* (*520*)
Vieweg, Johann Friedrich 71n., *291*, *293*, *305*, *323*, *476*, *503* (*510*)
Villanueva, Jaime *448* (*565*)
Villanueva Estengo, Joaquín Lorenzo *448* (*565*)
Villate, Eugene 52, 56, 316
Villeneuve, Alexandre-Louis Ducrest de *455*, *456* (*566*)
Villers, Charles François Dominique de *325*, *331*
Virgil 151
Virues, Cristóbal de *487* (*577*)
Vogt, Valentin *342* (*531*)
Volney, Constantin François de Chasseboeuf, Count *426* (*557*)
Voltaire (pseud. of François-Marie Arouet) 11, *426*, *449* (*557*)
Voß, Johann Heinrich *324*, *406*, *420*, *423* (*523*, *551–2*, *555*, *556*)

Index

Wackenroder, Wilhelm 98n.
Wagener, Johann Daniel *307* (515)
Wagenseil, Georg Christoph *336* (529)
Wagner, Adolf (549)
Wahlenberg, Georg Göran *335* (528)
Wasserhun, Rudolph *308* (515)
Weber, Carl Maria von *437* (561)
Weckherlin, Georg Rudolf *321, 328* (522)
Weeks, Andrew 91, 97
Weidner, Johann Jacob *326, 327* (524)
Weigel, Johann August Gottlob *309, 312, 332, 346*
Weigel, Valentin *326* (524)
Weinmann, Johannes Wilhelm *362* (537)
Weise, Christian (pseud. Sigismund Gleichviel) *318, 321* (521, 522)
Weisser, Friedrich Christoph *308* (515)
West, Carl August *384* (544)
Westmacott, Charles *475* (572)
Werner, Zacharias 89
Wernike, Christian *308* (515)
Wertheimer Bibel *313* (519)
Wetzel, Johann Caspar *321, 327* (522)
Wieland, Christoph 61
Wiener Jahrbücher der Literatur 386, 387, 393, 398, 400, 402, 411, 420, 432, 452, 463, 472, 480 (545, 547, 550, 555, 559, 570)
Wiffen, Jeremiah Holmes *468* (570)

Wilson, John (pseud. Christopher North) 200–1, *469, 470, 471* (570, 571)
Wolf, Ferdinand 58n., 209, 211, 236, 248, 249, 251, 252
Wolff, Christian Freiherr von 30, 91
Wöllner, Johann Christian 39n.
Wollstonecraft, Mary 52, 54, 56, 58n.
Wordsworth, William 11, 63, 71n., 76, 82, 83–5, 97, 137, 180–81, 199, 200, 237, *346, 364, 365, 369, 387, 392, 400, 403, 411–12, 418, 426, 431, 433, 443, 461, 469, 471, 498* (532, 538, 539, 545, 550, 555, 557, 559, 562, 570, 571, 579)
Wurm, Christoph Friedrich (578)

Young, Edward 71n., *343* (531)

Zachariä, Friedrich Wilhelm *317* (521)
Zavala y Zamora, Gaspar *299* (512)
Zesen, Philipp von *321, 327, 328* (523, 525)
Ziegler, Kaspar *321* (522)
Zimmermann, Friedrich Gottlieb *433, 438, 440* (559–60)
Zulueta, Cristobal 160–2, 165, 166, 171n., *394* (547)